INTERNATIONAL CRIMINAL LAW: CASES AND COMMENTARY

INTERNATIONAL CRIMINAL LAW: CASES AND COMMENTARY

ANTONIO CASSESE

GUIDO ACQUAVIVA

MARY FAN

AND

ALEX WHITING

OXFORD
UNIVERSITY PRESS

OXFORD

UNIVERSITY PRESS

Great Clarendon Street, Oxford ox2 6DP

Oxford University Press is a department of the University of Oxford.
It furthers the University's objective of excellence in research, scholarship,
and education by publishing worldwide in

Oxford New York

Auckland Cape Town Dar es Salaam Hong Kong Karachi
Kuala Lumpur Madrid Melbourne Mexico City Nairobi
New Delhi Shanghai Taipei Toronto

With offices in

Argentina Austria Brazil Chile Czech Republic France Greece
Guatemala Hungary Italy Japan Poland Portugal Singapore
South Korea Switzerland Thailand Turkey Ukraine Vietnam

Oxford is a registered trade mark of Oxford University Press
in the UK and in certain other countries

Published in the United States
by Oxford University Press Inc., New York

British Library Cataloguing-in-Publication Data
Data available

Library of Congress Cataloging in Publication Data
Data available

Typeset by Newgen Imaging Systems (P) Ltd, Chennai, India
Printed in Great Britain
on acid-free paper by
Ashford Colour Press Ltd, Gosport, Hampshire

ISBN 978-0-19-957678-4

1 3 5 7 9 10 8 6 4 2

PREFACE

This casebook is intended to offer a *concise and comprehensive* practice-oriented explanation of the development of major areas in substantive international criminal law through a selection of key illustrative cases from domestic and international jurisdictions. The focus is on the law related to individual criminal liability for war crimes, crimes against humanity, genocide, aggression, and the emerging practice on torture (as a discrete international crime) and terrorism, as well as the old and new practice relating to piracy. In the choice of cases, specific emphasis has been laid on fundamental principles of criminal responsibility as well as modes of international responsibility and defences. The casebook also briefly examines the interaction among domestic legal systems and between these systems and international courts or tribunals, including questions of primacy, complementarity, State cooperation, arrest or surrender, as well as some salient facets of international criminal procedural law.

Our purpose is not only to offer these decisions for discussion, but also to provide our readers with the conceptual tools for critically appraising them. This approach, we believe, is dictated by the very nature of international criminal law which results from the convergence of two different legal practices and traditions: that of common law countries and that of civil law States. Like the common law tradition, international criminal law relies heavily on case law and judicial precedent. Because of the paucity of national or international legal texts on international crimes, national and also international judicial decisions are at the origin of the gradual development of international criminal law and have potently contributed to making it a fully fledged body of criminal law. Hence their crucial importance. Also like the civil law tradition (particularly that bearing the imprint of the German school of thought), international criminal law has gradually built a set of rigorous legal constructs in an effort to conceptualize disparate trends in the case law. This tendency has been strengthened first by the important and ground-breaking case law of the International Criminal Tribunals for Yugoslavia (ICTY) and Rwanda (ICTR) (from 1995 onwards) and then by the adoption (in 1998) and the current application of the Statute of the International Criminal Court (ICC). The drafters of this Statute have for the first time laid down in a written text notions and concepts of criminal law that are spelled out in a rigorous manner and set forth within a logically stringent general structure.

Consistent with these characteristics of international criminal law and in order to reflect the unique nature of this body of law, we offer, in addition to the relevant case law, general introductions to each of the five Parts of this volume, with a view both to laying out the major problems arising in that area and to providing the theoretical background necessary for putting those issues in their proper perspective. In addition, each chapter or section relating to a set of judicial decisions is preceded by a historical and conceptual survey, which should help as an introduction to the reading of the cases reported.

To make the casebook a useful teaching instrument, we have also expounded (i) the circumstances of the most important cases cited, adding after the decision, where warranted, (ii) a commentary on its importance, with cross-references to other relevant decisions on similar issues, plus (iii) questions for discussion and (iv) a short list of references to scholarly articles and books on the issues raised in the decision.

The casebook is intended to provide a truly international perspective, with excerpts from decisions rendered by national courts of various countries (USA, Canada, France,

UK, Japan, Belgium, Lebanon, Germany, Italy, Kenya, Netherlands, Israel, and others), as well as judgments handed down by international or 'mixed' tribunals (Nuremberg and the World War II tribunals, ICTY, ICTR, ICC, SCSL, ECCC, STL, SPSC). Most of these decisions, though not all, are from criminal courts. Thus, the casebook offers a number of hard-to-find decisions (or decisions existing only in languages other than English) which are highly relevant for the present and future development of international criminal justice as well as the most important international judgments on the matter. Relevant decisions or reports by the ICJ, the ECtHR and other bodies are also offered to enhance the understanding of the various issues presented.

Of course, not all the cases excerpted in this casebook remain 'good law'. Alas, development of international criminal law through cases requires judicious discerning of the developments of the law, which is why we added questions and commentaries to prompt reflection and discussion in the classroom. Readers particularly interested in these cases, their background and their rationale, may refer to the *Oxford Companion to International Criminal Justice* (2009), which provides short summaries of most of them as well as cross-references to related entries.

The views expressed in this book are those of the authors and do not necessarily reflect the views of the institutions with which they are, or have been, affiliated.

While the co-authors have worked jointly on this volume, retrieving material and discussing many issues, A. Cassese drafted the introductions to each Part, and the sections on General Principles of Law, Necessity, Mistake of Fact, Mistake of Law, and Mental Disorder; G. Acquaviva drafted the sections on International Custom and the Value of Precedents, Treaties and Instruments Establishing International Tribunals, International Criminal Law and Human Rights, Immunities, War Crimes, Terrorism, Joint Criminal Enterprise, Co-Perpetration, Self-Defence, Superior Orders, Duress, and Tu Quoque; M. Fan drafted the sections on Nullum Crimen Sine Lege (Legality), Ne Bis In Idem, Genocide, Torture, Commission, Incitement to Commit Genocide, Ordering, and Superior Responsibility; A. Whiting drafted the sections on Crimes Against Humanity, Aggression, Piracy, Planning, and Aiding and Abetting, as well as Part V.

Each of the authors has benefited greatly from comments and suggestions from the others. When not otherwise indicated, translations of the cases excerpted in this volume were provided by the authors.

The format of decisions and judgments excerpted in this volume, especially those first issued in languages other than English, does not always correspond to the original version.

a.c., g.a., m.d.f., a.w.

SOURCE ACKNOWLEDGEMENTS

Grateful acknowledgement is made to all the authors and publishers of copyright material which appears in this book, and in particular to the following for permission to reprint material from the sources indicated:

American Society of International Law: extracts from Israel, Legality of the General Security Service Interrogation Methods, Supreme Court, Judgment of 6 September 1999, [1999] 38 ILM, starting at p. 1471.

British Institute of International and Comparative Law: extracts from *In Re Piracy Jure Gentium* [1934] AC 586 (*British International Law Cases*, Volume 3, at pp. 836–843).

Cambridge University Press: extracts from *Barbie* case, Judgment of 20 December 1985 [1985] 78 International Law Reports, starting at p. 78 (English language translation by A Oppenheimer); extracts from *Gaddafi* case, Judgment of 13 March 2001 [2004] 125 International law Reports, starting at p. 490 (English language translation by A Oppenheimer).

University of Chicago Press: extracts from John Langbein, *Torture and the Law of Proof: Europe and England in the Ancien Régime*, pp. 3–5 and 8–9.

Oxford University Press Journals: excerpts from *Hechingen* case [2009] 7 Journal of International Criminal Justice, pp. 131–154; excerpts from *Wolfgang* case [2006] 4 Journal of International Criminal Justice, pp. 862–865.

Every effort has been made to trace and contact copyright holders prior to publication. If notified, the publisher will undertake to rectify any errors or omissions at the earliest opportunity.

We further acknowledge the ECtHR, ICJ, ICTY, ICTR, ICC, STL, ECCC, SCSL, SPSC as sources of the judgments and decisions excerpted in the volume.

CONTENTS

PART I SOURCES AND PRINCIPLES OF INTERNATIONAL CRIMINAL LAW

PART II   CRIMES

PART III FORMS OF RESPONSIBILITY

PART IV CIRCUMSTANCES EXCLUDING CRIMINAL RESPONSIBILITY

PART V JURISDICTIONAL AND PROCEDURAL ISSUES

LIST OF COMMON ABBREVIATIONS

ABiH	*Armija Bosne i Hercegovine* – Army of Bosnia-Herzegovina [former Yugoslavia]
ACHR	American Convention on Human Rights
ACHPR	African Charter on Human and Peoples' Rights
Additional Protocol I	Protocol Additional to the Geneva Conventions of 12 August 1949, and relating to the Protection of Victims of International Armed Conflicts (Protocol I), 8 June 1977
Additional Protocol II	Protocol Additional to the Geneva Conventions of 12 August 1949, and relating to the Protection of Victims of Non-International Armed Conflicts (Protocol II), 8 June 1977
AFRC	Armed Forces Revolutionary Council [Sierra Leone]
ARK	*Autonomna Regija Krajina* – Autonomous Region of Krajina [former Yugoslavia]
ASP	Assembly of State Parties [ICC]
ATCA	Alien Torts Claims Act [US]
Cassese, *International Criminal Law*	A. Cassese, *International Criminal Law* (2nd edn, Oxford: OUP, 2008)
C.C. Law 10	Control Council Law Number 10 [World War II cases]
CDF	Civil Defence Force [Rwanda]
CERD	International Convention on the Elimination of All Forms of Racial Discrimination
CRC	Convention on the Rights of the Child
DRC	Democratic Republic of the Congo
ECCC	Extraordinary Chambers in the Courts of Cambodia
ECHR	European Convention on Human Rights
ECMM	European Community Monitor Mission
ECtHR	European Court of Human Rights
Einsatzgruppen case	*United States* v. *Ohlendorf et al.*, 10 April 1948, in TWC, vol. 4, at 411
EJIL	European Journal of International Law
ESCOR	Economic and Social Council Official Records
ETS	European Treaty Series
Fletcher, *Rethinking Criminal Law*	G. Fletcher, *Rethinking Criminal Law* (Boston and Toronto: OUP, 2000)

FPLC	*Forces patriotiques pour la libération du Congo* – Patriotic Forces for the Liberation of Congo [DRC]
FRY	Federal Republic of Yugoslavia
GCIII Commentary	J. de Preux (ed.), *Commentary: III Geneva Convention Relative to the Treatment of Prisoners of War* (Geneva: ICRC, 1960)
GCIV Commentary	J. Pictet (ed.), *Commentary: IV Geneva Convention Relative to the Protection of Civilian Persons in Time of War* (Geneva: ICRC, 1958)
Geneva Convention I	Convention (I) for the Amelioration of the Condition of the Wounded and Sick in Armed Forces in the Field, Geneva, 12 August 1949
Geneva Convention II	Convention (II) for the Amelioration of the Condition of Wounded, Sick and Shipwrecked Members of Armed Forces at Sea, Geneva, 12 August 1949
Geneva Convention III	Convention (III) relative to the Treatment of Prisoners of War, Geneva, 12 August 1949
Geneva Convention IV	Convention (IV) relative to the Protection of Civilian Persons in Time of War, Geneva, 12 August 1949
Hague Convention of 1899	Convention (II) with Respect to the Laws and Customs of War on Land and its annex: Regulations concerning the Laws and Customs of War on Land, The Hague, 29 July 1899
Hague Convention of 1907	Convention (IV) respecting the Laws and Customs of War on Land and its annex: Regulations concerning the Laws and Customs of War on Land, The Hague, 18 October 1907
HVO	*Hrvatsko vijeće obrane* – Bosnian Croat forces [former Yugoslavia]
IAD	Immigration and Refugee Board (Canada) (Abbreviation used in *Mugesera* v. *Canada (Minister of Citizenship and Immigration)*, Judgment of 28 June 2005)
ICC	International Criminal Court
ICCSt.	Statute of the International Criminal Court
ICCPR	International Covenant on Civil and Political Rights
ICJ	International Court of Justice
ICRC Commentary	Sandoz *et al.* (eds), *Commentary on the Additional Protocols of 8 June 1977 to the Geneva Conventions of 12 August 1949* (Geneva: ICRC, 1987)
ICRC Study	J.-M. Henckaerts and L. Doswald-Beck, *Customary International Humanitarian Law* (Cambridge: ICRC, Cambridge University Press, 2005), vol. 1
ICTR	International Criminal Tribunal for Rwanda
ICTRSt.	Statute of the International Criminal Tribunal for Rwanda

ICTY	International Criminal Tribunal for the Former Yugoslavia
ICTYSt.	Statute of the International Criminal Tribunal for the Former Yugoslavia
IFOR	Implementation Force [former Yugoslavia]
IMT	International Military Tribunal at Nüremberg
IMTFE	International Military Tribunal for the Far East
JAG	Judge Advocate General
JCE	Joint Criminal Enterprise
JICJ	Journal of International Criminal Justice
JNA	Jugoslovenska Narodna Armija – Yugoslav People's Army
Justice case	*United States* v. *Josef Altstöetter et al.*, 3–4 December 1947, in TWC, vol. 3, at 954.
KLA	Kosovo Liberation Army [former Yugoslavia]
LJIL	Leiden Journal of International Law
LRA	Lord's Resistance Army [Uganda]
McGill L.J.	McGill Law Journal
MuP	*Ministarstuo Unutrašnjih Poslova* – Ministry of Internal Affairs (Police) [former Yugoslavia]
Nuremberg Charter	London Charter of the International Military Tribunal
OG	Operations Group, an abbreviation used in cases stemming from the Bosnian Conflict [former Yugoslavia]
OTP	Office of the Prosecutor
Oxford Companion	A. Cassese (ed.), *Oxford Companion to International Criminal Justice* (Oxford: OUP, 2009)
POW	Prisoner of War
RPE	Rules of Procedure and Evidence
RUF	Revolutionary United Front [Sierra Leone]
RSK	*Republika Srpska Krajina* – Republic of Serbian Krajina [former Yugoslavia]
RTLM	*Radio Télévision Libres des Milles Collines* [Rwanda]
RUF	Revolutionary United Front [Rwanda]
RuSHA	*Rasse- und Siedlungshauptamt-SS* – SS Race and Resettlement Office [World War II cases]
RuSHA case	*US* v. *Greifelt et al.*, 10 March 1948, in TWC, vol. 5, at 88.
SA	*Stürmabteilung* – Storm Division or Stormtroopers or Brownshirts [World War II cases]
SAO	*Srpska Autonomna Oblast* – Serb Autonomous District [former Yugoslavia]
SCSL	Special Court for Sierra Leone
SFOR	Stabilisation Force [former Yugoslavia]

SIPO-SD	*Sicherheitspolizei-Sicherheitsdienst* – German State and National Socialist police [World War II cases]
SPSC	Special Panels for Serious Crimes [East Timor]
SRK	*Sarajevo-Romanija Korpus* – Sarajevo-Romanija Corps of the VRS [former Yugoslavia]
SS	*Schutzstaffel* – Paramilitary force under Adolf Hitler's control [World War II cases]
STL	Special Tribunal for Lebanon
SUA	Suppression of Unlawful Acts Against the Safety of Maritime Navigation
TO	*Teritorijalna odbrana* – Territorial Defence [former Yugoslavia]
TWC	*Trials of War Criminals before the Nürnberg Military Tribunals under Control Council Law no. 10*, 12 vols (Washington, DC: US Govt Printing Office, 1950)
UDHR	Universal Declaration of Human Rights
UN	United Nations
UNCLOS	United Nations Convention on the Law of the Sea
UNGA	United Nations General Assembly
UNICEF	United Nations Children's Fund
UNPROFOR	United Nations Protection Force [former Yugoslavia]
UNSC	United Nations Security Council
UNTAES	United Nations Transitional Administration for Eastern Slavonia, Baranja and Western Sirmium [former Yugoslavia]
UNTS	United Nations Treaty Series
UNWCC	United Nations War Crimes Commission
UPC	*Union des Patriotes Congolais* – Union of Congolese Patriots [DRC]
USC (also, U.S.C.)	United States Code
USCA	United States Code Annotated
VRS	*Vojska Srpske Republike Bosne i Herzegovine*, later *Vojska Republike Srpske* – Army of the Bosnian-Serb Republic [former Yugoslavia]
Werle, *Principles*	G. Werle, *Principles of International Criminal Law* (2nd edn, The Hague: Asser Press, 2009)
Zahar and Sluiter *International Criminal Law*	A. Zahar and G. Sluiter, *International Criminal Law* (Oxford: OUP, 2008)

TABLE OF CASES AND REPORTS

INTERNATIONAL MILITARY TRIBUNAL (NUREMBERG TRIBUNAL)

INTERNATIONAL MILITARY TRIBUNAL FOR THE FAR EAST (TOKYO TRIBUNAL)

ISRAEL

TABLE OF TREATIES AND CONVENTIONS

TABLE OF INTERNATIONAL INSTRUMENTS

TABLE OF STATUTES OF
INTERNATIONAL TRIBUNALS

TABLE OF RULES OF PROCEDURE AND EVIDENCE OF INTERNATIONAL COURTS

TABLE OF NATIONAL LEGISLATION

PART I

SOURCES AND PRINCIPLES OF INTERNATIONAL CRIMINAL LAW

INTRODUCTION

International criminal law is but a branch of public international law, though it shows some unique features. More than any other segment of international law, it simultaneously derives its origins from, and continuously draws upon, *international humanitarian law, human rights law* and *national criminal law*.

International humanitarian law embraces principles and rules designed to regulate warfare both by restraining States in the conduct of armed hostilities and by protecting those persons who do not take part, or no longer take part (having fallen into the hands of the enemy) in combat. Since international criminal law, at its origin, was chiefly concerned with offences committed during armed hostilities in time of war (war crimes), it was only natural for it to build heavily upon international humanitarian rules. Violations of these rules, which normally only generated State responsibility, gradually came to be considered as breaches of law also entailing individual criminal liability. For instance, the indiscriminate bombing of civilians, previously only considered a belligerent State's wrongful act entailing international responsibility of that State vis-à-vis the enemy belligerent, gradually came to be regarded also as a war crime for which those ordering and executing the indiscriminate attack had to bear individual criminal liability.

The description of the prohibited conduct that thus came to be criminalized was to be found in rules of international humanitarian law. Consequently those applying international criminal law had to refer to that body of law, designed to constrain States, to determine the definition and scope of individual crimes.

Human rights law essentially consists of customary rules or principles and international treaties granting fundamental rights to individuals by simultaneously restricting the authority of States over such individuals. It also includes the copious case law of international bodies such as the European Court of Human Rights (ECtHR), the Inter-American Court of Human Rights (IACHR) and the UN Human Rights Committee (HRC). This corpus of legal provisions and decisions has contributed to the development of criminal law in many respects. It has expanded, strengthened or created greater sensitivity to the values (human dignity, the need to safeguard life and limb as far as possible, etc.) to be protected through the imposition of individual criminal responsibility. Furthermore, human rights law lays down the fundamental rights of suspects, accused persons, victims and witnesses. It also sets out the basic safeguards of a fair trial. In short, this increasingly important segment of law has informed the whole area of international criminal law.

In addition, most customary rules of international criminal law have primarily evolved from *municipal* (*domestic intra-State*) *case law* relating to international crimes (chiefly war crimes). This element, as well as the paucity of treaty rules in this field, explain why international criminal law to a great extent results from the gradual *transposition* on to the international level of rules and legal constructs proper to national criminal law or to national trial proceedings.

The grafting of municipal law notions and rules on to international law has not, however, been a smooth process. National legal orders do not contain a uniform regulation of criminal law. On the contrary, they are split into many different systems, from among which two principal ones emerge: that prevailing in common law countries (the UK, the USA, Australia, Canada, many African and Asian countries), and that obtaining in civil law countries, chiefly based on a legal system of Romano-Germanic origin (they include States of continental Europe, such as France, Germany, Italy, Belgium, the countries of Northern Europe such as Norway, Sweden, Denmark, as well as Latin American countries, many Arab countries as well as Asian States including for instance China). The heterogeneous and composite origin of many international rules of both substantive and procedural criminal law, a real patchwork of normative standards, complicates matters, as we shall see.

It follows that international criminal law is essentially a *hybrid* branch of law: it is public international law impregnated with notions, principles and legal constructs derived from national criminal law, international humanitarian law as well as human rights law. However, the recent establishment of international criminal tribunals, and in particular of the ICC (International Criminal Court), has given a stupendous impulse to the evolution of a corpus of international criminal rules proper. It can therefore be safely maintained that we are now heading for the formation of a fully fledged body of law in this area.

Be that as it may, the fact remains that – as stated – international criminal law is a branch of international law. Hence it has to rely on the sources of international law. It follows that the sources of law from which one may derive the relevant rules of international criminal law (i) are *those proper to international law*, and (ii) must be resorted to in the *order of application* dictated by international law.

Consequently, courts can draw upon *primary* sources (treaties and customary law), *secondary* sources (law-making processes envisaged by customary rules or treaty provisions, such as United Nations Security Council resolutions, when for instance an international criminal tribunal has been established by a Security Council resolution), *general principles* of international criminal law or general principles of law, or in the final analysis such *subsidiary* sources as general principles of law recognized by the community of States.

The order of application of such sources may be derived from the structure of the sources of international law, which at present – as far as international criminal law is concerned – is largely codified in Article 21(1) ICCSt.:

The Court shall apply:

(a) In the first place, this Statute, Elements of Crimes and its Rules of Procedure and Evidence;

(b) In the second place, where appropriate, applicable treaties and the principles and rules of international law, including the established principles of the international law of armed conflict;

(c) Failing that, general principles of law derived by the Court from national laws of legal systems of the world including, where appropriate, the national laws of States that would normally exercise jurisdiction over the crime, provided that those principles are not inconsistent with this Statute and with international law and internationally recognized norms and standards.

Hence, courts should first look for treaty rules or rules laid down in such international instruments as binding resolutions of the UN Security Council when these treaty rules or resolutions contain the provisions conferring jurisdiction on the court and setting out the procedure (as is the case with the ICTY and the ICTR). When such rules are lacking or contain gaps, one should resort to customary law or to treaties implicitly or explicitly referred to in the aforementioned rules. When even this set of general or treaty rules is of no avail, one should apply general principles of international criminal law, such as, for example, the principle of non-retroactivity of criminal law or the principle of command responsibility. These principles can be inferred, by a process of induction and generalization, from treaty provisions or customary rules.

When even these principles do not prove helpful, one could rely, as a fallback, on general principles of law (such as the principle of respect for human rights). If one still does not find the applicable rule or, more often, if the rule contains a gap or is at any rate insufficient, one may have resort to general principles of criminal law common to the nations of the world (such as the ban on denial of justice and the doctrine of *res judicata*).

These questions regarding the sources of international criminal law are addressed in the first section of this Part. The second section deals with some of the fundamental principles shaping the work of international and 'hybrid' courts and tribunals: the principle of legality (*nullum crimen sine lege*), the question of immunities for international crimes, and the complex questions related to double jeopardy (*ne bis in idem*) and amnesties.

1

SOURCES OF INTERNATIONAL CRIMINAL LAW

(A) INTERNATIONAL CUSTOM AND THE VALUE OF PRECEDENTS

The two main sources of public international law – custom and treaties – also constitute part of the essential foundation of international criminal law. Treaty practice in the field of the law of armed conflicts has been extensive; however, customary international law, as interpreted and applied by international courts and tribunals, has been pre-eminent in the development of essential aspects of contemporary international criminal law.

Customary international law is the body of international law deriving from the practice of States accompanied by *opinio juris*. *Opinio juris* refers to State compliance with a practice out of a sense of obligation rather than, for instance, to further strategic, economic, political or military interests. State practice should be considered as comprising official acts of States: physical (e.g. battlefield behaviour), normative (national legislation, military manuals), diplomatic (protests, notifications) and judicial (domestic decisions). Such practice must be extensive and representative. The practice of international subjects other than States (e.g. the UN, EU, NATO, ICRC, insurgents) is also considered by international courts and tribunals when ascertaining the existence of rules of customary international law, though this approach is more disputed. The practice of all subjects of international law contributes to the creation of new custom. But constant practice not rooted in awareness of a legal obligation does not amount to custom.

Another more dynamic way of defining custom is that it is nothing more than the general acceptance of the claim, made by one or more subjects of international law, that a certain behaviour is lawful. What happens in reality is that one or more subjects of international law often behave in a certain way, essentially putting forth a claim of what they consider to be the law binding them (and others). Reactions to such claims by the other participants in international relations will determine whether a new rule of customary law is in the making. Thus, carefully ascertaining these trends is essential in establishing whether or not a certain rule has indeed reached the status of custom.

Whatever the exact terms of the definition, one feature of custom in international law relevant to the adjudication of international crimes is that it is unwritten law and is therefore somewhat difficult to establish. Unsurprisingly, therefore, international tribunals have used treaties and other written documents (such as UN resolutions), together with often scant State practice in this field, as evidence of customary international law.

Customary international law is relevant in international criminal proceedings because a founding statute of a tribunal will either refer to custom as a source (e.g. stating that a court has jurisdiction over 'violations of the laws or customs of war') or will be silent on a certain matter. In such instances judges will have to fill in the gaps left in the Statute by referring to customary rules. At the post-World War II tribunals and the ICTY and ICTR, where violations of the laws or customs of war were not identified in detail by the draftsmen, the judges had to identify the substantive rules related to crimes and individual criminal responsibility in custom. When treaty law is silent on specific issues raised during international criminal proceedings, judges will have to resort to custom with a view to avoiding a breach of the *nullum crimen sine lege* principle. Since the *nullum crimen* principle stands for the proposition that there can be no conviction without criminal provisions already existing at the time of the offence, the claims of the prosecuting authorities must be checked against treaties or customary rules existing at the time that the accused is alleged to have committed the crime.

Much of this section is devoted to introducing how the ICTY – the first international criminal tribunal since the World War-II era tribunals and undoubtedly the most important tribunal in developing and filling in the details of contemporary international law – has set out to do just that and, in doing so, has developed a doctrine of precedents. This is merely an introduction: much of the discussion in each section dealing with crimes and modes of liability will still be devoted to topics related to custom. In fact, pronouncements of international tribunals on the elements of the crimes and on other aspects relevant to their daily activities have greatly contributed to clarifying, and at times crystallizing, whole areas of international criminal law. As the Canadian Supreme Court stated '[t]hese tribunals have generated a unique body of authority which cogently reviews the sources, evolution and application of customary international law' (*Mugesera* v. *Canada (Minister of Citizenship and Immigration)* [2005] 2 S.C.R. 100, 2005 SCC 40).

The second part of this section will highlight the reasoning behind the adoption of a sort of *stare decisis* rule by the ICTY and the ICTR.

Two remarks are necessary in relation to the ICC. First, although custom is listed as a source of law in Article 21 of the ICCSt., the ICC has jurisdiction over crimes listed in the Statute and committed only after its entry into force, so the role of custom in adjudicating cases before the ICC is likely to be somewhat limited. Moreover, the ICCSt. (coupled with the Elements of Crimes) is rather detailed in relation to the elements of the crimes and the law of individual criminal responsibility. It follows that ICC judges will be less likely to refer to custom to ascertain the contours of crimes or individual criminal responsibility, as the ICTY and ICTR judges have routinely been required to do.

Second, although no rule of precedent is enshrined in the ICCSt. – nor have the first ICC decisions squarely addressed this issue – it is likely that a sort of rule of *stare decisis*, modelled upon that of the ICTY and ICTR, will gradually develop in practice in order to ensure uniformity of legal interpretation.

Cases

ICTY, Prosecutor *v.* Tadić, *Appeals Chamber, Jurisdiction Decision, 2 October 1995*

Duško Tadić was a reserve police officer in the municipality of Prijedor, in Bosnia-Herzegovina. In May and June 1992, during the ethnic cleansing of areas of Bosnia-Herzegovina that had fallen under the control of Bosnian Serb forces, Tadić participated in the collection and forced transfer of civilians. In February 1994, he was arrested in Germany and, upon request of the ICTY, transferred in April 1995 to become the first accused before the tribunal. During the preliminary phases of his proceedings, the Appeals Chamber issued a landmark decision dealing with various jurisdictional challenges brought by Tadić's lawyers. One of the issues was whether, at the time of Tadić's crimes in the early 1990s, customary international law contemplated individual responsibility for violations of the laws or customs of war in non-international armed conflicts. Article 3 of the ICTYSt. conferred jurisdiction 'to prosecute persons violating the laws or customs of war'. Tadić argued that since Article 3 was based on the 1907 Hague Convention (IV) Respecting the Laws and Customs of War on Land and the Regulations annexed to that Convention, as well as the Nuremberg Tribunal's interpretation of those Regulations – all of which are instruments regulating *interstate* armed conflict – Article 3 could not confer jurisdiction on the ICTY to adjudicate alleged violations stemming from what Tadić characterized as an *internal* conflict in the former Yugoslavia. The reasoning by the Appeals Chamber is instructive of the modalities that international courts use to ascertain custom.

(iii) Customary Rules of International Humanitarian Law Governing Internal Armed Conflicts

A. General

96. Whenever armed violence erupted in the international community, in traditional international law the legal response was based on a stark dichotomy: belligerency or insurgency. The former category applied to armed conflicts between sovereign States (unless there was recognition of belligerency in a civil war), while the latter applied to armed violence breaking out in the territory of a sovereign State. Correspondingly, international law treated the two classes of conflict in a markedly different way: interstate wars were regulated by a whole body of international legal rules, governing both the conduct of hostilities and the protection of persons not participating (or no longer participating) in armed violence (civilians, the wounded, the sick, shipwrecked, prisoners of war). By contrast, there were very few international rules governing civil commotion, for States preferred to regard internal strife as rebellion, mutiny and treason coming within the purview of national criminal law and, by the same token, to exclude any possible intrusion by other States into their own domestic jurisdiction. This dichotomy was clearly sovereignty-oriented and reflected the traditional configuration of the international community, based on the coexistence of sovereign States more inclined to look after their own interests than community concerns or humanitarian demands.

97. Since the 1930s, however, the aforementioned distinction has gradually become more and more blurred, and international legal rules have increasingly emerged or have been agreed upon to regulate internal armed conflict. There exist various reasons for this development. First, civil wars have become more frequent, not only because technological progress has made it easier for groups of individuals to have access to weaponry but also on account of increasing tension, whether ideological, inter-ethnic or economic; as a consequence the international community can no longer turn a blind eye to the legal regime of such wars. Secondly, internal armed conflicts have become more and more cruel and protracted, involving the whole population of the State where they occur: the all-out resort to armed violence has taken on such a magnitude that the difference with international wars has increasingly dwindled (suffice to think of the Spanish civil war, in 1936–39, of the civil war in the Congo, in 1960–1968, the Biafran conflict in Nigeria, 1967–70, the civil strife in Nicaragua, in 1981–1990 or El Salvador, 1980–1993). Thirdly, the large-scale nature of civil strife, coupled with the increasing interdependence of States in the world community, has made it more and more difficult for

third States to remain aloof: the economic, political and ideological interests of third States have brought about direct or indirect involvement of third States in this category of conflict, thereby requiring that international law take greater account of their legal regime in order to prevent, as much as possible, adverse spill-over effects. Fourthly, the impetuous development and propagation in the international community of human rights doctrines, particularly after the adoption of the Universal Declaration of Human Rights in 1948, has brought about significant changes in international law, notably in the approach to problems besetting the world community. A State-sovereignty-oriented approach has been gradually supplanted by a human-being-oriented approach. Gradually the maxim of Roman law *hominum causa omne jus constitutum est* (all law is created for the benefit of human beings) has gained a firm foothold in the international community as well. It follows that in the area of armed conflict the distinction between interstate wars and civil wars is losing its value as far as human beings are concerned. Why protect civilians from belligerent violence, or ban rape, torture or the wanton destruction of hospitals, churches, museums or private property, as well as proscribe weapons causing unnecessary suffering when two sovereign States are engaged in war, and yet refrain from enacting the same bans or providing the same protection when armed violence has erupted "only" within the territory of a sovereign State? If international law, while of course duly safeguarding the legitimate interests of States, must gradually turn to the protection of human beings, it is only natural that the aforementioned dichotomy should gradually lose its weight.

98. The emergence of international rules governing internal strife has occurred at two different levels: at the level of customary law and at that of treaty law. Two bodies of rules have thus crystallised, which are by no means conflicting or inconsistent, but instead mutually support and supplement each other. Indeed, the interplay between these two sets of rules is such that some treaty rules have gradually become part of customary law. This holds true for common Article 3 of the 1949 Geneva Conventions, as was authoritatively held by the International Court of Justice (Nicaragua Case, at para. 218), but also applies to Article 19 of the Hague Convention for the Protection of Cultural Property in the Event of Armed Conflict of 14 May 1954, and, as we shall show below (para. 117), to the core of Additional Protocol II of 1977.

99. Before pointing to some principles and rules of customary law that have emerged in the international community for the purpose of regulating civil strife, a word of caution on the law-making process in the law of armed conflict is necessary. When attempting to ascertain State practice with a view to establishing the existence of a customary rule or a general principle, it is difficult, if not impossible, to pinpoint the actual behaviour of the troops in the field for the purpose of establishing whether they in fact comply with, or disregard, certain standards of behaviour. This examination is rendered extremely difficult by the fact that not only is access to the theatre of military operations normally refused to independent observers (often even to the ICRC) but information on the actual conduct of hostilities is withheld by the parties to the conflict; what is worse, often recourse is had to misinformation with a view to misleading the enemy as well as public opinion and foreign Governments. In appraising the formation of customary rules or general principles one should therefore be aware that, on account of the inherent nature of this subject-matter, reliance must primarily be placed on such elements as official pronouncements of States, military manuals and judicial decisions.

B. Principal Rules

100. The first rules that evolved in this area were aimed at protecting the civilian population from the hostilities. As early as the Spanish Civil War (1936–39), State practice revealed a tendency to disregard the distinction between international and internal wars and to apply certain general principles of humanitarian law, at least to those internal conflicts that

constituted large-scale civil wars. The Spanish Civil War had elements of both an internal and an international armed conflict. Significantly, both the republican Government and third States refused to recognize the insurgents as belligerents. They nonetheless insisted that certain rules concerning international armed conflict applied. Among rules deemed applicable were the prohibition of the intentional bombing of civilians, the rule forbidding attacks on non-military objectives, and the rule regarding required precautions when attacking military objectives. Thus, for example, on 23 March 1938, Prime Minister Chamberlain explained the British protest against the bombing of Barcelona as follows:

"The rules of international law as to what constitutes a military objective are undefined and pending the conclusion of the examination of this question [...] I am not in a position to make any statement on the subject. The one definite rule of international law, however, is that the direct and deliberate bombing of non-combatants is in all circumstances illegal, and His Majesty's Government's protest was based on information which led them to the conclusion that the bombardment of Barcelona, carried on apparently at random and without special aim at military objectives, was in fact of this nature." (333 House of Commons Debates, col. 1177 (23 March 1938).)

More generally, replying to questions by Member of Parliament Noel-Baker concerning the civil war in Spain, on 21 June 1938 the Prime Minister stated the following:

"I think we may say that there are, at any rate, three rules of international law or three principles of international law which are as applicable to warfare from the air as they are to war at sea or on land. In the first place, it is against international law to bomb civilians as such and to make deliberate attacks upon civilian populations. That is undoubtedly a violation of international law. In the second place, targets which are aimed at from the air must be legitimate military objectives and must be capable of identification. In the third place, reasonable care must be taken in attacking those military objectives so that by carelessness a civilian population in the neighbourhood is not bombed." (337 House of Commons Debates, cols. 937–38 (21 June 1938).)

101. Such views were reaffirmed in a number of contemporaneous resolutions by the Assembly of the League of Nations, and in the declarations and agreements of the warring parties. [...]

102. Subsequent State practice indicates that the Spanish Civil War was not exceptional in bringing about the extension of some general principles of the laws of warfare to internal armed conflict. While the rules that evolved as a result of the Spanish Civil War were intended to protect civilians finding themselves in the theatre of hostilities, rules designed to protect those who do not (or no longer) take part in hostilities emerged after World War II. In 1947, instructions were issued to the Chinese "peoples' liberation army" by Mao Tse-Tung who instructed them not to "kill or humiliate any of Chiang Kai-Shek's army officers and men who lay down their arms." (*Manifesto of the Chinese People's Liberation Army,* in Mao Tse-Tung, 4 Selected Works (1961) 147, at 151.) He also instructed the insurgents, among other things, not to "ill-treat captives", "damage crops" or "take liberties with women." (*On the Reissue of the Three Main Rules of Discipline and the Eight Points for Attention – Instruction of the General Headquarters of the Chinese People's Liberation Army,* in *id.,* 155.)

In an important subsequent development, States specified certain minimum mandatory rules applicable to internal armed conflicts in common Article 3 of the Geneva Conventions of 1949. The International Court of Justice has confirmed that these rules reflect "elementary considerations of humanity" applicable under customary international law to any armed conflict, whether it is of an internal or international character (Nicaragua Case, at para. 218). Therefore, at least with respect to the minimum rules in common Article 3, the character of the conflict is irrelevant.

103. Common Article 3 contains not only the substantive rules governing internal armed conflict but also a procedural mechanism inviting parties to internal conflicts to agree to abide by the rest of the Geneva Conventions. As in the current conflicts in the former Yugoslavia, parties to a number of internal armed conflicts have availed themselves of this procedure to bring the law of international armed conflicts into force with respect to their internal hostilities. For example, in the 1967 conflict in Yemen, both the Royalists and the President of the Republic agreed to abide by the essential rules of the Geneva Conventions. Such undertakings reflect an understanding that certain fundamental rules should apply regardless of the nature of the conflict.

104. Agreements made pursuant to common Article 3 are not the only vehicle through which international humanitarian law has been brought to bear on internal armed conflicts. In several cases reflecting customary adherence to basic principles in internal conflicts, the warring parties have unilaterally committed to abide by international humanitarian law.

105. As a notable example, we cite the conduct of the Democratic Republic of the Congo in its civil war. In a public statement issued on 21 October 1964, the Prime Minister made the following commitment regarding the conduct of hostilities:

"For humanitarian reasons, and with a view to reassuring, in so far as necessary, the civilian population which might fear that it is in danger, the Congolese Government wishes to state that the Congolese Air Force will limit its action to military objectives.

In this matter, the Congolese Government desires not only to protect human lives but also to respect the Geneva Convention [sic]. It also expects the rebels – and makes an urgent appeal to them to that effect – to act in the same manner.

As a practical measure, the Congolese Government suggests that International Red Cross observers come to check on the extent to which the Geneva Convention [sic] is being respected, particularly in the matter of the treatment of prisoners and the ban against taking hostages." (Public Statement of Prime Minister of the Democratic Republic of the Congo (21 Oct. 1964), reprinted in American Journal of International Law (1965) 614, at 616.)

This statement indicates acceptance of rules regarding the conduct of internal hostilities, and, in particular, the principle that civilians must not be attacked. Like State practice in the Spanish Civil War, the Congolese Prime Minister's statement confirms the status of this rule as part of the customary law of internal armed conflicts. Indeed, this statement must not be read as an offer or a promise to undertake obligations previously not binding; rather, it aimed at reaffirming the existence of such obligations and spelled out the notion that the Congolese Government would fully comply with them.

106. A further confirmation can be found in the "Operational Code of Conduct for Nigerian Armed Forces", issued in July 1967 by the Head of the Federal Military Government, Major General Y. Gowon, to regulate the conduct of military operations of the Federal Army against the rebels. In this "Operational Code of Conduct", it was stated that, to repress the rebellion in Biafra, the Federal troops were duty-bound to respect the rules of the Geneva Conventions and in addition were to abide by a set of rules protecting civilians and civilian objects in the theatre of military operations. (See A.H.M. Kirk-Greene, 1 Crisis and Conflict in Nigeria, A Documentary Sourcebook 1966–1969, 455–57 (1971).) This "Operational Code of Conduct" shows that in a large-scale and protracted civil war the central authorities, while refusing to grant recognition of belligerency, deemed it necessary to apply not only the provisions of the Geneva Conventions designed to protect civilians in the hands of the enemy and captured combatants, but also general rules on the conduct of hostilities that are normally applicable in international conflicts. It should be noted that the code was actually applied by the Nigerian

authorities. Thus, for instance, it is reported that on 27 June 1968, two officers of the Nigerian Army were publicly executed by a firing squad in Benin City in Mid-Western Nigeria for the murder of four civilians near Asaba (see New Nigerian, 28 June 1968, at 1). In addition, reportedly on 3 September 1968, a Nigerian Lieutenant was court-martialled, sentenced to death and executed by a firing squad at Port-Harcourt for killing a rebel Biafran soldier who had surrendered to Federal troops near Aba. (See Daily Times, Nigeria, 3 September 1968, at 1; Daily Times, Nigeria, 4 September 1968, at 1.)

This attitude of the Nigerian authorities confirms the trend initiated with the Spanish Civil War and referred to above (see paras. 101–102), whereby the central authorities of a State where civil strife has broken out prefer to withhold recognition of belligerency but, at the same time, extend to the conflict the bulk of the body of legal rules concerning conflicts between States.

107. A more recent instance of this tendency can be found in the stand taken in 1988 by the rebels (the FMLN) in El Salvador, when it became clear that the Government was not ready to apply the Additional Protocol II it had previously ratified. The FMLN undertook to respect both common Article 3 and Protocol II:

"The FMLN shall ensure that its combat methods comply with the provisions of common Article 3 of the Geneva Conventions and Additional Protocol II, take into consideration the needs of the majority of the population, and defend their fundamental freedoms." (FMLN, *La legitimidad de nuestros metodos de lucha,* Secretaria de promocion y proteccion de lo Derechos Humanos del FMLN, El Salvador, 10 Octobre 1988, at 89; unofficial translation.)

108. In addition to the behaviour of belligerent States, Governments and insurgents, other factors have been instrumental in bringing about the formation of the customary rules at issue. [. . .]

109. [. . .] [T]he ICRC has promoted and facilitated the extension of general principles of humanitarian law to internal armed conflict. The practical results the ICRC has thus achieved in inducing compliance with international humanitarian law ought therefore to be regarded as an element of actual international practice; this is an element that has been conspicuously instrumental in the emergence or crystallization of customary rules.

110. The application of certain rules of war in both internal and international armed conflicts is corroborated by two General Assembly resolutions on "Respect of human rights in armed conflict." The first one, resolution 2444, was unanimously adopted in 1968 by the General Assembly: "[r]ecognizing the necessity of applying basic humanitarian principles in all armed conflicts," the General Assembly "affirm[ed]"

"the following principles for observance by all governmental and other authorities responsible for action in armed conflict: (a) That the right of the parties to a conflict to adopt means of injuring the enemy is not unlimited; (b) That it is prohibited to launch attacks against the civilian populations as such; (c) That distinction must be made at all times between persons taking part in the hostilities and members of the civilian population to the effect that the latter be spared as much as possible." (G.A. Res. 2444, U.N. GAOR., 23rd Session, Supp. No. 18 U.N. Doc. A/7218 (1968).)

It should be noted that, before the adoption of the resolution, the United States representative stated in the Third Committee that the principles proclaimed in the resolution "constituted a reaffirmation of existing international law" (U.N. GAOR, 3rd Comm., 23rd Sess., 1634th Mtg., at 2, U.N. Doc. A/C.3/SR.1634 (1968)). This view was reiterated in 1972, when the United States Department of Defence pointed out that the resolution was "declaratory of existing customary international law" or, in other words, "a correct restatement" of "principles of customary international law." (See 67 *American Journal of International Law* (1973), at 122, 124.)

111. Elaborating on the principles laid down in resolution 2444, in 1970 the General Assembly unanimously [with eight abstentions] adopted resolution 2675 on "Basic principles for the protection of civilian populations in armed conflicts." In introducing this resolution, which it co-sponsored, to the Third Committee, Norway explained that as used in the resolution, "the term 'armed conflicts' was meant to cover armed conflicts of all kinds, an important point, since the provisions of the Geneva Conventions and the Hague Regulations did not extend to all conflicts." (U.N. GAOR, 3rd Comm., 25th Sess., 1785th Mtg., at 281, U.N. Doc. A/C.3/ SR.1785 (1970); *see also* U.N. GAOR, 25th Sess., 1922nd Mtg., at 3, U.N. Doc. A/PV.1922 (1970) (statement of the representative of Cuba during the Plenary discussion of resolution 2675).) The resolution stated the following:

"Bearing in mind the need for measures to ensure the better protection of human rights in armed conflicts of all types, [. . . the General Assembly] Affirms the following basic principles for the protection of civilian populations in armed conflicts, without prejudice to their future elaboration within the framework of progressive development of the international law of armed conflict:

1. Fundamental human rights, as accepted in international law and laid down in international instruments, continue to apply fully in situations of armed conflict.

2. In the conduct of military operations during armed conflicts, a distinction must be made at all times between persons actively taking part in the hostilities and civilian populations.

3. In the conduct of military operations, every effort should be made to spare civilian populations from the ravages of war, and all necessary precautions should be taken to avoid injury, loss or damage to civilian populations.

4. Civilian populations as such should not be the object of military operations.

5. Dwellings and other installations that are used only by civilian populations should not be the object of military operations.

6. Places or areas designated for the sole protection of civilians, such as hospital zones or similar refuges, should not be the object of military operations.

7. Civilian populations, or individual members thereof, should not be the object of reprisals, forcible transfers or other assaults on their integrity.

8. The provision of international relief to civilian populations is in conformity with the humanitarian principles of the Charter of the United Nations, the Universal Declaration of Human Rights and other international instruments in the field of human rights. The Declaration of Principles for International Humanitarian Relief to the Civilian Population in Disaster Situations, as laid down in resolution XXVI adopted by the twenty-first International Conference of the Red Cross, shall apply in situations of armed conflict, and all parties to a conflict should make every effort to facilitate this application." (G.A. Res. 2675, U.N. GAOR., 25th Sess., Supp. No. 28 U.N. Doc. A/8028 (1970).)

112. Together, these resolutions played a twofold role: they were declaratory of the principles of customary international law regarding the protection of civilian populations and property in armed conflicts of any kind and, at the same time, were intended to promote the adoption of treaties on the matter, designed to specify and elaborate upon such principles.

113. That international humanitarian law includes principles or general rules protecting civilians from hostilities in the course of internal armed conflicts has also been stated on a number of occasions by groups of States. For instance, with regard to Liberia, the (then) twelve Member States of the European Community, in a declaration of 2 August 1990, stated:

"In particular, the Community and its Member States call upon the parties in the conflict, in conformity with international law and the most basic humanitarian principles, to safeguard from violence the embassies and places of refuge such as churches, hospitals, etc., where defenceless civilians have sought shelter." (6 European Political Cooperation Documentation Bulletin, at 295 (1990).)

114. A similar, albeit more general, appeal was made by the Security Council in its resolution 788 (in operative paragraph 5 it called upon "all parties to the conflict and all others concerned to respect strictly the provisions of international humanitarian law") (S.C. Res. 788 (19 November 1992)), an appeal reiterated in resolution 972 (S.C. Res. 972 (13 January 1995)) and in resolution 1001 (S.C. Res. 1001 (30 June 1995)).

Appeals to the parties to a civil war to respect the principles of international humanitarian law were also made by the Security Council in the case of Somalia and Georgia. As for Somalia, mention can be made of resolution 794 in which the Security Council in particular condemned, as a breach of international humanitarian law, "the deliberate impeding of the delivery of food and medical supplies essential for the survival of the civilian population") (S.C. Res. 794 (3 December 1992)) and resolution 814 (S.C. Res. 814 (26 March 1993)). As for Georgia, see Resolution 993, (in which the Security Council reaffirmed "the need for the parties to comply with international humanitarian law") (S.C. Res. 993 (12 May 1993)). [. . .]

116. It must be stressed that, in the statements and resolutions referred to above, the European Union and the United Nations Security Council did not mention common Article 3 of the Geneva Conventions, but adverted to "international humanitarian law", thus clearly articulating the view that there exists a corpus of general principles and norms on internal armed conflict embracing common Article 3 but having a much greater scope.

117. Attention must also be drawn to Additional Protocol II to the Geneva Conventions. Many provisions of this Protocol can now be regarded as declaratory of existing rules or as having crystallised emerging rules of customary law or else as having been strongly instrumental in their evolution as general principles.

This proposition is confirmed by the views expressed by a number of States. [. . .]

118. That at present there exist general principles governing the conduct of hostilities (the so-called "Hague Law") applicable to international and internal armed conflicts is also borne out by national military manuals. Thus, for instance, the German Military Manual of 1992 provides that:

"Members of the German army, like their Allies, shall comply with the rules of international humanitarian law in the conduct of military operations in all armed conflicts, whatever the nature of such conflicts." (Humanitäres Völkerrecht in bewaffneten Konflikten – Handbuch, August 1992, DSK AV207320065, at para. 211 in fine; unofficial translation.)

119. So far we have pointed to the formation of general rules or principles designed to protect civilians or civilian objects from the hostilities or, more generally, to protect those who do not (or no longer) take active part in hostilities. We shall now briefly show how the gradual extension to internal armed conflict of rules and principles concerning international wars has also occurred as regards means and methods of warfare. As the Appeals Chamber has pointed out above (see para. 110), a general principle has evolved limiting the right of the parties to conflicts "to adopt means of injuring the enemy." The same holds true for a more general principle, laid down in the so-called Turku Declaration of Minimum Humanitarian Standards of 1990, and revised in 1994, namely Article 5, paragraph 3, whereby "[w]eapons or other material or methods prohibited in international armed conflicts must not be employed in any circumstances." (Declaration of Minimum Humanitarian Standards, reprinted in Report of the Sub-Commission on Prevention of Discrimination and Protection of Minorities on its Forty-sixth Session, Commission on Human Rights, 51st Sess., Provisional Agenda Item 19, at 4, U.N. Doc. E/CN.4/1995/116 (1995).) It should be noted that this Declaration, emanating from a group of distinguished experts in human rights and humanitarian law, has been

indirectly endorsed by the Conference on Security and Cooperation in Europe in its Budapest Document of 1994 (Conference on Security and Cooperation in Europe, Budapest Document 1994: Towards Genuine Partnership in a New Era, para. 34 (1994)) and in 1995 by the United Nations Sub-Commission on Prevention of Discrimination and Protection of Minorities (*Report of the Sub-Commission on Prevention of Discrimination and Protection of Minorities on its Forty-sixth Session,* Commission on Human Rights, 51st Sess., Agenda Item 19, at 1, U.N. Doc. E/CN.4/1995/L.33 (1995)).

Indeed, elementary considerations of humanity and common sense make it preposterous that the use by States of weapons prohibited in armed conflicts between themselves be allowed when States try to put down rebellion by their own nationals on their own territory. What is inhumane, and consequently proscribed, in international wars, cannot but be inhumane and inadmissible in civil strife.

120. This fundamental concept has brought about the gradual formation of general rules concerning specific weapons, rules which extend to civil strife the sweeping prohibitions relating to international armed conflicts. By way of illustration, we will mention chemical weapons. [. . .]

125. State practice shows that general principles of customary international law have evolved with regard to internal armed conflict also in areas relating to methods of warfare. In addition to what has been stated above, with regard to the ban on attacks on civilians in the theatre of hostilities, mention can be made of the prohibition of perfidy. Thus, for instance, in a case brought before Nigerian courts, the Supreme Court of Nigeria held that rebels must not feign civilian status while engaging in military operations. (*See* Pius Nwaoga v. The State, 52 *International Law Reports*, 494, at 496–97 (Nig. S. Ct. 1972).)

126. The emergence of the aforementioned general rules on internal armed conflicts does not imply that internal strife is regulated by general international law in all its aspects. Two particular limitations may be noted: (i) only a number of rules and principles governing international armed conflicts have gradually been extended to apply to internal conflicts; and (ii) this extension has not taken place in the form of a full and mechanical transplant of those rules to internal conflicts; rather, the general essence of those rules, and not the detailed regulation they may contain, has become applicable to internal conflicts. (On these and other limitations of international humanitarian law governing civil strife, see the important message of the Swiss Federal Council to the Swiss Chambers on the ratification of the two 1977 Additional Protocols (38 *Annuaire Suisse de Droit International* (1982) 137 at 145–49).)

127. Notwithstanding these limitations, it cannot be denied that customary rules have developed to govern internal strife. These rules, as specifically identified in the preceding discussion, cover such areas as protection of civilians from hostilities, in particular from indiscriminate attacks, protection of civilian objects, in particular cultural property, protection of all those who do not (or no longer) take active part in hostilities, as well as prohibition of means of warfare proscribed in international armed conflicts and ban of certain methods of conducting hostilities.

(iv) Individual Criminal Responsibility In Internal Armed Conflict

128. Even if customary international law includes certain basic principles applicable to both internal and international armed conflicts, Appellant argues that such prohibitions do not entail individual criminal responsibility when breaches are committed in internal armed conflicts; these provisions cannot, therefore, fall within the scope of the International Tribunal's jurisdiction. It is true that, for example, common Article 3 of the Geneva Conventions contains no explicit reference to criminal liability for violation of its provisions. Faced with similar claims with respect to the various agreements and conventions that formed the basis of its jurisdiction, the International Military Tribunal at Nuremberg concluded that a finding of individual criminal responsibility is not barred by the absence of treaty provisions on punishment

of breaches. (See The Trial of Major War Criminals: Proceedings of the International Military Tribunal Sitting at Nuremberg Germany, Part 22, at 445, 467 (1950).) The Nuremberg Tribunal considered a number of factors relevant to its conclusion that the authors of particular prohibitions incur individual responsibility: the clear and unequivocal recognition of the rules of warfare in international law and State practice indicating an intention to criminalize the prohibition, including statements by government officials and international organizations, as well as punishment of violations by national courts and military tribunals (id., at 445–47, 467). Where these conditions are met, individuals must be held criminally responsible, because, as the Nuremberg Tribunal concluded:

"[c]rimes against international law are committed by men, not by abstract entities, and only by punishing individuals who commit such crimes can the provisions of international law be enforced." (id., at 447.)

129. Applying the foregoing criteria to the violations at issue here, we have no doubt that they entail individual criminal responsibility, regardless of whether they are committed in internal or international armed conflicts. Principles and rules of humanitarian law reflect "elementary considerations of humanity" widely recognized as the mandatory minimum for conduct in armed conflicts of any kind. No one can doubt the gravity of the acts at issue, nor the interest of the international community in their prohibition.

130. Furthermore, many elements of international practice show that States intend to criminalize serious breaches of customary rules and principles [in] internal conflicts. As mentioned above, during the Nigerian Civil War, both members of the Federal Army and rebels were brought before Nigerian courts and tried for violations of principles of international humanitarian law (see paras. 106 and 125).

131. Breaches of common Article 3 are clearly, and beyond any doubt, regarded as punishable by the Military Manual of Germany (Humanitäres Völkerrecht in bewaffneten Konflikten – Handbuch, August 1992, DSK AV2073200065, at para. 1209) (unofficial translation), which includes among the "grave breaches of international humanitarian law", "criminal offences" against persons protected by common Article 3, such as "wilful killing, mutilation, torture or inhumane treatment including biological experiments, wilfully causing great suffering, serious injury to body or health, taking of hostages", as well as "the fact of impeding a fair and regular trial". (Interestingly, a previous edition of the German Military Manual did not contain any such provision. See Kriegsvölkerrecht – Allgemeine Bestimmungen des Kriegführungsrechts und Landkriegsrecht, ZDv 15–10, March 1961, para. 12; Kriegsvölkerrecht – Allgemeine Bestimmungen des Humanitätsrechts, ZDv 15/5, August 1959, paras. 15–16, 30–2.) Furthermore, the "Interim Law of Armed Conflict Manual" of New Zealand, of 1992, provides that "while non-application [i.e. breaches of common Article 3] would appear to render those responsible liable to trial for 'war crimes', trials would be held under national criminal law, since no 'war' would be in existence" (New Zealand Defence Force Directorate of Legal Services, DM (1992) at 112, Interim Law of Armed Conflict Manual, para. 1807, 8). The relevant provisions of the manual of the United States (Department of the Army, The Law of Land Warfare, Department of the Army Field Manual, FM 27–10, (1956), at paras. 11 & 499) may also lend themselves to the interpretation that "war crimes", i.e., "every violation of the law of war", include infringement of common Article 3. A similar interpretation might be placed on the British Manual of 1958 (War Office, The Law of War on Land, Being Part III of the Manual of Military Law (1958), at para. 626).

132. Attention should also be drawn to national legislation designed to implement the Geneva Conventions, some of which go so far as to make it possible for national courts to try persons responsible for violations of rules concerning internal armed conflicts. This holds true for the Criminal Code of the Socialist Federal Republic of Yugoslavia, of 1990, as amended

for the purpose of making the 1949 Geneva Conventions applicable at the national criminal level. Article 142 (on war crimes against the civilian population) and Article 143 (on war crimes against the wounded and the sick) expressly apply "at the time of war, armed conflict or occupation"; this would seem to imply that they also apply to internal armed conflicts. (Socialist Federal Republic of Yugoslavia, Federal Criminal Code, arts. 142–43 (1990).) (It should be noted that by a decree having force of law, of 11 April 1992, the Republic of Bosnia and Herzegovina has adopted that Criminal Code, subject to some amendments.) (2 Official Gazette of the Republic of Bosnia and Herzegovina 98 (11 April 1992) (translation).) Furthermore, on 26 December 1978 a law was passed by the Yugoslav Parliament to implement the two Additional Protocols of 1977 (Socialist Federal Republic of Yugoslavia, Law of Ratification of the Geneva Protocols, Medunarodni Ugovori, at 1083 (26 December 1978)). As a result, by virtue of Article 210 of the Yugoslav Constitution, those two Protocols are "directly applicable" by the courts of Yugoslavia. (Constitution of the Socialist Federal Republic of Yugoslavia, art. 210.) Without any ambiguity, a Belgian law enacted on 16 June 1993 for the implementation of the 1949 Geneva Conventions and the two Additional Protocols provides that Belgian courts have jurisdiction to adjudicate breaches of Additional Protocol II to the Geneva Conventions relating to victims of non-international armed conflicts. Article 1 of this law provides that a series of "grave breaches" (infractions graves) of the four Geneva Conventions and the two Additional Protocols, listed in the same Article 1, "constitute international law crimes" ([c]onstituent des crimes de droit international) within the jurisdiction of Belgian criminal courts (Article 7). (*Loi du 16 juin 1993 relative à la répression des infractions graves aux Conventions internationales de Genève du 12 août 1949 et aux Protocoles I et II du 8 juin 1977, additionnels à ces Conventions,* Moniteur Belge, (5 August 1993).)

133. Of great relevance to the formation of *opinio juris* to the effect that violations of general international humanitarian law governing internal armed conflicts entail the criminal responsibility of those committing or ordering those violations are certain resolutions unanimously adopted by the Security Council. Thus, for instance, in two resolutions on Somalia, where a civil strife was under way, the Security Council unanimously condemned breaches of humanitarian law and stated that the authors of such breaches or those who had ordered their commission would be held "individually responsible" for them. (See S.C. Res. 794 (3 December 1992); S.C. Res. 814 (26 March 1993).)

134. All of these factors confirm that customary international law imposes criminal liability for serious violations of common Article 3, as supplemented by other general principles and rules on the protection of victims of internal armed conflict, and for breaching certain fundamental principles and rules regarding means and methods of combat in civil strife.

135. It should be added that, in so far as it applies to offences committed in the former Yugoslavia, the notion that serious violations of international humanitarian law governing internal armed conflicts entail individual criminal responsibility is also fully warranted from the point of view of substantive justice and equity. As pointed out above (*see* para. 132) such violations were punishable under the Criminal Code of the Socialist Federal Republic of Yugoslavia and the law implementing the two Additional Protocols of 1977. The same violations have been made punishable in the Republic of Bosnia and Herzegovina by virtue of the decree-law of 11 April 1992. Nationals of the former Yugoslavia as well as, at present, those of Bosnia-Herzegovina were therefore aware, or should have been aware, that they were amenable to the jurisdiction of their national criminal courts in cases of violation of international humanitarian law.

136. It is also fitting to point out that the parties to certain of the agreements concerning the conflict in Bosnia-Herzegovina, made under the auspices of the ICRC, clearly undertook to punish those responsible for violations of international humanitarian law. Thus, Article 5, paragraph 2, of the aforementioned Agreement of 22 May 1992 provides that:

"Each party undertakes, when it is informed, in particular by the ICRC, of any allegation of violations of international humanitarian law, to open an enquiry promptly and pursue it conscientiously, and to take the necessary steps to put an end to the alleged violations or prevent their recurrence and to punish those responsible in accordance with the law in force". (Agreement No. 1, art. 5, para. 2 (Emphasis added).)

Furthermore, the Agreement of 1st October 1992 provides in Article 3, paragraph 1, that

"All prisoners not accused of, or sentenced for, grave breaches of International Humanitarian Law as defined in Article 50 of the First, Article 51 of the Second, Article 130 of the Third and Article 147 of the Fourth Geneva Convention, as well as in Article 85 of Additional Protocol I, will be unilaterally and unconditionally released." (Agreement No. 2, 1 October 1992, art. 3, para. 1.)

This provision, which is supplemented by Article 4, paragraphs 1 and 2 of the Agreement, implies that all those responsible for offences contrary to the Geneva provisions referred to in that Article must be brought to trial. As both Agreements referred to in the above paragraphs were clearly intended to apply in the context of an internal armed conflict, the conclusion is warranted that the conflicting parties in Bosnia-Herzegovina had clearly agreed at the level of treaty law to make punishable breaches of international humanitarian law occurring within the framework of that conflict.

(v) Conclusion

137. In the light of the intent of the Security Council and the logical and systematic interpretation of Article 3 as well as customary international law, the Appeals Chamber concludes that, under Article 3, the International Tribunal has jurisdiction over the acts alleged in the indictment, regardless of whether they occurred within an internal or an international armed conflict. Thus, to the extent that Appellant's challenge to jurisdiction under Article 3 is based on the nature of the underlying conflict, the motion must be denied.

....

ICTY, Prosecutor v. Kupreškić et al., Trial Chamber, Judgment of 14 January 2000

Kupreškić involved charges against six Bosnian Croats that they helped prepare, and participated in, an attack on Bosnian Muslims in the area of the Ahmići-Šantići village (Lašva River Valley) in April 1993. The Defence argued, inter alia, that the Muslim population in Ahmići-Šantići was not civilian, since it encompassed persons who had previously taken part in the hostilities or had in any event taken up arms. Therefore, the attacks were justified militarily and civilian deaths were a form of collateral damage. The Trial Chamber discussed the principle of distinction between military targets and civilians or civilian objects as a rule of international customary law, the need to avoid needless injury to civilians and the absolute prohibition of reprisals against civilians during any type of armed conflict. In doing so, it presented interesting reflections on how custom is created in this field of law.

521. The protection of civilians in time of armed conflict, whether international or internal, is the bedrock of modern humanitarian law. In 1938, the Assembly of the League of Nations, echoing an important statement made, with reference to Spain, in the House of Commons by the British Prime Minister Neville Chamberlain, adopted a Resolution concerning the protection of civilian populations against bombing from the air, in which it stated that "the intentional bombing of [the] civilian population is illegal". Indeed, it is now a universally recognised

principle, recently restated by the International Court of Justice, that deliberate attacks on civilians or civilian objects are absolutely prohibited by international humanitarian law.[1]

522. The protection of civilians and civilian objects provided by modern international law may cease entirely or be reduced or suspended in three exceptional circumstances: (i) when civilians abuse their rights; (ii) when, although the object of a military attack is comprised of military objectives, belligerents cannot avoid causing so-called collateral damage to civilians; and (iii) at least according to some authorities, when civilians may legitimately be the object of reprisals. [...]

524. In the case of attacks on military objectives causing damage to civilians, international law contains a general principle prescribing that reasonable care must be taken in attacking military objectives so that civilians are not needlessly injured through carelessness. This principle, already referred to by the United Kingdom in 1938 with regard to the Spanish Civil War,[2] has always been applied in conjunction with the principle of proportionality, whereby any incidental (and unintentional) damage to civilians must not be out of proportion to the direct military advantage gained by the military attack. In addition, attacks, even when they are directed against legitimate military targets, are unlawful if conducted using indiscriminate means or methods of warfare, or in such a way as to cause indiscriminate damage to civilians. These principles have to some extent been spelled out in Articles 57 and 58 of the First Additional Protocol of 1977. Such provisions, it would seem, are now part of customary international law, not only because they specify and flesh out general pre-existing norms, but also because they do not appear to be contested by any State, including those which have not ratified the Protocol. Admittedly, even these two provisions leave a wide margin of discretion to belligerents by using language that might be regarded as leaving the last word to the attacking party. Nevertheless this is an area where the "elementary considerations of humanity" rightly emphasised by the International Court of Justice in the *Corfu Channel*, *Nicaragua* and *Legality of the Threat or Use of Nuclear Weapons* cases should be fully used when interpreting and applying loose international rules, on the basis that they are illustrative of a general principle of international law.

525. More specifically, recourse might be had to the celebrated Martens Clause which,[3] in the authoritative view of the International Court of Justice, has by now become part of customary international law.[4] True, this Clause may not be taken to mean that the "principles of humanity" and the "dictates of public conscience" have been elevated to the rank of independent sources of international law, for this conclusion is belied by international practice. However, this Clause enjoins, as a minimum, reference to those principles and dictates any time a rule of international humanitarian law is not sufficiently rigorous or precise: in those instances the

---

[1] [774] *Legality of the Threat or Use of Nuclear Weapons* (Advisory Opinion), ICJ Reports 1996, p. 257 (para. 78).

[2] [775] In his statement in the House of Commons on the Spanish civil war, the British Prime Minister stated that one of the rules applicable in any armed conflict was the rule whereby "[r]easonable care must be taken in attacking [...] military objectives so that by carelessness a civilian population in the neighbourhood is not bombed". (House of Commons, *Debates*, 21 June 1938, vol. 337, cols. 937–938).

[3] [779] The Martens Clause was first set forth in the preambular provisions of the 1899 Hague Convention concerning the Laws or customs of War on Land which reads as follows: 'Until a more complete code of the laws of war is issued, the High Contracting Parties think it right to declare that in cases not included in the Regulations adopted by them, populations and belligerents remain under the protection and empire of the principles of international law, as they result from the usages established between civilised nations, from the laws of humanity, and the requirements of the public conscience. [...] A modern version of this clause is to be found in Art. 1(2) of Additional Protocol I of 1977, which refers, instead, to "the principles of humanity and [...] the dictates of public conscience" ("principes de l'humanité et des exigences de la conscience publique").

[4] [780] *Legality of the Threat or Use of Nuclear Weapons* (Advisory Opinion), ICJ Reports 1996, at p. 259, para. 84.

scope and purport of the rule must be defined with reference to those principles and dictates. In the case under discussion, this would entail that the prescriptions of Articles 57 and 58 (and of the corresponding customary rules) must be interpreted so as to construe as narrowly as possible the discretionary power to attack belligerents and, by the same token, so as to expand the protection accorded to civilians. [. . .]

527. As for reprisals against civilians, under customary international law they are prohibited as long as civilians find themselves in the hands of the adversary. With regard to civilians in combat zones, reprisals against them are prohibited by Article 51(6) of the First Additional Protocol of 1977, whereas reprisals against civilian objects are outlawed by Article 52(1) of the same instrument. The question nevertheless arises as to whether these provisions, assuming that they were not declaratory of customary international law, have subsequently been transformed into general rules of international law. In other words, are those States which have not ratified the First Protocol (which include such countries as the U.S., France, India, Indonesia, Israel, Japan, Pakistan and Turkey), nevertheless bound by general rules having the same purport as those two provisions? Admittedly, there does not seem to have emerged recently a body of State practice consistently supporting the proposition that one of the elements of custom, namely *usus* or *diuturnitas* has taken shape. This is however an area where *opinio iuris sive necessitatis* may play a much greater role than *usus,* as a result of the aforementioned Martens Clause. In the light of the way States and courts have implemented it, this Clause clearly shows that principles of international humanitarian law may emerge through a customary process under the pressure of the demands of humanity or the dictates of public conscience, even where State practice is scant or inconsistent. The other element, in the form of *opinio necessitatis*, crystallising as a result of the imperatives of humanity or public conscience, may turn out to be the decisive element heralding the emergence of a general rule or principle of humanitarian law.

528. The question of reprisals against civilians is a case in point. It cannot be denied that reprisals against civilians are inherently a barbarous means of seeking compliance with international law. The most blatant reason for the universal revulsion that usually accompanies reprisals is that they may not only be arbitrary but are also not directed specifically at the individual authors of the initial violation. Reprisals typically are taken in situations where the individuals personally responsible for the breach are either unknown or out of reach. These retaliatory measures are aimed instead at other more vulnerable individuals or groups. They are individuals or groups who may not even have any degree of solidarity with the presumed authors of the initial violation; they may share with them only the links of nationality and allegiance to the same rulers.

529. In addition, the reprisal killing of innocent persons, more or less chosen at random, without any requirement of guilt or any form of trial, can safely be characterized as a blatant infringement of the most fundamental principles of human rights. It is difficult to deny that a slow but profound transformation of humanitarian law under the pervasive influence of human rights has occurred. As a result belligerent reprisals against civilians and fundamental rights of human beings are absolutely inconsistent legal concepts. This trend towards the humanisation of armed conflict is amongst other things confirmed by the works of the United Nations International Law Commission on State Responsibility. Article 50(d) of the Draft Articles on State Responsibility, adopted on first reading in 1996, prohibits as countermeasures any "conduct derogating from basic human rights".

530. It should be added that while reprisals could have had a modicum of justification in the past, when they constituted practically the only effective means of compelling the enemy to abandon unlawful acts of warfare and to comply in future with international law, at present they can no longer be justified in this manner. A means of inducing compliance with international law is at present more widely available and, more importantly, is beginning to prove

fairly efficacious: the prosecution and punishment of war crimes and crimes against humanity by national or international courts. This means serves the purpose of bringing to justice those who are responsible for any such crime, as well as, albeit to a limited extent, the purpose of deterring at least the most blatant violations of international humanitarian law.

531. Due to the pressure exerted by the requirements of humanity and the dictates of public conscience, a customary rule of international law has emerged on the matter under discussion. With regard to the formation of a customary rule, two points must be made to demonstrate that *opinio iuris* or *opinio necessitatis* can be said to exist.

532. First, even before the adoption of the First Additional Protocol of 1977, a number of States had declared or laid down in their military manuals that reprisals in modern warfare are only allowed to the extent that they consist of the use, against enemy armed forces, of otherwise prohibited weapons – thus *a contrario* admitting that reprisals against civilians are not allowed. In this respect one can mention the United States military manual for the Army (*The Law of Land Warfare*), of 1956, as well as the Dutch "Soldiers Handbook" (*Handboek voor de Soldaat*) of 1974. True, other military manuals of the same period took a different position, admitting reprisals against civilians not in the hands of the enemy belligerent. In addition, senior officials of the United States Government seem to have taken a less clear stand in 1978, by expressing doubts about the workability of the prohibition of reprisals against civilians. The fact remains, however, that elements of a widespread *opinio necessitatis* are discernible in international dealings. This is confirmed, first of all, by the adoption, by a vast majority, of a Resolution of the U.N. General Assembly in 1970 which stated that "civilian populations, or individual members thereof, should not be the object of reprisals".[5] A further confirmation may be found in the fact that a high number of States have ratified the First Protocol, thereby showing that they take the view that reprisals against civilians must always be prohibited.[6] It is also notable that this view was substantially upheld by the ICRC in its Memorandum of 7 May 1983 to the States parties to the 1949 Geneva Conventions on the Iran-Iraq war[7] and by Trial Chamber I of the ICTY in *Martić*.[8]

533. Secondly, the States that have participated in the numerous international or internal armed conflicts which have taken place in the last fifty years have normally refrained from claiming that they had a right to visit reprisals upon enemy civilians in the combat area. It would seem that such claim has been only advanced by Iraq in the Iran-Iraq war of 1980–1988 as well as[,] but only *in abstracto* and hypothetically, by a few States, such as France in 1974[9] and the United Kingdom in 1998.[10] The aforementioned elements seem to support the contention that the demands of humanity and the dictates of public conscience, as manifested in

---

5 [786] U.N. General Assembly Resolution 2675 (XXV) of 9 Dec. 1970.

6 [787] It should, however, be noted that in 1998 the United Kingdom, in ratifying the First Additional Protocol of 1977, made a reservation concerning the obligations of Articles 51 and 55 of the Protocol on the use of reprisals against civilians (see the letter sent on 28 January 1998 by the British Ambassador C. Hulse to the Swiss Government, and partially reproduced in M. Sassoli and A.A. Bouvier (eds.), *How Does Law Protect in War?*, ICRC, Geneva 1999, pp. 617–618).

7 [788] [...] [M]emorandum from the International Committee of the Red Cross to the States Parties to the Geneva Conventions of August 12, 1949 Concerning the Conflict Between the Islamic Republic of Iran and the Republic of Iraq, Geneva, May 7, 1983, partially reproduced in M. Sassoli and A.A. Bouvier (eds), *How Does Law Protect in War?*, ICRC, 1999 at 982 [...].

8 [789] *Prosecutor v. Milan Martić*, Review of Indictment Pursuant to Rule 61, ICTY Trial Chamber, Case No. IT-95-11-R61, 8 March 1996, at paras. 10–18.

9 [791] See Diplomatic Conference on the Reaffirmation and Development of International Humanitarian Law Applicable in Armed Conflict, Geneva 1974–77, *Official Records*, Vol. VI, 1977, at 162. France voted against the provision prohibiting reprisals, stating, *inter alia*, that it was "contrary to existing international law" (*idem*).

10 [792] See the British reservation to the First additional Protocol of 1977, *ibid.*

opinio necessitatis, have by now brought about the formation of a customary rule also binding upon those few States that at some stage did not intend to exclude the abstract legal possibility of resorting to the reprisals under discussion.

534. The existence of this rule was authoritatively confirmed, albeit indirectly, by the International Law Commission. In commenting on sub-paragraph d of Article 14 (now Article 50) of the Draft Articles on State Responsibility, which excludes from the regime of lawful countermeasures any conduct derogating from basic human rights, the Commission noted that Article 3 common to the four 1949 Geneva Conventions "prohibits any reprisals in non-international armed conflicts with respect to the expressly prohibited acts as well as any other reprisal incompatible with the absolute requirement of humane treatment".[11] It follows that, in the opinion of the Commission, reprisals against civilians in the combat zone are also prohibited. This view, according to the Trial Chamber, is correct. However, it must be supplemented by two propositions. First, Common Article 3 has by now become customary international law.[12] Secondly, as the International Court of Justice rightly held in *Nicaragua*, it encapsulates fundamental legal standards of overarching value applicable both in international and internal armed conflicts. Indeed, it would be absurd to hold that while reprisals against civilians entailing a threat to life and physical safety are prohibited in civil wars, they are allowed in international armed conflicts as long as the civilians are in the combat zone.

535. It should also be pointed out that at any rate, even when considered lawful, reprisals are restricted by: (a) the principle whereby they must be a last resort in attempts to impose compliance by the adversary with legal standards (which entails, amongst other things, that they may be exercised only after a prior warning has been given which has failed to bring about the discontinuance of the adversary's crimes); (b) the obligation to take special precautions before implementing them (they may be taken only after a decision to this effect has been made at the highest political or military level; in other words they may not be decided by local commanders); (c) the principle of proportionality (which entails not only that the reprisals must not be excessive compared to the precedent unlawful act of warfare, but also that they must stop as soon as that unlawful act has been discontinued) and; (d) "elementary considerations of humanity" (as mentioned above).

[After citing, among other authorities, a previous ICTY decision as support for its proposition that a certain rule of custom had formed (§532), the Trial Chamber then elaborated on the relevance of previous judicial practice in ascertaining the law applicable before it.]

540. Being international in nature and applying international law *principaliter*, the Tribunal cannot but rely upon the well-established sources of international law and, within this framework, upon judicial decisions. What value should be given to such decisions? The Trial Chamber holds the view that they should only be used as a "subsidiary means for the determination of rules of law" (to use the expression in Article 38(1)(d) of the Statute of the International Court of Justice, which must be regarded as declaratory of customary international law). Hence, generally speaking, and subject to the binding force of decisions of the Tribunal's Appeals Chamber upon the Trial Chambers, the International Tribunal cannot uphold the doctrine of binding precedent (*stare decisis*) adhered to in common law countries. Indeed, this doctrine among other things presupposes to a certain degree a hierarchical judicial system. Such a hierarchical system is lacking in the international community. Clearly, judicial precedent is not a distinct source of law in international criminal adjudication. The Tribunal is not bound by

---

[11] [793] See the Commission's comments on the former Article 14 of the [Second] Part of the Draft Articles in *Yearbook of the International Law Commission*, 1995, Volume II, Part Two, A/CN.4/SER.A/1995/Add.1 (Part 2) (State responsibility), para. 18, p. 72.

[12] [794] See in this regard *Military and Paramilitary Activities in and Against Nicaragua (Merits)*, Judgment of 27 June 1986, ICJ Reports 1986, p. 113, especially at para. 218.

precedents established by other international criminal courts such as the Nuremberg or Tokyo Tribunals, let alone by cases brought before national courts adjudicating international crimes. Similarly, the Tribunal cannot rely on a set of cases, let alone on a single precedent, as sufficient to establish a principle of law: the authority of precedents (*auctoritas rerum similiter judicatarum*) can only consist in evincing the possible existence of an international rule. More specifically, precedents may constitute evidence of a customary rule in that they are indicative of the existence of *opinio iuris sive necessitatis* and international practice on a certain matter, or else they may be indicative of the emergence of a general principle of international law. Alternatively, precedents may bear persuasive authority concerning the existence of a rule or principle, i.e. they may persuade the Tribunal that the decision taken on a prior occasion propounded the correct interpretation of existing law. Plainly, in this case prior judicial decisions may persuade the court that they took the correct approach, but they do not compel this conclusion by the sheer force of their precedential weight. Thus, it can be said that the Justinian maxim whereby courts must adjudicate on the strength of the law, not of cases (*non exemplis, sed legibus iudicandum est*) also applies to the Tribunal as to other international criminal courts.

541. As noted above, judicial decisions may prove to be of invaluable importance for the determination of existing law. Here again attention should however be drawn to the need to distinguish between various categories of decisions and consequently to the weight they may be given for the purpose of finding an international rule or principle. It cannot be gainsaid that great value ought to be attached to decisions of such international criminal courts as the international tribunals of Nuremberg or Tokyo, or to national courts operating by virtue, and on the strength, of Control Council Law no. 10, a legislative act jointly passed in 1945 by the four Occupying Powers and thus reflecting international agreement among the Great Powers on the law applicable to international crimes and the jurisdiction of the courts called upon to rule on those crimes. These courts operated under international instruments laying down provisions that were either declaratory of existing law or which had been gradually transformed into customary international law. In many instances no less value may be given to decisions on international crimes delivered by national courts operating pursuant to the 1948 Genocide Convention, or the 1949 Geneva Conventions or the 1977 Protocols or similar international treaties. In these instances the international framework on the basis of which the national court operates and the fact that in essence the court applies international substantive law, may lend great weight to rulings of such courts. Conversely, depending upon the circumstances of each case, generally speaking decisions of national courts on war crimes or crimes against humanity delivered on the basis of national legislation would carry relatively less weight.

542. In sum, international criminal courts such as the International Tribunal must always carefully appraise decisions of other courts before relying on their persuasive authority as to existing law. Moreover, they should apply a stricter level of scrutiny to national decisions than to international judgements, as the latter are at least based on the same *corpus* of law as that applied by international courts, whereas the former tend to apply national law, or primarily that law, or else interpret international rules through the prism of national legislation.

ICTY, Prosecutor v. Aleksovski, *Appeals Chamber, Judgment of 24 March 2000*

Just a few months later in *Aleksovski*, the ICTY Appeals Chamber developed an explicit doctrine of precedents. Zlatko Aleksovski, a former sociology student and prison commander in the Kaonik prison (Bosnia and Herzegovina) who had joined the Bosnian

Croat forces in 1993, had been convicted of violations of the laws or customs of war for the mistreatment of hundreds of prisoners. In responding to the Prosecutor's appeal based on the *Tadić* Appeal Judgment and relating to the international nature of the armed conflict, he argued that only customary international law – and not precedents – could form the basis for his conviction. Contrary to what the Prosecutor suggested, he submitted that the *Aleksovski* Appeal Chamber should not rely on the findings made in the *Tadić* Appeal Judgment. The Appeals Chamber reached the following conclusions.

97. The Appeals Chamber recognises that the principles which underpin the general trend in both the common law and civil law systems, whereby the highest courts, whether as a matter of doctrine or of practice, will normally follow their previous decisions and will only depart from them in exceptional circumstances, are the need for consistency, certainty and predictability. This trend is also apparent in international tribunals. Judge Shahabuddeen observes:

The desiderata of consistency, stability and predictability, which underlie a responsible legal system, suggest that the Court would not exercise its power to depart from a previous decision except with circumspection...The Court accordingly pursues a judicial policy of not unnecessarily impairing the authority of its decisions.[13]

The Appeals Chamber also acknowledges that that need is particularly great in the administration of criminal law, where the liberty of the individual is implicated.

98. References to the law and practice in various countries and in international institutions are not necessarily determinative of the question as to the applicable law in this matter. Ultimately, that question must be answered by an examination of the Tribunal's Statute and Rules, and a construction of them which gives due weight to the principles of interpretation (good faith, textuality, contextuality, and teleology) set out in the 1969 Vienna Convention on the Law of Treaties.

99. There is no provision in the Statute of the Tribunal that deals expressly with the question of the binding force of decisions of the Appeals Chamber. The absence of such a provision, however, does not mean that the Statute is of no assistance in this matter. Article 25 of the Statute provides as follows:

1. The Appeals Chamber shall hear appeals from persons convicted by the Trial Chambers or from the Prosecutor on the following grounds:
   (a) an error on a question of law invalidating the decision; or
   (b) an error of fact which has occasioned a miscarriage of justice.

2. The Appeals Chamber may affirm, reverse or revise the decisions taken by the Trial Chambers. [...]

101. The fundamental purpose of the Tribunal is the prosecution of persons responsible for serious violations of international humanitarian law. The Appeals Chamber considers that this purpose is best served by an approach which, while recognising the need for certainty, stability and predictability in criminal law, also recognises that there may be instances in which the strict, absolute application of that principle may lead to injustice.

105. An aspect of the fair trial requirement is the right of an accused to have like cases treated alike, so that in general, the same cases will be treated in the same way and decided [...] "possibly by the same reasoning."

---

[13] [238] [Shahabuddeen, *Precedents in the World Court* (1996)], pp. 131–2.

106. The right to a fair trial requires and ensures the correction of errors made at trial. At the hearing of an appeal, the principle of fairness is the ultimate corrective of errors of law and fact, but it is also a continuing requirement in any appeal in which a previous decision of an appellate body is being considered.

107. The Appeals Chamber, therefore, concludes that a proper construction of the Statute, taking due account of its text and purpose, yields the conclusion that in the interests of certainty and predictability, the Appeals Chamber should follow its previous decisions, but should be free to depart from them for cogent reasons in the interests of justice.

108. Instances of situations where cogent reasons in the interests of justice require a departure from a previous decision include cases where the previous decision has been decided on the basis of a wrong legal principle or cases where a previous decision has been given *per incuriam*, that is a judicial decision that has been "wrongly decided, usually because the judge or judges were ill-informed about the applicable law."[14]

109. It is necessary to stress that the normal rule is that previous decisions are to be followed, and departure from them is the exception. The Appeals Chamber will only depart from a previous decision after the most careful consideration has been given to it, both as to the law, including the authorities cited, and the facts.

110. What is followed in previous decisions is the legal principle (*ratio decidendi*), and the obligation to follow that principle only applies in similar cases, or substantially similar cases. This means less that the facts are similar or substantially similar, than that the question raised by the facts in the subsequent case is the same as the question decided by the legal principle in the previous decision. There is no obligation to follow previous decisions which may be distinguished for one reason or another from the case before the court.

111. Where, in a case before it, the Appeals Chamber is faced with previous decisions that are conflicting, it is obliged to determine which decision it will follow, or whether to depart from both decisions for cogent reasons in the interests of justice.

2. Whether the Decisions of the Appeals Chamber are Binding on Trial Chambers

112. Generally, in common law jurisdictions, decisions of a higher court are binding on lower courts. In civil law jurisdictions there is no doctrine of binding precedent. However, as a matter of practice, lower courts tend to follow decisions of higher courts. [. . .]

113. The Appeals Chamber considers that a proper construction of the Statute requires that the *ratio decidendi* of its decisions is binding on Trial Chambers for the following reasons:

(i) the Statute establishes a hierarchical structure in which the Appeals Chamber is given the function of settling definitively certain questions of law and fact arising from decisions of the Trial Chambers. Under Article 25, the Appeals Chamber hears an appeal on the ground of an error on a question of law invalidating a Trial Chamber's decision or on the ground of an error of fact which has occasioned a miscarriage of justice, and its decisions are final;

(ii) the fundamental mandate of the Tribunal to prosecute persons responsible for serious violations of international humanitarian law cannot be achieved if the accused and the Prosecution do not have the assurance of certainty and predictability in the application of the applicable law; and

(iii) the right of appeal is [. . .] a component of the fair trial requirement, which is itself a rule of customary international law and gives rise to the right of the accused to have like cases treated alike. This will not be achieved if each Trial Chamber is free to disregard decisions of law made

---

[14] [249] *Black's Law Dictionary* (7th ed., 1999).

by the Appeals Chamber, and to decide the law as it sees fit. In such a system, it would be possible to have four statements of the law from the Tribunal on a single legal issue – one from the Appeals Chamber and one from each of the three Trial Chambers, as though the Security Council had established not a single, but four, tribunals. This would be inconsistent with the intention of the Security Council, which, from a plain reading of the Statute and the Report of the Secretary-General, envisaged a tribunal comprising three trial chambers and one appeals chamber, applying a single, unified, coherent and rational corpus of law. The need for coherence is particularly acute in the context in which the Tribunal operates, where the norms of international humanitarian law and international criminal law are developing, and where, therefore, the need for those appearing before the Tribunal, the accused and the Prosecution, to be certain of the regime in which cases are tried is even more pronounced.

3. Whether the Decisions of the Trial Chambers are Binding on Each Other

114. The Appeals Chamber considers that decisions of Trial Chambers, which are bodies with coordinate jurisdiction, have no binding force on each other, although a Trial Chamber is free to follow the decision of another Trial Chamber if it finds that decision persuasive.

COMMENTARY

Unlike in common law systems, in international law, judicial decisions – even of the same court – are not per se a source of international criminal law. Formally speaking they may only amount to a 'subsidiary means for the determination of international rules of law' (Article 38(1)(d) of the ICJSt.).

Nevertheless, given the characteristics of international criminal law, one should set great store by national or international judicial decisions. They may prove of crucial importance not only for ascertaining whether a customary rule has evolved, but also as a means for establishing the most appropriate interpretation to be placed on a treaty rule.

The Appeals Chamber in *Aleksovski* purported to establish a rule of precedent at the Tribunal, which is somewhat looser than the rule of precedent in some domestic systems. According to the traditional and strict doctrine of precedent, decisions by higher courts or the same-level court are binding subsequently, though courts within the same level may revisit an issue and overrule precedent in exceptional cases. The rule of precedent set down in *Aleksovski*, in contrast, provides that one Appeals Chamber's decision is *persuasive authority* for another Appeals Chamber (which may depart for 'cogent reasons in the interests of justice'). Moreover, the ICTY abides by the notion that lower courts – Trial Chambers at the ICTY – are bound by the decisions of the Appeals Chamber.

The jurisprudence cited above comes from the ICTY, which is only one of the many existing international and 'mixed' jurisdictions now operating. However, the Appeals Chamber of the ICTY is composed of the same judges as the ICTR Appeals Chamber (though they are technically two distinct institutions) and this affords some horizontal harmonization between tribunals. Moreover, the SCSL has substantially adhered to the provision in its Statute that '[t]he judges of the Appeals Chamber of the Special Court shall be guided by the decisions of the Appeals Chamber of the International Tribunals for the former Yugoslavia and for Rwanda' (Article 20(3)). This approach mitigates the risk that with a proliferation of tribunals, international law may be interpreted differently, leading to potential horizontal inconsistency between tribunals.

The ICC is likely to interpret custom in much the same way, although the relevance of general rules of international law within the ICC context is reduced by the fact that Article 21 ICCSt. requires judges to apply the Statute, Elements of Crimes, and RPE first,

and only after that – 'where appropriate' – 'applicable treaties and the principles and rules of international law, including the established principles of the international law of armed conflict' and, failing that, general principles of law.

QUESTIONS

1. What is the role of actual State practice in establishing whether a customary rule has emerged? To what States does the ICTY refer in its analysis? Is the approach taken in *Tadić* and *Kupreškić* convincing?

2. How does the ICTY identify the *opinio juris* of States and other subjects of international law? Considering the reasoning in *Kupreškić* and *Aleksovski*, is there a tautological problem with using precedents – supposedly grounded in customary rules – to support findings that a certain customary rule exists?

3. What if a Trial Chamber does not agree with the finding by the Appeals Chamber in *Aleksovski* about the value of precedents? Is the rule nonetheless binding on it?

4. On the basis of *Tadić*, most commentators and even States are today convinced that certain violations of the laws or customs of war are criminalized in internal armed conflict as well. In this sense, did *Tadić* serve as a 'crystallizing' moment for a rule that had been long in the making?

FURTHER READING

G. Acquaviva and F. Pocar, 'Stare Decisis', in R. Wolfrum (ed.), *Max-Planck Encyclopedia of Public International Law* (Oxford: Oxford University Press, 2008–10).

D. Akande, 'Sources of International Criminal Law', in *Oxford Companion*, 41–53.

V.-D. Degan, 'On the Sources of International Criminal Law' (2005) 4 *Chinese Journal of International Law* 45, 63–64.

ICRC Study, xxxi–xlv.

(B)   TREATIES AND INSTRUMENTS ESTABLISHING INTERNATIONAL TRIBUNALS

Treaties and other instruments establishing international tribunals are important sources of international criminal law in addition to custom. Treaty sources of international criminal law include international conventions, i.e. multilateral treaties either aimed at creating a new institution (e.g. the ICCSt.) or containing substantive rules that are applied by international tribunals (e.g. the Geneva Conventions of 1949, referred to in various instruments establishing the jurisdiction of international tribunals). Other instruments setting up international tribunals include, for instance, UN Security Council Resolutions (such as Res. 827/1993 and 955/1994 establishing the ICTY and the ICTR).

As will be seen below, judges have tended to interpret these Resolutions – whether or not they technically are treaties – on the basis of the rules enshrined in the Vienna Convention on the Law of Treaties (1155 U.N.T.S. 331, entered into force on 27 January 1980), in particular Articles 31–33 on treaty interpretation. These rules are declaratory of international customary law. Among these provisions, the most important is the general clause stating that '[a] treaty shall be interpreted in good faith in accordance with the ordinary meaning to be given to the terms of the treaty in their context and in the light of its object and purpose'.

Two reasons explain why the Vienna Convention applies to the UN Security Council resolutions establishing international tribunals. First, these instruments are law-making documents similar to treaties (they are legally binding by virtue of Chapter VII and Article 25 of the UN Charter). Second, unlike in domestic systems, within the international realm there are no rules of interpretation other than those relating to the construction of treaties.

With respect both to treaties applicable to international criminal proceedings and to instruments establishing international criminal jurisdictions, certain interpretative considerations – such as the need to construe the relevant provisions in light of the purpose pursued by their drafters, or the importance of always taking into account the principles of fair trial and thus duly respecting the rights of the defendants – have played a major role in applying their provisions. Examples of such considerations will be shown throughout the following chapters.

A chief example is the (London) Agreement for the Prosecution and Punishment of the Major War Criminals of the European Axis, and Charter of the International Military Tribunal of 8 August 1945 between France, the United Kingdom, the United States of America, and the USSR, setting out the substantive and procedural law of the IMT of Nuremberg. Interpretation of the provisions of the London Agreement, especially in relation to the criminalization of certain conduct never before prosecuted, has clearly raised a host of legal and policy questions ever since the Nuremberg judgment. Similar issues, in particular those related to the question of the principle of legality (*nullum crimen sine lege*) (see below, Chapter 2(A)), have continued to arise before international criminal courts.

Cases

IMT Nuremberg, Göring et al., *Judgment of 30 September–1 October 1946*

The IMT was established in 1945 as a tribunal to try the major German war criminals during World War II. It was given jurisdiction to try (i) crimes against peace, (ii) war crimes, and (iii) crimes against humanity. The prosecutors, one from each of the Victorious Powers, charged 24 individuals – including such figures as Hermann Göring, Martin Bormann (*in absentia*), Albert Speer, Karl Dönitz, Rudolf Hess, Wilhelm Keitel, Alfred Jodl – considered representative of the leaders of the German National-Socialist party, Army, and Navy, as well as prominent civilian supporters of the regime. The IMT found all but three of the defendants (Hjalmar Schacht, Hans Fritzsche and Franz von Papen) guilty of at least one charge. In considering the challenges raised by the defendants, the IMT took into account not only the text of the London Charter, but also other existing treaty provisions binding Germany and other states.

The Law of the Charter

The jurisdiction of the Tribunal is defined in the Agreement and Charter, and the crimes coming within the jurisdiction of the Tribunal, for which there shall be individual responsibility, are set out in Article 6. The law of the Charter is decisive, and binding upon the Tribunal.

The making of the Charter was the exercise of the sovereign legislative power by the countries to which the German Reich unconditionally surrendered; and the undoubted right of these countries to legislate for the occupied territories has been recognised by the civilised world. The Charter is not an arbitrary exercise of power on the part of the victorious nations, but in the view of the Tribunal, as will be shown, it is the expression of international law existing at the time of its creation; and to that extent is itself a contribution to international law.

The Signatory Powers created this Tribunal, defined the law it was to administer, and made regulations for the proper conduct of the Trial. In doing so, they have done together what any one of them might have done singly; for it is not to be doubted that any nation has the right thus to set up special courts to administer law. With regard to the constitution of the court, all that the defendants are entitled to ask is to receive a fair trial on the facts and law. [. . .]

Murder and Ill-Treatment of Civilian Population

Article 6(b) of the Charter provides that "ill-treatment . . . of civilian population of or in occupied territory . . . killing of hostages . . . wanton destruction of cities, towns or villages" shall be a war crime. In the main these provisions are merely declaratory of the existing laws of war as expressed by the Hague Convention, Article 46, which stated: "Family honour and rights, the lives of persons and private property, as well as religious convictions and practices must be respected." The territories occupied by Germany were administered in violation of the laws of war. The evidence is quite overwhelming of a systematic rule of violence, brutality and terror. [. . .]

Article 49 of the Hague Convention provides that an occupying power may levy a contribution of money from the occupied territory to pay for the needs of the army of occupation, and for the administration of the territory in question. Article 52 of the Hague Convention provides that an occupying power may make requisitions in kind only for the needs of the army of occupation, and that these requisitions shall be in proportion to the resources of the country. These Articles, together with Article 48, dealing with the expenditure of money collected in taxes, and Articles 53, 55 and 56, dealing with public property, make it clear that under the rules of war, the economy of an occupied country can only be required to bear the expenses of the occupation, and these should not be greater than the economy of the country can reasonably be expected to bear. Article 56 reads as follows:

> "The property of municipalities, of religious, charitable, educational, artistic and scientific institutions, although belonging to the State, is to be accorded the same standing as private property. All pre-meditated seizure, destruction, or damage of such institutions[,] historical monuments, works of art and science, is prohibited and should be prosecuted."

The evidence in this case has established, however, that the territories occupied by Germany were exploited for the German war effort in the most ruthless way, without consideration of the local economy, and in consequence of a deliberate design and policy. There was in truth a systematic "plunder of public or private property", which was criminal under Article 6(b) of the Charter. The German occupation policy was clearly stated in a speech made by the defendant Goering on the 6th August, 1942, to the various German authorities in charge of occupied territories: "God knows, you are not sent out there to work for the welfare of the people in your charge, but to get the utmost out of them, so that the German people can live. That is what I expect of your exertions. This everlasting concern about foreign people must cease now, once and for all. I have here before me reports on what you are expected to deliver. It is nothing at all, when I consider your territories. It makes no difference to me in this connection if you say that your people will starve."

The methods employed to exploit the resources of the occupied territories to the full varied from country to country. [...]

Slave Labour Policy

Article 6 (b) of the Charter provides that the "ill-treatment, or deportation to slave labour or for any other purpose, of civilian population of or in occupied territory" shall be a war crime. The laws relating to forced labour by the inhabitants of occupied territories are found in Article 52 of The Hague Convention, which provides:–

"Requisition in kind and services shall not be demanded from municipalities or inhabitants except for the needs of the army of occupation. They shall be in proportion to the resources of the country, and of such a nature as not to involve the inhabitants in the obligation of taking part in military operations against their own country."

The policy of the German occupation authorities was in flagrant violation of the terms of this Convention. Some idea of this policy may be gathered from the statement made by Hitler in a speech on 9th November, 1941: "The territory which now works for us contains more than 250,000,000 men, but the territory which works indirectly for us includes now more than 350,000,000. In the measure in which it concerns German territory, the domain which we have taken under our administration, it is not doubtful that we shall succeed in harnessing the very last man to this work."

The actual results achieved were not so complete as this, but the German occupation authorities did succeed in forcing many of the inhabitants of the occupied territories to work for the German war effort, and in deporting at least 5,000,000 persons to Germany to serve German industry and agriculture. [...]

The Law Relating to War Crimes and Crimes Against Humanity

Article 6 of the Charter provides: "(b) War Crimes: namely, violations of the laws or customs of war. Such violations shall include, but not be limited to, murder, ill-treatment or deportation to slave labour or for any other purpose of civilian population of or in occupied territory, murder or ill-treatment of prisoners of war or persons on the seas, killing of hostages, plunder of public or private property, wanton destruction of cities, towns or villages or devastation not justified by military necessity; (c) Crimes against Humanity: namely, murder, extermination, enslavement, deportation, and other inhumane acts committed against any civilian population, before or during the war, or persecutions on political, racial or religious grounds in execution of or in connection with any crime within the jurisdiction of the Tribunal, whether or not in violation of the domestic law of the country where perpetrated."

As heretofore stated, the Charter does not define as a separate crime any conspiracy except the one set out in Article 6 (a), dealing with crimes against peace.

The Tribunal is of course bound by the Charter, in the definition which it gives both of war crimes and crimes against humanity. With respect to war crimes, however, as has already been pointed out, the crimes defined by Article 6, section (b), of the Charter were already recognised as war crimes under international law. They were covered by Articles 46, 50, 52, and 56 of the Hague Convention of 1907, and Articles 2, 3, 4, 46 and 51 of the Geneva Convention of 1929. That violations of these provisions constituted crimes for which the guilty individuals were punishable is too well settled to admit of argument.

But it is argued that the Hague Convention does not apply in this case, because of the "general participation" clause in Article 2 of the Hague Convention of 1907. That clause provided: "The provisions contained in the regulations (Rules of Land Warfare referred to in Article

1 as well as in the present Convention) do not apply except between contracting powers, and then only if all the belligerents are parties to the Convention."

Several of the belligerents in the recent war were not parties to this Convention.

In the opinion of the Tribunal it is not necessary to decide this question. The rules of land warfare expressed in the Convention undoubtedly represented an advance over existing international law at the time of their adoption. But the Convention expressly stated that it was an attempt "to revise the general laws and customs of war," which it thus recognised to be then existing, but by 1939 these rules laid down in the Convention were recognised by all civilised nations, and were regarded as being declaratory of the laws and customs of war which are referred to in Article 6 (b) of the Charter.

A further submission was made that Germany was no longer bound by the rules of land warfare in many of the territories occupied during the war, because Germany had completely subjugated those countries and incorporated them into the German Reich, a fact which gave Germany authority to deal with the occupied countries as though they were part of Germany. In the view of the Tribunal it is unnecessary in this case to decide whether this doctrine of subjugation, dependent as it is upon military conquest, has any application where the subjugation is the result of the crime of aggressive war. The doctrine was never considered to be applicable so long as there was an army in the field attempting to restore the occupied countries to their true owners, and in this case, therefore, the doctrine could not apply to any territories occupied after the 1st September, 1939. As to the war crimes committed in Bohemia and Moravia, it is a sufficient answer that these territories were never added to the Reich, but a mere protectorate was established over them. [. . .]

In referring to treaties enshrining violations of the laws or customs of war mentioned, the IMT does not point out that those treaties were meant to create obligations binding States, not individuals. Is this distinction relevant? Why or why not? This topic is further discussed in Chapter 2(A) in the discussion of *nullum crimen sine lege*.

ICTY, Prosecutor *v.* Delalić et al. *(Čelebići case)*, *Trial Chamber, Judgment of 16 November 1998*

> Zejnil Delalić, Zdravko Mučić, Hazim Delić and Esad Landžo were indicted in 1996 for their roles in the crimes committed against Serb civilians in the Čelebići camp in central Bosnia-Herzegovina between June and November 1992. The first-instance judgment that convicted three of the defendants (and acquitted Delalić) was one of the first handed down by the ICTY. As a general introduction to its legal findings, the Trial Chamber elaborated in a comprehensive way the methods of interpreting the ICTYSt. and, in general, international instruments applicable to international criminal proceedings.

158. The question of interpretation of the provisions of the Statute and Rules has continuously arisen throughout the proceedings in the present case. The Trial Chamber is aware that the meaning of the word "interpretation" in the context of statutes, including the Statute of the Tribunal, may be explained both in a broad and in a narrow sense. In its broad sense, it involves the creative activities of the judge in extending, restricting or modifying a rule of law contained in its statutory form. In its narrow sense, it could be taken to denote the role of a judge in explaining the meaning of words or phrases used in a statute. Within the context of the provisions of the Rules, the meaning of "interpretation" assumes a special complexity. This is

because of the approach adopted in the formulation of these provisions, which accommodate principles of law from the main legal systems of the world.

159. The Tribunal's Statute and Rules consist of a fusion and synthesis of two dominant legal traditions, these being the common law system, which has influenced the English-speaking countries, and the civil law system, which is characteristic of continental Europe and most countries which depend on the Code system. It has thus become necessary, and not merely expedient, for the interpretation of their provisions, to have regard to the different approaches of these legal traditions. It is conceded that a particular legal system's approach to statutory interpretation is shaped essentially by the particular history and traditions of that jurisdiction. However, since the essence of interpretation is to discover the true purpose and intent of the statute in question, invariably, the search of the judge interpreting a provision under whichever system, is necessarily the same. It is, therefore, useful at the outset to discuss some of the rules which could be usefully applied in the interpretation of our enabling provisions. [...]

160. It cannot be disputed that the cornerstone of the theory and practice of statutory interpretation is to ensure the accurate interpretation of the words used in the statute as the intention of the legislation in question. In all legal systems, the primary task of the court or judge interpreting a provision is to ascertain the meaning of that particular statutory provision.

161. In every legal system, whether common law or civil law, where the meaning of the words in a statute is clearly defined, the obligation of the judge is to give the words their clearly defined meaning and apply them strictly. This is the literal rule of interpretation. If only one construction is possible, to which the clear, plain or unambiguous word is unequivocally susceptible, the word must be so construed. In cases of ambiguity, however, all legal systems consider methods for determining how to give effect to the legislative intention.

162. Where the use of a word or expression leads to absurdity or repugnance, both common law and civil law courts will disregard the literal or grammatical meaning. Under the golden rule of interpretation, the common law court as well as the civil law court will modify the grammatical sense of the word to avoid injustice, absurdity, anomaly or contradiction, as clearly not to have been intended by the legislature. Where the grammatical meaning is ambiguous and suggests more than one meaning, the text of the provision in question may be construed under the logical interpretation approach of civil law jurisprudence, or the golden rule of common law jurisprudence. If the literal meaning of the provision does not resolve the issue, the civil law courts may resort to analogy to extract the meaning.

163. The 'teleological approach', also called the 'progressive' or 'extensive' approach, of the civilian jurisprudence, is in contrast with the legislative historical approach. The teleological approach plays the same role as the 'mischief rule' of common law jurisprudence. This approach enables interpretation of the subject matter of legislation within the context of contemporary conditions. The idea of the approach is to adapt the law to changed conditions, be they special, economic or technological, and attribute such change to the intention of the legislation.

164. The mischief rule (also known as the purposive approach) is said to have originated from *Heydon's case*, decided by the ancient English Court of Exchequer in 1584. In *Heydon's case*, four questions were posed in order to discover the intention of the legislation in question: (a) what was the common law before the making of the Act; (b) what was the mischief and defect for which the common law did not provide; (c) what remedy has Parliament resolved and appointed to cure the disease; and (d) the true reason for the remedy. According to the approach taken, the court is enjoined to suppress the mischief and advance the remedy. This requires looking at the legislative history for the "mischief" which may not be obvious on the face of the statute. This approach to interpretation is generously relied upon in Continental and American courts. In the important case of *AG v. Prince Ernest Augustus of Hanover,*

Viscount Simonds spelled out what he regarded as the meaning of context in the construction of statutes, as follows:

(a) other enacting provisions of the same Statute;

(b) its preamble;

(c) the existing state of the law;

(d) other statutes *in pari materia*;

(e) the mischief which the statute was intended to remedy.

In addition, the object of a statute or treaty is to be taken into consideration in arriving at the ordinary meaning of its provisions.

165. The method of judicial 'gap-filling', which may be adopted under the teleological interpretation of the civilian jurisprudence, would, under a common law approach, suggest two approaches. The first of these is to consider that, because the observation of the doctrine of the separation of powers preserves the judicial function to the judiciary, any judicial lawmaking would be an abuse of the legislative function by the judiciary. The second view is that courts are established to ascertain and give effect to the intention of the legislature. Filling any gap is also a means of securing this objective. The common law has rejected both views, despite an attempt to argue that the filling of gaps is part of the judicial role in the interpretation of statutes. The interpretative role of the judiciary is, however, never denied. [...]

166. The Trial Chamber would here refer to some other canons of interpretation, as illustrative in the interpretation of statutes. The five most common canons are:

(a) reading the text as a whole;

(b) giving technical words their technical meaning;

(c) reading words in their context *noscitur a sociis*;

(d) the *ejusdem generis* rule and the rank rule;

(e) the *expressio unius est exclusio alterius* rule.

167. In addition to the above, there are presumptions and precedents which are valuable aids to interpretation. The proper status of decided cases as judicial precedents and aids to interpretation is still not settled. The question is whether previous decisions involving words judicially interpreted are binding as to interpretation of the same words in a different statute. The general rule is that they are not. This view is based on the fact that the *ratio decidendi* of each case will be specific and confined to the particular piece of legislation being considered. The reasoning on the interpretation of the words of a statute will apply to cases decided on the same legislation. It does not necessarily relate to another statute. It might thus seem that decisions from the Appeals Chamber of the Tribunal on the provisions of the Statute ought to be binding on Trial Chambers, this being the fundamental basis of the appellate process. However, decisions from the same or other jurisdictions which have not construed the same provisions in their decisions as the case being considered, are of merely "persuasive" value.

168. Notwithstanding the similarity between the various systems, some of the significant differences in judicial attitudes towards the use of precedents as an aid to the interpretation of statutes ought to be mentioned. These are differences in:

(i)   materials used in argument;

(ii)   use of *travaux préparatoires*;

(iii) styles in judicial opinion;

(iv) styles of justification;

(v) levels of abstraction;

(vi) modes of rationality.

Materials used in argument consist of authoritative and non-authoritative materials, which correspond with the idea of binding and non-binding materials. Authoritative texts which are binding include the statute itself, related instruments, and general principles of law or customary law, whereas dictionaries, technical lexicons and other factors which might have led to the passing of the statute are non-authoritative.

169. It seems to the Trial Chamber that any *travaux préparatoires*, opinions expressed by members of the Security Council when voting on the relevant resolutions, and the views of the Secretary-General of the United Nations expressed in his Report, on the interpretation of the Articles of the Tribunal's Statute cannot be ignored in the interpretation of provisions which might be deemed ambiguous. The vast majority of members of the international community rely upon such sources in construing international instruments. [...]

170. The International Tribunal is an *ad hoc* international court, established with a specific, limited jurisdiction. It is *sui generis*, with its own appellate structure. The interpretation of the provisions of the Statute and Rules must, therefore, take into consideration the objects of the Statute and the social and political considerations which gave rise to its creation. The kinds of grave violations of international humanitarian law which were the motivating factors for the establishment of the Tribunal continue to occur in many other parts of the world, and continue to exhibit new forms and permutations. The international community can only come to grips with the hydra-headed elusiveness of human conduct through a reasonable as well as a purposive interpretation of the existing provisions of international customary law. Thus, the utilisation of the literal, golden and mischief rules of interpretation repays effort.

COMMENTARY

The standards for interpreting law-making instruments – treaties or others – are by now truly established by judicial practice in international adjudication. As the next sections of this book will show, however, this does not mean that in each case international courts and tribunals consistently follow the guidelines discussed above.

As for the ICC, in its first years of existence it appears to have adopted the same modalities when interpreting and applying the provisions of the Rome Statute and other legal instruments relevant to its work.

For instance, in proceedings leading up to the confirmation of the charges against Germain Katanga and Mathieu Ngudjolo Chui, the Prosecutor requested that the two cases against these individuals be joined on the basis that he had always sought to prosecute the suspects for their joint participation in the same attack. The Pre-Trial Chamber ruled that the ordinary meaning of Article 64(5) ICCSt. ('[...] the Trial Chamber may, as appropriate, direct that there be joinder or severance in respect of charges against more than one accused') provides that there shall be joint trials for persons accused jointly, and establishes a presumption for joint proceedings for persons prosecuted jointly. Mr Chui appealed, alleging an error because the power to authorize joinder under the rule appears to be confined to the Trial Chamber, and not to the Pre-Trial Chamber.

In an interesting application of the rule that 'the ordinary meaning [is] to be given to the terms of the treaty in their context and in the light of its object and purpose', the Appeals Chamber confirmed the interpretation of the Pre-Trial Chamber. It held that a comprehensive reading of Article 64(5), Rule 136 of the ICC RPE, and other relevant provisions 'tallies with the object of the Statute being, in this regard, the assurance of the efficacy of the criminal process, and promotes its purpose that proceedings should be held expeditiously'

(Judgment on the Appeal Against the Decision on Joinder rendered on 10 March 2008 by the Pre-Trial Chamber in the Germain Katanga and Mathieu Ngudjolo Chui Cases, 9 June 2008, para. 8).

When a number of substantive judgments are issued by the ICC it will be possible to assess how the ICC interprets its Statute in practice.

The ICJ recently elaborated on how to interpret Security Council resolutions, stating that '[t]he interpretation of Security Council resolutions may require the Court to analyse statements by representatives of members of the Security Council made at the time of their adoption, other resolutions of the Security Council on the same issue, as well as the subsequent practice of relevant United Nations organs and of States affected by those given resolutions' (ICJ, *Accordance with International Law of the Unilateral Declaration of Independence in Respect of Kosovo*, Advisory Opinion of 22 July 2010, para. 94).

QUESTIONS

1. Does it always make sense to resort to the principles enshrined in the Vienna Convention in order to interpret instruments other than treaties? Wouldn't it be better to develop specific provisions for these instruments to take into account their peculiarities, such as their origin (Security Council Resolutions or other)?

2. The relationship between custom and treaty law is a complex one. Already in the Nuremberg judgment above, the Judges referred to the text of the London Charter establishing aggression as a crime but, 'in view of the great importance of the questions of law involved', they added references to prior developments relevant to the formation of a treaty rule binding Germany and possibly of a rule of custom. Why did the judges make this choice? Was this necessary?

FURTHER READING

Cassese, *International Criminal Law*, 15–17.
Zahar and Sluiter, *International Criminal Law*, 79–105.

(C) GENERAL PRINCIPLES OF LAW

Whenever a court is unable to apply a provision of a treaty or other international instrument (such as a Security Council resolution laying down the Statute of an international criminal tribunal), and no customary rule of international law is available, it is permissible to draw upon general principles of law.

This category embraces (i) general principles of international criminal law; (ii) general principles of international law; and (iii) general principles of criminal law recognized by the community of nations, i.e. common to most countries of the world.

General principles of international criminal law include principles specific to criminal law, such as the principles of legality, the presumption of innocence, the principle of equality of arms and the principle of command responsibility (a corollary in international criminal law of the principle of responsible command existing in international humanitarian law). Except for the principle of command responsibility, the application of these principles at the international level normally results from their gradual transposition from national legal systems on to the international order. They are now firmly embedded in international criminal law.

General principles of international law also consist of principles inherent in to the international legal system. Hence, their identification can be carried out by way of generalization and induction from the main features of the international legal order.

It is only after looking for the existence of a principle belonging to one of these two categories that a court may then turn to general principles of criminal law recognized by the community of nations. This is because this last category is a *subsidiary* source of law, as was pointed out above, whereas general principles of international criminal law as well as general principles of international law derive from two *primary* sources of law, namely custom and treaty. In practice, however, international courts, once they find that no general rule exists on a specific issue, turn immediately to the subsidiary source and try to ascertain whether a general principle of criminal law common to all the countries of the world has evolved. The reasons behind this approach are clear: first, the distinction among the various categories of principles is not so clear; second and more importantly, the other two categories of principles (i.e. the general principles of international criminal law and those of international law) are very general; they may therefore prove of scant assistance in the search for a legal resolution of a specific issue. In contrast, the exploration of the principal criminal systems of the world is more likely to provide a normative standard applicable to the case at issue. Clearly, a principle of criminal law should be found to belong to this class only if a court finds that it is shared by common law and civil law systems as well as other legal systems such as those of the Islamic world, some Asian countries such as China and Japan and the African continent. (It is more and more frequently being pointed out in the legal literature that limiting comparative legal analysis to civil law and common law systems alone is too restrictive; however, in practice international courts tend not to rely on such broad review of national systems, and confine themselves to scrutinizing the criminal system of major civil law and common law countries.)

International courts have often relied upon these principles. For instance, the ICTY has had the opportunity to resort to this subsidiary source of law in a number of cases. In some, the ICTY found that there existed general principles common to the major legal systems of the world, and accordingly applied them.

Thus, in *Erdemović* (sentencing judgment), a Trial Chamber, in discussing the defences of duress, necessity, and superior orders, held that 'a rigorous and restrictive approach' to this matter should be taken, adding that such approach was in line with the 'general principles of law as expressed in numerous national laws and case law' (§19). However, it actually relied only on French law and case law (see ibid., n. 13).

In the same case, the Trial Chamber set about looking for the scale of penalties applicable for crimes against humanity. It found that among the various elements to be taken into account were 'the penalties associated with [crimes against humanity] under international law and national laws, which are expressions of general principles of law recognised by all nations' (§26). After a brief survey of international practice, it pointed out that '[a]s in international law, the states which included crimes against humanity in their national laws provided that the commission of such crimes would entail the imposition of the most severe penalties permitted in their respective systems' (§30). However, the Trial Chamber did not give any specific indication of these laws. It then concluded as follows:

The Trial Chamber thus notes that there is a general principle of law common to all nations whereby the severest penalties apply for crimes against humanity in national legal systems.

It thus concludes that there exists in international law a standard according to which a crime against humanity is one of extreme gravity demanding the most severe penalties when no mitigating circumstances are present. (§31)

Subsequently, after surveying the general practice regarding prison sentences in the case law of the former Yugoslavia, the Chamber found that reference to this practice was 'in fact a reflection of the general principle of law internationally recognised by the community of nations whereby the most severe penalties may be imposed for crimes against humanity' (§40). The Appeals Chamber judgment in this case provides for a vivid illustration of ways in which general principles have been 'discerned' from particular practices.

Cases

ICTY, **Prosecutor** *v.* **Erdemović**, *Appeals Chamber, Judgment of 7 October 1997 (Joint Separate Opinion of Judge McDonald and Judge Vorah)*

Dražen Erdemović was a member of the Bosnian Serb Army who had participated in the execution of approximately 1,200 unarmed Muslim men in Srebrenica during the summer of 1995. The defendant admitted to having personally killed about 70 men and pleaded guilty to crimes against humanity, adding however that he had acted under duress (see *infra*, section on duress, p. 472). Before the Trial Chamber and then the Appeals Chamber (judgment of 7 October 1997), the question was whether duress affords a complete defence to the killing of innocent persons. The majority of the Appeals Chamber held duress is not a defence in such a case under international law. Two of the Judges explained the import of the concept of general principles to the matter at issue.

55. [...] [I]t is our considered view that no rule may be found in customary international law regarding the availability or the non-availability of duress as a defence to a charge of killing innocent human beings. The post-World War Two military tribunals did not establish such a rule. We do not think that the decisions of these tribunals or those of other national courts and military tribunals constitute consistent and uniform state practice underpinned by *opinion juris sive necessitatis*.

D. General principles of law recognised by civilised nations (Article 38(1)(c) of ICJ Statute)

56. It is appropriate now to inquire whether the "general principles of law recognised by civilised nations", established as a source of international law in Article 38(1)(c) of the ICJ Statute, may shed some light upon this intricate issue of duress. Paragraph 58 of the Report of the Secretary-General of the United Nations presented on 3 May 1993 expressly directs the International Tribunal to this source of law:

"[T]he International Tribunal itself will have to decide on various personal defences which may relieve a person of individual criminal responsibility, such as minimum age or mental incapacity, drawing upon general principles of law recognised by all nations".

Further, Article 14 of the International Law Commission's Draft Code of Crimes Against the Peace and Security of Mankind provides:

"[T]he competent court shall determine the admissibility of defences in accordance with the general principles of law, in the light of the character of each crime".

57. A number of considerations bear upon our analysis of the application of "general principles of law recognised by civilised nations" as a source of international law. First, although
general principles of law are to be derived from existing legal systems, in particular, national
systems of Law, it is generally accepted that the distillation of a "general principle of law recognised by civilised nations" does not require the comprehensive survey of all legal systems
of the world as this would involve a practical impossibility and has never been the practice
of the International Court of Justice or other international tribunals which have had recourse
to Article 38(1)(c) of the ICJ Statute. Second, it is the view of eminent jurists, including Baron
Descamps, the President of the Advisory Committee of Jurists on Article 38(1)(c), that one
purpose of this article is to avoid a situation of *non-liquet*, that is, where an international tribunal is stranded by an absence of applicable legal rules. Third, a "general principle" must not
be confused with concrete manifestations of that principle in specific rules. As stated by the
Italian-Venezuelan Mixed Claims Commission in the *Gentini* case:

> "[A] rule...is essentially practical and, moreover, binding; there are rules of art as there are
> rules of government, while a principle expresses a general truth, which guides our action,
> serves as a theoretical basis for the various acts of our life, and the application of which to
> reality produces a given consequence".

In light of these considerations, our approach will necessarily not involve a direct comparison of
the specific rules of each of the world's legal systems, but will instead involve a survey of those
jurisdictions whose jurisprudence is, as a practical matter, accessible to us in an effort to discern
a general trend, policy or principle underlying the concrete rules of that jurisdiction which comports with the object and purpose of the establishment of the International Tribunal.
   As Lord McNair pointed out in his Separate Opinion in the *South-West Africa Case*,

> "[I]t is never a question of importing into international law private law institutions 'lock,
> stock and barrel', ready made and fully equipped with a set of rules. <u>It is rather a question
> of finding in the private law institutions indications of legal policy and principles appropri-
> ate to the solution of the international problem at hand</u>. It is not the concrete manifestation
> of a principle in different national systems – which are anyhow likely to vary – but the gen-
> eral concept of law underlying them that the international judge is entitled to apply under
> paragraph (c)". (Emphasis added.)

It is thus generally the practice of international tribunals to employ the general principle in its
formulation of a legal rule applicable to the facts of the particular case before it. This practice
is most evident in the treatment of the general principle of "good faith and equity" in cases
before the International Court of Justice and the Permanent Court of International Justice. For
example in the *North Sea Continental Shelf Cases* before the International Court of Justice, the
Court had regard to "equitable principles" in its formulation of the rule delimiting the boundaries of continental shelves. In the *Diversion of Water from the Meuse Case (Netherlands v.
Belgium)* before the Permanent Court of International Justice, Judge Hudson in his Individual
Opinion, after accepting that equity is a "general principle of law recognised by civilised
nations", stated:

> "[I]t would seem to be an important principle of equity that where two parties have
> assumed an identical or a reciprocal obligation, one party which is engaged in a continuing
> non-performance of that obligation should not be permitted to take advantage of a similar
> non-performance of that obligation by the other party".

In the *Chorzow Factory Case (Merits)*, the Permanent Court observed that "it is a principle of
international law, and even a general conception of law, that any breach of an engagement
involves an obligation to make reparation".

In the *Corfu Channel Case (Merits)*, the International Court stated that:

"[T]he other State, the victim of a breach of international law, is often unable to furnish direct proof of facts giving rise to responsibility. Such a State should be allowed a more liberal recourse to inferences of fact and circumstantial evidence. This indirect evidence is admitted in all systems of law, and its use is recognized by international decisions".

58. In order to arrive at a general principle relating to duress, we have undertaken a limited survey of the treatment of duress in the world's legal systems. This survey is necessarily modest in its undertaking and is not a thorough comparative analysis. Its purpose is to derive, to the extent possible, a "general principle of law" as a source of international law.

The two distinguished Judges concluded their survey of comparative criminal law by noting that no principle common to most countries of the world was discernible. Hence this source of law offered no rule on the matter. After that they decided to apply 'policy considerations' and in so doing they rejected the approach taken by an Italian court of law in the *Masetti* case. They said the following:

80. The *Masetti* approach proceeds from the starting point of strict utilitarian logic based on the fact that if the victim will die anyway, the accused is not at all morally blameworthy for taking part in the execution; there is absolutely no reason why the accused should die as it would be unjust for the law to expect the accused to die for nothing. It should be immediately apparent that the assertion that the accused is not morally blameworthy where the victim would have died in any case depends entirely again upon a view of morality based on utilitarian logic. This does not, in our opinion, address the true rationale for our rejection of duress as a defence to the killing of innocent human beings. The approach we take does not involve a balancing of harms for and against killing but rests upon an application in the context of international humanitarian law of the rule that duress does not justify or excuse the killing of an innocent person. Our view is based upon a recognition that international humanitarian law should guide the conduct of combatants and their commanders. There must be legal limits as to the conduct of combatants and their commanders in armed conflict. In accordance with the spirit of international humanitarian law, we deny the availability of duress as a complete defence to combatants who have killed innocent persons. In so doing, we give notice in no uncertain terms that those who kill innocent persons will not be able to take advantage of duress as a defence and thus get away with impunity for their criminal acts in the taking of innocent lives.

ICTY, **Prosecutor *v.* Furundžija**, *Trial Chamber, Judgment of 10 December 1998*

The defendant had been accused of rape and torture. In trying to define rape as a war crime, the Trial Chamber first surveyed international treaties and case law to determine whether there existed any rule of customary international law defining rape; having reached a negative conclusion, the Chamber moved directly to an examination of national legislation in order to identify a possible common definition of that offence. It concluded that such a common definition did exist, except for dissensus on one issue (whether or not the forced sexual penetration of the mouth by the male sexual organ amounted to rape), where a major discrepancy in the various legal systems could be discerned. Proceeding somewhat out of order in its consideration of sources of general principles of law, the Tribunal next held that it was appropriate to look for 'general principles of international criminal law or, if such principles are of no avail, to the general principles of international law' (§182). It then applied the 'general principle of respect for human dignity' both as a principle underpinning international humanitarian law and human rights law, and as a principle permeating the whole body of international law (§183). It also applied the principle of *nullum crimen sine lege* (§184), apparently as a general principle of criminal law.

177. This Trial Chamber notes that no elements other than those emphasised may be drawn from international treaty or customary law, nor is resort to general principles of international criminal law or to general principles of international law of any avail. The Trial Chamber therefore considers that, to arrive at an accurate definition of rape based on the criminal law principle of specificity (*Bestimmtheitgrundsatz*, also referred to by the maxim "*nullum crimen sine lege stricta*"), it is necessary to look for principles of criminal law common to the major legal systems of the world. These principles may be derived, with all due caution, from national laws.

178. Whenever international criminal rules do not define a notion of criminal law, reliance upon national legislation is justified, subject to the following conditions: (i) unless indicated by an international rule, reference should not be made to one national legal system only, say that of common-law or that of civil-law States. Rather, international courts must draw upon the general concepts and legal institutions common to all the major legal systems of the world. This presupposes a process of identification of the common denominators in these legal systems so as to pinpoint the basic notions they share; (ii) since "international trials exhibit a number of features that differentiate them from national criminal proceedings",[15] account must be taken of the specificity of international criminal proceedings when utilising national law notions. In this way a mechanical importation or transposition from national law into international criminal proceedings is avoided, as well as the attendant distortions of the unique traits of such proceedings.

179. The Trial Chamber would emphasise at the outset, that a trend can be discerned in the national legislation of a number of States of broadening the definition of rape so that it now embraces acts that were previously classified as comparatively less serious offences, that is sexual or indecent assault. This trend shows that at the national level States tend to take a stricter attitude towards serious forms of sexual assault: the stigma of rape now attaches to a growing category of sexual offences, provided of course they meet certain requirements, chiefly that of forced physical penetration.

180. In its examination of national laws on rape, the Trial Chamber has found that although the laws of many countries specify that rape can only be committed against a woman,[16] others provide that rape can be committed against a victim of either sex.[17] The laws of several jurisdictions state that the *actus reus* of rape consists of the penetration, however slight, of the female sexual organ by the male sexual organ.[18] There are also jurisdictions which interpret the

---

[15] [206] Para. 5, Separate and Dissenting Opinion of Judge Cassese, *Prosecutor v. Dražen Erdemović*, Judgement, Case No. IT-96-22-A, 7 Oct. 1997.

[16] [207] *See* Section 361 (2) of the Chilean Code; Art. 236 of the Chinese Penal Code (Revised) 1997; Art. 177 of the German Penal Code (StGB); Art. 177 of the Japanese Penal Code; Art. 179 of the SFRY Penal Code; Section 132 of the Zambian Penal Code.

[17] [208] *See* Art. 201 of the Austrian Penal Code (StGB); French Code Pénal Arts. 222–23; Art. 519 of the Italian Penal Code (as of 1978); Art. 119 of the Argentinian Penal Code.

[18] [209] *See* Section 375 of the Pakistani Penal Code 1995; Art. 375 of the Indian Penal Code; The Law of South Africa, W.A. Joubert 1996 at p. 257–8: "The *actus reus* of the crime consists in the penetration of the female by the male's sexual organ (*R. v. M.* 1961 2 SA 60 (O) 63). The slightest penetration is sufficient." (*R. v. Curtis* 1926 CPD 385 389); Section 117 of the Ugandan Penal Code: "[t]here must be 'carnal knowledge.' This means sexual intercourse. Sexual intercourse in turn means penetration of the man's penis into the woman's vagina".

actus reus of rape broadly.[19] The provisions of civil law jurisdictions often use wording open for interpretation by the courts.[20] Furthermore, all jurisdictions surveyed by the Trial Chamber require an element of force, coercion, threat, or acting without the consent of the victim:[21] force is given a broad interpretation and includes rendering the victim helpless.[22] Some jurisdictions indicate that the force or intimidation can be directed at a third person.[23] Aggravating factors commonly include causing the death of the victim, the fact that there were multiple perpetrators, the young age of the victim, and the fact that the victim suffers a condition, which renders him/her especially vulnerable such as mental illness. Rape is almost always punishable with a maximum of life imprisonment, but the terms that are imposed by various jurisdictions vary widely.

181. It is apparent from our survey of national legislation that, in spite of inevitable discrepancies, most legal systems in the common and civil law worlds consider rape to be the forcible sexual penetration of the human body by the penis or the forcible insertion of any other object into either the vagina or the anus.

183. The Trial Chamber holds that the forced penetration of the mouth by the male sexual organ constitutes a most humiliating and degrading attack upon human dignity. The essence of the whole corpus of international humanitarian law as well as human rights law lies in the protection of the human dignity of every person, whatever his or her gender. The general principle of respect for human dignity is the basic underpinning and indeed the very *raison d'être* of international humanitarian law and human rights law; indeed in modern times it has become of such paramount importance as to permeate the whole body of international law. This principle is intended to shield human beings from outrages upon their personal dignity, whether such outrages are carried out by unlawfully attacking the body or by humiliating and debasing the honour, the self-respect or the mental well being of a person. It is consonant with this principle that such an extremely serious sexual outrage as forced oral penetration should be classified as rape.

COMMENTARY

Due to the issues raised by general principles of law discussed above, and because of the delicate nature of a court's assessment when attempting to establish their existence and import, international judges have sounded a note of warning about resorting to them. They have emphasized that one ought not to transpose legal constructs typical of national legal systems into international law if those constructs do not harmonize with the specific features of the international legal system. This notion was forcefully stressed by Judge Cassese in his dissent in *Erdemović*, where he explained the legal grounds justifying great prudence in transposing domestic criminal notions on to the international plane (paras 2–6)

---

[19] [210] For a broad definition of sexual intercourse, *see* the Criminal Code of New South Wales s. 61 H (1). *See also* the U.S. Proposal to the U.N. Diplomatic Conference of Plenipotentiaries on the Establishment of an International Criminal Court (19 June 1998 A/CONF.183/C.1/L/10).

[20] [211] *See e.g.* the Dutch Penal Code stating in Art. 242: "A person who by an act of violence or another act or by threat of violence or threat of another act compels a person to submit to acts comprising or including sexual penetration of the body is guilty of rape and liable to a term of imprisonment of not more than twelve years or a fine of the fifth category." *See also* Art. 201 of the Austrian Penal Code (StGB); French Code Penal Arts. 222–23.

[21] [212] *See e.g.* in England and Wales the Sexual Offences Act 1956 to 1992.

[22] [213] *See* Art. 180 of the Dutch Penal Code; Art. 180 of the SFRY Penal Code.

[23] [214] The Penal Code of Bosnia and Herzegovina (1988) Ch. XI states that "[w]hoever coerces a female person with whom he is not married to, into sexual intercourse by force or threat to endanger her life or body or that of someone close to her will be sentenced to between one to ten years in prison".

and thus applied these methodological considerations to the notion of 'guilty plea' and the conditions under which it can be accepted at the international level (paras 7–10).

Moreover, international tribunals also need to be aware of the dangers of developing the law through recourse to policy arguments based on the rationale for criminal law and punishment, such as deterrence or retribution, because of the culturally contingent and variable nature of those policy concerns.

QUESTIONS

1. How many domestic systems should be analysed before drawing a conclusion about the existence of a general principle of law applicable in international criminal trials? And, more importantly, what kind of domestic systems should be looked at? Should systems that do not recognize the presumption of innocence and the principle of legality (*nullum crimen*), for instance, be afforded the same weight as other, more advanced ones?

2. Customary law and general principles are both non-written sources of law and need careful judicial interpretation. What are their main distinguishing features?

FURTHER READING

A. Cassese, 'The Contribution of the International Criminal Tribunal for the former Yugoslavia to the Establishment of General Principles of Law Recognized by the Community of Nations', in S. Yee and W. Tieya (eds), *International Law in the Post-Cold War World* (London: Routledge, 2001), 43.

G. Werle, 'General Principles of International Criminal Law', in *Oxford Companion*, 54–62.

(D) INTERNATIONAL CRIMINAL LAW AND HUMAN RIGHTS

Two of the major trends in international law after World War II have been the recognition of fundamental human rights at the international level on the one side, and the criminalization of particularly heinous conduct (leading to prosecutions for war crimes, crimes against humanity, genocide, and aggression) on the other. It is therefore no surprise that these two trends have mutually influenced and, to a certain extent, reinforced each other on a variety of levels.

As for the impact of human rights law on international criminal law, it should be noted that several crimes punishable under international law have developed to safeguard the fundamental rights of civilians and other protected categories, both in armed conflict and in times of peace. It is notable that international criminal rules on crimes against humanity (but not only those), which are discussed *infra*, in Part II, are largely predicated upon international human rights law. The progressive development of human rights law (for instance, the right to life; the right to be free from torture and other inhuman or degrading treatment; the right to equality and therefore to be free from discrimination and persecution based on political, racial or religious grounds; and so on) contributes to the enhancement and clarification of the scope of crimes against humanity. At the same time international criminal law jurisprudence sheds light on how fundamental human rights must be protected in times of armed conflict or other exceptional circumstances.

Cases

ICTY, Prosecutor v. Kupreškić et al., Trial Chamber, Judgment of 14 January 2000

The defendants, members of the Bosnian Croat HVO forces operating in Bosnia, were charged with crimes against humanity and war crimes for their role in the attack on the Bosnian Muslim village of Ahmići in the Lašva River valley region of Bosnia. The Trial Chamber, in determining the scope of crimes against humanity and therefore examining the various categories of acts that amount to such crimes, had to establish what is meant by 'other inhumane acts'. For this purpose the Chamber needed to have recourse to human rights provisions.

562. The expression "other inhumane acts" was drawn from Article 6(c) of the London Agreement and Article II(1)(c) of Control Council Law No. 10.

563. There is a concern that this category lacks precision and is too general to provide a safe yardstick for the work of the Tribunal and hence, that it is contrary to the principle of the "specificity" of criminal law. It is thus imperative to establish what is included within this category. The phrase "other inhumane acts" was deliberately designed as a residual category, as it was felt to be undesirable for this category to be exhaustively enumerated. An exhaustive categorization would merely create opportunities for evasion of the letter of the prohibition. The importance of maintaining such a category was elucidated by the ICRC when commenting on what would constitute a violation of the obligation to provide "humane treatment" contained in common Article 3 of the Geneva Conventions:[24]

> It is always dangerous to try to go into too much detail – especially in this domain. However great the care taken in drawing up a list of all the various forms of infliction, it would never be possible to catch up with the imagination of future torturers who wished to satisfy their bestial instincts; and the more specific and complete a list tries to be the more restrictive it becomes. The form of wording adopted is flexible and, at the same time, precise.

564. In interpreting the expression at issue, resort to the *ejusdem generis* rule of interpretation does not prove to be of great assistance. Under this rule, that expression would cover *actions similar* to those specifically provided for. Admittedly such a rule of interpretation has been relied upon by various courts with regard to Article 6(c) of the London Agreement. Thus, for instance, in the *Tarnek* case, the District Court of Tel-Aviv held in a decision of 14 December 1951 that the definition of "other inhumane acts" laid down in the Israeli Law on Nazi and Nazi Collaborators (Punishment) of 1950, which reproduced the definition of Article 6(c), was to apply only to such other inhumane acts as resembled in their nature and their gravity those

---

[24] [825] *ICRC Commentary on the IVth Geneva Convention Relative to the Protection of Civilian Persons in time of War* (1958, repr. 1994), p. 39.

specified in the definition. This interpretative rule lacks precision, and is too general to provide a safe yardstick for the work of the Tribunal.

565. The Statute of the International Criminal Court (ICC) (Article 7(k)) provides greater detail than the ICTY Statute as to the meaning of other inhumane acts: "other inhumane acts of a similar character intentionally causing great suffering, or serious injury to the body or to mental or physical health". However, this provision also fails to provide an indication, even indirectly, of the legal standards which would allow us to identify the prohibited inhumane acts.[25]

566. Less broad parameters for the interpretation of "other inhumane acts" can instead be identified in international standards on human rights such as those laid down in the Universal Declaration on Human Rights of 1948 and the two United Nations Covenants on Human Rights of 1966. Drawing upon the various provisions of these texts, it is possible to identify a set of basic rights appertaining to human beings, the infringement of which may amount, depending on the accompanying circumstances, to a crime against humanity. Thus, for example, serious forms of cruel or degrading treatment of persons belonging to a particular ethnic, religious, political or racial group, or serious widespread or systematic manifestations of cruel or humiliating or degrading treatment with a discriminatory or persecutory intent no doubt amount to crimes against humanity: inhuman or degrading treatment is prohibited by the United Nations Covenant on Civil and Political Rights (Article 7), the European Convention on Human Rights, of 1950 (Article 3), the Inter-American Convention on Human Rights of 9 June 1994 (Article 5) and the 1984 Convention against Torture (Article 1). Similarly, the expression at issue undoubtedly embraces the forcible transfer of groups of civilians (which is to some extent covered by Article 49 of the IVth Convention of 1949 and Article 17(1) of the Additional Protocol II of 1977), enforced prostitution (indisputably a serious attack on human dignity pursuant to most international instruments on human rights), as well as the enforced disappearance of persons (prohibited by General Assembly Resolution 47/133 of 18 December 1992 and the Inter-American Convention of 9 June 1994). Plainly, all these, and other similar acts, must be carried out in a systematic manner and on a large scale. In other words, they must be as serious as the other classes of crimes provided for in the other provisions of Article 5. Once the legal parameters for determining the content of the category of "inhumane acts" are identified, resort to the *ejusdem generis* rule for the purpose of comparing and assessing the gravity of the prohibited act may be warranted.

The Trial Chamber again relied on human rights instruments when it had to define the notion of 'persecution' (see *infra*, Part II(2), Crimes against humanity).

Human rights intertwine with international criminal law also in relation to the fundamental rights of the various *participants in international criminal proceedings*. This aspect of international criminal law has made great strides since the time of the Nuremberg and Tokyo trials; it is now considered 'axiomatic that the International Tribunal[s] must fully respect internationally recognised standards regarding the rights of the accused at all stages' of their proceedings (as the UN Secretary-General wrote in his report to the Security Council on the establishment of the ICTY).

---

[25] [828] The International Law Commission, commenting on Art. 18 of its Draft Code of Crimes further states that "[t]he Commission recognized that it was impossible to establish an exhaustive list of the inhumane acts which might constitute crimes against humanity. First, this category of acts is intended to include only additional acts that are similar in gravity to those listed in the preceding subparagraphs. Second, the act must in fact cause injury to a human being in terms of physical or mental integrity, health or human dignity" (*Report of the International Law Commission on the Work of its Forty-Eighth Session*, 6 May-26 July 1996, UNGAOR 51st Sess. Supp. No. 10 (A/51/10) (Crimes Against the Peace and Security of Mankind), at para. 17, p. 103).

While human rights law has traditionally focused on the relationship between *States* and individuals, it has been noted that 'the international human rights regime's aspiration to ensure the accountability of all major actors will be severely compromised [...] if it does not succeed in devising a considerably more effective framework than currently exists in order to take adequate account of the roles played by some non-state actors' (P. Alston, *Non-state Actors and Human Rights* (New York: Oxford University Press, 2005), at p. 6). International courts and tribunals may well have been among the first non-State actors to take it upon themselves to develop – despite a host of practical problems and hurdles – comprehensive protections for individuals affected by their conduct, protections extensively based on international human rights law. In this sense it has become essential to understand human rights law in the context of international criminal adjudication. The cases below provide a glimpse of this evolving regime and its development by judges in international courts and tribunals.

STL, **In re Hariri**, *President, Order on Conditions of Detention, 21 April 2009*

On 13 December 2005, the Government of the Republic of Lebanon requested the United Nations to establish a tribunal to investigate and try all individuals alleged to be responsible for the attack of 14 February 2005 in Beirut that killed the former Prime Minister Rafiq Hariri and 22 others. On 30 August 2005, four persons were arrested in Lebanon in connection with the attack of 14 February 2005. The United Nations and Lebanon negotiated an agreement on the establishment of the Special Tribunal for Lebanon (STL). Further to UNSC Resolution 1757(2007) of 30 May 2007, the provisions of the STL Statute entered into force on 10 June 2007. On 1 March 2009, the STL commenced its operation and immediately dealt with the case of the four persons who were still being detained and, among other things, lacked access to their lawyers in a manner that protected the attorney–client privilege.

2. On 27 March 2009, at the request of the Prosecutor of the Tribunal (the "Prosecutor"), the Pre-Trial Judge issued an order directing the Lebanese judicial authority seized with the case of the attack against Prime Minister Rafiq Hariri and others (the "*Hariri* case") to defer to the Tribunal within fourteen days of receipt of the order.

3. The Order of 27 March 2009 requested, in accordance with Rule 17, the Lebanese judicial authority seized of the *Hariri* case to continue to detain those persons held in Lebanon in connection with the case from the time of the Prosecutor's receipt of the results of the investigation by the Lebanese authority and the copy of the Lebanese court records until the issuance of a decision by the Pre-Trial Judge.

4. On 8 April 2009, the Lebanese judicial authorities referred the list of persons detained to the Pre-Trial Judge. According to this list, the persons detained are Mr Jamil Mohamad Amin El Sayed, Mr Ali Salah El Dine El Hajj, Mr Raymond Fouad Azar and Mr Mostafa Fehmi Hamdan (the "detained persons").

5. On 15 April 2009, the Pre-Trial Judge issued an order confirming that since 10 April 2009 the detained persons have been under the legal authority of the Tribunal, though they continue to be detained in Lebanon by the Lebanese authorities. He ordered that, pursuant to international standards on human rights and the general principles of international criminal law and procedure and considering the complexity of the matter at hand, the Prosecutor must file no later than 27 April 2009 his reasoned application according to Rule 17(B) on whether he requests the continuation of detention for the detained persons.

6. On 20 April 2009, the Head of the Defence Office, after visiting the detention facility where the detained persons are currently held pursuant to the Order of the Pre-Trial Judge of 15 April 2009, addressed a letter (the "Request") to me, in my capacity as President of the Tribunal, requesting an order that:

(i) any meetings between the lawyers and their clients be privileged and confidential, without any prison staff or other persons being able to listen to, or record, the communication.

(ii) the detainees be allowed to meet each other, subject to reasonable security restrictions, for a period of two hours a day; and

(iii) the Registrar, who is responsible for the conditions of detention while under the authority of the Tribunal, is requested to inform the relevant Lebanese authorities of this decision. [...]

III. APPLICABLE LAW

A) The Right Freely and Privately to Communicate with Counsel

13. The Statute of the Tribunal ("Statute") provides in Article 16(4)(b) that an accused is entitled, *inter alia*, "to communicate without hindrance with counsel of his or her own choosing". Moreover, Rule 163 – modelled upon Rule 97 of the ICTY Rules of Procedure and Evidence – expressly describes communications "made in the context of the professional relationship between a person and his legal counsel as privileged". Rule 65(F) of the Rules of Detention specifies that visits of counsel shall be conducted within sight but not within the hearing of the staff of the Detention Facility. The rights attaching to suspects or accused in detention under these provisions are necessarily to be considered applicable, *mutatis mutandis*, to all detained persons even if they have not formally been held to be suspects or accused.

14. The right of accused persons to communicate freely and privately with counsel is laid down in international instruments on human rights. It is enshrined expressly in the American Convention on Human Rights (Article 8(2)(d)), and implicitly in the UN Covenant on Civil and Political Rights (Article 14(3)(b)) ("ICCPR") and the European Convention on Human Rights (Article 6(3)(b)). When the right is simply implied in the text of the international instrument, it has been subsequently spelled out in the case law of the relevant supervisory body. This holds true in particular for the European Court of Human Rights.[26]

15. Article 14(3)(b) of the ICCPR – which was ratified by Lebanon on 3 November 1972 and entered into force on 23 March 1976 – provides for the right "to communicate with counsel of his own choosing". The Human Rights Committee has clarified that this provision "requires

---

[26] [8] In *S. v. Switzerland*, Judgment of 28 November 1991 ("*S. v. Switzerland*"), the Court said that "unlike some national laws and unlike Article 8 (2) (d) of the American Convention on Human Rights, the European Convention does not expressly guarantee the right of a person charged with a criminal offence to communicate with defence counsel without hindrance. That right is set forth, however, within the Council, in Article 93 of the Standard Minimum Rules for the Treatment of Prisoners (...) The Court considers that an accused's right to communicate with his advocate out of hearing of a third person is part of the basic requirements of a fair trial in a democratic society and follows from Article 6 para. 3 (c) (art. 6-3-c) of the Convention. If a lawyer were unable to confer with his client and receive confidential instructions from him without such surveillance, his assistance would lose much of its usefulness, whereas the Convention is intended to guarantee rights that are practical and effective" (para. 48). See also *Brennan* v. *The United Kingdom*, Judgment of 16 October 2001: "an accused's right to communicate with his advocate out of hearing of a third person is part of the basic requirements of a fair trial and follows from Article 6 § 3 (c). [...] The importance to be attached to the confidentiality of such consultations, in particular that they should be conducted out of hearing of third persons, is illustrated by the international provisions cited above" (para. 38) and *Lanz* v. *Austria*, Judgment of 21 January 2002, para. 50.

counsel to communicate with the accused in conditions giving full respect for the confidentiality of their communications. Lawyers should be able to counsel and to represent their clients in accordance with their established professional standards and judgement without any restrictions, influences, pressures or undue interference from any quarter."[27] In a similar vein, paragraph 93 of the UN Standard Minimum Rules for the Treatment of Detainees provides that "[i]nterviews between the [untried] prisoner and his legal adviser may be within sight but not within the hearing of a police or institution official."

16. The very broad recognition of the right to communicate freely and privately with counsel by the international community, and the general attitude taken by States and international judicial bodies as to its importance, show that the right is now accepted in customary international law as one of the fundamental human rights relating to due process. Indeed, the right of an accused person to freely and confidentially communicate with his or her counsel is an indispensable condition for the effective exercise of most [of] his or her other rights. As the European Court has aptly noted, "if a lawyer were unable to confer with his client and receive confidential instructions from him without [. . .] surveillance, his assistance would lose much of its usefulness".[28] The rights of the defence, of which this right is an indispensable component, are one of the foundations of the concept of a fair trial.

17. The right to communicate freely and privately with counsel also accrues to a person *suspected* of having committed a crime. Such persons may also find themselves in need of confidential legal assistance, particularly when held in detention.

18. The right at issue is not, however, unlimited. Other imperative exigencies relating to the good administration of justice or to the need to prevent crimes may make it necessary to temporarily restrict the right.[29] Thus, for instance, the European Court of Human Rights has acknowledged that restrictions may be justified when there is a risk of collusion between the accused and a defence counsel,[30] or when an accused may use a defence counsel to influence witnesses or tamper with evidence.

19. However, restrictions of the right may only be admissible if they fulfil certain conditions, namely, that: (i) they are envisaged by law; (ii) they are necessary (that is, they are rendered indispensable by the need to countervail possible negative effects); (iii) they are proportionate to the exigency that warrants them (that is, they are commensurate to and do not exceed the fulfilment of such exigency – this may imply that the restriction be of limited duration); and (iv) they are submitted to regular and judicial scrutiny.

20. Likewise, for any detained person, this fundamental right can be restricted only if such conditions as set out above in relation to accused persons are fulfilled. This notion is clearly spelled out in Principle 18 of the Body of Principles for the Protection of All Persons under Any Form of Detention or Imprisonment, which states that:

  1. A detained or imprisoned person shall be entitled to communicate and consult with his legal counsel.

---

[27] [9] HRC, General Comment No. 13: Equality before the courts and the right to a fair and public hearing by an independent court established by law (Art. 14), 13 April 1984, para. 9.

[28] [11] See *Artico* v. *Italy*, 13 May 1980, para. 33 as well as *S.* v. *Switzerland*, para. 48.

[29] [12] In *Brennan* v. *United Kingdom*, Judgment of 16 October 2001, the European Court of Human Rights stated that "[. . .] the Court's case-law indicates that the right of access to a solicitor may be subject to restrictions for good cause and the question in each case is whether the restriction, in the light of the entirety of the proceedings, has deprived the accused of a fair hearing. While it is not necessary for the applicant to prove, assuming such were possible, that the restriction had a prejudicial effect on the course of the trial, the applicant must be able to be claim to have been directly affected by the restriction in the exercise of the rights of the defence" (para. 58).

[30] [13] [*Lanz* v. *Austria*, Judgment of 21 January 2002, paras 52–53].

2. A detained or imprisoned person shall be allowed adequate time and facilities for consultation with his legal counsel.

3. The right of a detained or imprisoned person to be visited by and to consult and communicate, without delay or censorship and in full confidentiality, with his legal counsel may not be suspended or restricted save in exceptional circumstances, to be specified by law or lawful regulations, when it is considered indispensable by a judicial or other authority in order to maintain security and good order.

[...]

IV. GROUNDS FOR THE DECISION

A. The Right to Freely and Privately Communicate with Counsel

29. For the fundamental right of a detained person to communicate with his or her counsel to be effective, it is imperative that communication between the detained person and his or her lawyer be privileged, unless the detaining authorities demonstrate that extraordinary reasons exist to temporarily restrict the right.

30. Taking into account the legal considerations set out above in paragraphs 18 to 20, I find that, whatever the nature and impact of the original reasons for restricting the right to freely and privately communicate with counsel, at present any such restriction appears to be no longer justified. With the passage of time, and without any new evidence, any such restriction would be unreasonable and disproportionate to the need to prevent the risk of collusion, or further crimes.

31. In addition, the Prosecutor has not objected to restrictions of the detained persons' rights to freely and privately communicate with counsel.

V. DISPOSITION

On the strength of the above legal considerations, I hereby:

1) **GRANT** the request of the Head of Defence Office and accordingly;

2) **REQUEST** the Lebanese authorities

    (i) to ensure that the right of the detained persons to freely and privately communicate with their counsel be fully implemented. It is understood that the Lebanese authorities may take all security measures they consider necessary under the circumstances, including visual surveillance through remote video-camera, as long as the right to their privileged communication with counsel is respected; [...]

3) **REQUEST** the Registrar to notify the Lebanese authorities of this Order and to request their assistance in notifying it to the detained persons.

The Order by the President in the *Hariri* case was followed, a few days later, by the order of the Pre-Trial Judge to release the four detained persons for lack of evidence.

While human rights considerations in international criminal proceedings often relate to suspects, accused or detained persons, there are other individuals whose rights are to be taken into account. Over the past decade, victims of international crimes have been increasingly considered necessary participants in international proceedings. Article 68 of the ICCSt. provides that '[w]here the personal interests of the victims are affected, the Court shall permit their views and concerns to be presented and considered at stages of the proceedings determined to be appropriate by the Court', subject to several limitations.

ICC, Situation in the Democratic Republic of the Congo, *Pre-Trial Chamber I,*
Decision on the Applications for Participation in the Proceedings of VPRS 1,
VPRS 2, VPRS 3, VPRS 4, VPRS 5 and VPRS 6, 17 January 2006

> During proceedings related to the situation in the Democratic Republic of the Congo, in June 2005 the ICC received application from several persons requesting to participate in the proceedings as victims. One of the questions before the Pre-Trial Chamber was whether the Statute, the Rules of Procedure and Evidence and the Regulations of the Court accord victims the right to participate in the proceedings *at the stage of investigation* of a situation and, if so, what form such participation should take. Article 68 – which is placed in Part 6 of the ICCSt. dealing with 'Trial' – does not clarify the matter. After rejecting various arguments raised by the Prosecutor aimed at excluding victims' participation during the investigation stage, the Pre-Trial Chamber considered the 'teleological' interpretation of the provision in question, bringing to the fore the rights of victims recognized by international law.

50. The interpretation of article 68(3) as being applicable to the investigation stage is also consistent with the object and purpose of the victims participation regime established by the drafters of the Statute, which ensued from a debate that took place in the context of the growing emphasis placed on the role of victims by the international body of human rights law and by international humanitarian law.

51. In the Chamber's opinion, the Statute grants victims an independent voice and role in proceedings before the Court. It should be possible to exercise this independence, in particular, vis-à-vis the Prosecutor of the International Criminal Court so that victims can present their interests. As the European Court has affirmed on several occasions, victims participating in criminal proceedings cannot be regarded as "either the opponent – or for that matter necessarily the ally – of the prosecution, their roles and objectives being clearly different".

52. Furthermore, the Chamber notes, with regard to systems in which victims are authorised to participate in criminal proceedings,[31] that the European Court of Human Rights has applied article 6(1) of the European Convention on Human Rights to victims from the investigation stage, even before confirmation of the charges, particularly where the outcome of the criminal proceedings is of decisive importance for obtaining reparations for the harm suffered.[32]

---

[31] [51] Systems under which victims are not entitled to participate in criminal proceedings have other arrangements for giving them access to justice. For example, in England and Wales, in addition to victims' right to obtain reparations under the *Criminal Injuries Compensation Act* of 8 November 1995 (UK ST 1995 c 53 s l, amended on 1 July 1999), the Home Office published the *Code of Practice for Victims of Crime* on 18 October 2005 (which will enter into force in April 2006 and which replaces the *Victims Charter*, adopted in 1991 and amended in 1996), a document which accords victims of crimes rights before the law for the first time. The Code sets out the benefits that victims may expect from the criminal justice system, including the right to be notified within specific time limits of progress in the investigation of crimes committed against them (sections 5.9 to 5.12), the right to be notified of any arrest (sections 5.14 to 5.17) and the right to be informed of the status of cases before the courts (sections 5.18 to 5.35 and chapters VII and VIII). Moreover, in Ireland, in addition to victims' right to institute proceedings for reparations under the *Garda Siochana Compensation Act* of 7 August 1941 (No. 19, as amended on 21 February 1945), the *Criminal Justice Act* of 27 July 1993 (6/1993, sections 6 to 9) and the *Non-Statutory Scheme of Compensation for Personal Injuries Criminally Inflicted* (introduced in 1974 and amended in 1986), the *Charter for Victims of Crime*, promulgated in 1999 by the Ministry of Justice, Equality and Law Reform, also contains specific provisions aimed at keeping victims informed of action taken on their complaints, on the status of criminal proceedings and on their outcome.

[32] [52] European Court of Human Rights, *Moreira de Azevedo v. Portugal*, "Judgment", 23 October 1990, Series A No. 189; European Court of Human Rights, *Tomasi v. France*, "Judgment", 27 August 1992, Series

53. The Inter-American Court of Human Rights reached the same conclusion in the *Blake* case,[33] in which it applied article 8 (1) of the American Convention on Human Rights to victims participating in criminal proceedings from the investigation stage. The Inter-American Court decided that it was clear from the terms of article 8 of the Convention that victims of human rights violations or their relatives are entitled to take steps during criminal proceedings, from the investigation stage and prior to confirmation of the charges, to have the facts clarified and the perpetrators prosecuted, and are entitled to request reparations for the harm suffered. The Chamber considers that article 68 (3) of the Statute also gives victims the right to participate in the fight against impunity.

54. Having presented its terminological, contextual and teleological arguments, the Chamber finds that article 68 (3) is applicable to the stage of investigation of a situation.

An issue connected to the violation of fundamental human rights during international proceedings relates to the remedies that can be invoked by the persons concerned. The ICTY and the ICTR have dealt with several such cases.

ICTR, Prosecutor *v.* Rwamakuba, *Trial Chamber, Decision on Appropriate Remedy, 31 January 2007*

> André Rwamakuba was Minister for National Education in the Interim Government in the period of the genocide in Rwanda. He was arrested in Namibia on 21 October 1998 and transferred to the ICTR two days later to face allegations related to massacres of Tutsis. In September 2006, Rwamakuba was acquitted by a Trial Chamber, which considered the case was built on hearsay and unreliable evidence. After the acquittal, the Trial Chamber was called upon to deal with violations of the defendant's human rights during the proceedings, in particular, lack of legal assistance for several months.

1. On 20 September 2006, the Chamber rendered its Judgement in the present case, acquitting André Rwamakuba of all charges and consequently ordering his immediate release. [. . .]

4. In its Judgement of 20 September 2006, the Chamber held that in light of the previous finding of a violation of André Rwamakuba's right to legal assistance, he was at liberty to file an application seeking an appropriate remedy for the violation of his right to legal assistance between 22 October 1998 and 10 March 1999. [. . .]

32. The Chamber will first determine whether it has the power to provide for an effective remedy in case of violation of the rights of a person while he or she was an accused before this Tribunal. In particular, it will determine whether it has the power to order a financial compensation as an effective remedy. Finally, it will address the question of the effective remedy in view of the specific circumstances of the case. [. . .]

40. The Chamber agrees with the parties that neither the Statute, nor the Rules of this Tribunal provide for a right to an effective remedy for violations of human rights. However,

A No. 241-A; European Court of Human Rights, *Acquaviva v. France*, "Judgment", 21 November 1995, Series A No. 333-A; European Court of Human Rights, *Selmouni v. France*, "Judgment", 28 July 1999, Application No. 25803/94; European Court of Human Rights, *Calvelli and Ciglio v. Italy*, "Judgment", 17 January 2002, Application No. 32967/96; European Court of Human Rights, Grand Chamber, *Perez v. France*, "Judgment", 12 February 2004, Application No. 47287/99; European Court of Human Rights, *Antunes Rocha v. Portugal*, "Judgment", 31 May 2005, Application No. 64330/01.

[33] [53] Inter-American Court of Human Rights, *Blake v. Guatemala*, "Judgment", 24 January 1998, Series C No 36. [. . .]

this right undoubtedly forms part of customary international law and is expressly provided for in the following instruments: the Universal Declaration of Human Rights, the ICCPR, the Convention on the Elimination of All Forms of Racial Discrimination, the Convention against Torture and Other Cruel, Inhuman or Degrading Treatment, the Convention Concerning Indigenous and Tribal Peoples in Independent Countries, the UN Declaration of Basic Principles of Justice for Victims of Crime and Abuse of Power, the ECHR, the American Declaration of the Rights and Duties of Man and the American Convention of Human Rights.

41. Relying upon international human rights instruments, and particularly the International Covenant on Civil and Political Rights, the Appeals Chamber of this Tribunal has recognized on several occasions that an Accused has a right to an effective remedy.

42. In the *Kajelijeli* case, the Appeals Chamber relied upon the various sources of law applicable to the Tribunal, including the Statute, the Rules and customary international law as reflected in the ICCPR as well as referred to the provisions of regional human rights treaties as persuasive authority and evidence of international custom. It set out, on the basis of existing standards in international human rights law, that "any violation of the accused's rights entails the provision of an effective remedy pursuant to Article 2(3)(a) of the ICCPR." In that case, the Appeals Chamber ordered a reduction in sentence as the appropriate remedy with respect to the violations of the Appellant's rights.

43. In the *Barayagwiza* case, the Appeals Chamber also affirmed that all violations of rights demand a remedy. In his Separate Declaration, Judge Rafael Nieto-Navia shed further light on the Appeals Chamber decision by stating as follows:

> 28. Human rights treaties provide that when a state violates fundamental human rights, it is obliged to ensure that appropriate domestic remedies are in place to put an end to such violations and in certain circumstances to provide for fair compensation to the injured party.
>
> 29. Although the Tribunal is not a State, it is following such a precedent to compensate the Appellant for the violation of his human rights. As it is impossible to turn back the clock, I think that the remedy decided by the Appeals Chamber fulfills the international requirements.

44. In the present case, the Appeals Chamber has stated that "it [was] open to [Rwamakuba] to invoke the issue of the alleged violation of his fundamental human rights by the Tribunal in order to seek reparation as the case may be, at the appropriate time."

45. On the basis of the above Appeals Chamber decisions, the Chamber holds the view that its power to provide an accused or former accused with an effective remedy for violations of human rights arises out of the combined effect of the Tribunal's inherent powers and its obligation to respect generally accepted international human rights norms. [. . .]

47. In the Chamber's view, the power to give effect to the right to an effective remedy for violations of the rights of an accused or former accused accrues to the Chamber because this power is essential for the carrying out of judicial functions, including the fair and proper administration of justice. This is all the more true in the present case as the right at issue, the right to legal assistance, is one of the core fair trial rights held by an accused in criminal proceedings.

48. Moreover, this power accrues to the Chamber because the Tribunal, as a special kind of subsidiary organ of the U.N. Security Council, is bound to respect and ensure respect for generally accepted human rights norms. Indeed, the United Nations, as an international subject, is bound to respect rules of customary international law, including those rules which relate to the protection of fundamental human rights. This result is in keeping with the United Nations'

stated purposes as well as its internal practices. According to its constitutional instrument, one of the purposes of the United Nations is to achieve international co-operation in promoting and encouraging respect for human rights and for fundamental freedoms for all. In many instances, the U.N. Security Council has recalled this purpose by adopting resolutions aiming to promote and protect human rights. The Security Council and the Secretary-General have also recalled that the members of peacekeeping missions as well as transitional authorities for the administration of territory must observe fundamental human rights. In particular, when reporting to the Security Council on the establishment of the ICTY, the U.N. Secretary General underlined that: "It is axiomatic that the International Tribunal must fully respect internationally recognized standards regarding the rights of the accused at all stages of its proceedings." This result is furthermore in keeping with the principle that States cannot evade their obligations under international legal obligations by creating an international organization that would not be bound by the legal limits imposed upon them. As the Member States of the United Nations are bound to respect their international human rights obligations when prosecuting international crimes within their domestic national legal systems, they cannot establish an International Criminal Tribunal which would not be bound to respect the same human rights obligations.

49. In light of the above-mentioned principles and as there is no explicit provision of the Statute or the Rules providing for an organ of this Tribunal to grant an effective remedy, the Chamber finds that it has the inherent power to provide an accused or former accused with an effective remedy for violations of his or her human rights while being prosecuted or tried before this Tribunal. Such power necessarily accrues to the Chamber as it is essential both for the carrying out of its judicial functions and for complying with its obligation to respect generally accepted international human rights norms. [...]

COMMENTARY

In the *Rwamakuba* case, the Trial Chamber awarded the defendant US$2,000 for the violation of his right to legal assistance and, as further reparation for this violation, ordered the Registrar to provide an apology to him and to use his good offices to resettle him with his family and ensure his children's continued education. The ICTR Appeals Chamber affirmed this decision on 13 September 2007.

The ICCSt. contains provisions for compensation in case, inter alia, of unlawful arrest or detention, or of miscarriage of justice (Article 85 ICCSt.). If human rights violations are egregious and stem from culpable conduct of an organ of the Tribunal, the ad hoc Tribunals have even considered dismissal of the indictment with prejudice to the Prosecutor and immediate release of the accused (see, for instance, *Jean-Bosco Barayagwiza* v. *The Prosecutor*, Appeals Chamber's Decision of 3 November 1999, as revised by the Appeals Chamber's Decision (Prosecutor's Request for Review or Reconsideration) of 31 March 2000; *Prosecutor* v. *Dragan Nikolić*, Appeals Chamber's Decision on Interlocutory Appeal Concerning Legality of Arrest of 5 June 2003, excerpted in Part V(3), Surrenders and Arrests). These decisions, often criticized for how the tribunals have interpreted 'appropriate remedy', must however be commended for at least vindicating the *principle* that the existence of *effective* remedies constitutes the cornerstone of human rights protection. How such effective remedies are ensured in practice in each specific circumstance can be hardly decided a priori.

International tribunals composed of Judges coming from all the various cultural and legal traditions represented within the United Nations (Judges from Burkina Faso, China, Colombia, Egypt, France, Guyana, Italy, Malaysia, Turkey, United States of America and Zambia participated in issuing some of the decisions cited above) have time and again reiterated how essential the procedural and substantive due process protections are in criminal proceedings. This is a fact that cannot be overstated.

QUESTIONS

1. Human rights law is assumed to be a body of law in expansion, as existing rights are perfected and new rights are added. What issues can arise in applying this evolving body of law in international criminal proceedings?

2. Both the STL and the ICC orders above rely on pronouncements of the European Court of Human Rights for the purpose of interpreting provisions of their Statutes or of other human rights instruments. Why is this so? Can judgments of the European Court of Human Rights or the Inter-American Court of Human Rights, or findings by the UN Human Rights Committee, shed light on how Tribunals or, in the abovementioned case of the ICC, Congolese victims should interpret their rights and obligations?

3. The instruments cited in the *Rwamakuba* decision are treaties or declarations addressed to States. On what grounds did the ICTR find that they were binding in relation to proceedings held before it?

FURTHER READING

G. Acquaviva, 'Human Rights Violations before International Tribunals: Reflections of Responsibility of International Organizations' (2007) 20 *Leiden J. of Int'l L* 613–636.

J. Nilsson, 'Crimes Against Humanity', in *Oxford Companion*, 284–8.

W. Schomburg and J.C. Nemitz, 'The Protection of Human Rights of the Accused before the International Criminal Tribunal for Rwanda', in E. Decaux *et al.* (eds), *From Human Rights to International Criminal Law: Studies in Honour of an African Jurist, the Late Judge Laïty Kama* (Leyden: Martinus Nijhoff, 2007).

S. Starr, 'Rethinking "Effective Remedies": Remedial Deterrence in International Courts' (2008) 83 *NYU L. Rev.* 693.

Zahar and Sluiter, *International Criminal Law*, 275–322.

2

THE FUNDAMENTAL PRINCIPLES OF INTERNATIONAL CRIMINAL LAW

(A) *NULLUM CRIMEN SINE LEGE*

THE NOTION AND ITS ORIGINS

The principle of legality, expressed in the Latin maxim *nullum crimen sine lege, nulla poena sine lege* ('no crime without law, no punishment without law') haunts international criminal law – at once a fundamental principle of contemporary adjudication and an oft-raised accusation about the supposed illegitimacy of international criminal law's application. In its strict sense, legality is the idea that a person may only be convicted and punished for something that was a crime under law applicable at the time the conduct occurred. A criminal system with a strong and strict sense of legality privileges the interests of the individual accused over that of society in control and punishment. The rationale is that the individual must be protected against arbitrary government power and the vicissitudes of the majority's animosities.

The principle of legality entails three main corollaries: (1) specificity – the idea that criminal prohibitions must be sufficiently precise to give notice regarding what is criminalized, giving rise to the related principle of strict construction and the idea that ambiguities are resolved in favour of the accused; (2) non-retroactivity – barring retroactive criminal prohibitions; (3) and non-extension by analogy – the prohibition against expanding the scope of criminal prohibition by analogy beyond that set forth by law in advance. In addition, many democratic civil-law countries also construe legality as also requiring that criminal prohibitions be prescribed by written legislation passed by a parliamentary body in advance – a notion relaxed in those common-law countries that still permit judge-made law in the form of common-law crimes.[1]

The use of the Latin terms to express the maxim of legality may suggest Roman roots, but the notion of legality recognized in periods of ancient Roman law bears only rudimentary resemblance to its modern incarnation. An embryonic version of the principle appears in Article 39 of England's *Magna Charta libertatum* of 1215, an enumeration of

---

[1] In the interest of legality, however, even common-law jurisdictions like the USA have moved to mainly statutory crimes and have largely abolished the notion of common-law crimes or have frozen cognizable common-law crimes to those recognized in early colonial history.

protections and liberties limiting the monarch's prerogatives forced upon King John by a group of powerful barons. Article 39 limits the sovereign's power by forbidding dispossession or exile of any man 'except by the lawful judgment of his peers or by the law of the land'. It was not until the Enlightenment, however, that the principle's theoretical underpinnings developed, founded on concern over despotism when the monarch holds absolute power. Inspired by Enlightenment thinkers like Voltaire, Montesquieu and Rousseau, reformer Cesare Beccaria in 1764 cautioned in his *Dei Delitti e Delle Pene* (On Crimes and Penalties):

Nothing is more dangerous than the common axiom that one must consult the spirit of the law [...] Everyone has his own point of view, and everyone has a different one at different times. [...]

If the interpretation of laws is an evil, their obscurity which necessarily entails interpretation, is obviously another evil, one that will be all the greater if the laws are written in a language that is foreign to the common people. This places them at the mercy of a handful of men, for they cannot judge for themselves the prospect of their own liberty or that of others.

The German professor of criminal and international law, Franz von Liszt, explained the rationale of the *nullum crimen* principle in 1893, noting that it is 'the citizen's bulwark against the State's omnipotence' for it protects 'the individual against the ruthless power of the majority, against Leviathan' (Franz von Liszt, *The Rationale for the Nullum Crimen Principle*, reprinted in (2007) 5 JICJ 1009).

In the international criminal arena, the principle of legality poses several tensions. There is no super-legislature for the international community, and treaty law and customary rules may be underdeveloped to address grave crimes. In the aftermath of atrocity, the interest of the international community may be to condemn by adjudging acts criminal and to punish. In the absence of clear pre-existing law, however, this interest in justice for the community may conflict with a strong and strict sense of legality. Justice for the community may conflict with procedural justice for the accused.

Until recently, the interest in justice for the world community trumped strict legality. This approach was pronounced during the tribunals adjudicating World War II-era crimes – a key formative moment for international criminal law. Before the International Military Tribunal (IMT) at Nuremberg, Nazi war criminals protested that prosecutions for crimes against peace and crimes against humanity violated the principle of *nullum crimen sine lege*. The objection from Nazi defendants was ironic indeed because the Nazis infamously rejected the principle of *nulla crimen sine lege*, opting instead for the notion of *nullum crimen sine poena* ('no crime without punishment'). Prominent political theorist and Nazi Carl Schmitt argued that 'the bold and imaginatively endowed criminal' could rely on 'the phrase *nulla poena sine lege*' to render 'the *Rechtsstaat* a laughingstock' (Carl Schmitt, *On the Three Types of Juristic Thought* (Joseph W. Bedersky trans. [1934] 2004), at 93). Reich Minister of Justice Franz Gürtner proclaimed, 'Everyone who commits an act deserving of punishment shall receive due punishment regardless of the incompleteness of law. [...] National Socialism imposes a new and high task on Criminal Law, namely the realization of true justice.'

The international military tribunals at Nuremberg and Tokyo wrestled with the tension between legality and the call for prosecutions fully reflecting the nature of the defendants' wrongdoing. Prosecution for crimes against peace starkly posed the question because, as further discussed in the chapter on aggression, it is highly doubtful that waging aggressive war was a recognized international crime prior to the prosecution at Nuremberg. In the excerpts below, the Tribunals attempted to address the tensions.

Cases

IMT Nuremberg, Göring et al., *Judgment of 30 September–1 October 1946*

All the defendants before the Nuremberg Tribunal were charged with participating in the planning, preparation, initiation and waging of wars of aggression, and being part of a common plan or conspiracy to commit crimes against peace. In adjudicating the charges, the Tribunal at Nuremberg wrestled with the defendants' claim that the prosecution for the charges violated the *nullum crimen sine lege* principle.

The Law of the Charter

[...] [T]he crimes coming within the jurisdiction of the Tribunal, for which there shall be individual responsibility, are set out in Article 6 [of the Nuremberg Charter establishing the Tribunal]. The law of the Charter is decisive, and binding upon the Tribunal. [...]

It was urged on behalf of the defendants that a fundamental principle of all law international and domestic is that there can be no punishment of crime without a pre-existing law. "Nullum crimen sine lege, nulla poena sine lege." It was submitted that ex post facto punishment is abhorrent to the law of all civilized nations, that no sovereign power had made aggressive war a crime at the time that the alleged criminal acts were committed, that no statute had defined aggressive war, that no penalty had been fixed for its commission, and no court had been created to try and punish offenders.

In the first place, it is to be observed that the maxim nullum crimen sine lege is not a limitation of sovereignty, but is in general a principle of justice. To assert that it is unjust to punish those who in defiance of treaties and assurances have attacked neighboring states without warning is obviously untrue, for in such circumstances the attacker must know that he is doing wrong, and so far from it being unjust to punish him, it would be unjust if his wrong were allowed to go unpunished. Occupying the positions they did in the Government of Germany, the defendants, or at least some of them must have known of the treaties signed by Germany, outlawing recourse to war for the settlement of international disputes, they must have known that they were acting in defiance of all international law when in complete deliberation they carried out their designs of invasion and aggression. On this view of the case alone it would appear that the maxim has no application to the present facts.

This view is strongly reinforced by a consideration of the state of international law in 1939, so far as aggressive war is concerned. The General Treaty for the Renunciation of War of 27th August, 1928, more generally known as the Pact of Paris or the Kellogg-Briand Pact, was binding on sixty-three nations, including Germany, Italy and Japan at the outbreak of war in 1939. In the preamble, the signatories declared that they were:

"Deeply sensible of their solemn duty to promote the welfare of mankind; persuaded that the time has come when a frank renunciation of war as an instrument of national policy should be made to the end that the peaceful and friendly relations now existing between their peoples should be perpetuated.... all changes in their relations with one another should be sought only by pacific means.... thus uniting civilised nations of the world in a common renunciation of war as an instrument of their national policy...."

The first two Articles are as follows:–

"Article I: The High Contracting Parties solemnly declare in the names of their respective peoples that they condemn recourse to war for the solution of international controversies and renounce it as an instrument of national policy in their relations to one another."

"Article II: The High Contracting Parties agree that the settlement or solution of all disputes or conflicts of whatever nature or of whatever origin they may be, which may arise among them, shall never be sought except by pacific means."

The question is, what was the legal effect of this Pact? The nations who signed the Pact or adhered to it unconditionally condemned recourse to war for the future as an instrument of policy, and expressly renounced it. After the signing of the Pact, any nation resorting to war as an instrument of national policy breaks the Pact. In the opinion of the Tribunal, the solemn renunciation of war as an instrument of national policy necessarily involves the proposition that such a war is illegal in international law; and that those who plan and wage such a war, with its inevitable and terrible consequences, are committing a crime in so doing. War for the solution of international controversies undertaken as an instrument of national policy certainly includes a war of aggression, and such a war is therefore outlawed by the Pact. As Mr. Henry L. Stimson, then Secretary of State of the United States, said in 1932:

"War between nations was renounced by the signatories of the 'Kellogg-Briand Treaty. This means that it has become throughout practically the entire world.... an illegal thing. Hereafter, when nations engage in armed conflict, either one or both of them must be termed violators of this general treaty law.... We denounce them as law breakers."

But it is argued that the Pact does not expressly enact that such wars are crimes, or set up courts to try those who make such wars. To that extent the same is true with regard to the laws of war contained in the Hague Convention. The Hague Convention of 1907 prohibited resort to certain methods of waging war. These included the inhumane treatment of prisoners, the employment of poisoned weapons, the improper use of flags of truce, and similar matters. Many of these prohibitions had been enforced long before the date of the Convention; but since 1907 they have certainly been crimes, punishable as offences against the laws of war; yet the Hague Convention nowhere designates such practices as criminal, nor is any sentence prescribed, nor any mention made of a court to try and punish offenders. For many years past, however, military tribunals have tried and punished individuals guilty of violating the rules of land warfare laid down by this Convention. In the opinion of the Tribunal, those who wage aggressive war are doing that which is equally illegal, and of much greater moment than a breach of one of the rules of the Hague Convention. In interpreting the words of the Pact, it must be remembered that international law is not the product of an international legislature, and that such international agreements as the Pact have to deal with general principles of law, and not with administrative matters of procedure. The law of war is to be found not only in treaties, but in the customs and practices of states which gradually obtained universal recognition, and from the general principles of justice applied by jurists and practiced by military courts. This law is not static, but by continual adaptation follows the needs of a changing world. Indeed, in many cases treaties do no more than express and define for more accurate reference the principles of law already existing.

The view which the Tribunal takes of the true interpretation of the Pact is supported by the international history which preceded it. In the year 1923 the draft of a Treaty of Mutual Assistance was sponsored by the League of Nations. In Article I the Treaty declared "that aggressive war is an international crime," and that the parties would "undertake that no one of them will be guilty of its commission." The draft treaty was submitted to twenty-nine States, about half of whom were in favour of accepting the text. The principal objection appeared to be in the difficulty of defining the acts which would constitute "aggression," rather than any doubt as to the criminality of aggressive war.

The preamble to the League of Nations 1924 Protocol for the Pacific Settlement of International Disputes ("Geneva Protocol"), after "recognising the solidarity of the members of the international community," declared that "a war of aggression constitutes a violation of this

THE FUNDAMENTAL PRINCIPLES OF INTERNATIONAL CRIMINAL LAW   57

solidarity and is an international crime." It went on to declare that the contracting parties were "desirous of facilitating the complete application of the system provided in the Covenant of the League of Nations for the pacific settlement of disputes between the states and of ensuring the repression of international crimes." The Protocol was recommended to the members of the League of Nations by a unanimous resolution in the Assembly of the forty-eight members of the League. These members included Italy and Japan, but Germany was not then a member of the League.

Although the Protocol was never ratified, it was signed by the leading statesmen of the world, representing the vast majority of the civilised states and peoples, and may be regarded as strong evidence of the intention to brand aggressive war as an international crime.

At the meeting of the Assembly of the League of Nations on the 24th September, 1927, all the delegations then present (including the German, the Italian and the Japanese), unanimously adopted a declaration concerning wars of aggression. The preamble to the declaration stated:

"The Assembly:
Recognising the solidity which unites the community of nations;
Being "inspired by a firm desire for the maintenance of general peace;
Being convinced that a war of aggression can never serve as a means of settling international disputes, and is in consequence an international crime...."

The unanimous resolution of the 18th February, 1928, of twenty-one American Republics of the Sixth (Havana) Pan-American Conference, declared that "war of aggression constitutes an international crime against the human species."

All these expressions of opinion, and others that could be cited, so solemnly made, reinforce the construction which the Tribunal placed upon the Pact of Paris, that resort to a war of aggression is not merely illegal, but is criminal. The prohibition of aggressive war demanded by the conscience of the world, finds its expression in the series of pacts and treaties to which the Tribunal has just referred.

It is also important to remember that Article 227 of the Treaty of Versailles provided for the constitution of a special Tribunal, composed of representatives of five of the Allied and Associated Powers which had been belligerents in the first World War opposed to Germany, to try the former German Emperor "for a supreme offence against international morality and the sanctity of treaties." The purpose of this trial was expressed to be "to vindicate the solemn obligations of international undertakings, and the validity of international morality." In Article 228 of the Treaty, the German Government expressly recognised the right of the Allied Powers "to bring before military tribunals persons accused of having committed acts in violation of the laws and customs of war."

It was submitted that international law is concerned with the action of sovereign States, and provides no punishment for individuals; and further, that where the act in question is an act of state, those who carry it out are not personally responsible, but are protected by the doctrine of the sovereignty of the State. In the opinion of the Tribunal, both these submissions must be rejected. That international law imposes duties and liabilities upon individuals as well as upon States has long been recognised. In the recent case of Ex Parte Quirin (1942 317 US 1), before the Supreme Court of the United States persons were charged during the war with landing in the United States for purposes of spying and sabotage. The late Justice Stone, speaking for the Court, said:

"From the very beginning of its history this Court has applied the law of war as including that part of the law of nations which prescribes for the conduct of war the status, rights and duties of enemy nations as well as enemy individuals."

[...] Many other authorities could be quoted, but enough has been said to show that individuals can be punished for violations of international law. Crimes against international law are committed by men, not by abstract entities, and only by punishing individuals who commit such crimes can the provisions of international law be enforced. [...]

The principle of international law, which under certain circumstances protects the representatives of a state, cannot be applied to acts which are condemned as criminal by international law. The authors of these facts cannot shelter themselves behind their official position in order to be freed from punishment in appropriate proceedings. Article 7 of the Charter expressly declares:

> "The official position of defendants, whether as Heads of State, or responsible officials in government departments, shall not be considered as freeing them from responsibility, or mitigating punishment."

On the other hand the very essence of the Charter is that individuals have international duties which transcend the national obligations of obedience imposed by the individual State. He who violates the laws of war cannot obtain immunity while acting in pursuance of the authority of the State if the State in authorising action moves outside its competence under international law.

Defendants before the International Military Tribunal for the Far East (IMTFE), colloquially referred to as the Tokyo Tribunal, were also charged with crimes against peace. The Tokyo Tribunal adopted the rationale of the Nuremberg Tribunal regarding the principle of *nullum crimen sine lege*. The Tokyo Judgment sparked several separate opinions, of which two, by Judge Bernard V.A. Röling of the Netherlands and Radhabinod Pal of India, offer famously contrasting views and are excerpted below.

International Military Tribunal for the Far East, US et al. v. Araki et al., Separate Opinion of Bernard Victor Aloysius Röling, 12 November 1948 [pp. 44–9 of the original pagination]

The IMTFE was established by a special proclamation of General Douglas MacArthur on 19 January 1946 to try senior Japanese officials for war crimes, crimes against humanity and crimes against peace. While the majority of the IMTFE followed the rationale of the Nuremberg Tribunal in holding that crimes against peace were crimes at the relevant time, Judge Röling concluded that 'crimes against peace' were not viewed as 'true crimes' before the London Agreement constituting the Nuremberg Tribunal and squarely faced the question of legality.

The question has to be faced and answered whether the concept of these crimes was, and could be, created as such by the London Agreement of August 8, 1945, or by the Charter for the IMTFE.

The defence in this case has submitted that this question is of no consequence, in view of the rule invalidating ex post facto law. This argument, however, will not stand examination. If the principle of "nullum crimen sine preevia lege" were a principle of *justice*,[2] the Tribunal would be bound to exclude for that very reason every crime created in the Charter ex post facto, it being the first duty of the Tribunal to mete out justice. However, this maxim is not a principle of justice but a rule of policy, valid only if expressly adopted, so as to protect citizens against arbitrariness of courts (nullum crimen, nulla poena sine lege), as well as against arbitrariness of legislators (nullum crimen, nulla poena sine praevia lege). Nor does this rule

---

[2] [1] As the majority judgment, following the Judgment of Nuremberg, holds.

consider the question whether a certain act was criminally wrong at the moment it was committed, but only the question as to whether that act was or was not forbidden under penalty. As such, the prohibition of ex post facto law is an expression of political wisdom, not necessarily applicable in present international relations. This maxim of liberty may, if circumstances necessitate it, be disregarded even by powers victorious in a war fought for freedom. It is, however, neither the task nor within the power of the Tribunal to judge the wisdom of a certain policy. [...]

Positive international law, as existing at this moment, compels us to interpret the "crime against peace," as mentioned in the Charter, in a special way. It may be presupposed that the Allied Nations did not intend to create rules in violation of international law. This indicates that the Charter should be interpreted so that it is in accordance with International Law.

There is no doubt that powers victorious in a "bellum justum," and as such responsible for peace and order thereafter, have, according to international law, the right to counteract elements constituting a threat to that newly established order, and are entitled, as a means of preventing the recurrence of gravely offensive conduct, to seek and retain the custody of the pertinent persons. [...]

Mere political action, based on the responsibility of power, could have achieved this aim. That the judicial way is chose[n] to select those who were in fact the plan[n]ers, instigators and wagers of Japanese aggression is a novelty which cannot be regarded as a violation of international law in that it affords the vanquished more guarantees than mere political action could do. [...]

Crime in international law is applied to concepts with different meanings. Apart from those indicated above, it can also indicate acts comparable to political crimes in domestic law, where the decisive element is the danger rather than the guilt, where the criminal is considered an enemy rather than a villain, and where the punishment emphasizes the political measure rather than the judicial retribution.

In this sense should be understood the "crime against peace," referred to in the Charter. In this sense the crime against peace, as formulated in the Charter, is in accordance with international law. It goes without saying that this conception of the character of the "crime" has certain consequences with regard to the appropriate "punishment."

It appears to me that the Nuremberg Judgement is based upon a somewhat similar conception of the "crimes against peace." Although it qualified the "crime against peace" of initiating a war of aggression as "the supreme international crime," differing only from other war crimes in that it contains within itself the accumulated evil of the whole: yet those defendants found guilty of the crime against peace, who were not, or to a limited degree, found guilty of conventional war crimes, were given only prison sentences (Hess, Doenitz, Raeder, Funk, von Neurath).

As long as the dominant principle in the crime against peace is the dangerous character of the individual who committed this crime, the punishment should only be determined by considerations of security.

In this case, this means that no capital punishment should be given to anyone guilty of the crime against peace only.

International Military Tribunal for the Far East, US et al. v. Araki et al., Separate Opinion of Radhabinod Pal, 12 November 1948 [pp. 37, 61–4 of the original transcript]

Justice Pal of India also disagreed with the Tribunal's conclusion that waging a war of aggression was a crime at the time of commission. His view of how to address the issue of legality in prosecutions for crimes against peace differed sharply from Judge Röling, however. Pal was the only member of the 11-judge Tribunal who argued that Japan's top wartime leaders should be found not guilty.

The so-called trial held according to the definition of crime *now* given by the victors obliterates the centuries of civilization which stretch between us and the summary slaying of the defeated in a war. A trial with law thus prescribed will only be a sham employment of legal process for the satisfaction of a thirst for revenge. It does not correspond to any idea of justice. Such a trial may justly create the feeling that the setting up of a tribunal like the present is much more a political than a legal affair, an essentially political objective having thus been cloaked by a juridical appearance. Formalized vengeance can bring only an ephemeral satisfaction, with every probability of ultimate regret; but vindication of law through *genuine legal process* alone may contribute substantially to the re-establishment of order and decency in international relations. [...]

   Prisoners of war, so long as they remain so, are under the protection of international law. No national state, neither the victor nor the vanquished, can make any ex post facto law affecting their liability for past acts, particularly when they are placed on trial before *an international tribunal*. [...]

   Mr. Justice Jackson of the United States in his report as Chief of Counsel for the United States in prosecuting the principal war criminals of the European Axis observed:

   We could execute or otherwise punish them without a hearing. But undiscriminating executions or punishments without definite findings of guilt, fairly arrived at, would violate pledges repeatedly given, and would not sit easily on the American conscience or be remembered by our children with pride.

[...] I do not think that during recent centuries any victor has enjoyed any such right as is declared by Mr. Justice Jackson in his report. If the victor really had such a right then perhaps it might have been possible for him to give a new definition of a crime in respect of past acts and punish the prisoners as criminals according to such new definition after hearing them if that would ease the conscience of any nation. In that case it would have been mere adaptation of a particular method to the enforcement of an existing right. But I do not see anything anywhere in the existing international law conferring any such power on the victors. [...]

   Whatever the view of the legality or otherwise of a war may be taken, victory does not invest the victor with unlimited and undefined power now. International laws of war define and regulate the rights and duties of the victor over the individuals of the vanquished nationality. In my judgment, therefore, it is beyond the competence of any victor nation to go beyond the rules of international law as they exist, give new definitions of crimes and then punish the prisoners for having committed offences according to this new definition.

COMMENTARY

The Separate Opinions of Judges Röling and Pal are thought-provoking because of their frank realism and open acknowledgement of the considerations of political wisdom, legitimacy and the limits and prerogatives of victors' power. Their competing viewpoints also illustrate the contested status of the principle of *nullum crimen sine lege* at one of the most important formative moments for international criminal law – adjudication by the post-World War II military tribunals. Major systems of the world differed on the principle and its corollaries. For example, for centuries, China's Qing dynasty's legal code permitted punishment by analogy where conduct did not fall within the purview of the legal code detailing punishable acts. The nationalist Republic of China, which succeeded the Qing Dynasty and went on to govern Taiwan after being ousted by the Communists from China, did not proscribe retroactivity of criminal law in its constitution.

Among the Allied Powers, the Soviet Union, for example, rejected the notion of legality in criminal law. After the Russian Revolution, the earliest Communist decrees freed judges to define as criminal whatever their consciences indicated, guided by Marxist thought and remnants of the old imperial code deemed consistent with the new regime. In 1922 and 1926, new criminal codes permitted crime creation by analogy and the 'social defence' of punishing those 'who have committed socially dangerous acts'. Part of the political and theoretical basis for this approach was that legality hindered the proletariat in wielding the law as an instrument of class struggle and the view that societal interests should be privileged over individual rights.

In the decades since the military tribunals, however, the principle of legality has been enshrined in numerous human rights instruments. Very shortly after the Nuremberg and Tokyo judgments, the Universal Declaration of Human Rights of 1948 incorporated both the notions of *nullum crimen sine lege* and *nulla poena sine lege* as precepts of fair criminal process in Article 11, providing in part that:

No one shall be held guilty of any penal offence on account of any act or omission which did not constitute a penal offence, under national or international law, at the time when it was committed. Nor shall a heavier penalty be imposed than the one that was applicable at the time the penal offence was committed.

The International Covenant on Civil and Political Rights, among the most important of human rights treaties, similarly incorporates the notions of non-retroactivity of crime definitions or punishment in Article 15. Regional human rights treaties, such as the European Convention on Human Rights of 1950 and the American Convention on Human Rights of 1969, also prescribe protections based on the principle of legality.

Key major systems that formerly did not observe the maxim have moved towards recognition of the principle of *nullum crimen sine lege*. In 1958, the Soviet Union adopted new legislation that set the Soviet Republics on the path towards adopting aspects of the notion of legality. After the Soviet Union dissolved, most of the new states, including Russia, enshrined the principle of legality in their Constitutions. Since the 1997 revision of its criminal law, China's criminal code provides that punishment is permitted only for conduct 'explicitly defined as criminal acts in law.' More than four-fifths of the State members of the United Nations – 162 out of 192 States, approximately 84 per cent of the States – mandate non-retroactivity of crime definitions in their constitutions.

Before international criminal courts, the *nullum crimen* rule has also taken firm root and developed in sophistication. The approach taken by the Special Court for Sierra Leone (SCSL) in *Prosecutor* v. *Norman*, in adjudicating the crime of conscripting or enlisting children under the age of 15 years is illustrative.

SCSL, Prosecutor v. Norman, *Appeals Chamber, Decision on Preliminary Motion Based on Lack of Jurisdiction, 31 May 2004*

After a 1996 military coup, an alliance of the Revolutionary United Front (RUF) and Armed Forces Revolutionary Council (AFRC) took over Sierra Leone. The Civil

Defence Force (CDF) – an umbrella term for disparate militias including a band called the *kamajors* – fought to dislodge the RUF/AFRC alliance. Samuel Hinga Norman led the CDF during the bloody civil war and was indicted for, among other things, war crimes based on the recruitment of child soldiers under 15 by the CDF. The SCSL is the first international tribunal to consider war crimes charges based on the recruitment of child soldiers. Norman died of heart failure in 2007 before the Trial Chamber issued its judgment. In adjudicating pre-trial motions, however, the SCSL addressed the argument that war crimes charges based on the recruitment of child soldiers violated the principle of *nullum crimen sine lege*.

8. Under Article 4 of its Statute, the Special Court has the power to prosecute persons who committed serious violations of international humanitarian law including:

c. Conscripting or enlisting children under the age of 15 years into armed forces or groups using them to participate actively in hostilities ("child recruitment").

The original proposal put forward in the Secretary-General's Report on the establishment of the Special Court referred to the crime of "abduction and forced recruitment of children under the age of 15 years into armed forces or groups for the purpose of using them to participate actively in hostilities", reflecting some uncertainty as to the customary international law nature of the crime of conscripting or enlisting children as defined in the Rome Statute of the International Criminal Court and mirrored in the Special Court Statute. The wording was modified following a proposal by the President of the Security Council to ensure that Article 4(c) conformed "to the statement of the law existing in 1996 and as currently accepted by the international community". The question raised by the Preliminary Motion is whether the crime as defined in Article 4(c) of the Statute was recognised as a crime entailing individual criminal responsibility under customary international law at the time of the acts alleged in the indictments against the accused.

9. To answer the question before this Court, the first two sources of international law under Article 38(1) of the Statute of the International Court of Justice ("ICJ") have to be scrutinized:

1) international conventions, whether general or particular, establishing rules especially recognized by the contesting states

2) international custom, as evidence of a general practice accepted as law [...]

10. Given that the Defence does not dispute the fact that international humanitarian law is violated by the recruitment of children, it is not necessary to elaborate on this point in great detail. [...]

17. Prior to November 1996, the prohibition on child recruitment had also crystallised as customary international law. The formation of custom requires both state practice and a sense of pre-existing obligation (opinio iuris). "An articulated sense of obligation, without implementing usage, is nothing more than rhetoric. Conversely, state practice, without opinio iuris, is just habit." [...]

C. Nullum Crimen Sine Lege, Nullum Crimen Sine Poena

25. It is the duty of this Chamber to ensure that the principle of non-retroactivity is not breached. As essential elements of all legal systems, the fundamental principle *nullum crimen sine lege* and the ancient principle *nullum crimen sine poena*, need to be considered. In the ICTY case of *Prosecutor v Hadžihasanović*, it was observed that "In interpreting the principle *nullum crimen sine lege*, it is critical to determine whether the underlying conduct at the

time of its commission was punishable. The emphasis on conduct, rather than on the specific description of the offence in substantive criminal law, is of primary relevance." In other words it must be "foreseeable and accessible to a possible perpetrator that his concrete conduct was punishable". As has been shown in the previous sections, child recruitment was a violation of conventional and customary international humanitarian law by 1996. But can it also be stated that the prohibited act was criminalised and punishable under international or national law to an extent which would show customary practice?

26. In the ICTY case of *Prosecutor v. Tadić*, the test for determining whether a violation of humanitarian law is subject to prosecution and punishment is set out thus: [...]

(i)   the violation must constitute an infringement of a rule of international humanitarian law;

(ii) the rule must be customary in nature or, if it belongs to treaty law, the required conditions must be met;

(iii) the violation must be "serious", that is to say, it must constitute a breach of a rule protecting important values, and the breach must involve grave consequences for the victim [...];

(iv) the violation of the rule must entail, under customary or conventional law, the individual criminal responsibility of the person breaching the rule.

1. International Humanitarian Law

27. With respect to points i) and ii), it follows from the discussion above, where the requirements have been addressed exhaustively, that in this regard the test is satisfied.

2. Rule Protecting Important Values

28. Regarding point iii), all the conventions listed above deal with the protection of children and it has been shown that this is one of the fundamental guarantees articulated in Additional Protocol II. The Special Court Statute, just like the ICTR Statute before it, draws on Part II of Additional Protocol II entitled "Humane Treatment" and its fundamental guarantees, as well as Common Article 3 to the Geneva Conventions in specifying the crimes falling within its jurisdiction. "All the fundamental guarantees share a similar character. In recognising them as fundamental, the international community set a benchmark for the minimum standards for the conduct of armed conflict." Common Article 3 requires humane treatment and specifically addresses humiliating and degrading treatment. This includes the treatment of child soldiers in the course of their recruitment. Article 3(2) specifies further that the parties "should further endeavour to bring into force [...] all or part of the other provisions of the present convention", thus including the specific protection for children under the Geneva Conventions as stated above.

29. Furthermore, the UN Security Council condemned as early as 1996 the "inhumane and abhorrent practice" of recruiting, training and deploying children for combat. It follows that the protection of children is regarded as an important value. As can be verified in numerous reports of various human rights organizations, the practice of child recruitment bears the most atrocious consequences for the children.

3. Individual Criminal Responsibility

30. Regarding point iv), the Defence refers to the Secretary-General's statement that "while the prohibition on child recruitment has by now acquired a customary international law status, it is far less clear whether it is customarily recognised as a war crime entailing the individual criminal responsibility of the accused." The ICTY Appeals Chamber upheld the legality of prosecuting violations of the laws and customs of war, including violations of Common

Article 3 and the Additional Protocols in the *Tadić* case in 1995. In creating the ICTR Statute, the Security Council explicitly recognized for the first time that serious violations of fundamental guarantees lead to individual criminal liability and this was confirmed later on by decisions and judgments of the ICTR. In its Judgment in the *Akayesu* case, the ICTR Trial Chamber, relying on the *Tadić* test, confirmed that a breach of a rule protecting important values was a "serious violation" entailing criminal responsibility. The Trial Chamber noted that Article 4 of the ICTR Statute was derived from Common Article 3 (containing fundamental prohibitions as a humanitarian minimum of protection for war victims) and Additional Protocol II, "which equally outlines 'Fundamental Guarantees'". The Chamber concluded that "it is clear that the authors of such egregious violations must incur individual criminal responsibility for their deeds". Similarly, under the ICTY Statute adopted in 1993, a person acting in breach of Additional Protocol I to the Geneva Conventions may face criminal sanctions, and this has been confirmed in ICTY jurisprudence.

31. The Committee on the Rights of the Child, the international monitoring body for the implementation of the CRC, showed exactly this understanding while issuing its recommendations to Uganda in 1997. The Committee recommended that: "awareness of the duty to fully respect the rules of international humanitarian law, in the spirit of article 38 of the Convention, *inter alia* with regard to children, should be made known to the parties to the armed conflict in the northern part of the State Party's territory, and that **violations of the rules of international humanitarian law entail responsibility being attributed to the perpetrators.**"

32. In 1998 the Rome Statute for the International Criminal Court was adopted. It entered into force on 1 July 2002. Article 8 includes the crime of child recruitment in international armed conflict and internal armed conflict, the elements of which are elaborated in the Elements of Crimes adopted in 2000: [...]

33. [...] The discussion during the preparation of the Rome Statute focused on the codification and effective implementation of the existing customary norm rather than the formation of a new one.

34. Building on the principles set out in the earlier Conventions, the 1999 ILO Convention 182 Concerning the Prohibition and Immediate Action for the Elimination of the Worst Forms of Child Labour, provided:

Article 1

Each Member which ratifies this Convention shall take **immediate and effective measures** to secure the prohibition and elimination of the worst forms of child labour as a matter of urgency.

Article 2

For the purposes of this Convention, **the term "child" shall apply to all persons under the age of 18**.

Article 3

For the purposes of this Convention, the term "the worst forms of child labour" comprises:

(a) all forms of slavery or practices similar to slavery, such as the sale and trafficking of children, debt bondage and serfdom and forced or compulsory labour, **including forced or compulsory recruitment of children for use in armed conflict**.

It is clear that by the time Article 2 of this Convention was formulated, the debate had moved on from the question whether the recruitment of children under the age of 15 was prohibited or indeed criminalized, and the focus had shifted to the next step in the development of international law, namely the raising of the standard to include all children under the age of 18.

This led finally to the wording of Article 4 of the Optional Protocol II to the Convention on the Rights of the Child on the Involvement of Children in Armed Conflict.

35. The CRC Optional Protocol II was signed on 25 May 2000 and came into force on 12 February 2002. It has 115 signatories and has been ratified by 70 states. The relevant Article for our purposes is Article 4 which states:

1. Armed groups that are distinct from the armed forces of a State should not, under any circumstances, recruit or use in hostilities persons **under the age of 18 years**.
2. States Parties shall take all feasible measures to prevent such recruitment and use, including the adoption of legal measures necessary **to prohibit and criminalize such practices**. [...]

38. A norm need not be expressly stated in an international convention for it to crystallize as a crime under customary international law. What, indeed, would be the meaning of a customary rule if it only became applicable upon its incorporation into an international instrument such as the Rome Treaty? Furthermore, it is not necessary for the *individual criminal responsibility* of the accused to be explicitly stated in a convention for the provisions of the convention to entail individual criminal responsibility under customary international law. As Judge Meron in his capacity as professor has pointed out, "it has not been seriously questioned that some acts of individuals that are prohibited by international law constitute criminal offences, even when there is no accompanying provision for the establishment of the jurisdiction of particular courts or scale of penalties".[3]

39. The prohibition of child recruitment constitutes a fundamental guarantee and although it is not enumerated in the ICTR and ICTY Statutes, it shares the same character and is of the same gravity as the violations that are explicitly listed in those Statutes. The fact that the ICTY and ICTR have prosecuted violations of Additional Protocol II provides further evidence of the criminality of child recruitment before 1996.

40. The criminal law principle of specificity provides that criminal rules must detail specifically both the objective elements of the crime and the requisite *mens rea* with the aim of ensuring that all those who may fall under the prohibitions of the law know in advance precisely which behaviour is allowed and which conduct is instead proscribed.[4] Both the Elements of Crimes formulated in connection with the Rome Statute and the legislation of a large proportion of the world community specified the elements of the crime.

41. Article 38 of the CRC states that States Parties have to take "all feasible measures" to ensure that children under 15 do not take part in hostilities and Article 4 urges them to "undertake all appropriate legislative [...] measures" for the implementation of the CRC. As all "feasible measures" and "appropriate legislation" are at the disposal of states to prevent child recruitment, it would seem that these also include criminal sanctions as measures of enforcement. As it has aptly been stated: "Words on paper cannot save children in peril."

42. In the instant case, further support for the finding that the *nullum crimen* principle has not been breached is found in the national legislation of states which includes criminal sanctions as a measure of enforcement.

43. The Defence submitted during the oral hearing that there is not a single country in the world that has criminalized the practice of recruiting child soldiers and that child recruitment was not only not a war crime but it was doubtful whether the provisions of the CRC protected child soldiers. A simple reading of Article 38 of the CRC disposes of the latter argument. Concerning the former argument, it is clearly wrong. An abundance

---

[3] [64] Theodor Meron, *International Criminalization of Internal Atrocities*, (1995) 89 AJIL 554, p. 562.

[4] [65] Antonio Cassese, *International Criminal Law* (Oxford University Press, 2003), p. 145.

of states criminalized child recruitment in the aftermath of the Rome Statute, as for example Australia. In response to its ratification of the Rome Statute, Australia passed the *International Criminal Court (Consequential Amendments) Act*. Its purpose was to make the offences in the Rome Statute offences under Commonwealth law. Section 268.68(1) creates the offence of using, conscripting and enlisting children in the course of an international armed conflict and sets out the elements of the crime and the applicable terms of imprisonment. Section 268.88 contains similar provisions relating to conflict that is not an international armed conflict.

44. By 2001, and in most cases prior to the Rome Statute, 108 states explicitly prohibited child recruitment, one example dating back to 1902, and a further 15 states that do not have specific legislation did not show any indication of using child soldiers. The list of states in the 2001 Child Soldiers Global Report clearly shows that states with quite different legal systems – civil law, common law, Islamic law – share the same view on the topic.

45. It is sufficient to mention a few examples of national legislation criminalizing child recruitment prior to 1996 in order to further demonstrate that the *nullum crimen* principle is upheld. As set out in the UNICEF Amicus Brief, Ireland's Geneva Convention Act provides that any "minor breach" of the Geneva conventions [. . .], as well as any "contravention" of Additional Protocol II, are punishable offences. The operative Code of Military Justice of Argentina states that breaches of treaty provisions providing for special protection of children are war crimes. Norway's Military Penal Code states that [. . .] anyone who contravenes or is accessory to the contravention of provisions relating to the protection of persons or property laid down in [. . .] the Geneva Conventions [. . .] [and in] the two additional protocols to these Conventions [. . .] is liable to imprisonment.

46. More specifically in relation to the principle *nullum crimen sine poena*, before 1996 three different approaches by states to the issue of punishment of child recruitment under national law can be distinguished.

47. First, as already described, certain states from various legal systems have criminalized the recruitment of children under 15 in their national legislation. Second, the vast majority of states lay down the prohibition of child recruitment in military law. However, sanctions can be found in the provisions of criminal law as for example in Austria and Germany or in administrative legislation, criminalizing any breaches of law by civil servants. Examples of the latter include Afghanistan and Turkey. [. . .]

48. Even though a punishment is not prescribed, individual criminal responsibility may follow. [. . .]

50. Customary law, as its name indicates, derives from custom. Custom takes time to develop. It is thus impossible and even contrary to the concept of customary law to determine a given event, day or date upon which it can be stated with certainty that a norm has crystallised. One can nevertheless say that during a certain period the conscience of leaders and populations started to note a given problem. In the case of recruiting child soldiers this happened during the mid-1980s. One can further determine a period where customary law begins to develop, which in the current case began with the acceptance of key international instruments between 1990 and 1994. Finally, one can determine the period during which the majority of states criminalized the prohibited behaviour, which in this case, as demonstrated, was the period between 1994 and 1996. It took a further six years for the recruitment of children between the ages of 15 and 18 to be included in treaty law as individually punishable behaviour. The development process concerning the recruitment of child soldiers, taking into account the definition of children as persons under the age of 18, culminated in the codification of the matter in the CRC Optional Protocol II.

51. The overwhelming majority of states, as shown above, did not practise recruitment of children under 15 according to their national laws and many had, whether through criminal

or administrative law, criminalized such behaviour prior to 1996. The fact that child recruitment still occurs and is thus illegally practised does not detract from the validity of the customary norm. It cannot be said that there is a contrary practice with a corresponding opinio iuris as states clearly consider themselves to be under a legal obligation not to practise child recruitment.

4. Good Faith

52. The rejection of the use of child soldiers by the international community was widespread by 1994. In addition, by the time of the 1996 Graça Machel Report, it was no longer possible to claim to be acting in good faith while recruiting child soldiers (contrary to the suggestion of the Defence during the oral hearing). Specifically **concerning Sierra Leone, the Government acknowledged in its 1996 Report to the Committee of the Rights of the Child** that there was no minimum age for conscripting into armed forces "except the provision in the Geneva Convention that children below the age of 15 years should not be conscripted into the army." This shows that the Government of Sierra Leone was well aware already in 1996 that children below the age of 15 should not be recruited. Citizens of Sierra Leone, and even less, persons in leadership roles, cannot possibly argue that they did not know that recruiting children was a criminal act in violation of international humanitarian law.

53. Child recruitment was criminalized before it was explicitly set out as a criminal prohibition in treaty law and certainly by November 1996, the starting point of the time frame relevant to the indictments. As set out above, the principle of legality and the principle of specificity are both upheld.

Justice Geoffrey Robertson disagreed:

[...] [T]here was no common state practice of explicitly criminalizing child recruitment prior to the Rome Treaty. [...] The above analysis convinces me that it would breach the *nullen crimen* rule to impute the necessary intention to create an international law crime of child enlistment to states until 122 of them signed the Rome Treaty. From that point, it seems to me it was tolerably clear to any competent lawyer that a prosecution would be "on the cards" for anyone who enlisted children to fight for one party or another in an ongoing conflict, whether internal or international. It is not of course *necessary* that a norm should be embodied in a Treaty before it becomes a rule of international criminal law, but in the case of child enlistment the Rome Treaty provides a *sufficient* mandate – certainly no previous development will suffice. It serves as the precise point from which liability can be reckoned and charged against defendants in this court. It did, of course, take four years before the necessary number of ratifications were received to bring the treaty into force. But the normative status of the rule applicable to States prior to 1998, the overwhelming acceptance by states in the Rome Treaty of its penal application to individuals and the consequent predictability of prosecution from that point onwards, persuades me that the date of the Treaty provides the right starting point.

COROLLARY PRINCIPLES: SPECIFICITY, NON-RETROACTIVITY AND NON-EXTENSION BY ANALOGY

Increasingly, supranational and international courts are also clarifying the applicability and contours of the three main corollaries of the maxim of *nullum crimen sine lege* – specificity and strict construction in the face of ambiguity, non-retroactivity and non-extension by analogy. Courts are also confronting the challenge of clarifying and developing the law without affronting the corollary principles. When once-murky law is delineated and applied by courts, defendants often argue that the subsequent interpretations were not foreseeable. Such arguments raise questions about the line between interpretation and legislation, and the tensions between legality and competing urges for and visions of justice.

European Court of Human Rights, **Kononov v. Latvia,** *App. No. 36376/04,*
Grand Chamber, Judgment of 17 May 2010

This case involves a long journey through history and the Latvian courts. The case stems from a 1998 investigation by Latvia into the World War II-era killings of inhabitants of a Latvian village suspected of spying for Nazi Germany. The Latvian courts found that on 27 May 1944, the accused, Vassili Makarovich Kononov, led a platoon of the Red Partisans, a Soviet Commando unit, in taking reprisals against the villagers of Mazie Bati in Latvia, then a Soviet territory occupied by Nazi Germany. Suspecting the villagers of revealing the hiding place of executed Red Partisans to the Germans, Kononov's platoon entered the village dressed in German uniforms to avoid arousing suspicion. The platoon executed six male heads of households upon finding rifles and grenades given to the men by the Germans. They then set fire to two houses and adjoining buildings, causing the deaths of three women in the suspected collaborator households.

Kononov was prosecuted under Article 68–3 of the Latvian Criminal Code of 1993, which permitted punishment of those 'found guilty of a war crime as defined in the relevant legal conventions' against the 'civil population'. Article 6–1 of the Criminal Code permitted retrospective application of the criminal law with respect to war crimes. After much legal wrangling, the Latvian courts ultimately held that Kononov had committed war crimes against civilians in contravention of the Hague Convention of 18 December 1907, the Geneva Conventions of 12 August 1949, and the Additional Protocol to the Geneva Convention of 8 June 1977 and was therefore guilty under Article 68–3.

Kononov appealed his conviction to the European Court of Human Rights, arguing that this conviction violated Article 7 of the European Convention on Human Rights, which prohibits convicting and punishing for conduct that was not a crime at the time of commission. In a 2008 judgment, the ECtHR Chamber ruled that Kononov's conviction violated Article 7 because under the law of war in 1944 there was no plausible legal basis to convict for the killing of villagers who, as collaborators, could not be considered civilians and therefore were not covered by protections for civilians (*Kononov v. Latvia*, App. No. 36376/04, Judgment, 24 July 2008, paras. 127–48). The Latvian government successfully appealed the Chamber's ruling to the ECtHR Grand Chamber, which reversed the ECtHR Chamber in the judgment excerpted below.

143. The applicant complained under Article 7 of the Convention that he had been the victim of the retrospective application of criminal law. He maintained that the acts for which he was convicted did not, at the time of their commission in 1944, constitute an offence and that Article 7 § 2 did not apply because the alleged offences did not come within its scope. Article 7 reads as follows:

"1. No one shall be held guilty of any criminal offence on account of any act or omission which did not constitute a criminal offence under national or international law at the time when it was committed. Nor shall a heavier penalty be imposed than the one that was applicable at the time the criminal offence was committed.

2. This article shall not prejudice the trial and punishment of any person for any act or omission which, at the time when it was committed, was criminal according to the general principles of law recognised by civilised nations."

[. . .]

185. The guarantee enshrined in Article 7, an essential element of the rule of law, occupies a prominent place in the Convention system of protection, as is underlined by the fact that no derogation from it is permissible under Article 15 in time of war or other public emergency. It should be construed and applied, as follows from its object and purpose, so as to provide effective safeguards against arbitrary prosecution, conviction and punishment. Accordingly, Article 7 is not confined to prohibiting the retrospective application of the criminal law to an accused's disadvantage: it also embodies, more generally, the principle that only the law can define a crime and prescribe a penalty (*nullum crimen, nulla poena sine lege*) and the principle that the criminal law must not be extensively construed to an accused's detriment, for instance by analogy. It follows that an offence must be clearly defined in law. This requirement is satisfied where the individual can know from the wording of the relevant provision – and, if need be, with the assistance of the courts' interpretation of it and with informed legal advice – what acts and omissions will make him criminally liable.

When speaking of "law", Article 7 alludes to the same concept as that to which the Convention refers elsewhere when using that term, a concept which comprises written and unwritten law and which implies qualitative requirements, notably those of accessibility and foreseeability. As regards foreseeability in particular, the Court recalls that however clearly drafted a legal provision may be in any system of law including criminal law, there is an inevitable element of judicial interpretation. There will always be a need for elucidation of doubtful points and for adaptation to changing circumstances. Indeed, in certain Convention States, the progressive development of the criminal law through judicial law-making is a well-entrenched and necessary part of legal tradition. Article 7 of the Convention cannot be read as outlawing the gradual clarification of the rules of criminal liability through judicial interpretation from case to case, provided that the resultant development is consistent with the essence of the offence and could reasonably be foreseen [. . .]

186. Finally, the two paragraphs of Article 7 are interlinked and are to be interpreted in a concordant manner (*Tess v. Latvia* (dec.), no. 34854/02, 12 December 2002). Having regard to the subject matter of the case and the reliance on the laws and customs of war as applied before and during the Second World War, the Court considers it relevant to recall that the *travaux préparatoires* to the Convention indicate that the purpose of the second paragraph of Article 7 was to specify that Article 7 did not affect laws which, in the wholly exceptional circumstances at the end of the Second World War, were passed in order to punish, *inter alia*, war crimes so that Article 7 does not in any way aim to pass legal or moral judgment on those laws (*X. v. Belgium*, no 268/57, Commission decision of 20 July 1957, Yearbook 1, p. 241). In any event, the Court further notes that the definition of war crimes included in Article 6(b) of the IMT Nuremberg Charter was found to be declaratory of international laws and customs of war as understood in 1939 [. . .]

216. The Court [. . .] considers, having regard notably to Article 23(c) of the Hague Regulations 1907, that, even if the deceased villagers were considered combatants or civilians who had participated in hostilities, *jus in bello* in 1944 considered the circumstances of their murder and ill-treatment a war crime since those acts violated a fundamental rule of the laws and customs of war protecting an enemy rendered *hors de combat*. For this protection to apply a person had to be wounded, disabled or unable for another reason to defend him/herself (including not carrying arms), a person was not required to have a particular legal status and a formal surrender was not required. As combatants, the villagers would also have been entitled to protection as prisoners of war under the control of the applicant and his unit and their subsequent ill-treatment and summary execution would have been contrary to the numerous rules and customs of war protecting prisoners of war [. . .] Accordingly, the ill-treatment, wounding and killing of the villagers constituted a war crime.

217. Secondly, the Court finds that the domestic courts reasonably relied on Article 23(b) of the Hague Regulations 1907 to found a separate conviction as regards treacherous wounding

and killing. The concepts of treachery and perfidy were closely linked at the relevant time so that the wounding or killing was considered treacherous if it was carried out while unlawfully inducing the enemy to believe they were not under threat of attack by, for example, making improper use of an enemy uniform. [. . .] [T]he applicant and his unit were indeed wearing German uniforms during the operation in Mazie Bati. Article 23(b) clearly applies if the villagers are considered "combatants" and could also apply if they were considered civilians having participated in hostilities. [. . .]

218. Thirdly, the Latvian courts relied on Article 16 of the Geneva Convention (IV) 1949 to hold that burning a pregnant woman to death constituted a war crime in breach of the special protection afforded to women. That women, especially pregnant women, should be the object of special protection during war was part of the laws and customs of war as early as the Lieber Code 1863 (Articles 19 and 37). It was further developed through "Geneva" law on prisoners of war (women were considered especially vulnerable in this situation). The Court considers these expressions of "special protection", understood in conjunction with the protection of the Martens Clause (paragraphs 86–87 and 215 above), sufficient to find that there was a plausible legal basis for convicting the applicant of a separate war crime as regards the burning to death of Mrs Krupniks. The Court finds this view confirmed by the numerous specific and special protections for women included immediately after the Second World War in the Geneva Conventions (I), (II) and (IV) 1949, notably in Article 16 of the last-mentioned Convention. [. . .]

227. In conclusion, even assuming that the deceased villagers could be considered to have been "civilians who had participated in hostilities" or "combatants" [. . .] there was a sufficiently clear legal basis, having regard to the state of international law in 1944, for the applicant's conviction and punishment for war crimes as the commander of the unit responsible for the attack on Mazie Bati on 27 May 1944. [. . .]

234. The applicant further maintained that he could not have foreseen that the impugned acts constituted war crimes, or have anticipated that he would be subsequently prosecuted.

In the first place, he underlined that in 1944 he was a young soldier in a combat situation behind enemy lines and detached from the above-described international developments, in which circumstances he could not have foreseen that the acts for which he was convicted could have constituted war crimes. Secondly, he argued that it was politically unforeseeable that he would be prosecuted: his conviction following the independence of Latvia in 1991 was a political exercise by the Latvian State rather than any real wish to fulfil international obligations to prosecute war criminals.

235. As to the first point, the Court considers that, in the context of a commanding officer and the laws and customs of war, the concepts of accessibility and foreseeability must be considered together.

The Court recalls that the scope of the concept of foreseeability depends to a considerable degree on the content of the instrument in issue, the field it is designed to cover and the number and status of those to whom it is addressed. Persons carrying on a professional activity must proceed with a high degree of caution when pursuing their occupation and can be expected to take special care in assessing the risks that such activity entails (*Pessino v. France*, no. 40403/02, § 33, 10 October 2006).

236. As to whether the qualification of the impugned acts as war crimes, based as it was on international law exclusively, could be considered to be sufficiently accessible and foreseeable to the applicant in 1944, the Court recalls that it has previously found that the individual criminal responsibility of a private soldier (a border guard) was defined with sufficient accessibility and foreseeability by, *inter alia*, a requirement to comply with international fundamental human rights instruments, which instruments did not, of themselves, give rise to individual criminal responsibility and one of which had not been ratified by the relevant State at the

material time (*K.-H.W. v. Germany*, §§ 92–105, cited above). The Court considered that even a private soldier could not show total, blind obedience to orders which flagrantly infringed not only domestic law, but internationally recognised human rights, in particular the right to life, a supreme value in the international hierarchy of human rights (*K.-H.W. v. Germany*, at § 75).

237. It is true that the 1926 Criminal Code did not contain a reference to the international laws and customs of war (as in *K.-H. W v. Germany*) and that those international laws and customs were not formally published in the USSR or in the Latvian SSR (as in *Korbely v. Hungary* [GC], cited above, at §§ 74–75). However, this cannot be decisive. As is clear from the conclusions at paragraphs 213 and 227 above, international laws and customs of war were in 1944 sufficient, of themselves, to found individual criminal responsibility.

238. Moreover, the Court notes that in 1944 those laws constituted detailed *lex specialis* regulations fixing the parameters of criminal conduct in a time of war, primarily addressed to armed forces and, especially, commanders. The present applicant was a Sergeant in the Soviet Army assigned to the reserve regiment of the Latvian Division: at the material time, he was a member of a commando unit and in command of a platoon whose primary activities were military sabotage and propaganda. Given his position as a commanding military officer, the Court is of the view that he could have been reasonably expected to take such special care in assessing the risks that the operation in Mazie Bati entailed. The Court considers that, having regard to the flagrantly unlawful nature of the ill-treatment and killing of the nine villagers in the established circumstances of the operation on 27 May 1944 (paragraphs 15–20 above), even the most cursory reflection by the applicant, would have indicated that, at the very least, the impugned acts risked being counter to the laws and customs of war as understood at that time and, notably, risked constituting war crimes for which, as commander, he could be held individually and criminally accountable.

239. For these reasons, the Court deems it reasonable to find that the applicant could have foreseen in 1944 that the impugned acts could be qualified as war crimes.

240. As to his second submission, the Court notes the declarations of independence of 1990 and 1991, the immediate accession by the new Republic of Latvia to various human rights instruments (including the 1968 Convention in 1992) and the subsequent insertion of Article 68–3 into the 1961 Criminal Code in 1993.

241. It recalls that it is legitimate and foreseeable for a successor State to bring criminal proceedings against persons who have committed crimes under a former regime and that successor courts cannot be criticised for applying and interpreting the legal provisions in force at the material time during the former regime, but in the light of the principles governing a State subject to the rule of law and having regard to the core principles on which the Convention system is built. It is especially the case when the matter at issue concerns the right to life, a supreme value in the Convention and international hierarchy of human rights and which right Contracting parties have a primary Convention obligation to protect. As well as the obligation on a State to prosecute drawn from the laws and customs of war, Article 2 of the Convention also enjoins the States to take appropriate steps to safeguard the lives of those within their jurisdiction and implies a primary duty to secure the right to life by putting in place effective criminal law provisions to deter the commission of offences which endanger life (see *Streletz, Kessler and Krenz*, §§ 72 and 79–86, and *K.-H.W. v. Germany*, cited above, §§ 66 and 82–89). It is sufficient for present purposes to note that the above-cited principles are applicable to a change of regime of the nature which took place in Latvia following the declarations of independence of 1990 and 1991 (see paragraphs 27–29 and 210 above). [...]

244. In the light of all of the above considerations, the Court concludes that, at the time when they were committed, the applicant's acts constituted offences defined with sufficient accessibility and foreseeability by the laws and customs of war. [...]

245. For all of the above reasons, the Court considers that the applicant's conviction for war crimes did not constitute a violation of Article 7 § 1 of the Convention.

The foreseeability argument of the accused is particularly striking in light of the disagreement between the ECtHR Chamber and the ECtHR Grand Chamber on whether his acts were a crime under the law of war in 1944. If learned jurists with the benefit of hindsight and the clarifications of contemporary jurisprudence disagree, how foreseeable was criminal liability to a soldier in the heat and fray of battle?

Moreover, how can clarifications and developments in international criminal law be compatible with the restrictions of non-retroactivity, specificity and non-extension by analogy? The ICTY excerpt below is instructive. The ICTY explained how applying a mode of liability elucidated in jurisprudence postdating a crime developed through clarification and interpretation of scattered precedents predating the crime did not violate the principle of legality.

ICTY, Prosecutor v. Milutinović, Decision on Dragoljub Ojdanić's Motion Challenging Jurisdiction—Joint Criminal Enterprise, 21 May 2003

> Dragoljub Ojdanić, Chief of the General Staff of the Yugoslav Army from November 1998, and later Yugoslav Federal Minister of Defence, was charged with other co-accused in connection with a widespread and systematic attack on numerous Kosovo villages and hundreds of thousands of Kosovo Albanians by Yugoslav forces between March and June 1999. One of the modes of liability pursued against Ojdanić was being a member of a joint criminal enterprise (JCE) – a theory with a contested origin and history, as discussed further, *infra*, in Part III(2), Joint Criminal Enterprise. During the pre-trial phase of the proceedings, Ojdanić argued that to apply JCE liability – a theory he argued the ICTY cobbled together *after* the time of the alleged crimes – violated the principle of legality. The Appeals Chamber rejected his challenge on the reasoning below.

38. [The *nullum crimen sine lege* principle] "does not prevent a court from interpreting and clarifying the elements of a particular crime".[5] Nor does it preclude the progressive development of the law by the court.[6] But it does prevent a court from creating new law or from interpreting existing law beyond the reasonable limits of acceptable clarification. This Tribunal must therefore be satisfied that the crime or the form of liability with which an accused is charged was sufficiently foreseeable and that the law providing for such liability must be sufficiently accessible at the relevant time, taking into account the specificity of international law when making that assessment.

39. The meaning and scope of the concepts of "foreseeability" and "accessibility" of a norm will, as noted by the European Court of Human Rights, depend a great deal on "the content of the instrument in issue, the field it is designed to cover and the number and status of those to whom it is addressed".[7] [. . .]

40. Has Ojdanić had sufficient notice that if, as claimed in the indictment, he took part in the commission of very serious criminal offences as part of a joint criminal enterprise he could

---

5 [92] *Aleksovski* Appeal Judgment, paras 126–127; *Delalić* Appeal Judgment, para. 173.

6 [93] See, *inter alia*, *Kokkinakis v. Greece*, Judgment, 25 May 1993, Ser A 260-A (1993), pars 36 and 40 (*ECHR*) [. . .]

7 [95] *Groppera Radio AG and Others v. Switzerland*, Judgment, 22 Nov 1995, Ser A 335-C (1995).

be found criminally liable on that basis? This Tribunal does not apply the law of the former Yugoslavia to the definition of the crimes and forms of liability within its jurisdiction. It does, as pointed out above, apply customary international law in relation to its jurisdiction ratione materiae. It may, however, have recourse to domestic law for the purpose of establishing that the accused could reasonably have known that the offence in question or the offence committed in the way charged in the indictment was prohibited and punishable. In the present instance [...] the law of the Federal Republic of Yugoslavia in force at the time did provide for criminal liability for the foreseeable acts of others in terms strikingly similar to those used to define joint criminal enterprise. [...]

41. Although domestic law (in particular the law of the country of the accused) may provide some notice to the effect that a given act is regarded as criminal under international law, it may not necessarily provide sufficient notice of that fact. Customary law is not always represented by written law and its accessibility may not be as straightforward as would be the case had there been an international criminal code. But the rules of customary law may provide sufficient guidance as to the standard the violation of which could entail criminal liability.[8] In the present case, and even if such a domestic provision had not existed, there is a long and consistent stream of judicial decisions, international instruments and domestic legislation which would have permitted any individual to regulate his conduct accordingly and would have given him reasonable notice that, if infringed, that standard could entail his criminal responsibility.[9]

42. Also, due to the lack of any written norms or standards, war crimes courts have often relied upon the atrocious nature of the crimes charged to conclude that the perpetrator of such an act must have known that he was committing a crime [...] Although the immorality or appalling character of an act is not a sufficient factor to warrant its criminalisation under customary international law, it may in fact play a role in that respect, insofar as it may refute any claim by the Defence that it did not know of the criminal nature of the acts.

The Appeals Chamber found that charges of joint criminal enterprise liability could be pursued. On 26 February 2006, however, the Trial Chamber found that the evidence did not establish that Ojdanić was not responsible under this form of liability, and convicted him for aiding and abetting, a lesser form of liability.

COMMENTARY

The ECtHR and ICTY judgments show that the notion of legality and its corollary protections are now fundamental principles of contemporary international criminal law, influenced by the interpretation of human rights treaties adopted since World War II. Moreover, it is now well accepted that extension of the law by analogy is prohibited. Indeed, the rules of non-extension by analogy and strict construction in the face of ambiguity are now also viewed as customary law together with the prohibition against retroactivity in crime definitions. Article 22(2) ICCSt. accordingly provides: 'The definition of a crime shall be strictly construed and shall not be extended by analogy. In case of ambiguity, the definition shall be interpreted in favour of the person being investigated, prosecuted or convicted.'

There remains a tension between the principle of legality and its corollary precepts and the nature and development of international criminal law, however, as the excerpts above

---

[8]   [100] See *X Ltd and Y v. United Kingdom*, D and R 28 (1982), Appl 8710/79, pp 77, 80–81.

[9]   [102] See *Tadić* Appeal Judgment, paras. 195 *et seq*.

also suggest. Because the sources of international criminal law include the 'general principles of law recognised by civilised nations,' there is necessarily less determinacy and certainty in international criminal law than in domestic law. This characteristic is in tension with the principle of specificity, the notion that criminal rules should be as detailed as possible – construed in many national jurisdictions to require written legislation in advance – so that all may know in advance whether their conduct is criminal. If courts still wrestle and fracture over whether international law proscribed conduct at the time it occurred, how realistic or fair is it to pretend that the law was sufficiently specific so that the accused knew in advance that his conduct was criminal? Moreover, different courts may advance different interpretations of international criminal law, resulting in a cacophony of sometimes contradictory interpretations.

The nature of international crimes, often involving emotionally salient suffering and violence, may lead to the moral intuition that the accused *should have known* that his conduct was wrongful – a rationale that surfaced in the Nuremberg judgment excerpted at the outset of this chapter and addressed in more sophisticated form in the *Milutinović* excerpt above. But legality requires prior proscription of conduct; not just retrospective horror and a sense of affronted justice. What seems unjust and horrible, after all, is subjective; whereas law – or at least law as we aspire it to be – is objective and fixed in advance.

While the equities in Kononov's case may have elicited mixed emotions, other contemporary international crimes often elicit revulsion and horror and the temptation to blur the line between judicial interpretation and clarification of existing rules and retroactive expansion of the rules. The European Court of Human Rights has permitted expansive 'clarification' of the law through judicial interpretation so long as 'the resultant development is consistent with the essence of the offence and could reasonably be foreseen'. On such a rationale, the European Court of Human Rights ruled that the broad interpretation by German Courts of the definition of genocide to include intended destruction of a protected group as a social unit did not violate the principle of legality though, as further discussed in the genocide chapter (Part II(3)), the crafters of the Genocide Convention proscribed physical or biological destruction and rejected the notion of cultural genocide (*Jorgić* v. *Germany*, App. No. 74613/01, ECtHR, 12 October 2007).

The nature of international law also entails three important qualifications to the prohibition against extending the scope of prohibition by analogy. First, as discussed in detail in prior sections, where an issue is not specifically covered by a provision or rule, international courts regularly resort to general principles of international criminal law, general principles of criminal justice or principles common to major legal systems. The filling of gaps and *lacunae* in international law in this manner has been characterized as 'interpretation' instead of analogical application, but here again lines can blur. The mandate of legality means that the act of clarifying or spelling out prohibitions arising from general principles should never cross the line into creating new classes of criminal conduct.

Second, sometimes, the very definition of international crimes may require reasoning by analogy. For example, the definition of crimes against humanity in customary law and treaties includes a number of specific underlying crimes, such as murder, extermination and enslavement, committed as part of a widespread or systematic attack directed against any civilian population, with knowledge of the attack. Another underlying crime, however, may be '[o]ther inhumane acts of a similar character intentionally causing great suffering, or serious injury to body or to mental or physical health' (ICCSt., Art. 7.1(k)). Such a general crime definition authorizes analogical reasoning by comparison to assess whether conduct is similar to the specified inhumane acts.

Third, sometimes in analysing whether conduct is prohibited under a general principle of international law though not specifically covered by a treaty, the conduct may be compared against treaties that identify certain things as falling within the scope of the general prohibition. For example, in trying to determine whether a new weapon falls within the general proscription in international law against weapons that by their nature are inherently indiscriminate or cause superfluous suffering, jurists may compare the weapon to those already specifically banned because the international community has deemed them to meet the standard in general international law. Again, such a treaty provision invites reasoning by analogy.

Finally, while the notion of legality in terms of crime definitions has gained increasing ascendancy in contemporary international criminal law, the principle of legality of penalties is still being debated. The notion of legality of penalties, recognized in many national jurisdictions, requires that the sentence or sentencing range for a crime also be set out in advance to ensure relatively uniform, fair and non-arbitrary punishment, and to give people notice of the penalties they face for transgressions. Notions of just punishment differ sharply among States and legal cultures, however, as evidenced by the split among nations over the death penalty or what constitutes overly harsh punishment. Perhaps as a result, international criminal law has generally not set out tariffs of punishment for crimes, leaving judges to exercise discretion within loose constraints, such as the prohibition against meting out the death penalty that is explicit in the ICTYSt. and ICTRSt. and implicit in the ICCSt. (which generally caps punishment at a maximum of 30 years but permits life imprisonment 'when justified by the extreme gravity of the crime and the individual circumstances of the convicted person'). Thus while key components of legality have become fundamental to the notion of international justice, the nature of international law and relations has cabined the contours of the principle.

QUESTIONS

1. What competing visions and types of justice are at stake in the question of whether to recognize a strong version of strict legality in international criminal law?

2. At a sufficiently abstract level, political wisdom always influences the content of legal rules. Considering the continuing striving for legitimacy in international criminal law, which often confronts hostile jurisdictions, does political wisdom count for or against a strong notion of legality?

3. Should the notion of *nullum crimen sine lege* apply with the same force and effect in international proceedings as in the domestic jurisdiction? Why or why not?

4. Can you conceive of a clearer line between judicial clarification that leads to an expansive interpretation of criminal proscriptions and retroactive expansion of criminal liability? Is the line artificial or can you conceive of safeguards to distinguish between necessary interpretation and clarification and retroactive expansion of liability?

FURTHER READING

K.S. Gallant, *The Principle of Legality in International and Comparative Criminal Law* (Cambridge: Cambridge University Press, 2008).

J. Hall, 'Nulla Poena Sine Lege' (1937) 47 *Yale Law Journal* 165.

A. Mokhtar, 'Nullum Crimen, Nulla Poena Sine Lege: Aspects and Prospects' (2005) 26 *State Law Review* 41.

G. Pinzauti, 'The European Court of Human Rights' Incidental Application of International Criminal Law and Humanitarian Law: A Critical Discussion of *Kononov v. Latvia*' (2008) 6 JICJ 1043–60.

M. Shahabuddeen, 'Does the Principle of Legality Stand in the Way of Progressive Development of Law?' (2004) 2 JICJ 1007–17.

B. Van Schaack, 'Crime Sine Lege: Judicial Lawmaking at the Intersection of Law and Morals' (2008) 97 *Georgetown Law Journal* 119.

(B) IMMUNITIES

THE NOTION AND ITS ORIGINS

As exceptions to the general rule requiring accountability, international law allows certain individuals immunities from prosecution. Immunities based on international law should be kept conceptually distinct from the immunities that domestic systems often prescribe for Heads of State, members of Parliament, government officials and other classes of people. While there might be some overlap between the two types of immunity, their rationale and application are different. The main difference for our purposes is that immunities under international (customary or treaty) law are meant to be invoked by state officials vis-à-vis *foreign* tribunals. Domestic immunities, on the other hand, only apply within one's national legal system.

Under international law, two categories of immunities are often identified: functional immunities (or *ratione materiae*) and personal immunities (or *ratione personae*). Although, as will be made clear below, courts do not always specify which of these categories they intend to apply, for conceptual clarity, we will discuss the two categories separately in the following sections.

One preliminary caveat is that each State – despite international rules on immunities – is generally free to grant *more extensive* immunities to foreign diplomatic officials, Heads of State and other State agents. This is a political choice made by each State. Unless another (treaty or customary) rule requires prosecution, each State is free to limit its own jurisdiction by granting broader immunity than is strictly necessary.

FUNCTIONAL IMMUNITIES

Functional immunities can be a shield for public officials from liability for acts performed on behalf of a State and its organs. Functional immunity from foreign tribunals' jurisdiction is rooted in the assumption that official activities are performed by State organs on behalf of their State. Since no State is supposed to interfere in the structure of other States and in the allegiance that a State official normally owes to its own State, customary and treaty law recognize a plea of immunity covering activities performed in the exercise of the public official's functions and outlasting the period the official is in office. This is because the acts performed on behalf of a State (whence the expression 'Act of State') must be imputable to that State, and not to the individual who happened to hold a certain post in a specific period. The State official may of course be prosecuted for acts committed before or after his or her term in office, or for crimes committed *not in an official capacity* whilst in office (for instance, the murder of a spouse or of a servant, or the theft of jewels).

Functional immunities give rise to a host of issues. On a practical level, can soldiers – who are obviously agents of a State – plead functional immunity for crimes committed while serving in the military? Also, how does one distinguish 'Acts of State' from acts committed in a personal (or private) capacity, i.e. outside the scope of the agent's official duties?

Moreover, international law has shown a trend towards curtailing the scope of the plea of functional immunity. First, since Nuremberg, instruments establishing international tribunals have generally barred the plea of functional immunity. Thus, for instance, Article 7 IMT Charter, Article 7 ICTYSt. and Article 6 ICTRSt. all affirm that the official position of defendants shall not relieve them of responsibility. This position has been confirmed by decisions of these tribunals (see, for example, *Prosecutor* v. *Milošević*, Decision on Preliminary Motions, 8 November 2001, paras 26–34 and authorities cited). Second, functional immunity appears to be put into doubt in relation to certain particularly serious crimes, as seen in the cases below.

Cases

Israel, Eichmann v. Attorney-General, *Supreme Court, Judgment of 29 May 1962*

During World War II, Adolf Eichmann was a Lieutenant Colonel in the German Secret State Police dealing with 'Jewish Affairs' and responsible for the mass deportation and extermination of Jews pursuant to the 'Final Solution' approved by the Nazi regime. In 1960, he was abducted by Israeli agents in Argentina and flown to Israel where he was charged with crimes against the Jewish people (i.e. genocide against Jews), crimes against humanity and membership in a criminal organization under the 1950 Nazi and Nazi Collaborators (Punishment) Law. Eichmann's trial is undoubtedly one of the most momentous events in the domestic implementation of international criminal law.

The main defence raised by Eichmann was that he was a mere 'cog' in the Nazi machinery, just following superior orders.

14. The next submission to be considered is that the crimes of which the appellant was convicted were at the time within the definition of Acts of State and that therefore he is absolved from criminal responsibility in respect thereof. The theory of "Act of State" means that the act performed by a person as an organ of the State – whether he was head of State or a responsible official acting on the Government's orders – must be regarded as an act of the State alone. It follows that only the latter bears responsibility therefor, and it also follows that another State has no right to punish the person who committed the act, save with the consent of the State whose mission he performed. Were it not so, the first State would be interfering

in the internal affairs of the second, which is contrary to the conception of the equality of States based on their sovereignty [...] The contention of counsel for the appellant is therefore that the acts done by his client for the realization of the "Final Solution" had their origin in Hitler's decision to put that plan into effect and consequently they were purely "Acts of State", responsibility for which does not rest on the appellant.

We utterly reject this contention [...] Our reasons are as follows:

(a) The concept of "sovereignty", from which the doctrine of "Act of State" derives, is not considered today to be an absolute concept, as was made clear by Kunz in his article "The Nottebohm Judgment", in A.J.I.L., vol. 54, p. 545): "Any a priori or unlimited political concept of sovereignty must, with inescapable logic, lead to the non-existence of international law as law. Sovereignty is, therefore, essentially a *relative* notion."

This also applies to the "Act of State" doctrine. Even Chief Justice Marshall, who relied on it in Schooner Exchange v. McFaddon (3 L.Ed. 287), was particularly careful to base it on the sole foundation that the State within whose territory an illegal act was committed on behalf of another State had expressly or impliedly consented to waive its sovereign territorial right to punish for it. What is more he added the reservation that where implied consent is involved "its extent must be regulated by the nature of the case, and the views under which the parties requiring and conceding it must be supposed to act" (p. 296). [...]

(b) In any event, there is no basis for the doctrine when the matter pertains to acts prohibited by the law of nations, especially when they are international crimes of the class of "crimes against humanity" (in the wide sense). Of such odious acts it must be said that in point of international law they are completely outside the "sovereign" jurisdiction of the State that ordered or ratified their commission, and therefore those who participated in such acts must personally account for them and cannot shelter behind the official character of their task or mission, or behind the "Laws" of the State by virtue of which they purported to act. Their position may be compared with that of a person who, having committed an offence in the interests of a corporation which he represents, is not permitted to hide behind the collective responsibility of the corporation therefor. In other words, international law postulates that it is impossible for a State to sanction an act that violates its severe prohibitions, and from this follows the idea which forms the core of the concept of "international crime", that a person who was a party to such crime must bear individual responsibility for it. If it were otherwise, the penal provisions of international law would be a mockery.

"[I]n modern times a State is – ex hypothesi – incapable of ordering or ratifying acts which are not only criminal according to generally accepted principles of domestic penal law but also contrary to that international law to which all States are perforce subject. Its agents, in performing such acts, are therefore acting outside their legitimate scope; and must, in consequence, be held personally liable for their wrongful conduct." (Glueck [in *Harvard Law Review*, vol. 59, pp. 427–8].) This was written before the Nuremberg Tribunal delivered its judgment; and indeed, even before the Second World War the defence of "act of state" was not regarded as an adequate defence to the charge of an offence against the "laws of war" (a "conventional" war crime). [...]

(c) Whatever may be the value of the above doctrine in other cases, the principle laid down in Article 7 of the Charter of the International Military Tribunal at Nuremberg, to which the Tribunal (basing itself also on Ex parte Quirin) adhered, is that the doctrine cannot afford a defence in respect of international crimes, particularly those defined in the Charter. To quote the Court:

"[...] The authors of these acts cannot shelter themselves behind their official position in order to be freed from punishment in appropriate proceedings. [...] [T]he very essence of the Charter is that individuals have international duties which transcend the national obligations of obedience imposed by the individual State. He who violates the laws of war cannot obtain immunity while acting in pursuance of the authority of the State if the State in authorizing action moves outside its competence under international law." [. . .]

The principle expressed in these words, which totally negates the "Act of State" plea, is today one of the "Nuremberg Principles" which have become part of the law of nations and must [be] regarded as having been rooted in it also in the past, as explained [. . .] above [. . .] The result is that this plea, so far as it concerns the crimes in question, finds no support in international law and can in no way avail the appellant.

Eichmann's conviction was confirmed by the Supreme Court. He was sentenced to death and executed by hanging on 31 May 1962.

United Kingdom, R v. Bow Street Stipendiary Magistrate (Bartle) ex parte Pinochet Ugarte (No. 3), House of Lords, Judgment of 24 March 1999

In 1998 Augusto Pinochet, President of Chile from the 1973 coup against the lawfully elected President Salvador Allende until 1990, travelled to London for medical treatment. While Pinochet was in England, an English judge had him arrested for extradition upon the request of the Spanish judiciary for hostage taking, torture and genocide. The Divisional Court – which heard habeas corpus proceedings in the first instance – held that Pinochet was immune from jurisdiction because of his status as a former head of State. The decision was appealed before the House of Lords. A first decision of the House of Lords allowed the arrest warrant to stand and ruled that extradition to Spain would be proper for hostage taking and torture ('Pinochet (No. 1)'). This decision was however set aside because one of the Lords and his wife had links with Amnesty International, one of the interveners in the proceedings ('Pinochet (No. 2)'). As a result, the issue of extradition and immunity from criminal jurisdiction came up a second time before the House of Lords ('Pinochet (No. 3)'). Excerpts from the opinions of two of the Lords in the latter judgment are reproduced here.

Lord Phillips of Worth Matravers

The submission advanced on behalf of the respondent in respect of the effect of public international law can, I believe, be summarised as follows. (1) One state will not entertain judicial proceedings against a former head of state or other state official of another state in relation to conduct performed in his official capacity. (2) This rule applies even if the conduct amounts to a crime against international law. (3) This rule applies in relation to both civil and criminal proceedings.

For the reasons that I have given and if one proceeds on the premise that Part I of the State Immunity Act 1978 [domestic UK legislation on, inter alia, immunity of foreign states] correctly reflects current international law, I believe that the first two propositions are made out in relation to civil proceedings. The vital issue is the extent to which they apply to the exercise of criminal jurisdiction in relation to the conduct that forms the basis of the request for extradition. This issue requires consideration of the nature of that jurisdiction.

The development of international criminal law

In the latter part of this century there has been developing a recognition among states that some types of criminal conduct cannot be treated as a matter for the exclusive competence of the state in which they occur. [. . .]

The appellants, and those who have on this appeal been given leave to support them, contend […] that international law now recognises a category of criminal conduct with the following characteristics. (1) It is so serious as to be of concern to all nations and not just to the state in which it occurs. (2) Individuals guilty of it incur criminal responsibility under international law. (3) There is universal jurisdiction in respect of it. This means that international law recognises the right of any state to prosecute an offender for it, regardless of where the criminal conduct took place. (4) No state immunity attaches in respect of any such prosecution. My Lords, this is an area where international law is on the move and the move has been effected by express consensus recorded in or reflected by a considerable number of international instruments. Since the Second World War states have recognised that not all criminal conduct can be left to be dealt with as a domestic matter by the laws and the courts of the territories in which such conduct occurs. There are some categories of crime of such gravity that they shock the consciousness of mankind and cannot be tolerated by the international community. Any individual who commits such a crime offends against international law. The nature of these crimes is such that they are likely to involve the concerted conduct of many and liable to involve the complicity of the officials of the state in which they occur, if not of the state itself. In these circumstances it is desirable that jurisdiction should exist to prosecute individuals for such conduct outside the territory in which such conduct occurs.

I believe that it is still an open question whether international law recognises universal jurisdiction in respect of international crimes – that is the right, under international law, of the courts of any state to prosecute for such crimes wherever they occur. In relation to war crimes, such a jurisdiction has been asserted by the State of Israel, notably in the prosecution of Adolf Eichmann, but this assertion of jurisdiction does not reflect any general state practice in relation to international crimes. Rather, states have tended to agree, or to attempt to agree, on the creation of international tribunals to try international crimes. They have however, on occasion, agreed by conventions, that their national courts should enjoy jurisdiction to prosecute for a particular category of international crime wherever occurring.

The principle of state immunity provides no bar to the exercise of criminal jurisdiction by an international tribunal, but the instruments creating such tribunals have tended, none the less, to make it plain that no exception from responsibility or immunity from process is to be enjoyed by a head of state or other state official. Thus the Charter of the Nuremberg Tribunal 1945 provides by article 7: "The official position of defendants, whether as head of state or responsible officials in government departments, shall not be considered as freeing them from responsibility or mitigating punishment." The Tokyo Charter of 1946, the Statute of the International Criminal Tribunal for the Former Yugoslavia of 1993, the Statute of the International Criminal Tribunal for Rwanda 1994 and the Statute of the International Criminal Court 1998 all have provisions to like effect.

Where states, by convention, agree that their national courts shall have jurisdiction on a universal basis in respect of an international crime, such agreement cannot implicitly remove immunities ratione personae that exist under international law. Such immunities can only be removed by express agreement or waiver. Such an agreement was incorporated in the Convention on the Prevention and Suppression of the Crime of Genocide 1948, which provides: "Persons committing genocide or any of the other acts enumerated in article III shall be punished, whether they are constitutionally responsible rulers, public officials, or private individuals." Had the Genocide Convention not contained this provision, an issue could have been raised as to whether the jurisdiction conferred by the Convention was subject to state immunity ratione materiae. Would international law have required a court to grant immunity to a defendant upon his demonstrating that he was acting in an official capacity? In my view it plainly would not. I do not reach that conclusion on the ground that assisting in genocide can never be a function of a state official. I reach that conclusion on the simple basis that no established rule of international law requires state immunity ratione materiae to be accorded in respect of prosecution for an international crime. International crimes and extraterritorial jurisdiction in relation to them are both new arrivals in the field of public international law. I do not believe that state immunity ratione materiae can co-exist with them. The exercise of extra-territorial jurisdiction overrides the principle that one state will not intervene in the internal affairs of another. It does so because, where international crime is concerned, that principle cannot prevail. An international crime is as offensive, if not more offensive, to the international community when committed under colour of office. Once extraterritorial jurisdiction is established, it makes no sense to exclude from it acts done in an official capacity.

There can be no doubt that the conduct of which Senator Pinochet stands accused by Spain is criminal under international law. The Republic of Chile has accepted that torture is prohibited by international law and that the prohibition of torture has the character of jus cogens and or obligation erga omnes. It is further accepted that officially sanctioned torture is forbidden by international law. The information provided by Spain accuses Senator Pinochet not merely of having abused his powers as head of state by committing torture, but of subduing political opposition by a campaign of abduction, torture and murder that extended beyond the boundaries of Chile. When considering what is alleged, I do not believe that it is correct to attempt to analyse individual elements of this campaign and to identify some as being criminal under international law and others as not constituting international crimes. If Senator Pinochet behaved as Spain alleged, then the entirety of his conduct was a violation of the norms of international law. He can have no immunity against prosecution for any crime that formed part of that campaign.

It is only recently that the criminal courts of this country acquired jurisdiction, pursuant to section 134 of the Criminal Justice Act 1984, to prosecute Senator Pinochet for torture committed outside the territorial jurisdiction, provided that it was committed in the performance, or purported performance, of his official duties. Section 134 was passed to give effect to the rights and obligations of this country under the Convention against Torture and Other Cruel, Inhuman or Degrading Treatment or Punishment of 1984, to which the United Kingdom, Spain and Chile are all signatories. That Convention outlaws the infliction of torture "by or at the instigation of or with the consent or acquiescence of a public official or other person acting in an official capacity" (article 1). Each state party is required to make such conduct criminal under its law, wherever committed. More pertinently, each state party is required to prosecute any person found within its jurisdiction who has committed such an offence, unless it extradites that person for trial for the offence in another state. The only conduct covered by this Convention is conduct which would be subject to immunity ratione materiae, if such immunity were applicable. The Convention is thus incompatible with the applicability of immunity ratione materiae. There are only two possibilities. One is that the States parties to the Convention proceeded on the premise that no immunity could exist ratione materiae in respect of torture, a crime contrary to international law. The other is that the States parties to the Convention expressly agreed that immunity ratione materiae should not apply in the case of torture. I believe that the first of these alternatives is the correct one, but either must be fatal to the assertion by Chile and Senator Pinochet of immunity in respect of extradition proceedings based on torture.

The State Immunity Act 1978

I have referred earlier to Part I of the State Immunity Act 1978, which does not apply to criminal proceedings. Part III of the Act, which is of general application is headed "Miscellaneous and Supplementary." Under this Part, section 20 provides: "(1) Subject to the provisions of this section and to any necessary modifications, the Diplomatic Privileges Act 1964 shall apply to – (a) a sovereign or other head of state; (b) members of his family forming part of his household; and (c) his private servants, as it applies to the head of a diplomatic mission, to members of his family forming part of his household and to his private servants."

[. . .] All who have so far in these proceedings given judicial consideration to this problem have concluded that the provisions apply so as to confer the immunities enjoyed by a diplomat upon a head of state in relation to his actions wherever in the world they take place. This leads to the further conclusion that a former head of state continues to enjoy immunity in respect of acts committed "in the exercise of his functions" as head of state, wherever those acts occurred.

For myself, I would not accord section 20 of the Act of 1978 such broad effect. It seems to me that it does no more, than to equate the position of a head of state and his entourage visiting this country with that of a diplomatic mission within this country. Thus interpreted, section 20 accords with established principles of international law, is readily applicable and can appropriately be described as supplementary to the other Parts of the Act. As Lord Browne-Wilkinson has demonstrated, reference to the parliamentary history of the section discloses that this was precisely the original intention of section 20, for the section expressly provided that it applied to a head of state who was "in the United Kingdom at the invitation or with the consent of the Government of the United Kingdom." Those words were deleted by amendment. The mover of the amendment explained that the object of the amendment was to ensure that heads of state would be treated like heads of diplomatic missions "irrespective of presence in the United Kingdom."

Senator Pinochet and Chile have contended that the effect of section 20, as amended, is to entitle Senator Pinochet to immunity in respect of any acts committed in the performance of his functions as head of state anywhere in the world, and that the conduct which forms the subject matter of the extradition proceedings, in so far as it occurred when Senator Pinochet was head of state, consisted of acts committed by him in performance of his functions as head of state.

If these submissions are correct, the Act of 1978 requires the English court to produce a result which is in conflict with international law and with our obligations under the Torture Convention. I do not believe that the submissions are correct, for the following reasons.

As I have explained, I do not consider that section 20 of the Act of 1978 has any application to conduct of a head of state outside the United Kingdom. Such conduct remains governed by the rules of public international law. Reference to the parliamentary history of the section, which I do not consider appropriate, serves merely to confuse what appears to me to be relatively clear.

If I am mistaken in this view and we are bound by the Act of 1978 to accord to Senator Pinochet immunity in respect of all acts committed "in performance of his functions as head of state," I would not hold that the course of conduct alleged by Spain falls within that description. Article 3 of the Vienna Convention, which strangely is not one of those scheduled to the Act of 1964, defines the functions of a diplomatic mission as including "protecting in the receiving state the interests of the sending state and of its nationals, *within the limits permitted by international law.*" (The emphasis is mine.)

In so far as Part III of the Act of 1978 entitles a former head of state to immunity in respect of the performance of his official functions I do not believe that those functions can, as a matter of statutory interpretation, extend to actions that are prohibited as criminal under international law. In this way one can reconcile, as one must seek to do, the provisions of the Act of 1978 with the requirements of public international law.

For these reasons, I would allow the appeal in respect of so much of the conduct alleged against Senator Pinochet as constitutes extradition crimes. [. . .]

Lord Millet

Two overlapping immunities are recognised by international law; immunity ratione personae and immunity ratione materiae. They are quite different and have different rationales. Immunity ratione personae is a status immunity. An individual who enjoys its protection does so because of his official status. [. . .] The immunity of a serving head of state is enjoyed by reason of his special status as the holder of his state's highest office. He is regarded as the personal embodiment of the state itself. It would be an affront to the dignity and sovereignty of the state which he personifies and a denial of the equality of sovereign states to subject him to the jurisdiction of the municipal courts of another state, whether in respect of his public acts or private affairs. His person is inviolable; he is not liable to be arrested or detained on any ground whatever. The head of a diplomatic mission represents his head of state and thus embodies the sending state in the territory of the receiving state. While he remains in office he is entitled to the same absolute immunity as his head of state in relation both to his public and private acts. This immunity is not in issue in the present case. Senator Pinochet is not a serving head of state. If he were, he could not be extradited. It would be an intolerable affront to the Republic of Chile to arrest him or detain him.

Immunity ratione materiae is very different. This is a subject matter immunity. It operates to prevent the official and governmental acts of one state from being called into question in proceedings before the courts of another, and only incidentally confers immunity on the individual. It is therefore a narrower immunity but it is more widely available. It is available to former heads of state and heads of diplomatic missions, and any one whose conduct in the exercise of the authority of the state is afterwards called into question, whether he acted as head of government, government minister, military commander or chief of police, or subordinate public official. The immunity is the same whatever the rank of the office-holder. This too is common ground. It is an immunity from the civil and criminal jurisdiction of foreign national courts but only in respect of governmental or official acts. The exercise of authority by the military and security forces of the state is the paradigm example of such conduct. The immunity finds its rationale in the equality of sovereign states and the doctrine of noninterference in the internal affairs of other states [. . .] The immunity is sometimes also justified by the need to prevent the serving head of state or diplomat from being inhibited in the performance of his official duties by fear of the consequences after he has ceased to hold office. This last basis can hardly be prayed in aid to support the availability of the immunity in respect of criminal activities prohibited by international law.

Given its scope and rationale, it is closely similar to and may be indistinguishable from aspects of the Anglo-American act of state doctrine. As I understand the difference between them, state immunity is a creature of international law and operates as a plea in bar to the jurisdiction of the national court, whereas the act of state doctrine is a rule of domestic law which holds the national court incompetent to adjudicate upon the lawfulness of the sovereign acts of a foreign state. [. . .]

The charges brought against Senator Pinochet are concerned with his public and official acts, first as Commander-in-Chief of the Chilean army and later as head of state. He is accused of having embarked on a widespread and systematic reign of terror in order to obtain power and then to maintain it. If the allegations against him are true, he deliberately employed torture as an instrument of state policy. As international law stood on the eve of the Second World War, his conduct as head of state after he seized power would probably have attracted immunity ratione materiae. If so, I am of opinion that it would have been equally true of his conduct during the period before the coup was successful. He was not then, of course, head of state. But he took advantage of his position as Commander-in-Chief of the army and made use of the existing military chain of command to deploy the armed forces of the state against its constitutional government. These were not private acts. They were official and governmental or sovereign acts by any standard.

The immunity is available whether the acts in question are illegal or unconstitutional or otherwise unauthorised under the internal law of the state, since the whole purpose of state immunity is to prevent the legality of such acts from being adjudicated upon in the municipal courts of a foreign state. A sovereign state has the exclusive right to determine what is and is not illegal or unconstitutional under its own domestic law. Even before the end of the Second World War, however, it was questionable whether the doctrine of state immunity accorded protection in respect of conduct which was prohibited by international law. [. . .]

The landmark decision of the Supreme Court of Israel in *Attorney-General of Israel v. Eichmann,* 36 I.L.R. 5 is also of great significance. Eichmann had been a very senior official of the Third Reich. He was in charge of Department IV D-4 of the Reich Main Security Office, the department charged with the implementation of the Final Solution, and subordinate only to Heydrich and Himmler. He was abducted from Argentina and brought to Israel, where he was tried in the District Court for Tel Aviv. His appeal against conviction was dismissed by the Supreme Court. [. . .] Having disposed of the objections to its jurisdiction, the court rejected the defence of act of state. As formulated, this did not differ in any material respect from a plea of immunity ratione materiae. It was based on the fact that in committing the offences of which he had been convicted the accused had acted as an organ of the state, "whether as head of the state or a responsible official acting on the government's orders." The court applied article 7 of the Nuremberg Charter (which it will be remembered expressly referred to the head of state) and which it regarded as having become part of the law of nations.

The case is authority for three propositions. (1) There is no rule of international law which prohibits a state from exercising extraterritorial criminal jurisdiction in respect of crimes committed by foreign nationals abroad. (2) War crimes and atrocities of the scale and international character of the Holocaust are crimes of universal jurisdiction under customary international law. (3) The fact that the accused committed the crimes in question in the course of his official duties as a responsible officer of the state and in the exercise of his authority as an organ of the state is no bar to the exercise of the jurisdiction of a national court. [. . .]

Article 5 of the Universal Declaration of Human Rights of 1948 and article 7 of the International Covenant on Civil and Political Rights of 1966 both provided that no one shall be subjected to torture or to cruel, inhuman or degrading treatment or punishment. A resolution of the General Assembly in 1973 proclaimed the need for international cooperation in the detection, arrest, extradition and punishment of persons guilty of war crimes and crimes against humanity. A further resolution of the General Assembly in 1975 proclaimed the desire to make the struggle against torture more effective throughout the world. The fundamental human rights of individuals, deriving from the inherent dignity of the human person, had become a commonplace of international law. [. . .] By the time Senator Pinochet seized power, the international community had renounced the use of torture as an instrument of state policy. The Republic of Chile accepts that by 1973 the use of torture by state authorities was prohibited by international law, and that the prohibition had the character of jus cogens or obligation erga omnes. But it insists that this does not confer universal jurisdiction or affect the immunity of a former head of state ratione materiae from the jurisdiction of foreign national courts. [. . .]

In my opinion, the systematic use of torture on a large scale and as an instrument of state policy had joined piracy, war crimes and crimes against peace as an international crime of universal jurisdiction well before 1984. I consider that it had done so by 1973. For my own part, therefore, I would hold that the courts of this country already possessed extraterritorial jurisdiction in respect of torture and conspiracy to torture on the scale of the charges in the present case and did not require the authority of statute to exercise it.

By a vote of six to one, the House of Lords concluded that Pinochet did not enjoy immunity from extradition for at least *some* of the crimes in question – reducing considerably the scope of the charges originally brought by Spanish authorities – and allowed the appeal against the Divisional Court's decision. The reasons for which each Lord found that there was no immunity for (some of the charged acts of) torture varied (for a thorough summary, see R. Cryer, 'Pinochet', in *Oxford Companion*, at 872–5). After the judgment, the Home Secretary ruled, however, that Pinochet could in any event not be extradited due to health reasons. Pinochet returned to Chile, where he died in 2006, having been stripped of his (domestic) immunity but without any trial having been completed against him.

USA, **Matar v. Dichter,** *US Court of Appeals for the Second Circuit, Decision of 16 April 2009*

On 8 December 2005, the US Center for Constitutional Rights brought a civil claim against Avraham Dichter, former Director of the Israeli Security Agency, while he was in New York. Plaintiffs alleged that Dichter was involved in a 2002 aerial bombing of a Gaza residential neighbourhood, a 'targeted assassination' aimed at killing a person suspected of being a leader of the Palestinian organization Hamas. The person was indeed killed. The operation caused the death of 14 other persons – including 8 children – and the wounding of 150 more. The plaintiffs argued that Dichter, as a *former* foreign official acting outside the scope of his authority, was not entitled to immunity under the Foreign Sovereign Immunities Act (FSIA) or under US common law. The Southern District of New York District Court dismissed the case and the plaintiffs appealed the dismissal.

Appellants allege that they were injured or lost family members in the 2002 aerial bombing of a Gaza apartment complex by the Israeli Defense Force, and they allege that appellee Avraham Dichter, former head of the Israeli Security Agency, personally participated in the decision to bomb. The United States District Court for the Southern District of New York (Pauley, J.) dismissed appellants' complaint, ruling (1) that Dichter is immune from suit under the Foreign Sovereign Immunities Act of 1976 (FSIA), 28 U.S.C. §§ 1602–1611, or (2) that in the alternative, the complaint states a non-justiciable political question. On appeal, appellants argue that the FSIA does not extend to former foreign officials such as Dichter; that the FSIA does not immunize certain violations of domestic, foreign, and international law; and that the complaint is justiciable. We conclude that even if the FSIA does not apply, Dichter would nonetheless be immune under common law. We therefore affirm the judgment of the district court.

Background

On July 22, 2002, an Israeli Defense Force aircraft bombed an apartment complex in Gaza City in the Gaza Strip, a Palestinian territory then occupied by Israel. The attack was designed to kill Saleh Mustafah Shehadeh, an alleged leader of the terrorist organization Hamas, and it succeeded. Collateral damage included the deaths of fourteen people, as well as the destruction of the apartment building and surrounding structures. Appellants were injured in the attack, or represent others who were killed or injured. At the time of the attack, defendant Avraham Dichter was director of the Israeli Security Agency (the "Agency"), one of that country's main security and intelligence services. [...] The complaint, filed in December 2005, alleges that by committing war crimes and other violations of international law, Dichter is liable for damages pursuant to the Alien Tort Statute (ATS) and the Torture Victim Protection Act (TVPA), 28 U.S.C. § 1350 & note. At the time that suit was filed, Dichter had left the Agency and was no longer an official of the State of Israel. [...]

The district court granted Dichter's motion to dismiss. Rejecting the government's argument that the FSIA did not apply to individual foreign officials, the district court ruled that Dichter was an "agency or instrumentality of a foreign state" as defined in 28 U.S.C. § 1603. The court further rejected appellants' arguments that FSIA immunity does not extend to acts taken outside the scope of lawful authority and that FSIA immunity is trumped by liability under the TVPA. [...]

The FSIA "provides the sole basis for obtaining jurisdiction over a foreign state in federal court." Argentine Republic v. Amerada Hess Shipping Corp., 488 U.S. 428, 439 (1989). "Under the Act, a foreign state is presumptively immune from the jurisdiction of United States courts; unless a specified exception applies, a federal court lacks subject-matter jurisdiction over a claim against a foreign state." Saudi Arabia v. Nelson, 507 U.S. 349, 355 (1993). A defendant seeking dismissal for lack of subject matter jurisdiction under the FSIA must make a prima facie showing that it is a foreign sovereign. Virtual Countries, Inc. v. Republic of South Africa, 300 F.3d 230, 241 (2d Cir. 2002). The burden then shifts to the plaintiff to present evidence showing that an exception to the FSIA applies. Cargill Int'l S.A. v. M/T Pavel Dybenko, 991 F.2d 1012, 1016 (2d Cir. 1993). [. . .]

After the briefs were filed, but before oral argument, we had occasion to decide this question directly, and we concluded that "an individual official of a foreign state acting in his official capacity is the 'agency or instrumentality' of the state, and is thereby protected by the FSIA." In re Terrorist Attacks on September 11, 2001, 538 F.3d 71, 81 (2d Cir. 2008). [. . .] Appellants would distinguish In re Terrorist Attacks on the ground that the FSIA does not immunize former foreign government officials, and that Dichter – unlike the individual defendants in that case – was no longer an official of a foreign government when suit was filed. [. . .]

From Schooner Exchange until 1952, the Executive routinely called for immunity in all cases against friendly foreign sovereigns. Id. In 1952 the State Department adopted a "restrictive" theory of foreign sovereign immunity under which invocations of immunity were confined to a foreign sovereign's public acts, but did not extend to its strictly commercial acts. Id. at 486–87. In practice, this approach proved troublesome. In 1976, Congress enacted the FSIA in an effort to codify the rules governing foreign sovereign immunity, removing the immunity determination from the political branches by setting out a legal framework, including certain substantive standards and procedural rules, within which issues of immunity are to be decided by the judiciary. Altmann, 541 U.S. at 691; see Foreign Sovereign Immunities Act of 1976, Pub. L. No. 94–583, § 4, 90 Stat. 2891, 2891–97 (1976). [. . .]

The FSIA is silent with regard to former foreign government officials. Appellants argue that Congress therefore must have intended to strip former officials of the immunity they enjoyed under the Schooner Exchange scheme. But silence does not suffice; and appellants have identified no provision or feature of the FSIA that bespeaks intent to abrogate that common-law scheme with respect to former officials. It follows that if, as appellants contend, the FSIA does not apply to former government officials, we must look to common law to determine (a) whether former officials are entitled to immunity under the common-law Schooner Exchange scheme, and (b) if so, whether Dichter is entitled to immunity "in conformity to the principles accepted by the department of the government charged with the conduct of our foreign relations." Republic of Mexico v. Hoffman, 324 U.S. 30, 35 (1945). [. . .]

Common law recognizes the immunity of former foreign officials. At the time the FSIA was enacted, the common law of foreign sovereign immunity recognized an individual official's entitlement to immunity for "acts performed in his official capacity." Restatement (Second) of Foreign Relations Law of the United States § 66(f) (1965); see also Heaney v. Gov't of Spain, 445 F.2d 501, 504 (2d Cir. 1971) [. . .]

The United States – through the State Department and the Department of Justice – filed a Statement of Interest in the district court specifically recognizing Dichter's entitlement to immunity and urging that appellants' suit "be dismissed on immunity grounds." Accordingly, even if Dichter, as a former foreign official, is not categorically eligible for immunity under the FSIA (a question we need not decide here), he is nevertheless immune from suit under common-law principles that pre-date, and survive, the enactment of that statute. Appellants' two remaining arguments, raised in the FSIA context, are equally applicable in the common-law context. First, they argue that there can be no immunity – statutory or otherwise – for violations of jus cogens (international law norms). But we have previously held that there is no general jus cogens exception to FSIA immunity. See Smith v. Socialist People's Libyan Arab Jamahiriya, 101 F.3d 239, 242–45 (2d Cir. 1996) (considering, and rejecting, the argument that "a foreign state should be deemed to have forfeited its sovereign immunity whenever it engages in conduct that violates fundamental humanitarian standards..."). And in the common-law context, we defer to the Executive's determination of the scope of immunity. As Appellants also argue that any immunity Dichter might enjoy is overridden by his alleged violations of the TVPA, which makes liable "[any] individual who, under actual or apparent authority, or color of law, of any foreign nation... subjects an individual to extrajudicial killing." U.S.C. § 1350 note sec 2(a). Because the TVPA only applies to individuals acting under actual or apparent governmental authority, appellants argue that a grant of immunity to a former official such as Dichter would essentially write the TVPA out of existence. This is incorrect. As to statutory immunity, the TVPA applies to individual officials who fall into one of the enumerated exceptions listed in 28 U.S.C. § 1605. [...] And because the extension of common-law immunity is discretionary, the TVPA will apply to any individual official whom the Executive declines to immunize. In summary, we need not decide whether the FSIA applies to a former official of a foreign government (a close and interesting question), because if the FSIA does not apply, a former official may still be immune under common-law principles that pre-date, and survive, the enactment of the FSIA. Here, the Executive Branch has urged the courts to decline jurisdiction over appellants' suit, and under our traditional rule of deference to such Executive determinations, we do so. We therefore affirm the judgment of the district court dismissing appellants' complaint for lack of jurisdiction [...]

COMMENTARY

Dichter shows how US courts interpret US domestic law in relation to a civil suit (a tort based on a violation of the laws of nations, in this case an alleged war crime). Would the matter be different in proceedings directly related to criminal charges, for instance acts amounting to grave breaches of the Geneva Conventions? If not, would that expose the United States to international responsibility for failing to prosecute?

Interestingly, a letter from the Israeli Ambassador to the US Department of State introduced as evidence into the trial record read, in part:

[T]he cases [i.e. Dichter and one dealing with General Ya'alon] raise quintessentially political questions, in which judicial interference is improper, impracticable and risks complicating or undermining the important political and diplomatic avenues that are currently being pursued. While ostensibly brought against Mr. Dichter and Gen. Ya'alon personally, these cases challenge sovereign actions of the State of Israel, approved by the government of Israel in defence of its citizens against terrorist attacks. They attempt to circumvent Israel's sovereign immunity for official state acts. [...] [A]nything Mr. Dichter and Gen. Ya'alon did in connection with the events at issue in the suits was in the course of their official duties, and in furtherance of official policies of the State of Israel. To allow a suit against these former officials is to allow a suit against Israel itself. (Letter from Daniel Ayalon, Ambassador of Israel, to Nicholas Burns, Under-Secretary for Political Affairs, U.S. Department of State (6 February 2006).)

Is the reasoning of this letter persuasive? Is it fair to say that acts that might amount to war crimes are 'Acts of State' so that individuals are shielded from their legal consequences?

Another interesting question is whether a court in one country may make a finding that State officials of that same country (who do not therefore have immunity) have aided and abetted the commission of an international crime by officials of another country – officials who therefore do enjoy immunity before the courts of the first country. Is such a finding barred due to the fact that the conduct that might amount to a crime is an act of State? (See, for instance, *Habib v. Commonwealth of Australia* [2010] FCAFC 12, Judgment of 25 February 2010.)

As is clear from the above, often the issue in contention is whether the acts of the State agent are indeed *official* acts. In the *Bouterse* case for example, a Dutch Court found that the commission of very serious offences cannot be considered to be one of the official duties of a head of State (Gerechtshof Amsterdam, 20 November 2000, *Nederlandse Jurisprudentie* (2001) No. 51, 302). By implication, this would apply to any State official. Is this position convincing? What criteria should inform a decision on this matter? What about an agent acting in his official capacity but *ultra vires*?

PERSONAL IMMUNITIES

Personal immunities also arise from customary international law and attach to certain individuals holding a particular office. Unlike functional immunities (which are granted to *all* State agents acting in their official capacity), personal immunities only accrue to *some* categories of State organs because of the crucial relevance of their official position (diplomatic agents, Heads of States, heads of governments and ministers of foreign affairs). They cover *every* act performed by those who benefit from these rules, but they last *only while the person concerned remains in office*. Personal immunities include inviolability, that is to say immunity from arrest and detention, absolute immunity from criminal jurisdiction and immunity from civil jurisdiction (with very limited exceptions).

Rules on personal immunity are generally considered binding at the domestic level (i.e. in the 'horizontal' relation between State authorities), whereas international criminal tribunals are granted jurisdiction to indict and prosecute high State officials suspected of crimes under their jurisdiction, even if these are still in office. Indeed, the ICJ has made the following finding on the state of the law in *Yerodia* (*Congo* v. *Belgium*, also called the *Arrest Warrant* case):

60. The Court emphasizes [...] that the immunity from jurisdiction enjoyed by incumbent Ministers for Foreign Affairs does not mean that they enjoy *impunity* in respect of any crimes they might have committed, irrespective of their gravity. Immunity from criminal jurisdiction and individual criminal responsibility are quite separate concepts. While jurisdictional immunity is procedural in nature, criminal responsibility is a question of substantive law. Jurisdictional immunity may well bar prosecution for a certain period or for certain offences; it cannot exonerate the person to whom it applies from all criminal responsibility.

61. Accordingly, the immunities enjoyed under international law by an incumbent or former Minister for Foreign Affairs do not represent a bar to criminal prosecution in certain circumstances. First, such persons enjoy no criminal immunity under international law in their own countries, and may thus be tried by those countries' courts in accordance with the relevant rules of domestic law. Secondly, they will cease to enjoy immunity from foreign jurisdiction if the State which they represent or have represented decides to waive that immunity. Thirdly, after a person ceases to hold the office of Minister for Foreign Affairs, he or she will no longer enjoy all of the immunities accorded by international law in other States. Provided that it has jurisdiction under international law, a court of one State may try a former Minister for Foreign Affairs of another State in respect of acts committed prior or subsequent to his or her period of office, as well as in respect of acts committed during that period of office in a private capacity. Fourthly, an incumbent or former Minister for Foreign Affairs may be subject to criminal proceedings before certain international criminal courts, where they have jurisdiction. Examples include the International Criminal Tribunal for the former Yugoslavia, and the International Criminal Tribunal for Rwanda, established pursuant to Security Council resolutions under Chapter VII of the United Nations Charter, and the future International Criminal Court created by the 1998 Rome Convention. [...]

Examples of both categories (domestic and international prosecutions) follow below.

Spain, **Fidel Castro**, Audiencia Nacional *(Central Criminal Court), Decision of 4 March 1999*

> In October 1998, a criminal complaint for acts of genocide and terrorism was filed before a Spanish court against Fidel Castro, at the time President of the Republic of Cuba. The first instance judge rejected the complaint due to Castro's immunity as Head of State. The case was then brought before the *Audiencia National.*

FIRST. [...] The appeal expresses agreement with the opinion of the investigating judge not to allow jurisdictional immunity in relation to the accused, His Excellency Fidel Castro Ruz, despite his capacity as President of the Council of State of the Republic of Cuba. The appeal thus rejects the opinion of the Public Prosecutor. The Public Prosecutor had claimed that, although the complaint alleged criminal conduct [...], His Excellency Fidel Castro Ruz benefits, as from when he became Head of State of Cuba (a position he still continues to occupy) on the basis of the principle of immunity *'par in parem non habet imperium'*. Such immunity is recognized in Spanish legislation in Article 21(1) of the Organic Law on the Judicial Power (L.O.P.J.), which refers to international norms on the matter. [...]

The Plenum takes the view that logic requires it to consider first whether jurisdictional immunity applies. This is because the first task of any tribunal is to determine whether it has jurisdiction, and then competence, on the question brought before it by the party. Only if the answer to this question is positive, the tribunal is allowed to decide on the merits of the claim brought before it. [...] The issue to be determined is the question whether Spanish penal jurisdiction can, in the broad sense of embarking on judicial penal proceedings, judge the Head of State of a country that maintains diplomatic relations with Spain.

SECOND. In the seventh ground of the order appealed against, the investigating judge starts from Constitutional Court judgment No.107/92 of 1 July. This order is based on a reading of this judgment that leads the judge to conclude that the immunity of foreign States from enforcement is limited, not absolute.

In dealing with the question we are faced with, we must start from the following premises:

a) Jurisdictional immunity should not be confused with immunity from execution. It is the latter to which STC 107/92 refers, and, moreover, in reference to labour jurisdiction. Accordingly, saying that immunity from execution is limited in relation to foreign States in the labour sphere [...] has nothing to do with the problem of jurisdictional immunity in criminal matters in relation to a foreign Head of State for alleged criminal acts.

b) To be sure, the Constitutional Court judgment mentioned also refers to jurisdictional immunity, but it does so by way of *obiter dicta*, noting the difference from immunity from execution, in order to go on to answer the specific question before it, in the habeas corpus petition, with exclusive reference to immunity from enforcement in social matters.

Thus, [...] the Plenum must decide *ex officio* whether Spanish penal jurisdiction can take cognizance of supposedly criminal acts, and do so prior to pronouncing as to whether the same are covered by the principle of universality established by Article 23(4)(a) and (b) of the L.O.P.J for the crimes of genocide and terrorism, and in the Convention on the Repression of Torture and on the basis of Article 23(4)(g) for the crime of torture.

THIRD. In criminal matters Spanish jurisdiction covers cognizance of crimes referred to in Article 23 L.O.P.J. The Spanish judge has been granted jurisdiction based on the principle of territoriality, fundamentally, as well as on the principle of personality, the principle of protection, and the principle of universality, each of them contained in the four sections of Article 23 cited. The judgment of the Second Chamber of the Supreme Court of 1687 [*sic*] (st 87/4315) states 'however, the aforesaid principle of territoriality, proclaimed for fundamental legal bodies, and the ensuing principle of equality of all before the law, laid down in Article 14 of the Constitution, have important exceptions, some of domestic public law, others engendered by the nature of the act, and finally, the rest grounded in norms of public foreign law or international law, this point being reflected as regards these last exceptions in Article 334 of the former Organic Law of Judicial Power of 1870, where it is established.' Excepted from the provisions of the foregoing Article are Princes of ruling houses, Presidents or Heads of other States, Ambassadors, Ministers Plenipotentiary and Ministers Resident, *chargés d'affaires*, and foreign staff employees of embassies, who – should they commit crimes – are to be placed at the disposal of their respective governments.

There is accordingly no doubt, given the explicit mention of Presidents or Heads of other States in the aforesaid article 334 L.O.P.J. of 1870, that until the entry into force of the L.O.P.J. of 1785 [*sic*] the jurisdictional immunity of a foreign Head of State was an inevitable, legally binding reality.

In the current situation the starting point is Article 21(2) of the L.O.P.J. in force, the provisions of which state 'the cases of jurisdictional immunity and immunity from execution established by the norms of public international law are accepted,' which should be completed by the final phrase of Art 23 L.O.P.J.: 'without prejudice to the provisions of the international treaties to which Spain may be a party.'

FOURTH. In order to find the guiding principle on the matter before us, reference should again be made to the Supreme Court judgment 107/92 of 1 July 1992 since, as said above, it contains an *obiter dicta* reference to jurisdictional immunity. In the fourth judicial ground [of that judgment] it is indicated that: 'Given that jurisdictional immunity does not form part of the issues before us in the present habeas corpus appeal, it is enough to state in this respect that, from the traditional absolute rule of jurisdictional immunity based on the equal sovereignty of States expressed in the maxim *'par in parem imperium non habet'*, the international order has evolved beyond this formulation towards the crystallization of a limited rule of immunity that empowers national courts to exercise jurisdiction over those acts of a foreign State that have not been carried out in virtue of *imperium*, but subject to the ordinary rules of private transactions. The distinction between acts *iure imperium* [*sic*] and acts *iure gestionis*, however complex it may be to flesh out in specific cases and however diverse its development may be in the practice of States and in international codifications, has made its way to become a general international norm [. . .]'

These directives, applied to the case of judicial orders, allow us to assert the existence of jurisdictional immunity [. . .] having as its source not the Vienna Conventions on Diplomatic and Consular Relations, but the specific bilateral treaties signed by States and international customary law.

The quality as Head of State of His Excellency Fidel Castro Ruz cannot be doubted in the light of the post he holds. In fact Article 74 of the Constitution of the Republic of Cuba says that the President of the Council of State is Head of State and Head of Government, and the provisions of Article 93 of the aforesaid 1976 Constitution, amended in July 1992, provide that: 'The powers of the President of the Council of State and Head of Government are the following: (a) To represent the State and the Government and direct national policy.'

There are, then, jurisdictional exemptions in domestic law. Article 53(3) of the Spanish Constitution refers to this when it proclaims the inviolability of the King and jurisdictional exemptions in foreign law, such as that for a foreign Head of State. This exemption takes the form of an immunity of a general nature within the criminal and jurisdictional order of the receiving State, and constitutes an absolute jurisdictional exemption. This opinion is unanimous in penal and procedural legal literature. [. . .]

FIFTH. In conclusion, if Spain recognizes the sovereignty of the Cuban people and maintains diplomatic relations with that country, Spanish penal jurisdiction cannot take cognizance of the allegedly criminal acts (whether or not it be genocide, terrorism and torture that the complaint refers to as crimes) since one of the accused is His Excellency Fidel Castro Ruz, who represents vis-à-vis Spain the sovereignty of the Cuban people. The complaint cannot stand since the Plenum has determined that the ground for the inadmissibility of the complaint is the impossibility to pronounce on it under Spanish penal jurisdiction. Needless to say, the above solution in no way contradicts a recent resolution by this same Plenum in which the accused was General P., Senator of the Republic of Chile, given that he was not the head of a foreign State, having ceased to hold that office at the time when the appeal against the admission of the complaint was turned down.

SIXTH. From the foregoing arguments it follows that the non-admission of the complaint to proceedings is confirmed and the appeal rejected [...]

France, Gaddafi case, Cour de cassation, Judgment of 13 March 2001

On 19 September 1989, a bomb exploded on board a French aircraft, blowing it up over Chad and killing 171 people, including more than 50 French nationals. Victims and an NGO filed a criminal complaint against Muhammar Gaddafi – generally considered de facto Head of State of Libya – alleging his involvement in the attack. On 20 October 2000, the Court of Appeals of Paris allowed the case to proceed stating that treaty provisions as well as domestic and international case law from 1945 onwards showed the existence of an exception to the general rule granting immunity from criminal prosecution to heads of State. In this case, the exception was justified because ordering a terrorist attack involving the murder of 170 people on a civilian aircraft could never form part of the functions of a head of State, but rather was an act amounting to an international crime. The public prosecutor appealed this decision to the *Cour de cassation* – which issued a brisk judgment.

In the absence of any contrary international provision binding the concerned parties, international customary law prohibits the exercise of criminal jurisdiction over foreign Heads of State in office. [...]

  Moreover, and despite the contrary submissions of the Prosecution, in order to confirm the decision of the *Juge d'instruction*, the appeal judges consider that although the immunity of foreign Heads of State has always been accepted within the international community, including by France, immunity should not be granted for acts of complicity in destruction of property using an explosive substance which lead to the death of persons, in relation to a terrorist enterprise. However, in so judging, the *Chambre d'accusation* breached the principle discussed above, since the crime in question, serious as it may be, is not covered by one of the exceptions to the principle of immunity of jurisdiction of foreign Heads of States considering the present state of international law. [...]

  For these aforementioned reasons, the *Cour de cassation* quashes the decision of the *Chambre d'accusation* of the Paris Court of Appeal of 20 October 2000 [...]

This decision seems to be based on the finding that 'terrorism' is not an international crime providing an exception to immunity of foreign Heads of States. Is that so? Would the Court have reached a different result if the charged crime had been persecution or genocide?

Belgium, **Sharon and Yaron,** Cour de cassation, *Judgment of 12 February 2003*

In 2001 a number of survivors of the 1982 massacre in the Sabra and Shatila Palestinian refugee camps (Lebanon) lodged a criminal complaint with a Belgian court against Ariel Sharon (Minister of Defence at the time of the massacre) and Amos Yaron (commander of an Israeli army unit at the gates of the refugee camps of Sabra and Shatila), accusing them of genocide, crimes against humanity and war crimes. A Brussels pretrial Chamber (Court of appeal, *Chambre des mises en accusation*) held on 26 June 2002 that the defendants' presence in Belgium was a precondition for the application of the 1993 Belgian Statute granting extraterritorial jurisdiction to Belgian courts over some categories of international crimes. The Court of Cassation reversed the decision, holding that Belgian law on this type of crime extended its reach regardless of the presence of the defendant in Belgium. The reasoning of the Court, however, continued:

International custom does not allow heads of state or governments to be prosecuted before criminal courts of a foreign state, absent international rules binding upon the states concerned. Certainly, Article IV of the Convention on Genocide provides that persons who have committed one of the prohibited acts of genocide shall be punished without taking into account their official status. Nevertheless, Article VI of the same Convention only envisages prosecution of such persons before a competent tribunal of the state in the territory of which the act was committed or before the International Criminal Court. It follows from the joint reading of these two provisions that immunity from jurisdiction is excluded before the courts referred to in Article VI, but it is not when the person is brought before a court of a third state that intends to exercise jurisdiction not provided for in treaty law. On the other hand Article 27(2) of the Rome Statute of the International Criminal Court provides that "immunities [...] which may attach to the official capacity of a person, whether under national or international law, shall not bar the Court from exercising its jurisdiction over such a person". This provision therefore does not undermine or affect the principle of customary international law relating to the immunity from jurisdiction when the protected person is prosecuted, as in the case at issue, before national courts of a state exercising universal jurisdiction by default. The 1949 Geneva Conventions and the Additional Protocols I and II do not contain any provision impeding the immunity from jurisdiction of which the defendant may [avail] himself before Belgian courts. Admittedly, pursuant to Article 5(3) of the [Belgian] law of 16 June 1993 concerning the repression of serious breaches of international humanitarian law, the immunity attaching to the official quality of a person does not prevent the application of the law. However, this provision of national law would run against the aforementioned principle of international customary law if it were to be construed as removing the immunity granted by that principle. Hence, that Belgian provision may not pursue that purpose, but must be interpreted as only excluding that the official quality of a person may [exclude] criminal responsibility for crimes of international law enumerated in the law itself.

The decision here challenged states that the prosecution against the two defendants is not admissible. On the ground advanced by the Court in lieu of the ground that the complainants assail, the prosecution is indeed inadmissible to the extent that it is exercised against the defendant [Sharon] under the counts of genocide, crimes against humanity and war crimes.

The Court thus remitted the case to a lower court only with regard to Yaron, who at the relevant time was director general of the Israeli Defence Ministry, and therefore did not enjoy personal immunity. The proceedings were nevertheless discontinued when the Belgian Parliament, in 2003, amended the law on extraterritorial jurisdiction, requiring a special direct link of the criminal offender to the Belgian territory or State.

SCSL, Prosecutor v. Charles Taylor, Appeals Chamber, Decision on Immunity from Jurisdiction, 31 May 2004

In March 2003, the Special Court for Sierra Leone (SCSL) issued an indictment against Charles Taylor, at the time President of Liberia, for crimes against humanity and grave breaches of the Geneva Conventions, with intent 'to obtain access to the mineral wealth of the Republic of Sierra Leone, in particular the diamond wealth of Sierra Leone, and to destabilize the state'. In June 2003, the SCSL sent the warrant to the authorities of Ghana, where Taylor was visiting. In July 2003, Taylor filed an application to quash his Indictment and to set aside the warrant for his arrest on the grounds that he was immune from any exercise of the jurisdiction due to his status as Head of State. In August 2003, Mr Taylor stepped down from the Presidency of Liberia and was allowed to take up residence in Nigeria.

20. At the time of his indictment (7 March 2003) and of its communication to the authorities in Ghana (4 June 2003) and of this application to annul it (23 July 2003), Mr. Taylor was an incumbent Head of State. As such, he claims entitlement to the benefit of any immunity asserted by that state against exercise of the jurisdiction of this Court. These bare facts raise the issue of law that we are called upon to decide, namely, whether it was lawful for the Special Court to issue an indictment and to circulate an arrest warrant in respect of a serving Head of State. If it was unlawful and the warrant is quashed, the question may then arise as to the extent of Mr. Taylor's immunity as a former Head of state. [...]

28. On a combined reading of Article 1 and Article 6 of the Statute of the Special Court in which it is clear that the court has competence to prosecute persons who bear the greatest responsibility for serious violations of international humanitarian law and Sierra Leonean law (Article 1) and the official position (including as Head of State) of such persons shall not relieve them of criminal responsibility nor mitigate punishment (Article 6(2)) [sic]. In the Yerodia case similar provisions in the ICTY Statute and the Statute of the International Criminal Court ("ICC") were interpreted as making persons holding high office, including Heads of State, subject to criminal proceedings for certain offences "before certain criminal courts". But, then, to begin to apply that interpretation of the law as contained in the Yerodia case may indeed be tantamount to applying an interpretation that is challenged without first deciding the substance and merit of the application.

29. In the Yerodia case, the ICJ held that the mere issuance of a warrant of arrest by Belgium against the then incumbent Minister for Foreign Affairs of the Democratic Republic of Congo [DRC] constituted a violation of an obligation of Belgium towards the DRC and ordered Belgium to cancel the warrant. The matter was not raised as a jurisdictional issue in a Belgian court. [...]

34. As raised in the submissions of the parties and those of the amici curiae, the issues in this motion turn to a large extent on the legal status of the Special Court. The background to the establishment of the court has been amply narrated in several of the decisions of this Chamber [...]

35. The Special Court is established by the Agreement between the United Nations and Sierra Leone which was entered into pursuant to Resolution 1315 (2000) of the Security Council for

the sole purpose of prosecuting persons who bear the greatest responsibility for serious vio-lations of international humanitarian law and Sierra Leonean law committed in the territory of Sierra Leone. Subsequent to that resolution, the Security Council sent a mission to Sierra Leone from 7–14 October 2000. In its report, the mission, apart from recommending that '[i]n the context of the peace process, the Security Council and the Sierra Leonean authorities will need to reflect carefully before taking any final decisions on the scope of the Special Court', refrained from making a direct recommendation on the establishment of the Special Court, 'since this requires further discussion by the Security Council.' In the meantime, on 4 October 2000, the Secretary-General submitted a report on the implementation of Resolution 1315. In the report, the Secretary-General proposed a Special Court that is unlike the International Tribunals for the former Yugoslavia and Rwanda, which were established by resolutions of the Security Council and constituted as subsidiary organs of the United Nations, or national courts established by law; rather, he proposed a treaty-based organ not anchored in any existing system.

36. Correspondence and briefings between the Secretary-General and the President of the Security Council demonstrate the high level of involvement of the Security Council in the establishment of the court including, but not limited to, approving the Statute of the Special Court and initiating and facilitating arrangements for the funding of the Court. The com-mencement of the operations of the Special Court was authorized by the Secretary-General who notified his intention so to do to the President of the Security Council in a letter dated 2 March 2002. [. . .]

37. Although the Special Court was established by treaty, unlike the ICTY and the ICTR which were each established by resolution of the Security Council in its exercise of powers by virtue of Chapter VII of the UN Charter, it was clear that the power of the Security Council to enter into an agreement for the establishment of the court was derived from the Charter of the United Nations both in regard to the general purposes of the United Nations as expressed in Article I of the Charter and the specific powers of the Security Council in Articles 39 and 41. These powers are wide enough to empower the Security Council to initiate, as it did by Resolution 1315, the establishment of the Special Court by Agreement with Sierra Leone. Article 39 empowers the Security Council to determine the existence of any threat to the peace. In Resolution 1315, the Security Council reiterated that the situation in Sierra Leone continued to constitute a threat to international peace and security in the region.

38. Much issue had been made of the absence of Chapter VII powers in the Special Court. A proper understanding of those powers shows that the absence of the so-called Chapter VII powers does not by itself define the legal status of the Special Court. It is manifest from the first sentence of Article 41, read disjunctively, that (i) The Security Council is empowered to 'decide what measures not involving the use of armed force are to be employed to give effect to its decision;' and (ii) it may (at its discretion) call upon the members of the United Nations to apply such measures. The decisions referred to are decisions pursuant to Article 39. Where the Security Council decides to establish a court as a measure to maintain or restore international peace and security it may or may not, at the same time, contemporaneously, call upon the members of the United Nations to lend their cooperation to such court as a matter of obliga-tion. Its decision to do so in furtherance of Article 41 or Article 48, should subsequent events make that course prudent may be made subsequently to the establishment of the court. It is to be observed that in carrying out its duties under its responsibility for the maintenance of inter-national peace and security, the Security Council acts on behalf of the members of the United Nations. The Agreement between the United Nations and Sierra Leone is thus an agreement between *all* members of the United Nations and Sierra Leone. This fact makes the Agreement an expression of the will of the international community. The Special Court established in such circumstances is truly international.

39. By reaffirming in the preamble to Resolution 1315 'that persons who commit or authorize serious violations of international humanitarian law are individually responsible and account-able for those violations and that *the international community will exert every effort to bring those responsible to justice in accordance with international standards of justice, fairness and due process of law*', it has been made clear that the Special Court was established to fulfil an international mandate and is part of the machinery of international justice.

40. We reaffirm, as we decided in the Constitutionality Decision that the Special Court is not a national court of Sierra Leone and is not part of the judicial system of Sierra Leone exercis-ing judicial powers of Sierra Leone. This conclusion disposes of the basis of the submissions of counsel for the Applicant on the nature of the Special Court. [. . .]

42. We come to the conclusion that the Special Court is an international criminal court. The constitutive instruments of the court contain indicia too numerous to enumerate to justify that conclusion. To enumerate those indicia will involve virtually quoting the entire provisions of those instruments. It suffices that having adverted to those provisions, the conclusion we have arrived at is inescapable. [. . .]

43. The path of enquiry into the merit of the claim made by the Applicant essentially starts from the constitutive instruments of the Special Court and, particularly, the Statute. The Special Court cannot ignore whatever the Statute directs or permits or empowers it to do unless such provisions are void as being in conflict with a peremptory norm of general international law.

44. Article 6(2) of the Statute provides as follows: The official position of any accused per-sons, whether as Head of State or Government or as a responsible Government official, shall not relieve such a person of criminal responsibility nor mitigate punishment.

45. Article 6(2) is substantially in the same terms as Article 7(2) of the Statute of the ICTY and Article 6(2) of the Statute of the ICTR. [The Court then discussed Article 27 of the ICCSt., as well as Article 7 of the Nuremberg Charter and subsequent authorities showing that immunity has eroded before international tribunals.]

49. The nature of the offences for which jurisdiction was vested in these various tribunals is instructive as to the circumstances in which immunity is withheld. The nature of the Tribunals has always been a relevant consideration in the question whether there is an exception to the principle of immunity.

50. More recently in the *Yerodia* case, the International Court of Justice upheld immunities in national courts even in respect of war crimes and crimes against humanity relying on custom-ary international law. That court, after carefully examining "state practice, including national legislation and those few decisions of national higher courts such as the House of Lords or the French Court of Cassation", stated that it "has been unable to deduce from this practice that there exists under customary international law any form of exception to the rule according immunity from criminal jurisdiction and inviolability to incumbent Ministers of Foreign affairs, where they are suspected of having committed war crimes or crimes against humanity." [. . .]
But in regard to criminal proceedings before "certain international criminal courts" it held:

an incumbent or former Minister for Foreign Affairs may be subject to criminal proceedings before *certain international criminal courts*, where they have jurisdiction. Examples include the International Criminal tribunal for the former Yugoslavia, and the International Criminal tribunal for Rwanda, established pursuant to Security Council resolutions under Chapter VII of the United Nations Charter, and the future International Criminal Court created by the 1998 Rome Convention. The latter's statute expressly provides, in Article 27, paragraph 2, that '[I]mmunities or special procedural rules which may attach to the official capacity of a person, whether under national or international law, shall not bar the Court from exercising its jurisdiction over such person'.

51. A reason for the distinction, in this regard, between national courts and international courts, though not immediately evident, would appear [to be] due to the fact that the principle that one sovereign state does not adjudicate on the conduct of another state; the principle of state immunity derives from the equality of sovereign states and therefore has no relevance to international criminal tribunals which are not organs of a state but derive their mandate from the international community. Another reason is as put by Professor Orentlicher in her *amicus* brief that: states have considered the collective judgment of the international community to provide a vital safeguard against the potential destabilizing effect of unilateral judgment in this area.

52. Be that as it may, the principle seems now established that the sovereign equality of states does not prevent a Head of State from being prosecuted before an international criminal tribunal or court. [...]

53. In this result the Appeals Chamber finds that Article 6(2) of the Statute is not in conflict with any peremptory norm of general international law and its provisions must be given effect by this court. We hold that the official position of the Applicant as an incumbent Head of State at the time when these criminal proceedings were initiated against him is not a bar to his prosecution by this court. The Applicant was and is subject to criminal proceedings before the Special Court for Sierra Leone.

54. Since we have found that the Special Court is not a national court, it is unnecessary to discuss the cases in which immunity is claimed before national courts.

Taylor was arrested in Nigeria in March 2006 and transferred to the SCSL. On 3 April 2006 he pleaded not guilty to an amended indictment charging him with 11 counts. As of June 2010, he is on trial before the SCSL.

COMMENTARY

The SCSL Appeals Chamber attempted to follow carefully the *Yerodia* finding that 'certain' international tribunals are not bound by rules on personal immunity. Most of its reasoning appears to hinge on the fact that personal immunities are meant to protect incumbent Heads of State and other top officials from 'horizontal' prosecution (i.e. criminal proceedings initiated by other States). Since the SCSL was not a domestic court but, having received its mandate on the basis of an international agreement, was international in character, the rationale applicable to domestic courts did not hold true for it. Is this a convincing argument to strip a Head of State of immunity? Would this apply for any crime or only for international tribunals prosecuting *certain* crimes?

OTHER SOURCES OF 'IMMUNITIES'

Apart from immunities proper discussed above, there are analogous pleas that accused before international tribunals have attempted to make. Some of them stem from domestic acts of clemency or forgiveness for past offences (amnesties). In a 2004 decision, the SCSL ruled that it was not bound by amnesties pursuant to the Lomé Agreement between the warring parties for crimes under its jurisdiction (*Prosecutor* v. *Kallon, Norman and Kamara*, Decision on Challenge to Jurisdiction: Lomé Accord Amnesty, Appeals Chamber, 13 March 2004; see also *Prosecutor* v. *Kondewa*, Decision on Lack of Jurisdiction/Abuse of Process: Amnesty Provided by the Lomé Accord, 25 May 2004). Amnesty laws have also been found as not barring prosecution for certain serious crimes – such as enforced disappearances – by the Inter-American Court of Human Rights (*Barrios Altos*, Judgment of

14 March 2001), followed by the Supreme Courts of Argentina and Chile. See M. Frulli, 'Amnesty', in *Oxford Companion*, at 243–4).

As a final example, Radovan Karadžić claimed a sort of immunity before the ICTY on the basis of an alleged agreement he had reached with US negotiator Richard Holbrooke during the Dayton peace talks in 1995.

ICTY, **Prosecutor v. Karadžić,** *Decision on Karadžić's Appeal of Trial Chamber's Decision on Alleged Holbrooke Agreement, 12 October 2009*

On 25 July 1995, the ICTY issued an indictment and arrest warrant for genocide, crimes against humanity and war crimes against Radovan Karadžić, former President of Republika Srpska, an entity that attempted to break away from Bosnia and Herzegovina when the latter seceded from Yugoslavia. After about 13 years on the run, Karadžić was arrested by Serbian police and surrendered to the ICTY on 31 July 2008. Among the various challenges, he claimed that an agreement was reached between him and US negotiator Richard Holbrooke during the Dayton peace talks in November 1995 that, in exchange for completely withdrawing from public life, Karadžić would not be subject to prosecution by the Tribunal. The Trial Chamber dismissed his arguments, holding that even if an agreement did exist, Holbrooke would not have acted with the actual or apparent authority of the United Nations Security Council (UNSC), and on this basis observed that 'he was essentially a third party, unconnected to the Tribunal, promising immunity years before the Accused's transfer to the Tribunal'. While the existence of the agreement has not been established by the ICTY, on appeal one of the questions was whether an agreement without explicit endorsement by the UN Security Council could at least in theory provide a basis for Karadžić's immunity.

34. The Appeals Chamber recalls that the UNSC, acting under Chapter VII of the UN Charter, has adopted the Statute by means of resolution and established the Tribunal as a measure contributing to the restoration and maintenance of peace in the former Yugoslavia. The Statute, as the constitutive instrument of the Tribunal, defines the scope and limits of the Tribunal's substantive jurisdiction. In particular, Articles 1 to 9 of the Statute define the Tribunal's jurisdiction *ratione materiae, personae, loci* and *temporis*. Article 1 of the Statute confers a general power for the Tribunal to prosecute "persons responsible for serious violations of international humanitarian law committed in the territory of the former Yugoslavia since 1991". There is no provision of the Statute which excludes any specific individual from the jurisdiction of the Tribunal.

35. The Appeals Chamber considers that the Statute of the Tribunal can only be amended or derogated by means of UNSC resolution. This plainly derives from the *actus contrarius* doctrine, is established in the jurisprudence of the Tribunal, and is confirmed by the practice of the UNSC.[10]

36. As the ambit of the Tribunal's primary jurisdiction is defined in the Statute, it follows that the only basis for limiting or amending the Tribunal's jurisdiction is a UNSC resolution. Therefore, contrary to what the Trial Chamber appears to concede, the mere involvement

---

[10] [112] The UNSC has always acted by resolution when intervening in matters addressed in the Statute. *See* UNSC Resolution 827, S/RES/827, 25 May 1993 (establishing the Tribunal); UNSC Resolution 1534, S/RES/1534, 26 March 2005, para. 5 (calling on the Prosecution to focus on the most senior leaders responsible for crimes within the Tribunal's jurisdiction); UNSC Resolution 1786, S/RES/1786, 28 November 2007 (appointing the Prosecutor); UNSC Resolution 1837, S/RES/1837, 29 September 2008 (extending terms of office of Judges).

of the UNSC in concluding the alleged Agreement, without a ratification of the alleged Agreement by a UNSC resolution, could not limit the jurisdiction of the Tribunal. The Appeals Chamber notes that there is no UNSC resolution excluding the Appellant from the ambit [of] the Tribunal's jurisdiction.

37. In light of the foregoing, the Appeals Chamber finds that under no circumstance would the alleged Agreement in and of itself, even if its existence was proved, limit the jurisdiction of the Tribunal.

38. [...] As explained above, in the absence of a UNSC resolution, the alleged Agreement could not have any impact on the Tribunal's jurisdiction, even if it were made with the *actual* authority of the UNSC. *A fortiori*, even if one considered that the alleged Agreement was made with the apparent authority of the UNSC[, the Agreement] could not affect in any event the ambit of the Tribunal's jurisdiction. In his submissions, the Appellant attempts to rely on analogy with jurisdictional matters in international criminal law a theory typical of contract law protecting the legitimate expectations of a contracting party believing without fault that a contract was validly concluded with a legitimate representative of the other party. However, the Appellant ignores that one of the requirements for applying a doctrine by analogy is the existence of an *eadem ratio*, that is, the existence of sufficient similarities between two cases. The field of contract law is so distant from the question of jurisdiction in international criminal law that the two are effectively incomparable. Jurisdiction of criminal courts is not a negotiable matter. The power of a court to decide a criminal matter is defined by law rather than private contracting parties, and thus the expectation of a party on the validity of an agreement on criminal jurisdiction cannot have any impact on jurisdiction. The Appeals Chamber considers that the Appellant's submissions on apparent authority fall more squarely under the question of the applicability of the doctrine of abuse of process.

39. Additionally, the Appeals Chamber considers that the Appellant is not advancing an argument concerning the scope of the Tribunal's jurisdiction when he claims that the Prosecution's discretion not to prosecute an individual demonstrates that no UNSC resolution is necessary in order to limit the jurisdiction of the Tribunal. The Appellant confuses the two distinct notions of jurisdiction and prosecutorial discretion. The scope of the substantive jurisdiction of the Tribunal is entirely contingent upon the constitutive instrument of the Tribunal itself, that is, its Statute. On a different level, in systems of criminal law not based on the rule of compulsory prosecution, like that of the Tribunal, prosecutors possess the discretion not to bring before the court cases that theoretically fall within the court's jurisdiction. In other words, the fact that the Prosecution may decide not to prosecute an individual does not necessarily mean that, had the Prosecution decided to prosecute that individual, the Tribunal would not have jurisdiction over him or her. Jurisdiction and prosecutorial discretion are two independent issues.

41. [Moreover,] the alleged Agreement could not bind the Tribunal even if it were to be attributed to the Prosecution. The Appeals Chamber recalls that, while "[i]t is beyond question that the Prosecutor has a broad discretion in relation to the initiation of investigations and in the preparation of indictments", this discretion is not unlimited and must be exercised within the restrictions imposed by the Statute and the Rules. Pursuant to the restrictions to the Prosecution's discretion provided by Rule 51 of the Rules, the Prosecution was not in a position, at the time of the alleged Agreement, to withdraw the indictment against the Appellant without the leave of a Judge of the Tribunal. Consequently, even if the involvement of the Prosecution in the making of the alleged Agreement were proved, the alleged Agreement would not be binding on the Tribunal, as an indictment against the Appellant had already been confirmed at the time.

Was the ICTY right in stating that *only* a UN Security Council resolution can provide immunity before a Tribunal established by such a resolution? Was it right in stating that a UN Security Council resolution could actually have this effect, interfering *ex post* in the prosecutorial discretion of a Prosecutor mandated to act 'independently' and who 'shall not seek or receive instructions from any Government or from any other source' (Article 16 ICTYSt.) in order to investigate and prosecute the most serious international crimes?

QUESTIONS

1. In which cases do personal and functional immunities overlap? What would be the effect of this overlap?

2. The Spanish judgment in the *Castro* case makes much of the fact that the Head of State enjoys immunity because he or she represents the whole nation. Is this rationale convincing? What is the real rationale underpinning personal immunities?

3. If immunity is conceived as an exception to the general rule on State jurisdiction for criminal acts, courts should interpret it restrictively. How do you assess the way judges ascertained the contours of immunity in the cases above? Can you see trends developing and differences between the approaches of domestic and international tribunals?

FURTHER READING

A. Bianchi, 'Immunity Versus Human Rights: The Pinochet Case' (2002) 10 EJIL 237–77.

L. Sadat, 'Exile, Amnesty and International Law' (2006) 81 *Notre Dame Law Rev.* 955.

R. van Alebeek, *The Immunities of States and Their Officials in International Criminal Law and International Human Rights Law* (Oxford: Oxford University Press, 2008).

Werle, *Principles*, 234–41.

(C) *NE BIS IN IDEM*

THE NOTION AND ITS ORIGINS

The maxim *ne bis in idem* ('not twice for the same')[11] stands for the proposition that a person should not be tried twice for the same offence. The rule protects the individual from the anxiety, cost and potential abuse of power posed by successive prosecutions. From a pragmatic, system-efficiency perspective, the principle also has affiliations with the doctrine of *res judicata*, the notion that a final adjudication is binding and the costs and burdens of re-litigation should not be borne again.

---

[11] The ICTR and ICTY Statutes use the formulation *non bis in idem* while the drafters of the Rome Statute, after several hours of debate, opted for *ne bis in idem*. The latter formulation that will be used here.

Also commonly referred to in some national jurisdictions as the rule against double jeopardy[12] or *autrefois acquit/convict* ('formerly acquitted or convicted'), the protection has long roots in Greek and Roman law. The Latin phrase expressing the principle derives from the Roman law maxim '*nemo debet bis vexari pro una et eadem causa*', meaning 'no one shall be vexed twice for the same offence'.

The grant of the guarantee is widespread among national jurisdictions – albeit with widely varying approaches and qualifications, in part because of the complications of observing the principle when multiple sovereigns have overlapping jurisdictions, as discussed further in the next section. Perceptions of the values at stake also differ. While common law jurisdictions focus on abuse of process, civil law jurisdictions reason that the public prosecutor's 'right' to prosecute lapses after a final decision. The treatment of appeals of acquittals also differ – while the Prosecution often has the right to appeal acquittals in civil law jurisdictions, common law jurisdictions tend to deem appeals or re-opening of acquittals foreclosed by the double jeopardy bar, though this position is loosening, for example, in the United Kingdom after the Criminal Justice Act of 2003. The civil law position prevails among the international courts, which permit the Prosecution to appeal acquittals.

Because of disparate national approaches to the *ne bis in idem* principle, the main thrust of opinion is that it has not achieved the status of a general principle of international law applying to relations between States. In the *Zennaro* case, for instance, the Italian Constitutional Court explicitly stated that the principle has not turned into customary international law (Judgment of 8 April 1976, no. 69, in (1976) 59 *Rivista di diritto internazionale*, 584–8; English trans. in (1977) 3 *Italian Yearbook of International Law*, 300–2, at 301–2). Therefore a person tried in a State may be tried again in another State for the same criminal offence, unless the two States are bound by a treaty prohibiting such successive trials between the States. Nevertheless, contemporary international and hybrid tribunals generally recognize the protection with qualifications. As a threshold matter, for the protection to apply, there must have been a previous trial, not just the commencement of investigation that is deferred or stayed, or the paring down of charges in a lengthy indictment for a more efficient and effective trial. This is a source of repeated confusion among accused and defence counsel, as the next excerpts illustrate.

Cases

ICTY, Prosecutor v. Tadić*, Trial Chamber, Decision on the Defence Motion on the Principle of Non-Bis-In-Idem, 14 November 1995*

The son of a World War II hero, Duško Tadić had a more ignominious part to play in history. Tadić was the first to be prosecuted before the ICTY for war crimes and crimes

---

[12] Both the notion of *ne bis in idem* in civil law systems and the notion of double jeopardy in common law systems bar retrial for the same offence but their operation has a different scope, as the Special Court for Sierra Leone has explained: 'Unlike double jeopardy, [...] the principle of *ne bis in idem* prevents repeated prosecutions for the same conduct in the same or different legal systems, whereas the notion of double jeopardy "is a double exposure to sentencing which is applicable to all the different stages of the criminal justice process in the *same* legal system: prosecution, conviction, and punishment".' (*Prosecutor* v. *Norman, Fofana and Kondewa*, Case No. SCSL-04-14-T, Decision on the First Accused's Motion for Service and Arraignment on the Consolidated Indictment, 29 Nov. 2004, at p. 14 (quoting Kriangsak Kittichaisaree, *International Criminal Law* (Oxford: Oxford University Press, 2001) p. 289)).

against humanity stemming from violence against Omarska prison camp detainees during the Bosnian conflict.

In 1993, Tadić moved to Nuremberg, and then to Munich, in Germany, where he was arrested in 1994 by German police and held on charges of genocide and war crimes. At the ICTY Prosecutor's request, Germany deferred further proceedings against Tadić and transferred him to the ICTY where Tadić argued, among other things, that charges should be dismissed on the ground of *ne bis in idem*, denoted as *non bis in idem* in the ICTYSt. and below.

8. The deferral of the case [by Germany] took place after a German investigation of the charges against the accused had led to his indictment there but well before any trial of the accused in that country on those charges. While the proceedings may have passed beyond the purely investigative phase, it is undisputed that the accused had not been tried in the full sense, i.e., he was neither convicted nor acquitted by the German court.

2. No Violation of *Non-Bis-In-Idem* Within the Meaning of the Statute

9. The principle of *non-bis-in-idem* appears in some form as part of the internal legal code of many nations. Whether characterised as *non-bis-in-idem*, double jeopardy or autrefois acquit, autrefois convict, this principle normally protects a person from being tried twice or punished twice for the same acts. This principle has gained a certain international status since it is articulated in Article 14(7) of the International Covenant on Civil and Political Rights as a standard of a fair trial, but it is generally applied so as to cover only a double prosecution within the same State. The principle is binding upon this International Tribunal to the extent that it appears in [the] Statute, and in the form that it appears there.

(a) The Accused Has Not Already Been Tried in Germany

10. The deferral which occurred in this case does not raise a genuine issue of *non-bis-in-idem* according to the terms of the Statute, for this principle applies only in cases where a person has **already been tried**.

Article 10 [of the ICTYSt.] provides:

"*Non-bis-in-idem*

1. No person shall be tried before a national court for acts constituting serious violations of international humanitarian law under the present Statute, for which he or she has **already been tried** by the International Tribunal. (Emphasis added [by the Trial Chamber]).

2. A **person who has been tried** by a national court for acts constituting serious violations of international humanitarian law may be subsequently tried by the International Tribunal only if: . . ." (Emphasis added [by the Trial Chamber]).

11. The proceedings which were instituted against the accused in Germany do not constitute a trial. The Appeals Chamber correctly concluded in an earlier phase of this case that the accused was never actually tried in Germany. It noted, in reference to the stage of the proceedings in Germany at the time of the application of the Prosecutor, that "the matter has not yet passed the phase of investigation."

12. The defence has asserted that the accused was subsequently indicted and that, at the time of his transfer by Germany to the Tribunal, the proceedings against the accused had entered their "final phase". They are correct that the accused was indicted by the German authorities prior to the decision of the International Tribunal on deferral and transfer. The Defence does not explain what significance it attaches to the opening of the "final phase" of

the proceedings except to refer to the law of Germany which, it contends, demonstrates that the proceedings had opened. But, whatever its meaning, the Defence has admitted that the proceedings have not progressed so far that the accused has actually been tried as that term is used in the Statute. Thus a trial of the accused by this Tribunal would not violate the principle of *non-bis-in-idem* set forth in Article 10 of the Statute.

(b) The Accused Could Not Be Retried in Germany After Trial Before This Tribunal

13. The Defence has raised an issue of *non-bis-in-idem* by suggesting that the stage of the proceedings in Germany is such that there is a possibility that the accused might be retried in Germany after being tried by this International Tribunal. If true this would indeed raise an issue of *non-bis-in-idem* under of [*sic*] Article 10 of the Statute. But, having deferred the case of the accused to the International Tribunal, Germany could not proceed to retry him for the same acts after the disposition of his case here. Article 10(1) of the Statute makes this unequivocally clear.

14. If this were not already sufficient guarantee against double jeopardy, the German Government's own rulings on this matter make the situation in that country clear. On 10 April 1995 the German Bundestag, with the approval of the Bundesrat, passed the Yugoslavia Tribunal Law which provides in paragraph 2:

[. . .] (2) Criminal proceedings may no longer be conducted against a person against whom the Tribunal has taken or is taking action for a crime within its jurisdiction if a request has been submitted [. . .]

15. As a last guarantee against a retrial of an accused, Rule 13 empowers the Tribunal to issue an order requesting the discontinuance of subsequent retrial by any national court, and then if necessary to ask the United Nations Security Council to prevent such a second trial. Rule 13 provides:

"Non bis in idem

When the President receives reliable information to show that criminal proceedings have been instituted against a person before a court of any State for a crime for which that person has already been tried by the Tribunal, a Trial Chamber shall . . . issue a reasoned order requesting that court permanently to discontinue its proceedings. If that court fails to do so, the President may report the matter to the Security Council." [. . .]

3. No Violation of *Non-Bis-in-Idem* Within the Meaning of the International Covenant on Civil and Political Rights

17. While the *non-bis-in-idem* standard of the Statute is the only one which is directly applicable, it can also be confirmed that none of the *non-bis-in-idem* standards found in the other international instrument[s] cited by the Defence would bar the trial of the accused by this International Tribunal.

18. The International Covenant on Civil and Political Rights sets out a norm of *non-bis-in-idem* in its Article 14(7):

"No one shall be liable to be tried or punished again for an offence for which he has already been finally convicted or acquitted in accordance with the law and penal procedure of each country."

19. In interpreting this provision the Human Rights Committee has observed "that this provision prohibits double jeopardy only with regard to an offence adjudicated in a given State." (A.P. v. Italy, No. 204/1986, § 7.3) Thus, this provision is generally applied so as to cover only a

double prosecution within the same State, and has not received broad recognition as a mandatory norm of transnational application.

20. Furthermore, as with the Statute's *non-bis-in-idem* provision, this applies only to cases where an accused has already been tried. This essential precondition has not been met in this case.

4. No Violation of the Principle As Envisioned in the European Convention on the Transfer of Proceedings in Criminal Matters of 1992

21. The Defence has cited the European Convention on the Transfer of Proceedings in Criminal Matters of 1992 as evidence of the proper judicial procedure for the transfer of a criminal case from one country to another jurisdiction. Article 35 of this treaty sets out a rule of *ne-bis-in-idem* which applies between the States which are parties to that treaty. The relevant part of that article reads as follows:

"1. A person in respect of whom a final and enforceable criminal judgement has been rendered may for the same act neither be prosecuted nor sentenced nor subjected to enforcement of a sanction in another Contracting State:

(a) if he was acquitted;

(b) if the sanction imposed:

   (i) has been completely enforced or is being enforced, or

   (ii) has been wholly, or with respect to the part not enforced, the subject of a pardon or amnesty, or

   (iii) can no longer be enforced because of lapse of time;

(c) if the court convicted the offender without imposing a sanction."

22. The Defence conceded in oral argument that this treaty does not bind this Tribunal. The Trial Chamber notes, however, that even this broader transnational formulation of the principle of *non-bis-in-idem* applies only to a "person in respect of whom a final and enforceable criminal judgement has been rendered". So once again a *non-bis-in-idem* standard proposed by the Defence is inapplicable to the present case for that most basic of reasons.

5. No Violation of *Non-Bis-In-Idem* Under the Draft Statute of the International Criminal Court

23. The draft Statute of an International Criminal Court prepared by the International Law Commission also incorporates the notion of *non-bis-in-idem*. Like all the other *non-bis-in-idem* standards discussed above, Article 42(2) of that draft would preclude the proposed International Criminal Court from trying only a "person who has been tried by another court".

24. This review of the authorities leads to the unmistakeable conclusion that there can be no violation of *non-bis-in-idem*, under any known formulation of that principle, unless the accused has already been tried. Since the accused has not yet been the subject of a judgement on the merits on any of the charges for which he has not been indicted he has not yet been tried for those charges. As a result, the principle of *non-bis-in-idem* does not bar his trial before this Tribunal.

ICTY, Prosecutor *v.* Karadžić, *Trial Chamber, Decision on the Accused's Motion for a Finding on Non-Bis-In-Idem, 16 November 2009*

A long-time fugitive recently delivered to the ICTY for trial on charges of genocide, war crimes and crimes against humanity, Radovan Karadzić is considered one of the most notorious figures to be tried by the ICTY. From 1992 to 1996, he was the President of the self-declared Republika Srpska (Republic of the Serbs) established in Bosnia during the Bosnian conflict and Supreme Commander of the Bosnian Serb forces.

The risk posed by international criminal trials of ageing major figures and leaders charged with responsibility for numerous crimes at numerous crime sites is that the accused may die before judgment is delivered, as occurred in the case of former Serbian President Slobodan Milošević. A procedural innovation to address the problem of massive indictments and overly long trials is the grant to international judges of the power to pare down the Prosecution's indictment to representative charges, evidence and crime sites that capture the gravity of the crimes without bogging down proceedings. The judges in Karadžić's case pursued this course, and he erroneously seized on it to argue that *ne bis in idem* attached to the crime sites and incidents excised.

10. Article 10 of the Statute of the Tribunal ("Statute") provides that "no person shall be tried before a national court for acts constituting serious violations of international humanitarian law under the present Statute, for which he or she has already been tried by the International Tribunal."

11. Rule 73 *bis(D)* of the Rules empowers a Trial Chamber to invite the Prosecution to reduce the number of counts charged in an indictment, and to fix a number of crime sites or incidents in respect of which evidence may be presented by the Prosecution, in the interests of a fair and expeditious trial. When a Chamber exercises this power, it remains open to the Prosecution, after the commencement of trial, to apply under Rule 73 *bis(F)* to vary the Chamber's decision as to the number of crime sites or incidents in respect of which evidence may be presented. [...]

13. [...] [T]he principle of *non-bis-in-idem* applies only in cases where an accused has already been tried, and the trial of this Accused is far from completed. Furthermore, the removal of crime sites or incidents from an indictment pursuant to Rule 73 *bis(D)* cannot be interpreted as a finding on an accused's responsibility for those crime sites or incidents. The responsibilities of an accused with respect to specific charges can only be determined by way of a trial, including through the Chamber's assessment of all evidence presented by the parties in respect of those charges. Indeed, the Trial Chamber itself said that the removal of crime sites or incidents from the scope of the trial is not tantamount to any determination as to the responsibility of the Accused in relation to those charges. Therefore, the removal of crime sites or incidents from the Indictment cannot be said to constitute a completed trial of the Accused in respect of those crime sites or incidents for purposes of an application of the principle of *non-bis-in-idem*.

COMMENTARY

In the international domain, at least, the touchstone of the *ne bis in idem* principle in its diverse formulations is an adjudication on the merits. This reflects the affiliation of the *ne bis in idem* rule with the notion of *res judicata* and the import of the finality of judgments. The requirement of adjudication on the merits may come as a surprise to those from the United States where jeopardy attaches earlier; once the defendant is put in 'jeopardy' by the empanelment of a jury in a jury trial, or once the first witness is sworn in bench trials. The US rule, however, reflects an expansion of the notion of values served by the double jeopardy rule, including the interest in having the same jury decide the case, and the notion in a strong adversarial system that it is unfair that the prosecution with all its power should be allowed repeated tries. The original US constitutional protection derives from a narrower protection in English common law, however, which, as the US Supreme Court has acknowledged, follows 'then, as it does now, the relatively simple rule that a defendant has been put in jeopardy only when there has been a conviction or an acquittal – after a complete trial' (*Crist v. Bretz* 437 U.S. 28, 33 (1978)).

The *Tadić* excerpt on the effect of international adjudications on subsequent national adjudications also foregrounds a complex issue when it comes to implementation of *ne bis in idem* in international courts: the problem of multiple sovereigns, discussed in the next section. How does an international court have the power to tell a national court not to prosecute again for the same conduct after an international adjudication? How should international courts regard a prior national adjudication, and what factors are relevant in determining what weight international courts should give to prior national adjudications? How do different models of institutional structure influence these questions?

THE COMPLEXITY OF MULTIPLE SOVEREIGNS

So thorny is the question of incursion on sovereign power to prosecute where jurisdictions over crimes overlap that most of the main human rights treaties, including the ICCPR, the Seventh Protocol to the European Convention on Human Rights and the American Convention on Human Rights generally prohibit successive prosecutions only within a single State. One State's prosecution does not, therefore, limit the sovereign power of another State to prosecute.

Even in national jurisdictions, the *non bis in idem* principle is complicated by multiple sovereigns. For example, in the United States, the prohibition against double jeopardy guaranteed in the US Constitution's Fifth Amendment has been interpreted to accommodate dual sovereignty between the states and the federal systems, each with overlapping jurisdictions over certain crimes. The rationale for allowing a prosecution despite a previous prosecution by a separate state, the federal government or even a Native American tribe acting in its inherent sovereignty is that 'an act denounced as a crime by both national and state sovereignties is an offense against the peace and dignity of both and may be punished by each'. This approach formalistically treats prosecutions by separate sovereigns as prosecutions for different offences even though the proceedings stem from the same conduct.

In addition, there can be concerns that the interests of different sovereigns may diverge and that one sovereign may pursue criminal prosecution of a certain offence with inadequate vigour or even seek to protect an accused perpetrator through a sham prosecution. This anxiety was particularly acute during the 1960s in the United States when there was a suspicion that the authorities of certain states did not sufficiently prosecute violence committed against minority groups. Even today, the federal government will pursue a second prosecution if it concludes that a state effort was inadequate. The most famous example in recent times was the successive federal prosecution of the four police officers accused of beating Rodney King in Los Angeles. Nonetheless, despite this dual sovereign exception, some states in the United States have adopted provisions in their constitutions barring a state prosecution following a federal prosecution, and the US Justice Department has voluntarily adopted a policy, known as the 'Petite policy' following a Supreme Court case by that name, pursuant to which the Department will not authorize a successive federal prosecution following a state prosecution unless extraordinary circumstances obtain, such as when the state effort is inadequate or is a sham undertaking designed to protect the accused from true accountability.

The complexity of multiple sovereigns and competing interests is further compounded in the international domain. The concerns discussed in the context of the US rule are only heightened internationally where there may be even greater concerns about capacity or genuine willingness to prosecute. International courts typically step in when national jurisdictions are unable or unwilling to genuinely investigate and prosecute a grave crime. International cases therefore often include the element of a reluctant or downright recalcitrant national jurisdiction that may not want the case genuinely tried or that cannot fully and fairly try a case.

The Statutes of contemporary tribunals have tried to balance the competing concerns of sovereignty and procedural and substantive justice. The attempt to strike the balance is influenced by the structural relationship between each international court to national courts as a matter of institutional design, which in turn is shaped by decisions about the appropriate relationship between sovereign States and international bodies. As further discussed in the chapter on primacy and complementarity, *infra* (Part V(1)), the first wave of the second-generation international tribunals – the ICTR and ICTY – are in vertical relation above national courts, in a position of primacy, in part because they were adopted under the UN Security Council's Chapter VII power as measures to maintain peace and security. The Chapter VII power enables the UN Security Council to call for cooperation among UN Member States to uphold measures taken to ensure peace and security. In contrast, the ICC operates on a principle of complementarity that puts the court in a slanted horizontal relation to national courts, able to step in only when national courts are unwilling or unable to prosecute.

Below, the statutory provisions of the ICTR and ICC on *ne bis in idem* are provided. Apply your skills in statutory reading and analysis to identify the main contrasts before turning to the commentary. Take note of differences in approaches to the *ne bis in idem* principle when the question is the effect of a national judgment on the ability of an international court to render judgment versus the effect of an international judgment on the ability of national courts to prosecute. How does the structural design of whether a tribunal has primacy or complementarity to national courts influence these issues?

ICTR Statute Article 9

Non bis in idem

1. No person shall be tried before a national court for acts constituting serious violations of international humanitarian law under the present Statute, for which he or she has already been tried by the International Tribunal for Rwanda.

2. A person who has been tried before a national court for acts constituting serious violations of international humanitarian law may be subsequently tried by the International Tribunal for Rwanda only if:

   a) The act for which he or she was tried was characterised as an ordinary crime; or

   b) The national court proceedings were not impartial or independent, were designed to shield the accused from international criminal responsibility, or the case was not diligently prosecuted.

3. In considering the penalty to be imposed on a person convicted of a crime under the present Statute, the International Tribunal for Rwanda shall take into account the extent to which any penalty imposed by a national court on the same person for the same act has already been served.

ICC Statute, Article 20

Ne bis in idem

1. Except as provided in this Statute, no person shall be tried before the Court with respect to conduct which formed the basis of crimes for which the person has been convicted or acquitted by the Court.

2. No person shall be tried by another court for a crime referred to in article 5 [that is, genocide, crimes against humanity, war crimes and aggression] for which that person has already been convicted or acquitted by the Court.

3. No person who has been tried by another court for conduct also proscribed under article 6, 7 or 8 [that is, genocide, crimes against humanity and war crimes] shall be tried by the Court with respect to the same conduct unless the proceedings in the other court:

 (a) Were for the purpose of shielding the person concerned from criminal responsibility for crimes within the jurisdiction of the Court; or

 (b) Otherwise were not conducted independently or impartially in accordance with the norms of due process recognized by international law and were conducted in a manner which, in the circumstances, was inconsistent with an intent to bring the person concerned to justice.

The primacy of the ICTR and ICTY over national courts influences their incorporation of the *ne bis in idem* principle. Picture these international courts in a vertical relation above national courts. The ICTYSt. and ICTRSt. recognize a 'downward' *ne bis in idem* principle forbidding prosecution by national authorities for *acts* – not just the specific offence – tried by the international tribunal. This is a broad protection in the downward direction. In contrast, only a limited 'upward' *ne bis in idem* principle applies. International adjudication is permitted where national adjudication of the same conduct was for an 'ordinary crime' such as murder rather than genocide or a crime against humanity, or where 'the national court proceedings were not impartial or independent, were designed to shield the accused from individual criminal responsibility, or the case was not diligently prosecuted.'

While the ICTRSt. and ICTYSt. limit the notion of 'upward' *ne bis in idem*, they mitigate the impact by providing that any sentence imposed must take into consideration any sentence pronounced in the national proceeding. This reflects the influence of the notion of *ne bis poena in idem* ('not twice punished for the same'), which calls for the deduction of time served for the same conduct from any later penalty.

In contrast, the *ne bis in idem* principle in Article 20 ICCSt. is influenced by complementarity to national courts, which puts it in a horizontal rather than vertical relationship. Article 20 strikes a threefold balance. The first paragraph addresses *ne bis in idem* within the court, providing that no person shall be tried twice before the ICC. The last two paragraphs of Article 20 address the more complex questions of the effect of the interaction between decisions of national courts and the ICC.

In the international to national direction, the analogue to 'downward' *ne bis in idem*, adjudications by the ICC of crimes within its jurisdiction – genocide, crimes against humanity, war crimes and aggression – foreclose subsequent prosecution for those crimes in national courts. What is not foreclosed, however, is a subsequent national court prosecution for the same acts *on a different charge* – for example a prosecution for multiple murders instead of genocide. The notion in the ICCSt. of the '*idem*' – the thing for which the defendant cannot be tried twice – is therefore the narrower notion of the offence as defined by law rather than the factual conduct.

The *ne bis in idem* principle in the national to international direction – the analogue to 'upward' *ne bis in idem* in a vertical structure – is also qualified, as it is at the ad hoc Tribunals. Where there has been a prior national adjudication on three of the four headings of crimes within ICC jurisdiction – genocide, crimes against humanity or war crimes – the ICC may not prosecute again unless two qualifications apply. If, for example, an accused is acquitted of genocide in a national jurisdiction, the ICC cannot try the accused for crimes against humanity or war crimes for the same conduct unless the national proceedings were a sham or defective so as to meet one of the qualifications in Article 20(3)(a) or (b) of the ICCSt.

The reason for the odd omission of the fourth crime within the ICC's jurisdiction, aggression, from the *non bis in idem* protection where there has been a prior national proceeding is obscure. One explanation is that because the crime of aggression has not yet been defined in the ICCSt. and ICC jurisdiction has not yet vested over aggression (an issue further discussed in the chapter on aggression) the question of national to international *ne bis in idem* in relation to the crime has been postponed. Another explanation is that because it seems unlikely that national jurisdictions would prosecute for aggression, no provision was thought necessary.

AMNESTY AND *NE BIS IN IDEM*

A second delicate issue that complicates the implementation of the principle of *non bis in idem* in international criminal justice is how to treat amnesties conferred by national jurisdictions. Manifestly, an amnesty does not constitute an acquittal or conviction. Indeed, an amnesty averts such judgment altogether. Moreover, parliaments, truth commissions and other entities that typically grant amnesties are not courts nor judicial in character. Finally, in terms of the qualification in ICCSt., Article 20, it could be argued that amnesties are 'inconsistent with an intent to bring the person concerned to justice' – an exception to the *ne bis in idem* principle even if it otherwise applied. The question of an amnesty's relation to the *ne bis in idem* principle is unsettled, and implicates some of the substantive concerns of finality, fairness and reopening of old traumas that underlie the doctrine. The case below tries to navigate these tensions.

ECCC, Decision on Appeal Against Provisional Detention Order of Ieng Sary, 17 October 2008

> Between 1975 and 1979, the Khmer Rouge guerrillas of Cambodia seized power and under the Pol Pot regime turned Cambodia into a vast killing field. An estimated three million Cambodians died in a mere 3 years, 8 months and 20 days. Essentially anyone with an elementary school-level education was purged as a class enemy, often after brutal and crude torture. Cambodians were forced to denounce their family and friends as enemies. The cities were emptied and people forced into the countryside to toil and face more paranoid purges.
>
> The accused in this case, Ieng Sary – Pol Pot's brother-in-law – became Deputy Prime Minister and Minister of Foreign Affairs when the Khmer Rouge took over in 1975. Sary convinced educated Cambodians to return to the country, where many were then tortured and killed in purges. Sary was also implicated in planning and coordinating killings and forced labour.

When the Khmer Rouge fell, dislodged by the Vietnamese, Sary fled to Thailand. In absentia, he was convicted in 1979 of genocide and sentenced to death by the People's Revolutionary Tribunal of Phnom Penh. In 1996, however, Cambodian King Sihanouk granted him 'amnesty' for the conviction and from further prosecution under a 1994 law that outlawed the Khmer Rouge in exchange for Sary leaving the Khmer Rouge party with thousands of his followers.

In 2003, the Cambodian government reached an agreement with the United Nations to establish a hybrid tribunal with domestic and international cooperation to adjudicate serious crimes committed during the 1975–1979 Khmer Rouge regime. In 2007, Sary was arrested. He was charged with crimes against humanity and grave breaches of the Geneva Conventions of 1949. At issue in the portion of the decision below is whether the 1979 conviction and subsequent royal amnesties preclude his current prosecution.

a. Ne bis in idem

41. The principle of *ne bis in idem* provides that a court may not institute proceedings against a person for a crime that has already been the object of criminal proceedings and for which the person has already been convicted or acquitted. The principle of *ne bis in idem*, which derives from civil law, is similar to the concept of double jeopardy which is more frequently used in common law. The principle of *ne bis in idem* has been interpreted as meaning that the accused "shall not be tried twice for the same crime."

42. The Internal Rules of the ECCC make no direct provision in respect of the doctrine of *ne bis in idem*.

43. [. . .] The Pre-Trial Chamber notes that the principle is defined differently in the provisions in Cambodian law and at the international level. This is reflected in the consideration of what constitutes the "same crime". Under Cambodian law the "same crime" is provided as the "same act". The ICCPR prohibits successful trials for the "same offence".

44. Article 7 of the CPC [Cambodian Penal Code] provides as follows:

"Extinction of Criminal Actions

The reasons for extinguishing [*sic*] a charge in a criminal action are as follows: [. . .]

3. A grant of general amnesty [. . .]

5. The *res judicata*

When a criminal action is extinguished a criminal charge can no longer be pursued or shall be terminated."

45. Article 12 of the CPC provides:

"Res Judicata

In applying the principle of *res judicata*, any person who has been finally acquitted by a court judgment cannot be prosecuted again for the same act, even if such act is subject to different legal qualification."

46. Article 14(7) of the ICCPR provides:

"No one shall be liable to be tried or punished again for an offence for which he has already been finally convicted or acquitted in accordance with the law and penal procedure of each country."

47. The principle of *ne bis in idem* can be seen as very narrowly related to the doctrine of *res judicata* as the consequence of this doctrine is that no one can be convicted again for the same charges after a decision has become final. [...]

48. In the following, the Pre-Trial Chamber will consider whether the 1979 trial and conviction would evidently or manifestly prevent a conviction, applying the different interpretations of the principle advanced.

49. Decree Laws Nos. 1 and 2 and the Judgement of the People's Revolutionary Tribunal indicate that the Charged Person was tried and convicted for "genocide".

50. [...] "We advised this person that he was hereby placed under judicial investigation for the acts of which he has just been notified and specified the offences with which he was charged in relation thereto:

- **Crimes Against Humanity** (Murder, Extermination, Imprisonment, Persecution and Other Inhumane Acts), and

- **Grave Breaches of the Geneva Conventions of 12 August 1949** (Willful Killing, Wilfully Causing Great Suffering or Serious Injury to Body or Health, Wilful Deprivation of Rights to a Fair Trial of prisoners of war or civilians, unlawful deportation or transfer or unlawful confinement of a civilian) [...]

    for having, throughout Cambodia during the period from 17 April 1975 to 6 January 1979:

- in his capacity as Minister of Foreign Affairs [...] and as a full rights member of the Central and Standing Committees of the Communist Party of Kampuchea (CPK),

- instigated, ordered, failed to prevent or punish, or otherwise aided and abetted in the commission of the aforementioned crimes;

- by directing, encouraging, enforcing, or otherwise rendering support to CPK policy and practice which was characterised by murder, extermination, imprisonment, persecution on political grounds and other inhuman acts such as forcible transfers of the population, enslavement and forced labour;

- as part of a widespread or systematic attack targeting a civilian population;

- noting that there was a state of international armed conflict between Democratic Kampuchea and the Socialist Republic of Vietnam during all or part of the period between 17 April 1975 and 6 January 1979."

51. Since the Charged Person is not charged specifically with genocide, the Pre-Trial Chamber finds that the current prosecution might be for different "offences".

52. The Pre-Trial Chamber finds that the characterisation given by the Co-Investigating Judges, although sufficient to inform the Charged Person of the charges against him, is too vague to allow a proper consideration of whether the current prosecution is for the same "acts" as those 'acts' upon which the charges brought in 1979 were based. To specify such "acts" at the commencement of the investigation by the Co-Investigating Judges is not possible or proper. In the event of there being an indictment of the Charged Person, "the material facts and their legal characterisation" will be set out by the Co-Investigating Judges upon the issuance of the Closing Order at the conclusion of the investigation.

53. Therefore, when applying the *ne bis in idem* principle in the various proposed ways, the Pre-Trial Chamber finds it is not, at this stage of the proceedings, manifest or evident that the 1979 trial and conviction would prevent a conviction by the ECCC. The points may crystallise upon the indictment of the Charged Person, at which stage the precise charges and material facts relied upon will be known.

54. Given this finding the Pre-Trial Chamber will not consider the issue of whether the 1979 trial had to reach minimum standards in order for the principle of *ne bis in idem* to be applicable.

b. The Royal Decree

55. By Royal Decree NS/RKT/0996/72 [...] the following proclamation was made [by Preah Bat Norodom Sihanouk Varma, King of Cambodia:]

> **Article 1:** An amnesty to Mr. Ieng Sary, former Deputy Prime Minister in Charge of Foreign Affairs in the Government of Democratic Kampuchea, for the sentence of death and confiscation of all his property imposed by order of the People's Revolutionary Tribunal of Phnom Penh, dated 19 August 1979; and an amnesty for prosecution under the Law to Outlaw the Democratic Kampuchea Group [...]

57. The Pre-Trial Chamber finds that the meaning of the word "amnesty" [in the Royal decree] cannot necessarily be found by applying a grammatical interpretation. In this respect, the Pre-Trial Chamber notes that the use of the Khmer word for amnesty is used inconsistently. The word "amnesty" in the first sentence of Article 1 is used as "amnesty from a sentence" while in the second part of the article it is used as "amnesty from prosecution". Both amnesties mentioned in the Royal Decree are inconsistent with the provision on amnesty in Article 27 of the Constitution of Cambodia of 1993. The Pre-Trial Chamber further notes that at the time the Royal Decree was proclaimed, the death penalty had already been abolished in Cambodia by Article 32 of the Constitution.

58. In the light of these issues surrounding the amnesty for the sentence related to the conviction for genocide, the Pre-Trial Chamber considers that the validity of the amnesty is uncertain. The Pre-Trial Chamber finds that it is therefore not manifest or evident that this part of the Royal Decree will prevent a conviction for genocide before the ECCC.

59. In the context of the inconsistent use of the word "amnesty", the Pre-Trial Chamber finds that the second "amnesty" in the Royal Decree can be interpreted as meaning that the Charge Person "will not be proceeded against" in respect of the sentence given or breaches of [the 1994 law outlawing the Khmer Rouge]. [...]

61. The scope of this part of the amnesty is limited to the prosecution under the Law to outlaw the Democratic Kampuchea Group [...] The offences mentioned in this Law are not within the jurisdiction of the ECCC. The Pre-Trial Chamber finds therefore that this part of the amnesty in the Decree cannot be seen as having the possible effect of preventing a conviction by the ECCC. It is therefore not manifest or evident that it prevents a conviction by the ECCC.

COMMENTARY

Note that the ECCC considered the scope of the *ne bis in idem* protection only in connection with the 1979 conviction. The ECCC separately analysed whether the royal amnesty posed a bar to prosecution on *its own terms* rather than in view of the *ne bis in idem* principle. This freed the ECCC to consider whether the specific offences for which amnesty was granted were covered by the current prosecution. In contrast, in evaluating the impact of the prior conviction, the ECCC considered the *ne bis in idem* principle from both the perspective of specific prior offences tried as well as acts constituting the basis of the prior conviction. Why do you think the ECCC pursued these different analytical courses?

The context of the amnesty grant in this historical example shows the underlying tensions. On the one hand, amnesties are often, in a sense, extorted as the price of healing and relative peace. They can be the product of repugnant deals from the perspective of justice. On the other hand, the promise of amnesty must have some force and effect precisely for all the important reasons – the need for peace and healing – that amnesties are granted. Otherwise there is no incentive to take an amnesty, even in times when they can mitigate suffering and disorder. One approach is to tightly read amnesties and the scope of the *ne bis in idem* principle, as the ECCC did in this case.

QUESTIONS

1. Why do national jurisdictions – and even international courts – take such diverse and heterogeneous approaches to the *ne bis in idem* principle?

2. How does the structural relationship of an international court to national courts influence the scope of the *ne bis in idem* principle?

3. Even if successive prosecutions are sometimes permitted under a qualified or curtailed version of *ne bis in idem*, that does not mean they should occur as a policy matter. How can prosecutorial discretion ameliorate the potential for successive prosecutions? What factors should influence this exercise of prosecutorial discretion?

4. If a national jurisdiction convicts a defendant who planned and ordered the destruction of an ethnic group merely for the murder of a few individuals he personally killed, is the ICC foreclosed from exercising jurisdiction for genocide or crimes against humanity under Article 20 of the ICCSt.?

5. Should the principle of *ne bis in idem* apply after an alternative disposition through a truth commission or traditional restorative justice proceeding, such as Rwanda's gacaca courts? What factors surrounding these institutions of alternative justice – or alternatives to justice, depending on one's perspective – should be considered in determining the question?

FURTHER READING

Anthony J. Colangelo, 'Double Jeopardy and Multiple Sovereigns: A Jurisdictional Theory' (2009) 86 *Washington University Law Quarterly* 769–857.

Gerard Conway, '*Ne Bis in Idem* in International Law' (2003) 3 *International Criminal Law Review* 217–44.

M.L. Friedland, *Double Jeopardy* (Oxford: Clarendon Press, 1969).

C. Van den Wyngaert and T. Ongena, '*Ne bis in idem* Principle, Including the Issue of Amnesty', in A. Cassese, P. Gaeta and John R.W.D. Jones (eds), *The Rome Statue of the International Criminal Court: A Commentary*, Vol. I (2002), at 705–29.

PART II

CRIMES

INTRODUCTION

International criminal law is a relatively new branch of international law. The list of international crimes, that is of the acts for which international law makes the authors criminally responsible, has come into being by gradual accretion. Initially, in the late nineteenth century, and for a long time, only war crimes were punishable. It is only since World War II that new categories of crimes have developed, while that of war crimes has been restated: in 1945 and 1946, the Statutes of the International Military Tribunal at Nuremberg (IMT) and the International Military Tribunal for the Far East (IMTFE), respectively, were adopted, laying down new classes of international criminality. Thus, in 1945 crimes against humanity and crimes against peace (chiefly wars of aggression) were added, followed in 1948 by genocide as a special subcategory of crimes against humanity (soon to become an autonomous class of crimes), and then in the 1980s, by torture as a discrete crime.

What features must international crimes proper show to be classified as such? First of all, international crimes are breaches of international rules entailing the personal criminal liability of the individuals concerned (as opposed to the responsibility of the State of which the individuals may act as organs).

Second, international crimes result from the cumulative presence of the following elements. (1) They consist of violations of international *customary* rules (as well as treaty provisions, under certain circumstances, for instance where such provisions codify, spell out customary law or have contributed to its formation, or are otherwise applicable). (2) Such rules are intended to protect *values* considered important by the whole international community and are consequently binding on all states and individuals. The values at issue are not propounded by scholars or thought up by philosophers. Rather, they are laid down in a string of international instruments, which may not necessarily spell out the values fully or explicitly.[1] (3) There exists a universal interest in repressing these crimes. Subject to certain conditions, their alleged authors may in principle be prosecuted and punished *by any State*, regardless of any territorial or nationality link with the perpetrator or the victim. (4) Finally, if the perpetrator has acted in an official capacity, i.e. as a *de jure* or de

---

[1] They include the 1945 UN Charter, the 1948 Universal Declaration of Human Rights, the 1950 European Convention on Human Rights, the two 1966 UN Covenants on Human Rights, the 1969 American Convention on Human Rights, the UN Declaration on Friendly Relations of 1970 and the 1981 African Charter on Human and Peoples' Rights.

Other treaties also enshrine those values, although from another perspective: they do not proclaim the values directly, but prohibit conduct that infringes them: for instance, the 1948 Convention on Genocide, the 1949 Conventions on the protection of victims of armed conflict and the two Additional Protocols of 1977, the 1984 Convention against Torture, and the various treaties providing for the prosecution and repression of specific forms of terrorism.

facto State official, the State on whose behalf he has performed the prohibited act is *barred* from claiming enjoyment of functional immunity from the civil or criminal jurisdiction of foreign States.

Under this definition, as noted above, international crimes include war crimes, crimes against humanity, genocide and aggression – types of conduct that, in addition to being proscribed by international customary law, have also been discussed and pronounced upon by international judicial decisions. Torture – as a discrete crime distinct from torture as one of the subcategories of crimes against humanity or war crimes – has never been adjudicated as such by a criminal tribunal. Prosecutions have so far always focused on domestic provisions implementing in one system the international ban on torture.

Due to their impact at the transnational level within the past few years, international terrorism and piracy are also included in this casebook as relevant crimes. They have, however, never been dealt with as crimes by an international tribunal. Indeed, piracy is not punished for the sake of protecting a *community* value: all States are authorized to capture on the high seas and bring to trial pirates in order to safeguard their *joint interest* in fighting a common danger and consequent (real or potential) damage. Probably it was simply because piracy by definition occurred outside any State's territorial jurisdiction that a useful repressive mechanism evolved to allow any State to bring pirates to justice. On the other hand, as the cases below show, a general definition of piracy as a crime is clearly emerging at the international level and is being used by domestic courts directly.

Similarly, while heated discussions are continuing as to whether international terrorism has evolved into a discrete crime or not, it appears that recent events are forcing States to come to terms with this phenomenon in a more and more coherent and uniform way. No tribunal has, however, found a stand-alone discrete international crime of terrorism to date.

The notion of international crimes for the purpose of this casebook does not include acts often wrongly associated with this definition, such as (a) illicit traffic in narcotic drugs and psychotropic substances, (b) unlawful arms trade, (c) smuggling nuclear and other potentially deadly materials, (d) money laundering, (e) slave trade, or (f) traffic in women. For one thing, this broad range of crimes is only provided for in international *treaties* or *resolutions* of international organizations, not in customary law. These treaties require States to criminalize conduct falling within these definitions, but do not establish international judicial bodies entrusted with prosecuting alleged authors of those crimes. For another, normally these offences are perpetrated by private individuals or criminal organizations; States usually fight against them, often by joint official action. In other words, as a rule these offences are committed *against* States. They do not involve States as such or, if they involve State agents, these agents typically act for private gain, perpetrating what national legislation normally regards as ordinary crimes.

Nor does the list of international crimes include apartheid, provided for in a Convention of 1973 (which entered into force in 1976). It would seem that this offence has not yet reached the status of a customary law crime, probably because it was held to be limited in time and space. Moreover, the 101 States Parties to the Convention do not include any Western country: only two major segments of the international community (developing nations and what at the time were the Socialist countries) have agreed to label apartheid as an international crime, whereas Western States refused to do so. There is therefore a case for maintaining that under customary international law apartheid, although probably prohibited as a State delinquency, is not regarded as a crime entailing the criminal liability of individuals. Nevertheless, since Article 7(1)(j) ICCSt. grants the Court jurisdiction over apartheid as a crime against humanity and Article 7(2)(h) provides a definition of this crime, gradually a customary rule could evolve on the matter. This development could occur if cases concerning 'inhumane acts' 'committed in the context of an institutionalized regime of systematic oppression and domination by one racial group over any other racial group or groups and committed with the intention of maintaining that regime' are ever brought before the Court.

The gradual broadening of substantive criminal law has been a complex process. Among other things, when a new class of crime has emerged, its constituent elements (the objective and subjective conditions of the crime, or, in other words, the *actus reus* and *mens rea*) have not been immediately clear. Nor has any scale of penalties been laid down in international rules. This process can be easily explained. Three main features of the formation of international criminal law stand out.

The first is that, for a long time, either treaties or (more seldom) customary rules have confined themselves to prohibiting certain acts (for instance, killing prisoners of war or bombing civilians). These prohibitions were however addressed to States, not directly to individuals: belligerent Powers were legally obliged to prevent their officials (or, more generally, their nationals) from committing the prohibited acts. It followed that, if any such act was performed, the State to which the individual belonged was responsible under international law vis-à-vis the State of which the victims were nationals. Gradually, by bringing to trial before their courts enemy servicemen who had breached international rules of warfare, States made individuals directly and personally accountable, and gradually State responsibility was either accompanied or replaced by individual criminal liability. This development allowed the inference that international customary or treaty rules addressed themselves not only to States but also to individuals by criminalizing their deviant behaviour in time of war. However, this criminalization was insufficient and inadequate: international rules did not provide for either the objective and subjective requirements of the crimes or the criminal consequences of the prohibited conduct; in other words, they did not lay down the conditions of criminal repression and punishment.

It follows that international law left to national courts the task of prosecuting and punishing the alleged perpetrators of those acts. As a consequence, municipal courts of each State applied their procedural rules (legal provisions on jurisdiction and on the conduct of criminal proceedings) and rules on 'the general part' of substantive criminal law, that is, on the definition and character of the objective and subjective elements of crimes, on defences, etc. Among other things, very often national courts, faced with the *indeterminacy* of most criminal rules, found it necessary to flesh them out and give them legal precision by drawing upon their own criminal law. They thus refined notions initially left rather loose and woolly by treaty or customary law.

Finally (and this is the third of the features referred to above), when international criminal courts were set up (first in 1945–47, then in 1993–94 and more recently in 1998 and 2002–07), they did indeed lay down in their Statutes the various classes of crimes to be punished; however, these classes were couched merely as offences over which each court had jurisdiction. In other words, the crimes were not enumerated as in a criminal code, but simply as a specification of the jurisdictional authority of the relevant court. The value and scope of those enumerations were therefore only germane to the court's jurisdiction and did not purport to have a general reach.

Given these characteristics of the evolution of international criminal law, it should not be surprising that even the recent addition of the sets of written rules referred to above has not proved sufficient for building a coherent legal system, as is shown by the heavy reliance by the newly created *international* courts upon customary rules or unwritten general principles.

1

WAR CRIMES

(A) THE NOTION AND ITS ORIGINS

Under State practice and *opinio juris* war crimes are serious violations of international humanitarian law, the branch of international law dealing with the conduct of armed conflict whether international or non-international (such as civil wars or large-scale and protracted armed clashes within a State). As the ICTY Trial Chamber in *Haradinaj* explained:

37. [...] [A]n armed conflict exists whenever there is a resort to armed force between States or protracted armed violence between governmental authorities and organized armed groups or between such groups within a State. International humanitarian law applies from the initiation of such armed conflicts and extends beyond the cessation of hostilities until a general conclusion of peace is reached; or, in the case of internal conflicts, a peaceful settlement is achieved. Until that moment, international humanitarian law continues to apply in the whole territory of the warring States or, in the case of internal conflicts, the whole territory under the control of a party, whether or not actual combat takes place there.

38. This test serves to distinguish non-international armed conflict from banditry, riots, isolated acts of terrorism, or similar situations. The Trial Chamber must determine whether (i) the armed violence is protracted and (ii) the parties to the conflict are organized. [...]

Only serious violations of humanitarian law are considered war crimes that entail individual criminal responsibility of the perpetrator. In contrast, a number of rules relating to prisoners of war – such as the rules allowing prisoners of war to wear their own decorations (Article 19 of Geneva Convention III) or those on the distribution of collective consignments (Art. 43 of Geneva Convention III) – are merely obligations to provide for the general well-being of certain categories of protected persons. Their violation, although amounting to a breach of humanitarian law, does not entail individual criminal responsibility.

Serious violations – which amount to grave deviations from a rule protecting important values and involving serious consequences for the victim – can be divided into two categories. First, there are *violations of customary and treaty law applicable to armed conflicts*. This law evolved from the Hague Conventions of 1899 and 1907, which deal with means and methods of warfare and the treatment of persons who are no longer taking active part in the hostilities (primarily, prisoners of war). The central contemporary source of law in this category is the four Geneva Conventions of 1949 dealing with the sick, the wounded, civilians and prisoners of war. These four Conventions were complemented in 1977 by two Additional Protocols.

Second, while treaty law has been important in this field, most conventional rules have now attained the status of custom and are therefore often applicable regardless of the ratification by States of one specific convention. Each State has the *right* to prosecute this type of war crime (provided it has territorial jurisdiction, or jurisdiction based on the nationality of the perpetrator or of the victim, or universal jurisdiction).

The systematic prosecution of serious violations of the laws or customs of war at the international level took place for the first time after World War II (among the earlier instances of prosecution, the Leipzig trials of 1921 against German accused stand out). As discussed above,[1] 'war crimes' was one of the categories of crimes listed in the London Charter for the trial of Major War Criminals and Control Council Law No. 10, the instruments upon which several trials of German defendants were held. As explained below, these trials – and others conducted by other Occupying Powers, such as the USA, the UK and France, as well as trials conducted by German courts against Germans defendants – contributed to the refinement of important aspects of war crimes law.

(B) GRAVE BREACHES

A subset of the serious violations described above is the *grave breaches* regime contained in the Geneva Conventions and in Additional Protocol I (Article 85). A grave breach is a particularly serious violation of the Geneva Conventions or of Additional Protocol I, such as wilful killing, torture, cruel treatment, mutilations or extensive destruction of property. The particular regime of grave breaches imposes on all States the international *obligation* to prosecute (or extradite) persons accused of having committed them, regardless of the nationality of the perpetrator or the victim or the place of commission of the crime (so-called universal jurisdiction). However, since the Geneva Conventions and Additional Protocol I only apply to international armed conflict, the scope of this regime has historically been limited. The first prosecutions for grave breaches had to wait until the 1990s at the ICTY.

When the international community decided to establish the ICTY, the first international criminal tribunal after World War II, the notion of grave breaches of the Geneva Conventions was enshrined in Article 2 ICTYSt. which lists wilful killing; torture or inhuman treatment, including biological experiments; extensive destruction and appropriation of property not justified by military necessity and carried out unlawfully and wantonly; unlawful deportation or transfer or unlawful confinement of a civilian and other such grave breaches.

Moreover, Article 3 ICTYSt. goes on to list other 'violations of the laws or customs of war', including employment of poisonous weapons or other weapons calculated to cause unnecessary suffering; wanton destruction of cities, towns or villages, or devastation not justified by military necessity; attack, or bombardment, by whatever means, of undefended towns, villages, dwellings or buildings; and plunder. These other violations were meant to capture war crimes under customary law not enshrined in the grave breaches regime.

(C) WAR CRIMES IN NON-INTERNATIONAL ARMED CONFLICTS

The rationale for expanding the applicability of (Article 3 ICTYSt.) war crimes to non-international armed conflicts was propounded in 1995 by the ICTY Appeals Chamber in *Tadić*[2] and is now widely accepted. The ICTY Appeals Chamber (*Tadić* Interlocutory

---

[1] See *supra*, Part I(1)(B), p. 27.   [2] See *supra*, Part I(1)(A), p. 6.

Appeal, para. 95) further clarified that: (i) war crimes must constitute a breach of a rule of international humanitarian law; (ii) the rule in question must be of customary law or applicable treaty law; (iii) the violation must be serious, i.e. it must be a rule protecting important values and its breach must involve grave consequences for the victim; and (iv) the violation must entail, under either custom or treaty law, the individual criminal responsibility of the person breaching the rule (so-called 'four *Tadić* conditions', or '*Tadić* test'). Some of the most common war crimes, such as deliberate attacks against civilians or plunder of private property, infringe upon essential rules of international humanitarian law linked to the distinction between military and civilian objectives, one of the 'intransgressible principles of international humanitarian law' (ICJ, Advisory Opinion on *Nuclear Weapons*, para. 434).

At the ICTY most prosecutions for violations of the laws or customs of war were based on prohibited conduct found in common Article 3 of the four Geneva Conventions of 1949, which have been prosecuted under Article 3 of the ICTYSt. Common Article 3 proscribes the following acts at any time and in any place whatsoever with respect to persons taking no active part in the hostilities: '(a) violence to life and person, in particular murder of all kinds, mutilation, cruel treatment and torture; (b) taking of hostages; (c) outrages upon personal dignity, in particular humiliating and degrading treatment; (d) the passing of sentences and the carrying out of executions without previous judgment pronounced by a regularly constituted court, affording all the judicial guarantees which are recognized as indispensable by civilized peoples'. The corresponding crimes are nowadays considered applicable both to international and to internal armed conflict.

(D) LINK WITH THE ARMED CONFLICT

A separate issue is that not all serious crimes committed during an armed conflict constitute war crimes. There must be a link between the criminal conduct and the armed conflict. In *Kunarac*, the ICTY held:

57. There is no necessary correlation between the area where the actual fighting is taking place and the geographical reach of the laws of war. The laws of war apply in the whole territory of the warring states or, in the case of internal armed conflicts, the whole territory under the control of a party to the conflict, whether or not actual combat takes place there, and continue to apply until a general conclusion of peace or, in the case of internal armed conflicts, until a peaceful settlement is achieved. A violation of the laws or customs of war may therefore occur at a time when and in a place where no fighting is actually taking place. As indicated by the Trial Chamber, the requirement that the acts of the accused must be closely related to the armed conflict would not be negated if the crimes were temporally and geographically remote from the actual fighting. It would be sufficient, for instance, for the purpose of this requirement, that the alleged crimes were closely related to hostilities occurring in other parts of the territories controlled by the parties to the conflict.

58. What ultimately distinguishes a war crime from a purely domestic offence is that a war crime is shaped by or dependent upon the environment – the armed conflict – in which it is committed. It need not have been planned or supported by some form of policy. The armed conflict need not have been causal to the commission of the crime, but the existence of an armed conflict must, at a minimum, have played a substantial part in the perpetrator's ability to commit it, his decision to commit it, the manner in which it was committed or the purpose for which it was committed. Hence, if it can be established, as in the present case, that the

perpetrator acted in furtherance of or under the guise of the armed conflict, it would be sufficient to conclude that his acts were closely related to the armed conflict. The Trial Chamber's
finding on that point is unimpeachable.

59. In determining whether or not the act in question is sufficiently related to the armed conflict, the Trial Chamber may take into account, *inter alia*, the following factors: the fact that the
perpetrator is a combatant; the fact that the victim is a non-combatant; the fact that the victim
is a member of the opposing party; the fact that the act may be said to serve the ultimate goal of
a military campaign; and the fact that the crime is committed as part of or in the context of the
perpetrator's official duties.

Some defendants before the international tribunals have claimed the lack of such a link to
the armed conflict. In *Brđanin*, for example, the accused had been convicted, *inter alia*,
under Article 2 of the ICTYSt. (grave breaches of the Geneva Conventions of 1949) for a
series of rapes committed by Bosnian Serb police and the Bosnian Serb Army (VRS) during
military operations in the Teslić municipality of Bosnia-Herzegovina in 1992. The Appeals
Chamber rejected the arguments by Brđanin:

256. The first argument [raised by Brđanin] essentially states that a conviction under Article 2
of the Statute may not rely solely on the fact that the rapes were committed during a war. The
Appeals Chamber has previously stated that the jurisdictional prerequisites for the application of Article 2 of the Statute have been exhaustively considered in the jurisprudence. One of
those prerequisites, correctly stated by the Trial Chamber, is that the offence alleged to violate
Article 2 of the Statute must be committed in the context of an international armed conflict. The
Trial Chamber concluded that there was an international armed conflict in 1992 in the territory
of the ARK at the relevant time. When concluding that the members of the Bosnian Serb police
and the VRS committed rapes in Teslić municipality, the Trial Chamber cited witnesses who
described rapes associated with weapons searches. The Appeals Chamber considers that the
Trial Chamber clearly established the existence of an international armed conflict and furthermore reasonably concluded that the rapes in Teslić, committed as they were during weapons
searches, were committed in the context of the armed conflict, and were not "individual domestic crimes" as suggested by Brđanin. Crimes committed by combatants and by members of
forces accompanying them while searching for weapons during an armed conflict, and taking
advantage of their position, clearly fall into the category of crimes committed "in the context of
the armed conflict." The Trial Chamber did not err in concluding that the rapes at issue could
form a basis for conviction under Article 2 of the Statute.

(E) CATEGORIES OF WAR CRIMES

War crimes, which are among the most ancient international crimes, actually developed
to (i) regulate the methods and means of combat, weaponry and the control of occupied
territory and (ii) to protect persons not taking active part in the hostilities, such as civilians, prisoners of war, the wounded and the sick. These crimes find their source mostly in
treaties, which, however, usually just prohibit certain types of conduct rather than criminalize it. Thus, there is ample need for subsequent (judicial) interpretation in relation to
the elements constituting each specific war crime. The *Galić* discussion below, on how provisions from Additional Protocol I should be interpreted when assessing individual criminal responsibility, is a prime example of this process.

The most recent conventional restatement of existing war crimes is the ICCSt., which – at Article 8 – provides a long (though not necessarily exhaustive) list of criminal conduct falling under the jurisdiction of that Court under the rubric of war crimes. While many important States have not ratified the ICCSt. – including most Arab countries, the USA, China, Russia, India, Indonesia, Iran, Israel and Pakistan – 114 countries did ratify it (as of October 2010). This makes the ICCSt. a very important document for understanding the present *opinio juris* of the vast majority of States in this field.

Unfortunately, despite the value of this codification, Article 8 is extremely cumbersome. Among its various shortcomings, one should be underlined in particular, namely the fact that it addresses war crimes by dividing them up into four categories: (i) grave breaches of the 1949 Geneva Conventions; (ii) other serious violations of the laws and customs applicable in international armed conflict; (iii) serious violations of Common Article 3 of the four Geneva Conventions of 12 August 1949 (applicable to non-international armed conflicts); and (iv) other serious violations of the laws and customs applicable in non-international armed conflicts.

On a practical level, often the use of these categories is not very helpful to the persons striving to apply provisions contemplating these crimes, due to repetitions and duplications. For instance, if a prosecuting authority wishes to indict a person for attacks against protected property during an armed conflict, it will find that the ICCSt. contains several provisions on this matter, including, provisions under: (i), 'Extensive destruction [...] of property, not justified by military necessity and carried out unlawfully and wantonly'; (ii), '[i]ntentionally launching an attack in the knowledge that such attack will cause [...] damage to civilian objects[...]' and '[d]estroying [...] the enemy's property unless such destruction [...] be imperatively demanded by the necessities of war'; as well as (iv) '[d]estroying [...] the property of an adversary unless such destruction or seizure be imperatively demanded by the necessities of the conflict'. However, most of the cited provisions effectively require proof of the same *actus reus* and *mens rea* regardless of the nature of the conflict (international or non-international) and of whether the prohibited conduct amounts to a grave breach. This legal classification is thus bound to generate confusion for both prosecuting authorities and defendants.

A better categorization of war crimes would perhaps consist in considering *objective criteria* linking similar crimes. For example, it should be possible to list war crimes depending on the *subject matter* to which they relate. Thus, one could distinguish between various classes of war crimes depending on whether they are intended to deal with (i) attacks against *civilians or civilian objects*; (ii) unlawful taking of life (murder of civilians, murder of prisoners of war); (iii) unlawful attacks to *personal integrity* (for example, torture, wounding of civilians or prisoners of war, sexual violence); (iv) limitations of *personal freedoms* (for example, deportation, slavery, forced labour, forced enlisting, hostage taking); (v) illicit appropriation of *property* (for example, plunder, appropriation of cultural property); (vi) deportation and forcible *transfer of persons*; (vii) violations of rules on *means of combat* (for example, ordering that no quarter be given, use of human shields, use of prohibited weapons) and (viii) violations of rules on *belligerent occupation*. A further distinction would of course still need to be made within each category between crimes *only* applicable to international armed conflicts and those applicable to non-international armed conflicts as well (for which the legal regulation is more sparse and rudimentary). Arguably, a scheme along these lines would better allow interpreters to understand and apply the rules on war crimes.

(F) WAR CRIMES COMMITTED BY CIVILIANS

War crimes may be committed by military personnel against enemy combatants or civilians (or persons otherwise not taking active part in the hostilities). They may also be committed by civilians, as long as their conduct is linked to the armed conflict. Two cases explain how this may happen.

Cases

Superior Military Government Court of the French Occupation Zone in Germany, Röchling et al., *Judgment of 25 January 1949*

Hermann Röchling was one of the directors of the Röchling enterprises, leading German concerns in the coal, iron and steel industries. The French occupation authorities in Germany indicted him and other members of the board (including Hans Lothar von Gemmingen-Hornberg and Willem Rodenhauser) on the basis of Control Council Law No. 10, issued by the Allied Control Council in Germany for the punishment of persons guilty of crimes against peace, war crimes and crimes against humanity. Röchling was a militant member of the National-Socialist Party and participated in various meetings related to the re-armament of the German Reich and to the economic development of the country, both before and during the war, when he acceded to various administrative positions including Reich Commissioner for iron production in various occupied territories (including regions of France, Norway, Poland, Ukraine, and Serbia). While the charges related to crimes against peace were ultimately dismissed on appeal, this judgment is interesting in relation to the role of civilians – in this case, high-level industrialists – in committing war crimes of an economic nature.

War Crimes

A. War Crimes of an economic nature

As has been ascertained by the International Military Tribunal [also, IMT], the occupied countries were not only exploited for the requirements of the occupation army, but were also relentlessly exploited – in spite of the Hague Convention [of 18 October 1907, related to the laws and customs of war on land] – for the benefit of the entire war requirements, without any consideration being given to the economy of the country. [. . .]

Hermann Roechling, who was at first general commissioner for the control of the smelting works in the Moselle and Meurthe-et-Moselle areas, and later on, as emphasized by the judgment which has been contested [the first instance judgment by the General Tribunal of the Military Government of the French Zone of Occupation in Germany], the actual dictator of the iron production in Germany and the occupied countries as a result of his nomination as president of the Reich Association Iron, "RVE," and as Reich Plenipotentiary, commenced to carry out economic plundering – on the strength of his official positions and within the sphere of the instruction he received from the Reich Association – by means of the following actions:

a. Systematic plundering of industry, forcing the concerns of the occupied areas to work for the German war potential, and spoliation.

[...] The following clearly established facts must also be set forth to the charge of Hermann Roechling, which on the one hand, constitute simple economic spoliation in favor of the Reich and, on the other hand, spoliation and robbery in favor of his firm; but which in both cases constitute war crimes:

1. The removal of the rolling-mill power installation of the plant at Joeuf, (Meurthe-et-Moselle) which in 1943 were shipped to the Ukraine by order of Hermann Roechling. This case involved a considerable amount of material for, contrary to the assurance given by the defendant in the session of 19 March 1948, according to which it had been only one single generator requiring three or four freight cars, actually 40 freight cars were needed. [...]

In addition an electromotor was removed from the Joeuf plant and transferred to the Karlshuette at Thionville. Roechling regarded this plant as definitely his future property, so that this constitutes a robbery.

2. The removal of the rolling mill of Ymuiden (Holland), which was also dismantled at the request of Hermann Roechling in order to be transferred to Watenstedt (Brunswick) in 1943, required 12 ships because of its magnitude. This is an act of economic spoliation.

3. The removal of the "Halles D'Angleur-Arthus" (Belgium) which was effected on Roechling's initiative and which was dismantled in 1943 in order to be transferred to Russia, as appears from the statement made by Mr. Perret, constitutes an act of economic spoliation.

4. The removal of a 950 ton iron framework which belonged to the Société de Saint Gobain and which was dismantled in this company's plant at Cirey (Meurthe-et-Moselle) and shipped to Voelklingen despite the opposition of the owners, was intended to enable Hermann Roechling to produce a certain kind of war material in his Voelklingen plants.

The defendant alleges that this case involved a seizure by German authorities. From a letter dated 12 May 1942 addressed by the Roechling firm to the Société de Saint Gobain it is, however, apparent that the seizure was only effected after private negotiations between the "Société de Saint Gobain" and the Roechling firm had failed of their effect, and that at the time of the dismantling of the sheds on 9 July 1941 the owners wrote to Hermann Roechling in order to protest against this seizure which was carried out at his request and in his favor.

All these acts constitute unlawful seizure of property, which belonged to private persons in the occupied countries, in violation of the Hague Convention. On the other hand, the defense has advanced the argument that the returning of property after the war, which, incidentally, was not voluntary, should be taken into consideration; however, this argument is irrelevant and immaterial, as the restitution of unlawfully acquired property does not eliminate the fact that a punishable offense has been committed.

b. Systematic Financial and Commercial Spoliation.

[The Judgment recalls various instances of credits and goods illegally obtained from governments in occupied countries and from other sources in breach of the international law of military occupation].

B. Utilization of Labour

I. The policy of the Nazi government

The compulsory utilization of nationals of the occupied countries (prisoners of war, deported or allegedly voluntary workers) is one of the most important elements of the German policy of domination. [...]

1. *Deportation of civilians of an occupied country for compulsory employment.* The evidence submitted and the findings in the judgment of the IMT in the case against Goering, *et al.*, have shown that the program for deportation for the purpose of slave labour was worked out by the government of the Reich. It was an actual government program which had been arranged by the State and was carried out by its agencies. [...] It is a fact that the requirements reports [...] concerning the allocation of labor were in turn based on the requirements reports submitted by the responsible leaders of German war industries [...] In particular, Hermann Roechling, the chairman of the Reich Association Iron, RVE, was one of those leaders and, starting 29 May 1942, he was also the director of the Industrial Group for the Iron Producing Industry and Reich Plenipotentiary for Iron and Steel in the occupied territories.

It is interesting to note that he applied for these positions and at the same time for the dictatorial powers connected therewith. [...] The Court finds that Hermann Roechling's responsibility for the execution of the forced-labor program was of the same type as that with which the International Military Tribunal has charged Speer [Albert Speer, German Minister of Armament 1942–45 sentenced to 20 years' imprisonment at Nuremberg]. For, the applications which were forwarded by Speer to Sauckel [Fritz Sauckel, German Plenipotentiary General for the Utilisation of Labour 1942–45, sentenced to death at Nuremberg for war crimes and crimes against humanity], which were the cause for the deportation of civilian workers, were drafted at the behest of the Reich plenipotentiary Hermann Roechling, president of the RVE, in order to obtain workers for the iron industry. [...] Moreover, it should be emphasized that Herman Roechling did not confine himself to requisitioning workers, who were necessary for the realization of his objectives, from Sauckel through Speer and thus initiate the deportations; more than that, he repeatedly intervened personally not only in order to obtain more workers from the RVE at better conditions, but also in order to improve generally the efficiency of Sauckel's inhumane organization. In order to achieve this, he repeatedly took action by submitting numerous reports, proposals, and suggestions concerning the recruiting of forced labor to Speer, Sauckel, and other leading officials of the Reich. [...]

The court finds that Hermann Roechling, in order to execute his plan for raising the production of iron, sacrificed all human considerations and demonstrated a complete lack of respect for the rights of the civilian population in the occupied countries.

[The Court then discusses, under "2. *Allocation of deported workers*", the accused's responsibility for allocating deportees to forced labor, concluding that Hermann Roechling and two others were guilty of this count, too].

3. *The rough treatment and maltreatment of the deportees in order to force them to work.* The prosecution accused all defendants, in view of the positions held by them or their powers, of being responsible for the rough treatment accorded to the deportees with the intention of forcing them to work, either by consenting thereto or by instigating it.

The duty "to achieve the greatest possible output" (as Sauckel expressed it in his decree dated 29 May 1942) was imposed on the deportees under threat of rigorous punishment, and these punitive measures were employed when it was considered to be appropriate. The majority of these measures must be considered as rough treatment or ill treatment within the meaning of Law No. 10. In the first place it must be established that the deportees in the Voelklingen plants had to work under difficult and rigorous conditions. On this point the testimony of all witnesses, the workers, doctors, medical orderlies, and guards, agrees. (Some workers, so a medical orderly declared, collapsed from exhaustion at their work.) These difficult and rigorous conditions were in particular caused by insufficient food and too heavy work, and resulted in very poor health. However, in order to exact peak output from weak or even sick workers, who, moreover, had very little desire to perform work which was badly paid and opposed to the interests of their fatherland, the plant Directorate of the Voelklingen participated, on its own initiative, in the implementation of strict measures as prescribed in the regulations and ordinances of the Reich administration for the maintenance of working discipline and repeatedly took the initiative in a manner which exhibits conformity with the views, aims, and measures of that administration. [...] In addition, the Directorate neglected to exercise the necessary supervision over the methods employed to impose these measures on the convicted workers, and failed to make adequate protests when their scandalous misuses came to their knowledge. As the contested judgment states, the role of the plant police (Betriebspolizei) was played by the works police (Werkschutz), the chief of which, an SS officer called Rassner, was appointed by von Gemmingen-Hornberg. In April 1943, following an agreement between the leaders of the Roechling firm and the Gestapo, a summary court was set up to punish disciplinary offenses by the foreign workers, such as repeated absence, repeated tardiness, stoppage of work, refusal to perform additional work, undisciplined conduct. At the same time a punishment camp was set up about 15 kilometers away at Etzenhofen, by agreement between the leaders of the Roechling firm and the Gestapo, to which the foreigners sentenced by the summary court were to be consigned for a maximum period of 56 days. The persons undergoing sentence who spent the night in Etzenhofen were taken to the Roechling plant in the morning and back to the camp at night. The important advantage that Roechling gained from the creation of this camp lay in the fact that the convicted workers did not stop working in his plant, whereas previously they had been lost to him immediately they were handed over to the Gestapo. From the corroborative testimony of the former workers of the camp, the doctors, guards, and inhabitants of the village, it is shown that the situation of those undergoing punishment was inhuman. After a few hours sleep the inmates of the camp were often called out in the middle of the night and required, in a completely naked condition, to perform physical exercises. Thereafter they were taken into the Voelklingen plants and were then employed for 10 hours, even on Sundays, on the heaviest types of work, particularly in the coking plant or the pitch installation. In the evening at 1800 hours they were taken back to the camp where they were made to perform punishment exercises for several hours (crawling, running, jumping). Dogs were trained to bite the workers if they moved about the camp without running. The guards often struck the prisoners without reason. They were often locked in cellars half full of water. The food of the people who were called upon to perform this heavy work and these weakening exercises was completely inadequate; it consisted of a little bread and a soup usually made without vegetables. The inhabitants of Etzenhofen were outraged when they saw these exhausted people who could be recognized by their blue-and-white striped prisoners clothing, and who frequently collapsed when going through the streets.

Hermann Roechling and the other accused members of the Directorate of the Voelklingen works are not accused of having ordered this horrible treatment, but of having permitted it; and indeed supported it, and in addition, of not having done their utmost to put an end to these abuses. In adopting this attitude they permitted the continued existence and further development of this inhuman situation and thus, particularly through this tolerance, participated in the maltreatment within the meaning of Law No. 10. [...]

4. *Employment of prisoners of war in excessive work or in work connected with war operations – ill-treatment of prisoners of war.* The war crimes of which the defendants are accused include the employment of prisoners of war in excessive work or in work connected with war operations, as well as the ill treatment of prisoners of war. It has been proven and has furthermore not been denied, that many prisoners of war taken from the armies of the Allies were forced to work in the German iron industry. [...] It has furthermore been proved that production in this industry was directly and closely connected with the war operations. [...] The employment of prisoners of war in this industry was therefore prohibited in accordance with Article 6 of the Hague Convention, since this regulation decrees that prisoners of war may only be employed in work that is not connected with war operations. [...]

The Court is of the opinion that [...] the expression "war operations" is to be interpreted as meaning that the prohibition to employ prisoners of war refers to all work which might increase the war potential of their country's enemy.

On the other hand, the same Article 6 of the Hague Convention prohibits the employment of prisoners of war for excessively heavy work. In the Roechling steel works, however, the prisoners of war were employed for the heaviest work [...] This work must be considered as excessively heavy work and evaluated as constituting a breach of the Hague Convention, particularly if one considers the prisoners' state of health owing to the food which they received. In fact these prisoners received an entirely inadequate amount of food and were only able to exist as a result of the parcels which they received from the Red Cross and from their families, while the Italian and Russian prisoners who received no parcels were greatly reduced in number through illness. Conditions of this kind are absolutely contrary to the duties which Article 7, paragraph 2 of the Hague Convention imposes upon the government which has control of the prisoners, and furthermore constitute the crime of ill-treating prisoners of war according to Article II [paragraph] 1(b) of the law No. 10.

Hermann Roechling [...] participated in the above-discussed war crimes against the prisoners who were employed in the works subordinate to the RVE, and particularly in Voelklingen. Thus he actually agreed that the industry of which he was the leading administrator should employ prisoners of war who were placed at his disposal by the Reich government in contravention to the international agreement. He did this not only without raising the slightest protest, but he even demanded that such labor should be made available and submitted plans to his superior authorities for the better utilization of the prisoners of war [...]

Accordingly, the Superior Court, upon due deliberations, rules as follows:

2. *Hermann Roechling* [...] is guilty of having committed war crimes because, with a view to increasing the war potential of the Third Reich, he:

(a) Exploited to the highest possible degree the foundries of the occupied countries [...] and caused a great deal of material belonging to the industries of the occupied countries [...] to be taken away.

(b) Participated in the economic spoliation of the occupied countries in a financial and commercial respect [...]

(c) (1) Took an essential part in carrying out the program for deportation for purpose of forced labour by his persistent applications to this end and by the counsel given by him to the National Socialist government.
(2) Employed in his plants deported persons and prisoners of war for excessively hard labour bearing on war operations, and encouraged the ill-treatment inflicted on those persons with a view to compelling them to work. [...]

Hermann Roechling is sentenced to ten years' imprisonment, confiscation of his entire property, and loss of civil rights.

The trials following World War II are among the first examples of war crimes being prosecuted as international offences. The 'grave breaches' regime referred to above still did not exist, but customary law and various applicable treaties and conventions did regulate war and were used as a basis to find individuals guilty of serious violations of the laws of armed conflict.

While there might be doubts about some of the legal characterizations of the criminal conduct described above, it is easy to understand how, in cases such as *Röchling*, even civilians can be charged with war crimes. There are, however, other more complex instances where a court may be faced with facts that do not easily fit the ordinary course of events one would expect.

Israel, **Enigster,** *Tel-Aviv District Court, Judgment of 4 January 1952*

Ezekiel Enigster had been a persecuted Jew detained in two forced-labour camps in Upper Silesia in 1943 and 1944. During his detention, he had been selected as 'Kapo', i.e. an inmate appointed to discipline and police other inmates within the camps. In 1950, the Israel parliament adopted a law (the Law on Nazis and Nazi Collaborators Punishment) to prosecute, inter alia, any person who committed acts amounting to crimes against humanity ('murder, extermination, enslavement, starvation or deportation and other inhumane acts committed against *any civilian population*, and persecution on national, racial, religious or political grounds') and war crimes ('murder, ill-treatment or deportation to forced labour or for any other purpose, *of civilian population of or in occupied territory*; murder or ill-treatment of prisoners of war or persons on the seas; killing of hostages; plunder of public or private property; wanton destruction of cities, towns or villages; and devastation not justified by military necessity') in an enemy country. Enigster was charged under this law on the basis of his role as Kapo. He pleaded not guilty, arguing that he had not chosen to become a Kapo, but had rather been forced to, and also that he had actually attempted to use his authority to improve the living conditions of the other inmates. The excerpts of this judgment are interesting in assessing the scope of war crimes and in establishing some of the most important differences between this category of crimes, on the one side, and crimes against humanity, on the other.

1. The defendant is on trial subject to an indictment charging five violations of the Law on the Nazis and Nazi Collaborators Punishment, 1950 (hereinafter, for the purposes of brevity, the Law), of which one violation falls within the definition of war crime, one falls within the definition of a crime against humanity and three violations are causing grievous damage, caused with intent to a persecuted person, while being persecuted.

2. According to the charge sheet the aforementioned violation occurred in two work camps, Greiditz and Paulblick, located in Upper Silesia, during 1943 and 1944. Both of these camps were established by the German Nazi government during the Second World War and used to hold Jews from Poland and from other occupied countries, for the purpose of employing them in enforced labour. And the following is the picture of daily life in these camps, as it arises from the testimonies of the witnesses at this trial. The camp detainees would be awoken from their sleep between 3:30 and 5 a.m., and immediately everyone would hurry up and get dressed [...], get their serving of coffee and arrive at muster in the waiting yard. At muster the counting of people would be held, according to their various groups, and after determining the exact number, in order to check if anyone was missing, each group would leave to work, with a group leader heading it and accompanied by a German guard. Usually they would walk a certain distance on foot, until the railway, where they would wait for the train which carried freight cars, to bring these people to their places of employment. The train would leave this spot at about 6 a.m., and after the ride they still had to walk, usually a significant distance, to the place of employment. The people were organised in the camp according to work groups and at the head of every group there stood one of the detainees, known as a 'Schieber', and if a large place of employment required a very large group of people, several work groups would be put together to form a larger group, and at the head of it they would put one of the detainees, who would be called 'Kolonnenschieber', something like a main 'Schieber'. These 'Schiebers' and 'Kolonnenschiebers' were also called 'Kapos' or 'Hauptkapos' by the camp detainees, although the exact meaning of these phrases is 'concentration policeman'. The role

of the 'Schieber' was to lead his people to work and from work, to see that none of his men would be absent, and at the place of employment itself, his role was to keep an eye on the workers, to see that they do not become lax. They themselves would not work. The tasks at which the detainees were employed at were various, from simple work, such as digging, loading, and unloading, through to professional tasks at factories, and it would last throughout the hours of the day, excluding a short break for lunch. After work, between 4 and 5 in the afternoon, the people would return to the camp in the same order as they left it in the morning, and immediately after their return, and after the various 'Schiebers' gave their reports to the Jewish camp elder, the men would get in line to receive their dinner, which was very meagre and consisted of a plate of spinach soup, in most cases. After this meal the people were free to walk about in the camp yard for a while and do their business until the signal was sounded, at about 9 p.m., to get into their beds for a night's sleep. These beds were shelves arranged in three levels, one on top of the other, and each detainee had a sack of straw to lie upon, with the sacks laying one beside another, in very crowded conditions.

[...] In the places of employment the detainees were limited in their mobility and confined to the work space, and the guards would see to it that they would not leave it, and these limitations on mobility applied to the 'Schiebers', too. The food servings given to the detainees were starvation servings, and there is no doubt that these conditions, the deprivation of liberty, the enforced labour, walking great distances to work and from work, few hours of sleep and rest, poor nutrition both in terms of quantity and quality, all these could cause and did in fact cause the attrition of the detainees' physical and moral strengths, and as a result of this bring about horrifying mortality. At the Greiditz camp a typhoid epidemic broke out at the end of the summer of 1943, which covered almost the entire camp and wreaked havoc upon its inmates. Following this [...] the Greiditz camp was disbanded at the end of 1943 and the living detainees were all transferred to the Ollbrick camp. [...]

3. The defendant, along with several other people, was brought to the Greiditz camp around the middle of 1943, already serving in the position of 'Kolonnenschieber'. He remained in the Greiditz camp until its disbandment and then moved, along with the remnants of Greiditz, to Paulbrick camp, where he remained until a date which is in dispute. [...] The main opportunities for the defendant's wild rampages in the camp were, according to these witnesses, as follows: when the defendant was the 'Schieber' on duty, whose roles included awakening the detainees from their sleep, he would burst into the sleeping rooms and before he finished giving the whistle signifying the time to wake up he would storm through and beat the beds, indiscriminately. The next opportunity the defendant had to show his force was the time of the hurried descent of hundreds of detainees, who hurried down the single staircase and into the muster courtyard. At that time the defendant would stand by the stairs and use his baton to beat all the people who lagged behind. In the courtyard itself the defendant would also beat any detainee whose posture did not please him. As to the defendant's behaviour at the places of employment, the testimony does not indicate large scale rampages, but shows several specific cases of beatings and grievous damage, about which we shall focus on, hereafter. After the people returned from work in the evening, hungry, tired, worn out from the hard work and the wearisome walk, they could expect more of the defendant's beatings. While he was on duty, when one of his roles was to oversee the line standing by the kitchen windows to receive the small and flavourless serving of soup, which was usually a bowl of spinach soup mixed with sand, if he saw anyone hurrying or pushing in line, he immediately landed a baton-strike on his head or face or on any other part of his body, indiscriminately. In the event that any detainee was caught red-handed, trying to stand in line again and obtain an additional plate of soup, this would thereby enrage the defendant and the rubber baton would land on the detainee. [...] [H]e would sometimes also make use of his hands and his feet. [...] We must add here that, according to the witnesses for the prosecution, a detainee would not be forced

to accept the position of Schieber or Kolonnenschieber and that there were those who refused to accept this role and were not punished for this. Moreover, if a 'Schieber' sinned while fulfilling his role, he was usually punished only by demotion.

7. [...] After having weighted all the testimonies, both for the prosecution and of the defence, we determine as a fact that the defendant, when acting as Kolonnenschieber during the years 1943–1944 at the Greiditz and Paulbrick camps, would beat the detainees in the aforementioned camps morning and night, using a rubber baton, strikes with his hands and kicks, and in a cruel manner and at unaccountably many opportunities. We believe that the defendant beat the detainees mercilessly, whether there was a cause for that – that is, infractions of any of the cruel and criminal rules of discipline and order enforced upon the detainees by the Nazi government, or whether there was no such cause. With no hesitation we reject the defendant's testimony that he was forced to accept this position and that he beat only in order to separate fighting people or in similar cases. We determine as a fact that the position of Schieber or Kolonnenschieber or Kapo availed its owner of various privileges and benefits in terms of food, accommodations and movement, and at the same time the holders of these ranks were free of the work duty, which was usually crushing and exhausting. Acceptance of such a position would not be forced and, on the other hand, it seems that failure to live up to the demands of the role to the satisfaction of the Germans would not lead to any worse consequences than removal from the position and return to the regular life of a detainee. We were also convinced by the testimonies that some of the holders of these ranks succeeded in living up to their role without resorting to actions of severe violence. [...]

11. We shall now turn to the legal questions that arise in this trial. Mr. Tomkiewicz, representing the Attorney General, argues that the abuses proved about the defendant and described by us in paragraph 7 of this verdict comprise the violations defined in Article 1 of the law as a war crime and also as a crime against humanity. In respect to being a war crime, these actions are claimed to be ill-treatment of members of a civilian population in an occupied country for the purpose of enforced labour or for any other purpose, and this happened during the period of the Nazi government and in a hostile country. These acts amount to a crime against humanity, falling as they do within the description of 'other inhumane acts against a civilian population' during the Nazi government of a hostile country. Mr. Rosenberg, counsel for the defendant, argues in contrast that these actions comprise neither of the two aforementioned crimes, and this for the following grounds:

A. Concerning a war crime. The defendant's actions were not proven to fall within the definition of 'ill-treatment', and even if they could be included in that definition, this in itself would not be enough, as the definition of the crime requires ill-treatment and deportation together in order to comprise this crime, as the law states 'ill-treatment or deportation to slave labor or for any other purpose'. He argues further that a war criminal can only be a member of the conquering nation, in respect to his behaviour towards a member of the conquered nation, and in this case the defendant was himself persecuted, and a Polish Jew, just as were most of the detainees at camps Greiditz and Paulbrick.

B. Concerning a crime against humanity, the learned defence counsel argues that the words 'other inhumane acts committed against any civilian population' should be interpreted according to the principle of *eiusdem generis*, that is, these actions should be of the type specifically detailed in the definition before the aforementioned phrase, which are: murder, extermination, enslavement and deportation, while the conduct of the defendant was not of the type of action specifically set forth. He also argues that, considering the phrase 'and persecutions on political, racial or religious grounds', which appears at the end of the definition of a crime against humanity, a person should not be convicted of this crime unless it was proven that he acted for the aforementioned grounds, whereas here it was clear that the defendant did not act for this type of grounds.

12. As is common knowledge, the legislator had the Allied laws regarding the judging of Nazi war criminals before him, while phrasing the law. These included the Nuremberg Declaration, which formed part of the Allies' covenant signed in London on August 8th, 1945, and the law known as Law No. 10 of the Control Council. In both of those documents too, war crime and crime against humanity are defined, and apparently the definitions contained in our Law are, in their essential features, with changes of no concern to us here, taken from these two documents, with some changes that do not matter in our case. When we compare our definition of a war crime to the definition in those laws, we immediately note that the word 'ill treatment [negissa]' which appears twice in our laws, comes to replace [. . .] the phrase 'ill-treatment', which also appears twice in the definition of a war crime in both of the aforementioned laws. Therefore, there is no doubt in our mind that anything included in the English phrase 'ill-treatment' is included in the Hebrew word 'ill-treatment [negissa]', for the purposes of this crime. In addition, it is clear to us that the phrase 'ill-treatment and deportation' does not mean both of these items as one single action but that each of them is in its own right 'one of the conducts' which comprises a war crime, according to the definition. [. . .]

Therefore we have no hesitation in determining that the actions proven against the defendant as stated above in paragraph 7 of this verdict were acts of ill-treatment, in the sense of the definition of a war crime. However, we accept the plea of the defence that the accused ought not to be convicted since both he and his victims belonged to the same persecuted nation. True, a strict interpretation of the Law does not perhaps disclose such a restrictive intention, but comparison of the definition of war crime with that of crime against humanity shows that while, in the latter instance, the legislator referred simply to 'civilian population', in the former he chose a broader language – 'civilian population of or in occupied territory'. From this we infer that the victims of a war crime must always be citizens of an occupied country, which is not true regarding a crime against humanity: these can be committed against any civilian population whatsoever. True, these different formulations are not themselves sufficient to justify an assertion that they include a difference in regard to the national character of the criminal in relation to the national character of the victim. But the Allied Courts which functioned on the basis of the London Charter and Control Council Law No. 10, when faced with the problem of the distinction between war crime and crime against humanity, established this difference. [. . .] Indeed, it is possible to find a man guilty of a war crime even though he himself is of the population of the occupied territory and belongs to the same nation as his victims, if his actions make it clear that he identified with the Occupying Power. However, in the present case, that identification has not been proven. For all the aforementioned grounds, it is right to acquit the defendant of the first count in the charge sheet. [. . .]

As to a crime against humanity, [. . .] it is clear to us that the indication of the acts of murder, extermination, etc. of a civilian population shows two aspects:

A. That the action must be of a severe nature and one which could make a person's life a misery, humiliate him, or cause him severe physical or psychological harm.

B. The action must be perpetrated against civilians, in a wide scale and systematically, thus differing from individual actions, in such a manner as to arouse revolt by the human conscience and sensibility.

In this respect it should be stated that the Allied courts, who also came across the problem before us, that is, which inhuman actions comprise the crime against humanity, determined that systematic offences against human dignity also constitute such a crime.

We are convinced that strikes landed cruelly by means of a rubber baton, bare hands and feet, without distinguishing which part of the body the blow strikes, even if there were some cause for this – but especially when there was no cause whatsoever – and even more so when the victims were exhausted, helpless and in despair, and are perpetrated morning and evening, upon many detainees, are inhuman actions. Indeed, in order to convict a defendant of a crime against humanity it is necessary to show, according to the law's definition of this crime, not only that the actions in and of themselves were of an inhuman nature, but also that the victims are a population which is, by definition, a 'civilian population'. [. . .] We therefore state that the detainees at the Greiditz camp and the detainees at the Paulbrick camp consisted of a civilian population in the sense of the aforementioned definition.

It is right to add here that to our mind, even a person who is himself persecuted and jailed in the same camps as his victims can, in the legal sense, commit a crime against humanity when performing the inhuman actions described above upon his fellow detainees. Unlike a war criminal, a criminal against humanity does not necessarily have to be a person who identifies with the persecuting government, and with its evil intent.

The defendant, when performing the inhumane acts indicated above, allowed himself to become an instrument of the barbaric Nazi government, in its demonic plan to exterminate the Jewish people [. . .]

It is therefore unanimously determined to acquit the defendant of the charge of having committed a war crime, according to the first count in the charge sheet, and in addition to acquit him of the charge of causing injury to David Levkovitz, according to the fourth count in the charge sheet.

It was also decided by majority vote (Justices Avisar and Levine against the opinion of Justice Dr. Lem) to convict the defendant of a crime against humanity, in violation of Article 1 of the law, according to the second count in the charge sheet. [. . .]

Sentence

When we come to prepare the sentence in this trial, our heart trembles. [. . .]

[S]ince we have convicted the defendant of a crime against humanity, the law leaves us no alternative but to sentence the defendant to death. This result goes against our will, as we believe that the legislator should leave the court the authority to sentence a defendant convicted of a crime to a lighter punishment, as well, and this in two respects:

a) It is quite clear that the case of a criminal who is himself a Nazi or identified with the barbaric government of the evil Nazis is quite unlike a criminal such as this defendant, who was himself persecuted and lived in as inhuman conditions as his victims.

b) Not all the crimes against humanity are similar in their severity and cruelty and in this trial itself we heard that some of the other Kapos at the Greiditz and Paulbrick behaved with much greater cruelty than the defendant.

When setting only a death penalty, unless certain circumstances were proven, subject to Article 11 of the law, our legislator deviated from the Nuremberg Declaration and from Law [N]o. 10 – and it is beyond our power to understand why he did so – which both specifically stated that the court was free to inflict the death penalty or any other light penalty. [. . .]

Had we had the choice, when taking into account the severity of the actions proven against the defendant, and which comprise a crime against humanity, and the fact that he himself was persecuted, we would have sentenced the defendant to ten years imprisonment for the crime against humanity [. . .] And we would also take into account in this trial the proven fact that the defendant was already harshly punished by the divine force, his one leg was amputated due to a malignant illness, that his other leg was paralysed due to the same illness and that he is so ridden with other illnesses, to the point that the likelihood that he should live a long life are very meagre, and we would mitigate his punishment a great deal more. However, and as we have said before, we have no alternative and must sentence the defendant to the death penalty. [. . .]

It is therefore decided by majority opinion (Justices Avisar and Levine, against the opinion of Justice Dr. Lem), to sentence the defendant to death. Along with that, we recommend unanimously to the President of the State that he take into account the circumstances indicated above and mitigate the defendant's penalty as he should see fit.

COMMENTARY

The *Enigster* judgment points to one of the major differences between war crimes, on the one side, and crimes against humanity – that victims of war crimes have historically been understood to be members of the enemy forces or civilian population, while crimes against humanity developed as a response to mass atrocities against a civilian population, whether such population belongs to the very belligerent engaging in the criminal conduct or to the enemy. This and other differences are explored in more detail below.[3] In establishing these differences, the Israeli court makes extensive use of the Nuremberg Charter of the International Military Tribunal and the text of Control Council Law No. 10 discussed above.

(G) VIOLATIONS OF THE RULES ON THE CONDUCT OF WARFARE

MEANS OF WARFARE

Other courts, domestic and international, have dealt with massive attacks against civilians and have been called to assess whether these attacks – often consisting of the unlawful use of means of warfare, i.e. prohibited weapons – indeed constituted crimes.

Japan, **Shimoda et al. v. the State**, *Tokyo District Court, Judgment of 7 December 1963*[4]

Acts related to World War II not only gave rise to criminal prosecutions. In the 1960s, five Japanese citizens, survivors of the bombings of Hiroshima and Nagasaki in August 1945, brought a civil action for damages against their government for having unlawfully waived, in its 1951 Peace Treaty with the Allies, the rights and claims of Japan's citizens to compensation for the illegal use of atomic bombs by the USA. While this action was cloaked as a civil suit, the claimants mainly sought a finding on the legality of the use of atomic weapons under international law. The Tokyo district court examined the issue, assessing incidentally whether the use of atomic bombs could be considered a violation of international law in 1945.

2. Evaluation from a viewpoint of international law

(1) Whether or not an atomic bomb as a so-called nuclear weapon [...] is a weapon permitted under international law is undoubtedly an important and very difficult question in the field of international law. However, in this case, at issue is whether the act of dropping an atomic bomb in Hiroshima and Nagasaki by the United States is regarded as illegal under positive international law in force at the time. Therefore, it is sufficient to consider this point only.

---

  [3] See *infra*, the next chapter, on crimes against humanity.
  [4] This translation into English was prepared by Yohei Suda, Attorney at Law, the Law Office of Yohei Suda (Tokyo).

(2) First, as a premise for judging how the above-mentioned act of dropping an atomic bomb is evaluated under positive international law, we begin by considering what international law has existed among modern States since the latter half of the 19th Century with regard to warfare, in particular acts of hostilities.

The following are the rules relevant to this case listed in a chronological order:

1886: St. Petersburg Declaration Renouncing the Use, in Time of War, of Explosive Projectiles under 400 Grammes Weight.

1899: Convention with respect to the Laws and Customs of War on Land, adopted at the Fist Peace Conference at the Hague, and its annex: Regulations concerning the Laws and Customs of War on Land (the so-called Regulations respecting War on Land); Declaration on the Use of Bullets Which Expand or Flatten Easily in the Human Body (the so-called Declaration prohibiting dum-dum bullets); Declaration on the Launching of Projectiles and Explosives from Balloons (the so-called Declaration prohibiting aerial bombardment); Declaration on the Use of Projectiles the Object of Which is the Diffusion of Asphyxiating or Deleterious Gases (the so-called Declaration prohibiting poisonous gases).

1907: Convention with respect to the Laws and Customs of War on Land, adopted at the Second Peace Conference at the Hague (the revision of the Convention of the same title adopted at the First Peace Conference at the Hague); Declaration Prohibiting the Discharge of Projectiles and Explosives from Balloons.

1922: Treaty concerning Submarine and Poisonous Gases in Warfare.

1923: The Hague Rules of Air Warfare (Draft Rules of Air Warfare).

1925: Protocol for the Prohibition of the Use of Asphyxiating, Poisonous or Other Gases, and of Bacteriological Methods of Warfare (Protocol regarding the prohibitions of poisonous gases, etc.).

(3) In the above-mentioned laws and regulations, there is no provision that directly refers to the atomic bomb, a new weapon that appeared during the Second World War.

Raising this point, the Defendant State asserts that the question of a violation of positive international law cannot arise because there was neither customary international law, nor a treaty that banned the use of atomic bombs at that time. The use [of atomic bombs] was therefore not clearly prohibited by international law.

Of course, the use of a new weapon is naturally legal as long as international law does not prohibit it. However, prohibition in this context means not only the case where there is an express provision of direct prohibition but also the case where the prohibition is naturally implied by the interpretation and application by analogy of the existing international laws and regulations (customary international law and treaties). Moreover, we must understand that the prohibition includes the case where, in light of the principles of international law that constitute the basis of the above-mentioned international positive laws and regulations, the use is deemed to be contrary to such principles. This is because there is no reason why the interpretation of international law must be limited to literal interpretation, any more than the interpretation of domestic law is [...]

(4) Another argument is that a new weapon is always beyond the regulation of international law. However, this argument is just as insufficiently founded as the argument above. It is natural that any weapon contrary to the customs of civilised countries and to principles of international laws should be deemed to be prohibited even if there is no express provision in laws and regulations; a new weapon can be used as a legal means of conducting hostilities only where there is no express provision in statutory law and its use is not contrary to the principles of international law. On the other hand, some argue that while the invention and the use of a new weapon is always strongly opposed from various quarters, a new weapon is nonetheless soon regarded as one of the advanced weapons and its prohibition becomes altogether

meaningless. As civilisation advances, the weapon is deemed to be an effective means of injuring the enemy. This is what history shows and an atomic bomb is no exception. We cannot deny that, in the past, in spite of objections by various interested quarters to a new weapon at the time of its first appearance, the weapon nevertheless came to be considered lawful with the advancement of civilisation and the development of science and technology. This may be because international law had not yet been developed, or due to strong hostile feelings against citizens of an enemy State or those who believe in different religions, or, again, because the progress of weapons in general was gradual. However, it is clear that this was not always the case, especially in light of the above-mentioned existence of treaties prohibiting the use of dum-dum bullets or poisonous gases. Therefore, we cannot regard a weapon as legal just because it is a new weapon. It is naturally necessary to examine a new weapon in light of positive international law.

(5) Next, we will examine the international laws and regulations in force at the time relevant to the act of atomic bombing.

First, the question arises as to whether the act of atomic bombing is permissible under the laws and regulations regarding aerial bombardment since such act constitutes an aerial bombardment by military aircraft as an act of hostility.

No convention on aerial bombing has been concluded. However, according to customary rules generally recognised under international law relating to acts of hostility, a distinction is made between a defended town and an undefended town with regard to bombardment by land forces, and a defended area and an undefended area with regard to bombardment by naval forces. While indiscriminate bombardment against a defended town or area is permissible, with regard to an undefended town or area, only bombardment against combatants and military installations (military objectives) is permissible, and bombardment against non-combatants and non-military installations (non-military objectives) is impermissible. Any bombardment contrary to this principle constitutes an illegal act of hostility. [...] The existence of such a principle is evident in light of: Article 25 of Convention with respect to the Laws and Customs of War on Land, which provides that "[t]he attack or bombardment, by whatever means, of towns, villages, dwellings, or buildings which are undefended is prohibited"; Article 1 of Convention concerning Bombardment by Naval Forces in Time of War, adopted at the Hague Peace Conference of 1907, which provides that "[t]he bombardment by naval forces of undefended ports, towns, villages, dwellings, or buildings is forbidden..."; and Article 2 of the same convention, which provides that "[m]ilitary works, military or naval establishments, depots of arms or war *matériel*, workshops or plant which could be utilized for the needs of the hostile fleet or army, and the ships of war in the harbour, are not, however, included in this prohibition."

(6) With regard to air warfare, Article 24 of the Draft Rules of Air Warfare provides as follows:

(i) Aerial bombardment is legitimate only when directed at a military objective, that is to say, an object of which the destruction or damage would constitute a distinct military advantage to the belligerent.

(ii) Such bombardment is legitimate only when directed exclusively at the following objectives: military forces; military works; military establishments or depots; factories constituting important and well-known centres engaged in the manufacture of arms, ammunition, or distinctively military supplies; lines of communication or transportation used for military purposes.

(iii) The bombardment of cities, towns, villages, dwellings, or buildings not in the immediate neighbourhood of the operations of land forces is prohibited. In cases where the objectives specified in paragraph 2 are so situated, that they cannot be bombarded without the indiscriminate bombardment of the civilian population, the aircraft must abstain from bombardment.

(iv) In the immediate neighbourhood of the operations of land forces, the bombardment of cities, towns, villages, dwellings, or buildings is legitimate provided that there exists a reasonable presumption that the military concentration is sufficiently important to justify such bombardment, having regard to the danger thus caused to the civilian population. [. . .]

In addition, Article 22 of the Draft Rules of Air Warfare provides that "[a]erial bombardment for the purpose of terrorizing the civilian population, of destroying or damaging private property not of a military character, or of injuring non-combatants is prohibited." Thus, the Draft Rules of Air Warfare prohibit targetless aerial bombardment and establishes the doctrine of military objectives. They distinguish the immediate vicinity of the operations of land forces from other areas: indiscriminate aerial bombardment is allowed in the case of the former, while in the latter only aerial bombardment of military objectives is allowed. These rules appear to adopt a language that is much stricter than that used in the case of bombardment by land and naval forces. However, their meaning is considered to be the same as the distinction between a defended town (area) and an undefended town (area). While the Draft Rules of Air Warfare cannot be described as a part of international positive law because they have not come into effect yet as a treaty, they are regarded as authoritative with regard to air warfare among international law scholars. Some States adopt the substance of these rules as a code of activities of their own armed forces and the fundamental provisions of these rules are consistently in line with the international laws and regulations as well as customs in force at that time. Therefore, the prohibition of indiscriminate aerial bombardment of an undefended city and the doctrine of military objectives provided for in these rules form part of customary international law, also in light of the fact that they are in common with the principles of land and sea warfare. Further, whereas the distinction among land, sea and air warfare is based on the place and the purposes of hostilities, we think that it is warranted to state that laws and *regulations respecting war on land can be applicable by analogy to the aerial bombardment of a city, since this is nothing other than bombardment on land.*

(7) What is then the distinction between a defended city and an undefended city? Generally speaking, a defended city means a city resisting an attempt at occupation by land forces. Thus, a city that is far away from a battlefield and not in immediate danger of occupation by the enemy cannot be said to be a defended city even if defence installations or armed forces exist there, because there is no military necessity for indiscriminate bombardment. Therefore, in such a case, only bombardment of military objectives is permissible. Indiscriminate bombardment is however permissible on grounds of military necessity against a city resisting an attempt at occupation by the enemy, because in such a case an attack based on the distinction between military objectives and non-military objectives is of limited military effect and cannot accomplish the intended purposes. Thus, we can conclude that it is a generally recognised principle of international law with regard to air warfare that indiscriminate aerial bombardment of an undefended city is impermissible. Aerial bombardment of military objectives only is permitted with regard to an undefended city. [. . .]

Of course, it is anticipated that the aerial bombardment of military objectives might result in the destruction of non-military objectives as well as casualties of non-combatants; this is not illegal if it is an inevitable result of the aerial bombardment of military objectives. However, the aerial bombardment directed at non-military objectives or which does not distinguish between military objectives and non-military objectives (so-called blind aerial bombardment) against an undefended city is impermissible in light of the above-mentioned principle. [. . .]

As already stated, the power of damage and destruction of the atomic bomb is tremendous. Even such small-scale bombs as the ones dropped on Hiroshima and Nagasaki discharge energy equivalent to 20,000 tons of TNT bombs. An explosion of an atomic bomb with such power of destruction clearly results in an almost complete destruction of a medium-sized city, to say nothing of the distinction between military objectives and non-military objectives. Thus, the act of atomic bombing against an undefended city, if not against a defended city, should be regarded as tantamount to blind aerial bombardment and is an act of hostility contrary to international law in force at that time.

(8) It is a well-known fact that Hiroshima and Nagasaki were not cities resisting an attempt at occupation by land forces at that time. It is also clear from what has been stated that neither of them was qualified as a defended city since they were not in immediate danger of occupation by enemy, even if both cities were defended with anti-aircraft and other guns against air raids and did possess military installations. In addition, it is clear that some 330,000 civilians in Hiroshima and some 270,000 civilians in Nagasaki had their homes there, even though both cities had what can be defined as military objectives such as armed forces, military installations, munitions factories and so on. Therefore, it is proper to conclude that the aerial bombardment with an atomic bomb against Hiroshima and Nagasaki constituted an illegal act of hostility under international law at that time as the indiscriminate aerial bombardment of undefended cities. This is so because aerial bombardment with an atomic bomb – even if it targets only military objectives – brings about the same result as a blind aerial bombardment due to the tremendous destructive power of the atomic bomb.

(9) Against the conclusion above, a counter-argument is that the war in those days was a so-called "total war" in which it was difficult to distinguish between combatants and non-combatants as well as between military objectives and non-military objectives, and that the doctrine of military objectives was not necessarily maintained during the Second World War.

The concept of military objectives is prescribed by various provisions in the above-mentioned treaties. On the other hand, the substance of the concept of military objectives is not necessarily fixed and may change with time. It can hardly be denied that its scope is extended under total war. Nevertheless, we cannot say that the distinction between military objectives and non-military objectives has totally disappeared. For instance, schools, churches, temples, shrines, hospitals and private houses cannot be classified as military objectives even during a total war. If the concept of total war is to be understood to mean that everyone who is a national of a belligerent nation is a combatant and that all means of production are means of injuring the enemy, then it becomes necessary to destroy the whole population and all the property of the enemy. The distinction between military objectives and non-military objectives would thus be rendered meaningless. However, the concept of total war has been advocated in recent times to point out the fact that the outcome of a war is determined not just by armed forces or weapons, but that other factors, such as economic factors including energy, resources, productive capacity of industry, food and trade, as well as human factors including population and labour force, have a far-reaching effect on how a war is waged and on the war potential. The concept of total war is not advocated to have the above-mentioned vague meaning leading to a lack of distinction between combatants and non-combatants and describing all means of production as means of injuring the enemy; and no such cases have actually taken place. It is therefore incorrect to state that the distinction between military objectives and non-military objectives has disappeared under total war. [...]

(10) During the Second World War, aerial bombardment against the whole area where military objectives were concentrated did take place on the ground that it was impossible to identify and attack each military objective in places where munitions factories and military installations were concentrated in a relatively small area, and where defensive installations against air raids were strong. Some argue that such aerial bombardment is legal.

Such aerial bombardment is called target-area bombing. There may be room for regarding target-area bombing as legal even if it goes beyond the doctrine of military objectives, because the destruction of non-military objectives is small in proportion to the large military interests and necessity. However, Hiroshima and Nagasaki were clearly not areas where such military objectives were concentrated. Therefore, the doctrine of target-area bombing cannot be applied to these cities.

(11) In addition, the atomic bombing of both Hiroshima and Nagasaki is considered in breach of the principle of international law prohibiting means of injuring the enemy which cause unnecessary pain and are inhumane. [...]

However, in arguing this point, it goes without saying that we cannot easily conclude that an atomic bomb is necessarily prohibited because it has different characteristics from conventional weapons as regards the inhumanity of its effects. This is so because the international law of war is not formulated simply on the basis of humanitarian feelings. It is based on considerations of military necessity and effectiveness, on the one hand, and on humanitarian feelings, on the other, and is formulated on a balance of these two factors. To illustrate this point, scholars cite as an example the provision in the St. Petersburg Declaration of 1868 prohibiting the use of projectiles of a weight below 400 grams, which are either explosive or charged with combustible or inflammable substances. They explain the reason as follows. Such projectiles are so small that they are capable of killing or injuring one combatant. Since an ordinary bullet would suffice to achieve the same, purpose, there is no need to use such an inhumane weapon. On the other hand, the use of a weapon that has a great military effect, however great its inhumane effects are, is not necessarily prohibited under international law.

The question in this sense is whether the act of atomic bombing falls under the prohibition to "employ poison or poisoned weapons" of Article 23(a) of the Hague Regulations respecting War on Land or in the Declaration on the Use of Projectiles the Object of Which is the Diffusion of Asphyxiating or Deleterious Gases of 1899 or the Protocol for the Prohibition of the Use of Asphyxiating, Poisonous or Other Gases, and of Bacteriological Methods of Warfare of 1925. With regard to this point, international law scholars have not reached an agreement on the difference between poisons, poisonous gases, bacteria, etc., on the one hand, and an atomic bomb, on the other. However, in light of the fact that the St. Petersburg Declaration provides that "considering... that this object would be exceeded by the employment of arms which uselessly aggravate the sufferings of disabled men, or render their death inevitable; that [...] the employment of such arms would, therefore, be contrary to the laws of humanity... " and that Article 23(e) of the Hague Regulations respecting War on Land prohibits the use of "arms, projectiles, or material calculated to cause unnecessary suffering", it is safe to conclude that in addition to poisons, poisonous gases and bacteria, any means of injuring the enemy causing suffering at least as great or greater than those prohibited means is prohibited under international law. The destructive power of an atomic bomb is tremendous and it is doubtful whether it had appropriate military effect and was necessary at that time. It is indeed a regrettable fact that the atomic bombing of Hiroshima and Nagasaki took away the lives of many civilians and that among the survivors, there are those whose lives are still imperilled due to its radioactive effects even after 18 years. In this sense, it is not an exaggeration to state that the sufferings caused by an atomic bomb were greater than the pain caused by poisons and poisonous gases. Therefore, we can conclude that the act of dropping such a cruel bomb is contrary to the fundamental principle of the law of war that prohibits causing unnecessary suffering.

The Court however went on to find that individuals have no right to claim compensation directly under international law before a domestic court unless a treaty specifically provides for it. Absent an international agreement, and since Japan had waived 'all claims of Japan and its nationals against the Allied Powers and their nationals arising out of the war or out of actions taken because of the existence of a state of war' and considering the doctrine of sovereign immunity protecting the USA, the Court dismissed the claims.

COMMENTARY

While the *Shimoda* judgment touches upon several important features of war crimes – in particular the principle of distinction and the protection to be afforded persons not taking active part in the hostilities – it bears underscoring that it referred to the international rules relating to the lawful use of means of warfare only incidentally, within the framework of a tort case. In addition, it did not deal with the question of whether the use in 1945 of atomic bombs, in addition to being a breach of international law by the United States Government, also amounted to a war crime attributable to those who had ordered and executed that bombing (a question that can be resolved by inquiring into whether in that period international rules attached criminal law consequences to that violation of international law, namely the criminal liability of the persons responsible for the atomic attack). In other words, the Court incidentally dealt with State responsibility, not with individual criminal liability. In doing so, however, it discussed the state of the laws of war at the relevant time.

METHODS OF WARFARE

Murder and attacks against civilians – which often result in high casualties – are two of the most widespread war crimes to occur during both traditional combat operations and urban warfare. The following judgments explore how these offences come about and are assessed by *criminal* courts.

***USA*, US v. Calley,** *Court of Military Appeals, Judgment of 21 December 1973*

In March 1968, Lieutenant William L. Calley was in charge of a 25-man platoon within a Task Force of the US Army deployed in the Northern Quang Ngai province in Vietnam, an area largely controlled by local Viet Cong forces. On the morning of 16 March 1968, the Company including Calley's platoon was flown to the village of My Lai (the 'Pinkville Area' in US military jargon), made up of four hamlets. The platoon led by Calley murdered, raped and mutilated hundreds of Vietnamese non-combatants. Only about 18 months later, military authorities charged Calley and 11 other soldiers with the murder of various unknown civilians. Calley was convicted in the first instance to dismissal from the Army and confinement at hard labour for life, later reduced to 20 years' imprisonment, for the murder of 22 non-combatants and assault of a child. In his appeal, Calley argued that (i) he was just following orders, (ii) he had not enjoyed a fair trial due to pre-trial publicity, and (iii) there was insufficient evidence for a conviction. The excerpt below reproduces the portion of the appeal judgment on the last of these claims.

First Lieutenant Calley stands convicted of the premeditated murder of 22 infants, children, women, and old men, and of assault with intent to murder a child of about 2 years of age. All the killings and the assault took place on March 16, 1968 in the area of the village of May Lai in the Republic of South Vietnam. The Army Court of Military Review affirmed the findings of guilty and the sentence, which, as reduced by the convening authority, includes dismissal and confinement at hard labor for 20 years. The accused petitioned this Court for further review, alleging 30 assignments of error. We granted three of these assignments. [. . .]

In his second assignment of error the accused contends that the evidence is insufficient to establish his guilt beyond a reasonable doubt. Summarized, the pertinent evidence is as follows:

Lieutenant Calley was a platoon leader in C Company, a unit that was part of an organization known as Task Force Barker, whose mission was to subdue and drive out the enemy in an area in the Republic of Vietnam known popularly as Pinkville. Before March 16, 1968, this area, which included the village of My Lai 4, was a Viet Cong stronghold. C Company had operated in the area several times. Each time the unit had entered the area it suffered casualties by sniper fire, machine gun fire, mines, and other forms of attack. Lieutenant Calley had accompanied his platoon on some of the incursions.

On March 15, 1968, a memorial service for members of the company killed in the area during the preceding weeks was held. After the service Captain Ernest L. Medina, the commanding officer of C Company, briefed the company on a mission in the Pinkville area set for the next day. C Company was to serve as the main attack formation for Task Force Barker. In that role it would assault and neutralize May Lai 4, 5, and 6 and then mass for an assault on My Lai, 1. Intelligence reports indicated that the unit would be opposed by a veteran enemy battalion, and that all civilians would be absent from the area. The objective was to destroy the enemy. Disagreement exists as to the instructions on the specifics of destruction.

Captain Medina testified that he instructed his troops that they were to destroy My Lai 4 by "burning the hootches, to kill the livestock, to close the wells and to destroy the food crops." Asked if women and children were to be killed, Medina said he replied in the negative, adding that, "You must use common sense. If they have a weapon and are trying to engage you, then you can shoot back, but you must use common sense." However, Lieutenant Calley testified that Captain Medina informed the troops they were to kill every living thing – men, women, children, and animals – and under no circumstances were they to leave any Vietnamese behind them as they passed through the villages en route to their final objective. Other witnesses gave more or less support to both versions of the briefing.

On March 16, 1968, the operation began with interdicting fire. C Company was then brought to the area by helicopters. Lieutenant Calley's platoon was on the first lift. This platoon formed a defense perimeter until the remainder of the force was landed. The unit received no hostile fire from the village.

Calley's platoon passed the approaches to the village with his men firing heavily. Entering the village, the platoon encountered only unarmed, unresisting men, women, and children. The villagers, including infants held in their mothers' arms, were assembled and moved in separate groups to collection points. Calley testified that during this time he was radioed twice by Captain Medina, who demanded to know what was delaying the platoon. On being told that a large number of villagers had been detained, Calley said Medina ordered him to "waste them." Calley further testified that he obeyed the orders because he had been taught the doctrine of obedience throughout his military career. Medina denied that he gave any such order.

One of the collection points for the villagers was in the southern part of the village. There, Private First Class Paul D. Meadlo guarded a group of between 30 to 40 old men, women, and children. Lieutenant Calley approached Meadlo and told him, " 'You know what to do,' " and left. He returned shortly and asked Meadlo why the people were not yet dead. Meadlo replied he did not know that Calley had meant that they should be killed. Calley declared that he wanted them dead. He and Meadlo then opened fire on the group, until all but a few children fell. Calley then personally shot these children. He expended 4 or 5 magazines from his M-16 rifle in the incident.

Lieutenant Calley and Meadlo moved from this point to an irrigation ditch on the east side of My Lai 4. There, they encountered another group of civilians being held by several soldiers. Meadlo estimated that this group contained from 75 to 100 persons. Calley stated, " 'We got another job to do, Meadlo,' " and he ordered the group into the ditch. When all were in the ditch, Calley and Meadlo opened fire on them. Although ordered by Calley to shoot, Private First Class James J. Dursi refused to join in the killings, and Specialist Four Robert E. Maples refused to give his machine gun to Calley for use in the killings. Lieutenant Calley admitted that he fired into the ditch, with the muzzle of his weapon within 5 feet of people in it. He expended between 10 to 15 magazines of ammunition on this occasion.

With his radio operator, Private Charles Sledge, Calley moved to the north end of the ditch. There, he found an elderly Vietnamese monk, whom he interrogated. Calley struck the man with his rifle butt and then shot him in the head. Other testimony indicates that immediately afterwards a young child was observed running toward the village. Calley seized him by the arm, threw him into the ditch, and fired at him. Calley admitted interrogating and striking the monk, but denied shooting him. He also denied the incident involving the child.

Appellate defense counsel contend that the evidence is insufficient to establish the accused's guilt. They do not dispute Calley's participation in the homicides, but they argue that he did not act with the malice or *mens rea* essential to a conviction of murder; that the orders he received to kill everyone in the village were not palpably illegal; that he was acting in ignorance of the laws of war; that since he was told that only "the enemy" would be in the village, his honest belief that there were no innocent civilians in the village exonerates him of criminal responsibility for their deaths; and, finally, that his actions were in the heat of passion caused by reasonable provocation.

In assessing the sufficiency of the evidence to support findings of guilty, we cannot reevaluate the credibility of the witnesses or resolve conflicts in their testimony and thus decide anew whether the accused's guilt was established beyond a reasonable doubt. Our function is more limited; it is to determine whether the record contains enough evidence for the triers of the facts to find beyond a reasonable doubt each element of the offenses involved. [...]

The testimony of Meadlo and others provided the court members with ample evidence from which to find that Lieutenant Calley directed and personally participated in the intentional killing of men, women, and children, who were unarmed and in the custody of armed soldiers of C Company. If the prosecution's witnesses are believed, there is also ample evidence to support a finding that the accused deliberately shot the Vietnamese monk whom he interrogated, and that he seized, threw into a ditch, and fired on a child with the intent to kill.

Enemy prisoners are not subject to summary execution by their captors. Military law has long held that the killing of an unresisting prisoner is murder [*Winthrop's Military Law and Precedents*, 2nd edn, 1920 Reprint, at 788–91].

While it is lawful to kill an enemy "in the heat and exercise of war," yet "to kill such an enemy after he has laid down his arms...is murder" [Digest of Opinions of the Judge Advocates General of the Army, 1912, at 1074–75 n. 3].

Conceding for the purposes of this assignment of error that Calley believed the villagers were part of "the enemy," the uncontradicted evidence is that they were under the control of armed soldiers and were offering no resistance. In his testimony, Calley admitted he was aware of the requirement that prisoners be treated with respect. He also admitted he knew that the normal practice was to interrogate villagers, release those who could satisfactorily account for themselves, and evacuate the suspect among them for further examination. Instead of proceeding in the usual way, Calley executed all, without regard to age, condition, or possibility of suspicion. On the evidence, the court-martial could reasonably find Calley guilty of the offenses before us.

At trial, Calley's principal defense was that he acted in execution of Captain Medina's order to kill everyone in My Lai 4. Appellate defense counsel urge this defense as the most important factor in assessment of the legal sufficiency of the evidence. The argument, however, is inapplicable to whether the evidence is *legally* sufficient. Captain Medina denied that he issued any such order, either during the previous day's briefing or on the date the killings were carried out. Resolution of the conflict between his testimony and that of the accused was for the triers of the facts. [...] The general findings of guilty, with exceptions as to the number of persons killed, does not indicate whether the court members found that Captain Medina did not issue the alleged order to kill, or whether, if he did, the court members believed that the accused knew the order was illegal. For the purpose of the legal sufficiency of the evidence, the record supports the findings of guilty.

Calley's conviction was therefore affirmed. Later, however, the Secretary of the Army reduced the sentence to ten years' imprisonment. Calley ultimately spent, besides house arrest, less than five months in a military prison for the crimes in My Lai.

The *Calley* case deals with cases of murder as a war crime, where the *mens rea* of the accused was clear and the evidence definitively established the non-combatant status of the victims. Note the finding by the appellate court that, even if one were to consider the My Lai residents as 'part of the enemy', they could not be killed after they had fallen under the control of US armed soldiers and offered no resistance (they had become persons *hors de combat*). This principle of distinction between combatants and non-combatants has been discussed at length in several ICTY judgments, in particular those dealing with the crime of attacks against civilians, where the judges were confronted with evidence of attacks against civilians not taking active part in the hostilities.

***ICTY*, Prosecutor *v.* Galić,** *Trial Chamber, Judgment of 5 December 2003*

> Stanislav Galić was the commander of Bosnian Serb Sarajevo Romanija Corps (SRK), under Ratko Mladić and Radovan Karadžić, in and around Sarajevo (Bosnia-Herzegovina) between the second half of 1992 and August 1994, during part of the long siege of that city. He was charged by the ICTY Prosecutor with various counts related to a campaign of shelling and sniping against civilian areas of Sarajevo, thereby inflicting terror upon its civilian population. The Trial Chamber had to grapple not only with complex evidentiary issues related to a series of incidents of shelling and sniping, but also – preliminarily – with the very definition of the crime of 'attacks against civilians'. A prohibition to deliberately target civilians exists in Article 51(2) of Additional Protocol I ('[t]he civilian population as such, as well as individual civilians, shall not be the object of attack'). Article 85 of the same Additional Protocol makes a breach of this provision a grave breach and hence a war crime, at least in international armed conflict. Is this provision, however, enough to establish all of the necessary elements of a criminal offence? And how is this offence to be applied to specific factual situations?

2. Attack on Civilians as a Violation of the Laws or Customs of War

(a) Introduction

13. Count 4 of the Indictment reads:

Violations of the Laws or Customs of War (attacks on civilians as set forth in Article 51 of Additional Protocol I and Article 13 of Additional Protocol II to the Geneva Conventions of 1949) punishable under Article 3 of the Statute of the Tribunal.

14. The paragraph introducing Count 4 alleges that the Accused, General Galić, as commander of the SRK, "conducted a coordinated and protracted campaign of sniper attacks upon the civilian population of Sarajevo, killing and wounding a large number of civilians of all ages and both sexes, such attacks by their nature involving the deliberate targeting of civilians with direct fire weapons."

15. Count 7 of the Indictment is in terms identical to Count 4, except that the paragraph preceding Count 7 alleges that the Accused "conducted a coordinated and protracted campaign

of artillery and mortar shelling onto civilian areas of Sarajevo and upon its civilian population. The campaign of shelling resulted in thousands of civilians being killed or injured." [. . .]

(e) Material and Mental Elements

33. The Trial Chamber will now consider the material and mental elements of the offence of attack on civilians. [. . .]

41. Although the Indictment refers in general terms to Article 51 of Additional Protocol I, the Trial Chamber understands the first sentence of the second paragraph of that article to be the legal basis of the charges of attack on civilians in Counts 4 and 7. This sentence will hereinafter be referred to as "the first part" of the second paragraph of Article 51 of Additional Protocol I, or simply as the "first part of Article 51(2)".

42. The constitutive elements of the offence of attack on civilians have not yet been the subject of a definitive statement by the Appeals Chamber. In only two cases before the Tribunal have persons been charged and tried of attack on civilians under Article 3 of the Statute pursuant to Article 51(2) of Additional Protocol I. In each case a brief exposition was given of the offence, together with the offence of attacks on civilian property. In the *Blaškić* case the Trial Chamber observed in relation to the *actus reus* that "the attack must have caused deaths and/or serious bodily injury within the civilian population or damage to civilian property. [. . .] Targeting civilians or civilian property is an offence when not justified by military necessity." On the *mens rea* it found that "such an attack must have been conducted intentionally in the knowledge, or when it was impossible not to know, that civilians or civilian property were being targeted not through military necessity". The Trial Chamber in the *Kordić and Čerkez* case held that "prohibited attacks are those launched deliberately against civilians or civilian objects in the course of an armed conflict and are not justified by military necessity. They must have caused deaths and/or serious bodily injuries within the civilian population or extensive damage to civilian objects".

43. The Trial Chamber follows the above-mentioned jurisprudence to the extent that it states that an attack which causes death or serious bodily injury within the civilian population constitutes an offence. As noted above, such an attack when committed wilfully is punishable as a grave breach of Additional Protocol I.[5] The question remains whether attacks resulting in non-serious civilian casualties, or in no casualties at all, may also entail the individual criminal responsibility of the perpetrator under the type of charge considered here, and thus fall within the jurisdiction of the Tribunal, even though they do not amount to grave breaches of Additional Protocol I. The present Indictment refers only to killing and wounding of civilians; therefore the Trial Chamber does not deem it necessary to express its opinion on that question.

44. The Trial Chamber does not however subscribe to the view that the prohibited conduct set out in the first part of Article 51(2) of Additional Protocol I is adequately described as "targeting civilians when not justified by military necessity". This provision states in clear language that civilians and the civilian population as such should not be the object of attack. It does not mention any exceptions. In particular, it does not contemplate derogating from this rule by invoking military necessity.

45. The Trial Chamber recalls that the provision in question explicitly confirms the customary rule that civilians must enjoy general protection against the danger arising from hostilities. The prohibition against attacking civilians stems from a fundamental principle of international humanitarian law, the principle of distinction, which obliges warring parties to distinguish *at all times* between the civilian population and combatants and between civilian objects and

---

5 [75] See Article 85(3)(a) of Additional Protocol I.

military objectives and accordingly to direct their operations only against military objectives.[6] In its Advisory Opinion on the Legality of Nuclear Weapons, the International Court of Justice described the principle of distinction, along with the principle of protection of the civilian population, as "the cardinal principles contained in the texts constituting the fabric of humanitarian law" and stated that "States must never make civilians the object of attack [. . .]."[7]

46. Part IV of Additional Protocol I, entitled "Civilian Population" (articles 48 to 58), develops and augments earlier legal protections afforded to civilians through specific rules aimed at guiding belligerents to respect and protect the civilian population and individual civilians during the conduct of hostilities.[8] The general prohibition mentioned above forms integral part of and is complemented and reinforced by this set of rules. In order to properly define the conduct outlawed in the first part of Article 51(2) of Additional Protocol I, this rule must be interpreted in light of the ordinary meaning of the terms of Additional Protocol I, as well as of its spirit and purpose.

47. As already stated, the first part of Article 51(2) of Additional Protocol I proscribes making the civilian population as such, or individual civilians, the object of attack. According to Article 50 of Additional Protocol I, "a civilian is any person who does not belong to one of the categories of persons referred to in Article 4(A)(1), (2), (3) and (6) of the Third Geneva Convention and in Article 43 of Additional Protocol I." For the purpose of the protection of victims of armed conflict, the term "civilian" is defined negatively as anyone who is not a member of the armed forces or of an organized military group belonging to a party to the conflict. It is a matter of evidence in each particular case to determine whether an individual has the status of civilian.

48. The protection from attack afforded to individual civilians by Article 51 of Additional Protocol I is suspended when and for such time as they directly participate in hostilities.[9] To take a "direct" part in the hostilities means acts of war which by their nature or purpose are likely to cause actual harm to the personnel or matériel of the enemy armed forces.[10] [. . .] Combatants and other individuals directly engaged in hostilities are considered to be legitimate military targets.[11]

49. The civilian population comprises all persons who are civilians, as defined above.[12] The use of the expression "civilian population *as such*" in Article 51(2) of Additional Protocol I indicates that "the population must never be used as a target or as a tactical objective".[13]

50. The presence of individual combatants within the population does not change its civilian character.[14] In order to promote the protection of civilians, combatants are under the obliga-

---

[6] [79] See Article 48 of Additional Protocol I. This article enunciates the principle of distinction as a basic rule.

[7] [80] ICJ Advisory Opinion on the Legality of the Threat or Use of Nuclear Weapons, ICJ Report 1996, para. 78. [. . .]

[8] [81] Article 51(1) of Additional Protocol I states clearly that "the civilian population and individual civilians shall enjoy general protection against the dangers arising from military operations". [. . .] Among the instruments that provide rules for the protection of civilians are, *inter alia*, the Hague Regulations, annexed to the 1907 Hague Convention (IV) Respecting the Laws and Customs of War on Land and the Fourth Geneva Convention of 1949.

[9] [85] See Article 51(3) of Additional Protocol I.   [10] [86] ICRC Commentary, para. 1944.

[11] [88] Combatant status implies not only being considered a legitimate military objective, but also being able to kill or wound other combatants or individuals participating in hostilities, and being entitled to special treatment when hors-de-combat, *i.e.* when surrendered, captured or wounded (See Article 41(2) of Additional Protocol I).

[12] [89] See Article 50(1) of Additional Protocol I.

[13] [90] See ICRC Commentary, para. 1938. [. . .] The Appeals Chamber has considered these resolutions to be declaratory of customary international law in this field. See *Tadić* Decision on Jurisdiction, para. 112.

[14] [91] See Article 50(3) of Additional Protocol I. The Commentary to this paragraph notes that: "[i]n wartime condition it is inevitable that individuals belonging to the category of combatants become intermingled

tion to distinguish themselves at all times from the civilian population; the generally accepted practice is that they do so by wearing uniforms, or at least a distinctive sign, and by carrying their weapons openly. In certain situations it may be difficult to ascertain the status of particular persons in the population. The clothing, activity, age, or sex of a person are among the factors which may be considered in deciding whether he or she is a civilian. A person shall be considered to be a civilian for as long as there is a doubt as to his or her real status.[15] The Commentary to Additional Protocol I explains that the presumption of civilian status concerns "persons who have not committed hostile acts, but whose status seems doubtful because of the circumstances. They should be considered to be civilians until further information is available, and should therefore not be attacked".[16] The Trial Chamber understands that a person shall not be made the object of attack when it is not reasonable to believe, in the circumstances of the person contemplating the attack, including the information available to the latter, that the potential target is a combatant.

51. As mentioned above, in accordance with the principles of distinction and protection of the civilian population, only military objectives may be lawfully attacked. A widely accepted definition of military objectives is given by Article 52 of Additional Protocol I as "those objects which by their nature, location, purpose or use make an effective contribution to military action and whose total or partial destruction, capture or neutralization, in the circumstances ruling at the time, offers a definite military advantage". In case of doubt as to whether an object which is normally dedicated to civilian purposes is being used to make an effective contribution to military action, it shall be presumed not to be so used. The Trial Chamber understands that such an object shall not be attacked when it is not reasonable to believe, in the circumstances of the person contemplating the attack, including the information available to the latter, that the object is being used to make an effective contribution to military action.

52. "Attack" is defined in Article 49 of Additional Protocol I as "acts of violence against the adversary, whether in offence or in defence." The Commentary makes the point that "attack" is a technical term relating to a specific military operation limited in time and place, and covers attacks carried out both in offence and in defence. The jurisprudence of the Tribunal has defined "attack" as a course of conduct involving the commission of acts of violence.[17] In order to be punishable under Article 3 of the Statute, these acts have to be carried out during the course of an armed conflict.

53. In light of the discussion above, the Trial Chamber holds that the prohibited conduct set out in the first part of Article 51(2) is to direct an attack (as defined in Article 49 of Additional Protocol I) against the civilian population and against individual civilians not taking part in hostilities.

54. The Trial Chamber will now consider the mental element of the offence of attack on civilians, when it results in death or serious injury to body or health. Article 85 of Additional Protocol I explains the intent required for the application of the first part of Article 51(2). It expressly qualifies as a grave breach the act of *wilfully* "making the civilian population or individual civilians the object of attack". The Commentary to Article 85 of Additional Protocol I explains the term as follows:

> *wilfully*: the accused must have acted consciously and with intent, *i.e.*, with his mind on the act and its consequences, and willing them ('criminal intent' or 'malice aforethought');

with the civilian population, for example, soldiers on leave visiting their families. However, provided that these are not regular units with fairly large numbers, this does not in any way change the civilian character of a population." ICRC Commentary, para. 1922.

[15] [92] See Article 50(1) of Additional Protocol I.   [16] [93] ICRC Commentary, para. 1920.
[17] [98] *Krnojelac* Trial Judgment, para. 54; *Kunarac* Trial Judgment, para. 415.

this encompasses the concepts of 'wrongful intent' or 'recklessness', viz., the attitude of an agent who, without being certain of a particular result, accepts the possibility of it happening; on the other hand, ordinary negligence or lack of foresight is not covered, i.e., when a man acts without having his mind on the act or its consequences.[18]

The Trial Chamber accepts this explanation, according to which the notion of "wilfully" incorporates the concept of recklessness, whilst excluding mere negligence. The perpetrator who recklessly attacks civilians acts "wilfully".

55. For the *mens rea* recognized by Additional Protocol I to be proven, the Prosecution must show that the perpetrator was aware or should have been aware of the civilian status of the persons attacked. In case of doubt as to the status of a person, that person shall be considered to be a civilian. However, in such cases, the Prosecution must show that in the given circumstances a reasonable person could not have believed that the individual he or she attacked was a combatant.

56. In sum, the Trial Chamber finds that the crime of attack on civilians is constituted of the elements common to offences falling under Article 3 of the Statute, as well as of the following specific elements:

1. Acts of violence directed against the civilian population or individual civilians not taking direct part in hostilities causing death or serious injury to body or health within the civilian population.

2. The offender wilfully made the civilian population or individual civilians not taking direct part in hostilities the object of those acts of violence.

57. As regards the first element, the Trial Chamber agrees with previous Trial Chambers that indiscriminate attacks, that is to say, attacks which strike civilians or civilian objects and military objectives without distinction, may qualify as direct attacks against civilians. It notes that indiscriminate attacks are expressly prohibited by Additional Protocol I.[19] This prohibition reflects a well-established rule of customary law applicable in all armed conflicts.[20]

58. One type of indiscriminate attack violates the principle of proportionality. The practical application of the principle of distinction requires that those who plan or launch an attack take all feasible precautions to verify that the objectives attacked are neither civilians nor civilian objects, so as to spare civilians as much as possible.[21] Once the military character of a target has been ascertained, commanders must consider whether striking this target is "expected to cause incidental loss of life, injury to civilians, damage to civilian objectives or a combination

---

[18] [100] ICRC Commentary, para. 3474.

[19] [102] Article 51(4) of Additional Protocol I prohibits indiscriminate attacks and provides the first conventional definition of indiscriminate attacks. Paragraph (5) of the same provision provides examples of attacks considered to be indiscriminate. [...]

[20] [103] As recognized by the Appeals Chamber, among the customary rules that have developed to govern both international conflicts and non-international strife is the protection of the civilian population against indiscriminate attacks. *Tadić* Jurisdiction Decision, para. 127. [...] In its already cited Resolution 2444 (1968), the UN General Assembly affirmed that among the principles applicable to all armed conflicts was that "a distinction must be made at all times between persons taking part in the hostilities and members of the civilian population to the effect that the latter be spared as much as possible." (G.A. Res. 2444, U.N. GAOR, 23rd Session, Supp. No. 18 U.N. Doc A/7218(1968)). Resolution 2675(1970) also stated that "in the conduct of military operations, every effort should be made to spare the civilian populations from the ravages of war, and all necessary precautions should be taken to avoid injury loss or damage to the civilian populations." (G.A. Res. 2675, U.N. GAOR, 25th Session, Supp. No. 28 U.N. Doc A/8028 (1970).)

[21] [105] See Article 57(2) of Additional Protocol I. The precautions required by Article 57(2)(a) must be "feasible" and, in this context, "feasible" means that which is practicable or practically possible. The French version of this paragraph reads: "faire tout ce qui est *pratiquement possible* [...]" (emphasis added). [...]

thereof, which would be excessive in relation to the concrete and direct military advantage anticipated."[22] If such casualties are expected to result, the attack should not be pursued.[23] The basic obligation to spare civilians and civilian objects as much as possible must guide the attacking party when considering the proportionality of an attack.[24] In determining whether an attack was proportionate it is necessary to examine whether a reasonably well-informed person in the circumstances of the actual perpetrator, making reasonable use of the information available to him or her, could have expected excessive civilian casualties to result from the attack.

59. To establish the *mens rea* of a disproportionate attack the Prosecution must prove, instead of the above-mentioned *mens rea* requirement, that the attack was launched wilfully and in knowledge of circumstances giving rise to the expectation of excessive civilian casualties.[25]

60. The Trial Chamber considers that certain apparently disproportionate attacks may give rise to the inference that civilians were actually the object of attack. This is to be determined on a case-by-case basis in light of the available evidence.

61. As suggested by the Defence, the parties to a conflict are under an obligation to remove civilians, to the maximum extent feasible from the vicinity of military objectives and to avoid locating military objectives within or near densely populated areas.[26] However, the failure of a party to abide by this obligation does not relieve the attacking side of its duty to abide by the principles of distinction and proportionality when launching an attack.

(f) Conclusion

62. The Trial Chamber finds that an attack on civilian[s] can be brought under Article 3 by virtue of customary international law and, in the instant case, also by virtue of conventional law and is constituted of acts of violence wilfully directed against the civilian population or individual civilians not taking direct part in hostilities causing death or serious injury to body or health within the civilian population.

Thus, the Trial Chamber proceeded to consider on this legal basis various incidents alleged by the Prosecutor. One of them related to the shelling of a parking lot (car park) during an impromptu football (soccer) match, in the residential area of Dobrinjia. This area was situated alongside the airport to the south-west of the city, and the confrontation lines on the eastern side of Dobrinja ran approximately along a street separating the SRK-controlled settlements of Dobrinja I and IV from the settlements of Dobrinja II and III B, under the Army of Bosnia and Herzegovina (ABiH). Two of the three Judges considered the attack an example of indiscriminate attack against the civilian population, carefully considering and rejecting a series of arguments raised by the accused.

---

[22] [106] See Article 51(5)(b) of Additional Protocol I. The *travaux préparatoires* of Additional Protocol I indicate that the expression "concrete and direct" was intended to show that the advantage must be "substantial and relatively close", and that "advantages which are hardly perceptible and those which would only appear in the long term should be disregarded". ICRC Commentary, para. 2209. The Commentary explains that "a military advantage can only consist in ground gained or in annihilating or in weakening the enemy armed forces". ICRC Commentary, para. 2218. [...]

[23] [107] See Article 57(2)(b) of Additional Protocol I.

[24] [108] The ICRC Commentary acknowledges that "the disproportion between losses and damages caused and the military advantages anticipated raises a delicate problem; in some situations there will be no room for doubt, while in other situations there may be reason for hesitation. In such situations, the interests of the civilian population should prevail". ICRC Commentary, para. 1979.

[25] [111] See Article 85(3)(b) of Additional Protocol I.

[26] [112] See Article 58 of Additional Protocol I.

372. On 1 June 1993, some residents of Dobrinja decided to organize a football tournament in the community of Dobrinja IIIB. It was a beautiful, sunny day. Being aware of the danger of organising such an event, the residents looked for a safe place to hold the tournament. The football pitch was set up in the corner of a parking lot, which was bounded by six-storey apartment blocks on three sides and on the fourth side, which faced the north, by Mojmilo hill, and was not visible from any point on the SRK side of the confrontation line. Around 200 spectators, among whom were women and children, gathered to watch the teams play. Children aged between 10 to 15 years positioned themselves next to some old cars, damaged by previous shelling, that had been overturned and placed around the football pitch to mark the field. Some residents also came out onto the balconies of the apartment buildings surrounding the pitch to watch the football tournament.

373. The first match of the tournament began at around 9 am and the second one started an hour later. Some minutes after 10 am, during the second match, two shells exploded at the parking lot. Ismet Fažlić, a member of the civil defence, was the referee of the second game. He recounted that about 10 to 20 minutes into that game, as they carried out a penalty kick, the first shell landed among the players in the centre of the pitch. He was hit by shrapnel and sustained serious injuries in both legs as well as in other parts of his body. He immediately saw that there were eleven young men on the ground, eight of whom had died on the spot. Fažlić said that "three of my players [were] totally dismembered, their legs and arms; it was only their track suit that held them together" and that many people around the pitch were on the ground. Omer Hadziabdić, who was 15 years old at the time, was watching the match from the overturned cars when the first shell struck the football pitch. He heard a very strong explosion which knocked him down. He was wounded by shrapnel in his leg. Nedim Gavranović, who was 12 years old at the time, was standing behind one of the goals when he heard the first explosion and felt a very strong blow. He sustained an entry and exit wound in his right lower leg caused by shrapnel.

374. The witnesses recounted that a second shell landed at almost the same spot within seconds of the first shell. It fell in front of a young man and tore his leg off. After the second explosion, those who could began running away from the parking lot to take cover. As Hadziabdić ran from the site, he was able to see many wounded people on the ground.

375. The Majority is convinced that the shelling incident of 1 June 1993 in the residential settlement of Dobrinja IIIB occurred as recounted by eye-witnesses. It finds that two mortar shells landed at around 10.20am at the parking lot in the settlement of Dobrinja IIIB, where a crowd of approximately 200 people had gathered to watch the football tournament.

376. After the event, the wounded were taken to the Dobrinja auxiliary hospital. Some were later transferred to the Koševo hospital. While the witnesses agreed that the explosion on 1 June 1993 injured many people, there is disagreement as to the exact number of people killed or injured. Dr. Youssef Hajir, who worked at the Dobrinja hospital at the time, testified that he had never seen so many injured come to the hospital. The entire facility was filled with victims of the incident. Although he did not recall the exact number of casualties, Dr. Hajir estimated that there were approximately 130 to 140 injured and 13 to 14 dead. He stated that 90 of the injured were treated at the Dobrinja hospital and the rest was transferred to town, due to lack of capacity. The Dobrinja hospital records contain a list of 136 names of the casualties, twelve of which are recorded as killed. Gavranović, who was among the wounded at the Dobrinja hospital, recounted that he saw many people he knew there. He believed that 15 persons died and that approximately 50 to 70 were wounded. Hadziabdić was taken to the Dobrinja hospital to be given first aid. He also recognised many of those injured and killed and said that "mainly, those were men, most of them were civilians and children", and friends his age. Fažlić was among those transferred from the Dobrinja hospital to the Koševo hospital, where he underwent treatment and remained for almost two months. He believed that a total of 16 people

were killed and 82 or 83 wounded, including children. Ismet Hadžić, a resident of Dobrinja and the commander of the ABiH 5th Motorised Dobrinja Brigade, was not present when the incident occurred, but he recalled that the shells that fell that day killed 15 people, including children, and wounded 121 people, 56 of them severely. It is noted that Exhibit D25, an ABiH 5th Motorised Dobrinja Brigade command report dated 1 June 1993, signed by Commander Ismet Hadžić, indicated that there were 11 killed and 87 wounded (six combatants killed and fifty-five wounded and five civilians killed and thirty-two wounded). Dr. Janko Viličić, the Defence's expert in shelling, disagreed with the Prosecution's alleged number of casualties (12 killed and 101 wounded), and stated that, given the position of the spectators around the football pitch when the explosions occurred, a total of 43 persons would be expected to have been hit by fragments from the two shells. The Majority finds that the number of victims estimated by the theoretical model used by [expert witness called by the Defence] Viličić is contradicted by the evidence. It finds that there is sufficient specific and credible evidence to conclude that it has been shown beyond reasonable doubt that the explosion of 1 June 1993 in Dobrinja killed over 10 persons and injured approximately 100 others.

377. The Defence submits that the shells were not deliberately fired by SRK forces upon civilians. [...]

378. [...] The Majority [...] is convinced that the shells that hit the football pitch were of a calibre of at least 81–82mm and originated from the direction east-south-east.

379. [...] Having closely examined and verified the accuracy of the assessment made by [expert witness called by the Prosecution] Higgs on the bas[is] of the maps available to the Trial Chamber, it finds that the distance from the site of the event to the confrontation lines in the direction of the fire was approximately 300 metres.

380. [...] The Majority observes that, given the distance of the confrontation lines to the site of the event, even if the mortars had been fired with primary charge, as suggested by Viličić, their source would have been SRK-controlled territory. Had the shells been launched from a greater distance, as suggested by Higgs and Hamill [a Military Observer with the United Nations in Sarajevo], they would have been located well within the SRK side of the confrontation lines. Therefore, the Indictment's allegation that the origin of fire was SRK-held territory has been made out.

381. The Majority takes account of the previous testimonies of witnesses that recounted that the shelling of Dobrinja was a common occurrence. Witnesses also told the Trial Chamber that the area of the parking lot was shelled on previous occasions. Nedim Gavranović testified that shells landed at the parking lot "throughout the duration of the war, not every day, but occasionally". Ismet Fažlić said that the parking lot had been hit by shells on numerous occasions. He remembered that the evening prior to the occurrence of the incident, a shell had impacted only 10 metres north of a playground next to the parking lot.

382. The Defence submits, alternatively, that the intended target of this attack was a legitimate military objective. In support of this view, the Defence argues that the ABiH had headquarters located in the proximity of the parking lot and that a system of trenches ran only a dozen of metres away from this site. The evidence indicates that the ABiH 5th Motorised Dobrinja Brigade headquarters were not in the area of the parking lot, but in the Dobrinja II settlement. Two witnesses indicated, however, that there was a nuclear shelter of the Dobrinja IIIB community, located approximately 100 metres away from the parking lot behind a block of flats which was used by the ABiH forces. Other witnesses, all inhabitants of Dobrinja, testified that the nuclear shelters in Dobrinja were not used as military facilities or served any military purpose. The Majority finds that, regardless of whether the nuclear shelter located in the Dobrinja III settlement served as military facility, it is not reasonable to believe that it was the intended target of the attack, since an attack carried out with mortars shells cannot inflict

significant damage, if any, on such a facility. Considering that only two shells were fired, that these fell in quick succession and landed at almost the same spot on the parking lot, and that the second shell did not land any closer to the nuclear shelter, the Majority concludes that this was not the intended target of the attack.

383. The Majority heard contradictory evidence regarding the use of connecting trenches that existed in Dobrinja. Witness DP9 testified that a system of connecting trenches had been dug in the vicinity of the parking lot and that these were used by ABiH forces for "manpower and supplies". Ismet Hadžić and Witness R, on the other hand, testified that these connecting trenches were only used by civilians. The Majority cannot reasonably exclude the possibility that these connecting trenches, although used by civilians, were also used by ABiH soldiers. However, considering the pattern of the firing and that the second shell fired did not fall any closer to the location of the trenches indicated by Witness DP9, the Majority concludes that these trenches were not the intended target of the attack.

384. The Defence presented evidence that suggests the establishment of a second line of defence in Dobrinja. The witnesses heard by the Trial Chamber testified that this second line of defence did not exist. Considering that the evidence in the Trial Record insufficiently demonstrates the exact location, or even the existence, of the second line of defence in Dobrinja, the Trial Chamber concludes that the attack was not aimed at an alleged second line of defence.

385. No other evidence gives the Majority reason to believe that any other military facility in this area was targeted, and missed.

386. Witnesses heard by the Trial Chamber stated that a certain number of ABiH soldiers was present at the football match. Hadžić, the commander of the ABiH 5th Motorised Dobrinja Brigade, acknowledged that off-duty soldiers were among the casualties. He was of the opinion that the proportion of civilian and military killed or injured that day was roughly fifty-fifty. Exhibit D25, an ABiH 5th Motorised Dobrinja Brigade command report dated 1 June 1993 signed by Hadžić, indicates that there were "six combatants killed and fifty-five wounded and five civilians killed and thirty-two wounded". Two eye-witnesses of the event, Gavranović and Hadziabdić, recalled seeing soldiers in uniform, although unarmed, among the spectators. Hadziabdić believed that the soldiers made up approximately a third to one-half of the crowd present at the parking lot. Gavranović was of the opinion that approximately 20 to 30 percent of the crowd was made up of soldiers in uniform. Yet, Fažlić, another eye-witness of the shelling incident, said that the crowd gathered for the football tournament was composed mainly of children, young people and a few women. He told the Trial Chamber that no one present at the game was in military uniform or wearing a military insignia or carrying weapons, although some may have been off-duty police officers or soldiers. According to this witness, all the players were wearing jogging or sports outfits. The eye-witnesses of the event testified further that the football tournament took place on a quiet day when there was a lull in hostilities. The Majority understands the evidence to show that there were soldiers present at the parking lot, who were off-duty, unarmed and not engaged in any military activity. It finds that, although soldiers were present at the improvised football pitch, the crowd gathered there was carrying out a civilian activity, i.e., playing football.

387. The Defence submits that the football pitch was located very close to the confrontation lines, where a civilian gathering would not normally be expected to take place. According to the Defence, "the Bosnian-Serb forces could not see from any place whatsoever what was happening on the other side of the buildings", and "it is possible that soldiers heard noises and exclamations near the HQ location" and presumed that the ABiH was mounting an attack there. It alleges that "this hypothesis should obviously be held in discharge so that if a fire [. . .] had come from the areas under SRK control, the collateral damage would have been here perfectly understandable and explainable". The evidence confirms the Defence's submission

that, due to its location, the parking lot was not visible from SRK lines. One witness believed the crowd could not be heard from the SRK side of Dobrinja. The Majority notes that the parking lot was shelled well after the tournament began. It finds that the Defence's suggestion that, based on the noise made by the crowd yelling and cheering the game, the SRK forces could have suspected ABiH infantry troops to be preparing for attack is too improbable to accept, since these troops would not have normally revealed their presence to the enemy by making noise. Had the SRK forces launched two shells into a residential neighbourhood at random, without taking feasible precautions to verify the target of the attack, they would have unlawfully shelled a civilian area. The Majority notes that there is no evidence on the Trial Record that suggests that the SRK was informed of the event taking place in the parking lot. However, had the SRK troops been informed of this gathering and of the presence of ABiH soldiers there, and had intended to target these soldiers, this attack would nevertheless be unlawful. Although the number of soldiers present at the game was significant, an attack on a crowd of approximately 200 people, including numerous children, would clearly be expected to cause incidental loss of life and injuries to civilians excessive in relation to the direct and concrete military advantage anticipated. In light of its finding regarding the source and direction of fire, and taking account of the evidence that the neighbourhood of Dobrinja, including the area of the parking lot, was frequently shelled from SRK positions, the Majority finds that the first scheduled shelling incident constitutes an example of indiscriminate shelling by the SRK on a civilian area.

On the basis of almost 200 pages of findings similar to the ones above, the Trial Chamber proceeded to draw the following conclusions in relation to the siege of Sarajevo during the indictment period.

583. The Trial Chamber stated earlier that it understood the term "campaign" in the context of the Indictment to cover military actions in the area of Sarajevo involving widespread or systematic shelling and sniping of civilians resulting in civilian death or injury. The Majority believes that such a campaign existed for the reasons given below.

584. All residents of ABiH-held areas of Sarajevo who appeared before this Trial Chamber testified to the effect that no civilian activity and no areas of Sarajevo held by the ABiH seemed to be safe from sniping or shelling attacks from SRK-held territory. The Majority heard reliable evidence that civilians were targeted during funerals, in ambulances, in hospitals, on trams, on buses, when driving or cycling, at home, while tending gardens or fires or clearing rubbish in the city. [. . .] The most populated areas of Sarajevo seemed to be particularly subject to indiscriminate or random shelling attacks. Hadžić testified about every single part of Dobrinja, a very populated neighbourhood, exposed to severe shelling originating from SRK-controlled territory. A resident of Alipašino Polje, Diho, testified about entire façades of houses on Ante Babiča street "pock-marked" with shell pieces and grenades of all calibres and other apartment blocks targeted by SRK forces. Photographs adduced into evidence show the extensive destruction of civilian inhabitations in Sarajevo during the Indictment Period.

585. The natural and urban topography of the city of Sarajevo, such as ridges and high-rise buildings, provided vantage-points to SRK forces to target civilians moving around the city. The Trial Chamber heard evidence of the existence of specific areas throughout the city of Sarajevo which became notorious as sources of sniping fire directed at civilians. In the general area of Grbavica, witnesses testified that fire was opened against civilians from different high-rise buildings on the southern side of the Miljacka River, in the SRK-controlled neighbourhood of Grbavica. These positions allowed soldiers to "literally shoot down streets" in the central part of Sarajevo, exposing all pedestrians at intersections, as well as cars, buses and trams travelling from the east to the west of the city, to sniper fire. The main thoroughfare of Sarajevo, part

of which was called Marshal Tito Boulevard, became known as "Sniper Alley" as it was particularly prone to regular gunfire. The Trial Chamber recalls the testimony of Van Lynden, who said that from Grbavica the SRK "basically controlled a large chunk of the road that you had to travel to get to the western part of the city. So it was a case of picking up as much speed as you could in your car and going past there as fast as you possibly could". Containers were set up at intersections, such as near the Presidency and Energoinvest buildings and in the proximity of the Holiday Inn, to shield civilians against fire coming from the tall buildings in Grbavica. [...] The same pattern of regular fire at civilians from SRK-controlled positions or areas appears consistently throughout ABiH-held areas of the city of Sarajevo during the Indictment Period.

586. The evidence in the Trial Record also discloses that although civilians adapted to that hostile environment by closing schools, living at night, hiding during the day in their apartment or cellar, moving around the city of Sarajevo as little as possible, setting up containers and barricades to provide shelter against sniping fire, they were still not safe from sniping and shelling fire from SRK-controlled territory. Witnesses recounted how civilians tilled at night, fetched water or collected wood at night or when the visibility was reduced or developed alternative routes to traverse the city to avoid sniping fire directed against civilians seen from SRK-controlled territory. Nevertheless, they were still seen and targeted. Sniping incidents 5 (Novo Sarajevo) and 10 (in Hrasno) are representative of the targeting of civilians who were seen through gaps between containers set up along streets and main avenues in the city of Sarajevo and were targeted from SRK-controlled territory. The testimony of Akir Mukanović, an ABiH soldier, is speaking for itself: he felt safer at the frontline than anywhere else in Sarajevo.

587. The evidence of residents of Sarajevo or victims of attacks is supported by evidence from international military personnel present in Sarajevo during the Indictment Period, which testified uniformly that civilians in Sarajevo were targeted by small arm fire or shelling from SRK-controlled areas. The Majority particularly recalls the testimony of Hamill, an UNPROFOR officer present in Sarajevo almost throughout the Indictment Period, that few shelling incidents stand out in his mind because there was "a whole series of attacks that went on killing civilians in the city of Sarajevo". An UNPROFOR report concluded that in view of the unusually high volume of fire one day of 1993 in the area of Stari Grad (400 artillery and mortar impacts recorded), there was no doubt that civilians were targeted. UNPROFOR representatives who carried out investigations following shelling attacks in Dobrinja noticed that shelling affected very populated streets in Dobrinja.

588. Both Ashton and Hvaal, journalists, also observed that the majority of the targets they saw were civilians. They testified that they saw civilians being shot at almost every day. Ashton testified about SRK positions he visited and where gunners admitted firing indiscriminately in the city. He had no doubt that SRK forces shot civilians.

589. On many occasions, international military personnel, residents of ABiH-held areas of Sarajevo or visitors encountered difficulties to determine with certainty the source of fire on civilians. The Majority recalls that the conflict in the city of Sarajevo was mainly static; apart from some changes, most of the confrontation lines remained unchanged during the Indictment period. ABiH-held territory, including most of the city, was almost completely surrounded by SRK forces and distances were so short in some areas (see the map 1 attached in annex D to this Judgement [not reproduced in the present volume]) that one belligerent party could fire into the territory of the other party and also over that territory into its own positions. Evidence to the effect that ABiH forces attacked their own civilians was adduced at trial. UN representatives stationed in Sarajevo testified that, during the conflict, information had been gathered indicating that elements sympathetic or belonging to the ABiH *may* have shelled on occasions the Muslim population of Sarajevo. More generally, such elements would have engaged in behaviour objectively putting civilians in ABiH-controlled territory at risk in order

to draw international sympathy. The Majority cannot exclude that this firing occurred on some occasions to attract the attention of the international community. However, only a minimal fraction of attacks on civilians could be reasonably attributed to such conduct, which would be, in any case, difficult to carry out or keep secret for long. The protective barriers faced the SRK side. The Majority also accepts that stray bullets may have struck a number of civilians. But again, stray bullets, being by definition random in their direction and lacking a target, could not possibly explain but a fraction of incidents involving civilians. It is finally possible that some civilians were shot in the honest belief that they were combatants. Again, while not excluding this possibility, the Majority can think of few other examples of combat rivaling the 1992–94 Sarajevo conflict for close contact. In such circumstances, in the relatively cramped fighting conditions of Sarajevo, the accidental targeting of civilians could not be said to represent the whole real course of events that took place in Sarajevo. The evidence in the Trial Record conclusively establishes that the pattern of fire throughout the city of Sarajevo was that of indiscriminate or direct fire at civilians in ABiH-held areas of Sarajevo from SRK-controlled territory not that of combat fire where civilians were accidentally hit.

590. Fire into ABiH-held areas of Sarajevo followed a temporal pattern. Fire into that city was intense between September and December 1992, still important throughout the year 1993, with daily or weekly fluctuations (days of little shootings followed by days of extreme activity), with an intensification of fire in winter 1993 and up to the wake of the Markale shelling incident in February 1994 and then subsided. The Majority recalls the testimony of Mole, present in Sarajevo between September and December 1992, who said that there was a constant background noise of small arm, mortar and artillery fire. Witnesses emphasised that although there were periods of relative inactivity of shelling during the year 1994, people venturing outside were still targeted.

591. The Majority is convinced by the evidence in the Trial Record that civilians in ABiH-held areas of Sarajevo were directly or indiscriminately attacked from SRK-controlled territory during the Indictment Period, and that as a result and as a minimum, hundreds of civilians were killed and thousands others were injured.

592. The evidence in the Trial Record reveals the reason why civilians in ABiH-held areas of Sarajevo were targeted from SRK-controlled territory. The evidence, especially in relation to the nature of the civilian activities targeted, the manner in which the attacks on civilians were carried out and the timing and duration of the attacks on civilians, consistently shows that the aim of the campaign of sniping and shelling in Sarajevo was to terrorise the civilian population of the city. UN military personnel present in Sarajevo during the Indictment Period who observed and analysed the attacks launched into the city *not* made in relation to military objectives concluded that the purpose of the attacks was to spread terror among the civilian population. [. . .]

593. In view of the evidence in the Trial Record it has accepted and weighed, the Majority finds that the attacks on civilians were numerous, but were not consistently so intense as to suggest an attempt by the SRK to wipe out or even deplete the civilian population through attrition. The attacks on civilians had no discernible significance in military terms. They occurred with greater frequency in some periods, but very clearly the message which they carried was that no Sarajevo civilian was safe anywhere, at any time of day or night. The evidence shows that the SRK attacked civilians, men and women, children and elderly in particular while engaged in typical civilian activities or where expected to be found, in a similar pattern of conduct throughout the city of Sarajevo. The Majority finds that the only reasonable conclusion in light of the evidence in the Trial Record is that the primary purpose of the campaign was to instill in the civilian population a state of extreme fear.

594. In sum, the Majority finds that a series of military attacks on civilians in ABiH-held areas of Sarajevo and during the Indictment Period were carried out from SRK-controlled territories with the aim to spread terror among that civilian population. The Majority accepts the Prosecution's stand that as such, these attacks carried out with a specific purpose, constituted a campaign of sniping and shelling against civilians.

Galić was convicted to twenty years' imprisonment for having ordered this 'campaign of terror' through sniping and shelling. The Appeals Chamber, though applying a partly different reasoning, confirmed the conviction and modified the sentence into life imprisonment. Galić is presently serving his sentence in a German prison.

COMMENTARY

The *Galić* judgment – and, to a certain extent, the *Shimoda* case – explored one of the most important facets of the contemporary law of armed conflict: the need to distinguish between combatants (who may be targeted, as long as the weapons used are not meant to cause unnecessary suffering and destruction) and persons who are not (or no longer) actively participating in hostilities (who should be spared and can never be targeted). Attacks on legitimate targets are to limit incidental (collateral) damage and keep suffering to a minimum: disproportionate damage and unnecessary sufferings are unlawful.

QUESTIONS

1. Why are States generally reluctant to accept that war crimes may also be committed in non-international armed conflicts (i.e. civil wars)?

2. How does one define whether a person is a combatant or is taking no active part in the hostilities?

3. Is a terrorist taking part in an (international or internal) armed conflict subject to the laws of armed conflict? Can his acts be considered war crimes?

4. Can a person be convicted of both war crimes and crimes against humanity in relation to the same conduct?

FURTHER READING

Cassese, *International Criminal Law*, 81–97.

K. Dörmann, *Elements of War Crimes under the Rome Statute of the International Criminal Court* (Cambridge: Cambridge University Press, 2003).

W. Fenrick, 'Grave Breaches', in *Oxford Companion*, 336.

ICRC Study, 568–621.

2
CRIMES AGAINST HUMANITY

(A) THE NOTION AND ITS ORIGINS

Crimes against humanity occupy the space between war crimes and genocide. While war crimes can be isolated or singular events and are necessarily tied to armed conflict, crimes against humanity address serious crimes (such as murder, torture, persecutions, deportation, sexual violence, and other inhumane acts of similar character and gravity) committed as part of a 'widespread or systematic attack on a civilian population'. A perpetrator need only commit a single specific crime to be charged with a crime against humanity, but must do so in the context of a widespread or systematic attack and with an awareness of the link between his act and the larger attack. Accordingly, crimes against humanity address crimes committed against a civilian population on a massive scale, or repeatedly over time.

Moreover, in customary international law, and certain codifications of the concept (such as the ICCSt., but not the ICTYSt.), crimes against humanity can be committed absent an armed conflict, such as when a State commits atrocities against its own people. Although the ICTY reached this conclusion in the *Tadić* case, the statute of the ICTY in Article 5 limits the jurisdiction of the ICTY to crimes against humanity 'committed in armed conflict', and therefore adds an element beyond what is required by customary international law. When crimes against humanity *are* committed during the course of an armed conflict, there can be substantial overlap between war crimes and crimes against humanity, and frequently international criminal indictments will charge each specific crime as both a war crime and a crime against humanity. But even in these cases, the inclusion of the crimes against humanity charges provides a mechanism to put the individual crimes into a broader context, and to designate for particular condemnation (and more serious punishment) crimes that are part of a larger, organized and planned attack on civilians.

At the other end of the spectrum, crimes against humanity cover a broad range of conduct that does not necessarily satisfy the technical and narrow requirements of a genocide charge. For example, attacks on a civilian population for the purpose of driving that population out of a particular geographic area, frequently described as 'ethnic cleansing', may not evidence an intent to destroy (as opposed to displace) the group in whole or in part, as required by a genocide charge, but such conduct will typically fall squarely within crimes against humanity charges. In popular and political discourse, crimes against humanity must sometimes exist in the shadow of discussions about genocide, which often has the status of the 'ultimate' charge, but in fact it is crimes against humanity that are particularly well suited to address the kinds of wide-ranging ethnic conflicts that have led to the establishment of modern international war crimes tribunals.

In light of the broad utility of the law of crimes against humanity, it might be surprising to learn that crimes against humanity have perhaps the most tentative legal foundation, as a historical matter, of the three broad categories of crimes. Or perhaps it is precisely *because of* the broad utility of this law that its historical foundations are less certain. While war crimes derive largely from international humanitarian law and the self-interest of States in protecting their soldiers from unwarranted harm, and genocide from an international convention, crimes against humanity found its roots largely in international human rights law, which largely governs how States may treat individuals and is therefore particularly focused on the protection of civilians. Thus, concerns about State sovereignty will be at a maximum when it comes to crimes against humanity, which after all have a particular capacity to reach the internal conduct of States. At the same time, the gradual, cautious, and incremental development of the law of crimes against humanity has today put it on an unquestionably firm footing.

During the nineteenth century, States sometimes protested the brutal treatment by other States of their own minority populations, and at times even justified military intervention, in part, on this basis. In the *Altstötter* decision following World War II, excerpted below, the court relied in part on this history to find that crimes against humanity were established within international law, but of course one must consider whether States were always acting benevolently in these situations, and in any case it is certain that the purpose of these protests and interventions was not to promote individual criminal responsibility. Nonetheless, in this early history the seeds were planted for the later development of accountability for such crimes.

One of the first uses of the expression 'crimes against humanity' occurred in 1915 when the British, French and Russians protested the killings of Armenians in the Ottoman Empire. Although it was a political and diplomatic condemnation, and therefore in keeping with similar protests of the preceding century, the formulation that was used suggested at least the possibility of individual accountability. Four years later, in the lead-up to the Versailles Conference, diplomats from the Great Powers contemplated a tribunal to hold members of the German Empire and its allies accountable for violations of the laws and customs of war as well as the 'laws of humanity'. The American representatives, however, questioned both the existence and the possibility of this latter category of crimes:

As pointed out by the American representatives on more than one occasion, war was and is by its nature inhuman, but acts consistent with the laws and customs of war, although these acts are inhuman, are nevertheless not the object of punishment by a court of justice. A judicial tribunal only deals with existing law and only administers existing law, leaving to another forum infractions of the moral law and actions contrary to the laws and principles of humanity. A further objection lies in the fact that the laws and principles of humanity are not certain, varying with time, place, and circumstance, and according, it may be, to the conscience of the individual judge. There is no fixed and universal standard of humanity.[1]

This intervention helped defeat the proposal, but the idea of a body of crimes against humanity was nonetheless further concretized.

Following World War II, what began as a *political* expression of condemnation was further translated into a cognizable *legal* concept of individual responsibility. The Charter of the International Military Tribunal (IMT) at Nuremberg was, of course, the most significant step in this process; it included crimes against humanity among the potential charges and it provided some definition for these crimes. At the same time, it limited their scope by

---

[1] Robert Lansing and James Brown Scott, 'Memorandum of Reservations Presented by the Representatives of the United States to the Report of the Commission on Responsibilities' (4 April 1919), Annex II to Commission on the Responsibility of the Authors of the War and on Enforcement of Penalties, Report Presented to the Preliminary Peace Conference (Versailles, 29 March 1919) (1920) 14 *American Journal of International Law* 95, 144.

requiring a connection to the other crimes in the Charter (war crimes and crimes against peace). In its first incarnation, therefore, crimes against humanity were:

murder, extermination, enslavement, deportation, and other inhumane acts committed against any civilian population, before or during the war, or persecutions on political, racial, or religious grounds in execution of or in connexion with any crimes within the jurisdiction of the Tribunal, whether or not in violation of the domestic law of the country where perpetrated.

The IMT judgment further narrowed the work that was required of this new crime: it found that crimes committed before the war did not satisfy the 'connexion' requirement of the Charter, and with regard to crimes committed after the war it found in nearly all cases that the crimes against humanity were also war crimes. In fact, just 2 of the 24 accused, Julius Streicher and Baldur von Schirach, were convicted solely of crimes against humanity. Nonetheless, despite the narrow use of the concept of crimes against humanity by the IMT, these two particular cases from the IMT Judgment demonstrate the potential of the concept to reach conduct beyond that covered by war crimes, and therefore a brief excerpt of each case is warranted.

Cases

IMT Nuremberg, **Göring et al.**, *Judgment of 30 September–1 October 1946 (Streicher, von Schirach)*

Streicher was an early member of the Nazi party and the publisher and editor of *Der Stürmer*, an anti-Semitic weekly newspaper. His conviction for incitement to murder and extermination and for persecution resulted in a sentence of death for Streicher and foreshadows the prosecution of Ferdinand Nahimana and others (also known as the '*Media* Case') more than fifty years later by the ICTR, discussed later in this chapter.

For his twenty-five years of speaking, writing, and preaching hatred of the Jews, Streicher was widely known as "Jew-Baiter Number One." In his speeches and articles, week after week, month after month, he infected the German mind with the virus of anti-Semitism and incited the German people to active persecution. Each issue of "Der Stürmer", which reached a circulation of 600,000 in 1935, was filled with such articles, often lewd and disgusting.

Streicher had charge of the Jewish boycott of 1st April, 1933. He advocated the Nuremberg Decrees of 1935. He was responsible for the demolition on 10th August, 1938, of the Synagogue in Nuremberg. And on 10th November, 1938, he spoke publicly in support of the Jewish pogrom which was taking place at that time.

But it was not only in Germany that this defendant advocated his doctrines. As early as 1938 he began to call for the annihilation of the Jewish race. Twenty-three different articles of "Der Stürmer" between 1938 and 1941 were produced in evidence, in which the extermination "root and branch" was preached. Typical of his teachings was a leading article in September, 1938, which termed the Jew a germ and a pest, not a human being, but "a parasite, an enemy, an evil-doer, a disseminator of diseases who must be destroyed in the interest of mankind." Other articles urged that only when world Jewry had been annihilated would the Jewish problem have been solved, and predicted that fifty years hence the Jewish graves "will proclaim that this people of murderers and criminals has after all met its deserved fate." Streicher, in February, 1940, published a letter from one of "Der Stürmer's" readers which compared Jews with swarms of locusts which must be exterminated completely. Such was the poison Streicher injected into the minds of thousands of Germans which caused them to follow the National Socialists policy of Jewish persecution and extermination. A leading article of "Der Stürmer" in May, 1939, shows clearly his aim:

> A punitive expedition must come against the Jews in Russia. A punitive expedition which will provide the same fate for them that every murderer and criminal must expect: Death sentence and execution. The Jews in Russia must be killed. They must be exterminated root and branch.

As the war in the early stages proved successful [in] acquiring more territory for the Reich, Streicher even intensified his efforts to incite the Germans against the Jews. In the record are twenty-six articles from "Der Sturmer", published between August, 1941 and September, 1944, twelve by Streicher's own hand, which demanded annihilation and extermination in unequivocal terms. He wrote and published on 25th December, 1941:

> If the danger of the reproduction of that curse of God in the Jewish blood is to finally come to an end, then there is only one way - the extermination of that people whose father is the devil.

And in February, 1944, his own article stated:

> Whoever does what a Jew does is a scoundrel, a criminal. And he who repeats and wishes to copy him deserves the same fate, annihilation, death.

With knowledge of the extermination of the Jews in the Occupied Eastern Territory, this defendant continued to write and publish his propaganda of death. Testifying in this trial, he vehemently denied any knowledge of mass executions of Jews. But the evidence makes it clear that he continually received current information on the progress of the "final solution". His press photographer was sent to visit the ghettos of the East in the Spring of 1943, the time of the destruction of the Warsaw Ghetto. The Jewish newspaper, "Israelitisches Wochenblatt", which Streicher received and read, carried in each issue accounts of Jewish atrocities in the East, and gave figures on the number of Jews who had been deported and killed. For example, issues appearing in the summer and fall of 1942 reported the death of 72,729 Jews in Warsaw, 17,542 in Lodz, 18,000 in Croatia, 125,000 in Rumania, 14,000 in Latvia, 85,000 in Yugoslavia, 700,000 in all of Poland. In November, 1943, Streicher quoted verbatim an article from the "Israelitisches Wochenblatt" which stated that the Jews had virtually disappeared from Europe, and commented "This is not a Jewish lie." In December, 1942, referring to an article in the "London Times" about the atrocities, aiming at extermination, Streicher said that Hitler had given warning that the second World War would lead to the destruction of Jewry. In January, 1943, he wrote and published an article which said that Hitler's prophecy was being fulfilled, that world Jewry was being extirpated, and that it was wonderful to know that Hitler was freeing the world of its Jewish tormentors. [...]

Streicher's incitement to murder and extermination at the time when Jews in the East were being killed under the most horrible conditions clearly constitutes persecution on political and racial grounds in connection with war crimes as defined by the Charter, and constitutes a crime against humanity.

Baldur von Schirach was convicted of participating in the deportation of some 60,000 Jews from Vienna after he was appointed Governor and Gauleiter (head of the Nazi party) of Vienna in 1940, conduct that earned him a 20-year sentence from the IMT:

In July, 1940, von Schirach was appointed Gauleiter of Vienna. At the same time he was appointed Reichs Governor for Vienna and Reichs Defence Commissioner originally for Military District 17, including the Gaus of Vienna, Upper Danube and Lower Danube and, after 17th

November, 1942, for the Gau of Vienna alone. As Reichs Defence Commissioner, he had control of the civilian war economy. As Reichs Governor he was head of the municipal administration of the city of Vienna, and, under the supervision of the Minister of the Interior in charge of the governmental administration of the Reich in Vienna.

Von Schirach is not charged with the commission of war crimes in Vienna, only with the commission of crimes against humanity. As has already been seen, Austria was occupied pursuant to a common plan of aggression. Its occupation is, therefore, a "crime within the jurisdiction of the Tribunal," as that term is used in Article 6 (c) of the Charter. As a result, "murder, extermination, enslavement, deportation and other inhumane acts" and "persecutions on political, racial or religious grounds" in connection with this occupation constitute a crime against humanity under that Article.

As Gauleiter of Vienna, von Schirach came under the Sauckel decree dated 6th April, 1942, making the Gauleiters Sauckel's plenipotentiaries for manpower with authority to supervise the utilisation and treatment of manpower within their Gaus. Sauckel's directives provided that the forced labourers were to be fed, sheltered and treated so as to exploit them to the highest possible degree at the lowest possible expense.

When von Schirach became Gauleiter of Vienna the deportation of the Jews had already [...] begun, and [o]nly 60,000 out of Vienna's original 190,000 Jews remained. On 2nd October, 1940, he attended a conference at Hitler's office and told Frank that he had 50,000 Jews in Vienna which the General Government would have to take over from him. On 3rd December, 1940, von Schirach received a letter from Lammers stating that after the receipt of the reports made by von Schirach, Hitler had decided to deport the 60,000 Jews still remaining in Vienna to the General Government because of the housing shortage in Vienna. The deportation of the Jews from Vienna was then begun and continued until the early fall of 1942. On 15th September, 1942, von Schirach made a speech in which he defended his action in having driven "tens of thousands upon tens of thousands of Jews into the Ghetto of the East" as "contributing to European culture."

While the Jews were being deported from Vienna reports, addressed to him in his official capacity, were received in von Schirach's office from the office of the Chief of the Security Police and SD which contained a description of the activities of Einsatzgruppen in exterminating Jews. Many of these reports were initialled by one of von Schirach's principal deputies. On 30th June, 1944, von Schirach's office also received a letter from Kaltenbrunner informing him that a shipment of 12,000 Jews was on its way to Vienna for essential war work and that all those who were incapable of work would have to be kept in readiness for "special action."

The Tribunal finds that von Schirach, while he did not originate the policy of deporting Jews from Vienna, participated in this deportation after he had become Gauleiter of Vienna. He knew that the best the Jews could hope for was a miserable existence in the Ghettoes of the East. Bulletins describing the Jewish extermination were in his office.

One year later, in 1947, the US Military Tribunal sitting at Nuremberg provided a much more robust defence of the notion of crimes against humanity in the *Altstötter* case, excerpted below. The court, operating under Control Council Law No. 10 (which, unlike the IMT Charter, did not include a 'connection' requirement), concluded that acts committed by the German State against German nationals constituted crimes against humanity, even if they were not violations of the laws and customs of war. And in contrast to the conclusions of the American diplomats before the Versailles Conference, the court found that these crimes against humanity were established in international law *before* the war, invoking in part the history of protests and interventions during the previous century and early part of the twentieth century.

The history was further written (or rewritten) by the ICTY court in its first judgment in *Tadić*. At the ICTY, crimes against humanity are defined as follows in Article 5 of the ICTYSt.:

The International Tribunal shall have the power to prosecute persons responsible for the following crimes when committed in armed conflict, whether international or internal in character, and directed against any civilian population:

(a) murder;

(b) extermination;

(c) enslavement;

(d) deportation;

(e) imprisonment;

(f) torture;

(g) rape;

(h) persecutions on political, racial and religious grounds;

(i) other inhumane acts.

Although the *Altstötter* judgment sought to situate crimes against humanity in existing international law, nearly fifty years later the ICTY concluded in *Tadić*, excerpted below, that the IMT Charter had in fact 'created' a new crime. The *Tadić* court nonetheless found that by the time of the atrocities in the former Yugoslavia in the early 1990s, individual criminal responsibility for crimes against humanity had been firmly established in customary international law and did not require a connection to an armed conflict, even though the ICTYSt. imposed such a requirement for crimes against humanity within its jurisdiction. The other modern ad hoc tribunals – such as the ICTR, the Special Court of Sierra Leone, and the Extraordinary Chambers of Cambodia – do not require the existence of an armed conflict for crimes against humanity, and neither does the ICC.

US Military Tribunal Sitting in Nuremberg, US v. **Altstötter et al.** *(Justice Trial), Judgment of 3–4 December 1947*

The defendants in this trial were all judges or German Ministry of Justice officials charged with war crimes and crimes against humanity. They were accused of using the judicial process in furtherance of the persecution and extermination of opponents of the German regime. The court convicted 10 of the defendants of war crimes and crimes against humanity and acquitted four. The court found that the convicted defendants participated in the discriminatory enforcement of laws in order to imprison, terrorize and murder Jews, Poles and resisters of the regime.

(iii) *The Construction of the Provisions of Control Council Law No. 10 Regarding War Crimes and Crimes Against Humanity*

We next approach the problem of the construction of C.C. Law 10, for whatever the scope of international common law may be, the power to enforce it in this case is defined and limited by the terms of the jurisdictional act.

The first penal provision of Control Council Law No. 10 with which we are concerned is as follows:

Article II, I. – Each of the following acts is recognised as a crime: ... (b) War crimes. Atrocities or offences against persons or property constituting violations of the laws or customs of war, including, but not limited to, murder, ill-treatment or deportation to slave labour or for any other purpose, of civilian population from occupied territory, murder or ill-treatment of prisoners of war or persons on the seas, killing of hostages, plunder of public or private property, wanton destruction of cities, towns, or villages, or devastation not justified by military necessity.

Here we observe the controlling effect of common international law as such, for the statutes by which we are governed have adopted and incorporated the rules of international law as the rules by which war crimes are to be identified. This legislative practice by which the laws and customs of war are incorporated by reference into a statute is not unknown in the United States. [...]

The scope of inquiry as to war crimes is, of course, limited by the provisions, properly construed, of the Charter and C.C. Law 10. In this particular, the two enactments are in substantial harmony. Both indicate by inclusion and exclusion the intent that the term "war crimes" shall be employed to cover acts in violation of the laws and customs of war directed against non-Germans, and shall not include atrocities committed by Germans against their own nationals. It will be observed that Article VI of the Charter enumerates as war crimes acts against prisoners of war, persons on the seas, hostages, wanton destruction of cities and the like, devastation not justified by military necessity, plunder of public or private property (obviously not property of Germany or Germans), and "ill-treatment or deportation to slave labour, or for any other purpose, of civilian population *of, or in,* occupied territory." C.C. Law 10, *supra,* employs similar language. It reads: "ill-treatment or deportation to slave labour or for any other purpose *of civilian population from occupied territory.*"

This legislative intent becomes more manifest when we consider the provisions of the Charter and of C.C. Law 10 which deal with crimes against humanity. Article VI of the Charter defines crimes against humanity as follows: "...murder, extermination, enslavement, deportation and other inhumane acts committed against any civilian population, before or during the war; or persecutions on political, racial, or religious grounds in execution of or in connection with any crime within the jurisdiction of the Tribunal, whether or not in violation of the domestic law of the country where perpetrated."

C.C. Law 10 defines as criminal: "...Atrocities and offences, including but not limited to murder, extermination, enslavement, deportation, imprisonment, torture, rape, or other inhumane acts committed against any civilian population, or persecutions on political, racial or religious grounds whether or not in violation of the domestic laws of the country where perpetrated."

Obviously, these sections are not surplusage. They supplement the preceding sections on war crimes and include within their prohibition not only war crimes, but also acts not included within the preceding definition of war crimes. In place of atrocities committed against civilians of or in or from occupied territory, these sections prohibit atrocities "against any civilian population." Again, persecutions on racial, religious, or political grounds are within our jurisdiction "whether or not in violation of the domestic laws of the country where perpetrated." We have already demonstrated that C.C. Law 10 is specifically directed to the punishment of German criminals. It is, therefore, clear that the intent of the statute on crimes against humanity is to punish for persecutions and the like, whether in accord with or in violation of the domestic laws of the country where perpetrated, to wit: Germany. The intent was to provide that compliance with German law should be no defence. Article III of C.C. Law 10 clearly demonstrates that acts by Germans against German nationals may constitute crimes against humanity within the jurisdiction of this Tribunal to punish. That Article provides that each occupying authority within its zone of occupation shall have the right to cause persons suspected of having committed a crime to be arrested and...(d) shall have the right to cause all persons so arrested...to be brought to trial.... Such Tribunal may, in case of crimes committed by persons of German citizenship or nationality against other persons of German citizenship or nationality, or stateless persons, be a German court, if authorised by the occupying authorities. [...]

Our jurisdiction to try persons charged with crimes against humanity is limited in scope, both by definition and illustration, as appears from C.C. Law 10. It is not the isolated crime by a private German individual which is condemned, nor is it the isolated crime perpetrated by the German Reich through its officers against a private individual. It is significant that the enactment employs the words "against any civilian population" instead of "against any civilian individual." The provision is directed against offences and inhumane acts and persecutions on political, racial, or religious grounds systematically organised and conducted by or with the approval of government.

The opinion of the first International Military Tribunal in the case against Goering, *et al.*, lends support to our conclusion. That opinion recognised the distinction between war crimes and crimes against humanity, and said:

> "...in so far as the inhumane acts charged in the indictment and committed after the beginning of the war did not constitute war crimes, they were all committed in execution of, or in connection with, aggressive war and, therefore, constituted crimes against humanity." [...]

The evidence to be later reviewed established that certain inhumane acts charged in Count 3 of the indictment were committed in execution of, and in connection with, aggressive war and were, therefore, crimes against humanity even under the provisions of the I.M.T. Charter, but it must be noted that C.C. Law 10 differs materially from the Charter. The latter defines crimes against humanity as inhumane acts, etc., committed "...in execution of, or in connection with, any crime within the jurisdiction of the Tribunal...," whereas in C.C. Law 10 the words last quoted are deliberately omitted from the definition.

(iv) *The Ex Post Facto Principle Regarded as Constituting No Legal or Moral Barrier to the Present Trial*

The defendants claim protection under the principle *nullum crimen sine lege,* though they withheld from others the benefit of that rule during the Hitler regime. Obviously the principle in question constitutes no limitation upon the power or right of the Tribunal to punish acts which can properly be held to have been violations of international law when committed. By way of illustration, we observe that C.C. Law 10, Article II, 1 *(b)*, "War Crimes," has by reference incorporated the rules by which war crimes are to be identified. In all such cases it remains only for the Tribunal, after the manner of the common law, to determine the content of these rules under the impact of changing conditions. Whatever view may be held as to the nature and source of our authority under C.C. Law 10 and under common international law, the *ex post facto* rule, properly understood, constitutes no legal nor moral barrier to the prosecution in this case.

Under written constitutions the *ex post facto* rule condemns statutes which define as criminal acts committed before the law was passed, but the *ex post facto* rule cannot apply in the international field as it does under constitutional mandate in the domestic field. Even in the domestic field the prohibition of the rule does not apply to the decisions of common law courts, although the question at issue be novel. International law is not the product of statute for the simple reason that there is as yet no world authority empowered to enact statutes of universal application. International law is the product of multipartite treaties, conventions, judicial decisions and customs which have received international acceptance or acquiescence. It would be sheer absurdity to suggest that the *ex post facto* rule, as known to constitutional States, could be applied to a treaty, a custom, or a common law decision of an international tribunal, or to the international acquiescence which follows the event. To have attempted to apply the *ex post facto* principle to judicial decisions of common international law would have been to strangle that law at birth. As applied in the field of international law, the principle *nullum crimen sine lege* received its true interpretation in the opinion of the I.M.T. in the case *versus* Goering, *et al*. The question arose with reference to crimes against the peace, but the opinion expressed is equally applicable to war crimes and crimes against humanity. The Tribunal said:

"In the first place, it is to be observed that the maxim *nullum crimen sine lege* is not a limitation of sovereignty, but is in general a principle of justice. To assert that it is unjust to punish those who in defiance of treaties and assurances have attacked neighbouring States without warning is obviously untrue, for in such circumstances the attacker must know that he is doing wrong, and so far from it being unjust to punish him, it would be unjust if his wrong were allowed to go unpunished."

To the same effect we quote the distinguished statesman and international authority, Henry L. Stimson:

"A mistaken appeal to this principle has been the cause of much confusion about the Nuremberg trial.

It is argued that parts of the Tribunal's Charter, written in 1945, make crimes out of what before were activities beyond the scope of national and international law. Were this an exact statement of the situation we might well be concerned, but it is not. It rests on a misconception of the whole nature of the law of nations.

International law is not a body of authoritative codes or statutes; it is the gradual expression, case by case, of the moral judgments of the civilised world. As such, it corresponds precisely to the common law of Anglo-American tradition. We can understand the law of Nuremberg only if we see it for what it is – a great new case in the book of international law, and not a formal enforcement of codified statutes. A look at the charges will show what I mean.

It was the Nazi confidence that we would never chase and catch them, and not a misunderstanding of our opinion of them, that led them to commit their crimes. Our offence was thus that of the man who passed by on the other side. That we have finally recognised our negligence and named the criminals for what they are is a piece of righteousness too long delayed by fear." ('The Nuremburg Trial,' Landmark and Law; *Foreign Affairs,* January, 1947.) [. . .]

We quote with approval the words of Sir David Maxwell Fyfe:

"With regard to 'crimes against humanity,' this at any rate is clear: the Nazis, when they persecuted and murdered countless Jews and political opponents in Germany, knew that what they were doing was wrong and that their actions were crimes which had been condemned by the criminal law of every civilised State. When these crimes were mixed with the preparation for aggressive war and later with the commission of war crimes in occupied territories, it cannot be a matter of complaint that a procedure is established for their punishment." (Fyfe, Foreword to *The Nuremberg Trial,* by R. W. Cooper.)

Concerning the mooted *ex post facto* issue, Professor Wechsler of Columbia University writes:

"These are, indeed, the issues that are currently mooted: But there are elements in the debate that should lead us to be suspicious of the issues as they are drawn in these terms. For, most of those who mount the attack on one or another of these contentions hasten to assure us that their plea is not one of immunity for the defendants; they argue only that they should have been disposed of politically, that is, dispatched out of hand. This is a curious position indeed. A punitive enterprise launched on the basis of general rules, administered in an adversary proceeding under a separation of prosecutive and adjudicative powers, is, in the name of law and justice, asserted to be less desirable than an *ex parte* execution list or a drumhead court martial constituted in the immediate aftermath of war. I state my view reservedly when I say that history will accept no conception of law, politics or justice that supports a submission in these terms."

Again, he says:

"There is, indeed, too large a disposition among the defenders of Nuremberg to look for stray tags of international pronouncements and reason therefrom that the law of Nuremberg was previously fully laid down. If the Kellogg-Briand Pact or a general conception of international obligation sufficed to authorise England, and would have authorised us, to declare war on Germany in defence of Poland – and in this enterprise to kill countless thousands of German soldiers and civilians – can it be possible that it failed to authorise punitive action against individual Germans judicially determined to be responsible for the Polish attack? To be sure, we would demand a more explicit authorisation for punishment in domestic law, for we have adopted for the protection of individuals a prophylactic principle absolutely forbidding retroactivity that we can afford to carry to that extreme. International society, being less stable, can afford less luxury. We admit that in other respects. Why should we deny it here?" (Wechsler, "Issues of Nuremberg Trial" *Political Science Quarterly*, Vol. LXII, No.1, March, 1947, pages 23–25.)

Many of the laws of the Weimar era which were enacted for the protection of human rights have never been repealed. Many acts constituting war crimes or crimes against humanity as defined in C.C. Law 10 were committed or permitted in direct violation also of the provisions of the German criminal law. It is true that this Tribunal can try no defendant merely because of a violation of the German penal code, but it is equally true that the rule against retrospective legislation, as a rule of justice and fair play, should be no defence if the act which he committed in violation of C.C. Law 10 was also known to him to be a punishable crime under his own domestic law.

As a principle of justice and fair play, the rule in question will be given full effect. As applied in the field of international law that principle requires proof before conviction that the accused knew or should have known that in matters of international concern he was guilty of participation in a nationally organised system of injustice and persecution shocking to the moral sense of mankind, and that he knew or should have known that he would be subject to punishment if caught.

Whether it be considered codification or substantive legislation, no person who knowingly committed the acts made punishable by C.C. Law 10 can assert that he did not know that he would be brought to account for his acts. Notice of intent to punish was repeatedly given by the only means available in international affairs, namely, the solemn warning of the governments of the States at war with Germany. Not only were the defendants warned of swift retribution by the express declaration of the Allies at Moscow of 30th October, 1943. Long prior to the Second World War the principle of personal responsibility had been recognised. [. . .]

(v) *The Development of the Concept of Crimes Against Humanity as Violations of International Law*

C.C. Law 10 is not limited to the punishment of persons guilty of violating the laws and customs of war in the narrow sense; furthermore, it can no longer be said that violations of the laws and customs of war are the only offences recognised by common international law. The force of circumstance, the grim fact of worldwide interdependence, and the moral pressure of public opinion have resulted in international recognition that certain crimes against humanity committed by Nazi authority against German nationals constituted violations not alone of statute but also of common international law. We quote:

"If a State is unhampered in its activities that affect the interests of any other, it is due to the circumstance that the practice of nations has not established that the welfare of the international society is adversely affected thereby. Hence, that society has not been incited or aroused to endeavour to impose restraints; and by its law none are imposed. The Covenant of the League of Nations takes exact cognisance of the situation in its reference to disputes 'which arise out of a matter which by international law is solely within the domestic jurisdiction' of a party thereto. It is that law which as a product of the acquiescence of States permits the particular activity of the individual State to be deemed a domestic one.

"In as much as changing estimates are to be anticipated, and as the evolution of thought in this regard appears to be constant and is perhaps now more obvious than at any time since the United States came into being, the circumstance that at any given period the solution of a particular question is by international law deemed to be solely within the control or jurisdiction of one State gives frail assurance that it will always be so regarded." (Hyde, *International Law* (2nd rev. ed.), Vol. I, pages 7, 8.)

"The family of nations is not unconcerned with the life and experience of the private individual in his relationships with the State of which he is a national. Evidence of concern has become increasingly abundant since World War I, and is reflected in treaties through which that conflict was brought to a close, particularly in provisions designed to safeguard the racial, linguistic and religious minorities inhabiting the territories of certain States, and in the terms of Part XIII of the Treaty of Versailles, of 28th June, 1919, in respect to Labour, as well as in Article XXIII of that treaty embraced in the Covenant of the League of Nations." (Hyde, *International Law* (2nd rev. ed.), Vol. I, page 38.)

"The nature and extent of the latitude accorded a State in the treatment of its own nationals has been observed elsewhere. It has been seen that certain forms or degrees of harsh treatment of such individuals may be deemed to attain an international significance because of their direct and adverse effect upon the rights and interests of the outside world. For that reason it would be unscientific to declare at this day that tyrannical conduct, or massacres, or religious persecutions are wholly unrelated to the foreign relations of the territorial sovereign which is guilty of them. If it can be shown that such acts were immediately and necessarily injurious to the nationals of a particular foreign State, grounds for interference by it may be acknowledged. Again, the society of nations, acting collectively, may not unreasonably maintain that a State yielding to such excesses renders itself unfit to perform its international obligations, especially in so far as they pertain to the protection of foreign life and property within its domain. The propriety of interference obviously demands in every case a convincing showing that there is in fact a causal connection between the harsh treatment complained of, and the outside State that essays to thwart it." (Hyde, *International Law* (2nd rev. ed.), Vol. I, pages 249–250 (footnote deleted).)

"The international concern over the commission of crimes against humanity has been greatly intensified in recent years. The fact of such concern is not a recent phenomenon, however. England, France, and Russia intervened to end the atrocities in the Greco-Turkish warfare in 1827." (Oppenheim, *International Law*, Vol. I (3rd ed.) (1920), page 229.)

"President Van Buren, through his Secretary of State, intervened with the Sultan of Turkey in 1840 on behalf of the persecuted Jews of Damascus and Rhodes." *(State Department Publication No.9, pages 153–154.)*

"The French intervened and by force undertook to check religious atrocities in Lebanon in 1861." (Bentwich, "The League of Nations and Racial Persecution in Germany", Vol. 19, *Problems of Peace and War,* page 75, (1934).)

"Various nations directed protests to the governments of Russia and Roumania with respect to pogroms and atrocities against Jews. Similar protests were made to the government of Turkey on behalf of the persecuted Christian minorities. In 1872 the United States, Germany, and five other powers protested to Roumania; and, in 1915, the German government joined in a remonstrance to Turkey on account of similar persecutions." (Bentwich, *op. cit., supra.*)

In 1902 the American Secretary of State, John Hay, addressed to Roumania a remonstrance "in the name of humanity" against Jewish persecutions, saying: "This government cannot be a tacit party to such international wrongs."

Again, in connection with the Kishenef and other massacres in Russia in 1903, President Theodore Roosevelt stated: "Nevertheless, there are occasional crimes committed on a vast scale and of such peculiar horror as to make us doubt whether it is not our manifest duty to endeavour at least to show our disapproval of the deed and our sympathy with those who have suffered by it. The case must be extreme in which such a course is justifiable.... The cases in which we could interfere by force of arms, as we interfered to put a stop to the intolerable conditions in Cuba, are necessarily very few." (President's Message to Congress, 1904.)

Concerning the American intervention in Cuba in 1898, President McKinley stated: "First. In the cause of humanity and to put an end to the barbarities, bloodshed, starvation, and horrible miseries now existing there, and which the parties to the conflict are either unable or unwilling to stop or mitigate. It is no answer to say this is all in another country, belonging to another nation, and therefore none of our business. It is specially our duty, for it is right at our door." (President's Special Message of 11th April, 1898. Hyde, *International Law*, Vol. 1 (2nd ed.), page 259 (1945).)

The same principle was recognised as early as 1878 by a learned German professor of law, who wrote: "States are allowed to interfere in the name of international law if 'humanity rights' are violated to the detriment of any single race." (J. K. Bluntschel, Professor of Law, Heidelberg University, in *Das Moderne Volkerrecht der Civilisierten Staaten* (3rd ed.), page 270 (1878).)

Finally, we quote the words of Sir Hartley Shawcross, the British Chief Prosecutor at the trial of Goering, *et al.*: "The right of humanitarian intervention on behalf of the rights of man trampled upon by a State in a manner shocking the sense of mankind has long been considered to form part of the law of nations. Here too, the Charter merely develops a pre-existing principle." (*Transcript,* page 813.)

We hold that crimes against humanity as defined in C.C. Law 10 must be strictly construed to exclude isolated cases of atrocities or persecutions whether committed by private individuals or by a governmental authority. As we construe it, that section provides for the punishment of crimes committed against German nationals only where there is proof of conscious participation in systematic governmentally organised or approved procedures, amounting to atrocities and offences of that kind specified in the act and committed against populations or amounting to persecutions on political, racial, or religious grounds.

Thus the statute is limited by the construction of the type of criminal activity which prior to 1939 was and still is a matter of international concern. Whether or not such atrocities constituted technical violations of laws and customs of war, they were acts of such scope and malevolence, and they so clearly imperiled the peace of the world that they must be deemed to have become violations of international law. This principle was recognised although it was misapplied by the Third Reich. Hitler expressly justified his early acts of aggression against Czechoslovakia on the ground that the alleged persecution of the racial Germans by the government of that country was a matter of international concern warranting intervention by Germany. Organised Czechoslovakian persecution of racial Germans in Sudetenland was a fiction supported by "framed" incidents, but the principle invoked by Hitler was one which we have recognised, namely that governmentally organised racial persecutions are violations of international law.

As the prime illustration of a crime against humanity under C.C. Law 10, which by reason of its magnitude and its international repercussions has been recognised as a violation of common international law, we cite "genocide" which will receive our full consideration. A resolution recently adopted by the General Assembly of the United Nations [...]

The General Assembly is not an international legislature, but it is the most authoritative organ in existence for the interpretation of world opinion. Its recognition of genocide as an international crime is persuasive evidence of the fact.

We approve and adopt its conclusions. Whether the crime against humanity is the product of statute or of common international law, or, as we believe, of both, we find no injustice to persons tried for such crimes. They are chargeable with knowledge that such acts were wrong and were punishable when committed.

The *Altstötter* court was plainly aware of some of the criticism of the IMT that it had applied new law in violation of the *ex post facto* principle. While the IMT had provided a defence against this criticism with respect to crimes against peace, the *Altstötter* court extended the defence to crimes against humanity, and in doing so sought to provide an account of the operation of customary international law. It is worth considering whether the various arguments offered by the court regarding the status of the law of crimes against humanity are equally persuasive.

ICTY, Prosecutor *v.* Duško Tadić, *Trial Chamber, Judgment of 7 May 1997*

As mentioned above, the trial of Duško Tadić was the first at the ICTY and it resolved a number of fundamental questions. Tadić was a Bosnian Serb in Prijedor who was charged with grave breaches, war crimes and crimes against humanity for crimes committed against Bosnian Muslims and Croats in Prijedor and in the Omarska prison camp including murder, cruel treatment and inhumane acts. Tadić was convicted and sentenced to 20 years' imprisonment.

1. The Customary Status in International Humanitarian Law of the Prohibition Against Crimes Against Humanity

618. The Appeals Chamber Decision [on jurisdiction] discusses Articles 2 and 3 of the Statute [of the ICTY] at some length. In contrast, the discussion of Article 5 [regarding crimes against humanity] is confined to the requirement of a link to an armed conflict as provided in the Statute and thus now requires further discussion in considerable detail. The notion of crimes against humanity as an independent juridical concept, and the imputation of individual criminal responsibility for their commission, was first recognized in Article 6(c) of the Nürnberg Charter (Annex to the Agreement for the Prosecution and Punishment of Major War Criminals of the European Axis (London Agreement) ("Nürnberg Charter")), which granted the International Military Tribunal for the Trial of the Major War Criminals ("Nürnberg Tribunal") jurisdiction over this crime. The term "crimes against humanity", although not previously codified, had been used in a non-technical sense as far back as 1915 and in subsequent statements concerning the First World War and was hinted at in the preamble to the 1907 Hague

Convention in the so-called "Martens Clause". Thus when crimes against humanity were included in the Nürnberg Charter, although it was the first technical use of the term, it was not considered a novel concept. Nevertheless a new category of crime was created.

619. The decision to include crimes against humanity in the Nürnberg Charter and thus grant the Nürnberg Tribunal jurisdiction over this crime resulted from the Allies' decision not to limit their retributive powers to those who committed war crimes in the traditional sense but to include those who committed other serious crimes that fall outside the ambit of traditional war crimes, such as crimes where the victim is stateless, has the same nationality as the perpetrator, or that of a state allied with that of the perpetrator. The origins of this decision can be found in assertions made by individual governments, the London International Assembly and the United Nations War Crimes Commission.

620. Unlike the crime of aggression and war crimes, the Trial of the Major War Criminals before the International Military Tribunal ("Nürnberg Judgment") does not delve into the legality of the inclusion of crimes against humanity in the Nürnberg Charter and the pre-existence of the prohibition, noting only that "from the beginning of the War in 1939 War Crimes were committed on a vast scale, which were also Crimes against Humanity". Thus the inclusion of crimes against humanity in the Nürnberg Charter was justified by their relation to war crimes, the gaps in the traditional definition of which it was designed to fill, the customary nature of which is described. Additionally, the Nürnberg Judgment noted that, in regard to the law to be applied, the Nürnberg Charter was decisive and binding on the Nürnberg Tribunal and that it "is the expression of international law existing at the time of its creation; and to that extent is itself a contribution to international law". On the basis of the Nürnberg Charter the prohibition against crimes against humanity, and the attribution of individual criminal responsibility for their commission, was also contained in the Charter of the International Military Tribunal for the Far East of 19 January 1946 ("Tokyo Charter") and in Law No. 10 of the Control Council for Germany ("Control Council Law No. 10"), which were utilised for additional prosecutions for atrocities committed during the Second World War.

621. The prohibition of crimes against humanity was subsequently affirmed by the General Assembly in its resolution entitled Affirmation of the Principles of International Law recognized by the Charter of the Nürenberg Tribunal and thereafter confirmed in the Principles of International Law Recognized in the Charter of the Nürenberg Tribunal and in the Judgement of the Tribunal ("Nürenberg Principles"), adopted by the International Law Commission in 1950 and submitted to the General Assembly, Principle VI.c of which provides that a crime against humanity is punishable as a crime under international law. The attribution of individual criminal responsibility for the commission of crimes against humanity, as it was applied by the Nürnberg Tribunal, was also approved in Principle I of the Nürenberg Principles, which provides that "[a] person who commits an act which constitutes a crime under international law is responsible therefore and liable to punishment".

622. The customary status of the Nürnberg Charter, and thus the attribution of individual criminal responsibility for the commission of crimes against humanity, was expressly noted by the Secretary-General. Additional codifications of international law have also confirmed the customary law status of the prohibition of crimes against humanity, as well as two of its most egregious manifestations: genocide and apartheid.

623. Thus, since the Nürnberg Charter, the customary status of the prohibition against crimes against humanity and the attribution of individual criminal responsibility for their commission have not been seriously questioned. It would seem that this finding is implicit in *the Appeals Chamber Decision* which found that "[i]t is by now a settled rule of customary international law that crimes against humanity do not require a connection to international armed conflict". If customary international law is determinative of what type of conflict is required in order to

constitute a crime against humanity, the prohibition against crimes against humanity is necessarily part of customary international law. As such, the commission of crimes against humanity
violates customary international law, of which Article 5 of the Statute is, for the most part,
reflective. As stated by the Appeals Chamber: "[T]here is no question...that the definition of
crimes against humanity adopted by the Security Council in Article 5 comports with the principle of *nullum crimen sine lege*."

COMMENTARY

Unlike the *Altstötter* court, the *Tadić* court did not need to find that crimes against humanity formed a part of customary international law *before* World War II. Nonetheless, it is
striking how little the court has to rely upon, aside from the World War II cases themselves,
to establish the customary international law status of crimes against humanity.

(B) THE PERPETRATORS AND THE VICTIMS

Ordinarily, individuals who commit crimes against humanity will be state actors or members of an organized rebel or militia group. The Elements of Crimes of the ICC, adopted
by the Assembly of States Parties pursuant to Article 9 of the ICCSt., require, to prove
crimes against humanity, 'a State or organizational policy' to attack a civilian population,
meaning that 'the State or organization actively promote[d] or encourage[d] such an attack
against a civilian population'. While this requirement exceeds what is required by customary international law, as is discussed in the next section of this chapter, it nonetheless
captures the organizational component that is generally present when these crimes are
committed. The very notion of a 'widespread or systematic attack' on a civilian population
ordinarily requires coordination, or at least tacit acceptance or acquiescence, by a state or
organized group.

But the widespread or systematic attack on a civilian population provides only the *context* for a crime against humanity; there must also be a specific act by an individual perpetrator, and the nature of the relationship of that individual to the state or organization
may be a separate question. While in many cases individual perpetrators will themselves
be within the state or organizational entity promoting the attack on civilians, or in another
closely aligned group or organization (such as a paramilitary group), that is not necessarily
the case. All that is required is that the perpetrator commit an act that is *part of* the widespread or systematic attack, with knowledge of the link between his act and the broader
attack. When an individual's actions can be considered part of a broader attack may sometimes be a difficult question, and is touched on in the *Papon* judgment below.

With regard to the victims of crimes against humanity, the drafters of the London
Charter clearly had in mind that some of the worst acts perpetrated, in particular by
German officials, had not been committed against foreign nationals, but rather against
Germany's own citizens on racial, political or other discriminatory bases. They could
therefore not be considered criminal under the then-applicable laws or customs of war.
Crimes against humanity are therefore linked more to civilians than to combatants (*hors
de combat* or not). Accordingly, victims of crimes against humanity will ordinarily be
civilians, whether or not of the same nationality as the perpetrator, though one judgment of the US Military Tribunal found in 1948, in the prosecution of *Greifelt et al.*, that
euthanasia as a crime against humanity could *not* be committed by a state against its own
nationals.

US Military Tribunal Sitting in Nuremberg, US v. Greifelt et al. (RuSHA *Trial*), Judgment of 10 March 1948

Richard Hildebrandt was Higher SS and Police Leader at Danzig-West Prussia from October 1939 to February 1943, and simultaneously he was leader of the Administration District Danzig-West Prussia of the Allgemeine SS and deputy of the RKFDV [Reich Commissioner for the Strengthening of Germanism]. From 20 April 1943 to the end of the war, he was chief of RuSHA [the SS Race and Resettlement Main Office]. From 1939 to 1945, while serving in these capacities, he was deeply implicated in many measures put into force in the furtherance of the Germanization program, as has heretofore been set forth in detail in this judgment. [. . .]

Hildebrandt, as the sole defendant, is charged with special responsibility for and participation in the extermination of thousands of German nationals pursuant to the so-called "Euthanasia program." It is not contended that this program, insofar as Hildebrandt might have been connected with it, was extended to foreign nationals. It is urged by the prosecution, however, that notwithstanding this fact, the extermination of German nationals under such a program constitutes a crime against humanity; and in support of this argument the prosecution cites the judgment of the International Military Tribunal as well as the judgment in the case of the United States of America vs. Brandt, Case No. 1. Neither decision substantiated the contention of the prosecution. For instance, in holding defendants guilty in the Brandt judgment, the Tribunal expressly pointed out that the defendants, in participating in this program, were responsible for exterminating foreign nationals. The Tribunal expressly stated:

"Whether or not a state may validly enact legislation which imposes euthanasia upon certain classes of its citizens is likewise a question which does not enter into the issues. Assuming that it may do so, the Family of Nations is not obliged to give recognition to such legislation when it manifestly gives legality to plain murder and torture of defenseless and powerless human beings of other nations.

The evidence is conclusive that persons were included in the program who were non-German nationals. The dereliction of the defendant Brandt contributed to their extermination. That is enough to require this Tribunal to find that he is criminally responsible in the program."

It is our view that euthanasia, when carried out under state legislation against citizens of the state only, does not constitute a crime against humanity. Accordingly the defendant Hildebrandt is found not to be criminally responsible with regard to this specification of the indictment.

Although this chilling judgment contains no reasoning to support its conclusion, it appears to reflect lingering notions of national sovereignty. Since one theme in the development of the law of crimes against humanity has been to displace sovereignty concerns when such crimes have been perpetrated, and the *Altstötter* court had already found that Control Council Law No. 10 generally authorized prosecutions of Germans for crimes against humanity committed against other Germans, this decision has not been followed in subsequent judgments.

But what if a certain group of civilians is targeted for a particular reason, such as its perceived loyalty to an opponent in a conflict? Does that still amount to an attack on a *civilian* population? This was the question that an ICTY Trial Chamber confronted in the *Limaj* case. Moreover, is the victim class limited to civilians only, or could it include military targets, whether or not *hors de combat*? In the context of the crime of persecutions as a crime against humanity, the highest court in France seemed to suggest, in the *Barbie* case in 1985, that as a matter of customary international law, members of a military could also be the *intended* victims of crimes against humanity. But in the *Martić* case in 2008, the Appeals Chamber of the ICTY appears to have narrowed this possibility to include only *incidental* victims, both as a matter of customary international law and the ICTYSt.

France, Papon *case, Cour de cassation, Judgment of 23 January 1997*

Maurice Papon was charged with crimes against humanity for his role, as a member of the Vichy government, in deporting over 1,500 Jews to German concentration camps during World War II. Papon argued that he could not be charged with crimes against humanity because there was no evidence that he subscribed to the racial and hegemonic ideology of the Nazi regime which perpetrated the crimes that Papon was accused of being complicit in. Papon was convicted and sentenced to 10 years' imprisonment.

[Papon argued that] whereas we are dealing with crimes against humanity attributable principally to an institution or organization, individual complicity assumes the adherence of the accomplice (*complice*) to the hegemonic and racial ideology of the criminal institution; that it results from the findings of the appealed judgment that the orders of arrest, internment and deportation aimed at the extermination of victims have been issued by two Nazi organizations condemned by the Nuremberg tribunal; that the defendant has never been part of these organizations since the "facts" for which he has been accused are exclusively related to his functions as secretary general of the prefecture of the Gironde under the Vichy "Government" which has never had an hegemonic ideology striving for racial extermination; from which follows that the appealed judgment could not find the crime of complicity in crimes against humanity; [...]

[The court found that] the arrests and sequestrations, as well as the massive transfers of people aiming their deportation to Auschwitz, have had as victims persons chosen because of their membership in the "Jewish race" or in the Israelite religion and that these measures have been decided by the services of SIPO-SD, [the] organization of the national-socialist government declared criminal by judgment of the international military tribunal of Nuremberg of October 1st 1946; that the active help [...] provided by Maurice Y [...], through his personal acts, for the execution of criminal deeds committed by the abovementioned services, fall within the framework of a concerted plan for the account of Nazi Germany, Axis country practicing a policy of hegemonic ideology; [...]

In view of these arguments, which define, without insufficiency or contradiction, acts of complicity, in the meaning of former Article 60 and new Article 121–7 of the French Criminal Code, which have been committed to prepare or carry out arbitrary arrests and sequestrations (illegal detentions), as well as murders or attempt to murder, [...] the appealed decision does not reflect the alleged flaws.

[...] therefore, the arguments, particularly those invoking the last paragraph of article 6 of the statute of the international military tribunal, which does not require the accomplice of a crime against humanity to himself adhere to the hegemonic political ideology of the principals, nor to belong to one of the organizations declared criminal in Nuremberg, have to [be] rejected; [...]

ICTY, Prosecutor v. Limaj et al., *Trial Chamber, Judgment of 30 November 2005*

The three defendants in this case were charged with crimes against humanity and war crimes. All three defendants were members of the Kosovo Liberation Army and were accused of committing crimes against Albanian civilians suspected of collaborating with Serb authorities and Serbian civilians. Two of the defendants were acquitted while one was convicted only of war crimes and sentenced to 13 years' imprisonment. This excerpt is from the Trial Judgment. The acquittals for the crimes against humanity charges were not appealed by the Prosecution.

203. In addition to the abduction of Serbian civilians in areas of pitched battle, a number of civilians were abducted after the introduction of checkpoints in areas of strategic importance to the KLA. By May 1998 both the Serbian forces and the KLA had set up checkpoints on main roads. Kosovo Albanian civilians were apprehended at KLA checkpoints and detained for questioning or abducted from their homes in the night. Individuals abducted and detained were often blindfolded or placed in the boots of cars and driven either to Llapushnik/Lapusnik directly, or to other premises where they were interrogated before being conveyed to Llapushnik/Lapusnik, or to another place of detention. Those detained were subjected to interrogation; at times with physical abuse, many were accused of working as spies for the Serbian regime or accused of having knowledge of perceived collaborators operating in Kosovo. Detentions occurred not only at Llapushnik/Lapusnik. The barracks at Jabllanice/Jablanica also served as a makeshift prison for those accused of collaboration with Serbian forces. The barracks held those perceived to be collaborators and spies. The International Committee of the Red Cross was denied access to a number of KLA detainees, raising questions about detainees' safety.

204. The cumulative effect of this evidence demonstrates the use of insurgent tactics by the KLA in an attempt to gain the upper hand against the Serbian forces in Kosovo, which possessed superior military might and were able to deploy greater resources during the conflict. The evidence demonstrates the existence of a "course of conduct" that indicates that there was a military "attack" in the territory of Kosovo in the period relevant to the Indictment.

205. The Prosecution contends that the evidence of the duration and scope of the KLA attack demonstrates that the attack was "directed against" a civilian population. The Prosecution further contends that the civilian population was the "primary object of attack."

206. There appears to have been a number of abductions of Serbian civilians. As far as the evidence discloses, in most cases these occurred when an individual in a community or village was suspected of specific conduct adverse to KLA or Kosovo Albanian interests, or, in some instances, were undertaken by independent elements of the KLA not acting pursuant to a general KLA policy or direction. [. . .]

208. The Chamber accepts that particular Kosovo Albanians were abducted and detained because of their perceived associations with Serbian authorities. Kosovo Albanians suspected of collaboration were subjected to discrimination, harassment and abuse. It was those Kosovo Albanians with perceived links with the Serbian military or police regime who were singled out for especially severe treatment in detention. Those accused of collaboration were referred to as "spies" or as "traitors to their people." Both L06 and L10 [witnesses whose identities were protected] were asked, when being interrogated at Llapushnik/Lapusnik, about perceived spies and those alleged to have collaborated with Serbs in their village.

209. In total, the International Committee of the Red Cross documented the abduction of 138 Serbs, apparently civilians or those placed hors de combat, whom it was believed were in KLA custody. Human Rights Watch estimated that, from late February 1998 to late September 1998, between 100 and 140 Kosovo Albanians, Serbs and Roma, apparently civilians or those placed hors de combat, were abducted by KLA forces. [. . .]

210. History confirms, regrettably, that wartime conduct will often adversely affect civilians. Nevertheless, the Chamber finds that, even if it be accepted that those civilians of whatever ethnicity believed to have been abducted by the KLA in and around the relevant period were in truth so abducted, then, nevertheless, in the context of the population of Kosovo as a whole the abductions were relatively few in number and could not be said to amount to a "widespread" occurrence for the purposes of Article 5 of the Statute.

211. The evidence discloses that there was at most a "systematic" attempt by the KLA to target Kosovo Albanian individuals believed to be, or suspected of, collaborating with the Serbian authorities, but no attempt to target a civilian population as such.

212. The existence of a plan or policy can be indicative of the systematic character of offences charged as crimes against humanity. The existence of a "policy" to conduct an attack against a civilian population is most easily determined or inferred when a State's conduct is in question; but absence of a policy does not mean that a widespread or systematic attack against a civilian population has not occurred. Although not a legal element of Article 5, evidence of a policy or plan is an important indication that the acts in question are not merely the workings of individuals acting pursuant to haphazard or individual design, but instead have a level of organisational coherence and support of a magnitude sufficient to elevate them into the realm of crimes against humanity. It stands to reason that an attack against a civilian population will most often evince the presence of policy when the acts in question are performed against the backdrop of significant State action and where formal channels of command can be discerned.

213. Special issues arise, however, in considering whether a sub-state unit or armed opposition group, whether insurrectionist or transboundary in nature, evinces a policy to direct an attack. [...]

215. From the evidence before the Chamber, the KLA evinced no policy to target civilians per se. Peter Bouckaert stated that he never saw anything issued by the KLA which constituted an order to its members to target innocent civilians or to loot or destroy Serbian property. Susanne Ringgaard Pedersen stated that she could not discern a broad policy to target civilians. The Chamber accepts Jakup Krasniqi's statement that it was not part of KLA political or military policy to kidnap, torture or murder innocent civilians. The evidence does not establish, or even indicate, a general policy of targeting civilians as such, whether Serbian or Kosovo Albanian.

216. The Chamber accepts that there was evidence of a KLA policy to target perceived Kosovo Albanian collaborators who were believed to be or suspected of associating with Serbian authorities and interests. As early as 1997, the KLA warned the "stooges of the Serb regime" not to undermine the "liberation war." KLA communiqué number 43, published on 4 March 1998, contains the phrase "death to enemies and traitors." KLA communiqué number 53 of 19 September 1998 refers to "punitive measures of various kinds" undertaken against "collaborationist elements that continue to serve the occupying power." The Chamber accepts that communiqués were intended partly for propaganda purposes. However, there was a KLA policy, linked to its military objectives, to target those individuals thought to be collaborating with the Serbian forces. Nevertheless, in the guise of giving effect to this policy, a number of Kosovo Albanian civilians may have been abducted for other reasons, such as personal revenge of individual KLA members and other motives. The KLA did not have the resources or the command structure to adequately control the implementation of this policy by its forces at the time relevant to the Indictment, and the Chamber accepts that individual cases of abduction, for reasons not within the collaborator policy, were carried out by rogue elements of the KLA.

217. However, the effect of the evidence is to indicate that the KLA had a policy of targeting only those who were believed to have, or suspected of having, links with the Serbian regime. Evidence before the Chamber indicates there was a limited level of co-ordination and

organisation to such targeted attacks. The existence of the Llapushnik/Lapusnik prison camp itself demonstrates the co-ordinated and organised nature of the targeting of suspected collaborators. However, the Chamber concludes that, whether these perceived or suspected collaborators were correctly identified or not, they were targeted as individuals rather than as members of a larger targeted population. The Chamber accepts, however, that there were also instances of abduction undertaken by local elements of the KLA, who were acting independently of any central KLA control because, at the relevant time, the KLA had only limited capacity to exert effective control.

218. The requirement that a "civilian population" be targeted has, as its objective, the exclusion from the realm of crimes against humanity the perpetration of crimes against a limited and randomly selected number of individuals. In this sense, the requirement that a "civilian population" be the target of an attack may be seen as another way of emphasising the requirement that the attack be of large scale or exhibit systematic features.

219. For Article 5 to apply, it must be established that those targeted by the attack were "civilians" in the relevant sense. This involves consideration of the meaning of the term "civilian." In its Joint Final Brief, the Defence assert that any "collaborators" targeted by the KLA referred to those taking active part in hostilities and who were therefore disentitled to civilian status. They therefore contend that a "population" contemplated by Article 5 has not come under attack.

220. In support of their arguments, the Defence produced a number of examples in which KLA members in public statements and interviews distinguished between "civilians" and "collaborators." Rexhep Selimi stated that, by "collaborators", he intended to refer to persons involved in the structures of the Serbian secret services. Jakup Krasniqi defined a collaborator as a person who "was harmful to the KLA, when such a person is giving information on the movements of the KLA to the Belgrade regime." Peter Bouckaert of Human Rights Watch understood "collaborators" to mean people who were working with the Serbian authorities, or people who were suspected of being informants to Serbian officials.

221. In an interview, Jakup Krasniqi stated that the KLA never dealt with civilians, and that the KLA's rules of operation recognised the Geneva Conventions. Yet Jakup Krasniqi, while professing that the KLA followed "all international rules of warfare", stated that "[c]ollaborators are warned that we will kill them if they continue to follow the wrong path." Elsewhere, Jakup Krasniqi noted that "[e]ven if some people have suffered, these have been more Albanian collaborators than Serbian civilians. We do not deal with civilians, and we return those whom we take as prisoners of war . . . Those we have kidnapped are either announced in a list or reported to be executed, but we do not behave in a base fashion like Serbia."

222. By adducing a number of similar statements, the Defence contend that the KLA drew a fundamental distinction between civilians, which the KLA deemed entitled to protection, and collaborators, who were to be treated as combatants. However, the Chamber does not have sufficient evidence to conclude that those alleged to be collaborating with the Serbian regime possessed the characteristics that would deny them membership of the civilian population.

223. The Chamber is satisfied that the KLA definition of "collaborators" encompassed civilians as well as perceived combatants. The Chamber recalls that Article 50, paragraph 1 of Additional Protocol I to the Geneva Conventions (which the Defence invite the Chamber to apply in the present situation) states that "[i]n case of doubt whether a person is a civilian, that person shall be considered a civilian." The provisions of Article 50 have been considered by the Appeals Chamber to reflect customary international law. [. . .]

224. Taking account of these considerations, and in light of the evidence before the Chamber concerning those apprehended and detained because of their alleged or suspected acts of

collaboration, the Chamber concludes that, at least as a general rule, perceived collaborators abducted by the KLA were entitled to civilian status.

225. To acknowledge the abduction of specific civilians, whether Serbian or Kosovo Albanian, as discussed and identified above, does not demonstrate, however, at least in the established circumstances of this case, that the KLA had a policy to target a "civilian population." [...]

226. In the particular context of this case, the majority of identified detainees in the prison camp were Kosovo Albanian. The evidence does not enable any conclusion as to the overall proportion of civilians abducted and detained by the KLA as between Serbian and Kosovo Albanian victims. What has been established in respect of those abducted and detained, indicates that the abductions occurred in diverse geographic locations, were relatively limited in number and involved relatively few abductees in comparison to the civilian population of Kosovo, such that it is not possible to discern from them that the civilian population itself was the subject of an attack, or that Kosovo Albanian collaborators and perceived or suspected collaborators and other abductees were of a class or category so numerous and widespread that they themselves constituted a "population" in the relevant sense.

227. The means and methods used by the KLA in the period relevant to the Indictment, in the abduction of Serbian and Kosovo Albanian civilians (whether considered together or separately) do not evince characteristics of an attack directed against a civilian population. At least in most cases of which there is evidence, the individuals who were abducted and then detained were singled out as individuals because of their suspected or known connection with, or acts of collaboration with, Serbian authorities – and not because they were members of a general population against which an attack was directed by the KLA.

228. Upon consideration of the evidence before it, the Chamber finds that at the time relevant to the Indictment there was no attack by the KLA directed against a "civilian population", whether Kosovo Albanian or Serbian in ethnicity, and no attack that could be said to indicate a "widespread" scale; however, as indicated earlier there is evidence of a level of systematic or coordinated organisation to the abduction and detention of certain individuals. While the KLA evinced a policy to target those Kosovo Albanians suspected of collaboration with the Serbian authorities, the Chamber finds that there was no attack directed against a civilian population, whether of Serbian or Albanian ethnicity.

The requirement that the attack on the civilian population be 'widespread or systematic' is discussed in the next section of this chapter. Ordinarily, in crimes against humanity cases, both elements are proven or not proven together. The *Limaj* case is a rare crimes against humanity case where the court found that only one of the two elements, the 'systematic' requirement, had been satisfied, but ultimately the court found that there could be no convictions for crimes against humanity because civilians had not been targeted as such.

France, Barbie case, *Cour de cassation, Judgment of 20 December 1985*

Barbie was a Nazi SS officer known as the 'Butcher of Lyon'. He was charged with crimes against humanity for his role in the torture and murder of thousands of Jews during World War II. One issue in the case was whether members of the French Resistance could be included in the victim group. Barbie was found guilty and was sentenced to life imprisonment.

By application of these principles, the *Chambre d'accusation* ordered that an indictment should be drawn up against Klaus Barbie and he should be sent for trial by the *Cour d'assises* for crimes against humanity, but only for those acts established by the examining magistrate which constituted "persecution against innocent Jews", carried out for racial and religious motives with a view to their extermination, that is to say in furtherance of the "final solution" sought by the leaders of the Nazi regime. In this regard, the judgment under appeal is final since no appeal has been lodged against its provisions seising the trial court. In addition the judgment under appeal, in considering the appeal of the civil parties, confirmed the order of the examining magistrate by which he held that [. . .] the prosecution is barred by statutory limitation to the extent that it relates to the unlawful imprisonment without judgment, torture, deportation and death of combatants who were members of the Resistance, or persons whom Barbie supposed to be members of the Resistance, even if they were Jewish. Even if such acts were heinous and were committed in violation of human dignity and the laws of war, they could only constitute war crimes, whose prosecution was barred by statutory limitation.

It is evident that the combatants in the Resistance were particularly effective in their struggle against the German armed forces, in particular in creating insecurity over the whole of the territory and in neutralizing or destroying entire units. Furthermore the combatants constituted dangerous adversaries requiring elimination and this was the view of all Germans, whether Nazis or not and regardless of any ideology. The security police known as SIPOSD, of which the Gestapo in Lyons directed by Klaus Barbie was a part, fought the combatants by the heinous means which are well known.

The combatants in the Resistance were motivated firstly by the desire to chase out the invader of their country and give freedom to their children. Their political ideology, by comparison with their patriotism, was merely a secondary impetus for their action, inseparable from their patriotism. On the other hand, when the Nazis took into account the political philosophies of their adversaries, they classified them without distinction as "Judéo-Bolsheviks and Communists" in order to render their fight against these "combatants of darkness" more effective.

Finally the judgment under appeal adds that the deportation of persons with regard to whom there was information allowing Barbie to think that they were members of the Resistance was to be considered as a war crime whose prosecution was barred by statutory limitation and not as a crime against humanity, in the absence of the element of intention necessary for the latter crime. With regard to Professor Gompel, a Jewish member of the Resistance, the judgment under appeal states that proof has not been furnished that he was arrested and tortured to death because he was Jewish and the accused was rightly given the benefit of the doubt on this point.

[This Court considers] however that the judgment under appeal states that the "heinous" crimes committed systematically or collectively against persons who were members or could have been members of the Resistance were presented, by those in whose name they were perpetrated, as justified politically by the national socialist ideology. Neither the driving force which motivated the victims, nor their possible membership of the Resistance, excludes the possibility that the accused acted with the element of intent necessary for the commission of crimes against humanity. In pronouncing as it did and excluding from the category of crimes against humanity all the acts imputed to the accused committed against members or possible members of the Resistance, the *Chambre d'accusation* misconstrued the meaning and the scope of the provisions listed in these grounds of appeal.

ICTY, **Prosecutor v. Martić,** *Appeals Chamber, Judgment of 8 October 2008*

Milan Martić became the highest Serbian official within the Serb breakaway republic in Croatia from 1991 to 1995. Martić was charged with crimes against humanity and war crimes for his role in a range of crimes committed during this period, in particular the ethnic cleansing of virtually all Croat civilians living within the self-declared Serb territory. Martić was convicted and sentenced to 35 years' imprisonment. This excerpt is from the Appeals Judgment and addresses who may properly be within the victim class of crimes against humanity.

1. The definition of "civilian"

291. The Prosecution's central argument is that the Trial Chamber erred in defining "civilian" [pursuant to Article 5 of the ICTY Statute, relating to crimes against humanity] too narrowly as not including other categories of individuals protected by international humanitarian law, such as persons *hors de combat*.

292. In Blaškić, the Appeals Chamber overturned the Trial Chamber's holding that the specific situation of the victim at the time of the crime may be determinative of his civilian or non-civilian status and held that members of the armed forces and other combatants (militias, volunteer corps and members of organised resistance groups) cannot claim civilian status. In its reasoning, the Appeals Chamber considered that:

[i]n determining the scope of the term "civilian population," the Appeals Chamber recalls its obligation to ascertain the state of customary law in force at the time the crimes were committed. In this regard, it notes that the Report of the Secretary General states that the Geneva Conventions "constitute rules of international humanitarian law and provide the core of the customary law applicable in international armed conflicts." Article 50 of Additional Protocol I to the Geneva Conventions contains a definition of civilians and civilian populations, and the provisions in this article may largely be viewed as reflecting customary law. As a result, they are relevant to the consideration at issue under Article 5 of the Statute, concerning crimes against humanity.

The Appeals Chamber went on to find that:

Read together, Article 50 of Additional Protocol I and Article 4A of the Third Geneva Convention establish that members of the armed forces, and members of militias or volunteer corps forming part of such armed forces, cannot claim civilian status. Neither can members of organized resistance groups, provided that they are commanded by a person responsible for his subordinates, that they have a fixed distinctive sign recognizable at a distance, that they carry arms openly, and that they conduct their operations in accordance with the laws and customs of war.

It therefore concluded that the Trial Chamber had erred in its characterization of the civilian population and of civilians under Article 5 of the Statute by holding that the specific situation of the victim at the moment the crimes were committed, rather than his status, must be taken into account in determining whether the victim is a "civilian". [...]

294. [...] In determining the scope of the term "civilian population," the Appeals Chamber recalls its obligation to ascertain the state of customary law in force at the time the crimes were committed. The Appeals Chamber considers that Article 50 of Additional Protocol I contains a definition of civilians and civilian populations, and the provisions in this article may largely be viewed as reflecting customary law. As a result, they are relevant to the consideration at issue under Article 5 of the Statute, concerning crimes against humanity. [...]

297. With respect to the argument of the Prosecution that the definition of civilian enshrined in Article 50(1) of Additional Protocol I is not applicable to the distinctive context of crimes against humanity, the Appeals Chamber recalls that the Tribunal has consistently held, since

its first cases, that provisions of the Statute must be interpreted according to the "natural and ordinary meaning in the context in which they occur", taking into account their object and purpose. In this regard, the Appeals Chamber observes that the definition of civilian found in Article 50(1) of Additional Protocol I accords with the ordinary meaning of the term "civilian" (in English) and "civil" (in French) as persons who are not members of the armed forces. As such, the definition of civilians relied upon by the Prosecution is contrary to the ordinary meaning of the term "civilian."

298. As for the Prosecution's reference to case-law considering whether or not victims of Article 3 crimes were participating in the hostilities at the time of the offence, the Appeals Chamber notes that this jurisprudence does not redefine the meaning of the term "civilian", but merely refers to the rule laid down in Article 51(3) of Additional Protocol I, according to which civilians enjoy "general protection against dangers arising from military operations" unless and for such time as they take a direct part in hostilities.

299. The Appeals Chamber considers that while certain terms have been defined differently in international humanitarian law and in the context of crimes against humanity, the fundamental character of the notion of civilian in international humanitarian law and international criminal law militates against giving it differing meanings under Article 3 and Article 5 of the Statute. Such definitional consistency also accords with the historical development of crimes against humanity, intended as they were to fill the gap left by the provisions pertaining to crimes against peace and war crimes in the Charter of the International Military Tribunal of 8 August 1945 ("Nuremberg Charter").

300. As for the Prosecution's argument that the definition in Article 50 of Additional Protocol I is not directly transferable to non-international armed conflicts (where the notion of "combatant" does not exist), the Appeals Chamber notes that Article 13 of Additional Protocol II refers to the protection of civilians and the civilian population. According to the ICRC Commentary, this provision corresponds with Article 50 of Additional Protocol I and, as a result, civilians in the context of non-international armed conflicts can be defined as those persons who do not belong to the armed forces, militias or volunteer corps forming part of such armed forces, organised resistance groups or a levée en masse.

301. The Prosecution also refers to post World-War II jurisprudence, which holds that victims of crimes against humanity can include members of the armed forces and resistance fighters. Insofar as this argument tends to demonstrate that members of the armed forces and resistance fighters hors de combat are civilians, it is rejected on the basis of the foregoing discussion. However, if this contention by the Prosecution challenges the Trial Chamber's finding that any victim of crimes against humanity must necessarily be civilian, the Appeals Chamber will address it in the next section.

302. In light of the above, the Appeals Chamber finds that the definition of civilian contained in Article 50 of Additional Protocol I reflects the definition of civilian for the purpose of applying Article 5 of the Statute and that the Trial Chamber did not err in finding that the term civilian in that context did not include persons *hors de combat*. This does not, however, answer the second contention raised by the Prosecution, i.e., whether the fact that persons *hors de combat* are not civilians for the purpose of Article 5 means that only civilians may be victims of crimes against humanity. The Appeals Chamber will turn to this second argument in the next section.

2. Individual victims as civilians

303. The second issue raised by the Prosecution is whether the condition under the chapeau of Article 5 of the Statute – that the attack be directed against a civilian population – also requires that all victims of each individual crime under Article 5 have civilian status, and in

particular, whether the chapeau excludes persons *hors de combat* who are present within the civilian population from constituting victims of a crime against humanity. In response, Martić argues that a proper reading of the Statute requires that individual victims also be civilians in order to fall under the jurisdiction of the Tribunal pursuant to Article 5 of the Statute. In this respect, he argues that the reference to "civilians" in Article 5 should be considered as meaning that both the chapeau requirement of a widespread or systematic attack and the individual crimes listed in that provision must target civilians. [. . .]

305. [. . .] [O]n the face of it, the requirement that the acts of an accused must be part of a widespread or systematic attack directed against any civilian population does not necessarily imply that the criminal acts within this attack must be committed against civilians only. The chapeau rather requires a showing that an attack was primarily directed against a civilian population, rather than "against a limited and randomly selected number of individuals."

306. Relevant interpretative sources tend to show that the drafters of the Statute did not in fact intend to exclude persons *hors de combat* from the purview of victims under Article 5. In its discussion of crimes against humanity, the Report of the Secretary-General recommending the establishment of the Tribunal expressly referred to Common Article 3. Moreover, in its report, the Commission of Experts Established Pursuant to Security Council Resolution 780 referred to Common Article 3 and noted as well that article 4 of Additional Protocol II addressed "fundamental guarantees" and included in the protected group "all persons who do not take a direct part or who have ceased to take part in hostilities."

307. Indeed, in the cases cited by the parties to support their interpretations of the meaning of "civilian" referenced above, the issue at stake was whether a population as a whole could be regarded as "civilian", while single individuals in its midst – the exact number depending on the circumstances – could still be combatants without modifying the status of the population as a whole. These statements were made by the Appeals Chamber in the context of illustrating the scope of the "well-established jurisprudence regarding the chapeau element of 'civilian population'." Thus, the authorities cited by the Trial Chamber in order to exclude persons *hors de combat* from the victims of crimes against humanity (as opposed to the category of persons who may be [the] object of the attack according to the chapeau of Article 5) are misleading. There is nothing in the text of Article 5 of the Statute, or previous authorities of the Appeals Chamber that requires that individual victims of crimes against humanity be civilians. [. . .]

309. The Appeals Chamber is satisfied that this approach reflects customary international law. The Nuremberg Charter and Allied Control Council Law No. 10 identified crimes against humanity of murder, extermination, enslavement, and deportation as crimes being committed against "any civilian population", but subsequent practice established that the status of a victim of a crime against humanity was not restricted to "civilians". This practice includes the High Command Case before the United States Military Tribunal, cases of the Supreme Court in the British Occupied zone, and the French cases of Barbie and Touvier.

310. Further, the Appeals Chamber notes that while post-World War II case-law generally considered war crimes and crimes against humanity together, when military tribunals did distinguish between them, they did so not on the basis of the status of their victims, but on the element of scale or organisation involved in crimes against humanity:

> It is not the isolated crime by a private German individual which is condemned, nor is it the isolated crime perpetrated by the German Reich through its officers against a private individual. It is significant that the enactment employs the words "against any civilian population" instead of "against any civilian individual." The provision is directed against offenses and inhumane acts and persecutions on political, racial, or religious grounds systematically organized and conducted by or with the approval of government.

311. In light of the above, the Appeals Chamber finds that the interpretation of the Statute according to which persons *hors de combat* fall within the purview of Article 5 of the Statute as victims is consistent with the status of applicable customary international law.

312. As for Martić's argument that extending Article 5 of the Statute to persons *hors de combat* would encompass offences already punishable under Article 2 or 3 of the Statute and would thus obviate the need for these provisions, the Appeals Chamber recalls its pronouncement in the *Tadić* Appeal Judgement, according to which "those who drafted the Statute deliberately included both classes of crimes, thereby illustrating their intention that those war crimes which, in addition to targeting civilians as victims, present special features such as the fact of being part of a widespread or systematic practice, must be classified as crimes against humanity and deserve to be punished accordingly." The Appeals Chamber has indeed consistently held that crimes against humanity constitute crimes which are distinct from the offences encompassed in Articles 2 and 3 of the Statute.

COMMENTARY

Ordinarily, crimes committed against combatants *hors de combat* will be covered by the laws and customs of war and so there is arguably little need to consider whether such crimes could, under particular circumstances, also constitute crimes against humanity. The *Barbie* court faced a peculiar situation, however, because under French law any potential war crimes charges were barred by a 20-year statute of limitations. Moreover, the French Resistance victims of Barbie included the famous Jean Moulin. The court therefore did a purposive reading of the law of crimes against humanity to conclude that members of the Resistance could be victims of crimes against humanity because of Barbie's *intent*, which was to target his victims as 'Judéo-Bolsheviks and Communists'. The *Martić* court reached the question from a different route. The Trial Chamber found that combatants could not even be the incidental victims of crimes against humanity. In addressing the Prosecution's appeal of this finding, the Appeals Chamber rejected, on more formalist grounds, the approach of the *Barbie* court, but nonetheless concluded that combatants could be *incidental* victims of crimes against humanity.

(C) THE 'CHAPEAU' ELEMENTS

With respect to crimes against humanity, there exist certain 'chapeau', or contextual, elements concerning the attack on the civilian population, and the alleged perpetrator's connection to that attack, that must be proven in every case, in addition to the elements of the specific crime (such as murder and torture). The chapeau elements establish the context for the specific crime and thereby identify what it is about that crime that merits particular condemnation and punishment. The law of crimes against humanity focuses on massive crime, but does so by targeting individual contributions, no matter how specific, to a widespread attack on civilians. In other words, the law recognizes that large-scale crimes against civilians are committed only through the particular (and intentional) acts of numerous individuals, each of whom must bear some responsibility for the final result. As the *Tadić* court found, 'the reason that crimes against humanity so shock the conscience of mankind and warrant intervention by the international community is because they are not isolated, random acts of individuals but rather result from a deliberate attempt to target a civilian population' (*Tadić* Trial Judgment, para. 653).

Crimes against humanity have always been conceived, from the beginning, as crimes committed on an enormous scale. While early codifications of crimes against humanity in the IMT Charter, the Control Council No. 10 law, or even the ICTYSt. did not explicitly contain a requirement that the attack on the civilian population be on a large scale, it was understood that this law was intended to address massive attacks and that this was implicit in the requirement that the crimes be committed against 'a civilian population'. The *Altstötter* decision, excerpted above, describes Control Council No. 10 law as 'directed against offences and inhumane acts and persecutions on political, racial, or religious grounds *systematically* organised and conducted by or with the approval of government' (emphasis added).

Nonetheless, it was left to the ICTY to articulate a precise requirement, based on sparse descriptions of crimes against humanity in international law, that would capture the required scale of the attack on the civilian population. The *Tadić* judgment settled on the following formulation: 'While this issue has been the subject of considerable debate, it is now well established that the requirement that the acts be directed against a civilian "population" can be fulfilled if the acts occur on either a widespread basis or in a systematic manner' (*Tadić* Trial Judgment, para. 646). That the attack be 'widespread or systematic' became a requirement at the ICTY, and was explicitly included in the definition of crimes against humanity in Article 7 of the Rome Statute.

A parallel question arose concerning whether the attack on a civilian population had to be perpetrated by a government. The *Altstötter* opinion reflected the understanding at the time that a policy of a government had to underlie such an attack. In *Tadić*, the Trial Chamber raised a doubt about whether a policy was required, and found that the entity behind the attack could be a State or a non-State actor: '[T]he law in relation to crimes against humanity has developed to take into account forces which, although not those of the legitimate government, have de facto control over, or are able to move freely within, defined territory' (*Tadić* Trial Judgment, para. 654). By the time of *Kunarac*, excerpted below, any requirement of a 'policy' or 'plan' was definitively abandoned. The ICC appears, however, to have retreated a little from this advance, requiring the existence of a policy, though on behalf of *either* a state or a non-state entity: '"Attack directed against any civilian population" means a course of conduct involving the multiple commission of acts referred to in paragraph 1 against any civilian population, pursuant to or in furtherance of a State or organizational policy to commit such attack' (Article 7(2)(a) ICCSt.).

In considering whether to authorize the ICC Prosecutor's request under Article 15 of the ICCSt. to investigate alleged crimes against humanity in Kenya, a Pre-Trial Chamber at the ICC split sharply on the meaning of 'organizational' within this Article. The majority of the Pre-Trial Chamber focused on the *acts* of the organization, finding that a non-State organization qualifies if it 'has the capability to perform acts which infringe on basic human values'.[2] The dissent, however, concluded that the Article requires more, and includes only those organizations that 'partake of some characteristics of a State', that 'act like a State' or that have 'quasi-State abilities'.[3] In thinking about the scope of this Article, it is worth thinking about the risks of these two different formulations. Is one too broad while the other too narrow?

Certain of the modern ad hoc tribunals have added an additional chapeau requirement. At the ICTR and the ECCC, the attack on the civilian population must be carried out on

---

[2] Decision Pursuant to Article 15 of the Rome Statute on the Authorisation of an Investigation into the Situation in the Republic of Kenya, Pre-Trial Chamber II, 31 March 2010, para. 90 (majority opinion).

[3] Ibid at para. 51 (dissenting opinion).

national, political, ethnic, racial or religious grounds. In the context of these conflicts, this requirement does not significantly narrow the scope of the crime. At the ICTY, Special Court for Sierra Leone and ICC, the requirement of this particular animus exists only with respect to the specific crime of persecutions within crimes against humanity, which is further discussed in the next section.

ICTY, Prosecutor v. Kunarac et al., Appeals Chamber, Judgment of 12 June 2002

The defendants, members of a unit within the Bosnian Serb Army, were accused of crimes against humanity and war crimes for their role in the ethnic cleansing of Bosnian Muslims from the area of Foča within Bosnia. The defendants were convicted and sentenced to terms ranging from 28 to 12 years' imprisonment. The Appeals Chamber defined the chapeau elements of crimes against humanity.

2. Legal Requirement of an "attack"

85. In order to amount to a crime against humanity, the acts of an accused must be part of a widespread or systematic attack "directed against any civilian population". This phrase has been interpreted by the Trial Chamber, and the Appeals Chamber agrees, as encompassing five elements:

(i)   There must be an attack.

(ii) The acts of the perpetrator must be part of the attack.

(iii) The attack must be directed against any civilian population.

(iv) The attack must be widespread or systematic.

(v)   The perpetrator must know that his acts constitute part of a pattern of widespread or systematic crimes directed against a civilian population and know that his acts fit into such a pattern.

86. The concepts of "attack" and "armed conflict" are not identical. As the Appeals Chamber has already noted when comparing the content of customary international law to the Tribunal's Statute, "the two – the 'attack on the civilian population' and the 'armed conflict' – must be separate notions, although of course under Article 5 of the Statute the attack on 'any civilian population' may be part of an 'armed conflict'". Under customary international law, the attack could precede, outlast, or continue during the armed conflict, but it need not be a part of it. Also, the attack in the context of a crime against humanity is not limited to the use of armed force; it encompasses any mistreatment of the civilian population. The Appeals Chamber recognises, however, that the Tribunal will only have jurisdiction over the acts of an accused pursuant to Article 5 of the Statute where the latter are committed "in armed conflict". [. . .]

90. As was correctly stated by the Trial Chamber, the use of the word "population" does not mean that the entire population of the geographical entity in which the attack is taking place must have been subjected to that attack. It is sufficient to show that enough individuals were targeted in the course of the attack, or that they were targeted in such a way as to satisfy the Chamber that the attack was in fact directed against a civilian "population", rather than against a limited and randomly selected number of individuals.

91. As stated by the Trial Chamber, the expression "directed against" is an expression which "specifies that in the context of a crime against humanity the civilian population is the primary object of the attack". In order to determine whether the attack may be said to have been so directed, the Trial Chamber will consider, inter alia, the means and method used in the course

of the attack, the status of the victims, their number, the discriminatory nature of the attack, the nature of the crimes committed in its course, the resistance to the assailants at the time and the extent to which the attacking force may be said to have complied or attempted to comply with the precautionary requirements of the laws of war. To the extent that the alleged crimes against humanity were committed in the course of an armed conflict, the laws of war provide a benchmark against which the Chamber may assess the nature of the attack and the legality of the acts committed in its midst. [. . .]

4. The Attack must be Widespread *or* Systematic

93. The requirement that the attack be "widespread" or "systematic" comes in the alternative. Once it is convinced that either requirement is met, the Trial Chamber is not obliged to consider whether the alternative qualifier is also satisfied. Nor is it the role or responsibility of the Appeals Chamber to make supplementary findings in that respect. As stated by the Trial Chamber, the phrase "widespread" refers to the large-scale nature of the attack and the number of victims, while the phrase "systematic" refers to "the organized nature of the acts of violence and the improbability of their random occurrence". The Trial Chamber correctly noted that "patterns of crimes – that is the non-accidental repetition of similar criminal conduct on a regular basis – are a common expression of such systematic occurrence". [. . .]

95. As stated by the Trial Chamber, the assessment of what constitutes a "widespread" or "systematic" attack is essentially a relative exercise in that it depends upon the civilian population which, allegedly, was being attacked. A Trial Chamber must therefore "first identify the population which is the object of the attack and, in light of the means, methods, resources and result of the attack upon the population, ascertain whether the attack was indeed widespread or systematic". The consequences of the attack upon the targeted population, the number of victims, the nature of the acts, the possible participation of officials or authorities or any identifiable patterns of crimes, could be taken into account to determine whether the attack satisfies either or both requirements of a "widespread" or "systematic" attack vis-à-vis this civilian population.

96. As correctly stated by the Trial Chamber, "only the attack, not the individual acts of the accused, must be widespread or systematic". In addition, the acts of the accused need only be a part of this attack and, all other conditions being met, a single or relatively limited number of acts on his or her part would qualify as a crime against humanity, unless those acts may be said to be isolated or random.

97. The Trial Chamber thus correctly found that the attack must be either "widespread" or "systematic", that is, that the requirement is disjunctive rather than cumulative. It also correctly stated that the existence of an attack upon one side's civilian population would not disprove or cancel out that side's attack upon the other's civilian population. In relation to the circumstances of this case, the Appeals Chamber is satisfied that the Trial Chamber did not err in concluding that the attack against the non-Serb civilian population of Foča was systematic in character. The Appellants' arguments on those points are all rejected and this part of their common grounds of appeal accordingly fails.

5. The Requirement of a Policy or Plan and Nexus with the Attack

98. Contrary to the Appellants' submissions, neither the attack nor the acts of the accused needs to be supported by any form of "policy" or "plan". There was nothing in the Statute or in customary international law at the time of the alleged acts which required proof of the existence of a plan or policy to commit these crimes.[4] As indicated above, proof that the attack

---

4 [114] There has been some debate in the jurisprudence of this Tribunal as to whether a policy or plan constitutes an element of the definition of crimes against humanity. The practice reviewed by the Appeals

was directed against a civilian population and that it was widespread or systematic, are legal elements of the crime. But to prove these elements, it is not necessary to show that they were the result of the existence of a policy or plan. It may be useful in establishing that the attack was directed against a civilian population and that it was widespread or systematic (especially the latter) to show that there was in fact a policy or plan, but it may be possible to prove these things by reference to other matters. Thus, the existence of a policy or plan may be evidentially relevant, but it is not a legal element of the crime.

99. The acts of the accused must constitute part of the attack. In effect, as properly identified by the Trial Chamber, the required nexus between the acts of the accused and the attack consists of two elements:

(i) the commission of an act which, by its nature or consequences, is objectively part of the attack; coupled with

(ii) knowledge on the part of the accused that there is an attack on the civilian population and that his act is part thereof.

100. The acts of the accused must be part of the "attack" against the civilian population, but they need not be committed in the midst of that attack. A crime which is committed before or after the main attack against the civilian population or away from it could still, if sufficiently connected, be part of that attack. The crime must not, however, be an isolated act. A crime would be regarded as an "isolated act" when it is so far removed from that attack that, having considered the context and circumstances in which it was committed, it cannot reasonably be said to have been part of the attack.

101. The Appeals Chamber is satisfied that the Trial Chamber identified and applied the proper test for establishing the required nexus between the acts of the accused and the attack and that the Trial Chamber was correct in concluding that there is no requirement in the Statute or in customary international law that crimes against humanity must be supported by a policy or plan to carry them out. The Appeals Chamber is also satisfied that the acts of the Appellants were not merely of a military sort as was claimed, but that they were criminal in kind, and that the Trial Chamber did not err in concluding that these acts comprised part of the attack against the non-Serb civilian population of Foča. This part of the Appellants' common grounds of appeal therefore fails.

6. *Mens rea* for Crimes against Humanity

102. Concerning the required *mens rea* for crimes against humanity, the Trial Chamber correctly held that the accused must have had the intent to commit the underlying offence or offences with which he is charged, and that he must have known "that there is an attack on the civilian population and that his acts comprise part of that attack, or at least [that he took] the risk that his acts were part of the attack." This requirement, as pointed out by the Trial Chamber, does not entail knowledge of the details of the attack.

Chamber overwhelmingly supports the contention that no such requirement exists under customary international law. [...] Some of the decisions which suggest that a plan or policy is required in law went, in that respect, clearly beyond the text of the statute to be applied [...] Other references to a plan or policy which have sometimes been used to support this additional requirement in fact merely highlight the *factual* circumstances of the case at hand, rather than impose an independent constitutive element [...] Finally, another decision, which has often been quoted in support of the plan or policy requirement, has been shown not to constitute an authoritative statement of customary international law (see *In re Altstötter*, ILR 14/1947, 278 and 284 and comment thereupon in *Ivan Timofeyevich Polyukhovich* v *The Commonwealth of Australia and Anor*, (1991) 172 CLR 501, pp 586–587).

103. For criminal liability pursuant to Article 5 of the Statute, "the motives of the accused for taking part in the attack are irrelevant and a crime against humanity may be committed for purely personal reasons." Furthermore, the accused need not share the purpose or goal behind the attack. It is also irrelevant whether the accused intended his acts to be directed against the targeted population or merely against his victim. It is the attack, not the acts of the accused, which must be directed against the target population and the accused need only know that his acts are part thereof. At most, evidence that he committed the acts for purely personal reasons could be indicative of a rebuttable assumption that he was not aware that his acts were part of that attack.

COMMENTARY

From the spare language of Article 5 ICTYSt., quoted at the beginning of this chapter, the courts at the ICTY have had to derive particular elements, which are fully articulated in the *Kunarac* case and which are designed to distinguish individual or random crimes from crimes against humanity. Thus, while an individual perpetrator need only commit a single crime, it must be in the context of, and with the knowledge of, a larger widespread or systematic attack on a civilian population.

(D) THE SPECIFIC CRIMES WITHIN CRIMES AGAINST HUMANITY

In addition to the chapeau elements, crimes against humanity require proof that the individual perpetrator committed a particular crime within a specified list. The IMT Charter identified, as potential crimes against humanity, 'murder, extermination, enslavement, deportation, and other inhumane acts [...]' as well as 'persecutions on political, racial or religious grounds'. The ICTYSt. included these and added imprisonment, torture and rape. The ICC expanded the list even further to include other sexual crimes such as sexual slavery and enforced prostitution or pregnancy (which were found by the ICTY to fall under 'inhumane acts'), enforced disappearance of persons and the crime of apartheid.

Persecution is the crime of violating a person's 'fundamental rights' with a discriminatory purpose as specified in the applicable statute. It is a crime that can encompass numerous other violations, and therefore it has the capacity to capture within a single charge a wide range of atrocities committed against a population. For this reason, it has been particularly useful in addressing ethnic cleansing, which is typically accomplished by means of a series of escalating measures targeted at an identifiable victim group, beginning with restrictions on movement and employment, and finishing with deportation, imprisonment, torture and murder. All of these acts, if found to be pursued with a specified discriminatory purpose, can fall under a persecutions charge. Regarding purpose, the IMT Charter and the ICTYSt. specified 'political, racial and religious grounds', while the ICCSt. dramatically expanded the list to include also 'national, ethnic, cultural, [...] gender [...], or other grounds that are universally recognized as impermissible under international law'. Because the crime of persecutions requires a double *mens rea* (the intent to commit the underlying violation and the intent to do it for a prohibited purpose), its structure resembles the crime of genocide, discussed in the next chapter of this book, and it is the charge that will frequently apply where there is inadequate proof of a genocide.

The more difficult question regarding the crime of persecutions is to determine what is included within 'fundamental rights'. In the *Tadić* Trial Judgment, the court focused on the discriminatory purpose element and suggested that it was the prohibited purpose that rendered the conduct criminal. Therefore the court did not provide any significant definition of what it meant to violate 'fundamental rights'. Later decisions of the ICTY clarified that the fundamental right deprivations had to be of equal severity to the other deprivations listed in Article 5 ICTYSt., that is, murder, extermination, enslavement, and so forth. The ICTY and ICTR tribunals have recognized conduct such as the denial of freedom of movement, the denial of employment, the denial of the right to judicial process, and the denial of equal access to public services as constituting persecutory acts, at least when in conjunction with other acts of similar gravity.

Although the ICCSt. broadened the list of discriminatory purposes, it narrowed what can qualify as the underlying violation by specifying that it must be an 'act referred to in this paragraph [the crimes against humanity article] or any crime within the jurisdiction of the court'.

The ICTR confronted the question of whether hate speech by itself can constitute the crime of persecutions. Hate speech and propaganda are commonly fundamental features of atrocities committed against civilians, providing the mechanism by which groups are mobilized to commit massive crimes against others. There is little dispute that such speech can constitute 'incitement' to commit crimes, but sharp controversy about whether it can be a crime itself, falling under persecutions.

Apart from the charge of persecutions, the other broad crime within crimes against humanity is the charge of 'inhumane acts', which has served as a kind of residual crime to capture conduct not specified by the other specific crimes contained within crimes against humanity. Decisions of the ICTY have also narrowed this provision, requiring that inhumane acts be of equal seriousness to the other crimes within the list of crimes against humanity:

234. [...] The crime of inhumane acts, like inhumane treatment under Article 3, and cruel treatment under Article 2, functions as a residual category for serious charges which are not otherwise enumerated under Article 5. All of these offences require proof of the same elements. The elements to be proved are:

(i) the occurrence of an act or omission of similar seriousness to the other enumerated acts under the Article;

(ii) the act or omission caused serious mental or physical suffering or injury or constituted a serious attack on human dignity; and

(iii) the act or omission was performed deliberately by the accused or a person or persons for whose acts and omissions he bears criminal responsibility.

235. To assess the seriousness of an act, consideration must be given to all the factual circumstances. These circumstances may include the nature of the act or omission, the context in which it occurred, the personal circumstances of the victim including age, sex and health, as well as the physical, mental and moral effects of the act upon the victim. While there is no requirement that the suffering imposed by the act have long term effects on the victim, the fact that an act has had long term effects may be relevant to the determination of the seriousness of the act.

236. The *mens rea* of inhumane acts is satisfied where the offender, at the time of the act or omission, had the intention to inflict serious physical or mental suffering or to commit a serious attack on the human dignity of the victim, or where he knew that his act or omission was likely to cause serious physical or mental suffering or a serious attack upon human dignity and was reckless thereto.[5]

---

[5] *Prosecutor* v. *Vasiljević*, ICTY, Trial Chamber, 29 November 2002.

The ICCSt. similarly defines other inhumane acts as acts 'of a similar character intentionally causing great suffering, or serious injury to body or to mental or physical health'.

Finally, rape and other sexual abuse were crimes that were largely neglected by the World War II tribunals. The modern international tribunals have taken an enormous step forward in defining and enforcing these crimes and in recognizing that they are not incidental violations, but are in fact frequently employed as tools of warfare to subjugate and destroy a particular population. Therefore these crimes have been identified within the context not just of crimes against humanity, but of war crimes and genocide as well. An important question has been how to define the elements of these crimes, and in particular whether to require a particular showing of coercion on the part of the individual perpetrator or whether coercion can be inferred from the wider circumstances when rape or sexual abuse occurs in, for example, a detention camp or during a widespread attack on a village or town.

ICTY, Prosecutor *v.* Kupreškić et al., *Trial Chamber, Judgment of 14 January 2000*

> The defendants, members of the Bosnian Croat HVO forces operating in Bosnia, were charged with crimes against humanity and war crimes for their role in the attack on the Bosnian Muslim village of Ahmići in the Lašva River valley region of Bosnia. The Trial Chamber convicted five of the defendants and acquitted one, but the Appeals Chamber later reversed the convictions of three of the defendants, finding inadequate evidence to support convictions, and reduced the sentences of the remaining two defendants. This excerpt is from the Trial Chamber judgment.

3. The Definition of Persecution

616. In the Judgement of *Prosecutor v. Tadić*, Trial Chamber II held that persecution is a form of discrimination on grounds of race, religion or political opinion that is intended to be, and results in, an infringement of an individual's fundamental rights. It is not necessary to have a separate act of an inhumane nature to constitute persecution, but rather, the discrimination itself makes the act inhumane. The Trial Chamber held that the crime of persecution encompasses a wide variety of acts, including, *inter alia*, those of a physical, economic, or judicial nature that violate an individual's basic or fundamental rights. The discrimination must be on one of the listed grounds to constitute persecution.

617. As mentioned above, this is a broad definition which could include acts prohibited under other subheadings of Article 5, acts prohibited under other Articles of the Statute, and acts not covered by the Statute. The same approach has been taken in Article 7(2)(g) of the ICC Statute, which states that "[p]ersecution means the intentional and severe deprivation of fundamental rights contrary to international law by reason of the identity of the group or collectivity" (emphasis added).

618. However, this Trial Chamber holds the view that in order for persecution to amount to a crime against humanity it is not enough to define a core assortment of acts and to leave peripheral acts in a state of uncertainty. There must be clearly defined limits on the types of acts which qualify as persecution. Although the realm of human rights is dynamic and expansive, not every denial of a human right may constitute a crime against humanity.

619. Accordingly, it can be said that at a minimum, acts of persecution must be of an equal gravity or severity to the other acts enumerated under Article 5. This legal criterion has already been resorted to, for instance, in the *Flick* case.

620. It ought to be emphasised, however, that if the analysis based on this criterion relates only to the <u>level of seriousness</u> of the act, it does not provide guidance on <u>what types of acts</u> can constitute persecution. The *ejusdem generis* ["of the same kind"] criterion can be used as a supplementary tool, to establish whether certain acts which generally speaking fall under the proscriptions of Article 5(h), reach the <u>level of gravity</u> required by this provision. The only conclusion to be drawn from its application is that only <u>gross or blatant denials</u> of fundamental human rights can constitute crimes against humanity.

621. The Trial Chamber, drawing upon its earlier discussion of "other inhumane acts", holds that in order to identify those rights whose infringement may constitute persecution, more defined parameters for the definition of human dignity can be found in international standards on human rights such as those laid down in the Universal Declaration on Human Rights of 1948, the two United Nations Covenants on Human Rights of 1966 and other international instruments on human rights or on humanitarian law. Drawing upon the various provisions of these texts it proves possible to <u>identify a set of fundamental rights appertaining to any human being, the gross infringement of which may amount, depending on the surrounding circumstances, to a crime against humanity</u>. Persecution consists of a severe attack on those rights, and aims to exclude a person from society on discriminatory grounds. The Trial Chamber therefore defines persecution as <u>the gross or blatant denial, on discriminatory grounds, of a fundamental right, laid down in international customary or treaty law, reaching the same level of gravity as the other acts prohibited in Article 5</u>.

622. In determining whether particular acts constitute persecution, the Trial Chamber wishes to reiterate that acts of persecution must be evaluated not in isolation but in context, by looking at their cumulative effect. Although individual acts may not be inhumane, their overall consequences must offend humanity in such a way that they may be termed "inhumane". This delimitation also suffices to satisfy the principle of legality, as inhumane acts are clearly proscribed by the Statute.

623. The Trial Chamber does not see fit to identify which rights constitute fundamental rights for the purposes of persecution. The interests of justice would not be served by so doing, as the explicit inclusion of particular fundamental rights could be interpreted as the implicit exclusion of other rights (*expressio unius est exclusio alterius*). This is not the approach taken to crimes against humanity in customary international law, where the category of "other inhumane acts" also allows courts flexibility to determine the cases before them, depending on the forms which attacks on humanity may take, forms which are ever-changing and carried out with particular ingenuity. Each case must therefore be examined on its merits.

624. In its earlier conclusions the Trial Chamber noted that persecution was often used to describe a series of acts. However, the Trial Chamber does not exclude the possibility that a single act may constitute persecution. In such a case, there must be clear evidence of the discriminatory intent. For example, in the former Yugoslavia an individual may have participated in the single murder of a Muslim-person. If his intent clearly was to kill him because he was a Muslim, and this occurred as part of a wide or systematic persecutory attack against a civilian population, this single murder may constitute persecution. But the discriminatory intent of the perpetrator must be proved for this crime to qualify as persecution.

625. Although acts of persecution are often part of a discriminatory policy, the Trial Chamber finds that it is not necessary to demonstrate that an accused has taken part in the formulation of a discriminatory policy or practice by a governmental authority. An example is that of the defendant *Streicher*: "In his speeches and articles [. . .] he infected the German mind with the virus of anti-Semitism, and incited the German People to active persecution". He did so not in any official capacity but as the publisher of an anti-Semitic journal, *Der Stürmer*. The Tribunal concluded that his "incitement to murder and extermination at the time when Jews in the East

were being killed under the most horrible conditions clearly constitutes persecution" and sentenced him to death.

626. The Trial Chamber observes that in the light of its broad definition of persecution, the Prosecution cannot merely rely on a general charge of "persecution" in bringing its case. This would be inconsistent with the concept of legality. To observe the principle of legality, the Prosecution must charge particular acts (and this seems to have been done in this case). These acts should be charged in sufficient detail for the accused to be able to fully prepare their defence.

627. In sum, a charge of persecution must contain the following elements:

(a)　those elements required for all crimes against humanity under the Statute;

(b)　a gross or blatant denial of a fundamental right reaching the same level of gravity as the other acts prohibited under Article 5;

(c)　discriminatory grounds.

The discussion of persecutions in *Kupreškić* reflects the tension that faces modern tribunals seeking to give further definition to specific crimes, in particular open-ended crimes like that of persecutions. On the one hand, the court seeks a broad definition that will capture all conduct that might be seen to fall within persecutions. On the other hand, the court tries to identify certain limiting principles in order to cabin the notion and provide notice to potential defendants. These same concerns arise in the partial dissent of Judge Meron in the *Nahimana* case below.

ICTR, Nahimana et al. *v.* Prosecutor *(the* Media *case)*, Appeals Chamber, Judgment of 28 November 2007

> The three defendants were charged with having roles in the media in Rwanda, in particular the *Radio Television Libre des Mille Collines* (RTLM) and the newspaper *Kangura*, and in using these positions to promote genocide. The three were convicted of genocide and crimes against humanity. The following excerpt is from the Appeals Judgment and the portial dissents of Judges Pocar and Meron.

983. The Trial Chamber defined the crime of persecution as " 'a gross or blatant denial of a fundamental right reaching the same level of gravity' as the other acts enumerated as crimes against humanity under the Statute." The Chamber then stated:

> It is evident that hate speech targeting a population on the basis of ethnicity, or other discriminatory grounds, reaches this level of gravity and constitutes persecution under Article 3(h) of its Statute. In *Ruggiu*, the Tribunal so held, finding that the radio broadcasts of RTLM, in singling out and attacking the Tutsi ethnic minority, constituted a deprivation of "the fundamental rights to life, liberty and basic humanity enjoyed by members of the wider society." Hate speech is a discriminatory form of aggression that destroys the dignity of those in the group under attack. It creates a lesser status not only in the eyes of the group members themselves but also in the eyes of others who perceive and treat them as less than human. The denigration of persons on the basis of their ethnic identity or other group membership in and of itself, as well as in its other consequences, can be an irreversible harm.

984. The Trial Chamber explained that the speech itself constituted the persecution and that there was therefore no need for the speech to contain a call to action, or for there to be a link

between persecution and acts of violence. It recalled that customary international law prohibits discrimination and that hate speech expressing ethnic and other forms of discrimination violates this prohibition. It found that the expressions of ethnic hatred in the RTLM broadcasts, *Kangura* publications and the activities of the CDR constituted persecution under Article 3(h) of the Statute.

985. The Appeals Chamber reiterates that "the crime of persecution consists of an act or omission which discriminates in fact and which: denies or infringes upon a fundamental right laid down in international customary or treaty law (the *actus reus*); and was carried out deliberately with the intention to discriminate on one of the listed grounds, specifically race, religion or politics (the *mens rea*)." However, not every act of discrimination will constitute the crime of persecution: the underlying acts of persecution, whether considered in isolation or in conjunction with other acts, must be of a gravity equal to the crimes listed under Article 3 of the Statute. Furthermore, it is not necessary that these underlying acts of persecution amount to crimes in international law. Accordingly, there is no need to review here the Appellants' arguments that mere hate speech does not constitute a crime in international criminal law.

986. The Appeals Chamber considers that hate speech targeting a population on the basis of ethnicity, or any other discriminatory ground, violates the right to respect for the dignity of the members of the targeted group as human beings, and therefore constitutes "actual discrimination". In addition, the Appeals Chamber is of the view that speech inciting to violence against a population on the basis of ethnicity, or any other discriminatory ground, violates the right to security of the members of the targeted group and therefore constitutes "actual discrimination". However, the Appeals Chamber is not satisfied that hate speech alone can amount to a violation of the rights to life, freedom and physical integrity of the human being. Thus other persons need to intervene before such violations can occur; a speech cannot, in itself, directly kill members of a group, imprison or physically injure them.

987. The second question is whether the violation of fundamental rights (right to respect for human dignity, right to security) is as serious as in the case of the other crimes against humanity enumerated in Article 3 of the Statute. The Appeals Chamber is of the view that it is not necessary to decide here whether, in themselves, mere hate speeches not inciting violence against the members of a group are of a level of gravity equivalent to that for other crimes against humanity. As explained above, it is not necessary that every individual act underlying the crime of persecution should be of a gravity corresponding to other crimes against humanity: underlying acts of persecution can be considered together. It is the cumulative effect of all the underlying acts of the crime of persecution which must reach a level of gravity equivalent to that for other crimes against humanity. Furthermore, the context in which these underlying acts take place is particularly important for the purpose of assessing their gravity.

988. In the present case, the hate speeches made after 6 April 1994 were accompanied by calls for genocide against the Tutsi group and all these speeches took place in the context of a massive campaign of persecution directed at the Tutsi population of Rwanda, this campaign being also characterized by acts of violence (killings, torture and ill-treatment, rapes . . .) and of destruction of property. In particular, the speeches broadcast by RTLM – all of them by subordinates of Appellant Nahimana, considered as a whole and in their context, were, in the view of the Appeals Chamber, of a gravity equivalent to other crimes against humanity. The Appeals Chamber accordingly finds that the hate speeches and calls for violence against the Tutsi made after 6 April 1994 (thus after the beginning of a systematic and widespread attack against the Tutsi) themselves constituted underlying acts of persecution. In addition, as explained below, some speeches made after 6 April 1994 did in practice substantially contribute to the commission of other acts of persecution against the Tutsi; these speeches thus also instigated the commission of acts of persecution against the Tutsi.

XIX. PARTLY DISSENTING OPINION OF JUDGE FAUSTO POCAR

[…] 3. With respect to the Appeals Chamber's findings on persecution as a crime against humanity, I would like to make the following clarifications. Paragraph 987 of the Appeal Judgement does not appear to rule definitively on the question whether a hate speech can *per se* constitute an underlying act of persecution. In my opinion, the circumstances of the instant case are, however, a perfect example where a hate speech fulfils the conditions necessary for it to be considered as an underlying act of persecution. Indeed, the hate speeches broadcast on RTLM by Appellant Nahimana's subordinates were clearly aimed at discriminating against the Tutsi and led the population to discriminate against them, thus violating their basic rights. Taken together and in their context, these speeches amounted to a violation of equivalent gravity as other crimes against humanity. Consequently, the hate speeches against the Tutsi that were broadcast after 6 April 1994 – that is, after the beginning of the systematic and widespread attack against this ethnic group – were *per se* underlying acts of persecution.

XXII. PARTLY DISSENTING OPINION OF JUDGE MERON

B. Nahimana's Conviction for Persecution (RTLM Broadcasts)

3. The Trial Chamber convicted Appellant Nahimana for persecution pursuant to Articles 3(h), 6(1), and 6(3) of the Statute, and the Appeals Chamber has affirmed the conviction based on Articles 3(h) and 6(3). The conviction rests on Appellant Nahimana's superior responsibility for the post-6 April RTLM broadcasts. My objections to the conviction for persecution are two-fold: first, from a strictly legal perspective, the Appeals Chamber has improperly allowed hate speech to serve as the basis for a criminal conviction; second, the Appeals Chamber has misapplied the standard that it articulates by failing to link Appellant Nahimana directly to the widespread and systematic attack.

4. By way of clarification, when I refer to "mere hate speech," I mean speech that, however objectionable, does not rise to the level of constituting a direct threat of violence or an incitement to commit imminent lawless action. Hate speech, by definition, is vituperative and abhorrent, and I personally find it repugnant. But because free expression is one of the most fundamental personal liberties, any restrictions on speech—and especially any criminalization of speech—must be carefully circumscribed.

1. Mere Hate Speech is Not Criminal

5. Under customary international law and the Statute of the Tribunal, mere hate speech is not a criminal offense. Citing the obligation to ban hate speech under the International Covenant on Civil and Political Rights (ICCPR) and the Convention on the Elimination of all Forms of Racial Discrimination (CERD), the Trial Chamber held that "hate speech that expresses ethnic and other forms of discrimination violates the norm of customary international law prohibiting discrimination." Although the Appeals Chamber does not address the accuracy of this statement, the Trial Chamber incorrectly stated the law. It is true that Article 4 of the CERD and Article 20 of the ICCPR require signatory states to prohibit certain forms of hate speech in their domestic laws, but do not criminalize hate speech in international law. However, various states have entered reservations with respect to these provisions. Several parties to the CERD objected to any obligation under Article 4 that would encroach on the freedom of expression embodied in Article 5 of the CERD and in their own respective laws. For example, France stated: "With regard to article 4, France wishes to make it clear that it interprets the reference made therein to the principles of the Universal Declaration of Human Rights and to the rights set forth in article 5 of the Convention as releasing the States Parties from the obligation to enact anti-discrimination legislation which is incompatible with the freedoms of opinion and

expression and of peaceful assembly and association guaranteed by those texts." With respect to Article 20 of the ICCPR, several states reserved the right not to introduce implementing legislation precisely because such laws might conflict with those states' protections of political liberty. The United States has entered arguably the strongest reservations in light of the fact that the American Constitution protects even "vituperative" and "abusive" language that does not qualify as a "true threat" to commit violence. Critically, no state party has objected to such reservations. The number and extent of the reservations reveal that profound disagreement persists in the international community as to whether mere hate speech is or should be prohibited, indicating that Article 4 of the CERD and Article 20 of the ICCPR do not reflect a settled principle. Since a consensus among states has not crystallized, there is clearly no norm under customary international law criminalizing mere hate speech.

6. The drafting history of the Genocide Convention bolsters this conclusion. An initial provision, draft Article III, stated: "All forms of public propaganda tending by their systematic and hateful character to provoke genocide, or tending to make it appear as a necessary, legitimate or excusable act shall be punished." As the commentary to draft Article III made clear, the provision was not concerned with direct and public incitement to commit genocide, which fell under the purview of draft Article II; rather, draft Article III was aimed unequivocally at mere hate speech. Importantly, the final text of the Convention did not include draft Article III or subsequent proposals by the Soviet delegation that also would have codified a ban on mere hate speech. As a result, the Genocide Convention bans only speech that constitutes direct incitement to commit genocide; it says nothing about hate speech falling short of that threshold.

7. Furthermore, the only precedent of either International Tribunal to address this precise question notes that hate speech is not prohibited under the relevant statute or customary international law. The language of the *Kordić* Trial Judgement of the International Criminal Tribunal for the former Yugoslavia (ICTY) is instructive.

> The Trial Chamber notes that the Indictment against Dario Kordić is the first indictment in the history of the International Tribunal to allege [hate speech] as a crime against humanity. The Trial Chamber, however, finds that this act, as alleged in the Indictment, does not by itself constitute persecution as a crime against humanity. It is not enumerated as a crime elsewhere in the International Tribunal Statute, but most importantly, it does not rise to the same level of gravity as the other acts enumerated in Article 5. Furthermore, the criminal prohibition of this act has not attained the status of customary international law. Thus to convict the accused for such an act as is alleged as persecution would violate the principle of legality.

The Prosecution did not appeal this important determination, and the Appeals Chamber did not intervene to correct a perceived error, lending credence to the notion that the *Kordić* Trial Judgement accurately reflects the law on hate speech. Notably, Article 5 of the Statute of the ICTY, including the prohibition against persecution, is virtually identical in scope to Article 3 of the Statute of the ICTR under which Nahimana was convicted.

8. In light of the reservations to the relevant provisions of the CERD and the ICCPR, the drafting history of the Genocide Convention, and the *Kordić* Trial Judgement, it is abundantly clear that there is no settled norm of customary international law that criminalizes hate speech. Similarly, a close textual analysis demonstrates that the Statute of the ICTR does not ban mere hate speech. This is as it should be because the Statute codifies established principles of international law, including those reflected in the Genocide Convention. Were it otherwise, the Tribunal would violate basic principles of fair notice and legality. The Appeals Chamber asserts that finding that hate speech can constitute an act of persecution does not violate the principle of legality as the crime of persecution itself "is sufficiently precise in international law."

I find this statement puzzling. In international criminal law, a notion must be precise, not just "sufficiently precise." The Brief of *Amicus Curiae* correctly observes that "[i]n contrast to most other crimes against humanity...'persecution' by its nature is open to broad interpretation." Citing *Kordić*, which is given short shrift by the Appeals Chamber, the Brief of *Amicus Curiae* continues: "Mindful of the attendant risks to defendants' rights, international courts have sought to ensure the 'careful and sensitive development' of the crime of persecution 'in light of the principle of *nullem crimen sine lege*'." The Tribunal must proceed with utmost caution when applying new forms of persecution because, of the various crimes against humanity, persecution is one of the most indeterminate. There are difficulties with the rubric or definition of persecution itself, and even more so with the vagueness of its constituent elements. The combined effect of this indeterminacy and the Tribunal's desire to address effectively such an egregious crime as persecution is to gravitate towards expansion through judicial decisions. Understandable as such tendency is, it may clash, as in the present case, with the fundamental principle of legality. [...]

12. The Statute of the ICTR explicitly prohibits genocide and incitement to commit genocide. When hate speech rises to the level of inciting violence or other imminent lawless action, such expression does not enjoy protection. But for the reasons explained above, an attempt, under the rubric of persecution, to criminalize unsavory speech that does not constitute actual imminent incitement might have grave and unforeseen consequences. Thus, courts must remain vigilant in preserving the often precarious balance between competing freedoms.

3. Mere Hate Speech May Not Be the Basis of a Criminal Conviction

13. In upholding Appellant Nahimana's conviction, the Appeals Chamber has impermissibly predicated the conviction on mere hate speech. As noted above, my colleagues do not decide whether hate speech, without more, can be the *actus reus* of persecution under the Statute, but hate speech nonetheless is an important and decisive factor in the conviction for persecution. In effect, the Appeals Chamber conflates hate speech and speech inciting to violence and states that both kinds of speech constitute persecution. This, to my mind, is a distinction without a meaningful difference.

14. I agree with the Appeals Chamber that under the Tribunal's jurisprudence, cumulative convictions under different statutory provisions are permissible as long as each provision has at least one distinct element that the Prosecution must prove separately. The same act – here, Nahimana's responsibility for the post-6 April RTLM broadcasts – may form the basis for convictions of direct and public incitement to commit genocide as well as persecution; however, the unique element of persecution is that the acts must be part of a widespread and systematic attack on a civilian population. Because of Nahimana's responsibility for the post-6 April broadcasts, the only remaining question concerns whether the unique element of persecution existed.

15. One might argue that the post-6 April broadcasts in themselves are enough to establish the existence of a widespread and systematic attack on a civilian population. The Appeals Chamber recognizes the weakness of such a conclusion; otherwise, the analysis would have been much more straightforward and would not have required a finessing of the hate speech question. Clearly, then, the existence of mere hate speech contributed to the Appeals Chamber's finding of a widespread and systematic attack. My distinguished colleagues defend this approach by noting (1) that "underlying acts of persecution can be considered jointly" and (2) that "it is not necessary that...underlying acts of persecution amount to crimes in international law." According to this view, hate speech, though not criminal, may be considered along with other acts in order to establish that the Appellant committed persecution.

16. The fundamental problem with this approach is that it fails to appreciate that speech is unique – expression which is not criminalized is protected. As Justice Oliver Wendell Holmes

has observed: "Every idea is an incitement." But in the case of conflicting liberties, a balance must be struck, and speech that falls on the non-criminal side of that balance enjoys special protection. This stands in stark contrast to other non-criminal acts that have no such unique status and indeed may contribute to the aggregate circumstances a court can consider. The Appeals Chamber, even without deciding whether hate speech alone can justify a conviction, nevertheless permits protected speech to serve as a basis for a conviction for persecution. Such a tack abrogates the unique status accorded to non-criminal expression and, in essence, criminalizes non-criminal speech.

4. Nexus Between Nahimana and the Widespread and Systematic Attack

17. Having discussed my objections to the legal question of what role, if any, mere hate speech may play in justifying a conviction for persecution, I turn now to a factual problem. In describing the widespread and systematic attack on a civilian population that must underpin the conviction, the Appeals Chamber takes cognizance of a campaign "characterised by acts of violence (killings, ill-treatments, rapes, ...) and of destruction of property." Nowhere in the Judgement, however, does the Appeals Chamber establish a nexus between these vile acts and Appellant Nahimana. Unless there is a causal nexus between the underlying acts committed by an accused and the systematic attack to which they contributed, a conviction for persecution would be based on guilt by association.

18. The Appeals Chamber notes that mere hate speech "contributed" to the other acts of violence and thus constituted an instigation to persecution. It also observes that the hate speech occurred in the midst of a "broad campaign of persecution against the Tutsi population." While the Appeals Chamber has thus correctly recognized the necessity of establishing a causal nexus between Nahimana's actions and the widespread and systematic attack, it has marshaled no evidence to this effect. The supposed nexus rests on nothing more than *ipse dixit* declarations that Nahimana's hate speech "contributed" to a larger attack.

19. It is true that Nahimana's responsibility for the post-6 April broadcasts occurred within the same temporal and geographic context as the wider Rwandan genocide. Generalizations about the atrocities that took place, though, cannot convert Nahimana's conviction for direct and public incitement to commit genocide into a conviction for persecution as well. It is quite possible that a direct link exists between Nahimana's actions and the wider attack, but a vague appeal to various killings, rapes, and other atrocities does not pass muster under norms of legality and due process.

20. The conclusion, then, is that the evidence of Nahimana's connection to a widespread attack rests on only two sources: first, certain post-6 April broadcasts, which the Appeals Chamber itself deemed insufficient when considered alone, to establish that such an attack took place; and, second, non-criminal hate speech, which I have argued should not form the basis, in whole or in part, of any conviction. Nahimana's conviction for persecution is thus left on extremely weak footing and cannot stand.

21. For the foregoing reasons, I believe that the Appeals Chamber should have reversed Nahimana's conviction for persecution.

Hate speech will continue to be a thorny issue because the values that crimes against humanity law seeks to protect fall on both sides of the debate. On the one hand, hate speech and propaganda have proven to be essential ingredients to the commission of widespread atrocity. On the other hand, as Judge Meron points out in his partial dissent, repressive regimes can use speech laws to suppress legitimate criticism. Moreover, there is no consensus on the topic internationally. While some countries are extremely protective of hate speech, others are more willing to tolerate some regulation. In most instances, international tribunals will consider speech in connection with other crimes, either as incitement to commit another specific crime or as proof of a perpetrator's intent or discriminatory motive. But it is likely that courts will also have to face again the question addressed in *Nahimana*, whether speech alone can rise to the level of persecutions. The issue of hate speech is further examined in the chapter on incitement to commit genocide, *infra* in this casebook.

ICTY, **Prosecutor** *v.* **Kunarac et al.,** *Trial Chamber, Judgment of 22 February 2001*

This case has already been introduced in connection with the definition by the Appeals Chamber of the chapeau elements. A tool used by the defendants in the attack on Foča was rape and sexual abuse. In its judgment, the Trial Chamber set forth the required elements of rape.

D. Rape

436. Rape has been charged against the three accused as a violation of the laws or customs of war under Article 3 and as a crime against humanity under Article 5 of the Statute. The Statute refers explicitly to rape as a crime against humanity within the Tribunal's jurisdiction in Article 5(g). The jurisdiction to prosecute rape as an outrage against personal dignity, in violation of the laws or customs of war pursuant to Article 3 of the Statute, including upon the basis of common Article 3 to the 1949 Geneva Conventions, is also clearly established. The elements common to each of those Articles are set out above.

437. The specific elements of the crime of rape, which are neither set out in the Statute nor in international humanitarian law or human rights instruments, were the subject of consideration by the Trial Chamber in the Furundžija case. There the Trial Chamber noted that in the International Criminal Tribunal for Rwanda [ICTR] judgement in the Akayesu proceedings the Trial Chamber had defined rape as "a physical invasion of a sexual nature, committed under circumstances which are coercive". It then reviewed the various sources of international law and found that it was not possible to discern the elements of the crime of rape from international treaty or customary law, nor from the "general principles of international criminal law or [. . .] general principles of international law". It concluded that "to arrive at an accurate definition of rape based on the criminal law principle of specificity ("Bestimmtheitsgrundsatz", also referred to by the maxim "nullem crimen sine lege stricta"), it is necessary to look for principles of criminal law common to the major legal systems of the world. These principles may be derived, with all due caution, from national laws". The Trial Chamber found that, based on its review of the national legislation of a number of states, the actus reus of the crime of rape is:

(i) the sexual penetration, however slight:

    (a) of the vagina or anus of the victim by the penis of the perpetrator or any other object used by the perpetrator; or

    (b) of the mouth of the victim by the penis of the perpetrator;

(ii) by coercion or force or threat of force against the victim or a third person.

438. This Trial Chamber agrees that these elements, if proved, constitute the actus reus of the crime of rape in international law. However, in the circumstances of the present case the Trial Chamber considers that it is necessary to clarify its understanding of the element in paragraph (ii) of the Furundžija definition. The Trial Chamber considers that the Furundžija definition, although appropriate to the circumstances of that case, is in one respect more narrowly stated than is required by international law. In stating that the relevant act of sexual

penetration will constitute rape only if accompanied by coercion or force or threat of force against the victim or a third person, the Furundžija definition does not refer to other factors which would render an act of sexual penetration non-consensual or non-voluntary on the part of the victim, which, as foreshadowed in the hearing and as discussed below, is in the opinion of this Trial Chamber the accurate scope of this aspect of the definition in international law.

439. As observed in the Furundžija case, the identification of the relevant international law on the nature of the circumstances in which the defined acts of sexual penetration will constitute rape is assisted, in the absence of customary or conventional international law on the subject, by reference to the general principles of law common to the major national legal systems of the world. The value of these sources is that they may disclose "general concepts and legal institutions" which, if common to a broad spectrum of national legal systems, disclose an international approach to a legal question which may be considered as an appropriate indicator of the international law on the subject. In considering these national legal systems the Trial Chamber does not conduct a survey of the major legal systems of the world in order to identify a specific legal provision which is adopted by a majority of legal systems but to consider, from an examination of national systems generally, whether it is possible to identify certain basic principles, or in the words of the Furundžija judgement, "common denominators", in those legal systems which embody the principles which must be adopted in the international context.

440. As noted above, the Trial Chamber in the Furundžija case considered a range of national legal systems for assistance in relation to the elements of rape. In the view of the present Trial Chamber, the legal systems there surveyed, looked at as a whole, indicated that the basic underlying principle common to them was that sexual penetration will constitute rape if it is not truly voluntary or consensual on the part of the victim. The matters identified in the Furundžija definition – force, threat of force or coercion – are certainly the relevant considerations in many legal systems but the full range of provisions referred to in that judgement suggest that the true common denominator which unifies the various systems may be a wider or more basic principle of penalising violations of sexual autonomy. The relevance not only of force, threat of force, and coercion but also of absence of consent or voluntary participation is suggested in the Furundžija judgement itself where it is observed that:

[…] all jurisdictions surveyed by the Trial Chamber require an element of force, coercion, threat, or acting without the consent of the victim: force is given a broad interpretation and includes rendering the victim helpless.

441. A further consideration of the legal systems surveyed in the Furundžija judgement and of the relevant provisions of a number of other jurisdictions indicates that the interpretation suggested above, which focuses on serious violations of sexual autonomy, is correct.

442. In general, domestic statutes and judicial decisions which define the crime of rape specify the nature of the sexual acts which potentially constitute rape, and the circumstances which will render those sexual acts criminal. The relevant law in force in different jurisdictions at the time relevant to these proceedings identifies a large range of different factors which will classify the relevant sexual acts as the crime of rape. These factors for the most part can be considered as falling within three broad categories:

(i) the sexual activity is accompanied by force or threat of force to the victim or a third party;

(ii) the sexual activity is accompanied by force or a variety of other specified circumstances which made the victim particularly vulnerable or negated her ability to make an informed refusal; or

(iii) the sexual activity occurs without the consent of the victim.

1. Force or threat of force

443. The definition of rape in a number of jurisdictions requires that the sexual act occurs by force or is accompanied by force or threat of force. Typical provisions of this nature include the Penal Code of Bosnia and Herzegovina, which provided relevantly:

[...w]hoever coerces a female not his wife into sexual intercourse by force or threat of imminent attack upon her life or body or the life or body of a person close to her, shall be sentenced to a prison term of one to ten years.

In Germany, the Criminal Code in force at the relevant time provided:

Rape (1) Whoever compels a woman to have extramarital intercourse with him, or with a third person, by force or the threat of present danger to life or limb, shall be punished by not less than two years' imprisonment.

444. The Criminal Code of Korea defines rape as sexual intercourse with a female "through violence or intimidation". Other jurisdictions with definitions of rape similarly requiring violence, force or a threat of force include China, Norway, Austria, Spain and Brazil.

445. Certain jurisdictions require proof of force or threat of force (or equivalent concepts) and that the act was non-consensual or against the will of the victim. This includes some jurisdictions in the United States of America.

2. Specific circumstances which go to the vulnerability or deception of the victim

446. A number of jurisdictions provide that specified sexual acts will constitute rape not only where accompanied by force or threat of force but also in the presence of other specified circumstances. These circumstances include that the victim was put in a state of being unable to resist, was particularly vulnerable or incapable of resisting because of physical or mental incapacity, or was induced into the act by surprise or misrepresentation.

447. The penal codes of a number of continental European jurisdictions contain provisions of this type. The Swiss Penal Code provides that anyone who compels a woman to have sexual intercourse "notably by threat or by violence, by putting psychological pressure on the victim or rendering her unable to resist" commits rape. The provision on rape in the Portuguese Penal Code contains a similar reference to the perpetrator making it impossible for the victim to resist. The relevant provision of the French Penal Code defines rape as "[a]ny act of sexual penetration of whatever nature, committed through violence, coercion, threat or surprise [...]". The Italian Penal Code contains the crime of compelling a person to have sexual intercourse by violence or threats but applies the same punishment to anyone who has intercourse with any person who, inter alia, was "mentally ill, or unable to resist by reason of a condition of physical or mental inferiority, even though this was independent of the act of the offender" or "was deceived because the offender impersonated another person".

448. In Denmark, section 216 of the Criminal Code provides that rape is committed by any person who "enforces sexual intercourse by violence or under threat of violence", but specifies that "the placing of a person in such a position that that person is unable to resist the act shall be equivalent to violence." The Penal Codes of Sweden and Finland, contain similar provisions. In Estonia, rape is defined in the Criminal Code as sexual intercourse "by violence or threat of violence or by taking advantage of the helpless situation of the victim".

449. The Japanese Criminal Code provides that "[a] person who by violence or threat, obtains carnal knowledge of a female person of thirteen years or over shall be guilty of rape [...]". Article 178 of the Code however, effectively widens the conduct which will be considered to amount to rape by providing that where a person "by taking advantage of loss of reason or

incapacity to resist or by causing such loss of reason or incapacity to resist, commits an indecent act or obtains carnal knowledge of a woman" is to be punished in the same way as provided for in the article relating to rape.

450. The Criminal Code of Argentina defines rape as sexual penetration where there is force or intimidation, where the victim is "of unsound mind or effect, or when due to illness or whatever other reason, they are incapable of resisting" or where the victim is under twelve. Similar provisions apply in Costa Rica, Uruguay and the Philippines.

451. Some States of the United States of America provide in their criminal codes that sexual intercourse constitutes rape if committed in the presence of various factors as an alternative to force, such as that the victim is drugged or unconscious, has been fraudulently induced to believe the perpetrator is the victim's spouse, or is incapable of giving legal consent because of a mental disorder or developmental or physical disability.

452. The emphasis of such provisions is that the victim, because of an incapacity of an enduring or qualitative nature (eg mental or physical illness, or the age of minority) or of a temporary or circumstantial nature (eg being subjected to psychological pressure or otherwise in a state of inability to resist) was unable to refuse to be subjected to the sexual acts. The key effect of factors such as surprise, fraud or misrepresentation is that the victim was subjected to the act without the opportunity for an informed or reasoned refusal. The common denominator underlying these different circumstances is that they have the effect that the victim's will was overcome or that her ability freely to refuse the sexual acts was temporarily or more permanently negated.

3. Absence of consent or voluntary participation

453. In most common law systems, it is the absence of the victim's free and genuine consent to sexual penetration which is the defining characteristic of rape. The English common law defined rape as sexual intercourse with a woman without her consent. In 1976 rape was also defined by statute. Under the provision in force at the time relevant to these proceedings, a man committed rape where "(a) he has unlawful sexual intercourse with a woman who at the time of the intercourse does not consent to it; and (b) at that time he knows that she does not consent to the intercourse or he is reckless as to whether she consents to it [...]". Force or threat or fear of force need not be proven; however where apparent consent is induced by such factors it is not real consent. Similar definitions apply in other Commonwealth countries including Canada, New Zealand and Australia. In these jurisdictions it is also clear that the consent must be genuine and voluntarily given. In Canada, consent is defined in the Criminal Code as "the voluntary agreement of the complainant to engage in the sexual activity in question". The Code also explicitly identifies circumstances in which no consent will be considered to have been obtained, including that "the agreement is expressed by the words or conduct of a person other than the complainant" or that the accused "induces the complainant to engage in the activity by abusing a position of trust, power or authority". In Victoria, Australia, consent is defined as "free agreement" and the statute defines circumstances in which free agreement is not given, including where a person submits because of the use of force, fear of force or harm, or because the person is in unlawful detention; where the person is asleep or unconscious or is mistaken as to, or is incapable of understanding, the nature of the act.

454. The Indian Penal Code provides that sexual intercourse with a woman will constitute rape in any of six defined circumstances. These include that it occurs "[a]gainst her will"; "without her consent", or with her consent if such consent is negated by various circumstances including that it was "obtained by putting her or any person in whom she is interested in fear of death or being hurt". The provision on rape in the Bangladesh Penal Code is materially almost identical.

455. Rape is defined in South Africa at common law as a man intentionally having unlawful sexual intercourse with a woman without her consent. The Zambian Penal Code provides that rape is committed by any person

[...] who has unlawful carnal knowledge of a woman or girl, without her consent, or with her consent, if the consent is obtained by force or by means of threats or intimidation of any kind, or by fear of bodily harm, or by means of false representation as to the nature of the act, or, in the case of a married woman, by impersonating her husband.

456. Certain non-common law jurisdictions also define rape in terms of non-consensual sexual intercourse. The Belgian Penal Code provides: "Any act of sexual penetration, whatever its nature, and by whatever means, committed on someone who does not consent to it, constitutes the crime of rape." There is no consent in particular when the act has been imposed through violence, coercion or ruse, or was made possible by the infirmity or the mental or physical incapacity of the victim.

4. The basic principle underlying the crime of rape in national jurisdictions

457. An examination of the above provisions indicates that the factors referred to under the first two headings are matters which result in the will of the victim being overcome or in the victim's submission to the act being non-voluntary. The basic principle which is truly common to these legal systems is that serious violations of sexual autonomy are to be penalised. Sexual autonomy is violated wherever the person subjected to the act has not freely agreed to it or is otherwise not a voluntary participant.

458. In practice, the absence of genuine and freely given consent or voluntary participation may be evidenced by the presence of the various factors specified in other jurisdictions – such as force, threats of force, or taking advantage of a person who is unable to resist. A clear demonstration that such factors negate true consent is found in those jurisdictions where absence of consent is an element of rape and consent is explicitly defined not to exist where factors such as use of force, the unconsciousness or inability to resist of the victim, or misrepresentation by the perpetrator.

459. Given that it is evident from the Furundžija case that the terms coercion, force, or threat of force were not to be interpreted narrowly and that coercion in particular would encompass most conduct which negates consent, this understanding of the international law on the subject does not differ substantially from the Furundžija definition.

460. In light of the above considerations, the Trial Chamber understands that the actus reus of the crime of rape in international law is constituted by: the sexual penetration, however slight: (a) of the vagina or anus of the victim by the penis of the perpetrator or any other object used by the perpetrator; or (b) of the mouth of the victim by the penis of the perpetrator; where such sexual penetration occurs without the consent of the victim. Consent for this purpose must be consent given voluntarily, as a result of the victim's free will, assessed in the context of the surrounding circumstances. The mens rea is the intention to effect this sexual penetration, and the knowledge that it occurs without the consent of the victim.

COMMENTARY

In *Furundžija*, an earlier ICTY case, the Trial Chamber defined rape to require a showing of coercion, force or threat of force. In this case, the Trial Chamber broadened this definition to include a showing that the penetration occurred without the consent of the victim. How did the Trial Chamber in *Kunarac* accomplish this step? Did it, as it claimed, derive this broader approach from the 'principles' or 'common denominator' of the national laws it reviewed? Or did it instead adopt an approach that included all of the various options in these different national laws? Regardless of how it reached this conclusion, the court's approach represented an important step in war crimes and crimes against humanity cases where coercion of a victim often derives from the broader circumstances rather than the particular acts of an individual.

QUESTIONS

1. What, if any, correspondence must exist between the acts that comprise the widespread or systematic attack on the civilian population and the alleged individual perpetrator's crimes? What if the broader attack was largely comprised of property crimes while the individual engaged in a violent act such as rape or murder?

2. To what degree should prosecutors take into account the fragile origins of crimes against humanity and possible lingering sovereignty concerns in making charging decisions? In other words, should prosecutors be cautious in their use of crimes against humanity charges, particularly in circumstances where war crimes charges might also be available?

3. To what extent do the open-ended components of crimes against humanity law, e.g. persecutions and other inhumane acts, threaten to undermine the legitimacy of the broader concept?

FURTHER READING

G. Acquaviva and F. Pocar, 'Crimes against Humanity', in R. Wolfrum (ed.), *Max Planck Encyclopedia of Public International Law* (Oxford: Oxford University Press, 2008–2010).

Cassese, *International Criminal Law*, 98–127.

Zahar and Sluiter, *International Criminal Law*, 197–219.

3

GENOCIDE

(A) THE NOTION AND ITS ORIGINS

Frequently called the 'crime of crimes' in contemporary international criminal law cases, genocide is infamous because of its association with the Shoah, translated into English as 'Holocaust'. What gives genocide its particular odiousness is its *dolus specialis* (special intent element, also referred to as genocidal intent): the specific intent to destroy a national, racial, religious or ethnical group as such, in whole or in part, through one of five listed categories of criminal conduct. When mass slaughter targeting a racial, religious or ethnical group flares there often is a legal and political battle over whether the term genocide applies because the label conveys deep condemnation and particular expressive force. Contemporary adjudicated cases of genocide such as the mass slaughter of more than half a million Rwandan Tutsis in 1994 and the mass killings of more than 7,000 men and boys in Srebrenica, Bosnia in 1995 demonstrate that attempts to eradicate groups of people need not be on the vast, sustained and systematic scale of the Shoah to be termed genocide.

Genocide was a 'crime without a name' as Winston Churchill put it in describing the Nazi Final Solution until Polish lawyer Raphaël Lemkin, a refugee fleeing Nazi occupation of his homeland, coined the term genocide. The term merges the ancient Greek word *genos*, meaning race or tribe, and *caedere*, the Latin word for killing. The term was meant to capture the grave offence of extinguishing a group, thereby robbing the world of the group and its future contributions.

The rapid ascension of the newly coined term in treaty law did not occur until after the prototypical contemporary genocide and the main World War II-era adjudications. Under the Charter of the International Military Tribunal, large-scale slaughter of ethnic, racial or religious groups was encompassed in the definition of crimes against humanity, which, as detailed in the previous chapter, included murder, extermination, and persecutions on political, racial or religious grounds, among other crimes. In analysing the crime of persecution, the International Military Tribunal referred to the extermination of the Jews. Some of the subsequent military tribunal prosecutions discussed the extermination of the Jews as a crime against humanity. In two later judgments of a US Military Tribunal, *Altstötter et al.* in 1947, and *Greifelt et al.* in 1948, the word 'genocide' was used, but the contours of the term were not fleshed out as a distinct crime.

The UN Genocide Convention defining and outlawing genocide as a specific crime was not adopted by the General Assembly until 9 December 1948. Now widely viewed as expressing customary law, at least in its main provisions, the Genocide Convention provides for the criminal responsibility of individuals and States for acts of genocide and imposes on Contracting States the duty to prevent and repress genocide. The Convention has been influential (see ICJ, Reservations to Genocide Convention, Advisory Opinion of 28 May 1951, p. 23) and widely subscribed to, with 137 States parties. The definition of genocide in Article 2 of the Convention has been incorporated verbatim into the statutes of the ad hoc tribunals – the ICTY and ICTR – as well as, in part, in the ICCSt.

(B) THE ELEMENTS OF GENOCIDE

The key components of genocide are threefold. First, there must be an underlying offence committed with the requisite *mens rea*. Second, the underlying offence must be directed against a protected national, racial, religious or ethnical group. Third, the underlying offence against a protected group must be committed with genocidal intent – the specific intent to destroy the group. Genocide thus has two layers of *mens rea*. The first layer of *mens rea* depends on the nature of the underlying crime. The second overarching *mens rea*, specific intent to destroy, is what sets genocide apart from all other crimes.

Article 2 of the Genocide Convention prescribes five categories of underlying acts:

(a) Killing members of the group;

(b) Causing serious bodily or mental harm to members of the group;

(c) Deliberately inflicting on the group conditions of life calculated to bring about its physical destruction in whole or in part;

(d) Imposing measures intended to prevent births within the group;

(e) Forcibly transferring children of the group to another group.

The terms of the Genocide Convention have been interpreted and enforced in national as well as international courts, which have filled in the meaning of the elements of genocide.

THE UNDERLYING ACTS

The five well-defined underlying acts of genocide reflect a focus on physical destruction. As discussed further in the section on cultural genocide below, the drafters of the Genocide Convention considered and rejected the idea of cultural genocide – the destruction of the language and culture of a group – because of the vagueness and malleability of the concept. The only vestige of the notion of cultural genocide is the recognition that the forced transfer of children might be an underlying act of genocide.

The interpretation of what conduct falls into the five underlying acts of genocide must therefore be seen through the lens of the focus on physical or biological destruction. While reading the excerpt below from *Prosecutor* v. *Akayesu* – the first international trial where genocide was charged as an autonomous crime – consider whether the ICTR was faithful in construing the meaning of the five underlying acts in keeping with the focus on physical or biological destruction.

Cases

....

***ICTR*, Prosecutor *v.* Akayesu, *Trial Chamber, Judgment of 2 September 1998*

During the Rwandan genocide in 1994, Jean-Paul Akayesu was *bourgmestre* (mayor) of Taba Commune and responsible for maintaining public order. Between April and June 1994, at least 2,000 Tutsis were slaughtered in the Commune. The Prosecutor alleged that Akayesu ordered and participated in brutal interrogations and killings of Tutsis and encouraged the slaughter. Akayesu was charged with genocide, complicity in genocide and incitement to commit genocide, among other crimes. In the excerpt below, the ICTR analysed the elements of the underlying acts of genocide.

494. The definition of genocide, as given in Article 2 of the Tribunal's Statute, is taken verbatim from Articles 2 and 3 of the Convention on the Prevention and Punishment of the Crime of Genocide (the "Genocide Convention"). [...]

495. The Genocide Convention is undeniably considered part of customary international law, as can be seen in the opinion of the International Court of Justice on the provisions of the Genocide Convention, and as was recalled by the United Nations' Secretary-General in his Report on the establishment of the International Criminal Tribunal for the former Yugoslavia. [...]

497. Contrary to popular belief, the crime of genocide does not imply the actual extermination of [a] group in its entirety, but is understood as such once any one of the acts mentioned in Article 2(2)(a) through 2(2)(e) is committed with the specific intent to destroy "in whole or in part" a national, ethnical, racial or religious group. [...]

Killing members of the group (paragraph (a))

500. With regard to Article 2(2)(a) of the Statute, like in the Genocide Convention, the Chamber notes that the said paragraph states "*meurtre*" in the French version while the English version states "killing". The Trial Chamber is of the opinion that the term "killing" used in the English version is too general, since it could very well include both intentional and unintentional homicides, whereas the term "*meurtre*", used in the French version, is more precise. It is accepted that there is murder when death has been caused with the intention to do so, as provided for, incidentally, in the Penal Code of Rwanda. [...]

501. Given the presumption of innocence of the accused, and pursuant to the general principles of criminal law, the Chamber holds that the version more favourable to the accused should be upheld and finds that Article 2(2)(a) of the Statute must be interpreted in accordance with the definition of murder given in the Penal Code of Rwanda, according to which "*meurtre*" (killing) is homicide committed with the intent to cause death. The Chamber notes in this regard that the *travaux préparatoires* of the Genocide Convention, show that the proposal by certain delegations that premeditation be made a necessary condition for there to be genocide, was rejected, because some delegates deemed it unnecessary for premeditation to be made a requirement; in their opinion, by its constitutive physical elements, the very crime of genocide, necessarily entails premeditation.

Causing serious bodily or mental harm to members of the group (paragraph b)

502. Causing serious bodily or mental harm to members of the group does not necessarily mean that the harm is permanent and irremediable.

503. In the Adolf Eichmann case, who was convicted of crimes against the Jewish people, genocide under another legal definition, the District Court of Jerusalem stated in its judgment of 12 December 1961, that serious bodily or mental harm of members of the group can be caused

"by the enslavement, starvation, deportation and persecution [...] and by their detention in ghettos, transit camps and concentration camps in conditions which were designed to cause their degradation, deprivation of their rights as human beings, and to suppress them and cause them inhumane suffering and torture".

504. For purposes of interpreting Article 2(2)(b) of the Statute, the Chamber takes serious bodily or mental harm, without limiting itself thereto, to mean acts of torture, be they bodily or mental, inhumane or degrading treatment, persecution.

Deliberately inflicting on the group conditions of life calculated to bring about its physical destruction in whole or in part (paragraph c)

505. The Chamber holds that the expression deliberately inflicting on the group conditions of life calculated to bring about its physical destruction in whole or in part, should be construed as the methods of destruction by which the perpetrator does not immediately kill the members of the group, but which, ultimately, seek their physical destruction.

506. For purposes of interpreting Article 2(2)(c) of the Statute, the Chamber is of the opinion that the means of deliberate inflicting on the group conditions of life calculated to bring about its physical destruction, in whole or part, include, *inter alia*, subjecting a group of people to a subsistence diet, systematic expulsion from homes and the reduction of essential medical services below minimum requirement.

Imposing measures intended to prevent births within the group (paragraph d)

507. For purposes of interpreting Article 2(2)(d) of the Statute, the Chamber holds that the measures intended to prevent births within the group, should be construed as sexual mutilation, the practice of sterilization, forced birth control, separation of the sexes and prohibition of marriages. In patriarchal societies, where membership of a group is determined by the identity of the father, an example of a measure intended to prevent births within a group is the case where, during rape, a woman of the said group is deliberately impregnated by a man of another group, with the intent to have her give birth to a child who will consequently not belong to its mother's group.

508. Furthermore, the Chamber notes that measures intended to prevent births within the group may be physical, but can also be mental. For instance, rape can be a measure intended to prevent births when the person raped refuses subsequently to procreate, in the same way that members of a group can be led, through threats or trauma, not to procreate.

Forcibly transferring children of the group to another group (paragraph e)

509. With respect to forcibly transferring children of the group to another group, the Chamber is of the opinion that, as in the case of measures intended to prevent births, the objective is not only to sanction a direct act of forcible physical transfer, but also to sanction acts of threats or trauma which would lead to the forcible transfer of children from one group to another.

COMMENTARY

International tribunals have generally followed the discussion of the elements of genocide – particularly the five types of conduct that may amount to genocide (*actus reus*) – discussed in *Akayesu*, though its language is sometimes overbroad. For instance, scholars have noted that 'subjecting a group of people to a subsistence diet' does not amount to 'conditions of life calculated to bring about its physical destruction in whole or in part', despite the overbroad language of para. 506 of the *Akayesu* Trial Judgment (TJ) (see A. Zahar, 'The ICTR's "Media" Judgment and the Reinvention of Direct and Public Incitement to

Commit Genocide' (2005) 16 *Criminal Law Forum* 33, n. 44). Also despite the overly sweep-ing language of para. 506 of the *Akayesu* TJ, most courts have found that forced expulsion of persons belonging to a particular protected group (and, more generally, ethnic cleansing) should be excluded from the notion of genocide, if not coupled at least with the creation of circumstances that would lead to a slow death, such as lack of proper housing, clothing and hygiene or excessive work or physical exertion (see for instance *Jelisić* TJ, paras 107–8 and *Brđanin* TJ, para. 691). Displacement may disrupt community and cultural bonds, but it arguably does not destroy the group in a physical or biological sense unless conducted in a manner that leads to destruction, such as shelling or starving a group to force it out of a region.

PROTECTED GROUPS

In adjudicating cases of genocide, difficult questions often centre on whether a targeted group fits within the protected categories of the definition of genocide. In limiting the pro-tected groups to national, racial, religious or ethnical groups, the framers of the Genocide Convention considered and decided against including political and economic groups, focusing instead on groups with more 'stable' characteristics. Leaving out political and eco-nomic groups also helped ensure more widespread acceptance of the Genocide Convention because nations engaged in political purges – such as the Soviet Union, a strong opponent of including political groups – or in class-based maltreatment, would find the Convention less threatening.

The concepts of national, racial, or religious or ethnical groups are not objectively fixed and certain, however. In contemporary times, we are increasingly realizing that race, eth-nicity, nationality and religion are subjective cultural constructs rather than fixed bio-logical facts. A group targeted for harm is often subjectively perceived and defined by the perpetrators and may even be castigated by the members of the same group, as in the case of the mass killings of Cambodians by Cambodians during the Khmer Rouge era. Fixed objective distinguishing criteria might be difficult to identify. A targeted group sharing many commonalities with the perpetrators of genocide may nonetheless be perceived as separate, foreign and distinct. Moreover, multiple groups of people may be targeted for destruction because they are perceived as *not* of the dominant group rather than because of their particular distinctive national, racial, religious or ethnic identity. The definition of genocide, however, is focused on the destruction of a group with a positive identity rather than the destruction of peoples defined negatively as lacking a particular identity.

Moreover, campaigns of destruction may be focused on pockets of a particular national, racial, religious or ethnic group in a particular region, rather than the entire group. The question becomes whether targeted regional subunits, such as the Bosnian Muslims of the municipality of Srebrenica, fall within the scope of the definition of groups under the Genocide Convention. The excerpt below considers these questions.

ICTY, Prosecutor *v.* Krstić, *Trial Chamber, Judgment of 2 August 2001*

As the ICTY Trial Chamber put it, General Radoslav Krstić's 'story is one of a respected professional soldier who could not balk at his superiors' insane desire to forever rid the Srebrenica area of Muslim civilians' and who ultimately reluctantly acceded to his superiors and allowed his men to help implement the plan. General Krstić was inserted by the order of his commander into a tragedy – the mass slaughter of more than 7,000 Bosnian Muslim men and boys after the fall of the UN 'safe area' of Srebrenica.

By 11 July 1995, the city of Srebrenica – a predominantly Muslim city in largely Bosnian Serb-held territory – had fallen to Bosnian Serb forces. Between 11 and 13 July 1995, Muslims were fleeing the city, with civilians interspersed with some Muslim combatants. Between 12 and 13 July 1995, Bosnian Serb forces separated males from females at the city of Potočari, a few kilometres from Srebrenica. While the separation was couched as culling military-aged males from the group as prisoners, many boys and elderly men were also taken prisoner. Women and children were taken by bus to Bosnian Muslim-held territory.

Amidst these tumultuous events, on 13 July 1995, General Krstić was ordered by his commander, General Ratko Mladić, to assume command of the Drina Corps, a Bosnian Serb force in eastern Bosnia. The military-aged males taken prisoner were straining the capacity of their captors, whose ranks were stretched thin because many soldiers were away conducting warfare in another area. The Muslim military-aged men were held prisoner in brutal conditions in places of ordinary life converted into places of extraordinary horror, such as schoolrooms, gymnasiums and warehouses. Between 14 and 19 July 1995 the Drina Corps was involved in the mass execution of prisoners.

General Krstić was the first senior official associated with the Srebrenica killings to be brought before the ICTY, where he was prosecuted on charges of war crimes, crimes against humanity and genocide.

553. The [Genocide] Convention [...] seeks to protect the right to life of human groups, as such. This characteristic makes genocide an exceptionally grave crime and distinguishes it from other serious crimes, in particular persecution, where the perpetrator selects his victims because of their membership in a specific community but does not necessarily seek to destroy the community as such.

554. However, the Genocide Convention does not protect all types of human groups. Its application is confined to national, ethnical, racial or religious groups.

555. National, ethnical, racial or religious group are not clearly defined in the Convention or elsewhere. In contrast, the preparatory work on the Convention and the work conducted by international bodies in relation to the protection of minorities show that the concepts of protected groups and national minorities partially overlap and are on occasion synonymous. European instruments on human rights use the term "national minorities", while universal instruments more commonly make reference to "ethnic, religious or linguistic minorities"; the two expressions appear to embrace the same goals. In a study conducted for the Sub-Commission on Prevention of Discrimination and Protection of Minorities in 1979, F. Capotorti commented that "the Sub-Commission on Prevention of Discrimination and Protection of Minorities decided, in 1950, to replace the word 'racial' by the word 'ethnic' in all references to minority groups described by their ethnic origin". The International Convention on the Elimination of All Forms of Racial Discrimination defines racial discrimination as "any distinction, exclusion, restriction or preference based on race, colour, descent, or national or ethnic origin". The preparatory work on the Genocide Convention also reflects that the term "ethnical" was added at a later stage in order to better define the type of groups protected by the Convention and ensure that the term "national" would not be understood as encompassing purely political groups.

556. The preparatory work of the Convention shows that setting out such a list was designed more to describe a single phenomenon, roughly corresponding to what was recognised,

before the second word war, as "national minorities", rather than to refer to several distinct prototypes of human groups. To attempt to differentiate each of the named groups on the basis of scientifically objective criteria would thus be inconsistent with the object and purpose of the Convention.

557. A group's cultural, religious, ethnical or national characteristics must be identified within the socio-historic context which it inhabits. As in the *Nikolić* and *Jelisić* cases, the Chamber identifies the relevant group by using as a criterion the stigmatisation of the group, notably by the perpetrators of the crime, on the basis of its perceived national, ethnical, racial or religious characteristics.

558. Whereas the indictment in this case defined the targeted group as the Bosnian Muslims, the Prosecution appeared to use an alternative definition in its pre-trial brief by pleading the intention to eliminate the "Bosnian Muslim population of Srebrenica" through mass killing and deportation. In its final trial brief, the Prosecution chose to define the group as the Bosnian Muslims of Srebrenica, while it referred to the Bosnian Muslims of Eastern Bosnia in its final arguments. The Defence argued in its final brief that the Bosnian Muslims of Srebrenica did not form a specific national, ethnical, racial or religious group. In particular, it contended that "one cannot create an artificial 'group' by limiting its scope to a geographical area". According to the Defence, the Bosnian Muslims constitute the only group that fits the definition of a group protected by the Convention.

559. Originally viewed as a religious group, the Bosnian Muslims were recognised as a "nation" by the Yugoslav Constitution of 1963. The evidence tendered at trial also shows very clearly that the highest Bosnian Serb political authorities and the Bosnian Serb forces operating in Srebrenica in July 1995 viewed the Bosnian Muslims as a specific national group. Conversely, no national, ethnical, racial or religious characteristic makes it possible to differentiate the Bosnian Muslims residing in Srebrenica, at the time of the 1995 offensive, from the other Bosnian Muslims. The only distinctive criterion would be their geographical location, not a criterion contemplated by the Convention. In addition, it is doubtful that the Bosnian Muslims residing in the enclave at the time of the offensive considered themselves a distinct national, ethnical, racial or religious group among the Bosnian Muslims. Indeed, most of the Bosnian Muslims residing in Srebrenica at the time of the attack were not originally from Srebrenica but from all around the central Podrinje region. Evidence shows that they rather viewed themselves as members of the Bosnian Muslim group.

560. The Chamber concludes that the protected group, within the meaning of Article 4 of the Statute, must be defined, in the present case, as the Bosnian Muslims. The Bosnian Muslims of Srebrenica or the Bosnian Muslims of Eastern Bosnia constitute a part of the protected group under Article 4. [. . .]

561. The Prosecution and the Defence, in this case, concur in their belief that the victims of genocide must be targeted *by reason of* their membership in a group. This is the only interpretation coinciding with the intent which characterises the crime of genocide. The intent to destroy a group as such, in whole or in part, presupposes that the victims were chosen by reason of their membership in the group whose destruction was sought. Mere knowledge of the victims' membership in a distinct group on the part of the perpetrators is not sufficient to establish an intention to destroy the group as such. As the ILC noted:

> [. . .] the intention must be to destroy a group and not merely one or more individuals who are coincidentally members of a particular group. The [. . .] act must be committed against an individual because of his membership in a particular group and as an incremental step in the overall objective of destroying the group.

COMMENTARY

As the excerpt highlights, an important criterion in defining whether a targeted group falls within the Genocide Convention's protections is the subjective stigmatization of a group based on perceived national, ethnical, racial or religious characteristics. Subjective definitions are difficult to apply in law because their content will vary depending on the socio-historical context of the crime – and perhaps even from perpetrator to perpetrator. The advantage of such an approach, however, is that it accounts for the socially constructed nature of categories like race and ethnicity.

Issues relating to the identification of the protected group have also arisen before the ICTR. How racial or ethnic separateness can be a function of social construction and subjective perception, rather than fixed biological fact, is dramatically demonstrated by the Hutu and Tutsi of Rwanda. During its colonial period, Rwanda had about 18 clans defined primarily by kinship lines. The distinction between Hutu and Tutsi was based on lineage, not ethnicity, and the boundaries were fluid rather than fixed because people could move between statuses in the course of a lifetime as their fortunes changed or they married. In the early 1930s, Belgian colonial authorities imposed a permanent division of the population into three groups – the Hutu, Twa and Tutsi, the group favoured by colonial authorities at the outset because of their height and skin colour. Every person was required to carry an identity card bearing their 'identity' and this practice persisted until after the Rwandan genocide of 1994. These identity cards – imposed as a way to codify subjective perceptions of group divisions – became such an entrenched part of life that they were used by the ICTR as 'objective' evidence of separate ethnic identity. In *Kayishema and Ruzindana*,[1] the ICTR Trial Chamber reasoned:

98. [...] An ethnic group is one whose members share a common language and culture; or, a group which distinguishes itself, as such (self identification); or, a group identified as such by others, including perpetrators of the crimes (identification by others). A racial group is based on hereditary physical traits often identified with geography. A religious group includes denomination or mode of worship or a group sharing common beliefs. [...]

522. The Prosecution submitted that the targeted group was the Tutsi population in Kibuye that was attacked on the grounds of ethnicity. [...] The evidence proves, beyond a reasonable doubt, that the victims of the acts for which Kayishema and Ruzindana are charged were Tutsis.

523. The Chamber further accepts that the Tutsis were an ethnic group. In support of this contention the Prosecution provided evidence that since 1931, Rwandans were required to carry identification cards which indicated the ethnicity of the bearer as Hutu, Tutsi or Twa. The government-issued identification cards specified the individual bearer's ethnicity. It should be noted that, in accordance with Rwandan custom, the ethnicity of a Rwandan child is derived from that of her or his father.

524. The Prosecution's expert witnesses, Professor Guichaoua and Mr. Nsanzuwera, also offered information on this issue. Through Mr. Nsanzuwera a copy of an identity card was tendered into evidence. He confirmed that all Rwandans were required to identify themselves by ethnicity on official documents. He added that identification based on ethnicity was a highly divisive issue in Rwanda. Therefore, the matter was addressed in the Arusha Peace Accords, which categorically resolved that there would be no mention of ethnicity on the identification cards of Rwandans from that period forth. Identification cards identifying the victims as Tutsis were found on those exhumed from mass graves in Kibuye.

---

[1] *Prosecutor* v. *Kayishema and Ruzindana*, Trial Chamber, Judgment of 21 May 1999.

525. Additionally, the scores of survivors who testified before this Chamber stated that they were Tutsis and that those whom they saw massacred during the time in question were also Tutsis.

526. In *Akayesu*, Trial Chamber I found that the Tutsis are an ethnic group, as such. Based on the evidence presented in the present case, this Trial Chamber concurs. The Trial Chamber finds beyond a reasonable doubt that the Tutsi victims of the massacres were an ethnical group as stipulated in Article 2(2) of the Statute, and were targeted as such.

Though group identity is socially constructed and may be subject to re-engineering, the types of groups singled out for protection by the Genocide Convention were deemed relatively stable. The *Akayesu* Trial Chamber Judgment, excerpted above, explained:

510. Since the special intent to commit genocide lies in the intent to "destroy, in whole or in part, a national, ethnical, racial or religious group, as such", it is necessary to consider a definition of the group as such. Article 2 of the Statute, just like the Genocide Convention, stipulates four types of victim groups, namely national, ethnical, racial or religious groups.

511. On reading through the *travaux préparatoires* of the Genocide Convention, it appears that the crime of genocide was allegedly perceived as targeting only "stable" groups, constituted in a permanent fashion and membership of which is determined by birth, with the exclusion of the more "mobile" groups which one joins through individual voluntary commitment, such as political and economic groups. Therefore, a common criterion in the four types of groups protected by the Genocide Convention is that membership in such groups would seem to be normally not challengeable by its members, who belong to it automatically, by birth, in a continuous and often irremediable manner.

512. Based on the *Nottebohm* decision rendered by the International Court of Justice, the Chamber holds that a national group is defined as a collection of people who are perceived to share a legal bond based on common citizenship, coupled with reciprocity of rights and duties.

513. An ethnic group is generally defined as a group whose members share a common language or culture.

514. The conventional definition of racial group is based on the hereditary physical traits often identified with a geographical region, irrespective of linguistic, cultural, national or religious factors.

515. The religious group is one whose members share the same religion, denomination or mode of worship.

516. Moreover, the Chamber considered whether the groups protected by the Genocide Convention, echoed in Article 2 of the Statute, should be limited to only the four groups expressly mentioned and whether they should not also include any group which is stable and permanent like the said four groups. In other words, the question that arises is whether it would be impossible to punish the physical destruction of a group as such under the Genocide Convention, if the said group, although stable and membership is by birth, does not meet the definition of any one of the four groups expressly protected by the Genocide Convention. In the opinion of the Chamber, it is particularly important to respect the intention of the drafters of the Genocide Convention, which according to the *travaux préparatoires*, was patently to ensure the protection of any stable and permanent group.

517. As stated above, the crime of genocide is characterized by its *dolus specialis*, or special intent, which lies in the fact that the acts charged, listed in Article 2(2) of the Statute, must have been "committed with intent to destroy, in whole or in part, a national, ethnical, racial or religious group, as such".

518. Special intent is a well-known criminal law concept in the Roman-continental legal systems. It is required as a constituent element of certain offences and demands that the perpetrator have the clear intent to cause the offence charged. According to this meaning, special intent is the key element of an intentional offence, which offence is characterized by a psychological relationship between the physical result and the mental state of the perpetrator.

519. As observed by the representative of Brazil during the *travaux préparatoires* of the Genocide Convention,

"genocide [is] characterised by the factor of particular intent to destroy a group. In the absence of that factor, whatever the degree of atrocity of an act and however similar it might be to the acts described in the convention, that act could still not be called genocide."

520. With regard to the crime of genocide, the offender is culpable only when he has committed one of the offences charged under Article 2(2) of the Statute with the clear intent to destroy, in whole or in part, a particular group. The offender is culpable because he knew or should have known that the act committed would destroy, in whole or in part, a group.

521. In concrete terms, for any of the acts charged under Article 2(2) of the Statute to be a constitutive element of genocide, the act must have been committed against one or several individuals, because such individual or individuals were members of a specific group, and specifically because they belonged to this group. Thus, the victim is chosen not because of his individual identity, but rather on account of his membership of a national, ethnical, racial or religious group. The victim of the act is therefore a member of a group, chosen as such, which, hence, means that the victim of the crime of genocide is the group itself and not only the individual.

GENOCIDAL INTENT

Genocidal intent – also called *dolus specialis*, special intent and specific intent in the jurisprudence – is frequently the most complex issue in a case of alleged genocide. The specific intent to destroy a national, racial, religious or ethnic group as such is the hallmark of genocide and gives the crime its particular gravity. Discerning genocidal intent can be difficult. Mass killing often takes many hands. Some may harbour the intent to destroy a group as such, and some may lack that special intent element; aiming instead to kill for such manifold reasons as revenge, to obey orders, or out of generalized hatred and sadism short of genocidal intent. Some may also contribute to the commission of genocide without sharing the intent to destroy the group.

Because there is rarely direct evidence of genocidal intent, it is often hard to discern such intent absent a policy or plan of genocide. Moreover, even when there is a policy in place, in cases of modern-day ethnic cleansing the goal may be to displace, rather than destroy a group. Acts of violence and intimidation aimed at displacement may be deemed to fall short of intent to destroy the group, in which case the conduct constitutes crimes against humanity (usually the specific crime of persecutions) rather than genocide. The excerpts below illustrate how courts adjudicating cases of alleged genocide have dealt with difficulties in discerning genocidal intent to destroy a protected group.

ICTY, **Prosecutor v. Jelisić,** *Trial Chamber, Judgment of 14 December 1999*

Goran Jelisić's case presents a portrait of how ordinary people can become extraordinarily brutal in war when put in positions of power over lives. Formerly an agricultural machinery mechanic, Jelisić held a position of de facto authority at Luka prison camp during the Bosnian conflict and styled himself the 'Serb Adolf'. For the brutalities and murders that Jelisić committed at Luka camp, the Prosecution charged him with genocide as well as war crimes and crimes against humanity. On 29 October 1998, Jelisić pleaded guilty to the war crimes and crimes against humanity charges but not the genocide charges. He was tried on the genocide charges and the case against him hinged on whether he harbored genocidal intent while brutalizing and murdering Muslim and Croatian detainees.

64. In her pre-trial brief, the Prosecutor alleges that throughout the time Luka operated, the Serbian authorities, including the accused, killed hundreds of Muslim and Croatian detainees. The number of the victims would thus be much higher than the figure given for only those crimes to which the accused pleaded guilty.

65. Although the Trial Chamber is not in a position to establish the precise number of victims ascribable to Goran Jelisić for the period in the indictment, it notes that, in this instance, the material element of the crime of genocide [that is, the underlying act of killing members of the group] has been satisfied. Consequently, the Trial Chamber must evaluate whether the intent of the accused was such that his acts must be characterised as genocide.

B. The *mens rea* of the offence: the intent to destroy, in whole or in part, a national, ethnical, racial or religious group

66. It is in fact the *mens rea* which gives genocide its speciality and distinguishes it from an ordinary crime and other crimes against international humanitarian law. The underlying crime or crimes must be characterised as genocide when committed with the intent to destroy, in whole or in part, a national, ethnical, racial or religious group as such. Stated otherwise, "[t]he prohibited act must be committed against an individual because of his membership in a particular group and as an incremental step in the overall objective of destroying the group". Two elements which may therefore be drawn from the special intent are:

- that the victims belonged to an identified group;
- that the alleged perpetrator must have committed his crimes as part of a wider plan to destroy the group as such. [. . .]

72. In this case, it is the positive approach towards a group which has been advanced by the Prosecution. The genocide charge states that the murders committed by the accused targeted the Bosnian Muslim population. [. . .]

2. The intent to destroy, in whole or in part, the group as such

78. In examining the intentionality of an attack against a group, the Trial Chamber will first consider the different concepts of the notion of destruction of a group as such before then reviewing the degree of intent required for a crime to be constituted. In other words, the Trial Chamber will have to verify that there was both an intentional attack against a group and an intention upon the part of the accused to participate in or carry out this attack. [. . .]

(a) Definition

79. Apart from its discriminatory character, the underlying crime is also characterised by the fact that it is part of a wider plan to *destroy*, in whole or in part, the group *as such*. As indicated by the ILC, "the intention must be to destroy the group "as such', meaning as a separate

and distinct entity, and not merely some individuals because of their membership in a particular group'. [...]

80. Notwithstanding this, it is recognised that the destruction sought need not be directed at the whole group which, moreover, is clear from the letter of Article 4 of the Statute. The ILC also states that "[i]t is not necessary to intend to achieve the complete annihilation of a group from every corner of the globe". The question which then arises is what proportion of the group is marked for destruction and beyond what threshold could the crime be qualified as genocide? In particular, the Trial Chamber will have to verify whether genocide may be committed within a restricted geographical zone. [...]

82. Given the goal of the Convention to deal with mass crimes, it is widely acknowledged that the intention to destroy must target at least a *substantial* part of the group. [...]

(b) The degree of intention required

84. The accused is charged with committing genocide or aiding and abetting therein. [...]

87. Before even ruling on the level of intention required, the Trial Chamber must first verify whether an act of genocide has been committed as the accused cannot be found guilty of having aided and abetted in a crime of genocide unless that crime has been established.

(i) The intention to commit "all-inclusive" genocide

88. As has already been seen, the collection of the population in centres located at different points around the town, their subsequent transfer to detention camps and the interrogations always conducted in an identical manner over a short period of time demonstrate that the operation launched by the Serbian forces against the Muslim population of Brcko was organised. Consequently, whether this organisation meant to destroy in whole or in part the Muslim group must be established.

89. The Trial Chamber notes in this regard that one witness related how a Serbian friend had told him that he had planned for only 20% of the Muslims to remain. Another witness declared that he was told during an interrogation at the mosque that 5% of the Muslims and Croats would be allowed to live but that this 5% would have to perform back-breaking work. Some witnesses even declared that on several occasions during their time at Luka they had carried up to twenty bodies.

90. During the exhumations which took place in summer 1997, approximately 66 bodies were discovered scattered about in four mass graves. The positions of the bodies indicate that they were piled haphazardly into the graves. Most were the bodies of males of fighting age and most of them had been shot dead.

91. The Prosecutor also tendered lists of names of persons who were reputedly killed at the time of the acts ascribed to the accused. In particular, the Prosecutor submitted a list of thirty-nine persons who for the most part were either members of the local administrative or political authorities, well-known figures in town, members of the Muslim Youth Association, members of the SDA or simply SDA sympathisers.

92. One witness described how the police detectives who interrogated the detainees at Luka camp appeared to decide which detainees were to be executed upon the basis of a document. Another detainee claimed at the hearing to have seen a list of numbered names headed "people to execute" in one of the administrative building offices in Luka camp. According to this witness, about fifty names appeared on the list and they were mostly Muslim.

93. However, the reason for being on these lists and how they were compiled is not clear. Nor has it been established that the accused relied on such a list in carrying out the executions. One witness stated *inter alia* that Goran Jelisić seemed to select the names of persons

at random from a list. Other witnesses suggested that the accused himself picked out his victims from those in the hangar. In no manner has it been established that the lists seen by Witness K or by Witness R at Luka camp correspond to that submitted by the Prosecutor. It is not therefore possible to conclude beyond all reasonable doubt that the choice of victims arose from a precise logic to destroy the most representative figures of the Muslim community in Brčko to the point of threatening the survival of that community.

94. In addition, it has been established that many detainees at Luka camp had a laissez-passer [a pass out of the camp]. According to Witness F, eighty to a hundred persons out of a total of six to seven hundred detainees were reputedly released in this way on the day they arrived, 8 May 1992. Other laissez-passer were reportedly issued subsequently. Allegedly, the detainees were also exchanged as of 19 May 1992.

95. It has also not been established beyond all reasonable doubt whether the accused killed at Luka camp under orders. Goran Jelisić allegedly presented himself to the detainees as the Luka camp commander. The detainees believed that he was the chief or at least a person in authority because he gave orders to the soldiers at the camp who appeared to be afraid of him. The Trial Chamber does not doubt that the accused exercised a *de facto* authority over the staff and detainees at the camp.

96. However, no element establishing the chain of command within which he operated has been presented. In particular, no clear information has been provided concerning the authority to which he answered. Some testimony did however make reference to a man who supposedly presented himself as being Jelisić's superior. This commander, who wore the uniform of the Yugoslav National Army (JNA), supposedly came to Luka camp on about 16 or 18 May 1992 with other military personnel and reported that an order had been given for the detainees not to be killed but kept alive for use in exchanges. Several witnesses attested to Goran Jelisić's being present in Luka camp up until 18 or 19 May 1992 and reported that there was a change of regime following his departure. Cruel treatment allegedly became less frequent and there were supposedly no more murders.

97. The Trial Chamber thus considers it possible that Goran Jelisić acted beyond the scope of the powers entrusted to him. Some of the testimony heard would appear to confirm this conclusion since it describes the accused as a man acting as he pleased and as he saw fit. One witness even recounted that Goran Jelisić had an altercation with a guard and told him that he should not subject the detainees to such treatment.

98. In consequence, the Trial Chamber considers that, in this case, the Prosecutor has not provided sufficient evidence allowing it to be established beyond all reasonable doubt that there existed a plan to destroy the Muslim group in Brcko or elsewhere within which the murders committed by the accused would allegedly fit.

(ii) Jelisić's intention to commit genocide

99. It is therefore only as a perpetrator that Goran Jelisić could be declared guilty of genocide.

100. Such a case is theoretically possible. The murders committed by the accused are sufficient to establish the material element of the crime of genocide and it is *a priori* possible to conceive that the accused harboured the plan to exterminate an entire group without this intent having been supported by any organisation in which other individuals participated. In this respect, the preparatory work of the Convention of 1948 brings out that premeditation was not selected as a legal ingredient of the crime of genocide, after having been mentioned by the *ad hoc* committee at the draft stage, on the grounds that it seemed superfluous given the special intention already required by the text and that such precision would only make the burden of proof even greater. It ensues from this omission that the drafters of the Convention did not deem the existence of an organisation or a system serving a genocidal objective as a

legal ingredient of the crime. In so doing, they did not discount the possibility of a lone individual seeking to destroy a group as such.

101. The Trial Chamber observes, however, that it will be very difficult in practice to provide proof of the genocidal intent of an individual if the crimes committed are not widespread and if the crime charged is not backed by an organisation or a system.

102. Admittedly, the testimony makes it seem that during this period Goran Jelisić presented himself as the "Serbian Adolf" and claimed to have gone to Brcko to kill Muslims. He also presented himself as "Adolf" at his initial hearing before the Trial Chamber on 26 January 1998. He allegedly said to the detainees at Luka camp that he held their lives in his hands and that only between 5 to 10 % of them would leave there. According to another witness, Goran Jelisić told the Muslim detainees in Luka camp that 70% of them were to be killed, 30% beaten and that barely 4% of the 30% might not be badly beaten. Goran Jelisić remarked to one witness that he hated the Muslims and wanted to kill them all, whilst the surviving Muslims could be slaves for cleaning the toilets but never have a professional job. He reportedly added that he wanted "to cleanse" the Muslims and would enjoy doing so, that the "balijas" had proliferated too much and that he had to rid the world of them. Goran Jelisić also purportedly said that he hated Muslim women, that he found them highly dirty and that he wanted to sterilise them all in order to prevent an increase in the number of Muslims but that before exterminating them he would begin with the men in order [to] prevent any proliferation.

103. The statements of the witnesses bring to light the fact that, during the initial part of May, Goran Jelisić regularly executed detainees at Luka camp. According to one witness, Goran Jelisić declared that he had to execute twenty to thirty persons before being able to drink his coffee each morning. The testimony heard by the Trial Chamber revealed that Goran Jelisić frequently informed the detainees of the number of Muslims that he had killed. Thus, on 8 May 1992 he reputedly said to one witness that it was his sixty-eighth victim, on 11 May that he had killed one hundred and fifty persons and finally on 15 May to another witness following an execution that it was his "eighty-third case".

104. Some witnesses pointed out that Goran Jelisić seemed to take pleasure from his position, one which gave him a feeling of power, of holding the power of life or death over the detainees and that he took a certain pride in the number of victims that he had allegedly executed. According to another testimony, Goran Jelisić spoke in a bloodthirsty manner, he treated them like animals or beasts and spittle formed on his lips because of his shouts and the hatred he was expressing. He wanted to terrorise them.

105. The words and attitude of Goran Jelisić as related by the witnesses essentially reveal a disturbed personality. Goran Jelisić led an ordinary life before the conflict. This personality, which presents borderline, anti-social and narcissistic characteristics and which is marked simultaneously by immaturity, a hunger to fill a "void" and a concern to please superiors, contributed to his finally committing crimes. Goran Jelisić suddenly found himself in an apparent position of authority for which nothing had prepared him. It matters little whether this authority was real. What does matter is that this authority made it even easier for an opportunistic and inconsistent behaviour to express itself.

106. Goran Jelisić performed the executions randomly. In addition, Witness R, an eminent and well-known figure in the Muslim community was allegedly forced to play Russian roulette with Goran Jelisić before receiving a laissez-passer directly from him. Moreover, on his own initiative and against all logic, Goran Jelisić issued laissez-passer to several detainees at the camp, as shown *inter alia* by the case of Witness E whom Goran Jelisić released after having beaten.

107. In conclusion, the acts of Goran Jelisić are not the physical expression of an affirmed resolve to destroy in whole or in part a group as such.

108. All things considered, the Prosecutor has not established beyond all reasonable doubt that genocide was committed in Brcko during the period covered by the indictment. Furthermore, the behaviour of the accused appears to indicate that, although he obviously singled out Muslims, he killed arbitrarily rather than with the clear intention to destroy a group. The Trial Chamber therefore concludes that it has not been proved beyond all reasonable doubt that the accused was motivated by the *dolus specialis* of the crime of genocide. The benefit of the doubt must always go to the accused and, consequently, Goran Jelisić must be found not guilty on this count.

ICTY, **Prosecutor *v.* Jelisić,** *Appeals Chamber, Judgment of 5 July 2001*

> The Prosecution appealed Jelisić's acquittal on the genocide count and Jelisić appealed his sentence of 40 years of imprisonment on the war crimes and crimes against humanity charges to which he pleaded guilty. The Prosecution argued that the Trial Chamber erred in law by applying an overly narrow conception of genocidal intent (*dolus specialis*) and in its factual inferences that genocidal intent was lacking.

C. Prosecution's third ground of appeal: intent to commit genocide

44. [...] Before discussing the Trial Chamber's interpretation of the term *dolus specialis*, the Appeals Chamber considers it necessary to clarify the requisite *mens rea* under Article 4 of the Statute [...]

45. Article 4, paragraphs (2) and (3) of the Statute largely reflect Articles II and III of the Convention on the Prevention and Punishment of the Crime of Genocide. As has been seen, Article 4(2) of the Statute defines genocide to mean any of certain "acts committed with intent to destroy, in whole or in part, a national, ethnical, racial or religious group, as such". The Statute itself defines the intent required: the intent to accomplish certain specified types of destruction. This intent has been referred to as, for example, special intent, specific intent, *dolus specialis,* particular intent and genocidal intent. The Appeals Chamber will use the term "specific intent" to describe the intent to destroy in whole or in part, a national, ethnical, racial or religious group, as such.

46. The specific intent requires that the perpetrator, by one of the prohibited acts enumerated in Article 4 of the Statute, seeks to achieve the destruction, in whole or in part, of a national, ethnical, racial or religious group, as such.

47. As to proof of specific intent, it may, in the absence of direct explicit evidence, be inferred from a number of facts and circumstances, such as the general context, the perpetration of other culpable acts systematically directed against the same group, the scale of atrocities committed, the systematic targeting of victims on account of their membership of a particular group, or the repetition of destructive and discriminatory acts.

48. The Appeals Chamber is of the opinion that the existence of a plan or policy is not a legal ingredient of the crime. However, in the context of proving specific intent, the existence of a plan or policy may become an important factor in most cases. The evidence may be consistent with the existence of a plan or policy, or may even show such existence, and the existence of a plan or policy may facilitate proof of the crime.

49. The Appeals Chamber further recalls the necessity to distinguish specific intent from motive. The personal motive of the perpetrator of the crime of genocide may be, for example, to obtain personal economic benefits, or political advantage or some form of power. The existence of a personal motive does not preclude the perpetrator from also having the specific

intent to commit genocide. In the *Tadic* appeal judgement the Appeals Chamber stressed the irrelevance and "inscrutability of motives in criminal law". [. . .]

53. The remaining issue is whether under the correct standard, that is, upon consideration of all relevant evidence submitted by the prosecution in its case-in-chief, the Trial Chamber was entitled to conclude that no reasonable trier of fact could find the evidence sufficient to sustain a conviction, beyond reasonable doubt, for genocide.

57. Having reviewed the evidence in the appeal record, the Appeals Chamber cannot validate the Trial Chamber's conclusion that it was not sufficient to sustain a conviction. It is not necessary in explaining reasons for this conclusion that the Appeals Chamber evaluates every item of evidence in the record. Rather, the Appeals Chamber can first assess the Trial Chamber's own reasons for its conclusion that acquittal was required in light of the evidence on record which was relevant to those reasons and, secondly, the Appeals Chamber can assess other evidence on the record which was not specifically referred to by the Trial Chamber but to which it has been directed in the course of the appeal. [. . .]

66. The Appeals Chamber turns first to evidence on the record that was presented by the prosecution during the appeal to demonstrate both that the respondent believed himself to be following a plan sent down by superiors to eradicate the Muslims in Brcko and that, regardless of any such plan, he was himself a one-man genocide mission, intent upon personally wiping out the protected group in whole or part. Some of this evidence was specifically cited by the Trial Chamber itself and summarised in its Judgement: threats by the respondent to kill 70%, to beat 30%, and spare only 5–10% of the Muslim detainees, statements by the respondent that he wanted to rid the world of the Muslims, announcements of his quota of daily killings, and his desire to sterilise Muslims in order to prevent proliferation of the group.

67. However, during the appeal the prosecution has also pointed to other material on the record which in its view supplements this evidence considerably, including extended interviews with the respondent himself which, though often contradictory, contained critical evidence as to his state of mind in committing the murders. A lengthy Annex A compiled by the prosecution contains citations from the evidence that the respondent operated from lists designating prominent Muslims to be killed; he referred to a "plan" for eradicating them; he wanted to "cleanse [. . .] the extremist Muslims and balijas like one cleans the head of lice". Witness I said of him: "[h]e carried out orders but he also selected his victims through his own free will" and that "[h]e could have not shot dead someone even if he were told to do so, but he did quite a few things on his own". There is additional evidence of the regular visits of a Bimeks refrigerated truck to the camp to pick up 10–20 dead bodies a day; nightly killings in which the respondent commented after each one "[a]nother balija less"; his repeated references to himself as the "Adolf the second" and comments like "I've killed 80 Muslims so far, and I'll finish all of you too" and "as many Muslims as possible had to be killed and that Brcko should become a Serbian town".

68. The Appeals Chamber considers that this evidence and much more of a similar genre in the record could have provided the basis for a reasonable Chamber to find beyond a reasonable doubt that the respondent had the intent to destroy the Muslim group in Brcko. To reiterate, the proper lens through which the Appeals Chamber must view such evidence is not whether it is convinced that the respondent was guilty of genocide beyond reasonable doubt but whether, giving credence to such evidence, no reasonable Trial Chamber could have found that he had such an intent. The Appeals Chamber is not able to conclude that that was the case.

69. The Appeals Chamber also considers whether the Trial Chamber reasonably concluded that, even on the basis of the evidence it cited and discussed, the respondent should be acquitted for lack of the requisite intent by any reasonable trier of fact.

70. The Trial Chamber essentially relied on the following evidence for its reasonable doubt conclusion: that the respondent had a disturbed personality; that he was immature, narcissistic, desirous of pleasing superiors and that, when placed in a position of authority, those traits manifested themselves in an obsession with power over the lives of those he commanded. This, the Trial Chamber said, was not the same as "an affirmed resolve" to destroy a protected group, in this case the Brcko Muslims. It bears noting that the psychiatric underpinnings of this conclusion come from expert reports prepared for the purpose of deciding whether the respondent was competent to stand trial (he was found to be) and in particular not for evaluating his mental capacity to commit the crimes with which he was charged. He did not plead a defence of insanity and indeed the Trial Chamber itself found him capable of a discriminatory intent in a separate finding. It is sufficient for our purposes here to point out that there is no *per se* inconsistency between a diagnosis of the kind of immature, narcissistic, disturbed personality on which the Trial Chamber relied and the ability to form an intent to destroy a particular protected group. Indeed, as the prosecution points out, it is the borderline unbalanced personality who is more likely to be drawn to extreme racial and ethnical hatred than the more balanced modulated individual without personality defects. The Rules visualise, as a defence, a certain degree of mental incapacity and in any event, no such imbalance was found in this case.

71. The Trial Chamber also placed heavy reliance on the randomness of the respondent's killings. It cited examples of where he let some prisoners go, played Russian roulette for the life of another, and picked his victims not just off lists allegedly given to him by others, but according to his own whim. Entitled though it may have been to consider such evidence, the Trial Chamber, in the view of the Appeals Chamber, was not entitled to conclude that these displays of "randomness" negated the plethora of other evidence recounted above as to the respondent's announced intent to kill the majority of Muslims in Brcko and his quotas and arrangements for so doing. A reasonable trier of fact could have discounted the few incidents where he showed mercy as aberrations in an otherwise relentless campaign against the protected group. Similarly, the fact that he took "pleasure" from the killings does not detract in any way from his intent to perform such killings; as has been mentioned above, the Tribunal has declared in the *Tadic* appeal judgement the irrelevance and "inscrutability of motives in criminal law" insofar as liability is concerned, where an intent – including a specific intent – is clear.

72. Thus, even if the Trial Chamber's conclusion that there was insufficient evidence to show an intent to destroy the group on the respondent's part is examined on the basis of the evidence specifically referred to by the Trial Chamber itself, it does not pass the approved standard for acquittal under Rule 98*bis*(B) and, consequently, this part of the prosecution's third ground of appeal is sustained.

73. With regard to remedy, counsel for the respondent argues that the Appeals Chamber has discretion, and that, in all the circumstances of this case, there should be no retrial. The Appeals Chamber agrees that the choice of remedy lies within its discretion. Article 25 of the Statute (relating to appellate proceedings) is wide enough to confer such a faculty; this discretion is recognised as well in the wording of Rule 117(C) of the Rules which provides that in "appropriate circumstances the Appeals Chamber may order that the accused be retried according to law". Similarly, national case law gives discretion to a court to rule that there should be no retrial. [...]

74. For the purpose of determining that question, the Appeals Chamber considers the following factors to be of relevance. The respondent pleaded guilty to certain criminal conduct that was set out in the agreed factual basis. On the basis of that criminal conduct he was found guilty of 31 counts of violations of the laws or customs of war and crimes against humanity. The Trial Chamber imposed a sentence of 40 years' imprisonment. A potential retrial would deal with a count of genocide, charging the respondent with genocide by killing. In respect

of this count, the prosecution has brought no further charges of killing. The genocide count is therefore based on the killings to which he has already pleaded guilty. Accordingly, a retrial would be limited to the question of whether he possessed the special intent to destroy in whole or in part, a national, ethnical, racial or religious group, as such. The definition of specific intent has been clarified in the context of the prosecution appeal above.

75. Also, it was through no fault of the accused that the Trial Chamber erred in law – it was not the case that arguments advanced by the defence led to the Trial Chamber's decision to enter a judgement of acquittal. Considerable time will have elapsed between the date that the offences were committed in May 1992 and the date of any potential retrial. The *ad hoc* nature of the International Tribunal which, unlike a national legal system, means resources are limited in terms of man-power and the uncertain longevity of the Tribunal. [. . .]

77. Rule 117(C) of the Rules provides that in "appropriate circumstances the Appeals Chamber may order that the accused be retried according to law". The Appeals Chamber recognizes the prosecution's right to request a retrial as a remedy on appeal. However, as has been stated above, whether or not such a request is granted, lies within the discretion of the Appeals Chamber based on the facts of the case before it. It is not obliged, having identified an error, to remit for retrial. Considering the exceptional circumstances of the present case, the Appeal Chamber considers that it is not in the interests of justice to grant the prosecution's request and accordingly declines to reverse the acquittal entered by the Trial Chamber and remit the case for further proceedings. [. . .]

While the facts of *Jelisić* posed the problem of distinguishing sadism from genocidal intent, the facts of *Krstić* posed the problem of distinguishing intent to displace *part* of a group from a particular region with intent to destroy. In the post-World War II era, episodes of what has been dubbed 'ethnic cleansing' have flared repeatedly in regions such as Bosnia, Rwanda and Sudan. Ethnic cleansing is not a formal legal term. It is shorthand used to signify various strategies aimed at ridding a region of a particular ethnic group. One of the struggles in contemporary genocide jurisprudence is determining whether acts of violence with the goal of displacing a population amount to genocide. Is intent to displace a group different from intent to destroy the group and why? When might ethnic cleansing and efforts aimed at intimidating a population into leaving a region rise to the level of genocide?

ICTY, **Prosecutor v. Krstić**, *Trial Chamber, Judgment of 2 August 2001*

After analysing whether the military-aged men of Srebrenica met the definition of a protected group (see the excerpt, *supra*, subsection (b)(1) on protected groups), the Krstić Trial Chamber analysed whether General Krstić – thrust into a genocidal course of action he probably would not have chosen – harboured the requisite *mens rea*. Consider whether the ICTY Trial Chamber takes sufficient care to avoid conflating intent to displace with intent to destroy.

563. The accused himself defined the objective of the campaign in Bosnia during an interview in November 1995, when he explained that the Podrinje region should remain "Serbian for ever, while the Eastern part of Republika Srpska and the Drina river would be an important meeting point for the entire Serbian people from both sides of the Drina".

564. In this goal, the cleansing of Bosnian Muslims from Srebrenica had special advantages. Lying in the central Podrinje region, whose strategic importance for the creation of a Bosnian

Serb Republic has frequently been cited in testimony, Srebrenica and the surrounding area was a predominantly Muslim pocket within a mainly Serbian region adjoining Serbia. Given the war objectives, it is hardly surprising that the Serbs and Bosnian Muslims fought each other bitterly in this region from the outbreak of the conflict.

565. Many attacks were launched by both parties against villages controlled by the other side in the region. The Bosnian Muslim forces committed apparent violations of humanitarian law directed against the Bosnian Serb inhabitants of the region, especially from May 1992 to January 1993. In response, operations were conducted by the Bosnian Serb forces, notably, a large-scale attack launched in January 1993. The attack forced the Bosnian Muslim population from the surrounding villages to flee to the areas of Srebrenica and Žepa. As a result, the population of Srebrenica climbed from 37,000 in 1991 to 50,000 or 60,000 in 1993 while, at the same time, the territory shrank from 900 to 150 square km. [. . .]

567. However, the Trial Chamber has found that, on its face, the operation Krivaja 95 did not include a plan to overrun the enclave and expel the Bosnian Muslim population. The Trial Chamber heard credible testimony on the chronic refusal of Bosnian Muslim forces to respect the demilitarisation agreement of 1993. Defence witnesses accused the Bosnian Muslim forces of using the safe area as a fortified base from which to launch offensives against the Bosnian Serb forces. In particular, on 26 June 1995, several weeks prior to the offensive of the VRS on Srebrenica, the Bosnian Muslim forces launched an assault from the enclave on the Serbian village of Visnica 5km away. Such acts could well have motivated an attack designed to cut communications between the enclaves of Žepa and Srebrenica.

568. The operation, however, was not confined to mere retaliation. Its objective, although perhaps restricted initially to blocking communications between the two enclaves and reducing the Srebrenica enclave to its urban core, was quickly extended. Realising that no resistance was being offered by the Bosnian Muslim forces or the international community, President Karadžić broadened the operation's objective by issuing, on 9 July, the order to seize the town. By 11 July, the town of Srebrenica was captured, driving 20,000 to 25,000 Muslim refugees to flee towards Potočari. Operation Krivaja 1995 then became an instrument of the policy designed to drive out the Bosnian Muslim population. The humanitarian crisis caused by the flow of refugees arriving at Potočari, the intensity and the scale of the violence, the illegal confinement of the men in one area, while the women and children were forcibly transferred out of the Bosnian Serb held territory, and the subsequent death of thousands of Bosnian Muslim civilian and military men, most of whom clearly did not die in combat, demonstrate that a purposeful decision was taken by the Bosnian Serb forces to target the Bosnian Muslim population in Srebrenica, by reason of their membership in the Bosnian Muslim group. It remains to determine whether this discriminatory attack sought to destroy the group, in whole or in part, within the meaning of Article 4 of the Statute.

(b) Intent to destroy the group in whole or in part

(i) Intent to destroy

571. [. . .] The preparatory work of the Genocide Convention clearly shows that the drafters envisaged genocide as an enterprise whose goal, or objective, was to destroy a human group, in whole or in part. [. . .] Moreover, the Chamber notes that the domestic law of some States distinguishes genocide by the existence of a plan to destroy a group. Some legal commentators further contend that genocide embraces those acts whose foreseeable or probable consequence is the total or partial destruction of the group without any necessity of showing that destruction was the goal of the act. Whether this interpretation can be viewed as reflecting the status of customary international law at the time of the acts involved here is not clear. For the purpose of this case, the Chamber will therefore adhere to the characterisation of

genocide which encompass[es] only acts committed with the *goal* of destroying all or part of a group.

572. Article 4 of the Statute does not require that the genocidal acts be premeditated over a long period. It is conceivable that, although the intention at the outset of an operation was not the destruction of a group, it may become the goal at some later point during the implementation of the operation. For instance, an armed force could decide to destroy a protected group during a military operation whose primary objective was totally unrelated to the fate of the group. The Appeals Chamber, in a recent decision, indicated that the existence of a plan was not a legal ingredient of the crime of genocide but could be of evidential assistance to prove the intent of the authors of the criminal act(s). Evidence presented in this case has shown that the killings were planned: the number and nature of the forces involved, the standardised coded language used by the units in communicating information about the killings, the scale of the executions, the invariability of the killing methods applied, indicate that a decision was made to kill all the Bosnian Muslim military aged men.

573. The Trial Chamber is unable to determine the precise date on which the decision to kill all the military aged men was taken. Hence, it cannot find that the killings committed in Potočari on 12 and 13 July 1995 formed part of the plan to kill all the military aged men. Nevertheless, the Trial Chamber is confident that the mass executions and other killings committed from 13 July onwards were part of this plan.

574. The manner in which the destruction of a group may be implemented so as to qualify as a genocide under Article 4 must also be discussed. The physical destruction of a group is the most obvious method, but one may also conceive of destroying a group through purposeful eradication of its culture and identity resulting in the eventual extinction of the group as an entity distinct from the remainder of the community.

575. The notion of genocide, as fashioned by Raphael Lemkin in 1944, originally covered all forms of destruction of a group as a distinct social entity. As such, genocide closely resembled the crime of persecution. In this regard, the ILC stated, in its 1996 report, that genocide as currently defined corresponds to the second category of crime against humanity established under Article 6(c) of the Nuremberg Tribunal's Statute, namely the crime of persecution. There is consensus that the crime of persecution provided for by the Statute of the Nuremberg Tribunal was not limited to the physical destruction of the group but covered all acts designed to destroy the social and/or cultural bases of a group. Such a broad interpretation of persecution was upheld *inter alia* in the indictment against *Ulrich Greifelt et al.*, before the United States Military Tribunal in Nuremberg. The accused were charged with implementing a systematic programme of genocide which sought to destroy foreign nations and ethnic groups. The indictment interpreted destruction to mean not only the extermination of the members of those groups but also the eradication of their national characteristics. It should be noted that this interpretation was supported by the working group established to report on the human rights violations in South Africa in 1985. While recognising that the Convention literally covered only the physical or material destruction of the group, the report explained that it was adopting a broader interpretation that viewed as genocidal any act which prevented an individual "from participating fully in national life", the latter being understood "in its more general sense".

576. Although the Convention does not specifically speak to the point, the preparatory work points out that the "cultural" destruction of a group was expressly rejected after having been seriously contemplated. The notion of cultural genocide was considered too vague and too removed from the physical or biological destruction that motivated the Convention. The ILC noted in 1996:

> As clearly shown by the preparatory work for the Convention, the destruction in question
> is the material destruction of a group either by physical or by biological means, not the

destruction of the national, linguistic, religious, cultural or other identity of a particular group. The national or religious element and the racial or ethnic element are not taken into consideration in the definition of the word "destruction", which must be taken only in its material sense, its physical or biological sense.

577. Several recent declarations and decisions, however, have interpreted the intent to destroy clause in Article 4 so as to encompass evidence relating to acts that involved cultural and other non physical forms of group destruction.

578. In 1992, the United Nations General Assembly labelled ethnic cleansing as a form of genocide.

579. The Federal Constitutional Court of Germany said in December 2000 that:

the statutory definition of genocide defends a supra-individual object of legal protection, i.e. the *social* existence of the group [...] the intent to destroy the group [...] extends beyond physical and biological extermination [...] The text of the law does not therefore compel the interpretation that the culprit's intent must be to exterminate physically at least a substantial number of the members of the group.

580. The Trial Chamber is aware that it must interpret the Convention with due regard for the principle of *nullum crimen sine lege*. It therefore recognises that, despite recent developments, customary international law limits the definition of genocide to those acts seeking the physical or biological destruction of all or part of the group. Hence, an enterprise attacking only the cultural or sociological characteristics of a human group in order to annihilate these elements which give to that group its own identity distinct from the rest of the community would not fall under the definition of genocide. The Trial Chamber however points out that where there is physical or biological destruction there are often simultaneous attacks on the cultural and religious property and symbols of the targeted group as well, attacks which may legitimately be considered as evidence of an intent to physically destroy the group. In this case, the Trial Chamber will thus take into account as evidence of intent to destroy the group the deliberate destruction of mosques and houses belonging to members of the group.

(ii) "In part"

581. Since in this case primarily the Bosnian Muslim men of military age were killed, a second issue is whether this group of victims represented a sufficient part of the Bosnian Muslim group so that the intent to destroy them qualifies as an "intent to destroy the group in whole or in part" under Article 4 of the Statute. [...]

583. The Defence contends that the term "in part" refers to the scale of the crimes actually committed, as opposed to the intent, which would have to extend to destroying the group as such, *i.e.* in its entirety. [...]

584. The Trial Chamber does not agree. Admittedly, by adding the term "in part", some of the Convention's drafters may have intended that actual destruction of a mere part of a human group could be characterised as genocide, only as long as it was carried out with the intent to destroy the group as such. The debates on this point during the preparatory work are unclear, however, and a plain reading of the Convention contradicts this interpretation. Under the Convention, the term "in whole or in part" refers to the intent, as opposed to the actual destruction, and it would run contrary to the rules of interpretation to alter the ordinary meaning of the terms used in the Convention by recourse to the preparatory work which lacks clarity on the issue. The Trial Chamber concludes that any act committed with the intent to destroy a part of a group, as such, constitutes an act of genocide within the meaning of the Convention.

585. The Genocide Convention itself provides no indication of what constitutes intent to destroy "in part". The preparatory work offers few indications either. The draft Convention submitted by the Secretary-General observes that "the systematic destruction even of a fraction of a group of human beings constitutes an exceptionally heinous crime". Early commentaries on the Genocide Convention opined that the matter of what was substantial fell within the ambit of the Judges' discretionary evaluation. Nehemia Robinson was of the view that the intent to destroy could pertain to only a region or even a local community if the number of persons targeted was substantial. Pieter Drost remarked that any systematic destruction of a fraction of a protected group constituted genocide.

586. A somewhat stricter interpretation has prevailed in more recent times. According to the ILC, the perpetrators of the crime must seek to destroy a quantitatively substantial part of the protected group:

It is not necessary to intend to achieve the complete annihilation of a group from every corner of the globe. None the less the crime of genocide by its very nature requires the intention to destroy at least a substantial part of a particular group. [...]

587. Benjamin Whitaker's 1985 study on the prevention and punishment of the crime of genocide holds that the partial destruction of a group merits the characterisation of genocide when it concerns a large portion of the entire group or a significant section of that group.

'In part' would seem to imply a reasonably significant number, relative to the total of the group as a whole, or else a significant section of a group, such as its leadership.

The "Final Report of the Commission of Experts established pursuant to Security Council resolution 780 (1992)" (hereinafter "Report of the Commission of Experts") confirmed this interpretation, and considered that an intent to destroy a specific part of a group, such as its political, administrative, intellectual or business leaders, "may be a strong indication of genocide regardless of the actual numbers killed". The report states that extermination specifically directed against law enforcement and military personnel may affect "a significant section of a group in that it renders the group at large defenceless against other abuses of a similar or other nature". However, the Report goes on to say that "the attack on the leadership must be viewed *in the context of the fate of what happened to the rest of the group*. If a group suffers extermination of its leadership and in the wake of that loss, a large number of its members are killed or subjected to other heinous acts, for example deportation, the cluster of violations ought to be considered in its entirety in order to interpret the provisions of the Convention in a spirit consistent with its purpose".

588. Judge Elihu Lauterpacht, the *ad hoc* Judge nominated by Bosnia-Herzegovina in the case before the International Court of Justice regarding the application of the Convention on the Prevention and Punishment of the Crime of Genocide, spoke similarly in his separate opinion. Judge Lauterpacht observed that the Bosnian Serb forces had murdered and caused serious mental and bodily injury to the Bosnian Muslims and had subjected the group to living conditions meant to bring about its total or partial physical destruction. He went on to take into account "the forced migration of civilians, more commonly known as 'ethnic cleansing' " in order to establish the intent to destroy all or part of the group. In his view, this demonstrated the Serbs' intent "to eliminate Muslim control of, and presence in, substantial parts of Bosnia-Herzegovina". Judge Lauterpacht concluded that the acts which led to the group's physical destruction had to be characterised as "acts of genocide" since they were "directed against an ethnical or religious group as such, and they were intended to destroy that group, if not in whole certainly in part, to the extent necessary to ensure that that group would no longer occupy the parts of Bosnia-Herzegovina coveted by the Serbs".

589. Several other sources confirm that the intent to eradicate a group within a limited geographical area such as the region of a country or even a municipality may be characterised as genocide. The United Nations General Assembly characterised as an act of genocide the murder of approximately 800 Palestinians detained at Sabra and Shatila, most of whom were women, children and elderly. The *Jelisić* Judgement held that genocide could target a limited geographic zone. Two Judgements recently rendered by German courts took the view that genocide could be perpetrated within a limited geographical area. The Federal Constitutional Court of Germany, in the *Nikola Jorgic* case, upheld the Judgement of the Düsseldorf Supreme Court, interpreting the intent to destroy the group "in part" as including the intention to destroy a group within a limited geographical area. In a Judgement against Novislav Djajic on 23 May 1997, the Bavarian Appeals Chamber similarly found that acts of genocide were committed in June 1992 though confined within the administrative district of Foča.

590. The Trial Chamber is thus left with a margin of discretion in assessing what is destruction "in part" of the group. But it must exercise its discretionary power in a spirit consonant with the object and purpose of the Convention which is to criminalise specified conduct directed against the existence of protected *groups*, as such. The Trial Chamber is therefore of the opinion that the intent to destroy a group, even if only in part, means seeking to destroy a distinct part of the group as opposed to an accumulation of isolated individuals within it. Although the perpetrators of genocide need not seek to destroy the entire group protected by the Convention, they must view the part of the group they wish to destroy as a distinct entity which must be eliminated as such. A campaign resulting in the killings, in different places spread over a broad geographical area, of a finite number of members of a protected group might not thus qualify as genocide, despite the high total number of casualties, because it would not show an intent by the perpetrators to target the very existence of the group as such. Conversely, the killing of all members of the part of a group located within a small geographical area, although resulting in a lesser number of victims, would qualify as genocide if carried out with the intent to destroy the part of the group as such located in this small geographical area. Indeed, the physical destruction may target only a part of the geographically limited part of the larger group because the perpetrators of the genocide regard the intended destruction as sufficient to annihilate the group as a distinct entity in the geographic area at issue. In this regard, it is important to bear in mind the total context in which the physical destruction is carried out.

591. The parties have presented opposing views as to whether the killings of Bosnian Muslim men in Srebrenica were carried out with intent to destroy a substantial part of the Bosnian Muslim group. It should be recalled that the Prosecution at different times has proposed different definitions of the group in the context of the charge of genocide. In the Indictment, as in the submission of the Defence, the Prosecution referred to the group of the Bosnian Muslims, while in the final brief and arguments it defined the group as the Bosnian Muslims of Srebrenica or the Bosnian Muslims of Eastern Bosnia. The Trial Chamber has previously indicated that the protected group, under Article 4 of the Statute, should be defined as the Bosnian Muslims.

594. The Trial Chamber concludes from the evidence that the VRS forces sought to eliminate all of the Bosnian Muslims in Srebrenica as a community. Within a period of no more than seven days, as many as 7,000–8,000 men of military age were systematically massacred while the remainder of the Bosnian Muslim population present at Srebrenica, some 25,000 people, were forcibly transferred to Kladanj. [. . .]

595. Granted, only the men of military age were systematically massacred, but it is significant that these massacres occurred at a time when the forcible transfer of the rest of the Bosnian Muslim population was well under way. The Bosnian Serb forces could not have failed to know, by the time they decided to kill all the men, that this selective destruction of the

group would have a lasting impact upon the entire group. Their death precluded any effective attempt by the Bosnian Muslims to recapture the territory. Furthermore, the Bosnian Serb forces had to be aware of the catastrophic impact that the disappearance of two or three generations of men would have on the survival of a traditionally patriarchal society, an impact the Chamber has previously described in detail. The Bosnian Serb forces knew, by the time they decided to kill all of the military aged men, that the combination of those killings with the forcible transfer of the women, children and elderly would inevitably result in the physical disappearance of the Bosnian Muslim population at Srebrenica. Intent by the Bosnian Serb forces to target the Bosnian Muslims of Srebrenica as a group is further evidenced by their destroying homes of Bosnian Muslims in Srebrenica and Potočari and the principal mosque in Srebrenica soon after the attack.

596. Finally, there is a strong indication of the intent to destroy the group as such in the concealment of the bodies in mass graves, which were later dug up, the bodies mutilated and reburied in other mass graves located in even more remote areas, thereby preventing any decent burial in accord with religious and ethnic customs and causing terrible distress to the mourning survivors, many of whom have been unable to come to a closure until the death of their men is finally verified.

597. The strategic location of the enclave, situated between two Serb territories, may explain why the Bosnian Serb forces did not limit themselves to expelling the Bosnian Muslim population. By killing all the military aged men, the Bosnian Serb forces effectively destroyed the community of the Bosnian Muslims in Srebrenica as such and eliminated all likelihood that it could ever re-establish itself on that territory.

598. The Chamber concludes that the intent to kill all the Bosnian Muslim men of military age in Srebrenica constitutes an intent to destroy in part the Bosnian Muslim group within the meaning of Article 4 and therefore must be qualified as a genocide.

After the Trial Chamber sentenced him to 46 years in prison, Krstić appealed his genocide conviction to the Appeals Chamber, which held that the Trial Chamber erred in deeming Krstić to be a principal perpetrator of genocide because he personally lacked the specific intent to destroy the targeted group. That is, while genocide occurred in Srebrenica, Krstić did not commit it. The Appeals Chamber held that because Krstić knew of the genocidal intent of others, however, when he allowed men to join the killing operation, he was liable as an accomplice – an aider and abettor of genocide. Krstić was ultimately sentenced to 35 years of imprisonment and is now serving his sentence in the United Kingdom.

....

Report of the International Commission of Inquiry on Darfur to the United Nations Secretary-General, 25 January 2005 (UN Doc. S/2005/60)

Another example of the complexities of discerning between intent to displace versus to destroy, and the interaction between the notion of a 'protected group' and the necessary specific intent to commit genocide, is posed by the widespread attacks against civilians in the Darfur region of Sudan. In 2004, the United Nations commissioned a report on Darfur. The Commission of Inquiry, chaired by Antonio Cassese, reached the following findings in relation to genocide.

507. *General.* There is no doubt that some of the objective elements of genocide materialized in Darfur. As discussed above, the Commission has collected substantial and reliable material which tends to show the occurrence of systematic killing of civilians belonging to particular

tribes, of large-scale causation of serious bodily or mental harm to members of the population belonging to certain tribes and of massive and deliberate infliction on those tribes of conditions of life bringing about their physical destruction in whole or in part (for example, by systematically destroying their villages and crops, by expelling them from their homes and by looting their cattle). However, two other constitutive elements of genocide require a more in-depth analysis, namely, whether the target groups amount to one of the groups protected by international law and, if so, whether the crimes were committed with a genocidal intent. These elements are considered separately below.

508. *Do members of tribes that are victims of attacks and killing objectively constitute a protected group?* The various tribes that have been the object of attacks and killings (chiefly the Fur, Masalit and Zaghawa tribes) do not appear to make up ethnic groups distinct from the ethnic group to which persons or militias that attack them belong. They speak the same language (Arabic) and embrace the same religion (Islam). In addition, owing to the high incidence of intermarriage, they can hardly be distinguished in their outward physical appearance from the members of tribes that allegedly attacked them. Furthermore, intermarriage and coexistence in both social and economic terms have over the years tended to blur the distinction between the groups. Apparently, the sedentary and nomadic character of the groups constitutes one of the main distinctions between them. It is also notable that members of the African tribes speak their own dialects in addition to Arabic, while members of Arab tribes speak only Arabic.

509. *If not, may one hold that they subjectively constitute distinct groups?* If objectively the two sets of persons at issue do not constitute two distinct protected groups, the question arises as to whether they may nevertheless be regarded as such subjectively in that they perceive each other and themselves as constituting distinct groups.

510. As noted above, in recent years the perception of differences has heightened and has extended to distinctions that earlier were not the predominant basis for identity. The rifts between tribes and the political polarization around the rebel opposition to the central authorities have been extended to issues of identity. Those tribes in Darfur which support rebels have increasingly come to be identified as "African", and those supporting the Government as "Arab". Clearly, however, not all "African" tribes support the rebels and not all "Arab" tribes support the Government. Some so-called Arab tribes appear to be either neutral or even support the rebels. For example, the Gimmer, a pro-Government African tribe, and how it is seen by the African tribes opposed to the Government as having been Arabized. Other measures contributing to a polarization of the two groups include the 1987–1989 conflict over access to grazing lands and water sources between nomads of Arab origin and the sedentary Fur. The Arab-African divide has also been fanned by the growing insistence on such a divide in some circles and in the media. All this has contributed to the consolidation of the contrast and gradually created a marked polarization in the perception and self-perception of the groups concerned. At least those most affected by the conditions explained above, including those directly affected by the conflict, have come to perceive themselves as either African or Arab.

511. There are other elements that tend to indicate the self-perception of two distinct groups. In many cases militias attacking "African" villages tend to use derogatory epithets, such as "slaves", "blacks", *nuba*, or *zurga* that might imply a perception of the victims as members of a distinct group. However, in numerous other instances they use derogatory language that is not linked to ethnicity or race. As for the victims, they often refer to their attackers as *Janjaweed*, a derogatory term that normally designates "a man (a devil) with a gun on a horse". However, in this case the term Janjaweed clearly refers to "militias of *Arab* tribes on horseback or camelback". In other words, the victims perceive the attackers as persons belonging to a different and hostile group.

512. For these reasons it may be considered that the tribes that have been victims of attacks and killings subjectively make up a protected group.

513. *Was there a genocidal intent?* Some elements emerging from the facts, including the scale of atrocities and the systematic nature of the attacks, killing, displacement and rape, as well as racially motivated statements by perpetrators that have targeted members of the African tribes only, could be indicative of the genocidal intent. However, there are other more indicative elements that show a lack of genocidal intent. An important element is the fact that in a number of villages attacked and burned by both militias and Government forces, the attackers refrained from exterminating the whole population that had not fled, but instead selectively killed groups of young men. A telling example is the attack of 22 January 2004 on Wadi Saleh, a group of 25 villages inhabited by about 11,000 Fur. According to credible accounts of eyewitnesses questioned by the Commission, after occupying the villages, the Government Commissioner and the leader of the Arab militias that had participated in the attack and burning gathered all those who had survived or had not managed to escape into a large area. Using a microphone, they selected 15 persons (whose names they read from a written list), as well as 7 *omdas* (local leaders), and executed them on the spot. They then sent many men, including all elderly men, all boys and all women to a nearby village where they held them for some time, whereas they executed 205 young villagers who they asserted were rebels (*Torabora*). According to male survivors interviewed by the Commission, about 800 persons were not killed (most of the young men spared by the attackers were detained for some time in the Mukjar prison).

514. This case clearly shows that the intent of the attackers was not to destroy an ethnic group as such or part of the group. Instead, the intention was to murder all those men they considered as rebels, as well as forcibly expel the whole population so as to vacate the villages and prevent rebels from hiding among or getting support from the local population.

515. Another element that tends to show the Sudanese Government's lack of genocidal intent can be seen in the fact that persons forcibly dislodged from their villages are collected in camps for internally displaced persons. In other words, the populations surviving attacks on villages are not killed outright in an effort to eradicate the group; they are rather forced to abandon their homes and live together in areas selected by the Government. While this attitude of the Government of the Sudan may be held to be in breach of international legal standards on human rights and international criminal law rules, it is not indicative of any intent to annihilate the group. This is all the more true because the living conditions in those camps, although open to strong criticism on many grounds, do not seem to be calculated to bring about the extinction of the ethnic group to which the internally displaced persons belong. Suffice it to note that the Government of the Sudan generally allows humanitarian organizations to help the population in camps by providing food, clean water, medicine and logistical assistance (construction of hospitals, cooking facilities, latrines, etc.).

516. Another element that tends to show a lack of genocidal intent is the fact that in contrast with other instances described above, in a number of instances villages with a mixed composition (African and Arab tribes) have not been attacked. This holds true, for instance, for the village of Abaata (north-east of Zalinguei in Western Darfur), consisting of Zaghawa and members of Arab tribes.

517. Furthermore, it has been reported by a reliable source that one inhabitant of the Jabir village (situated about 150 km from Abu Shouk Camp) was among the victims of an attack carried out by Janjaweed on the village on 16 March 2004. He stated that he did not resist when the attackers took 200 camels from him, although they beat him up with the butts of their guns. Prior to his beating, however, his younger brother, who possessed only one camel, had resisted when the attackers had tried to take his camel, and he had been shot dead. Clearly,

in this instance the special intent to kill a member of a group *to* destroy the group as such was lacking, the murder being motivated only by the desire to appropriate cattle belonging to the inhabitants of the village. Irrespective of the motive, had the attackers' intent been to annihilate the group, they would not have spared one of the brothers.

518. *Conclusion.* On the basis of the foregoing observations, the Commission concludes that the Government of the Sudan has not pursued a policy of genocide. Arguably, two elements of genocide might be deduced from the gross violations of human rights perpetrated by Government forces and the militias under their control. These two elements are, first, the *actus reus* consisting of killing, causing serious bodily or mental harm or deliberately inflicting conditions of life likely to bring about physical destruction, and second, on the basis of a subjective standard, the existence of a protected group being targeted by the perpetrators of criminal conduct. Recent developments have led to the perception and self-perception of members of African tribes and members of Arab tribes as making up two distinct ethnic groups. However, one crucial element appears to be missing, at least as far as the central Government authorities are concerned: genocidal intent. Generally speaking, the policy of attacking, killing and forcibly displacing members of some tribes does not evince a specific intent to annihilate, in whole or in part, a group distinguished on racial, ethnic, national or religious grounds. Rather, it would seem that those who planned and organized attacks on villages pursued the intent to drive the victims from their homes primarily for purposes of counter-insurgency warfare.

519. However, as pointed out above, the Government also entertained the intent to drive a particular group out of an area on persecutory and discriminatory grounds for political reasons. In the case of Darfur, this discriminatory and persecutory intent may be found, on many occasions, in some Arab militias, as well as in the central Government: the systematic attacks on villages inhabited by civilians (or mostly by civilians) belonging to some "African" tribes (Fur, Masalit and Zaghawa), the systematic destruction and burning down of those villages and the forced displacement of civilians from the villages attest to a manifestly persecutory intent. In this respect, in addition to murder as a crime against humanity, the Government may be held responsible for persecution as a crime against humanity. This would not affect the conclusion of the Commission that the Government of the Sudan has not pursued a policy of genocide in Darfur.

520. One should not rule out the possibility that in some instances *single individuals*, including Government officials, may entertain a genocidal intent or, in other words, attack the victims with the specific intent of annihilating, in part, a group perceived as a hostile ethnic group. If any single individual, including any Government official, has such an intent, it would be up to a competent court to make such a determination on a case-by-case basis. Should the court determine that in some instances certain individuals pursued a genocidal intent, the issue would arise of establishing any criminal responsibility of senior officials either for complicity in genocide or for failure to investigate, or to suppress and punish, such possible acts of genocide.

521. Similarly, it would be for a competent court to determine whether some individual members of the militias supported by the Government, or even single Government officials, pursued a policy of extermination as a crime against humanity or whether the murder of civilians was so widespread and systematic as to acquire the legal features proper to extermination as a crime against humanity.

522. The conclusion that no genocidal policy has been pursued and implemented in Darfur by the Government authorities, directly or through the militias under their control, should not be taken as in any way detracting from, or belittling, the gravity of the crimes perpetrated in that region. As stated above, genocide is not necessarily the most serious international crime. Depending on the circumstances, such international offences as crimes against humanity or large-scale war crimes may be no less serious and heinous than genocide. This is exactly what

happened in Darfur, where massive atrocities were perpetrated on a very large scale and have so far gone unpunished.

On 31 March 2005, the UN Security Council referred the situation in Darfur to the ICC. While the ICCSt. reproduces the definition of genocide in the Genocide Convention, the ICC Elements of Crimes, an aid to interpretation and application of the ICC's subject-matter jurisdiction, adds as an element of genocide that:

[t]he conduct took place in the context of a manifest pattern of similar conduct directed against that group or was conduct that could itself effect such destruction.[2]

This element may help distinguish genocide cases from those that should be charged instead as crimes against humanity. What this element will mean for the ICC's interpretation of the Genocide Convention in practice has yet to be determined.

In the *Al Bashir* arrest warrant decision, an ICC Pre-Trial Chamber – like the Commission of Inquiry in 2004 – ruled that the Prosecution failed to establish reasonable grounds to believe that the Government of Sudan (GoS) acted with genocidal intent to destroy in whole or in part the Fur, Masalit and Zaghawa groups of the Sudan. The Pre-Trial Chamber reasoned:

203. [...] [T]he Majority agrees with the Prosecution in that the [A]rticle 58 evidentiary standard would be met only if the materials provided by the Prosecution in support of the Prosecution Application show that the only reasonable conclusion to be drawn therefrom is the existence of reasonable grounds to believe that the GoS acted with a *dolus specialis*/specific intent to destroy, in whole or in part, the Fur, Masalit and Zaghawa groups. [...]

205. In the view of the Majority [...] the existence of reasonable grounds to believe that the GoS acted with a *dolus specialis*/specific intent to destroy in whole or in part the Fur, Masalit and Zaghawa groups is not the only reasonable conclusion that can be drawn therefrom.

206. As a result, the Majority finds that the materials provided by the Prosecution in support of the Prosecution Application fail to provide reasonable grounds to believe that the GoS acted with *dolus specialis*/specific intent to destroy in whole or in part the Fur, Masalit, and Zaghawa groups, and consequently no warrant of arrest for Omar Al Bashir shall be issued in relation to counts 1 to 3.

207. Nevertheless, the Majority considers that, if, as a result of the ongoing Prosecution's investigation into the crimes allegedly committed by Omar Al Bashir, additional evidence on the existence of a GoS's genocidal intent is gathered, the Majority's conclusion in the present decision would not prevent the Prosecution from requesting, pursuant to [A]rticle 58(6) of the Statute, an amendment to the arrest warrant for Omar Al Bashir so as to include the crime of genocide.

The Pre-Trial Chamber decision was reversed by the Appeals Chamber on 3 February 2010 on the grounds that the Pre-Trial Chamber had applied an erroneous standard when evaluating the evidence submitted for the purpose of issuing an arrest warrant. The Pre-Trial Chamber had put too high a burden on the prosecutor in requiring that genocidal intent be 'the only reasonable conclusion' to draw from the evidence. The analysis of the law of genocide in the decision is still instructive, however.

COMMENTARY

The ICC has demonstrated that it will distinguish between acts intended to displace rather than destroy to preserve the core of what is understood as constituting genocide. Regardless of whether one agrees or disagrees with the ICC's reading of the evidence, a promising feature of the ICC's analysis is its reference to ICJ jurisprudence, which in part is consonant

---

[2] International Criminal Court, Elements of Crimes, Art. 6.

with ICTY jurisprudence. This approach to giving substantial weight to ICTY and ICJ jurisprudence on genocide will help provide horizontal consistency in the interpretation of the Genocide Convention in the contemporary era of active interpretation after decades of dormancy.

(C) CULTURAL GENOCIDE?

The notion of cultural genocide is an amorphous and politically freighted one that was explicitly rejected during the framing of the Genocide Convention. The problem with vague concepts is that they are often capacious enough to be seized upon for various political projects, thereby loosening and weakening the concept of genocide from its baseline horror – the effort to physically or biologically eradicate the existence of a group. Moreover, the idea of cultural genocide would have opened a nettlesome rash of questions in light of colonial history in which languages and cultures of indigenous peoples have been repeatedly eradicated. There would also be line-drawing problems between assimilation measures and the contested concept of cultural genocide.

The association of cultural destruction with genocide may nonetheless enter through the back door by other means. In *Krstić*, even as the ICTY acknowledged that the framers of the Genocide Convention rejected the idea of cultural genocide, it considered evidence of attacks on the cultural and religious property and symbols of the targeted group as *evidence* of genocidal intent. Moreover, though Srebrenica women and children were bussed to Bosnian Muslim-held territory and survived, the *Krstić* Trial Chamber reasoned that killing military-aged men disrupted 'the bedrock social and cultural foundations of the group', and therefore constituted genocide.

The notion of cultural genocide may also enter by the front door through interpretation by national courts. German courts have expanded the definition of genocide to embrace destruction of a group as a social unit – an expansion upheld by the European Court of Human Rights. The *Jorgić* case, which is often invoked as showing this trend towards 'cultural genocide', is excerpted below.

Germany, Jorgić *case, Federal Court of Justice* (Bundesgerichtshof), *Judgment of 30 April 1999*

Nikola Jorgić was a Bosnian Serb who murdered and ill-treated Bosnian Muslim civilians during the Bosnian conflict between 1992 and 1995. In a ruling later upheld by Germany's Federal Court of Justice and Federal Constitutional Court, the Düsseldorf Court of Appeal held in Jorgić's case that destruction of a group within the meaning of German Penal Code Article 220a meant destruction of the group as a social unit in its distinctiveness, particularity and feeling of belonging together, and that biological-physical destruction was not necessary. The Federal Court of Justice upheld the reasoning, focusing on the notion of intent.

Contrary to its essential meaning based on the term of genocide, the statutory definition of the offence in § 220 of the Criminal Code does not necessarily require that the perpetrator intended the physical extermination and destruction of the group. It is sufficient to act in order to destroy the group in its social existence ("as such"), in its uniqueness and distinctiveness as a social unit, and in its sense of belonging together. [. . .] The Higher Regional Court of Appeal correctly based its decision on that. Admittedly, the destructive intent is particularly clearly exhibited in acts of deliberate killing and inflicting serious bodily harm (§ 220a, section 1 of the Criminal Code); but according to § 220a, section 1 of the Criminal Code other measures also suffice which are suitable to accomplish the intent or goal of destroying the social identity and existence of the group by forcibly transferring children of the group to another group (§ 220a, section 1, no. 5 of the Criminal Code) or by imposing rules to prevent births within the group (§ 220a, section 1, no. 4 of the Criminal Code). Considering the perpetrator's intent to commit genocide, the same holds true for endangering the physical existence of the group which is achieved by inflicting on the group conditions of life calculated to bring about its physical destruction in whole or in part (§ 220a, section 1, no. 3 of the Criminal Code). Such calculated conditions of life include not only causing physical or mental injury to members of the group or deliberately killing members of the group, but also the creation of inhumane conditions of life, e.g., in detention camps, by refusing to provide sufficient food or the necessary medical aid, as well as the systematic expulsion of the group from its homeland.

Jorgić appealed his conviction to the European Court of Human Rights (ECtHR). In *Jorgić v. Germany*, Jorgić argued to the ECtHR that the internationally accepted definition of genocide requires intent to destroy in a biological-physical sense and that therefore the German courts' broader interpretation in his case to include destruction of the group as a social unit was not foreseeable. Jorgić argued his conviction was in breach of Article 7(1) of the European Convention on Human Rights, which provides in pertinent part: 'No one shall be held guilty of any criminal offence on account of any act or omission which did not constitute a criminal offence under national or international law at the time when it was committed'.

The ECtHR ruled that the protection of Article 7 of the European Convention on Human Rights 'cannot be read as outlawing the gradual clarification of the rules of criminal liability through judicial interpretation' so long as 'the resultant development is consistent with the essence of the offence and could reasonably be foreseen'. As long as the national courts' interpretation of genocide 'could reasonably be regarded as consistent with the essence of that offence and could reasonably be foreseen' then 'it was for the German courts to decide which interpretation of the crime of genocide under domestic law they wished to adopt'. The ECtHR opined that the broader interpretation of intent to destroy 'does not appear unreasonable' when read in context of the definition of genocide, which includes imposition of measures intended to prevent births in a group and forcible transfer of children of the group to another group – conduct that does not necessitate a physical destruction of the living members of the group. (See *Jorgić* v. *Germany*, ECtHR, Judgment, 12 October 2007.)

(D) PREVENTION OF GENOCIDE VS. COMPLICITY IN GENOCIDE

After the Shoah, the world said 'never again' to genocide – but genocide has flared time and again in the contemporary era. The international community has been slow to intervene to prevent genocide, as the Rwandan case demonstrates, though under the Genocide Convention, States undertake to prevent as well as punish genocide. The duty to prevent genocide is less well fleshed out in the Convention than the obligation to punish. Punishment is often conceived as a deterrent to future such crimes. More muscular forms of prevention, however, include intervention, which the international community has historically proved loath to undertake.

Genocide expert William Schabas has termed prevention the Genocide Convention's 'greatest failure'. The politics of intervention are complicated and often hinder efforts to prevent genocide. As a matter of legal design, moreover, the enforcement mechanism of the Genocide Convention is subject to critique. Article VI of the Convention leaves enforcement to courts of the State where the genocide occurred or before an international penal tribunal – which in 1948 was still a distant dream. The flaw of leaving enforcement to the States on which territory the genocide occurred is that the officials of those States are precisely those which are likely to have a strong interest in non-prosecution.

Article VIII of the Convention permits contracting parties to 'call upon the competent organs of the United Nations to take such action under the Charter of the United Nations as they consider appropriate for the prevention and suppression of acts of genocide' – but the United Nations General Assembly has only once denounced what it found to be genocide, the massacres of Palestinians in the Sabra and Shatila refugee camps in Beirut (*The Situation in the Middle East*, U.N. Res. 37/123D (16 December 1982)).

The Genocide Convention also contemplates that the International Court of Justice may adjudicate disputes between States over the interpretation, application or fulfilment of Convention obligations. For decades after its enactment, the Genocide Convention remained dormant in terms of enforcement, until events in the Balkans and Rwanda – belatedly and largely in the aftermath – galvanized the international community to action.

The ICJ has had the occasion to rule on the interpretation of the Genocide Convention – and of its prevention provisions – in the *Bosnia v. Serbia* case, decided in 2007. In this Judgment, the Court tackled the distinction between the obligation to prevent genocide incumbent on all States and the concept of complicity in genocide. While the ICJ, like the ICTY, found that the Srebrenica mass killings constituted acts of genocide, the ICJ concluded that Bosnia and Herzegovina did not establish that Serbia (or the Federal Republic of Yugoslavia (FRY), the political entity created when Serbia formed a federation with Montenegro) had genocidal intent. The ICJ ruled, however, that Serbia failed in its obligation to prevent genocide.

....

ICJ, Application of the Convention on the Prevention and Punishment of the Crime of Genocide (Bosnia and Herzegovina v. Serbia and Montenegro), Judgment of 26 February 2007

The ICJ's first occasion to interpret the substantive provisions of the Genocide Convention, including the duty of Contracting States to prevent and punish genocide, came when Bosnia and Herzegovina sued Serbia and Montenegro alleging state responsibility for genocide. Among the allegations against Respondent Serbia was complicity in the Srebrenica massacre, which the ICTY had ruled amounted to genocide and the ICJ agreed amounted to genocide. The question became whether Serbia could be held responsible for the genocidal acts in Srebrenica.

428. As regards the obligation to prevent genocide, the Court thinks it necessary to begin with the following introductory remarks and clarifications, amplifying the observations already made above.

429. First, the Genocide Convention is not the only international instrument providing for an obligation on the States parties to it to take certain steps to prevent the acts it seeks to prohibit. [. . .] The content of the duty to prevent varies from one instrument to another, according to the wording of the relevant provisions, and depending on the nature of the acts to be prevented. The decision of the Court does not, in this case, purport to establish a general jurisprudence applicable to all cases where a treaty instrument, or other binding legal norm, includes an obligation for States to prevent certain acts. Still less does the decision of the Court purport to find whether, apart from the texts applicable to specific fields, there is a general obligation on States to prevent the commission by other persons or entities of acts contrary to certain norms of general international law. The Court will therefore confine itself to determining the specific scope of the duty to prevent in the Genocide Convention, and to the extent that such a determination is necessary to the decision to be given on the dispute before it. This will, of course, not absolve it of the need to refer, if need be, to the rules of law whose scope extends beyond the specific field covered by the Convention.

430. Secondly, it is clear that the obligation in question is one of conduct and not one of result, in the sense that a State cannot be under an obligation to succeed, whatever the circumstances, in preventing the commission of genocide: the obligation of States parties is rather to employ all means reasonably available to them, so as to prevent genocide so far as possible. A State does not incur responsibility simply because the desired result is not achieved; responsibility is however incurred if the State manifestly failed to take all measures to prevent genocide which were within its power, and which might have contributed to preventing the genocide. In this area the notion of "due diligence", which calls for an assessment *in concreto*, is of critical importance. Various parameters operate when assessing whether a State has duly discharged the obligation concerned. The first, which varies greatly from one State to another, is clearly the capacity to influence effectively the action of persons likely to commit, or already committing, genocide. This capacity itself depends, among other things, on the geographical distance of the State concerned from the scene of the events, and on the strength of the political links, as well as links of all other kinds, between the authorities of that State and the main actors in the events. The State's capacity to influence must also be assessed by legal criteria, since it is clear that every State may only act within the limits permitted by international law; seen thus, a State's capacity to influence may vary depending on its particular legal position vis-à-vis the situations and persons facing the danger, or the reality, of genocide. On the other hand, it is irrelevant whether the State whose responsibility is in issue claims, or even proves, that even if it had employed all means reasonably at its disposal, they would not have sufficed to prevent the commission of genocide. As well as being generally difficult to prove, this is irrelevant to the breach of the obligation of conduct in question, the more so since the possibility remains that the combined efforts of several States, each complying with its obligation to prevent, might have achieved the result – averting the commission of genocide – which the efforts of only one State were insufficient to produce.

431. Thirdly, a State can be held responsible for breaching the obligation to prevent genocide only if genocide was actually committed. It is at the time when commission of the prohibited act (genocide or any of the other acts listed in Article III of the Convention) begins that the breach of an obligation of prevention occurs. [. . .] This obviously does not mean that the obligation to prevent genocide only comes into being when perpetration of genocide commences; that would be absurd, since the whole point of the obligation is to prevent, or attempt to prevent, the occurrence of the act. In fact, a State's obligation to prevent, and the corresponding duty to act, arise at the instant that the State learns of, or should normally have learned of, the existence of a serious risk that genocide will be committed. From that moment onwards, if the State has available to it means likely to have a deterrent effect on those suspected of preparing

genocide, or reasonably suspected of harbouring specific intent *(dolus specialis)*, it is under a duty to make such use of these means as the circumstances permit. However, if neither genocide nor any of the other acts listed in Article III of the Convention are ultimately carried out, then a State that omitted to act when it could have done so cannot be held responsible *a posteriori*, since the event did not happen which, under the rule set out above, must occur for there to be a violation of the obligation to prevent. In consequence, in the present case the Court will have to consider the Respondent's conduct, in the light of its duty to prevent, solely in connection with the massacres at Srebrenica, because these are the only acts in respect of which the Court has concluded in this case that genocide was committed.

432. Fourth and finally, the Court believes it especially important to lay stress on the differences between the requirements to be met before a State can be held to have violated the obligation to prevent genocide – within the meaning of Article I of the Convention – and those to be satisfied in order for a State to be held responsible for "complicity in genocide" – within the meaning of Article III, paragraph (e) – as previously discussed. There are two main differences; they are so significant as to make it impossible to treat the two types of violation in the same way. In the first place, as noted above, complicity always requires that some positive action has been taken to furnish aid or assistance to the perpetrators of the genocide, while a violation of the obligation to prevent results from mere failure to adopt and implement suitable measures to prevent genocide from being committed. In other words, while complicity results from commission, violation of the obligation to prevent results from omission; this is merely the reflection of the notion that the ban on genocide and the other acts listed in Article III, including complicity, places States under a negative obligation, the obligation not to commit the prohibited acts, while the duty to prevent places States under positive obligations, to do their best to ensure that such acts do not occur. In the second place, as also noted above, there cannot be a finding of complicity against a State unless at the least its organs were aware that genocide was about to be committed or was under way, and if the aid and assistance supplied, from the moment they became so aware onwards, to the perpetrators of the criminal acts or to those who were on the point of committing them, enabled or facilitated the commission of the acts. In other words, an accomplice must have given support in perpetrating the genocide with full knowledge of the facts. By contrast, a State may be found to have violated its obligation to prevent even though it had no certainty, at the time when it should have acted, but failed to do so, that genocide was about to be committed or was under way; for it to incur responsibility on this basis it is enough that the State was aware, or should normally have been aware, of the serious danger that acts of genocide would be committed. As will be seen below, this latter difference could prove decisive in the present case in determining the responsibility incurred by the Respondent.

433. In light of the foregoing, the Court will now consider the facts of the case. For the reasons stated above (paragraph 431), it will confine itself to the FRY's conduct vis-à-vis the Srebrenica massacres.

434. The Court would first note that, during the period under consideration, the FRY was in a position of influence, over the Bosnian Serbs who devised and implemented the genocide in Srebrenica, unlike that of any of the other States parties to the Genocide Convention owing to the strength of the political, military and financial links between the FRY on the one hand and the Republika Srpska and the VRS on the other, which, though somewhat weaker than in the preceding period, nonetheless remained very close.

435. Secondly, the Court cannot but note that, on the relevant date, the FRY was bound by very specific obligations by virtue of the two Orders indicating provisional measures delivered by the Court in 1993. In particular, in its Order of 8 April 1993, the Court stated, *inter alia*, that although not able, at that early stage in the proceedings, to make "definitive findings of fact or of imputability" *(I.C.J. Reports 1993*, p. 22, para. 44) the FRY was required to ensure:

"that any military, paramilitary or irregular armed units which may be directed or supported by it, as well as any organizations and persons which may be subject to its control, direction or influence, do not commit any acts of genocide, of conspiracy to commit genocide, of direct and public incitement to commit genocide, or of complicity in genocide..." (*ibid.*, p. 24, para. 52 A.(2)).

The Court's use, in the above passage, of the term "influence" is particularly revealing of the fact that the Order concerned not only the persons or entities whose conduct was attributable to the FRY, but also all those with whom the Respondent maintained close links and on which it could exert a certain influence. Although in principle the two issues are separate, and the second will be examined below, it is not possible, when considering the way the Respondent discharged its obligation of prevention under the Convention, to fail to take account of the obligation incumbent upon it, albeit on a different basis, to implement the provisional measures indicated by the Court.

436. Thirdly, the Court recalls that although it has not found that the information available to the Belgrade authorities indicated, as a matter of certainty, that genocide was imminent (which is why complicity in genocide was not upheld above: paragraph 424), they could hardly have been unaware of the serious risk of it once the VRS forces had decided to occupy the Srebrenica enclave. Among the documents containing information clearly suggesting that such an awareness existed, mention should be made of the above-mentioned report (see paragraphs 283 and 285 above) of the United Nations Secretary-General prepared pursuant to General Assembly resolution 53/35 on the "fall of Srebrenica" (United Nations doc. A/54/549), which recounts the visit to Belgrade on 14 July 1995 of the European Union negotiator Mr. Bildt to meet Mr. Milošević. Mr. Bildt, in substance, informed Mr. Milošević of his serious concern and "pressed the President to arrange immediate access for the UNHCR to assist the people of Srebrenica, and for the ICRC to start to register those who were being treated by the BSA [Bosnian Serb Army] as prisoners of war".

437. The Applicant has drawn attention to certain evidence given by General Wesley Clark before the ICTY in the *Milošević* case. General Clark referred to a conversation that he had had with Milošević during the negotiation of the Dayton Agreement. He stated that "I went to Milošević and I asked him. I said, 'If you have so much influence over these [Bosnian] Serbs, how could you have allowed General Mladić to have killed all those people at Srebrenica?' And he looked to me – at me. His expression was very grave. He paused before he answered, and he said, 'Well, General Clark, I warned him not to do this, but he didn't listen to me.' And it was in the context of all the publicity at the time about the Srebrenica massacre." (*Milošević,* IT-02-54-T, Transcript, 16 December 2003, pp. 30494–30495). General Clark gave it as his opinion, in his evidence before the ICTY, that the circumstances indicated that Milošević had foreknowledge of what was to be "a military operation combined with a massacre" (*ibid.*, p. 30497). The ICTY record shows that Milošević denied ever making the statement to which General Clark referred, but the Trial Chamber nevertheless relied on General Clark's testimony in its Decision of 16 June 2004 when rejecting the Motion for Judgment of Acquittal (*Milošević,* IT-02-54-T, Decision on Motion for Judgment of Acquittal, 16 June 2004, para. 280).

438. In view of their undeniable influence and of the information, voicing serious concern, in their possession, the Yugoslav federal authorities should, in the view of the Court, have made the best efforts within their power to try and prevent the tragic events then taking shape, whose scale, though it could not have been foreseen with certainty, might at least have been surmised. The FRY leadership, and President Milošević above all, were fully aware of the climate of deep-seated hatred which reigned between the Bosnian Serbs and the Muslims in the Srebrenica region. As the Court has noted in paragraph 423 above, it has not been shown that the decision to eliminate physically the whole of the adult male population of

the Muslim community of Srebrenica was brought to the attention of the Belgrade authorities. Nevertheless, given all the international concern about what looked likely to happen at Srebrenica, given Milošević's own observations to Mladić, which made it clear that the dangers were known and that these dangers seemed to be of an order that could suggest intent to commit genocide, unless brought under control, it must have been clear that there was a serious risk of genocide in Srebrenica. Yet the Respondent has not shown that it took any initiative to prevent what happened, or any action on its part to avert the atrocities which were committed. It must therefore be concluded that the organs of the Respondent did nothing to prevent the Srebrenica massacres, claiming that they were powerless to do so, which hardly tallies with their known influence over the VRS. As indicated above, for a State to be held responsible for breaching its obligation of prevention, it does not need to be proven that the State concerned definitely had the power to prevent the genocide; it is sufficient that it had the means to do so and that it manifestly refrained from using them.

Such is the case here. In view of the foregoing, the Court concludes that the Respondent violated its obligation to prevent the Srebrenica genocide in such a manner as to engage its international responsibility.

(E) DOMESTIC IMPLEMENTATION

Under Article 5 of the Genocide Convention, '[t]he Contracting Parties undertake to enact, in accordance with their respective Constitutions, the necessary legislation to give effect to the' Genocide Convention and to 'provide effective penalties for persons guilty of genocide or any of the other acts enumerated in article III'. Many signatory States reproduced verbatim the Genocide Convention's definition of genocide into their criminal codes upon ratification.

Some States have even expanded on the definition, for example adding protections for political groups or deploying a potentially elastic definition of protected groups. Canada's Crimes Against Humanity and War Crimes Act 2000, for example, defines genocide as 'an act or omission committed with intent to destroy, in whole or in part, an identifiable group of persons, as such, that, at the time and in the place of its commission, constitutes genocide according to customary international law or conventional international law or by virtue of its being criminal according to the general principles of law recognized by the community of nations, whether or not it constitutes a contravention of the law in force at the time and in the place of its commission'.

Since international tribunals intervene when domestic institutions are not able or willing to act, it is logical that national courts deal with genocide as with any other crime. However, when no specific statutory provision exists domestic courts have often proven reluctant to apply the provisions of the Genocide Convention – despite ratification of the Convention – or to enforce obligations to prevent and punish genocide arising from customary international law. The reluctance may be heightened by lawsuits that strain the notion of genocide. The following case provides an example.

Australia, **Nulyarimma v. Thompson**, *Federal Court of Australia, Judgment of 1 September 1999*

Wadjularbinna Nulyarimma and others challenged an Australian governmental plan concerning land ownership that they alleged would constitute genocide against the Aboriginal people. The Supreme Court of the Australian Capital Territory upheld the refusal of the Registrar of the Magistrates Court, Phillip Thompson, to issue warrants of arrest for the Prime Minister and other government officials. Justice Wilcox wrote the Reasons for Judgment denying the appeal.

18. I accept that the prohibition of genocide is a peremptory norm of customary international law, giving rise to a non-derogatable obligation by each nation State to the entire international community. This is an obligation independent of the *Convention on the Prevention and Punishment of the Crime of Genocide*. It existed before the commencement of that Convention in January 1951, probably at least from the time of the United Nations General Assembly resolution in December 1946. I accept, also, that the obligation imposed by customary law on each nation State is to extradite or prosecute any person, found within its territory, who appears to have committed any of the acts cited in the definition of genocide set out in the Convention. It is generally accepted [that] this definition reflects the concept of genocide, as understood in customary international law.

19. It follows from the obligation to prosecute or extradite, imposed by international customary law on Australia as a nation State, that it would be constitutionally permissible for the Commonwealth Parliament to enact legislation providing for the trial within Australia of persons accused of genocide, wherever occurring. In *Polyukhovitch v the Commonwealth* [...] the High Court held that legislation providing for the trial in Australia of persons alleged to have committed war crimes outside Australia during the Second World War was a valid exercise of the Commonwealth Parliament's power to make laws with respect to external affairs. None of the Justices thought it necessary that Australia be under an **obligation** to enact the legislation; it was enough that it **pertained to conduct** external to Australia: see per Mason CJ at 530–531, per Deane J at 599–604, per Dawson J at 632–638, per Toohey J at 652–656, per Gaudron J at 695–696, per McHugh J at 712–714. Where there is a positive obligation to provide a trial, pursuant to international customary law, the argument in favour of legislative validity is even more compelling. [...]

20. However, it is one thing to say Australia has an international legal obligation to prosecute or extradite a genocide suspect found within its territory, and that the Commonwealth Parliament may legislate to ensure that obligation is fulfilled; it is another thing to say that, without legislation to that effect, such a person may be put on trial for genocide before an Australian court. If this were the position, it would lead to the curious result that an international obligation incurred pursuant to customary law has greater domestic consequences than an obligation incurred, expressly and voluntarily, by Australia signing and ratifying an international convention. Ratification of a convention does not directly affect Australian domestic law unless and until implementing legislation is enacted. This seems to be the position even where the ratification has received Parliamentary approval, as in the case of the *Genocide Convention*. In *Minister for Immigration and Ethnic Affairs v Teoh* [...] at 286–287, Mason CJ and Deane J said:

> *"It is well established that the provisions of an international treaty to which Australia is a party do not form part of Australian law unless those provisions have been validly incorporated into our municipal law by statute. This principle has its foundation in the proposition that in our constitutional system the making and ratification of treaties fall within the province of the Executive in the exercise of its prerogative power whereas the making and the alteration of the law fall within the province of Parliament, not the Executive. So, a treaty which has not been incorporated into our municipal law cannot operate as a direct source of individual rights and obligations under that law."*

21. Counsel for the appellants and Mr Buzzacott point out that genocide is one of a handful of "international crimes", along with piracy, torture, slavery and – more debatably – crimes against peace, war crimes and crimes against humanity. Hannikainen *Peremptory Norms*

(Jus Cogens) in International Law (1988) at 285 defines an "international crime" as "a grave offence against international law which the international community of States recognises as a crime and for the committing of which the responsible individuals can be punished under international law **even if the domestic law of a particular State does not declare it to be punishable**" [...] In support of the latter assertion, Hannikainen cites several sources, notably Art 6(c) of the *Statute of the Nuremberg Tribunal,* Art V(I) of the *Statute of the Tokyo Tribunal* and Art 15 of the *International Covenant on Civil and Political Rights.* It is not clear to me that these sources justify the statement. The Articles in the two War Crimes Tribunal statutes merely define the jurisdiction of the particular tribunals. Article 15 of the International Covenant is concerned to prohibit retrospective criminality. Its only present relevance is sub-article 2 which reads:

"2. Nothing in this article shall prejudice the trial and punishment of any person for any act or omission which, at the time when it was committed, was criminal according to the general principles of law recognized by the community of nations."

22. However, even if Hannikainen's statement is correct, it is not enough to say that, **under international law**, an international crime is punishable in a domestic tribunal even in the absence of a domestic law declaring that conduct to be punishable. If genocide is to be regarded as punishable in Australia, on the basis that it is an international crime, it must be shown that **Australian law** permits that result. [...]

26. Perhaps this is only another way of saying that domestic courts face a policy issue in deciding whether to recognise and enforce a rule of international law. If there is a policy issue, I have no doubt it should be resolved in a criminal case by declining, in the absence of legislation, to enforce the international norm.

QUESTIONS

1. The track record of the international community of States in implementing the duty to prevent and punish genocide has been spotty. What obstacles do you see in fulfilling these obligations?

2. Social psychologist Paul Slovic has posited that there may be a social psychological basis for the neglect of the duty to prevent genocide. Slovic argues that we may be 'numbed by numbers' – studies show that polities are more moved by the personalized plight of a particular individual than by large numbers of people being killed. Statistics of large numbers of death numb the affective emotion or feeling that triggers people to act. For example, Slovic found that donations to aid a starving 7-year-old in Africa dropped sharply when accompanied by a statistical summary stating there are millions of other needy children like her in Africa. If Slovic is right that the sheer statistical scale of mass slaughter that is often involved in genocide numbs our desire to act, what approaches should law and policy take to implement the duty to prevent genocide?

3. Assuming lack of a written plan to destroy (at least part of) a protected group, what type of evidence should be used by prosecutors to prove the existence of genocidal intent?

4. Various ICTR and ICTY judgments have stated that an accused is liable as an accomplice to genocide even if he lacked the intent to destroy if he knowingly aided

or abetted or instigated one or more persons in the commission of genocide, know-ing of the perpetrators' genocidal intent even if he did not share it. Is it just to convict someone as an aider and abettor of genocide even if the hallmark of genocide – the intent to destroy – is lacking?

5. Can a person be convicted of crimes against humanity and genocide in relation to the same conduct?

FURTHER READING

A. Cassese, 'Genocide', in *Oxford Companion*.

P. Gaeta, *The UN Genocide Convention: A Commentary* (Oxford: Oxford University Press, 2009).

P. Gourevich, *We Wish to Inform You that Tomorrow We Will Be Killed Together with Our Families: Stories from Rwanda* (New York: Picador, 1998).

J. Hagan and W. Rymond-Richmond, *Darfur and the Crime of Genocide* (Cambridge: Cambridge University Press, 2008).

R. Lemkin, *Axis Rule in Occupied Europe* (Washington DC: Carnegie Endowment for International Peace, 1944), 79.

L. Newman and R. Erber (eds), *Understanding Genocide: The Social Psychology of the Holocaust* (Oxford: Oxford University Press, 2002).

W.A. Schabas, *Genocide in International Criminal Law: The Crime of Crimes* (Cambridge: Cambridge University Press, 2000).

4

AGGRESSION

It is a paradox of the history of the International Military Tribunal (IMT) at Nuremberg that the crime that was its primary focus, aggression (or crime against peace), is also the one crime that, to date, has not prospered in modern times. Since World War II, no court has prosecuted a case of aggression. However, the Rome Statute offers at least the possibility that the ICC will one day enforce this crime. As initially adopted, the Rome Statute deferred the question of aggression. Article 5 provided for jurisdiction over the crime, but only 'once a provision [was] adopted in accordance with articles 121 and 123 defining the crime and setting out the conditions under which the Court shall exercise jurisdiction with respect to this crime'. The ICC's 2010 Review Conference adopted a definition of the crime of aggression, but deferred its enforcement until after 2017 at the earliest and narrowed the means by which the court could exercise jurisdiction.

The crime of aggression was set out first among the crimes listed in the London Charter and was charged in the first two counts of the IMT indictment. The Judgment of the IMT declared that '[t]o initiate a war of aggression, therefore, is not only an international crime; it is the supreme international crime differing only from other war crimes in that it contains within itself the accumulated evil of the whole' (Nuremberg Judgment at 186). Although central to the IMT Judgment, the inclusion of the crime of aggression in the London Charter was not without controversy. France and the Soviet Union initially sought to avoid any suggestion that aggression was an international crime, proposing instead that the Charter criminalize only the aggression of the Axis powers over other nations. France in particular contended that the crime of aggression had not been established in international law. Both countries may have recognized the challenge of identifying when aggression has occurred (as opposed to self-defence), a difficulty that has continued to impede the inclusion of this crime among those enforced by the modern tribunals. At Nuremberg, it was the United States that insisted that the crime be included in its broad formulation, an enthusiasm for the notion that has not been repeated in modern times. In the end, the London Charter gave the IMT jurisdiction over 'Crimes against peace: namely, planning, preparation, initiation or waging of a war of aggression, or a war in violation of international treaties, agreements or assurances, or participation in a common plan or conspiracy for the accomplishment of any of the foregoing'. (For an account of the debates surrounding the inclusion of the crime of aggression in the London Charter, see Telford Taylor, *The Anatomy of the Nuremberg Trials* (New York: Alfred A. Knopf, 1992), at 65–74).

In considering the charges under this provision, the IMT faced two principal issues: whether the crime of aggression was established in international law (the *nullum crimen sine lege* question), and the scope and definition of the crime. The portion of the judgment resolving the first question is excerpted in Part I of this book (Part I(2)(A) on Nullum Crimen). With regard to scope, the IMT had little difficulty concluding that Hitler had a preconceived plan of territorial conquest to create a greater Germany and that in pursuit of this plan he had waged aggressive war against 12 separate states. The more challenging question was, who could be held liable for these crimes of aggression? The IMT rejected the argument that *only* Hitler could be held responsible for crimes against peace:

The argument that such common planning cannot exist where there is complete dictatorship is unsound. A plan in the execution of which a number of persons participate is still a plan, even though conceived by only one of them; and those who execute the plan do not avoid responsibility by showing that they acted under the direction of the man who conceived it. Hitler could not make aggressive war by himself. He had to have the co-operation of statesmen, military leaders, diplomats, and business men. When they, with knowledge of his aims, gave him their co-operation, they made themselves parties to the plan he had initiated. They are not to be deemed innocent because Hitler made use of them, if they knew what they were doing. That they were assigned to their tasks by a dictator does not absolve them from responsibility for their acts. The relation of leader and follower does not preclude responsibility here any more than it does in the comparable tyranny of organized domestic crime.

This language begs, however, the essential question: if a State engages in aggressive war, are all those who participate in the war on behalf of the State individually criminally liable? Or are only the commanders liable? And if so, which commanders? Although the IMT did not address these questions directly, in evaluating the individual criminal responsibility of the individual defendants – who represented the most senior members of the German government, Nazi party and military – it insisted on proof of both *knowledge of*, and *participation in*, Hitler's plans for aggressive war. Of the 22 verdicts rendered by the IMT, 12 defendants were convicted of one or both counts related to aggressive war, while 10 were acquitted of the aggression charges.[1]

The US and French military tribunals subsequently considered charges of aggressive war against less senior political, military and financial leaders. They reaffirmed the IMT's stance on the status of the crime of aggression in international law and, because of the positions of the accused, were forced to confront more squarely the question of which individuals in a State may be held responsible for aggressive war. In all of these cases except the *Ministries* case, which was brought against a number of former high-level government officials, the defendants were acquitted of the aggression charges, and in the *Ministries* case only 3 of the 17 defendants charged with aggression were convicted. These cases, excerpted below, held that only the most senior leaders who knew of plans of aggressive war and, with that knowledge, acted to shape or advance them could be held criminally liable. With respect to war crimes and crimes against humanity, a principal challenge of prosecutors is to determine whether, in addition to the actual perpetrators of the crimes, senior commanders and leaders should be held responsible. With respect to the crime of aggression, it seems that *only* the most senior leaders may be held responsible.

Although, as stated above, there have been no prosecutions for aggression since World War II, efforts have continued to define the notion, both as a legal principle for States to respect and as a concept of international criminal law. In 2006, in the case of *R* v. *Jones*, the House of Lords in England had to consider the status in international law of the crime of aggression in the context of a prosecution of war protesters who committed trespass and property damage at British military installations, claiming that they were acting to stop an illegal war (in Iraq). The decision of Lord Bingham, excerpted below, reviewed these developments and found, much as the *Tadić* court found with respect to crimes against humanity, see Part 2(2)(A), *supra*, that while it was unlikely that the crime of aggression

---

[1] The Tokyo Tribunal convicted all 25 defendants against which it rendered a verdict of charges relating to aggressive war.

was established in international law *before* World War II (as claimed by the IMT and the subsequent World War II military tribunals), it certainly was by the end of the twentieth century. However, while the developments cited by the House of Lords plainly solidified the customary international law status of the crime of aggression, none provided any further definition of the crime itself.

As the States Parties to the ICC met in 2010 to consider the future of the crime of aggression, two issues emerged. First, what is the relationship between the crime, which denotes individual responsibility, and State responsibility, and how would ICC jurisdiction over the crime be triggered? The individual crime of aggression presupposes an aggressive war by a State or non-State organization (such as a rebel group). Yet the United Nations system assigns the Security Council the responsibility to determine when a State has engaged in aggressive war. Article 2(4) of the UN Charter requires '[a]ll Members [to] refrain in their international relations from the threat or use of force against the territorial integrity or political independence of any state', and Article 39 states that '[t]he Security Council shall determine the existence of any threat to the peace, breach of the peace, or act of aggression and shall make recommendations, or decide what measures shall be taken in accordance with Articles 41 and 42, to maintain or restore international peace and security'. What then should be the relationship between such a determination by the Security Council (or failure to make such a determination) and the prosecution of individual crimes of aggression by the ICC? Should an individual prosecution by the ICC be dependent on a determination of aggressive war by the Security Council? Or could the ICC make its own determination independent of the judgment of the Security Council?

Second, the ICC had to decide on the precise definition and elements of the *crime* of aggression. Not every act of aggression need constitute a crime, and not every participant in the aggression need be liable. As it had come to be defined, the crime required an act of aggression by a State or non-State actor and both knowledge of, and participation in, the policy or plans of aggression on the part of the accused, who must also have direct and high-level responsibility for the conduct of the war. Would the crime also include a scale requirement to ensure that only large-scale unlawful armed attacks become the focus of the court? Such a requirement would be consistent with Article 5(1) ICCSt. which states that '[t]he jurisdiction of this Court shall be limited to the most serious crimes of concern to the international community as a whole'. And, further, would the definition be designed to exclude from coverage humanitarian interventions? These questions of jurisdiction and definition are interrelated, because States anxious about a court enforcing any crime of aggression might be assuaged by either a provision granting limited jurisdiction over the crime or a narrow definition of the crime itself.

In the end, the Review Conference adopted a broad definition of aggression, but narrowed the *crime* of aggression to cover only serious violations, limited the court's jurisdiction over the crime, and deferred ultimate implementation of the aggression provisions until after 2017. The definition of aggression will be included in a new Article 8 *bis* of the ICCSt. and will track UN General Assembly Resolution 3313 (1974), which defined aggression to be 'the use of armed force by a State against the sovereignty, territorial integrity or political independence of another State, or in any other manner inconsistent with the Charter of the United Nations'. Article 8 *bis* further includes seven examples of aggression from the UN General Assembly Resolution, though is not explicit whether this list is exhaustive or illustrative:

a) The invasion or attack by the armed forces of a State of the territory of another State, or any military occupation, however temporary, resulting from such invasion or attack, or any annexation by the use of force of the territory of another State or part thereof;

b) Bombardment by the armed forces of a State against the territory of another State or the use of any weapons by a State against the territory of another State;

c) The blockade of the ports or coasts of a State by the armed forces of another State;

d) An attack by the armed forces of a State on the land, sea or air forces, or marine and air fleets of another State;

e) The use of armed forces of one State which are within the territory of another State with the agreement of the receiving State, in contravention of the conditions provided for in the agreement or any extension of their presence in such territory beyond the termination of the agreement;

f) The action of a State in allowing its territory, which it has placed at the disposal of another State, to be used by that other State for perpetrating an act of aggression against a third State;

g) The sending by or on behalf of a State of armed bands, groups, irregulars or mercenaries, which carry out acts of armed force against another State of such gravity as to amount to the acts listed above, or its substantial involvement therein.

The 'crime of aggression' is defined in Article 8 *bis* as the 'planning, preparation, initiation or execution, by a person in a position effectively to exercise control over or to direct the political or military action of a State, of an act of aggression which, by its character, gravity and scale, constitutes a manifest violation of the Charter of the United Nations'. In keeping with the definition of the crime developed by the World War II courts, this formulation focuses on the senior leaders responsible for planning and advancing war policy, and is limited to serious acts of aggression. In addition, Articles 15 *bis* and *ter* will provide for narrower jurisdiction by the ICC over the crime of aggression than it has over other crimes. States Parties to the ICCSt. may opt out of jurisdiction for any case of aggression initiated by the Prosecutor or referred by another State Party, and if a case is initiated by one of these two means then the ICC may not bring a charge of aggression against a national of a non-State party. However, when a case is referred to the ICC by the UN Security Council pursuant to Article 13(b), none of these limiting provisions apply. Finally, the aggression provisions will come into force only after 2017 and only after the provisions are adopted by two-thirds of the States Parties, and will only apply to acts that occur more than one year after 30 States Parties ratify the provisions.

The cases below trace the development of the crime of aggression and engage the challenges of this particular crime that continue to be reflected in the complex provisions regarding the crime adopted by the ICC Review Conference.

Cases

US Military Tribunal Sitting in Nuremberg, US v. von Weizsäcker et al. *(Ministries case), Judgment of 11–13 April 1949*

In this case, 17 of the 21 defendants, all high-level officials in the German Government and the Nazi party, were charged with aggression, but only three were ultimately convicted: Hans Lammers sentenced to 20 years' imprisonment, Paul Koerner sentenced to 15 years, and Wilhelm Keppler sentenced to 10 years. Various of the defendants were also charged with war crimes and crimes against humanity, and all but two of the defendants were convicted of at least one count.

Aggressive wars and invasions. – The question, therefore, is whether or not the London Charter and Control Council Law No. 10 define new offenses or whether they are but definitive statements of preexisting international law. That monarchs and states, at least those who considered themselves civilized, have for centuries recognized that aggressive wars and invasions violated the law of nations is evident from the fact that invariably he who started his troops on the march or his fleets over the seas to wage war has endeavored to explain and justify the act by asserting that there was no desire or intent to infringe upon the lawful rights of the attacked nation or to engage in cold-blooded conquest, but on the contrary that the hostile acts became necessary because of the enemy's disregard of its obligations; that it had violated treaties; that it held provinces or cities which in fact belonged to the attacker; or that it had mistreated or discriminated against his peaceful citizens.

Often these justifications and excuses were offered with cynical disregard of the truth. Nevertheless, it was felt necessary that an excuse and justification be offered for the attack to the end the attacker might not be regarded by other nations as acting in wanton disregard of international duty and responsibility. From Caesar to Hitler the same practice has been followed. It was used by Napoleon, was adopted by Frederick the Great, by Philip II of Spain, by Edward I of England, by Louis XIV of France, and by the powers who seized lands which they desired to colonize and make their own. Every and all of the attackers followed the same time-worn practice. The white, the blue, the yellow, the black, and the red books had only one purpose, namely, to justify that which was otherwise unjustifiable.

But if aggressive invasions and wars were lawful and did not constitute a breach of international law and duty, why take the trouble to explain and justify? Why inform neutral nations that the war was inevitable and excusable and based on high notions of morality, if aggressive war was not essentially wrong and a breach of international law? The answer to this is obvious. The initiation of wars and invasions with their attendant horror and suffering has for centuries been universally recognized by all civilized nations as wrong, to be resorted to only as a last resort to remedy wrongs already or imminently to be inflicted. We hold that aggressive wars and invasions have, since time immemorial, been a violation of international law, even though specific sanctions were not provided.

The Kellogg-Briand Pact [an international treaty ratified by 65 countries before World War II] not only recognized that aggressive wars and invasions were in violation of international law, but proceeded to take the next step, namely, to condemn recourse to war (otherwise justifiable for the solution of international controversies), to renounce it as an instrumentality of national policy, and to provide for the settlement of all disputes or conflicts by pacific means. Thus war as a means of enforcing lawful claims and demands became unlawful. The right of self-defense, of course, was naturally preserved, but only because if resistance was not immediately offered, a nation would be overrun and conquered before it could obtain the judgment of any international authority that it was justified in resisting attack. [...]

Is there personal responsibility for those who plan, prepare, and initiate aggressive wars and invasions? The defendants have ably and earnestly urged that heads of states and officials thereof cannot be held personally responsible for initiating or waging aggressive wars and invasions because no penalty had been previously prescribed for such acts. History, however, reveals that this view is fallacious. Frederick the Great was summoned by the Imperial Council to appear at Regensburg and answer, under threat of banishment, for his alleged breach of the public peace in invading Saxony.

When Napoleon, in alleged violation of his international agreement, sailed from Elba to regain by force the Imperial Crown of France, the nations of Europe, including many German princes in solemn conclave, denounced him, outlawing him as an enemy and disturber of the peace, mustered their armies, and on the battlefield of Waterloo, enforced their decree, and applied the sentence by banishing him to St. Helena. By these actions they recognized and declared that personal punishment could be properly inflicted upon a head of state who violated an international agreement and resorted to aggressive war.

But even if history furnished no examples, we would have no hesitation in holding that those who prepare, plan, or initiate aggressive invasions, and wage aggressive wars; and those who knowingly participate therein are subject to trial, and if convicted, to punishment.

By the Kellogg-Briand Treaty, Germany as well as practically every other civilized country of the world, renounced war as an instrumentality of governmental policy. The treaty was entered into for the benefit of all. It recognized the fact that once war breaks out, no one can foresee how far or to what extent the flames will spread, and that in this rapidly shrinking world it affects the interest of all.

No one would question the right of any signatory to use its armed forces to halt the violator in his tracks and to rescue the country attacked. Nor would there be any question but that when this was successfully accomplished sanctions could be applied against the guilty nation. Why then can they not be applied to the individuals by whose decisions, cooperation, and implementation the unlawful war or invasion was initiated and waged? Must the punishment always fall on those who were not personally responsible? May the humble citizen who knew nothing of the reasons for his country's action, who may have been utterly deceived by its propaganda, be subject to death or wounds in battle, held as a prisoner of war, see his home destroyed by artillery or from the air, be compelled to see his wife and family suffer privations and hardships; may the owners and workers in industry see it destroyed, their merchant fleets sunk, the mariners drowned or interned; may indemnities result which must be derived from the taxes paid by the ignorant and the innocent; may all this occur and those who were actually responsible escape? The only rationale which would sustain the concept that the responsible shall escape while the innocent public suffers, is a result of the old theory that "the King can do no wrong," and that "war is the sport of Kings." We may point out further that the [Hague and] Geneva Conventions relating to rules of land warfare and the treatment of prisoners of war provide no punishment for the individuals who violate those rules, but it cannot be questioned that he who murders a prisoner of war is liable to punishment. To permit such immunity is to shroud international law in a mist of unreality. We reject it and hold that those who plan, prepare, initiate, and wage aggressive wars and invasions, and those who knowingly, consciously, and responsibly participate therein violate international law and may be tried, convicted, and punished for their acts. [...]

Our task is to determine which, if any, of the defendants, knowing there was an intent to so initiate and wage aggressive war, consciously participated in either plans, preparations, initiations of those wars, or so knowing, participated or aided in carrying them on. Obviously, no man may be condemned for fighting in what he believes is the defense of his native land, even though his belief be mistaken. Nor can he be expected to undertake an independent investigation to determine whether or not the cause for which he fights is the result of an aggressive act of his own government. One can be guilty only where knowledge of aggression in fact exists, and it is not sufficient that he have suspicions that the war is aggressive. Any other test of guilt would involve a standard of conduct both impracticable and unjust. [...]

We concur in and shall apply the following principles laid down by the International Military Tribunal [...]

While we hold that knowledge that Hitler's wars and invasions were aggressive is an essential element of guilt under count one of the indictment, a very different situation arises with respect to counts three, five, six, and seven, which deal with war crimes and crimes against humanity. He who knowingly joined or implemented, aided, or abetted in their commission as principal or accessory cannot be heard to say that he did not know the acts in question were criminal. Measures which result in murder, ill-treatment, enslavement, and other inhumane acts perpetrated on prisoners of war, deportation, extermination, enslavement, and persecution on political, racial, and religious grounds, and plunder and spoliation of public and private property are acts which shock the conscience of every decent man. These are criminals *per se*.

The court in the *Ministries* case reprised certain of the arguments relied upon by the IMT regarding the established status of the crime of aggression in international law, but made even grander claims based on the history of wars from prior centuries to find that 'aggressive wars and invasions have, since time immemorial, been a violation of international law'. The court relied upon a noteworthy form of argumentation, claiming that the efforts of past leaders to justify their military interventions, even if for propagandistic purposes, demonstrated the existence of a norm in international law prohibiting aggressive war. With regard to individual responsibility, the court drew an important contrast with war crimes and crimes against humanity. With respect to these latter crimes, it is usually impossible to engage in the conduct without knowledge that a crime is being committed. Not so, found the court, regarding the crime of aggression, where only the top leaders might know of the illegal nature of the war. The following case emphasizes that in addition to knowledge, the accused must be in a position to affect the aggressive policy underlying the war.

US Military Tribunal Sitting in Nuremberg, US v. von Leeb et al. (High Command case), Judgment of 27 October 1948

This case charged 14 high-level officers in the German military with crimes against peace (as well as other crimes). All of the defendants were acquitted on this charge.

Count one of the indictment, heretofore set out, charges the defendants with crimes against peace. Before seeking to determine the law applicable it is necessary to determine with certainty the action which the defendants are alleged to have taken that constitutes the crime. As a preliminary to that we deem it necessary to give a brief consideration to the nature and characteristics of war. We need not attempt a definition that is all-inclusive and all-exclusive. It is sufficient to say that war is the exerting of violence by one state or politically organized body against another. In other words, it is the implementation of a political policy by means of violence. Wars are contests by force between political units but the policy that brings about their initiation is made and the actual waging of them is done by individuals. What we have said thus far is equally as applicable to a just as to an unjust war, to the initiation of an aggressive and, therefore, criminal war as to the waging of a defensive and, therefore, legitimate war against criminal aggression. The point we stress is that war activity is the implementation of a predetermined national policy. [. . .]

   The initiation of war or an invasion is a unilateral operation. When war is formally declared or the first shot is fired the initiation of the war has ended and from then on there is a waging of war between the two adversaries. Whether a war be lawful, or aggressive and therefore unlawful under international law, is and can be determined only from a consideration of the factors that entered into its initiation. In the intent and purpose for which it is planned, prepared, initiated and waged is to be found its lawfulness or unlawfulness. As we have pointed out, war whether it be lawful or unlawful is the implementation of a national policy. If the policy under which it is initiated is criminal in its intent and purpose it is so because the individuals at the policy-making level had a criminal intent and purpose in determining the policy. If war is the means by which the criminal objective is to be attained then the waging of the war is but an implementation of the policy, and the criminality which attaches to the waging of an aggressive war should be confined to those who participate in it at the policy level.

This does not mean that the Tribunal subscribes to the contention made in this trial that since Hitler was the Dictator of the Third Reich and that he was supreme in both the civil and military fields, he alone must bear criminal responsibility for political and military policies. No matter how absolute his authority, Hitler alone could not formulate a policy of aggressive war and alone implement that policy by preparing, planning, and waging such a war. Somewhere between the Dictator and Supreme Commander of the Military Forces of the nation and the common soldier is the boundary between the criminal and the excusable participation in the waging of an aggressive war by an individual engaged in it. Control Council Law No. 10 does not definitely draw such a line. It points out in paragraph 2 of Article II certain fact situations and established relations that are or may be sufficient to constitute guilt and sets forth certain categories of activity that do not establish immunity from criminality. Since there has been no other prosecution under Control Council Law No. 10 with defendants in the same category as those in this case, no such definite line has been judicially drawn. This Tribunal is not required to fix a general rule but only to determine the guilt or innocence of the present defendants.

The judgment of the IMT held that:

"The Charter is not an arbitrary exercise of power on the part of the victorious nations, but in view of the Tribunal, as will be shown, it is the expression of international law existing at the time of its creation; and to that extent is itself a contribution to international law."

We hold that Control Council Law No. 10 likewise is but an expression of international law existing at the time of its creation. We cannot therefore construe it as extending the international common law as it existed at the time of the Charter to add thereto any new element of criminality, for so to do would give it an *ex post facto* effect which we do not construe it to have intended. Moreover, that this was not intended is indicated by the fact that the London Charter of 8 August 1945, is made an integral part of the Control Council Law. Since international common law grows out of the common reactions and the composite thinking with respect to recurring situations by the various states composing the family of nations, it is pertinent to consider the general attitude of the citizens of states with respect to their military commanders and their obligations when their nations plan, prepare for and initiate or engage in war.

While it is undoubtedly true that international common law in case of conflict with state law takes precedence over it and while it is equally true that absolute unanimity among all the states in the family of nations is not required to bring an international common law into being, it is scarcely a tenable proposition that international common law will run counter to the consensus within any considerable number of nations.

Furthermore, we must not confuse idealistic objectives with realities. The world has not arrived at a state of civilization such that it can dispense with fleets, armies, and air forces, nor has it arrived at a point where it can safely outlaw war under any and all circumstances and situations. In as much as all war cannot be considered outlawed then armed forces are lawful instrumentalities of state, which have internationally legitimate functions. An unlawful war of aggression connotes of necessity a lawful war of defense against aggression. There is no general criterion under international common law for determining the extent to which a nation may arm and prepare for war. As long as there is no aggressive intent, there is no evil inherent in a nation making itself militarily strong. An example is Switzerland which for her geographical extent, her population and resources is proportionally stronger militarily than many nations of the world. She uses her military strength to implement a national policy that seeks peace and to maintain her borders against aggression.

There have been nations that have initiated and waged aggressive wars through long periods of history, doubtless there are nations still disposed to do so; and if not, judging in the light of history, there may be nations which tomorrow will be disposed to do so. Furthermore, situations may arise in which the question whether the war is or is not aggressive is doubt-ful and uncertain. We may safely assume that the general and considered opinions of the people within states – the source from which international common law springs are not such as to hamper or render them impotent to do the things they deem necessary for their national protection.

We are of the opinion that as in ordinary criminal cases, so in the crime denominated aggressive war, the same elements must all be present to constitute criminality. There first must be actual knowledge that an aggressive war is intended and that if launched it will be an aggressive war. But mere knowledge is not sufficient to make participation even by high ranking military officers in the war criminal. It requires in addition that the possessor of such knowledge, after he acquires it shall be in a position to shape or influence the policy that brings about its initiation or it continuance after initiation, either by furthering, or by hindering or preventing it. If he then does the former, he becomes criminally responsible; if he does the latter to the extent of his ability, then his action shows the lack of criminal intent with respect to such policy.

If a defendant did not know that the planning and preparation for invasions and wars in which he was involved were concrete plans and preparations for aggressive wars and for wars otherwise in violation of international laws and treaties, then he cannot be guilty of an offense. If, however, after the policy to initiate and wage aggressive wars was formulated, a defendant came into possession of knowledge that the invasions and wars to be waged, were aggressive and unlawful, then he will be criminally responsible if he, being on the policy level, could have influenced such policy and failed to do so.

If and as long as a member of the armed forces does not participate in the preparation, planning, initiating, or waging of aggressive war on a policy level, his war activities do not fall under the definition of crimes against peace. It is not a person's rank or status, but his power to shape or influence the policy of his state, which is the relevant issue for determining his criminality under the charge of crimes against peace.

International law condemns those who, due to their actual power to shape and influence the policy of their nation, prepare for, or lead their country into or in an aggressive war. But we do not find that, at the present stage of development, international law declares as criminals those below that level who, in the execution of this war policy, act as the instruments of the policy makers. Anybody who is on the policy level and participates in the war policy is liable to punishment. But those under them cannot be punished for the crimes of others. The misdeed of the policy makers is all the greater in as much as they use the great mass of the soldiers and officers to carry out an international crime; however, the individual soldier or officer below the policy level is but the policy makers' instrument, finding himself, as he does, under the rigid discipline which is necessary for and peculiar to military organization.

We do not hesitate to state that it would have been eminently desirable had the command-ers of the German armed forces refused to implement the policy of the Third Reich by means of aggressive war. It would have been creditable to them not to contribute to the cataclysmic catastrophe. This would have been the honorable and righteous thing to do; it would have been in the interest of their State. Had they done so they would have served their fatherland and humanity also.

But however much their failure is morally reprimandable, we are of the opinion and hold that international common law, at the time they so acted, had not developed to the point of making the participation of military officers below the policy making or policy influencing level into a criminal offense in and of itself.

International law operates as a restriction and limitation on the sovereignty of nations. It may also limit the obligations which individuals owe to their states, and create for them international obligations which are binding upon them to an extent that they must be car-ried out even if to do so violates a positive law or directive of state. But the limitation which international common law imposes on national sovereignty, or on individual obligations, is a limitation self-imposed or imposed by the composite thinking in the international community, for it is by such democratic processes that common law comes into being. If there is no generality of opinion among the nations of the world as to a particular restriction on national sovereignty or on the obligations of individuals toward their own state, then there is no international common law on such matter.

By the Kellogg-Briand Pact 63 nations, including Germany, renounced war as an instrument of *national policy*.

If this, as we believe it is, is evidence of a sufficient crystallization of world opinion to authorize a judicial finding that there exist crimes against peace under international common law, we cannot find that law to extend further than such evidence indicates.

The nations that entered into the Kellogg-Briand Pact considered it imperative that existing international relationships should not be changed by force. In the preamble they state that they are:

> "...persuaded that the time has come when...all changes in their relationships with one another should be sought only by pacific means."

This is a declaration that from that time forward each of the signatory nations should be deemed to possess and to have the right to exercise all the privileges and powers of a sovereign nation within the limitations of international law, free from all interference by force on the part of any other nation. As a corollary to this, the changing or attempting to change the international relationships by force of arms is an act of aggression and if the aggression results in war, the war is an aggressive war. It is, therefore, aggressive war that is renounced by the pact. It is aggressive war that is criminal under international law.

The crime denounced by the law is the use of war as an instrument of national policy. Those who commit the crime are those who participate at the policy making level in planning, preparing, or in initiating war. After war is initiated, and is being waged, the policy question then involved becomes one of extending, continuing or discontinuing the war. The crime at this stage likewise must be committed at the policy making level.

The making of a national policy is essentially political, though it may require, and of necessity does require, if war is to be one element of that policy, a consideration of matters military as well as matters political.

It is self-evident that national policies are made by man. When men make a policy that is criminal under international law, they are criminally responsible for so doing. This is the logical and inescapable conclusion.

The acts of commanders and staff officers below the policy level, in planning campaigns, preparing means for carrying them out, moving against a country on orders and fighting a war after it has been instituted, do not constitute the planning, preparation, initiation, and waging of war or the initiation of invasion that international law denounces as criminal.

Under the record we find the defendants were not on the policy level, and are not guilty under count one of the indictment. With crimes charged to have been committed by them in the *manner* in which they behaved in the waging of war, we deal in other parts of this judgment.

COMMENTARY

The court in the *High Command* case provided further articulation of both the meaning of aggressive war, and the elements to be found to hold a military commander responsible for the crime of aggressive war. The court focused on the 'intent and purpose' of a war to determine its lawfulness. This perspective on the meaning of aggressive war also largely answered the question of individual criminal liability, because only those who were in a position to *shape* the intent and purpose of the war could be held accountable for aggressive war. It was not sufficient to be a high-level military commander responsible for the conduct of hostilities: only those in high-level *policy-making* positions could be convicted of the crime of aggressive war.

....

US Military Tribunal Sitting in Nuremberg, US v. Krauch et al. *(*I.G. Farben *case),* Judgment of 30 July 1948

> This case charged 24 high-level members of the German industrial firm I.G. Farben which was responsible, among other things, for the production and distribution of poison gas used in the concentration camps. Ultimately 23 of the accused stood trial, and all were acquitted of the aggression charges. Thirteen of the accused were convicted of either plunder, enslavement, or both and were sentenced to terms of imprisonment ranging from one and a half to eight years.

[T]he IMT approached a finding of guilty of any defendant under the charges of participation in a common plan or conspiracy or planning and waging aggressive war with great caution. It made findings of guilty under counts one and two only where the evidence of both knowledge and active participation was conclusive. No defendant was convicted under the charge of participating in the common plan or conspiracy unless he was, as was the defendant Hess, in such close relationship with Hitler that he must have been informed of Hitler's aggressive plans and took action to carry them out, or attended at least one of the four secret meetings at which Hitler disclosed his plans for aggressive war. [. . .]

The record is also clear that Krauch had no connection with the *initiation* of any of the specific wars of aggression or invasions in which Germany engaged. He was informed of neither the time nor method of initiation. The evidence that most nearly approaches Krauch is that pertaining to the *preparation* for aggressive war. After World War I, Germany was totally disarmed. She was stripped of war material and the means of producing it. Immediately upon the acquisition of power by the Nazis, they proceeded to rearm Germany, secretly and inconspicuously at first. As the rearmament program grew, so also did the boldness of Hitler with reference to rearmament. Rearmament took the course, not only of creating an army, a navy, and an air force, but also of coordinating and developing the industrial power of Germany so that its strength might be utilized in support of the military in event of war. The Four Year Plan, initiated in 1936, was a plan to strengthen Germany as both a military and an economic power, although, in its introduction to the German people, the military aspect was kept in the background.

In order to conceal Germany's growing military power, strict measures were undertaken to impose secrecy, not only regarding military matters, but also regarding Germany's growing industrial strength. This served two purposes: it tended to conceal the true facts from the world and from the German public; it also kept the people who were actually participating in rearmament from learning of the progress being made outside of their own specific fields of endeavor, and kept them in ignorance of the actual state of Germany's military strength. The dictatorial system was in full control. Even people in high places were kept in ignorance and were not permitted to disclose to each other the extent of their individual activities in behalf of the Reich. A striking example of this is Keitel's objection to Krauch's appointment as Plenipotentiary General for Special Questions of Chemical Production, on the ground that Krauch, as a man *of* industry and not of the military, should not obtain insight into the armament fields. He pointed out that anyone in that position might learn how many divisions were being set up in the army and what plans were being made for bomber squadrons. The evidence shows that, although Krauch was appointed over the objection of Keitel, he was never fully trusted by the military. His functions and authority were limited to fields bordering on military affairs. He could not act without the cooperation of the Army Ordnance Office. The evidence does not show that anyone told Krauch that Hitler had a plan or plans to plunge Germany into aggressive war. Moreover, the positions that Krauch held with reference to the government did not, necessarily, result in the acquisition by him of such knowledge.

The IMT stated that "Rearmament of itself is not criminal under the Charter." It is equally obvious that participation in the rearmament of Germany was not a crime on the part of any of the defendants in this case, unless that rearmament was carried out, or participated in, with knowledge that it was a part of a plan or was intended to be used in waging aggressive war. Thus we come to the question which is decisive of the guilt or innocence of the defendants under counts one and five – the question of knowledge.

We have already discussed common knowledge. There was no such common knowledge in Germany that would apprise any of the defendants of the existence of Hitler's plans or ultimate purpose.

It is contended that the defendants must have known from events transpiring within the Reich that what they did in aid of rearmament was preparing for aggressive war. It is asserted that the magnitude of the rearmament effort was such as to convey that knowledge. Germany was rearming so rapidly and to such an extent that, when viewed in retrospect in the light of subsequent events, armament production might be said to impute knowledge that it was in excess of the requirements of defense. If we were trying military experts, and it was shown that they had knowledge of the extent of rearmament, such a conclusion might be justified.

None of the defendants, however, were military experts. They were not military men at all. The field of their life work had been entirely within industry, and mostly within the narrower field of the chemical industry with its attendant sales branches. The evidence does not show that any of them knew the extent to which general rearmament had been planned, or how far it had progressed at any given time. There is likewise no proof of their knowledge as to the armament strength of neighboring nations. Effective armament is relative. Its efficacy depends upon the relative strength with respect to the armament of other nations against whom it may be used either offensively or defensively.

The opinion considers all of the defendants separately and finds that with respect to each there is insufficient evidence of knowledge.

There remains the question as to whether the evidence establishes that any of the defendants are guilty of "waging a war of aggression" within the meaning of Article II, 1, *(a)* of Control Council Law No. 10. This calls for an interpretation of the quoted clause. Is it an offense under international law for a citizen of a state that has launched an aggressive attack on another country to support and aid such war efforts of his government, or is liability to be limited to those who are responsible for the formulation and execution of the policies that result in the carrying on of such a war?

It is to be noted in this connection that the express purpose of Control Council Law No. 10, as declared in its preamble, was to "give effect to the terms of the Moscow Declaration of 30 October 1943, and the London Agreement of 8 August 1945, and the charter issued pursuant thereto." The Moscow Declaration gave warning that the "German officers and men and members of the Nazi Party" who were responsible for "atrocities, massacres and cold-blooded mass executions" would be prosecuted for such offenses. Nothing was said in that declaration about criminal liability for waging a war of aggression. The London Agreement is entitled an agreement "for the Prosecution and Punishment of the Major War Criminals of the European Axis." There is nothing in that agreement or in the attached Charter to indicate that the words "waging a war of aggression," as used in Article II (a) of the latter, were intended to apply to any and all persons who aided, supported, or contributed to the carrying on of an aggressive war; and it may be added that the persons indicted and tried before the IMT may fairly be classified as "major war criminals" insofar as their activities were concerned. Consistent with the express purpose of the London Agreement to reach the "major war criminals," the judgment of the IMT declared that "mass punishments should be avoided." To depart from the concept that only major war criminals – that is, those persons in the political, military, and industrial fields, for example, who were responsible for the formulation and execution of policies – may be held liable for waging wars of aggression, would lead far afield. Under such circumstances there could be no practical limitation on criminal responsibility that would not include, on principle, the private soldier on the battlefield, the farmer who increased his production of foodstuffs to sustain the armed forces, or the housewife who conserved fats for the making of munitions. Under such a construction the entire manpower of Germany could, at the uncontrolled discretion of the indicting authorities, be held to answer for waging wars of aggression. That would, indeed, result in the possibility of mass punishments.

There is another aspect of this problem that may not be overlooked. It was urged before the IMT that international law had theretofore concerned itself with the actions of sovereign states and that to apply the Charter to individuals would amount to the application of *ex post facto* law.

After observing that the offenses with which it was concerned had long been regarded as criminal by civilized peoples, the High Tribunal said: "Crimes against international law are committed by men, not by abstract entities, and only by punishing individuals who commit such crimes can the provisions of international law be enforced." The extension of punishment for crimes against peace by the IMT to the leaders of the Nazi military and government was, therefore, a logical step. The acts of a government and its military power are determined by the individuals who are in control and who fix the policies that result in those acts. To say that the government of Germany was guilty of waging aggressive war but not the men who were in fact the government and whose minds conceived the plan and perfected its execution would be an absurdity. The IMT, having accepted the principle that the individual could be punished, then proceeded to the more difficult task of deciding which of the defendants before it were responsible in fact.

In this case we are faced with the problem of determining the guilt or innocence with respect to the waging of aggressive war on the part of men of industry who were not makers of policy but who supported their government during its period of rearmament and who continued to serve that government in the waging of war, the initiation of which has been established as an act of aggression committed against a neighboring nation. Hitler launched his war against Poland on 1 September 1939. The following day France and Britain declared war on Germany. The IMT did not determine whether the latter were waged as aggressive wars on the part of Germany. Neither must we determine that question in this case. We seek only the answer to the ultimate question: Are the defendants guilty of crimes against peace by waging aggressive war or wars? Of necessity, the great majority of the population of Germany supported the waging of war in some degree. They contributed to Germany's power to resist, as well as to attack. Some reasonable standard must, therefore, be found by which to measure the degree of participation necessary to constitute a crime against peace in the waging of aggressive war. The IMT fixed that standard of participation high among those who lead their country into war.

The defendants now before us were neither high public officials in the civil government nor high military officers. Their participation was that of followers and not leaders. If we lower the standard of participation to include them, it is difficult to find a logical place to draw the line between the guilty and the innocent among the great mass of German people. It is, of course, unthinkable that the majority of Germans should be condemned as guilty of committing crimes against peace. This would amount to a determination of collective guilt to which the corollary of mass punishment is the logical result for which there is no precedent in international law and no justification in human relations. We cannot say that a private citizen shall be placed in the position of being compelled to determine in the heat of war whether his government is right or wrong, or, if it starts right, when it turns wrong. We would not require the citizen, at the risk of becoming a criminal under the rules of international justice, to decide that his country has become an aggressor and that he must lay aside his patriotism, the loyalty to his homeland, and the defense of his own fireside at the risk of being adjudged guilty of crimes against peace on the one hand, or of becoming a traitor to his country on the other, if he makes an erroneous decision based upon facts of which he has but vague knowledge. To require this of him would be to assign to him a task of decision which the leading statesmen of the world and the learned men of international law have been unable to perform in their search for a precise definition of aggression.

Strive as we may, we are unable to find, once we have passed below those who have led a country into a war of aggression, a rational mark dividing the guilty from the innocent. Lest it be said that the difficulty of the task alone should not deter us from its performance, if justice should so require, here let it be said that the mark has already been set by that Honorable Tribunal in the trial of the international criminals. It was set below the planners and leaders, such as Goering, Hess, von Ribbentrop, Rosenberg, Keitel, Frick, Funk, Doenitz, Raeder, Jodl, Seyss-Inquart, and von Neurath, who were found guilty of waging aggressive war, and above those whose participation was less and whose activity took the form of neither planning nor guiding the nation in its aggressive ambitions. To find the defendants guilty of waging aggressive war would require us to move the mark without finding a firm place in which to reset it. We leave the mark where we find it, well satisfied that individuals who plan and lead a nation into and in an aggressive war should be held guilty of crimes against peace, but not those who merely follow the leaders and whose participations, like those of Speer, "were in aid of the war effort in the same way that other productive enterprises aid in the waging of war." (IMT judgment, vol. 1, p. 330.).

COMMENTARY

The *I.G. Farben* case demonstrates the difficulty of attempting to assign liability for aggressive war outside of the top governmental and military policy makers. Here, the court considers the role of key leaders in industry who were indisputably essential to Germany's war effort. Yet the court invokes a slippery slope argument; why did it do so? Was this a strictly legal decision, or a decision based on policy considerations? The result does not mean that individuals outside of the spheres of government and the military could never be liable for aggression. In a second case charging industrialists with aggression, *US* v. *Alfried Krupp et al.*, the US Military Tribunal emphasized that '[w]e do not hold that industrialists, as such, could not under any circumstances be found guilty upon such charges'. In that case, however, all 12 defendants, who all held high-level management positions in their businesses, were acquitted. A French Military Tribunal ultimately reached the same result with respect to five accused industrialists in the case of *Röchling* (excerpted above, in Part II(1) (F) War Crimes). Initially, the General Tribunal convicted Hermann Röchling alone for aggression after finding that once the aggressive war was under way, he undertook a leadership position in ensuring the continued production of steel and iron in the occupied countries to support the war effort. At that point, the court found that Röchling 'stepped out of his role of industrialist, demanded and accepted high administrative positions in order to develop the German ferrous production'. This judgment was reversed, however, by the Superior Military Government Court of France, which cited both the IMT Judgment and the decision in the *I.G. Farben* case in concluding that 'the degree of participation necessary to make an originator of a crime against peace punishable [is]...very high, in order to avoid "mass sentences," that is to say, in order not to go as far as the lowest ranks, namely, the ordinary soldier'.

Domestic tribunals have seldom dealt with the issue of aggression as a crime, and usually only incidentally. On 21 June 2005, for instance, in the case *Germany* v. *N.*, the German Federal Administrative Court (*Bundesverwaltungsgericht*, Decision No. 2 WD 12.04, available at www.bverwg.de) acquitted a soldier charged with refusing to participate in a military software project that he feared could support Operation Iraqi Freedom, the war against Iraq launched in 2003, which the soldier considered illegal. The Court, without making a definite finding on the legality of Operation Iraqi Freedom, reached its finding on the basis of the right of freedom of conscience enshrined in the German Constitution, and made specific reference to the serious legal concerns raised by the military operation in question, including whether it amounted to an act of aggression.

Another case related to the war in Iraq was dealt with by the UK House of Lords.

United Kingdom, R v. Jones, *House of Lords, Judgment of 29 March 2006*

The 20 defendants in this case were charged with breaking into British and NATO military bases in three different incidents during 2003 to protest against the war in Iraq. The defendants contended that they were legally justified because they were acting to prevent the British government from committing the international crime of aggression. This claim required the court to consider the international law status of the crime of aggression, and then to determine whether there existed a mechanism under British law for the accused to assert their defence.

LORD BINGHAM OF CORNHILL

[...] (2) *At all times relevant to these appeals customary international law has recognised a crime of aggression.*

12. I would question whether, as ruled by the United States Military Tribunal in *United States of America v Ernst von Weizsäcker et al* at p 319 of its judgment of 11–13 April, 1949, "aggressive wars and invasions have, since time immemorial, been a violation of international law, even though specific sanctions were not provided". It may, I think, be doubtful whether such wars were recognised in customary international law as a crime when the 20th century began. But whether that be so or not, it seems to me clear that such a crime was recognized by the time the century ended.

13. It is, I think, enough to identify the major milestones along the road leading to this conclusion. A draft Treaty of Mutual Assistance, sponsored by the League of Nations, described aggressive war as an international crime in 1923. In the following year the same description was used in the preamble to a protocol recommended by the League of Nations Assembly but not ratified. In 1927 the League of Nations Assembly unanimously adopted a preamble which used that description. The Pan-American Conference in 1928 unanimously resolved that "war of aggression constitutes an international crime against the human species". In the same year the General Treaty for the Renunciation of War (94 LNTS 57, the "Kellogg-Briand Pact") condemned recourse to war as an instrument of international policy.

14. The Second World War gave new impetus to this movement. The Charter of the United Nations, in its preamble and in article 2(4), set its face against the threat and use of force. Article 6 of the Charter of the International Military Tribunal established to try major war criminals of the European Axis at Nuremberg defined its jurisdiction as including

"(a) Crimes against peace. Namely, planning, preparation, initiation, or waging of a war of aggression or a war in violation of international treaties, agreements or assurances, or participation in a common plan or conspiracy for the accomplishment of any of the foregoing."

The International Military Tribunal convicted a number of defendants of offences under this head. By General Assembly Resolution 95(1) of 11 December 1946 the principles recognised by the Charter of the International Military Tribunal and its judgment were affirmed. The Charter of the International Military Tribunal for the Far East was, save for an immaterial difference of wording, to the same effect as article 6(a). Law No 10 of the Control Council for Germany (20 December 1945) recognised a crime against peace in very similar terms.

15. The condemnation of aggressive war found further expression in General Assembly Resolutions 2131(xx) of 21 December 1965, 2625(xxv) of 24 October 1970 and 3314 (xxix) of 14 December 1974, in the last of which the definition of an act of aggression in contravention of the Charter was approved as including:

"(a) The invasion or attack by the armed forces of a State of the territory of another State, or any military occupation, however temporary, resulting from such invasion or attack . . .
(b) Bombardment by the armed forces of a State against the territory of another State or the use of any weapons by a State against the territory of another State."

In 1954 the International Law Commission, in a Draft Code of Offences against the Peace and Security of Mankind, defined as such offences

"(1) Any act of aggression, including the employment by the authorities of a State of armed force against another State for any purpose other than national or collective self defence or in pursuance of a decision or recommendation of a competent organ of the United Nations."

16. In a further ILC draft code of 1996, article 1(2) declares that "Crimes against the peace and security of mankind are crimes under international law and punishable as such, whether or not they are punishable under national law". Thus, as the commentary (paragraph (9)) makes clear, they are crimes "irrespective of the existence of any corresponding national law". Article 2 of the code provides, as was established at Nuremberg, that individuals are personally responsible for crimes committed under international law. Article 16 addresses the crime of aggression and provides that "An individual who, as leader or organizer, actively participates in or orders the planning, preparation, initiation or waging of aggression committed by a State shall be responsible for a crime of aggression". Paragraph (14) of the commentary on article 8 makes plain that

"An individual cannot incur responsibility for this crime in the absence of aggression committed by a State. Thus, a court cannot determine the question of individual criminal responsibility for this crime without considering as a preliminary matter the question of aggression by a State."

But article 16 establishes, as was held at Nuremberg and other post-war trials, that aggression is a leadership crime: it cannot be committed by minions and footsoldiers. Article 8, addressing jurisdiction, provides that jurisdiction over the crime of aggression shall rest with an international criminal court, but without precluding trial of its own nationals alleged to have committed that crime by a state whose leaders participated in an act of aggression.

17. In the Rome Statute of the International Criminal Court 1998 the jurisdiction of the court is limited by article 5 to "the most serious crimes of concern to the international community as a whole". These are: the crime of genocide; crimes against humanity; war crimes; and the

crime of aggression. But, by article 5(2), the court is not to exercise jurisdiction over the crime of aggression until a provision is adopted defining the crime and setting out the conditions under which the court may exercise jurisdiction with respect to it.

18. In the *Case Concerning Military and Paramilitary Activities in and against Nicaragua (Merits) (Nicaragua v United States)* [1986] ICJ Reports 14, para 190, the prohibition on the use of force in article 2(4) of the United Nations Charter was accepted as jus cogens, a universally recognised principle of international law. As Professor Brownlie has observed (*Principles of Public International Law*, 5th ed (1998), p 566), "whatever the state of the law in 1945, Article 6 of the Nuremberg Charter has since come to represent general international law".

19. It was suggested, on behalf of the Crown, that the crime of aggression lacked the certainty of definition required of any criminal offence, particularly a crime of this gravity. This submission was based on the requirement in article 5(2) of the Rome statute that the crime of aggression be the subject of definition before the international court exercised jurisdiction to try persons accused of that offence. This was an argument which found some favour with the Court of Appeal (in para 43 of its judgment). I would not for my part accept it. It is true that some states parties to the Rome statute have sought an extended and more specific definition of aggression. It is also true that there has been protracted discussion of whether a finding of aggression against a state by the Security Council should be a necessary pre-condition of the court's exercise of jurisdiction to try a national of that state accused of committing the crime. I do not, however, think that either of these points undermines the appellants' essential proposition that the core elements of the crime of aggression have been understood, at least since 1945, with sufficient clarity to permit the lawful trial (and, on conviction, punishment) of those accused of this most serious crime. It is unhistorical to suppose that the elements of the crime were clear in 1945 but have since become in any way obscure. [. . .]

LORD HOFFMANN

[. . .] 44. All these defences thus depend upon the proposition that the war in Iraq was a crime as well as a mistake. What was that crime? Various offences were suggested but all except one have either fallen by the wayside or been left for further consideration at a later stage. The one which remains is the crime of aggression, the unlawful use of war as an instrument of national policy. There is no doubt that this is a recognized crime in international law. Twelve of the major German war criminals were convicted of aggression in one form or another by the International Military Tribunal at Nuremberg and eight of them were executed. This decision has since received general international approbation. Article 5 of the Rome Statute of the International Criminal Court lists "the crime of aggression" together with genocide, crimes against humanity and war crimes as the crimes over which the Court is to have jurisdiction, these being "the most serious crimes of concern to the international community as a whole". But the Statute postpones the exercise of jurisdiction over the crime of aggression until the adoption of a provision which defines the crime and sets out the conditions under which the jurisdiction is to be exercised. [. . .]

COMMENTARY

Although the House of Lords found, based on its review of the development of the law since World War II, that the crime of aggression was established in customary international law, it did not find that aggression was a crime (or a defence to a crime) under British law, absent a specific statutory enactment. While some national codes (for instance, in Germany) do provide for the crime of aggression, no prosecutions have been brought for this crime before national courts. Therefore, whatever the status of the crime in international law, its future enforcement is likely to remain theoretical without further enactment at the ICC.

QUESTIONS

1. In light of the actions of the 2010 ICC Review Conference, is there a real prospect that future individuals will be investigated and prosecuted for the crime of aggression, or do the limitations contained in the definition and jurisdiction provisions mean that it will remain an unused crime? Is there any role for national courts to consider enforcing the crime?

2. The court in the *Ministries* case drew a sharp distinction between the crime of aggression on the one hand and war crimes and crimes against humanity on the other, contending that it was possible for ordinary soldiers and civilians to participate in an aggressive war without being aware of its illegality. Is this distinction persuasive as a matter or principle or is it more justified as a pragmatic accommodation?

FURTHER READING

J.A. Bush, ' "The Supreme . . . Crime" and Its Origins: The Lost Legislative History of the Crime of Aggressive War' (2002) 102 *Columbia Law Review* 2324ff.

Cassese, *International Criminal Law*, 152–61.

G. Dawson, 'Defining Substantive Crimes within the Subject Matter Jurisdiction of the International Criminal Court: What is the Crime of Aggression?' (2000) 19 *NY Law School J. Int'l and Comp. Law* 413.

C. Kress, 'The German Chief Federal Prosecutor's Decision not to Investigate the Alleged Crime of Preparing Aggression against Iraq' (2004) 2 JICJ 245ff.

C. Villarino Villa, 'The Crime of Aggression before the House of Lords' (2006) 4 JICJ 866ff.

Werle, *Principles*, 474–95.

5

TORTURE

(A) OVERVIEW: THE PRACTICE AND THE PROHIBITION

The problem of torture underscores the disparity between law's aspirations and actual practice. Widely proscribed, torture is 'the most universally condemned and repudiated' of 'all human rights violations.'[1] A single incident constitutes a discrete international crime. When committed in the context of war, torture is also a war crime, and when part of a widespread or systematic practice, may also constitute a crime against humanity. Numerous treaties and regional conventions ban torture, from general human rights instruments such as the 1948 Universal Declaration of Human Rights to the 1984 UN Convention Against Torture (the 'Torture Convention').

Under the Torture Convention, states have the duty to prevent and punish torture. The ban on torture is absolute: Article 2(2) of the Torture Convention provides that '[n]o exceptional circumstances whatsoever, whether a state of war or a threat or war, internal political instability or any other public emergency, may be invoked as a justification of torture'. In a famous formulation, a US Court of Appeals concluded, 'the torturer has become, like the pirate and slave trader before him, *hostis humani generis*, an enemy of all mankind'.[2] Yet some of the major powers of the world and proclaimed leaders in human rights, such as the United States, Britain and Israel, wrestle with accusations of engaging in torture or complicity in torture, and respond by quibbling with the definitions. Many other countries routinely engage in torture in the dark of their prisons, police stations and other similar places.

The temptation to make a suspect speak through torture is an age-old problem. The ban on torture is a relatively new development. Some of the great ancient legal systems of the world have institutionalized torture. In Europe, the twelfth-century turn to basing convictions on evidence instead of divine judgment by ordeals such as withstanding infection from application of a hot iron, or floating when cast into water meant there was greater pressure to get a confession, dubbed 'the queen of proofs'. Legal historian John Langbein explains:

From the late Middle Ages and throughout the ancien régime, torture was an incident of the legal systems of all the great states of continental Europe. Torture was part of the ordinary criminal procedure, regularly employed to investigate and prosecute routine crime before the ordinary courts. The system was one of *judicial torture*.

---

[1] Juan E. Méndez, 'Foreword' to William F. Schulz (ed.), *The Phenomenon of Torture: Readings and Commentary* (University of Pennsylvania Press, 2007), at xiii.
[2] *Filártiga* v. *Pena-Irala*, 630 F.2d 876, 878–9 (2d Cir. 1980).

There was in fact a jurisprudence of torture, with its own rules, treatises and learned doctors of law. This law of torture developed in northern Italy in the thirteenth century within the Roman-canon inquisitorial tradition, and it spread through Europe [...] Well into the eighteenth century the law of torture was still current everywhere, and it survived into the nineteenth century in some corners of central Europe. [...]

It is universally acknowledged that judicial torture as it existed in the national legal systems of Western Europe in early modern times was the creature of the so-called statutory system of proofs – the Roman-canon law of evidence. [...]

The Roman-canon law of proof governed judicial procedure in cases of serious crime, cases where blood sanctions (death or severe physical maiming) could be imposed. In brief, there were three fundamental rules.

First, the court could convict and condemn an accused upon the testimony of two eyewitnesses to the gravamen of the crime.

Second, if there were not two eyewitnesses, the court could convict and condemn the accused only upon the basis of his own confession.

Third, circumstantial evidence, so-called *indicia*, was not an adequate basis for conviction and condemnation, no matter how compelling. It does not matter, for example, that the suspect is seen running away from the murdered man's house and that the bloody dagger and the stolen loot are found in his possession. The court cannot convict him of the crime.

At least, the court cannot convict him without his confession, and that is where torture fitted into the system. In certain cases where there was neither the voluntary confession nor the testimony of the two eyewitnesses, the court could order that the suspect be examined about the crime under torture in order to secure his confession.

However, examination under torture was permitted only when there was a so-called half proof against the suspect. That meant either (1) one eyewitness, or (2) circumstantial evidence of sufficient gravity, according to a fairly elaborate tariff of gravity worked out by the later jurists. [...]

[T]he threshold requirement of half proof [...] amounted to what Anglo-American lawyers would call a rule of probable cause. It was designed to assure that only those persons highly likely to be guilty would be examined under torture. [...]

From a purely practical standpoint, laying aside moral objections to the use of coercion, there were a number of things wrong with the system. [...] Because torture tests an accused's capacity to endure pain, not his veracity, innocent persons might yield to 'the pain and torment and confess things they never did.'

Further the safeguards that were designed to prevent the condemnation of an innocent man on the basis of a false confession extracted from him were quite imperfect. [...]

Long before Voltaire, French writers of the sixteenth and seventeenth centuries are pointing to cases in which an innocent person confesses and is executed after which the real culprit is discovered. [...][3]

Langbein argues that pragmatic factors rather than moral outrage accounted for torture's abolition in Europe by the eighteenth century. The abolition of torture was possible because there was a lessening of a perceived need for torture because the Roman-canon law of proof no longer reigned supreme. Free judicial evaluation of evidence, including circumstantial evidence, was emerging.[4]

In contemporary times, pragmatic notions of need continue to inform the torture debate and controversial interrogation practices. The dilemma is often presented through the 'ticking time bomb' scenario – imagery with particular salience in these times of terrorism.

---

[3] John Langbein, *Torture and the Law of Proof* (2nd edn, University of Chicago Press, 2006), 3–5, 8–9.
[4] Ibid., 11–12.

The argument, fundamentally, is that the ban on torture cannot be absolute as a matter of principle because necessity may call for torture as an extraordinary measure – for example, to forestall a ticking time bomb in a school, or train, or plane.

Before examining how the necessity argument has been addressed in contemporary jurisprudence, it is first important to understand what torture means in international criminal law. Definitions are important because although States today do not unabashedly claim entitlement to torture, some States vigorously contest that certain of their practices constitute torture. The stakes in the definitional debate are exemplified, for example, in the debate over whether the practice of water-boarding constitutes torture. The next subsections explain the elements of torture before turning to the definitional debate regarding whether certain forms of harsh interrogation amount to torture and the argument regarding necessity.

(B) ELEMENTS OF THE CRIME OF TORTURE

As noted above, torture can be a war crime, a crime against humanity and a discrete crime. The shared core among the three forms is the proscription of intentionally inflicting severe mental or physical pain or suffering. Generally, an instrumental purpose is also required, though the ICC Elements of Crimes dispenses with the purpose requirement in defining torture as a crime against humanity. Article 7(1)(F) of the ICC Elements of Crimes defines torture as a crime against humanity thus:

1. The perpetrator inflicted severe physical or mental pain or suffering upon one or more persons.

2. Such person or persons were in the custody or under the control of the perpetrator.

3. Such pain or suffering did not arise only from, and was not inherent in or incidental to, lawful sanctions.

4. The conduct was committed as part of a widespread or systematic attack directed against a civilian population.

5. The perpetrator knew that the conduct was part of or intended the conduct to be part of a widespread or systematic attack directed against a civilian population.

Article 8(2)(a)(ii)-1 of the ICC Elements of Crimes prescribes the following elements for the war crime of torture:

1. The perpetrator inflicted severe physical or mental pain or suffering upon one or more persons.

2. The perpetrator inflicted the pain or suffering for such purposes as: obtaining information or a confession, punishment, intimidation or coercion or for any reason based on discrimination of any kind.

3. Such person or persons were protected under one or more of the Geneva Conventions of 1949.

4. The perpetrator was aware of the factual circumstances that established that protected status.

5. The conduct took place in the context of and was associated with an international armed conflict.

6. The perpetrator was aware of factual circumstances that established the existence of an armed conflict.

While the definitions of torture as a discrete crime vary between international instruments and domestic implementing instruments, the most influential definition of torture comes from Article 1(1) of the Convention Against Torture and Other Cruel, Inhuman, or Degrading Treatment or Punishment:

[T]he term 'torture' means any act by which severe pain or suffering, whether physical or mental, is intentionally inflicted on a person for such purposes as obtaining from him or a third person information or a confession, punishing him for an act he or a third person has committed or is suspected of having committed, or intimidating or coercing him or a third person, or for any reason based on discrimination of any kind, when such pain or suffering is inflicted by or at the instigation of or with the consent or acquiescence of a public official or other person acting in an official capacity. It does not include pain or suffering arising only from, inherent in or incidental to lawful sanctions.

As the ICTY has explained, 'there is now general acceptance of the main elements contained in the definition' (*Furundžija*, Appeal Judgment, para. 111), which can be divided into four elements, two objective – *actus reus* – and two subjective – *mens rea*:

Objective Elements

1. *Severe Pain or Suffering*: Infliction of severe pain or suffering, whether physical or mental, on a person, that is not merely stemming from, or inherent in or incident to, lawful sanctions.
2. *Public Official as Actor*: The infliction is at the instigation, or with the consent or acquiescence, of a public official or other person acting in an official capacity.

Subjective Elements

3. *Intent*: The infliction of severe pain or suffering must be intentional.
4. *Purpose*: The intentional infliction of severe pain or suffering must be for 'such purposes as' obtaining information or a confession, punishment not stemming from a lawful sanction, intimidation or coercion or discrimination.

The meaning and import of the four elements in the most influential definition of torture are explicated in the commentary and cases below. These cases often refer to torture as a war crime or as a crime against humanity, but their relevance in defining torture as a discrete crime stems from the existence of 'core' elements of torture.

SEVERITY OF PAIN OR SUFFERING

Deciding what counts as severe pain or suffering is a macabre exercise in line-drawing between torture and other forms of violence, such as cruel, inhuman or degrading treatment. The line-drawing is important, however, because the duties of States and the content of criminal prohibitions can turn on the characterization of conduct as torture. Even the serious crime of cruel, inhuman and degrading treatment is subject to fewer strictures in international law. For example, the Convention Against Torture prohibits both crimes but only requires states to criminalize torture. The excerpt below explains the meaning of severe pain and suffering under customary international law – and contrasts it with the definition proffered in the infamous and now rescinded 2002 'Torture Memo' by the Office of Legal Counsel in the US Department of Justice.

Cases

ICTY, Prosecutor v. Brđanin, Appeals Chamber, Judgment of 3 April 2007

During the Bosnian conflict, in 1992, Radoslav Brđanin became President of the self-declared Bosnian Serb-held Autonomous Region of Krajina (ARK). He was convicted of, among other things, torture as a crime against humanity, committed in the course of implementing a strategic plan to link Serb-populated areas of Bosnia to create a separate Serb state from which non-Serbs would be excluded. He was sentenced to 32 years of imprisonment and appealed against, among other things, his conviction for torture as a crime against humanity.

241. The Trial Chamber convicted Brđanin of aiding and abetting numerous acts of torture. It divided these acts into two categories: acts of torture committed "in [the] context of the armed attacks [by] Bosnian Serb forces on non-Serb towns, villages and neighbourhoods", and acts of torture committed in "camps and detention facilities" run by Bosnian Serb authorities.

242. The Trial Chamber pointed out that, under the Tribunal's jurisprudence, torture consists of "the infliction, by act or omission, of severe pain or suffering, whether physical or mental" and that "the threshold level of suffering or pain required for the crime of torture [. . .] depends on the individual circumstances of each case." The Trial Chamber further held that, in assessing whether that threshold level of suffering or pain has been met, "the objective severity of the harm inflicted must be considered," as must "[s]ubjective criteria, such as the physical or mental condition of the victim, the effect of the treatment and, in some cases, factors such as the victim's age, sex, state of health and position of inferiority". The Trial Chamber noted that "[p]ermanent injury is not a requirement for torture". [. . .]

244. Brđanin submits that the Trial Chamber erred in law in its determination of what acts constitute torture. Brđanin asserts that current customary international law on the amount of harm that must have been caused by the act "is best exemplified by a pronouncement from the Office of Legal Counsel of the United States Justice Department." He then quotes this "pronouncement", which is in fact a memorandum [from] the Counsel to the President of the United States ("Bybee Memorandum"), for the proposition that:

[F]or an act to constitute torture. . . it must inflict pain that is difficult to endure. Physical pain amounting to torture must be equivalent in intensity to the pain accompanying serious physical injury, such as organ failure, impairment of bodily function, or even death.[5]

Asserting that the Trial Chamber erred by failing to apply this newly recognized standard, Brđanin asks that "all alleged acts of torture in this case should be reviewed in light of it." [. . .]

246. The Appeals Chamber has previously explained that the definition of the crime of torture, as set out in the Convention against Torture and Other Cruel, [Inhuman] or Degrading

---

5 [466] Brđanin Appeal Brief, para. 256. The only citation provided for the block quote on paragraph 256 of the Appellant's Brief is "Hersh, *Chain of Command: The Road from 9/11 to Abu Ghraib*, Harper Collins, New York, 2004, p. 4–5." *See* Brđanin Appeal Brief, fn. 227. The quoted text is originally from: Memorandum from Jay S. Bybee, Assistant Attorney General, U.S. Dept of Justice, to Alberto R. Gonzales, Counsel to the President, 1 August 2002, p. 1, available at: http://www.humanrightsfirst.org/us_law/etn/gonzales/memos_dir/memo_20020801_JD_%20Gonz_.pdf.

Treatment or Punishment ("Convention against Torture") "may be considered to reflect customary international law." Accordingly, the Appeals Chamber has drawn verbatim from the Convention against Torture when explaining the amount of harm an act must cause in order to constitute torture: it must cause "severe pain or suffering, whether physical or mental". By examining if the acts charged in the indictment as torture caused "severe pain or suffering, whether physical or mental" – and not if they caused some greater amount of pain or suffering – the Trial Chamber was not only applying clear Appeals Chamber jurisprudence, it was also properly determining whether a conviction would be consistent with customary international law. In the discussion that follows, the Appeals Chamber will focus on developments relating to the law of torture after the indictment period, considering whether the definition of torture has, as suggested by Brđanin, changed to his benefit. Therefore, this discussion should not be in any way construed as an application of *ex post facto* law that could be prejudicial to Brđanin.

247. To support his argument that the requisite amount of harm has increased, Brđanin cites only the 2002 Bybee Memorandum – a memorandum in which the U.S. Department of Justice interpreted the criminal prohibition on torture found in U.S. federal law. Yet even if the U.S. executive branch determined that, for an act causing physical pain or suffering to amount to torture, it must "inflict pain . . . equivalent in intensity to the pain accompanying serious physical injury, such as organ failure, impairment of bodily function, or even death", this would not suffice to make pain of such intensity a requirement for conviction under customary international law. No matter how powerful or influential a country is, its practice does not automatically become customary international law.

248. Not only does Brđanin merely cite one memorandum for the proposition that there is a new customary international law standard for the amount of harm required for a torture conviction: he cites a memorandum that was withdrawn.[6] The Levin memorandum, which superseded the Bybee memorandum, did not endorse the view that physical torture consists only of those acts that "inflict pain . . . equivalent in intensity to the pain accompanying serious physical injury, such as organ failure, impairment of bodily function, or even death." To the contrary, the Levin memorandum suggested that the criminal prohibition on torture found in U.S. federal law was not intended "to reach only conduct involving excruciating and agonizing pain or suffering." Moreover, this memorandum concluded that the criminal prohibition on torture found in U.S. law covers some acts that cause severe physical suffering even if the acts do not also cause severe physical pain.

249. The Convention against Torture's requirement of "severe" pain or suffering was not itself meant to require "pain . . . equivalent in intensity to the pain accompanying serious physical injury, such as organ failure, impairment of bodily function, or even death". Indeed, during negotiations over the text of the Convention against Torture, the United Kingdom (seeking to make the definition of torture more restrictive) proposed that the infliction of "extreme pain or suffering" should be required. This wording was rejected. Hence, the Convention against Torture's drafting history makes clear that "severe pain or suffering" is not synonymous with "extreme pain or suffering", and that the latter is a more intense level of pain and suffering – one that might come closer to "pain . . . equivalent in intensity to the pain accompanying serious physical injury, such as organ failure, impairment of bodily function, or even death" – not required by the Convention against Torture. As the Convention against Torture is recognized to be declarative of customary international law on torture, it is therefore clear that, under customary international law, physical torture can include acts inflicting physical pain or suffering less severe than "extreme pain or suffering" or "pain . . . equivalent in intensity to the pain accompanying serious physical injury, such as organ failure, impairment of bodily function, or even death".

---

[6] [479] Levin Memorandum, p. 1 (formally withdrawing the Bybee Memorandum).

250. Article 3 of the European Convention on Human Rights and Fundamental Freedoms ("ECHR") declares that torture is prohibited, without defining it. Nonetheless, cases decided by the European Court of Human Rights ("ECtHR") applying the ECHR have shed light on the degree of harm that Court considers is required for an act to amount to torture.[7] In a decision the ECtHR observed that "what might have been inhumane treatment in the past is now seen as torture in the light of the increasingly higher standard of human rights protections."[8] ECtHR's more recent judgements, moreover, have endorsed the definition of torture contained in the Convention against Torture.[9] This Court's approach thus confirms that no more than "severe" pain or suffering is required under customary international law.

251. The amount of harm required under customary international law for an act to constitute torture has not increased since 2000, when the Appeals Chamber endorsed the above-mentioned standards in *Furundžija*.[10] Acts inflicting physical pain may amount to torture even when they do not cause pain of the type accompanying serious injury. An act may give rise to a conviction for torture when it inflicts severe pain or suffering. Whether it does so is a fact-specific inquiry. As the Appeals Chamber explained in the *Naletilić and Martinović* Appeal Judgement:

> torture is constituted by an act or an omission giving rise to severe pain or suffering, whether physical or mental, but there are no more specific requirements which allow an exhaustive classification and enumeration of acts which may constitute torture. Existing case-law has not determined the absolute degree of pain required for an act to amount to torture. Thus, while the suffering inflicted by some acts may be so obvious that the acts amount *per se* to torture, in general allegations of torture must be considered on a case-by-case basis so as to determine whether, in light of the acts committed and their context, severe physical or mental pain or suffering was inflicted.

252. Thus, in assessing whether the harm caused by the acts charged suffices to support a torture conviction, the Trial Chamber applied principles that the Appeals Chamber has endorsed and that reflect customary international law. Brđanin has failed to demonstrate that the Trial Chamber made an error of law which invalidated the decision.

COMMENTARY

Though the prohibition of torture is universal and accepted as *jus cogens* – that is, as an international peremptory norm from which no derogation by way of treaty or national legislation is admissible – the devil is in the details. States in incorporating the international definition of torture may vary it in domestic implementing legislation or tightly constrain the definition to permit a wide ambit of coercive practices. The withdrawn Bybee Memo referenced in the above excerpt interpreted US legislation implementing the obligation to criminalize torture under the Convention Against Torture. The implementing legislation specifies that "severe pain and suffering" means:

the prolonged mental harm caused by or resulting from –

(A) the intentional infliction or threatened infliction of severe physical pain or suffering;

---

[7] [487] *See*, among others, *Aydın v. Turkey*, Judgement of 25 September 1997, *Reports of Judgments and Decisions* 1997-VI, para. 82. For examples of acts constituting torture, *see also* Report of the Special Rapporteur Kooijmans, UN Doc. Res. 1985/33, E/CN.4/1986/15, 19 February 1986, para. 119.

[8] [488] *Selmouni v. France* [GC], no. 25803/94, para. 101, ECHR 1999-V.

[9] [489] Knut Dörmann, *Elements of War Crimes under the Rome Statute of the International Criminal Court: Sources and Commentary* (Cambridge: Cambridge University Press 2002), p. 51, fn. 23 pointing to *Ilhan v. Turkey* [GC], no. 22277/93, para. 85, ECHR 2000-VII; *Salman v. Turkey* [GC], no. 21986/93, para. 114, ECHR 2000-VII and *Akkoç v. Turkey*, nos. 22947/93 and 22948/93, para. 115, ECHR 2000-X.

[10] *Furundzija* Appeal Judgment, para. 111.

(B) the administration or application, or threatened administration or application, of mind-altering substances or other procedures calculated to disrupt profoundly the senses or the personality;

(C) the threat of imminent death; or

(D) the threat that another person will imminently be subjected to death, severe physical pain or suffering, or the administration or application of mind-altering substances or other procedures calculated to disrupt profoundly the senses or personality.[11]

The Bybee memo referenced by the ICTY above reasoned that this statutory definition 'prohibits only the most extreme acts by reserving criminal penalties solely for torture and declining to require such penalties for "cruel, inhuman, or degrading treatment or punishment"' (Bybee Memo, at 1–2). Examples of conduct egregious enough to constitute torture, according to the memo, are 'severe beatings using instruments such as iron barks, truncheons, and clubs', 'mock executions', and 'electronic shocks to genitalia or threats to do so' (Bybee Memo, at 24). The memo opines that 'interrogation techniques would have to be similar to these in their extreme nature and in the type of harm caused to violate the law' (Bybee Memo, at 24).

Also dubbed the 'Torture Memo', the Bybee Memo responds to a request by the CIA regarding use of 'enhanced interrogation techniques' on terrorism suspect Abu Zubaydah. The techniques included such methods as 'walling' (slamming the prisoner headlong into a wall while wearing a collar to prevent a broken neck), stress positions, slaps on the face, sleep deprivation, placement in a 'confinement box' with an insect to exploit Zubaydah's fear of insects and the experience of simulated drowning induced by water-boarding. The memo concludes that these techniques do not inflict the 'prolonged mental harm' required to constitute the 'severe pain or suffering' necessary for torture.

Politics can mediate in definitional difficulties. The politics of securing widespread consensus and adoption of the Torture Convention arguably contributed to the ambiguity of the notion of 'severe pain and suffering'. Subscribing jurisdictions were left to flesh out the meaning – and thereby retained some ambit to decide the scope of constraints. Politics can also reshape interpretations that permit practices that shock the polity. As the *Brđanin* Appeals Chamber noted, for example, when the Torture Memo came to light, the disgusted reaction of a nation finding its values sullied led to the eventual repudiation of the controversial interpretation.

The problem of pushing the line in using coercive techniques is not a new dilemma born of the War on Terror or troubles with jihadists. A 1983 CIA manual on coercive techniques is instructive. The manual had been hand-edited at some point in the mid-1980s, when Congress was investigating reported CIA abuses in the Central Americas. Here are some excerpts, with the deletions denoted by being struck out and the insertions italicized:

I. The Theory of Coercion

A. The purpose of all coercive techniques is to induce psychological regression in the subject [. . .] Regression is basically a loss of autonomy, a reversion to an earlier behavioral level. [. . .] *The use of most coercive techniques is improper and violates laws.*

B. There are three major principles involved in the successful application of coercive techniques:

---

[11] 18 U.S.C. §2340(2).

Debility (Physical Weakness)

For centuries 'questioners' have employed various methods of inducing physical weakness: prolonged constraint; prolonged exertion; extremes of heat, cold or moisture; and deprivation of food or sleep. [...] Many psychologists consider the threat of inducing debility to be more effective than debility itself. Prolonged constraint or exertion, sustained deprivation of food or sleep, etc. often become patterns to which a subject adjusts by becoming apathetic and withdrawing into himself [...] In this case, debility would be counter productive. [...] *Another coercive technique is* to manipulate the subject's environment to disrupt patterns [...] *This* [...] *is done to* disorient the subject and [...] destroy [...] his capacity to resist. *However if successful it causes serious psychological damage and therefore is a form of torture.*

Dependency

He is helplessly dependent on the 'questioner' for the satisfaction of all basic needs.

Dread (Intense Fear and Anxiety)

Sustained long enough, a strong fear of anything vague or unknown induces regression. [...] If the debility-dependency-dread state is unduly prolonged, the subject may sink into a defensive apathy from which it is hard to arouse him. ~~It is advisable to have a psychologist available whenever regression is induced~~ *This illustrates why this coercive technique may produce torture.*

II. Objections to Coercion

A. There is a profound moral objection to applying duress beyond the point of irreversible psychological damage such as occurs during brainwashing. [...] ~~Aside from this extreme, we will not judge the validity of other ethical arguments~~ *This technique is illegal and may not be used.*[12]

Defining the legalities of pain is not just difficult for a State sitting in judgment of its own practices and State organs deciding the scope of their agents' power. In a leading case, *Ireland* v. *United Kingdom*, the European Court of Human Rights ruled that the following techniques used in combination constituted inhuman and degrading treatment but not torture:

- Wall standing – requiring the prisoner to stand spread-eagled against a wall perched slanted on his toes so that his full weight is borne by fingers held high above his head;
- Hooding – sensory deprivation by placing a dark hood over the prisoner's head;
- Subjection to a loud and continuous hissing noise;
- Sleep deprivation; and
- Reduced diet.[13]

The European Court of Human Rights therefore overruled the determination by the then-existing European Commission on Human Rights that the five 'techniques' amounted to torture proper.

In the violence-saturated disorder of war, in contrast, the case is often clearer. The ICTY Appeals Chamber has held, for example, that the 'rubbing of a knife on a naked

---

[12] Central Intelligence Agency, *Human Resource Exploitation Training Manual* (1983), L-1 through L-6, available at http://www.gwu.edu/~nsarchiv/NSAEBB/NSAEBB122/#hre.

[13] Series A No. 25 (1978) 2 EHRR 25, para. 96.

woman's thighs and stomach, coupled with a threat to insert the knife into her vagina' caused severe pain or suffering sufficient for torture.[14]

PUBLIC OFFICIAL AS ACTOR

One of the most notable features of torture when connected to a wider context, such as a widespread or systematic practice, or armed conflict, is that there is not an across-the-board requirement that the perpetrator be a state official. Torture connected to an armed conflict is proscribed by international law when committed by private individuals as well as combatants, if committed against enemy lawful combatants or protected persons of the enemy's nationality or under the enemy's control. Torture, even by private actors, is a matter of international concern when connected to a systematic practice, or when armed conflict puts people at particular risk and vulnerability.

In contrast, torture as a stand-alone crime requires perpetration by an official actor or instigation, acquiescence or condoning by a state official to make it a matter of international concern. This reflects the provenance of the prohibition against torture as a discrete crime in human rights law – directed at the misconduct of states – and the notion that the international community cannot be mobilized to interfere each time in the infinite array of private cruelties and sadism.

In *Prosecutor* v. *Kunarac*, involving the rapes of women detained in houses around the area of Foča by Bosnian Serb military and paramilitary forces, the ICTY explained the blurry status of the state actor element for torture in customary international law.

ICTY, Prosecutor v. Kunarac, Trial Chamber, Judgment of 22 February 2001

> The first international case to focus wholly on wartime crimes of sexual violence and issue a conviction for rape as a crime against humanity, *Kunarac* involved systematized rape of women and girls in the town of Foča, captured by Bosnian Serb forces in 1992. Detained in deplorable conditions in apartments, houses and a sports centre, Muslim women and girls as young as 12 were subject to sexual servitude, including repeated rapes at knifepoint. In the excerpt below the Trial Chamber, preceding its holding that two of the accused were guilty of torture based on acts of sexual violence, analysed the status of the state actor element when torture is charged as a war crime and a crime against humanity rather than a discrete crime.

466. Torture is prohibited under both conventional and customary international law and it is prohibited both in times of peace and during an armed conflict. The prohibition can be said to constitute a norm of *jus cogens*. However, relatively few attempts have been made at defining the offence of torture. This has been done in Article 1 of the 1975 Declaration on the Protection of All Persons from Being Subjected to Torture and Other Cruel, Inhuman or Degrading Treatment or Punishment ("Declaration on Torture"), Article 1 of the 1984 Convention against Torture and Other Cruel, Inhuman or Degrading Treatment or Punishment ("Torture Convention") and Article 2 of the Inter-American Convention to Prevent and Punish

---

[14] *Prosecutor* v. *Furundžija*, ICTY Case No. IT-95–17/1-A, Appeals Chamber Judgment, 21 July 2000, at §§112–14.

Torture of 9 December 1985 ("Inter-American Torture Convention"). All three are, as is obvious, human rights instruments. [. . .]

469. [. . .] The absence of an express definition of torture under international humanitarian law does not mean that this body of law should be ignored altogether. The definition of an offence is largely a function of the environment in which it develops. Although it may not provide its own explicit definition of torture, international humanitarian law does provide some important definitional aspects of this offence.

470. In attempting to define an offence under international humanitarian law, the Trial Chamber must be mindful of the specificity of this body of law. In particular, when referring to definitions which have been given in the context of human rights law, the Trial Chamber will have to consider two crucial structural differences between these two bodies of law:

  (i)   Firstly, the role and position of the state as an actor is completely different in both regimes. Human rights law is essentially born out of the abuses of the state over its citizens and out of the need to protect the latter from state-organised or state-sponsored violence. Humanitarian law aims at placing restraints on the conduct of warfare so as to diminish its effects on the victims of the hostilities.

        In the human rights context, the state is the ultimate guarantor of the rights protected and has both duties and a responsibility for the observance of those rights. In the event that the state violates those rights or fails in its responsibility to protect the rights, it can be called to account and asked to take appropriate measures to put an end to the infringements.

        In the field of international humanitarian law, and in particular in the context of international prosecutions, the role of the state is, when it comes to accountability, peripheral. Individual criminal responsibility for violation of international humanitarian law does not depend on the participation of the state and, conversely, its participation in the commission of the offence is no defence to the perpetrator.[15] Moreover, international humanitarian law purports to apply equally to and expressly bind all parties to the armed conflict whereas, in contrast, human rights law generally applies to only one party, namely the state involved, and its agents. This distinction can be illustrated by two recent American decisions of the Court of Appeals for the Second Circuit rendered under the Alien Torts Claims Act. The Act gives jurisdiction to American district courts for any civil action by an alien for a tort committed in violation of the law of nations or a treaty of the United States. In the first decision, *In re Filártiga,* the Court of Appeals of the Second Circuit held that "deliberate torture perpetrated under colour of official authority violates universally accepted norms of the international law of human rights, regardless of the nationality of the parties".[16] This decision was only concerned with the situation of an individual *vis-à-vis* a state, either his national state or a foreign state. In a later decision in *Kadic v Karadžić,*[17] the same court made it clear that the body of law which it applied in the *Filártiga* case was customary international law *of human rights* and that, according to the Court of Appeals, in the human rights context torture is proscribed by international law only when committed by state officials or under the colour of the law. The court added, however, that atrocities including torture are actionable under the Alien Tort Claims Act regardless of state participation to the extent that the criminal acts were committed in pursuit of genocide or war crimes. [. . .]

---

  [15] [1175] Art 7(2) of the [ICTY] Statute states that: "The official position of any accused person, whether as Head of State or Government or as a responsible Government official, shall not relieve such person of criminal responsibility nor mitigate punishment."

  [16] [1176] *Filártiga v Pena-Irala,* 630 F.2d 876, 878–879 (2d Cir. 1980).

  [17] [1178] *Kadic v Karadžić,* 70 F.3d 232 (2d Cir 1995), *cert denied,* 64 US 3832 (18 June 1996).

471. The Trial Chamber is therefore wary not to embrace too quickly and too easily concepts and notions developed in a different legal context. The Trial Chamber is of the view that notions developed in the field of human rights can be transposed in international humanitarian law only if they take into consideration the specificities of the latter body of law. [. . .]

472. The Trial Chamber in the *Delalic* case, considered that the definition contained in the Torture Convention "reflects a consensus which the Trial Chamber considers to be representative of customary international law." The Trial Chamber in the *Furundžija* case shared that view and held that there was general acceptance of the main elements contained in the definition set out in Article 1 of the Torture Convention.

473. This Trial Chamber notes, however, that Article 1 of the Torture Convention makes it abundantly clear that its definition of torture is limited in scope and was meant to apply only "for the purposes of this Convention". In addition, paragraph 2 of Article 1 of the Torture Convention states that this Article is "without prejudice to any international instrument or national legislation which does or may contain provisions of wider application." Therefore, insofar as other international instruments or national laws give the individual broader protection, he or she shall be entitled to benefit from it. This, and the fact that the definition was meant to apply only in the context of the Convention are elements which should be kept in mind when considering the possibility that the definition of the Torture Convention produced an extra-conventional effect. [. . .]

477. Other international human rights instruments prohibit the act of torture without providing an express definition of the offence. Article 5 of the 1948 Universal Declaration of Human Rights provides that no one shall be subjected to torture or to cruel treatment. Article 30 of that Declaration in turn holds that "nothing in this Declaration may be interpreted as implying for any State, *group or person* any right to engage in any activity or to perform any act aimed at the destruction of any of the rights and freedoms set forth herein." This general statement is also valid with respect to the principle of freedom of torture expressed in Article 5.

478. Article 3 of the 1950 European Convention for the Protection of Human Rights and Fundamental Freedoms ("European Convention" or "Convention") provides that no one shall be subjected to torture or to inhuman or degrading treatment or punishment. The European Court of Human Rights ("ECHR") held that the concept of torture attaches a special stigma to deliberate inhuman treatment causing very serious and cruel suffering. The European Commission of Human Rights held that torture constitutes an aggravated and deliberate form of inhuman treatment which is directed at obtaining information or confessions, or at inflicting a punishment. The three main elements of the definition of torture under the European Convention are thus the level of severity of the ill-treatment, the deliberate nature of the act and the specific purpose behind the act. The requirement that the state or one of its officials take part in the act is a general requirement of the Convention – not a definitional element of the act of torture – which applies to each and every prohibition contained in the Convention. Article 1 of the Convention, which provides that the High Contracting Parties shall secure to everyone within their jurisdiction the rights and freedoms defined in Section I of the Convention, is clearly addressed to member states, not to individuals. The ECHR is not a criminal court which determines individual criminal responsibility, but an organ whose mandate is to determine state compliance with its obligations under the Convention.

479. The Trial Chamber notes, however, the ECHR's jurisprudence which has held that Article 3 of the Convention may also apply in situations where organs or agents of the state

are *not* involved in the violation of the rights protected under Article 3. For example, in *HLR v France*, the Court held that

> Owing to the absolute character of the right guaranteed, the Court does not rule out the possibility that Article 3 of the Convention (art. 3) may also apply where the danger emanates from persons or groups of persons who are not public officials.[18]

480. Article 7 of the 1966 International Covenant on Civil and Political Rights ("ICCPR") provides that no one shall be subject to torture or to cruel, inhuman or degrading treatment or punishment. The Human Rights Committee held that the protection offered by Article 7 of the ICCPR was not limited to acts committed by or at the instigation of public officials but that it also possessed horizontal effects, and that states should therefore protect individuals from interference by private parties. The Committee stated the following: "It is also the duty of public authorities to ensure protection by law against such treatment even when committed by persons acting outside or without any official authority".

481. In a later Comment of 3 April 1992, the Human Rights Committee stated that

> [i]t is the duty of the State party to afford everyone protection through legislative and other measures as may be necessary against the acts prohibited by article 7, whether inflicted by people acting in their official capacity, outside their official capacity or in a private capacity.

482. [...] In view of the international instruments and jurisprudence reviewed above, the Trial Chamber is of the view that the definition of torture contained in the Torture Convention cannot be regarded as the definition of torture under customary international law which is binding regardless of the context in which it is applied. The definition of the Torture Convention was meant to apply at an inter-state level and was, for that reason, directed at the states' obligations. The definition was also meant to apply only in the context of that Convention, and only to the extent that other international instruments or national laws did not give the individual a broader or better protection. The Trial Chamber, therefore, holds that the definition of torture contained in Article 1 of the Torture Convention can only serve, for present purposes, as an interpretational aid.

483. Three elements of the definition of torture contained in the Torture Convention are, however, uncontentious and are accepted as representing the status of customary international law on the subject:

(i) Torture consists of the infliction, by act or omission, of severe pain or suffering, whether physical or mental.

(ii) This act or omission must be intentional.

(iii) The act must be instrumental to another purpose, in the sense that the infliction of pain must be aimed at reaching a certain goal.

484. On the other hand, three elements remain contentious[, including:]

(iii) The requirement, if any, that the act be inflicted by or at the instigation of or with the consent or acquiescence of a public official or other person acting in an official capacity.

COMMENTARY

The Torture Convention's definition of torture has been influential in a field where torture is often proscribed but less frequently defined. The provenance of the source of criminalization – for example, stemming from human rights law versus international

---

[18] [1191] *HLR v France*, 29 Apr 1997, Reports 1997-III, p 758, par 40.

humanitarian law – must be taken into account, however, in understanding which elements are required for torture.

Reviewing the ICTY Trial Chamber's analysis, the ICTY Appeals Chamber in *Kunarac* further clarified the status of the state actor element:

146. [...] The Torture Convention was addressed to States and sought to regulate their conduct, and it is only for that purpose and to that extent that the Torture Convention deals with the acts of individuals acting in an official capacity. Consequently, the requirement set out by the Torture Convention that the crime of torture be committed by an individual acting in an official capacity may be considered as a limitation of the engagement of States; they need prosecute acts of torture only when those acts are committed by "a public official... or any other person acting in a non-private capacity." So the Appeals Chamber in the *Furundija* case was correct when it said that the definition of torture in the Torture Convention, inclusive of the public official requirement, reflected customary international law.

147. [...] This assertion, which is tantamount to a statement that the definition of torture in the Torture Convention reflects customary international law as far as the obligation of States is concerned, must be distinguished from an assertion that this definition wholly reflects customary international law regarding the meaning of the crime of torture generally.

148. The Trial Chamber in the present case was therefore right in taking the position that the public official requirement is not a requirement under customary international law in relation to the criminal responsibility of an individual for torture outside of the framework of the Torture Convention. [...][19]

In short: under customary international law, the duty of States to prosecute torture only applies with regard to acts of torture by public officials. The notion of torture, however, has a broader scope that extends beyond acts by State officials where the source of criminalization is external to the Torture Convention, such as international humanitarian law.

INTENT AND PURPOSE

The *mens rea* portion of the crime of torture consists of two components: the intent to inflict severe pain or suffering and the purpose for doing so. The infliction of severe pain or suffering must be done intentionally. One cannot recklessly or negligently commit torture. The intentionality requirement obtains under all three definitions of torture as a discrete crime, a war crime and a crime against humanity.

The purpose requirement ensures that the pain or suffering is being inflicted for an instrumental end, and not just out of an isolated incident of sadism that is more properly the province of domestic criminal law. Notably, while the purpose requirement is part of the definition of torture as a discrete crime and war crime, it is not part of the definition of torture as a crime against humanity, at least under the ICC Elements of Crimes. Arguably, when there is a practice of torture connected to a widespread or systematic attack directed against civilians, there is less ambiguity about whether severe pain or suffering is being imposed for instrumental ends.

Where it obtains, the purpose requirement is open-ended and, therefore, typically not a hard element to satisfy. The Torture Convention, for example, gives suggestive examples of 'such purposes as' obtaining information or a confession; punishment not stemming from a lawful sanction; intimidation or coercion or discrimination. The ICTY Trial Chamber in *Prosecutor* v. *Furundžija* has held that another cognizable purpose of torture may be to

---

[19] *Kunarac* Appeal Judgment, 12 June 2002.

humiliate the victim.[20] The excerpt below considers whether sexual violence satisfies the intent and purpose requirements.

ICTY, Prosecutor v. Kunarac, Appeals Chamber, Judgment of 12 June 2002

Kunarac's import in international criminal law in developing the international law against rape and sexual violence was discussed previously. Two of the accused, Dragoljub Kunarac and Zoran Vuković, were convicted of war crimes and crimes against humanity based on torture as well as rape.

The torture convictions were predicated on acts of sexual violence accompanied by threats. Kunarac tried to obtain information from a woman about her alleged sending of messages to Muslim forces and the whereabouts of her valuables. Kunarac threatened the woman, designated Witness FWS-183, and her son with death, and then participated in her rape by multiple men in succession. Kunarac also participated in the rapes of other women and held two women in sexual servitude, treating one of the women as his personal property. The second accused, Vuković, participated in multiple rapes, including gang rape. When a victim tried to hide, he threatened to kill the other women in the house.

The accused appealed. Among their challenges was the contention that sexual violence for sexual gratification does not satisfy the *mens rea* (subjective) elements required for torture.

(c) Subjective Elements

153. The Appellants argue that the intention of the perpetrator was of a sexual nature, which, in their view, is inconsistent with an intent to commit the crime of torture. In this respect, the Appeals Chamber wishes to assert the important distinction between "intent" and "motivation". The Appeals Chamber holds that, even if the perpetrator's motivation is entirely sexual, it does not follow that the perpetrator does not have the intent to commit an act of torture or that his conduct does not cause severe pain or suffering, whether physical or mental, since such pain or suffering is a likely and logical consequence of his conduct. In view of the definition, it is important to establish whether a perpetrator intended to act in a way which, in the normal course of events, would cause severe pain or suffering, whether physical or mental, to his victims. The Appeals Chamber concurs with the findings of the Trial Chamber that the Appellants did intend to act in such a way as to cause severe pain or suffering, whether physical or mental, to their victims, in pursuance of one of the purposes prohibited by the definition of the crime of torture, in particular the purpose of discrimination.

154. The Appellant Kunarac claims that the requisite intent for torture, alleged by the Prosecutor, has not been proven. Vuković also challenges the discriminatory purpose ascribed to his acts. The Appeals Chamber finds that the Appellants have not demonstrated why the conclusions of the Trial Chamber on this point are unreasonable or erroneous. The Appeals Chamber considers that the Trial Chamber rightly concluded that the Appellants deliberately committed the acts of which they were accused and did so with the intent of discriminating against their victims because they were Muslim. Moreover, the Appeals Chamber notes that in addition to a discriminatory purpose, the acts were committed against one of the victims with

---

[20] *Prosecutor* v. *Furundžija*, ICTY Case No. IT-95-17/1-T, Judgment, 10 December 1998, at para. 162.

the purpose of obtaining information. The Appeals Chamber further finds that, in any case, all acts were committed for the purpose of intimidating or coercing the victims.

155. Furthermore, in response to the argument that the Appellant's avowed purpose of sexual gratification is not listed in the definition of torture, the Appeals Chamber restates the conclusions of the Trial Chamber that acts need not have been perpetrated solely for one of the purposes prohibited by international law. If one prohibited purpose is fulfilled by the conduct, the fact that such conduct was also intended to achieve a non-listed purpose (even one of a sexual nature) is immaterial.

COMMENTARY

The rape centres of Foča involved a less complicated question of purpose because sexual violence was used as an instrument of ethnic cleansing. Muslim women were targeted to be sullied and sometimes impregnated based on the notion that they would then bear Serb children. The sexual violence therefore had a larger instrumental purpose beyond sexual gratification. As the scope of international crimes widens to recognize harms against women in conflict situations, the open-ended purpose requirement may also be expanded to capture the kinds of harms women suffer in war.

Consider, however, harder cases that are also prevalent and quotidian. Take, for example, a band of soldiers who, for their sexual gratification, kidnap a girl from a village to rape her, slaughtering her family in front of her in the process. In picking their victim, they target a member of the village suspected to sympathize with the enemy group. Let us assume the trauma of being wrested from one's murdered family, forced to march with the murderers, and repeatedly raped by them constitutes severe mental pain and suffering, both mental and physical. Should the infliction of the pain and suffering be deemed intentional or simply incidental to the aim of sexual gratification? Is rape under these circumstances necessarily dependent, or inextricably intertwined, with intent to inflict pain?

(C) NECESSITY?

The absolute ban on torture is hotly contested and subject to slippage. The spectre of the 'ticking time bomb' needing to be defused by wresting information from an individual suspected of having pertinent information is often marshalled to argue that the ban cannot be absolute. How should the law address concerns of necessity? The excerpt below from the Israeli Supreme Court addresses the question in connection with methods involving physical force that, while not amounting to torture, were nonetheless prohibited under Israeli law.

Israel, Legality of the General Security Service Interrogation Methods, Supreme Court, Judgment of 6 September 1999

In this judgment the nine justices of the Israeli Supreme Court unanimously invalidated the interrogation methods involving physical force used by the Israeli General Security Service. President Aharon Barak, writing for the Court, rejected the notion that necessity could be a licence for an exception to the prohibition – but provided an outlet for necessity to be a potential justification *ex post*.

President A. Barak:

Background:

1. The State of Israel has been engaged in an unceasing struggle for both its very existence and security, from the day of its founding. Terrorist organizations have established as their goal Israel's annihilation. Terrorist acts and the general disruption of order are their means of choice. In employing such methods, these groups do not distinguish between civilian and military targets. They carry out terrorist attacks in which scores are murdered in public areas, public transportation, city squares and centers, theaters and coffee shops. They do not distinguish between men, women and children. They act out of cruelty and without mercy [...]

The facts presented before this Court reveal that one hundred and twenty one people died in terrorist attacks between 1.1.96 to 14.5.98. Seven hundred and seven people were injured. A large number of those killed and injured were victims of harrowing suicide bombings in the heart of Israel's cities. Many attacks – including suicide bombings, attempts to detonate car bombs, kidnappings of citizens and soldiers, attempts to highjack buses, murders, the placing of explosives, etc. – were prevented due to the measures taken by the authorities responsible for fighting the above described hostile terrorist activities on a daily basis. The main body responsible for fighting terrorism is the GSS.

In order to fulfill this function, the GSS also investigates those suspected of hostile terrorist activities. The purpose of these interrogations is, among others, to gather information regarding terrorists and their organizing methods for the purpose of thwarting and preventing them from carrying out these terrorist attacks. In the context of these interrogations, GSS investigators also make use of physical means. The legality of these practices is being examined before this Court in these applications. [...]

The Physical Means

8. The physical means employed by the GSS investigators were presented before this Court by the GSS investigators. The State's attorneys were prepared to present them for us behind closed doors (in camera). The applicants' attorneys were opposed to this proposal. Thus, the information at the Court's disposal was provided by the applicants and was not tested in each individual application. This having been said, the State's position, which failed to deny the use of these interrogation methods, and even offered these and other explanations regarding the rationale justifying the use of [one] interrogation [method] or another, provided the Court with a picture of the GSS' interrogation practices. [...]

Shaking

9. [...] Among the investigation methods outlined in the GSS' interrogation regulations, shaking is considered the harshest. The method is defined as the forceful shaking of the suspect's upper torso, back and forth, repeatedly, in a manner which causes the neck and head to dangle and vacillate rapidly. According to an expert opinion submitted in one of the applications (H.C. (motion) 5584/95 and H.C. 5100/95), the shaking method is likely to cause serious brain damage, harm the spinal cord, cause the suspect to lose consciousness, vomit and urinate uncontrollably and suffer serious headaches.

The State entered several countering expert opinions into evidence. It admits the use of this method by the GSS. To its contention, there is no danger to the life of the suspect inherent to shaking; the risk to life as a result of shaking is rare; there is no evidence that shaking causes fatal damage; and medical literature has not to date listed a case in which a person died directly as a result of having been only shaken. In any event, they argue, doctors are present in all interrogation compounds, and instances where the danger of medical damage presents itself are investigated and researched.

All agree that in one particular case (H.C. 4054/95) the suspect in question expired after being shaken. According to the State, that case constituted a rare exception. Death was caused by an extremely rare complication resulting in the atrophy of the neurogenic lung. In addition, the State argues in its response that the shaking method is only resorted to in very particular cases, and only as a last resort. The interrogation directives define the appropriate circumstances for its application and the rank responsible for authorizing its use. The investigators were instructed that in every case where they consider resorting to shaking, they must probe the severity of the danger that the interrogation is intending to prevent; consider the urgency of uncovering the information presumably possessed by the suspect in question; and seek an alternative means of preventing the danger. Finally, the directives respecting interrogation state, that in cases where this method is to be used, the investigator must first provide an evaluation of the suspect's health and ensure that no harm comes to him. According to the respondent, shaking is indispensable to fighting and winning the war on terrorism. It is not possible to prohibit its use without seriously harming the GSS' ability to effectively thwart deadly terrorist attacks. Its use in the past has lead to the thwarting of murderous attacks.

Waiting in the "Shabach" Position

10. [. . .] As per applicants' submission, a suspect investigated under the "Shabach" position has his hands tied behind his back. He is seated on a small and low chair, whose seat is tilted forward, towards the ground. One hand is tied behind the suspect, and placed inside the gap between the chair's seat and back support. His second hand is tied behind the chair, against its back support. The suspect's head is covered by an opaque sack, falling down to his shoulders. Powerfully loud music is played in the room. According to the affidavits submitted, suspects are detained in this position for a prolonged period of time, awaiting interrogation at consecutive intervals.

The aforementioned affidavits claim that prolonged sitting in this position causes serious muscle pain in the arms, the neck and headaches. The State did not deny the use of this method before this Court. They submit that both crucial security considerations and the investigators' safety require tying up the suspect's hands as he is being interrogated. The head covering is intended to prevent contact between the suspect in question and other suspects. The powerfully loud music is played for the same reason.

The "Frog Crouch"

11. [. . .] This refers to consecutive, periodical crouches on the tips of one's toes, each lasting for five minute intervals. The State did not deny the use of this method, thereby prompting [the] Court to issue an order *nisi* [preliminary order] in the application where this method was alleged. Prior to hearing the application, however, this interrogation practice ceased.

Excessive Tightening of Handcuffs

12. [. . .] [V]arious applicants have complained of excessive tightening of hand or leg cuffs. To their contention, this practice results in serious injuries to the suspect's hands, arms and feet, due to the length of the interrogations. The applicants invoke the use of particularly small cuffs, ill fitted in relation to the suspect's arm or leg size. The State, for its part, denies any use of unusually small cuffs, arguing that those used were both of standard issue and properly applied. They are, nonetheless, prepared to admit that prolonged hand or foot cuffing is likely to cause injuries to the suspect's hands and feet. To the State's contention, however, injuries of this nature are inherent to any lengthy interrogation.

Sleep Deprivation

13. [. . .] [A]pplicants have complained of being deprived of sleep as a result of being tied in the "Shabach" position, being subjected to the playing of powerfully loud music, or intense non-stop interrogations without sufficient rest breaks. They claim that the purpose of depriving them of sleep is to cause them to break from exhaustion. While the State agrees that suspects are at times deprived of regular sleep hours, it argues that this does not constitute

an interrogation method aimed at causing exhaustion, but rather results from the prolonged amount of time necessary for conducting the interrogation. [. . .]

The State's Arguments

15. [. . .] With respect to the physical means employed by the GSS, the State argues that these do not violate International Law. Indeed, it is submitted that these methods cannot be qualified as "torture," "cruel and inhuman treatment" or "degrading treatment," that are strictly prohibited under International Law. Instead, the practices of the GSS do not cause pain and suffering, according to the State's position.

Moreover, the State argues that these means are equally legal under Israel's internal (domestic) law. This is due to the "necessity" defence outlined in article 34(11) of the Penal Law (1977). Hence, in the specific cases bearing the relevant conditions inherent to the "necessity" defence, GSS investigators are entitled to use "moderate physical pressure" as a last resort in order to prevent real injury to human life and well being. Such "moderate physical pressure" may include shaking, as the "necessity" defence provides in specific instances. Resorting to such means is legal, and does not constitute a criminal offence. In any case, if a specific method is not deemed to be a criminal offence, there is no reason not to employ it even for interrogation purposes. As per the State's submission, there is no reason for prohibiting a particular act, in specific circumstances, *ab initio* if it does not constitute a crime. This is particularly true with respect to the GSS investigators' case, who, according to the State, are after all responsible for the protection of lives and public safety. In support of their position, the State notes that the use of physical means by GSS investigators is most unusual and is only employed as a last resort in very extreme cases. Moreover, even in these rare cases, the application of such methods is subject to the strictest of scrutiny and supervision, as per the conditions and restrictions set forth in the Commission of Inquiry's Report. This having been said, when the exceptional conditions requiring the use of these means are in fact present, the above described interrogation methods are fundamental to saving human lives and safeguarding Israel's security. [. . .]

The Means Employed for Interrogation Purposes

22. An interrogation, by its very nature, places the suspect in a difficult position. "The criminal's interrogation," wrote Justice Vitkon over twenty years ago, "is not a negotiation process between two open and fair vendors, conducting their business on the basis of maximum mutual trust" (Cr. A 216/74 *Cohen v The State of Israel*) 29(1) P.D. 340 at 352). An interrogation is a "competition of minds", in which the investigator attempts to penetrate the suspect's thoughts and elicit from him the information the investigator seeks to obtain. [. . .]

[. . .] In crystallizing the interrogation rules, two values or interests clash. On the one hand, lies the desire to uncover the truth, thereby fulfilling the public interest in exposing crime and preventing it. On the other hand, is the wish to protect the dignity and liberty of the individual being interrogated. This having been said, these interests and values are not absolute. A democratic, freedom-loving society does not accept that investigators use any means for the purpose of uncovering the truth. "The interrogation practices of the police in a given regime," noted Justice Landau, "are indicative of a regime's very character" (Cr. A. 264/65 *Artzi v. The Government's Legal Advisor,* 20(1) P.D. 225 at 232). At times, the price of truth is so high that a democratic society is not prepared to pay it. [. . .]

Our concern, therefore, lies in the clash of values and the balancing of conflicting values. The balancing process results in the rules for a 'reasonable interrogation' [. . .] These rules are based, on the one hand, on preserving the "human image" of the suspect (See Cr. A. 115/82 *Mouadi v. The State of Israel* 35 (1) P.D. 197 at 222–4) and on preserving the "purity of arms" used during the interrogation (Cr. A. 183/78, *supra, ibid.*). On the other hand, these rules take into consideration the need to fight the phenomenon of criminality in an effective manner generally, and terrorist attacks specifically. [. . .]

First, a reasonable investigation is necessarily one free of torture, free of cruel, inhuman treatment of the subject and free of any degrading handling whatsoever. There is a prohibition on the use of "brutal or inhuman means" in the course of an investigation. Human dignity also includes the dignity of the suspect being interrogated. This conclusion is in perfect accord with (various) International Law treaties – to which Israel is a signatory – which prohibit the use of torture, "cruel, inhuman treatment" and "degrading treatment". These prohibitions are "absolute". There are no exceptions to them and there is no room for balancing. Indeed, violence directed at a suspect's body or spirit does not constitute a reasonable investigation practice. The use of violence during investigations can potentially lead to the investigator being held criminally liable. (See, for example, article 277 of the Penal Law: Pressure on a Public Servant; *supra* at 130, 134; Cr. A. 64/86 *Ashash v. The State of Israel* (unpublished)). Second, a reasonable investigation is likely to cause discomfort; It may result in insufficient sleep; The conditions under which it is conducted risk being unpleasant. Indeed, it is possible to conduct an effective investigation without resorting to violence. Within the confines of the law, it is permitted to resort to various machinations and specific sophisticated activities which serve investigators today [. . .] In the end result, the legality of an investigation is deduced from the propriety of its purpose and from its methods. Thus, for instance, sleep deprivation for a prolonged period, or sleep deprivation at night when this is not necessary to the investigation time wise may be deemed a use of an investigation method which surpasses the least restrictive means.

From the General to the Particular

24. We shall now turn from the general to the particular. Plainly put, shaking is a prohibited investigation method. It harms the suspect's body. It violates his dignity. It is a violent method which does not form part of a legal investigation. It surpasses that which is necessary. Even the State did not argue that shaking is an "ordinary" investigation method which every investigator (in the GSS or police) is permitted to employ. [. . .]

25. It was argued before the Court that one of the investigation methods employed consists of the suspect crouching on the tips of his toes for five minute intervals. The State did not deny this practice. This is a prohibited investigation method. It does not serve any purpose inherent to an investigation. It is degrading and infringes upon an individual's human dignity.

26. The "Shabach" method is composed of a number of cumulative components: the cuffing of the suspect, seating him on a low chair, covering his head with an opaque sack (head covering) and playing powerfully loud music in the area. [. . .] Our point of departure is that there are actions which are inherent to the investigation power. Therefore, we accept that the suspect's cuffing, for the purpose of preserving the investigators' safety, is an action included in the general power to investigate. Provided the suspect is cuffed for this purpose, it is within the investigator's authority to cuff him. [. . .] Notwithstanding, the cuffing associated with the "Shabach" position is unlike routine cuffing. The suspect is cuffed with his hands tied behind his back. One hand is placed inside the gap between the chair's seat and back support, while the other is tied behind him, against the chair's back support. This is a distorted and unnatural position. The investigators' safety does not require it. Therefore, there is no relevant justification for handcuffing the suspect's hands with particularly small handcuffs, if this is in fact the practice. The use of these methods is prohibited. As was noted, "Cuffing causing pain is prohibited". Moreover, there are other ways of preventing the suspect from fleeing from legal custody which do not involve causing the suspect pain and suffering.

27. This is the law with respect to the method involving seating the suspect in question in the "Shabach" position. We accept that seating a man is inherent to the investigation. This is not the case when the chair upon which he is seated is a very low one, tilted forward facing the

ground, and when he is sitting in this position for long hours. This sort of seating is not encom-passed by the general power to interrogate. Even if we suppose that the seating of the suspect on a chair lower than that of his investigator can potentially serve a legitimate investigation objective (for instance, to establish the "rules of the game" in the contest of wills between the parties, or to emphasize the investigator's superiority over the suspect), there is no inher-ent investigative need for seating the suspect on a chair so low and tilted forward towards the ground, in a manner that causes him real pain and suffering. [...] All these methods do not fall within the sphere of a "fair" interrogation. They are not reasonable. They impinge upon the suspect's dignity, his bodily integrity and his basic rights in an excessive manner (or beyond what is necessary). [...]

28. We accept that there are interrogation related considerations concerned with preventing contact between the suspect under interrogation and other suspects and his investigators, which require means capable of preventing the said contact. The need to prevent contact may, for instance, flow from the need to safeguard the investigators' security, or that of the sus-pects and witnesses. It can also be part of the "mind game" which pins the information pos-sessed by the suspect, against that found in the hands of his investigators. For this purpose, the power to interrogate – in principle and according to the circumstances of each particular case – includes preventing eye contact with a given person or place. In the case at bar, this was the explanation provided by the State for covering the suspect's head with an opaque sack, while he is seated in the "Shabach" position. From what was stated in the declarations before us, the suspect's head is covered with an opaque sack throughout his "wait" in the "Shabach" position. It was argued that the sack (head covering) is entirely opaque, causing the suspect to suffocate. The edges of the sack are long, reaching the suspect's shoulders. All these methods are not inherent to an interrogation. They do not confirm the State's position, arguing that they are meant to prevent eye contact between the suspect being interrogated and other sus-pects. Indeed, even if such contact should be prevented, what is the purpose of causing the suspect to suffocate? Employing this method is not connected to the purpose of preventing the said contact and is consequently forbidden. Moreover, the statements clearly reveal that the suspect's head remains covered for several hours, throughout his wait. For these purposes, less harmful means must be employed, such as letting the suspect wait in a detention cell. Doing so will eliminate any need to cover the suspect's eyes. In the alternative, the suspect's eyes may be covered in a manner that does not cause him physical suffering. For it appears that at present, the suspect's head covering – which covers his entire head, rather than eyes alone, – for a prolonged period of time, with no essential link to the goal of preventing con-tact between the suspects under investigation, is not part of a fair interrogation. It harms the suspect and his (human) image. It degrades him. It causes him to lose sight of time and place. It suffocates him. All these things are not included in the general authority to investigate. In the cases before us, the State declared that it will make an effort to find [a] "ventilated" sack. This is not sufficient. The covering of the head in the circumstances described, as distinguished from the covering of the eyes, is outside the scope of authority and is prohibited.

29. [...] Being exposed to powerfully loud music for a long period of time causes the sus-pect suffering. Furthermore, the suspect is tied (in place) in an uncomfortable position with his head covered (all the while). [...] Powerfully loud music is a prohibited means for use in the context described before us.

30. To the above, we must add that the "Shabach" position includes all the outlined methods employed simultaneously. Their combination, in and of itself gives rise to particular pain and suffering. This is a harmful method, particularly when it is employed for a prolonged period of time. For these reasons, this method does not form part of the powers of interrogation. It is an unacceptable method. "The duty to safeguard the detainee's dignity includes his right not to

be degraded and not to be submitted to sub-human conditions in the course of his detention, of the sort likely to harm his health and potentially his dignity". [. . .]

A similar – though not identical – combination of interrogation methods were discussed in the case of *Ireland v. United Kingdom* (1978) 2 EHRR 25. In that case, the Court probed five interrogation methods used by England for the purpose of investigating detainees suspected of terrorist activities in Northern Ireland. The methods were as follows: protracted standing against the wall on the tip of one's toes; covering of the suspect's head throughout the detention (except during the actual interrogation); exposing the suspect to powerfully loud noise for a prolonged period and deprivation of sleep, food and drink. The Court held that these methods did not constitute "torture". However, since they treated the suspect in an "inhuman and degrading" manner, they were nonetheless prohibited.

31. The interrogation of a person is likely to be lengthy, due to the suspect's failure to cooperate or due to the information's complexity or in light of the imperative need to obtain information urgently and immediately. Indeed, a person undergoing interrogation cannot sleep as does one who is not being interrogated. The suspect, subject to the investigators' questions for a prolonged period of time, is at times exhausted. This is often the inevitable result of an interrogation, or one of its side effects. This is part of the "discomfort" inherent to an interrogation. This being the case, depriving the suspect of sleep is, in our opinion, included in the general authority of the investigator. [. . .]

The above described situation is different from those in which sleep deprivation shifts from being a "side effect" inherent to the interrogation, to an end in itself. If the suspect is intentionally deprived of sleep for a prolonged period of time, for the purpose of tiring him out or "breaking" him – it shall not fall within the scope of a fair and reasonable investigation. Such means harm the rights and dignity of the suspect in a manner surpassing that which is required. [. . .]

Physical Means and the "Necessity" Defence

33. [. . .] As noted, an explicit authorization permitting [the] GSS to employ physical means is not to be found in our law. An authorization of this nature can, in the State's opinion, be obtained in specific cases by virtue of the criminal law defense of "necessity", prescribed in the Penal Law. The language of the statute is as follows: (Article 34 (1)):

"A person will not bear criminal liability for committing any act immediately necessary for the purpose of saving the life, liberty, body or property, of either himself or his fellow person, from substantial danger of serious harm, imminent from the particular state of things [circumstances], at the requisite timing, and absent alternative means for avoiding the harm."

The State's position is that by virtue of this "defence" to criminal liability, GSS investigators are also authorized to apply physical means, such as shaking, in the appropriate circumstances, in order to prevent serious harm to human life or body, in the absence of other alternatives. The State maintains that an act committed under conditions of "necessity" does not constitute a crime. Instead, it is deemed an act worth committing in such circumstances in order to prevent serious harm to a human life or body. We are therefore speaking of a deed that society has an interest in encouraging, as it is deemed proper in the circumstances. It is choosing the lesser evil. Not only is it legitimately permitted to engage in the fighting of terrorism, it is our moral duty to employ the necessary means for this purpose. This duty is particularly incumbent on the state authorities – and for our purposes, on the GSS investigators – who carry the burden of safeguarding the public peace. As this is the case, there is no obstacle preventing the investigators' superiors from instructing and guiding them with regard to when the conditions of the "necessity" defence are fulfilled and the proper boundaries in those circumstances. From

this flows the legality of the directives with respect to the use of physical means in GSS interrogations. In the course of their argument, the State's attorneys submitted the "ticking time
bomb" argument. A given suspect is arrested by the GSS. He holds information respecting
the location of a bomb that was set and will imminently explode. There is no way to diffuse
the bomb without this information. If the information is obtained, however, the bomb my be
diffused. If the bomb is not diffused, scores will be killed and maimed. Is a GSS investigator
authorized to employ physical means in order to elicit information regarding the location of
the bomb in such instances? The State's attorneys answers in the affirmative. The use of physical means shall not constitute a criminal offence, and their use is sanctioned, to the State's
contention, by virtue of the "necessity" defence.

34. We are prepared to assume that – although this matter is open to debate – (See
A. Dershowitz, *Is it Necessary to Apply 'Physical Pressure' to Terrorists- And to Lie About
It?*, [1989] 23 Israel L. Rev. 193; Bernsmann, *Private Self-Defence and Necessity in German
Penal Law and in the Penal Law Proposal[l]* – *Some Remarks*, [1998] 30 Israel L. Rev. 171,
208–210) – the "necessity" defence is open to all, particularly an investigator, acting in an
organizational capacity of the State in interrogations of that nature. Likewise, we are prepared
to accept – although this matter is equally contentious – (See M. Kremnitzer, *The Landau
Commission Report – Was the Security Service Subordinated to the Law or the Law to the
Needs of the Security Service?*, [1989] 23 Israel L. Rev. 216, 244–247) – that the "necessity"
exception is likely to arise in instances of "ticking time bombs", and that the immediate need
("necessary in an immediate manner" for the preservation of human life) refers to the imminent nature of the act rather than that of the danger. Hence, the imminence criteria is satisfied
even if the bomb is set to explode in a few days, or perhaps even after a few weeks, provided
the danger is certain to materialize and there is no alternative means of preventing its mater-
ialization. In other words, there exists a concrete level of imminent danger of the explosion's
occurrence.

Consequently we are prepared to presume, as was held by the Inquiry Commission's Report,
that if a GSS investigator – who applied physical interrogation methods for the purpose of
saving human life – is criminally indicted, the "necessity" defence is likely to be open to him in
the appropriate circumstances. [. . .]

35. Indeed, we are prepared to accept that in the appropriate circumstances, GSS investigators may avail themselves of the "necessity" defence, if criminally indicted. This however, is
not the issue before this Court. We are not dealing with the potential criminal liability of a
GSS investigator who employed physical interrogation methods in circumstances of "necessity." Moreover, we are not addressing the issue of admissibility or probative value of evidence
obtained as a result of a GSS investigator's application of physical means against a suspect.
We are dealing with a different question. The question before us is whether it is possible to
infer the authority to, in advance, establish permanent directives setting out the physical interrogation means that may be used under conditions of "necessity". Moreover, we are asking
whether the "necessity" defence constitutes a basis for the GSS investigator's authority
to investigate, in the performance of his duty. According to the State, it is possible to imply
from the "necessity" defence, available (*post factum*) to an investigator indicted of a criminal
offence, an advance legal authorization endowing the investigator with the capacity to use
physical interrogation methods. Is this position correct?

36. In the Court's opinion, a general authority to establish directives respecting the use of
physical means during the course of a GSS interrogation cannot be implied from the "necessity" defence. The "necessity" defence does not constitute a source of authority, allowing
GSS investigators to make use [of] physical means during the course of interrogations. The
reasoning underlying our position is anchored in the nature of the "necessity" defence. This

defence deals with deciding those cases involving an individual reacting to a given set of facts; It is an ad hoc endeavour, in reaction to a event. It is the result of an improvisation given the unpredictable character of the events (See Feller, *ibid.* at 209). Thus, the very nature of the defence does not allow it to serve as the source of a general administrative power. The administrative power is based on establishing general, forward looking criteria, as noted by Professor Enker:

> "Necessity is an after-the-fact judgment based on a narrow set of considerations in which we are concerned with the immediate consequences, not far-reaching and long-range consequences, on the basis of a clearly established order of priorities of both means and ultimate values…The defence of Necessity does not define a code of primary normative behaviour. Necessity is certainly not a basis for establishing a broad detailed code of behaviour such as how one should go about conducting intelligence interrogations in security matters, when one may or may not use force, how much force may be used and the like (Enker, "The Use of Physical Force in Interrogations and the Necessity Defense," in Israel and International Human Rights Law: The Issue of Torture 61, 62 (1995)).

In a similar vein, Kremnitzer and Segev note:

> "[t]he basic rationale underlying the necessity defence is the absence of the possibility to establish accurate rules of behaviour in advance, appropriate in concrete emergency situations, whose circumstances are varied and unexpected. From this it follows, that the necessity defence is not well suited for regulation [of] a general situation, the circumstances of which are known and (often) repeat themselves. In similar cases, there is no reason for not setting the rules of behaviour in advance, in order that their content be determined in a thought out and well-planned manner, in advance, permitting them to apply in a uniform manner to all" (*supra*, at 705).

Moreover, the "necessity" defence has the effect of allowing one who acts under the circumstances of "necessity" to escape criminal liability. The "necessity" defence does not possess any additional normative value. In addition, it does not authorize the use of physical means for the purposes of allowing investigators to execute their duties in circumstances of necessity. The very fact that a particular act does not constitute a criminal act (due to the "necessity" defence) does not in itself authorize the administration to carry out this deed, and in doing so infringe upon human rights. The Rule of Law (both as a formal and substantive principle) requires that an infringement on a human right be prescribed by statute, authorizing the administration to this effect. The lifting of criminal responsibility does not imply authorization to infringe upon a human right. It shall be noted that the Commission of Inquiry did not hold that the "necessity" defence is the source of authority for employing physical means by GSS investigators during the course of their interrogations. All that the Commission of Inquiry determined is that if an investigator finds himself in a situation of "necessity", constraining him to choose the "lesser evil" – harming the suspect for the purpose of saving human lives – the "necessity" defence shall be available to him. Indeed, the Commission of Inquiry noted that, "the law itself must ensure a proper framework governing the [security] service's actions with respect to the interrogation of hostile terrorist activities and the related problems particular to it" (*ibid.* at 328).

37. In other words, general directives governing the use of physical means during interrogations must be rooted in an authorization prescribed by law and not from defences to criminal liability. The principle of "necessity" cannot serve as a basis of authority (See Kremnitzer, *ibid.* at 236). If the State wishes to enable GSS investigators to utilize physical means in interrogations, they must seek the enactment of legislation for this purpose. This authorization would

also free the investigator applying the physical means from criminal liability. This release would flow not from the "necessity" defence but from the "justification" defense which states:

"A person shall not bear criminal liability for an act committed in one of the following cases:

(1) He was obliged or authorized by law to commit it. "

(Article 34(13) of the Penal Law)

The defence to criminal liability by virtue of the "justification" is rooted in [an] area outside of the criminal law. This "external" law serves as a defence to criminal liability. This defence does not rest upon the "necessity", which is "internal" to the Penal Law itself. Thus, for instance, where the question of when an officer is authorized to apply deadly force in the course of detention arises, the authority is found in a provision of the Law of Detention, external to the Penal Law. If a man is killed as a result of the application of force, the provision is likely to give rise to a defence, by virtue of the "Justification" (See Cr. A. 486/88, *Ankonina v. The Chief Army Prosecutor* 34(2) P.D. 353). The "necessity" defence cannot constitute the basis for the determination of rules respecting the needs of an interrogation. It cannot constitute a source of authority on which the individual investigator can rely [...] for the purpose of applying physical means in an investigation that he is conducting. The power to enact rules and to act according to them requires legislative authorization, by legislation whose object is the power to conduct interrogations. Within the boundaries of this legislation, the Legislator, if he so desires, may express his views on the social, ethical and political problems, connected to authorizing the use of physical means in an interrogation. These considerations did not, from the nature of things, arise before the Legislature at the time when the "necessity" defence was enacted (See Kremnitzer, *supra*, at 239–40). The "necessity" defence is not the appropriate place for laying out these considerations (See Enker, *supra*, at 72). Endowing GSS investigators with the authority to apply physical force during the interrogation of suspects suspected of involvement in hostile terrorist activities, thereby harming the latters' dignity and liberty, raise basic questions of law and society, of ethics and policy, and of the Rule of Law and security. These questions and the corresponding answers must be determined by the Legislative branch. This is required by the principle of the Separation of Powers and the Rule of Law, under our very understanding of democracy (See H.C. 3267/97 *Rubinstein v. Minister of Defence* (has yet to be published)).

38. Our conclusion is therefore the following: According to the existing state of the law, neither the government nor the heads of security services possess the authority to establish directives and bestow authorization regarding the use of liberty infringing physical means during the interrogation of suspects suspected of hostile terrorist activities, beyond the general directives which can be inferred from the very concept of an interrogation. Similarly, the individual GSS investigator – like any police officer – does not possess the authority to employ physical means which infringe upon a suspect's liberty during the interrogation, unless these means are inherently accessory to the very essence of an interrogation and are both fair and reasonable.

An investigator who insists on employing these methods, or does so routinely, is exceeding his authority. His responsibility shall be fixed according to law. His potential criminal liability shall be examined in the context of the "necessity" defence, and according to our assumptions (See paragraph 35 *supra*.), the investigator may find refuge under the "necessity" defence's wings (so to speak), provided this defence's conditions are met by the circumstances of the case. Just as the existence of the "necessity" defence does not bestow authority, so too the lack of authority does not negate the applicability of the necessity defense or that of other defences from criminal liability. The Attorney General can instruct himself regarding the circumstances in which investigators shall not stand trial, if they claim to have acted from a feeling of "necessity". Clearly, a legal statutory provision is necessary for the purpose of authorizing the government to instruct in the use of physical means during the course of an interrogation, beyond what is permitted by the ordinary "law of investigation", and in order to provide the individual GSS investigator with the authority to employ these methods. The "necessity" defence cannot serve as a basis for this authority.

A Final Word

39. [. . .] Although a democracy must often fight with one hand tied behind its back, it nonetheless has the upper hand. Preserving the Rule of Law and recognition of an individual's liberty constitutes an important component in its understanding of security. At the end of the day, they strengthen its spirit and its strength and allow it to overcome its difficulties. This having been said, there are those who argue that Israel's security problems are too numerous, thereby requiring the authorization to use physical means. If it will nonetheless be decided that it is appropriate for Israel, in light of its security difficulties to sanction physical means in interrogations (and the scope of these means which deviate from the ordinary investigation rules), this is an issue that must be decided by the legislative branch which represents the people. [. . .]

40. Deciding these applications weighed heavy on this Court. True, from the legal perspective, the road before us is smooth. We are, however, part of Israeli society. Its problems are known to us and we live its history. We are not isolated in an ivory tower. We live the life of this country. We are aware of the harsh reality of terrorism in which we are, at times, immersed. Our apprehension is that this decision will hamper the ability to properly deal with terrorists and terrorism, disturbs us. We are, however, judges. Our brethren require us to act according to the law.

COMMENTARY

In the remove of the classroom or courtroom, it is easier to dismiss the 'ticking time bomb' scenario and insist that we adhere absolutely to unadulterated principle. But law must govern in reality. Justice Barak's opinion offers hard statistics and a personally experienced depiction of a reality lived in the shadow of terrorism. The opinion prohibits, however, tactics that dilute the commitments of society – at least as a matter of law *ex ante*. The opinion leaves open the possibility, however, that necessity may be a complete defence *ex post*.

Whether this solution is brilliant or deemed sleight of hand depends on one's worldview. A moral absolutist might deplore the approach as sophistry that does not avoid the trammelling of a value that should be inviolate. A pragmatist or someone with more of an instrumentalist bent might, however, admire the approach for its setting of incentives. An agent who might face criminal consequences for improper tactics has strong incentive to be very certain that necessity demands the transgression because she or he bears the risk of being wrong. The approach may cut down on routinized brutality while leaving open a route when extreme circumstances may demand extraordinary action. The incentives argument depends, however, on the assumption that juries and jurists will not afford torturers the benefits of the necessity argument even when the agent is wrong. An open question is whether juries and jurists living in the fear and shadow of terrorism will be so sympathetic to the dilemma of law enforcement that an *ex post* defence becomes so certain that it begins to operate like an implicit exception.

The issue is also complicated by serious questions about the reliability of any information obtained pursuant to extreme methods. Is the marginal benefit of gleaning any information through torture of such low value that it is not worth the cost, even if one adopts a balancing perspective? Reality does not operate like a television drama. We operate under uncertainty about the probability that an individual will have relevant information. A danger of the ticking time bomb scenario is that it will be defined and applied broadly and an exception meant to be narrow will begin to gape. In the United States for example extreme interrogation techniques – in many instances amounting to torture – were applied to suspected accomplices long after their capture and therefore absent any plausible claim that they could literally have information about a ticking time bomb. Moreover, interrogations in the interest of security rarely involve a *discrete* ticking bomb – rather, investigations cobble together bits and pieces of information in hopes of averting the very planting of a bomb or fruition of a similar scheme.

An alternative approach to that taken by the Israeli Supreme Court is presented in a 2004 judgment by the German Regional Court of Frankfurt am Main in the *Daschner Wolfgang and E.* case. There, the court held that even in an emergency situation torture – or even the mere threat of torture – is prohibited, and state officials who engage in such action are criminally liable, although the special circumstances of the case must then be taken into account at the level of penalty.

Germany, **Daschner Wolfgang and E.** *case, Regional Court* (Landgericht) *of Frankfurt am Main, Decision of 20 December 2004*[21]

On 27 September 2002, a law student, Magnus Gäfgen, kidnapped and killed 11-year-old Jakob von Metzler, the son of a senior bank executive. Gäfgen hid the boy's body close to a lake near Frankfurt. He sent a letter to the boy's family in which he demanded one million Euros for the release of the child. Three days after the boy's disappearance, Gäfgen was arrested after being observed picking up the ransom. During his interrogation, the suspect gave evasive answers concerning his involvement in the abduction and provided no information about the whereabouts of the boy. The day after the arrest, Frankfurt Police Vice-President, Wolfgang Daschner, who was responsible for the investigation, ordered that pain be inflicted on the suspect, without causing injuries, under medical supervision and subject to prior warning, in order to save the life of the boy. Accordingly, a subordinate police officer [E.] told Gäfgen that the police were prepared to inflict pain on him that 'he would never forget', if he continued to withhold information concerning the whereabouts of the boy. Gäfgen disclosed the whereabouts of the boy. The actual infliction of pain, which in fact had been arranged by fetching a specially trained police officer, was not necessary. Shortly thereafter, police officers found the body of the boy. On 28 July 2003, Gäfgen was convicted of extortionate abduction and murder, and sentenced to life imprisonment. Both Daschner and the police officer were then indicted by the Prosecution and brought to court. They were both found guilty: E. of coercion (*Nötigung*), and Daschner of instructing a subordinate to commit coercion. The Frankfurt Court held that in the case neither justifications nor excuses were admissible. In particular, the defendants could not rely upon self-defence (that includes the defence of another person) or necessity.

[...] Under Article 1 paragraph 1(1) of the *Grundgesetz*, human dignity is inviolable. The state authority may not make any person an object, a paragon of fear of pain. This legal principle has also been laid down in international treaties and conventions, for instance in Article 3 of the European Convention on Human Rights, which in Germany has the legally binding value of a law.

Respect for human dignity is the basis of this state, which is based on the rule of law. The framers of the Constitution have deliberately put such notion at the outset of the Constitution.

---

[21] Translated by A. Cassese (who wishes to thank Florian Jessberger for painstakingly revising his translation).

In contrast, the right to life and to physical inviolability is only laid down in Article 2 paragraph 2 of the *Grundgesetz*. The motivation behind that lies in the history of this state. Documents relating to the origin of the German Federal Republic make it absolutely clear that the members of the Parliamentary Council had very much in mind the cruelties of the National Socialist regime. They pursued the fundamental purpose of preventing anything similar from recurring and clearly to bar any such temptation through the drafting of the *Grundgesetz*. The human being was not to be treated for the second time as somebody having information that the state would wring out of him, even if for the purpose of serving justice. This is the reason why Article 1 paragraph 1(1) of the *Grundgesetz* is unalterable. The draughtsmen of the Constitution enunciated in Article 79 paragraph 3 of the *Grundgesetz* the notion 'beware of the beginning' and ruled out any change of the constitutional rule enshrined in Article 1 paragraph 1, even if the requisite majority for a constitutional amendment were to exist. It is for this reason that Article 79 paragraph 3 of the *Grundgesetz* is also characterized as an 'everlasting clause'. The strict prohibition even to threaten the use of force against a suspect, is already the result of a balancing of all relevant interests at stake. Such balancing was undertaken when the *Grundgesetz* was drafted. What essentially is at stake here is also the protection of the administration of criminal justice and its capacity to discharge its functions.

The judgments of criminal courts are based on the correct work of the police applying a procedure which is based on the rule of law. A state based on the rule of law would abdicate its essence if it did not fully comply with this strict principle. [. . .]

The same holds true for the applicability of Section 240 paragraph 2 of the criminal court, relating to reprehensible conduct. It was reprehensible to threaten the infliction of pain for the purpose of extracting information. The internal link between means of constraint and purpose of the constraint (relation between purpose and means) rests upon a full appraisal of such standards as ethical disapproval and anti-social conduct. This appraisal also takes into account the commands of the *Grundgesetz* together with the peremptory value of Article 1 paragraph 1(1) of the *Grundgesetz*. Consequently, any act contrary to respect for human dignity must be regarded as reprehensible even when the subjective purpose of the act is to save the life of a child. [. . .]

In the instant case the intensity of the means of coercion was not insignificant. To cause suffering without wounding, at the hand of a special official who knows the areas of the body that are particularly sensitive to pain and who can purposefully attack those areas, is bound to produce anxiety and intimidation. To call in a medical doctor does not have a calming effect. The causing of pain was to be so strong that it could leave no chance of resisting. Its purpose was to break the will of the suspect. There was no question of simply suggesting an abstract possibility. Concrete preparations were indeed made. The doctor was summoned to the police station and asked whether he was prepared to proceed. The special official was to be taken by helicopter from the place where he had been on holiday.

To make an exception to this pellucid legal condition would mean that the constitutional protection of human dignity, which is absolute, would be breached. It would be made subject to a balancing amounting to a breach of the legal taboo. Such exceptions have been discussed in the context of terrorist attacks. Borderline cases have been set forth where the protection of the human dignity of the perpetrator is contrasted with the possible death and, therefore, the protection of the lives of thousands of people. In these discussions among others, the view has been put forward that the victim's human dignity demands that the state must do everything to save the life of the person threatened, if necessary by also applying mental or physical coercion. According to this view, in the balancing of concerns the human dignity of the perpetrator is less important. [The opinion of various authorities follows.]

In sum, it can be stated that even the supporters of the need to qualify human dignity are in the event very cautious and strict in suggesting the conditions for such an extreme exceptional situation. Fundamental doubts remain and all the abstract cases put forward have this in common, that means of coercion are accepted only as *ultima ratio* and on condition that their use promises to be successful against an indubitable perpetrator. A comparison with the right of state agents to shoot and kill a hostage-taker on the spot in order to save the life of the hostage (*finaler Rettungsschuss*), which is acknowledged under certain conditions, is not convincing. In that case, an immediate danger caused by a well-identified attacker is removed definitively. To shoot the hostage-taker is the only and last means to remove a concrete danger. In addition, in the cases where a '*finaler Rettungsschuss*' may be allowed, the hostage-taker is not requested to do anything [e.g. give information], but only to omit something [namely to threaten and eventually kill the hostage].

This Chamber must not take part in the abstract discussion of constitutional principles, as this is not necessary for adjudicating the instant case. The law is clear. The exceptional cases that have been discussed are theoretical borderline cases; in appraising them one may come up against a legal grey zone and arrive at the frontier of jurisprudence. The present case, however, does not constitute one of such extreme exceptional situations. Rather, it belongs to a different category. The use of means of coercion cannot be taken into account because all the suspicious elements had not yet been satisfactorily investigated and the admissible means of investigation had not been exhausted.

Similarly there does not exist any ground for excusing criminal responsibility. [...][22]

Gäfgen also complained to the European Court of Human Rights that the interrogation violated the prohibition against torture in Article 3 of the European Convention on Human Rights. Concluding that the interrogation amounted to inhuman treatment, also prohibited by Article 3, though not torture, the Grand Chamber underscored that

Torture, inhuman or degrading treatment cannot be inflicted even in circumstances where the life of an individual is at risk. No derogation is allowed even in the event of a public emergency threatening the life of the nation. Article 3, which has been framed in unambiguous terms, recognises that every human being has an absolute, inalienable right not to be subjected to torture or to inhuman or degrading treatment under any circumstances, even the most difficult. The philosophical basis underpinning the absolute nature of the right under Article 3 does not allow for any exceptions or justifying factors or balancing of interests, irrespective of the conduct of the person concerned and the nature of the offence at issue.[23]

QUESTIONS

1. Why do you think torture is often proscribed but relatively rarely defined? Is torture something susceptible of a legal definition, or is it something that we know viscerally when we hear about it?

2. What are the core elements in the various forms of torture as a discrete crime, a crime against humanity and a war crime? What elements constitute the essence of torture?

3. US legislation defining torture requires, among other elements, that the torturer 'specifically intended to inflict severe physical or mental pain or suffering' – a variation

[22] On this judgment, see in particular F. Jessberger, 'Bad Torture – Good Torture? What International Criminal Lawyers May Learn from the Recent Trial of Police Officers in Germany' (2005) *J. Int'l Crim. Justice* 1059–73.

[23] *Gäfgen* v. *Germany* App. No. 22978/05, European Court of Human Rights, Grand Chamber, Judgment, 1 June 2010, at para. 107.

from the international definition of torture requiring 'intentional infliction' of such pain or suffering. Does this variation in formulation create a loophole or potential defence for torturers? Even if coercive tactics like water-boarding are deemed to inflict severe mental or physical pain or suffering, do interrogators have a defence if a jury or jurist finds that the torturer believed – even if unreasonably – that the techniques would not cause the 'prolonged mental harm' that is the hallmark of severe physical or mental pain or suffering under the US definition of torture?

4. What is the point of requiring that torture be directed towards an instrumental purpose? Why do we wish to exclude sadism for sadism's sake from the definition of torture as an international crime?

5. Is the scenario of the ticking time bomb with a suspect who holds the code to disarming it a fantasy that fails to capture the true dilemmas of reality? In what ways does the scenario fail to capture the hard questions surrounding the notion of necessity?

FURTHER READING

A. Cassese, *The Human Dimension of International Law: Selected Papers* (edited by P. Gaeta and S. Zappala) (Oxford: Oxford University Press, 2008), at 295–374.

D. Cole (ed.), *The Torture Memos: Rationalizing the Unthinkable* (New York and London: The Free Press, 2009).

A. Dershowitz, *Why Terrorism Works: Understanding the Threat, Responding to the Challenge* (New Haven: Yale University Press, 2003).

R.A. Fothergill, 'The Dershowitz Protocol', in *Public Lies and Other Plays* (2008) (performed as an off-off-Broadway play in 2007).

P. Gaeta, 'When is the Involvement of State Officials a Requirement for the Crime of Torture?' (2008) 6 *J. Int'l Crim. Justice* 183–93.

Y. Ginbar, *Why Not Torture Terrorists? Moral, Practical and Legal Aspects of the 'Ticking Bomb' Justification for Torture* (Oxford: Oxford University Press, 2008).

R. Imre, 'Torture Works, but Not on Terrorists', in R. Imre, T.B. Mooney and B. Clarke (eds), *Responding to Terrorism: Political, Philosophical and Legal Perspectives* (Farnham, UK: Ashgate, 2008), at 57–63.

J.H. Langbein, *Torture and the Law of Proof: Europe and England in the Ancien Regime* (2nd edn, Chicago: Chicago University Press, 2006). The 2006 edition updated the original 1977 edition with a commentary in light of recent events.

D. Luban, 'The Torture Lawyers of Washington', in D. Luban (ed.), *Legal Ethics and Human Dignity* (New York: Cambridge University Press, 2007), at 162–206.

J. Marshall, 'Torture Committed by Non-State Actors: The Developing Jurisprudence from the Ad Hoc Tribunals', in Andrea Bianchi (ed.), *Non-State Actors and International Law* (Farnham, UK: Ashgate, 2009), 493–504.

R. Matthews, *The Absolute Violation: Why Torture Must Be Prohibited* (Montreal: McGill-Queen's University Press, 2008).

6

TERRORISM

(A) THE NOTION AND ITS ORIGINS

In *Galić*, the ICTY case mentioned in Part II(1), an international tribunal for the first time convicted an accused of the crime of 'acts or threats of violence the primary purpose of which is to spread terror among the civilian population'. This conclusion was based on the prohibition of Article 51(2) of Additional Protocol I and Article 13(2) of Additional Protocol II. Both the Trial and the Appeal Judgments contain a careful assessment of the development of the notion of terrorism in armed conflict from the end of World War I onwards. In cases before the ICTY, and later the SCSL, 'terrorism' was considered as a war crime, i.e. unlawful attacks against civilians with the additional specific intent of spreading terror among the civilian population. Specific acts committed for the purpose of terrorizing civilians may also fall under the category of crimes against humanity when all other requirements for this type of crime are met.

A different – though somewhat related – question relates to terrorism as a discrete crime, which can be committed both in armed conflict and in times of peace. Despite the interest aroused by transnational criminal acts often imprecisely defined as terrorism, the international community has been struggling for decades to reach a consensus on whether a crime of terrorism indeed exists under international law.

The main bone of contention for a definition of terrorism lies in the oft-cited aphorism according to which 'one person's terrorist is another person's freedom fighter'. Many countries have been reluctant to accept a binding international definition of terrorism that might run counter to their own perceived interests. Thus, until the 1990s the *opinio juris* requirement necessary to reach a norm of customary international law prohibiting and criminalizing a clear set of conduct as 'terrorism' had not materialized.

(B) OUTLAWING TERRORIST ACTS

During the 1960s and 1970s, various treaties aimed at banning *specific conduct* normally considered as falling within the notion of terrorism were adopted at the universal level. These included conventions on (i) the safety of civil aviation (such as: Tokyo Convention on Offences and Certain Other Acts Committed on Board Aircraft (1963; 704 UNTS 219); The Hague Convention for the Suppression of Unlawful Seizure of Aircraft (1970; 860 UNTS 105); Montreal Convention for the Suppression of Unlawful Acts against the Safety of Civil Aviation (1971; (1971) 10 ILM 1151)); (ii) the protection of diplomats (Convention on the Prevention and Punishment of Crimes against Internationally Protected Persons, Including Diplomatic Agents (1977; UNGA Res. 3166 (1973)); (iii) the taking of hostages (Convention On Taking of Hostages (1979; UNGA Res. 34/146)) and others. Efforts to promote a general ban on terrorism also achieved some results at the regional level (European Convention on the Suppression of Terrorism (1977; ETS, No. 90), but were no more successful in setting out a satisfactory comprehensive definition.

It was only in the 1990s that this trend was partially reversed. In 1999, in particular, a UN-sponsored International Convention for the Suppression of the Financing of Terrorism (UNGA Res. 54/109 (1999) ('1999 Convention'), entered into force on 10 April 2002) which, in addition to dealing with some specifically enumerated 'terrorist' acts, addressed

[a]ny other act intended to cause death or serious bodily injury to a civilian, or to any other person not taking an active part in the hostilities in a situation of armed conflict, when the purpose of such act, by its nature or context, is to intimidate a population, or to compel a Government or an international organization to do or to abstain from doing any act.

This Convention is often mentioned or referred to in the context of other UN initiatives on this subject, such as the 1994 Declaration on Measures to Eliminate International Terrorism (UNGA Res. 46/90 (1994)), adopted by consensus, which states that

[c]riminal acts intended or calculated to provoke a state of terror in the general public, a group of persons or particular persons for political purposes are in any circumstance unjustifiable, whatever the considerations or a political, philosophical, ideological, racial, ethnic, religious or any other nature that may be invoked to justify them.

These two instruments, despite their different normative values and distinct emphases on the aims of the criminal acts considered, show that a generalized *opinio juris* on the prohibition of certain criminal and violent acts is indeed consolidating around a core concept.

Similarly, following the attacks of 11 September 2001, the UNSC passed Res. 1373 (2001) – which states that 'any act of international terrorism [constitutes] a threat to international peace and security'. This resolution requires states to prevent, suppress, freeze and criminalize terrorist financing (i.e. to implement provisions of the 1999 Convention, at the time not yet in force), to refrain from supporting terrorists, to prevent terrorist acts and the use of their territory for international terrorism and to deny safe haven to terrorists. Moreover, States are required to criminalize the financing, planning, preparation, commission and support of terrorism, to bring culprits of such acts to justice and to assist other States in criminal investigations and proceedings related to terrorism.

In 2004, the UNSC further adopted Res. 1566 (2004), which mentions certain acts that are never justifiable, by recalling that

criminal acts committed with the intent to cause death or serious bodily injury, or taking of hostages, with the purpose to provoke a state of terror in the general public or in a group of persons or particular persons, intimidate a population or compel a government or an international organization to do or to abstain from doing any act, which constitute offences within the scope of and as defined in the international conventions and protocols relating to terrorism, are under no circumstances justifiable by considerations of a political, philosophical, ideological, racial, ethnic, religious or other similar nature [...]

In spite of these attempts at formulating a widely acceptable definition of terrorism, there remains in the world community a major divide along two questions: (i) Should 'freedom fighters' engaged in national liberation movements be classified as terrorists? (ii) Should the articulation of international rules on terrorism be made contingent upon delving into the root causes of this phenomenon? Many States have asserted that as long as no agreement is reached on these two contentious issues, no consent can evolve on the very notion of terrorism itself.

The question of investigating the historical, social and economic causes of terrorism has been put on the backburner, although recently the UN Secretary General (SG) has again drawn attention to the need to 'address conditions conducive to exploitation by terrorists'.[1] Importantly, broad agreement has been reached on the definition of terrorism *in time of peace*, while major dissensions persist on the meaning of terrorism *in time of armed conflict* (a debate that turns on the following questions: (i) whether freedom fighters must be labelled terrorists, as opposed to war criminals, when they attack civilians, and (ii) whether actions of State armies attacking civilians may be characterized as terrorist).

(C) CRIMINALIZING TERRORISM

The international instruments mentioned above clearly aim at ensuring that terrorist acts are outlawed and criminalized at the *domestic* level. However, they fall short of explicitly imposing individual criminal responsibility under international law for the acts mentioned. While, therefore, there is little doubt that a general consensus has emerged that violent acts already criminalized under domestic law, if politically or ideologically motivated and committed with the specific intent to spread terror or to coerce a state or an international organization to act in a certain manner, are unlawful under international law, no consensus has emerged that this necessarily entails individual criminal responsibility under international law. The fact that terrorism was not included as a separate crime under the jurisdiction of the ICC also reinforces the impression that States are not yet ready to agree on its criminalization under international law.

As will be seen below, however, this does not mean that terrorist acts have not been considered at the domestic level, at times with a view to harmonizing national legal systems with international obligations. Domestic courts have also been called upon to make findings on the difference between terror during armed conflict and terrorism in time of peace.

Cases

Lebanon, **In re Dany Chamoun et al.,** *Judicial Council, Judgment No. 5/1995 of 24 June 1995*

> Dany Chamoun was a Lebanese politician, of Christian (Maronite) faith and allegiance during the civil war (1975–90). In 1988, he became President of a coalition of mainly Christian parties, the Lebanese front. On 21 October 1990, Chamoun, along with his wife and his two sons, was killed. A rival Christian politician, Samir Geagea, was accused of the attack and tried.

The facts of the case

On 15 January 1986 the defendant Mr. Samir Geagea carried out a military operation in which he achieved victory over Minister Elie Hobeika, head of the Executive Committee of the

---

[1] See his Report to the General Assembly of 27 April 2006 (A/60/825), *Uniting against Terrorism: Recommendations for a Global Counter-Terrorism Strategy*, at §§20–37).

Lebanese Forces at the time. The latter was compelled to leave what was known as the Eastern Region and seek refuge in Zahle with some of his supporters. Mr. Geagea then took over the leadership of the Lebanese Forces without contest, implemented a radical military reorganization programme and placed all components of the Forces under the authority of persons who had a special and close relationship with the leader, serving him devotedly and faithfully carrying out his orders.

[. . .] After the 15 January 1986 operation, the Lebanese Front, composed of leaders of political parties and movements, expanded. The late Dany Chamoun, the defendant Samir Geagea, Gibran Tueni and others joined the Front.

Early on, a form of alliance existed between the late Dany and Mr. Geagea, since they had a single political position. However, subsequent developments led to a divergence of views between Dany and the Forces on many questions relating to politics, the administration of the Eastern Region and the treatment of the Liberal Party, which had been led by the late Dany since 1985.

Relations between them began to deteriorate. When the office of leader of the Lebanese Front fell vacant after the death of the late President Camille Chamoun, the late Dany felt that custom dictated that he should lead the Front, since the Lebanese Forces were led by a Phalangist. But Mr. Geagea supported the candidacy of the Phalangist Georges Saadeh, preventing the late Dany from becoming the leader of the Front. This gave rise to a certain amount of touchiness between the two men, but that did not prevent Mr. Geagea from nominating the late Dany in 1988 to head the transitional government after the end of Sheikh Amine Gemayel's term of office.

The crisis between Geagea and Chamoun escalated in 1989 when clashes broke out between the Army and the armed members of the Forces. The late Dany Chamoun sided with the Army and this had a major impact on Mr. Geagea's state of mind, since he felt that it was the duty of all leaders in the Eastern Region to coordinate with him at all times and to stand by him, or at least to remain neutral, especially since the military, social, financial and political status of the Lebanese Forces had been considerably enhanced under his leadership. [. . .]

The antagonism between the late Dany and Mr. Geagea increased as the battles between the Army and the Lebanese Forces escalated. In statements by the late Dany against Samir Geagea published in the newspapers, he described him as harbouring feelings of hatred against some people and as aspiring to become the governor of the Eastern Region. Dany remained in the Lebanese Front after it was renamed the New Lebanese Front and became its leader.

The Front adopted a number of decisions expressing full support for General Aoun [another Christian politician and military commander] and condemning the conduct of the Forces, accusing them of carrying out the Nahr al-Mott and Boustat al-Mathaf massacre and of deviating from their principles. It instructed the members of the Liberal Party, the Guardians of the Cedars and Al-Tanzeem to withdraw from the Lebanese Forces, and decided to dissolve the Forces and to transfer their military equipment and materiel to the Lebanese Army.

Mr. Geagea knew that a large number of Lebanese, especially Christians, were influenced by the views of the National Liberal Party, especially those of the leader of the Party, the late Dany Chamoun, who grew up in the home of an old and venerated political family, inheriting great popularity from his father, the late Camille Chamoun, in addition to his personal record.

Mr. Geagea perceived the late Dany as a major obstacle to his ambitions to be the sole Christian decision-maker and hence to control the Eastern Region. He therefore decided to eliminate him, especially since he knew and all the evidence indicated that General Aoun's day was coming to an end.

In July 1990 Mr. Geagea ordered his security departments to prepare an operation to assassinate Dany Chamoun. Forces member Georges Khirat got in touch with Youssef Ghalayini who lived in Bouar, counting on the latter's need for money, and asked him whether he wanted to carry out the operation for a considerable sum of money. He put him in contact with security officer Rafik al-Fahl who asked him to cooperate with the Forces Security Department for the purpose. [. . .]

On 13 October 1990 Lebanese and Syrian armies entered the area of influence of General Aoun and overthrew him, ending the war between the Lebanese Forces and the Army. Moreover, parties and organizations whose political positions were opposed to those of the National Liberal Party entered the region. The late Dany tried to show flexibility in the new circumstances and met with Mr. Elie Hobeika, the leader of the Waed Party, who was allied with the party that opposed General Aoun. He stated that he wished to cooperate with all parties and he made contact with all the leaders. [. . .]

Furthermore, Mr. Dany Chamoun was pursuing a new policy based on burying the past and on openness and building bridges with the General Staff of the new authorities. He began to forge closer relations with Mr. Elie Hobeika so that it was easier for the latter's group to spread out among Chamoun's supporters. Moreover, the policy of openness to the legally established General Staff and its institutions secured official support for the areas that were loyal to General Aoun and Dany Chamoun.

All these new developments made it extremely urgent for Geagea to address them even if they were not in his interest. He had to take steps, before it was too late, to deal with new and different circumstances, imposing himself (i.e. Geagea) on the new political environment and preventing his marginalization should that idea occur to anybody.

At the evaluation meeting convened by Mr. Geagea in Ghadras after the 13 October 1990 operation, the entry of the Syrian Nationalists and Elie Hobeika's followers into the two Metn districts was discussed in the presence of Mr. Ghassan Touma, the head of the Security Department, and the other department heads, including Robert Abi Saab, the head of the Foreign Intelligence Department. The question of the assassination of Dany Chamoun was not discussed at the meeting, but it was not absent from the mind of Mr. Geagea, who alluded to it after the meeting, without mentioning it openly, in a private conversation with Ghassan Touma that was overheard by Mr. Abi Saab, whom Mr. Geagea had asked to stay behind in order to give him a fax message to send abroad.

The assassination plan was carried out by members of the Protection and Intervention Division, who wore Army uniforms. The defendant Jean Youssef Chahine was instructed to supply uniforms from among those looted by the Lebanese Forces when they had occupied the Army barracks in Sarba. Jean Chahine went to Kesrouan and dispatched a carton of military uniforms after telling Rafik Saadeh to be ready to pick up the carton, which was to be transported by ship. When the carton arrived, the operations room called to inform him of its arrival and he went to pick it up and place it in the warehouse.

Three days before the murder of Dany, Tony Obeid, Jean Chahine and Atef al-Haber picked up the carton containing the military uniforms and transported it to the office of Georges Feghali opposite the warehouse in Karantina.

On the evening of Saturday 20 October 1990, the defendant Tony Obeid called Rafik Saadeh and asked him to provide Atef al-Haber with Ingram submachine guns and five handguns when he arrived at around 7 p.m.

At dawn on 21 October 1990, a meeting was held in the office of the defendant Georges Feghali in the Protection and Intervention Division building, which was attended by the other defendants, Atef al-Haber, Camille Karam, Elie Akiki, Jean Chahine, Naja Kaddoum, Elias Awad, also known as Giuliano, and Farid Saadeh. Feghali told the defendants that they must now execute the task for which they had been trained, i.e. to assassinate Dany Chamoun in accordance with the plan, and that they must wear army uniforms during the operation. He then distributed the military uniforms and the weapons.

They left Karantina for Baabda in three cars led by Atef al-Haber, who was wearing the insignia of a first lieutenant and was carrying a Motorola two-way radio – a trade mark used by the official forces – as evidence of the official military status he claimed for himself and his companions. The radio had been among the equipment looted by the Lebanese Forces when they occupied the building of the General Directorate of the Internal Security Forces on 4 February 1990 at the beginning of their war with General Aoun. It had previously been in the possession of Security Forces First Lieutenant As'ad Nahra.

When the group arrived at the specified location, Atef al-Haber parked the car 20 metres from the Chahine Centre buildings and the other cars parked behind him. Then Atef al-Haber drove on and parked his car in front of the building in which Dany Chamoun's home is located and the group got out of their cars.

At the entrance to the building Atef al-Haber met the concierge, witness Nabih Aref Nakhleh. He placed his hand on his neck and ordered him to go upstairs with him, after inquiring whether Dany Chamoun was at home. The concierge answered: "I haven't seen him for three days." Atef al-Haber was accompanied upstairs by Naja Kaddoum and Elie Awad, who were carrying Ingram submachine guns and handguns fitted with silencers hidden beneath their uniforms. Jean Samia and Georges Feghali took up a protective position at the entrance to the building, while Camille Karam, Farid Saadeh and Elie Akiki remained in the vicinity of the cars.

When Atef al-Haber and his companions reached Dany Chamoun's home, which is an apartment on the fifth floor of the building, they told the concierge Nabih Nakhleh to knock on the door. He did so and the door was opened by the maid, Jeannette Dakkash, who first asked who was there. The concierge replied: "Open the door, Jeannette, it's Abou Georges." It was then around 6.30 a.m.

When Jeannette opened the door, where she had been joined by the two boys Tarek and Julian, Atef al-Haber and Elie Awad entered and Naja Kaddoum remained outside the door, telling the concierge to go back downstairs. The concierge went back to his room at the entrance to the building.

On entering the apartment, Atef al-Haber asked for the late Dany. At that moment the latter entered the living room and asked him what he wanted. He replied: "I just want to have a word with you." When Dany turned round to sit down with him in the small living room, he suspected what was going on and pushed him away. They began to fight and fell onto the couch. Elie Awad had told the witness Jeannette and the Sri Lankan maid to go into the bathroom and he had pushed the two boys in another direction.

But the fight between Chamoun and Al-Haber and Kaddoum, the arrival of Ingrid, Dany's wife, and the screaming of the children made it necessary to speed up the operation. So Naja Kaddoum went inside to assist his two companions and the three of them opened fire on Dany and his wife and also fired at the two boys, Tarek and Julian. They then left the apartment and went back to their cars, returning to the security building in Karantina, where they took off their military uniforms and returned them together with the weapons to Atef al-Haber and Georges Feghali.

Atef al-Haber had forgotten his Motorola radio, which had fallen on the couch in the small living-room while he was fighting with Dany. The radio was picked up by Army First Lieutenant Hossein Aasy, who travelled to the site of the incident immediately after its occurrence. He handed it over to the responsible officers in the Internal Security Forces.

At about 5 a.m. on the same morning, 21 October 1990, Ghassan Touma and Tony Obeid went to the "Al-Sana" building in Ashrafiyeh, where the operations room of the Lebanese Forces Security Department was located. They did not leave the building until 7.30 a.m., returning to the security centre in Karantina after being informed of the success of the assassination operation that they had ordered.

The late Dany was shot fourteen times with 9 mm bullets; his wife Ingrid was shot ten times with 7 mm bullets; Tarek was shot three times and Julian four times with 9 mm bullets. However, Julian did not die immediately but was taken to hospital, where he passed away. [. . .]

The applicable law

I. Application of the law and customs of war

Mr. Geagea argues through the oral and written submissions of his counsel, Attorney Naim, that the crime is not punishable under the law and customs of war.

If we assume that the situation in Lebanon during the period prior to the murder of Dany Chamoun can be described as a situation of war or civil war and that the norms of international law pertaining to war and the customs of war are applicable thereto, all related questions are unclear and call for closer scrutiny of Lebanese events and recent developments.

Attorney Naim presents an article by a foreign legal authority, [...] according to which the law of war is governed by two principles: (i) The principle of necessity, which justifies all violent acts designed to achieve the aims of the war provided that they take humanitarian considerations into account; (ii) The principle of humanity, according to which, since war occurs between states, acts of war should not extend to non-combatants.

Based on these two principles, a prisoner shall not be killed, and a person who has been rendered unable to fight or resist shall not be put to death;

And, as noted in this case:

(a) The Lebanese Forces, under the leadership of the defendant, Mr. Geagea, waged war with the Lebanese Army under General Aoun, who had held the office of Prime Minister since April 1988.

(b) This war ended on 13 October 1990, i.e. eight days before the murder of Dany Chamoun, with the defeat of General Aoun and the regular forces that were under his orders, and the integration of these troops into the forces under the leadership of the new lawful regime stemming from the Taif Agreement, to which the "Lebanese Forces" proclaimed their loyalty, largely with a view to bringing down General Aoun.

(c) The late Dany Chamoun – who had stood by General Aoun politically in his struggle with the "Lebanese Forces" – was one of thousands of Lebanese non-combatants who supported General Aoun as the representative of the state against outlaws, militias and those who imposed their authority on the ground by force of arms. He had no militia fighting the "Forces" and no military status or combatant role.

(d) Dany Chamoun and all those who sided with General Aoun and fought for him belonged to the faction that suffered political defeat following the military defeat of General Aoun.

He and the others sought protection, like any other losing faction, from a confrontation which was characterized by violence and was decided by military means. The rapid victory, which occurred within a matter of hours, gave rise to rumours of the settlement of scores on a massive scale during the takeover.

Chamoun himself, as is clear from the evidence in the case file, sought protection from the faction that had taken over politically and militarily. Thus, he appealed to the President of the Republic, the Prime Minister, the President of the Chamber of Deputies, the head of the army and a member of the new political alliance, Mr. Elie Hobeika, for protection by the lawful forces.

It was in these circumstances that Dany Chamoun, his wife and his two sons were assassinated;

These murders, under the circumstances prevailing at the time, were not required by the war of the "Forces" who are charged with this crime, since the persons they targeted presented no military danger to them, especially since they benefited from the outcome of the armed struggle which they had entered on the pretext of frustrating an attempt to eliminate them;

There were thus no war-related circumstances of necessity that might have warranted the killing of Dany Chamoun, his wife and his two children;

It follows that the murder of all those persons was an ordinary heinous crime, contrary to all humanitarian principles, whether the purpose was to take revenge on a person who had sided with the enemy, to eliminate a political rival in an area in which the perpetrator aspired to uncontested leadership, or any other personal aim. The argument pertaining to the norms and customs of war invoked to remove this crime from the scope of the internal Criminal Code is baseless and must be dismissed.

It remains to consider the articles of the Code applicable to the crime:

II. The Criminal Code and the articles applicable to the crime

The defendants are being prosecuted under article 6 of the Law of 11 January 1958, article 549, paragraph 1, of the Criminal Code and article 72 of the Weapons and Ammunition Act;

1. Article 6 of the Law of 11 January 1958

This article stipulates that any terrorist act shall be punishable by a life sentence of hard labour and shall be punishable by a death sentence if it leads to the death of a person…

> "Terrorist acts are all acts which are aimed at creating panic, which are perpetrated by means of explosives, incendiary materials, poisonous or combustible products, or contagious or microbial substances, and which are designed to bring about a public emergency."

While it may be true that the crime that is being prosecuted was intended and succeeded in creating panic, it was not perpetrated by any of the means referred to in the article, and the means used (handguns and submachine guns), the place in which they were used, a private and closed apartment, and the persons targeted were not designed to bring about a public emergency;

It follows that the crime does not come under article 6 of the Law of 11 January 1958.

2. Article 549 of the Criminal Code[2]

A. The homicide of Dany Chamoun

[…] Concerning the defendants Samir Geagea, Ghassan Touma and Tony Obeid

It has been established that the defendant Samir Geagea decided and was determined to assassinate his political opponent Dany Chamoun, using the Security Department of the Lebanese Forces under his leadership, which carried out his orders, and that he instructed the head of the Department, the defendant Ghassan Touma, to make arrangements for the assassination. The latter told his assistant, the defendant Tony Obeid, to carry out the mission and Tony Obeid ordered his subordinates in the Protection and Intervention Division to perpetrate the crime. The decision and orders to eliminate Dany Chamoun were preceded by planning, preparations and determination to proceed with what had been decided.

Article 218 of the Criminal Code concerning incitement does not specify the means whereby this crime is committed, giving the judges absolute discretion in this regard;

The Council finds that the defendants Samir Geagea, Ghassan Touma and Tony Obeid took steps to create a determination among their subordinates and pressed them to commit the

---

[2] [Article 549, para. 1 provides: "Intentional murder shall be punished by the death penalty if committed: (i) with premeditation".]

crime, or to participate in its commission, by issuing orders to them which, given their power over them, amounted to incitement, so that their act constitutes the crime defined in and punishable under article 549, paragraph 1, in conjunction with paragraphs 217 and 218 of the Criminal Code;

It is untrue that their act corresponds in any way to complicity in the crime, inasmuch as the Lebanese legislature enacted a special provision applicable to such acts, designating them as incitement, which is a separate crime from complicity, and devoted a special section of the Criminal Code to this crime, namely Section II of Chapter II in Part 1 of Book IV (articles 217 and 218), while Section I deals with complicity. The elements of the two crimes are different. In this case, the defendants Samir Geagea, Ghassan Touma and Tony Obeid cannot legally be characterized as perpetrators. [...]

For these reasons, the Judicial Council unanimously decides,

[...] To convict the defendants Samir Geagea, Ghassan Antoine Touma and Antonios Elias Elias, also known as Antonios Elias Obeid and Tony Obeid, of the crime defined in and punishable under article 549, paragraph 1, in conjunction with articles 217 and 218 of the Criminal Code, and to impose the death penalty on all three of them, commuted, pursuant to article 253 of the Criminal Code, to a life sentence of hard labour in each case, for incitement to the murder of the late Dany Chamoun; [...]

An *Amnesty International* report described Geagea's trial 'to be in violation of international standards of fair trial, and [his] conditions of detention to be cruel, inhuman and degrading'.[3] Regardless of the substance of the conviction, the Lebanese Judicial Council – while dealing with terrorist acts that were, on their face, exclusively domestic in nature – did refer to international law when dealing with the arguments on the applicability of humanitarian law to the case. This shows how the international dimension of the law on terrorism is often relevant in even purely national contexts.

Unsurprisingly, international law – and the way it is implemented in various countries – plays an even more important role when terrorist acts are transnational in nature, as the next cases show.

USA, US v. Fawaz Yunis, US Court of Appeals, District of Columbia Circuit, Judgment of 29 January 1991

On 11 June 1985, Fawaz Yunis, a Lebanese national, and four other armed men boarded a Jordanian airliner, took control of the cockpit, and forced the pilot to take off immediately. They tied up Jordanian air marshals assigned to the flight and held the civilian passengers, including two American citizens, captive in their seats. The hijackers explained to the crew and passengers that they wanted the plane to fly to Tunis, where a conference of the Arab League was under way. They wanted a meeting with delegates to the conference and their ultimate goal was removal of all Palestinians from Lebanon. After a refuelling stop in Cyprus, the aircraft headed for Tunis but turned away when authorities blocked the airport runway. Following various other stops the plane returned to Beirut, where more hijackers came aboard. These reinforcements included an official of Lebanon's Amal Militia, the group at whose direction Yunis claimed to act. The plane then took off for Syria, but was turned away and went back to Beirut. There, the hijackers released the passengers, held a press conference reiterating

---

[3] *Lebanon: Samir Gea'gea' and Jirjis al-Khouri: Torture and Unfair Trial*, 23 November 2004, Index Number: MDE 18/003/2004.

their demand that Palestinians leave Lebanon, blew up the plane, and fled from the airport. An American investigation identified Yunis as the likely leader of the hijackers and prompted US civilian and military agencies, led by the FBI, to plan his arrest. After obtaining an arrest warrant, undercover FBI agents lured Yunis on to a yacht in the eastern Mediterranean Sea with promises of a drug deal, and arrested him once the vessel entered international waters. The agents transferred Yunis to a United States Navy ship and interrogated him for several days as the vessel steamed toward a second rendezvous with an aircraft carrier. Yunis was flown to Washington, DC. There, Yunis was arraigned on an indictment charging him with conspiracy, hostage taking, and aircraft damage. A grand jury subsequently returned a superseding indictment adding additional aircraft damage counts and a charge of air piracy.

Yunis admitted participation in the hijacking at trial but denied parts of the government's account and offered the affirmative defence of obedience to military orders, asserting that he acted on instructions given by his superiors in Lebanon's Amal Militia. The jury convicted Yunis of conspiracy, hostage taking and air piracy. However, it acquitted him of three other charged offences (violence against people on board an aircraft, aircraft damage and placing a destructive device aboard an aircraft). The district court imposed concurrent sentences of five years for conspiracy, 30 years for hostage taking, and 20 years for air piracy. Yunis appealed against his conviction and sought the dismissal of the indictment.

Before the Court of Appeals, Yunis argued that: (i) the district court lacked subject matter and personal jurisdiction to try him on the charges of which he was convicted; (ii) the indictment should have been dismissed because the government seized him unlawfully and withheld classified materials useful to his defence; and that (iii) the judge had made errors when instructing the jury.

A. Jurisdictional Claims

[...] Appellant's principal claim is that, as a matter of domestic law, the federal hostage taking and air piracy statutes do not authorize assertion of federal jurisdiction over him. Yunis also suggests that a contrary construction of these statutes would conflict with established principles of international law, and so should be avoided by this court. Finally, appellant claims that the district court lacked personal jurisdiction because he was seized in violation of American law.

1. Hostage Taking Act

The Hostage Taking Act provides, in relevant part:

(a) [W]hoever, whether inside or outside the United States, seizes or detains and threatens to kill, to injure, or to continue to detain another person in order to compel a third person or a governmental organization to do or to abstain from any act...shall be punished by imprisonment by any term of years or for life.

(b) (1) It is not an offense under this section if the conduct required for the offense occurred outside the United States unless –

(A) the offender or the person seized or detained is a national of the United States;

(B) the offender is found in the United States; or

(C) the governmental organization sought to be compelled is the Government of the United States. 18 U.S.C. Sec. 1203.

Yunis claims that this statute cannot apply to an individual who is brought to the United States by force, since those convicted under it must be "found in the United States." But this ignores the law's plain language. Subsections (A), (B), and (C) of section 1203(b)(1) offer independent bases for jurisdiction where "the offense occurred outside the United States." Since two of the passengers on Flight 402 were U.S. citizens, section 1203(b)(1)(A), authorizing assertion of U.S. jurisdiction where "the offender or the person seized or detained is a national of the United States," is satisfied. The statute's jurisdictional requirement has been met regardless of whether or not Yunis was "found" within the United States under section 1203(b)(1)(B).

Appellant's argument that we should read the Hostage Taking Act differently to avoid tension with international law falls flat. Yunis points to no treaty obligations of the United States that give us pause. Indeed, Congress intended through the Hostage Taking Act to execute the International Convention Against the Taking of Hostages, which authorizes any signatory state to exercise jurisdiction over persons who take its nationals hostage "if that State considers it appropriate." International Convention Against the Taking of Hostages, opened for signature Dec. 18, 1979, art. 5, para. 1, 34 U.N. GAOR Supp. (No. 39), 18 I.L.M. 1456, 1458. See H.R. CONF. REP. No. 1159, 98th Cong., 2d Sess. 418 (1984), reprinted in 1984 U.S.CODE CONG. & ADMIN.NEWS 3182, 3710, 3714.

Nor is jurisdiction precluded by norms of customary international law. The district court concluded that two jurisdictional theories of international law, the "universal principle" and the "passive personal principle," supported assertion of U.S. jurisdiction to prosecute Yunis on hijacking and hostage-taking charges. See Yunis, 681 F.Supp. at 899–903. Under the universal principle, states may prescribe and prosecute "certain offenses recognized by the community of nations as of universal concern, such as piracy, slave trade, attacks on or hijacking of aircraft, genocide, war crimes, and perhaps certain acts of terrorism," even absent any special connection between the state and the offense. See Restatement (THIRD) of the Foreign Relations Law of the United States Secs. 404, 423 (1987) [hereinafter RESTATEMENT]. Under the passive personal principle, a state may punish non-nationals for crimes committed against its nationals outside of its territory, at least where the state has a particularly strong interest in the crime. See id. at Sec. 402 comment g; United States v. Benitez, 741 F.2d 1312, 1316 (11th Cir.1984) (passive personal principle invoked to approve prosecution of Colombian citizen convicted of shooting U.S. drug agents in Colombia), cert. denied, 471 U.S. 1137, 105 S.Ct. 2679, 86 L.Ed.2d 698 (1985).

Relying primarily on the Restatement, Yunis argues that hostage taking has not been recognized as a universal crime and that the passive personal principle authorizes assertion of jurisdiction over alleged hostage takers only where the victims were seized because they were nationals of the prosecuting state. Whatever merit appellant's claims may have as a matter of international law, they cannot prevail before this court. Yunis seeks to portray international law as a self-executing code that trumps domestic law whenever the two conflict. That effort misconceives the role of judges as appliers of international law and as participants in the federal system. Our duty is to enforce the Constitution, laws, and treaties of the United States, not to conform the law of the land to norms of customary international law. See U.S. CONST. art. VI. As we said in Committee of U.S. Citizens Living in Nicaragua v. Reagan, 859 F.2d 929 (D.C.Cir.1988): "Statutes inconsistent with principles of customary international law may well lead to international law violations. But within the domestic legal realm, that inconsistent statute simply modifies or supersedes customary international law to the extent of the inconsistency." Id. at 938. See also Federal Trade Comm'n v. Compagnie de Saint-Gobain-Pont-a-Mousson, 636 F.2d 1300, 1323 (D.C.Cir.1980) (U.S. courts "obligated to give effect to an unambiguous exercise by Congress of its jurisdiction to prescribe even if such an exercise would exceed the limitations imposed by international law").

To be sure, courts should hesitate to give penal statutes extraterritorial effect absent a clear congressional directive. See Foley Bros. v. Filardo, 336 U.S. 281, 285, 69 S.Ct. 575, 577, 93

L.Ed. 680 (1949); United States v. Bowman, 260 U.S. 94, 98, 43 S.Ct. 39, 41, 67 L.Ed. 149 (1922). Similarly, courts will not blind themselves to potential violations of international law where legislative intent is ambiguous. See Murray v. The Schooner Charming Betsy, 6 U.S. (2 Cranch) 64, 118, 2 L.Ed. 208 (1804) ("[A]n act of congress ought never to be construed to violate the law of nations, if any other possible construction remains...."). But the statute in question reflects an unmistakable congressional intent, consistent with treaty obligations of the United States, to authorize prosecution of those who take Americans hostage abroad no matter where the offense occurs or where the offender is found. Our inquiry can go no further.

2. Antihijacking Act

The Antihijacking Act provides for criminal punishment of persons who hijack aircraft operating wholly outside the "special aircraft jurisdiction" of the United States, provided that the hijacker is later "found in the United States." 49 U.S.C. App. Sec. 1472(n). Flight 402, a Jordanian aircraft operating outside of the United States, was not within this nation's special aircraft jurisdiction. See 49 U.S.C. App. Sec. 1301. Yunis urges this court to interpret the statutory requirement that persons prosecuted for air piracy must be "found" in the United States as precluding prosecution of alleged hijackers who are brought here to stand trial. But the issue before us is more fact-specific, since Yunis was indicted for air piracy while awaiting trial on hostage-taking and other charges; we must determine whether, once arrested and brought to this country on those other charges, Yunis was subject to prosecution under the Antihijacking Act as well.

The Antihijacking Act of 1974 was enacted to fulfill this nation's responsibilities under the Convention for the Suppression of Unlawful Seizure of Aircraft (the "Hague Convention"), which requires signatory nations to extradite or punish hijackers "present in" their territory. Convention for the Suppression of Unlawful Seizure of Aircraft, Dec. 16, 1970, art. 4, para. 2, Dec. 16, 1970, [...] This suggests that Congress intended the statutory term "found in the United States" to parallel the Hague Convention's "present in [a contracting state's] territory," a phrase which does not indicate the voluntariness limitation urged by Yunis. Moreover, Congress interpreted the Hague Convention as requiring the United States to extradite or prosecute "offenders in its custody," evidencing no concern as to how alleged hijackers came within U.S. territory. S. REP. No. 13, 93d Cong., 1st Sess. at 3; see H. REP. No. 885, 93d Cong., 2d Sess. at 10, 1974 U.S.Code Cong. & Admin.News 3978 (Hague Convention designed to close "gap" in Tokyo Convention, which did not require states to prosecute or extradite hijackers "in [their] custody"). From this legislative history we conclude that Yunis was properly indicted under section 1472(n) once in the United States and under arrest on other charges.

The district court correctly found that international law does not restrict this statutory jurisdiction to try Yunis on charges of air piracy. See Yunis, 681 F.Supp. at 899–903. Aircraft hijacking may well be one of the few crimes so clearly condemned under the law of nations that states may assert universal jurisdiction to bring offenders to justice, even when the state has no territorial connection to the hijacking and its citizens are not involved. See id. at 900–01; United States v. Georgescu, 723 F.Supp. 912, 919 (E.D.N.Y.1989); RESTATEMENT Sec. 404 & reporters' note 1, Sec. 423; Randall, Universal Jurisdiction under International Law, 66 TEX.L.REV. 785, 815–34 (1988). But in any event we are satisfied that the Antihijacking Act authorizes assertion of federal jurisdiction to try Yunis regardless of hijacking's status vel non as a universal crime. Thus, we affirm the district court on this issue. [...]

D. Jury Instructions

Lastly, Yunis challenges the district court's instructions to the jury insofar as they relate to intent requirements of the federal hostage taking, hijacking, and conspiracy statutes and to appellant's affirmative defense of obedience to military orders. In so doing, appellant does not come before an "impregnable citadel[ ] of technicality." United States v. Hasting, 461 U.S. 499, 509, 103 S.Ct. 1974, 1980, 76 L.Ed.2d 96 (1983) [...] Trial courts, not the courts of appeals, are the principal bulwarks against injustice in our judicial system, and their resolution of the myriad questions that arise in the course of a criminal trial must be afforded deference. As the Supreme Court has "stressed on more than one occasion, the Constitution entitles a criminal defendant to a fair trial, not a perfect one." Delaware v. Van Arsdall, 475 U.S. 673, 681, 106 S.Ct. 1431, 1436, 89 L.Ed.2d 674 (1986). [...] In particular, appellate judges ought not substitute their prejudices regarding jury instructions or their notions of apt phraseology for the experience of trial judges in such matters; our more limited responsibility is to ensure that the law is correctly stated for jurors to apply. Where the indispensable prerequisites for a fair trial have been afforded, we will not overturn a conviction just because an awkward word was used in instructing the jury, or even because we would have sustained a defense objection that was overruled. Instead, we look at the entire record of the proceedings below and ignore errors that do not undermine confidence in the conviction when viewed in light of all that took place. See Rose v. Clark, 478 U.S. 570, 576-79, 106 S.Ct. 3101, 3105–07, 92 L.Ed.2d 460 (1986); Hasting, 461 U.S. at 507-09, 103 S.Ct. at 1979–81; Chapman v. California, 386 U.S. 18, 21-24, 87 S.Ct. 824, 826–28, 17 L.Ed.2d 705 (1967); Kotteakos v. United States, 328 U.S. 750, 762-65, 66 S.Ct. 1239, 1246–48, 90 L.Ed. 1557 (1946). With these precepts in mind, we now turn to appellant's specific allegations of error in the instructions given by the trial judge.

1. Intent Requirements

Yunis claims that the Antihijacking Act, 49 U.S.C.App. Sec. 1472(n), and the Hostage Taking Act, 18 U.S.C. Sec. 1203, make specific intent an element of the offenses they establish, and that the district court erred in failing to adopt jury instructions offered by the defense that would have made this clear. In appellant's view, the trial judge's instruction that Yunis could be convicted on these counts only if he acted "intentionally, deliberately and knowingly" was inadequate. Transcript of Jury Instructions, March 10, 1989, at 17–18, 20 [hereinafter "Instructions"].

49 U.S.C. App. Sec. 1472(n) suggests no specific intent requirement on its face, criminalizing any "unlawful" hijacking of an aircraft. Nor do judicial interpretations of related statutes support appellant's position. In fact, courts have interpreted a companion provision criminalizing domestic hijacking, 49 U.S.C. App. Sec. 1472(i), as requiring only general criminal intent, even though (unlike section 1472(n)) it specifies that hijackers must act with "wrongful intent." See United States v. Castaneda-Reyes, 703 F.2d 522, 525 (11th Cir.), cert. denied, 464 U.S. 856, 104 S.Ct. 174, 78 L.Ed.2d 157 (1983); United States v. Busic, 592 F.2d 13, 21 (2d Cir.1978); United States v. Bohle, 445 F.2d 54, 60 (7th Cir.1971). In light of these decisions, and absent any encouragement from Congress, we decline Yunis' invitation to graft a specific intent requirement onto the Antihijacking Act.

Yunis' claim that the Hostage Taking Act requires specific intent also fails. The statutory language suggests no intent requirement other than that the offender must act with the purpose of influencing some third person or government through the hostage taking, a point on which the jury received proper instructions. See Instructions at 17 (quoting 18 U.S.C. Sec. 1203(a)). Nor are we aware of any legislative history suggesting that Congress meant to impose a specific intent requirement. Thus, we conclude that the trial judge's instructions on this count of the indictment accorded with law.

We find no merit in Yunis' objection (not raised at trial) that the district court failed to instruct the jury that specific intent is a necessary element of the crime of conspiracy. True, "the specific intent required for the crime of conspiracy is in fact the intent to advance or further the unlawful object of the conspiracy." United States v. Haldeman, 559 F.2d 31, 112 (D.C.Cir.1976) (footnote omitted), cert. denied, 431 U.S. 933, 97 S.Ct. 2641, 53 L.Ed.2d 250

(1977). But the jury received instructions that the government "must show beyond a reasonable doubt that the conspiracy was knowingly formed and that the defendant willfully participated in the unlawful plan with the intent to advance or further some object or purpose of the conspiracy." Instructions at 10. We discern no defect in this instruction. [. . .]

2. Obedience to Military Orders

The final issues before us concern jury instructions relating to Yunis' affirmative defense of obedience to military orders. Yunis and the government agree on the elements of this common law defense, which are established by several civilian court decisions of rather ancient vintage and by military practice. These precedents generally accord with a formulation approved by the Court of Military Appeals in United States v. Calley, 22 C.M.A. 534, 48 C.M.R. 19 (1973):

> The acts of a subordinate done in compliance with an unlawful order given him by his superior are excused and impose no criminal liability upon him unless the superior's order is one which a man of ordinary sense and understanding would, under the circumstances, know to be unlawful, or if the order in question is actually known to the accused to be unlawful. Id. at 542, 48 C.M.R. at 27 (opinion of Quinn, J.) (emphasis deleted); see United States v. Clark, 31 F. 710, 716–17 (C.C.E.D. Mich.1987); McCall v. McDowell, 15 F.Cas. 1235, 1240 (C.C.D. Cal.1867) (No. 8,673); Neu v. McCarthy, 309 Mass. 17, 33 N.E.2d 570, 573 (1941); U.S. DEP'T OF DEFENSE, MANUAL FOR COURTS-MARTIAL, UNITED STATES, 1984, R.C.M. 916(d) at II-128 ("It is a defense to any offense that the accused was acting pursuant to orders unless the accused knew the orders to be unlawful or a person of ordinary sense and understanding would have known the orders to be unlawful.").

Appellant does not disagree with the district court's jury instructions on the general elements of this affirmative defense. Instead, Yunis claims that the district court erred as a matter of law when it instructed the jury that Yunis could prevail on this defense only if the Amal Militia – to which Yunis belonged and which, he claimed, ordered the hijacking – is a "military organization." The court further instructed the jury that it could find that the Amal Militia is a military organization only if the group has a hierarchical command structure and "[c]onducts its operations in accordance with the laws and customs of war," and if its members have a uniform and carry arms openly. Instructions at 34.

Yunis disputes the district court's position that members of a legitimate military organization must have a uniform. Since the hijackers wore civilian clothes and there was evidence that members of the Amal Militia often dressed this way, appellant concludes that the instruction was prejudicial to his defense. Yunis argues that the relevance of uniforms to the ultimate factual question of whether or not the Amal Militia is a military organization is itself a factual question for the jury, not a question of law. He notes that U.S. courts have not developed any test for determining whether or not defendants who invoke the obedience defense actually belong to bona fide military organizations. But the government responds that courts have not developed such a test simply because the issue has not arisen in U.S. courts; heretofore, the defense has been raised only by members of the United States armed forces. In the government's view, the district court properly adapted its instructions on the obedience defense when faced with novel factual circumstances.

We agree that the district court did not commit legal error when it looked beyond domestic precedents to give jurors guidance in evaluating the Amal Militia's military credentials. Moreover, we find that the test of a bona fide military organization adopted by the district court reflects international practice, providing assurance that Yunis did not suffer from parochial projection of American norms onto the issue of whether he should be treated as a soldier for purposes of the obedience defense.

Specifically, the district court's uniform instruction finds sufficient support in international agreements that bear on the question. See Geneva Convention Relative to the Treatment of Prisoners of War, opened for signature Aug. 12, 1949, art. 4(A)(2), [...] [hereinafter Geneva Convention]; Hague Convention No. IV Respecting the Law and Customs of War on Land, Oct. 18, 1907, annex Sec. I, ch. I, art. 1, [...] [hereinafter Hague Convention No. IV]. The Geneva Convention, signed by 167 nations including the United States and Lebanon, establishes "having a fixed and distinctive signal recognizable at a distance" as one of four necessary conditions that qualify the members of a militia for treatment as prisoners of war. The Hague Convention No. IV, to which the United States and forty-two other nations are parties, uses having "a fixed distinctive emblem recognizable at a distance" as a test for whether militiamen and members of volunteer corps have the rights and responsibilities of national armies. See 36 Stat. at 2295–96. At oral argument, counsel for appellant disavowed reliance on the district court's substitution of "uniform" for "signal" or "emblem," and we agree that this free interpretation of the treaty language did not prejudice the defense.

Yunis' second objection to the district court's "military organization" test relates to the instruction, tracking language found in article 4 of the Geneva Convention and chapter I of the annex to the Hague Convention No. IV, that militias must "conduct [their] operations in accordance with the laws and customs of war" to qualify as military organizations. Instructions at 34. Appellant alleges that this instruction must be considered in tandem with the trial judge's statement to the jury that the hijacking of Flight 402 violated international law. Together, he says, these instructions directed the jury to conclude that the defense of obedience to military orders was unavailable to Yunis because no organization could have given the instruction to hijack Flight 402 without violating "the laws and customs of war."

We disagree with appellant's reading of the record, however, and find that when the district court's instructions are considered as a whole, it is highly improbable that a reasonable juror would have understood them to direct a verdict on the affirmative defense. See United States v. Lemire, 720 F.2d 1327, 1339 (D.C.Cir.1983), cert. denied, 467 U.S. 1226, 104 S.Ct. 2678, 81 L.Ed.2d 874 (1984). In the first place, appellant ignores the trial judge's charge to the jury that it was responsible for determining, based on the evidence, whether or not the Amal Militia is a military organization. Instructions at 34. So too, the court told jurors that if they found that Yunis was a soldier in a military organization under the definition given them, they would then have to address the issue of whether or not Yunis knew that his orders were illegal. Id. at 35. Both of these instructions contradict appellant's suggested reading, leading us to conclude that the jury would not have understood the question of whether or not the Amal Militia is a military organization to be foreclosed.

Appellant's interpretation becomes even more attenuated in light of the government's closing argument, during which the prosecution told jurors that they would have to determine whether the Amal Militia is "a military organization that basically plays by the rules." Trial Transcript, March 9, 1989, at 106–07 [...] See United States v. Park, 421 U.S. 658, 674-75 & n. 16, 95 S.Ct. 1903, 1912 & n. 16, 44 L.Ed.2d 489 (1975) (jury instructions must be viewed in context of trial as a whole). This statement framed the issue correctly, albeit informally, providing additional assurance that any ambiguity arising from the court's juxtaposition of the illegality instruction and the adherence to international law instruction did not prejudice Yunis' defense. Because the jury instructions, read as a whole and in light of the evidence and arguments at trial, leave us confident that no prejudicial error occurred, we find that the district court acted within the scope of its discretion.

For the foregoing reasons, the convictions are affirmed.

An example of prosecution of terrorist acts under US laws not specifically targeting terrorism is provided by *US* v. *Rahman* 854 F. Supp. 254 (S.D.N.Y. 1994).

(D) TERRORISTS AND INTERNATIONAL HUMANITARIAN LAW

Terrorism poses a challenge to the application of rights and duties prescribed by international humanitarian law, and its most prominent contemporary edifice, the Geneva Conventions. As introduced in Part II(1) on war crimes, the Geneva Conventions and Additional Protocols are a major source of regulation of combatants and protections for prisoners of war, among others. What protections, if any should terrorists receive under the Geneva Conventions? It is hard to fit terrorists, who fight in stealth and as part of transnational networks, under the rubric of combatants acting under the authority of a particular state. What aspects of the law of war should bind states struggling with terrorists who do not 'play fair'? In the excerpt below, the US Supreme Court addressed, among other things, the protections due to an alleged terrorist under the Geneva Conventions.

USA, Hamdan v. Rumsfeld, *Supreme Court, Judgment of 29 June 2006*

Salim Ahmed Hamdan was captured by Afghani militia forces in Afghanistan and detained by US forces in Guantánamo Bay for more than a year before the US authorities decided to try him by military commission. After another year passed, the authorities charged him with one count of conspiracy 'to commit [...] offenses triable by military commission'. His attorneys filed petitions for writs of habeas corpus and mandamus challenging the decision to try him by military commission. In the excerpt below, the Supreme Court considered how to classify Hamdan – who had been termed by the United States Government an 'enemy combatant' – under international humanitarian law and what protections of the Geneva Conventions applied.

Justice Stevens announced the judgment of the Court and delivered the opinion of the Court with respect to Parts I through IV, Parts VI through VI–D–iii, Part VI–D–v, and Part VII, and an opinion with respect to Parts V and VI–D–iv, in which Justice Souter, Justice Ginsburg, and Justice Breyer join. [...]

ii

[...] As an alternative to its holding that Hamdan could not invoke the Geneva Conventions at all, the Court of Appeals concluded that the Conventions did not in any event apply to the armed conflict during which Hamdan was captured. The court accepted the Executive's assertions that Hamdan was captured in connection with the United States' war with al Qaeda and that that war is distinct from the war with the Taliban in Afghanistan. It further reasoned that the war with al Qaeda evades the reach of the Geneva Conventions. See 415 F. 3d, at 41–42. We, like Judge Williams, disagree with the latter conclusion.

The conflict with al Qaeda is not, according to the Government, a conflict to which the full protections afforded detainees under the 1949 Geneva Conventions apply because Article 2 of those Conventions (which appears in all four Conventions) renders the full protections applicable only to "all cases of declared war or of any other armed conflict which may arise between two or more of the High Contracting Parties." 6 U. S. T., at 3318.[4] Since Hamdan

---

[4] [59] For convenience's sake, we use citations to the Third Geneva Convention only.

was captured and detained incident to the conflict with al Qaeda and not the conflict with the Taliban, and since al Qaeda, unlike Afghanistan, is not a "High Contracting Party" – *i.e.*, a signatory of the Conventions, the protections of those Conventions are not, it is argued, applicable to Hamdan.[5]

We need not decide the merits of this argument because there is at least one provision of the Geneva Conventions that applies here even if the relevant conflict is not one between signatories.[6] Article 3, often referred to as Common Article 3 because, like Article 2, it appears in all four Geneva Conventions, provides that in a "conflict not of an international character occurring in the territory of one of the High Contracting Parties, each Party[7] to the conflict shall be bound to apply, as a minimum," certain provisions protecting "[p]ersons taking no active part in the hostilities, including members of armed forces who have laid down their arms and those placed *hors de combat* by…detention." *Id.*, at 3318. One such provision prohibits "the passing of sentences and the carrying out of executions without previous judgment pronounced by a regularly constituted court affording all the judicial guarantees which are recognized as indispensable by civilized peoples." *Ibid.*

The Court of Appeals thought, and the Government asserts, that Common Article 3 does not apply to Hamdan because the conflict with al Qaeda, being " 'international in scope,' " does not qualify as a " 'conflict not of an international character.' " 415 F. 3d, at 41. That reasoning is erroneous. The term "conflict not of an international character" is used here in contradistinction to a conflict between nations. So much is demonstrated by the "fundamental logic [of] the Convention's provisions on its application." *Id.*, at 44 (Williams, J., concurring). Common Article 2 provides that "the present Convention shall apply to all cases of declared war or of any other armed conflict which may arise between two or more of the High Contracting Parties." 6 U. S. T., at 3318 (Art. 2, ¶1). High Contracting Parties (signatories) also must abide by all terms of the Conventions vis-á-vis one another even if one party to the conflict is a nonsignatory "Power," and must so abide vis-á-vis the nonsignatory if "the latter accepts and applies" those terms. *Ibid.* (Art. 2, ¶3). Common Article 3, by contrast, affords some minimal protection, falling short of full protection under the Conventions, to individuals associated with neither a signatory nor even a nonsignatory "Power" who are involved in a conflict "in the territory of" a signatory. The latter kind of conflict is distinguishable from the conflict described in Common Article 2 chiefly because it does not involve a clash between nations (whether signatories or not). In context, then, the phrase "not of an international character" bears its literal meaning. See, *e.g.*, J. Bentham, Introduction to the Principles of Morals and Legislation 6, 296 (J. Burns & H. Hart eds. 1970) (using the term "international law" as a "new though not inexpressive appellation" meaning "betwixt nation and nation"; defining "international" to include "mutual transactions between sovereigns as such"); Commentary on the Additional Protocols to the Geneva Conventions of 12 August 1949, p. 1351 (1987)

---

[5] [60] The President has stated that the conflict with the Taliban is a conflict to which the Geneva Conventions apply. See White House Memorandum, Humane Treatment of Taliban and al Qaeda Detainees 2 (Feb. 7, 2002), available at http://www.justicescholars.org/pegc/archive/White_House/bush_memo_20020207_ed.pdf (hereinafter White House Memorandum).

[6] [61] Hamdan observes that Article 5 of the Third Geneva Convention requires that if there be "any doubt" whether he is entitled to prisoner-of-war protections, he must be afforded those protections until his status is determined by a "competent tribunal." 6 U. S. T., at 3324. See also Headquarters Depts. of Army, Navy, Air Force, and Marine Corps, Army Regulation 190–8, Enemy Prisoners of War, Retained Personnel, Civilian Internees and Other Detainees (1997), App. 116. Because we hold that Hamdan may not, in any event, be tried by the military commission the President has convened pursuant to the November 13 Order and Commission Order No. 1, the question whether his potential status as a prisoner of war independently renders illegal his trial by military commission may be reserved.

[7] [62] The term "Party" here has the broadest possible meaning; a Party need neither be a signatory of the Convention nor "even represent a legal entity capable of undertaking international obligations." GCIII Commentary 37.

("[A] non-international armed conflict is distinct from an international armed conflict because of the legal status of the entities opposing each other").

Although the official commentaries accompanying Common Article 3 indicate that an important purpose of the provision was to furnish minimal protection to rebels involved in one kind of "conflict not of an international character," *i.e.*, a civil war, see GCIII Commentary 36–37, the commentaries also make clear "that the scope of the Article must be as wide as possible," *id.*, at 36.[8] In fact, limiting language that would have rendered Common Article 3 applicable "especially [to] cases of civil war, colonial conflicts, or wars of religion," was omitted from the final version of the Article, which coupled broader scope of application with a narrower range of rights than did earlier proposed iterations. See GCIII Commentary 42–43.

iii

Common Article 3, then, is applicable here and, as indicated above, requires that Hamdan be tried by a "regularly constituted court affording all the judicial guarantees which are recognized as indispensable by civilized peoples." 6 U. S. T., at 3320 (Art. 3, ¶1(d)). While the term "regularly constituted court" is not specifically defined in either Common Article 3 or its accompanying commentary, other sources disclose its core meaning. The commentary accompanying a provision of the Fourth Geneva Convention, for example, defines " 'regularly constituted' " tribunals to include "ordinary military courts" and "definitely exclud[e] all special tribunals." GCIV Commentary 340 (defining the term "properly constituted" in Article 66, which the commentary treats as identical to "regularly constituted");[9] see also *Yamashita*, 327 U. S., at 44 (Rutledge, J., dissenting) (describing military commission as a court "specially constituted for a particular trial"). And one of the Red Cross' own treatises defines "regularly constituted court" as used in Common Article 3 to mean "established and organized in accordance with the laws and procedures already in force in a country." Int'l Comm. of Red Cross, 1 Customary International Humanitarian Law 355 (2005); see also GCIV Commentary 340 (observing that "ordinary military courts" will "be set up in accordance with the recognized principles governing the administration of justice").

The Government offers only a cursory defense of Hamdan's military commission in light of Common Article 3. See Brief for Respondents 49–50. As Justice Kennedy explains, that defense fails because "[t]he regular military courts in our system are the courts-martial established by congressional statutes." *Post*, at 8 (opinion concurring in part). At a minimum, a military commission "can be 'regularly constituted' by the standards of our military justice system only if some practical need explains deviations from court-martial practice." *Post*, at 10. As we have explained, see Part VI–C, *supra*, no such need has been demonstrated here.[10]

---

[8] [63] See also GCIII Commentary 35 (Common Article 3 "has the merit of being simple and clear.... Its observance does not depend upon preliminary discussions on the nature of the conflict"); GCIV Commentary 51 ("[N]obody in enemy hands can be outside the law"); U. S. Army Judge Advocate General's Legal Center and School, Dept. of the Army, Law of War Handbook 144 (2004) (Common Article 3 "serves as a 'minimum yardstick of protection in all conflicts, not just internal armed conflicts'" (quoting Nicaragua v. United States, 1986 I. C. J. 14, ¶218, 25 I. L. M. 1023)); Prosecutor v. Tadić, Case No. IT-94-1, Decision on the Defence Motion for Interlocutory Appeal on Jurisdiction, ¶102 (ICTY App. Chamber, Oct. 2, 1995) (stating that "the character of the conflict is irrelevant" in deciding whether Common Article 3 applies).

[9] [64] The commentary's assumption that the terms "properly constituted" and "regularly constituted" are interchangeable is beyond reproach; the French version of Article 66, which is equally authoritative, uses the term "régulirement constitués" in place of "properly constituted."

[10] [65] Further evidence of this tribunal's irregular constitution is the fact that its rules and procedures are subject to change midtrial, at the whim of the Executive. See Commission Order No. 1, §11 (providing that the Secretary of Defense may change the governing rules "from time to time").

iv

Inextricably intertwined with the question of regular constitution is the evaluation of the procedures governing the tribunal and whether they afford "all the judicial guarantees which are recognized as indispensable by civilized peoples." 6 U. S. T., at 3320 (Art. 3, ¶1(d)). Like the phrase "regularly constituted court," this phrase is not defined in the text of the Geneva Conventions. But it must be understood to incorporate at least the barest of those trial protections that have been recognized by customary international law. Many of these are described in Article 75 of Protocol I to the Geneva Conventions of 1949, adopted in 1977 (Protocol I). Although the United States declined to ratify Protocol I, its objections were not to Article 75 thereof. Indeed, it appears that the Government "regard[s] the provisions of Article 75 as an articulation of safeguards to which all persons in the hands of an enemy are entitled." Taft, The Law of Armed Conflict After 9/11: Some Salient Features, 28 Yale J. Int'l L. 319, 322 (2003). Among the rights set forth in Article 75 is the "right to be tried in [one's] presence." Protocol I, Art. 75(4)(e).[11]

We agree with Justice Kennedy that the procedures adopted to try Hamdan deviate from those governing courts-martial in ways not justified by any "evident practical need," *post*, at 11, and for that reason, at least, fail to afford the requisite guarantees. See *post*, at 8, 11–17. We add only that, as noted in Part VI–A, *supra*, various provisions of Commission Order No. 1 dispense with the principles, articulated in Article 75 and indisputably part of the customary international law, that an accused must, absent disruptive conduct or consent, be present for his trial and must be privy to the evidence against him. See §§6(B)(3), (D).[12] That the Government has a compelling interest in denying Hamdan access to certain sensitive information is not doubted. Cf. *post*, at 47–48 (Thomas, J., dissenting). But, at least absent express statutory provision to the contrary, information used to convict a person of a crime must be disclosed to him.

v

Common Article 3 obviously tolerates a great degree of flexibility in trying individuals captured during armed conflict; its requirements are general ones, crafted to accommodate a

---

[11] [66] Other international instruments to which the United States is a signatory include the same basic protections set forth in Article 75. See, e.g., International Covenant on Civil and Political Rights, Art. 14, ¶3(d), Mar. 23, 1976, 999 U. N. T. S. 171 (setting forth the right of an accused "[t]o be tried in his presence, and to defend himself in person or through legal assistance of his own choosing"). Following World War II, several defendants were tried and convicted by military commission for violations of the law of war in their failure to afford captives fair trials before imposition and execution of sentence. In two such trials, the prosecutors argued that the defendants' failure to apprise accused individuals of all evidence against them constituted violations of the law of war. See 5 U. N. War Crimes Commission 30 (trial of Sergeant-Major Shigeru Ohashi), 75 (trial of General Tanaka Hisakasu).

[12] [67] The Government offers no defense of these procedures other than to observe that the defendant may not be barred from access to evidence if such action would deprive him of a "full and fair trial." Commission Order No. 1, §6(D)(5)(b). But the Government suggests no circumstances in which it would be "fair" to convict the accused based on evidence he has not seen or heard. Cf. Crawford v. Washington, 541 U. S. 36, 49 (2004) ("'It is a rule of the common law, founded on natural justice, that no man shall be prejudiced by evidence which he had not the liberty to cross examine'" (quoting State v. Webb, 2 N. C. 103, 104 (Super. L. & Eq. 1794) (per curiam)); Diaz v. United States, 223 U. S. 442, 455 (1912) (describing the right to be present as "scarcely less important to the accused than the right of trial itself"); Lewis v. United States, 146 U. S. 370, 372 (1892) (exclusion of defendant from part of proceedings is "contrary to the dictates of humanity" (internal quotation marks omitted)); Joint Anti-Fascist Refugee Comm. v. McGrath, 341 U. S. 123 , n. 17, 171 (1951) (Frankfurter, J., concurring) ("[t]he plea that evidence of guilt must be secret is abhorrent to free men" (internal quotation marks omitted)). More fundamentally, the legality of a tribunal under Common Article 3 cannot be established by bare assurances that, whatever the character of the court or the procedures it follows, individual adjudicators will act fairly.

wide variety of legal systems. But *requirements* they are nonetheless. The commission that the President has convened to try Hamdan does not meet those requirements.

A different aspect in the interaction between the law applicable to armed conflict and terrorism was discussed by the Italian Supreme Court in 2007.

Italy, **Bouyahia Maher Ben Abdelaziz et al.,** *Supreme Court, Judgment No. 1072 of 17 January 2007*

Article 270-bis of the Italian Penal Code ('Associations in furtherance of domestic or international terrorist aims or of subversion of the democratic structure of the state'), as amended on 15 December 2001, reads in part: 'Anyone promoting, instituting, organizing, managing or financing associations whose purpose is to commit acts of violence for purposes of terrorism or to subvert the democratic order shall be punished by a term of imprisonment between 7 and 15 years. Anyone participating in the afore-mentioned associations shall be punished by a term of imprisonment between 5 and 10 years.'

A number of foreign nationals were charged on the basis of this provision with having participated in recruiting and dispatching volunteers to Iraq and other conflict areas to be trained as fighters within *Ansar-al-Islam*, a transnational Islamic group. A pre-trial judge in Milan dismissed the case, holding that the activities carried out by the accused were not terrorist in nature. According to the judge, they were acts of guerrilla warfare forming part of a struggle against foreign military occupation and did not have the purpose of spreading terror among civilians. The Prosecutor appealed against the dismissal of the charges, but the Appeals Court upheld the decision in the first instance. It held that violent acts by 'freedom fighters' could be deemed terrorist only if aimed *exclusively* at harming the civilian population. If, as the evidence showed, the acts were legitimate combatant actions merely causing *collateral* damage amongst civilians, then a terrorist purpose could not be established. Lacking specific intent, the charge had to be dismissed. The Prosecutor appealed once again, this time to the Supreme Court (*Corte di cassazione*). During this period, Parliament had approved Article 270-sexies, which criminalized international terrorism as defined in the EU Council Framework Decision on Combating Terrorism of 13 June 2002. While this provision was *ex post facto* law in relation to the facts of the case, the Court deemed useful to refer to it in order to elucidate the terms of Article 270-bis.

[. . .] 2.1 First, it is necessary to note that, when trying to identify a general category [of terrorism] the host of international conventions ratified by Italy relating to the repression of terrorist acts in specific sectors (such as, among others, the conventions of Tokyo of 1963, The Hague of 1970, Montreal of 1971 on air transport, the Convention of Rome of 1988 on Safety of Maritime Navigation, and the Vienna Convention of 1980 on Physical Protection of Nuclear Material) are of limited importance. The quest for a general definition of terrorism is instead to be based on two international instruments in particular: (i) the 1999 New York Convention adopted by UN General Assembly in order to fight the financing of terrorism; (ii) the EU Framework Decision 2002/475/JHA.

Due to the decades-long disagreements among UN member states on terrorist acts perpetrated during liberation wars and armed struggles for self-determination, a global convention on terrorism does not exist. Having said that, it should be noted that the wording of the

1999 Convention, which was implemented in Italy through law No. 7 of 27 January 2003, is so broad that it can be considered a general definition, capable of being applied in both times of peace and times of war. This definition includes all conduct intended to cause death or serious bodily harm to a civilian or, in wartime, 'to any other person not taking an active part in the hostilities in a situation of armed conflict' with the aim of spreading terror among the population or to compel a government or an international organization to do or to abstain from doing any act. In order for conduct to be qualified as a 'terrorist act', it must be characterized not only by the actus reus and the mens rea, as well as by the identity of victims (civilians or persons not engaged in war operations), but it is generally understood that it must also include a political, religious, or ideological purpose. This is pursuant to the rule of customary international law embodied in various resolutions by the UNGA and the UNSC, as well as in the 1997 Convention for the Suppression of *Terrorist* Bombings.

The definition of terrorist acts in Article 1 of the EU Framework Decision is based instead upon a list of specified crimes, as they exist under national laws, which may entail serious harm to a State or an international organization and are committed with the aim of seriously intimidating a population, unduly compelling a government or international organization to perform or abstain from performing any act, or seriously destabilising or destroying the fundamental political, constitutional, economic or social structures of a country or an international organization.

Despite similarities, this definition of the 2002 EU Framework Decision is different from that of the 1999 UN Convention in two respects. On the one hand, the Framework Decision provides a more limited contextual scope by applying only to acts perpetrated in times of peace: the eleventh "Considering" precludes a legal regulation of "actions by armed forces during periods of armed conflict", according to the definition given to these terms by international humanitarian law. Thus, the definition does not relate to acts committed in times of war that are subject to the rules of international humanitarian law and, in particular, to the Geneva Conventions and the Additional Protocols thereto. On the other hand, the Framework Decision provides a broader definition of terrorist activities, adding those activities that are characterized by subversive purposes. These are acts with the purpose of "destabilizing or destroying the fundamental political, constitutional, economic or social structures of a country or an international organization", a category of activities that does not appear in the 1999 Convention text.

Both definitions, however, recognize as emblematic of terrorist acts, the characteristic identified by leading scholars as the "depersonalization of the victim". This is evidenced by the fact that the persons targeted are generally unknown, the real objective of these acts being that of instilling indiscriminate fear in the collectivity and of compelling a government or an international organization to perform or abstain from performing a specific act.

Finally, the reference to situations of armed conflict – which is included in the 1999 Convention but is absent from the Framework decision – shows two contexts in which terrorist acts are committed and the necessity of separating their legal treatment depending on the identities of the perpetrators and the victims. Thus, international humanitarian law should apply when the perpetrators are "combatants" and the targets are civilians or are persons not taking active part in the hostilities, while ordinary law applies when these features are not present. The implication is that, when the definition of personal identity changes, the qualification of terrorist acts as war crimes or crimes against humanity also changes.

2.2. Article 15 of legislative Decree N. 144 of 27 July 2005, converted into Law No. 155 of 31 July 2005 has incorporated the legal characterization found in the Framework Decision into the domestic legal order pursuant to the obligation to do so in order to implement EU law. Thus, "acts in furtherance of terrorist aims" are now defined as those "that, due to their nature or context, may entail serious harm to a State or an international organization and are committed with the aim of seriously intimidating a population, unduly compelling a government or international organisation to perform or abstain from performing any act, or seriously destabilising or destroying the fundamental political, constitutional, economic or social structures of a country or an international organisation, as well as other acts defined as terrorist or perpetrated in furtherance of terrorist aims by conventions or by other international law rules binding upon Italy."

By making an explicit reference to the binding character of international sources, the definition in Article 270-sexies of the Penal Code necessarily becomes dynamic because it will expand or restrict not only on the basis of the international conventions already ratified, but also on the basis of future conventions to which Italy will adhere. Thus, the law has created a mechanism that ensures automatic state harmonization with respect to the means necessary for common action against transnational terrorist criminality.

From the above, the following can be deduced: the definition in Article 270-sexies must be read together with that of the 1999 Convention, implemented by law No. 7 of 2003. This means that the constitutive elements of acts in furtherance of terrorist aims – provided for in the domestic provision based upon the EU Framework Decision – must be integrated into the principles contained in that convention. A joint reading of the domestic provision with the aforementioned international rule shows that the terrorist aim can also be ascertained when the acts are perpetrated in the context of an armed conflict – thus qualified by international law even where the conflict is an internal civil war – and target civilians and persons not taking active part in the hostilities. This leaves out only those acts targeting combatants, which remain subject to international humanitarian law.

3. Having identified the essential traits of the activities in furtherance of terrorist aims, it is necessary to examine the characteristics of the crime in Article 270-bis of the Penal Code [Associations in furtherance of domestic or international terrorist aims or of subversion of the democratic structure of the state] [. . .], which targets prodromal or preparatory activities before the perpetration of planned violent acts [. . .] [T]he provision in question [Article 270-bis of the criminal code] is aimed at punishing the mere establishment of an association, whether or not the criminal acts envisaged in the common plan and instrumental to the association's aim are actually committed. Undoubtedly, however, the association must be effective enough for execution of the criminal plan to be a realistic possibility. The required level of harm is only reached if the association is capable of committing the crimes for which it was established. If, on the other hand, the association is only conceived in vague and abstract terms, to make its establishment criminal would punish the mere commitment to an abstract idea. However appalling its calls to indiscriminate violence and the spreading of terror may be, since such an idea is not accompanied by the possibility of implementing the plan, punishing such commitment would result in criminalizing opinions and not acts [. . .]

As far as the act of participating in a terrorist association is concerned, it is necessary to recall the principles enunciated by the Grand Chamber of this Court regarding the crime of association provided for in Article 416-bis of the Penal Code [criminalizing mafia-type criminal associations]. [In sum,] the participation of an individual in a terrorist association may also be substantiated by conduct which is instrumental and provides logistical support to the activities of the association – as long as this conduct demonstrates that the individual is a member of the association and that a part of his or her conduct takes place in Italy.

As far as mens rea is concerned, the crime provided for in Article 270-bis of the Penal Code is a typical specific-intent crime. The wilfulness and the awareness of the prohibited conduct must also include a pursuit of the specific terrorist aim characterizing the activity of the association, which the law identifies as either the aim of terrorizing amongst the population or that of compelling States or international organizations to do or to abstain from doing any act. [. . .]

4.1 The Prosecutor General was correct in alleging the erroneous application of criminal law by the Appeals Court [. . .] The Appeals Court considered terrorist "only the acts exclusively directed against the civilian population", thus excluding suicidal acts of the so-called 'kamikaze' [suicide-bombers] perpetrated against military objectives in armed conflict, even if such attacks also inflict serious damage and spread fear amongst the civilian population. Such a generalization may not be accepted and requires a more detailed analysis. First, this view is clearly at odds with the text of the 1999 Convention, which was nonetheless referred to in the impugned judgment. This international instrument defines as terrorist "any conduct intended to cause death or serious bodily harm to a civilian or to any other person not taking an active part in the hostilities in a situation of armed conflict". Thus, this category also includes attacks directed against military who are engaged in tasks unrelated to military operations, including those tasks not even indirectly connected to military operations, such as humanitarian assistance.

The view of the Appeals Court is also to be rejected, however, for another reason. During an armed conflict (whether between States or a civil war) there may be cases where acts of violence are aimed both at the military and at the civilian population. This happens when, due to the nature of the acts, the means employed and the specific circumstances surrounding their commission, the acts result in serious harm not just to soldiers but also to civilians. The consequence of this is that the letter and rationale of the international provisions defining 'terrorist aim' in war contexts unquestionably lead us to conclude that an attack planned against a military target must be considered a terrorist act when – having regard to the specific and concrete circumstances – its consequences would entail certain and inevitable harm to life and limb of civilians, simultaneously spreading fear and panic amongst the population at large. An example would be that of a bomb explosion against a military vehicle located in a crowded market. Such a scenario demonstrates that it would be absurd and irrational to read the provision in question as precluding the act from being terrorist in nature simply because victims are both military and civilians. On the contrary, the certainty (rather than the prospect or probability) of the consequences of the act on civilians unquestionably shows that the specific intent includes both the willingness to cause the event and the aim of attaining results that are characterized as terrorist purposes.

The consequences of this error of interpretation of the law by the court of merit will have to be considered when re-assessing the events on the basis of the evidence. [. . .]

5. [. . .] Thus, the appeal must be allowed as discussed above.

At the outset, it should be noted that the findings of the court of merit are upheld insofar as it found that adhering to religious radicalism and Islamic fundamentalism – and even good will towards political and military struggles – do not as such demonstrate connections aimed at perpetrating terrorist acts as long as they remain in the realm of opinion. This is because our legal system recognizes, among others, the right to freely speak one's mind. Conforming to an ideology (even if subversive) can therefore never qualify as a crime as long as it does not lead to the establishment of an organizational structure or to actual perpetration of violent acts [. . .]

The impugned judgment, together with the first-instance one, can be criticized, as the Prosecutor General has done, because it did not delve into the relationships between the group established by the accused, on the one hand, and the transnational association identified in the indictment, on the other. Such an analysis on the basis of the available evidence would have been necessary, since the investigation should have focussed on the existence of the 'cell' in Milan of which the accused were allegedly members, the tasks undertaken by this cell, the degree of autonomy of this cell vis-à-vis the other cells operating in Italy [. . .] and, finally, the links among these cells and between such cells and the organizations abroad engaged in terrorist activities. [. . .]

Moreover, having clarified these matters on the basis of the evidence, the judges should have established whether the logistical support activities for the organization working abroad – fundraising, provision of false documents, aiding and abetting [*favoreggiamento*] illegal immigration into Italy of the persons intending to subsequently fight abroad – may form an adequate basis for reaching a conclusion on whether the cells were indeed part of a trans-national organization and whether the organization had terrorist aims. Thus, the fact that the cell in Milan was not directly involved in terrorist activities but supported the militants that were carrying out such activities abroad does not exclude liability in relation to the crime provided for in Article 272-bis of the Penal Code, taking into account the undeniable functional relationship among the groups.

Moreover, even such an analysis should not have brought the inquiry to an end. Lacking evidence of structural and organizational links of the Milan cell with the more extended organization operating abroad, the judges should also have considered whether the evidence showed the individual criminal responsibility of a person who, while not being a member of a criminal association or participant in any criminal conspiracy, had nevertheless intentionally aided and abetted such criminal association [*concorso esterno nel delitto associativo*] [...] This leads us to the conclusion that the evaluations made by the lower courts are deficient and incomplete due to lack of analysis of certain essential evidentiary matters as well as of legal questions.

5.1 Having established what is to be proven, this Court is now required to evaluate the reasoning of the challenged judgment, first with respect to the procedural rules dealing with the gathering of evidence.

At the start it should be noted that, in the struggle against international terrorism, the Italian legal system has chosen to follow the procedural and substantive guarantees essential to respecting our Constitutional values. This has meant refusing to adopt repressive measures falling outside the legal system, which negate the very basis of the judicial process [...] Such measures taken by other countries in opposition to Islamic terrorism have been characterized pursuant to the concept of "criminal law of the enemy". This is a system that does not recognize common guarantees (starting with habeas corpus rights), for those who are suspected of terrorism, and which deprives those persons of the civil and political rights to which all individuals are generally entitled.

Thus, in our legal system, trials dealing with international terrorist acts are still subject to the ordinary regime, except for those specific – and specifically identified – matters that are regulated differently on the basis of the law (starting from Legislative Decree No. 374 of 2001, converted into law by Law No. 438 of 2001). These new laws have added specific provisions modelled upon those existing for mafia-type organized crime and relating, in particular, to the preliminary inquiries – without subverting the fundamental principles of the criminal process and the provisions of Article 111 of the Constitution on fair trial [a lengthy provision which regulates in detail all the elements of fair trial]. The impugned judgment followed these rules scrupulously when it found that information on the transnational organization Ansar Al Islam that was received from intelligence sources could not be put on the record. This is because such information was gathered by authorities who had no power to make inquiries within legal proceedings and without following the prescribed procedures. Thus, the evidence so seriously threatened the legality of the proceedings that it was considered 'pathologically unusable' [...]

The Prosecutor General has also appealed against lower court's failure to take into account the fact that UNSC Resolution 1267/99 listed the organization Ansar Al Islam among the terrorist associations. He alleges that, due to this circumstance, the aims of the group – with which the accused had repeated contacts – could not have been unknown.

This is incorrect, since the mere inclusion by international organizations of an association in a list of terrorist persons or groups may not by itself demonstrate the terrorist nature of the association in question. This is an assessment that, during trial, must be left for the judge to freely consider, and the legal characterization provided by those organizations is not binding. [...] The listing of a group is, according to most scholars, merely an administrative act, which may form the basis of the sanctions foreseen, but this does not make such a finding evidence [in criminal proceedings]. [...] The fact that an association is added to such lists may be an element to be taken into account for investigative purposes, but proof of the terrorist aims must be shown according to the rules on admissibility and evaluation in procedural law. [...]

6.4 The reasoning followed by the lower court is also flawed because it relied on the assumption that proof of the terrorist aims was to be based in a decisive way on the fact that the civilian population was the initial target of the attacks. In this respect, this Court has already clarified that a terrorist act includes any act targeting a military objective, as long as the specific circumstances of the case make serious consequences for life or limb of civilians inevitable and certain, thus contributing to the spread of fear and panic among the general population. It follows that the lower courts, in assessing the terrorist objectives, should not have limited themselves to considering the military nature of the target. They also should have verified whether such attacks would have caused serious harm to life and limb among civilians, in circumstances that would have made such harm certain and inevitable due to the nature of the conduct, the means employed and the specific circumstances of the case.

An additional mistake of the impugned decision is the fact that the lower court considered that no responsibility could attach to the defendants since the acts described in the charges were committed before terrorist attacks by car-bombs and suicide bombs started in Iraq. On the contrary, the essential elements of the crime provided for in Article 270-bis of the Penal Code do not require the commission of the subsequent crimes towards which the association aims. In order to meet the elements of the crime in question, it is sufficient that a suitable association is created and that this association is based on a plan with international terrorist aims, whether or not the planned crimes are actually carried out.

Thus, on the basis of the evidence, the lower court should have ascertained whether the defendants had direct links with Ansar Al Islam or if they were criminally responsible because, while not being a member of a criminal association or participant in any criminal conspiracy, they nevertheless intentionally aided and abetted such criminal association. Moreover, in both cases, the court should have made a finding on whether the defendants knew that Ansar Al islam pursued a program which included terrorist attacks, bearing in mind that similar actions had been undertaken in Kurdistan prior to the war in Iraq. On this last point, which refers to mens rea, the lower court failed to provide adequate reasoning. It merely excluded, without any analysis, the fact that the defendants acted with intent; it did not discuss the issue of the defendants' knowledge of the means to engage in the struggle and of the aims of the association supported by their conduct. [...]

For these reasons, the Supreme Court of Cassation, First Penal Chamber, quashes the impugned judgment and remits the matter to a new Section of the Appeals Court in Milan, in relation to Count 1.

COMMENTARY

Another interesting example of a case dealing with terrorism is the *Lockerbie* judgment of 31 January 2001[13] by a Scottish Court sitting in the Netherlands. This court convicted one of the two defendants, Al Megrahi, to life imprisonment for the bombing of Pan Am flight 103 over the town of Lockerbie, resulting in the death of 270 people.

The case had been the object of Security Council Resolution 748 (1992), which required Libya to surrender the suspects in the attack to the USA or the UK. Libya invoked the provisions of the 1971 Montreal Convention for the Suppression of Unlawful Acts against the Safety of Civil Aviation, which gave it two options: either extradite the suspects or submit the case to its own competent authorities (*aut dedere aut judicare*). Libya argued that because the case had been considered by Libyan authorities, there was no obligation

---

[13] Case No. 1475/99, *Her Majesty's Advocate* v. *Abdelbaset Ali Mohmed Al Megrahi and Al Amin Khalifa Fhimah*, Court of Justiciary at Camp Zeist.

to extradite. The ICJ, called upon by Libya to rule on the matter, held that the binding UNSC Resolution superseded the provisions of the Montreal Convention.[14] At trial, the two defendants were charged with destroying a civil passenger aircraft and murdering its occupants to further the purposes of the Libyan Intelligence Services. In this judgment, the Court found that '[t]he clear inference which we draw from this evidence is that the conception, planning and execution of the plot which led to the planting of the explosive device was of Libyan origin' (para. 82). The judges however did not discuss the law applicable to terrorism in the verdict; as a consequence the case does not shed much light on the legal aspects of the fight against international terrorism. (Al Megrahi was released in 2009 on health grounds by the Scottish authorities.)

So far, no judgment on terrorism has been issued by an international tribunal. Nonetheless, international terrorism is often confronted at the domestic level, as shown by the US and Italian judgments reported above. Due to the differences existing among the various systems, however, it is difficult to compare these judgments, as they are based on the particular law and procedures of each country. Closer cooperation in matters of terrorism is, however, arguably leading to convergent approaches and comparable definitions when dealing with international terrorism.

QUESTIONS

1. Consider the – very different – judgments above. Do you see a pattern in how the legal issues are assessed? Or are the judges only applying their own domestic doctrines and disregarding the international dimension of terrorism?

2. The *Chamoun* court makes a clear finding that international humanitarian law is not applicable to the situation before it. Is this a fair conclusion? How did the Italian Supreme Court see the relationship between terrorism in time of war and terrorism as an 'ordinary' crime? Are these matters only to be discussed by looking at the domestic penal codes?

3. Do you think it advisable to prosecute and try terrorism cases in the country of nationality of the victims, rather than where the conduct took place? What are the advantages of one choice over the other?

FURTHER READING

A. Cassese, 'The Multifaceted Criminal Notion of Terrorism in International Law' (2006) 4 JICJ 933–58.

J. Friedrichs, 'Defining the International Public Enemy: The Political Struggle behind the Legal Debate on International Terrorism' (2006) 19 *Leiden J. of Int'l L.* 69–91.

B. Saul, *Defining Terrorism in International Law* (Oxford: Oxford University Press, 2006).

---

[14] Questions of Interpretation and Application of the 1971 Montreal Convention arising from the Aerial Incident at Lockerbie (*Libyan Arab Jamahiriya* v. *United Kingdom*), Provisional Measures, Order of 14 April 1992, I.C.J. Reports 1992, p. 3.

7

PIRACY

Piracy is the original crime of universal jurisdiction. Long before war crimes, crimes against humanity and genocide achieved this status, piracy that occurred on the high seas was prosecutable, pursuant to customary international law and later treaty law, anywhere in the world. In this regard piracy was, as Justice Moore of the Permanent Court of International Justice stated in his dissent in the 1927 *Lotus* case, '*sui generis*'.

After World War II, piracy was cited as precedent for the extension of universal jurisdiction to other crimes. For example, in the *Eichmann* case, the Supreme Court of Israel drew on the example of piracy in finding universal jurisdiction for crimes against humanity:

In other words, the basic reason for which international law recognizes the right of each State to exercise such jurisdiction in piracy offences – notwithstanding the fact that its own sovereignty does not extend to the scene of the commission of the offence (the high seas) and the offender is a national of another State or is stateless – applies with even greater force to the above-mentioned crimes [against humanity]. That reason is, it will be recalled, that the interest to prevent bodily and material harm to those who sail the seas and to persons engaged in trade between nations, is a vital interest common to all civilized States and of universal scope […][1]

This use of piracy as precedent for universal jurisdiction raises an important question: *why* precisely was universal jurisdiction recognized first for this crime? In the quotation above, the *Eichmann* court suggests that it was in the nature of the crime and the harm it caused all nations. Judges Higgins, Kooijmans and Buergenthal of the ICJ expressed this same view in a joint separate opinion in *Arrest Warrant of 11 April 2000*:[2]

60. It is equally necessary that universal criminal jurisdiction be exercised only over those crimes regarded as the most heinous by the international community.

61. Piracy is the classical example. This jurisdiction was, of course, exercised on the high seas and not as an enforcement jurisdiction within the territory of a non-agreeing State. But this historical fact does not mean that universal jurisdiction only exists with regard to crimes committed on the high seas or in other places outside national territorial jurisdiction. Of decisive importance is that this jurisdiction was regarded as lawful because the international community regarded piracy as damaging to the interests of all.

But is this view persuasive? Is it especially heinous as compared to other crimes? Although a questionable rationale for piracy, heinousness is certainly a more convincing justification for the extension of universal jurisdiction to war crimes, crimes against humanity and genocide.

A more compelling explanation for the long-standing recognition of universal jurisdiction for piracy is the difficulty of prosecuting cases occurring on the high seas outside of any state territorial jurisdiction. Although the flag state of the victim ship will

---

[1] *Eichmann* Judgment, para. 12.
[2] *Case Concerning the Arrest Warrant of 11 April 2000 (Democratic Republic of the Congo v. Belgium)*, ICJ, 14 February 2002.

have jurisdiction, as a practical matter the ship may be far from its flag country, making investigation and prosecution impracticable. As Judge Guillaume stated in his separate opinion in the *Arrest Warrant* case, 'universal jurisdiction is accepted in cases of piracy because piracy is carried out on the high seas, outside all State territory' (para. 5). This rationale also supports the extension of universal jurisdiction to war crimes, crimes against humanity and genocide; while these crimes do not typically occur outside of a state jurisdiction, they often occur in a context in which the territorial state is unable to enforce the law, and therefore there may be an equivalent absence of law justifying universal jurisdiction.

The definition of piracy has been a matter of debate. There has always been a consensus that it includes an attack on the high seas by a private ship on another ship *animo furandi* (i.e. with the intent to commit robbery), but disagreement about whether the crime should be expanded to cover additional conduct. Some have argued that robbery should not be a required element: whatever the reason universal jurisdiction was recognized for piracy, the inclusion of robbery hardly seems a critical feature. But at the same time there has been, among some, a reluctance to include within piracy *any* crime that occurs on the high seas. As Judge Moore further stated in the *Lotus* case, 'nations have shown the strongest repugnance to extending the scope of the offence, because it carried with it not only the principle of universal jurisdiction but also the right of visit and search on the high seas in time of peace'.

A second point of debate has been whether piracy includes within it attacks on state vessels by insurgents or rebels who are unrecognized belligerents. On the one hand, to the extent such attacks occurred on the high seas, they shared some of the features of piracy that have warranted its special consideration, but on the other hand rebel attacks are usually focused on a particular State and therefore are not necessarily 'damaging to the interests of all' nations.

Some of these definitional debates were resolved by law of the sea treaties. Article 15 of the 1958 Geneva Convention on the High Seas and Article 101 of the 1982 UN Convention on the Law of the Sea (UNCLOS) both defined piracy as follows:

(a) any illegal acts of violence or detention, or any act of depredation, committed for private ends by the crew or the passengers of a private ship or a private aircraft, and directed:

    (i) on the high seas, against another ship or aircraft, or against persons or property on board such ship or aircraft;

    (ii) against a ship, aircraft, persons or property in a place outside the jurisdiction of any State;

(b) any act of voluntary participation in the operation of a ship or of an aircraft with knowledge of facts making it a pirate ship or aircraft;

(c) any act of inciting or of intentionally facilitating an act described in subparagraph (a) or (b).

Notably, this definition was not limited to robbery; but as it was restricted to acts 'for private ends', it did not appear to apply to attacks by insurgents.

In 1985, a group called the Palestine Liberation Front hijacked the *Achille Lauro*, an Italian flag ship, on the high seas and demanded the release of some 50 Palestinian prisoners. When these demands were not met, they murdered one American passenger, Leon Klinghoffer, and threw his body and wheelchair overboard. The United States claimed this attack to be an act of piracy, but some commentators disagreed. The attack was the impetus for the adoption of the Convention for the Suppression of Unlawful Acts against the Safety of Maritime Navigation (SUA), which broadly commits nations to the prosecution or extradition of individuals responsible for violent attacks on vessels on the high seas.

Until a few years ago, it was thought that the crime of piracy, as conventionally defined, had essentially disappeared. Since 2008, however, pirates operating out of Somalia have attacked ships in the Gulf of Aden and beyond, demanding (and often receiving) enormous ransoms. Despite international efforts to counter these attacks, they have continued, costing billions of dollars in ransoms and protection measures. Universal jurisdiction for these crimes have proven to be just the beginning of a response, however. Since pirates often avoid capture on the high seas by retreating into Somalia's waters, the UNSC adopted, pursuant to Chapter VII, Resolution 1851 (2008), allowing States to pursue pirates onto Somali territory.

Nonetheless, countering this new spate of piracy has continued to pose enormous practical and logistical challenges. At most, the authorities have been able to capture only the pirates themselves, the 'foot soldiers', but not those organizing the ongoing attacks. Moreover, even with regard to the captured pirates, there have been difficult questions about how evidence will be gathered and where the accused will be tried. Some countries have been reluctant to bring the alleged pirates back to their own territory for prosecution because of the costs of such an effort and the fear that the pirates will claim asylum if acquitted or once they are released from prison. Kenya has agreed to prosecute some of the pirates, but many have simply been released on shore after capture, a recognition that the logistical challenges of prosecution can be insurmountable. The persistent practical difficulties of prosecuting the pirates, despite the availability of universal jurisdiction, have led some to consider expanding the jurisdiction of the ICC to include these cases or assigning them to a specially created tribunal for this crime.

Cases

USA, US v. Smith, *Supreme Court, Judgment of 25 February 1820*

> Thomas Smith was accused of an act of piracy as described by the court. The charge required the court to determine if, at the time, the alleged crime was sufficiently defined in international law. But since the conduct involved robbery, the court, in an opinion of Justice Story, did not have to define the outer definitional limits of the crime.

The jury found a special verdict as follows: 'We, of the jury, find, that the prisoner, Thomas Smith, in the month of March, 1819, and others, were part of the crew of a private armed vessel, called the Creollo, (commissioned by the government of Buenos Ayres, a colony then at war with Spain,) and lying in the port of Margaritta; that in the month of March, 1819, the said prisoner and others of the crew mutinied, confined their officer, left the vessel, and in the said port of Margaritta, seized by violence a vessel called the Irresistible, a private armed vessel, lying in that port, commissioned by the government of Artigas, who was also at war with Spain; that the said prisoner and others, having so possessed themselves of the said vessel, the Irresistible, appointed their officers, proceeded to sea on a cruize, without any documents or commission whatever; and while on that cruize, in the month of April, 1819, on the high seas, committed the offence charged in the indictment, by the plunder and robbery of the Spanish vessel therein mentioned. If the plunder and robbery aforesaid be piracy under the act of the Congress of the United States, entitled, 'An act to protect the commerce of the United States,

and punish the crime of piracy,' then we find the said prisoner guilty; if the plunder and robbery, above stated, be not piracy under the said act of Congress, then we find him, not guilty.'

The Circuit Court divided on the question, whether this be piracy as defined by the law
of nations, so as to be punishable under the act of Congress, of the 3d of March, 1819, and
thereupon the question was certified to this Court for its decision. [. . .]

It is next to be considered, whether the crime of piracy is defined by the law of nations
with reasonable certainty. What the law of nations on this subject is, may be ascertained by
consulting the works of jurists, writing professedly on public law; or by the general usage and
practice of nations; or by judicial decisions recognising and enforcing that law. There is scarcely
a writer on the law of nations, who does not allude to piracy as a crime of a settled and deter-
minate nature; and whatever may be the diversity of definitions, in other respects, all writers
concur, in holding, that robbery, or forcible depredations [. . .] upon the sea, *animo furandi*, is
piracy. The same doctrine is held by all the great writers on maritime law, in terms that admit
of no reasonable doubt. The common law, too, recognises and punishes piracy as an offence,
not against its own municipal code, but as an offence against the law of nations, (which is
part of the common law,) as an offence against the universal law of society, a pirate being
deemed an enemy of the human race. Indeed, until the statute of 28th of Henry VIII. ch. 15.
piracy was punishable in England only in the admiralty as a civil law offence; and that statute,
in changing the jurisdiction, has been universally admitted not to have changed the nature of
the offence. Sir Charles Hedges, in his charge at the Admiralty sessions, in the case of Rex v.
Dawson, (5 *State Trials*,) declared in emphatic terms, that 'piracy is only a sea term for robbery,
piracy being a robbery committed within the jurisdiction of the admiralty.' Sir Leoline Jenkins,
too, on a like occasion, declared that 'a robbery, when committed upon the sea, is what we
call piracy;' and he cited the civil law writers, in proof. And it is manifest from the language of
Sir William Blackstone, in his comments on piracy, that he considered the common law definition as distinguishable in no essential respect from that of the law of nations. So that, whether
we advert to writers on the common law, or the maritime law, or the law of nations, we shall
find that they universally treat of piracy as an offence against the law of nations, and that its
true definition by that law is robbery upon the sea. And the general practice of all nations in
punishing all persons, whether natives or foreigners, who have committed this offence against
any persons whatsoever, with whom they are in amity, is a conclusive proof that the offence is
supposed to depend, not upon the particular provisions of any municipal code, but upon the
law of nations, both for its definition and punishment. We have, therefore, no hesitation in
declaring, that piracy, by the law of nations, is robbery upon the sea, and that it is sufficiently
and constitutionally defined by the fifth section of the act of 1819.

USA, The Ambrose Light, *Federal District Court of New York, Judgment of 30 September 1885*

This case arose out of an action to forfeit the ship, *The Ambrose Light*, which had been
used by Colombian insurgents seeking to attack a port in Colombia. The ship was
seized by a US naval ship and brought back to the United States. The court found that
the insurgents had not been recognized either by the Colombian or US governments as
having belligerent rights, and that a state of war had not been recognized between the
insurgents and the Colombian government.

The legality of the original seizure of the Ambrose Light depends upon the answer to be given
to the inquiry whether the cruise of the vessel under the commission of the insurgent leaders,
to assist in the so-called blockade of Cartagena, must be regarded, under the circumstances
of this case, as lawful warfare or as piratical. She was owned by one of the insurgents that

signed her commission. None of her officers or crew were residents of this country. The question must therefore be adjudged according to the law of nations.

Neither the causes, nor the objects, nor the merits of the revolt are understood by the court; nor is its extent or probability of success known. It is said to be, not for independence, nor for any division of the republic, but rather a personal or party struggle for the possession of the reins of government, such as, unhappily, has too often arisen in the southern republics. The few ports and provinces that have passed under the control of the insurgents have been acquired, it is said, partly by force of arms and partly by the former loyal officials recognizing the insurgent leaders as their superior officers. But these circumstances, as well as the general merits or demerits of the struggle, are, in the view of the court, wholly immaterial here; because, as will be seen, it is not within the province of this court to inquire into them, or to take any cognizance of them, except in so far as they have been previously recognized by the political or executive department of the government.

The consideration that I have been able to give to the subject leads me to the conclusion that the liability of the vessel to seizure, as piratical, turns wholly upon the question whether the insurgents had or had not obtained any previous recognition of belligerent rights, either from their own government or from the political or executive department of any other nation; and that, in the absence of recognition by any government whatever, the tribunals of other nations must hold such expeditions as this to be technically piratical. This result follows logically and necessarily, both from the definition of piracy in the view of international law, and from a few well-settled principles. Wheaton defines piracy as 'the offense of depredating on the high seas without being authorized by any sovereign state, or with commissions from different sovereigns at war with each other.' Dana's Wheat. Int. Law, Sec. 122. Rebels who have never obtained recognition from any other power are clearly not a sovereign state in the eye of international law, and their vessels sent out to commit violence on the high seas are therefore piratical within this definition. The general principles of international right and of self-protection lead to the same conclusion. (1) All nations are entitled to the peaceful pursuit of commerce through the ports of all other civilized nations, unobstructed, save by the incidents of lawful war, or by the just restrictions of the sovereign. (2) Maritime warfare, with its burdens and inconveniences to nations not engaged in it, is the lawful prerogative of sovereigns only. Private warfare is unlawful. International law has no place for rebellion; and insurgents have strictly no legal rights, as against other nations, until recognition of belligerent rights is accorded them. (3) Recognition of belligerency, or the accordance of belligerent rights to communities in revolt, belongs solely to the political and executive departments of each government. (4) Courts cannot inquire into the internal condition of foreign communities in order to determine whether a state of civil war, as distinguished from sedition or armed revolt, exists there or not. They must follow the political and executive departments, and recognize only what those departments recognize; and, in the absence of any recognition by them, must regard the former legal conditions as unchanged.

From these principles it necessarily follows that in the absence of recognition by any government of their belligerent rights, insurgents that send out vessels of war are, in legal contemplation, merely combinations of private persons engaged in unlawful depredations on the high seas; that they are civilly and criminally responsible in the tribunals for all their acts of violence; that in blockading ports which all nations are entitled to enter, they attack the rights of all mankind, and menace with destruction the lives and property of all who resist their unlawful acts; that such acts are therefore piratical, and entitle the ships and tribunals of every nation whose interests are attacked or menaced, to suppress, at their discretion, such unauthorized warfare by the seizure and confiscation of the vessels engaged in it. The right of seizure by other nations arises in such cases, ex necessitate, from the very nature of the case. There is no other remedy except open war; and nations are not required to declare war against individual rebels whom they are unwilling and are not required to recognize as a belligerent power. Nor are other nations required, for their own security, in such a case, to make any alliance with the parent state. By the right of self-defense, they may simply seize such law-breakers as come in their way and menace them with injury. Without this right, insurgents, though recognition were rightly refused them, and however insignificant their cause, or unworthy their conduct, might violate the rights of all other nations, harass their commerce, and capture or sink their ships with impunity. The whole significance and importance of the doctrine of recognition of belligerency would be gone, since the absence of recognition could be safely disregarded; the distinction between lawful and unlawful war would be practically abolished; and the most unworthy revolt would have the same immunities for acts of violence on the high seas, without any recognition of belligerent rights, as the most justifiable revolt would have with it. The right to treat unlawful and unauthorized warfare as piratical, seems to me, therefore, clearly imbedded in the very roots of international law.

United Kingdom, In Re Piracy Jure Gentium, *Judicial Committee of the Privy Council, Judgment of 26 July 1934*

This case involved the prosecution of accused Chinese pirates in Hong Kong. The question of the definition of piracy was referred to the Judicial Committee of the Privy Council in the United Kingdom, which hears final appeals from UK territories overseas. The Privy Council engaged in an extensive analysis of the scope of the crime of piracy in international law.

On January 4, 1931, on the high seas, a number of armed Chinese nationals were cruising in two Chinese junks. They pursued and attacked a cargo junk which was also a Chinese vessel. The master of the cargo junk attempted to escape, and a chase ensued during which the pursuers came within 200 yards of the cargo junk. The chase continued for over half an hour, during which shots were fired by the attacking party, and while it was still proceeding, the steamship *Hang Sang* approached and subsequently also the steamship *Shui Chow*. The officers in command of these merchant vessels intervened and through their agency, the pursuers were eventually taken in charge by the Commander of H.M.S. *Somme,* which had arrived in consequence of a report made by wireless. They were brought as prisoners to Hong Kong and indicted for the crime of piracy. The jury found them guilty subject to the following question of law: "Whether an accused person may be convicted of piracy in circumstances where no robbery has occurred." The Full Court of Hong Kong on further consideration came to the conclusion that robbery was necessary to support a conviction of piracy and in the result the accused were acquitted.

The decision of the Hong Kong Court was final and the present proceedings are in no sense an appeal from that Court, whose judgment stands.

Upon November 10, 1933, His Majesty in Council made the following Order:

"The question whether actual robbery is an essential element of the crime of piracy *jure gentium*, or whether a frustrated attempt to commit a piratical robbery is not equally piracy *jure gentium*, is referred to the Judicial Committee for their hearing and consideration."

It is to this question that their Lordships have applied themselves, and they think it will be convenient to give their answer at once and then to make some further observations upon the matter.

The answer is as follows: "Actual robbery is not an essential element in the crime of piracy *jure gentium*. A frustrated attempt to commit a piratical robbery is equally piracy *jure gentium*." [...]

Their Lordships have been referred to a very large number of Acts of Parliament, decided cases and opinions of jurisconsults or text-book writers, some of which lend colour to the contention that robbery is a necessary ingredient of piracy, others to the opposite contention. Their Lordships do not propose to comment on all of them [...]

The conception of piracy according to the civil law is expounded by Molloy (1646–1690) *De Jure Maritimo et Navali* or *A Treatise of affairs Maritime and of Commerce*. That book was first published in 1676 and the ninth edition in 1769. Chapter 4 is headed "Of Piracy." The author defines a pirate as "a sea thief or *hostis humani generis* who to enrich himself either by surprize or open face sets upon merchants or other traders by sea". He clearly does not regard piracy as necessarily involving successful robbery or as being inconsistent with an unsuccessful attempt. [...]

But in certain trials for piracy held in England under the Act of Henry VIII, a narrower definition of piracy seems to have been adopted.

Thus in 1696, the trial *R. v. Joseph Dawson* took place. The prisoners were indicted for "feloniously and piratically taking and carrying away from persons unknown a certain ship called the *Gunsway*... upon the high seas ten leagues from the Cape St. Johns near Surat in the East Indies." The Court was comprised of Sir Charles Hedges, then judge in the High Court of Admiralty, Lord Chief Justice Holt, Lord Chief Justice Treby, Lord Chief Baron Ward and a number of other judges. Sir Charles Hedges gave the charge to the grand jury. In it he said "now piracy is only a sea-term for robbery, piracy being a robbery committed within the jurisdiction of the Admiralty. If any man be assaulted within that jurisdiction, and his ship or goods violently taken away without legal authority, this is robbery and piracy."

Dawson's case was described as the sheet-anchor for those who contend that robbery is an ingredient of piracy. It must be remembered, however, that every case must be read *secundum subjectam materiam* and must be held to refer to the facts under dispute. In *Dawson's* case, the prisoners had undoubtedly committed robbery in their piratical expeditions. The only function of the Chief Judge was to charge the grand jury and in fact to say to them: "Gentlemen, if you find the prisoners have done these things, then you ought to return a true bill against them." The same criticism applies to certain charges given to grand juries by Sir Leoline Jenkins (1623–1685) judge of the Admiralty Court (1685): see *Life of Leoline Jenkins,* vol. 1, p. 94. It cannot be suggested that these learned judges were purporting to give an exhaustive definition of piracy, and a moment's reflection will show that a definition of piracy as sea robbery is both too narrow and too wide. Take one example only. Assume a modern liner with its crew and passengers, say of several thousand aboard, under its national flag, and suppose one passenger robbed another. It would be impossible to contend that such a robbery on the high seas was piracy and that the passenger in question had committed an act of piracy when he robbed his fellow passenger, and was therefore liable to the penalty of death. "That is too wide a definition which would embrace all acts of plunder and violence in degree sufficient to constitute piracy simply because done on the high seas. As every crime can be committed at sea, piracy might thus be extended to the whole criminal code. If an act of robbery or murder were committed upon one of the passengers or crew by another in a vessel at sea, the vessel being at the time and continuing under lawful authority and the offender were secured and confined by the master of the vessel to be taken home for trial, this state of things would not authorize seizure and trial by any nation that chose to interfere or within whose limits the offender might afterwards be found": Dana's Wheaton, p. 193, note 83, quoted in Moore's *Digest of International Law* (Washington, 1906) Article "Piracy," p. 953.

But over and above that, we are not now in the year 1696; we are now in the year 1934. International law was not crystallized in the 17th century, but is a living and expanding code. In his treatise on international law, the English textbook writer Hall (1835–94) says at p. 25 of his preface to the third edition (1889): "Looking back over the last couple of centuries we see international law at the close of each fifty years in a more solid position than that which it occupied at the beginning of the period. Progressively it has taken firmer hold, it has extended its sphere of operation, it has ceased to trouble itself about trivial formalities, it has more and more dared to grapple in detail with the fundamental facts in the relations of states. The area within which it reigns beyond dispute has in that time been infinitely enlarged, and it has been greatly enlarged within the memory of living man." Again another example may be given. A body of international law is growing up with regard to aerial warfare and aerial transport, of which Sir Charles Hedges in 1696 could have had no possible idea.

A definition of piracy which appears to limit the term to robbery on the high seas was put forward by that eminent authority Hale (1609–76), in his *Pleas of the Crown* ed. 1737, cap. 27, p. 305, where he states, "it is out of the question that piracy by the statute is robbery." It is not surprising that subsequent definitions proceed on these lines.

The court then cites various commentaries as well as decisions, some of them requiring the robbery element, others denying it.

However that may be, their Lordships do not themselves propose to hazard a definition of piracy. They remember the words of M. Portalis, one of Napoleon's commissioners, who said:

> "We have guarded against the dangerous ambition of wishing to regulate and to foresee everything. . . . A new question springs up. Then how is it to be decided? To this question it is replied that the office of the law is to fix by enlarged rules the general maxims of right and wrong, to establish firm principles fruitful in consequences, and not to descend to the detail of all questions which may arise upon each particular topic." (Quoted by Halsbury L.C. in Halsbury's *Laws of England*, Introduction, p. ccxi.)

A careful examination of the subject shows a gradual widening of the earlier definition of piracy to bring it from time to time more in consonance with situations either not thought of or not in existence when the older jurisconsults were expressing their opinions.

All that their Lordships propose to do is to answer the question put to them, and having examined all the various cases, all the various statutes and all the opinions of the various jurisconsults cited to them, they have come to the conclusion that the better view and the proper answer to give to the question addressed to them is that stated at the beginning – namely, that actual robbery is not an essential element in the crime of piracy *jure gentium,* and that a frustrated attempt to commit piratical robbery is equally piracy *jure gentium.*

The debate about whether a required element of piracy is robbery or an intent to rob seems less about robbery itself than about finding some limiting principle so that piracy, and universal jurisdiction, apply only to a limited class of serious crimes and do not encompass all criminal activity occurring on the high seas. The decision about *where* to place this line is shaped in part by the rationale for assigning universal jurisdiction to the crime of piracy in the first place, i.e. whether it is due to the nature of the crime or because of where the crime occurs. Regarding universal jurisdiction, there is debate about whether nations *may* prosecute acts of piracy or are *required* to do so. This question will be of particular importance in cases of alleged attacks by insurgents where there might be disputes about the status of the perpetrators as criminals or belligerents.

Kenya, **Hassan M. Ahmed et al. *v.* Republic,** *High Court of Kenya, Judgment of 12 May 2009*

The accused in this case were charged with piracy for attacking an Indian flag ship. They were arrested by the US navy participating in a multinational effort to protect ships from pirates in the area and brought to Kenya for prosecution.

[...] The particulars of the offence were that the appellants, on 16th January 2006, upon the High Seas of the Indian Ocean, jointly attacked and detained a Machine Sailing Vessel called Safina Al Bisarat-M.N.V.-723 (hereinafter the Indian Ship) and, at the time of, or immediately after such acts, assaulted and put in fear of their lives, the crew of the said vessel and made demands upon its captain Akbar Ali Suleman for a ransom payment of US $50,000.

The appellants pleaded not guilty. After a full trial, the appellants were convicted of the offence charged and each was sentenced to serve seven (7) years imprisonment. [...]

I turn now to the ground that the Learned Principal Magistrate had no jurisdiction to try the case. That complaint is raised in grounds 1 and 2 of the Memorandum of Appeal. The basis of this contention is that none of the parties involved is Kenyan and that the offence was committed miles away from the Kenyan Coast. Piracy is described in Churchill & Lowe "The Law of the Sea" 3rd Edition at page 209 to include "any illegal act of violence detention or depredation committed for private ends by the crew or passengers of a private ship (or aircraft) against another ship (or aircraft) or persons or property on board (or over) the high seas." The actions of the appellants clearly fitted this description. They were crew members of private vessels. They attacked the crew of the Indian ship and detained them. They even deprived them of food and demanded from one of them USD 50,000 and an International mobile phone. Those demands were clearly for private gain. The attack took place about 300 kilometers off the Somalia coast on International waters of the Indian Ocean. I have no doubt in mind that an act of piracy was committed by the appellants. Section 69 (1) and (3) of the Penal Code reads as follows:

"69(1) Any person who, in territorial waters or upon the high seas, commits any act of piracy jure gentium is guilty of the offence of piracy. [...]

(3) Any person who is guilty of the offence of piracy is liable to imprisonment for life."

Under this Section, the offence of piracy is triable and punishable in this country. There are no limitations under the Section. [...]

Even if the Penal Code had been silent on the offence of piracy, I am of the view that the Learned Principal Magistrate would have been guided by the United Nations Convention on the Law of the Sea which defines piracy in Articles 101 as consisting of any of the following acts [The opinion then quotes the text of Article 101].

At the trial Mrs. Mwangi, the Learned Assistant Deputy Public Prosecutor informed the Learned Principal Magistrate that the United Nations Convention on the Law of the Sea had been ratified by Kenya and that Kenya had domesticated the Convention. At the hearing of these appeals, Mr. Onserio relied upon Mrs. Mwangi's submissions at the trial on her contention that the said Convention had been ratified and domesticated. A contrary view was not given by counsel for the appellants. Indeed that status of the Convention in Kenya seems to have been accepted by counsel for the appellants. In the circumstances, I must hold that the Learned Principal Magistrate was bound to apply the provisions of the Convention should there have been deficiencies in our Penal Code and Criminal Procedure Code.

I would go further and hold that even if the Convention had not been ratified and domesticated, the Learned Principal Magistrate was bound to apply international norms and Instruments since Kenya is a member of the civilized world and is not expected to act in contradiction to expectations of member states of the United Nations. That is the view expressed in the Text book on International Law by Martin Dixon NA at page 76. The Learned author writes at paragraph 5.2.3 page 76 as follows: –

"Under international Law, there are certain crimes which are regarded as so destructive of the international order that any state may exercise jurisdiction in respect of them. This is a jurisdiction which exists irrespective of where the act constituting the crime takes place and the nationality of the person committing it [...]

It seems clear that piracy, war crimes and crimes against humanity (e.g. genocide) are crimes susceptible to universal jurisdiction under customary international Law."

The Learned author adds at page 77 as follows:

"The universal principle of jurisdiction rests then, on the nature of the 'crime' committed rather than the identity of the perpetrator or the place of commission."

In the premises, the grounds of Appeals on want of jurisdiction must fail.

COMMENTARY

The accused in this case claimed that they were fishermen whose ship had broken down. They further maintained that they sought assistance from the Indian ship but that then the American Navy arrived, arrested and tortured them, and called them 'Islamic extremists'. The trial required the testimony of crew members from the victim Indian ship, as well as that of officers from the American Navy ship, illustrating some of the practical and logistical costs of prosecuting these cases.

QUESTIONS

1. How, if at all, does piracy inform the broader debate about when and why universal jurisdiction is appropriate? Should it properly be considered as precedent, or as a special case?
2. What are the advantages and disadvantages of assigning piracy cases to the ICC? Of creating a special tribunal for such cases instead?

FURTHER READING

A. Cassese, *Terrorism, Politics and the Law – The* Achille Lauro *Affair* (Princeton, NJ: Princeton University Press, 1989).

M. Halberstam, 'Terrorism on the High Seas: The Achille Lauro, Piracy and the IMO Convention on Maritime Safety' (1988) 82 *The American Journal of International Law* 269–310.

E. Kontorovich, 'The Piracy Analogy: Modern Universal Jurisdiction's Hollow Foundation' (2004) 45 *Harvard International Law Journal* 183–237.

M. Paparinskis, 'Piracy', in *Oxford Companion*, 455–6.

PART III

FORMS OF
RESPONSIBILITY

INTRODUCTION

As in any national legal system, also in international criminal law, responsibility arises not only when a person materially commits a crime, but also when he or she engages in other forms of criminal conduct (for example, provides a weapon to the prospective killer or looks out for intruders while another person is raping a woman, receives money stolen from servicemen who have plundered enemy property).

National legal systems converge in holding that, where a crime involves more than one person, all performing the same act, all are equally liable as co-perpetrators, or principals. In contrast, national laws and case law differ when it comes to the punishment of two or more persons participating in a crime, where these persons do not perform the same act but in one way or another contribute to the realization of a criminal design. Many systems (for instance those of the United States, France, Austria, Italy, Uruguay, Australia) do not provide for different categories of participants, and consequently do not attach different penalties to each of the classes (principals or accessories) under which a person may eventually fall. They provide that each participant, whatever his or her degree of participation, must be considered as a principal; consequently the same penalty *may* be meted out to each of them (though actual sentencing will often take account of the defendant's role in the offence). As the California Penal Code provides at §31, all those 'concerned in the commission of a crime' including those who aid and abet the crime, are to be held liable as principals. (A similar provision exists in the US federal code, see 18 U.S.C. §2.)

Nonetheless, a distinction in these systems is often drawn between three categories of participation: perpetration, on the one side, and two categories of accomplice liability, on the other, namely instigation and aiding and abetting. This distinction is based on the difference in *actus reus* and *mens rea* for each class (see below). In spite of the difference in such objective and subjective elements, the law does not however attach to each of these categories *different consequences* as far as penalties are concerned; or, at least, under the general sentencing tariff no formal distinction is made. It is only provided that for accomplices or accessories, extenuating circumstances may be taken into account if their participation in the offence is less serious than that of the principal or principals. In fact, as noted, for the purposes of sentencing, judges often draw a distinction between principals, instigators, and aiders and abettors.

In other national legal systems (for instance, Germany and Russia) the law draws instead a *normative* distinction between two categories, principals and accomplices (or accessories), formally providing that the persons falling under the latter category must be punished less severely. Thus, for instance, in German law, the scale of penalties for accomplices (at least in the case of aiders and abettors) is less harsh than for the perpetrator.

In addressing these complex interactions of motives, acts, omissions and results, international judges have had to interpret and apply rather anodyne provisions contained in the founding instruments conferring international criminal jurisdiction. In Control Council Law No. 10, for example, Article 2(2) provided:

Any person [...] *is deemed to have committed a crime* as defined in paragraph 1 of this Article, if he was (a) a principal or (b) was an accessory to the commission of any such crime or ordered or abetted the same or (c) took a consenting part therein or (d) was connected with plans or enterprises involving its commission or (e) was a member of any organization or group connected with the commission of any such crime or (f) with reference to paragraph 1 (a) if he held a high political, civil or military (including General Staff) position in Germany or in one of its Allies, co-belligerents or satellites [...]

Article 7(1) of ICTYSt. instead reads:

A person who planned, instigated, ordered, committed or otherwise aided and abetted in the planning, preparation or execution of a crime [...] shall be individually responsible for the crime.

Control Council Law No. 10 clearly follows a *unitary model* of criminal responsibility, under which anybody who participates in criminal conduct 'is deemed to have committed the crime'. The degree of each accused's responsibility is in other words considered only at the stage of sentencing and not when imputing liability. Apart from the doubts about guilt by association under points (e) and (f) above, the system is clear and apparently easy to apply.

In contrast, the ICTY approach (which is the one accepted by contemporary international and mixed tribunals) rests on a *differentiated model*, i.e. a model requiring judges to make a finding on the mode of participation in order to impute responsibility. If a person 'orders' a crime, then, he will presumably be considered more responsible than an individual who has merely 'aided and abetted' the crime. This model ensures that an accused knows from the start what role is attributed to him by the prosecuting authorities, but – at the same time – risks simplifying with a 'label' the often complex interactions of acts and omissions through which a person participates in criminal conduct. Is it fair to say that only the person driving the bus full of civilians beyond a national border commits deportation, while those devising the appropriate legal instruments (a decree on deportation of all Muslims from a Bosnian municipality, for example) are 'ordering', 'planning', or 'aiding and abetting' deportation? Are they not all, in a sense, engaging in 'deportation'?

In international criminal law neither treaties nor case law (as indicative of customary rules) make any legal distinction between the various categories, at least as far as the consequent penalties are concerned. This lack of distinction follows both from (i) the absence of any agreed scale of penalties in international criminal law and (ii) the general character of this body of law, namely its still rudimentary nature and the ensuing lack of formalism.

Consequently, the differentiation between the various classes of participation in crimes (perpetration, co-perpetration, aiding and abetting, ordering, planning, instigation, joint criminal enterprise and so on) is merely based on the intrinsic features of each modality of participation. It serves a descriptive and conceptual or classificatory purpose only. It is in practice devoid of any relevance as far as sentencing is concerned. It is for judges to decide in each case on the *degree of culpability* of a participant in an international crime and assign the penalty accordingly, whatever the modality of participation of the offender in the crime.

1

COMMISSION

Commission is a capacious concept in international criminal law because international crimes often involve mass action. One of the challenges is attributing and defining individual responsibility in the heat and complexity of collective criminality. International criminal law has made significant strides in this task since the World War II-era military tribunals, which only rudimentarily and amorphously articulated the conceptual boundaries and interrelationships of modes of responsibility such as commission, participation in a common plan and being an accomplice.[1] In contemporary international criminal law, the term 'commission' embraces not only the simple schema of an individual committing a crime personally, for example, one person shooting another. The notion of commission also includes more complex forms that capture the culpability of a plurality of persons who contribute to the commission of the crime in differentiated ways – even if they do not physically execute the crime.

Article 25(3) of the ICCSt. is viewed as reflecting, in some respects, customary international law regarding modes of individual responsibility. The first heading holds a person responsible for a crime if that person:

(a) Commits such a crime, whether as an individual, jointly with another or through another person, regardless of whether that other person is criminally responsible.

Thus, liability for commission is contemplated for individual commission, joint commission and commission through another person. The third form of commission, through another person, is recognized by most of the major legal systems of the world and addresses the situation where another person is used as a tool to commit an international crime. While the human tool is typically envisioned as an innocent, liability can attach whether or not the intermediary is also held criminally responsible.

The excerpts below address the evidentiary and conceptual complexities of discerning individual commission in the context of crimes committed by numerous persons. Contemporary international criminal law has evolved such sophisticated doctrines to cover joint commission that the two main approaches, joint criminal enterprise doctrine and co-perpetration, are sufficiently intricate to warrant separate treatment in the following sections of this chapter.

---

[1] Article VI of the Nuremberg Charter, for example, conferred jurisdiction to try individuals who 'committed' crimes against peace, crimes against humanity and war crimes and further provided: 'Leaders, organizers, instigators and accomplices participating in the formulation or execution of a common plan or conspiracy to commit any of the foregoing crimes are responsible for all acts performed by any persons in execution of such plan.' The conceptual boundaries of the notion of commission thus appeared capacious enough to embrace commission by multiple persons through participation in the execution or formulation of a common plan. Whether this was conceived of as a form of commission or some alternative form of participation or accomplice liability was unclear, however.

Cases

USA, **US v. Potter,** *US Navy Board of Review, Judgment of 5 June 1968*

This Vietnam War-era case involves the murder and rape of inhabitants of a Vietnamese hamlet during a raid by nine US Marines on patrol. Though the task of the Marines was to set up an ambush, the accused, Private First Class John D. Potter, told his fellow Marines Monroe, Henderson, Hobson, Sullivan, Bretag, McGhen, Vogel and Boyd that plans had changed and they were to raid a hamlet instead and 'beat up the people, tear up the hooches, rape and kill if necessary'. The excerpt below details what ensued and how the individual commission of acts must often be discerned from the heat and confusion of group action.

The government's view of the scene is portrayed in its brief. We find it persuasive on the issue:

"At the last house in the hamlet, the squad discovered a number of people, the family of Dao Thinh. It was composed of Thinh, his wife (Bui Thi Huong, aged 18), his child (Dao Thien, aged 3), his sister (Pham Thi Tan), her child (Dao Thi Dao, aged 5), and his mother Nguyen Thi Lanh). Thinh was routed from the house by Monroe, who tackled him on the patio. Monroe exhibited a grenade and said to the corpsman, 'This man is VC . . .' [Viet Cong]. Then he, Potter and two others beat the man up. During the beating a woman came out of the house and approached the group. Monroe pushed her aside and knocked her down. The four men took Thinh over to the right-hand corner of the courtyard (as one would face the house) and set Bretag to guard him. Sullivan then appeared from the left side of the house with a woman and child (probably the sister and her child). An old lady (Thinh's mother) appeared in the courtyard. Then either Hobson or Henderson brought a child (Thinh's baby) from the right side of the house. All were settled in the courtyard and several members of the squad, including Sgt Vogel and Bretag, left to guard them. At some point in the foregoing train of events, the accused, Monroe, Henderson, Hobson and Sullivan went around the right side of the house, behind a detached kitchen and pigpen. Bretag was called to the area, where he found the men gathered around Thinh's wife, Bui Thi Huong; Huong had been dragged back there, thrown to the ground and her trousers removed. Once more, Bretag carried out his examination for venereal disease. On his announcement that he was uncertain whether she was infected or not, the group discussed the matter. Monroe mounted the girl. Three more persons had intercourse with her, with Potter finishing it up.

Thinh, who was still out on the patio, apparently realized what was happening to his wife; he began talking and then screaming. Bretag and another Marine tried to quiet him, but their efforts, including use of a gag, were unsuccessful. Thinh's sister, also screaming, started towards Thinh and the right side of the court. The commotion attracted most of the squad, who gathered in a bunch in the court. Potter or Monroe said, 'Let's get out of here.' The group started to move off, and then Potter or Monroe said, 'We better shoot 'em.' Pfc Boyd recounted what then happened:

'At this time they stopped, Potter, Monroe, myself turned around to see . . . .

That's when I saw Potter shoot the man, the Vietnamese man and the old lady.

He aimed his rifle in and fired off a three or four round burst which hit the man and the Vietnamese woman. [. . .]

Then I watched Potter aim his rifle towards this young girl . . . and the baby, and fire a three or four round burst at them which knocked the woman down . . . .

When he fired at her, it knocked her down on her stomach, and the baby she had went flying off the patio into the rice paddy. . . .'

Boyd and Monroe then opened up on the body of Thinh's mother and the body of Thinh, respectively. [. . .]

Bretag, who had been off to the right of the house, came into the courtyard and approached Thinh's mother. He saw a 'large visceration,' which he described as "a large hole in the peritoneum with the intestines coming out." Her aorta appeared to have been severed.

Potter came over and turned over the body of the old woman. She moaned, and Bretag exclaimed 'Damn, she's still alive.' The accused backed away a few paces and raised his rifle. Bretag moved out of the line of fire and heard him trigger a 5-round burst. [. . .]

Sometime during the latter part of the business, the rape victim, Huong, staggered onto the patio. [. . .] The Marines, hearing her, fired. Huong, was only wounded in the arm, but she lay still. They examined her, decided she was dead and moved off.

The squad had reached the outskirts of the yard when Potter decided they should go back and throw a grenade, to make the carnage 'look good.' One man – Bretag said it was the accused – ran back into the courtyard and tossed a grenade. The squad left the scene, but Potter stopped them again and he, Monroe and Hobson concocted a false account of what had happened. [. . .]"

On the ample evidence adduced the triers of fact were convinced beyond a reasonable doubt that the named victims, as pleaded in the two specifications of Charge I, were murdered as that term was defined to them by the Law Officer, we can require no more. Likewise, this Board is convinced. [. . .]

IV

Appellant's fourth assignment [of error] brings into question the government counsel's opening argument. In concluding his opening argument, trial counsel stated:

"The government feels the evidence is clear and convincing. It feels that the evidence points directly at the accused, Pfc Potter, as the instigator, architect and chief perpetrator of the crimes that occurred on the evening of the 23rd of September in the Xuan Ngoc area village." [. . .]

At bar, the prosecutor merely told the court that the government "feels" the evidence is sufficient to prove its case against the accused, like the situation in Meisch, supra. This is merely a statement that the government believes it has introduced enough evidence to warrant a finding of guilty – or enough evidence to take to the triers. We find no prejudice to the accused and no merit to the assignment.

V

Appellant's fifth assignment of error is a claim that the evidence fails to support the charge of the rape of Huong beyond a reasonable doubt. We simply do not agree. An eyewitness testified he saw the accused, Potter, on Huong and she had her legs locked behind him. She testified she had intercourse with four persons forcibly and against her will. Appellant questions the "unlikely posture for resistance," which the crossed legs of the complaining witness implies. The suggestion is not without some force. However, the triers of fact found the offense as delineated to them by the law officer's instruction beyond a reasonable doubt and we, being without doubt, are not willing to upset the findings.

Potter was convicted of, among other, things, the premeditated murders of Dao Quan Thinh, Dao Thien, Nguyen Thi Lanh, Pham Tai Tan and the rape of Bui Thi Huong. He was sentenced to a dishonorable discharge, forfeitures, reduction in pay grade and confinement at hard labour for life.

The schema of perpetration in *Potter* is relatively simple compared to most international crimes. The accused, Potter, personally shot the victims, together with other members of his squad, and was the fourth man to rape Huong. He personally committed the elements of the crimes of which he was convicted. Rather than conceptual, the main complexities in this case are of proof. When multiple actors are involved in the murders and rape – each with incentive to shift the blame – how do we reliably determine who did what? Even when there are survivors, how can the victim identify one fearsome stranger from another? In the heat and confusion of such crimes and ensuing fragmentary impressions, how can we be sure who did what?

In other cases, involving larger-scale crimes, the conceptual boundaries of the notion of commission may be the indistinct matter. When multiple actors are involved in a crime, people may have different roles and take varying degrees and measures of actions. A frequent paradox is that those dealing the death blows may not be the most culpable actor in the perpetration of the crime. The excerpt below illustrates how the ICTR has tried to adjust the concept of commission to account for this complexity.

ICTR, Gacumbitsi v. Prosecutor, Appeals Chamber, Judgment of 7 July 2006

During the Rwandan genocide, the accused, Sylvestre Gacumbitsi was *bourgmestre* (mayor) of Rusumo Commune and the highest-ranking local administrative official. The Trial Chamber convicted Gacumbitsi of, among other things, committing, planning, ordering, instigating and aiding and abetting genocide. The conviction was based on findings that Gacumbitsi urged officials in his commune to incite the Hutu to kill the Tutsi, directly urged Hutu crowds to arm themselves with machetes and kill all the Tutsi, instigated the rape of Tutsi women and girls and personally killed a Tutsi surnamed Murefu on 15 April 1994. That murder signalled the beginning of Hutu attacks on Tutsis at Nyarubuye Parish leading to the massacre of thousands of Tutsis who had sought refuge over three days.

Gacumbitsi was sentenced to 30 years in prison. On appeal, Gacumbitsi challenged, among other things, his conviction for committing genocide. The Appeals Chamber rejected Gacumbitsi's challenge, adding that even if the finding that Gacumbitsi personally killed a victim, Mr Murefu, were set aside, he should be convicted for commission.

59. In addition, by a differently composed majority, the Appeals Chamber holds, Judge Güney dissenting, that even if the killing of Mr. Murefu were to be set aside, the Trial Chamber's conclusion that the Appellant "committed" genocide would still be valid. The Trial Chamber convicted the Appellant of "ordering" and "instigating" genocide on the basis of findings of fact detailing certain conduct that, in the view of the Appeals Chamber, should be characterized not just as "ordering" and "instigating" genocide, but also as "committing" genocide.

60. As the Trial Chamber observed, the term "committed" in Article 6(1) of the Statute has been held to refer "generally to the direct and physical perpetration of the crime by the offender himself." In the context of genocide, however, "direct and physical perpetration" need not mean physical killing; other acts can constitute direct participation in the actus reus of the crime.[2] Here, the accused was physically present at the scene of the Nyarubuye Parish

---

2 [145] For instance, it has been recognized that selection of prisoners for extermination played an integral role in the Nazi genocide. *See, e.g.*, Judgment of the International Military Tribunal for the Trial of German

massacre, which he "directed" and "played a leading role in conducting and, especially, supervising". It was he who personally directed the Tutsi and Hutu refugees to separate – and that action, which is not adequately described by any other mode of Article 6(1) liability, was as much an integral part of the genocide as were the killings which it enabled. [...]

61. The Appeals Chamber is persuaded that in the circumstances of this case, the modes of liability used by the Trial Chamber to categorize this conduct – "ordering" and "instigating" – do not, taken alone, fully capture the Appellant's criminal responsibility. The Appellant did not simply "order" or "plan" genocide from a distance and leave it to others to ensure that his orders and plans were carried out; nor did he merely "instigate" the killings. Rather, he was present at the crime scene to supervise and direct the massacre, and participated in it actively by separating the Tutsi refugees so that they could be killed. The Appeals Chamber finds by majority, Judge Güney dissenting, that this constitutes "committing" genocide.

Partially Dissenting Opinion of Judge Güney

2. I agree with the present judgement that the Appellant committed genocide through his killing of Mr. Murefu. However, I disagree with the conclusion that "even if the killing of Mr. Murefu were to be set aside, the Trial Chamber's conclusion that the Appellant 'committed' genocide would still be valid" because the Appellant "was present at the crime scene to supervise and direct the massacre, and participated in it actively by separating the Tutsi refugees so that they could be killed". [...]

4. According to the *Tadic* Appeal Judgement, "committing" refers to a) "the physical perpetration of a crime by the offender himself, or the culpable omission of an act that was mandated by a rule of criminal law"; or b) "participation in the realization of a common design or purpose" (or participation in a joint criminal enterprise). Until the present case, "committing" has always been understood in one of those two ways, and attempts to extend the meaning of "committing" further have not been accepted.

5. [...] In the present case, a majority of the Appeals Chamber concludes that joint criminal enterprise was not properly pleaded [in the Indictment], and that the Appellant can therefore not be convicted on this basis, a conclusion with which I agree. As to physical perpetration, the Appellant can be convicted of having committed genocide pursuant to Article 2(2) (a) of the Statute for the killing of Mr. Murefu. However, even if the Appellant was present at Nyarubuye Parish, played a leading role in conducting and supervising the attack and directed the Tutsi and Hutu refugees to separate, this does not entail that, in addition to "ordering" and "instigating" genocide, he also "committed" genocide. Plainly, "playing a leading role in conducting and [...] supervising" the attack and directing the refugees to separate do not constitute the physical perpetration by the Appellant of one of the acts listed at Article 2(2) of the Statute.[3]

Major War Criminals, Nuremberg, 30th September and 1st October, 1946, p. 63 (London: His Majesty's Stationary Office, 1946) (Reprinted Buffalo, New York: William S. Hein & Co., Inc., 2001) (describing the selection process at Auschwitz) [...]

[3] [7] Article 2(2) of the Statute reads as follows:
Genocide means any of the following acts committed with intent to destroy, in whole or in part, a national, ethnical, racial or religious group, [as such]:
(a) Killing members of the group;
(b) Causing serious bodily or mental harm to members of the group;
(c) Deliberately inflicting on the group conditions of life calculated to bring about its physical destruction in whole or in part;
(d) Imposing measures intended to prevent births within the group;
(e) Forcibly transferring children of the group to another group.

COMMENTARY

Consider Judge Güney's critique of the majority's rationale: how does Gacumbitsi's presence supervising the massacres and separating the Tutsi refugees for slaughter constitute one of the five forms of underlying genocidal acts, which, as discussed in the chapter on genocide (Part II(3)), are:

(a) Killing members of the group.

(b) Causing serious bodily or mental harm to members of the group.

(c) Deliberately inflicting on the group conditions of life calculated to bring about its physical destruction in whole or in part.

(d) Imposing measures intended to prevent births within the group.

(e) Forcibly transferring children of the group to another group?

Is Judge Güney's dissent overly formalistic, or is the majority straining to expand the notion of commission to get around a charging error, the omission of the charge of participation in a joint criminal enterprise? When someone stirs the crowd to carry out the crime that involves killing as the underlying *actus reus*, is it fair to say they have committed the crime though they never personally bloodied their hands?

The equities in this case may elicit sympathy with the majority's conclusion that Gacumbitsi, a leader who stirred the crowd to act, can be said to have committed the crime of genocide without physically perpetrating the underlying act of mass killings. But what if at issue was an ordinary person, swept up in the mob frenzy and hatred, who helped separate out Tutsis from Hutus? Would it be fair to say that this contribution to the crime is sufficient to deem the individual to have committed genocide or is this form of participation more accurately characterized as aiding and abetting genocide? How does the *mens rea* of the individual matter in weighing this question?

Or to take another example drawn from real-life situations, consider crimes, such as the deportation or forcible transfer of people from their home nations or regions. Would it be fair to consider someone who drove the buses carrying away forcibly displaced civilians as 'committing' deportation? What about the person putting people on the bus or the person issuing a call for the deportation or forcible transfer?

How you view the situation – and your perception of the import of the question – may vary depending on whether you are socialized in a legal culture with a 'unitary perpetrator' model or a 'differential participation' model. The distinctions between the two models are described in the Introduction to Part III.

QUESTIONS

1. As you learned in Part I(2) on the principle of *nullum crimen sine lege*, international criminal law does not prescribe a scale of penalties for crimes, much less calibrate penalties to modes of participation. What is at stake, then, in finding that an accused not only ordered and instigated a crime like genocide, but actually 'committed' it? What is the expressive force of saying someone 'committed' a crime like genocide?

2. What are the risks and benefits of expanding the notion of commission in international criminal law to include those who do not physically perpetrate the *actus reus* of the crime?

3. Criminal responsibility for omissions are not specified in the ICCSt. as a basis of individual criminal responsibility except for military commanders who fail to exercise proper control or take measures to prevent or repress the commission of crimes by their forces. The general eschewal regarding omissions is viewed as a refusal to impose individual criminal responsibility for commission by omission. Why would the drafters of the Rome Statute decline to specify that omissions may be a form of commission of international crimes?

FURTHER READING

A. Eser, 'Individual Criminal Responsibility', in Antonio Cassese *et al.* (eds), *The Rome Statute of the International Criminal Court: A Commentary*, Vol. I (Oxford: Oxford University Press, 2002), 767–821.

B. Swart, 'Modes of International Criminal Liability', in *Oxford Companion*, 82–93.

Werle, *Principles*, 166–71.

2

JOINT CRIMINAL ENTERPRISE

As introduced in the preceding chapter on commission, crimes – and international crimes in particular – are often committed by a group of people acting together. The contribution to a specific crime by each of these persons may be difficult to ascertain, although these persons all acted in furtherance of a common criminal purpose.

In addressing the general question of co-perpetrators, international courts do not have a general doctrine or crime of conspiracy at their disposal. As the US Supreme Court remarked,[1] conspiracy is not a crime under customary law – except in specific circumstances (e.g. conspiracy to commit genocide in Article 3(b) of the Genocide Convention, also reproduced in Articles 4(3) of the ICTYSt. and 2(3) of the ICTRSt.). Scholars have noted that no such crime has emerged in international law because, inter alia, domestic legal systems around the world do not provide a uniform answer to the question of group criminality: with some important exceptions, the civil law tradition does not consider merely entering into an agreement to commit a crime to be punishable as such, until and unless a crime is actually perpetrated.

In its seminal and landmark *Tadić* case in 1999, the ICTY, not being endowed with an all-encompassing crime of conspiracy, developed the doctrine of 'common purpose' or 'joint criminal enterprise' (JCE). In that case, the ICTY construed JCE as a form of 'commission'. The contours of this doctrine, and its rooting in customary international law, will become apparent when assessing how the ICTY Appeals Chamber described, and later refined, the concept of JCE. The ICTY identified three forms of JCE (often referred to as 'basic', 'systemic' and 'extended'), which share the *actus reus* requirements that a person significantly – but not necessarily substantially – participate in a common plan involving the commission of a crime under the ICTYSt. The *mens rea* requirements are different for each form, as will be seen below.

Scholars and dissenting judges have criticized JCE, suggesting that its application may result in 'guilt by association'. This risk would be greatest in large-scale cases, where the contribution of an accused might in fact be rather remote from the actual crime; think, for example, of the politician concerned with the organization of transport and security for convoys in a war zone, including (but not limited to) the convoys of deported persons. The issues of (i) the degree of participation in the criminal enterprise of each participant in this type of situation and of (ii) the *mens rea* required to incur liability are indeed valid questions raised in all cases of joint criminal conduct, including the common law concept of conspiracy. The danger of convicting a person who associated with (alleged) criminals but did not actually contribute to crimes in any meaningful way should never be underestimated. However, it must also be recognized that the ICTY has so far shown restraint in its application of JCE to individual cases, declining to attribute responsibility on the basis

---

[1] *Hamdan* v. *Rumsfeld* 548 U.S. 557, 606–12 (2006))

of this doctrine when the contribution of the accused to the crime was too remote or his *mens rea* could not be established.

Cases

ICTY, Prosecutor v. Tadić, *Appeals Chamber, Judgment of 15 July 1999*

Duško Tadić was a reserve police officer in the municipality of Prijedor, in Bosnia and Herzegovina. In May and June 1992, during the ethnic cleansing of areas of Bosnia and Herzegovina that had fallen under the control of Bosnian Serb forces, Tadić participated in the collection and forced transfer of civilians. The Prosecutor charged him with individual criminal responsibility for his role both in detention camps and during certain attacks on villages and hamlets near Prijedor. While convicting him of various counts of persecution as a crime against humanity for various killings and beatings, the Trial Chamber acquitted Tadić, inter alia, of two counts of murder in the village of Jaskići. The Trial Chamber reasoned that, while Tadić was indeed part of the group of Serbs who rounded up the men in the village, his personal role in certain killings had not been proved beyond reasonable doubt. The Appeals Chamber, in its Judgment of 15 July 1999, reversed with the following reasoning.

178. The Trial Chamber found, amongst other facts, that on 14 June 1992, the Appellant, with other armed men, participated in the removal of men, who had been separated from women and children, from the village of Sivci to the Keraterm camp, and also participated in the calling-out of residents, the separation of men from women and children, and the beating and taking away of men in the village of Jaskići. It also found that five men were killed in the latter village. [. . .]

185. The question therefore arises whether under international criminal law the Appellant can be held criminally responsible for the killing of the five men from Jaskići even though there is no evidence that he personally killed any of them. The two central issues are:

(i) whether the acts of one person can give rise to the criminal culpability of another where both participate in the execution of a common criminal plan; and

(ii) what degree of *mens rea* is required in such a case.

186. The basic assumption must be that in international law as much as in national systems, the foundation of criminal responsibility is the principle of personal culpability: nobody may be held criminally responsible for acts or transactions in which he has not personally engaged or in some other way participated (*nulla poena sine culpa*). In national legal systems this principle is laid down in Constitutions, in laws, or in judicial decisions. In international criminal law the principle is laid down, *inter alia*, in Article 7(1) of the Statute of the International Tribunal [. . .]

Article 7(1) [. . .] sets out the parameters of personal criminal responsibility under the Statute. Any act falling under one of the five categories contained in the provision may entail the criminal responsibility of the perpetrator or whoever has participated in the crime in one of the ways specified in the same provision of the Statute.

187. Bearing in mind the preceding general propositions, it must be ascertained whether criminal responsibility for participating in a common criminal purpose falls within the ambit of Article 7(1) of the Statute.

188. This provision covers first and foremost the physical perpetration of a crime by the offender himself, or the culpable omission of an act that was mandated by a rule of criminal law. However, the commission of one of the crimes envisaged in Articles 2, 3, 4 or 5 of the Statute might also occur through participation in the realisation of a common design or purpose.

189. An interpretation of the Statute based on its object and purpose leads to the conclusion that the Statute intends to extend the jurisdiction of the International Tribunal to *all* those "responsible for serious violations of international humanitarian law" committed in the former Yugoslavia (Article 1). As is apparent from the wording of both Article 7(1) and the provisions setting forth the crimes over which the International Tribunal has jurisdiction (Articles 2 to 5), such responsibility for serious violations of international humanitarian law is not limited merely to those who actually carry out the *actus reus* of the enumerated crimes but appears to extend also to other offenders (see in particular Article 2, which refers to committing or *ordering* to be committed grave breaches of the Geneva Conventions and Article 4 which sets forth various types of offences in relation to genocide, including *conspiracy*, *incitement*, *attempt* and *complicity*).

190. It should be noted that this notion is spelled out in the Secretary General's Report, according to which:

> The Secretary-General believes that *all* persons who *participate* in the planning, preparation or execution of serious violations of international humanitarian law in the former Yugoslavia are individually responsible for such violations.

Thus, all those who have engaged in serious violations of international humanitarian law, whatever the manner in which they may have perpetrated, or participated in the perpetration of those violations, must be brought to justice. If this is so, it is fair to conclude that the Statute does not confine itself to providing for jurisdiction over those persons who plan, instigate, order, physically perpetrate a crime or otherwise aid and abet in its planning, preparation or execution. The Statute does not stop there. It does not exclude those modes of participating in the commission of crimes which occur where several persons having a common purpose embark on criminal activity that is then carried out either jointly or by some members of this plurality of persons. Whoever contributes to the commission of crimes by the group of persons or some members of the group, in execution of a common criminal purpose, may be held to be criminally liable, subject to certain conditions, which are specified below.

191. The above interpretation is not only dictated by the object and purpose of the Statute but is also warranted by the very nature of many international crimes which are committed most commonly in wartime situations. Most of the time these crimes do not result from the criminal propensity of single individuals but constitute manifestations of collective criminality: the crimes are often carried out by groups of individuals acting in pursuance of a common criminal design. Although only some members of the group may physically perpetrate the criminal act (murder, extermination, wanton destruction of cities, towns or villages, etc.), the participation and contribution of the other members of the group is often vital in facilitating the commission of the offence in question. It follows that the moral gravity of such participation is often no less – or indeed no different – from that of those actually carrying out the acts in question.

192. Under these circumstances, to hold criminally liable as a perpetrator only the person who materially performs the criminal act would disregard the role as co-perpetrators of all those who in some way made it possible for the perpetrator physically to carry out that criminal act. At the same time, depending upon the circumstances, to hold the latter liable only as aiders and abettors might understate the degree of their criminal responsibility.

193. This interpretation, based on the Statute and the inherent characteristics of many crimes perpetrated in wartime, warrants the conclusion that international criminal responsibility

embraces actions perpetrated by a collectivity of persons in furtherance of a common criminal design. It may also be noted that – as will be mentioned below – international criminal rules on common purpose are substantially rooted in, and to a large extent reflect, the position taken by many States of the world in their national legal systems.

194. However, the Tribunal's Statute does not specify (either expressly or by implication) the objective and subjective elements (*actus reus* and *mens rea*) of this category of collective criminality. To identify these elements one must turn to customary international law. Customary rules on this matter are discernible on the basis of various elements: chiefly case law and a few instances of international legislation.

195. Many post-World War II cases concerning war crimes proceed upon the principle that when two or more persons act together to further a common criminal purpose, offences perpetrated by any of them may entail the criminal liability of all the members of the group. Close scrutiny of the relevant case law shows that broadly speaking, the notion of common purpose encompasses three distinct categories of collective criminality.

196. The first such category is represented by cases where all co-defendants, acting pursuant to a common design, possess the same criminal intention; for instance, the formulation of a plan among the co-perpetrators to kill, where, in effecting this common design (and even if each co-perpetrator carries out a different role within it), they nevertheless all possess the intent to kill. The objective and subjective prerequisites for imputing criminal responsibility to a participant who did not, or cannot be proven to have, effected the killing are as follows: (i) the accused must voluntarily participate in one aspect of the common design (for instance, by inflicting non-fatal violence upon the victim, or by providing material assistance to or facilitating the activities of his co-perpetrators); and (ii) the accused, even if not personally effecting the killing, must nevertheless intend this result.

197. With regard to this category, reference can be made to the *Georg Otto Sandrock et al.* case (also known as the *Almelo Trial*).[2] There a British court found that three Germans who had killed a British prisoner of war were guilty under the doctrine of "common enterprise". It was clear that they all had had the intention of killing the British soldier, although each of them played a different role. They therefore were all co-perpetrators of the crime of murder. Similarly, in the *Hoelzer et al.* case, brought before a Canadian military court, in his summing up the Judge Advocate spoke of a "common enterprise" with regard to the murder of a Canadian prisoner of war by three Germans, and emphasised that the three all knew that the purpose of taking the Canadian to a particular area was to kill him.[3]

198. Another instance of co-perpetratorship of this nature is provided by the case of *Jepsen and others*.[4] A British court had to pronounce upon the responsibility of Jepsen (one of several accused) for the deaths of concentration camp internees who, in the few weeks leading up to the capitulation of Germany in 1945, were in transit to another concentration camp. In this regard, the Prosecutor submitted (and this was not rebutted by the Judge Advocate) that:

[I]f Jepsen was joining in this voluntary slaughter of eighty or so people, helping the others by doing his share of killing, the whole eighty odd deaths can be laid at his door and at the door of any single man who was in any way assisting in that act.

---

[2] [233] *Trial of Otto Sandrock and three others*, British Military Court for the Trial of War Criminals, held at the Court House, Almelo, Holland, on 24th–26th November, 1945, UNWCC, vol. I, p. 35.

[3] [235] *Hoelzer et al.*, Canadian Military Court, Aurich, Germany, Record of Proceedings 25 March–6 April 1946, vol. I, pp. 341, 347, 349 (RCAF Binder 181.009 (D2474); copy on file with the International Tribunal's Library).

[4] [236] *Trial of Gustav Alfred Jepsen and others, Proceedings of a War Crimes Trial held at Luneberg, Germany* (13–23 August, 1946), judgement of 24 August 1946 (original transcripts in Public Record Office, Kew, Richmond; on file with the International Tribunal's Library).

In a similar vein, the Judge Advocate noted in *Schonfeld* that:

> if several persons combine for an unlawful purpose or for a lawful purpose to be effected
> by unlawful means, and one of them in carrying out that purpose, kills a man, it is murder
> in all who are present [...] provided that the death was caused by a member of the party in
> the course of his endeavours to effect the common object of the assembly.[5]

199. It can be noted that some cases appear broadly to link the notion of common purpose
to that of causation. In this regard, the *Ponzano* case,[6] which concerned the killing of four
British prisoners of war in violation of the rules of warfare, can be mentioned. Here, the Judge
Advocate adopted the approach suggested by the Prosecutor, and stressed:

> [...] the requirement that an accused, before he can be found guilty, must have been con-
> cerned in the offence. [T]o be concerned in the commission of a criminal offence [...] does
> not only mean that you are the person who in fact inflicted the fatal injury and directly
> caused death, be it by shooting or by any other violent means; it also means an indirect
> degree of participation [...]. [I]n other words, he must be the cog in the wheel of events
> leading up to the result which in fact occurred. He can further that object not only by giv-
> ing orders for a criminal offence to be committed, but he can further that object by a vari-
> ety of other means [...].

Further on, the Judge Advocate submitted that while the defendant's involvement in the criminal acts must form a link in the chain of causation, it was not necessary that his participation be a *sine qua non,* or that the offence would not have occurred but for his participation.
Consonant with the twin requirements of criminal responsibility under this category, however,
the Judge Advocate stressed the necessity of knowledge on the part of the accused as to the
intended purpose of the criminal enterprise.

200. A final case worthy of mention with regard to this first category is the *Einsatzgruppen*
case.[7] With regard to common design, a United States Tribunal sitting at Nuremberg noted
that:

> the elementary principle must be borne in mind that neither under Control Council Law
> No. 10 nor under any known system of criminal law is guilt for murder confined to the man
> who pulls the trigger or buries the corpse. In line with recognized principles common to
> all civilized legal systems, paragraph 2 of Article II of Control Council Law No. 10 specifies
> a number of types of connection with crime which are sufficient to establish guilt. Thus,
> not only are principals guilty but also accessories, those who take a consenting part in the
> commission of crime or are connected with plans or enterprises involved in its commis-
> sion, those who order or abet crime, and those who belong to an organization or group
> engaged in the commission of crime. These provisions embody no harsh or novel principles
> of criminal responsibility [...].

201. It should be noted that in many post-World War II trials held in other countries, courts
took the same approach to instances of crimes in which two or more persons participated with
a different degree of involvement. However, they did not rely upon the notion of common

---

[5] [238] *Trial of Franz Schonfeld and others*, British Military Court, Essen, June 11th–26th, 1946, UNWCC,
vol. XI, p. 68 (summing up of the Judge Advocate).

[6] [239] *Trial of Feurstein and others*, Proceedings of a War Crimes Trial held at Hamburg, Germany (4–24
August, 1948), judgement of 24 August 1948 (original transcripts in Public Record Office, Kew, Richmond; on
file with the International Tribunal's Library).

[7] [244] *The United States of America v. Otto Ohlenforf et al., Trials of War Criminals before the Nuremberg
Military Tribunals under Control Council Law No. 10*, United States Government Printing Office, Washington,
1951, vol. IV, p. 3.

purpose or common design, preferring to refer instead to the notion of co-perpetration. This applies in particular to Italian and German cases.

202. The second distinct category of cases is in many respects similar to that set forth above, and embraces the so-called "concentration camp" cases. The notion of common purpose was applied to instances where the offences charged were alleged to have been committed by members of military or administrative units such as those running concentration camps; i.e., by groups of persons acting pursuant to a concerted plan. Cases illustrative of this category are *Dachau Concentration Camp*,[8] decided by a United States court sitting in Germany and *Belsen*,[9] decided by a British military court sitting in Germany. In these cases the accused held some position of authority within the hierarchy of the concentration camps. Generally speaking, the charges against them were that they had acted in pursuance of a common design to kill or mistreat prisoners and hence to commit war crimes. In his summing up in the *Belsen* case, the Judge Advocate adopted the three requirements identified by the Prosecution as necessary to establish guilt in each case: (i) the existence of an organised system to ill-treat the detainees and commit the various crimes alleged; (ii) the accused's awareness of the nature of the system; and (iii) the fact that the accused in some way actively participated in enforcing the system, i.e., encouraged, aided and abetted or in any case participated in the realisation of the common criminal design. The convictions of several of the accused appear to have been explicitly based upon these criteria.

203. This category of cases (which obviously is not applicable to the facts of the present case) is really a variant of the first category, considered above. The accused, when they were found guilty, were regarded as co-perpetrators of the crimes of ill-treatment, because of their objective "position of authority" within the concentration camp system and because they had "the power to look after the inmates and make their life satisfactory" but failed to do so. It would seem that in these cases the required *actus reus* was the active participation in the enforcement of a system of repression, as it could be inferred from the position of authority and the specific functions held by each accused. The *mens rea* element comprised: (i) knowledge of the nature of the system and (ii) the intent to further the common concerted design to ill-treat inmates. [...]

204. The third category concerns cases involving a common design to pursue one course of conduct where one of the perpetrators commits an act which, while outside the common design, was nevertheless a natural and foreseeable consequence of the effecting of that common purpose. An example of this would be a common, shared intention on the part of a group to forcibly remove members of one ethnicity from their town, village or region (to effect "ethnic cleansing") with the consequence that, in the course of doing so, one or more of the victims is shot and killed. While murder may not have been explicitly acknowledged to be part of the common design, it was nevertheless foreseeable that the forcible removal of civilians at gunpoint might well result in the deaths of one or more of those civilians. Criminal responsibility may be imputed to all participants within the common enterprise where the risk of death occurring was both a predictable consequence of the execution of the common design and the accused was either reckless or indifferent to that risk. Another example is that of a common plan to forcibly evict civilians belonging to a particular ethnic group by burning their houses; if some of the participants in the plan, in carrying out this plan, kill civilians by setting their houses on fire, all the other participants in the plan are criminally responsible for the killing if these deaths were predictable.

---

[8] [248] *Trial of Martin Gottfried Weiss and thirty-nine others*, General Military Government Court of the United States Zone, Dachau, Germany, 15th November–13th December, 1945, UNWCC, vol. XI, p. 5.

[9] [249] *Trial of Josef Kramer and 44 others*, British Military Court, Luneberg, 17th September–17th November, 1945, UNWCC, vol. II, p. 1.

205. The case-law in this category has concerned first of all cases of mob violence, that is, situations of disorder where multiple offenders act out a common purpose, where each of them commit offences against the victim, but where it is unknown or impossible to ascertain exactly which acts were carried out by which perpetrator, or when the causal link between each act and the eventual harm caused to the victims is similarly indeterminate. Cases illustrative of this category are *Essen Lynching* and *Borkum Island*.

206. As is set forth in more detail below, the requirements which are established by these authorities are two-fold: that of a criminal intention to participate in a common criminal design and the foreseeability that criminal acts other than those envisaged in the common criminal design are likely to be committed by other participants in the common design.

207. The *Essen Lynching* (also called *Essen West*) case was brought before a British military court, although, as was stated by the court, it "was not a trial under English law".[10] Given the importance of this case, it is worth reviewing it at some length. Three British prisoners of war had been lynched by a mob of Germans in the town of Essen-West on 13 December 1944. Seven persons (two servicemen and five civilians) were charged with committing a war crime in that they were concerned in the killing of the three prisoners of war. They included a German captain, Heyer, who had placed the three British airmen under the escort of a German soldier who was to take the prisoners to a *Luftwaffe* unit for interrogation. While the escort with the prisoners was leaving, the captain had ordered that the escort should not interfere if German civilians should molest the prisoners, adding that they ought to be shot, or would be shot. This order had been given to the escort from the steps of the barracks in a loud voice so that the crowd, which had gathered, could hear and would know exactly what was going to take place. According to the summary given by the United Nations War Crimes Commission:

> [w]hen the prisoners of war were marched through one of the main streets of Essen, the crowd around grew bigger, started hitting them and throwing sticks and stones at them. An unknown German corporal actually fired a revolver at one of the airmen and wounded him in the head. When they reached the bridge, the airmen were eventually thrown over the parapet of the bridge; one of the airmen was killed by the fall; the others were not dead when they landed, but were killed by shots from the bridge and by members of the crowd who beat and kicked them to death.

208. [...] The Prosecutor then went on to add:

> the allegation of the prosecution is that every person who, following the incitement to the crowd to murder these men, voluntarily took aggressive action against any one of these three airmen *is guilty in that he is concerned in the killing*. It is impossible to separate any one of these from another; they all make up what is known as lynching. In my submission from the moment they left those barracks those men were doomed and the crowd knew they were doomed and *every person in that crowd who struck a blow is both morally and criminally responsible for the deaths of those three men*.

Since Heyer was convicted, it may be assumed that the court accepted the Prosecution arguments as to the criminal liability of Heyer (no Judge Advocate had been appointed in this case). As for the soldier escorting the airmen, he had a duty not only to prevent the prisoners from escaping but also of seeing that they were not molested; he was sentenced to imprisonment for five years (even though the Prosecutor had suggested that he was not criminally liable). According to the Report of the United Nations War Crimes Commission, three civilians "were found guilty [of murder] because every one of them had in one form or another taken part in

---

[10] [255] *Trial of Erich Heyer and six others*, British Military Court for the Trial of War Criminals, Essen, 18th–19th and 21st–22nd December, 1945, UNWCC, vol. I, p. 88, at p. 91.

the ill-treatment which eventually led to the death of the victims, though against none of the accused had it been exactly proved that they had individually shot nor given the blows which caused the death".

209. It would seem warranted to infer from the arguments of the parties and the verdict that the court upheld the notion that all the accused who were found guilty took part, in various degrees, in the killing; not all of them intended to kill but all intended to participate in the unlawful ill-treatment of the prisoners of war. Nevertheless they were all found guilty of murder, because they were all "concerned in the killing". The inference seems therefore justified that the court assumed that the convicted persons who simply struck a blow or implicitly incited the murder could have foreseen that others would kill the prisoners; hence they too were found guilty of murder.

210. A similar position was taken by a United States military court in *Kurt Goebell et al.* (also called the *Borkum Island* case). On 4 August 1944, a United States Flying Fortress was forced down on the German island of Borkum. Its seven crew members were taken prisoner and then forced to march, under military guard, through the streets of Borkum. They were first made to pass between members of the Reich's Labour Corps, who beat them with shovels, upon the order of a German officer of the *Reichsarbeitsdienst*. They were then struck by civilians on the street. Later on, while passing through another street, the mayor of Borkum shouted at them inciting the mob to kill them "like dogs". They were then beaten by civilians while the escorting guards, far from protecting them, fostered the assault and took part in the beating. When the airmen reached the city hall one was shot and killed by a German soldier, followed by the others a few minutes later, all shot by German soldiers. The accused included a few senior officers, some privates, the mayor of Borkum, some policemen, a civilian and the leader of the Reich Labour Corps. All were charged with war crimes, in particular both with "wilfully, deliberately and wrongfully encourag[ing], aid[ing], abett[ing] and participat[ing] in the killing" of the airmen and with "wilfully, deliberately and wrongfully encourag[ing], aid[ing], abett[ing] and participat[ing] in assaults upon" the airmen.[11] In his opening statement the Prosecutor developed the doctrine of common design. [. . .]

In short, noted the Prosecutor, the accused were "cogs in the wheel of common design, all equally important, each cog doing the part assigned to it. And the wheel of wholesale murder could not turn without all the cogs". As a consequence, according to the Prosecutor, if it were proved beyond a reasonable doubt "that each one of these accused played *his part* in mob violence which led to the unlawful killing of the seven American flyers, [. . .] under the law *each and every one of the accused* [was] guilty of murder".

211. It bears emphasising that by taking the approach just summarised, the Prosecutor substantially propounded a doctrine of common purpose which presupposes that all the participants in the common purpose shared the same criminal intent, namely, to commit murder. In other words, the Prosecutor adhered to the doctrine of common purpose mentioned above with regard to the first category of cases. It is interesting to note that the various defence counsel denied the applicability of this common design doctrine, not, however, on principle, but merely on the facts of the case. [. . .]

212. In this case too, no Judge Advocate stated the law. However, it may be fairly assumed that in the event, the court upheld the common design doctrine, but in a different form, for it found some defendants guilty of both the killing and assault charges while others were only found guilty of assault.

213. It may be inferred from this case that all the accused found guilty were held responsible for pursuing a criminal common design, the intent being to assault the prisoners of war.

---

[11] [261] *See* Charge Sheet, in U.S. National Archives Microfilm Publications, I (on file with the International Tribunal's Library).

However, some of them were also found guilty of murder, even where there was no evidence that they had actually killed the prisoners. Presumably, this was on the basis that the accused, whether by virtue of their status, role or conduct, were in a position to have predicted that the assault would lead to the killing of the victims by some of those participating in the assault.

The Appeals Chamber further analysed other post-World War II cases before Italian courts.

220. In sum, the Appeals Chamber holds the view that the notion of common design as a form of accomplice liability is firmly established in customary international law and in addition is upheld, albeit implicitly, in the Statute of the International Tribunal. As for the objective and subjective elements of the crime, the case law shows that the notion has been applied to three distinct categories of cases. First, in cases of co-perpetration, where all participants in the common design possess the same criminal intent to commit a crime (and one or more of them actually perpetrate the crime, with intent). Secondly, in the so-called "concentration camp" cases, where the requisite *mens rea* comprises knowledge of the nature of the system of ill-treatment and intent to further the common design of ill-treatment. Such intent may be proved either directly or as a matter of inference from the nature of the accused's authority within the camp or organisational hierarchy. With regard to the third category of cases, it is appropriate to apply the notion of "common purpose" only where the following requirements concerning *mens rea* are fulfilled: (i) the intention to take part in a joint criminal enterprise and to further – individually and jointly – the criminal purposes of that enterprise; and (ii) the foreseeability of the possible commission by other members of the group of offences that do not constitute the object of the common criminal purpose. Hence, the participants must have had in mind the intent, for instance, to ill-treat prisoners of war (even if such a plan arose extemporaneously) and one or some members of the group must have actually killed them. In order for responsibility for the deaths to be imputable to the others, however, everyone in the group must have been able to *predict* this result. It should be noted that more than negligence is required. What is required is a state of mind in which a person, although he did not intend to bring about a certain result, was aware that the actions of the group were most likely to lead to that result but nevertheless willingly took that risk. In other words, the so-called *dolus eventualis* is required (also called "advertent recklessness" in some national legal systems).

221. In addition to the aforementioned case law, the notion of common plan has been upheld in at least two international treaties. The first of these is the International Convention for the Suppression of Terrorist Bombing, adopted by consensus by the United Nations General Assembly through resolution 52/164 of 15 December 1997 and opened for signature on 9 January 1998. Pursuant to Article 2(3)(c) of the Convention, offences envisaged in the Convention may be committed by any person who:

[i]n any other way [other than participating as an accomplice, or organising or directing others to commit an offence] contributes to the commission of one or more offences as set forth in paragraphs 1 or 2 of the present article by a group of persons acting with a common purpose; such contribution shall be intentional and either be made with the aim of furthering the general criminal activity or purpose of the group or be made in the knowledge of the intention of the group to commit the offence or offences concerned. [...]

222. A substantially similar notion was subsequently laid down in Article 25 of the Statute of the International Criminal Court, adopted by a Diplomatic Conference in Rome on 17 July 1998 ("Rome Statute"). [...]

224. As pointed out above, the doctrine of acting in pursuance of a common purpose is rooted in the national law of many States. Some countries act upon the principle that where

multiple persons participate in a common purpose or common design, all are responsible for the ensuing criminal conduct, whatever their degree or form of participation, provided all had the intent to perpetrate the crime envisaged in the common purpose. If one of the participants commits a crime not envisaged in the common purpose or common design, he alone will incur criminal responsibility for such a crime. These countries include Germany and the Netherlands. Other countries also uphold the principle whereby if persons take part in a common plan or common design to commit a crime, all of them are criminally responsible for the crime, whatever the role played by each of them. However, in these countries, if one of the persons taking part in a common criminal plan or enterprise perpetrates another offence that was outside the common plan but nevertheless foreseeable, those persons are all fully liable for that offence. These countries include civil law systems, such as that of France and Italy. They also embrace common law jurisdictions such as England and Wales, Canada, the United States, Australia and Zambia.

225. It should be emphasised that reference to national legislation and case law only serves to show that the notion of common purpose upheld in international criminal law has an underpinning in many national systems. [...]

226. The Appeals Chamber considers that the consistency and cogency of the case law and the treaties referred to above, as well as their consonance with the general principles on criminal responsibility laid down both in the Statute and general international criminal law and in national legislation, warrant the conclusion that case law reflects customary rules of international criminal law.

227. In sum, the objective elements (*actus reus*) of this mode of participation in one of the crimes provided for in the Statute (with regard to each of the three categories of cases) are as follows:

  i.   *A plurality of persons.* They need not be organised in a military, political or administrative structure, as is clearly shown by the *Essen Lynching* and the *Kurt Goebell* cases.

  ii. *The existence of a common plan, design or purpose which amounts to or involves the commission of a crime provided for in the Statute.* There is no necessity for this plan, design or purpose to have been previously arranged or formulated. The common plan or purpose may materialise extemporaneously and be inferred from the fact that a plurality of persons acts in unison to put into effect a joint criminal enterprise.

  iii. *Participation of the accused in the common design* involving the perpetration of one of the crimes provided for in the Statute. This participation need not involve commission of a specific crime under one of those provisions (for example, murder, extermination, torture, rape, etc.), but may take the form of assistance in, or contribution to, the execution of the common plan or purpose.

228. By contrast, the *mens rea* element differs according to the category of common design under consideration. With regard to the first category, what is required is the intent to perpetrate a certain crime (this being the shared intent on the part of all co-perpetrators). With regard to the second category (which, as noted above, is really a variant of the first), personal knowledge of the system of ill-treatment is required (whether proved by express testimony or a matter of reasonable inference from the accused's position of authority), as well as the intent to further this common concerted system of ill-treatment. With regard to the third category, what is required is the *intention* to participate in and further the criminal activity or the criminal purpose of a group and to contribute to the joint criminal enterprise or in any event to the commission of a crime by the group. In addition, responsibility for a crime other than the one agreed upon in the common plan arises only if, under the circumstances of the case, (i) it was *foreseeable* that such a crime might be perpetrated by one or other members of the group and (ii) the accused *willingly took that risk*. [...]

231. The Appellant actively took part in the common criminal purpose to rid the Prijedor region of the non-Serb population, by committing inhumane acts. The common criminal purpose was not to kill all non-Serb men; from the evidence adduced and accepted, it is clear that killings frequently occurred in the effort to rid the Prijedor region of the non-Serb population. That the Appellant had been aware of the killings accompanying the commission of inhumane acts against the non-Serb population is beyond doubt. That is the context in which the attack on Jaskići and his participation therein, as found by the Trial Chamber as well as the Appeals Chamber above, should be seen. [...]

232. The Appellant was an armed member of an armed group that, in the context of the conflict in the Prijedor region, attacked Jaskići on 14 June 1992. The Trial Chamber found the following:

> Of the killing of the five men in Jaskići, the witnesses Draguna Jaskić, Zemka Sahbaz and Senija Elkasović saw their five dead bodies lying in the village when the women were able to leave their houses after the armed men had gone; Senija Elkasović saw that four of them had been shot in the head. She had heard shooting after the men from her house were taken away.

The Appellant actively took part in this attack, rounding up and severely beating some of the men from Jaskići. As the Trial Chamber further noted:

> [t]hat the armed men were violent was not in doubt, a number of these witnesses were themselves threatened with death by the armed men as the men of the village were being taken away. Apart from that, their beating of the men from the village, in some cases beating them into insensibility, as they lay on the road, is further evidence of their violence.

Accordingly, the only possible inference to be drawn is that the Appellant had the intention to further the criminal purpose to rid the Prijedor region of the non-Serb population, by committing inhumane acts against them. That non-Serbs might be killed in the effecting of this common aim was, in the circumstances of the present case, foreseeable. The Appellant was aware that the actions of the group of which he was a member were likely to lead to such killings, but he nevertheless willingly took that risk.

233. [...] The Appeals Chamber therefore holds that under the provisions of Article 7(1) of the Statute, the Trial Chamber should have found the Appellant guilty.

....

ICTY, **Prosecutor *v.* Brđanin,** *Appeals Chamber, Judgment of 3 April 2007*

Radoslav Brđanin was a politician in Bosnia Herzegovina. In May 1992, he was elected President of a regional 'crisis staff', a civilian-military structure set up for emergency periods which soon evolved into a "War Presidency" of the Autonomous Region of Krajina (ARK), which in turn included various municipalities. The crisis staff and the War Presidency brought together civilian, police, and military authorities at a regional level. The Trial Chamber convicted Brđanin of persecution and other crimes against humanity as well as various war crimes (but acquitted him of the charge of genocide). However, due to the large scale of the enterprise, it ruled that the most appropriate mode of responsibility to define Brđanin's conduct was not JCE, but 'aiding and abetting'. It reasoned that the Prosecutor had failed to show (i) that all of the principal perpetrators (the individuals who 'pulled the trigger') were members of the JCE together with Brđanin and (ii) that there had been an agreement or understanding between Brđanin and them to commit the crimes in furtherance of the common criminal purpose. Thus, Brđanin could not be considered responsible for their crimes as if he had specifically foreseen, or agreed to them. The rationale for this finding was that the doctrine of JCE had been articulated in *Tadić* and subsequent cases in order to target small groups acting together, not extended political-military structures that make use of other people to further their criminal goals. The Appeals Chamber, in its Judgment of 3 April 2007, for the first time explicitly dealt with the question of how to apply JCE to a large-scale enterprise.

After discussing the ambiguities in *Tadić*, as well as two post-World War II cases – the *Justice* and the *RuSHA* cases – and other ICTY judgments where the Appeals Chamber had implicitly accepted that members of a JCE could use other individuals to further the common criminal purpose, the Appeals Chamber reached the following conclusions.

410. In light of the above discussion of relevant jurisprudence, persuasive as to the ascertainment of the contours of joint criminal enterprise liability in customary international law, the Appeals Chamber is of the view that what matters in a first category JCE is not whether the person who carried out the *actus reus* of a particular crime is a member of the JCE, but whether the crime in question forms part of the common purpose. In cases where the principal perpetrator of a particular crime is not a member of the JCE, this essential requirement may be inferred from various circumstances, including the fact that the accused or any other member of the JCE closely cooperated with the principal perpetrator in order to further the common criminal purpose. In this respect, when a member of the JCE uses a person outside the JCE to carry out the *actus reus* of a crime, the fact that the person in question knows of the existence of the JCE – without it being established that he or she shares the *mens rea* necessary to become a member of the JCE – may be a factor to be taken into account when determining whether the crime forms part of the common criminal purpose. However, this is not a *sine qua non* for imputing liability for the crime to that member of the JCE.

411. When the accused, or any other member of the JCE, in order to further the common criminal purpose, uses persons who, in addition to (or instead of) carrying out the *actus reus* of the crimes forming part of the common purpose, commit crimes going beyond that purpose, the accused may be found responsible for such crimes provided that he participated in the common criminal purpose with the requisite intent and that, in the circumstances of the case, (i) it was foreseeable that such a crime might be perpetrated by one or more of the persons used by him (or by any other member of the JCE) in order to carry out the *actus reus* of the crimes forming part of the common purpose; and (ii) the accused willingly took that risk – that is the accused, with the awareness that such a crime was a possible consequence of the implementation of that enterprise, decided to participate in that enterprise. [. . .]

413. Considering the discussion of post-World War II cases and of the Tribunal's jurisprudence above, the Appeals Chamber finds that, to hold a member of a JCE responsible for crimes committed by non-members of the enterprise, it has to be shown that the crime can be imputed to one member of the joint criminal enterprise, and that this member – when using a principal perpetrator – acted in accordance with the common plan. The existence of this link is a matter to be assessed on a case-by-case basis.

414. For the aforementioned reasons, the Appeals Chamber considers that the Trial Chamber erred in stating that, in order to hold the Accused criminally responsible for the crimes charged in the Indictment pursuant to the first category of JCE, the Prosecution must, *inter alia*, establish that the persons who carried out the *actus reus* of the crimes in question were members of a joint criminal enterprise. Therefore, the Appeals Chamber, Judge Shahabuddeen

dissenting, grants Ground 1 of the Prosecution's appeal but emphasizes that, for the reasons set out above, it will not examine the consequences of this finding on the facts of the case.

415. The post-World War II jurisprudence mentioned above, which has been interpreted as a valid source for the ascertainment of the contours of joint criminal enterprise liability in customary international law, also supports the contention that the imposition of liability upon an accused for his participation to further a common criminal purpose does not require an understanding or an agreement between the accused and the principal perpetrator of the crime to commit that particular crime. [...]

418. [...] What JCE requires in any case is the existence of a common purpose which amounts to, or involves, the commission of a crime. The common purpose need not be previously arranged or formulated; it may materialize extemporaneously. The Appeals Chamber recalls that, as far as the basic form of JCE is concerned, an essential requirement in order to impute to any accused member of the JCE liability for a crime committed by another person is that the crime in question *forms part of the common criminal purpose*. In cases where the principal perpetrator shares that common criminal purpose of the JCE or, in other words, is a member of the JCE, and commits a crime in furtherance of the JCE, it is superfluous to require an additional agreement between that person and the accused to commit that particular crime. In cases where the person who carried out the *actus reus* of the crime is not a member of the JCE, the key issue remains that of ascertaining whether the crime in question forms part of the common criminal purpose. This is a matter of evidence. [...]

420. Finally, the Appeals Chamber turns to the issue of whether JCE liability is a doctrine that applies, or should apply, only to relatively small-scale cases. [...]

422. The Appeals Chamber recalls that, in *Tadić*, it explicitly envisaged the possibility of a JCE as large as the one in the present case. When providing an example of a JCE of the third category, where the common purpose is no different from the first category of JCE, it spoke of a "common, shared intention on the part of a group to forcibly remove members of one ethnicity from their town, village or *region*". The reference to the ethnic cleansing of a "region" covers exactly cases like the one at hand, which relates to the ARK. Furthermore, among the cases the Appeals Chamber discussed when defining the first category of JCE, it pointed to the *Einsatzgruppen* case, which, given the large mass killings in which the Einsatz units were involved, is based on a common purpose which is far from small.[12] [...]

427. Although *Tadić* and subsequent Trial and Appeal Judgements make it clear that, to be held responsible for a crime committed pursuant to a JCE, the accused need not have performed any part of the *actus reus* of the perpetrated crime, they also clearly require that the accused have participated in furthering the common purpose at the core of the JCE. The Appeals Chamber considers that not every type of conduct would amount to a significant enough contribution to the crime for this to create criminal liability for the accused regarding the crime in question,[13] and that the pleading practice of the Prosecution, at least in cases

---

[12] [900] *Einsatzgruppen* Case, reprinted in Trials of War Criminals Before the Nuremberg Military Tribunals Under Control Council Law No. 10, Vol. IV, pp. 427–433. The Einsatzgruppen is estimated to have been responsible for the deaths of more than one million people across an area of Europe stretching from Estonia to Crimea [...]

[13] [909] *Tadić* Appeal Judgement, para. 192 (considering that it would be wrong to disregard the role of "all those who in some way made it possible" to commit a crime); *Kvočka* Trial Judgement, para. 311 in light of the discussion in *Kvočka* Appeal Judgement, paras 95–98. *See also* the language and examples in *Tadić* Appeal Judgement, para. 191 and in *Vasiljević* Appeal Judgement, para. 119. This was also the view expressed in the case *Trial of Feurstein and others*, by the Judge Advocate who stated that, in order to be found responsible, an accused "must be the cog in the wheel of events leading up to the result which in fact occurred." Proceedings of a War Crimes Trial held at Hamburg, Germany (4–24 August, 1948), judgement of 24 August 1948 (original transcripts in Public Record Office, Kew, Richmond; on file with the Tribunal's Library), p. 7.

where the Appeals Chamber has had an opportunity to rule on the judgement, has followed this principle.

428. The Appeals Chamber emphasizes that JCE is not an open-ended concept that permits convictions based on guilt by association. On the contrary, a conviction based on the doctrine of JCE can occur only where the Chamber finds all necessary elements satisfied beyond a reasonable doubt. In light of the concerns raised by the [Association of Defence Counsel, ADC] about the scope of JCE, the Appeals Chamber briefly reiterates these elements here.

429. To begin with, as explained above, the accused must possess the requisite intent. Moreover, a Chamber can only find that the accused has the requisite intent if this is the only reasonable inference on the evidence.

430. The other requirements for a conviction under the JCE doctrine are no less stringent. A trier of fact must find beyond reasonable doubt that a plurality of persons shared the common criminal purpose; that the accused made a contribution to this common criminal purpose; and that the commonly intended crime (or, for convictions under the third category of JCE, the foreseeable crime) did in fact take place. Where the principal perpetrator is not shown to belong to the JCE, the trier of fact must further establish that the crime can be imputed to at least one member of the joint criminal enterprise, and that this member – when using the principal perpetrator – acted in accordance with the common plan. In establishing these elements, the Chamber must, among other things: identify the plurality of persons belonging to the JCE (even if it is not necessary to identify by name each of the persons involved); specify the common criminal purpose in terms of both the criminal goal intended and its scope (for example, the temporal and geographic limits of this goal, and the general identities of the intended victims); make a finding that this criminal purpose is not merely the same, but also common to all of the persons acting together within a joint criminal enterprise; and characterize the contribution of the accused in this common plan. On this last point, the Appeals Chamber observes that, although the contribution need not be necessary or substantial, it should at least be a significant contribution to the crimes for which the accused is to be found responsible.

431. Where all these requirements for JCE liability are met beyond a reasonable doubt, the accused has done far more than merely associate with criminal persons. He has the intent to commit a crime, he has joined with others to achieve this goal, and he has made a significant contribution to the crime's commission. Pursuant to the jurisprudence, which reflects standards enshrined in customary international law when ascertaining the contours of the doctrine of joint criminal enterprise, he is appropriately held liable not only for his own contribution, but also for those actions of his fellow JCE members that further the crime (first category of JCE) or that are foreseeable consequences of the carrying out of this crime, if he has acted with *dolus eventualis* (third category of JCE). It is not decisive whether these fellow JCE members carried out the *actus reus* of the crimes themselves or used principal perpetrators who did not share the common objective.

432. The Appeals Chamber recognizes that, in practice, this approach may lead to some disparities, in that it offers no formal distinction between JCE members who make overwhelmingly large contributions and JCE members whose contributions, though significant, are not as great. However, the Appeals Chamber recalls that any such disparity is adequately dealt with at the sentencing stage.

ICTY, Prosecutor v. Martić, Appeals Chamber, Judgment of 8 October 2008

From 1991 to 1995, Milan Martić held various positions within the government of the Serbian Autonomous Region of Krajina (SAO Krajina), which later evolved into the

Republic of Serbian Krajina (RSK) within the territory of Croatia. His posts included, in the period relevant to the JCE charges, Chief of the Police in Knin, Secretary for Internal Affairs of the SAO Krajina, Deputy Commander of the Territorial Defence (TO) of the SAO Krajina, Minister of Defence of the SAO Krajina, Minister of the Interior of the SAO Krajina and President of the RSK. The Trial Chamber found Martić responsible, inter alia, for persecution and other crimes against humanity, as well as war crimes, due to his participation in a JCE, the common purpose of which was to establish an ethnically Serb territory through the displacement of the non-Serb population. Martić appealed against all of these findings, alleging in particular that no specific link had been established between him and these crimes or their principal perpetrators, which included a variety of forces – such as the JNA (the Yugoslav army), MUP forces (police, including a special militia), TO forces (grass-root territorial defence units gradually integrated into the armed forces) – as well as various paramilitary organizations.

Martić essentially argued that the mere fact that he had held high-level posts had been used by the Trial Chamber to attribute most of the crimes committed in the area to him, regardless of his actual contribution to the JCE or to the crimes. The Appeals Chamber considered his arguments, first explaining how the various political and military institutions worked and interacted one with the other, then evaluating whether the Trial Chamber's finding that Martić's conduct contributed to each of the crimes committed in the various municipalities had been reasonable.

173. In light of the characterization of the common purpose of the JCE [...], the Appeals Chamber will [...] discuss whether the Trial Chamber correctly applied the above-mentioned principles in the instant case.

174. Before reviewing the Trial Chamber's factual findings on the link between Martić and the principal perpetrators of the crimes falling within the scope of the JCE, the Appeals Chamber will recall the Trial Chamber's findings on Martić's role and responsibilities in the SAO Krajina and RSK governments. This way, while bearing in mind the deference afforded to triers of fact in reaching factual findings, the Appeals Chamber will consider whether the factual findings in the Trial Judgement as a whole warrant the conclusion that the interaction of the members of the JCE in the implementation of the common criminal objective, together with other elements of proof, can serve as a basis for establishing a link between the crimes committed and Martić.

175. The Trial Chamber found that, on 4 January 1991, the Executive Council of the SAO Krajina established the Regional Secretariat for Internal Affairs ("SUP") in Knin and appointed Martić Secretary for Internal Affairs. On 1 April 1991, Milan Babić ordered the mobilisation of the TO and volunteer units of the SAO Krajina. In practice, however, volunteers and the *Milicija Krajina* (see below) were to remain the SAO Krajina's only effectively functioning armed forces until August 1991.

176. The Trial Chamber further established that on 29 May 1991, Babić became the President of the newly constituted SAO Krajina government. He appointed Martić as Minister of Defence. On the same day, the Assembly of the SAO Krajina established "special purpose police units" named *Milicija Krajine*, in addition to the previously established Public Security Service ("SJB") police and State Security Service ("SDB") police. The Trial Chamber accepted the evidence of a witness who testified that the SJB was responsible for maintaining law and order and the SDB handled political crime, terrorism, extremism, and intelligence work, while the *Milicija Krajine* units defended the territorial integrity of the SAO Krajina, secured vital facilities, infiltrated

sabotage groups, and could be used in military operations. The *Milicija Krajine* was established within the MUP [the Ministry of Interior], but was at first put under the authority of the Ministry of Defence – this was at the insistence of Martić himself, who did not want to lose his control over the special police units. [. . .]

177. According to the Trial Chamber, as Minister of Defence of the SAO Krajina government from 29 May 1991 to 27 June 1991, Martić held authority over the *Milicia Krajine*. On 27 June, he was then appointed Minister of Interior. The Trial Judgement established that, even before 29 May and after 27 June, however, Martić exercised control over the *Milicia Krajine*. [. . .] Martić was also the Minister of the Interior in the new government formed on 26 February 1992.

178. The Trial Chamber established that, after 1 August 1991, the *Milicija Krajine* units and the TO were combined into the "armed forces" of the SAO Krajina. On 8 August 1991, Martić was appointed Deputy Commander of the TO, in which position he remained until 30 September 1991. He continued to serve as Minister of the Interior while he was TO Deputy Commander. The Trial Chamber found that, after the summer of 1991, the SAO Krajina TO could be subordinated to the JNA for combat operations and that there was operational cooperation between the JNA and the armed forces of the SAO Krajina. The Trial Chamber relied on Babić's testimony that, in August and September 1991, Martić cooperated with the 9th JNA Corps concerning coordination between JNA and MUP units. Moreover, beginning in August 1990 and through the summer of 1991, officials of the MUP of Serbia [. . .] met with the SAO Krajina leadership, in particular with Martić, concerning financial, logistical, and military assistance.

179. The Trial Chamber found that, as Minister of the Interior, Martić "exercised absolute authority over the MUP", with the power to intervene and punish perpetrators who committed crimes against the non-Serb population. He was kept informed about military activities during the fall of 1991 and maintained "excellent communications" with the units subordinated to the MUP. His authority over the armed forces in the SAO Krajina during this period was established by the Trial Chamber, based on evidence that included testimony from several witnesses that Martić was *de jure* and *de facto* in control of the SAO Krajina and RSK police from 1991 through 1993.

180. With respect to JNA forces active in the region, the Trial Chamber found that the JNA was under the control of a number of the members of the JCE, in particular Ratko Mladić, the Commander of the 9th Corps of the JNA, and General Blagoje Adžić, JNA Chief of the General Staff. [. . .] The Trial Chamber further found that the SFRY Federal Secretariat of National Defence of the JNA had made unit and personnel changes within the SAO Krajina armed forces, and that the former cooperated with the latter in joint operations.

181. The Trial Chamber considered that the JNA, the police and other Serb forces active on the territory of the SAO Krajina and the RSK were structured hierarchically and closely coordinated one with the other. In conjunction with such findings, and its conclusions regarding the plurality of people sharing the common criminal purpose and Martić's contribution to it, the Trial Chamber explicitly found that the objective of establishing a unified Serb territory was implemented "through widespread and systematic armed attacks [. . .] and through the commission of acts of violence and intimidation". Considering in addition the "scale and gravity of the crimes [. . .] committed against the non-Serb population", the attacks could not have been carried out by members of the JCE individually, but only by using the forces under their control. Therefore, the only reasonable interpretation of these findings is that the Trial Chamber was satisfied beyond reasonable doubt that members of the JCE, when using these forces, were acting in accordance with the common purpose, *i.e.*, the establishment of a unified Serb territory through the forcible removal of the non-Serb population. The Appeals Chamber finds that, while the Trial Chamber should have made an explicit finding on this question, this omission, in such circumstances, does not invalidate the Trial Judgement. However, in relation to

some armed structures and paramilitary units, including those referred to as "Martić's men" or "Martić's police" (*Martićevci*), the Trial Chamber did not reach any definite finding on their link with Martić. The Appeals Chamber will take this into account when reviewing the Trial Chamber's findings.

182. The Appeals Chamber will now proceed to analyse the Trial Chamber's findings on the crimes for which it held Martić responsible as a participant in the JCE, bearing in mind that if a crime falling within the common purpose is imputable to one of the members of the JCE, and all other elements are met, it would be open to a reasonable trier of fact to find that Martić bore criminal responsibility for that crime.

The following are two examples from the many findings by the Appeals Chamber on the link between Martić and the forces on the ground actually 'pulling the trigger'. Note how they take into account the evidence on any link as well as the 'contextual' evidence on Martić's authority over the various forces.

191. The Trial Chamber [. . .] found that on 13, 21 and 24 September 1991, armed Serbs from Živaja led by Nikola Begović burnt ten houses and damaged the Catholic church in the village of Cerovljani. The Trial Chamber concluded that the elements of persecution as a crime against humanity (Count 1), wanton destruction of villages, or devastation not justified by military necessity, as a violation of the laws or customs of war (Count 12) and destruction or wilful damage done to institutions dedicated to education or religion as a violation of the laws or customs of war (Count 13) had been established in relation to these acts and convicted Martić on the basis that the commission of the crimes was a natural and foreseeable consequence of the implementation of the common purpose of the JCE.

192. The Appeals Chamber finds that a reasonable trier of fact could not have reached the conclusion that Martić was responsible for the acts of destruction perpetrated by armed Serbs from Živaja led by Nikola Begović. Having due regard to the Trial Chamber's findings and the evidence on which they relied, the Appeals Chamber concludes that the Trial Chamber erred in establishing a link between Martić and these perpetrators. In particular, Exhibit 273, a witness statement of Antun Blažević, on which much of these findings depend, only suggests that the armed men under Begović had received weapons from the JNA, without any evidence of additional control or influence by Martić or other members of the JCE. Without any further elaboration on the link between these forces and the JNA, no reasonable trier of fact could have held that the only reasonable conclusion in the circumstances was that these crimes could be imputed to a member of the JCE. The link between the principal perpetrators of these crimes and members of the JCE is therefore too tenuous to support Martić's conviction.

193. The Appeals Chamber considers that this error resulted in a miscarriage of justice and accordingly reverses Martić's conviction for Counts 1, 12 and 13 in respect of the acts of destruction committed in Cerovljani by armed Serbs from Živaja led by Nikola Begović.

194. The Trial Chamber found that Serb paramilitary forces intentionally killed seven civilians in Lipovača towards the end of October 1991. The Trial Chamber concluded that all the elements of persecution as a crime against humanity (Count 1), murder as a crime against humanity (Count 3) and murder as a violation of the laws or customs of war (Count 4) had been established in relation to these killings and convicted Martić on the basis that these crimes were a natural and foreseeable consequence of the implementation of the common purpose of the JCE.

195. The Appeals Chamber finds that a reasonable trier of fact could have reached the conclusion that Martić was responsible for the killings perpetrated in Lipovača by Serb paramilitary forces. The Appeals Chamber notes that, in its findings on the killings in Lipovača, the Trial

Chamber referred to evidence establishing that the JNA had warned the villagers to beware of Serb paramilitary units that would arrive after the JNA left, that the Serb paramilitary units arrived after the JNA as warned and that these paramilitary units were called "reserve forces, Martić's troops or Martić's army" and wore uniforms like those of the army. The Appeals Chamber is therefore satisfied that a reasonable trier of fact could have been satisfied beyond a reasonable doubt that the Serb paramilitary forces in question were in fact JNA or TO soldiers or were at least acting in concert with the JNA. Taking into account the warning provided by the JNA, the denomination of these troops and their uniforms, as well as the general pattern of take-over and criminal conduct in the area, it was reasonable for the Trial Chamber to conclude that these crimes were committed by a member of a paramilitary group with a link to a member of the JCE, and, therefore, that they were imputable to Martić as a participant in that JCE.

196. In light of the above, and of [the] Trial Chamber's findings that the common purpose was implemented through widespread and systematic armed attacks, the sub-ground of appeal relating to these crimes is dismissed.

COMMENTARY

The doctrine of joint criminal enterprise has been adopted by various other international and hybrid tribunals, in particular the ICTR,[14] the SCSL,[15] and the East Timorese Special Panel for Serious Crimes.[16] ECCC Judges also considered the matter, and found JCE I and JCE II applicable to events that occurred in the 1970s.[17]

QUESTIONS

1. Is the reasoning in para. 190 of the *Tadić* Appeal Judgment, above, convincing? Why isn't aiding and abetting enough to cover the responsibility of 'all those who have engaged in serious violations of international humanitarian law'?

2. Is the ICTY's tracing of contemporary JCE doctrine to strands of World War II-era jurisprudence convincing? Is there a danger in having judge-made law in relation to forms of responsibility? Would you consider joint criminal enterprise established under customary law?

3. The third ('extended') form of JCE essentially requires the intent to participate in, and further the criminal purpose of, the joint criminal enterprise and the acceptance of the risk that a foreseeable crime might be perpetrated by members of the group. Does this amount to 'guilt by association'? Is it fair to impute criminal liability in this type of situation?

4. Can a person be convicted under the third form of JCE, as developed by ICTY case law, for a specific-intent crime such as genocide? If so, what are the conceptual problems in doing it?

---

[14] *Rwamakuba* Decision of 22 October 2004, ICTR-98-44C, and *Ntakirutimana* Appeals Judgment, ICTR-96-10-A and ICTR-96-17-A.

[15] *Norman*, Decision of 21 October 2005.

[16] *José Cardoso* (4c/2003), Judgment of 5 April 2003, paras 367ff.

[17] Decision on the Appeals against the Co-Investigative Judges Order on Joint Criminal Enterprise (JCE), Case File No: 002/19-09-2007-ECCC-OCIJ, Pre-Trial Chamber, 20 May 2010.

FURTHER READING

Cassese, *International Criminal Law*, 187–213.

G. Sluiter (ed.), 'Symposium' (2007) 5 JICJ 67–227.

Werle, *Principles*, 172–8.

Zahar and Sluiter, *International Criminal Law*, 221–57.

3

CO-PERPETRATION

As suggested above, the State delegates at the Rome Conference working on the ICCSt. chose a different, and probably wiser, path than the drafters of the Statutes of previous international tribunals and decided to flesh out in detail the provisions on individual criminal responsibility. In particular, apart from provisions on aiding and abetting, ordering, planning and other such modes of responsibility, Article 25 ICCSt. states:

3. In accordance with this Statute, a person shall be criminally responsible and liable for punishment for a crime within the jurisdiction of the Court if that person:

(a) Commits such a crime, whether as an individual, jointly with another or through another person, regardless of whether that other person is criminally responsible; [...]

(d) In any other way contributes to the commission or attempted commission of such a crime by a group of persons acting with a common purpose. Such contribution shall be intentional and shall either:

(i) Be made with the aim of furthering the criminal activity or criminal purpose of the group, where such activity or purpose involves the commission of a crime within the jurisdiction of the Court; or

(ii) Be made in the knowledge of the intention of the group to commit the crime [...]

Thus, unlike Article 7 ICTYSt., the ICCSt. expressly identifies three forms of perpetration: (i) committing a crime as an individual; (ii) committing a crime jointly with another; and (iii) committing a crime 'through another person'. In cases akin to those addressed through JCE at the ad hoc Tribunals (that is, when more persons participate in a common criminal plan), the ICC relies on explicit provisions addressing the matter. One of these provisions is Article 25(3)(a) ICCSt., which deals with joint commission or commission through another person (what is often referred to as 'perpetrator behind the perpetrator'). The other is Article 25(3)(d), which refers to intentional contribution to the commission of a crime by a group of persons acting with a common purpose.

The main difference between these theories of responsibility and JCE, according to the case law and most scholars, is that the ICCSt. focuses primarily on 'control over the crime' by an individual. In the case of co-perpetration, a finding of 'joint control' (rooted in the division of essential tasks among group members) must be made. While JCE also requires a 'significant contribution' for an individual to be considered responsible,[1] the focus at the ICTY is more on the *mens rea* (participation *to further a common criminal purpose*).

The ICC dealt for the first time at some length with this matter in the *Lubanga* case and then in the *Katanga and Chui* case. With the caveat that the Pre-Trial Chamber's decisions in this matter are not final, the first of these decisions is interesting for the light

---

[1] See *supra*, Part III(2) on JCE (in particular *Brđanin*, Appeal Judgment, paras 427 and 430).

that it throws on how the Judges are interpreting Article 25 ICCSt. It also shows how Article 25(3)(a) and Article 25(3)(d) ICCSt. may interact with each other.

Cases

ICC, **Prosecutor *v.* Lubanga,** *Pre-Trial Chamber, Decision on the Confirmation of Charges of 29 January 2007*

On 17 March 2006, in Kinshasa, Democratic Republic of the Congo (DRC), Thomas Lubanga Dyilo, a Congolese national and alleged founder and leader of the rebel group Union des Patriotes Congolais (UPC), was arrested and transferred to the International Criminal Court. He was charged by the ICC Prosecutor for his role as commander-in-chief of the Forces Patriotiques pour la Libération du Congo (FPLC), the military wing of the UPC during the period from September 2002, when the movement was founded, to 13 August 2003. On 28 August 2006, the ICC Prosecutor formally charged him. Pursuant to the ICCSt., the Prosecutor then requested the Pre-Trial Chamber to confirm the charges against Lubanga, alleging that he was a co-perpetrator of the war crimes of enlisting and conscripting children under the age of 15 into the FPLC and using them to participate actively in hostilities in Ituri (DRC). Between 9 and 17 November 2006, the Pre-Trial Chamber held a hearing on the confirmation of charges to determine whether there was enough evidence to establish substantial grounds to believe that Lubanga committed the crimes with which he was charged. The Judges issued their landmark decision on 29 January 2007. While the decision covers various interesting topics, excerpted below is the bulk of the reasoning in relation to the concept of 'co-perpetration' (or 'co-perpetratorship') and to the differences between this approach and JCE.

2. The concept of co-perpetration as embodied in the Statute

326. The Chamber is of the view that the concept of co-perpetration is originally rooted in the idea that when the sum of the co-ordinated individual contributions of a plurality of persons results in the realisation of all the objective elements of a crime, any person making a contribution can be held vicariously responsible for the contributions of all the others and, as a result, can be considered as a principal to the whole crime.[2]

327. In this regard, the definitional criterion of the concept of co-perpetration is linked to the distinguishing criterion between principals and accessories to a crime where a criminal offence is committed by a plurality of persons.

328. The objective approach to such a distinction focuses on the realisation of one or more of the objective elements of the crime. From this perspective, only those who physically carry out one or more of the objective elements of the offence can be considered principals to the crime.

329. The subjective approach – which is the approach adopted by the jurisprudence of the ICTY through the concept of joint criminal enterprise or the common purpose doctrine – moves the focus from the level of contribution to the commission of the offence as the distinguishing criterion between principals and accessories, and places it instead on the state of mind in which the contribution to the crime was made. As a result, only those who make

---

2 [417] AMBOS K., "Article 25: Individual Criminal Responsibility", in *Commentary on the Rome Statute of the International Criminal Court*, Baden-Baden, 1999, p. 479, margin No. 8.

their contribution with the shared intent to commit the offence can be considered principals to the crime, regardless of the level of their contribution to its commission.

330. The concept of control over the crime constitutes a third approach for distinguishing between principals and accessories which, contrary to the Defence claim, is applied in numerous legal systems.[3] The notion underpinning this third approach is that principals to a crime are not limited to those who physically carry out the objective elements of the offence, but also include those who, in spite of being removed from the scene of the crime, control or mastermind its commission because they decide whether and how the offence will be committed.

331. This approach involves an objective element, consisting of the appropriate factual circumstances for exercising control over the crime, and a subjective element, consisting of the awareness of such circumstances.

332. According to this approach, only those who have control over the commission of the offence – and are aware of having such control – may be principals because:

i.   they physically carry out the objective elements of the offence (commission of the crime in person, or direct perpetration);

ii. they control the will of those who carry out the objective elements of the offence (commission of the crime through another person, or indirect perpetration); or

iii. they have, along with others, control over the offence by reason of the essential tasks assigned to them (commission of the crime jointly with others, or co-perpetration).

333. Article 25(3)(a) of the Statute does not take into account the objective criterion for distinguishing between principals and accessories because the notion of committing an offence through another person – particularly when the latter is not criminally responsible – cannot be reconciled with the idea of limiting the class of principals to those who physically carry out one or more of the objective elements of the offence.

334. Article 25(3)(a) of the Statute, read in conjunction with article 25(3)(d), also does not take into account the subjective criteria for distinguishing between principals and accessories. In this regard, the Chamber notes that, by moving away from the concept of co-perpetration embodied in article 25(3)(a), article 25(3)(d) defines the concept of (i) contribution to the commission or attempted commission of a crime by a group of persons acting with a common purpose, (ii) with the aim of furthering the criminal activity of the group or in the knowledge of the criminal purpose.

335. The Chamber considers that this latter concept – which is closely akin to the concept of joint criminal enterprise or the common purpose doctrine adopted by the jurisprudence of the ICTY – would have been the basis of the concept of co-perpetration within the meaning of article 25(3)(a), had the drafters of the Statute opted for a subjective approach for distinguishing between principals and accessories.

336. Moreover, the Chamber observes that the wording of article 25(3)(d) of the Statute begins with the words "[i]n any other way contributes to the commission or attempted commission of such a crime."

337. Hence, in the view of the Chamber, article 25(3)(d) of the Statute provides for a residual form of accessory liability which makes it possible to criminalise those contributions to a crime which cannot be characterised as ordering, soliciting, inducing, aiding, abetting or assisting

---

[3] [418] *The Prosecutor* v. *Gacumbitsi*, Case No. ICTR-2001–64-A, Separate Opinion of Judge Schomburg, 7 July 2006, para. 16, footnote 30. See also FLETCHER G.P., *Rethinking Criminal Law*, New York, Oxford University Press, 2000, p. 639; WERLE G., *Principles of International Criminal Law*, The Hague, T.M.C. Asser Press, 2005, margin No. 354.

within the meaning of article 25(3)(b) or article 25(3)(c) of the Statute, by reason of the state of mind in which the contributions were made.

338. Not having accepted the objective and subjective approaches for distinguishing between principals and accessories to a crime, the Chamber considers, as does the Prosecution and, unlike the jurisprudence of the ad *hoc* tribunals, that the Statute embraces the third approach, which is based on the concept of control over the crime.

339. In this regard, the Chamber notes that the most typical manifestation of the concept of control over the crime, which is the commission of a crime through another person, is expressly provided for in article 25(3)(a) of the Statute. In addition, the use of the phrase "regardless of whether that other person is criminally responsible" in article 25(3)(a) of the Statute militates in favour of the conclusion that this provision extends to the commission of a crime not only through an innocent agent (that is, through another person who is not criminally responsible), but also through another person who is fully criminally responsible.[4]

340. The Chamber considers that the concept of co-perpetration embodied in article 25(3)(a) of the Statute by the reference to the commission of a crime "jointly with [...] another person" must cohere with the choice of the concept of control over the crime as a criterion for distinguishing between principals and accessories.

341. Hence, as stated in its *Decision to Issue a Warrant of Arrest*, the Chamber considers that the concept of co-perpetration embodied in article 25(3)(a) of the Statute coincides with that of joint control over the crime by reason of the essential nature of the various contributions to the commission of the crime.

3. Elements of co-perpetration based on joint control over the crime

342. The concept of co-perpetration based on joint control over the crime is rooted in the principle of the division of essential tasks for the purpose of committing a crime between two or more persons acting in a concerted manner. Hence, although none of the participants has overall control over the offence because they all depend on one another for its commission, they all share control because each of them could frustrate the commission of the crime by not carrying out his or her task.[5]

a. Objective Elements

i) Existence of an agreement or common plan between two or more persons

343. In the view of the Chamber, the first objective requirement of co-perpetration based on joint control over the crime is the existence of an agreement or common plan between two or more persons.[6] Accordingly, participation in the commission of a crime without co-ordination with one's co-perpetrators falls outside the scope of co-perpetration within the meaning of article 25(3)(a) of the Statute.

344. The common plan must include an element of criminality, although it does not need to be specifically directed at the commission of a crime. It suffices:

i.   that the co-perpetrators have agreed (a) to start the implementation of the common plan to achieve a non-criminal goal, and (b) to only commit the crime if certain conditions are met; or

---

[4] [419] ESER A., "Individual Criminal Responsibility", in *The Rome Statute of the International Criminal Court: A Commentary*, Oxford, Oxford University Press, 2002, Vol. I, p. 795.

[5] [422] *The Prosecutor v. Milomir Stakić*, Case No. IT-97–24-T, Trial Judgement, 31 July 2003, para. 440.

[6] [423] In *Stakić*, the first objective requirement for co-perpetration is divided into two sub-criteria: i) a common goal and ii) an agreement or silent consent, *The Prosecutor v. Milomir Stakić*, Case No. IT-97-31-T [*sic*], Trial Judgement, 24 July 2003 [*sic*], paras. 470–477.

ii. that the co-perpetrators (a) are aware of the risk that implementing the common plan (which is specifically directed at the achievement of a non-criminal goal) will result in the commission of the crime, and (b) accept such an outcome.

345. Furthermore, the Chamber considers that the agreement need not be explicit and that its existence can be inferred from the subsequent concerted action of the co-perpetrators.

ii) Co-ordinated essential contribution by each co-perpetrator resulting in the realisation of the objective elements of the crime

346. The Chamber considers that the second objective requirement of co-perpetration based on joint control over the crime is the co-ordinated essential contribution made by each co-perpetrator resulting in the realisation of the objective elements of the crime.[7]

347. In the view of the Chamber, when the objective elements of an offence are carried out by a plurality of persons acting within the framework of a common plan, only those to whom essential tasks have been assigned – and who, consequently, have the power to frustrate the commission of the crime by not performing their tasks – can be said to have joint control over the crime.

348. The Chamber observes that, although some authors have linked the essential character of a task – and hence the ability to exercise joint control over the crime – to its performance at the execution stage of the crime, the Statute does not contain any such restriction.

b. Subjective Elements

i) The suspect must fulfil the subjective elements of the crime in question

349. The Chamber considers that co-perpetration based on joint control over the crime requires above all that the suspect fulfil the subjective elements of the crime with which he or she is charged, including any requisite *dolus specialis* or ulterior intent for the type of crime involved.[8]

350. Article 30 of the Statute sets out the general subjective element for all crimes within the jurisdiction of the Court by specifying that "[u]nless otherwise provided, a person shall be criminally responsible and liable for punishment for a crime within the jurisdiction of the Court only if the material elements are committed with intent and knowledge",[9] that is:

i. if the person is "[aware] that a circumstance exists or a consequence will occur in the ordinary course of events"; and

ii. if the person means to engage in the relevant conduct and means to cause the relevant consequence or is aware that it will occur in the ordinary course of events.

351. The cumulative reference to "intent" and "knowledge" requires the existence of a volitional element on the part of the suspect. This volitional element encompasses, first and foremost, those situations in which the suspect (i) knows that his or her actions or omissions will bring about the objective elements of the crime, and (ii) undertakes such actions or omissions with the concrete intent to bring about the objective elements of the crime (also known as *dolus directus* of the first degree).

---

    [7] [424] *In Stakić*, the second objective requirement for co-perpetration is divided into two sub-criteria: i) co-ordinated co-operation and ii) joint control over criminal conduct, *The Prosecutor v. Milomir* Stakić, Case No. IT-97-24-T, Trial Judgement, 31 July 2003, paras. 478–491.

    [8] [426] *The Prosecutor v. Milomir* Stakić, Case No. IT-97-24-T, Trial Judgement, 31 July 2003, para. 495.

    [9] [427] Article 30(1) of the Statute.

352. The above-mentioned volitional element also encompasses other forms of the concept of *dolus*, which have already been resorted to by the jurisprudence of the *ad hoc* tribunals, that is:

i.   situations in which the suspect, without having the concrete intent to bring about the objective elements of the crime, is aware that such elements will be the necessary outcome of his or her actions or omissions (also known as *dolus directus* of the second degree); and

ii. situations in which the suspect (a) is aware of the risk that the objective elements of the crime may result from his or her actions or omissions, and (b) accepts such an outcome by reconciling himself or herself with it or consenting to it (also known as *dolus eventualis*). [. . .]

355. Where the state of mind of the suspect falls short of accepting that the objective elements of the crime may result from his or her actions or omissions, such a state of mind cannot qualify as a truly intentional realisation of the objective elements,[10] and hence would not meet the "intent and knowledge" requirement embodied in article 30 of the Statute.[11]

356. As provided for in article 30(1) of the Statute, the general subjective element ("intent and knowledge") therein contemplated applies to any crime within the jurisdiction of the Court "[u]nless otherwise provided", that is, as long as the definition of the relevant crime does not expressly contain a different subjective element.

357. In this regard, the Chamber observes that the definitions of the war crimes of conscripting and enlisting children under the age of fifteen years and using them to participate actively in hostilities set forth in article 8 of the Statute do not contain any subjective element. However, the Chamber notes that the third element listed in the Elements of Crimes for these specific crimes requires that, in relation to the age of the victims, "[t]he perpetrator knew or should have known that such person or persons were under the age of 15 years."

358. The "should have known" requirement set forth in the Elements of Crimes – which is to be distinguished from the "must have known" or constructive knowledge requirement – falls within the concept of negligence because it is met when the suspect:

i.   did not know that the victims were under the age of fifteen years at the time they were enlisted, conscripted or used to participate actively in hostilities; and

---

[10] [437] For instance, where the suspect is aware of the likelihood that the objective elements of the crime would occur as a result of his actions or omissions, and in spite of that, takes the risk in the belief that his or her expertise will suffice in preventing the realisation of the objective elements of the crime. This would be the case of a taxi driver taking the risk of driving at a very high speed on a local road, trusting that nothing would happen on account of his or her driving expertise.

[11] [438] The concept of recklessness requires only that the perpetrator be aware of the existence of a risk that the objective elements of the crime may result from his or her actions or omissions, but does not require that he or she reconcile himself or herself with the result. In so far as recklessness does not require the suspect to reconcile himself or herself with the causation of the objective elements of the crime as a result of his or her actions or omissions, it is not part of the concept of intention. According to Fletcher, "Recklessness is a form of *culpa* – equivalent to what German scholars call 'conscious negligence'. The problem of distinguishing 'intention' and 'recklessness' arises because in both cases the actor is aware that his conduct might generate a specific result." FLETCHER, G.P., *Rethinking Criminal Law*, New York, Oxford University Press, 2000, p. 443. Hence, recklessness does not meet the "intent and knowledge" requirement embodied in article 30 of the Statute. The same conclusion is reached by ESER, A., "Mental Elements – Mistakes of Fact and Law", in *The Rome Statute of the International Criminal Court: A Commentary*, Oxford, Oxford University Press, 2002, Vol. I, pp. 898–899, and PIRAGOFF, D.K., "Article 30: Mental Element", in *Commentary on the Rome Statute of the International Criminal Court*, Baden Baden, Nomos, 1999, p. 535. Negligence likewise does not meet the "intent and knowledge" requirement embodied in article 30 of the Statute.

ii.   lacked such knowledge because he or she did not act with due diligence in the relevant circumstances (one can only say that the suspect "should have known" if his or her lack of knowledge results from his or her failure to comply with his or her duty to act with due diligence).

359. As a result, the "should have known" requirement as provided for in the Elements of Crimes in relation to articles 8(2)(b)(xxvi) and 8(2)(e)(vii) is an exception to the "intent and knowledge" requirement embodied in article 30 of the Statute. Accordingly, as provided for in article 30(1) of the Statute, it will apply in determining the age of the victims, whereas the general "intent and knowledge" requirement will apply to the other objective elements of the war crimes set forth in articles 8(2)(b)(xxvi) and 8(2)(e)(vii) of the Statute, including the existence of an armed conflict and the nexus between the acts charged and the armed conflict. [...]

ii) The suspect and the other co-perpetrators must all be mutually aware and mutually accept that implementing their common plan may result in the realisation of the objective elements of the crime

361. The theory of co-perpetration based on joint control over the crime requires two additional subjective elements. The suspect and the other co-perpetrators (a) must all be mutually aware of the risk that implementing their common plan may result in the realisation of the objective elements of the crime, and (b) must all mutually accept such a result by reconciling themselves with it or consenting to it.[12]

362. The Chamber considers that it is precisely the co-perpetrators' mutual awareness and acceptance of this result which justifies (a) that the contributions made by the others may be attributed to each of them, including the suspect, and (b) that they be held criminally responsible as principals to the whole crime. [...]

365. Consequently, although, in principle, the war crime of enlisting or conscripting children under the age of fifteen years or using them to participate actively in hostilities requires only a showing that the suspect "should have known" that the victims were under the age of fifteen years, the Chamber considers that this subjective element is not applicable in the instant case. Indeed, the theory of co-perpetration based on joint control over the crime requires that all the co-perpetrators, including the suspect, be mutually aware of, and mutually accept, the likelihood that implementing the common plan would result in the realisation of the objective elements of the crime.

iii) The suspect must be aware of the factual circumstances enabling him or her to jointly control the crime

366. The Chamber considers that the third and last subjective element of co-perpetration based on joint control of the crime is the awareness by the suspect of the factual circumstances enabling him or her to jointly control the crime.

367. In the view of the Chamber, this requires the suspect to be aware (i) that his or her role is essential to the implementation of the common plan, and hence in the commission of the crime, and (ii) that he or she can – by reason of the essential nature of his or her task – frustrate the implementation of the common plan, and hence the commission of the crime, by refusing to perform the task assigned to him or her.

At paras 368–410, on the basis of a meticulous analysis of the evidence offered by the Prosecutor, the Pre-Trial Chamber went on to find that there was sufficient evidence to

---

[12] [440] *The Prosecutor v. Milomir Stakić*, Case No. IT-97-24-T, Trial Judgement, 31 July 2003, para. 496.

establish substantial grounds to believe that Lubanga was criminally responsible as a co-perpetrator within the meaning of Article 25(3)(a) ICCSt. for the crimes with which he was charged.

COMMENTARY

The *Lubanga* Pre-Trial Chamber, following a somewhat different approach from the one seen in the ICTY decisions (*Tadić* and others), breaks novel ground using interesting arguments.

Most of the differences in approach might be explained by the fact that the Pre-Trial Chamber in this case is not attempting to ascertain the customary rules applicable to individual responsibility, as the ICTY was called upon to do, but is just interpreting the ICCSt. and its provisions. As discussed above, the ICCSt. provides textual support for joint perpetration, while the ICTYSt. does not.

Note that most of the authorities cited in the decision are international and criminal law scholars. The Judges even go so far as to provide just one scholar's view as the sole basis for their legal finding on recklessness (their n. 438 (n. 11 above)): no inquiry into domestic or international practice is attempted to support this pronouncement. Also, the examples provided in some footnotes (see their n. 437, about the taxi driver (n. 10 above)) might appear a bit out of place in a war crimes trial.

Be that as it may, the Judges in this case needed to assess how to interpret the concept of joint perpetration and reached the conclusion that this must be equated to 'joint control over the crime'. The Pre-Trial Chamber appears to base its reasoning upon a conceptual distinction between 'principals' and 'accessories', a distinction known to several domestic systems but not necessarily valid before international jurisdictions. For instance, the JCE doctrine elaborated by the ICTY does not appear to be premised on such a distinction.

Under the ICC model, as understood by the *Lubanga* Pre-Trial Chamber, co-perpetrators are persons acting together with joint control over the crime, since each of them plays an essential role in its commission. Each perpetrator is therefore able to frustrate the commission of the crime by not carrying out his or her tasks. In other words, what the ICC appears to require is a level of contribution to the crime by each participant that is higher than the (significant) one required by the ICTY Appeals Chamber for JCE. Moreover, each co-perpetrator must be aware of the fact that he or she is providing this essential contribution and must possess the requisite *mens rea* for the crime at issue. In any event the real issue, at least from the perspective of an accused, will be what trial judges consider to be an 'essential' contribution and, therefore, what kind of evidence is deemed sufficient to base a conviction beyond reasonable doubt for co-perpetration.

ICC, Prosecutor v. Katanga and Chui, Pre-Trial Chamber, Decision on the Confirmation of Charges of 30 September 2008

In a subsequent decision, ICC Judges further elaborated on the issue of co-perpetration, reading into the ICCSt. the possibility of charging *joint commission through another person* to capture the case of a person acting jointly with another, who in turns uses yet another individual to carry out the crime. This is how the Pre-Trial Judges envisaged the doctrine in question.

493. An individual who has no control over the person through whom the crime would be committed cannot be said to commit the crime by means of that other person. However,

if he acts jointly with another individual – one who controls the person used as an instrument – these crimes can be attributed to him on the basis of mutual attribution. [...]

521. Co-perpetration based on joint control over the crime involves the division of essential tasks between two or more persons, acting in a concerted manner, for the purposes of committing that crime. As explained, the fulfillment of the essential task(s) can be carried out by the co-perpetrators physically or they may be executed through another person. [...]

522. In the view of the Chamber, the first objective requirement of co-perpetration based on joint control over the crime is the existence of an agreement or common plan between the persons who physically carry out the elements of the crime or between those who carry out the elements of the crime through another individual. Participation in the crimes committed by the latter without coordination with one's co-perpetrators falls outside the scope of co-perpetration within the meaning of article 25(3)(a) of the Statute. [...]

524. The Chamber considers that the second objective requirement of co-perpetration based on joint control over the crime is the coordinated essential contribution made by each co-perpetrator resulting in the realisation of the objective elements of the crime.

525. When the objective elements of an offence are carried out by a plurality of persons acting within the framework of a common plan, only those to whom essential tasks have been assigned – and who, consequently, have the power to frustrate the commission of the crime by not performing their tasks – can be said to have joint control over the crime. Where such persons commit the crimes through others, their essential contribution may consist of activating the mechanisms which lead to automatic compliance with their orders and, thus, the commission of crimes.

526. Although some authors have linked the essential character of a task – and hence, the ability to exercise joint control over the crime – to its performance at the execution stage, the Statute does not encompasses [*sic*] any such restriction. Designing the attack, supplying weapons and ammunitions, exercising the power to move the previously recruited and trained troops to the fields; and/or coordinating and monitoring the activities of those troops, may constitute contributions that must be considered essential regardless of when they are exercised (before or during the execution stage of the crime). [...]

527. The Chamber finds that the commission of the crimes requires that the suspects carry out the subjective elements of the crimes with which they are charged, including any required *dolus specialis* or ulterior intent for the type of crime involved.

QUESTIONS

1. Why do you think the ICC took such a different approach in interpreting a provision like Article 25 ICCSt.? Is it fair to state, as the Pre-Trial Chamber does, that under JCE 'those who make their contribution with the shared intent to commit the offence can be considered principals to the crime, *regardless of the level of their contribution*' (emphasis added)?

2. In the *Katanga and Chui* decision, much is made of the requirement that the contribution be essential to the realization of the *actus reus*. Does this mean that a person whose contribution can be replaced by another (and therefore a person who cannot frustrate the commission of the crime by withdrawing his contribution) can never be considered a co-perpetrator in this sense? If this is so, would a soldier at a

concentration camp escape conviction as a co-perpetrator before the ICC, as he is just one of 100 guards committing, for instance, the extermination of 100,000 inmates? After all, wouldn't his contribution never amount to an 'essential' contribution, since the other 99 guards could always replace him?

3. What is the difference between commission (as understood in *Gacumbitsi*), JCE (as applied in *Martić*) and co-perpetration? Are there examples where a person would be convicted under the JCE doctrine at the ICTY, but acquitted under Article 25 ICCSt.? What kind of evidence would be sufficient to convict a person under JCE that is insufficient under co-perpetration?

FURTHER READING

Cassese, *International Criminal Law*, 212–13.

H. Olasolo, *The Criminal Responsibility of Senior Political and Military Leaders as Principals to International Crimes* (Oxford: Oxford University Press, 2009).

T. Weigend, 'Intent, Mistake of Law, and Co-perpetration in the *Lubanga* Decision on Confirmation of Charges' (2008) 6 JICJ 471–87.

G. Werle, 'International Criminal Responsibility in Article 25 ICC Statute' (2007) 5 JICJ 953–75.

Werle, *Principles*, 178–80.

4

PLANNING

Planning as a mode of liability in international criminal law is defined according to its everyday meaning and entails devising, preparing or arranging for the commission of a crime. It was included in Article 6(2)(a) of the London Charter, which criminalized the 'planning, preparation, initiation or waging of a war of aggression'. It was then listed as a potential mode of individual criminal liability in the statutes of the ICTY (Art. 7(1)), ICTR (Art. 6(1)), Special Court of Sierra Leone (Art. 6(1)) and the Extraordinary Chambers of the Courts of Cambodia (Art. 29). Although the ICCSt. includes a variety of modes of liability within Article 25 (including committing, ordering, soliciting, inducing and aiding and abetting), it does not explicitly include planning. However, an individual who makes an essential contribution to the commission of a crime by *planning* the crime could be liable as a co-perpetrator under Article 25(3)(a) if he did so with the requisite *mens rea*. The Pre-Trial Chamber in the *Lubanga* confirmation decision, excerpted in the previous chapter, made it clear that a co-perpetrator could make an essential contribution to a crime before the execution of the crime itself, which would include planning (see, e.g. para. 348 of that decision).

An unresolved question is whether planning *alone*, absent the commission of a crime, is sufficient for liability. As reflected in the excerpts below, courts from the ICTR and the ICTY have answered this question differently. Liability for planning alone would largely resemble conspiracy liability, which is generally not an available mode of liability in international criminal law outside the crime of genocide, except that planning can be done by one person acting alone whereas conspiracy requires a minimum of two persons. To the extent that international criminal law seeks to deter the commission of offences, the criminalization of planning alone might seem warranted. On the other hand, if one focuses on the costs of criminalization as well as the difficulty of proving the criminal nature of planning absent the actual commission of a crime, there might be reasons to limit jurisdiction to those cases where the planning has in fact led to criminal conduct. This debate is, however, largely academic. Although some courts have held that planning alone is sufficient for liability, no international tribunal has convicted an accused simply for planning a crime when the crime was not in fact committed. Moreover, to the extent that the ICC regime governs the future prosecution of international crimes, planning can be charged only under a co-perpetration theory, which requires the actual commission of the crime. Finally, even in those circumstances when planning alone is sufficient for liability, it will rarely be detected or prosecuted absent the commission of the crime itself. In fact, planning is generally not proven directly, because such evidence is usually not available, but is instead inferred from the nature of committed criminal conduct itself.

Regarding this last point about how planning is proven, the Appeals Chamber of the ICTY sounded a cautionary note about what inferences are permissible. There is no question that large-scale atrocities do not occur spontaneously without planning, but a finding of liability for planning requires *specific* evidence allowing the inference, beyond a reasonable doubt, that the particular accused participated in the planning of the criminal conduct. That is the focus of the *Dragomir Milošević* excerpt below.

Cases

ICTY, Prosecutor v. Kordić and Čerkez, Trial Chamber, Judgment of 26 February 2001 and Appeals Chamber, Judgment of 17 December 2004

Dario Kordić, a Bosnian Croat political leader, and Mario Čerkez, a Bosnian Croat military commander, were both tried for grave breaches, war crimes and crimes against humanity for crimes committed against Bosnian Muslims in the Lašva Valley region of Central Bosnia in 1992 and 1993. Kordić was convicted of most of the charges and was sentenced to 25 years' imprisonment, a sentence that was affirmed on appeal. Čerkez was sentenced to a smaller number of crimes. He was initially sentenced to 15 years' imprisonment but on appeal his sentence was reduced to six years. Although the trial judgment suggested that an accused could be convicted for planning alone, the Appeals Chamber cast doubt on this notion, and in any event neither accused was in fact convicted of only planning crimes.

Trial judgment

386. Referring to the Akayesu Trial Judgement [which held that an individual could be held liable for 'planning' a crime only if the crime was in fact committed], the Trial Chamber in Blaškić held that "planning implies that 'one or several persons contemplate designing the commission of a crime at both the preparatory and execution phases'". The Blaškić Trial Chamber also found that the existence of a plan may be demonstrated through circumstantial evidence. The Trial Chamber finds that planning constitutes a discrete form of responsibility under Article 7(1) of the Statute, and thus agrees that an accused may be held criminally responsible for planning alone. However, a person found to have committed a crime will not be found responsible for planning the same crime. Moreover, an accused will only be held responsible for planning, instigating or ordering a crime if he directly or indirectly intended that the crime be committed.

Appeal Judgment

25. The Appeals Chamber notes that the Trial Chamber convicted Kordić for planning, instigating, and ordering crimes pursuant to Article 7(1) of the Statute. The Trial Chamber's legal definitions of these modes of responsibility have not been appealed by any of the Parties. However, the Appeals Chamber deems it necessary to set out and clarify the applicable law in relation to these modes of responsibility insofar as it is necessary for its own decision.

26. The actus reus of "planning" requires that one or more persons design the criminal conduct constituting one or more statutory crimes that are later perpetrated. It is sufficient to demonstrate that the planning was a factor substantially contributing to such criminal conduct. [...]

29. The mens rea for these modes of responsibility is established if the perpetrator acted with direct intent in relation to his own planning, instigating, or ordering. [...]

31. The Appeals Chamber similarly holds that in relation to "planning", a person who plans an act or omission with the awareness of the substantial likelihood that a crime will be committed

in the execution of that plan, has the requisite mens rea for establishing responsibility under Article 7(1) of the Statute pursuant to planning. Planning with such awareness has to be regarded as accepting that crime.

ICTY, Prosecutor *v.* Dragomir Milošević, *Appeals Chamber, Judgment of 12 November 2009*

Dragomir Milošević was the second Serb general in charge of the siege of Sarajevo from August 1994 until November 1995. He succeeded General Stanislav Galić who was tried and convicted before Milošević for war crimes and crimes against humanity in connection with the siege and was sentenced to life imprisonment. Milošević was also convicted of both war crimes and crimes against humanity for his role in continuing and maintaining the siege. He was initially sentenced to 33 years' imprisonment, but his term was reduced to 29 years by the Appeals Chamber. While it was clear that the sniping and shelling of civilians that characterized the siege was 'planned', the Appeals Chamber considered carefully Milošević's specific role in planning, considering that he inherited the siege from Galić, that he was not the most senior figure in the Bosnian Serb Army, and that it is likely that some of the crimes were planned by subordinate soldiers.

268. Although Milošević does not explicitly challenge his responsibility for planning the crimes under this ground of appeal, the Appeals Chamber takes note of his relevant submissions under other grounds and decides to address the issue within the present Section of the Judgement. In this regard, the Appeals Chamber recalls that the actus reus of "planning" requires that one or more persons design the criminal conduct constituting one or more statutory crimes that are later perpetrated. It is sufficient to demonstrate that the planning was a factor substantially contributing to such criminal conduct. The mens rea for this mode of responsibility entails the intent to plan the commission of a crime or, at a minimum, the awareness of the substantial likelihood that a crime will be committed in the execution of the acts or omissions planned.

269. The Appeals Chamber reiterates that the campaign of sniping and shelling civilians in Sarajevo was already in place when Milošević took the [Bosnian Serb Sarajevo Romanija Corps] SRK command over from Galić. Although this cannot be determinative in the present case, the Appeals Chamber finds it instructive to note that Galić was held responsible for ordering the indicted crimes, but not for planning them. Conversely, Milošević, although found not [to have] "devise[d] a strategy for Sarajevo on his own"[,] and having "acted in furtherance of orders by the VRS Main Staff", was convicted for both planning and ordering the campaign of shelling and sniping of civilians in Sarajevo during the Indictment period, subsequent to Galić's term in command.

270. With respect to the actus reus of planning, the Trial Chamber held that Milošević "was able to implement the greater strategy in a manner he saw fit". It is unclear from these findings whether Milošević was found to have participated in the design of the military strategy concerning the ongoing campaign as such or whether he planned each and every incident for which he is held responsible by the Trial Chamber. The Appeals Chamber further finds that it is unclear what specific evidence was relied upon by the Trial Chamber to come to these conclusions. In light of these uncertainties, the Appeals Chamber finds that Milošević's responsibility for planning of the campaign of sniping and shelling of civilians in Sarajevo as such could not be established beyond reasonable doubt.

271. The Appeals Chamber emphasizes that its findings above pertain strictly to Milošević's individual criminal responsibility for ordering and planning the campaign of shelling and sniping of civilians in Sarajevo as such, given that not all the legal requirements necessary for these modes of liability have been established at trial. These findings do not affect the conclusions of the Trial Chamber or those of the Galić Trial and Appeal Chambers that such a campaign took place in Sarajevo during the relevant period.

(b) Shelling incidents

272. The Trial Chamber established that Milošević ordered air bombs and distributed them between different SRK brigades, and that he ordered the construction of launchers of modified air bombs that were used by the SRK throughout its zone of responsibility in Sarajevo. The Trial Chamber further concluded that Milošević controlled the SRK shelling activities in general and, in particular, issued orders pertaining to positions of artillery pieces and to artillery ammunition. The Trial Chamber also heard evidence with respect to medium and heavy mortars that they would not be moved "unless this is ordered 'by the commander' ". Finally, the Trial Chamber established on the basis of direct evidence that Milošević planned and ordered the shelling in two specific incidents – the shelling of the TV Building and the shelling of Hrasnica neighbourhood on 7 April 1995.

273. On the basis of this evidence coupled with the established fact that Milošević was directly involved in the use and deployment of air modified bombs and issued orders regarding their use from as early as August 1994, the Appeals Chamber finds that it was not unreasonable for the Trial Chamber to conclude beyond reasonable doubt that all the shelling involving modified air bombs and mortars fired by the SRK in Sarajevo during the Indictment period could only occur pursuant to Milošević's orders. Furthermore, considering that modified air bombs were a highly inaccurate weapon, sometimes even described as uncontrollable, yet with extremely high explosive force, the Appeals Chamber finds that it was not unreasonable to establish that Milošević possessed the required mens rea for ordering the crimes of terror and crimes against humanity, either deliberately targeting civilians or attacking them indiscriminately.

274. However, the Appeals Chamber notes that the Trial Chamber's conclusions that Milošević planned the shelling incidents are based on essentially the same set of facts. In the circumstances of this case, the Appeals Chamber proprio motu finds that Milošević's responsibility for ordering fully encompasses his criminal conduct and thus does not warrant a conviction for planning the same crimes.

(c) Sniping incidents

275. The Trial Chamber inferred that Milošević planned and ordered sniping incidents from the fact that he was in charge of sniping activities in general. To illustrate this conclusion, the Trial Chamber referred to the fact that "sniping occurred over an extended period of time in different areas of Sarajevo on territory under control of different SRK brigades", thus showing that the operation of snipers was coordinated by Milošević, and that he issued "numerous orders relating to training, equipment and the deployment of snipers". The Trial Chamber noted that it had not been presented with "any written order [from Milošević] unequivocally ordering the sniping of civilians" but concluded that "the entire sniping campaign was under [Milošević's] control. The Appeals Chamber has already overturned the Trial Chamber's findings with respect to ordering and planning such a campaign as a whole due to the lack of evidence allowing [it] to establish beyond reasonable doubt the existence of such order in any form.

276. To establish that Milošević ordered all the sniping incidents attributed to the SRK by the Trial Judgement, the Trial Chamber further took into account the facts that Milošević (i) signed the Anti-sniping agreement of 14 August 1994 as one of his first actions when he became the commander of the SRK and had been involved in the negotiations before then; and (ii) signed an order to stop sniping. The Appeals Chamber finds that the Trial Chamber abused its discretion by taking into account instances where Milošević acted towards preventing the sniping as proof of him planning and ordering the sniping of civilians. The Trial Chamber also referred to "an order for combat readiness and to draw up a firing plan onto the Old Town" as examples of Milošević planning and ordering the sniping. However, in the absence of any mention of an exhibit or witness testimony, the Appeals Chamber is unable to discern what exactly the Trial Chamber was citing to.

277. Unlike the manner in which control was exercised over shelling activities, the Trial Chamber noted that Milošević "would issue general orders as to how to engage a target and the lower level commander would then organise the firing position. The organisation of firing systems at the positions was done by the squad, regiment, battalion or platoon commanders." Unlike the use of "uncontrollable" modified air bombs, snipers are generally precise in hitting the target. Moreover, the Trial Chamber heard "evidence that not all the sniping of civilians was intentional". In these circumstances, the Appeals Chamber concludes that the inference that Milošević ordered all sniping incidents attributed to the SRK snipers by the Trial Judgement is not the only reasonable one on the ground that he generally controlled the sniping activity and training. The Appeals Chamber therefore quashes Milošević's convictions for ordering and planning the crimes related to the sniping incidents.

COMMENTARY

Planning can seem like an essential mode of liability, but it also poses a paradox. Planning will often be inferred from the organized and systematic nature of the conduct that constitutes the crime, but often when the crime has in fact occurred the accused will be liable for ordering or participating in some way, the commission of the crime. In such a case, planning liability is subsumed under commission liability. Perhaps the better way to think about planning is to regard it rather as an aggravating factor. A crime that is planned and then executed is more grave and should be punished more seriously than one that is not. In any case, while planning is frequently not difficult to infer from large-scale atrocities, the specific role of each accused in the planning may be more difficult to discern.

QUESTIONS

1. If planning is allowed as a mode of liability regardless of whether the crime is in fact committed, should there be any additional elements required? For example, liability for planning alone could be limited to those cases where a large-scale crime is being contemplated, or when there is a specific degree of intent, or where there is direct proof of the planning. Why might such additional requirements be important?

2. Are there advantages to the ICC regime, which appears to subsume planning under the concept of co-perpetration?

FURTHER READING

Cassese, *International Criminal Law*, 225–7.

S. Manacorda, 'Planning', in A. Cassese (ed.), *Oxford Companion to International Criminal Justice* (Oxford: Oxford University Press, 2009), 456–7.

5

ORDERING

(A) OVERVIEW

Sometimes regarded as a form of instigation – participating in a crime before its perpetration by inducing it[1] – ordering liability involves the particularly dangerous spark of a superior in a civilian or military hierarchy directing a subordinate to commit a crime. The de facto or *de jure* superior must have the authority to order, thus posing the risk of, or causing, the commission of the crime. The requirement of an order – an affirmative act – is what distinguishes ordering responsibility (liability for commission) from the broader reach of superior responsibility based on culpable omissions – the failure to prevent or punish – (liability for omission), discussed in the later section of this chapter.[2]

The notion of a superior is elastic and does not hinge on formal status because in the chaotic context in which international crimes tend to occur, there may be a superior-subordinate relationship without a formal hierarchy. Similarly, the order need not take a particular form or be in writing, accounting for the fluidity of realities on the ground, which may not pause for formal niceties.

Indeed, in the prosecution of Bosnian Serb Major General Stanislav Galić for the havoc wreaked on Sarajevo by Bosnian Serb sniping and shelling during the Bosnian conflict, a majority of an ICTY Trial Chamber reasoned that the existence of orders could be inferred:

740. The Defence's argument that there is no evidence of written orders establishing that General Galić ordered fire against civilians in Sarajevo is not persuasive. First, [...] an order need not to be in a particular form, it can be given in a wide variety of manners. Secondly, the Trial Chamber received reliable evidence that oral orders were issued on a daily basis by General Galić or the chain of command during the Sarajevo Romanija Corps briefings. [...]

741. [...] The Majority has already noted above that the manner of commission of these crimes reveals a striking similarity of pattern throughout. All this has led the Majority to draw the conclusion that the criminal acts were not sporadic acts of soldiers out of control but were carried out pursuant to a deliberate campaign of attacking civilians, which must have emanated from a higher authority or at least had its approval.

742. The Trial Chamber has already found that the Bosnian Serb troops positioned in and around Sarajevo were under the command of General Galić, who exerted control over them. The

---

[1] Sometimes in common law jurisdictions, instigators are termed accessories before the fact because they participate in the crime before its commission. The notion of instigation is an umbrella concept that captures an array of modes of participation, including ordering, soliciting or inducing the commission of a crime.

[2] Where the superior issues an order to commit a crime, the prosecution can proceed under both an ordering theory and a theory of superior responsibility. As discussed further in the next section, superior responsibility is conceptually distinct from, and covers a broader swathe of conduct than, liability for ordering because superior responsibility can also attach in certain circumstances even absent an order.

Trial Chamber has also found that General Galić was fully appraised of the criminal acts committed by forces under his command and within his zone of responsibility, which, at the least, he did not prevent the commission nor did he punish the perpetrator(s) thereof. According to the Majority, there is an irresistible inference to be drawn from the evidence on the Trial Record that what the Trial Chamber has found to be widespread and notorious attacks against the civilian population of Sarajevo could not have occurred without it being the will of the commander of those forces which perpetrated it [...][3]

Two questions that have arisen in ordering cases concern (i) whether an order must be executed for liability to ensue – a question that relates to the *actus reus* of the crime of ordering; and (ii) the baseline *mens rea* standard where direct intent to order crimes is lacking. The cases in the next two sections address these questions.

(B) MUST THE ORDER BE EXECUTED?

When subordinates resist compliance with an order to engage in criminality, leaving the order unexecuted, can a superior escape liability for issuing the order? Or does an order to commit a crime by someone with authority pose such a risk of commission that the order, even if unexecuted, constitutes a crime, to be condemned to deter such abuses of power? The approach in the excerpt below has been taken by a number of military courts.

Cases

USA, Court-Martial of General Jacob H. Smith, Sen. Doc. No. 213, 57th Cong., 2s Sess. 3, 3 March 1903

> After participating in the brutal campaign against Native Americans, and taking part in the infamous massacre of the Sioux at Wounded Knee, Jacob H. Smith went to the Philippine islands, where he was promoted to Brigadier General in the US Army and put in charge of the military campaign in the island of Samar. The court-martial proceeding below was based on his notorious order to take no prisoners and kill all over the age of 10.

Office of the Judge-Advocate-General, War Department, Washington, June 19, 1902

General Smith was arraigned upon the following charge and specification:

CHARGE. – Conduct to the prejudice of good order and military discipline.

Specification. – In that Brig. General Jacob H. Smith, U.S. Army, commanding general of the Sixth Separate Brigade, Division of the Philippines, did give instructions in regard to the conduct of hostilities in the island of Samar, P.I. [Philippine Islands], to his subordinate officer, Maj. L.W.T. Waller, U.S. Marine Corps, the said Waller being under his command and commanding at the time a subterritorial district in the island of Samar, P.I., in language and words, to wit: "I want no prisoners" (meaning thereby that giving of quarter was not desired or required) and "I wish you to kill and burn. The more you kill and burn, the better you will please me," and

---

[3] *Prosecutor* v. *Galić*, ICTY Trial Chamber Case No. IT-98-29-T, Trial Judgment, 5 December 2003.

"the interior of Samar must be made a howling wilderness" and did further give instructions to said Major Waller that he, (General Smith), wanted all persons killed who were capable of bearing arms, and did, in reply to a question by said Major Waller, asking for an age limit, designate the age limit as 10 years of age. This at or near the island of Samar, P.I., between the 23d day of October, 1901, [and] the 30th day of November, 1901. [. . .]

General Smith's Orders

In the statement which accompanied his plea [of not guilty to the charges conduct to the prejudice of good order and military discipline], General Smith expressly admits that he instructed Major Waller "not to burden himself with prisoners, of which he, General Smith, already had so many that the efficiency of his command was impaired;" that "he wanted him to kill and burn in the interior and hostile country;" and the "interior of Samar must be made a howling wilderness," and that "he wanted all persons killed who were capable of bearing arms and were actively employed in hostilities against the United States," and that he did "designate the age limit of 10 years, as boys of that age were actively engaged in hostilities [. . .]"

The Judge-Advocate-General also detailed how the order was further corroborated by eye-witness testimony.

[The orders] were in direct opposition to the requirements of paragraph 60 of the instructions for the government of armies in the field, which declares it to be "against the usage of modern war to resolve, in hatred and revenge, to give no quarter. No body of troops has the right to declare that it will not give, and therefore will not expect, quarter;" and the testimony shows that there was no occasion to bring into operation the qualifying clause of that paragraph, which provides that "a commander is permitted to direct his troops to give no quarter, in great straits, when his own salvation makes it impossible to encumber himself with prisoners."

The refusal of quarter is an act of serious importance, and is determined upon by the general commander in chief after full consideration of all the circumstances which seem to call for an exercise of the right of retaliation – a right which is rarely resorted to in modern war. It is a power which should never be delegated to subordinates, for the reason that such a delegation would be calculated to introduce as many different policies in respect to the refusal of quarter as there were separate subordinate commanders, and uniformity of policy throughout the entire theater of military operations would thus become impossible of attainment. That the instructions were not executed is due [. . .] to the good sense of his subordinates, whose better judgment of the emergency made such execution unnecessary.

The findings of the court are as follows: [. . .]

Of the charge, "Guilty."

Upon the foregoing findings the following sentence was imposed by the court: [. . .] to be admonished by the reviewing authority.

The court is thus lenient in view of the undisputed evidence that the accused did not mean everything that his unexplained language implied; that his subordinates did not gather such a meaning; and that the orders were never executed in such sense, notwithstanding the fact that a desperate struggle was being conducted with a cruel and savage foe.

War Department, Washington, July 12, 1902 [from Elihu Root, Secretary of War to President Theodore Roosevelt]

[. . .] An examination of the evidence has satisfied me that the conviction was just, and the reasons for the very light sentence imposed are sustained by the facts. General Smith, in his conversation with Major Waller, was guilty of intemperate, inconsiderate, and violent expressions, which, if accepted literally, would grossly violate the humane rules governing American armies in the field, and if followed, would have brought lasting disgrace upon the military service of the United States. Fortunately they were not taken literally and were not followed. No women or children or helpless persons or noncombatants or prisoners were put to death in pursuance of them. [. . .]

It is due, however, to the good sense and self-restraint of General Smith's subordinates, and their regard for the laws of war, rather than his own self-control and judgement, that his intemperate and unjustifiable verbal instructions were not followed, and that he is relieved from the indelible stain which would have resulted from literal compliance with them. [. . .]

[. . .] Although the sentence imposed is exceedingly light, it carries with it a condemnation which, for an officer of his rank and age, is really a severe punishment. [. . .]

White House, Washington, July 14, 1902 [From President Theodore Roosevelt]

[. . .] The findings and sentence of the court are approved. [. . .] I am well [aw]are of the danger and great difficulty of the task our Army has had in the Philippine Islands and of the well-nigh intolerable provocations it has received from the cruelty, treachery, and total disregard of the rules and customs of civilized warfare on the part of its foes. [. . .] It would be culpable to show weakness in dealing with such foes or to fail to use all legitimate and honorable methods to overcome them. But the very fact that warfare is of such character as to afford infinite provocation for the commission of acts of cruelty by junior officers and the enlisted men, must make the officers in high and responsible position peculiarly carefully [*sic*] in their bearing and conduct so as to keep a moral check over any acts of improper character by their subordinates [. . .] Loose and violent talk by an officer of high rank is always likely to excite to wrongdoing those among his subordinates whose wills are weak or whose passions are strong. [. . .]

COMMENTARY

While harm is mitigated when an order is not carried out, the issuance of an order to commit illegal acts is an *actus reus* that still poses sufficient risk to warrant criminal liability. Even if not implemented, it creates an atmosphere in which illegality and breaches may seem to be condoned by authority. Indeed Major Littleton Waller went on to be tried by court-martial for executing 11 Filipino guides without trial. Major Waller did not try to rely on General Smith's order as a defence but the content of the order came out during Waller's court-martial proceeding.

Paradoxically, the greater the degree of apparent criminality of the order, the less may be the risk of realization because subordinates are alerted that something is wrong with the order and the usual obedience cannot obtain. Yet because punishment in part vindicates the harm to victims, and an unexecuted order means there were no victims as a consequence of it, the punishment may be less though the culpable act and intent may be particularly aggravated.

While criminal liability *may* attach for unexecuted orders, the International Criminal Court only takes within its purview ordering as a mode of liability when the crime occurs or is attempted.[4] This reflects the logic of assuming jurisdiction over the most serious crimes, defined by realized social harm or proximity to realized social harm. The risk posed by unexecuted orders may be better addressed in the domestic context.

Recall that in certain circumstances, contemporary international criminal law may criminalize even the issuance of orders that are lawful on their face. Such orders, while

---

[4] Art. 25.3(b) ICCSt.

lawful on their face, may in context be illegal or pose a substantial risk that malfeasance will occur in the execution. When criminal liability is pursued for orders where there is no explicit exhortation of unlawful acts nor direct intent to order unlawful acts, the question of what level of *mens rea* is acceptable for liability becomes particularly important, as considered in the next section.

(C) *MENS REA*

Plainly intent to have a subordinate commit a crime is a culpable mental state. The difficult question arises where direct intent to order a crime is lacking. The excerpts below address the question of whether those with authority to order may be held liable based on a form of recklessness or its civil-law analogue of *dolus eventualis*, defined and contrasted in the excerpts below.

ICTY, Prosecutor v. Blaškić, *Trial Chamber, Judgment of 3 March 2000*

During the three-way civil war that ravaged Bosnia in the 1990s, the accused, Tihomir Blaškić, commanded the armed forces of the Croatian Defence Council (HVO) of the Croatian Community of Herzeg-Bosna in the central Bosnian region of conflict. The Croatian Community aimed to eventually unite Bosnian areas that were majority ethnic Croatian with neighbouring Croatia.

The events in the indictment against General Blaškić stem from fighting between HVO forces and the majority-Muslim Bosnian Army (ABiH) in central Bosnia between May 1992 and January 1994. The excerpt below analyses whether General Blaškić may be held criminally responsible for war crimes and crimes against humanity based on an order that, on its face, was concerned with establishing a defensive counterattack in the event of a Muslim attack, when HVO forces subsequently killed Muslim civilians and burned their homes in Ahmići village, and other areas.

281. The *Akayesu* Trial Chamber was of the opinion that ordering

implies a superior-subordinate relationship between the person giving the order and the one executing it. In other words, the person in a position of authority uses it to convince another to commit an offence.

There is no requirement that the order be in writing or in any particular form; it can be express or implied. That an order was issued may be proved by circumstantial evidence. [...]

282. [...] [I]t is irrelevant whether the illegality of the order was apparent on its face. [...]

i) The orders issued by the accused

[...] 434. The second order is dated 15 April at 15:45 hours. According to the witness Marin, that "order for action" was given in response to information from the HVO intelligence services pointing to a general mobilisation in Zenica of Muslim forces assumed to be arriving via Mount Kuber. The accused further referred to the abduction of [HVO] Commander Totic by the ABiH at Zenica on 15 April, which allegedly caused a great frenzy in the population and was described by the accused as "pure terrorism" designed to eliminate the Commanders of the HVO brigades. The enemy designated in that order was the seventh Muslim brigade which the order accused of being responsible for a new wave of terrorist activities. That order was addressed to the *Viteška* brigade of the HVO and to the Military Police Fourth Battalion. They were asked to ensure that "combat readiness [...] be increased to the highest level" and that they were ready "to take defensive action". [...] Even though the order was not an order to carry out combat operations, the accused admitted that action could be taken by virtue of that order in particular to combat terrorist activities.

435. A third order, which again referred to "planned terrorist activities" on the part of the enemy and to the risk of its engaging in an open offensive designed to destroy everything Croatian, was given on 16 April at 01:30 hours and addressed to the *Viteška* brigade and to the Tvrtko independent units. That "combat command order to prevent attack activity by the enemy" ordered Commander Cerkez and the Tvrtko independent units "to occupy the defence region, blockade villages and prevent all entrances to and exits from the villages". The order stated that "in the event of open attack activity by the Muslims", those units should "neutralize them and prevent their movement with precise fire" in counterattack. That order indicated that the forces of the Military Police Fourth Battalion, the N. Š. Zrinski unit and the civilian police would also take part in the combat. The order required the forces to be ready to open fire at 05:30 hours and, by way of combat formation, provided for blockade (observation and ambush), search and attack forces. [...]

ii) The accused ordered the attack of 16 April 1993

437. The Trial Chamber finds that the third order [designated D269], dated 16 April at 01:30 hours is very clearly an order to attack. That order, which was addressed in particular to the *Viteška* brigade, also expressly mentions other units, such as the Military Police Fourth Battalion, the forces of the N.Š. Zrinski unit and the forces of the civilian police which were recognised on the ground as being those which had carried out the attack. The time to commence hostilities which is set out in that order corresponds very precisely to the start of fighting on the ground. Admittedly, the order is presented as "a combat command order to prevent attack activity by the enemy". Accordingly, the attack purportedly formed part of a defensive rather than offensive strategy. However the Trial Chamber has already concluded that no military objective justified that attack [after finding there was insufficient evidence of an imminent attack justifying the attack order.] [...]

469. The Trial Chamber observes that the reasons adduced in order to justify the order of 16 April (D269) are based on propaganda designed to incite racial hatred. [...] Order D269 refers to the intention of the Muslim forces to destroy everything Croatian. Several international observers have stated that those words gave a very exaggerated picture as compared with the real situation. [...]

470. The Trial Chamber further notes that those orders recommend the modes of combat that were actually used on the ground on 16 April. [...] Order D269 refers to blocking (observation and ambush), search and offensive forces. The main (mountain and valley) roads between Vitez and Zenica were in fact blocked by HVO blocking forces on the morning of 16 April, in particular by the *Viteška* brigade. According to witness Landry, the area was subjected to a so-called "cleansing" operation, which was carried out by establishing a cordon outside the village by means of check points on the roads leading to the villages, whilst lighter, more mobile troops, notably search troops, carried out the "cleansing" of the village. [...]

472. The testimony of the victims of the massacres tended to show that the civilians were killed in response to orders. Accordingly, witness Fatima Ahmic testified that she heard an HVO soldier in a van say by walkie-talkie: "Yes, the operation was successful, they are lying in front of houses like pigs". When she asked them why they had killed her son, the soldiers said that "it was the *force majeure* who ordered it...the orders came from above". Witness Abdullah Ahmic testified that he saw a soldier say to another soldier who refused to

kill a man: "do as you are ordered". Witness Cazim Ahmic testified to what an officer, Ibrica Kupreškic, said to him: "go and run for your life. No Muslim may stay here. If they learn that I let you go, I will be executed". According to witness F, the Djokeri and the Vitezovi said that they had been given orders to kill all the Muslims so that Muslims would never ever live there again. Witness A said that he heard a person named Cicko speak in these terms with regard to the events of 16 April: "everyone is washing their hands now as regards Ahmici, but we all know that Blaškic has ordered that no prisoners of war were of interest to him, only dead bodies". [...]

vi) The risk taken by the accused

474. Even if doubt were still cast in spite of everything on whether the accused ordered the attack with the clear intention that the massacre would be committed, he would still be liable under Article 7(1) of the Statute for ordering the crimes. As has been explained above, any person who, in ordering an act, knows that there is a risk of crimes being committed and accepts that risk, shows the degree of intention necessary (recklessness) so as to incur responsibility for having ordered, planned or incited the commitment of the crimes. In this case, the accused knew that the troops which he had used to carry out the order of attack of 16 April had previously been guilty of many crimes against the Muslim population of Bosnia. The order given by the accused on 4 November 1992 expressly prohibiting the troops from burning the houses proves this. Moreover, the accused admitted before the Trial Chamber that he had been informed about the crimes committed by troops acting in the area for which he was responsible. In particular, the disciplinary reports were forwarded to him. Likewise, the accused stated that he asked the Commander of the main general staff and the head of the Defence Department in January 1993 that the independent units be withdrawn from the Central Bosnia Operative Zone on account of the troubles they were causing. Furthermore, the accused was aware that there were criminals acting in the ranks of the Military Police. [...] Admittedly, the accused did give an order on 18 January 1993 for the attention of the regular units of the HVO, the independent units and the Military Police Fourth Battalion instructing them to make sure that all soldiers prone to criminal conduct were not in a position to do any harm. However, that order remained without effect, even though the accused issued a reminder on 6 February 1993. On the contrary, according to the witness Marin the situation deteriorated thereafter. The Defence also presented an order issued by the accused on 17 March 1993 requiring the commanders of all HVO brigades to identify their members who were prone to criminal conduct. Nevertheless, the Trial Chamber finds that the accused did not ensure himself, before calling on their services on 16 April, that measures had indeed been taken so as to be sure that those criminal elements were not in a position to do any harm. On the contrary, according to the accused it was not until he received the letter from Colonel Stewart on 22 April 1993 that he realised that he could not rely on the reports sent to him by the Military Police commander Ljubicic. It was not until 30 April that the accused asked the commander of the main staff to replace Paško Ljubicic and to change the structure of that unit.

The Trial Chamber found Blaškić guilty of war crimes and crimes against humanity. Discounting General Blaškić's expressions of deep remorse over his inability to constrain his troops from committing the crimes, the Trial Chamber sentenced him to 45 years in prison.

General Blaškić appealed his conviction and sentence. Among the errors he alleged on appeal was the Trial Judgment's incorrect interpretation of order D269 as a basis for holding him liable for killings of Muslims in the Ahmići area. In the excerpt below the Appeals Chamber agreed that the Trial Chamber had erred.

ICTY, Prosecutor *v.* Blaškić, *Appeals Chamber, Judgment of 29 July 2004*

27. According to the Appellant, the standards set forth in the Trial Judgement concerning the forms of criminal participation consisting of planning, instigating, and ordering under Article 7(1) of the Statute deviate from those established by the jurisprudence of the International Tribunal and the ICTR, customary international law, and national legislation. The Appellant submits that the correct standard of *mens rea* for these three forms of criminal participation is "direct or specific intent," rather than the "indirect" or recklessness standard adopted by the Trial Chamber in this case. In addition, he alleges that the Trial Chamber failed to differentiate between the recklessness standard and that of *dolus eventualis*, and improperly applied these concepts.

28. The Appellant further claims that his conviction has been erroneously based on a strict liability theory. He submits that the Trial Chamber erroneously considered that a lawful order can become unlawful circumstantially "because unlawful acts have occurred in its implementation." He also claims that, under that standard, a commander may be held responsible for "anything that takes place once his order has begun," regardless of whether these acts were within the scope of actions intended by the commander himself. [...]

32. [...] The issue which the Appeals Chamber will address is whether a standard of *mens rea* that is lower than direct intent may apply in relation to ordering under Article 7(1) of the Statute, and if so, how it should be defined. [...]

34. In further examining the issue of whether a standard of *mens rea* that is lower than direct intent may apply in relation to ordering under Article 7(1) of the Statute, the Appeals Chamber deems it useful to consider the approaches of national jurisdictions. In common law systems, the *mens rea* of recklessness is sufficient to ground liability for serious crimes such as murder or manslaughter. In the United States, for example, the concept of recklessness in criminal cases has been defined in the Model Penal Code[5] as follows:

> a conscious disregard of a substantial and unjustifiable risk that the material element exists or will result from the [actor]'s conduct. The risk must be of such a nature and degree that, considering the nature and purpose of the actor's conduct and the circumstances known to him, its disregard involves a gross deviation from the standard of conduct that a law-abiding person would observe in the actor's situation.

According to the Model Penal Code, therefore, the degree of risk involved must be substantial and unjustifiable; a mere possibility of risk is not enough.

35. In the United Kingdom, the House of Lords in the case of *R v. G and another* considered the ambit of recklessness within the meaning of section 1 of the Criminal Damage Act of 1971. Lord Bingham's opinion, with which his colleagues agreed, was that

> [A] person acts recklessly within the meaning of section 1 of the Criminal Damage Act 1971 with respect to – (i) a circumstance when he is aware of a risk that it exists or will exist; (ii) a result when he is aware of a risk that it will occur; and it is, in the circumstances known to him, unreasonable to take the risk [...]

---

5 [63] In his Foreword to the Model Penal Code, Herbert Wechsler (Director of the American Law Institute from 1963 to 1984) writes: "The Model Penal Code of the American Law Institute, completed in 1962, played an important part in the widespread revision and codification of the substantive criminal law of the United States that has been taking place in the last twenty years. [...] It is fair to say that [the] thirty-four [state] enactments were all influenced in some part by the positions taken in the Model Code, though the extent to which particular formulations or approaches of the Model were adopted or adapted varied extensively from state to state." Foreword, May 30, 1985.

According to this opinion, the risk involved must be unreasonable; furthermore, with respect to a particular result, the actor in question must be aware of a risk that such a result will occur, not merely that it may occur.

36. In the Australian High Court decision of *R v. Crabbe,* the Court considered "whether the knowledge which an accused person must possess in order to render him guilty of murder when he lacks an actual intent to kill or to do grievous bodily harm must be knowledge of the probability that his acts will cause death or grievous bodily harm (...) or whether knowledge of a possibility is enough." The High Court determined that:

> The conclusion that a person is guilty of murder if he commits a fatal act knowing that it will probably cause death or grievous bodily harm but (absent an intention to kill or do grievous bodily harm) is not guilty of murder if he knew only that his act might possibly cause death or grievous bodily harm is not only supported by a preponderance of authority but is sound in principle. The conduct of a person who does an act, knowing that death or grievous bodily harm is *a probable consequence*, can naturally be regarded for the purposes of the criminal law as just as blameworthy as the conduct of one who does an act intended to kill or to do grievous bodily harm.

37. The High Court in *R v. Crabbe* also considered the situation where a person's knowledge of the probable consequence of his act is accompanied by indifference, finding that:

> A person who does an act causing death knowing that it is probable that the act will cause death or grievous bodily harm is...guilty of murder, although such knowledge is accompanied by indifference whether death or grievous bodily harm might not [sic] be caused or not, or even by a wish that death or grievous bodily harm might not be caused. That does not mean that reckless indifference is an element of the mental state necessary to constitute the crime of murder. It is not the offender's indifference to the consequences of his act but his knowledge that those consequences will probably occur that is the relevant element.

38. In the common law jurisdictions examined above, the *mens rea* of recklessness incorporates the awareness of a risk that the result or consequence will occur or will probably occur, and the risk must be unjustifiable or unreasonable. The mere possibility of a risk that a crime or crimes will occur as a result of the actor's conduct generally does not suffice to ground criminal responsibility.

39. In civil law systems, the concept of *dolus eventualis* may constitute the requisite *mens rea* for crimes. In French law, for example, this has been characterized as the taking of a risk and the acceptance of the eventuality that harm may result. Although the harm in question was not desired by the actor, it was caused by his dangerous behaviour, which was carried out deliberately and with the knowledge that harm may occur. In Italian law, the principle is expressed as follows: the occurrence of the fact constituting a crime, even though it is not desired by the perpetrator, is foreseen and accepted as a possible consequence of his own conduct. The German Federal Supreme Court (Bundesgerichtshof, BGH) has found that acting with *dolus eventualis* requires that the perpetrator perceive the occurrence of the criminal result as possible and not completely remote, and that he endorse it or at least come to terms with it for the sake of the desired goal.[6] It has further stated that in the case of extremely

---

6 [73] BGHSt 36, 1–20 [9–10]: "According to the established jurisprudence of the Federal Supreme Court on the delimitation of *dolus eventualis* and conscious/advertent negligence, the perpetrator is acting intentionally if he recognizes as possible and not entirely unlikely the fulfilment of the elements of an offence and agrees to it in such a way that he approves the fulfilment of the elements of the offence or at least reconciles himself with it in order to reach the intended result, even if he does not wish for the fulfilment of the elements of the crime; conscious negligence means that the perpetrator does not agree with the fulfilment

dangerous, violent acts, it is obvious that the perpetrator takes into account the possibility of the victim's death and, since he continues to carry out the act, accepts such a result. The volitional element denotes the borderline between *dolus eventualis* and advertent or conscious negligence. [. . .]

41. Having examined the approaches of national systems as well as International Tribunal precedents, the Appeals Chamber considers that none of the Trial Chamber's above articulations of the *mens rea* for ordering under Article 7(1) of the Statute, in relation to a culpable mental state that is lower than direct intent, is correct. The knowledge of any kind of risk, however low, does not suffice for the imposition of criminal responsibility for serious violations of international humanitarian law. The Trial Chamber does not specify what degree of risk must be proven. Indeed, it appears that under the Trial Chamber's standard, any military commander who issues an order would be criminally responsible, because there is always a possibility that violations could occur. The Appeals Chamber considers that an awareness of a higher likelihood of risk and a volitional element must be incorporated in the legal standard.

42. The Appeals Chamber therefore holds that a person who orders an act or omission with the awareness of the substantial likelihood that a crime will be committed in the execution of that order, has the requisite *mens rea* for establishing liability under Article 7(1) pursuant to ordering. Ordering with such awareness has to be regarded as accepting that crime.

On the facts, the Appeals Chamber found that the Trial Chamber's finding that General Blaškić issued Order D269 with 'clear intention' that the later massacre would occur was wholly erroneous. The Appeals Chamber next considered whether the evidence established awareness of a substantial likelihood that civilians would be harmed.

344. The Trial Chamber concluded that since the Appellant knew that some of the troops engaged in the attack on Ahmići and the neighbouring villages had previously participated in criminal acts against the Muslim population of Bosnia or had criminals within their ranks, when ordering those troops to launch an attack on 16 April 1993 pursuant to D269, the Appellant deliberately took the risk that crimes would be committed against the Muslim civilian population in the Ahmići area and their property. [. . .]

346. The evidence underlying [. . .] the Trial Judgement [finding] consists of orders issued by the Appellant with the aim of deterring criminal conduct, *i.e.*, orders prohibiting looting, the burning of Muslim houses, and instructing the identification of soldiers prone to criminal conduct. The analysis of the evidence relied upon by the Trial Chamber supports the conclusion that concrete measures had been taken to deter the occurrence of criminal activities, and for the removal of criminal elements once they had been identified. For instance, approximately a month before the attack of 16 April 1993 took place, the Appellant had ordered the commanders of HVO brigades and independent units to identify the causes of disruptive conduct, and to remove, arrest and disarm conscripts prone to criminal conduct.

347. The Appeals Chamber considers that the orders and reports outlined above, may be regarded at most, as sufficient to demonstrate the Appellant's knowledge of the mere possibility that crimes could be committed by some elements. However, they do not constitute sufficient evidence to prove, under the legal standard articulated by the Appeals Chamber, awareness on the part of the Appellant of a substantial likelihood that crimes would be committed in the execution of D269.

of the elements of the crime – which he recognizes as possible – and seriously – not only vaguely – trusts that the fulfilment will not come about." Confirmed in BGH v. 7. 6. 1994 – 4 StR 105/94, reproduced in *Strafverteidiger* (StV) 1994, 654 (and BGH v. 22. 2. 2000 – 5 StR 573/99, reproduced in *Neue Zeitschrift für Strafrecht – Rechtsprechungsreport* [NStZ-RR] 2000, 165).

348. Therefore, the Appeals Chamber is not satisfied that the relevant trial evidence and the additional evidence admitted on appeal prove beyond reasonable doubt that the Appellant is responsible under Article 7(1) of the Statute for ordering the crimes committed in the Ahmići area on 16 April 1993.

Based on these errors of the Trial Chamber and other errors, the Appeals Chamber reduced General Blaškić's sentence to nine years.

COMMENTARY

In war, there is always a risk that things will go terribly wrong and many people will die. Plainly, therefore, the Trial Chamber's *mens rea* standard holding an officer or other person in a position to order liable merely because he 'knows that there is a risk of crimes being committed and accepts that risk' is problematic. How can it be a practicable standard to guide judgment in the grim realities of combat situations?

Consider Blaškić's contention that the Trial Chamber's standard verged on strict liability for crimes that may ensue in executing a lawful order. Is his argument far off the mark or is the Trial Chamber's *mens rea* standard so elastic that it allows essentially open discretion to hold an officer liable if things go wrong? One of the challenges after the kinds of affectively charged violence that are often the stuff of international crimes is to adhere to standards of individual responsibility that ensure that punishment is tied to individual moral desert and culpability. Does the Appeals Chamber's stronger standard, requiring, at a minimum, awareness of a substantial likelihood that crimes may be committed in carrying out the order, better accomplish this objective?

Also consider the distinction between how the Trial Chamber and the Appeals Chamber interpreted the evidence. The Trial Chamber judgment pointed to Blaškić's orders trying to address and prevent misconduct among unruly troops as evidence of guilt. If a superior's attempts to manage and mitigate unruliness among subordinates are used as evidence of guilt, does this create a perverse incentive? What *should* Blaškić have done?

QUESTIONS

1. Is it just to impose criminal liability for an order that is lawful on its face where direct intent to order criminal conduct is lacking? Is there a principled way to distinguish liability in such circumstances from virtual strict liability when things go wrong in the execution of an order and, in the grim light of retrospect, we are apt to see substantial risk in the issuance of the order?

2. On the other hand, imagine a situation where a military commander's order is to achieve a military objective that is not per se criminal. Due to the circumstances, however, both he and any reasonable observer know perfectly well that the only way to reach that military objective is by committing crimes. Is it fair to allow a commander to escape liability in such circumstances?

3. While a hierarchy of crimes and modes of liability have yet to be established in international criminal law, if you were to generate a sentencing scheme to reflect relative degrees of culpability, would you put ordering as a mode of liability near the top?

4. Should the relative seniority of the person with authority to order be an aggravating circumstance for the purposes of ascribing culpability and sentencing? When might the rule of thumb of aggravating culpability based on the seniority of the person issuing the order be misguided?

FURTHER READING

I. Bantekas, *Principles of Direct and Superior Responsibility in International Humanitarian Law* (Manchester: Manchester University Press, 2002).

A. Eser, 'Individual Criminal Responsibility', in A. Cassese *et al.* (eds), *The Rome Statute of the International Criminal Court: A Commentary*, Vol. I (Oxford: Oxford University Press, 2002), 795–7.

G. Mettraux, 'U.S. Courts-Martial and the Armed Conflict in the Philippines (1899–1902): Their Contribution to National Case Law on War Crimes', (2003) 1 JICJ 135.

6

AIDING AND ABETTING

Although aiding and abetting as a mode of liability addresses the most marginal form of criminal participation, it can be a powerful weapon in the international prosecutor's arsenal. Considerable attention has been paid to the potentially broad reaches of joint criminal enterprise liability, or even co-perpetration, but aiding and abetting also has the particular ability to touch conduct at the edges of criminal activity. Because of the lower showing required (depending on the court) both for the *actus reus* and the *mens rea* of aiding and abetting, this mode of liability can capture the acts of perpetrators who play a more peripheral, but nonetheless important, role in the commission of atrocities.

Perhaps a better way to think about aiding and abetting, though, is not as a mode of liability that operates at the periphery, but rather as one that has the potential to fill gaps in the liability scheme. While other modes of liability directly address the conduct of those at the top of a criminal organization (who order, plan or organize criminal conduct) or that of direct perpetrators at the bottom of the group (who commit the acts), aiding and abetting can reach the participation of actors *in between*: those many individuals who contribute in small but cumulatively essential ways to the commission of mass crimes. In the excerpts below, the courts frequently show an acute understanding of how large-scale international crimes occur; they require not just planners and perpetrators, but numerous actors who participate – sometimes simply by doing their 'job' or because they want to get along or are unwilling to object to those more powerful – and who together make it possible for the crime to occur on a massive level. Thus, through the analysis of the most exiguous mode of liability, courts grapple with some of the hardest and most essential questions about the responsibility of small and ordinary actors in international crimes.

Aiding and abetting can fill other gaps as well. Sometimes senior leaders will participate in the commission of crimes simply by giving their tacit approval and encouragement, conduct that may best be characterized as aiding and abetting. Additionally, aiding and abetting can sometimes fill evidentiary gaps. Investigators and prosecutors of massive crimes often have limited access to evidence and few investigative tools (particularly as compared to domestic authorities). Accordingly, even with regard to more central participants, sometimes the *available* evidence will support no more than a charge of aiding and abetting.

The evolution of the concept of aiding and abetting has seen expansion followed by some arguable retrenchment, as one can note in the excerpts below. The World War II cases applied the concept of aiding and abetting as accessory liability, but did not fully articulate its contours and sometimes applied it unevenly. The modern ad hoc international tribunals fully fleshed out the concept, ultimately holding that an aider and abetter is one who makes a *substantial* contribution to the commission of a crime, with the *knowledge* that his or her acts will assist in the commission of the crime in question, but not necessarily with an *intent* to promote the crime. This articulation of the concept was particularly useful to prosecutors because it perfectly captured the conduct of actors who participated in crimes because doing so fitted in with their bureaucratic or organizational function, but without any actual desire or intent to further the crimes. Additionally, intent can often be the most difficult element to prove, since it usually must be inferred, and so the diminished intent requirement of aiding and abetting at the ad hoc tribunals allowed it to serve as a useful backup charge to charges of more direct and intentional participation in crimes.

The ICCSt., however, appears to have retreated somewhat from the broad concept developed at the ad hoc tribunals. Article 25(3)(c) assigns liability to a person who, '[f]or the purpose of facilitating the commission of [...] a crime [under the Statute], aids, abets or otherwise assists in its commission or its attempted commission, including providing the means for its commission'. On its face, this formulation does not include a requirement that the contribution be 'substantial', but it appears to require that an aider and abettor not simply have 'knowledge' of the main perpetrator's intent, but share it. While the ICC has yet to litigate the concept of aiding and abetting, it appears that this version may allow for a more minimal *actus reus* but require a higher *mens rea* than at the ad hoc tribunals. On the other hand, Article 25(3) further contains section (d) which, while not called 'aiding and abetting', might capture conduct (particularly in its subsection (ii)) that would fall under aiding and abetting liability at the ad hoc tribunals:

(d) In any other way contributes to the commission or attempted commission of such a crime by a group of persons acting with a common purpose. Such contribution shall be intentional and shall either:

   (i)   Be made with the aim of furthering the criminal activity or criminal purpose of the group, where such activity or purpose involves the commission of a crime within the jurisdiction of the Court; or

   (ii) Be made in the knowledge of the intention of the group to commit the crime.

These questions await the further elucidation by future decisions of the ICC.

Cases

Federal Republic of Germany, S. and others (Hechingen and Haigerloch Deportation *case*), *Tribunal (Landgericht) Hechingen, Judgment of 28 June 1947*[1]

Five accused in this case were charged with assisting the Gestapo with the deportation of Jews from two towns in Germany, Hechingen and Haigerloch, to concentration camps in 1941–42. One of the accused was acquitted while four were convicted. None of these four accused devised or ordered the deportations. The principal accused was S., who was a senior administrative and police official who transmitted orders that he received from the Gestapo on to those responsible in the villages, while the other three – H., Ho. and K – were women who held no official positions but who were required to search the deportees to determine if they were holding any valuables. The first excerpt is from the trial judgment. The second excerpt is from the Court of Appeal which reversed the convictions of the three women and granted a new trial to S. In the second trial, S. was acquitted.

---

[1] English translation in (2009) 7 JICJ 131.

[. . .] On the basis of the trial and the hearing of the evidence, the following is established:

(a) The accused S., as then *Landrat* ['county president', senior administrative and police official of a County] of Hechingen, received the order of 14 August 1942 of the Stuttgart Head Office of the Gestapo [abbreviation of Geheime Staatspolizei, Secret State Police – the German text uses the full form throughout]. On 17 August 1942, he gave the mayors of Haigerloch and Hechingen the necessary instructions in writing for carrying out this order, in particular to have the Jews directed to 'deportation' and their luggage searched in the prescribed manner, and to ready these persons for transport on 19 August 1942. He further instructed persons officially subordinate to him to cooperate in the physical search of the persons to be deported; he gave this instruction to, among others, co-defendant Ms Ho., who carried it out on 19 August 1942 together with Mrs M., appointed for the purpose by the mayor of Haigerloch, in relation to the Jewish women concerned. These findings are based, to the extent that they relate to the accused Mr S., on his own statements; otherwise they result from the statements of co-defendant Ms Ho. The detail of how the physical search of the Jewish women by Ms Ho. occurred will be presented below in another context.

(b) A total of 138 people, 136 from Haigerloch and 2 from Hechingen, were affected by this fourth deportation. These 138 people were transported under police escort on 19 August 1942 from Haigerloch to Stuttgart, nine of the particularly infirm in road vehicles, the rest by rail. In Stuttgart they were brought to the Gestapo collecting point, and from there transported to Theresienstadt. Of the 138 people deported, only a single victim remained alive and returned to Haigerloch; all the others, it must be regarded as certain, either died or were killed during the deportation. Information on the circumstances in Theresienstadt has been provided by the testimony of Senior State Attorney Mr D. of Stuttgart. [. . .]

(2) The accused S., by executing himself in part the orders that reached him from the Gestapo and in part having them executed by people under him, participated in persecution on racial grounds and thus in a crime against humanity.

(a) Accused S. objectively, to be sure, acted neither as perpetrator (*Täter*) nor co-perpetrator (*Mittäter*) but as accessory (*Gehilfe*), since his participation was confined to executing the orders of the Gestapo in his capacity as *Landrat* of *Kreis* Hechingen, to the detriment of the Jews concerned, without departing from these orders on the basis of decisions of his own.

The consideration that the Gestapo orders would have been executed even if accused S. had not been involved in their execution, that is, the consideration that his participation was not causal for their success, does not exonerate the accused. The causality concept (*Ursachenbegriff*) in legal science is not – unlike that in natural science – mechanistically oriented, but teleologically, in the sense of the purpose of the legal system. Accordingly, no accessory can escape penal responsibility by showing that the main perpetrator (*Haupttäter*) could have carried out the act even without his assistance. In the great mechanism of the persecution of the Jews, every single cog was interchangeable at all times. Were one, given that fact, to seek to exclude the criminal responsibility of each interchangeable participant because of the absence of causality of his participation, then ultimately only the main perpetrators would be liable; all accessories would get off scot-free, even if they had acted on racial grounds, for even in the latter case their participation would, on a mechanistic view, not have been causal.

The accused S. has further appealed to the fact that it could not be within the intention of Control Council Law No. 10 to punish absolutely all participation in the carrying out of persecution of the Jews; for instance, a typist typing out the Gestapo deportation orders and posting them, or the driver of a locomotive pulling the train the deported Jews were to be transported by, could not be punishable. This consideration is just as wrong as the previous one, though in the opposite direction; while the previous consideration couched the concept of causality too narrowly, it is now too broad. From the impunity of participation by a typist or train driver, the impunity of the *Landrat*'s participation does not follow; to that extent, his argument does not prove what it is supposed to prove. The range of duties (*Pflichtenkreis*) of a typist or train driver is quite different from a *Landrat*'s. A typist's official duty is fulfilled in her accurately and punctually typing what she is asked to; a train driver's in bringing the rail transport punctually and safely to its destination; neither the one nor the other commits a breach of duty if their activity happened to be part of the persecution of the Jews. Things are quite different with a *Landrat*. As the senior administrative and police official of the *Kreis*, he is entrusted with the administrative and police protection of its population against unlawful interference with their liberty and property; he infringes his set of duties if he participates in interference with the very legal goods he is called on to protect.

(b) In subjective respects, the punishability of accused S. depends on his having acted intentionally as an accessory. Intent as an accessory (*Gehilfenvorsatz*) requires, first, that the accused knew what act he was furthering by his participation; he must have been aware that the actions ordered from him by the Gestapo served persecution on racial grounds. He had this awareness, as the Court hereby finds, as the outcome of the trial and taking of evidence, on the basis of the wording and content of the Gestapo orders he received, even if, as he has credibly assured, he did not reckon on the possibility that the deported Jews might be killed. The accused may also be believed to have assumed that the forced deportation of the Jews was in the interest of the defence of the Reich, and that he formed a too favourable conception of the fate awaiting the Jews after deportation ('resettlement') and was strengthened therein by hopes expressed by some of the Jews concerned themselves. The fact nonetheless remains that the forced deportation of the Jews as such, taken together with the confiscation and seizure of their assets, was seen by the accused as 'persecution on racial grounds'. The accused himself stated at the trial that he regarded the Gestapo measures as 'unjust' to the Jews, and struggled with himself whether to carry out the measures or not; these statements by the accused himself enable and support the finding made above.

Intent as an accessory (*Gehilfenvorsatz*) requires, second, that the accused knew that through his participation he was furthering the principal act. He had this awareness too, as the Court hereby finds, as an outcome of the trial and taking of evidence. This awareness is not excluded by the consideration brought up by the accused that if he himself had refused to execute the Gestapo measures someone else would have carried them out in his place, but on the contrary shown to be present; for this consideration shows that the accused took it upon himself, for reasons the scope of which is still to be discussed, to carry out the Gestapo orders himself instead of leaving it to someone else.

Intent as an accessory does not, by contrast, require the accused himself to have acted from racial considerations or from inhumane attitudes at all. Nor is it required that the accused had an awareness of the illegality of his action, since Control Council Law No. 10 declares persecution on racial grounds punishable irrespective of whether it infringes the national law of the country in which it was committed; it is thus immaterial what notion the person had as to the legality of his actions. That, finally, the fact that the accused was acting on orders does not exclude penal responsibility as an accessory is explicitly stated in Article II(4)(b) of Control Council Law No. 10.

(3) It remains to be discussed whether accused S. can appeal to grounds excluding guilt or punishment.

(a) Accused S. has asserted that he weighed against each other the facts that he could not prevent the carrying out of the Gestapo measures; that these measures would be carried out all the same even if he refused to do so; that his participation in these measures would accordingly not spare any of the Jews concerned the evils threatening them; and on the other the facts that his participation in these measures enabled him to remain in his post as *Landrat*, that his remaining in office was both in the interest of the Jewish population to the extent that he could mitigate some things, and in the interest of the non-Jewish part of the population with a negative attitude to National Socialism, in so far as he could uphold or procure facilitations for this part of the *Kreis* population too; from this weighing up, he had arrived at the conclusion that preponderant interests justified his carrying out, in order to remain in office, the orders of the Gestapo; he was strengthened in this view by the fact that his remaining in office was desired both on the Jewish side and by respectable figures in the non-Jewish part of the *Kreis* population, and even explicitly asked for: if in this weighing up he had based himself on inaccurate expectations or if the weighing up as such was incorrect, this was at most a political error, not a criminal fault.

That accused S., and with him the circles supporting him in his resolution, were making a severe political mistake in this consideration, even if the premises of the weighing up be supposed to be correct, is plain. During the rule of National Socialism, the temptation was – it may be admitted – indeed great to come to terms with the unbearable, whether out of fear of worse yet to come or in the hope of being able to maintain for oneself and others a 'party-free' reservation – however small. This fear and this hope, both of these elements in the thinking of accused S., were very well recognized by National Socialism, which used them and abused them as a psychological and political factor. Inside the official apparatus, in general only the key positions were occupied by ideologically committed and reliable party comrades. That was quite enough. The rest of the officials could be left with the illusion of freedom in little things, indeed even a certain actual freedom; that was a cheap price to pay for their compliance in all important matters, and they were willing to pay it for they knew very well that all those who – like accused S. – pursued opportunist policies in order to maintain their freedom of action ultimately became prisoners of their own policies.

Thus it could not fail to happen, and, as this case showed actually did happen, that part of the civil service bowed to immoral and illegal impositions; what began as a political error ended as moral and criminal guilt. When politics comes into conflict with law and morality, this conflict can be solved only in the sense that law and morality must never be adjusted to politics, but politics must always be to law and morality. This principle applies to the State as a whole; it applies to every official as an individual. Each citizen has a right to have an official, from whom an immoral and illegal action is demanded, refrain from that action; each citizen must be protected against officials, irrespective of the considerations they base themselves on, committing such acts. An official who fails to see this is acting not simply unwisely politically because he is undermining trust in the lawfulness of the administration, but at the same time unlawfully. That is why accused S. must be refused the appeal to the balancing of interests he did; an error as to the admissibility of this balancing of interests counts against him. [. . .]

(2) The accused Ho., K. and B., by undertaking the search of the Jewish women for deportation, objectively took part, specifically as accessories (*Gehilfen*), in a persecution on racial grounds and thus in a crime against humanity within the meaning of Article II(1)(c), (2)(b) and (3) of Control Council Law No. 10. Their involvement was admittedly, considered in the context of the whole, only of a subordinate nature, and the three accused did not, by contrast with co-defendant S., infringe any special set of duties. What nonetheless makes their involvement punishable is the fact that the body search taken together with the removal of the valuables found thereby was particularly degrading for the Jewish women affected. In subjective respects, the punishability of the three accused depends on whether they deliberately (*vorsätzlich*) acted as accessories (*Gehilfen*). This condition is met for all three of these accused. The accused recognized (accused K. and B. at the latest by the time they were at the station in Haigerloch and accused Ho. earlier, when she received the order given to her) that they were being called on to take part in a persecution on racial grounds; this finding is hereby made on the basis of the oral proceedings. That these three accused did not know the contents

of the Gestapo decrees and could not therefore fully perceive what measures of persecution the Jews would individually be exposed to is irrelevant; what they did know, namely that
Jews were being forcibly deported and in this connection searched and made to hand over
jewelry, suffices to establish intention in their cases. This knowledge (*Wissen*) was also inevitably associated with the insight that through their actions the accused were furthering the
principal offence. Intentionality as accessory (*Gehilfenvorsatz*) did not require that the accused
acted from racial motives and further did not require that they had an awareness of the illegality (*Bewusstsein der Rechtswidrigkeit*) of their actions, as has already been explained in the
judgment on accused S. It is similarly irrelevant that if an individual accused or all the accused
had refused their participation, the search would still have been carried out by the remaining
accused, or by other persons.

Federal Republic of Germany, S. and others (Hechimgen and Haigerloch Deportation case), *Court of Appeal (*Oberlandesgericht*) Tübingen, Judgment of 20 January 1948*

The Court of Appeal found that the Trial Court made inadequate findings with respect
to the letter ordering S. to facilitate and implement the deportation, and therefore it
ordered that S. be granted a new trial. It addressed therefore the scope of accessory
liability, and in particular the required *mens rea*, in the context of the case against the
three women.

Persecution on political, racial and religious grounds is listed in Article II(1)(c) of the Law as the
last explanatory example of a crime against humanity. This crime too must accordingly be carried out inhumanely. The perpetrator must have acted out of an inhumane mindset, derived
from a politically, racially or religiously determined ideology [. . .]
    [Control Council] Law No. 10, in Article II(2)(a)–(e), equates all conceivable forms of commis-
sion or participation. It does not distinguish between perpetration (*Täterschaft*) and participation (*Teilnahme*). The accessory (*Gehilfe*) to a crime against humanity is 'regarded as guilty
of a crime against humanity, without regard to the capacity in which he acted' (Clause 2 of
the Introductory Act). From this complete equation with the perpetrator it follows that the
accessory must have acted from the same mindset as the perpetrator himself, that is, from
an inhumane mindset and in persecutions under politically, racially or religiously determined
ideologies. The Criminal Division rightly took it that as regards the punishability of participation, Law No. 10 is of plain interpretation.

The trial court plainly struggles with the limits of accessory liability. While it eloquently
articulates why 'cogs' in the machine of mass crime must be held to account, it also recognizes the potential breadth of this approach and seeks to find a line between the 'typist'
and the 'senior administrative and police official' who both assist in the execution of a
criminal scheme. With respect to S., the court seizes on the question of 'duty', finding that
S.'s transmission of Gestapo orders amounted to accessory liability because he had a duty
to protect the people of his village. This distinction falls away, however, when it comes to
the responsibility of the three women who had no duty. Nonetheless the trial court finds
that they are different from the 'typist', it seems, because of their physical and proximate
(and degrading) participation in the deportation itself. For the Court of Appeal, though,
the line was elsewhere; only those who assisted the crime *and* shared the intent of the main
perpetrators could be held liable. This question of where to draw the line of liability is a
central theme in the ongoing debates on aiding and abetting.

US Military Tribunal Sitting in Nuremberg, US v. Ernst von Weizsäcker et al., (Ministries *case*), Judgment of 11–13 April 1949

> This case is primarily known for its holding on the crime of aggression, and is excerpted in the chapter (Part I(4)) dealing with aggression, but in addition all but 2 of the 21 defendants were convicted of war crimes and crimes against humanity. The following excerpt pertains to the responsibility of two officials in the German Foreign Office for the deportation of 6,000 Jews from France in March 1942: Ernst von Weizsaecker, the State Secretary of the Foreign Office, and Ernst Woermann, the Ministerial Director and Chief of the Political Division of the German Foreign Office. Both Accused were sentenced to a term of imprisonment of seven years.

On 9 March 1942 [Adolf] Eichmann of the SS wrote [to] the Foreign Office [saying] that it was intended to deport to Auschwitz 1,000 French and stateless Jews who had been arrested in France in 1941, asking if there was any objection.

On 11 March the SS again wrote [to] the Foreign Office [saying] that it was desired to include 5,000 more Jews from France. On the same day [Hans] Luther [Under Secretary in charge of Deutschland] wired the German Embassy in Paris, forwarding the request and asking for comment, and Paris replied, "No objection."

On 20 March [Franz] Rademacher [subordinate to Luther], by order, informed the SS that the Foreign Office had no objections to these 6,000 Jews being deported. This was initialed by Woermann and von Weizsaecker, and contains the latter's comment, "to be selected by the police."

There remains no shadow of doubt that both Woermann and von Weizsaecker were informed of this nefarious plan and that it received their official approval. There is nothing in the record to show that they questioned its propriety, objected to or protested against it, or availed themselves of the opportunity to suggest to von Ribbentrop that even from the viewpoint of German foreign policy its execution would be a catastrophic mistake in that it would not only alienate public sentiment in France, but would arouse a wave of horror and resentment throughout the world. Neither claims that there was any legal justification for this deportation or suggests it was other than a flagrant violation of international law and of the provisions of the Hague Convention.

Woermann's excuse is that he was not able to do anything and that his cosignature meant that he saw no valid political reason which could be urged against it and that the reason that the Foreign Office communication was signed by the State Secretary and by two other state secretaries, including himself, was that it was an important matter.

However, his own witness, Lehmann, an old civil servant in the Foreign Office, called as an expert on Foreign Office practice, does not bear him out. He testified, somewhat reluctantly, that when a Foreign Office official initialed a draft he thereby outwardly approved it, even though he may have had mental reservations as to its propriety.

The defendant Woermann knew that there were cogent reasons of a political nature why the measure should be disapproved; he knew that it was in violation of every principle of international law and in direct contradiction of the Hague Convention.

Von Weizsaecker asserts that this occurred at a time of repeated attempted attacks on members of the Wehrmacht and Hitler had ordered frequent shootings of hostages in France; that these Jews were already interned and were in danger, and one could very easily come to the conclusion that the deportations to the East might involve less danger to them than remaining where they were; that the name Auschwitz did not mean anything to anybody at that time. He does not state that this was, in fact, his reason for not objecting, but that it was probably his reason. He further asserts that the Foreign Office did not instigate or execute these measures and its point of view or opinion could not prevent them. The latter contention, however, is hardly tenable, in view of the fact that Eichmann of the SS made specific inquiries as to whether the Foreign Office had objections.

While we are ready and anxious to accord to every defendant the benefit of any reasonable doubt to which he may be entitled, it is difficult to find any such doubt here, even though we assume that neither defendant, at that time, had knowledge that Auschwitz was a death camp. Nevertheless they knew and were well informed of the fate of any Jew who came into the tender hands of the SS and Gestapo; they knew what had been the fate of the Jews of Poland, the Baltic states, and Russia; they knew what had been the horrible fate of German Jews.

While admitting that many things passed over his desk and received his initials of approval as to which he harbored mental reservations and objections, he states he remained in office for two reasons: first, that he might thereby continue to be at least a cohesive factor in the underground opposition to Hitler by occupying an important listening post, maintaining members of the opposition in strategic positions, distributing information between opposition groups in the Wehrmacht, the various governmental departments, and in civil life; and second, that he might be in a position to initiate or aid in attempts to negotiate peace. We believe him, but this, while it may and should be considered in mitigation, cannot constitute a defense to charges of war crimes or crimes against humanity. One cannot give consent to or implement the commission of murder because by so doing he hopes eventually to be able to rid society of the chief murderer. The first is a crime of imminent actuality while the second is but a future hope.

When the SS inquired whether the Foreign Office had any objections, it was the defendant's duty to point them out. That is the function of a political department and a state secretary of a foreign office. It is not performed by saying or doing nothing. Even the defendant's witness, von Schlabrendorff, himself an active leader in the resistance movement, and a participant in the plot of 20 July 1944, testified that being a member of that movement did not justify one in becoming a party to the program of the murder of Jews. As to these and like instances, we find the defendants von Weizsaecker and Woermann guilty.

COMMENTARY

The court here finds that Woermann and von Weizsaecker had a legal and political duty to object to the deportation plan and that their failure to object, even if they were not aware of the ultimate fate of the deportees and did not instigate the plan or share its aims, amounted to aiding and abetting the crime of deportation. Although the accused in fact *approved* the plan, the court suggests that the result would have been the same had they simply done nothing in the face of the deportation proposal. The court, therefore, seems to embrace the notion of aiding and abetting through omission whereby an individual becomes liable if he fails to fulfil a duty that is his, acts with the requisite intent (either knowledge that his failure allows for the crime to occur or for the purpose of furthering the crime), and thereby allows for, or contributes to, the commission of a crime. The court's analysis – and the fact that it was carried out by US Judges – raises interesting questions about contemporary debates (for example in the United States) concerning the responsibility of government officials, and in particular legal advisers, to act affirmatively to stop the conduct of government actors that might amount to international crimes.

The court in the *Ministries* case was arguably not completely consistent, however, in its application of the notion of aiding and abetting. Another defendant was Karl Rasche, a member and later speaker of the *Vorstand* (management board) of the Dresdner bank.

At issue was whether he could be held criminally liable for approving loans that he knew would be used by the SS to finance enterprises that used slave labour:

[Rasche's] participation in the loans made by the Dresdner Bank to various SS enterprises which employed slave labor and to those engaged in the resettlement program presents a more difficult problem.

The defendant is a banker and businessman of long experience and is possessed of a keen and active mind. Bankers do not approve or make loans in the number and amount made by the Dresdner Bank without ascertaining, having, or obtaining information or knowledge as to the purpose for which the loan is sought, and how it is to be used. It is inconceivable to us that the defendant did not possess that knowledge, and we find that he did.

The real question is, is it a crime to make a loan, knowing or having good reason to believe that the borrower will us[e] the funds in financing enterprises which are employed in using labor in violation of either national or international law? Does he stand in any different position than one who sells supplies or raw materials to a builder building a house, knowing that the structure will be used for an unlawful purpose? A bank sells money or credit in the same manner as the merchandiser of any other commodity. It does not become a partner in enterprise, and the interest charged is merely the gross profit which the bank realizes from the transaction, out of which it must deduct its business costs, and from which it hopes to realize a net profit. Loans or sale of commodities to be used in an unlawful enterprise may well be condemned from a moral standpoint and reflect no credit on the part of the lender or seller in either case, but the transaction can hardly be said to be a crime. Our duty is to try and punish those guilty of violating international law, and we are not prepared to state that such loans constitute a violation of that law, nor has our attention been drawn to any ruling to the contrary.

The defendant Rasche should be and is found not guilty under count five.

Although the court's approach seems different with respect to Rasche as compared to von Weizsaecker and Woermann, perhaps the distinction is that Rasche, acting in his capacity as a banker, owed no duty to any person to ensure that the funds he was responsible for loaning were not being used for any criminal purpose.

A French court had, however, a different approach in the *Röchling* case, in which five German industrialists were tried for their role in aggressive war, war crimes and crimes against humanity. It found the accused Hans Lothar von Gemmingen-Hornberg, the President of the Board of Directors of the Röchling steel plants and a plant manager, guilty of inhuman treatment because of the horrific conditions faced by the foreign workers and prisoners of war forced to work in the plants. The court found that although the Gestapo was principally responsible for the conditions and treatment of the workers, von Gemmingen-Hornberg's high position in the corporation and his close relationship to Röchling himself (von Gemmingen-Hornberg was Röchling's son-in-law) gave the accused 'sufficient authority to obtain an alleviation in the treatment of these workers'. The court concluded that there is 'cause under these circumstances to hold von Gemmingen-Hornberg responsible for the inhuman treatment of the foreign workers and prisoners of war in the firm of Röchling, which he aided by his negligence and his lack of courage towards the Gestapo'.[2]

Therefore, while the World War II courts embraced the concept of aiding and abetting liability (while not always identifying it in those terms), they did not necessarily reach a uniform definition of the concept. The modern tribunals took further steps to define the notion as demonstrated in the following excerpt.

---

[2] General Tribunal at Rastadt of the Military Government for the French Zone of Occupation of Germany, 16 June 1948, English summary in *Annual Digest 1948*, 398–404.

ICTY, **Prosecutor** *v.* **Furundžija,** *Trial Chamber, Judgment of 10 December 1998*

Anto Furundžija was the commander of a special unit, known at the 'Jokers', of the Bosnian-Croat army (the HVO). He was tried and convicted of the war crimes of torture and outrages on personal dignity, including rape. Specifically, Furundžija was accused of interrogating a Muslim woman while a fellow officer first rubbed his knife all over her body and thigh, threatening to cut out her private parts if she did not cooperate, and then raped her. Furundžija was convicted of being a co-perpetrator of torture and aiding and abetting outrages on personal dignity and sentenced to 10 years. The excerpt below is from the trial judgment.

D. Aiding and Abetting

1. Introduction

190. The accused is charged with torture and outrages upon personal dignity, including rape. For the purposes of the present case however, it is necessary to define "aiding and abetting" as used in Article 7(1) of the Statute.

191. Since no treaty law on the subject exists, the Trial Chamber must examine customary international law in order to establish the content of this head of criminal responsibility. In particular, it must establish both whether the accused's alleged presence in the locations where Witness A was assaulted would be sufficient to constitute the *actus reus* of aiding and abetting, and also the relevant *mens rea* required to accompany this action for responsibility to ensue.

2. Actus Reus

192. With regard to the *actus reus*, the Trial Chamber must examine whether the assistance given by the aider and abettor need be tangible in nature or may consist only of encouragement or moral support. The Trial Chamber must also examine the proximity required between the assistance provided and the commission of the criminal act. In particular, it will have to consider whether the actions of the aider and abettor need to have a causal effect, so that without his contribution the offence would not be committed, or whether the acts of the aider and abettor need simply facilitate the commission of the offence in some way.

(a) International Case Law

(i) Introduction

193. Little light is shed on the definition of aiding and abetting by the international instruments providing for major war trials: the London Agreement, the Charter of the International Military Tribunal for the Far East, establishing the Tokyo Tribunal, and Control Council Law No. 10. It therefore becomes necessary to examine the case law.

194. For a correct appraisal of this case law, it is important to bear in mind, with each of the cases to be examined, the forum in which the case was heard, as well as the law applied, as these factors determine its authoritative value. In addition, one should constantly be mindful of the need for great caution in using national case law for the purpose of determining whether customary rules of international criminal law have evolved in a particular matter.

195. First of all, there are the cases stemming from US military commissions or, in territory occupied by US forces, by courts and tribunals set up by the military government. While the

military commissions operated under different directives within each theatre of US military operations, each applied a provision identical to that of the London Agreement with relation to complicity. In occupied territories, the courts and tribunals operated under the terms of Control Council Law No. 10.

196. The Trial Chamber will also rely on case law from the British military courts for the trials of war criminals, whose jurisdiction was based on the Royal Warrant of 14 June 1945, which provided that the rules of procedure to be applied were those of domestic military courts, unless otherwise specified. In fact, unless otherwise provided, the law applied was domestic, thus rendering the pronouncements of the British courts less helpful in establishing rules of international law on this issue. However, there is sufficient similarity between the law applied in the British cases and under Control Council Law No. 10 for these cases to merit consideration. The British cases deal with forms of complicity analogous to that alleged in the present case. The term used to describe those liable as accomplices (in killing) is that they were "concerned in the killing".

197. Cases heard under Control Council Law No. 10, either by the German Supreme Court in the British Occupied Zone, or by German courts in the French Occupied Zone are also material to the Trial Chamber's analysis.

198. Finally, the International Tribunal has on a previous occasion examined the question of complicity under its Statute, namely in the Opinion and Judgment of 7 May 1997 in the case of *Prosecutor v. Duško Tadić*, hereafter "*Tadić Judgement*".

(ii) Nature of Assistance

199. The Trial Chamber will first examine the nature of the assistance required to establish *actus reus*. The cases which follow indicate that in certain circumstances, aiding and abetting need not be tangible, but may consist of moral support or encouragement of the principals in their commission of the crime.

200. In the British case of *Schonfeld*, four of the ten accused were found guilty of being "concerned in the killing of" three Allied airmen, who had been found hiding in the home of a member of the Dutch resistance. All four claimed that their purpose in visiting the scene had been the investigation and arrest of the Allied airmen. One admitted to shooting the three airmen but claimed it was in self-defence; he was found guilty and sentenced to death. The roles of the three others were less direct. One drove a car to the scene and was the first to enter the house. Another had obtained the original information, searched a different house for the airmen earlier and claimed to have stood guard at the back entrance to the house along with the fourth convicted person. All except one denied having fired any shots themselves.

201. The court did not make clear the grounds on which it found these three to have been "concerned in the killing". However, the Advocate General, citing the position in English law, outlined the role of an accessory who is not present at the scene but procures, counsels, commands or abets another to commit the offence, and that of an aider and abettor, either of which could have formed the basis of the court's decision. In doing so he gave an example of how an individual may participate without giving tangible assistance:

> if he watched for his companions in order to prevent surprise, or remained at a convenient distance in order to favour their escape, if necessary, or was in such a situation as to be able readily to come to their assistance, the knowledge of which was calculated to give additional confidence to his companions, he was, in contemplation of law, present, aiding and abetting.

202. Again, in giving "additional confidence to his companions" the defendant facilitates the commission of the crime, and it is this which constitutes the *actus reus* of the offence.

203. In the British case of *Rohde* six persons were found guilty of being "concerned in the killing" of four British women prisoners in German hands. The women were executed by lethal injection and their bodies disposed of in the prison camp crematorium. In defining the term "concerned in the killing", the Judge Advocate explained that actual presence at the crime scene was not necessary to be "concerned in the killing". He gave the example of a lookout, who would be "concerned in the killing" by providing a service to the commission of the crime in the knowledge that the crime was going to be committed.

204. In the case of one of the accused, assistance *ex post facto* was found to be sufficient for criminal responsibility. As this was not the position under English law, the inference is warranted that the court applied a different law to these international crimes. The service provided by the cremator may be analogous to that of the lookout, in that the knowledge that the bodies will be disposed of, in the same way that the knowledge that they will be warned of impending discovery in the lookout scenario, reassures the killers and facilitates their commission of the crime in some significant way.

205. Guidance can also be derived from the following cases, which were heard under the terms of Control Council Law No. 10. In the *Synagogue* case, decided by the German Supreme Court in the British Occupied Zone, one of the accused was found guilty of a crime against humanity (the devastation of a synagogue) although he had not physically taken part in it, nor planned or ordered it. His intermittent presence on the crime-scene, combined with his status as an *"alter Kämpfer"* (long-time militant of the Nazi party) and his knowledge of the criminal enterprise, were deemed sufficient to convict him.

206. The accused was convicted at first instance of a crime against humanity under the provision on co-perpetration of a crime (*"Mittäterschaft"*) of the then German penal code (Art. 47 *Strafgesetzbuch*). The conviction was confirmed on appeal. The appellate decision noted that the accused was a militant Nazi. The court went on to find that he knew of the plan at least two hours before the commission of the crime.

207. It may be inferred from this case that an approving spectator who is held in such respect by the other perpetrators that his presence encourages them in their conduct, may be guilty of complicity in a crime against humanity.

208. The *Synagogue* case may be contrasted with the *Pig-cart parade* case, also from the German Supreme Court in the British Occupied Zone. The accused, P had attended, as a spectator in civilian dress, a SA (*Stürmabteilung*) "parade" in which two political opponents of the NSDAP (*Nationalsozialistische Deutsche Arbeiterpartei*) were exposed to public humiliation. P had followed the "parade" without taking any active part. The court found that P,

> followed the parade only as a spectator in civilian clothes, although he was following a service order by the SA for a purpose yet unknown...His conduct cannot even with certainty be evaluated as objective or subjective approval. Furthermore, silent approval that does not contribute to causing the offence in no way meets the requirements for criminal liability.

P was found not guilty. He may have lacked the necessary *mens rea*. But in any event, his insignificant status brought the effect of his "silent approval" below the threshold necessary for the *actus reus*.

209. It appears from the *Synagogue* and *Pig-cart parade* cases that presence, when combined with authority, can constitute assistance in the form of moral support, that is, the *actus reus* of the offence. The supporter must be of a certain status for this to be sufficient for criminal responsibility. This emphasis on the accused's authority was also affirmed in *Akayesu*. Jean-Paul Akayesu was the *bourgmestre*, or mayor, of the Commune in which atrocities, including rape and sexual violence, occurred. That Trial Chamber considered this position of authority highly significant for his criminal liability for aiding and abetting: "The Tribunal finds, under

Article 6(1) of its Statute, that the Accused, having had reason to know that sexual violence was occurring, aided and abetted the following acts of sexual violence, by allowing them to take place on or near the premises of the bureau communal and by facilitating the commission of such sexual violence through his words of encouragement in other acts of sexual violence which, *by virtue of his authority*, sent a clear signal of official tolerance for sexual violence, without which these acts would not have taken place: [...]". Furthermore, it can be inferred from this finding that assistance need not be tangible. In addition, assistance need not constitute an indispensable element, that is, a *conditio sine qua non* for the acts of the principal.

210. Mention should also be made of several cases which enable us to distinguish aiding and abetting from the case of co-perpetration involving a group of persons pursuing a common design to commit crimes.

211. The *Dachau Concentration Camp* case was held before a US Tribunal under Control Council Law No. 10. All the accused held some position in the hierarchy running the Dachau concentration camp. While allegations of direct participation in instances of ill-treatment were made against certain accused, and allegations of command responsibility against others, the real basis of the charges was that all the accused had "acted in pursuance of a common design" to kill and mistreat prisoners, and hence to commit war crimes.

212. The organised and official nature of the system by which war crimes were perpetrated in this case adds a specific element to the "complicity" of the accused. The report of the case by the United Nations War Crimes Commission isolates three elements necessary to establish guilt in each case. The first was the existence of a system to ill- treat the prisoners and commit the various crimes alleged; the second was the accused's knowledge of the nature of this system; and the third was that the accused "encouraged, aided and abetted or participated" in enforcing the system. Once the existence of the system had been established, a given accused was potentially liable for his participation in this system. The roles of the accused ranged from camp commanders to guards and prisoner functionaries and all were found guilty, with the difference in the levels of participation reflected in the sentences. It would seem that the holding of any role in the administration of the camps was sufficient to constitute encouraging, aiding and abetting or participating in the enforcement of the system.

213. The prosecution in the *Dachau Concentration Camp* case, did not base its case on the direct participation of the accused in the crime. Regardless of whether the accused themselves had beaten or murdered the concentration camp inmates, the assistance they afforded to those who did, or the system, formed the basis of their guilt. The level of assistance required was low: any participation in the enterprise was sufficient, although as the accused were all members of staff of the camps, their contribution to the commission of the crimes was tangible – the carrying out of their respective duties – so that none were convicted on the basis of having lent moral support or encouragement alone. [...]

(iii) Effect of Assistance on the Act of the Principal

217. Back to aiding and abetting, in the *Einsatzgruppen* case, heard by a US Military Tribunal sitting at Nuremberg, all of the accused except for one (Graf) were officers charged with war crimes and crimes against humanity pursuant to Control Council Law No. 10. The Tribunal held that the acts of the accomplices had to have a substantial effect on those of the principals to constitute the *actus reus* of the war crimes and crimes against humanity charged. This conclusion is illustrated by the cases of four of the accused: Klingelhoefer, Fendler, Ruehl and Graf. Klingelhoefer held a variety of positions, the least important of which was that of interpreter. The court said that even if this were his only function,

> it would not exonerate him from guilt because in locating, evaluating and turning over lists of Communist party functionaries to the executive of his organisation he was aware that the people listed would be executed when found.

218. Fendler served in one of the *Kommandos* of the *Einsatzgruppen* for a period of seven months. The prosecution case against him was not that he himself conducted an execution but rather "that he was part of an organisation committed to an extermination programme". The Court noted that:

> The defendant knew that executions were taking place. He admitted that the procedure which determined the so-called guilt of a person which resulted in him being condemned to death was "too summary". But, there is no evidence that he ever did anything about it. As the second highest ranking officer in the *Kommando*, his views could have been heard in complaint or protest against what he now says was a too summary procedure, but he chose to let the injustice go uncorrected.

Both of these defendants were found guilty.

219. The cases of Ruehl and Graf provide a contrast which helps delineate the *actus reus* of the offence. The Tribunal held that both had the requisite knowledge of the criminal activities of the organisations of which they were a part. Ruehl's position, however, was not such as to "control, prevent, or modify" those activities. His low rank failed to "place him automatically into a position where his lack of objection in any way contributed to the success of any executive operation". He was found not guilty.

220. Graf was a non-commissioned officer. The court held that:

> Since there is no evidence in the record that Graf was at any time in a position to protest against the illegal actions of the others, he cannot be found guilty as an accessory under counts one and two [war crimes and crimes against humanity] of the indictment.

221. It is clear, then, that knowledge of the criminal activities of the organisation combined with a role in that organisation was not sufficient for complicity in this case and that the defendants' acts in carrying out their duties had to have a substantial effect on the commission of the offence for responsibility to ensue. This might be because their failure to protest made some difference to the course of events, or, in the case of Klingelhoefer, that his transmission of the lists of names led directly to the execution of the members of those lists.

222. In the British case of *Zyklon B*, the three accused were charged with supplying poison gas used for the extermination of allied nationals interned in concentration camps, in the knowledge that the gas was to be so used. The owner and second-in-command of the firm were found guilty; Drosihn, the firm's first gassing technician, was acquitted. The Judge Advocate set out the issue of Drosihn's complicity as turning on,

> whether there was any evidence that he was in a position either to influence the transfer of gas to Auschwitz or to prevent it. If he were not in such a position, no knowledge of the use to which the gas was put could make him guilty.

223. This clearly requires that the act of the accomplice has at least a substantial effect on the principal act – the use of the gas to murder internees at Auschwitz – in order to constitute the *actus reus*. The functions performed by Drosihn in his employment as a gassing technician were an integral part of the supply and use of the poison gas, but this alone could not render him liable for its criminal use even if he was aware that his functions played such an important role in the transfer of gas. Without influence over this supply, he was not guilty. In other words, *mens rea* alone is insufficient to ground a criminal conviction.

224. In *S. et al.*, hereafter "*Hechingen Deportation*", heard by a German court in the French occupied zone, five accused were charged with complicity in the mass deportation of Jews in 1941 and 1942 as a crime against humanity under Control Council Law No. 10. The accused, S, was the local administrative authority responsible for organising the execution of Gestapo orders. He had complied with a Gestapo decree concerning the deportations. The court of

first instance found S guilty of aiding and abetting the Gestapo in its criminal activity. His objection that his conduct in no way contributed to the crimes, because others would have taken his place if he had refused to comply with the Gestapo decree, was dismissed. The court pointed out that the culpability of an aider and abettor is not negated by the fact that his assistance could easily have been obtained from another. [. . .]

The court reviewed relevant 'international instruments' and found that both the 1996 Draft Cod[e] of Crimes against Peace and Security of Mankind, drafted by the International Law Commission, and the Rome Statute supported the notion that aiding and abetting could include either physical or moral support and that the assistance need only be substantial or facilitating but not necessary or essential.

(c) Conclusion

232. On the issue of the nature of assistance rendered, the German cases suggest that the assistance given by an accomplice need not be tangible and can consist of moral support in certain circumstances. While any spectator can be said to be encouraging a spectacle – an audience being a necessary element of a spectacle – the spectator in these cases was only found to be complicit if his status was such that his presence had a significant legitimising or encouraging effect on the principals. This is supported by the provisions of the International Law Commission Draft Code. In view of this, the Trial Chamber believes the use of the term "direct" in qualifying the proximity of the assistance and the principal act to be misleading as it may imply that assistance needs to be tangible, or to have a causal effect on the crime. This may explain why the word "direct" was not used in the Rome Statute's provision on aiding and abetting.

233. On the effect of the assistance given to the principal, none of the cases above suggests that the acts of the accomplice need bear a causal relationship to, or be a *conditio sine qua non* for, those of the principal. The suggestion made in the *Einsatzgruppen* and *Zyklon B* cases is that the relationship between the acts of the accomplice and of the principal must be such that the acts of the accomplice make a significant difference to the commission of the criminal act by the principal. Having a role in a system without influence would not be enough to attract criminal responsibility, as demonstrated by the case of the defendant Ruehl in the *Einsatzgruppen* case. This interpretation is supported by the German cases cited.

234. The position under customary international law seems therefore to be best reflected in the proposition that the assistance must have a substantial effect on the commission of the crime. This is the position adopted by the Trial Chamber.

235. In sum, the Trial Chamber holds that the *actus reus* of aiding and abetting in international criminal law requires practical assistance, encouragement, or moral support which has a substantial effect on the perpetration of the crime.

3. Mens Rea

(a) International Case Law

236. With regard to *mens rea*, the Trial Chamber must determine whether it is necessary for the accomplice to share the *mens rea* of the principal or whether mere knowledge that his actions assist the perpetrator in the commission of the crime is sufficient to constitute *mens rea* in aiding and abetting the crime. The case law indicates that the latter will suffice.

237. For example in the *Einsatzgruppen* case, knowledge, rather than intent, was held to be the requisite mental element.

238. The same position was taken in *Zyklon B* where the prosecution did not attempt to prove that the accused acted with the intention of assisting the killing of the internees. It was

accepted that their purpose was to sell insecticide to the SS (for profit, that is a lawful goal pursued by lawful means). The charge as accepted by the court was that they knew what the buyer in fact intended to do with the product they were supplying.

239. Two of the not guilty verdicts in *Schonfeld* also provide an indication of the *mens rea* necessary to amount to being "concerned in the killing". Both concerned drivers who claimed to have followed instructions without knowing the purpose of the mission, and were therefore found not guilty. Despite having made a physical contribution to the commission of the offence, they had no knowledge that they were doing so.

240. In the *Hechingen Deportation* case, the court of first instance considered the *mens rea* required for aiding and abetting and concluded that this mental element encompassed both the knowledge of the crime being committed by the principals and the awareness of support- ing, by aiding and abetting, the criminal conduct of the principals.

As mentioned above, the subsequent acquittal of the accused Ho., K., and B. on appeal was based on a different legal standard concerning the *mens rea* of those accused, requiring the aider and abettor to have acted out of the same cast of mind as the principal.

241. Finally, in the *Tadić Judgment* it was found that the test of *mens rea* which emerged from the post-Second World War trials is "awareness of the act of participation coupled with a conscious decision to participate". The requirement adopted by the Trial Chamber was that the mental element for aiding and abetting consists of a knowing participation in the commission of an offence.

(b) International Instruments

242. Article 2(3)(d) of the International Law Commission's Draft Code on Crimes and Offences Against Mankind, provides that the *mens rea* required is that the assistance be given "know- ingly". The Commentary adds:

Thus, an individual who provides some assistance to another individual without knowing that this assistance will facilitate the commission of a crime would not be held accountable under the present sub-paragraph.

243. Therefore, it is not necessary for an aider and abettor to meet all the requirements of *mens rea* for a principal perpetrator. In particular, it is not necessary that he shares and identi- fies with the principal's criminal will and purpose, provided that his own conduct was with knowledge. That conduct may in itself be perfectly lawful; it becomes criminal only when combined with the principal's unlawful conduct.

244. Reference should also be made to article 30 of the Rome Statute, which provides that, "[u]nless otherwise provided, a person shall be criminally responsible and liable for punish- ment for a crime within the jurisdiction of the Court only if the material elements are commit- ted with intent and *knowledge*".

(c) Conclusions

245. The above analysis leads the Trial Chamber to the conclusion that it is not necessary for the accomplice to share the *mens rea* of the perpetrator, in the sense of positive intention to commit the crime. Instead, the clear requirement in the vast majority of the cases is for the accomplice to have knowledge that his actions will assist the perpetrator in the commission of the crime. This is particularly apparent from all the cases in which persons were convicted for having driven victims and perpetrators to the site of an execution. In those cases the prosecution did not prove that the driver drove for the purpose of assisting in the killing, that is, with an intention to kill. It was the knowledge of the criminal purpose of the executioners that rendered the driver liable as an aider and abettor. Consequently, if it were not proven that a driver would reasonably have known that the purpose of the trip was an unlawful execution, he would be acquitted.

246. Moreover, it is not necessary that the aider and abettor should know the precise crime that was intended and which in the event was committed. If he is aware that one of a number of crimes will probably be committed, and one of those crimes is in fact committed, he has intended to facilitate the commission of that crime, and is guilty as an aider and abettor.

247. Knowledge is also the requirement in the International Law Commission Draft Code, which may well reflect the requirement of *mens rea* in customary international law. This is the standard adopted by this Tribunal in the *Tadić Judgement*, although sometimes somewhat misleadingly expressed as "intent".

[...]

249. In sum, the Trial Chamber holds the legal ingredients of aiding and abetting in international criminal law to be the following: the *actus reus* consists of practical assistance, encouragement, or moral support which has a substantial effect on the perpetration of the crime. The *mens rea* required is the knowledge that these acts assist the commission of the offence. This notion of aiding and abetting is to be distinguished from the notion of common design, where the *actus reus* consists of participation in a joint criminal enterprise and the *mens rea* required is intent to participate.

E. How to Distinguish Perpetration of Torture from Aiding and Abetting Torture

250. The definitions and propositions concerning aiding and abetting enunciated above apply equally to rape and to torture, and indeed to all crimes. Nevertheless, the Trial Chamber deems it useful to address the issue of who may be held responsible for torture as a perpetrator and who as an aider and abettor, since in modern times the infliction of torture typically involves a large number of people, each performing his or her individual function, and it is appropriate to elaborate the principles of individual criminal responsibility applicable thereto.

251. Under current international law, individuals must refrain from perpetrating torture or in any way participating in torture.

252. To determine whether an individual is a perpetrator or co-perpetrator of torture or must instead be regarded as an aider and abettor, or is even not to be regarded as criminally liable, it is crucial to ascertain whether the individual who takes part in the torture process also *partakes of the purpose behind torture* (that is, acts with the intention of obtaining information or a confession, of punishing, intimidating, humiliating or coercing the victim or a third person, or of discriminating, on any ground, against the victim or a third person). If he does not, but gives some sort of assistance and support with the knowledge however that torture is being practised, then the individual may be found guilty of aiding and abetting in the perpetration of torture. Arguably, if the person attending the torture process neither shares in the purpose behind torture nor in any way assists in its perpetration, then he or she should not be regarded as criminally liable (think for example of the soldier whom a superior has ordered to attend a torture session in order to determine whether that soldier can stomach the sight of torture and thus be trained as a torturer).

253. These legal propositions, which are based on a logical interpretation of the customary rules on torture, are supported by a teleological construction of these rules. To demonstrate this point, account must be taken of some modern trends in many States practicing torture: they tend to "compartmentalise" and "dilute" the moral and psychological burden of perpetrating torture by assigning to different individuals a partial (and sometimes relatively minor) role in the torture process. Thus, one person orders that torture be carried out, another organises the whole process at the administrative level, another asks questions while the detainee is being tortured, a fourth one provides or prepares the tools for executing torture, another physically inflicts torture or causes mental suffering, another furnishes medical assistance so as

to prevent the detainee from dying as a consequence of torture or from subsequently showing physical traces of the sufferings he has undergone, another processes the results of interrogation known to be obtained under torture, and another procures the information gained as a result of the torture in exchange for granting the torturer immunity from prosecution.

254. International law, were it to fail to take account of these modern trends, would prove unable to cope with this despicable practice. The rules of construction emphasising the importance of the object and purpose of international norms lead to the conclusion that international law renders all the aforementioned persons equally accountable, although some may be sentenced more severely than others, depending upon the circumstances. In other words, the nature of the crime and the forms that it takes, as well as the intensity of international condemnation of torture, suggest that in the case of torture all those who in some degree participate in the crime and in particular take part in the pursuance of one of its underlying purposes, are equally liable.

255. This, it deserves to be stressed, is to a large extent consistent with the provisions contained in the Torture Convention of 1984 and the Inter-American Convention of 1985, from which it can be inferred that they prohibit not only the physical infliction of torture but also any deliberate participation in this practice.

256. It follows, *inter alia*, that if an official interrogates a detainee while another person is inflicting severe pain or suffering, the interrogator is as guilty of torture as the person causing the severe pain or suffering, even if he does not in any way physically participate in such infliction. Here the criminal law maxim *quis per alium facit per se ipsum facere videtur* (he who acts through others is regarded as acting himself) fully applies.

257. Furthermore, it follows from the above that, at least in those instances where torture is practiced under the pattern described *supra*, that is, with more than one person acting as co-perpetrators of the crime, accomplice liability (that is, the criminal liability of those who, while not partaking of the purpose behind torture, may nevertheless be held responsible for encouraging or assisting in the commission of the crime) may only occur within very narrow confines. Thus, it would seem that aiding and abetting in the commission of torture may only exist in such very limited instances as, for example, driving the torturers to the place of torture in full knowledge of the acts they are going to perform there; or bringing food and drink to the perpetrators at the place of torture, again in full knowledge of the activity they are carrying out there. In these instances, those aiding and abetting in the commission of torture can be regarded as accessories to the crime. By contrast, at least in the case we are now discussing, all other varying forms of direct participation in torture should be regarded as instances of co-perpetration of the crime and those co-perpetrators should all be held to be principals. Nevertheless, the varying degree of direct participation as principals may still be a matter to consider for sentencing purposes.

Thus to summarise the above:

(i)   to be guilty of torture as a perpetrator (or co-perpetrator), the accused must participate in an integral part of the torture and partake of the purpose behind the torture, that is the intent to obtain information or a confession, to punish or intimidate, humiliate, coerce or discriminate against the victim or a third person.

(ii) to be guilty of torture as an aider or abettor, the accused must assist in some way which has a substantial effect on the perpetration of the crime and with knowledge that torture is taking place.

In a subsequent case, the Appeals Chamber in *Blaškić* endorsed the notion that aiding and abetting could occur through omission:

47. The Trial Chamber further stated that the actus reus of aiding and abetting may be perpetrated through an omission, "provided this failure to act had a decisive effect on the commission of the crime and that it was coupled with the requisite mens rea." It considered:

In this respect, the mere presence at the crime scene of a person with superior authority, such as a military commander, is a probative indication for determining whether that person encouraged or supported the perpetrators of the crime.

The Appeals Chamber leaves open the possibility that in the circumstances of a given case, an omission may constitute the actus reus of aiding and abetting.

In relation to aiding and abetting by omission, the first clear-cut case of conviction by a contemporary international tribunal for failure to carry out a duty incumbent upon the accused on the basis of the laws of war came on 5 May 2009, with the *Mrkšić* Appeal Judgment. In that Judgment, the ICTY Appeals Chamber found (§102) that the accused Veselin Šljivančanin's 'failure to act pursuant to his duty [to protect prisoners of war] substantially contributed to the killing of the prisoners of war'.

USA, Khulumani *v. Barclay National Bank Ltd. et al., US Court of Appeals for the Second Circuit, Judgment of 12 October 2007*

Three groups of plaintiffs brought a civil action in United States federal court under the Alien Tort Claims Act (ATCA) against various international corporations that did business in South Africa alleging that the corporations aided and abetted the apartheid regime in South Africa in the commission of torture and extrajudicial killings. In order to prevail on their claim, the plaintiffs were required to demonstrate that the principle of aiding and abetting is established in customary international law. The case is still pending. The following is from the concurring opinion of Judge Katzmann.

[...] I conclude that the recognition of the individual responsibility of a defendant who aids and abets a violation of international law is one of those rules "that States universally abide by, or accede to, out of a sense of legal obligation and mutual concern." Recognized as part of the customary law which authorized and was applied by the war crimes trials following the Second World War, it has been frequently invoked in international law instruments as an accepted mode of liability. During the second half of the twentieth century and into this century, it has been repeatedly recognized in numerous international treaties, most notably the Rome Statute of the International Criminal Court, and in the statutes creating the International Criminal Tribunal for the Former Yugoslavia ("ICTY") and the International Criminal Tribunal for Rwanda ("ICTR"). Indeed, the United States concedes, and the defendants do not dispute, that the concept of criminal aiding and abetting liability is "well established" in international law.

Judge Katzmann engages in a comprehensive review of international criminal law sources to support this conclusion before turning to an examination of the *mens rea* requirement.

Still the Rome Statute's *mens rea* standard is entirely consistent with the application of accomplice liability under the sources of international law discussed above. For example, in the *Ministries Case* conducted under Control Council Law No. 10, the tribunal declined to impose criminal liability on a bank officer who was alleged to have "made a loan, knowing or having good reason to believe that the borrower w[ould] use the funds in financing enterprises [conducted] in violation of either national or international law," but was not proven to have made the loan with the purpose of facilitating the enterprises' illegal activities. Meanwhile, those who assist in the commission of a crime with the purpose of facilitating that crime would be subject to aiding and abetting liability under the statutes governing the ICTY and ICTR.[3] My research has revealed no source of international law that recognizes liability for aiding and abetting a violation of international law but would not authorize the imposition of such liability on a party who acts with the purpose of facilitating that violation (provided, of course, that the *actus reus* requirement is also satisfied).

With respect to the *actus reus* component of the aiding and abetting liability, the international legislation is less helpful in identifying a specific standard. However, in the course of its analysis of customary international law, the ICTY concluded that "the *actus reus* of aiding and abetting in international criminal law requires practical assistance, encouragement, or moral support which has a *substantial effect* on the perpetration of the crime." *Furundzija,* Trial Chamber Judgment, ¶ 235 (second emphasis added). My research has uncovered nothing to indicate that a standard other than "substantial assistance" should apply.

Accordingly, I conclude that a defendant may be held liable under international law for aiding and abetting the violation of that law by another when the defendant (1) provides practical assistance to the principal which has a substantial effect on the perpetration of the crime, and (2) does so with the purpose of facilitating the commission of that crime. Furthermore, based on this review of international law's treatment of aiding and abetting liability over the past sixty years, I conclude that aiding and abetting liability, so defined, is sufficiently "well-established[ ] [and] universally recognized" to be considered customary international law for the purposes of the ATCA.

QUESTIONS

1. Normatively where is the right place to draw the line between innocent and culpable contributions to mass crimes? Should the focus be on the *actus reus* or on the *mens rea*?

2. Aiding and abetting by omission requires, inter alia, the failure to fulfil a duty. What kinds of duties should give rise to the possibility of such liability?

3. Given the potentially broad scope of aiding and abetting liability, does it necessarily depend on the judicious exercise of prosecutorial discretion?

---

[3] [12] These Tribunals would also extend liability to individuals who merely had "knowledge that [their] acts assist the commission of the specific crime of the principal." Any individual who acts with the purpose to facilitate the commission of a crime would necessarily act with such knowledge. Thus, I do not view the articulation of a broader definition by the ICTY as detracting from my position that liability in accordance with the purposefulness standard is well-established and universally recognized under international law. The critical question is whether there is a discernable core definition that commands the same level of consensus as the 18th-century crimes identified by the Supreme Court in [*United States* v. *Sosa*]. I believe that the standard I adopt is such a definition.

FURTHER READING

Cassese, *International Criminal Law*, 214–18.

A. Eser, 'Individual Criminal Responsibility', in A. Cassese *et al.* (eds), *International Criminal Court Commentary*, vol. 1 (Oxford: Oxford University Press, 2002), 798–801.

O. Triffterer (ed.), *Commentary on the Rome Statute of the International Criminal Court* (The Netherlands: IOS Press, 2008), 754–7.

Werle, *Principles*, 182–5.

7

INCITEMENT TO COMMIT GENOCIDE

(A) THE NOTION AND ITS ORIGINS

Criminalizing incitement pushes the line of prohibition to the stage when criminal acts are being encouraged or induced. Among national jurisdictions, common-law systems tend to treat incitement as an inchoate offence – criminal regardless of whether the incited offence ensues or is caused by the incitement – while civil-law systems tend to address incitement as a form of complicity in the incited offence. In international criminal law, the conception of criminal incitement is tightly circumscribed in part because incitement often involves exhortatory speech and criminalization of incitement risks the suppression of unpopular speech. In general, direct and explicit incitement followed by the commission of a war crime, a crime against humanity or an act of genocide is punished. Incitement is not punished as an inchoate offence per se, however, with one exception: incitement to commit genocide.

The criminalization of incitement of genocide is founded on the understanding that such conduct is so dangerous that the law should intercede earlier, at the inchoate stage. Although not a genocide case, the World War II-era case of Julius Streicher is instructive. Dubbed 'Jew-Baiter Number One', Streicher, the publisher of the anti-Semitic newspaper *Der Stürmer*, demonstrated the virulence of incitement. Streicher's incitement was direct and explicit and his intent clear and unequivocal – numerous articles of *Der Stürmer* preached extermination 'root and branch', and advocated solution of the 'Jewish problem' through annihilation. Streicher personally penned several of the articles directly calling for the extermination of the Jewish people, writing for example, 'there is only one way – the extermination of that people whose father is the devil'. In 1943, with knowledge that Jewish people in the Eastern Occupied Territories were being destroyed, Streicher wrote in celebration 'that world Jewry was being extirpated, and that it was wonderful to know that Hitler was freeing the world of its Jewish tormentors'. In the excerpt that appears in the chapter on crimes against humanity (see p. 156), the IMT ruled that 'Streicher's incitement to murder and extermination at the time when Jews in the East were being killed under the most horrible conditions clearly constitutes persecution on political and racial grounds in connection with war crimes as defined by the Charter, and constitutes a crime against humanity' and sentenced Streicher to hang.

In contrast, the Tribunal ruled that Hans Fritzsche, the supervisor of the German press who funnelled directives to the newspapers to promulgate Nazi themes, lacked the intent to incite war crimes and aggression and therefore was not guilty of those charges:

Excerpts in evidence from his speeches show definite anti-Semitism on his part. He broadcast, for example, that the war had been caused by Jews and said their fate had turned out "as unpleasant as the Fuehrer predicted." But these speeches did not urge persecution or extermin-ation of Jews. There is no evidence that he was aware of their extermination in the East. The evidence moreover shows that he twice attempted to have publication of the anti-Semitic "Der Sturmer" suppressed, though unsuccessfully. [...]

It appears that Fritzsche sometimes made strong statements of a propagandistic nature in his broadcasts. But the Tribunal is not prepared to hold that they were intended to incite the German people to commit atrocities on conquered peoples, and he cannot be held to have been a participant in the crimes charged. His aim was rather to arouse popular sentiment in support of Hitler and the German war effort.[1]

Fritzsche's case is an early illustration of the line-drawing questions posed by criminal liability on an incitement theory.

While incitement was the prosecution theory in the cases of Streicher and Fritzsche, it was not a codified and formally charged offence at the time. Not until 1948, when the 'crime without a name' became the subject of the Genocide Convention, was incite-ment of genocide also expressly proscribed in treaty law. Article III of the Genocide Convention criminalizes '[d]irect and public incitement to commit genocide' as well as attempted genocide and conspiracy to commit genocide. The goal of criminalizing these acts on the path to genocide was to better facilitate prevention of genocide before it happens.

The framing of incitement of genocide as a crime was controversial. The original *Draft Convention on the Crime of Genocide* provided that 'direct public incitement to any act of genocide, whether the incitement be successful or not' was punishable.[2] This roused the concern of the United States, which objected that '[u]nder Anglo-American rules of law the right of free speech is not to be interfered with unless there is a clear and present danger that the utterance might interfere with a right of others'.[3] The objection presaged the US standard for incitement later set out in the oft-quoted case of *Brandenburg* v. *Ohio* 395 U.S. 444 (1969), which involved the prosecution of a white supremacist Klu Klux Klan leader for making speeches at anti-Black and anti-Jewish gatherings. The US Supreme Court ruled that criminal laws may not 'forbid or proscribe advocacy of the use of force or of law violation except where such advocacy is directed to inciting or producing imminent lawless action and is likely to incite or produce such action' (*ibid.* at 447).

The body created to review the draft Convention, the ad hoc Committee on Genocide, sent an even broader provision on incitement to the General Assembly, making punishable 'direct public or private incitement to commit the crime of genocide whether such incite-ment be successful or not'. In subsequent debates, the United States moved that the incite-ment provision be struck out altogether because it might impinge on freedom of the press. The United Kingdom, Iran, Chile, the Dominican Republic and Brazil were also among the nations supporting striking out incitement of genocide.

Though it also initially supported striking out incitement from the Genocide Convention, Belgium crafted a compromise that comprises the current Genocide Convention's provi-sion regarding incitement. In the compromise, the phrases 'or in private' and 'whether such incitement be successful or not' were excised. Belgium reasoned that striking out the clause regarding success would permit 'the legislature of each country to decide, in accordance with its own laws on incitement, whether incitement to commit genocide

---

[1] IMT Nuremberg, *Göring et al.*, Judgment, 30 September–1 October 1946.

[2] U.N. ESCOR, U.N. Doc. E/447, at Art. II(II) (1947).

[3] *Prevention and Punishment of Genocide: Comments by Governments on the Draft Convention Prepared by the Secretariat*, U.N. ESCOR, U.N. Doc. E/623, at 14 (1948).

had to be successful in order to be punishable'.[4] The Belgian compromise language was adopted while the American amendment to simply delete the provision on incitement was defeated.[5]

Despite these contested foundations, the prohibition against incitement of genocide has passed firmly into contemporary international criminal law. The notion that direct and public incitement of genocide incurs criminal responsibility has also been incorporated in the Statutes of the ICTY, ICTR and ICC. While the ICTYSt. and ICTRSt. make incitement of genocide a crime unto itself, Article 25.3(e) ICCSt. treats incitement as a mode of responsibility, albeit restricted to genocide. Whether this difference in wording will lead to interpretive divergence remains to be seen – the ICC has not confirmed incitement of genocide charges to date.

(B) THE MEANING OF DIRECT AND PUBLIC INCITEMENT

The three key *actus reus* terms in the criminalization of incitement are (i) direct, (ii) public and (iii) incitement. The requirements that incitement be direct and public limit the scope of the offence to the zone of greater danger. Odious words are not always criminal words. Diatribes that play on hatred may not be criminal, though there may be areas of overlap. It is not necessary, however, that incitement be followed by the actual commission of acts of genocide.

The jurisprudence on precisely how the requirement of direct and public incitement limits the scope of the offence did not begin until fifty years after the codification of the crime in the Genocide Convention. The first conviction for incitement of genocide came in 1998 in *Prosecutor* v. *Akayesu* – the first international trial where genocide and incitement of genocide were formally charged as such. Portions of the *Akayesu* trial judgment were excerpted in the chapter on genocide (Part II(3)). The *Akayesu* Trial Chamber explained that:

556. The public element of incitement to commit genocide may be better appreciated in light of two factors: the place where the incitement occurred and whether or not assistance was selective or limited. A line of authority commonly followed in Civil law systems would regard words as being public where they were spoken aloud in a place that were [sic] public by definition. According to the International Law Commission, public incitement is characterized by a call for criminal action to a number of individuals in a public place or to members of the general public at large by such means as the mass media, for example, radio or television. It should be noted in this respect that at the time [the] Convention on Genocide was adopted, the delegates specifically agreed to rule out the possibility of including private incitement to commit genocide as a crime, thereby underscoring their commitment to set aside for punishment only the truly public forms of incitement.

557. The "direct" element of incitement implies that the incitement assume a direct form and specifically provoke another to engage in a criminal act, and that more than mere vague or indirect suggestion goes to constitute direct incitement. [...] [T]he Chamber is of the opinion that the direct element of incitement should be viewed in the light of its cultural and linguistic

---

[4] U.N. GAOR, Sixth Committee, 3d Sess., 85th Mtg., U.N. Doc. A/C.6/SR.85, at 220 (1948).

[5] Misgivings about the criminalization of incitement of genocide were among the reasons the United States did not ratify the Genocide Convention until 1986.

content. Indeed, a particular speech may be perceived as "direct" in one country, and not so in another, depending on the audience. The Chamber further recalls that incitement may be direct, and nonetheless implicit. Thus, at the time the Convention on Genocide was being drafted, the Polish delegate observed that it was sufficient to play skillfully on mob psychology by casting suspicion on certain groups, by insinuating that they were responsible for economic or other difficulties in order to create an atmosphere favourable to the perpetration of the crime.

In the decade after the *Akayesu* judgment, the ICTR has further developed a robust jurisprudence tackling the difficult task of distinguishing criminal incitement of genocide from the wider universe of hate speech. The Appeal Chamber's decision in one of the most famous incitement cases, excerpted below, offers a lesson in close textual analysis to distinguish direct incitement of genocide from hate speech.

Cases

ICTR, Nahimana et al. *v.* Prosecutor *(Media case), Appeals Chamber, Judgment of 28 November 2007*

Dubbed the '*Media* Case', the prosecution of media executives for the Rwandan genocide is a landmark in the law of incitement of genocide. Among the accused were Ferdinand Nahimana and Jean-Bosco Barayagwiza, founders of the infamous *Radio Télévision Libres des Milles Collines* (RTLM), and Hassan Ngze, owner and editor of the Hutu extremist newspaper *Kangura*. Because radio was the medium of mass communication with broadest reach in Rwanda, RTLM was an important instrument in mobilizing the population and whipping them into a frenzied hatred that led to the slaughter of hundreds of thousands of people in less than four months. *Kangura* also helped foment hatred by portraying the Tutsi as an evil dishonest enemy and promulgating messages of violence.

All three media executives were convicted by the Trial Chamber of inciting genocide among other crimes and appealed. Based on the reasoning below, the Appeals Chamber limited the basis of the incitement conviction of Nahimana to RTLM broadcasts after 6 April 1994; reversed the conviction of Barayagwiza for incitement based on RTLM broadcasts because his effective control over RTLM journalists and employees predated 6 April 1994; and affirmed Ngeze's conviction for incitement based on 1994 publications in *Kangura*.

(a) Hate speech and direct incitement to commit genocide

692. The Appeals Chamber considers that there is a difference between hate speech in general (or inciting discrimination or violence) and direct and public incitement to commit genocide. Direct incitement to commit genocide assumes that the speech is a direct appeal to commit an act referred to in Article 2(2) of the Statute; it has to be more than a mere vague or indirect suggestion. In most cases, direct and public incitement to commit genocide can be preceded or accompanied by hate speech, but only direct and public incitement to commit genocide is prohibited under Article 2(3)(c) of the Statute. This conclusion is corroborated by the *travaux préparatoires* to the Genocide Convention.

693. The Appeals Chamber therefore concludes that when a defendant is indicted pursuant to Article 2(3)(c) of Statute, he cannot be held accountable for hate speech that does not directly call for the commission of genocide. [. . .]

(b) Speeches that are open to several interpretations

698. In conformity with the *Akayesu* Trial Judgement, the Trial Chamber considered that it was necessary to take account of Rwanda's culture and language in determining whether a speech constituted direct incitement to commit genocide. [...]

700. The Appeals Chamber agrees that the culture, including the nuances of the Kinyarwanda language, should be considered in determining what constitutes direct and public incitement to commit genocide in Rwanda. For this reason, it may be helpful to examine how a speech was understood by its intended audience in order to determine its true message.

701. The principal consideration is thus the meaning of the words used in the specific context: it does not matter that the message may appear ambiguous to another audience or in another context. On the other hand, if the discourse is still ambiguous even when considered in its context, it cannot be found beyond reasonable doubt to constitute direct and public incitement to commit genocide. [...]

703. The Appeals Chamber therefore concludes that it was open to the Trial Chamber to hold that a speech containing no explicit appeal to commit genocide, or which appeared ambiguous, still constituted direct incitement to commit genocide in a particular context. [...]

(c) Reliance on the intent of the speech's author, its potential dangers and the author's political and community affiliation

(i) Intent

704. [...] Appellants Nahimana and Ngeze contend that the Trial Chamber erred in holding that speech containing no direct appeal to extermination could nevertheless constitute the *actus reus* of the crime of incitement simply because its author had a criminal intent.

705. [...] The relevant paragraph[ ] of the Trial Judgement read[s] as follows:

> 1001. Editors and publishers have generally been held responsible for the media they control. In determining the scope of this responsibility, the importance of intent, that is the purpose of the communications they channel, emerges from the jurisprudence – whether or not the purpose in publicly transmitting the material was of a *bona fide* nature (e.g. historical research, the dissemination of news and information, the public accountability of government authorities). The actual language used in the media has often been cited as an indicator of intent. For example, in the *Faurisson* case, the term "magic gas chamber" was seen by the UN Human Rights Committee as suggesting that the author was motivated by anti-Semitism rather than pursuit of historical truth. In the *Jersild* case, the comments of the interviewer distancing himself from the racist remarks made by his subject were a critical factor for the European Court of Human Rights in determining that the purpose of the television program was the dissemination of news rather than propagation of racist views. [...]

706. It is apparent from Paragraph 1001 of the Trial Judgement that the Trial Chamber employed the term "intent" with reference to the purpose of the speech, as evidenced, *inter alia*, by the language used, and not to the intent of its author. The Appeals Chamber is of the opinion that the purpose of the speech is indisputably a factor in determining whether there is direct and public incitement to commit genocide, and it can see no error in this respect on the part of the Trial Chamber. It is plain that the Trial Chamber did not find that a speech constitutes direct and public incitement to commit genocide simply because its author had criminal intent.

707. Appellants Barayagwiza and Ngeze further submit that the Trial Chamber erred in find-ing in paragraph 1029 of the Judgement that the media's intention to cause genocide was evidenced in part by the fact that genocide did occur. [...]

709. The Appeals Chamber is not persuaded that the mere fact that genocide occurred demonstrates that the journalists and individuals in control of the media intended to incite the commission of genocide. It is, of course, possible that these individuals had the intent to incite others to commit genocide and that their encouragement contributed significantly to the occurrence of genocide (as found by the Trial Chamber), but it would be wrong to hold that, since genocide took place, these individuals necessarily had the intent to incite genocide, as the genocide could have been the result of other factors. However, the Appeals Chamber notes that paragraph 1029 of the Judgement concludes that the fact that "the media intended to [cause genocide] is evidenced *in part* by the fact that it did have this effect". The Appeals Chamber cannot conclude that this reasoning was erroneous: in some circumstances, the fact that a speech leads to acts of genocide could be an indication that in that particular context the speech was understood to be an incitement to commit genocide and that this was indeed the intent of the author of the speech. The Appeals Chamber, notes, however, that this cannot be the only evidence adduced to conclude that the purpose of the speech (and of its author) was to incite the commission of genocide.

(ii) Potential dangers

710. As noted above, Appellant Nahimana contends that the Trial Chamber erred in relying on the potential dangers of a speech in determining whether it constitutes direct incitement to commit genocide. He argues that, even though some speeches inciting hatred may contain inherent dangers, they do not necessarily qualify as direct and public incitement to commit genocide, which, he contends, presupposes an unequivocal call for extermination.

711. The Appeals Chamber is not persuaded that the Trial Chamber took the view that any potentially dangerous hate speech constitutes direct incitement to commit genocide. The Trial Chamber referred to the possible impact of certain remarks in its analysis of the context in which such remarks were made. As explained above, the meaning of a message can be intrin-sically linked to the context [in] which it is formulated. In the opinion of the Appeals Chamber, the Trial Chamber was correct in concluding that it was appropriate to consider the potential impact in context – notably, how the message would be understood by its intended audi-ence – in determining whether it constituted direct and public incitement to commit genocide. The appeal on this point is dismissed. [...]

C. Application of the legal principles to the facts of the case [...]

1. The RTLM broadcasts

[...] 739. The Appeals Chamber would begin by pointing out that the broadcasts must be considered as a whole and placed in their particular context. Thus, even though the terms *Inyenzi* [cockroaches] and *Inkotanyi* [tenacious fighters] may have various meanings in various contexts (as with many words in every language), the Appeals Chamber is of the opinion that it was reasonable for the Trial Chamber to conclude that these expressions could in certain cases be taken to refer to the Tutsi population as a whole. The Appeals Chamber further con-siders that it was reasonable to conclude that certain RTLM broadcasts had directly equated the Tutsi with the enemy.

740. The Judgement specifically considers the following broadcasts made between 1 January and 6 April 1994:

- The broadcast of 1 January 1994[6]

741. [...] The Trial Chamber found that this RTLM broadcast "heated up heads". The Appeals Chamber agrees with the Trial Chamber: the broadcast of 1 January 1994 encouraged ethnic hatred. The Appeals Chamber notes that the broadcast also wanted to "warn" the Hutu majority against an impending "threat". The implicit message was perhaps that the Hutu had to take action to counter that "threat". However, in the absence of other evidence to show that the message was actually a call to commit acts of genocide against the Tutsi, the Appeals Chamber cannot conclude beyond reasonable doubt that the broadcast was a direct and public incitement to commit genocide.

- The broadcast of 5 January 1994[7]

742. [...] The Trial Chamber found that the broadcast was an "example of inflammatory speech", that the journalist's obvious intention "was to mobilize anger against the Tutsis" and to make fun of them. However, the broadcast contains no direct and public incitement to commit genocide against the Tutsi. [...]

- The broadcast of 14 March 1994[8]

744. [...] The broadcast named a person said to be an RPF member and his family members. The broadcast did not directly call on anyone to kill the children, although it was perhaps an implicit call to do so. However, in the absence of other evidence to that effect, the Appeals

---

6 [1738] The Judgement cites the following excerpt [...]:
Very small children, Tutsi small children came and said: "Good morning Kantano. We like you but do not heat up our heads." [...] They said: "You see, we are few and when you talk of Tutsis, we feel afraid. We see that CDR people are going to pounce on us. Leave that and do not heat up our heads."
  You are really very young... That is not what I mean. However, in this war, in this hard turn that Hutus and Tutsis are turning together, some colliding on others, some cheating others in order to make them fall fighting [...] If Tutsis want to seize back the power by tricks... Everybody has to say: "Mass, be vigilant... Your property is being taken away. What you fought for in '59 is being taken away."... So kids, do not condemn me. I have nothing against Tutsis, or Twas, or Hutus. I am a Hutu but I have nothing against Tutsis. But in this political situation I have to explain: "Beware, Tutsis want to take things from Hutus by force or tricks." So, there is not any connection in saying that and hating the Tutsis. [...]

7 [1740] The Judgement cites the following excerpt [...]:
The *Inkotanyi* said, "Kantano hates the *Inkotanyi* so much; he hates the Tutsi. We really want him. We must get that Kantano of RTLM. We must argue with him and make him change his mind. He has to become a partisan of the *Inkotanyi* ideology." All the *Inkotanyi* wanted to see that Hutu who "hates the Tutsi." I do not hate the Tutsi! I do not think it is their real opinion. It is not. Why should I hate the Tutsi? Why should I hate the *Inkotanyi*? The only object of misunderstanding was that the *Inkotanyi* bomb shelled us. They chased us out of our property and compelled us to live at a loss on wastelands like Nyacyonga. That was the only reason for the misunderstanding. There is no reason for hating them anymore. They have now understood that dialogue is capital. They have given up their wickedness and handed in their weapons. [...]

8 [1743] The Judgement cites the following extracts [...]:
At RTLM, we have decided to remain vigilant. I urge you, people of Biryogo, who are listening to us, to remain vigilant. Be advised that a weevil has crept into your midst. Be advised that you have been infiltrated, that you must be extra vigilant in order to defend and protect yourself. You may say: "Gahigi, aren't you trying to scare us?" This is not meant to scare you. I say that people must be told the truth. That is useful, a lot better than lying to them. I would like to tell you, inhabitants of Biryogo, that one of your neighbors, named Manzi Sudi Fadi, alias Bucumi, is no longer among you. He now works as a technician for Radio Muhabura. We have seized a letter he wrote to Ismael Hitimana, alias Safari, ... heads a brigade of *Inkotanyi* there the [sic] in Biryogo area, a brigade called *Abatiganda*. He is their coordinator. It's a brigade composed of *Inkotanyi* over there in Biryogo. [...]
  You must know that the man Manzi Sudi is no longer among you, that the brigade is headed by a man named Hitimana Ismaël, coordinator of the *Abatiganda* brigade in Biryogo. [...]

Chamber cannot conclude beyond reasonable doubt that the broadcast directly and publicly incited the commission of genocide. [...]

Editorial note: other analyses of specific broadcasts are excised in the interest of brevity. An illustrative and instructive sampling is provided.

- The broadcast of 3 April 1994[9]

751. [...] Even if this broadcast was calculated to cause fear among the population by predicting an imminent attack by the RPF, the Appeals Chamber cannot conclude beyond reasonable doubt that it was a direct and public incitement to commit genocide. [...]

(iv) Conclusion

754. The Appeals Chamber thus finds that, although it is clear that RTLM broadcasts between 1 January and 6 April 1994 incited ethnic hatred, it has not been established that they directly and publicly incited the commission of genocide.

(c) Broadcasts after 6 April 1994

755. Appellant Barayagwiza submits that the RTLM broadcasts made from 7 April 1994 did not amount to direct and public incitement to commit genocide against the Tutsi. The only specific argument that Appellant Barayagwiza raises is that the broadcast of 4 June 1994 could not be interpreted as a call to kill the Tutsi, because this broadcast used the term *Inkotanyi*, and that was not synonymous with Tutsi. For the reasons cited earlier, the Appeals Chamber considers that it was reasonable to find that, in certain contexts, the term *Inkotanyi* was used to refer to the Tutsi. In particular, the Appeals Chamber considers that it was reasonable to find that the broadcast of 4 June 1994, which described the *Inkotanyi* as having the physical features popularly associated with the Tutsi, equated the *Inkotanyi* with the Tutsi, and that it amounted to direct and public incitement to commit genocide against the Tutsi.

756. The Appeals Chamber further notes that, although paragraph 1032 of the Judgement only mentions the broadcast of 4 June 1994 to illustrate the incitement engaged in by RTLM, the Trial Chamber also considered that other broadcasts made after 6 April 1994 explicitly called for the extermination of the Tutsi:

Many of the RTLM broadcasts explicitly called for extermination. In the 13 May 1994 RTLM broadcast, Kantano Habimana spoke of exterminating the *Inkotanyi* so as "to wipe them from human memory", and exterminating the Tutsi "from the surface of the earth...to make them disappear for good". In the 4 June 1994 RTLM broadcast, Habimana again talked of exterminating the *Inkotanyi*, adding "the reason we will exterminate them is that they belong to one ethnic group". In the 5 June 1994 RTLM broadcast, Ananie Nkurunziza acknowledged that this extermination was underway and expressed the hope that "we continue exterminating them at the same pace". On the basis of all the programming he listened to after 6 April 1994, Witness GO testified that RTLM was constantly asking people to kill other people, that no distinction was made between the *Inyenzi* and the Tutsi, and that listeners were encouraged to continue killing them so that future generations would have to ask what *Inyenzi* or Tutsi looked like.

These broadcasts constitute, as such, direct and public incitement to commit genocide. [...]

---

[9] [1756] The Judgement cites the following excerpt [...]:
They want to carry out a little something during the Easter period. In fact, they're saying: "We have the dates hammered out." They have the dates, we know them too. [...]

3. Kangura

[...] 765. The Trial Chamber found that "[m]any of the writings published in *Kangura* combined ethnic hatred and fear-mongering with a call to violence to be directed against the Tutsi population, who were characterized as the enemy or enemy accomplices". As examples, it mentioned "The *Appeal to the Conscience of the Hutu*" (published in December 1990) and the cover of *Kangura* No. 26 (November 1991), and it noted the "increased attention in 1994 issues of *Kangura* to the fear of an RPF attack and the threat that [the] killing of innocent Tutsi civilians [...] would follow as a consequence". The Trial Chamber then recognized that not all of the writings published in *Kangura* and highlighted by the Prosecutor constituted direct incitement. Finally, it considered that, as founder, owner and editor of *Kangura*, Appellant Ngeze was responsible for the content of *Kangura*, and it found him guilty of direct and public incitement to commit genocide.

766. The Appeals Chamber summarily dismisses Appellant Ngeze's argument that the genocide would have occurred even if the *Kangura* articles had never existed, because it is not necessary to show that direct and public incitement to commit genocide was followed by actual consequences. Regarding the argument that *Kangura* was not being published at the time of the genocide, this is not relevant in deciding whether the *Kangura* publications constituted direct and public incitement to commit genocide. [...]

770. However, the Appeals Chamber notes that the Trial Chamber did not clearly identify all the extracts from *Kangura* which, in its view, directly and publicly incited genocide, confining itself to mentioning only extracts from *Kangura* published before 1 January 1994 to support its findings. The Appeals Chamber has already found that the Trial Chamber erred in basing the convictions of the Appellant on pre-1994 issues [before the date of the ICTR's temporal jurisdiction]. Moreover, as explained previously, the lack of particulars concerning the acts constituting direct and public incitement to commit genocide represented an error, and obliges the Appeals Chamber to examine the 1994 issues of *Kangura* mentioned in the Judgement in order to determine, beyond reasonable doubt, whether one or more of them constituted direct and public incitement to commit genocide.

- "The Last Lie"

771. In an article headed the "Last Lie", which appeared in issue No. 54 of *Kangura* (January 1994), Appellant Ngeze wrote:

Let's hope the *Inyenzi* will have the courage to understand what is going to happen and realize that if they make a small mistake, they will be exterminated; if they make the mistake of attacking again, there will be none of them left in Rwanda, not even a single accomplice. All the Hutus are united...

The Appeals Chamber agrees with the Trial Chamber that the term "accomplice" refers to the Tutsi in general, in light of the sentence which immediately follows this reference and which was written by the Appellant: "All the Hutus are united...". The Appeals Chamber considers that this article called on the Hutu to stand united in order to exterminate the Tutsi if the RPF were to attack again. In the view of the Appeals Chamber, the fact that this call was conditional on there being an attack by RPF does nothing to lessen its impact as a direct call to commit genocide if the condition should be fulfilled; the Appeals Chamber finds that this article constituted direct and public incitement to commit genocide.

- "Who will survive the war of March?"

772. An article headed "Who Will Survive the War of March?", which appeared in issue No. 55 (January 1994) and was signed *Kangura*, included the following passage:

If the *Inkotanyi* have decided to massacre us, the killing should be mutually done. This boil must be burst. The present situation warrants that we should be vigilant because they are difficult. The presence of U.N. forces will not prevent the *Inkotanyi* to start the war (. . .). These happenings are possible in Rwanda, too. When the *Inkotanyi* must have surrounded the capital of Kigali, they will appeal to those of Mulindi and their accomplices within the country, and the rest will follow. It will be necessary for the majority people and its army to defend itself. . . On that day, blood will be spilled. On that day, much blood must have been spilled.

The Appeals Chamber notes that this article contains an appeal to "the majority people" to kill the *Inkotanyi* and their "accomplices within the country" (meaning the Tutsi) in case of an attack by the RPF. Accordingly, the Appeals Chamber finds that this article constituted direct and public incitement to commit genocide.

- "How Will the UN Troops Perish?"

773. An editorial signed by Appellant Ngeze and published in issue No. 56 of *Kangura* (February 1994) stated that, after the departure of the United Nations troops, "[a]ll the Tutsis and cowardly Hutus will be exterminated". The Trial Chamber found that this editorial was both a prediction and a threat. In the opinion of the Appeals Chamber, this article goes even further: it implicitly calls on its readers to exterminate Tutsi (and "cowardly Hutus") after the departure of the United Nations troops. The Appeals Chamber finds that this article constituted direct and public incitement to commit genocide against the Tutsi.

- "One Would Say That Tutsis Do Not Bleed, That Their Blood Does Not Flow"

774. Paragraphs 227 to 229 of the Judgement also refer to an extract from an article headed "One Would Say That Tutsis Do Not Bleed, That Their Blood Does Not Flow", published in issue No. 56 of *Kangura* (February 1994). This article does not appear to threaten all the Tutsi, but only the Tutsi who acclaimed Tito Rutaremara and who, in doing so, demonstrated their support for an armed insurrection. In the absence of any element demonstrating that all the Tutsi were actually targeted by this article, or that some Tutsi were targeted on the sole basis of their ethnicity, the Appeals Chamber cannot find that this article constituted direct incitement to commit genocide.

(c) Conclusion

775. The Appeals Chamber finds that *Kangura* articles published in 1994 directly and publicly incited the commission of genocide[.]

Whether incitement is public is usually more straightforward than whether it is direct. The question of how broadly to interpret the concept of direct incitement is inflected with the countervailing concerns of not unduly chilling or suppressing speech while ensuring that liability is not evaded through euphemisms or veiled calls that are just as insidious and dangerous.

The *Media* case shows how the ICTR has attempted to strike a careful middle path that takes into account the realities and cultural context of communication and the fact that what may seem obscure to someone from a different culture and historical moment may be a clarion call to violence to the audience at the time. Euphemisms and implicit calls may be direct when construed in linguistic, cultural and historical context. Careful identification and analysis of the alleged incitement is required, however, to ensure that general expressions of hatred and fear-mongering are not conflated with incitement of genocide. This might be particularly difficult when international judges are requested to rule on speech made in foreign contexts and in languages in which they are not proficient.

In the next case, the ICTR tackled head-on whether criminalization of incitement of genocide is consistent with free speech values enshrined in numerous human rights instruments.

ICTR, Prosecutor v. Bikindi, *Trial Chamber, Judgment of 2 December 2008*

Famous Rwandan singer-songwriter Simon Bikindi, an ethnic Hutu, was accused of using his music to incite genocide against the Tutsis. The Trial Chamber found that three of Bikindi's songs, *Twasezereye, Nanga Abahutu* and *Bene Sebahinzi*, 'manipulated the history of Rwanda to extol Hutu solidarity' and 'were deployed in a propaganda campaign in 1994 in Rwanda to incite people to attack and kill Tutsi'. The extremist radio station RTLM broadcast the songs repeatedly during the genocide and machete-wielding slaughterers of Tutsis would sing the songs.

The Trial Chamber ruled that there was insufficient evidence to find that Bikindi composed the songs with the specific intent that they incite attacks. There was also insufficient proof that Bikindi was responsible for the broadcasts by extremists in 1994 that incited attacks. Bikindi was instead convicted of incitement not for his music but for an incident in June 1994 when he used a vehicle with a public broadcast system to incite people to exterminate the Tutsi. He was sentenced to 15 years in prison.

CHAPTER III: FREEDOM OF EXPRESSION BEFORE THE TRIBUNAL

378. Simon Bikindi has been charged with offences based upon acts of expression, namely musical compositions, musical disseminations using a vehicle outfitted with a public address system, as well as musical performances and speeches given both in person and broadcast over the radio. [...]

1. FREEDOM OF EXPRESSION, THE RIGHT AND ITS LIMITS

379. There is a right to freedom of expression under customary international law. This is demonstrated by numerous international instruments which incorporate the right to freedom of expression, the widespread integration of such protections into domestic legal systems and the dispositions of numerous international, regional, and domestic courts that have interpreted such a right. Notably, all of the following international and regional instruments contain provisions protecting freedom of expression: the Universal Declaration of Human Rights ("UDHR"); the International Covenant on Civil and Political Rights ("ICCPR"); the International Convention on the Elimination of All Forms of Racial Discrimination ("CERD"); the European Convention for the Protection of Human Rights and Fundamental Freedoms ("ECHR"); the American Convention on Human Rights ("ACHR"); and the African Charter on Human and Peoples' Rights ("ACHPR"). These provisions have been widely incorporated into numerous domestic legal systems, and there exists widespread domestic jurisprudence supporting the right to freedom of expression.

380. However, this right is not absolute. It is restricted by the very same conventions and international instruments that provide for it. For example, the UDHR states that everyone should be free from incitement to discrimination. Similarly, the ICCPR prohibits war propaganda, as well as the advocacy of national, racial or religious hatred that constitutes incitement to discrimination, hostility, or violence, and the CERD aims to outlaw all forms of expression that explicitly lead to discrimination. Each of the regional conventions mentioned above also restrict the freedom of expression: the ECHR recognises that there are "duties and responsibilities" that accompany the freedom of expression and thus limit its application; the ACHR allows for legal liability regarding acts that harm the rights or reputations of others, or that threaten the protection of national security, public order, or public health or morals and considers as offences punishable by law any propaganda for war and advocacy of national,

racial or religious hatred that constitute incitements to lawless violence; and the ACHPR restricts the right to that which is "within the law". The Chamber notes that the restrictions on this right have been interpreted in the jurisprudence of the various adjudicating bodies created from the international and regional instruments above. The Chamber also notes that a large number of countries have banned the advocacy of discriminatory hate in their domestic legislation.

381. Prohibited expression can take different forms including incitement to hatred alone, to discrimination, or to violence. Given the varied approaches cited above, for the purposes of this Judgement the Chamber will use "hate speech" as an umbrella term for these forms of expression.

382. Hate speech is not criminalised *per se* under the Statute of the Tribunal, and the Chamber recognises the importance of protecting the right to freedom of expression. Protecting free expression is widely considered to allow for open debate on societal values, encourage artistic and scholarly endeavors, and lead to freedom of conscience and self-fulfilment. Due to such benefits, freedom of expression is widely considered to be the very foundation of successful democracies. In fact, a failure to protect expression may allow repressive regimes to flourish.

383. Nevertheless, the Chamber is of the opinion that there is a discernable hierarchy of expression, one which requires the Chamber to treat different forms of expression differently. Whereas most forms of expression clearly remain within the limits of the legality, others are unequivocally of a criminal nature and should be sanctioned as such.

384. The Chamber considers that international definitions of expression and speech are broad enough to include artistic expression such as songs. Expression has been defined as the freedom to "impart information and ideas", "either orally, in writing or in print, in the form of art, or through any other media of his choice"; and "express and disseminate his opinions". The speech prohibited has been defined broadly as "propaganda", "advocacy of [...] hatred", and the "dissemination of ideas". The Chamber therefore considers that the words accompanying a score of music are comparable from a legal perspective to the words used in a speech. [...]

2.1 Hate Speech and Direct and Public Incitement to Commit Genocide

387. In order to be considered direct and public incitement to commit genocide, a speech must be a public and direct appeal to commit an act referred to in Article 2(2) of the Statute; it must be more than a vague or indirect suggestion. To determine whether a speech rises to the level of direct and public incitement to commit genocide, context is the principal consideration, specifically: the cultural and linguistic content; the political and community affiliation of the author; its audience; and how the message was understood by its intended audience, *i.e.* whether the members of the audience to whom the message was directed understood its implication. A direct appeal to genocide may be implicit; it need not explicitly call for extermination, but could nonetheless constitute direct and public incitement to commit genocide in a particular context.

388. While most direct and public incitements to commit genocide would be preceded or accompanied by hate speech, only the former, which actually calls for genocide, is punishable under Article 2(3)(c) of the Statute. The *travaux préparatoires* of the Genocide Convention supports this conclusion as the Genocide Convention was only intended to criminalise direct appeals to commit acts of genocide and not all forms of hatred.

389. Depending on the nature of the message conveyed and the circumstances, the Chamber does not exclude the possibility that songs may constitute direct and public incitement to commit genocide. [...]

419. A person commits the crime of direct and public incitement to commit genocide if he directly and publicly incites the commission of genocide with the intent to directly and publicly incite others to commit genocide, which presupposes a genocidal intent. As an inchoate crime, public and direct incitement to commit genocide is punishable even if no act of genocide has resulted therefrom.

420. In the absence of direct evidence, the genocidal intent may be inferred from relevant facts and circumstances of a case, such as the overall context in which the crime occurred, the systematic targeting of the victims on account of their membership of a protected group, the exclusion of members of other groups, the scale and scope of the atrocities committed, the frequency of destructive and discriminatory acts, or the political doctrine that gave rise to the acts referred to.

421. Based on its factual findings as to the meaning of the songs *Twasezereye*, *Nanga Abahutu* and *Bene Sebahinzi*, the Chamber concludes that none of these three songs constitute direct and public incitement to commit genocide *per se*. The Chamber also recalls that it has found above that the Prosecution failed to prove that Bikindi played any role in the dissemination or deployment of these songs in 1994.

422. The Chamber has found that the Prosecution proved beyond reasonable doubt that towards the end of June 1994, in Gisenyi *préfecture*, Bikindi travelled on the main road between Kivumu and Kayove as part of a convoy of *Interahamwe*, in a vehicle outfitted with a public address system broadcasting songs, including Bikindi's. When heading towards Kayove, Bikindi used the public address system to state that the majority population, the Hutu, should rise up to exterminate the minority, the Tutsi. On his way back, Bikindi used the same system to ask if people had been killing Tutsi, who he referred to as snakes.

423. The Chamber finds that both statements, broadcast over loudspeaker, were made publicly. The Chamber also finds that Bikindi's call on "the majority" to "rise up and look everywhere possible" and not to "spare anybody" immediately referring to the Tutsi as the minority unequivocally constitutes a direct call to destroy the Tutsi ethnic group. Similarly, the Chamber considers that Bikindi's address to the population on his way back from Kayove, asking "Have you killed the Tutsis here?" and whether they had killed the "snakes" is a direct call to kill Tutsi, pejoratively referred to as snakes. In the Chamber's view, it is inconceivable that, in the context of widespread killings of the Tutsi population that prevailed in June 1994 in Rwanda, the audience to whom the message was directed, namely those standing on the road, could not have immediately understood its meaning and implication. The Chamber therefore finds that Bikindi's statements through loudspeakers on the main road between Kivumu and Kayove constitute direct and public incitement to commit genocide.

COMMENTARY

Bikindi's case – the first prosecution of an entertainer based on the theory that popular music can constitute incitement of genocide – posed particularly stark questions about the tension between free speech values and broad interpretations of what constitutes direct and public incitement. The Trial Chamber took the clearer course of finding Bikindi guilty on the basis of his loudspeaker statements about killing Tutsis rather than his music. While Bikindi's loudspeaker statements were a relatively transparent goading of genocide, more veiled euphemisms and implicit calls present interpretative challenges. The following speech made by government official Leon Mugesera a year and a half before the Rwandan genocide provides an example:

1. Militants of our movement, as we are all met here, I think you will understand the meaning of the word I will say to you. [...]

9. [...] At all costs, you will leave here taking these words with you, that you should not let yourselves be invaded. [...]

13. Something else which may be called [TRANSLATION] "not allowing ourselves to be invaded" in the country, you know people they call "Inyenzis" (cockroaches), no longer call them "Inkotanyi" (tough fighters), as they are actually "Inyenzis". These people called Inyenzis are now on their way to attack us. [...]

15. You know what it is, dear friends, "not letting ourselves be invaded", or you know it. You know there are "Inyenzis" in the country who have taken the opportunity of sending their children to the front, to go and help the "Inkotanyis". [...] So I will tell you now, it is written in the law, in the book of the Penal Code: [TRANSLATION] "Every person who recruits soldiers by seeking them in the population, seeking young persons everywhere whom they will give to the foreign armed forces attacking the Republic, shall be liable to death". It is in writing.

16. Why do they not arrest these parents who have sent away their children and why do they not exterminate them? Why do they not arrest the people taking them away and why do they not exterminate all of them? Are we really waiting till they come to exterminate us?

17. I should like to tell you that we are now asking that these people be placed on a list and be taken to court to be tried in our presence. If they (the judges) refuse, it is written in the Constitution that "ubutabera bubera abaturage". In English, this means that [TRANSLATION] "JUSTICE IS RENDERED IN THE PEOPLE'S NAME". If justice therefore is no longer serving the people, as written in our Constitution which we voted for ourselves, this means that at that point we who also make up the population whom it is supposed to serve, we must do something ourselves to exterminate this rabble. I tell you in all truth, as it says in the Gospel, "When you allow a serpent biting you to remain attached to you with your agreement, you are the one who will suffer".

18. [...] The representatives of those parties who collaborate with the "Inyenzis", those who represent them [...] I am telling you, and I am not lying, it is [...] they only want to exterminate us. They only want to exterminate us: they have no other aim. [...]

25. Recently, I told someone who came to brag to me that he belonged to the P.L. – I told him [TRANSLATION] "The mistake we made in 1959, when I was still a child, is to let you leave". I asked him if he had not heard of the story of the Falashas, who returned home to Israel from Ethiopia? He replied that he knew nothing about it! I told him [TRANSLATION] "So don't you know how to listen or read? I am telling you that your home is in Ethiopia, that we will send you by the Nyabarongo [river] so you can get there quickly".

28. [...] So in order to conclude, I would remind you of all the important things I have just spoken to you about: the most essential is that we should not allow ourselves to be invaded, lest the very persons who are collapsing take away some of you. Do not be afraid, know that anyone whose neck you do not cut is the one who will cut your neck. [...]

Can a call to genocide be fairly read from the rhetorical tactic of pitting of group against group – a tactic racial supremacists groups deploy in their quotidian hate speech? Is your judgment coloured by the harsh light of retrospect, because genocide came to pass in Rwanda? Does it matter whether there was actually a causal link between this speech and the genocide that occurred a year and a half later? Consider these questions as you read the next section on intent and causation and the excerpt of the Canadian Supreme Court's judgment in *Mugesera*.

(C) INTENT AND CAUSATION

Canada, **Mugesera v. Canada** (Minister of Citizenship and Immigration), *Judgment of 28 June 2005*

In 1993, Mugesera ('M' in the text) obtained permanent residence in Canada. After Canadian officials learned of Mugesera's past conduct, deportation proceedings began based on a Canadian Criminal Code provision permitting deportation of a permanent resident who has committed criminal acts or offences. On the theory that Mugesera's speech was criminal incitement of murder, genocide and hatred and that Mugesera had committed a crime against humanity, an immigration adjudicator issued a deportation order that was affirmed by the Immigration and Refugee Board (IAD). The Federal Court of Appeal (FCA) reversed several findings of fact by the IAD, however, and ruled that the allegations against Mugesera were unfounded and that the deportation order had to be set aside. In the decision below, the Canadian Supreme Court reversed the FCA and upheld the deportation order.

82. Genocide is a crime originating in international law. International law is thus called upon to play a crucial role as an aid in interpreting domestic law, particularly as regards the elements of the crime of incitement to genocide. Section 318(1) of the *Criminal Code* incorporates, almost word for word, the definition of genocide found in art. II of the *Genocide Convention*, and the Minister's allegation B makes specific reference to Rwanda's accession to the *Genocide Convention*. Canada is also bound by the *Genocide Convention*. In addition to treaty obligations, the legal principles underlying the *Genocide Convention* are recognized as part of customary international law: see International Court of Justice, Advisory Opinion of May 28, 1951, *Reservations to the Convention on the Prevention and Punishment of the Crime of Genocide*, I.C.J. Reports 1951, at p. 15. The importance of interpreting domestic law in a manner that accords with the principles of customary international law and with Canada's treaty obligations was emphasized in *Baker v. Canada (Minister of Citizenship and Immigration)*, [1999] 2 S.C.R. 817, at paras. 69–71. In this context, international sources like the recent jurisprudence of international criminal courts are highly relevant to the analysis. [. . .]

83. Section 318(1) of the *Criminal Code* proscribes the offence of advocating genocide: "Every one who advocates or promotes genocide is guilty of an indictable offence and liable to imprisonment for a term not exceeding five years." [. . .]

(i) Is Proof of Genocide Required?

84. In *Prosecutor v. Akayesu*, 9 IHRR 608 (1998), the Trial Chamber of the International Criminal Tribunal for Rwanda ("ICTR") drew a distinction between the constituent elements of the crimes of complicity in genocide and incitement to genocide. In the case of a charge of complicity, the prosecution must prove that genocide has actually occurred. A charge of incitement to genocide, however, does not require proof that genocide has in fact happened:

In the opinion of the Chamber, the fact that such acts are in themselves particularly dangerous because of the high risk they carry for society, even if they fail to produce results, warrants that they be punished as an exceptional measure. The Chamber holds that genocide clearly falls within the category of crimes so serious that direct and public incitement to commit such a crime must be punished as such, even where such incitement failed to produce the result expected by the perpetrator. [para. 562]

85. In the case of the allegation of incitement to genocide, the Minister does not need to establish a direct causal link between the speech and any acts of murder or violence. Because

of its inchoate nature, incitement is punishable by virtue of the criminal act alone irrespective of the result. It remains a crime regardless of whether it has the effect it is intended to have: see also *Prosecutor v. Nahimana, Barayagwiza and Ngeze*, Case No. ICTR-99-52-T (Trial Chamber I) ("*Media Case*"), 3 December 2003, at para. 1029. The Minister is not required, therefore, to prove that individuals who heard Mr. Mugesera's speech killed or attempted to kill any members of an identifiable group.

(ii) The Criminal Act: Direct and Public Incitement

86. The criminal act requirement for incitement to genocide has two elements: the act of incitement must be direct and it must be public: *Akayesu*, Trial Chamber, at para. 559. See also art. III(c) of the *Genocide Convention*. The speech was public. We need only consider the meaning of the requirement that it be direct.

87. In *Akayesu*, the Trial Chamber of the ICTR held that the *direct element* "implies that the incitement assume a direct form and specifically provoke another to engage in a criminal act, and that more than mere vague or indirect suggestion goes to constitute direct incitement" (para. 557). The direct element of incitement "should be viewed in the light of its cultural and linguistic content" (para. 557). *Depending on the audience*, a particular speech may be perceived as direct in one country, and not so in another. The determination of whether acts of incitement can be viewed as direct necessarily focusses mainly on the issue of whether the persons for whom the message was intended immediately grasped the implication thereof (para. 558). The words used must be clear enough to be immediately understood by the intended audience. Innuendo and obscure language do not suffice.

(iii) The Guilty Mind for Direct and Public Incitement to Genocide

88. The guilty mind required for the crime of incitement to genocide is an "intent to directly prompt or provoke another to commit genocide" (*Akayesu*, Trial Chamber, at para. 560). It implies a desire on the part of the perpetrator to cause another to have the state of mind necessary to commit the acts enumerated in s. 318(2) of the *Criminal Code*. The person who incites must also have the specific intent to commit genocide: an intent to destroy in whole or in part any identifiable group, namely, any section of the public distinguished by colour, race, religion, or ethnic origin (s. 318(2) and (4) of the *Criminal Code*).

89. Intent can be inferred from the circumstances. Thus, the court can infer the genocidal intent of a particular act from the systematic perpetration of other culpable acts against the group; the scale of any atrocities that are committed and their general nature in a region or a country; or the fact that victims are deliberately and systematically targeted on account of their membership in a particular group while the members of other groups are left alone: *Akayesu*, Trial Chamber, at para. 523. A speech that is given in the context of a genocidal environment will have a heightened impact, and for this reason the environment in which a statement is made can be an indicator of the speaker's intent (*Media Case*, at para. 1022).

(b) *Findings in Respect of the Criminal Act*

90. Mr. Duquette's conclusion[10] that Mr. Mugesera advocated genocide in his speech of November 22, 1992, is based on a number of findings of fact. The most important of them is Mr. Duquette's interpretation of para. 25 of the speech, the infamous "river passage":

[TRANSLATION] Recently, I told someone who came to brag to me that he belonged to the P.L. – I told him [TRANSLATION] "The mistake we made in 1959, when I was still a child, is to let you leave". I asked him if he had not heard of the story of the Falashas, who returned home to Israel from Ethiopia? He replied that he knew nothing about it! I told him

---

[10] Pierre Duquette was the author of the main reasons for the Immigration and Refugee Board's decision.

[TRANSLATION] "So don't you know how to listen or read? I am telling you that your home is in Ethiopia, that we will send you by the Nyabarongo so you can get there quickly".

91. The first relevant finding of fact is that the individual to whom Mr. Mugesera was speaking in this story was a Tutsi. As Mr. Duquette explained, Mr. Mugesera was speaking to a member of an opposition party, the PL. He referred specifically to the events of 1959 when many Tutsi went into exile, and he mentioned Ethiopia. It is common lore in Rwanda that the Tutsi originated in Ethiopia. This belief was even taught in primary and secondary schools.

92. The second relevant finding of fact is that Mr. Mugesera was suggesting at this point that Tutsi corpses be sent back to Ethiopia. Mr. Mugesera argued that he was only telling his audience that, just as the Falasha had left Ethiopia to return to their place of origin, Israel, so should the Tutsi return to Ethiopia. In their case, the return trip would be by way of the Nyabarongo River, which runs through Rwanda toward Ethiopia. This river is not navigable, however, so the return would not be by boat. In earlier massacres, Tutsi had been killed and their bodies thrown into the Nyabarongo River.

93. The reference to 1959 is also important, because the group that was exiled then was essentially Tutsi. The "Inyenzi" and the "Inkotanyi" were recruited from this group. Throughout his speech, as we have seen, Mr. Mugesera drew connections between the two groups. Mr. Duquette also found that the speech clearly advocated that these "invaders" and "accomplices" should not be allowed to "get out", suggesting that the mistake made in 1959 was to drive the Tutsi out of Rwanda, with the result that they were now attacking the country.

94. Summarizing his findings on the meaning of this paragraph, Mr. Duquette wrote:

It is therefore clear that the speaker [the individual Mr Mugesera says he will send back to Ethiopia via the Nyabarongo] is a Tutsi and that when Mr. Mugesera says "we will send you down the Nyabarongo", "you" means the Tutsi and "we", means the Hutu. It is also obvious that the speaker [Mr Mugesera] is impressing on the audience that it was a mistake to drive the Tutsi out of Rwanda in 1959, since they are now attacking the country. Finally, it is clear that he is suggesting that the Tutsi corpses be sent back via the Nyabarongo River. [para. 201]

This message was delivered in a public place at a public meeting and would have been clearly understood by the audience.

95. Mr. Duquette concluded that the individual elements of the "river passage" were inconclusive, but that, taken together, they contained a deliberate call for the murder of Tutsi. "When a person says that Tutsis should be thrown into the river as [sic] and is making references to 1959, he is sending out a clear signal" (para. 323). Drawing on these findings of fact, Mr. Duquette held that Mr. Mugesera had advocated the killing of members of an identifiable group distinguished by ethnic origin, namely the Tutsi, with intent to destroy the group in part.

(c) Findings in Respect of the Guilty Mind

96. On the issue of whether Mr. Mugesera had the requisite mental intent, Mr. Duquette found that "[s]ince he knew approximately 2,000 Tutsis had been killed since October 1, 1990, the context leaves no doubt as to his intent" (para. 323), and that "he intended specifically to provoke citizens against one another" (para. 324). The *mens rea* for incitement to genocide would not be made out if the finding were that Mr. Mugesera had intended to destroy, in whole or in part, members of his political opposition only. Members of a political group do not fit within the definition set out in s. 318(4) of the *Criminal Code*. The IAD went further than this and held that Mr. Mugesera had advocated the destruction of Tutsi, a distinct and identifiable ethnic group.

97. In discussing the elements of the crime, Mr. Duquette concluded that Mr. Mugesera had attempted to incite citizens to act against each other (which is an element of the offence under s. 166 of the Rwandan *Penal Code*). He specified that the citizens in question were "either MRND supporters against opposition parties or Hutu against Tutsi" (para. 324). This finding, coupled with the holding that Mr. Mugesera was aware of the ethnic massacres that were taking place, is sufficient to infer the necessary mental element of the crime of incitement to genocide.

98. The allegation of incitement to the crime of genocide is well founded. The IAD came to the correct legal conclusion on this question.

COMMENTARY

The intent standard further helps to distinguish between general hate speech and criminal incitement of genocide. The hate-monger politician who tries to build solidarity by pitting one group against another may stoke the risk of violence, but is not guilty of incitement if intent to destroy is lacking. The accused must have intended to provoke or prompt genocidal intent – and thus must have harboured such genocidal intent himself. While this strong intent standard does not create an incentive for care in tactics or speech, that may be a virtue as well as a vice – free-wheeling speech in the messy arena of debate is not chilled. The excerpts above also demonstrate that thus far, courts interpreting the crime of incitement of genocide have not required proof of success – despite the deletion of the original language in the Genocide Convention specifying that incitement is punishable 'whether the incitement be successful or not'. Holding inciters of genocide liable regardless of whether a genocidal act ensued makes sense from the perspective of the prevention of dangerous acts. While we may not wish to risk curbing free-wheeling debate, we do wish to deter the particularly dangerous and morally blameworthy subspecies of direct and public incitement undertaken with intent to destroy a protected group. The interpretation also coheres with how incitement of genocide has been framed in the Statutes of the ad hoc tribunals, as an inchoate crime.

Moreover, dispensing with proof of a causal link or contribution to the crime has thus far been a way of distinguishing incitement of genocide from modes of responsibility like instigation or complicity, and thus avoids redundancy. The ICTR Appeals Chamber in *Nahimana* explained the distinction between instigation and incitement of genocide:

678. The Appeals Chamber considers that a distinction must be made between instigation under Article 6(1) of the [ICTR] Statute and public and direct incitement to commit genocide under Article 2(3)(c) of the Statute. In the first place, instigation under Article 6(1) of the Statute is a mode of responsibility; an accused will incur criminal responsibility only if the instigation in fact substantially contributed to the commission of one of the crimes under Articles 2 to 4 of the Statute. By contrast, direct and public incitement to commit genocide under Article 2(3)(c) is itself a crime, and it is not necessary to demonstrate that it in fact substantially contributed to the commission of acts of genocide. In other words, the crime of direct and public incitement to commit genocide is an inchoate offence, punishable even if no act of genocide has resulted therefrom. This is confirmed by the *travaux préparatoires* to the Genocide Convention, from which it can be concluded that the drafters of the Convention intended to punish direct and public incitement to commit genocide, even if no act of genocide was committed, the aim being to forestall the occurrence of such acts. The Appeals Chamber further observes – even if this is not decisive for the determination of the state of customary international law in 1994 – that the Statute of the International Criminal Court also appears to provide that an accused incurs criminal responsibility for direct and public incitement to commit genocide, even if this is not followed by acts of genocide.

679. The second difference is that Article 2(3)(c) of the Statute requires that the incitement to commit genocide must have been direct and public, while Article 6(1) does not so require.[11]

It remains to be seen whether the ICC will adopt a similar interpretation, though the ICCSt. appears to list incitement of genocide as a mode of incurring criminal responsibility rather than an inchoate offence.

QUESTIONS

1. How does incitement of genocide differ from hate speech and when do the categories overlap?

2. 'Information intervention' strategies such as jamming the broadcasts of radio or television stations inciting genocide, or broadcasting competing views can be alternatives or complements to criminal prosecution to mitigate the danger of incitement of genocide. When should information intervention strategies be deployed? What concerns are implicated by deployment of such strategies?

3. Should the ICC pursue the jurisprudential course forged thus far, dispensing with requiring proof that incitement of genocide was successful?

4. Should international criminalization of incitement expand beyond incitement of genocide to other international crimes? If so, which crimes? All international crimes? How would you draw the line?

FURTHER READING

Cassese, *International Criminal Law*, 229–30.

W.A. Schabas, 'Hate Speech in Rwanda: The Road to Genocide' (2000) 46 *McGill L.J.* 141.

A, Zahar, 'The *ICTR's* "Media" Judgment and the Reinvention of Direct and Public Incitement to Commit Genocide' (2005) 16 *Criminal Law Forum* 33–48.

[11] ICTR, *Ferdinand Nahimana, Jean-Bosco Barayagwiza and Hassan Ngeze v. Prosecutor*, Appeals Chamber, Judgment of 28 November 2007.

8

SUPERIOR RESPONSIBILITY

(A) THE NOTION

Superior responsibility is an innovation of international criminal law to address the culpability of superiors who fail to prevent or punish the commission of international crimes by their subordinates. The doctrine is remarkable in several respects. While criminal acts typically involve affirmative commission, superior responsibility criminalizes omissions. In addition, while most international norms and doctrines diffuse from practices in national jurisdictions, superior responsibility doctrine emerged in international cases and could be informative for national practices and legislation. Germany's Code of Crimes Against International Law adopted in 2002, for example, codified a version of superior responsibility for military and civilian superiors drawing from concepts such as effective command and control that have evolved in international criminal law.

Though the early landmark cases of contemporary superior responsibility doctrine were controversial, the doctrine of superior responsibility evolved rapidly and soon crystallized in the years after World War II into an international customary rule. This rule reflects the pragmatic import of the notion in a world scene where criminality often involves group or collective action that is at least condoned or tolerated by superiors. In contemporary international criminal law, superior responsibility doctrine includes liability for both military and civilian superiors. A superior can be held liable for international crimes by subordinates, even if subordinates are not direct perpetrators and are guilty under alternative bases such as, for example, aiding and abetting or joint criminal enterprise liability.

The following key elements must be met for superior responsibility to attach:

(a) *Subordination: Effective Command and Control.* The accused must be a superior with *effective command and control* over the subordinates about to commit, committing or who committed the crimes.

(b) *Mens rea.* The accused must know that subordinates have committed or are about to commit crimes or have information permitting him to so conclude – that is, have *knowledge or constructive knowledge.* As further discussed in section (C) below, the notion of constructive knowledge has been diluted by some lower and looser formulations and sometimes stretched to something more akin to recklessness or negligence.

(c) *Culpable omission (actus reus).* The accused failed to prevent or punish (or to request that the competent authorities to punish) the commission of crimes by the subordinates.

The sections below begin with the history of contemporary superior responsibility doctrine and then turn to cases elaborating on the key elements.

(B) A CONTROVERSIAL START

After World War I, efforts were made to sketch a notion of superior responsibility. The 1919 Treaty of Versailles contained a provision relating to the trial and punishment of the former German Kaiser Wilhelm II for not mitigating the barbarities of the war though he had the power to do so. Article 227(1) of the Treaty announced that '[t]he Allied and Associated Powers publicly arraign' the former Emperor 'for a supreme offence against international morality and the sanctity of treaties'. In fact, however, the Emperor escaped to the Netherlands, which refused to extradite him to the Allies. It was not until after World War II that the notion of superior responsibility evolved into a basis for the successful prosecution of superiors.

Early post-World War II precursors of the doctrine began by treating the failure of military commanders to prevent or punish crimes by subordinates as a form of complicity in the crime. French and Chinese war crimes legislation, for example, conceived of hierarchical superiors as accomplices to their subordinates perpetrating the crime. Soon, however, superior responsibility doctrine would shed its affiliation with a notion of complicity and begin to take its contemporary mode of articulation. In an early precursor, United States military commissions recognized superior responsibility for the 'omission of a superior officer to prevent war crimes when he knows of, or is on notice as to their commission or contemplated commission and is in a position to prevent them'.

The first judgment that began to flesh out the notion of a contemporary superior responsibility doctrine concerned General Tomoyuki Yamashita of the Japanese Army, tried by a United States Military Commission in Manila, the Philippines, the scene of widespread atrocities by Japanese troops. To understand the contours and contested questions of contemporary superior responsibility doctrine it is important to know this key formative moment and precursor, for 'in many ways, the evolution of command responsibility doctrine has consisted of reactions and counter-reactions to *Yamashita*'.[1]

Cases

US Military Commission in Manila, Trial of General Tomoyuki Yamashita, *Case No. 21, United States Military Commission, Manila, 8 October–7 December 1945*

Japanese forces occupying Manila, Batangas Province and the island of Luzon in the Philippines near the end of World War II tortured and brutally slaughtered thousands of civilians, including women and children, and engaged in mass rapes. At the time of the worst of the slaughter, shortly before the Japanese surrender, General Tomoyuki Yamashita was commanding general of the Japanese Army in the Philippines.

General Yamashita surrendered to the United States in September 1945 and was originally set to be tried by the Military Tribunal for the Far East, scheduled to begin operations in 1946. General Douglas MacArthur opted, however, instead to try General Yamashita earlier by military commission on the charge that General Yamashita had,

---

[1] A. M. Danner and J. S. Martinez, 'Guilty Associations: Joint Criminal Enterprise, Command Responsibility, and the Development of International Criminal Law' (2005) 93 *Cal. L. Rev.* 75, 124.

between the time of his assumption of command of Japanese forces in the Philippines on 9 October 1944 and his eventual surrender in September 1945:

unlawfully disregarded and failed to discharge his duty as commander to control the operations of the members of his command, permitting them to commit brutal atrocities and other high crimes against people of the United States and of its allies and dependencies, particularly in the Philippines; and he, General Tomoyuki Yamashita, thereby violated the laws of war.

The summary of proceedings excerpted below is by the United Nations War Crimes Commission, which, in its reporting capacity, summarized the parties' positions and evidence to derive the basis of the judgment of military commissions, which often did not issue written judgments.

[T]he President of the Commission in delivering judgment [...] pointed out that: "The crimes alleged to have been permitted by the accused in violation of the laws of war may be grouped into three categories:

(1) Starvation, execution or massacre without trial and maladministration generally of civilian internees and prisoners of war;

(2) Torture, rape, murder and mass execution of very large numbers of residents of the Philippines, including women and children and members of religious orders, by starvation, beheading, bayoneting, clubbing, hanging, burning alive, and destruction by explosives;

(3) Burning and demolition without adequate military necessity of large numbers of homes, places of business, places of religious worship, hospitals, public buildings, and educational institutions. In point of time, the offences extended throughout the period the accused was in command of Japanese troops in the Philippines. In point of area, the crimes extended throughout the Philippine Archipelago, although by far the most of the incredible acts occurred on Luzon." [...]

Those stated to have been the victims of these atrocities were unarmed non-combatant civilians, civilian internees and prisoners of war; and unspecified hospital patients. The civilians included Austrian, French, Russian, Chinese and German nationals as well as United States citizens. [...]

The Charge alleged that the accused failed in his duty to control his troops, permitting them to commit certain alleged crimes. The Bill of Particulars, however, set forth no instance of neglect of duty by the accused. Nor did it set forth any acts of commission or omission by the accused as amounting to a "permitting" of the crimes in question. What then was the substance of the Charge against the accused? It was submitted by the Defence that, on the three documents now before the Commission, the Charge and the two Bills of Particulars, the accused was not accused of having done something or having failed to do something, but solely of having been something, namely commander of the Japanese forces. It was being claimed that, by virtue of that fact alone, he was guilty of every crime committed by every soldier assigned to his command.

American jurisprudence recognised no such principle so far as its own military personnel was concerned. The Articles of War denounced and punished improper conduct by military personnel, but they did not hold a commanding officer responsible for the crimes committed by his subordinates. No one would even suggest that the Commanding General of an American occupation force became a criminal every time an American soldier violated the law. It was submitted that neither the Laws of War nor the conscience of the world upon which they were founded would countenance any such charge. It was the basic premise of all civilised criminal justice that it punished not according to status but according to fault, and that one man was not held to answer for the crime of another. [...]

The Defence maintained that the Manila atrocities were committed by the naval troops, and that these troops were not under General Yamashita's command. How, it was asked, could he be held accountable for the actions of troops which had passed into his command only one month before, at a time when he was 150 miles away – troops whom he had never seen, trained or inspected, whose commanding officers he could not change or designate, and over whose actions he had only the most nominal control?

It was pointed out that General Yamashita arrived in Manila on 9th October and left on 26th December. Until 17th November, General Yamashita was not even the highest commander in the City of Manila since his immediate superior, Count Terauchi, was there and in charge. It was Count Terauchi and not General Yamashita who was handling affairs concerning the civilian population, relations with the civil government and the discouragement and suppression of anti-Japanese activities. The crucial period, therefore, was from 17th November to 26th December, a matter of a mere five weeks, during which General Yamashita was in Manila and in charge of civilian affairs. Could it be seriously contended that a commander who was beset and harassed by the enemy and was staggering under a successful enemy invasion to the south and expecting at any moment another invasion in the north could in such a short period gather in all the strings of administration? Even so, the accused took some steps in an attempt to curb the activities of the Japanese military police who were terrorising the civilian population. [...]

The Defence anticipated that the Prosecution would claim that there were so many of these atrocities, that they covered so large a territory, that General Yamashita must have known about them. The reply of the Defence was that, in the first place, a man was not convicted on the basis of what someone thought he must have known but on what he has been proved beyond reasonable doubt to have known; and in the second place, General Yamashita did not know and could not have known about any of these atrocities.

Practically all of the atrocities took place at times when and in areas where the communication of news of such matters was practically impossible. Further, the accused's orders were clear: to attack armed guerrillas and to befriend and win the co-operation of other civilians. When atrocities occurred, they were committed in violation of General Yamashita's orders, and it was quite natural that those who violated these orders would not inform him of their acts. [...]

The Judgment of the Commission was delivered by the President in the following words:

"[...] Clearly, assignment to command military troops is accompanied by broad authority and heavy responsibility. This has been true in all armies throughout recorded history. It is absurd, however, to consider a commander a murderer or rapist because one of his soldiers commits a murder or a rape. Nevertheless, where murder and rape and vicious, revengeful actions are widespread offences, and there is no effective attempt by a commander to discover and control the criminal acts, such a commander may be held responsible, even criminally liable, for the lawless acts of his troops, depending upon their nature and the circumstances surrounding them. Should a commander issue orders which lead directly to lawless acts, the criminal responsibility is definite and has always been so understood. The *Rules of Land Warfare*, Field Manual 27–10, United States Army, are clear on these points. It is for the purpose of maintaining discipline and control, among other reasons, that military commanders are given broad powers of administering military justice. The tactical situation, the character, training and capacity of staff officers and subordinate commanders as well as the traits of character, and training of his troops are other important factors in such cases. These matters have been the principal considerations of the Commission during its deliberations.

"General Yamashita: The Commission concludes: (1) That a series of atrocities and other high crimes have been committed by members of the Japanese armed forces under your command against people of the United States, their allies and dependencies throughout the Philippine Islands; that they were not sporadic in nature but in many cases were methodically supervised by Japanese officers and non-commissioned officers; (2) That during the period in question you failed to provide effective control of your troops as was required by the circumstances.

"Accordingly upon secret written ballot, two-thirds or more of the members concurring, the Commission finds you guilty as charged and sentences you to death by hanging." [...]

USA, In re Application of Yamashita, Supreme Court, Judgment of 4 February 1946

During the Military Commission adjudication, Yamashita's defence counsel filed a petition for writ of habeas corpus and writ of prohibition in the Supreme Court for the Philippines. Defence counsel argued that the US Military Commission was improperly constituted and lacked jurisdiction, the proceedings violated due process of law and the charge against General Yamashita did not constitute a violation of the laws of war. On 4 December 1945, the Philippine Supreme Court denied the petitions for writ of habeas corpus and writ of prohibition.

Three days later came the Military Commission's judgment and sentence on the fourth anniversary of the Japanese attack on Pearl Harbor, 7 December 1945. That same day, General Yamashita's defence counsel appealed from the denial of the petition for writ of habeas corpus and writ of prohibition to the US Supreme Court, and petitioned for writ of certiorari. In the opinion excerpted below, the Supreme Court denied the petitions for writ of habeas corpus and prohibition, emphasizing that its task was not to review the guilt or innocence of the defendant but rather only to determine the lawful power of the commission to try an enemy belligerent on the charge alleged.

Mr. Chief Justice STONE delivered the opinion of the Court.

[...] The extent to which the power to prosecute violations of the law of war shall be exercised before peace is declared rests, not with the courts, but with the political branch of the Government, and may itself be governed by the terms of an armistice or the treaty of peace. [...] The conduct of the trial by the military commission has been authorized by the political branch of the Government, by military command, by international law and usage, and by the terms of the surrender of the Japanese government.

The Charge. Neither Congressional action nor the military orders constituting the commission authorized it to place [the] petitioner on trial unless the charge preferred against him is of a violation of the law of war. The charge, so far as now relevant, is that [the] petitioner, between October 9, 1944 and September 2, 1945, in the Philippine Islands, 'while commander of armed forces of Japan at war with the United States of America and its allies, unlawfully disregarded and failed to discharge his duty as commander to control the operations of the members of his command, permitting them to commit brutal atrocities and other high crimes against people of the United States and of its allies and dependencies, particularly the Philippines; and he [...] thereby violated the laws of war.' [...]

It is not denied that such acts directed against the civilian population of an occupied country and against prisoners of war are recognized in international law as violations of the law of war. Articles 4, 28, 46, and 47, Annex to Fourth Hague Convention, 1907, 36 Stat. 2277, 2296, 2303, 2306, 2307. But it is urged that the charge does not allege that [the] petitioner has either committed or directed the commission of such acts, and consequently that no violation is charged as against him. But this overlooks the fact that the gist of the charge is an unlawful breach of duty by [the] petitioner as an army commander to control the operations of the members of his command by 'permitting them to commit' the extensive and widespread atrocities specified. The question then is whether the law of war imposes on an army commander a duty to take such appropriate measures as are within his power to control the troops under his command for the prevention of the specified acts which are violations of the law of war and which are likely to attend the occupation of hostile territory by an uncontrolled soldiery, and whether he may be charged with personal responsibility for his failure to take such measures when violations result. [...]

It is evident that the conduct of military operations by troops whose excesses are unrestrained by the orders or efforts of their commander would almost certainly result in violations which it is the purpose of the law of war to prevent. Its purpose to protect civilian populations and prisoners of war from brutality would largely be defeated if the commander of an invading army could with impunity neglect to take reasonable measures for their protection. Hence the law of war presupposes that its violation is to be avoided through the control of the operations of war by commanders who are to some extent responsible for their subordinates.

This is recognized by the Annex to [the] Fourth Hague Convention of 1907, respecting the laws and customs of war on land. Article I lays down as a condition which an armed force must fulfill in order to be accorded the rights of lawful belligerents, that it must be 'commanded by a person responsible for his subordinates.' 36 Stat. 2295. Similarly Article 19 of the Tenth Hague Convention, relating to bombardment by naval vessels, provides that commanders in chief of the belligerent vessels 'must see that the above Articles are properly carried out.' 36 Stat. 2389. And Article 26 of the Geneva Red Cross Convention of 1929, 47 Stat. 2074, 2092, for the amelioration of the condition of the wounded and sick in armies in the field, makes it 'the duty of the commanders-in-chief of the belligerent armies to provide for the details of execution of the foregoing articles (of the convention), as well as for unforeseen cases.' And, finally, Article 43 of the Annex of the Fourth Hague Convention, 36 Stat. 2306, requires that the commander of a force occupying enemy territory, as was [the] petitioner, 'shall take all the measures in his power to restore, and ensure, as far as possible, public order and safety, while respecting, unless absolutely prevented, the laws in force in the country.'

These provisions plainly imposed on [the] petitioner, who at the time specified was military governor of the Philippines, as well as commander of the Japanese forces, an affirmative duty to take such measures as were within his power and appropriate in the circumstances to protect prisoners of war and the civilian population. This duty of a commanding officer has heretofore been recognized, and its breach penalized by our own military tribunals.[2] A like principle has been applied so as to impose liability on the United States in international arbitrations. Case of Jenaud, 3 Moore, International Arbitrations, 3000; Case of 'The Zafiro,' 5 Hackworth, Digest of International Law, 707.

We do not make the laws of war but we respect them so far as they do not conflict with the commands of Congress or the Constitution. There is no contention that the present charge, thus read, is without the support of evidence, or that the commission held [the] petitioner responsible for failing to take measures which were beyond his control or inappropriate for a commanding officer to take in the circumstances. We do not here appraise the evidence on which [the] petitioner was convicted. We do not consider what measures, if any, [the] petitioner took to prevent the commission, by the troops under his command, of the plain violations of the law of war detailed in the bill of particulars, or whether such measures as he may

---

[2] [3] Failure of an officer to take measures to prevent murder of an inhabitant of an occupied country committed in his presence. Gen.Orders No. 221, Hq.Div. of the Philippines, August 17, 1901. And in Gen.Orders No. 264, Hq.Div. of the Philippines, September 9, 1901, it was held that an officer could not be found guilty for failure to prevent a murder unless it appeared that the accused had 'the power to prevent' it.

have taken were appropriate and sufficient to discharge the duty imposed upon him. These are questions within the peculiar competence of the military officers composing the commission and were for it to decide. See Smith v. Whitney, 116 U.S. 167, 178, 6 S.Ct. 570, 576, 29 L.Ed. 601. It is plain that the charge on which [the] petitioner was tried charged him with a breach of his duty to control the operations of the members of his command, by permitting them to commit the specified atrocities. This was enough to require the commission to hear evidence tending to establish the culpable failure of [the] petitioner to perform the duty imposed on him by the law of war and to pass upon its sufficiency to establish guilt. [. . .]

Mr. Justice MURPHY, dissenting.

The failure of the military commission to obey the dictates of the due process requirements of the Fifth Amendment is apparent in this case. The petitioner was the commander of an army totally destroyed by the superior power of this nation. While under heavy and destructive attack by our forces, his troops committed many brutal atrocities and other high crimes. [. . .]

A military commission was appointed to try the petitioner for an alleged war crime. The trial was ordered to be held in territory over which the United States has complete sovereignty. No military necessity or other emergency demanded the suspension of the safeguards of due process. Yet [the] petitioner was rushed to trial under an improper charge, given insufficient time to prepare an adequate defense, deprived of the benefits of some of the most elementary rules of evidence and summarily sentenced to be hanged. In all this needless and unseemly haste there was no serious attempt to charge or to prove that he committed a recognized violation of the laws of war. He was not charged with personally participating in the acts of atrocity or with ordering or condoning their commission. Not even knowledge of these crimes was attributed to him. It was simply alleged that he unlawfully disregarded and failed to discharge his duty as commander to control the operations of the members of his command, permitting them to commit the acts of atrocity. The recorded annals of warfare and the established principles of international law afford not the slightest precedent for such a charge. [. . .]

In my opinion, such a procedure is unworthy of the traditions of our people or of the immense sacrifices that they have made to advance the common ideals of mankind. The high feelings of the moment doubtless will be satisfied. But in the sober afterglow will come the realization of the boundless and dangerous implications of the procedure sanctioned today. No one in a position of command in an army, from sergeant to general, can escape those future [consequences.] Indeed, the fate of some future President of the United States and his chiefs of staff and military advisers may well have been sealed by this decision. But even more significant will be the hatred and ill-will growing out of the application of this unprecedented procedure. That has been the inevitable effect of every method of punishment disregarding the element of personal culpability. The effect in this instance, unfortunately, will be magnified infinitely for here we are dealing with the rights of man on an international level. [. . .]

[. . .] I find it impossible to agree that the charge against the petitioner stated a recognized violation of the laws of war. [. . .]

[. . .] Nowhere was it alleged that the petitioner personally committed any of the atrocities, or that he ordered their commission, or that he had any knowledge of the commission thereof by members of his command.

The findings of the military commission bear out this absence of any direct personal charge against the petitioner. The commission merely found that atrocities and other high crimes 'have been committed by members of the Japanese armed forces under your command. . . that they were not sporadic in nature but in many cases were methodically supervised by Japanese officers and noncommissioned officers. . . that during the period in question you failed to provide effective control of your troops as was required by the circumstances.'

In other words, read against the background of military events in the Philippines subsequent to October 9, 1944, these charges amount to this: 'We, the victorious American forces, have done everything possible to destroy and disorganize your lines of communication, your effective control of your personnel, your ability to wage war. In those respects we have succeeded. We have defeated and crushed your forces. And now we charge and condemn you for having been inefficient in maintaining control of your troops during the period when we were so effectively besieging and eliminating your forces and blocking your ability to maintain effective control. Many terrible atrocities were committed by your disorganized troops. Because these atrocities were so widespread we will not bother to charge or prove that you committed, ordered or condoned any of them. We will assume that they must have resulted from your inefficiency and negligence as a commander. In short, we charge you with the crime of inefficiency in controlling your troops. We will judge the discharge of your duties by the disorganization which we ourselves created in large part. Our standards of judgment are whatever we wish to make them.'

Nothing in all history or in international law, at least as far as I am aware, justifies such a charge against a fallen commander of a defeated force. To use the very inefficiency and disorganization created by the victorious forces as the primary basis for condemning officers of the defeated armies bears no resemblance to justice or to military reality.

International law makes no attempt to define the duties of a commander of an army under constant and overwhelming assault; nor does it impose liability under such circumstances for failure to meet the ordinary responsibilities of command. The omission is understandable. Duties, as well as ability to control troops, vary according to the nature and intensity of the particular battle. To find an unlawful deviation from duty under battle conditions requires difficult and speculative calculations. Such calculations become highly untrustworthy when they are made by the victor in relation to the actions of a vanquished commander. Objective and realistic norms of conduct are then extremely unlikely to be used in forming a judgment as to deviations from duty. The probability that vengeance will form the major part of the victor's judgment is an unfortunate but inescapable fact. So great is that probability that international law refuses to recognize such a judgment as a basis for a war crime, however fair the judgment may be in a particular instance. [...]

The Court's reliance upon vague and indefinite references in certain of the Hague Conventions and the Geneva Red Cross Convention is misplaced. Thus the statement in Article 1 of the Annex to Hague Convention No. IV of October 18, 1907, 36 Stat. 2277, 2295, to the effect that the laws, rights and duties of war apply to military and volunteer corps only if they are 'commanded by a person responsible for his subordinates,' has no bearing upon the problem in this case. Even if it has, the clause 'responsible for his subordinates' fails to state to whom the responsibility is owed or to indicate the type of responsibility contemplated. The phrase has received differing interpretations by authorities on international law. In Oppenheim, International Law (6th ed., rev. by Lauterpacht, 1940, vol. 2, p. 204, fn. 3) it is stated that 'The meaning of the word "responsible" ... is not clear. It probably means "responsible to some higher authority," whether the person is appointed from above or elected from below;....' Another authority has stated that the word 'responsible' in this particular context means 'presumably to a higher authority,' or 'possibly it merely means one who controls his subordinates and who therefore can be called to account for their acts.' Wheaton, International Law (14th ed., by Keith, 1944, p. 172, fn. 30). Still another authority, Westlake, International Law (1907, Part II, p. 61), states that 'probably the responsibility intended is nothing more than a capacity of exercising effective control.' Finally, Edwards and Oppenheim, Land Warfare (1912, p. 19, par. 22) state that it is enough 'if the commander of the corps is regularly or temporarily commissioned as an officer or is a person of position and authority.' It seems apparent beyond dispute that the word 'responsible' was not used in this particular Hague Convention to hold the commander of a defeated army to any high standard of efficiency when he is under destructive attack; nor was it used to impute to him any criminal responsibility for war crimes committed by troops under his command under such circumstances.

The provisions of the other conventions referred to by the Court are on their face equally devoid of relevance or significance to the situation here in issue. Neither Article 19 of Hague Convention No. X, 36 Stat. 2371, 2389, nor Article 26 of the Geneva Red Cross Convention of 1929, 47 Stat. 2074, 2092, refers to circumstances where the troops of a commander commit atrocities while under heavily adverse battle conditions. Reference is also made to the requirement of Article 43 of the Annex to Hague Convention No. IV, 36 Stat. 2295, 2306, that the commander of a force occupying enemy territory 'shall take all the measures in his power to restore, and ensure, as far as possible, public order and safety, while respecting, unless absolutely prevented, the laws in force in the country.' But the petitioner was more than a commander of a force occupying enemy territory. He was the leader of an army under constant and devastating attacks by a superior re-invading force. This provision is silent as to the responsibilities of a commander under such conditions as that.

Even the laws of war heretofore recognized by this nation fail to impute responsibility to a fallen commander for excesses committed by his disorganized troops while under attack. Paragraph 347 of the War Department publication, Basic Field Manual, Rules of Land Warfare, FM 27–10 (1940), states the principal offenses under the laws of war recognized by the United States. This includes all of the atrocities which the Japanese troops were alleged to have committed in this instance. Originally this paragraph concluded with the statement that 'The commanders ordering the commission of such acts, or under whose authority they are committed by their troops, may be punished by the belligerent into whose hands they may fall.' The meaning of the phrase 'under whose authority they are committed' was not clear. On November 15, 1944, however, this sentence was deleted and a new paragraph was added relating to the personal liability of those who violate the laws of war. Change 1, FM 27–10. The new paragraph 345.1 states that 'Individuals and organizations who violate the accepted laws and customs of war may be punished therefor. However, the fact that the acts complained of were done pursuant to order of a superior or government sanction may be taken into consideration in determining culpability, either by way of defense or in mitigation of punishment. The person giving such orders may also be punished.' From this the conclusion seems inescapable that the United States recognizes individual criminal responsibility for violations of the laws of war only as to those who commit the offenses or who order or direct their commission. Such was not the allegation here. Cf. Article 67 of the Articles of War, 10 U.S.C. s 1539, 10 U.S.C.A. s 1539.

There are numerous instances, especially with reference to the Philippine Insurrection in 1900 and 1901, where commanding officers were found to have violated the laws of war by specifically ordering members of their command to commit atrocities and other war crimes. [. . .] And in other cases officers have been held liable where they knew that a crime was to be committed, had the power to prevent it and failed to exercise that power. Pedro Abad Santos, G.O. 130, June 19, 1901, Hq. Div. Phil. Cf. Pedro A. Cruz, G.O. 264, Sept. 9, 1901, Hq. Div. Phil. In no recorded instance, however, has the mere inability to control troops under fire or attack by superior forces been made the basis of a charge of violating the laws of war.

The Government claims that the principle that commanders in the field are bound to control their troops has been applied so as to impose liability on the United States in international arbitrations. Case of Jeannaud, 1880, 3 Moore, International Arbitrations (1898) 3000; Case of The Zafiro, 1910, 5 Hackworth, Digest of International Law (1943) 707. The difference between arbitrating property rights and charging an individual with a crime against the laws of war is too obvious to require elaboration. But even more significant is the fact that even these arbitration cases fail to establish any principle of liability where troops are under constant assault and demoralizing influences by attacking forces. [. . .] No one denies that inaction or negligence may give rise to liability, civil or criminal. But it is quite another thing to say that the inability to control troops under highly competitive and disastrous battle conditions renders one guilty of a war crime in the absence of personal culpability. Had there been some element of knowledge or direct connection with the atrocities the problem would be entirely different. Moreover, it must be remembered that we are not dealing here with an ordinary tort or criminal action; precedents in those fields are of little if any value. Rather we are concerned with a proceeding involving an international crime, the treatment of which may have untold effects upon the future peace of the world. [. . .]

The only conclusion I can draw is that the charge made against the petitioner is clearly without precedent in international law or in the annals of recorded military history. This is not to say that enemy commanders may escape punishment for clear and unlawful failures to prevent atrocities. But that punishment should be based upon charges fairly drawn in light of established rules of international law and recognized concepts of justice.

But the charge in this case, as previously noted, was speedily drawn and filed but three weeks after the petitioner surrendered. The trial proceeded with great dispatch without allowing the defense time to prepare an adequate case. [The] [p]etitioner's rights under the due process clause of the Fifth Amendment were grossly and openly violated without any justification. All of this was done without any thorough investigation and prosecution of those immediately responsible for the atrocities, out of which might have come some proof or indication of personal culpability on [the] petitioner's part. Instead the loose charge was made that great numbers of atrocities had been committed and that [the] petitioner was the commanding officer; hence he must have been guilty of disregard of duty. Under that charge the commission was free to establish whatever standard of duty on [the] petitioner's part that it desired. By this flexible method a victorious nation may convict and execute any or all leaders of a vanquished foe, depending upon the prevailing degree of vengeance and the absence of any objective judicial review. [. . .]

Mr. Justice RUTLEDGE, dissenting.

[. . .] This trial is unprecedented in our history. Never before have we tried and convicted an enemy general for action taken during hostilities or otherwise in the course of military operations or duty. Much less have we condemned one for failing to take action. The novelty is not lessened by the trial's having taken place after hostilities ended and the enemy, including the accused, had surrendered. Moreover, so far as the time permitted for our consideration has given opportunity, I have not been able to find precedent for the proceeding in the system of any nation founded in the basic principles of our constitutional democracy, in the laws of war or in other internationally binding authority or usage.

The novelty is legal as well as historical. We are on strange ground. Precedent is not all-controlling in law. There must be room for growth, since every precedent has an origin. But it is the essence of our tradition for judges, when they stand at the end of the marked way, to go forward with caution keeping sight, so far as they are able, upon the great landmarks left behind and the direction they point ahead. If, as may be hoped, we are now to enter upon a new era of law in the world, it becomes more important than ever before for the nations creating that system to observe their greatest traditions of administering justice, including this one, both in their own judging and in their new creation. The proceedings in this case veer so far from some of our time-tested road signs that I cannot take the large strides validating them would demand. [. . .]

It is not in our tradition for anyone to be charged with crime which is defined after his conduct, alleged to be criminal, has taken place; or in language not sufficient to inform him of the nature of the offense or to enable him to make defense. Mass guilt we do not impute to individuals, perhaps in any case but certainly in none where the person is not charged or shown actively to have participated in or knowingly to have failed in taking action to prevent the wrongs done by others, having both the duty and the power to do so. [. . .]

COMMENTARY

To criminalize an omission, there must first be a duty to act. In *Yamashita*, US prosecutors and the US Supreme Court inferred the duty to prevent and punish international crimes by subordinates – and criminal consequences for failing in these duties – from a collage of scattered provisions of international humanitarian law that were not directly on point and heightened duties placed on those standing in responsible relation to dangerous instrumentalities. *Yamashita* is both a landmark in the evolution of superior responsibility doctrine and a murk posing more questions than answers.

As the dissents of Justices Murphy and Rutledge capture, the case illustrates the pitfalls of the notion of superior responsibility, if not constrained by clear standards of law. When liability is based on omissions rather than affirmative misconduct, the *mens rea* standard becomes all the more important to ensure personal culpability. Yet the *mens rea* standard in *Yamashita* was unclear. The facts of *Yamashita* – involving a besieged commander with disobedient troops in disarray and communications cut off – were not ideal for the imposition of superior responsibility. Was General Yamashita found guilty on the basis of strict liability because of his official position, as Justice Murphy suggested in dissent? Or was culpability founded on mere negligence? Alternatively, the Military Commission's judgment might be construed as treating General Yamashita's approach of operating in a seeming 'vacuum, almost in another world' from what was being done by his troops, as a form of deliberate ignorance treated constructively as knowledge.

One of the main critiques of *Yamashita* was that it was a case in want of a legal standard and that Yamashita was in essence held liable paradoxically because of a *lack* of effective command and control. From a utilitarian perspective, we may well wish to penalize the failure of commanders having effective command and control to prevent and punish crimes because we want to give them incentive to act to mitigate harm. This utilitarian goal weakens when it comes to those who lack such ability to prevent crimes because of a confluence of circumstances beyond the superior's control. From the vantage of moral desert, moreover, while we may fault those with the power to act and mitigate harm and fail to do so, how can we blame an officer for not doing something he lacked the ability to do? Certainly, many Japanese were guilty for the terrible atrocities. *Yamashita* illustrates, however, a recurring danger in the application of superior responsibility doctrine: in the wake of horrific acts, an official easily on hand becomes an emblem for blame in lieu of doing the difficult job of assessing through the fog of war who or what is actually most culpable.[3]

(C) CRYSTALLIZATION AND CODIFICATION

Despite its controversial debut, superior responsibility doctrine began its progress towards its contemporary form. Superior responsibility was applied to civilian as well as military commanders. In *United States* v. *Friedrich Flick et al.*, and the *Röchling* case, for example, Nazi industrialists were convicted on the basis of superior responsibility for enslavement and other war crimes and crimes against humanity. The International Military Tribunal for the Far East (IMTFE), colloquially dubbed the Tokyo Tribunal, convicted such civilian

---

[3] Perversities of justice can ensue. For example, while General Yamashita was executed as the figurehead in the immediate aftermath of war, the infamous Lieutenant-Colonel Masanobu Tsuji, responsible for brutalizing and killing prisoners of war during the Bataan death march, and massacring civilians in occupied territories in Asia, enjoyed impunity and a subsequent political career in Japan after the first flush of desire for accountability subsided.

superiors and senior Cabinet members as Foreign Ministers Koki Hirota and Mamoru Shigemitsu and Prime Minister Hideki Tojo.

An eminent member of the Tokyo Tribunal, Judge Bernard Victor Aloysius Röling of the Netherlands, wrote separately in dissent regarding the conviction of Cabinet members for failing to prevent the abuse of prisoners of war and civilian internees. Judge Röling's dissent is important because it began to articulate some of the minimum prerequisites to ensure that superior responsibility for omissions is tied to culpability:

The problem which has to be faced here is the question whether there are some persons responsible for the fact that they did not prevent the commission of crimes. This responsibility for "omission" is a very restricted one, in domestic law recognized only in special cases where the legal duty was clearly indicated. This duty to act varies in different countries with the degree of liberal individualism. The modern trend in most countries is to emphasize the duty of the individual towards his fellow citizens or the community. However, there does not appear to be a similar trend in international law. The American Rules of Land Warfare until 1944 carried this provision: "The commanders ordering the commission of such acts, or under whose authority they are committed by their troops, may be punished by the belligerent into whose hands they may fall." (Art. 347, last sentence.) The meaning of the words, "under whose authority they were committed," was not considered sufficiently clear. Therefore, this phrase was deleted in 1944, and replaced by ['The persons giving such orders may also be punished']. This new provision could indicate a reluctance to accept responsibility for "omission". [...]

[...] The "Commission on the Responsibility of the Authors of War and On Enforcement of Penalties" suggested as one of the groups to be dealt with by the proposed High Tribunal: "All authorities, civil or military, belonging to enemy countries, however high their position may have been, without distinction of rank, including the heads of states who ordered, or, with knowledge thereof and with power to intervene, abstained from preventing or taking measures to prevent, putting an end to, or repressing, violations of the laws or customs of war." As explained in the Report, and especially in the Memorandum of Reservations of the American delegates Lansing and Scott, these two restrictions of the responsibility, knowledge and power to intervene, were inserted at the suggestion of the American members. In the Memorandum of Reservations, Lansing and Scott further deal with the criminal liability for crimes committed by others, stating: "To establish responsibility in such cases it is elementary that the individual[ ] sought to be punished should have knowledge of the commission of the acts of a criminal nature and that he should have possessed the power as well as the authority to prevent, to put an end to, or repress them. Neither knowledge of commission nor ability to prevent is alone sufficient. The duty or obligation to act is essential." [...] This third element, the duty or obligation to act is apparently related with the authority to prevent violations of the laws of war. [...]

The three elements seem to be essential in relation to liability for "omissions", viz., knowledge, power, and duty. These elements, however, are correlated in that the duty may imply the duty to know. Ignorance is no excuse in case the person in charge could and should have known. On the other hand, "power" means power in relation with legal duty. The three elements combined may lead to criminal responsibility. To hold an official criminally responsible for certain acts which he himself did not order or permit, it will be necessary that the following conditions are fulfilled:

1. That he knew, or should have known of the acts.

Not only the knowledge, but also the lack of knowledge resulting from criminal negligence matters. If his function, and the duties involved[,] place upon the official concerned the obligation to know what is happening, lack of knowledge – if he could have known provided only he was normally alert – cannot be claimed in defense.

2. That he had the power to prevent the acts.

It is a generally recognized fact that in every war – war crimes are committed by soldiers of every army. No government or commander will be able to prevent all war crimes. There is criminal responsibility only where all possible steps to prevent war crimes have not been taken. But since it is a matter of common knowledge that war crimes are likely to be omitted, the authority vested in an official position should be exercised with due regard to this possibility.

3. That he had the duty to prevent these acts.

One could argue that this duty exists, as soon as knowledge and power are apparent. International law may develop to this point. At this moment, however, one has to look for the specific obligation, placed on government officials or military commanders, which makes them criminally responsible for "omissions." The scope of this responsibility is extensive. The majority judgment may be generally referred to with regard to the extension of its implications. It must be stated, however. That it seems that the judgment goes too far where it assumes the responsibility of every member of the government for the atrocities committed in the field or against POW or civilian internees. [...]

In every government a division of labor is established, and where, as in Japan, special departments of the government were charged with a special task, e.g., the War and Navy Ministries with the care for POW and civilian internees in occupied territory, the Home Ministry with the care for civilian internees in Japan proper, the Ministry of Overseas Affairs with the care for civilian internees in Formosa, Korea and Saghalin – the responsibility for not preventing violations of the rules of war should be limited to these officials especially indicated in the pertinent domestic law.[4]

Judge Röling's separate opinion was an important precursor to contemporary superior responsibility doctrine because it articulated one of the most important safeguards to ensure culpability: culpable *mens rea*, the power to prevent crimes and the duty to act.

The *mens rea* standard for superior responsibility also began to be articulated in post-*Yamashita* decisions, with some decisions requiring a finding of knowledge of crimes committed by subordinates. A US Tribunal at Nuremberg in *Wilhelm von Leeb et al.* (the *High Command* case) held that 'the occupying commander must have knowledge' of offences by his troops and 'acquiesce or participate or criminally neglect to interfere in their commission'.

Some tribunals, however, stretched the notion of *constructive knowledge* – an approach that presumes knowledge as a matter of law because of factors like ample notice or information or wilful blindness to sufficiently alarming information – into a lower standard more akin to recklessness or negligence. The Tokyo Tribunal in *Araki and others* ruled outright that superiors could be liable on the basis of 'negligence or supineness' where the superior 'knew or should have known' about the commission of crimes by subordinates but failed to take 'adequate steps' to prevent the crimes.

Despite some blurriness in the details of the doctrine, however, in just a few years after World War II there crystallized an international customary rule that superiors have the

---

[4] International Military Tribunal for the Far East, *Separate Opinion of Bernard Victor Aloysius Röling*, 12 November 1948, pp. 54–61 of the original pagination of the opinion.

duty, backed by criminal sanctions for omissions, to prevent and punish crimes by subordinates about which they knew, actually or constructively. The Geneva Conventions of 1949, however, did not codify the doctrine of superior responsibility because the Geneva Convention drafters assumed that domestic jurisdictions would apply their own approaches to liability.

Not until 1977 did Protocol I to the Geneva Conventions codify, at Articles 86 and 87, a version of the superior responsibility standard that emerged in the World War II-era cases. Article 86(2) of Additional Protocol I provides:

The fact that a breach of the Conventions or of this Protocol was committed by a subordinate does not absolve his superiors from penal or disciplinary responsibility, as the case may be, if they knew, or had information which should have enabled them to conclude in the circumstances at the time, that he was committing or was going to commit such a breach and if they did not take all feasible measures within their power to prevent or repress the breach.

Note that the provision applies to superiors generally, including a civilian superior. The provision eschews a 'should have known' standard, which was rejected by the drafters as too broad. The standard of 'knew, or had information which should have enabled them to conclude in the circumstances at the time' was a higher standard of actual or constructive knowledge based on information before the superior.

Additional Protocol I, Article 87 contains more specific duties for military commanders:

1. The High Contracting Parties and the Parties to the conflict shall require military commanders, with respect to members of the armed forces under their command and other persons under their control, to prevent and, where necessary, to suppress and to report to competent authorities breaches of the Conventions and of this Protocol.

2. In order to prevent and suppress breaches, High Contracting Parties and Parties to the conflict shall require that, commensurate with their level of responsibility, commanders ensure that members of the armed forces under their command are aware of their obligations under the Conventions and this Protocol.

3. The High Contracting Parties and Parties to the conflict shall require any commander who is aware that subordinates or other persons under his control are going to commit or have committed a breach of the Conventions or of this Protocol, to initiate such steps as are necessary to prevent such violations of the Conventions or this Protocol, and, where appropriate, to initiate disciplinary or penal action against violators thereof.

Note that the *mens rea* standard in Article 87(3) is specified as awareness – again eschewing the negligence standard that haunted *Yamashita*.

Superior responsibility is also set forth in the Statutes of the 'second-generation' international criminal tribunals responsible for some of the major doctrinal developments in international criminal law. The ICTYSt., in language similar to the ICTRSt., provides in Article 7(3):

The fact that any of the [criminal] acts [...] [within the Tribunal's jurisdiction] was committed by a subordinate does not relieve his superior of criminal responsibility if he knew or had reason to know that the subordinate was about to commit such acts or had done so and the superior failed to take the necessary and reasonable measures to prevent such acts or to punish the perpetrators thereof.

The ICTY and the ICTR do not distinguish between civilian and military superiors and have expanded the notion of superior responsibility by holding that it obtains in cases of *internal* as well as international armed conflicts.

Notably, the *mens rea* standard in the Statutes of the ad hoc tribunals contemplates liability based on actual knowledge and what the superior 'had reason to know'. This standard is similar to that proposed by the International Law Commission's 1996 Draft Code, which departed in form, at least, from the 'knew or had information enabling them to conclude' language in the Commission's 1991 Draft Code that was similar to Article 86(2) of Additional Protocol I. The International Law Commission explained that the 1996 change in language was not intended to constitute a substantive difference. Yet, as will be examined further below, there is a risk of a lower and looser notion of 'reason to know' that is more akin to negligence or recklessness than constructive knowledge.

The meaning of the term 'necessary and reasonable measures' was spelled out in the *Halilović* Appeal Judgment:

> The general duty of commanders to take the necessary and reasonable measures is well rooted in customary international law and stems from their position of authority. The Appeals Chamber stresses that "necessary" measures are the measures appropriate for the superior to discharge his obligation (showing that he genuinely tried to prevent or punish) and "reasonable" measures are those reasonably falling within the material powers of the superior.[5] What constitutes "necessary and reasonable" measures to fulfil a commander's duty is not a matter of substantive law but of evidence.

Against this backdrop of precedents, the ICCSt. took an approach that differentiates between military and non-military superiors. Article 28, on the responsibility of commanders and other superiors provides:

(a) A military commander or person effectively acting as a military commander shall be criminally responsible for crimes within the jurisdiction of the Court committed by forces under his or her effective command and control, or effective authority and control as the case may be, as a result of his or her failure to exercise control properly over such forces, where:

    (i) That military commander or person either knew or, owing to the circumstances at the time, should have known that the forces were committing or about to commit such crimes; and

    (ii) That military commander or person failed to take all necessary and reasonable measures within his or her power to prevent or repress their commission or to submit the matter to the competent authorities for investigation and prosecution.

---

[5] [167] Article 86 of Additional Protocol I provides that superiors are responsible if, *inter alia* "[t]hey did not take all feasible measures within their power to prevent or repress the breach"; in this respect, the ICRC Commentary explains that, for a superior to be found responsible, it must be demonstrated that the superior "did not take the *measures within his power* to prevent it" and elaborates that these measures must be " 'feasible' measures, since it is not always possible to prevent a breach or punish the perpetrators" (ICRC Commentary, paras 3543 and 3548, emphasis added); Article 87 adds the duty to "initiate such steps as are necessary to prevent such violations [...] and, where appropriate, to initiate disciplinary or penal action against violators thereof." *See* also the US Supreme Court's holding in *In re Yamashita*, 327 US 1 (1945), at 16 ("such measures [...] within his power and appropriate in the circumstances") and *US v. Karl Brandt et al.*, in TWC, Vol. II, p. 212 ("The law of war imposes on a military officer in a position of command an affirmative duty to take such steps as are within his power and appropriate to the circumstances to control those under his command...").

(b) With respect to superior and subordinate relationships not described in paragraph (a), a superior shall be criminally responsible for crimes within the jurisdiction of the Court committed by subordinates under his or her effective authority and control, as a result of his or her failure to exercise control properly over such subordinates, where:

(i) The superior either knew, or consciously disregarded information which clearly indicated, that the subordinates were committing or about to commit such crimes;

(ii) The crimes concerned activities that were within the effective responsibility and control of the superior; and

(iii) The superior failed to take all necessary and reasonable measures within his or her power to prevent or repress their commission or to submit the matter to the competent authorities for investigation and prosecution.

The distinction in treatment is pronounced at the level of *mens rea*. The ICCSt. is harder on military than non-military commanders, electing to employ a standard of 'should have known' that might be interpreted in a manner more akin to negligence or recklessness than constructive knowledge. For non-military superiors, however, liability is permitted only where the superior had knowledge or consciously disregarded information clearly indicating that subordinates were committing or about to commit crimes. The notion of conscious disregard is usually affiliated with the notion of willful blindness – akin to being an ostrich to information that would put the superior on notice – and properly treated as constructive knowledge.

Despite the variations in codified approaches and in the history of superior responsibility doctrine, its key elements can be discerned and have been fleshed out by contemporary jurisprudence. The next subsections and cases explain the key elements required for superior responsibility.

(D) ELEMENTS

SUBORDINATION: EFFECTIVE COMMAND AND CONTROL

A salutary progression from *Yamashita* in contemporary superior responsibility doctrine is the threshold requirement of subordination and effective command and control. Both the duty to act that gives rise to direct liability for the omission to act, and the indirect liability for crimes committed by others, flow from the fact of subordination. The notion of subordination in superior responsibility doctrine is a functional one that accounts more fully for on-the-ground realities. The hallmark is effective command and control rather than formal designations.

In the chaotic context in which international criminal crimes tend to arise, lines of subordination may not always be clear or formal. Subordination may be de facto rather than *de jure* – a matter of factual practice, rather than formal designation. Someone who is not formally designated a superior may nonetheless have effective command and control and be liable as a superior for purposes of superior responsibility. Conversely, someone who may be formally designated a superior may lack the effective command and control that is an aspect of subordination in the full functional sense required for liability. In the *Delalić* prison camp case – involving the first conviction based on superior responsibility before an international tribunal since the World War II-era cases – the ICTY Appeals Chamber addressed the responsibility of a civilian prison camp warden for abuses by guards against detainees and explained:

197. In determining questions of responsibility it is necessary to look to effective exercise of power or control and not to formal titles. [...] In general, the possession of *de jure* power in itself may not suffice for the finding of command responsibility if it does not manifest in effective control, although a court may presume that possession of such power *prima facie* results in effective control unless proof to the contrary is produced. [...] Although the degree of control wielded by a *de jure* or *de facto* superior may take different forms, a *de facto* superior must be found to wield substantially similar powers of control over subordinates to be held criminally responsible for their acts. The Appeals Chamber therefore agrees with the Trial Chamber's conclusion:

[...] *The doctrine of command responsibility is ultimately predicated upon the power of the superior to control the acts of his subordinates.* A duty is placed upon the superior to exercise this power so as to prevent and repress the crimes committed by his subordinates, and a failure to do so in a diligent manner is sanctioned [...]. While the Trial Chamber must at all times be alive to the realities of any given situation and be prepared to pierce such veils of formalism that may shield those individuals carrying the greatest responsibility for heinous acts, *great care must be taken lest an injustice be committed in holding individuals responsible for the acts of others in situations where the link of control is absent or too remote.*

Accordingly [...] in order for the principle of superior responsibility to be applicable, *it is necessary that the superior have effective control over the persons committing the underlying violations of international humanitarian law, in the sense of having the material ability to prevent and punish the commission of these offences.* [...]

266. The Appeals Chamber considers, therefore, that customary law has specified a standard of *effective* control, although it does not define precisely the means by which the control must be exercised. It is clear, however, that substantial influence as a means of control in any sense which falls short of the possession of effective control over subordinates, which requires the possession of material abilities to prevent subordinate offences or to punish subordinate offenders, lacks sufficient support in State practice and judicial decisions. [...][6]

The *Halilović* Appeals Chamber later elaborated on the concept of effective control:

[...] [T]he Appeals Chamber recalls that the necessity of proving that the perpetrator was the "subordinate" of the accused (against whom charges have been brought under Article 7(3) of the Statute) does not require direct or formal subordination. Rather, the accused has to be, by virtue of his position, senior in some sort of formal or informal hierarchy to the perpetrator. The ability to exercise effective control in the sense of a material power to prevent or punish, which the Appeals Chamber considers to be a minimum requirement for the recognition of a superior-subordinate relationship for the purpose of superior responsibility, will almost invariably not be satisfied unless such a relationship of subordination exists. The Appeals Chamber considers that a material ability to prevent and punish may also exist outside a superior-subordinate relationship relevant for Article 7(3) of the Statute. For example, a police officer may be able to "prevent and punish" crimes under his jurisdiction, but this would not as such make him a superior (in the sense of Article 7(3) of the Statute) vis-à-vis any perpetrator within that jurisdiction. [...]

The ICTR and ICTY have ruled that civilian superiors, like military commanders, may incur superior responsibility for acts by subordinates under their effective control so long as they exercise a degree of control similar to the degree of control exercised by military

---

[6] *Prosecutor* v. *Delalić*, Case No. IT-96-21-A, Appeals Chamber Judgment, 20 February 2001.

commanders.[7] The kind of control exercised by a civilian leader need not be of the same kind as that of a military commander – the operative requirement is that there is a similar *degree* of effective control.[8] In practice, however, because non-military structures such as political hierarchies involve different modes and methods of power, and lack the salient feature of a superior wielding power over a dangerous instrumentality of armed troops, courts may be more hesitant, whether rightly or wrongly, to impose superior responsibility.

Even in the military context, discerning lines of subordination and effective command and control can be difficult in the circumstances of modern warfare. Regular troops may ally with irregular forces. Lines of authority may crosscut. The cases below illustrate some of the problems that arise in assessing effective command and control.

ICTY, Prosecutor *v.* Hadžihasanović, *Appeals Chamber, Judgment of 22 April 2008*

Brigadier General Enver Hadžihasanović of the majority-Muslim Army of Bosnia and Herzegovina (ABiH) was convicted on the basis of superior responsibility for crimes committed by foreign Muslim (*Mujahedin*) combatants. This case was the first judgment of the ICTY to consider crimes by *Mujahedin* combatants fighting alongside Bosnian Muslim forces during the Bosnian conflict.

Hadžihasanović was sentenced to five years for, among other crimes, failing to take necessary and reasonable measures to prevent or punish crimes by *Mujahedin* who brutally beat and psychologically abused five civilians and murdered a Bosnian Serb hostage named Dragan Popović. Hadžihasanović appealed against, among other things, the finding that he had superior responsibility for crimes by *Mujahedin* fighters.

188. [...] Hadžihasanović argues that he could not incur responsibility for the murder of Dragan Popović and the cruel treatment of the civilians because there was no superior-subordinate relationship between the 3rd Corps and the members of the *El Mujahedin* detachment between 13 August and 1 November 1993, when he left his position as commander of the 3rd Corps. [...]

189. The ultimate question under this ground of appeal is whether Hadžihasanović exercised effective control over the *El Mujahedin* detachment. Since *de jure* authority is only one factor that helps to establish effective control, and because the present question is resolvable on the basis of effective control alone, the Appeals Chamber declines to address whether Hadžihasanović had *de jure* authority over the *El Mujahedin* detachment. [...]

190. The Appeals Chamber recalls that a showing of effective control is required in cases involving both *de jure* and *de facto* superiors and that the burden of proving beyond reasonable doubt that the accused had effective control over his subordinates ultimately rests with the Prosecution. [...]

197. The Trial Chamber found that Hadžihasanović exercised effective control over the *El Mujahedin* detachment on the basis that the evidence before it showed that three types of indicia of effective control were satisfied, namely: (i) the power to give orders to the *El Mujahedin* detachment and have them executed; (ii) the conduct of combat operations involving the *El Mujahedin* detachment; and (iii) the absence of any other authority over

---

[7] Ibid. at §197; *Prosecutor* v. *Bagilishema*, Case No. ICTR-95-1A-A, Appeals Chamber Judgment, 3 July 2002, at §52.

[8] *Bagilishema* Appeal Judgment, at §55.

the *El Mujahedin* detachment. The Trial Chamber also took into account the fact that criminal proceedings were initiated in autumn 1993 in a Travnik court against a member of the *El Mujahedin* detachment. The Appeals Chamber will examine each of these bases in turn to determine whether they support the Trial Chamber's conclusion that effective control existed.

(a) The power to give orders to the *El Mujahedin* detachment and have them executed

[. . .] 199. The Appeals Chamber recognises that the power to give orders and have them executed can serve as an indicium of effective control. The Trial Chamber took certain orders of re-subordination into account, though to varying degrees, as indicia of effective control. Specifically, the Trial Chamber indicated that three re-subordination orders were sent to the *El Muja*hedin detachment by the 3rd Corps: an order from Hadžihasanović, dated 28 August 1993, addressed to the OG *Bosanska Krajina*, the 306th Brigade and the *El Mujahedin* detachment, to "re-subordinate the detachment to the 306th Brigade in order to effectively coordinate combat operations" ("28 August Order"); an order from Džermal Merdan (3rd Corps Deputy Commander), on behalf of Hadžihasanović, dated 6 September 1993, addressed to the OG *Bosanska Krajina* and the *El Mujahedin* detachment, to re-subordinate this detachment to the OG *Bosanska Krajina* for forthcoming combat activities ("6 September Order"); and an order dated 4 December 1993, addressed by the then 3rd Corps Commander Mehmed Alagić to the OG *Bosanska Krajina* and the *El Mujahedin* detachment, to re-subordinate this detachment to the OG *Bosanska Krajina* ("4 December Order"). The Trial Chamber found that the 28 August Order was never carried out because the *El Mujahedin* detachment refused to obey it, and that the 4 December Order, though carried out, was issued a month after Hadžihasanović had left his position as 3rd Corps Commander. These orders are of limited value to the determination of Hadžihasanović's responsibility as a superior for crimes he failed to prevent in October 1993.

200. By issuing the 6 September Order, the 3rd Corps sought to re-subordinate the *El Mujahedin* detachment to the OG *Bosanska Krajina*. The Trial Chamber found that this order had been carried out and that the *El Mujahedin* detachment "took part in several combat operations along with other units in the [OG *Bosanska Krajina*]". In the Appeals Chamber's view, the 6 September Order alone is not sufficient for a showing that the relationship between the 3rd Corps and the *El Mujahedin* detachment was one of effective control rather than one of mere cooperation, as it was prior to 13 August 1993. The 6 September Order was an attempt on the part of the 3rd Corps to exercise control over the *El Mujahedin* detachment, not its realisation. Thus, none of the re-subordination orders, either individually or collectively, is sufficient to establish the existence of effective control. [. . .]

(b) The conduct of combat operations involving the *El Mujahedin* detachment

[. . .] 203. At the outset, the Appeals Chamber points out that, if taken literally, there is little basis in the jurisprudence of this International Tribunal for considering what the Trial Chamber termed as the "conduct of combat operations involving the forces in question" as an indicium of effective control. A reading of the relevant sections of the Trial Judgement suggests that what the Trial Chamber sought to demonstrate by defining this criterion was the degree of subordination of the *El Mujahedin* detachment to the OG *Bosanska Krajina* during combat operations. Accordingly, the Appeals Chamber will discuss the Trial Chamber's findings within this latter context.

204. The Trial Chamber found that, during the combat operations of September and October 1993, there were "no indications that the detachment fought outside the framework established by the [OG *Bosanska Krajina*] commanders" or "conduct[ed] independent operations on its own initiative". The Trial Chamber concluded that the *El Mujahedin* detachment fought

during this period "under the command of the OG *Bosanska Krajina*". This was based on a number of findings, the most significant of which are recalled below.

205. The Trial Chamber found that the *El Mujahedin* detachment took part in combat operations in the zone of responsibility of the OG *Bosanska Krajina* between 5 and 7 September 1993 and that, on 5 September 1993, the 306th Brigade led a coordinated attack with the 27th Brigade, the 325th Brigade and the *El Mujahedin* detachment. On 7 September 1993, when the 325th Brigade experienced difficulties in fighting in the Grbavica sector and sought the help of the *El Mujahedin* detachment to repel an HVO [Bosnian Croat Army] attack, the OG *Bosanska Krajina* responded favourably and organised the means to assist them, including the deployment of the *El Mujahedin* detachment to fight alongside the 325th Brigade.

206. Further, the Trial Chamber found that, around 18 September 1993, the *El Mujahedin* detachment also took part in combat operations in the Krušica sector, in the vicinity of Vareš. The Trial Chamber found that Mehmed Alagić "ordered the mujahedin to fight in the combat operations alongside the 17th Brigade". The Trial Chamber noted, however, that during these operations, "the ABiH sustained heavy losses because of the *mujahedin*'s combat methods". Witness Čuškić testified to the behaviour of the members of the *El Mujahedin* detachment during these operations as follows:

> [R]egardless of the plan of operation, the issued order, and everything else, because we had done our best to prepare it properly, during the operation itself, they acted independently, and this caused considerable losses in my own unit. That day, I think I had 78 wounded and 16 dead, which had never happened to me as a brigade commander up until then, nor after that.

207. On 9 October 1993, the commander of the OG *Zapad* sent a letter to Hadžihasanović. In this letter, the commander of the OG *Zapad* sought permission to use part of the *El Mujahedin* detachment in combat operations because the representatives of the detachment had informed him that "they were ready to take part in combat but that they believed this required an order from the 3rd Corps". The next day, Hadžihasanović seemingly denied that request. He replied that "the [*El Mujahedin*] detachment was still attached to OG *Bosanska Krajina* and engaged in combat operations in the Lašva valley". While the Trial Chamber did not indicate whether the detachment ultimately fought with the OG *Zapad*, it nevertheless took into account Hadžihasanović's reply to underscore that the *El Mujahedin* detachment did not believe it could conduct combat operations on its own initiative.

208. Lastly, the Trial Chamber found that the war diaries and the operational logbook of the OG *Bosanska Krajina* mentioned that the *El Mujahedin* detachment participated in combat operations with the 308th Brigade in the Novi Travnik – Gornji Vakuf region – on 24 October 1993. The result of the combat was 4 dead and 17 wounded for the 308th brigade and 3 dead and 8 wounded for the *El Mujahedin* detachment.

209. These findings confirm that the *El Mujahedin* detachment took part in several combat operations in September and October 1993 and that this occurred within the framework established by the OG *Bosanska Krajina* and the 3rd Corps. This, however, does not in itself necessarily provide sufficient support for the conclusion that Hadžihasanović had effective control over the *El Mujahedin* detachment in the sense of having the material ability to prevent or punish its members should they commit crimes. Further, several findings of the Trial Chamber demonstrate that the *El Mujahedin* detachment maintained on various issues a significant degree of independence from the units it fought alongside. This belies the Trial Chamber's conclusion that the *El Mujahedin* detachment was under the effective control of the 3rd Corps.

210. The Appeals Chamber notes that the *El Mujahedin* detachment took part in combat operations alongside 3rd Corps formations, including the OG *Bosanska Krajina*, as of the

second half of 1992. The Appeals Chamber stresses that, with respect to the period before 13 August 1993, the Trial Chamber found that the relationship between the *El Mujahedin* detachment and the 3rd Corps was one of cooperation, not effective control. [...]

211. In addition to these considerations, the Trial Chamber made several findings regarding the *El Mujahedin* detachment's combat conditions and methods. The Trial Chamber found, for example, that "the detachment members were anxious to maintain their independence and reserved the right to decide whether they would take part in combat operations". Members of the detachment "demanded special missions" and "groups of negotiators had to be used to determine if they would take part in combat". [...] In addition, the Trial Chamber noted that "[c]ontact and communication with its members were difficult", that "there was no information on the identity of the detachment members [or] other aspects of its operations", and that the *El Mujahedin* detachment "sometimes left the battlefield without submitting reports on the outcome of combat". The Appeals Chamber also notes that the *El Mujahedin* detachment was not stationed within the premises of the 3rd Corps or that of the OG *Bosanska Krajina*, but was stationed on its own in a separate camp. [...]

212. Finally, the independence of the *El Mujahedin* detachment in respect of the 3rd Corps is reflected by the detachment's abduction of civilians, a practice that was conducted in reckless disregard of the directives of the 3rd Corps, which sought to prevent and stop these abductions. As the Trial Chamber did not discuss these abductions in its section dedicated to effective control, the Appeals Chamber will first discuss the other considerations developed by the Trial Chamber with regard to whether Hadžihasanović had effective control. It will then discuss the significant relevance of that practice and the surrounding circumstances as an indicator of the independence of the *El Mujahedin* detachment in respect of the 3rd Corps.

213. In its concluding remarks on the issue of Hadžihasanović's effective control, the Trial Chamber stated the following:

> It must be noted, however, that this exceptional position was in fact accepted by the 3rd Corps, insofar as it did not in effect prevent the 3rd Corps and its units from using the detachment in combat and benefiting militarily from its existence. It should also be noted that nothing forced the 3rd Corps commanders to use the detachment in combat. In so doing, they accepted all the consequences of their decisions and inevitably assumed full responsibility for them.

The Appeals Chamber does not dispute that the 3rd Corps may have benefited from the *El Mujahedin* detachment, and that a circumstance of this kind may entail some form of responsibility, if the particulars of such responsibility are adequately pleaded in an Indictment. The Appeals Chamber nevertheless questions the relevance of that consideration for demonstrating the existence of Hadžihasanović's effective control over the *El Mujahedin* detachment. [...]

214. Thus, while these Trial Chamber's findings indicate that the 3rd Corps cooperated with the *El Mujahedin* detachment, they are insufficient to establish the existence of effective control. [...]

(c) The absence of any other authority over the *El Mujahedin* detachment

215. The Trial Chamber concluded that there was no authority over the *El Mujahedin* detachment other than the authority of the 3rd Corps. According to Hadžihasanović, the *El Mujahedin* detachment was not under the command of the 3rd Corps, but under the command of some "mujahedin leaders". He affirms that the *El Mujahedin* detachment refused to be placed under the command and control of the 3rd Corps and wanted to be assigned tasks from another authority.

216. Some of the Trial Chamber's findings suggest that the *El Mujahedin* detachment was more under the influence of Muslim clerics, than under that of the 3rd Corps. The Trial

Chamber noted that, in June 1993, Hadžihasanović informed Rasim Delić and Sefer Halilović that the mujahedin "had the support of certain state organs and high-ranking clergymen". On two occasions, at the end of October 1993, the circle of Muslim clerics was able to exercise influence over the members of the detachment while the OG *Bosanska Krajina* was unable to have its orders carried out. Despite these findings, the Trial Chamber nevertheless concluded that the *El Mujahedin* detachment was subject to no other authority.

217. Assuming that the Trial Chamber's conclusion that there was no other authority over the *El Mujahedin* detachment is correct, the Appeals Chamber disputes the relevance of the criterion identified by the Trial Chamber as an indicator of the existence of effective control. Hadžihasanović's effective control cannot be established by process of elimination. The absence of any other authority over the *El Mujahedin* detachment in no way implies that Hadžihasanović exercised effective control in this case.

(d) The prosecution of a member of the *El Mujahedin* detachment

218. In its analysis of whether Hadžihasanović exercised effective control over the members of the *El Mujahedin* detachment, the Trial Chamber took into consideration the testimony of Witness Šiljak that a member of the *El Mujahedin* detachment was "prosecuted by the Travnik District Military Court and sentenced for having run the witness' wife out of the village of Kljaci in the fall of 1993 because she was the offspring of a mixed marriage". [. . .]

219. [. . .] Even if it were true that the said individual had been brought before the Travnik District Military Court, there is no indication in the Trial Judgement as to what role Hadžihasanović would have had in bringing about the initiation of proceedings against that perpetrator. Nor does Witness Šiljak's testimony demonstrate that the perpetrator was prosecuted following measures taken or initiated by the 3rd Corps. [. . .]

(e) The abduction of civilians by the *El Mujahedin* detachment and the non-use of force by the 3rd Corps to rescue them

222. Hadžihasanović submits that, given that the only way for the 3rd Corps to obtain the release of the five civilians who had been abducted by members of the *El Mujahedin* detachment on 19 October 1993 was to use force against the detachment, he could not be found to have had effective control over it. According to Hadžihasanović, a commander who has no other option but to attack a group, with a view to preventing its members from committing a crime, cannot exercise effective control over that group. [. . .]

224. The Trial Chamber made the following findings regarding the *El Mujahedin* detachment's abduction of civilians. On 15 October 1993, members of the *El Mujahedin* detachment abducted six Croatian civilians, though the detachment had been explicitly warned against such action by Mehmed Alagić, Hadžihasanović's deputy. On 15 or 16 October 1993, the OG *Bosanska Krajina* Command threatened to attack the *El Mujahedin* detachment should they refuse to release the civilians who were still being kept hostage. The Trial Chamber noted that these first threats to use force against the *El Mujahedin* detachment did not have the expected deterrent effect. On the contrary, the *El Mujahedin* detachment responded by abducting five more civilians on 19 October 1993. On 20 October 1993, a member of the OG *Bosanska Krajina* command handed out a list of persons abducted by the *El Mujahedin* detachment to representatives of the ICRC, the ECMM [European Community Monitor Mission] and the UNHCR. That same day, Mehmed Alagić ordered the *El Mujahedin* detachment to release the prisoners who had been abducted the previous day, and communicated with the circle of Muslim clerics and naturalised Bosnian Muslims with a view to influencing the mujahedin. A member of the OG *Bosanska Krajina* went to the mujahedin camp in Poljanice, where he met Abu Haris, the head of the *El Mujahedin* detachment. He transmitted Mehmed Alagić's order to release the prisoners immediately. On 21 October 1993, however, Dragan Popović,

one of the five hostages kidnapped on 19 October 1993, was killed. Another hostage, Kazimir Pobrić, was released on 22 or 23 October 1993. Between 20 and 29 October 1993, a representative of the ICRC tried, with the assistance of an officer from the OG *Bosanska Krajina* Command, to pay a visit to the abducted civilians. The mujahedin refused to let them enter their camp. Finally, on 29 October 1993, Mehmed Alagić threatened for a second time to attack the detachment if the prisoners were not released. The last hostage was released on 7 December 1993.

225. Furthermore, the Appeals Chamber notes that the 3rd Corps was unable to obtain the release of one of its soldiers who was abducted by members of the *El Mujahedin* detachment on 23 October 1993. Emir Kuduzović, a 17th Brigade soldier, was detained for several days and mistreated at the Poljanice Camp by members of the detachment because he had consumed alcohol. The Trial Chamber found that the "mujahedin did not release the soldier in spite of Alagić's order" and that the 17th Brigade was "only able to obtain his release by sending a message through the Mufti of Travnik." The message indicated that the 17th Brigade would attack the camp if the mujahedin did not release the soldier.

226. The Trial Chamber dealt with these events with a view to determining whether Hadžihasanović had taken necessary and reasonable measures as a superior to prevent or punish crimes committed by the *El Mujahedin* detachment on the premise that Hadžihasanović had effective control over the detachment. In the Appeals Chamber's view, these events confirm that Hadžihasanović did not have effective control over the *El Mujahedin* detachment. They demonstrate that there were areas, in addition to the examples already provided in paragraph 224 above, in which the *El Mujahedin*'s detachment acted independently from the 3rd Corps. [. . .]

228. The Appeals Chamber agrees with the Trial Chamber that the fact that a superior is compelled to use force to control some of his subordinates does not automatically lead to the conclusion that this superior does not exercise effective control over them. The Appeals Chamber concurs with the Trial Chamber's finding that this issue must be evaluated on a case-by-case basis. Further, there might be situations in which a superior has to use force against subordinates acting in violation of international humanitarian law. A superior may have no other alternative but to use force to prevent or punish the commission of crimes by subordinates. This kind of use of force is legal under international humanitarian law insofar as it complies with the principles of proportionality and precaution and may even demonstrate that a superior has the material ability to prevent and punish the commission of crimes. The issue in the present case, however, is whether those modalities in which force should have been used, in the Trial Chamber's view, to rescue the hostages, confirm the absence of Hadžihasanović's effective control over the *El Mujahedin* detachment.

229. The military operation that the Trial Chamber expected the 3rd Corps to launch in order to rescue the hostages was not simply a type of police operation over a few recalcitrant subordinates. Rather, it would have amounted to a full-fledged armed attack against the camp where the *El Mujahedin* detachment was based. [. . .]

230. [. . .] [T]he above scenario reveals a situation in which the relationship between the *El Mujahedin* detachment and the 3rd Corps was not one of subordination. It was quite close to overt hostility since the only way to control the *El Mujahedin* detachment was to attack them as if they were a distinct enemy force. This scenario is at odds with the premise of the Trial Chamber that the *El Mujahedin* detachment was subordinated to the 3rd Corps. This conclusion further confirms that Hadžihasanović did not have effective control over the *El Mujahedin* detachment.

Various accused have also challenged the imposition of superior responsibility on the ground that they lacked effective command and control because of unruly subordinates or because concurrent command with another superior superseded their control. The excerpt below – the first appeals judgment of the Special Court for Sierra Leone – considers such claims.

SCSL, Prosecutor v. Brima (AFRC case), Appeals Chamber, Judgment of 22 February 2008

The excerpt below addresses an appeal by the accused, Brima Bazzy Kamara, a former leader of the Armed Forces Revolutionary Council (AFRC), of his conviction for crimes against humanity and war crimes under a superior responsibility theory. The AFRC was formed after a breakaway group of soldiers staged a coup against the elected Sierra Leone government in 1997. Allied with the rebel Revolutionary United Front (RUF), the AFRC sought to gain control over the entire territory of Sierra Leone and particularly over diamond-mining areas. After being dislodged from power in March 1998, the AFRC continued to fight until hostilities ceased in 2002. The fighting was marked by brutal attacks against civilians, including sexual violence against men, women and children. Women and girls were used as sex slaves and forced labour and boys and girls were conscripted as child soldiers. Kamara commanded AFRC/RUF forces fighting in various areas of Sierra Leone, including the Kono and Bombali Districts and Freetown.

1. Trial Chamber findings

253. The Trial Chamber found Kamara criminally responsible as a superior under Article 6(3) of the Statute for crimes committed by his subordinates in Kono District, Bombali District, Port Loko District and Freetown and other parts of the Western Area. Regarding Kamara's superior responsibility in Kono District, the Trial Chamber found that after the departure of Johnny Paul Koroma from Kono District, Kamara became the highest ranking AFRC soldier in this location and that he exercised effective control over some mixed battalion[s] of AFRC and RUF troops. It also found that battalions consisting of both AFRC and RUF soldiers were under AFRC command in several locations in Kono District including Tombodu; that [commander Mohamed] Savage committed crimes in Tombodu and that Kamara had effective control over Savage. [...]

255. Under his Seventh Ground of Appeal, Kamara submits:

(i) That he did not have effective control or the ability to control the actions of Savage and consequently could not be liable for crimes committed by Savage in Kono District;

(ii) That he did not have effective control over AFRC troops in Kono District [...]

3. Discussion

257. In addition to military commanders, superior responsibility under Article 6(3) of the Statute encompasses political leaders and other civilian superiors in positions of authority. A superior is one who possesses the power or authority to either prevent a subordinate's crimes or punish the subordinate after the crime has been committed. The power or authority may arise from a *de jure* or a *de facto* command relationship. Whether it is *de jure* or *de facto*, the superior-subordinate relationship must be one of effective control, however short or temporary in nature. Effective control refers to the material ability to prevent or punish criminal conduct. The test of effective control is the same for both military and civilian superiors.

258. Kamara submits that a finding of superior responsibility requires proof of both command and control which he claims are inseparable. The Appeals Chamber rejects this assertion. The

terms "command" and "control" are two related but distinct concepts. The term "command" refers to powers that attach to a military superior, while the term "control," which has a wider meaning encompasses both military and civilian superiors.

(a) Kamara's Responsibility for Crimes Committed by Savage

259. Kamara contends that the Trial Chamber erred in finding him liable as a superior for crimes committed by Savage in Kono District. According to Kamara, he did not have the material ability to control the acts of Savage because Savage was unruly in character. The Trial Chamber noted that there was evidence that Savage was very difficult to control and that he was unpredictable. The Trial Chamber was satisfied that Savage's unpredictable character was not a bar to finding that Kamara had effective control over him. The Appeals Chamber finds no reason to disturb the Trial Chamber's finding that Kamara is liable as a superior for crimes committed by Savage in Kono District.

(b) Kamara's Effective Control in Kono District and the Testimony of Witness TF1–334 on AFRC Muster Parades in Kono District

260. With respect to Kamara's responsibility for the crimes committed by AFRC troops in Kono, the Trial Chamber found that after the departure of Johnny Paul Koroma from Kono District, the AFRC was subordinate to the RUF and that Kamara became the highest ranking AFRC soldier in the District. [. . .] It held that despite the AFRC's subordination to the RUF, including Kamara's subordination to the RUF's Denis Mingo, Kamara still had effective control over some mixed battalions of AFRC and RUF troops. [. . .]

262. Subordination of the AFRC to the RUF and substantial cooperation between the AFRC and RUF may have diminished the distinction between the two command structures. Nonetheless, the Appeals Chamber considers that concurrent command does not vitiate the individual responsibility of any of the commanders. In its evaluation of concurrent command in Kono District, the Trial Chamber concluded that Denis Mingo's command in Kono District over joint units of the AFRC/RUF force did not preclude a finding of superior responsibility on the part of Kamara. The Trial Chamber noted Denis Mingo's position of authority over Kamara, but also noted that Kamara continued to issue orders to AFRC subordinates which were followed, and remained the most senior AFRC commander in Kono until Brima's arrival in mid-May 1998. The Appeals Chamber finds no error in the Trial Chamber's approach [. . .]

COMMENTARY

Consider this hypothetical scenario, based on defences mounted by military officers charged with superior responsibility during the Bosnian conflict. The accused was trained in elite military academies and rose through the ranks of the Yugoslav People's Army. After the disintegration of the former Yugoslavia, he was ordered to return to Bosnia to command a brigade of the Bosnian Serb Army, cobbled together from a motley collection of people whose day jobs were as factory workers, farmers and the like, and lacked military discipline and training. These men occasionally mustered to fight, were often drunk, and then returned home to their everyday lives. When the accused tried to impose military rules of discipline and training, some of the soldiers, riding tractors and brandishing guns, chased him and his deputy officer, shooting at them.

Aggravating the troubles of the accused was a political–military structure that further undermined his authority by placing a security officer among his ranks, who, though nominally his subordinate, had the power to bypass him and channel commands from higher authorities to his men in the interest of security. The accused argues that when he was away trying to defend Bosnian Serb villages from a wedge of advancing Bosnian Muslim forces with his poorly trained and insufficient troops, the security officer ordered the slaughter of thousands of prisoners because of insufficient manpower and space to maintain security.

If this account is credited, should the accused be deemed to lack sufficient effective command and control to have prevented the slaughter of the prisoners? Or do you think the law should make the accused bear the risk that his unruly subordinates would commit crimes and the responsibility for forestalling them? If you believe the superior should bear the risk despite unruly subordinates, then do you think *Hadžihasanović*, involving an alliance with the *Mujahedin*, was rightly decided? Should regular disciplined officers who ally with unpredictable and hard-to-control elements bear responsibility for the crimes that ensue to chill such dangerous alliances and the potentially explosive instrumentalities that such alliances and formations create? Contemporary warfare, involving patchwork armies, sometimes allied uneasily with local militias and other irregular fighters, and complicated politics of mistrust, pose such dilemmas of adjudication.

MENS REA

From *Yamashita* to the present, the question of the minimum *mens rea* sufficient for culpability has been contested and the standard subject to variation. Section (B) surveyed differences in the codified *mens rea* standards between Additional Protocol I to the Geneva Conventions, the Statutes of the ad hoc Tribunals and the Rome Statute of the International Criminal Court. Culpable *mens rea* is predicated on actual or constructive knowledge of crimes committed or about to be committed by subordinates. The notion of constructive knowledge is both amorphous and capacious, however, and risks being stretched to something more akin to recklessness or even mere negligence, as the case below illustrates.

ICTY, Prosecutor v. Strugar, *Appeals Chamber, Judgment of 17 July 2008*

This case arises out of the shelling of the Old Town of Dubrovnik, a beautiful UNESCO World Heritage site on the Adriatic seacoast in Croatia, in October, November and December 1991 when Yugoslavia was beginning to dissolve. The unit that shelled the Old Town, the 3rd Battalion of the 472nd Motorized Brigade (abbreviated 3/472 mtbr in the text), was subordinated to the Second Operational Group (abbreviated 2nd OG) commanded by the accused, General Pavle Strugar of the Yugoslav People's Army (JNA). General Strugar ordered an attack on Srđ, a legitimate military target, neighbouring the Old Town. In the course of the attack on Srđ on 6 December 1991, the Old Town was shelled. The Trial Chamber held that General Strugar lacked the requisite minimum *mens rea* for superior responsibility before the shelling began and did not have the requisite *mens rea* until around 7 a.m. on 6 December 1991, when he was informed that the ECMM was protesting about the shelling of the Old Town. The Trial Chamber also found that General Strugar could not be held guilty on an ordering theory because he was not aware of a substantial likelihood that in attacking the legitimate military target of Srđ the Old Town would be shelled. General Strugar was convicted, however, on a superior responsibility theory for failing to prevent further shelling of the Old Town after the 7 a.m. notice by the ECMM and for failing to punish the acts.

At issue in the portion of the appeal excerpted below is the Prosecution's challenge of the Trial Chamber's finding that General Strugar did not have the requisite 'reason to know' that his subordinates were unlawfully shelling or would unlawfully shell the Old

Town before 7 a.m. The Prosecution argued that this dispute regarding when General Strugar had culpable *mens rea* for superior liability mattered, even though it was only a difference of a few hours, because the crime was not simply of failing to intervene once the shelling had started, but of failing to *prevent* the shelling of the Old Town altogether during the attack on Srđ.

297. Pursuant to Article 7(3) of the Statute, the knowledge required to trigger a superior's duty to prevent is established when the superior "knew or had reason to know that [his] subordinate was about to commit [crimes]". The Trial Chamber in *Čelebići* interpreted this requirement in light of the language used in Article 86(2) of Additional Protocol I and held that, under the "had reason to know" standard, it is required to establish that the superior had "information of a nature, which at the least, would put him on notice of the risk of [...] offences by indicating the need for additional investigation in order to ascertain whether such crimes were committed or were about to be committed by his subordinates". As a clarification, the Trial Chamber added that "[i]t is sufficient that the superior was put on further inquiry by the information, or, in other words, that it indicated the need for additional investigation in order to ascertain whether offences were being committed or about to be committed by his subordinates".

298. The Appeals Chamber in *Čelebići* endorsed this interpretation and held that the rationale behind the standard set forth in Article 86(2) of Additional Protocol I is plain: "failure to conclude, or conduct additional inquiry, in spite of alarming information constitutes knowledge of subordinate offences". It noted that this information may be general in nature and does not need to contain specific details on the unlawful acts which have been or are about to be committed. It follows that, in order to demonstrate that a superior had the mens rea required under Article 7(3) of the Statute, it must be established whether, in the circumstances of the case, he possessed information sufficiently alarming to justify further inquiry.

299. In *Krnojelac*, the Trial Chamber found that "[t]he fact that the Accused witnessed the beating of [a detainee, inflicted by one of his subordinates], ostensibly for the prohibited purpose of *punishing* him for his failed escape, is not sufficient, in itself, to conclude that the Accused knew or [...] had reason to know that, other than in that particular instance, beatings were inflicted for any of the prohibited purposes". The Appeals Chamber rejected this finding and held that "while this fact is indeed insufficient, in itself, to conclude that Krnojelac *knew* that acts of torture were being inflicted on the detainees, as indicated by the Trial Chamber, it may nevertheless constitute sufficiently alarming information such as to alert him to the risk of other acts of torture being committed, meaning that Krnojelac *had reason to know* that his subordinates were committing or were about to commit acts of torture". The Appeals Chamber also reiterated that "an assessment of the mental element required by Article 7(3) of the Statute should, in any event, be conducted in the specific circumstances of each case, taking into account the specific situation of the superior concerned at the time in question".

300. In *Hadžihasanović and Kubura*, the Trial Chamber found that "the Accused Kubura, owing to his knowledge of the plunder committed by his subordinates in June 1993 and his failure to take punitive measures, could not [ignore] that the members of the 7th Brigade were likely to repeat such acts". The Appeals Chamber in that case found that the Trial Chamber had erred in making this finding as it implied "that the Trial Chamber considered Kubura's knowledge of and past failure to punish his subordinates' acts of plunder in the Ovnak area as automatically entailing that he had reason to know of their future acts of plunder in Vareš". The Appeals Chamber thus applied the correct legal standard to the evidence on the trial record: "While Kubura's knowledge of his subordinates' past plunder in Ovnak

and his failure to punish them did not, in itself, amount to actual knowledge of the acts of plunder in Vareš, the Appeals Chamber concurs with the Trial Chamber that the orders he received on 4 November 1993 constituted, at the very least, sufficiently alarming information justifying further inquiry."

301. As such, while a superior's knowledge of and failure to punish his subordinates' past offences is insufficient, in itself, to conclude that the superior knew that similar future offences would be committed by the same group of subordinates, this may, depending on the circumstances of the case, nevertheless constitute sufficiently alarming information to justify further inquiry under the 'had reason to know' standard. In making such an assessment, a Trial Chamber may take into account the failure by a superior to punish the crime in question. Such failure is indeed relevant to the determination of whether, in the circumstances of a case, a superior possessed information that was sufficiently alarming to put him on notice of the risk that similar crimes might subsequently be carried out by subordinates and justify further inquiry. In this regard, the Appeals Chamber stresses that a superior's failure to punish a crime of which he has actual knowledge is likely to be understood by his subordinates at least as acceptance, if not encouragement, of such conduct with the effect of increasing the risk of new crimes being committed.

302. In the present case, the Appeals Chamber observes that the Trial Chamber recalled the approach taken in the *Čelebići* Trial Judgement and upheld in the related Appeal Judgement, according to which "a superior will be criminally responsible by virtue of the principles of superior responsibility only if information was available to him which would have put him on notice of offences committed by subordinates, or about to be committed". The Trial Chamber also recalled "that even general information in [the superior's] possession, which would put him on notice of possible unlawful acts by his subordinates would be sufficient". However, the Appeals Chamber also notes that the Trial Chamber referred to the standard as requiring that a superior be "in possession of sufficient information to be on notice of the likelihood of illegal acts by his subordinates". Consequently, the Appeals Chamber cannot conclude with certainty that the Trial Chamber properly interpreted the standard of "had reason to know" as requiring an assessment, in the circumstances of the case, of whether a superior possessed information that was sufficiently alarming to put him on notice of the risk that crimes might subsequently be carried out by subordinates and justify further inquiry. The Appeals Chamber must therefore determine whether the Trial Chamber erred in law by applying an incorrect legal standard in its findings on Strugar's criminal responsibility as a superior.

303. The Appeals Chamber observes that the Trial Chamber found that prior to the commencement of the attack against Srđ, Strugar had reason to know of the risk that the forces under his command might repeat their previous conduct and unlawfully shell the Old Town. The Trial Chamber characterised this risk as "a real and obvious prospect", "a clear possibility", "a risk that was not slight or remote", and a "real risk". The Appeals Chamber moreover notes that the Trial Chamber found that the mens rea element of Article 7(3) of the Statute was not met before the commencement of the attack against Srđ because it found that it had not been established that Strugar "had reason to know that 'unlawful shelling' would occur", that the risk of such shelling was shown "to have been so strong as to give rise, in the circumstances, to *knowledge* that his forces were about to commit an offence" or that "there was a *substantial likelihood* of the artillery" unlawfully shelling the Old Town. In addition, the Trial Chamber held that it was "not apparent that additional investigation before the attack could have put the Accused in any better position". The Appeals Chamber finally notes that the Trial Chamber found that Strugar's notice, after the commencement of the attack against Srđ, of a "clear and strong risk" or a "clear likelihood" that his forces were repeating its previous conduct and unlawfully shelling the Old Town did however meet the *mens rea* requirement under Article 7(3).

304. Taking into consideration the relevant factual findings of the Trial Chamber, the Appeals Chamber finds that the Trial Chamber committed an error of law by not applying the correct legal standard regarding the mens rea element under Article 7(3) of the Statute. The Trial Chamber erred in finding that Strugar's knowledge of the risk that his forces might unlawfully shell the Old Town was not sufficient to meet the *mens rea* element under Article 7(3) and that only knowledge of the "substantial likelihood" or the "clear and strong risk" that his forces would do so fulfilled this requirement. In so finding, the Trial Chamber erroneously read into the *mens rea* element of Article 7(3) the requirement that the superior be on notice of a strong risk that his subordinates would commit offences. In this respect, the Appeals Chamber recalls that under the correct legal standard, sufficiently alarming information putting a superior on notice of the risk that crimes might subsequently be carried out by his subordinates and justifying further inquiry is sufficient to hold a superior liable under Article 7(3) of the Statute.

305. Having found that the Trial Chamber erred in law, the Appeals Chamber must apply the correct legal standard to the facts as found by the Trial Chamber and determine whether it is itself convinced beyond reasonable doubt that Strugar possessed, prior to the commencement of the attack against Srđ, sufficiently alarming information to meet the "had reason to know" standard under Article 7(3) of the Statute. The Appeals Chamber recalls that the Trial Chamber established the following facts in relation to Strugar's knowledge prior to the commencement of the attack against Srđ:

- Strugar ordered the attack against Srđ and knew that the attack against Srđ necessarily contemplated some shelling of the wider city of Dubrovnik;
- Strugar knew that in the course of previous JNA [Yugoslav People's Army] military action in October and November 1991 seeking to capture further territory in the vicinity of Dubrovnik, including Srđ in November, there was unauthorised shelling of the Old Town;
- Strugar knew that the forces in the attack on 6 December 1991 included the forces involved in the November shelling of the Old Town, and that the unit directly located around Srđ on 6 December was the 3/472 mtbr which, under the same commander, had been identified as a likely participant in the November shelling;
- Strugar knew that the 3/472 mtbr, and the 3/5 mtbr located to the immediate north of the 3/472 mtbr, were each equipped with substantial artillery capacity on 6 December 1991, as they had been in November 1991;
- Strugar knew that existing orders precluding shelling of the Old Town in October and November 1991 had not proved effective as a means of preventing his troops from shelling the Old Town on these two occasions;
- Strugar knew that no adverse action had been taken against the perpetrators of previous acts of shelling the Old Town and thus that there were no examples of adverse disciplinary or other consequences for those who breached existing preventative orders or international law.

306. In light of the Trial Chamber's factual findings regarding Strugar's knowledge prior to the attack against Srđ, the Appeals Chamber is satisfied beyond a reasonable doubt that Strugar had notice of sufficiently alarming information such that he was alerted of the risk that similar acts of unlawful shelling of the Old Town might be committed by his subordinates as well as of the need to undertake further enquiries with respect to this risk.

307. In the opinion of the Appeals Chamber, the only reasonable conclusion available on the facts as found by the Trial Chamber was that Strugar, despite being alerted of a risk justifying further enquiries, failed to undertake such enquiries to assess whether his subordinates properly understood and were inclined to obey the order to attack Srđ and existing preventative orders precluding the shelling of the Old Town.

308. Consequently, the Appeals Chamber is satisfied beyond a reasonable doubt that as of 12:00 a.m. on 6 December 1991, Strugar possessed sufficiently alarming information to meet the "had reason to know" standard under Article 7(3) of the Statute.

COMMENTARY

In conflict situations, risk is rampant. A realistic commander is always aware of a risk that things might go wrong. The Trial Chamber's standard requiring knowledge of a substantial likelihood of crimes by subordinates or a clear and strong risk of such crimes is one way to distinguish criminally culpable disregard from the ordinary risk that inheres in conflict situations. One might agree with the Trial Chamber's standard even if one disagrees with how the Trial Chamber applied it in holding the facts insufficient to demonstrate a substantial likelihood that the Old Town would be shelled again under the circumstances.

The Appeals Chamber, however, vitiated the Trial Chamber's *legal standard*, rather than just the questionable analysis of the facts under the standard, and discarded the requirement of a substantial likelihood of crimes or a clear and strong risk. The Appeals Chamber instead ruled that 'sufficiently alarming information putting a superior on notice of the risk' that crimes might be committed by subordinates suffices for liability. Is this a better or worse formulation to guide action by superiors in the field, dealing with on-the-ground realities? Surely knowledge of the risk that inheres in any combat situation is insufficient. To read the standard as one capable of discerning between the ordinary and the criminal, weight must be put on the requirement of 'sufficiently alarming information' – such information is what supplies the superior with constructive knowledge. *Strugar* illustrates the difficulty in formulating a practicable *mens rea* standard that is not so high that the culpable go free but not so low and broad as to be hardly a standard at all but rather a licence to impose liability retrospectively when things go wrong.

ACTUS REUS: OMISSION

The *actus reus* for superior liability is based on omission: the failure to prevent or punish the crimes of subordinates. The omissions are defined in the disjunctive: failure either to prevent or to punish crimes can be the basis of liability. As a practical matter, cases often involve both kinds of omission because superiors have a self-interest in not drawing attention to the crimes of subordinates that they failed to prevent. Sometimes, however, superiors may not have had sufficient alarming information before the commission of crimes to trigger the duty to prevent but may fail in the aftermath, upon discovery, to punish the crimes or report the crimes to the relevant authorities for prosecution.

One contested issue is whether there is a duty to punish or report crimes committed before a superior takes command or control of the subordinates. Over vigorous dissents by Judges Shahabuddeen and Hunt, the ICTY has declined to hold commanders responsible for not reporting to relevant authorities crimes committed by subordinates *before* assumption of command over the subordinates.[9] Where a duty to act exists, a culpable omission may sometimes be found even where effort is made to prevent or punish and investigate crimes by subordinates. The excerpt below, drawn from another portion of the *Strugar* Appeal Judgment (see the previous subsection), is illustrative.

---

[9] See ICTY Appeals Chamber, *Hadžihasanović, Alagić and Kubura*, Decision on Interlocutory Appeal Challenging Jurisdiction in Relation to Command Responsibility, para. 16.

ICTY, Prosecutor *v.* Strugar, *Appeals Chamber, Judgment of 17 July 2008*

This portion of the *Strugar* Appeal Judgment rejects General Strugar's argument that an investigation into the illegal shelling on 6 December 1991 ordered by Yugoslav Federal Secretary of National Defense, General Veljko Kadijević, satisfied the duty to punish. The investigation was conducted by Admiral Miodrag Jokić, commander of the Ninth Military Naval Sector. The Third Battalion of the 472nd Motorized Brigade, which engaged in the illegal shelling, was directly subordinated to Admiral Jokić's Ninth Military Naval Sector, which in turn was subordinated to General Pavle Strugar's Second Operational Group.

223. Strugar impugns the Trial Chamber's finding that he failed to initiate an investigation and take action and undertake punitive measures against the perpetrators of the shelling of the Old Town.

224. [. . .] According to Strugar, Jokić informed [Croatian Prime Minister] Rudolf at 11:45 a.m. that Kadijević had ordered an investigation. Rudolf, in turn, informed Strugar that Kadijević had ordered an investigation, and that he was certain that it would be fair and that he would be informed of its results. In addition, at a meeting on 6 December 1991, Kadijević told five ambassadors from Western countries that he would immediately start an investigation and that every person responsible for violating the ceasefire would be punished.

225. Strugar secondly argues that the Trial Chamber failed to consider all of the measures taken by Jokić in accordance with Kadijević's order. In particular, the Trial Chamber failed to mention the following measures: (i) Jokić took statements from the company commanders who had taken part in the attack, in particular from those who were in a position to attack the Old Town, such as Nešić, commander of an anti-armour detachment from Žarkovica, and Captain Jeremić ("Jeremić"), commander of the 120 mm mortar battery; (ii) Jokić also called Kovačević for explanations and the two met with Nešić and Jeremić on 8 December 1991 so that the three lower officers could provide explanations for the shelling of 6 December 1991; (iii) the commander of the 3/5 mtbr, Jovanović, was asked to give a statement on the events of 6 December 1991; and (iv) Jovanović gave his statement at the Command of the 9 VPS already at 14:00 p.m. on 6 December 1991. In addition, Strugar avers that Jokić formed a commission composed of higher officers of the 9 VPS and sent them to Dubrovnik to establish the damages caused.

226. Strugar also submits that he was excluded from the process of investigating the events of 6 December 1991 because the JNA [Yugoslav People's Army] Supreme Command had ordered Jokić to conduct an investigation and report on its results. Strugar argues that he could not therefore have had the material ability to punish the perpetrators, a prerequisite for having failed to punish them. His argument rests on two main submissions. Strugar submits that there is no evidence to prove that he was ordered to take part in the investigation. He argues that the Trial Chamber erroneously held that the order issued by Kadijević to Jokić was of no significance to him as he should have conducted his own investigation. According to Strugar, the effect of the order given by the JNA Supreme Command to Jokić made it impossible for him to conduct a parallel investigation of his own. [. . .]

227. In addition, Strugar maintains that the Trial Chamber erroneously found that he should have conducted an investigation and concluded that he participated "at the very least by acquiescence" in Jokić's sham investigation and sham disciplinary action. Strugar argues that he was never informed about the content of Jokić's report and that the JNA Supreme Command had accepted the report on the investigation. Indeed, on the basis of Jokić's report,

Admiral Brovet informed the ambassadors of the United States, Russia and the Netherlands on 12 December 1991 that those responsible for the shelling of the Old Town were under criminal investigation and had been relieved of their command. [. . .]

(b) Discussion

230. [. . .] The Trial Chamber ultimately considered that assurances were given to international authorities as part of "a damage control exercise by the JNA as a consequence of the adverse international reaction to the shelling". The Appeals Chamber finds that it was open to a reasonable trier of fact to reach this conclusion, given the evidence surrounding the circumstances in which the investigation was initiated and the results and outcome of the investigation. [. . .]

231. [. . .] The Appeals Chamber notes that the Trial Chamber found that:

- "the JNA deliberately put in place false records to indicate that the attack was undertaken spontaneously by Captain Kovačević by virtue of Croatian 'provocations' during the night of 5–6 December 1991" and that this "position was in fact taken by the JNA, including the command of the 2 OG, publicly and when dealing with Croatian representatives after the attack";

- Jokić's report to the SFRY [Socialist Federal Republic of Yugoslavia] Secretariat on his ongoing investigation was "quite out of keeping with the facts as revealed by the evidence in this case, so as to put the conduct of the JNA forces in a more favourable light";

- the report produced by a Commission of three 9 VPS officers on damage to the Old Town and endorsed by Jokić "sought to minimise the nature and extent of the damage and deflect responsibility for its cause from the JNA";

- no disciplinary action was taken against any officers of the 9 VPS or 2 OG, save for Jovanović, who was relieved from his temporary command of the 3/5 mtbr, despite the fact that this unit was not in a position to shell the Old Town on 6 December 1991;

- only a limited number of reports and statements were obtained after 6 December 1991, which supported the view that Kovačević of the 3/472 mtbr had "acted alone and contrary to orders in carrying out the attack on Srđ" and in which the "extent of the shelling and the damage it caused, especially to the Old Town, were significantly downplayed".

232. Moreover, the Appeals Chamber recalls that the Trial Chamber established that following the shelling of the Old Town, the JNA was in "damage control mode" and furthermore noted that Jokić testified that at a meeting between Strugar, Kadijević, and himself, "he felt that he was being portrayed as the main perpetrator" of the shelling. In the opinion of the Appeals Chamber, taking also into consideration that "only a few written statements and reports were obtained in the day or two after 6 December 1991", it was open to a reasonable trier of fact to conclude, on the basis of the whole of the evidence, that the investigation undertaken by Jokić was a "sham".

233. The Appeals Chamber will now address Strugar's challenges to the Trial Chamber's findings regarding the impossibility for him to conduct a parallel investigation and his participation in, and knowledge of, Jokić's investigation.

234. The Appeals Chamber notes that the Trial Chamber explicitly considered and rejected Strugar's submissions to the effect that the order given by the JNA Supreme Command to Jokić had excluded him from the investigation of the events of 6 December 1991 and had made it impossible for him to conduct a parallel investigation of his own. In this regard, the Appeals Chamber recalls that the Trial Chamber found that:

- in a meeting in Belgrade on 6 December 1991, Kadijević accepted Jokić's suggestion that the latter investigate the shelling of the Old Town;

- there was no explicit order from Kadijević to Jokić to conduct an investigation into the shelling of the Old Town, "although an acceptance that he should do so was implicit";

- "the nature of Admiral Jokić's reporting was NOT to provide General Kadijević with information and/or recommendation for action and decision by General Kadijević in respect of the events of 6 December 1991 and consequent disciplinary action", but served rather to inform the Federal Secretariat of what had occurred and what actions and decision he had taken as Commander of the 9 VPS;

- during the meeting in Belgrade, Kadijević was equally critical of both Strugar and Jokić;

- Strugar was present throughout the meeting and did not object to, nor resist in any way, Jokić's proposal that he should investigate or Kadijević's "apparent acceptance" of that proposal;

- Strugar "effectively" knew that Jokić's investigation was meant "to smooth over the events of 6 December 1991 as best he could with both the Croatian and ECMM interests, while providing a basis on which it could be maintained by the JNA that it had taken appropriate measures";

- Strugar's direct role in the launching of the attack against Srđ and ongoing sympathy with the military objectives of this attack as well as the critical view taken by Kadijević "provided clear reasons why [Strugar] would not be minded to have the events of 6 December fully investigated, or to take disciplinary or other adverse action himself against those who directly participated";

- "[t]here is no suggestion in the evidence that at any time [Strugar] proposed or tried to investigate or to take any action against any subordinate for the shelling of the Old Town, or that he was prevented from doing so by General Kadijević or any other authority";

- "[w]ithin a week or so of 6 December 1991, effect was given to a proposal commenced in November, and which necessarily had the endorsement of the Accused as Commander of the 2 OG, for the promotion of Captain Kovačević who led the actual attack on 6 December 1991";

- "on the occasion of a visit to 3/472 mtbr by General Panić, the JNA Deputy Chief of General Staff, when both [Strugar] and Admiral Jokić were present, [Strugar] invited Captain Kovačević to nominate outstanding participants in the events of 6 December 1991".

235. In addition, the Appeals Chamber notes the following passages from Jokić's testimony, which the Trial Chamber found credible in relation to the initiation of the investigation and the damage control exercise conducted by the JNA:

Q. On the return from Podgorica, did you discuss with General Strugar the measures to be taken in relation to the shelling?

A. Yes, I did. [. . .] As we travelled, we talked, especially at his command post in Trebinje, about the further steps that were to be taken. *It was accepted that the official version of the events of the 6th of December, which was composed at the command of the 2nd Operational Group on the basis of information provided by Captain Kovacevic, which was given by his officers, that this official version of the event should be sent to Belgrade to the General Staff, and that I should stand by that story, that version, at the press conference on the following day.* [. . .] Likewise, I suggested, and General Strugar agreed, that on the following day, I sign the peace agreement, initial the peace agreement, or rather the ceasefire, and that I send my team of officers to Dubrovnik to assess the damage in the Old Town.

Q. [. . .] What did you mean by "accepted"? Who accepted it? Who gave the instructions to adopt a certain version of the facts?

A. *General Strugar instructed me as to what we should accept, what we should do. It was this official version of the events that took place on the 6th of December. That is to say, that I should stand by that at the press conference.* [. . .]

Q. What was the reason in your view that a thorough, complete investigation was not conducted by you? Why did you not complete a thorough investigation?

A. *First of all, this unit, the 3rd Battalion, was temporarily resubordinated to me. It was not within my establishment. It was within the establishment of the 472nd Brigade, which was subordinated to the 2nd Operational Group. So for an investigation that I would carry out with my authorities, I would have to receive orders from the commander of the 2nd Operational Group.*

Q. Did such orders come through? Did you receive such orders for an investigation?

A. No. No. *A thorough and real investigation regarding this case was not wanted.*

Q. By whom?

A. *I think everybody from the General Staff – let me start from there, and the commander of the operational group, and at my level, my level, including me.* [. . .]

236. In view of the Trial Chamber's findings, the Appeals Chamber dismisses Strugar's argument that there is no evidence to prove that he was ordered to take part in the investigation. Indeed, the Trial Chamber found that Strugar knew that Jokić's investigation was a sham undertaken as part of a damage control exercise by the JNA and that Jokić's task was merely to report to the Federal Secretariat on the measures he had taken as part of this investigation. As such, Strugar need not have been ordered to take part in the investigation for him to be liable for failure to punish as his material and legal authority to investigate and punish remained intact. [. . .]

238. With respect to Strugar's other submissions regarding his exclusion from the process of investigation, the impossibility for him to conduct a parallel investigation and his lack of knowledge of the results of Jokić's investigation, the Appeals Chamber finds that Strugar has merely asserted that the Trial Chamber should have drawn a particular conclusion on the basis of the evidence without explaining why the Trial Chamber's conclusion was unreasonable. In this regard, the Appeals Chamber finds that it was open to a reasonable trier of fact to conclude, on the basis of the whole of the evidence, including most notably the evidence relating to the meeting in Belgrade and the actions undertaken subsequent to this meeting, that Strugar had not been excluded from the process of investigation, but had rather been "at the least, prepared to accept a situation in which he would not become directly involved, leaving all effective investigation, action and decisions concerning disciplinary [*sic*] of other adverse action to his immediate subordinate, Admiral Jokić, whose task effectively was known to [Strugar] to be to smooth over the events of 6 December 1991 as best he could with both the Croatian and ECMM interests, while providing a basis on which it could be maintained by the JNA that it had taken appropriate measures". The Appeals Chamber also finds that it was reasonable for the Trial Chamber to conclude that Strugar "was, at the very least by acquiescence, a participant in the arrangement by which Admiral Jokić undertook his sham investigation and sham disciplinary action, and reported to the First Secretariat in a way which deflected responsibility for the damage to the Old Town from the JNA".

Joint Dissenting Opinion of Judge Meron and Judge Kwon

1. [. . .] We cannot agree with the majority's decision to uphold the Trial Chamber's finding that Strugar did not fulfil his duty to take measures to punish those responsible for the unlawful shelling of the Old Town on 6 December 1991. [. . .]

A. Singleness of Command

3. We are of the opinion that Kadijević's order, albeit an implicit one, that Jokić should investigate the events of 6 December 1991 prevented Strugar in both a *de jure* and *de facto* sense from conducting his own parallel investigation. We note in this regard that the oral submissions made by the Prosecution on Appeal that an officer retains his obligation to investigate even where that officer's superior has ordered that officer's subordinate to conduct a legitimate investigation is unacceptable.

4. The principle of singleness of command, adopted as one of the basic principles of command and control within the JNA creates a single, direct channel through which orders will be formulated, received and carried out. It follows that where an officer's competent superior orders an investigation, any attempt by that officer to interfere with or undermine the order by carrying out a parallel investigation would not be tolerated. The fact that Strugar might have become the subject of an investigation actually strengthens the notion that he should not have interfered with any investigation ordered by his superior. Under such circumstances, it would have been especially inappropriate for Strugar to have become involved. Given the singleness of command doctrine, we do not consider it necessary and reasonable in this case to say that Strugar was obliged to conduct an investigation parallel to the one ordered by the JNA Supreme Command, i.e., Kadijević.

5. In order to find Strugar guilty under Article 7(3) for failure to punish his subordinates for the unlawful shelling of Old Town, despite Kadijević's order, it must be established that the following situation exists, which the prosecution must prove beyond a reasonable doubt:

(i)   the investigation ordered by Kadijević was a sham;

(ii) Strugar knew that the investigation was a sham; and

(iii) Strugar was complicit, with Kadijević and Jokić, in conducting a sham investigation. [. . .]

7. The Trial Chamber has chosen to focus on the absence of proof that Kadijević's order for Jokić to investigate effectively prevented Strugar from conducting a parallel investigation. We consider this to be an inappropriate reversal of the burden of proof. The burden of proof rests squarely with the Prosecution to prove Strugar's guilt beyond a reasonable doubt. As noted above, in order to prove Strugar's guilt, the prosecution must show that Strugar was both aware of the sham nature of the investigation ordered by Kadijević and part of the conspiracy with Kadijević and Jokić to conduct the sham investigation. We consider that the Trial Chamber erred by focusing on the absence of evidence that Strugar was prevented from conducting a parallel investigation, as this constitutes a reversal of the burden of proof.

COMMENTARY

The notion of a culpable omission begs the question of what we expect superiors reasonably to do under the circumstances. What efforts to prevent and punish are deemed sufficient? Recall from the excerpt in the preceding subsection of the *Strugar* Appeal Judgment that there were standing orders not to shell the Old Town of Dubrovnik that had proved insufficient in the past to restrain shelling. Before ordering the attack on Srđ, what more should General Strugar have done? Reiterated the standing orders not to shell the Old Town? Bench the 472nd Motorized Brigade and preclude them from battle – or at least bar the Brigade's commander Captain Kovačević? Refrain from attacking Srđ altogether because it neighboured the Old Town of Dubrovnik? In the remove of courtroom or classroom proceedings, it is important to keep in mind the realities of conflict situations in framing the duties the criminal law implies, while not letting the practicalities of conflict be an excuse for everything.

How far superiors are expected to go also intertwines with the issue of the scope of a superior's authority within the hierarchy. The question of whether there was a culpable omission may also bleed into an accused's defence regarding lack of the material ability to prevent and punish under the circumstances. Here again, realism is in order because criminal liability should not be founded on fictions. What does the Appeals Chamber expect General Strugar to have done despite the investigation ordered by higher authorities? What could he realistically have done? Who has the better of the argument regarding whether General Strugar should be convicted of failure to punish despite the investigation ordered by higher authorities – the two dissenting judges or the three-judge majority?

QUESTIONS

1. How does *Yamashita* still haunt the lingering doctrinal questions regarding effective command and control, the *mens rea* standard for superior liability, and what counts as a culpable omission?

2. Does superior liability doctrine place defendants in a damned-if-you-do and damned-if-you-don't dilemma because attempts to mitigate wrongdoing by others are used as evidence of effective command and control while the failure to issue such orders is taken as a culpable omission? Or is this argument specious? Consider this question by contrasting the approaches taken by the ICTY Appeals Chamber in *Hadžihasanović* and in *Strugar*.

3. Justice Murphy's *Yamashita* dissent raised the spectre of prosecution of a US President and his chiefs of staff and military advisers on a superior responsibility theory. Is this prospect more colourful than probable? What barriers do you see to such a suit? To see the grounds of dismissal of suit in the United States on a superior responsibility theory against US military and civilian supervisors, including former Secretary of State Donald Rumsfeld, for torture by US personnel, see *In re Iraq and Afghanistan Detainees Litigation* 479 F. Supp. 2d 85 (DDC 2007).

4. Why do you think the drafters of the Rome Statute created a looser and lower standard for military commanders than for civilian superiors? Beyond political pragmatics, is there a principled reason why we place a higher burden, reflected in a lower *mens rea* standard, on military superiors?

5. For military commanders, the duty to prevent crimes developed in customary law from the Hague Conventions of the early 1900s. What is the source of the corresponding duties upon civilian superiors?

FURTHER READING

K. Ambos, 'Superior Responsibility', in A. Cassese *et al.* (eds), *The Rome Statute of the International Criminal Court: A Commentary* (Oxford: Oxford University Press, 2002), 823–72.

G. Mettraux, *The Law of Command Responsibility* (Oxford: Oxford University Press, 2009).

W.H. Parks, 'Command Responsibility for War Crimes' (1973) 62 *Military Law Review* 1–104.

Greg Vetter, 'Command Responsibility of Non-Military Superiors in the International Criminal Court (ICC)' (2000) 25 *Yale J. Int'l L.* 89.

Werle, *Principles*, 185–97.

J.A. Williamson, 'Some Considerations on Command Responsibility and Criminal Liability' (2008) 90 *International Review of the Red Cross* 303–17.

PART IV

CIRCUMSTANCES EXCLUDING CRIMINAL RESPONSIBILITY

INTRODUCTION

Criminal law systems normally provide for circumstances where, although an offence is committed, no criminal responsibility ensues. When the law provides for a *justification*, an action that would ordinarily be considered contrary to law, because it causes harm or damage to individuals or society is regarded instead as lawful, because of larger interests at stake. Such an act does not therefore amount to a crime. Society, and the legal system it has created, positively want a person to do the otherwise illegal act because (i) the act, though criminal, is the lesser of two evils (for instance, when one kills in lawful self-defence, the death of the attacker is regarded as a lesser evil than that of the person unlawfully attacked), or (ii), in the case of execution of a sentence of imprisonment or of the death penalty the taking of liberty or life is a measure positively required by law. Take also the case of lawful belligerent reprisals (for example, the use of prohibited weapons). The commander ordering the reprisals as well as those carrying them out do not act contrary to law, although the weapons used are prohibited by international law. Resort to these weapons is warranted by the need to stop gross breaches of international law by the adversary, or to respond to those breaches with a view to preventing their recurrence.

In these and other similar cases, society and its legal system make a positive appraisal of what would otherwise be misconduct. The international community wants the person to behave so, because in weighing two conflicting values (for instance, the need not to use prohibited weapons and the necessity to induce the enemy belligerent to comply with law) it gives pride of place to one of them, although this entails the exceptional infringement of the legal rules designed to satisfy the other need. The person acting under a justification intends to attain the result caused by his action and is aware that by undertaking the conduct he will bring about that result (e.g. he intends to cause the death or wounding of enemy combatants through the use of prohibited weapons). However, this frame of mind is not considered culpable *mens rea*, that is as intent to murder, for that action and the attendant mental element are deemed to be legally authorized.

By contrast, *excuses* may be raised in defence when, although the law regards as *unlawful* an action that causes harm and is contrary to a criminal norm, the wrongdoer is nevertheless *not punished*. Here the positive appraisal of the conduct excused is *less strong* than that relating to conduct covered by a justification. In other words, the value judgment enshrined in law is not so favourable as to consider the conduct as authorized. Indeed, although conduct is blameworthy and unlawful, the agent is not punished because account ought to be taken of special circumstances. Furthermore, in the case of excuses the required subjective element of the crime is lacking. Think, for instance, of the following case: a captain acts under a mistake of fact, in that he orders the shooting of a number of civilians in occupied territory who, he had been told, had committed war crimes and had been duly court-martialled, whereas in fact they either had not committed the crimes or had not been duly tried as required by international humanitarian law. In this case the agent believes himself to be engaged in conduct (lawful execution of war criminals) different from that prohibited by the criminal rule (execution of enemy civilians not duly tried and sentenced). The *actus reus* cannot be called into doubt, whereas the *mens rea* is lacking (he did not intend to kill enemy civilians). True, he was aware that by his order he would bring about their death. However, he did not mean to act contrary to international prescriptions and therefore lacked the requisite *culpable* mental element. In short, he intended to bring about the *lawful death* of those civilians, not their (unlawful) *murder*.

The distinction between the two categories at issue should be clear, although in both cases the author performing an act that normally would fall foul of the law is not punished. Plainly, the law-making bodies of each community (national or international) choose between a justification and an excuse on the basis of an appraisal of the various values at stake.

In international criminal law justifications embrace (i) the *lawful punishment* of enemy civilians or combatants guilty of war crimes or other international crimes such as crimes against humanity (e.g. the execution, after conviction and sentencing by a duly constituted Court Martial, of civilians who had engaged in prohibited attacks on the belligerents, amounting to war crimes or other international crimes); (ii) the taking of *lawful belligerent reprisals* against war crimes (as stated before, they may include the use of prohibited weapons as a response to a serious violation of international humanitarian law by the adversary, for instance, the killing of prisoners of war or the intentional shelling of civilians); and (iii) *self-defence*. Due to its interesting dimensions, self-defence will be separately discussed. The customary restrictions on reprisals developed by the ICTY were discussed in the chapter on sources of international criminal law, above (see the *Kupreškić* case under International Custom and the Value of Precedents, Part I(1)(A), p. 17).

The excuses provided for in international criminal law include: superior orders, duress, mistake of fact, mistake of law and necessity, as well as mental disorder, involuntary intoxication and physical compulsion. *Tu quoque*, though repeatedly pleaded in war crimes trials, has succeeded only in very specific circumstances.

A number of interesting cases dealing with some of these excuses will be dealt with in the forthcoming pages. It should be noted that necessity – one of the excuses discussed below – may actually be more properly described as a justification under certain circumstances.[1]

---

[1] For an interesting application of the concepts to a real situation, see J. D. Ohlin, 'The Torture Lawyers' (2010) 51 *Harvard International Law Journal* 193–256.

1
JUSTIFICATIONS: SELF-DEFENCE

Under customary international law a person who commits an international crime may plead self-defence on the ground that he was trying to prevent or halt a crime by another person against him or a third person. Self-defence is lawful provided it fulfils the following requirements: (i) the action in self-defence is taken in response to an imminent or actual unlawful attack on the life of the person or of another person; (ii) there is no other way of preventing or stopping the offence; (iii) the unlawful conduct of the other has not been caused by the person acting in self-defence; (iv) the conduct in self-defence is proportionate to the offence to which the person reacts.

Examples of self-defence include the killing by a prison guard of an enemy prisoner of war who was about to murder the guard, or the wounding of an enemy serviceman by a civilian woman in the hands of the enemy occupant, for the purpose of preventing or halting torture or rape.

Self-defence under international criminal law must not be confused with self-defence under public international law. The latter relates to conduct by States or State-like entities, whereas the former concerns actions by individuals against other individuals. This confusion often occurs. For instance, in the ICTY case *Kordić and Čerkez*, defence counsel argued that the Bosnian Croat forces engaging in armed action under the authority of the two accused were acting in self-defence in response to a policy of aggression by Muslim forces (§448). An ICTY Trial Chamber rightly rejected the argument, noting that 'military operations in self-defence do not provide a justification for serious violations of international humanitarian law' (§452).

Cases

US General Military Court in Ludwigsburg (Germany), **Erich Weiss and Wilhelm Mundo,** *Decision of 10 November 1945, Report of the Judge Advocate*

An American airman who in May 1944 had safely parachuted from his military aircraft over Germany was captured and turned over to two policemen. During an air raid, a crowd gathered around the policemen demanding that the prisoner be killed. When the airman suddenly moved his right hand in his pocket, the two policemen fired at him and he was instantly killed. The two defendants pleaded that they had felt threatened by the prisoner's movement of his hand in his pocket and had fired in self-defence. The US Court upheld the plea (149–50). The US Staff Judge Advocate charged with revising the decision recommended that 'the record of trial be affirmed and approved'. He gave the following reasons with regard to the defence invoked by the accused.

The defence of these accused was justifiable killing on the grounds of self-defence. The accused as guards of a prisoner of war are under a duty to accord the prisoner proper treatment, even protection if necessary. Conversely, as guards they would be authorized to use force, but only that force reasonably necessary under all the circumstances either to secure the custody of the prisoner or to protect themselves from an attack by their prisoner. Under these rules, and considering all the surrounding circumstances – the war, the air raid, the hostile crowd, the fact that the prisoner was an enemy alien – the court must have concluded the sudden motion of the captive in reaching in his pocket did in fact constitute sufficient threat to justify the shooting; that the force used was not unreasonably excessive. This being so the acquittal of these accused was proper. Further, the only evidence establishing the facts surrounding the actual killing is contained in the numerous confessions of the accused and their testimony at the trial. Each such statement also contains all the evidence in justification of the killing on the grounds of self-defence. In the absence of any other evidence, if the court accorded these statements that probative value necessary to convict these accused, the court would be bound to accord the balance of the statements with reference to self-defence that same weight. Under this basic rule of weighing evidence, even if a finding of guilty had been made, it could not thereafter be sustained on review.

COMMENTARY

The plea failed in *Yamamoto Chusaburo*, brought before a British Military Court sitting in Kuala Lumpur. A Japanese sergeant, charged with a war crime for killing a Malayan civilian who was stealing rice from a military store, claimed among other things that he had acted in self-defence: after arresting the civilian, he had been surrounded by a hostile crowd; fearing a grave danger to life, the more so because he was in pitch darkness, he had lost control of himself and in a rage killed the civilian with a bayonet. The Prosecutor rebutted that there was evidence that the act had not been committed in defence of property or person while the civilian was in the process of looting; rather, it had been committed after the civilian had been taken from his house into custody.[2]

Similarly, in *Frank C. Schultz*, heard in 1969 by a US Court of Military Appeals, the plea, while implicitly admitted in theory, failed on the facts. Schultz, a US marine, was a member of a four-man patrol commonly referred to as a hunter-killer team designed to ambush and kill Viet Cong. He killed an innocent Vietnamese farmer in a Vietnamese village. Before the Appellate Court he pleaded that he believed that the individual killed was a member of the Viet Cong, or that he was in communication with the enemy and was signalling the enemy and attempting to lead the appellant and his patrol into an ambush; he claimed that he did 'what he was instructed to do and what he felt he had to do to survive'. The court rejected the defence, noting that '[t]he testimony of the accused shows his actions to be intentional. Thus removed is the possibility that death of the victim resulted from accident or misadventure [...] Moreover, self-defence is unavailable for it is a plea of necessity not available, normally speaking, to one who is an aggressor'.[3]

The ICCSt. upholds a broader definition of self-defence. Article 31(c) provides that a person shall not be criminally responsible if, at the time of that person's conduct,

[t]he person acts reasonably to defend himself or herself or another person or, in the case of war crimes, property which is essential for the survival of the person or another person or property which is essential for accomplishing a military mission, against an imminent and unlawful use of force in a manner proportionate to the degree of danger to the person or the other person

---

[2] Decision of 1 February 1946, in *Law Reports of Trials of War Criminals*, vol. III, at 76–9).
[3] Decision of 7 March 1969, in 18 USCMA 133; 1969 CMA LEXIS 563; 39 CMR 133.

or property protected. The fact that the person was involved in a defensive operation conducted by forces shall not in itself constitute a ground for excluding criminal responsibility under this subparagraph.

It has been argued that the right to invoke self-defence in a war crime case when defending 'property which is essential for the survival of the person or another person or property which is essential for accomplishing a military mission' goes beyond what is established under customary law.

As for other types of justifications – lawful reprisals and lawful punishments under international humanitarian law – they are more related to the applicable law of armed conflicts than to actual procedural defences and are more properly assessed when analysing the elements of each crime.

QUESTIONS

1. Why is self-defence considered a justification and not an excuse? What consequences does this classification have on accomplices and other persons participating in the conduct?

2. What would be the reasons for the ICCSt. to take a broader approach in relation to self-defence? What kind of balancing exercise is involved?

FURTHER READING

Cassese, *International Criminal Law*, 259–62.

G.P. Fletcher, *A Crime of Self-Defence* (Chicago: University of Chicago Press, 1988).

J.D. Ohlin, 'Self-Defence', in *Oxford Companion*, 506–8.

2

EXCUSES

(A) SUPERIOR ORDERS

The foundation of 'superior orders' as an excuse lies in the general assumption that soldiers have a duty to obey orders received from their superiors. In general, in keeping with the principle of responsible command informing armed groups (even in non-international armed conflicts, see Article 1(1) of Additional Protocol II), military subordinates must abide by superior orders. This assumption is the basic condition not only of the efficiency of armed forces, but also of the orderly and responsible discharge of their duties. It is therefore understandable that subordinates – who must presume the lawfulness of the orders they receive – at least try to shield themselves from responsibility otherwise attributable to them based on the obedience they are trained and required to give to superiors.

A dilemma is, however, posed when the order from a superior is unlawful: should the subordinate in such circumstances choose not to abide by the (unlawful) superior order – risking disciplinary and, if necessary, criminal consequences due to his refusal – or is he instead excused from having followed the unlawful order? Case law related to war crimes and other international crimes over the past decades has addressed various aspects of this problem.

One caveat is necessary when reading the cases dealing with superior orders: while often in practice intertwined with the issue of duress, and even of mistake of fact and law, the doctrine of 'superior orders' should be kept conceptually distinct from other excuses that can be pleaded in international criminal proceedings. The defence does not concern coercion of any kind directed to the subordinate – other than the aforementioned presumptions and duties engrained in every military structure – but is premised on the balancing of different duties when a soldier is faced with an illegal order.

Cases

Germany, Llandovery Castle *case* (Dithmar and Boldt case), *Supreme Court (Reichsgericht) at Leipzig, Judgment of 16 July 1921*

The *Llandovery Castle* was a British hospital ship sunk by a German submarine in the Atlantic Ocean on 27 June 1918. Patzig, commander of the German submarine U-86, while aware of the protected status of the ship, suspected that it carried ammunition and US military personnel and ordered it sunk. Between three and five lifeboats with survivors were launched from the ship. The Germans proceeded to capture the ship's captain and two other officers from the lifeboats and subjected them to interrogation about the nature of the cargo. No proof of improper use of the ship was found. In any event, commander Patzig ordered Lieutenants Dithmar and Boldt, first and second officers of the watch on the submarine, to fire against the lifeboats. On 29 June, another British ship picked up one of the lifeboats with survivors, but all other lifeboats had disappeared or were empty. Since Patzig had not been brought to trial (probably he had escaped) nor was he tried in absentia, Dithmar and Boldt were indicted for their involvement in the firing against the lifeboats which had resulted in the death of several crew members of the *Llandovery Castle*. The court found that the two could at most be considered accessories to multiple homicides, since there was no proof of their agreement with the commander's intentions. Both accused, however, argued that they had acted on superior orders and sought to be excused on the basis of Article 47 of the German Penal Code providing for such defence.

Patzig's order does not free the accused from guilt. It is true that according to Article 47 of the Military Penal Code, if the execution of an order in the ordinary course of duty involves a punishable violation of the law, the superior officer issuing such an order is the only [person] responsible. According to sub-article 2, however, the subordinate obeying such an order is punishable, if it was known to him that the order of the superior involved the infringement of civil or military law. This applies in the case of the defendant. It is certainly to be considered in favour of the military subordinates that they were under no obligation to question the order by their superior officer, and they can be confident of its legality. But no such confidence can be held to exist, if such an order is universally known to everybody, including also the accused, to be without any doubt whatsoever in breach of the law. This happens only in rare and exceptional circumstances. But this case was precisely one of them, since [...] it was perfectly clear to the accused that killing defenceless persons in the lifeboats could be nothing else than a violation of the law. As professional naval officers they were well aware, as naval expert Saalwachter strikingly stated, that it is unlawful to kill defenceless persons. They well knew that this was the case here. They quickly found out the facts by questioning the occupants of the boats when these were halted. From Patzig's order they could have only reached the conclusion that he intended to use his subordinates to carry out a breach of the law. They should, therefore, have refused to obey. As they did not do so, they must be punished.

The witnesses [a former Vice-Admiral and a legal adviser to the Navy] admitted frankly that in the German fleet, the impression prevailed that a naval officer, who in the course of a fight exceeded the boundaries of the law, was not thereby punishable, although he might be called to answer for his actions to his superiors. The statements of these two witnesses relate, however, to the point of view held by the fleet's higher command at the time. They did not state that the accused shared this opinion. It seems that neither of the witnesses discussed these concepts in relation to the incidents in question. These opinions are based on a misunderstanding of the law and are irrelevant here. They are of no use to the accused, because the sinking of the lifeboats was not done in the course of a fight, during an attack on the enemy or in defence [...]

The accused were eventually sentenced to four years' imprisonment and dismissal from service.

The US Military Tribunal in the *Einsatzgruppen* case (*US v. Ohlendorf et al.*) also found that if a subordinate 'accepts a criminal order and executes it with a malice of his own, he may not plead superior orders' – not even in mitigation (4 TMWC, at 471). In this case, the *mens rea* of the subordinate fully justifies holding him responsible.

A different matter is how to prove the order of the superior, especially when there is conflicting evidence as to whether an order had been given, as well as the apparent illegality of the order.

....

US Military Commission, Csihas et al., *Report of the Judge Advocate*, September 1946

In early March 1945, three US air force officers and five enlisted men parachuted near the town of Sur (Hungary) and were captured by a unit of Hungarian SS (so-called 'SS-Kampfgruppe Ney'). While the unit, under the command of Karoly Ney, handed over the three officers to the Germans, they executed the remaining downed men. In 1946, a US Military Commission tried six members of this SS unit in Salzburg (Austria) for the murder of the five prisoners of war. Four of them (Karoly Ney, Ferenc Karolyi, Miklos Bakos and Istvan Csihas) were sentenced to death by the Commission, while the remaining two (Istvan Eros and Istvan Langyel) were sentenced to life imprisonment. Review proceedings were carried out in September 1946.

[...] The reason given for the failure to deliver all the prisoners was that the car ordered for the purpose proved to be a passenger car rather than a truck and was too small. [Ferenc] Karolyi inquired of Captain Grund, Fourth Corps Headquarters, as to the disposition of the five enlisted men remaining at Sur and it was ordered that they be delivered to either the Corps Headquarters at Inota or the Fourth Wehrmacht Cavalry Brigade at Aka [...] Subsequently in the discussion Captain Grund made the remark to Karolyi that they must have too much gasoline at the unit [and] Karolyi got the impression that the flyers' execution was desirable to the SS Headquarters, but no direct order was given by that headquarters to Karolyi for their execution [...] Karolyi and Lieutenant Schmidt returned to their headquarters and Karolyi went into the room occupied by Ney, who at the time was ill and had a high fever, and reported the delivery of the three officers to the higher headquarters. He told Ney of the order for the disposition of the five enlisted men [...] He then told Ney that he had gotten the impression the officers were to be executed and it was the desire of the Corps Headquarters that the enlisted men actually be executed instead of taken to Aka [...] Either Karolyi or Ney gave Bakos [commanding officer of the troops of the Gendarmerie] an order to have the five enlisted men taken to the Fourth Cavalry Brigade at Aka the next morning by escort [...]

According to Bakos, shortly after he returned to his quarters from Ney's room he received a telephone call from a Captain Peter, Ney's adjutant, to return to the castle to receive important orders [...] Thereupon Bakos returned to the castle to Captain Peter's office where, in the presence of Lieutenant Schmidt, Captain Peter told Bakos that he had received a telephone call from Corps Headquarters inquiring what was being done about the American flyers. Peter had replied in the conversation with Corps that Major Ney had ordered the prisoners taken to Aka, at which Corps Headquarters was upset and said that they had sent orders through Lieutenant Schmidt that were very easy to understand and if Ney was unwilling or unable to execute these orders they would take the necessary steps to carry the orders through. The order was "The American enlisted men are meant not to be brought to Aka and handed over to the command post in Aka but they were to be executed by shooting", before the next noon.

Bakos replied to Peter upon receipt of the new order that he had shortly before received contrary orders from Karolyi. Peters replied that the last order had arrived shortly before and had to be executed. Lieutenant Schmidt interrupted to say that he had already brought such orders with him and that the Corps Headquarters does not consider the airmen as prisoners of war. [...] The next morning detailed orders for the execution were given by Bakos to Csihas [second Lieutenant] and he was told to summon four men for the 'escort' [including Eros and Langyel].

No receipt for the prisoners of war was brought to Ney nor did he ask for one [. . .] Between three days and a week after the incident, rumors reached Ney that the prisoners had not reached their destination as he had ordered; yet, he did not investigate those rumors. [. . .]

The defence of 'superior orders' was squarely presented to the commission in the cases of four of the accused, and it therefore calls for special consideration. It was a rule in both American and English courts from the earliest cases until 1914 that obedience to a superior order was not a defence in a prosecution for a criminal act. In 1914, however, both the United States and England adopted a rule of absolute non-liability, and this rule was originally published in FM [Basic Field Manual, Rules of Land Warfare] 27–10, paragraph 347. This rule was not in accordance with pre-existing judicial decisions, so on 15 November 1944 the non-liability clause was struck out and the following was substituted:

'Individuals and organizations who violate the accepted laws and customs of war may be punished therefor. However, the fact that the acts complained of were done pursuant to order of a superior or government sanction may be taken into consideration in determining culpability, either by way of defence or in mitigation of punishment. The person giving such orders may also be punished.' (FM27–10, par 345.1)

That the rule as thus stated is based on sound logic is recognized by most writers on the subject [. . .]

It is interesting to note that even the German military Penal Code, which was in full force and effect at the time of this offence, likewise incorporates this principle. Section IV, paragraph 47, Deutsches Militarstrafgesetzbuch, states as follows:

'(1) If in the execution of an order relating to service matters a penal law is violated, the commanding officer is solely responsible. Nevertheless, the subordinate obeying the order is subject to penalty as accomplice: (1) if he transgressed the order given, or (2) if he knew that the order of the commanding officer concerned an action the purpose of which was to commit a general or military crime or misdemeanor. (2) If the guilt of the subordinate is minor, his punishment may be suspended.'

This principle was followed by a German court in Leipzig after World War I in the *LLandovery Castle* case [. . .] It must be admitted, however, that to deprive an officer or a soldier completely of the defence of superior orders may place him 'between the devil and the deep blue sea.' Under order[s] issued by Adolph Hitler [*sic*], any officer or soldier who refused to obey an order was to be summarily shot to death by any officer or solider who had knowledge of such refusal. In discussing the difficult position of a subordinate officer or solider, Dr. Sheldon Glueck, Professor of Criminal Law and Criminology at Harvard University, in his recent book, 'War Crimes, Their Prosecution and Punishment' (September 1944), states: 'Yet in time of hostilities, a soldier – certainly a German or Japanese officer or soldier – may hesitate to disobey even the most glaringly unlawful order. Suppose, for example, his captain orders him to commit wholesale homicide by machine-gunning unoffending enemy civilians, old men, women and children or unarmed and surrendered troops, as many a German and Japanese soldier has been ordered to do. This is so patently unlawful that either he actually knows it to be or, as a reasonable man, he ought to be held to know such acts to be prohibited not only by international law but by the criminal law of all civilized peoples. He is then, however, between the Charybdis of defying an order patently and shockingly unlawful and being disciplined (perhaps shot on the spot) and the Scylla of obeying it and being later charged with murder.' [. . .]

From the foregoing it may be concluded that members of military organizations are bound to obey lawful orders only, but that a plea of superior orders may be taken into consideration in determining culpability, either by way of defence or in mitigation of punishment, dependent on the facts in each particular case. Before the plea is taken into consideration, the facts should show at least the following: (1) That an actual order was given by a superior, (2) that it was not obviously illegal and contrary to the principles of humanity, or if obviously illegal,

(3) that the subordinate was bound to obedience under penalty of immediate and severe punishment. [. . .]

Sufficiency of Evidence

[. . .] The participation of Bakos in the execution has been established beyond doubt. The sole question raised by his testimony and the argument of his special counsel [. . .] is the defence of superior orders. There is evidence to support a conclusion that the order of the Corps Headquarters described by Bakos was never given. The issue raised by Bakos was simple. He testified that he had received no order for the execution from Ney or Karolyi (his immediate commanding officer), but that the order was a Corps order transmitted to him by Peter or from Corps to Schmidt to Peter to Bakos. Neither Peter nor Schmidt are available as witnesses. [. . .] A finding that there was no superior order from Corps Headquarters changing the original order of Major Ney is well supported.

Assuming without conceding that Bakos believed that Corps Headquarters had expressed a desire to have the flyers shot, yet by his own testimony he never received orders to that effect directly from his commanding officer or from an officer of the superior headquarters, the Corps. Peter and Schmidt were both officers serving with the Group. [. . .] Neither of them had any command responsibility or authority to issue orders [. . .] Bakos sought to overcome this difficulty by testifying to his repeated attempts to speak to his superior officers, Ney and Karolyi, but his failure to speak to them and receive clear, definite orders, under the circumstances of this case vitiates the argument that in ordering the executions he was simply obeying the orders of a superior.

Assuming that the order was originally given as claimed by Bakos, however [. . .] [t]here is no doubt that the order, if given, was known to him to be illegal. He testified that he questioned it repeatedly [. . .]

The defence was therefore dismissed on the facts for all the accused, because it was not proven that the order in question had been given and that, in any event, such an order should not have been implemented. Ney's and Karolyi's death sentences were commuted to life imprisonment; Eros and Lengyel were sentenced to life imprisonment; Bakos and Csihas were executed.

The discussion in the *LLandovery* Castle case – as well as in other cases – relies on three principles: (i) as a general rule, a subordinate committing a criminal act following an order by a superior should not be criminally responsible; (ii) however, the general rule on non-responsibility does not apply when the subordinate knew that the order was unlawful and nonetheless acted upon the order; (iii) to prove knowledge of the unlawful nature of the order, the judges may use the test of 'manifest illegality', which would therefore exclude a plea of superior orders. This does not amount to saying that superior orders may not be a valid defence whenever the orders are manifestly unlawful. The issue appears to turn on the *knowledge* by the accused of the unlawful nature of the order. What becomes pivotal for the prosecuting authorities in this type of case is, therefore, how to prove such knowledge. At times courts have assessed the circumstances in relation to superior orders with surprising deference to the defendant's claims.

Italy, **Kappler et al.,** *Military Tribunal, Judgment No. 631 of 20 July 1948*

Herbert Kappler was an SS officer and head of the German Security Services in Rome (Italy) during 1944. After the war he and four other officers were charged with the murder of 335 Italian civilians at the Ardeatine caves on 24 March 1944. The killing of

320 civilians had been ordered by Adolf Hitler himself – through the German Military Commander in Rome, Mältzer – as a reprisal for the killing, a day earlier, of 32 German soldiers, all members of an SS unit, by Italian partisans in Via Rasella (Rome). Ten civilians were to be executed for each German SS; hence 320 persons were to be killed. Kappler added ten Italian Jews due to the subsequent death of one more German soldier wounded in the same incident. Five more persons were apparently killed either by mistake or because, having being brought by mistake to the execution site, had witnessed the massacre and could not be freed. Kappler raised the defence of superior orders.

[T]he Chamber finds that although the order to kill ten Italians per each German killed in Via Rasella [...] was unlawful – since the executions constituted murders for the reasons discussed above –, Kappler may not be said in all certainty to have considered it so. The modalities in which the executions were carried out, cruel towards the victims [...], do constitute an objective element of proof that the order was unlawful. But it cannot be excluded that these modalities were linked to a kind of camaraderie towards the killed Germans, which led to cruelties because of the hatred against other Italians, compatriots [of the ones who carried out the action in Via Rasella], rather than being based on the intent to implement an unlawful order.

This consideration, the mental habit of prompt obedience that the accused had developed working in an organization based on very strict discipline, the fact that orders with the same gist had been previously executed in the various areas of military operation, the fact that an order from the Head of State and Supreme Commander of the armed forces, due to the great moral force inherent in it, cannot but diminish, especially in a military official, that freedom of judgment necessary for an accurate appraisal, all these elements lead this Chamber to find that it may not be held with certainty that Kappler was aware and willed to obey an unlawful order.

The execution of the ten Jews, ordered by him, as discussed above, following the death of another German soldier and without having received any order is a different matter. For this conduct, he bears full responsibility in relation to both the *actus reus* and the *mens rea*.

Kappler was sentenced to life imprisonment for the killing of these ten individuals and because of his negligence leading to the execution of the five additional victims.

In another case relating to World War II and concerning a Dutch resistance member who had executed Dutch collaborators, a Dutch Court Martial[1] held the following:

Considering in respect of the accused's criminal liability, that the accused, as a member of the *Binnenlandse Strijdkrachten* [i.e., the resistance underground armed forces], owed a duty of obedience to his commanding officer, that, given the circumstances in which the order was given, the accused was entitled to assume in good faith that his commanding officer was authorized to give that order for the liquidation of the prisoners, and that this order was within the scope of his subordination, [...] the accused is therefore not criminally liable.

The language of the IMT Charter and Control Council Law No. 10 – providing that '[t]he fact that any person acted pursuant to the order of his Government or of a superior does not free him from responsibility for a crime, but may be considered in mitigation' – also does not squarely address the issue of whether the unlawful nature of the order prevents an accused from raising the defence per se. Similarly, according to the ICTYSt. (Art. 7(4))

---

[1] *E. Van E.*, 2 January 1951, (1951) 246 *NederJ.*

and the ICTRSt. (Art. 6(4)), 'the fact that an accused person acted pursuant to an order of a Government or of a superior shall not relieve him of criminal responsibility, but may be considered in mitigation of punishment if the International Tribunal determines that justice so requires.' In all such cases, while the order as such may not excuse, it is clearly left open to consider the *mens rea* of the accused.

When, however, the question is not one of an order coupled with compulsion (duress), or of mistake of law or fact on the part of the accused, the issue often actually comes down to an assessment of whether the order was manifestly unlawful.

Israel, Jamal Abd El-Kader Mahmud et al. *v.* The Military Advocate General et al. (*Meir* case), *Supreme Court, Judgment of 27 December 1989*

In January 1988, during the so-called 'first intifada', various soldiers under Colonel Yehuda Meir's direct command physically kidnapped, brought to a remote location, blindfolded, and assaulted 20 young men in Palestinian occupied territories. Following a complaint by the ICRC and a military investigation, the Military Advocate General initiated internal proceedings which led to Meir's discharge and forced retirement. The petitioners, including four victims of the assault, claimed that Meir should have been tried before a military tribunal for injuries. The case heard before the Israeli Supreme Court sheds some light on how to understand 'unlawful' orders negating individual criminal responsibility.

[...] [T]he JAG [Judge Advocate General] notes that he had originally thought that, in view of his grave and intolerable behaviour, it would be just and proper to bring [Meir] to trial before a special military tribunal and adds: 'My decision...to refrain from [a military trial of Meir], notwithstanding the severity of his action, results from the following rationales:

a. The events took place on 19 and 22 January 1988, that is at the start of the uprising and only a few days after a decision had been made to use force against violators of public order and insurgents, with a view to calming the situation in the territories.

b. The obscurity and lack of clarity which prevailed at the time, in the field, with regard to the instructions concerning the procedures for the use of force, whether as a result of various declarations which had been made to the press or due to the lack of unequivocal instructions in the chain of command in relation to what was allowed and forbidden in all matters as far as the use of force was concerned [...]

c. The decision by the Chief of Main Staff that, in view of his conduct in the incident in question, Col. Yehuda Meir's position [...] would be terminated and that he would not be transferred to any other position, and would actually terminate his active service in the Israel Defence Forces (IDF) [...]

Let us examine these rationales one by one. [First, the Court found that the time elapsed and the different circumstances prevailing later on in the occupied territories did not warrant choosing disciplinary proceedings over criminal ones]. [...]

We must begin with the assumption that the initial period of the uprising was especially difficult for both officers and enlisted men, who did not know how to cope with it. However, it is impossible to accept the reason based on the 'obscurity and lack of clarity which prevailed at the time in the field, in relation to the instructions on how to use force'. May we speak of lack of clarity and obscurity in a case where an instruction was given to remove people from their homes, bind and gag them, and beat them with clubs so as to break their arms and legs? What obscurity could possibly exist with regard to an a priori illegal order of this type – one which, as the JAG himself stated, was 'marked, as it were, by a "black flag" ', and which it was compulsory to disobey?

Conduct of this kind is an outrage to any civilized person, and no obscurity or lack of clarity can shield them, certainly not when such an order is given by a senior officer, who should have been aware that the ethical standards of the IDF obviously prohibit such behavior. This, too, was stated in a report by the JAG stating that enlisted men had difficulty carrying out the order; one of the officers 'expressed his opinion in the matter before Lt. Col. Yehuda Meir that, in his mind, the matter was unethical... asked the enlisted men not to lose their humanity in enforcing the order, "which had been transmitted from above"'.

The court further addressed the third reason advanced by the JAG, that is that the dismissal of Meir from the IDF was sufficient to address Meir's conduct:

[T]his retirement was necessary, not as a punishment for the criminal act which [Meir] committed, but on another level – because the IDF desire to remain clean, and anyone committing this type of actions does not belong in the IDF, but should be immediately dismissed from service. Nonetheless, [Meir] still owes a duty to society and to the rule of law in respect of the actual criminal conduct imputed to him.

The court instructed the Military Advocate General to prosecute Meir before a military court. In his separate opinion, Justice Levin added that 'it was the responsibility of [Meir] as a senior and responsible officer – his responsibility and not that of his subordinates – to subject the order to the text of criticism and to comment to that effect to his superiors, and not to land that order on his subordinates... It is obvious to me that, the higher the rank of the commanding officer and the more comprehensive and more decisive his authority, the greater the responsibility incumbent upon him to examine and determine the justification and legality of the order'.

COMMENTARY

The ICCSt. has surprisingly split war crimes, for which a plea of superior orders is possible, from crimes against humanity and genocide, which are considered per se 'manifestly unlawful' – and therefore never excused if carried out in execution of orders. On the other hand, the ICCSt. expands the availability of the defence to civilians (as long as the subordinate is under a legal obligation to obey), thus signalling a clear departure from the *origins* of the doctrine in question, which was limited to military personnel. Article 33 reads:

1. The fact that a crime within the jurisdiction of the Court has been committed by a person pursuant to an order of a Government or of a superior, whether military or civilian, shall not relieve that person of criminal responsibility unless:

    (a) The person was under a legal obligation to obey orders of the Government or the superior in question;

    (b) The person did not know that the order was unlawful; and

    (c) The order was not manifestly unlawful.

2. For the purposes of this article, orders to commit genocide or crimes against humanity are manifestly unlawful.

QUESTIONS

1. Does a superior order (though unlawful) negate as such the *mens rea* of the subordinate? What considerations should be taken into account by a court dealing with this issue?

2. What type of legal obligation to obey a superior order would be necessary for a civilian to be able to invoke this defence? Would a contractual obligation suffice? An administrative regulation?

3. Aggression is not listed among the crimes that are 'manifestly unlawful' in Article 33 ICCSt. Could a plea of superior orders succeed in relation to this crime, when and if the ICC is able to exercise its jurisdiction over it? Or is the situation different because charges of aggression are usually limited to high-level accused?

FURTHER READING

P. Gaeta, 'The Defence of Superior Orders: the Statute of the International Criminal Court versus Customary International Law' (1999) 10 EJIL 172–91.

M. Minow, 'Living Up to the Rules: Holding Soldiers Responsible for Abusive Conduct and the Dilemma of the Superior Orders Defence' (2007) 52 *McGill L.J.* 1.

A. Zahar, 'Superior Orders', in *Oxford Companion*, 525–7.

(B) DURESS

Duress is an excuse that can be invoked when a person is compelled to commit a crime as a result of a serious threat to life or limb by another person. This is different from necessity, where the threat emanates *from objective circumstances* such as exigencies arising from natural forces like shipwreck after a storm.

As discussed above, a typical example of the plea of duress is when a subordinate is ordered to commit a crime *under threat* by a superior – in this case, separate from the defence of superior orders, the subordinate could argue that he should not be held criminally responsible because he could not be expected to resist the threat to his life or limb.

Despite the differences between duress and necessity, the basic requirements prescribed by international rules for each of these two defences are the same. Four strict conditions are required: (i) the act charged is done under an immediate threat of severe and irreparable harm to life or limb, (ii) there is no adequate means of averting such evil, (iii) the crime committed is not disproportionate to the evil threatened (as would, for example, occur in case of killing in order to avert unlawful appropriation or cruel treatment), and (iv) the situation leading to duress or necessity must not have been voluntarily brought about by the person coerced. The cases below serve to highlight various facets of how tribunals have interpreted and applied duress in the context of international crimes.

Cases

US Military Court Sitting in Nuremberg, US *v.* Ohlendorf et al. *(*Einsatzgruppen *case), Judgment of 10 April 1948*

The 24 defendants in this case were officers in the *Einsatzgruppen,* death squads within the Nazi SS, which followed the advance of the German Army in Eastern Europe kill- ing Jews, Roma, communists, disabled people and other targeted groups. This case was the single largest murder case in history, with the defendants convicted for more than 1 million murders. The defendants were charged with 'actively superintending, con- trolling, directing, and taking an active part' in the massacres. As the Tribunal put it '[o]ne cannot grasp the full cumulative terror of murder one million times repeated. It is only when this grotesque total is broken down into units capable of mental assimil- ation that one can understand the monstrousness of the things we are in this trial con- templating' (p. 413).

Among the various defences raised by the accused was duress.

One either justifies the Fuehrer Order or one does not. One supports the killing of the Jews or denounces it. If the massacres are admitted to be unsupportable and if the defendants assert that their participation was the result of physical and moral duress, the issue is clear and it becomes only a question of determining how effective and oppressive was the force exerted to compel the reluctant killer. If, however, the defendants claim that the killing of the Jews was justified, but this claim does not commend itself to human reason and does not meet the requirements of law, then it is inevitable that the defendants committed a crime. [. . .] [p. 468]

[. . .] [I]t is stated that in military law even if the subordinate realizes that the act he is called upon to perform is a crime, he may not refuse its execution without incurring serious conse- quences, and that this, therefore, constitutes duress. Let it be said at once that there is no law which requires that an innocent man must forfeit his life or suffer serious harm in order to avoid committing a crime which he condemns. The threat, however, must be imminent, real, and inevitable. No court will punish a man who, with a loaded pistol at his head, is compelled to pull a lethal lever. Nor need the peril be that imminent in order to escape punishment. But were any of the defendants coerced into killing Jews under the threat of being killed them- selves if they failed in their homicidal mission? The test to be applied is whether the subor- dinate acted under coercion or whether he himself approved of the principle involved in the order. If the second proposition be true, the plea of superior orders fails. The doer may not plead innocence to a criminal act ordered by his superior if he is in accord with the principle and intent of the superior. When the will of the doer merges with the will of the superior in the execution of the illegal act, the doer may not plead duress under superior orders.

If the mental and moral capacities of the superior and subordinate are pooled in the plan- ning and execution of an illegal act, the subordinate may not subsequently protest that he was forced into the performance of an illegal undertaking.

Superior means superior in capacity and power to force a certain act. It does not mean superiority only in rank. It could easily happen in an illegal enterprise that the captain guides the major, in which case the captain could not be heard to plead superior orders in defense of his crime.

If the cognizance of the doer has been such, prior to the receipt of the illegal order, that the order is obviously but one further logical step in the development of a program which he knew to be illegal in its very inception, he may not excuse himself from responsibility for an illegal act which could have been foreseen by the application of the simple law of cause and effect. From 1920, when the Nazi Party program with its anti-Semitic policy was published, until 1941 when the liquidation order went into effect, the ever-mounting severity of Jewish persecution was evident to all within the Party and especially to those charged with its execution. One who participated in that program which began with Jewish disenfranchisement and depatriation and led, step by step, to deprivation of property and liberty, followed with beatings, whippings, and measures aimed at starvation, may not plead surprise when he learns that what has been done sporadically; namely, murder, now is officially declared policy. On 30 January 1939, Hitler publicly declared in a speech to the Reichstag that if war should come it would mean "the obliteration of the Jewish race in Europe".

One who embarks on a criminal enterprise of obvious magnitude is expected to anticipate what the enterprise will logically lead to. In order successfully to plead the defense of superior orders the opposition of the doer must be constant. It is not enough that he mentally rebel at the time the order is received. If at any time after receiving the order he acquiesces in its illegal character, the defense of superior orders is closed to him.

Many of the defendants testified that they were shocked with the order when they first heard it. This assertion is, of course, contradicted by the other assertion made with equal insistence, and already disposed of, that the Fuehrer Order was legal because the ordered executions were needed for the defense of the Fatherland. But if they were shocked by the order, what did they do to oppose it? Many said categorically that there was nothing to do. It would be enough, in order to escape legal and moral stigmatization to show the order was parried every time there was a chance to do so. The evidence indicates that there was no will or desire to depreciate its fullest intent. When the defendant Braune testified that he inwardly opposed the Fuehrer Order, he was asked as to whether, only as a matter of salving his conscience in the multiplicitous executions he conducted, he ever released one victim. The interrogation follows:

"Q. But you did not in compliance with that order attempt to salve your conscience by releasing one single individual human creature of the Jewish race, man, woman, or child?

"A. I have already said that I did not search for children. I can only say the truth. There were no exceptions, and I did not see any possibility."

One may accuse the Nazi military hierarchy of cruelty, even sadism of one will. But it may not be lightly charged with inefficiency. If any of these Kommando leaders had stated that they were constitutionally unable to perform this cold-blooded slaughter of human beings, it is not unreasonable to assume that they would have been assigned to other duties, not out of sympathy or for humanitarian reasons, but for efficiency's sake alone. In fact Ohlendorf himself declared on this very subject –

"In two and a half years I had sufficient occasion to see how many of my Gruppe [group] did not agree to this order in their inner opinion. Thus, I forbade the participation in these executions on the part of some of these men, and I sent some back to Germany."

Ohlendorf himself could have got out of his execution assignment by refusing cooperation with the army. He testified that the Chief of Staff in the field said to him that if he, Ohlendorf, did not cooperate, he would ask for his dismissal in Berlin.

The witness Hartel testified that Thomas, Chief of Einsatzgruppe B, declared that all those who could not reconcile their conscience to the Fuehrer Order, that is, people who were too soft, as he said, would be sent back to Germany or assigned to other tasks, and that, in fact, he did send a number of people including commanders back to the Reich.

This might not have been true in all Einsatzgruppen, as the witness pointed out, but it is not enough for a defendant to say, as did Braune and Klingelhoefer, that it was pointless to ask to be released, and, therefore, did not even try. Exculpation is not so easy as that. No one can shrug off so appalling a moral responsibility with the statement that there was no point in trying. The failure to attempt disengagement from so catastrophic an assignment might well spell the conclusion that the defendant involved had no deep-seated desire to be released. He may have thought that the work was unpleasant but did it nonetheless. Even a professional murderer may not relish killing his victim, but he does it with no misgivings. A defendant's willingness may have been predicated on the premise that he personally opposed Jews or that he wished to stand well in the eyes of his comrades, or by doing the job well he might earn rapid promotion. The motive is unimportant if he killed willingly.

The witness Hartel also related how one day as he and Blobel were driving through the country, Blobel pointed out to him a long grave and said, "Here my Jews are buried." One can only conclude that Blobel was proud of what he had done. "Here my Jews are buried." Just as one might speak of the game he had bagged in a jungle.

Despite the sustained assertion on the part of the defendants that they were straight-jacketed in their obedience to superior orders, the majority of them have, with testimony and affidavits, demonstrated how on numerous occasions they opposed decrees and orders handed down by their superiors. In an effort to show that they were not really Nazis at heart, defendant after defendant related his dramatic clashes with his superiors. If one concentrated only on this latter phase of the defense, one would conclude that these defendants were all ardent rebels against National Socialism and valiantly fought against the inhuman proposals put to them. Thus, one affiant says of the defendant Willy Seibert that he "was strongly opposed to the measures taken by the Party and the government".

Of Steimle an affiant said, "Many a time he opposed the Party agencies and so-called superior leaders." Another affidavit not only states that Steimle opposed violence but that in his zeal for justice he shrewdly joined the SD in order to be able "to criticize the shortcomings in the Party". Again it was stated that "repeatedly his sense of justice led him to oppose excesses, corruptions, and symptoms of depravity by Party officers."

Of Braune an affiant states, "over and over again Dr. Braune criticized severely our policy in the occupied territories (especially in the East, Ukraine, and Baltic States)". During the time he served in Norway, Braune was a flaming sword of opposition to tyranny and injustice in his own camp. He bitterly opposed the Reich Commissioner Terboven, cancelled his orders, condemned large-scale operations, released hostages, and freed the Norwegian State Minister Gerhardsen. One affidavit said that in these actions "Braune nearly always went beyond his authority." And yet in spite of this open rebellion Braune was not shot or even disciplined. Why is it that in Norway he acted so differently from the manner in which he performed in Russia? Was he more the humanitarian in Norway? The answer is not difficult to find. One of the affiants very specifically states –

"Right from the beginning of our conferences, Braune opposed the large-scale operations which Terboven and Fehlis continually carried out. He did not expect the slightest success from such measures, and saw in them only the danger of antagonizing the Norwegian population more and more against German policy and the danger of increasing their spirit of resistance."

Thus, the defendants could and did oppose orders when they did not agree with them. But when they ideologically espoused an order such as the Fuehrer Order they had no interest in opposing it. [pp. 480–3]

While in some cases duress might not be proven on the facts, the matter might become even more complicated when an accused is able to show that he did act under a threat of the type discussed above: how do international judges balance, for instance, such a danger to the life of one person with conduct affecting dozens of potential victims?

ICTY, **Prosecutor *v.* Erdemović,** *Appeals Chamber, Judgment of 7 October 1997*

The defendant, Dražen Erdemović, was a member of the Bosnian Serb Army who had participated in the execution of approximately 1,200 unarmed Muslim men in Srebrenica during the summer of 1995. The defendant admitted to personally killing about 70 men and pleaded guilty to crimes against humanity. He added, however, that he had acted under duress. Before the Trial Chamber and then the Appeals Chamber (judgment of 7 October 1997), the question arose as to whether the guilty plea was ambiguous (one cannot plead guilty if in fact the crime is justified by a defence and as a consequence no criminal responsibility arises). If the defence of duress was to be upheld, then the guilty plea must be regarded as ambiguous. The Chamber had therefore to determine whether duress affords a complete defence to the killing of innocent persons. For the reasons set out in the Joint Separate Opinion of Judge McDonald and Judge Vohrah and in the Separate and Dissenting Opinion of Judge Li, the majority of the Appeals Chamber found that duress did not afford a complete defence to a soldier charged with a crime against humanity or a war crime involving the killing of innocent human beings. Judges Stephen and Cassese took a different view in their Dissenting Opinions.

Judges McDonald and Vohrah:

[. . .] 47. A number of war crimes cases have been brought to our attention as supporting the position that duress is a complete defence to the killing of innocent persons in international law: the *Llandovery Castle case* before the German Supreme Court at Leipzig; *Mueller et al.* before the Belgium Military Court of Brussels and the Belgium Court of Cassation; the *Eichmann* case before the Supreme Court of Israel; the *Papon* case before the French Court of Cassation; *Retzlaff et al.* before the Soviet Military Tribunal in Kharkov; *Sablic et al.* before the Military Court of Belgrade; the cases *Bernadi and Randazzo, Srà et. al* and *Masetti* before the Italian Courts of Assize and the Court of Cassation; the German cases *S. and K.* before the Landesgericht of Ravensburg; the *Warsaw ghetto* case before the Court of Assize attached to the District Court of Dortmund; and *Wetzling et al.* before the Court of Assize of Arnsberg.

(a) Questionable relevance and authority of a number of these cases

48. The cases set out in paragraph 62 touch upon the issue of duress in varying degrees. In our view, however, these cases are insufficient to support the finding of a customary rule providing for the availability of the defence of duress to the killing of innocent persons. We would note that a number of the cases are of questionable relevance and authority. Firstly, in the *Papon* case, the accused was not charged with murder as a principal in the first degree but merely as an accomplice in the extermination of Jews during the World War Two by his actions as a police officer who rounded up and deported French Jews to Germany. Secondly, in the *Retzlaff* and *Sablic* cases, the defence of duress did not succeed and there was no clear statement by the courts as to the reason for this failure. Thirdly, the decision in the *S. and K.* case was in fact quashed by the superior court in the French Zone for contravening Control Council Law No.10 and thus is of doubtful authority. Finally, the accused in the *Warsaw ghetto* case were held merely to be accomplices in murder and thus the application of duress in that case is only authoritative in respect of complicity to murder and not murder in the first degree.

(b) No consistent and uniform state practice underpinned by *opinio juris*

49. Although some of the above mentioned cases may clearly represent the positions of national jurisdictions regarding the availability of duress as a complete defence to the killing of

innocent persons, neither they nor the principles on this issue found in decisions of the post-World War Two military tribunals are, in our view, entitled to be given the status of customary international law. For a rule to pass into customary international law, the International Court of Justice has authoritatively restated in the *North Sea Continental Shelf* cases that there must exist extensive and uniform state practice underpinned by *opinio juris sive necessitatis*. To the extent that the domestic decisions and national laws of States relating to the issue of duress as a defence to murder may be regarded as state practice, it is quite plain that this practice is not at all consistent. The defence in its Notice of Appeal surveys the criminal codes and legislation of 14 civil law jurisdictions in which necessity or duress is prescribed as a general exculpatory principle applying to all crimes. The surveyed jurisdictions comprise those of Austria, Belgium, Brazil, Greece, Italy, Finland, the Netherlands, France, Germany, Peru, Spain, Switzerland, Sweden and the former Yugoslavia. Indeed, the war crimes decisions cited in the Separate Opinion of Judge Cassese are based upon the acceptance of duress as a general defence to all crimes in the criminal codes of France, Italy, Germany, the Netherlands and Belgium. In stark contrast to this acceptance of duress as a defence to the killing of innocents is the clear position of the various countries throughout the world applying the common law. These common law systems categorically reject duress as a defence to murder. The sole exception is the United States where a few states have accepted Section 2.09 of the United States Penal Code which currently provides that duress is a general defence to all crimes. Indeed, the rejection of duress as a defence to the killing of innocent human beings in the *Stalag Luft III* and the *Feurstein* cases, both before British military tribunals, and in the *Hölzer* case before a Canadian military tribunal, reflects in essence the common law approach.

50. Not only is State practice on the question as to whether duress is a defence to murder far from consistent, this practice of States is not, in our view, underpinned by *opinio juris*. Again to the extent that state practice on the question of duress as a defence to murder may be evidenced by the opinions on this question in decisions of national military tribunals and national laws, we find quite unacceptable any proposition that States adopt this practice because they "feel that they are conforming to what amounts to a legal obligation" at an international level.

51. To answer the Prosecution's submission regarding conspiracy during oral argument, we are of the view that conspiracy owes its status as customary international law to the fact that it was incorporated in the Nuremberg Charter which subsequently obtained recognition as custom and not to the fact that the objections of the civil law system were rejected in the process. Moreover, conspiracy was clearly established as a principle in the Nuremberg Charter. In the present case, duress, either as a general notion or specifically as it applies to murder, is not contained in any international treaty or instrument subsequently recognised to have passed into custom.

Having found that no rule of custom allowed duress as a defence, the two judges discussed the import of general principles of law to the issue – see the text *supra*, General Principles of Law, Part I(1)(C), at p. 36.

79. It was suggested during the hearing of 26 May 1997 that neither the English national cases nor the post-World War Two military tribunal decisions specifically addressed the situation in which the accused faced the choice between his own death for not obeying an order to kill or participating in a killing which was inevitably going to occur regardless of whether he participated in it or not. It has been argued that in such a situation where the fate of the victim was already sealed, duress should constitute a complete defence. This is because the accused is then not choosing that one innocent human being should die rather than another. In a situation where the victim or victims would have died in any event, such as in the present case where the victims were to be executed by firing squad, there would be no reason for the

accused to have sacrificed his life. The accused could not have saved the victim's life by giving his own and thus, according to this argument, it is unjust and illogical for the law to expect an accused to sacrifice his life in the knowledge that the victim/s will die anyway. The argument, it is said, is vindicated in the Italian case of *Masetti* which was decided by the Court of Assize in L'Aquila. The accused in that case raised duress in response to the charge of having organised the [execution] of two partisans upon being ordered to do so by the battalion commander. The Court of Assize acquitted the accused on the ground of duress and said:

> [...] the possible sacrifice [of their lives] by Masetti and his men [those who comprised the execution squad] would have been in any case to no avail and without any effect in that it would have had no impact whatsoever on the plight of the persons to be shot, who would have been executed anyway even without him [the accused].

We have given due consideration to this approach which, for convenience, we will label "the *Masetti* approach". For the reasons given below we would reject the *Masetti* approach.

80. The *Masetti* approach proceeds from the starting point of strict utilitarian logic based on the fact that if the victim will die anyway, the accused is not at all morally blameworthy for taking part in the execution; there is absolutely no reason why the accused should die as it would be unjust for the law to expect the accused to die for nothing. It should be immediately apparent that the assertion that the accused is not morally blameworthy where the victim would have died in any case depends entirely again upon a view of morality based on utilitarian logic. This does not, in our opinion, address the true rationale for our rejection of duress as a defence to the killing of innocent human beings. The approach we take does not involve a balancing of harms for and against killing but rests upon an application in the context of international humanitarian law of the rule that duress does not justify or excuse the killing of an innocent person. Our view is based upon a recognition that international humanitarian law should guide the conduct of combatants and their commanders. There must be legal limits as to the conduct of combatants and their commanders in armed conflict. In accordance with the spirit of international humanitarian law, we deny the availability of duress as a complete defence to combatants who have killed innocent persons. In so doing, we give notice in no uncertain terms that those who kill innocent persons will not be able to take advantage of duress as a defence and thus get away with impunity for their criminal acts in the taking of innocent lives.

(a) Proportionality?

81. The notion of proportionality is raised with great frequency in the limited jurisprudence on duress. Indeed, a central issue regarding the question of duress in the *Masetti* decision was whether the proportionality requirement in Article 54 of the Italian Penal Code was satisfied where innocent lives were taken. By the *Masetti* approach, the killing of the victims by the accused is apparently proportional to the fate faced by the accused if the victims were going to die anyway. Proportionality is merely another way of referring to the utilitarian approach of weighing the balance of harms and adds nothing to the debate when it comes to human lives having to be weighed and when the law must determine, because a certain legal consequence will follow, that one life or a set of lives is more valuable than another. The Prosecution draws attention to the great difficulty in judging proportionality when it is human lives which must be weighed in the balance:

> [O]ne immediately sees even from a philosophical point of view the immensely difficult balancing which a court would have to engage in [in] such a circumstance. It would be really a case of a numbers game, if you like, of: "Is it better to kill one person and save ten? Is it better to save one small child, let us say, as opposed to elderly people? Is it better to save a lawyer as opposed to an accountant?" One could engage in all sorts of highly

problematical philosophical discussions. These difficulties are clear where the court must decide whether or not duress is a defence by a straight answer, "yes" or "no". Yet, the difficulties are avoided somewhat when the court is instead asked not to decide whether or not the accused should have a complete defence but to take account of the circumstances in the flexible but effective facility provided by mitigation of punishment.

4. Mitigation of punishment as a clear, simple and uniform approach

82. An argument often advanced by proponents within the common law itself in favour of allowing duress as a defence to murder rests upon the assertion that the law cannot demand more of a person than what is reasonable, that is, what can be expected from an ordinary person in the same circumstances. [. . .] The commentary to the Model Penal Code of the United States states that:

> law is ineffective in the deepest sense, indeed . . . hypocritical, if it imposes on the actor who has the misfortune to confront a delemmatic choice, a standard that his judges are not prepared to affirm that they should and could comply with if their turn to face the problem should arise. Condemnation in such a case is bound to be an ineffective threat; what is, however, more significant is that it is divorced from any moral base and is unjust.

83. A number of comments are called for at this point. Firstly, the *Masetti* approach, if it is confined to the factual situation where the accused merely participates in the killing of victims whose lives would be lost in any case, is no answer to the stricture levelled against our approach whereby the law "expects" from its subjects what no reasonable person can live up to. This is because it is equally unrealistic to expect a reasonable person to sacrifice his own life or the lives of loved ones in a duress situation even if by this sacrifice, the lives of the victims would be saved. Either duress should be admitted as a defence to killing innocent persons generally based upon an objective test of how the ordinary person would have acted in the same circumstances or not admitted as a defence to murder at all. The *Masetti* approach is, in our view, a half-way house which contributes nothing to clarity in international humanitarian law. The approach, by a strict application of utilitarian logic, rejects duress for murder but for this one exception where the victims would have died in any event, and yet comes down hard on an accused who, when faced with a threat to his child's life, acts reasonably in deciding to obey a command to shoot innocent persons in order to save the life of his child. Thus, our rejection of duress as a defence to the killing of innocent human beings does not depend upon what the reasonable person is expected to do. We would assert an absolute moral postulate which is clear and unmistakable for the implementation of international humanitarian law.

84. Secondly, as we have confined the scope of our inquiry to the question whether duress affords a complete defence to a soldier charged with killing innocent persons, we are of the view that soldiers or combatants are expected to exercise fortitude and a greater degree of resistance to a threat than civilians, at least when it is their own lives which are being threatened. Soldiers, by the very nature of their occupation, must have envisaged the possibility of violent death in pursuance of the cause for which they fight. The relevant question must therefore be framed in terms of what may be expected from the ordinary soldier in the situation of the Appellant. What is to be expected of such an ordinary soldier is not, by our approach, analysed in terms of a utilitarian approach involving the weighing up of harms. Rather, it is based on the proposition that it is unacceptable to allow a trained fighter, whose job necessarily entails the occupational hazard of dying, to avail himself of a complete defence to a crime in which he killed one or more innocent persons.

85. Finally, we think, with respect, that it is inaccurate to say that by rejecting duress as a defence to the killing of innocent persons, the law "expects" a person who knows that the victims will die anyway to throw his life away in vain. If there were a mandatory life sentence

which we would be bound to impose upon a person convicted of killing with only an executive pardon available to do justice to the accused, it may well be said that the law "expects" heroism from its subjects. Indeed, such a mandatory life-term was prescribed for murder in England at the time the relevant English cases were decided and featured prominently in the considerations of the judges. We are not bound to impose any such mandatory term. One cannot superficially gauge what the law "expects" by the existence of only two alternatives: conviction or acquittal. In reality, the law employs mitigation of punishment as a far more sophisticated and flexible tool for the purpose of doing justice in an individual case. The law, in our view, does not "expect" a person whose life is threatened to be [a] hero and to sacrifice his life by refusing to commit the criminal act demanded of him. The law does not "expect" that person to be a hero because in recognition of human frailty and the threat under which he acted, it will mitigate his punishment. In appropriate cases, the offender may receive no punishment at all. We would refer again to the opinion of Lord Simon in *Lynch v. DPP for Northern Ireland* where he stated:

> Any sane and humane system of criminal justice must be able to allow for all such situations as the following, and not merely for some of them. A person, honestly and reasonably believing that a loaded pistol is at his back which will in all probability be used if he disobeys, is ordered to do and [sic] act *prima facie* criminal. Similarly, a person whose child has been kidnapped, and whom as a consequence of threats he honestly and reasonably believes to be in danger of death or mutilation if he does not perform an act *prima facie* criminal. Or his neighbour's child in such a situation. Or any child. Or any human being? Or his home, a national heritage, threatened to be blown up? Or a stolen masterpiece of art destroyed. Or his son financially ruined? Or his savings for himself and his wife put in peril. <u>In other words, a sane and humane system of criminal justice needs some general flexibility, and not merely some quirks of deference to certain odd and arbitrarily defined human weaknesses. In fact our own system of criminal justice has such flexibility, provided that it is realised that it does not consist only in the positive prohibitions and injunctions of the criminal law, but extends also to its penal sanctions. May it not be that the infinite variety of circumstances in which the lawful wish of the actor is overborne could be accommodated with far greater flexibility, with much less anomaly, and with avoidance of the social evils which would attend acceptance of the appellant's argument (that duress is a general criminal defence), by taking those circumstances into account in the sentence of the court?</u> Is not the whole rationale of duress as a criminal defence that it recognises that an act prohibited by the criminal law may be morally innocent? Is not an absolute discharge just such an acknowledgement of moral innocence? (Emphasis added.)

86. In other words, the fact that justice may be done in ways other than admitting duress as a complete defence was always apparent to judges in England who rejected duress as a defence to murder. They have consistently argued that in cases of murder, duress could in appropriate cases be taken into account in mitigation of sentence, executive pardon or recommendations to the Parole Board [...]

87. Indeed, we would note that Stephen in his classic work argued that duress should never constitute a defence to any crime but merely as a ground in mitigation. The merit of this view was acknowledged by Lord Morris of Borth-y-Gest in *D.P.P for Northern Ireland v. Lynch* where he stated:

> A tenable view might be that duress should never be regarded as furnishing an excuse from guilt but only where established as providing reasons why after conviction a court could mitigate its consequences or absolve from punishment. Some writers including Stephen...have so thought.

E. Our conclusions

88. After the above survey of authorities in the different systems of law and exploration of the various policy considerations which we must bear in mind, we take the view that duress cannot afford a complete defence to a soldier charged with crimes against humanity or war crimes in international law involving the taking of innocent lives. We do so having regard to our mandated obligation under the Statute to ensure that international humanitarian law, which is concerned with the protection of humankind, is not in any way undermined.

89. In the result, we do not consider the plea of the Appellant was equivocal as duress does not afford a complete defence in international law to a charge of a crime against humanity or a war crime which involves the killing of innocent human beings.

90. Our discussion of the issues relating to the guilty plea entered by the Appellant is sufficient to dispose of the present appeal. It is not necessary for us to engage ourselves in the remaining issues raised by the parties. We would observe, however, that in rejecting the evidence of the Appellant that he had committed the crime under a threat of death from his commanding officer and consequently in refusing to take the circumstance of duress into account in mitigation of the Appellant's sentence, the Trial Chamber appeared to require corroboration of the Appellant's testimony as a matter of law. There is, with respect, nothing in the Statute or the Rules which requires corroboration of the exculpatory evidence of an accused person in order for that evidence to be taken into account in mitigation of sentence.

91. We would allow the appeal on the ground that the plea was not informed. The case is hereby remitted to another Trial Chamber where the Appellant must be given the opportunity to replead in full knowledge of the consequences of pleading guilty *per se* and of the inherent difference between the alternative charges.

As noted above, Judges Sir Ninian Stephen and Antonio Cassese appended their Dissenting Opinions. Judge Stephen pointed out that, since there was no rule of customary international law on the matter, it was necessary to establish whether there was nevertheless a general principle of law recognized in the major legal systems of the world. To this effect, after noting that civil law countries accept duress across the board, without distinguishing between the case of murder and other cases, he carefully perused the case law of common law countries. He concluded that such case law excludes the applicability of duress as a defence for the killing of an individual only when there is a choice between the loss of the life of the person acting under duress (if he refused to kill a third person) and the killing of the third person: the perpetrator tells the victim, if you do not fire at that man and kill him I shall kill you. For that eventuality the common law case law was grounded on the notion that an accused ought rather to die than to kill an innocent. The case before the ICTY, noted Sir Ninian, was different: here the choice the defendant had faced was between the death of innocent civilians and their death plus his own. The choice was not between one life or another, between one innocent or another, but between the sure loss of the life of many innocents and the taking of the life of the accused in addition to the death of those innocents. It followed, according to the distinguished Judge, that, despite the aforementioned exception to duress envisaged in common law countries, one may hold the view that there exists in international law a defence derived from a general principle of law recognized in the major legal systems of the world, and that this principle does apply in international criminal law at least when the circumstances giving rise to the common law exception do not arise.

In his Opinion, Judge Cassese reached a similar conclusion, based however on international case law.

18. [. . .] Before I enunciate the reasons for my dissent, I should briefly recall that the Office of the Prosecutor (the "Prosecution") and the majority of the Appeals Chamber take a different view of the international legal regulation of duress in cases involving the killing of innocent persons. According to the Prosecution a customary rule, or exception, has evolved in international law specifically excluding the applicability of duress as a defence to such crimes. By contrast, the majority of the Appeals Chamber holds the view that no such special rule has come into being; however they contend that in the absence of such a rule one ought to apply general policy considerations; the result of this application is the same as the one reached by the Prosecution through a different path: also for the majority of the Appeals Chamber duress <u>cannot be admitted</u> as a defence for crimes involving killing, but might only be urged in mitigation.

I disagree with both views. [. . .]

41. I shall delve below into what I regard – with respect – as the flaws in the majority's view. For now I shall elaborate on the logical conclusion I have just enunciated. This conclusion is that even in case of war crimes and crimes against humanity involving killing, if confronted with the defence of duress, an international criminal court must apply, as a minimum, the four criteria enunciated above (*see* paragraph 16, *supra*), namely (1) a severe threat to life or limb; (2) no adequate means to escape the threat; (3) proportionality in the means taken to avoid the threat; (4) the situation of duress should not have been self-induced.

42. The third criterion – proportionality (meaning that the remedy should not be disproportionate to the evil or that the lesser of two evils should be chosen) – will, in practice, be the hardest to satisfy where the underlying offence involves the killing of innocents. Perhaps – although that will be a matter for a Trial Chamber or a Judge to decide – it will <u>never</u> be satisfied where the accused is saving his own life <u>at the expense of</u> his victim, since there are enormous, perhaps insurmountable, philosophical, moral and legal difficulties in putting one life in the balance against that of others in this way: how can a judge satisfy himself that the death of one person is a lesser evil that the death of another? Conversely, however, where it is <u>not</u> a case of a direct choice between the life of the person acting under duress and the life of the victim – in situations, in other words, where there is a high probability that the person under duress will not be able to save the lives of the victims whatever he does – then duress may succeed as a defence. Again, this will be a matter for the judge or court hearing the case to decide in the light of the evidence available in this regard. The court may decide, in a given case, that the accused did not do all he could to save the victims before yielding to duress, or that it is too speculative to assert that they would have died in any event. The important point, however – and this is the fundamental source of my disagreement with the majority – is that this question should be for the Trial Chamber to decide with all the facts before it. The defence should not be cut off absolutely and *a priori* from invoking the excuse of duress by a ruling of this International Tribunal whereby, in law, the fact of acting under duress can <u>never</u> be a defence to killing innocents. This is altogether too dogmatic and, moreover, it is a stance unsupported by international law, where there is no rule to this effect; in international law there only exists a general rule stating that duress may be a defence when certain requirements are met.

43. These inferences, which I have drawn from the case-law, find support in the following considerations:

<u>Firstly</u>, it is extremely difficult to meet the requirements for duress where the offence involves killing of innocent human beings. This I infer from the fact that courts have very rarely allowed the defence of duress to succeed in cases involving unlawful killing even where they have <u>in principle</u> admitted the applicability of this defence. But for the Italian and German cases mentioned above (paragraphs 35–39, *supra*), which stand out as exceptional, the only cases where national courts have upheld the plea of duress in relation to violations of

Article 31(1)(d) ICCSt. seems to uphold the view set out by the two dissenting Judges of the ICTY (see *infra*, under Necessity, at p. 499).

The issue of duress when an accused has been able to show that he fired his weapon because he had a gun pointed at his head – coupled with the complex factual circumstances in 'common purpose' situations – led to a somewhat troubling conclusion in the *Leki* case, discussed below.

East Timorese Transitional Administration, **Prosecutor v. Leki**, *Special Panels for Serious Crimes (SPSC), Judgment of 11 June 2001 (English original)*

After the Portuguese withdrew from the territory of East Timor (Timor-Leste) in 1974, Indonesia occupied the territory, starting a 25-year long period of massive human rights abuses. Following international pressure, a referendum was finally allowed to take place on the status of the territory in 1999. The Indonesian military and the civilian administrations in East Timor, however, opposed this policy and increased the persecution of pro-independence organizations and intimidation of the general population. When, in September 1999, the results of the referendum showed that the overwhelming majority of the Timorese people opted for outright independence – instead of simple autonomy within Indonesia – the military started a campaign of vengeance against those who supported independence. The violence left at least 1,300 people dead and many more raped or seriously injured, and resulted in near total devastation of the territory's property and infrastructure, in particular in the main town of Dili. Under increasing international pressure, Indonesia finally ceded control of East Timor to the UN at the end of September 1999. After the Indonesian withdrawal, the UN Security Council placed Timor-Leste under the control of a UN Transitional Administration for East Timor (UNTAET), with the objective of preparing the territory for independence. In mid-2000 UNTAET took steps to establish Special Panels of the Dili District Court (Special Panels for Serious Crimes, or SPSC) to try cases of 'serious criminal offences' that had occurred in 1999. The panels were composed of one national and two international judges and applied UNTAET Regulations, international law and the domestic law applied in East Timor prior to 25 October 1999 (i.e. the Penal Code of Indonesia). Amidst logistical and practical difficulties – caused in particular by a complete lack of cooperation by Indonesia – trials resulted in dozens of convictions and contributed to the compilation of a chronological record of the systematic nature of the crimes and violence of 1999. The Special Panels in the District Court of Dili ceased to operate in 2005.

In June 1999, Joseph Leki had allegedly joined a pro-Indonesian militia group ('Laksaur') engaged in violent acts in the Cova Lima District of East Timor. On 25 and 26 September 1999, two groups of people who had escaped previous attacks were ambushed by the Laksaur militia. During the first attack, three men (Titus Mali, Damiao Ximenes and Januario Maia) were killed, while Paulino Cardoso was hit and killed during the second raid. Leki was accused of participating in the two attacks.

[. . .] *The conduct of the accused*

The accused declared before the Court he was a member of Laksaur militia. He joined the group in June 1999 because he was forced to. His first duty was to keep guard at the Militia post. "I [had] to report periodically in the morning and afternoon. Nighttime I was guarding. I sat down all night and then slept", he clarified his duty when asked by the Prosecutor (p. 179, lines 15, 18, 19 and 37). He declared that militia leaders Olivio Moruk and Egidio Manek ordered him to provide security. Those leaders required him as guard because "they carried and kept the guns (...) to be distributed to people" (p. 179, line 33). [...]

From the comparison between [his various] statements the Court deems that the accused really carried a gun during the attack. Not any of the eyewitnesses imputes to him as the main perpetrator of the murder of Damiao Ximenes, Titus Mails and Januario Maya. He refused, at the beginning of the trial, to admit he used guns before the incident on 25 September 1999, but the contradictions came soon as long as he was invited to give further informations [sic] about the performance of his duties as security guard to the militia. His phrases reveal, as a whole, that he was given a gun much time before the operation in September 1999. Right after his joining in prior June, he symptomatically [sic] was entitled to have a gun, since his duty was to protect the militia post in West Timor. It is far beyond the common sense that someone in charge of security activities in a paramilitary group could not be allowed to hold and to use guns. Also it sounds pathetic his statements that, in performing his duties as security guard he just "sat down all night and then slept" (p. 179, line 37). After being allegedly constrained to join the militia, he should not complain by spending many nights along [sic] sitting down and sleeping.

The first conclusion is that the accused was indeed carrying guns all the time since he joined the militia, otherwise he should not be in charge of security service for those who "carried and kept guns" (p. 179, line 25). The accused cannot explain why his duty was to provide security and keep guns [...] even though he was not given a gun. His confused deposition almost immediately revealed that, some months before the three-day operation in September, he was already carrying guns.

Along the first day of that operation, he continued to use the guns, as stated by both witnesses. However, there is no evidence that he could have fired a single shot on September 25. [...]

On the second day of the operation, the accused admitted he was carrying a gun and fired a shot, a fatal gunshot at the victim Paulino Cardoso. His shot, nevertheless, was not the single one; it was fired after that Egidio and Norberto had also shot at the victim. Joseph Leki stands [by] his act by imputing to the militiaman Norberto a[n] unavoidable pressure to shoot at the victim. The accused reports this pressure: "(...) Because I was ordered, [I shot Paulino Cardoso]. (...) I was forced by Norberto. Norberto put the gun to me. (...) If I didn't, I would die." (p. 187, excerpts).

The witnesses C and E also detail this fact. They report that Joseph Leki actually received a strict order to fire his gun at the victim Paulino Cardoso. "Norberto Ximenes jumped and aimed his rifle at Joseph Leki and said: 'Shoot him or I'll shoot you!'," testified Amaral, one of the villagers who were forced to hide in the forest and in the company of the victim and E. This witness C also confirmed that, hiding in the bush and at 20 meters far from the crime scene, he could see and hear what was going on (p. 195, lines 20/43). After an apparent misunderstanding on cross-examination by the defense, he agreed: "I saw Norberto pointing the gun to Joseph Leki and saying: 'Shoot him or I'll shoot you!' " (p. 196, lines 9/10).

The testimony about the same scene came through the statement of the witness C, also one of the escapees of the militia's actions that day [...]

The second conclusion is that the accused, under pressure from a gun pointed to his own head, fired the last and lethal shot at the victim Paulino Cardoso, who previously was wounded by other gunshots fired by his fellowmen. Both accused and witnesses have unchallenged versions for this fact and its circumstances. The Court will assess them in appropriate framework.

The victims' cause of death and the link between the conduct and the outcome proved

It is undisputed that the four victims' cause of the death was the gunshots fired the length of the operation carried out by the militia group on 25 and 26 September 1999. On the first day, there is no evidence that the accused fired one of the bullets that resulted in the death of Damiao Ximenes, Titus Malis and Januario Maya; but, it is acknowledged that Joseph Leki was taking part of the operation, providing and carrying guns, supporting, frightening and forcing the hidden villagers to flee. The operation has its successful results with his help. He was not a security guard any more; he had already joined an operation, which objectives and reasons he was fully aware [of]. The main purpose of this widespread and organized strategy was in fact to kill the villagers and to burn their houses in retaliation to the results from the popular consultation in the preceding month. In addition, the plan outlined and executed by Indonesian military forces and its supported local militia groups was the forced deportation of hundreds of thousands of East Timorese. Those facts do not call for any formal evidence in the light of what even the humblest and the most candid man in the world can assess.

On the second day, the final bullet fired at Paulino Cardoso really came from the rifle pointed by Joseph Leki. Regardless [of] any consideration about which bullet caused the fatal wound that killed the victim, there are no doubts Leki fired and <u>also</u> killed Cardoso.

Two controversial points at this moment raise and demand a meticulous assessment: the individual criminal responsibility and its exemption by the duress. The Court shall point out its belief according to what it has been proved by both parties and pursuant to the legal provisions on the matter.

About the incidents related to both counts, the defense relies on the following evidence:

(a) the fact that the shots that caused the death of Damiao Ximenes, Titus Malis and Januario Maya were not fired by the accused, regardless he were carrying or not a gun; and

(b) the circumstance that, in the following day, the accused was allegedly under duress so that he could not avoid shooting at Paulino Cardoso.

This Court, however, has a different sight from [sic] the same facts and circumstances relied on by the defense.

About the three victims on September 25, the accused did participate in their killings, pursuant to what is considered as individual criminal responsibility according to UNTAET Regulations.

By supporting morally and in logistic, carrying guns and with immediate involvement in both attacks held on 25 and 26 September 1999, the accused had deliberate intent to provide sufficient means to accomplish the purposes of the militia group. The killings of Damiao Ximenes, Titus Malis and Januario Maya was [sic] not a casual fact; they were carried out as a part of a longer planning to terminate any opponent to the *establishment*.

Section 14.3(d) of UR-2000/15 provides that "a person shall be individually responsible and liable for punishment for a crime within the jurisdiction of the panels if that person, in any other way contributes to the commission or attempted commission of such a crime by a group of persons acting with a common purpose. Such contribution shall be intentional and shall be made with the aim of furthering the criminal activity or criminal purpose of the group, where such activity or purpose involves the commission of a crime within the jurisdiction of the panels; or be made in the knowledge of the intention of the group to commit the crime" (...). Since he joined the militia, the accused obviously knew about the purposes of the group. To participate in those operations, regardless he was carrying a gun or not, was his contribution to the killings of the first three victims. The evidence he was carrying a gun, as the Court could assess above, enhances his performance to the results. Just holding a gun during a siege maneuver against unarmed civilians, he played an undoubting role to the commission of the three deaths.

The alleged duress can be assessed not only the day the accused shot Paulino Cardoso, as stressed by the Defense, but also along his whole activity in the militia group.

The accused joined the militia in June 1999; he did it supposedly to avoid threats to himself and his family, as his statements underline. However, such constraint is not plenty to put aside his criminal responsibility for the acts, he was later involved. He alleged that the militia could kill him or his family if he refused to join (p. 179, line 46). Asked why he didn't take his family and fled to hide in the places the population was forced to, he just answered that "there was a big number of familiars" (p. 180, line 38). No one should be supposed to stand a heroic behavior by challenging the alleged constraint to join. However, the Court is persuaded that the accused had several choices to do as long as he was with his family and worked as house security guard as he informed when the militia leaders came before him (p. 185, line 16). Leki admitted that many other persons resisted joining the militia (p. 178, line 15) and recognized that they were forced to hide in the forests (p. 180, lines 30/32). The Accused chose to be in line with the guns.

From the time when he joined until the operation came after the ballot in August 1999, he had many chances to refuse to share the purposes of the militia group. The retaliation would come as soon as the results pro-independence were confirmed. More than two months after he joined, would Leki still be afraid to be killed? The Court is convinced that his personal condition was not worse nor better than what forced the rest of the population who fled to the forests.

The Defense emphasizes that the accused could not avoid killing Paulino Cardoso on the second day of the operation. "He had no voluntarily shot, he had a gun pointed at his head to shoot Cardoso", justifies the Defense in final statement. The Court agrees that this specific circumstance was really sufficient to exclude his criminal responsibility for the murder as principal perpetrator. However even so remains his individual responsibility as one of those who provided the opportunity and the means for the result, considering that he had prior joined the militia plans to make possible the attack. The killings, burnings and forced deportation came as a corollary of the militia campaigns he joined to. Even before having a gun pointed at his head − specific circumstance that by itself should be duress − the accused had already agreed with and accepted that the rifle he was entitled to hold and his performance in the attacks were necessary to the acts committed by the main perpetrators. Both the rules above are appropriate to consider his responsibility in the two counts.

Therefore, the alleged − and proved − duress on the accused at the very last time he fired his gun at Paulino Cardoso would exclude his responsibility, since he could not necessarily and reasonably avoid that threat, as says Sect. 19.1(d) of UR-2000/15. However, the undisputed fact that he, prior to the very last moment of duress, could avoid that circumstance endows the Court sufficient grounds to believe that Joseph Leki was able to avoid such threat simply by refusing to contribute to the attacks. [. . .]

For the aforementioned reasons, the Special Panel is satisfied that the Public Prosecutor has proved the case against the accused beyond reasonable doubt and therefore finds Joseph Leki guilty of murder, as a violation of Sect. 8 U.R. 2000/15 and article 340 of PCI. [. . .]

For the aforementioned reasons, having considered all the evidences (statements from transitional rules of Criminal Procedure, the Special Panel finds and imposes sentence as follows:

With respect to the defendant JOSEPH LEKI:

(1) GUILTY for both of the charges of murder, in violation of Section 8 of UNTAET Regulation 2000/15 and Article 340 of the Penal Code of Indonesia;

(2) In punishment of the continued crimes, sentences JOSEPH LEKI to an imprisonment of 13 (thirteen) years.

(3) Orders the defendant to pay the costs of the criminal procedure.

QUESTIONS

1. The utilitarian logic is indeed appealing when deciding on issues of duress – is the Majority's view in *Erdemović* convincing in rejecting it?

2. In time of war, can one really distinguish between the plea of superior orders, on the one side, and duress, on the other, considering the likely consequences of not obeying an order?

3. A soldier knows that by participating in combat operations he puts his life in danger. One of these dangers is arguably that of being punished for not obeying illegal orders. Should this be a consideration to be taken into account when deciding whether duress can be pleaded as a defence?

FURTHER READING

Cassese, *International Criminal Law*, 284–9.

A. Fichtelberg, 'Liberal Values in International Criminal Law: A Critique of *Erdemović*' (2008) 6 JICJ 3–19.

G. Fletcher, *Rethinking Criminal Law* (Oxford: Oxford University Press, 2009), 817–34.

(C) NECESSITY

Necessity as a defence is broader than duress. As discussed above, it concerns threats to life and limb emanating *from objective circumstances*, and not from another person.

In the case of necessity the agent intends to cause an unlawful harmful effect. In other words, he does entertain the criminal intent required by the criminal rule: he is not only aware that by his action he causes the death of another person but he indeed wills that death, because achieving this result is the only means for him to avert a serious imminent threat to his life. For instance, he wills the death of the other shipwrecked person who is attempting to climb into the small boat capable of carrying only one person; nevertheless, the law considers that he must be excused by not being punished.

In contrast, duress to a large extent negates the subjective element of the person under coercion (he does not will the death of the prisoner of war he is constrained by another person to kill). The criminal intent of the person causing duress in a way substitutes for his *mens rea*. Hence, with duress, unlike necessity, a third person, that is, the person threatening the agent, is held criminally responsible for the harm caused by the person acting under duress (for instance, a lieutenant is responsible for the death of an innocent civilian he has constrained a soldier to kill).

Cases

US Military Tribunal Sitting in Nuremberg, **US v. Flick et al.,** *Judgment of 22 December 1947*

> In this case the question was whether some defendants (Steinbrinck, Burkart, Kaletsch and Terberger), managers of various companies belonging to the 'Flick Konzern' were guilty of having employed conscripted foreign workers, concentration camp inmates, or prisoners of war allocated to them through the slave-labour programme of the German Government. The defendants claimed that they had done so 'under the circumstances of compulsion under which such employment came about'. The US Military Tribunal upheld the plea.

[Page 1199:] Recognizing the criminality of the Reich labor program, as such, the only question remaining for our decision with respect to this count is whether the defendants are guilty of having employed conscripted foreign workers, concentration camp inmates or prisoners of war allocated to them through the slave-labor program of the Reich under the circumstances of compulsion under which such employment came about. The circumstances have hereinbefore been discussed. The prosecution has called attention to the fact that defendants Walter Funk and Albert Speer were convicted by IMT because of their participation in the slave-labor program. It is clear, however, that [the] relation of Speer and Funk to such program differs substantially from the nature of the participation in such program by the defendants [in] this case. Speer and Funk were numbered among the group of top public officials responsible for the slave-labor program.

We are not unmindful of the provision of paragraph 2 of Article II of Control Council Law No. 10 which states that –

> "2. Any person without regard to the nationality or the capacity in which he acted, is deemed to have committed a crime as defined in paragraph 1 of this Article, if he was (a) principal or (b) was an accessory to the commission of any such crime or ordered or abetted the same or (c) took a consenting part therein or (d) was connected with plans or enterprises involving its commission. . . ."

Nor have we overlooked the provision in paragraph 4(b) Article II of such Control Council Law No. 10 which states –

> "(b) The fact that any person acted pursuant to the order of his Government or of a superior does not free him from responsibility for a crime, but may be considered in mitigation."

In our opinion, it is not intended that these provisions are to be employed to deprive a defendant of the defense of necessity – such circumstances as obtained in this case with respect to defendants Steinbrinck, Burkart, Kaletsch, and Terberger.

This Tribunal might be reproached for wreaking vengeance rather than administering justice if it were to declare as unavailable to defendants the defense of necessity here urged in their behalf. This principle has had wide acceptance in American and English courts and is recognized elsewhere.

Wharton's *Criminal Law*, volume I, chapter III, subdivision VII, paragraph 126 contains the following statement with respect to the defense of necessity citing cases in support thereof:

"Necessity is a defense when it is shown that the act charged was done to avoid an evil both serious and irreparable; that there was no other adequate means of escape; and that the remedy was not disproportioned to the evil."

A note under paragraph 384 in chapter XIII, Wharton's *Criminal Law*, volume I, gives the underlying principle of the defense of necessity as follows:

"Necessity forcing a man to do an act justifies him, because no man can be guilty of a crime without the will and intent in his mind. When a man is absolutely, by natural necessity, forced, his will does not go along with the act. Lord Mansfield in *Stratton's* Case, 21 How. St. Tr. (Eng.) 1046–1223."

The prosecution, on final argument, contended that the defendants are barred from interposing the defense of necessity. In the course of its argument, the prosecution referred to paragraph 4*(b)*, of Article II of Control Council Law No. 10 and stated:

"This principle has been most frequently applied and interpreted in military cases...."

Further on in the argument, it was said:

"The defendants in this case, as they have repeatedly and plaintively told us, were not military men or government officials. None of the acts with which they are charged under any count of the indictment were committed under 'orders' of the type we have been discussing. By their own admissions, it seems to us they are in no position to claim the benefits of the doctrine of 'superior orders' even by way of mitigation."

The foregoing statement was then closely followed by another, as follows:

"The defense of 'coercion' or 'duress' has a certain application in ordinary civilian jurisprudence. But despite the most desperate efforts, the defendants have not, we believe, succeeded in bringing themselves within the purview of these concepts,"

The prosecution then asserted that this defense has no application unless the defendants acted under what is described as "clear and present danger." Reference was made to certain rules and cases in support of such position.

The evidence with respect to defendants Steinbrinck, Burkart, Kaletsch, and Terberger in our opinion, however, clearly established that there was in the instant case "clear and present danger" within the contemplation of that phrase. We have already discussed the Reich reign of terror. The defendants lived within the Reich. The Reich, through its hordes of enforcement officials and secret police, was always "present," ready to go into instant action and to mete out savage and immediate punishment against anyone doing anything that could be construed as obstructing or hindering the carrying out of governmental regulations or decrees.

In considering the application of rules to the defense of necessity, attention may well be called to the following statement:

The law of cases of necessity is not likely to be well furnished with precise rules; necessity creates the law, it supersedes rules, and whatever is reasonable and just in such cases is likewise legal. It is not to be considered as [a] matter of surprise, therefore, if much instituted rule is not to be found on such subject. (Wharton's *Criminal Law*, vol. I, Chapter III, subdivision VII, par.126 and cases cited.)

In this case, in our opinion, the testimony establishes a factual situation which makes clearly applicable the defense of necessity as urged in behalf of the defendants Steinbrinck, Burkart, Kaletsch, and Terberger.

The active steps taken by Weiss with the knowledge and approval of Flick to procure for the Linke-Hofmann Works increased production quota of freight cars which constitute military

equipment within the contemplation of the Hague Convention, and Weiss's part in the pro-
curement of a large number of Russian prisoners of war for work in the manufacture of such
equipment deprive the defendants Flick and Weiss of the complete defense of necessity. In
judging the conduct of Weiss in this transaction, we must, however, remember that obtaining
more materials than necessary was forbidden by the authorities just as falling short in filling
orders was forbidden. The war effort required all persons involved to use all facilities to bring
the war production to its fullest capacity. The steps taken in this instance, however, were initiated not in Governmental circles but in the plant management. They were not taken as a result
of compulsion or fear, but admittedly for the purpose of keeping the plant as near capacity
production as possible.

It is, accordingly, adjudged that the defendants Steinbrinck, Burkart, Kaletsch, and Terberger
are not guilty on count one and that defendants Flick and Weiss are guilty on this count.

Federal Republic of Germany, Sch. and Dr. L. (Gestapo members case), German Federal High Court (Bundesgerichtshof), Judgment of 14 October 1952

Two Gestapo officers on many occasions executed a secret order of the Main Office
of the Reich Security Service (*Reichssichereheitshauptamt*, or RSHA) of 5 November
1942. Under this order, they were allowed to undertake against workers from Eastern
countries (*Ostarbeiter*) a 'short treatment' (*Kurzbehandlung*, which consisted in fustigating – beating with an implement – instead of briefly imprisoning, workers who
had refused to work or committed disciplinary violations), or a 'special treatment'
(*Sonderbehandlung*, that is, the hanging, without any prior trial, of workers who had
committed criminal offences). The two accused had taken part in both categories of
action. Brought before a Munich court of assize (*Schwurgericht*), the accused pleaded
two defences: (i) they were not aware of the unlawfulness of the Order; (ii) they had
acted under necessity. The Court held that, since the Order had not the value of a
binding law justifying their actions, the two were responsible for bodily harm resulting from their actions ('short treatment'), and for aiding and abetting murder, as far
as their participation in the 'special treatment' was concerned. However, the court
acquitted them, on the grounds of having acted under necessity. Both they and the
Prosecution appealed against the decision. The Federal High Court upheld the Court
of Assize's decision that the first defence was not applicable, for the accused were aware
of the unlawfulness of their actions. It then moved on to the second defence.

Although the Court of Assize reaffirmed the objective and subjective elements of abetting
unlawful killing, it nonetheless acquitted the accused. This was based on its opinion that the
accused had acted under necessity as described in Article 52 [on necessity, *Nötigungsstand*]
of StGB [*Strafgesetzbuch*, German Criminal Code]. The appeal correctly stated that what had
been established could not be covered by recourse to Article 52.

The legal error, in any case, does not lie in the fact that in a case in which the accused, like
those here, committed a punishable act on instructions from his superior, that is, acted on
orders of a superior, and that recourse to Article 52 StGB is fundamentally excluded. In addition, Article 2 of Bavarian Law 22 on the punishment of the crimes of the National Socialists,
which does not recognize orders of superiors as grounds for acquittal of criminal charges but
only as grounds for mitigation. It only states that the order as such is not grounds for acquittal
though it is not clearly stated that Article 52 StGB should remain inapplicable if a situation of

necessity, as described in Article 52 StGB, arises. The above provision of Law 22 corresponds, even if its wording refers back to Article II 4b of the KRG 10, to a principle which, in German criminal law, has long been held as valid for military personnel and officials (Article 47 MStGB; Article 7 DBG of 26 January 1936) and which was also valid at the time of the crime. In addition, according to these provisions, it was not excluded that in respect of an act of a subordinate who, by executing an unlawful order given to him, made himself liable to punishment, Article 52 StGB would be applied if, because of an order, he was placed in a position of constraint as understood in Article 52 StGB. Should one therefore seek to understand Article 2 para 2 of Bavarian Law 22 as meaning that this provision should also preclude the application of Article 52 StGB, if because of that order a situation of constraint in the sense of Article 52 was created, resulting in conduct which until that time was not punishable, would have been declared punishable additionally and retrospectively. Completely aside from the constitutional considerations against the validity of such a provision, nothing permits the conclusion that the lawmakers intended to link that meaning with the terms of Article 2 para 2.

Therefore, although the application of Article 52 StGB was in itself possible, as the judgment shows, the Court of Assize failed to appreciate its sense and consequences. It established that, in view of the "special treatment", the accused were subject to specific instructions, since they were officials of the State police. From 1943 until the end of the war, the National Socialists took out their fury with the greatest of measures intended to terrorize not only political opponents and so-called enemies of the State but also their own followers and colleagues who had sabotaged the State orders. If the accused had failed to cooperate with the "special treatment" which had been ordered, they would have been threatened with being placed in a concentration camp and, as members of the SS, according to the laws of war applicable at that time, with the death penalty. Other than by compliance with the service orders given to them, this danger could not be avoided, and, at the very least, they cannot be reproached for having had that conviction. These findings are insufficient for the application of Article 52 StGB. Whoever carries out an order which appears unreasonable to him, even if it exposes him to danger to life and limb should he not comply, need not carry it out in order to escape that danger. He could also have had other compelling reasons than an attempt to avoid the danger. In that case, however, Article 52 StGB is not applicable. What is much more relevant is the fact that the perpetrator is compelled to commit the acts because of the threat of a present danger to life and limb, and hence his will too is thus bent by the threat *(OGHSt. J, 310, 313)*. This was not appreciated by the Court of Assize, which was satisfied, with no reasons given, as to why the accused were prepared to cooperate with the "special treatment" of eastern workers since they realized that, had they refused to cooperate, they would have been threatened with internment in a concentration camp or sentenced to death and had no illusions as to that fact. The meaning of Article 52 StGB is not that all those who, under the power of the National Socialists, for years *voluntarily* served crime and terror – some, like the accused, in influential and leading positions – could then escape responsibility by the mere indication that they had to fear for life and limb if they failed in their further co-operation in criminal conduct.

As the findings made so far do not support the acquittal of the two accused and the judgment must therefore be reversed, in the new proceedings the Court of assize shall also better clarify on what grounds the accused showed to be prepared to participate in the "special treatment" of the eastern workers. Only if it appears that this occurred for the purpose of escaping a danger that was otherwise threatening their life or limb, can the application of Article 52 be taken into account. The current findings already contain numerous probative indicia that the accused possibly were ready to participate in the actions on grounds other than that of evading a danger threatening their life or limb. Both of them had long belonged, as a result of a voluntary decision, to the Gestapo. To decide the question of the reasons for their actions, a question that the Court of assize has not tackled nor answered, it may be significant to establish the following: whether the application of the secret Order of 5 November 1942 was the first time the accused were requested to undertake illegal conduct, as instead the Court of Assize seems to believe contrary to the general experience. Already, many years before, the Gestapo had evolved into a dreaded tool of oppression and abuse of the Nazi state. There are no signs that these circumstances remained concealed to the accused, who already in early times had occupied influential and senior positions within the State police. Even assuming that, as the Court of Assize believes, under the war conditions existing in 1943 it was not possible for them to quit the Gestapo without endangering their life and limb, the question arises why they had not taken such a step already at a time when that action could be undertaken without danger. The fact that they, since joining the Gestapo, in a quick sequence were called upon to occupy more and more influential and important positions, similarly does not show that in this whole period they acted as coerced and recalcitrant participants. As the Court of Assize has held without committing any legal mistake, in the end they had participated in the "short treatment" on their own free will. On that occasion, according to the findings of the decision, the accused Dr. L. stood out for his particular zeal and brutality. In its new proceedings the Court of Assize shall have to appraise what weight must be attributed to all these circumstances, when deciding the question remaining and so far neglected, that of the reasons for the conduct taken by the accused.

Israel, **Eichmann v. Attorney General**, *Supreme Court, Judgment of 29 May 1962*

> Before the Court, Eichmann raised, among other things, the plea of necessity. The Court first ruled that he could not rely upon the plea of superior orders, and then addressed the issue of necessity.

In point of fact, the appellant did not receive orders 'from above' at all; he was the high and mighty one, the commander of all that pertained to Jewish affairs. He ordered and commanded, not only without orders from his superiors in the hierarchy of the service, but also at times completely contrary to such orders, as already shown above. The following illustrates how far he was possessed by the concept of the 'Final Solution' and to what extent he attempted to surpass even his 'illustrious masters'. In April 1945, about a month before Germany's complete collapse, when even the Reichsfuehrer S.S., in the quest of an alibi for himself, had already begun to consider 'more humane methods' of persecuting the Jews, he – Eichmann – was still uneasy about these methods and only with deep regret and emotional self-restraint did he comply with Himmler's instructions, as he told the representative of the International Red Cross (T/865). It is clear that the *idea* of the 'Final Solution' was not his own but the Fuehrer's. Yet that idea might not have assumed so satanic and infernal a manifestation – in the blood of millions of tortured and martyred Jews – but for the thorough planning, the zeal, the fanatical enthusiasm and the insatiable bloodthirstiness of the appellant and those who did his bidding. We do not minimize even by one jot the terrible guilt that rests on the heads of many, many others; no one who lent the least assistance – active or passive, direct or indirect – to Nazi gangsterism in Europe, is to be exculpated. But here in this trial we are concerned with the appellant's individual guilt, and as to him it has been proved with unchallengeable certainty that he took his place not only among those who were active in but also those who activated the implementation of the 'Final Solution', the total extermination of the Jews of Europe. The appellant was no petty killer in this undertaking, but took a leading part and had a central and decisive role.

[The Plea of 'Necessity']

18. Thus the fourth submission of counsel for the appellant, the plea of 'necessity' falls to the ground. He (the appellant) was not coerced into doing what he did and was not in any danger of his life, since, as we have seen above, he did far more than was demanded or expected of him by his superiors in the chain of command. No one would have taken him to task, and he would certainly not have been brought to the gallows, had he – to give one example – based himself on the consent of Hitler and Ribbentropp to the emigration to Sweden and Switzerland of a few score thousand Jews (see paragraph 16 *(e)* above) and not undermined the proposal so wickedly and guilefully. As we have seen above, he was lavish in such 'volunteer acts'. In the upper echelons of their organization, the Nazis did not need the services of those who acted like unwilling ciphers. That would have impaired operational efficiency, and they had no shortage of zealous followers, people with unshaken nerve, in other words people lacking all human feeling. This is proved by the thousands of arch-murderers, the members of the Operation Units and execution squads, who operated in Riga, Minsk, Kiev (Babi Yar) and other places and wiped out about a million Jews by shooting – isolated, individual shooting at point blank range – without hesitation or failure of nerves (see the statement of Otto Ohlendorf at Nuremberg, T/312). Had the appellant exhibited at any stage the slightest displeasure or heart-searching or even mere lack of enthusiasm for the implementation of the 'Final Solution', his superiors would willingly have relieved him of his post and replaced him by some other person more 'qualified' than he. Thus on October 4, 1943, Himmler delivered a long address in Posen in which he said, *inter alia*:

"If anyone thinks that he cannot undertake to carry out an order (given him) he must say honestly: 'I cannot undertake this task, please relieve me of it.' Then, in most cases, the order would probably be: 'You must nevertheless carry this out'. Or (the commander) might think, 'This man's nerves are shaken, he is weak', in which case he would be told, 'All right, you had better resign.' " (T/1288.)

The appellant never displayed any remorse or weakness or sapping of strength or weakening of will in performing the task he had undertaken. He was 'the right man in the right place', and he carried out his unspeakably horrible crimes with genuine wholehearted joy and pleasure, to his own gratification and the satisfaction of all his superiors. Here certainly were not present the conditions of 'necessity' mentioned in Section 18 of the [Israeli] Criminal Code Ordinance, and the appellant would be liable to the death penalty under Section 1 of the [Israeli] Law for the Punishment of Nazis and Nazi Collaborators, 1950, even if the defence under Section 18 of the Ordinance had not been taken away by Section 8 of the Law in respect of offences set out in that Law. All the more so now that this defence has been excluded. For no one has even as much as suggested that the appellant 'did his best to reduce the gravity of the consequences' of the offence or that he did what he did with intent 'to avert...consequences more serious than those which resulted from the offence' (sub-sections *(a)* and *(b)* of Section 11 of the Law).

There was here therefore neither any 'necessity' within the meaning of Section 18 of the Ordinance, nor any 'extenuating circumstances' within the meaning of Section 11 of the Law, and the appellant deserves the punishment to which he was sentenced by the District Court.

France, **Touvier case,** *Court of Appeal, Versailles, Judgment of 2 June 1993*

In 1943 and 1944 Paul Touvier, a French citizen, acted as the regional chief of a special section (*Deuxième Service*, or second department) of the *Milice* (the French militia established by the Vichy regime), a section that specialized in combating members of the resistance movement and other opponents of Vichy France. Arrested in 1989 in

Nice, he was accused of crimes against humanity in connection with the killing, on 28 June 1944, at Rillieux, near Lyon, of seven civilians, all of them Jewish, as a reprisal for the murder of Philippe Henriot (the Vichy Minister for Information and Propaganda) by members of the resistance movement. It should be noted that the seven victims had been killed because they were Jewish and not because they belonged to the Resistance (a member of the movement, Louis Goudard, testified before the Court of Versailles that he had not been included into the group of victims because he was not Jewish).

The defendant raised among other things the defence of necessity. The Versailles Court of Appeal rejected it, as follows.

Touvier does not hesitate to invoke the pressures exercised by the Germans, relying on necessity as a justification. According to his defence counsel, the execution of the seven hostages at Rillieux allowed to save a much greater number of human lives. Indeed, Touvier has steadily argued that "he had to surrender to the inevitable", and that by his personal action he saved the life of 23 hostages out of the 30 granted by de Bourmont [the regional chief of the *Milice*] after negotiations with [Werner] Knab [chief of the *Einsatzkommando*, or operational unit, of Lyon]. Thus we may read in his correspondence: "faced with the certainty of the tragedy, de Bourmont and I have chosen to avoid the greater evil"; and "We were dogged by time and absolutely unable to totally oppose the will of the occupant".

However, the impact of the constraints thus relied upon may be questioned, if one recalls the testimonies of two witnesses, Gilberte Duc and Jean Reynaudon. The former, who was a secretary at the *"Deuxième Service"* [of the Lyon *Milice*] has stated: "I remember having heard this sentence uttered by Touvier: 'Philippe Henriot has been revenged.' " While recalling this utterance, she has however been unable to remember the date. As for the latter witness, he has stated the following: "I know that Touvier and Reynaud had directed and ordered this execution, because the same day they boasted of that".

One should emphasize that Touvier has not always been accurate as to the number of executions demanded by Knab. In a draft letter of 17 February 1960 intended for Father [Blaise] Arminjon [former Provincial of the Jesuits in Lyon], he suggested the number of 60 hostages. Four months later, in writing again to Father Arminjon, he set the number of hostages at 100, a number from which he did not depart later.

It is also necessary to recall the circumstances of the pillage of the assets of one of the executed hostages, Émile Zeizig, in the afternoon of 29 June 1944. This action ordered by Touvier, according to a member of the *Milice*, Fayolle, cannot easily been connected to orders given by Knab, and further diminishes the plausibility of the alleged necessity.

More generally, reliance on a justification is difficult to propound in the case at issue, from the viewpoint of principles of law. Where the sacrifice of human lives is at stake, one cannot engage in quantitative evaluations to decide if the lives saved represented a superior interest, given that crimes against humanity, while admittedly targeting individuals as victims, essentially entail that fundamental values of the civilized nations are infringed.

What is even more important, no legal justification – whether grounded in necessity or the self-defence of other persons – can be validly invoked by a leader of the *Milice* such as Touvier, who, on account of his functions, was all too naturally under the obligation to satisfy the requests of the Nazi authorities. The very exercise of this activity, freely chosen by him, involved a habitual cooperation with such services as the SD (*Sicherheitsdienst*, Security Service) and the Gestapo (*Geheime Staatspolizei*, State secret police). These relations existed both at the local and at the national level.

The French *Milice* had already participated in a number of so-called operations for the maintenance of public order, together with the German police or military. On 6 June 1944, when the Allies' landing in Normandy had been announced, Joseph Darnand had called upon the *Milice* to mobilize by getting in touch with the SD. The same Darnand, in August 1943, upon being appointed *Sturmbannführer* [commander of an SS unit] of the Waffen SS [military section of the SS], had taken an oath of allegiance and obedience to Hitler. This act clearly involved a total adherence to the Nazi ideology, and one of the watchwords of the *Milice* was that it had to fight "against the Jewish plague (*la lèpre juive*), for French purity." Nevertheless Touvier continued to exercise his functions as an official of the *Milice* under the orders of Darnand, while many other members of this organization chose to move away from it. Touvier himself, on account of his functions as the chief of the *Deuxième Service*, was in normal contact with SIPO[*Sicherheitspolizei*, or security police]-SD. Thus, together with regional chief de Bourmont, he periodically called on Commander Knab. Witness Feuz, who was his driver, has testified that he had a general laissez-passer issued by the German security services, which enabled him to move around by car day and night. Feuz has equally reported a meeting between Touvier and an official of the *Einsatzkommando* named Floreck, during which it was envisaged to step up the actions against the Jews. Although Touvier disputes that such meeting occurred, the relations between the *Milice* and the SIPO-SD were of such a nature that they would suffice to nullify any defence relying on an alleged necessity removing criminal liability.

In 1994 Touvier (born in 1915) was sentenced to life imprisonment. He died of cancer in prison in 1996.

COMMENTARY

From the last cases mentioned, it is clear that the pleas of duress and necessity are often confused one with the other and operate in a very similar way – in international criminal practice, they are often conflated into one defence. In particular, the ICCSt. has adopted this approach in Article 31, which provides as follows:

1. In addition to other grounds for excluding criminal responsibility provided for in this Statute, a person shall not be criminally responsible if, at the time of that person's conduct:

   [...]

   (d) The conduct which is alleged to constitute a crime within the jurisdiction of the Court has been caused by duress resulting from a threat of imminent death or of continuing or imminent serious bodily harm against that person or another person, and the person acts necessarily and reasonably to avoid this threat, provided that the person does not intend to cause a greater harm than the one sought to be avoided. Such a threat may either be:

   (i)   Made by other persons; or

   (ii) Constituted by other circumstances beyond that person's control.

QUESTIONS

1. Is the gravity of the coercion exercised by external circumstances a decisive factor for upholding the plea of necessity?

2. How can one appraise whether the mere fear or expectation of a serious threat to the life or limb of a person, following from external circumstances, can amount to a defence?

3. Under what conditions could one downgrade seriously threatening circumstances to a mitigating factor rather than a defence?

FURTHER READING

J. Ohlin, 'Necessity and Duress', in *Oxford Companion*, 431–3.
Werle, *Principles*, 203–10.

(D) MISTAKE OF FACT

Mistake of fact operates as a defence even when the defendant commits the *actus reus* of a crime but the requisite *mens rea* is lacking because the person mistakenly believed that there existed factual circumstances making the conduct lawful. The logic of mistake of fact as a defence is that there is a failure of proof of an element of the crime. That is, the defendant's mistake negates the requisite *mens rea* for the offence. According to ICCSt. Article 32(1), 'A mistake of fact shall be a ground for excluding criminal responsibility only if it negates the mental element required by the crime'.

What kind of mistake will negate *mens rea* therefore depends on the *mens rea* prescribed for the crime. Where the defendant must have specific intent to commit a crime, even an honest but unreasonable mistake will negate the requisite *mens rea* because so long as the finder of fact believes that the defendant was honestly labouring under a mistake, the specific intent is lacking. In contrast, where the *mens rea* standard is lower, providing, for example, that the defendant is culpable if he should have known of a risk, then an unreasonable mistake of fact is no defence because the defendant still should have known of the risk and was unreasonable in failing to be aware of the risk. The defendant therefore had the requisite *mens rea* for the offence. In contrast, if the defendant's mistake was reasonable, then *mens rea* is negated because we cannot say that the defendant should have known. The cases below illustrate.

Cases

USA, **US v. Schwarz**, *Navy Court of Military Review, Judgment of 29 October 1971*

The accused, a member of a five-man night patrol called the 'killer team', had gone out on 19 February 1970 to search out, locate, and kill enemy Viet Cong in South Vietnam. They had soon entered a small hamlet, Son Thang, where there were three huts, occupied by civilian women and children. The team killed 16 civilians. When they surrounded the first hut, four women came out and lined up on the patio in front of it. The accused Schwarz went inside the empty hut to search it. While inside he heard the team leader yell outside, 'Shoot them, shoot them all, kill them'. He jumped up and ran out, and participated in killing the four women. His defence counsel argued that Schwarz had mistakenly believed that they were under attack because the people standing on the patio were performing hostile acts.

The accused was charged with premeditated murder of Vietnamese civilians. The Military Judge instructed the jury that if they found that the accused mistakenly believed that he was returning fire, and shot the victims they must acquit – and even an unreasonable belief would exonerate the accused.

The military judge submitted this issue to the court as follows:

"In determining this issue you must consider all relevant facts and circumstances including but not limited to the accused's testimony that he believed himself and his teammates to have been under enemy attack at all three sites where the alleged victims were allegedly shot. And that the accused was on all these occasions in fear of his personal safety and that of his teammates. The court should also consider the evidence of the nature, condition, and configuration of the area in question. The general disposition of the inhabitants of this area and the disposition and activity of friendly and enemy forces during the time in question. Particularly as these factors might have been known to or believed to be by the accused. The court is advised that if the accused was of the honest belief that he and his teammates were being attacked by enemy forces he cannot be found guilty of any offense charged or the lesser included offenses thereto. Such belief no matter how unreasonable will exonerate the accused. In determining whether the accused was of the belief that enemy forces were attacking him and his teammates you should consider the accused's age, education, military training, and combat experience together will [sic] all other evidence bearing upon this issue. The burden is upon the prosecution to establish the accused's guilt of each offense charged by legal and competent evidence beyond a reasonable doubt. The accused committed no crime unless he knew that the enemy forces were not attacking him. I repeat – the accused committed no crime unless he knew that the enemy forces were not attacking him and his teammates at the time the alleged victims were allegedly shot. Consequently, unless you are satisfied beyond reasonable doubt that the accused was not under the belief that enemy forces were attacking him and his teammates you must acquit the accused of all offenses charged and the lesser included offenses thereto."

Counsel now argue that the foregoing instructions unduly restricted the members of the court in their consideration of the issue of alleged mistake of fact. It is claimed that the instructions required acquittal of the accused only if the court found that he did not honestly believe that he was under enemy attack but prejudicially failed to require acquittal unless the court found that he did not believe that the killer team was attacking the enemy at the time the victims were killed.

In the setting of this case we are certain that the instructions conveyed to the court the direction that the accused must be acquitted unless they found beyond a reasonable doubt that he did not honestly believe that he was in immediate contact with the enemy either offensively or defensively.

COMMENTARY

Schwarz illustrates that where the *mens rea* requires premeditation – which includes the intent to kill – even an unreasonable mistake of fact negates *mens rea* and operates as a defence. If the jury credited the defence that the accused honestly – albeit unreasonably – believed he was engaging with enemy fighters, the accused lacked the intent to kill civilians and could not be convicted of premeditated murder of civilians.

USA, US v. McMonagle, *US Court of Military Appeals, Judgment of 27 September 1993*

In 1990, US Army private McMonagle was deployed with his unit to Panama. After hostilities had ended, McMonagle and two members of his squad, Finsel and Gussen, went to a bar or brothel known as the Fenix Club. Finsel left a pistol which he had borrowed from Captain Seider on a table while he went to a back room with a Panamanian woman. As he rejoined his squad members, someone shouted that the military police (MPs) were nearby, causing the three soldiers to hide in a back room. When they came out of hiding about 15 minutes later, the pistol was missing. Finsel and McMonagle agreed to stage a sham firefight so that they could claim that the pistol was lost as a result. All three soldiers fired their M-16 rifles into the air while standing outside the Fenix Club and then ran toward a local school where the unit command post was located. On the way back, they met several other members of the unit who were responding to the sound of gunfire. Finsel told them that he had been fired upon by men with AK-47 rifles in a car and from a rooftop. He then began firing up at a three-story building. As the sham firefight continued, McMonagle yelled and ran down an alley into a courtyard. He began kicking in doors. The platoon sergeant Cavello followed McMonagle into the courtyard and told him to cool down. Captain Sieder ordered the unit to fall back to the school and directed McMonagle to remain behind as part of a rear security force, along with Finsel and Verrender. As the unit withdrew, Finsel ordered the rear security squad to stay and watch the house, from which – he said – fire had originated. A second firefight erupted, during which McMonagle shot Mrs. Panay, a civilian Panamanian woman. After hearing the commotion, Verrender entered the courtyard and saw McMonagle and the wounded victim. Mrs. Panay died shortly thereafter. McMonagle argued that he had acted upon a mistake of fact. The military panel convicted McMonagle for unlawful killing through an act inherently dangerous, but acquitted him of premeditated or intentional unlawful killing. The Court of Military Appeals reasoned as follows.

The military judge agreed to give an instruction on mistake of fact, as it relates to the unlawful nature of the killing, with respect to "all of these murder charges and the lesser included," but he neglected to repeat the instruction with respect to Article 118(3) [unlawful killing when the killer 'is engaged in an act that is inherently dangerous to another and evinces a wanton disregard of human life']. Appellant argues that mistake of fact goes to two elements of the offense: (1) the heedless or indifferent state of mind required for wanton disregard for human life and (2) the unlawfulness of the killing. The Court of Military Review held that appellant was not entitled to a mistake-of-fact instruction with respect to Article 118(3) because a mistake of fact would not negate the mental state of mind required to commit the offense. We hold that appellant was entitled to an instruction on mistake of fact with respect to Article 118(3).
    RCM 916(j) provides:

Except as otherwise provided in this subsection, it is a defense to an offense that the accused held, as a result of ignorance or mistake, an incorrect belief of the true circumstances such that, if the circumstances were as the accused believed them, the accused would not be guilty of the offense. If the ignorance or mistake goes to an element requiring premeditation, specific intent, willfulness, or knowledge of a particular fact, the ignorance or mistake need only have existed in the mind of the accused. If the ignorance or mistake goes to any other element requiring only general intent or knowledge, the ignorance or mistake must have existed in the mind of the accused and must have been reasonable under all the circumstances. However, if the accused's knowledge or intent is immaterial as to an element, then ignorance or mistake is not a defense.

The Court of Military Review held that "mistake...must negate a mental state of the accused that the prosecution must necessarily prove to establish the offense." [...] That court further held that the only two "mental state" elements involved in this case were (1) the intentional act of shooting and (2) knowledge that death or great bodily harm was a natural and probable consequence of shooting. Finally, that court held that "wanton disregard" characterized by "heedlessness or indifference" is not measured subjectively by the state of an accused's mind but is measured objectively by a "qualitative judgment" of the circumstances of his conduct. [...]

The Court of Military Review's interpretation of the state of mind required for a violation of Article 118(3) is inconsistent with the concept of a "depraved heart" which underlies Article 118(3). The terms "wanton," "disregard," "heedless," and "indifferent" all describe an attitude, a mental state. [...] In a depraved-heart murder, the killer's attitude is "not measured in the abstract, but is evaluated in light of the surrounding circumstances that are apparent and known to the perpetrator, or at least should reasonably be apparent and known by him." [...]

Although some courts have held that guilt of a depraved-heart murder should be founded on "an objective assessment of the risk created, regardless of whether the perpetrator actually realized it," [...] the weight of authority holds that a person should not be convicted of depraved-heart murder "unless he was subjectively aware of the risk he created." [...] This Court follows the majority view. See *United States v. Berg*, 30 MJ 195, 199 (CMA 1990) (Article 118(3) intended to cover cases where acts "are calculated to put human lives in jeopardy"); *United States v. Stokes*, supra (accused must know that acts endangered human life). See also para. 43c(4)(b), Part IV, Manual for Courts-Martial, United States, 1984; Milhizer, supra at 235–36.

The holding of the court below represents a minority view and is contrary to the decisions of this Court. Accordingly, we hold that the court below erred in holding that mistake of fact cannot rebut the state of mind required for a violation of Article 118(3).

The court below also held that appellant's mistaken belief would not negate the element of unlawfulness. This holding also is incorrect. The military judge correctly deduced that mistake of fact in this case gave rise to a defense of justification. Under the specific facts of this case, the two special defenses of mistake and justification are interrelated. A mistake of fact can negate unlawfulness because ignorance or mistake a [sic] fact can produce "a mental state which in turn supports a defense of justification." [...]

Murder under Article 118(3) is a general-intent crime. [...] Mistake of fact is not a defense to a general intent crime unless it is both honest and reasonable. [...] Accordingly, appellant's mistake as to the identity of the victim must have been both honest and reasonable to raise the defense of justification.

The military judge in this case instructed the court members on justification as a defense to murder under Article 118(2) [i.e. intentional killing]. He commented during the hearing on instructions that he intended to instruct on justification "as far as all of these murder charges and the lesser included." Based on this comment, we agree with the Court of Military Review's observation that the military judge intended to instruct on justification under Article 118(3) as well, but that he "inadvertently omitted instructing the members that 'unlawfulness' means without justification or excuse." [...]

We certainly do not believe that a military judge must define a term every time it is used. Nevertheless, in this case the military judge compartmentalized and separated his instructions on Article 118(2) and 118(3) to the extent that his failure to specifically advise the members that justification was a defense to Article 118(3) amounted to failure to give an instruction on a special defense as required by RCM 920(e)(3). He instructed separately on Article 118(2) and 118(3); he did not instruct that the defense of justification based on mistaken identity of the victim was available under Article 118(3) or remind the court members that the same definitions of "unlawful" and "without legal justification or excuse" were also applicable to Article 118(3); and he required the members to vote separately on the two theories of murder.

The net effect of the military judge's compartmentalized instructions was to tell the members that the special defense of justification based on an honest and reasonable mistake as to the identity of the victim was limited to Article 118(2) and not applicable to Article 118(3). Accordingly, we hold that the military judge erred by failing to advise the court members with respect to Article 118(3) that the killing was justified if appellant honestly and reasonably thought that he was shooting at a combatant.

IV. Conclusions

After reviewing the instructions in this case as a whole, we hold that the military judge correctly denied the request for an instruction on accident, because there was no evidence that death or grievous bodily harm was an unintended or unexpected consequence. The military judge correctly ruled that mistake of fact and the justification based on that mistake of fact were raised by the evidence. Unfortunately, the military judge presented his instructions in a manner suggesting that mistake of fact and justification were only applicable to unpremeditated murder under Article 118(2). There was no issue regarding appellant's knowledge that death or grievous bodily harm was a probable consequence of his acts, but there was a factual issue whether appellant thought he was receiving hostile fire and thought he was firing at a combatant when he shot and killed Mrs. Panay. Based on the evidence of record, we hold that the defense of justification based on mistake of fact was raised, because there is some evidence from which the court members could have concluded that appellant was laboring under an honest and reasonable mistake of fact when he shot and killed Mrs. Panay.

We hold further that the failure of the military judge to instruct on mistake of fact and justification with respect to Article 118(3) was prejudicial error. The theory of the defense was justification based on mistake of fact. The military judge's omission deprived appellant of the opportunity to have his defense theory considered by the members. [...]

Finally, because instructions on special defenses are not waived by failure to request them or to object to their omission, we hold that the military judge's error was not waived.

COMMENTARY

In contrast to the premeditated murder charge at issue in *Schwarz*, at issue here is a lesser form of murder, which only requires general intent. That is, the defendant need not have specifically intended to kill, nor specifically intended to harm a civilian. To negate this lower *mens rea* standard of general intent what kind of mistake is required?

Federal Republic of Germany, **Polish prisoner of war case,** *Federal Court of Justice* (Bundesgerichtshof), *Judgment of 12 December 1950*

As discussed above, very often the defence of mistake of fact is raised in connection with the execution of a superior order. An illustration of this category of case is a German decision rendered in 1950. On 10 October 1940 the accused, the commander of a detachment of border guards also entrusted with assignments by the Gestapo, had his men execute K., a Polish prisoner of war, on the orders of the Gestapo officer superior to him. K. in fact had not been court-martialled and duly sentenced. The Court of

Assize of Flensburg acquitted the accused. It found that he lacked the intent or culpable negligence required for the charge of 'intentional killing'. On appeal, the Federal Court of Justice dismissed the Prosecutor's appeal and upheld the acquittal.

The acquittal of the accused is based exclusively on the rejection of the accused's guilt in respect of intent and negligence.

[1] As regards the issue of guilt, the Trial Chamber considered that, in addition to knowledge and will regarding the circumstances relating to the legal elements of the case, in the sense of Article 59 of the StGB [German Criminal Code], [intent] includes the awareness of unlawfulness of an offence or the possibility of such awareness. Thus, the Trial Chamber agreed with an opinion which appears frequently in the recent literature of individual regional appellate courts. This contradicts the RG [*Reichsgericht*, Supreme Court of the Reich], which, in its regular decisions in force until the last days it was operative, considered that the awareness of unlawfulness did not pertain to intent (RGSt 2. 269: 58. 249; 61. 258; 63. 218; 73, 278).

It is not necessary to settle this fundamental legal issue, if the lack of the awareness of unlawfulness was based on an error in fact or on a non-criminal error in law, since the RG treated non-criminal errors in law in the same manner as it did errors in fact. i.e. it denied intent even if it was established that the perpetrator, as the result of a non-criminal error in law, was not aware of the unlawfulness of his act. This applies here.

At the time of the offence, the accused was aware of the fact that the judgments, as well as the carrying out of sentences, of citizens of Eastern peoples, were handled by offices of the Gestapo [*Geheime Staatspolizei*, or Secret State police]. At the time of the offence, he also assumed that K. had been sentenced to death in this manner. As the Trial Chamber explicitly stated, the accused had "no doubt that the judgment was issued by the appropriate authority in accordance with properly conducted proceedings which are final and conclusive". The accused's conviction was based on the content of a telex which he received in October 1944 from the *Gau* [District] Office of the Gestapo superior to him, and which was signed by the head of that office, a senior civil official. The contents of the telex were more or less that the Pole K. had been sentenced to death for a violation of the "Order for the Protection of Agents of the Law" and that the Main Office of the Reich Security Service had ordered the execution to take place in the district where the offence had been committed. Such an order did not in fact exist; but that is immaterial. The crucial fact is that the accused, according to the evidence presented in the contested judgment, believed in some type of formal "judgment" based on legal requirements (even if not rendered by a regular court). He also knew that fully qualified lawyers were employed at the higher office of the Gestapo. In a prior conversation in the Gestapo office it had been explicitly pointed out that the conviction of foreigners by the Gestapo occurred with the participation of fully qualified lawyers in something akin to a "chamber of judges".

The established facts concerning the accused's belief that there had been some sort of prior proceedings in relation to the facts as well as the lawfulness of those proceedings and of the guilty verdict and judgment of K., led the Trial Chamber to conclude that, at the time of the offence, the accused was convinced of the lawfulness of the writ of execution which he received from the Gestapo office as his immediate superior and also of the existence of grounds for the justification of his own participation in the killing. The Trial Chamber therefore correctly acquitted the accused of the charge of intentional killing based on his lack of awareness that his assessment of the offence might have been incorrect, even if one assumes the stricter interpretation of the RG. In this respect, the appeal is unfounded.

[2] The major thrust of the appeal runs counter to the determination of the Trial Chamber that, as regards the accused's assumption that the Pole had been lawfully convicted and that

the writ of execution against him was lawful, he did not act negligently in either a factual or a legal sense. The appeal's objection in this regard is unfounded as well.

The first issue, whether the legal provisions and administrative regulations issued by the Hitler government during the war regarding the conviction of Polish prisoners of war by offices of the Gestapo outside of ordinary legal proceedings, need not be resolved. This legal issue is a matter of international law. It was not at all clear, at least at the time of the offence, that it was to be decided negatively, as the appeal claims. In the judgment of Military Court V against the former General Field Marshal Wilhelm von Leeb and his associates after the war, this issue is characterized as dubious.

The issue depends solely on whether the accused could and should have, based on his personal circumstances, recognized the legal invalidity of such provisions. The Trial Chamber, after assuming that the offence was unlawful, denied this. It pointed out that, at the time of the offence, the accused, based on his personal circumstances, could not have been expected to recognize the illegality, according to international law, as well as the resulting invalidity of the death sentence which the Gestapo had issued and the execution of which he had been charged with. This was so especially because the accused, based on records of the police interrogation of K. which had been presented to him, was convinced, and could have been convinced, that the Pole had attacked the Superintendent of Police, and seized him by the neck, thereby committing an offence punishable by death. Although the accused may have been a capable, knowledgeable and experienced official within a group of criminal investigators to which he had belonged for 24 years before the offence, he nevertheless, according to the legally incontrovertible evidence presented to the Trial Chamber, did not have the knowledge necessary for appreciating these issues of State and international law. There are no indications that, at the time of the offence, the accused had any reason to mistrust the academically trained head of the Gestapo office. Moreover, the accused had learned from experience prior to the offence that the administration of criminal justice against Poles had passed from the hands of the judiciary to the offices of the Gestapo, and that, according to his observations, the Public Prosecutor's offices and ordinary criminal courts had generally not resisted this. In this respect, it does not matter if there were also courts and prosecutors that, exceptionally, resisted this, inasmuch as it has not been established that the accused had knowledge of such exceptions. Nor did the accused, based on the wartime laws in effect then and based on the critical situation that Schleswig-Holstein was in at the time, have any reason to doubt the factual legality of a death sentence against a Polish prisoner of war who physically attacked a police superintendent.

QUESTIONS

1. How does the *mens rea* standard for an offence determine whether an accused's mistake of fact is a defence?

2. The main issue at stake when evaluating a claim of mistake of fact often appears to be that of the reasonableness of the error. Are the mistakes by the defendants in the cases discussed above all reasonable? What elements should be considered in such an assessment?

3. Is mistake of fact always linked to a superior order?

FURTHER READING

A. Cassese, *International Criminal Law*, 290–3.

J. Ohlin, 'Mistake of Fact', in *Oxford Companion*, 421.

(E) MISTAKE OF LAW

International criminal law, like all national legal systems, upholds the principle that no one is allowed to ignore the law (*ignorantia legis non excusat*). Compliance with this principle is required by law and order. Indeed, if ignorance of law were admitted as a defence, the applicability of criminal norms would differ from person to person, depending on their degree of knowledge of law. Moreover, the admission of such a defence would eventually constitute an incentive for persons to break the law and then simply try to prove that they were not actually aware of the existence of a legal prohibition.

Nevertheless, in international criminal law there may be cases where a mistake of law may become relevant as an excuse. This occurs not when the offender was unaware of the unlawfulness of his conduct, but (i) he had no knowledge of an essential element of law referred to in the international prohibition of a certain conduct; (ii) this lack of knowledge did not result from negligence; (iii) consequently the person, when he took a certain action, did not possess the requisite *mens rea*. For instance, a low-ranking member of an occupying army, genuinely believing that his action is allowed by international humanitarian law, sets fire to private property following an order to take reprisals against civilians who have committed a war crime against the occupying army. Under certain circumstances, this situation may give rise to an error of law excusing the low-ranking soldier for his (criminal) conduct.

This notion is codified in ICCSt. Article 32(2), under which '[a] mistake of law as to whether a particular type of conduct is a crime within the jurisdiction of the Court shall not be a ground for excluding criminal responsibility. A mistake of law may, however, be a ground for excluding criminal responsibility if it negates the mental element required by such a crime, or as provided for in article 33 [on superior orders]'. Scholars have argued that this provision opens the door for mistakes with regard to normative elements and evaluations.[2] This might have an enormous impact on the prosecution of crimes within ICC jurisdiction.

Cases

Germany, Llandovery Castle (Dithmar and Boldt *case*), *Supreme Court* (Reichsgericht*) at Leipzig, Judgment of 16 July 1921

First Lieutenant Patzig, a senior officer on a German submarine, ordered his men to fire on lifeboats full of shipwrecked marines after the submarine sank a British hospital

---

[2] A. Eser, 'Mental Elements – Mistake of Fact and Mistake of Law', in A. Cassese *et al.* (eds), *The Rome Statute of the International Criminal Court: A Commentary*, vol. I (Oxford: OUP, 2002), 889, at 941.

ship suspected of transporting troops (for further details about the facts of the case, see *supra*, under Superior Orders, Part IV(2)(A), at p. 264). The court discussed the issue of whether ignorance of law could be raised as a defence to this war crime.

The fact that his [the First Lieutenant's] deed is a violation of international law must be well-known to the doer, apart from acts of carelessness, in which careless ignorance is a sufficient excuse. In examining the question of the existence of this knowledge, the ambiguity of many of the rules of international law, as well as the actual circumstances of the case, must be borne in mind, because in war time decisions of great importance have frequently to be made on very insufficient material. This consideration, however, cannot be applied to the case at present before the court. The rule of international law, which is here involved, is simple and is universally known. No possible doubt can exist with regard to the question of its applicability. The court must in this instance affirm [First Lieutenant] Patzig's guilt of killing contrary to international law.

As is evident from the *Llandovery Castle* case, the plea of mistake of law is often intertwined with the defence of superior orders, because one of the elements of the latter might hinge on the awareness that the order was illegal. Examples of this type of mistake in such a context are discussed below.

Netherlands, In re Wintgen, *Special Court of Cassation, Judgment of 6 July 1949*

Wintgen, a member of the German Security Police during the occupation of the Netherlands, acting under orders, set fire to a number of houses near Amsterdam as a reprisal for acts of sabotage committed by unknown persons on a nearby railway line. Convicted of a war crime by the Amsterdam Special Criminal Court on 11 February 1949, he appealed, stating, among other things, that his acts did not constitute a war crime. The Court rejected this, stating that the tribunal below had rightly held that the arson came under the provision of 'devastation not justified by military necessity' contained in Article 6(b) of the Charter of the International Military Tribunal and at the same time constituted a violation of Article 50 of the Hague Regulations of 1907. The Court rejected the distinction sometimes made by writers between reprisals and ordinary penalties, if only on the ground that penalties are never imposed on persons other than those who are actually guilty; and every so-called punishment which is directed against innocent persons comes within the term 'acts of vengeance' expressly prohibited by Article 50 of the Hague Regulations for the protection of the population of occupied territory.

However, even though it is admitted that the acts of the accused were correctly termed war crimes, it does not necessarily follow that he must be punished for his acts. In situations such as this, committing a war crime may be excused by the defence that *"ihm nich bekannt gewesen ist, dass der Befehl des Vorgesetzten eine handlung betraf, welche ein [...] militärisches verbrechen [...] bezweckte"* (he was unaware that the orders given to him by a superior related to an act that aimed at committing a military crime, Article 47, para. 1, of the German Military Criminal Code). Such a plea should not be lightly accepted. Its acceptability depends, on the one hand, on the intellectual level and rank in the military hierarchy of the individual concerned and, on the other hand, on the nature of the acts committed. In connection with the latter, the killing of defenceless prisoners or innocent civilians has, in the view of every civilized person, a much more serious character than the destruction of property. In this case, and taking into account the above with regard to the punishment of the war crime of arson, it should be held that the person committing the crime, a low-ranking police officer, was not aware of the criminal nature of his act under military law. Therefore he should not be held criminally liable for the war crime he committed.

Netherlands, B., Court Martial, Judgment of 2 January 1951

The accused B. was the commander of a unit of the Dutch Resistance movement (*Nederlandse Binnenlandse Strijdkrachten*) which had been granted the status of armed forces as part of the Royal Dutch Army, by a Dutch royal decree of 1944. In April 1945 the unit joined with a detachment of French parachutists that had landed in the Netherlands. Shortly thereafter the group took prisoner four Dutch Nazis, members of the NSB (*Nationaal-Socialistische Beweging in Nederland*, a Dutch fascist and later national socialist party) in civilian clothes; they regarded those Dutch Nazis as *franc-tireurs* (i.e. members of irregular military formations, not entitled to prisoners-of-war status in case of capture) and traitors. One of the captives escaped. Meanwhile the group had captured other Dutch Nazis and released some others. There was a danger that with the help of the escaped prisoner, the Germans would attack them. Under these circumstances the presence of the remaining prisoners presented a serious danger to the unit.

  B. consulted with the French commander, who did not instruct him to kill the prisoners. However, B. did gather from his behaviour, and also from that of the other French parachutists who were present, consisting of pointing to their Sten guns and drawing their hands across their throats, that, in his position, they would have proceeded to liquidate the prisoners. B. then ordered v. E. (another member of the Dutch Resistance movement) to kill the prisoners with the assistance of other members of the unit.

  When the case was brought before a Dutch Field Court Martial in 1950, the Prosecuting Officer, in his statement, argued that the conduct of the accused was unlawful. However, with regard to the accused's defence that he was mistaken as to the unlawfulness of the offence, he stated that this was 'not in itself sufficient to relieve him of responsibility; for that the error must also have been pardonable. Only if there was no intent and no negligence as to the unlawfulness, is the accused not liable criminally'. In conclusion he asked the court to find the accused guilty of being an accomplice to manslaughter and to sentence him to six months' imprisonment. The Court Martial agreed with the Prosecuting Officer that the action by B. was unlawful, for, although the prisoners' legal status was 'even inferior to that of *franc-tireurs*', they nevertheless could not be shot and killed immediately after being captured.

Considering furthermore the issue of the accused's criminal liability:

  The Court Martial is of the opinion that it cannot be argued, as the Prosecuting Officer does, that an offence which, had it been committed against subjects of the other side, would constitute a war crime, would *a fortiori* not be permitted against fellow-countrymen.

  In the opinion of the Court Martial, fellow-countrymen who attack members of their own armed forces or betray them to the enemy, place themselves in a position such that they clearly cannot rely on the rights which are due to subjects of the other side, but their position in certain circumstances must even be subordinated to that of *franc-tireurs*; this does not, however, mean that it is permitted to kill such people, not at the time they are caught committing their deed, but only after they have been taken prisoner for some time, as in the present case. Therefore the accused acted unlawfully.

However, in the opinion of the Court Martial, the accused was entitled to assume with virtual certainty that the four arrested persons were persons who, if they had been able to, would have attacked his K.P. group and the French parachutists or betrayed them to the enemy.

The situation in which B. and his K.P. group found themselves was such that, if one of them had fallen into the hands of the Germans, this would certainly have cost this person his life, it being general knowledge that the enemy did not regard persons belonging to such groups as legal combatants and would not have treated them as such; the views of the members of his group and of the French parachutists, as has emerged from the examinations, were such that liquidation of the members of the N.S.B. taken prisoner was not regarded as unlawful; this attitude is confirmed by the instructions which applied to the *Binnenlandse Strijdkrachten* at the time.

It is general knowledge that the broadcasts of Radio Orange from England were also intended to give the impression that members of the N.S.B. were to be regarded as traitors and that it was unnecessary to show them any consideration, nor would they be shown any.

The Court Martial has become convinced, on the strength of the accused's statement and of the facts referred to above, that the accused believed that he was entitled to act as he did and that the accused's intent was not therefore directed at the unlawfulness of his actions.

The accused had to take his decision without being able to consult a superior; he was placed in a position for which he was not trained and in circumstances in which it was practically impossible quietly to consider the relative merits of the various interests, so that he also cannot be held responsible for the unlawfulness of his actions.

Therefore, it is true that the accused was acting unlawfully when he instructed v. E. to liquidate the four members of the N.S.B., but he was mistaken as to the unlawfulness of his actions [. . .]

The accused is therefore not criminally liable and must be acquitted.

Federal Republic of Germany, Sch. and Dr. L. (Gestapo members *case*), Federal High Court (Bundesgerichtshof*), Judgment of 14 October 1952*

As stated above (under Necessity, Part IV(2)(C), at p. 494), on many occasions two Gestapo officers executed a secret Order of the Main Office of the Reich Security Service of 5 November 1942. Under this Order, it was permitted to subject workers from Eastern countries to a 'short treatment' (which consisted of fustigating, instead of briefly imprisoning, workers who had refused to work or committed disciplinary violations), or a 'special treatment' (that is, hanging, without any prior trial, workers who had committed criminal offences). The two accused had taken part in both categories of action. A Munich Court of Assize (*Schwurgericht*) held that, since the Order did not have the value of a binding law justifying their actions, the two were responsible for bodily harm in the exercise of their actions, with regard to the 'short treatment', and for aiding and abetting murder, in connection with their participation in the 'special treatment'. On appeal, the Federal High Court upheld the Court of Assize's decision that the first excuse was not applicable, for the accused were aware of the unlawfulness of their actions.

As regards the mental element of the offence, the Court of Assize was concerned with the appellants' assertion that they considered their conduct lawful and legal on the basis of the RSHA (*Main Office of the Reich Security Service*) decree of 5 November 1942. The Court of Assize is of the opinion that, in addition to the knowledge and will included in the elements of an offence in its statutory definition, the awareness of the unlawfulness of an offence also constitutes a part of intent. However, it considers it proven that the accused were aware of the injustice of their actions, because [they] did not believe in the legality of the decree of 5 November 1942. Nevertheless, the legal starting point of the Court of Assize requires correction. The Higher Appeals Chamber, in *BGHSt*, 2, 194 = *NJW 52*, 593 decided further that in cases where illegality is not a special element of an offence but a general characteristic thereof, the perpetrator, assuming he committed all elements of the crime knowingly and willingly, must be punished for the intentional commission of an offence not only if he was aware of its unlawfulness but also if, because of pangs of conscience, he could have been aware that he was committing an injustice. For the particular case when the elements of a punishable offence are established by a court judgment, and such judgment is enforced, the Appeals Chamber, [...] has stated that the participant may be held criminally responsible for the offence only if he knew that the judgment was contrary to the true legal situation, or at least considered that possibility and was willing to participate in that case. The Appeals Chamber also decided in this manner for the case of the attempt to commit intentional murder, where the elements of the offence do not include illegality as an element of the offence. However, the facts of the case, which have been considered as proven by the Court of Assize, differ from that case. The Court of Assize has ruled out the assumption that the accused could have erroneously considered facts as given, which, had they been present, could have provided grounds for the justification of his actions. In the whole situation, he could, at most, have erroneously believed in a justification that did not exist in reality and that could not be recognised in any legal order. A possible error by the accused would have been in the ambit of the legal appreciation of his actions. It thus follows that such an error does not necessarily release the perpetrator from responsibility for the intentional realisation of the elements of the offence of bodily harm while exercising his functions and of grievous bodily harm, but that such an error would have to be handled according to the principles concerning errors as to the prohibited nature of an act specified in *BGHSt*. 2, 194 = NJW 52, 593. Considering the fact that the Court of Assize holds the accused's defence to be refuted and that it regards it as proven that they were aware of the unlawfulness of their actions, this issue requires no further discussion here.

QUESTIONS

1. What factors did the courts take into account in order to conclude that in these specific cases a mistake of law could (or could not) be pleaded? In particular, with regard to *B.*, were the criticisms of B.V.A. Röling (a distinguished Dutch international lawyer and judge) justified when he noted that summary executions are never lawful, and every reasonable person is or must be fully aware of this prohibition?

2. Is it always easy to distinguish mistakes of law from mistakes of fact? What about, for instance, the question of whether targeted victims belong to a 'protected group' for the purpose of the definition of genocide? Is this a question of law or fact?

FURTHER READING

G. Fletcher, *Rethinking Criminal Law* (Oxford: Oxford University Press, 730–6.

K.J. Heller, 'Mistake of Legal Element, the Common Law, and Article 32 of the Rome Statute – A Critical Analysis', (2008) 6 JICJ 419–45.

J. Ohlin, 'Mistake of Law', in *Oxford Companion*, 422–3.

(F) MENTAL DISORDER

Insanity or mental disorder (or mental incapacitation or mental disease) can be pleaded as an excuse whenever this state of mind entails that the person is deprived of the mental capability necessary for deciding whether an act is right or wrong. The plea may be urged when at the time of commission of the crime the accused was unaware of what he or she was doing and hence unable to form a rational judgment about his or her conduct. As a consequence, the accused, while committing an unlawful act, lacked the requisite *mens rea* and may not be held responsible for the behaviour.

Article 31(1)(a) ICCSt. provides that '[a person shall not be criminally responsible if, at the time of that person's conduct, he or she] suffers from a mental disease or defect that destroys that person's capacity to appreciate the unlawfulness or nature of his or her conduct, or capacity to control his or her conduct to conform to the requirements of law'.

Cases

***Germany,* Stenger and Crusius,** *German Imperial Court* (Reichsgericht) *in Leipzig, Judgment of 6 July 1921*

During World War I the German Captain Benno Crusius, commander of a company, was accused of passing on to his subordinates, in the battle of 26 August 1914 against French troops in the forest near Sainte Barbe (Alsace), what he construed as an order from Major General Karl Stenger not to take prisoners of war – in other words to kill all captured enemy soldiers (so-called denial of quarter). The Supreme Court of Leipzig found that, while in a state of mental disorder, Captain Crusius had misunderstood that order and hence wrongly ordered the killing of prisoners of war.

During the following days, the 58th Infantry Brigade continued its pursuit of the enemy towards the southwest through the villages of Hessen, Frackelfingen, Cireh, Merville. On 25 August, it captured Thiaville. The French retreated to the forest of Ste. Barbe to the south and west where they entrenched themselves solidly. Infantry Regiment No. 142 suffered significant losses when it tried to mop up the forest. The 112th Infantry Regiment's 1st Battalion was used as a support. In the afternoon, an attack by the 142nd Infantry Regiment's 2nd Battalion and the 112th Infantry Regiment's 1st Battalion failed. Defending themselves against an enemy who kept appearing from all sides of a wooded area which was difficult to see through, the troops suffered heavy losses and had to retreat.

During an investigation of Stenger regarding the events of 26 August 1914 conducted before the Military Investigation Office for Breaches of the Laws of War, Crusius was questioned as a witness on 28 January 1915 and testified under oath. He said: [']We were the corps reserve and were moved forward between 1400 and 1500 hours. Major General Stenger was up ahead with First Lieutenant Neubauer, the regiment leader. Stenger first listened to the orders which Neubauer issued to the battalion leaders. Shortly before the last of them left to implement the orders, Stenger said, "We are not taking any prisoners." Since I was among the company leaders up front, I heard those words clearly and understood them to be an order. Then I passed the order on to the two companies which were subordinated to me at the time. The troops became extremely embittered because we heard that our men up-front were again being shot at from the trees. Major Müller probably passed on the order as I did.[']

Even today the accused stands behind this account and adds: 'In the afternoon at around 1500 hours, Stenger discussed the tactical situation with Neubauer, Müller, the brigade and the regiment adjutants near the forest hut and, agitated, made disparaging remarks about the enemy's way of fighting. Following Neubauer's issuing of the combat order, Stenger went on to tell the officers present, "No prisoners are to be taken; there will be no mercy, and no one shall ask for mercy." ' Soon after that, Crusius passed the order on to the 3rd and 4th Companies and led them into battle. He heard Stenger call out to them once again, "Don't you dare bring any prisoners back!"

Contrary to this account, the accused Stenger described the event of the afternoon of 26 August as follows: His task was to mop up the forest and block the enemy's retreat. By afternoon, he had received numerous reports about how the French fought – they pretended to be dead, wounded or surrendering, only to start shooting at the passing troops from behind and from up in the trees with rifles and machine guns. One of the reports said that a man from a bicycle patrol was found with his throat cut, and another with his eyes gouged out. As the commander responsible for the well-being of the troops, he needed both to talk to the people around him and to call out warnings and encouragement to the troops by pointing out the dangers to their own safety which, under such circumstances, were the result of an effort to bring back as many prisoners as possible. Although he did not explicitly give an order to kill, he did say something like "The French are said to be sitting on the trees and shooting down from above; even the wounded are shooting from behind. Watch out! It is not important to take prisoners (or possibly: We have no use for prisoners today), but to defend yourselves and guard against the enemy's treachery. Shoot these guys off the trees like sparrows!" His words were only meant to alert everybody to be cautious, to proceed resolutely against fighting enemies, and to be especially aware of insidious attacks. They were however by no means intended to refer to the enemies who were wounded, defenceless or who seriously offered to surrender. In view of how clearly the words were expressed, they could not have referred to those enemies either. He believes that such an order would certainly not be permissible under international law, even under the critical conditions which had developed by the afternoon of 26 August.

The accused Stenger also noted that his two regiment commanders at least should have known of such an order, and that, in fact, on 26 August, just as on the previous days, many prisoners were taken and led past him and, in particular, past the forest hut (which Crusius mentioned) without his having expressed any criticism. He did not know of a possible passing on of the questionable "order" to one or more of the companies, not on instructions from the accused Crusius or from Major Müller.

The Court then reported the testimonies given by a number of military personnel.

There are no indications that the witness mistook the accused Stenger for the accused Crusius, who, according to witness Dominik, was later heard to have had three French prisoners who had been taken past Stenger shot. Furthermore, in his description, Oberdorf cannot have referred to the count of the indictment against Crusius based on Dr. Wenger's testimony about the shooting of two French Alpine Troops in the evening of 26 August.

The evidence for the accusation against Stenger, as it relates to the events on 26 August, is thus essentially exhausted. It does not establish that the accused committed a crime pursuant to Article 212 of the Criminal Code or an offence pursuant to Article 116 of the Military Criminal Code, or any other criminal act with which the accused can be charged; rather, in this case, like in case 1 on 21 August, it has been proved again that the accused is not guilty. Likewise, on 26 August, Stenger issued neither a written nor a verbal brigade order whose content appears in the extradition list. The cautions, encouragements and warnings he addressed both to the people around him and to troops walking past him referred unmistakably in form and content to defence and attacks against fighting enemies, particularly those fighting insidiously. Since it would have seriously put them in harm's way, they were instructed not to spend time, for instance because of personal ambition, on capturing enemies who were shooting from trees or on those continuing their armed fight behind the back of the German troops even though they were wounded. The situation that day was not conducive for that. The typical final words used to summarize what had been said before, "Shoot these guys (sitting in the trees) down like sparrows," could not have been taken as referring to defenceless enemies or to those who seriously offered to surrender.

The accused Crusius does not deny that an order to take no prisoners and to show no mercy was passed on to his company as an order from Major General Stenger which was carried out by the troops on several occasions during the ensuing battle in the forest in the afternoon of 26 August.

In order to make a decision about the charges raised against him for that reason, it would be necessary to begin to examine and to acknowledge the existing evidence as well as to have a discussion based on the established facts of the matter as to whether the accused should be charged from the point of view of premeditation or culpable negligence for the proved cases of killing or wounding of enemies who were defenceless or who had laid down their arms, insofar as the killing or wounding were the result of his conduct. Furthermore, the question of the accused having overstepped the alleged order in some cases – in premeditation or negligence – would have to be raised. Encouraging the troops not to take any prisoners and not to have mercy, i.e. to reject serious offers by the enemy to surrender, and to force them to fight until some of them were destroyed, does not necessarily imply an order to kill the enemies who were captured contrary to this instruction or those unfit for battle because they were wounded. While under any circumstances the latter runs contrary to the prevailing views and provisions of more recent laws of war, legal opinion does find that, although a rejection of an offer to be taken prisoner conflicts with the "guidelines" of Article 23 c, d of the Order on Land Warfare, it can nevertheless be justified by the necessity of war and as an exception in individual cases.

The Court cites other testimonies on the issue of Crusius' mental state.

Admittedly, according to the testimony of Dr. Döhner, Laule, Schreiber and Dominik, and also Gretz, Eldagsen and others, a complete mental and psychological collapse, i.e. a state of utter mental confusion, which would unequivocally preclude responsibility pursuant to criminal law, only emerged with certainty in the late afternoon of 26 August, at around the time when the accused, distraught, with a bright red face and swollen eyes, came running out of the forest, screaming and rushing towards Dr. Döhner, grabbing his arm, desperately uttering calls, and leaving the overall impression of a maniac. However, the expert witnesses, Anton, Bumke, Sernau and Döhner, agreed that this state did not occur suddenly and abruptly but rather gradually worsened after having developed from an already existing nervous condition induced by a psychopathic disposition and by the particular disturbances of the battle days in Mülhausen, Saarburg and Ste. Barbe. Naturally, the exact time this so-called diminished responsibility, which according to current law is inconsequential for determining the question of guilt, turned into a mental state as defined in Article 51 of the Criminal Code, cannot be determined. The expert witnesses Anton, Bumke and Sernau (who differ from Dr. Döhner insofar as they did not maintain a similar presumption for 21 August) all demonstrated with convincing justification that a possibility, indeed an overwhelming likelihood, existed for claiming that in the afternoon of 26 August when the supposed brigade order was passed on (not when it was carried out, Reich Legal Gazette Vol. 22, p. 414), the accused was suffering from a mental disorder rendering him incapable of forming a rational intention. The court agrees with their expert opinions. However, since established practice of the courts (Reich Legal Gazette Vol. 21, p. 131) precludes a guilty judgment if there is reasonable doubt about the perpetrator's ability to exercise his will, no judgment can be passed on count I of the indictment (Article 116 of the Military Criminal Code) in relation to 26 August and on count 3 of the same (Article 212 of the Criminal Code). The accused Crusius is thus acquitted.

COMMENTARY

It is notable that in the same case the Court rejected the same plea with respect to a previous episode. Captain Crusius had been accused of transmitting unlawful orders of Major General Stenger to his subordinates on 21 August 1914. The Court found that in fact he had misunderstood the superior orders; when he passed them on to his subordinates, he was in 'extreme agitation and psychological suffering'; however, his mental state was not such as to preclude his 'free determination of will'. Crusius was therefore found guilty on that count.

The defence of complete insanity – to be distinguished from diminished mental capacity, which might be relevant at the stage of sentencing as mitigating circumstance – has been recognized also by the ICTY (*Delalić et al.* Appeal Judgment of 20 February 2001, para. 582).

QUESTIONS

1. In many contemporary conflicts, combatants are under the influence of various drugs or substances, often with the connivance or even at the prompting of their superiors. How does this affect the possibility of pleading an altered mental state in case of crimes committed during the conflict?

2. When in doubt about the level or gravity of mental trouble of the accused at the time of the commission of a crime, may a court consider his diminished mental state as an extenuating circumstance?

FURTHER READING

P. Krug, 'The Emerging Mental Incapacity Defence in International Criminal Law: Some Initial Questions of Implementation' (2000) 94 AJIL 317.

J. Ohlin, 'Mental Disease', in *Oxford Companion*, 415–16.

(G) *TU QUOQUE*

The *tu quoque* (Latin for 'you, too') defence, which is hardly conceivable in domestic criminal trials, appears to have a certain appeal in international proceedings. This is probably due to the often-perceived political nature of certain prosecutions: a defendant often feels entitled to ask why he should be prosecuted and punished when other participants in the same conflicts behaved in a similar way.

Strictly speaking, the *tu quoque* argument is only made when a defendant argues that since one side has committed certain crimes, it has no authority to prosecute or punish nationals of the other side for similar crimes. However, the expression is today also used to characterize those defences based on a general invocation by an individual that his adversaries, while engaging in practices similar to those on which his indictment is based, have escaped prosecution. Thus, judges in international criminal proceedings have often been faced with arguments that the conduct of the accused should be excused because the other party to the conflict in question also engaged in the same behaviour.

Cases

IMT Nuremberg, **Göring et al.,** *Judgment of 30 September–1 October 1946 (Dönitz)*

Karl Dönitz held various high-level positions in the German Navy during World War II, in particular that of *Befehlshaber der Unterseeboote* (Commander of Submarines) and, from 1943, *Oberbefehlshaber der Kriegsmarine* (Commander in Chief of the Navy). Following Hitler's death, on 1 May 1945 he became Head of State and Supreme Commander of the Armed Forces. He was indicted and tried, together with Göring and the other major war criminals before the International Military Tribunal at Nuremberg, on count 1 (common plan or conspiracy), count 2 (aggression), and count 3 (war crimes). The IMT found him guilty of waging aggressive war but not guilty of conspiracy. The following excerpt discusses his responsibility for war crimes.

Dönitz is charged with waging unrestricted submarine warfare contrary to the Naval Protocol of 1936, to which Germany acceded, and which reaffirmed the rules of submarine warfare laid down in the London Naval Agreement of 1930.

The Prosecution has submitted that on 3 September 1939 the German U-boat arm began to wage unrestricted submarine warfare upon all merchant ships, whether enemy or neutral, cynically disregarding the Protocol; and that a calculated effort was made throughout the war to disguise this practice by making hypocritical references to international law and supposed violations by the Allies.

Dönitz insists that at all times the Navy remained within the confines of international law and of the Protocol. He testified that when the war began, the guide to submarine warfare was the German Prize Ordinance, taken almost literally from the Protocol, that pursuant to the German view, he ordered submarines to attack all merchant ships in convoy, and all that refused to stop or used their radio upon sighting a submarine. When his reports indicated that British merchant ships were being used to give information by wireless, were being armed, and were attacking submarines on sight, he ordered his submarines on 17 October 1939 to attack all enemy merchant ships without warning on the ground that resistance was to be expected.

Orders already had been issued on 21 September 1939 to attack all ships, including neutrals, sailing at night without lights in the English Channel.

On 24 November 1939, the German Government issued a warning to neutral shipping that, owing to the frequent engagements taking place in the waters around the British Isles and the French coast between U-boats and Allied merchant ships which were armed and had instructions to use those arms as well as to ram U-boats, the safety of neutral ships in those waters could no longer be taken for granted. On 1 January 1940, the German U-boat command, acting on the instructions of Hitler, ordered U-boats to attack all Greek merchant ships in the zone surrounding the British Isles which was banned by the United States to its own ships and also merchant ships of every nationality in the limited area of the Bristol Channel. Five days later a further order was given to U-boats to "make immediately unrestricted use of weapons against all ships" in an area of the North Sea, the limits of which were defined. Finally on 18 January 1940, U-boats were authorized to sink, without warning, all ships "in those waters near the enemy coasts in which the use of mines can be pretended." Exceptions were to be made in the cases of United States, Italian, Japanese, and Soviet ships.

Shortly after the outbreak of war the British Admiralty, in accordance with its *Handbook of Instructions* of 1938 to the Merchant Navy, armed its merchant vessels, in many cases convoyed them with armed escort, gave orders to send position reports upon sighting submarines, thus integrating merchant vessels into the warning network of naval intelligence. On 1 October 1939 the British Admiralty announced that British merchant ships had been ordered to ram U-boats if possible.

In the actual circumstances of this case, the Tribunal is not prepared to hold Dönitz guilty for his conduct of submarine warfare against British armed merchant ships.

However, the proclamation of operational zones and the sinking of neutral merchant vessels which enter those zones presents a different question. This practice was employed in the war of 1914–18 by Germany and adopted in retaliation by Great Britain. The Washington Conference of 1922, the London Naval Agreement of 1930 and the Protocol of 1936 were entered into with full knowledge that such zones had been employed in the First World War. Yet the Protocol made no exception for operational zones. The order of Dönitz to sink neutral ships without warning when found within these zones was therefore, in the opinion of the Tribunal, therefore a violation of the Protocol.

It is also asserted that the German U-boat arm not only did not carry out the warning and rescue provisions of the Protocol but that Dönitz deliberately ordered the killing of survivors of shipwrecked vessels, whether enemy or neutral. The Prosecution has introduced much evidence surrounding two orders of Dönitz, War Order Number 154, issued in 1939, and the so-called "Laconia" order of 1942. The Defense argues that these orders and the evidence supporting them do not show such a policy and introduced much evidence to the contrary. The Tribunal is of the opinion that the evidence does not establish with the certainty required that Dönitz deliberately ordered the killing of shipwrecked survivors. The orders were undoubtedly ambiguous, and deserve the strongest censure.

The evidence further shows that the rescue provisions were not carried out and that the Defendant ordered that they should not be carried out. The argument of the Defense is that the security of the submarine is, as the first rule of the sea, paramount to rescue and that the development of aircraft made rescue impossible. This may be so, but the Protocol is explicit. If the commander cannot rescue, then under its terms he cannot sink a merchant vessel and should allow it to pass harmless before his periscope. These orders, then, prove Dönitz is guilty of a violation of the Protocol.

In view of all of the facts proved and in particular of an order of the British Admiralty announced on 8 May 1940, according to which all vessels should be sunk at night in the Skagerrak, and the answer to interrogatories by Admiral Nimitz stating that unrestricted submarine warfare was carried on in the Pacific Ocean by the United States from the first day that nation entered the war, the sentence of Dönitz is not assessed on the ground of his breaches of the international law of submarine warfare.

The *Dönitz* case appears to have been a rare instance where invoking *tu quoque* actually worked to the benefit of the defendant – although the expression used by the tribunal ('the sentence of Doenitz is not assessed') does not conclusively tell us whether the judges (i) recognized the claim as a justification proper, (ii) simply felt that – despite Doenitz's undeniable criminal responsibility – it would have been unfair to impose a sentence for a conduct their side had also engaged in, or (iii) decided that the rule in question had become obsolete due to the contrary practice of all sides involved. The ICTY has also routinely faced claims amounting to, or at least hinting at, *tu quoque*. Two examples are discussed below.

ICTY, Prosecutor v. Kupreškić, *Trial Chamber, Judgment of 14 January 2000*

In *Kupreškić*, six Bosnian Croats faced charges that they had helped prepare, and had participated in, an attack against Bosnian Muslims in the area of the Ahmići-Šantići village (Lašva River Valley) in April 1993. The Defence put forth, among other arguments, the suggestion that the attacks against the Muslim population in the Lašva River Valley were justifiable because similar attacks were allegedly being perpetrated by Muslims against the Croat population elsewhere. For instance, during cross-examination of a witness, Defence counsel gave a list of Croatian villages from which Croats had allegedly been expelled and their houses burnt, which the judges understood as an attempt to suggest that the Ahmići massacres were justified.

515. Defence counsel have indirectly or implicitly relied upon the *tu quoque* principle, i.e. the argument whereby the fact that the adversary has also committed similar crimes offers a valid defence to the individuals accused. This is an argument resting on the allegedly reciprocal nature of obligations created by the humanitarian law of armed conflict. This argument may amount to saying that breaches of international humanitarian law, being committed by the enemy, justify similar breaches by a belligerent. Or it may amount to saying that such breaches, having been perpetrated by the adversary, legitimise similar breaches by a belligerent in response to, or in retaliation for, such violations by the enemy. Clearly, this second approach to a large extent coincides with the doctrine of reprisals, and is accordingly assessed below. Here the Trial Chamber will confine itself to briefly discussing the first meaning of the principle at issue.

516. It should first of all be pointed out that although *tu quoque* was raised as a defence in war crimes trials following the Second World War, it was universally rejected. The US Military Tribunal in the *High Command* trial, for instance, categorically stated that under general principles of law, an accused does not exculpate himself from a crime by showing that another has committed a similar crime, either before or after the commission of the crime by the accused. Indeed, there is in fact no support either in State practice or in the opinions of publicists for the validity of such a defence.

517. Secondly, the *tu quoque* argument is flawed in principle. It envisages humanitarian law as based upon a narrow bilateral exchange of rights and obligations. Instead, the bulk of this body of law lays down absolute obligations, namely obligations that are unconditional or in other words not based on reciprocity. This concept is already encapsulated in Common Article 1 of the 1949 Geneva Conventions, which provides that "The High Contracting Parties

undertake to respect [...] the present Convention *in all circumstances*" (emphasis added). Furthermore, attention must be drawn to a common provision (respectively Articles 51, 52, 131 and 148) which provides that "No High Contracting party shall be allowed to absolve itself or any other High Contracting Party of any liability incurred by itself or by another High Contracting Party in respect of breaches referred to in the preceding Article [i.e. grave breaches]". Admittedly, this provision only refers to State responsibility for grave breaches committed by State agents or *de facto* State agents, or at any rate for grave breaches generating State responsibility (e.g. for an omission by the State to prevent or punish such breaches). Nevertheless, the general notion underpinning those provisions is that liability for grave breaches is absolute and may in no case be set aside by resort to any legal means such as derogating treaties or agreements. *A fortiori* such liability and, more generally, individual criminal responsibility for serious violations of international humanitarian law may not be thwarted by recourse to arguments such as reciprocity.

518. The absolute nature of most obligations imposed by rules of international humanitarian law reflects the progressive trend towards the so-called 'humanisation' of international legal obligations, which refers to the general erosion of the role of reciprocity in the application of humanitarian law over the last century. After the First World War, the application of the laws of war moved away from a reliance on reciprocity between belligerents, with the consequence that, in general, rules came to be increasingly applied by each belligerent despite their possible disregard by the enemy. The underpinning of this shift was that it became clear to States that norms of international humanitarian law were not intended to protect State interests; they were primarily designed to benefit individuals *qua* human beings. Unlike other international norms, such as those of commercial treaties which can legitimately be based on the protection of reciprocal interests of States, compliance with humanitarian rules could not be made dependent on a reciprocal or corresponding performance of these obligations by other States. This trend marks the translation into legal norms of the "categorical imperative" formulated by Kant in the field of morals: one ought to fulfil an obligation regardless of whether others comply with it or disregard it.

519. As a consequence of their absolute character, these norms of international humanitarian law do not pose synallagmatic obligations, i.e. obligations of a State *vis-à-vis* another State. Rather – as was stated by the International Court of Justice in the *Barcelona Traction* case (which specifically referred to obligations concerning fundamental human rights) – they lay down obligations towards the international community as a whole, with the consequence that each and every member of the international community has a "legal interest" in their observance and consequently a legal entitlement to demand respect for such obligations.

520. Furthermore, most norms of international humanitarian law, in particular those prohibiting war crimes, crimes against humanity and genocide, are also peremptory norms of international law or *jus cogens*, i.e. of a non-derogable and overriding character. One illustration of the consequences which follow from this classification is that if the norms in question are contained in treaties, contrary to the general rule set out in Article 60 of the Vienna Convention on the Law of Treaties, a material breach of that treaty obligation by one of the parties would not entitle the other to invoke that breach in order to terminate or suspend the operation of the treaty. Article 60(5) provides that such reciprocity or in other words the principle *inadimplenti non est adimplendum* does not apply to provisions relating to the protection of the human person contained in treaties of a humanitarian character, in particular the provisions prohibiting any form of reprisals against persons protected by such treaties.

In a similar vein, in the *Martić* Appeal Judgment, the Appeals Chamber rejected the claim, adding other grounds to discard this type of defence in war situations.

ICTY, **Prosecutor *v.* Martić,** *Appeals Chamber, Judgment of 8 October 2008*

As discussed above (under Joint Criminal Enterprise, Part III(2), at p. 347) a Trial Chamber found Milan Martić responsible, inter alia, for persecution and other crimes against humanity, as well as war crimes, due to his participation in a Joint Criminal Enterprise (JCE), the common purpose of which was the establishment of an ethnically Serb territory through the displacement of the non-Serb population. Some of these crimes occurred on 26 August 1991, when the Croat village of Kijevo, situated 15 kilometres east of Knin, was attacked upon Martić's orders. Other subsequent clashes produced several more casualties. Martić appealed against his conviction, alleging, inter alia, that the Trial Chamber had not considered these clashes, for instance the attack on Kijevo, in the historical context of the region and in light of the unlawful declaration of independence by Croatia from Yugoslavia and of the crimes committed by Croats. The Appeals Chamber dealt with these arguments from various perspectives, including an expanded notion of *tu quoque.*

108. Martić appeals [against] the decision of the Trial Chamber not to make certain factual findings on the basis that it considered them irrelevant because, in his view, they are important to understanding the Kijevo ultimatum, the objectives of the Serbian leadership and the cooperation of its members, as well as the overall "coercive atmosphere" in the territory now comprising Croatia.

109. Martić argues that Serbs in SAO [Serbian Autonomous Oblast] Krajina, for historical reasons, had a right to claim self-determination in accordance with international law and that instead of being able to exercise this right, they ended up being persecuted by the Croatian authorities in the 1990s in a way similar to the persecutions and massacres of Serbs by Croats during the 1940s. After the HDZ [Croatian Democratic Union] won the first multi-party elections in Croatia, it "started the process of separation from the rest of Yugoslavia and discrimination on ethnic grounds" by, *inter alia,* establishing paramilitary units and adopting Ustasha symbols and discourse. Martić submits that the aim of the new Croat authorities was that of killing and expelling almost the entire Serb population of Croatia. The terrorisation of Serbs proceeded, according to Martić, with the canonisation of Archbishop Stepinac – an important Catholic backer of the Ustasha regime – by the Roman Pontiff and with racist and inflammatory statements by important Croatian politicians, including President Franjo Tuđman. Finally, Martić highlights statements related to the Croatian offensive (denominated "Storm") against Serb-held Croatian Krajina in 1995, averring that this operation was "a final phase of the realization of Croatian policy towards Serbs in Croatia", *i.e.,* their slaughter. In sum, Martić argues that had the Trial Chamber taken into account the preceding historical context, it would have reached different findings on the goals and objectives of the Serb leadership and on the lack of existence of a JCE. In particular, it would have understood that Martić advocated an independent Serb state or at least a substantial degree of autonomy within Croatia as a response to the aims of the Croatian authorities. [...]

111. To the extent that Martić's argument is an attempt to plead a defence of *tu quoque, i.e.,* to plead that the acts for which he was found responsible should not be considered criminal because they were in response to crimes committed against him and his people, it must be rejected. It is well established in the jurisprudence of the Tribunal that arguments based on

reciprocity, including the *tu quoque* argument, are no defence to serious violations of international humanitarian law.[3]

112. To the extent that Martić argues that the Trial Chamber erred in failing to take into account relevant contextual factors or erred in its findings on such factors, in particular the political objectives of the Serb leadership, the Appeals Chamber is not persuaded that the Trial Chamber erred in either respect. In the Trial Judgement, the Trial Chamber carefully considered that the political aims of the Serb leadership "to unite Serb areas in Croatia and in BiH with Serbia in order to establish a unified territory" did not "amount to a common purpose within the meaning of the law on JCE pursuant to Article 7(1) of the Statute". The Trial Chamber rather held that "where the creation of such territories is intended to be implemented through the commission of crimes within the Statute this may be sufficient to amount to a common criminal purpose." As such, Martić's submissions fail to show any error in findings of relevance to his conviction, including the Trial Chamber's findings that the objectives of the Serb leadership were "implemented through widespread and systematic armed attacks on predominantly Croat and other non-Serb areas and through the commission of acts of violence and intimidation", which "necessitated the forcible removal of the non-Serb population from the SAO Krajina and RSK territory."

113. Martić's argument may also be understood as alleging that the Trial Chamber failed to consider the possibility that the prevailing circumstances in the SAO Krajina, and in Croatia in general, created the conditions for acts of violence erupting throughout the territory relevant to the Indictment period, despite Martić's willingness to deal with the situation in a legal and peaceful way. In this respect, the Appeals Chamber notes that

> [e]vidence of an attack by the other party on the accused's civilian population may not be introduced unless it tends "to prove or disprove any of the allegations made in the indictment", notably to refute the Prosecutor's contention that there was a widespread or systematic attack against a civilian population.[4]

Further, if Martić is arguing that the Croatian leadership started a process of separation and discrimination unacceptable to the Serb population and that this process, together with ancestral fears due to past animosity and conflicts, led to the commission of decentralised and uncoordinated crimes, the Appeals Chamber notes that this argument was carefully considered and rejected by the Trial Chamber at trial. As Martić has failed to show that the Trial Chamber's finding was unreasonable, this argument stands to be rejected.

QUESTIONS

1. Contemporary international tribunals have generally rejected *tu quoque* defences on the assumption that norms of international humanitarian law are today absolute; that is, they are no longer based on reciprocity. The question, however, remains: is it always fair to prosecute a person for conduct that is condoned when carried out by the other side?

---

[3] [266] See, for example, *Kupreškić et al.* Trial Judgement, paras 515–520, as confirmed by *Kupreškić et al.* Appeal Judgement, para. 25.

[4] [270] *Kunarac et al.* Appeal Judgement, para. 88 (footnotes omitted).

2. While *tu quoque* proper is unacceptable in contemporary international criminal trials, judges should be careful not to discard too lightly claims that the other side behaved in a way similar to the defendant. International criminal law, as part and parcel of public international law, is based on a network of claims and counterclaims about the normative value of certain conduct. As discussed above, in the section on custom (Part I(1)(A)), reactions by other international actors to such claims will determine whether a new rule of customary law has emerged or, possibly, waned. Is it conceivable that, by demonstrating that all parties to a conflict accepted the legality of a specific conduct, an accused could show that a rule change had indeed occurred? Could this lead to a finding that no criminal responsibility attaches to his conduct? If so, under which conditions?

FURTHER READING

F. Harhoff, '*Tu Quoque* Principle', in *Oxford Companion*, 553.

S. Yee, 'The *Tu Quoque* Argument as a Defence to International Crimes, Prosecution or Punishment' (2004) 3 *Chinese Journal Int'l L.* 87–134.

PART V

JURISDICTIONAL AND PROCEDURAL ISSUES

INTRODUCTION

The modern commitment to the prosecution of international crimes has resulted in the development of substantive international criminal law, as detailed in the earlier chapters in this volume, as well as the creation and definition of both institutions and procedure. Different institutional models have been used to seek criminal accountability: purely international tribunals (the ICTY and ICTR), hybrid courts (the SCSL, the ECCC and the STL), and national tribunals. The ICCSt. establishes what may be described as an international *system*, combining within the complementarity principle a preference for national proceedings with the establishment of a permanent international court which serves both as a backstop and as a spur to domestic efforts to prosecute international crimes.

The development of international institutions (of all of these types) to enforce international criminal law has presented both external and internal challenges. Externally, a central task has been to define the relationship of these international institutions to Nation States. The tribunals share jurisdiction over the international crimes with the countries where those crimes happened (and in many cases with other countries as well), and therefore there will always be a preliminary question about which forum, international or domestic, has primacy.

In addition, international tribunals lack a supranational police force to investigate crimes, collect evidence and effectuate arrests. They are therefore necessarily dependent on Nation States to do their work or to allow their work to be done, and that includes both the States where the crimes occurred and any States where evidence of criminality might reside. This dependent relationship necessarily raises questions about the power of the tribunals to demand assistance and cooperation from nations in gathering evidence and obtaining arrests.

Looking inward, the international tribunals require procedures to regulate the investigation and prosecution of crimes. The tribunals have generally adopted a hybrid procedural system combining elements of the common law adversarial and civil law inquisitorial systems (though with a definite tilt towards the common law model, except for the ECCC which is substantially based on French-derived Cambodian criminal procedure). In theory, this approach allows for a *sui generis* 'international' procedural system that is tailored to the specific requirements and challenges of international criminal cases. As with any criminal procedural system, however, one must ask whether the procedures strike the right balance between the need to prosecute mass atrocities fairly, and efficiently and the rights of the accused.

1

PRIMACY VERSUS COMPLEMENTARITY

The ICTY and ICTR share concurrent jurisdiction with national courts, but also by statute enjoy primacy over those courts and can therefore assert exclusive jurisdiction over any case that falls within their mandates. This arrangement made sense with these tribunals, at least at the beginning of their existence, as they were established precisely because of an anticipated failure of national courts to address the crimes. The SCSL and STL also have concurrent jurisdiction, but have primacy only over the courts of Sierra Leone and Lebanon, respectively. These courts were established pursuant to agreements between the UN and their respective countries, and therefore cannot bind any other states. Nonetheless, the SCSL and STL are empowered to seek the deferral of cases, as a matter of comity, from other States.

As a general matter, the primacy (or limited primacy) of the ad hoc tribunals follows from their focus on crimes arising out of a single conflict (or set of related conflicts). The fear that these tribunals will encroach on national sovereignty will be at a minimum because of their specific jurisdiction. Moreover, within their area of focus, they have the mandate and capacity to investigate and prosecute a broad range of cases, or at least those persons most responsible for the crimes. Under these circumstances, it was important to give the tribunals the possibility of control over all cases to ensure that national prosecutions would not disrupt a broader prosecutorial strategy.

At the ICC, the situation is reversed and primacy rests with the national courts. Following the principle of complementarity encapsulated in Article 17 of the Rome Statute, a case will be admissible at the ICC *only if* the State (or the States) which has (or have) jurisdiction over the case is 'unwilling or unable genuinely to carry out the investigation or prosecution'. The insertion of the word 'genuinely' into the test allows the ICC to assert jurisdiction if the national or territorial State is investigating or prosecuting in bad faith, e.g. to shield the accused while giving the appearance of accountability. The domestic courts, therefore, have primary responsibility for investigating and prosecuting international crimes, and the ICC can step in only if those courts fail or cannot do so. This arrangement is just as unsurprising in the context of the ICC as the opposite is with the ad hoc tribunals. Unlike the ad hoc tribunals, the ICC is a permanent court that could potentially investigate and prosecute cases occurring all over the world. Accordingly, States will have a greater concern about protecting their sovereignty and ensuring that they have a first opportunity to investigate and prosecute alleged crimes occurring in their jurisdiction. In addition, there are strong arguments that national prosecutions are more meaningful – for the gathering of evidence, as well as for the victims, deterrence and reconciliation – than international prosecutions occurring in The Hague. Therefore, as long as there exists the possibility of national prosecutions, they should be preferred. Finally, simple resource constraints dictate that investigations and prosecutions should occur nationally, if possible. The annual budget of the ICC is comparable to the budgets of the ICTY and the ICTR, but its jurisdiction is far broader.

Cases

***ICTR*, Prosecutor *v.* Kanyabashi**, *Trial Chamber, Decision on the Defence Motion on Jurisdiction, 18 June 1997*

> Joseph Kanyabashi was *Bourgemestre* of Ngoma commune in Rwanda and was indicted for participation in the genocide, crimes against humanity, and war crimes. His trial is still ongoing. In this challenge, the accused offers a familiar challenge to the ad hoc tribunals, that they are 'political' institutions established to prosecute individuals from a particular conflict.

30. Although the Defence Counsel did not explicitly challenge the primacy of the Tribunal's jurisdiction over national courts, this objection is implied in the Defence Counsel's contention that establishment of the Tribunal violated the principle of *jus de non evocando*.

31. This principle, originally derived from constitutional law in civil law jurisdictions, establishes that persons accused of certain crimes should retain their right to be tried before the regular domestic criminal Courts rather than by politically founded ad-hoc criminal tribunals which, in times of emergency, may fail to provide impartial justice. As stated by the Appeals Chamber in the Tadić [...] case: "As a matter of fact and of law the principle advocated by the Appellant aims at one very specific goal: to avoid the creation of special or extraordinary courts designed to try political offenses in times of social unrest without guarantees of a fair trial." In the Trial Chamber's opinion, however, the Tribunal is far from being an institution designed for the purpose of removing, for political reasons, certain criminal offenders from fair and impartial justice and have them prosecuted for political crimes before prejudiced arbitrators.

32. It is true that the Tribunal has primacy over domestic criminal Courts and may at any stage request national Courts to defer to the competence of the Tribunal pursuant to article 8 of the Statute of the Tribunal, according to which the Tribunal may request that national Courts defer to the competence of the Tribunal at any stage of their proceedings. The Tribunal's primacy over national Courts is also reflected in the principle of *non bis in idem* as laid down in Article 9 of the Statute and in Article 28 of the Statute which establishes that States shall comply without undue delay with any request for assistance or an order issued by a Trial Chamber. The primacy thereby entrenched for the Tribunal, however, is exclusively derived from the fact that the Tribunal is established under Chapter VII of the UN Charter, which in turn enables the Tribunal to issue directly binding international legal orders and requests to States, irrespective of their consent. Failure of States to comply with such legally binding orders and requests may, under certain conditions, be reported by the President of the Tribunal to the Security Council for further action. The Trial Chamber concludes, therefore, that the principle of *jus de non evocando* has not been violated.

***ICTR*, In the Matter of Théoneste Bagosora**, *Trial Chamber, Decision on the Application by the Prosecutor for a Formal Request for Deferral, 17 May 1996*

> Théoneste Bagosora was the 'directeur de cabinet' in the Ministry of Defence in Rwanda and was therefore the highest civil servant within the military. In the *Military I*

trial, he was convicted of genocide, crimes against humanity and war crimes and was sentenced to life imprisonment. His conviction is currently on appeal. At the beginning of the case, the ICTR sought the deferral of Belgium's investigation to the ICTR. Although the ICTRSt. gave the tribunal primacy, it was left to the judges to devise in the rules how and under what conditions such requests would be made and considered.

I – The Request

1. This is an application by the Prosecutor of the International Criminal Tribunal for Rwanda, made pursuant to article 8(2) of the Statute of the International Criminal Tribunal for the Prosecution of Persons Responsible for Genocide and other Serious Violations of International Humanitarian Law Committed in the Territory of Rwanda and Rwandan citizens responsible for such acts or violations committed in the territory of neighbouring States, between 1 January 1994 and 31 December 1994, and in accordance with Rule 9 (iii) of the Rules of Procedure and Evidence, seeking an order from the Trial Chamber in relation to investigations and criminal proceedings being conducted by the Kingdom of Belgium respecting serious violations of International Humanitarian Law committed in the Prefecture of Kibuye in the territory of Rwanda between April 1994 and July 1994 by Théoneste Bagosora, for a formal request to be made to the Kingdom of Belgium for its courts to defer to the competence of the Tribunal.

2. Pursuant to Rule 10 of the Rules, the Prosecutor has requested the Trial Chamber to issue a formal request to the Kingdom of Belgium in the following terms:

a) The courts of Belgium defer to the competence of the Tribunal in regard to all investigations and all criminal proceedings in respect of Théoneste Bagosora,

b) In regards to all such investigations and criminal proceedings of Théoneste Bagosora, the Tribunal requests that the Kingdom of Belgium forward to the Tribunal the results of said investigations, criminal proceedings, copies of the courts' records and judgements concerning Théoneste Bagosora, if any.

c) The reasons advanced by the Prosecutor in support of his proposal are:

1) Investigations have been instituted against Théoneste Bagosora by the Kingdom of Belgium for murder and violations of the Geneva Conventions of 12 August 1949 and of Additional Protocols I and II of 8 June 1977, which were allegedly committed in the territory of Rwanda during 1994.

2) 'The Prosecutor has been conducting investigations into crimes allegedly committed by Théoneste Bagosora which fall within the jurisdiction of the Tribunal.

3) The national investigations instituted by the Kingdom of Belgium closely relate to, or otherwise involve, significant factual and legal questions which have implications for investigations or prosecutions before the Tribunal.

3. In his request the Prosecutor has furnished facts which, in brief, are that as early as 8 April 1994, the Belgian military office opened an investigation against Colonel Théoneste Bagosora, Director of the Cabinet of the Ministry of Defense under the regime of former President Habyarimana. The Belgian civilian courts carried on the investigation, pursuant to an order from the Tribunal of First Instance in Brussels, dated 24 April 1995. The Examining Magistrate, Judge D. Vandermeersch, issued an international warrant of arrest for Colonel Théoneste Bagosora on 29 May 1995. On 9 March 1996, Colonel Théoneste Bagosora was apprehended by the Cameroonian authorities. To this day, he is still being held by the Cameroonian authorities, pending a decision on his extradition.

4. The current investigations of the Kingdom of Belgium against Colonel Théoneste Bagosora involve allegations of murder and crimes of international law which constitute serious violations of the Geneva Conventions of 12 August 1949 and of additional Protocols I and II of 8 June 1977. Théoneste Bagosora is alleged, <u>inter alia</u>, to have been directly responsible for the massacres which followed the attack against President Habyarimana on 6 April 1994, and for the murder, on 7 April 1994, of 10 soldiers from the [B]elgian contingent of the United Nations Assistance Mission to Rwanda.

5. The Prosecutor has submitted that in order to develop the ongoing investigations, he must collect further essential evidence and obtain full access to the statements, documents and other findings of the investigations conducted by the Kingdom of Belgium in relation to Théoneste Bagosora. In his investigations, the Prosecutor is collecting evidence in order to determine the merits of the allegations that the massacres were planned and led to the mass murder of a great many victims who were protected under international law. The investigations by the Prosecutor focus mainly on persons in position of authority, who were responsible for serious violations of international humanitarian law. To the extent that the investigations relate to persons in positions of authority, Colonel Théoneste Bagosora's alleged criminal responsibility seems most important. Indeed, Théoneste Bagosora, born in 1941 in Gicyie commune, was successively Second in Command of the *École Supérieure Militaire* in Kigali, Commander of the military camp in Kanombe and Director of the Cabinet of the Ministry of Defense, a position he continued to hold during the April 1994 events, though he had already retired in September 1993. A native of the same region as former President Habyarimana, he had become one of his close associates and participated in the Arusha accords as a military advisor. The aim of the Prosecutor's investigations is to assess Théoneste Bagosora's responsibility for the events and massacres which followed the attack on the presidential plane on 6 April. It is stated in the request that within six hours of the attack against the presidential plane on 6 April 1994, while the massacres were starting in Rwanda, Théoneste Bagosora allegedly assumed de facto control of the army and the country. The aim of the Prosecutor's investigations is therefore to assess Théoneste Bagosora's responsibility for said massacres.

6. According to the Prosecutor, if the Kingdom of Belgium continues investigations which are similar to his investigations, a number of confusions and complications might occur. It could turn out to be detrimental to investigations before the Tribunal, in particular in relation to testimonies. It is indeed to be feared that witnesses might become reluctant to appear before successive investigators and would no longer be willing to cooperate fully and effectively in the questioning. Testimonies might thus lose credibility as the number of questionings in different conditions increases, whereas some other witnesses might even be exposed to threats and see their lives put in danger.

II – Analysis of the merits of the request

7. Article 7 of the Statute of the International Tribunal extends its jurisdiction to the prosecution of persons responsible for serious violations of international humanitarian law committed in the territory of Rwanda and Rwandan citizens responsible for such violations committed in the territory of neighbouring States, between 1 January 1994 and 31 December 1994.

  Article 8 of the 3 Statute states that:

"1. The International Tribunal for Rwanda and national courts shall have concurrent jurisdiction to prosecute persons for serious violations of international humanitarian law committed in the territory of Rwanda and Rwandan citizens for such violations committed in the territory of neighbouring States, between 1 January 1994 and 31 December 1994.

2. The International Tribunal for Rwanda shall have primacy over the national courts of all States. At any stage of the procedure, the International Tribunal for Rwanda may formally

request national courts to defer to its competence in accordance with the present Statute and the Rules of Procedure and Evidence of the International Tribunal for Rwanda."

Such primacy, however, can only be exercised if a formal request is addressed to the national court to defer to the competence of the International Tribunal. The Rules specify the modalities for exercising this right.

Rule 9 of the Rules states that:

"Where it appears to the Prosecutor that in any such investigations or criminal proceedings instituted in the courts of any State: (i) (. . .) (ii) (. . .) (iii) what is in issue is closely related to, or otherwise involves, significant factual or legal questions which may have implications for investigations or prosecutions before the Tribunal, (. . .).

9. In order to meet the conditions for a deferral, the Prosecutor therefore must demonstrate:

a) that national investigations or criminal proceedings have been instituted against said Théoneste Bagosora by the Kingdom of Belgium respecting crimes which come under the jurisdiction of the International Tribunal;

b) that investigations are being conducted by the Prosecutor on serious violations of international humanitarian law allegedly committed in the territory of Rwanda or in the territory of neighbouring States between 1 January 1994 and 31 December 1994, in particular in respect of violations allegedly committed by Théoneste Bagosora;

c) that these investigations or criminal proceedings are closely related and otherwise involve significant factual or legal questions which may have implications for the Prosecutor's investigations or prosecutions.

10. The Prosecutor states that an investigation has been instituted by the Kingdom of Belgium in respect of acts allegedly committed by Théoneste Bagosora, which might also come within the jurisdiction of the Tribunal. This is supported by documents provided by the Prosecutor in support of his case, including: the order for an investigation against Théoneste Bagosora, under the charges of murder and serious violations of the Geneva Conventions of 12 August 1949 and of additional Protocols I and II of 8 June 1977, issued by the Prosecutor of the King of Belgium on 21 April 1995, the Order of 24 April 1995 issued by the President of the Tribunal of First Instance of Brussels nominating an Examining Magistrate to pursue the case, and the international warrant of arrest issued on 29 May 1995 by the [B]elgian Examining Magistrate responsible for the case against Théoneste Bagosora.

11. The Prosecutor indicates that his Office is investigating the crimes allegedly committed by Théoneste Bagosora.

12. The Prosecutor considers, not without reason, that the continuation of parallel investigations by the [B]elgian courts and the International Tribunal might be detrimental to the investigations, including the testimonies. As they are repeated, testimonies can indeed lose their credibility, not to mention the risk of causing the witnesses to be distrustful; moreover the witnesses might be traumatised and even threatened of bodily harm.

13. Moreover, the Prosecutor rightly observes that Article 9.2 of the Tribunal's Statute, concerning the principle of *non bis in idem*, sets limits to the subsequent prosecution by the Tribunal of persons who have been tried by a national court for acts constituting serious violations of international humanitarian law. And, in the case of Théoneste Bagosora, as [B]elgian law does not contain any provision concerning genocide or crimes against humanity, it was only for murder and serious violations of the Geneva Conventions of 12 August 1949 and Additional Protocols I and II of 8 June 1977 that the [B]elgian authorities were able to prosecute him, given the facts that he is charged with. Therefore, should the Prosecutor subsequently wish to prosecute Théoneste Bagosora for the same facts, characterising them as

genocide and crimes against humanity, he would not be able to do so, if Théoneste Bagosora had already been tried by [B]elgian jurisdictions.

14. Finally and in addition, according to the Prosecutor's request the Kingdom of Belgium has always been cooperative and it is expected that the latter would not be reluctant to accede to this request. Moreover, at the hearing on 16 May 1996, the representative of the Prosecutor stated that, in a telephone conversation with the authorities of the [B]elgian Ministry of Justice, the Government of the Kingdom of Belgium indicated its goodwill and its willingness to comply fully with the decisions of the International Tribunal, including in the case concerning Théoneste Bagosora. The representative of the Prosecutor has confirmed that to that end, a law was enacted on 22 March 1996 by the Kingdom of Belgium.

15. In the light of the foregoing, the Judges of the Trial Chamber are of the opinion that the request for deferral by the Belgian judicial authorities in the case of Théoneste Bagosora complies [with] the provisions of Rule 9 of the Rules of Procedure and Evidence, and that such request should be favourably received.

In a similar manner, the ICTY also took over the *Tadić* case from German prosecutors and certain investigations from the national authorities in Macedonia. In reality, though, there was not a frequent need for either the ICTY or the ICTR to invoke primacy as national courts did not, in the early days, take up many cases from these conflicts. As the life of these international tribunals exceeded initial expectations and pressures grew to end their work, and as courts in the republics that once comprised the former Yugoslavia began to gain credibility, the ICTY in particular began to send cases back to the region for prosecution pursuant to Rule 11 *bis* of the Rules of Procedure and Evidence. In its last days, then, the ICTY followed a model that more closely resembles the likely procedure of the ICC: an international tribunal prosecutes the most responsible perpetrators, leaving the lower-level accused to the national courts. To date the judges at the ICTR have refused requests from the prosecution to refer pending cases back to the courts of Rwanda, finding insufficient evidence to conclude that the accused would receive a fair trial there. The ICTR did refer one case, against Michel Bagaragaza, to the Netherlands for prosecution, but the transfer was revoked on 17 August 2007 after a Dutch District Court ruled that the Netherlands did not have jurisdiction over a Rwandan individual accused of genocide in Rwanda where there was no allegation that there were any victims of Dutch nationality.

***ICC*, Prosecutor *v.* Kony et al., *Pre-Trial Chamber, Decision on the Admissibility of the Case under Article 19(1) of the Statute, 10 March 2009**

In 2005, the ICC issued arrest warrants for Joseph Kony, Vincent Otti, Okot Odhiambo and Dominic Ongwen, all leaders of the Lord's Resistance Army (LRA), for crimes against humanity and war crimes. They are still at large. There has been discussion in Uganda about creating special courts to try accused war criminals. Accordingly, in 2009 the Pre-Trial Chamber exercised its *proprio motu* power to consider whether the case against the accused was still 'admissible' under Article 17, that is whether it was still the case that the government of Uganda, which had referred the investigation of the LRA to the ICC, was still 'unwilling or unable genuinely to carry out the investigation or prosecution'. Ultimately it concluded that despite moves to create war crimes courts in Uganda, it remained speculative whether the accused in this case could be prosecuted in the State and therefore the case remained admissible.

14. Article 19(1), second sentence of the Statute vests "the Court" (i.e., its Chambers in the exercise of their judicial functions) with a broad power: it "may, on its own motion, determine the admissibility of a case in accordance with article 17". The broadness of such power, and the wide discretion which presides over its exercise, are made apparent by the use of the term "may": the authority to decide whether the determination of admissibility should be made, and, in the affirmative, at what specific stage of the proceedings such determination should occur, resides exclusively with the relevant Chamber. The sole limit entailed by the lean wording of the provision appears to be that the proceedings must have reached the stage of a case (including "specific incidents during which one or more crimes within the jurisdiction of the Court seem to have been committed by one or more identified suspects"), as opposed to the preceding stage of the situation following the Prosecutor's decision to commence an investigation pursuant to article 53 of the Statute. Apart from this procedural boundary, the Statute and the other statutory texts are silent as to the criteria which may or should guide a Chamber in deciding whether and when to resort to the power vested in it by article 19(1), second sentence, of the Statute. Accordingly, it is for the Court, in the exercise of its judicial functions and when appropriate, to establish appropriate criteria for determining whether the actual exercise of this *proprio motu* power is warranted in a given case.

The Pre-Trial Chambers' practice in assessing proprio motu the admissibility of a case

15. It has already become the established practice of the Court to wield its power under article 19(1) at a number of specific procedural stages.

16. First and foremost, in most cases all three Pre-Trial Chambers of the Court have assessed admissibility on their own motion upon deciding on a Prosecutor's application for a warrant for arrest under article 58, albeit to varying degrees in scope and depth. At the time of the issuance of the Warrants, this Chamber stated that, based upon the application, the evidence and other information submitted by the Prosecutor, the Case "appear[ed] to be admissible", without further elaboration.

17. Acting against a different factual background, which included the existence of judicial initiatives at the national level, Pre-Trial Chamber I, upon issuing warrants of arrest for Thomas Lubanga Dyilo and Bosco Ntaganda in the situation of the Democratic Republic of the Congo ("DRC"), pointed out that "for a case arising from the investigation of a situation to be inadmissible, national proceedings must encompass both the person and the conduct which is the subject of the case before the Court". Since the warrants of arrest issued in the DRC contained no reference to the charges brought by the Prosecutor and no other State with jurisdiction was investigating, prosecuting or had investigated and prosecuted the same crimes, the case was considered admissible.

18. Pre-Trial Chamber I followed the same approach in the case against Germain Katanga and Mathieu Ngujolo Chui. While finding that the case was admissible, it clarified that its determination was "without prejudice to any subsequent determination on jurisdiction or admissibility concerning this case pursuant to article 19(1), (2) and (3) of the Statute".

19. Both in the situation in Darfur and in the situation in the Central African Republic, Pre-Trial Chamber I and Pre-Trial Chamber IIP3 respectively found that the circumstances of the case warranted the exercise of their discretion to determine admissibility under article 19(1) within the context of the issuance of warrants of arrest. Both Pre-Trial Chambers clarified that their determination that the case was admissible was however without prejudice to either any challenge to the admissibility under article 19 or any subsequent determination.

Assessment of the Pre-Trial Chambers' practice by the Appeals Chamber: limited relevance for the purposes of the Proceedings

20. The practice of assessing admissibility within the context of proceedings under article 58 initiated by Pre-Trial Chamber I was scrutinised by the Appeals Chamber in an appeal seeking to reverse the decision on the Prosecutor's application for a warrant of arrest against Mr Bosco Ntaganda. In its decision dated 13 July 2006, the Appeals Chamber stated that the use of the word "may" in article 19(1), second sentence, of the Statute indicated that a Chamber was vested with discretion as to whether making a determination of the admissibility of a case and that it "accept[ed] that the Pre-Trial Chamber may on its own motion address admissibility". By the same token, however, it qualified its statement by pointing out that, within the context of *ex parte* Prosecutor only proceedings triggered by an application for a warrant of arrest, the Pre-Trial Chamber should exercise its discretion on the matter "only when…appropriate in the circumstances of the case bearing in mind the interests of the suspect". Elaborating on the issue, the Appeals Chamber listed a number of instances in which such appropriateness would be satisfied: namely, "instances where a case is based on the established jurisprudence of the Court, uncontested facts that render a case clearly inadmissible or an ostensible cause impelling the exercise of *proprio motu* review".

21. The Chamber wishes to clarify that the judgment by the Appeals Chamber referred to the very specific procedural scenario of a Prosecutor's application for a warrant of arrest, by its nature triggering *ex parte* proceedings where the suspect is not represented. Such a scenario profoundly differs from the one at stake in the Proceedings, where a counsel for the defence has been appointed, the relevant State is a participant and *amici curiae* observations have been submitted. Accordingly, the determinations by the Appeals Chamber as to the conditions warranting the exercise of a Chamber's *proprio motu* powers under article 19(1) are not of direct relevance to the Proceedings. For the purposes of the present decision, the judgment by the Appeals Chamber appears nevertheless to shed light on the meaning of the second sentence of article 19(1) of the Statute in two ways: first, it confirms that the exercise of the *proprio motu* power under this provision falls within the realm of a Chamber's discretion; second, it clarifies that the criteria presiding over the actual exercise of such discretion are to be inferred to a great extent from the circumstances of each individual case.

The need to "bear in mind the interests of the suspect" and the arguments raised by the Defence

22. A critical element of the guidance provided by the Appeals Chamber regarding the advisability and appropriateness of exercising the power enshrined in article 19(1), albeit in a different context, is the reference to the need to "bear in mind the interests of the suspect". The relevance of this element for the purposes of this decision stems from the fact that concern for these interests seems to underlie the Defence's submissions questioning the legitimacy of opening proceedings under article 19(1) at the present stage, in the absence of any of the persons sought by the Court. The Chamber is of the view that the Defence's arguments are of a preliminary nature and, as such, need to be addressed prior to the assessment of the factual circumstances of the Case.

23. In the view of the Defence, a determination of the admissibility of the Case at this stage, when none of the persons sought by the Court is in custody, would jeopardize their right to bring a challenge pursuant to article 19(2) at a later stage, i.e. once they are apprehended and appear before the Court. More specifically, the Defence argues that opening *proprio motu* proceedings under article 19(1) under these circumstances might entail that the persons sought in the Case might face "a heightened risk of judicial pre-determination" in the context of future challenges to the admissibility of the Case.

24. The arguments of the Defence seem to stem from a partial and inaccurate view of the relevance of the Chamber's determination of admissibility at this stage, as well as from a misconstruction of the function and role of counsel appointed to represent the interests of the Defence in the absence of the persons sought by the Court. The Chamber will address the two issues separately.

Relevance of the Chamber's determination of admissibility at this stage and need to review the determination on admissibility as a consequence of a change in circumstances

25. With regard to the relevance of the determination of admissibility at this stage, the Chamber wishes to highlight that the Statute does not rule out the possibility that multiple determinations of admissibility may be made in a given case. Whilst as a general rule the accused may only raise issues of admissibility once, and that is at the commencement of the trial or prior to it, the power to bring a challenge under this heading is vested with the accused and a State which has jurisdiction over the case or whose acceptance of jurisdiction is required under article 13 of the Statute. Nowhere is it said that a challenge brought by either of these parties forecloses the bringing of a challenge by another equally legitimate party, nor that the right of either of the parties to bring a challenge is curtailed or otherwise affected by the Chamber's exercise of its *proprio motu* powers.

26. On the contrary, the existence of a plurality of parties vested with the power to raise challenges in matters of admissibility *per se* entails that, during proceedings in a given case, the Court may need to address the issue of the admissibility of the case more than once, including as a result of multiple challenges brought by different parties at different points in time. Article 19(4), second sentence explicitly allows for a challenge to jurisdiction or admissibility to be brought "more than once" prior to the commencement of the trial, on leave to be granted by the Court "in exceptional circumstances". Furthermore, no provision is made for a compulsory joinder of challenges to admissibility by different parties. On the basis of the foregoing, it appears beyond controversy that the accused will always be entitled to raise a challenge under article 19(2) of the Statute, whether or not the Chamber has exercised its powers under article 19(1).

27. By its very nature, the determination of the admissibility of a case is subject to change as a consequence of a change in circumstances. This idea underlies the whole regime of complementarity at the pre-trial stage, as may be evinced from several provisions of the Statute. According to article 18(7), "a State which has challenged a ruling of the Pre-Trial Chamber under this article (i.e., following the Prosecutor's determination that there would be a reasonable basis to commence an investigation on a situation) may challenge the admissibility of a case under article 19 on the grounds of additional significant facts or significant change in circumstances"; article 19(4) lays down the principle that a State or the accused may bring a challenge only once, but nevertheless provides that "in exceptional circumstances, the Court may grant leave for a challenge to be brought more than once or at a time later than the commencement of a trial"; article 19(5) enables the Prosecutor having deferred an investigation to the State to "request that the State concerned periodically inform the Prosecutor of the progress of its investigations and any subsequent prosecutions", to which request the State concerned "shall respond ... without undue delay"; according to article 19(10), when the Court has decided that a case is inadmissible, "the Prosecutor may submit a request for a review of the decision when he or she is fully satisfied that new facts have arisen which negate the basis on which the case had previously been found inadmissible under article 17".

28. Considered as a whole, the *corpus* of these provisions delineates a system whereby the determination of admissibility is meant to be an ongoing process throughout the pre-trial

phase, the outcome of which is subject to review depending on the evolution of the relevant factual scenario. Otherwise stated, the Statute as a whole enshrines the idea that a change in circumstances allows (or even, in some scenarios, compels) the Court to determine admissibility anew.

29. Based upon the above provisions, it appears hardly debatable that the statutory framework envisages as a possible scenario that the issue of admissibility may be discussed more than once in the course of the proceedings. That may be the case either as a result of challenges brought by the various parties entitled to do so, or as a consequence of the Chamber exercising its *proprio motu* power under article 19(1), which does not provide for any restriction as to the number of times in which this power may be exercised.

COMMENTARY

As this decision makes clear, the question of admissibility is an ongoing one, and therefore it is conceivable that even after an accused is charged by the ICC, a national State could begin proceedings and reassert jurisdiction over a case. This possibility has already arisen in relation to the ICC cases in Uganda and Darfur, and in time is certain to raise difficult questions of whether such national proceedings are in good faith or are in fact designed to derail the ICC proceedings. What if a national State is genuinely supportive of investigations and prosecutions of accused perpetrators, but for various reasons wishes that they be undertaken by the ICC? In other words, if a national State is not investigating or prosecuting the case, must the court consider the *reasons* that the State is not acing? In the case of Germain Katanga and Ngudjolo Chui, the ICC Appeals Chamber held that under Article 17 of the Statute, where a national jurisdiction is not investigating or prosecuting the case at issue, the case is admissible before the ICC regardless of motivation. It is only when the naional State undertakes an investigation or prosecution that the ICC must inquire into the ability or genuine willingness of that State to perform its undertaking.

2

STATE COOPERATION

As the first President of the ICTY, one of the authors of this volume, Judge Cassese, told the UN General Assembly on 7 November 1995, that '[o]ur tribunal is like a giant who has no arms and legs. To walk and work, he needs artificial limbs. These artificial limbs are the state authorities'. Article 29 ICTYSt. and Article 28 ICTRSt. require states to 'cooperate' in the 'investigation and prosecution of persons accused of committing serious violations of international humanitarian law' and oblige them to comply with any request for assistance from a Trial Chamber pertaining to the identification and location of persons, taking of testimony, service of documents and the arrests and surrenders of accused persons. As these courts were established pursuant to Chapter VII of the UN Charter, these obligations have the force of law. The Rome Statute also obliges States Parties, in Articles 86–93, to cooperate with the court in all fundamental matters related to the investigation and prosecution of perpetrators, including arrests, surrenders and the taking of evidence. The difficult question, though, is how to enforce these obligations.

Cases

ICTY, Prosecutor v. Blaškić, Appeals Chamber, Judgment on the Request of the Republic of Croatia for Review of the Decision of Trial Chamber II of 18 July 1997, 29 October 1997

Tihomir Blaškić was a commander in the Bosnian Croat armed forces, the HVO, in Central Bosnia from 1992 to 1994. He was indicted for crimes against humanity and war crimes for crimes committed against Bosnian Muslims by members of the HVO. He was convicted at trial and sentenced to 45 years' imprisonment. On appeal, the Appeals Chamber considered an enormous quantity of new evidence that became available only at the end of the Accused's trial. The Appeals Chamber reversed the Trial Chamber's judgment and sentenced Blaškić to nine years' imprisonment. During the trial, the prosecution sought a *subpoena duces tecum*, that is a subpoena seeking documents, from the government of Croatia, the Minister of Defence of Croatia, the government of Bosnia and Herzegovina and the Custodian of Records of the Central Archive of the Ministry of Defence of the Croatian Community of Herceg-Bosna. Thus the Trial Chamber and eventually the Appeals Chamber had to consider the authority of the ICTY to issue a 'subpoena' to a government or individuals within the government.

B. Whether The International Tribunal Is Empowered To Issue Binding Orders To States

1. Can the International Tribunal issue subpoenas to States?

25. The Appeals Chamber holds the view that the term "subpoena" (in the sense of injunction accompanied by threat of penalty) cannot be applied or addressed to States. This finding rests on two grounds.

First of all, the International Tribunal does not possess any power to take enforcement measures against States. Had the drafters of the Statute intended to vest the International Tribunal with such a power, they would have expressly provided for it. In the case of an international judicial body, this is not a power that can be regarded as inherent in its functions. Under current international law States can only be the subject of countermeasures taken by other States or of sanctions visited upon them by the organized international community, i.e., the United Nations or other intergovernmental organizations.

Secondly, both the Trial Chamber and the Prosecutor have stressed that, with regard to States, the 'penalty' attached to a subpoena would not be penal in nature. Under present international law it is clear that States, by definition, cannot be the subject of criminal sanctions akin to those provided for in national criminal systems.

With regard to States, the Appeals Chamber therefore holds that the term "subpoena" is not applicable and that only binding "orders" or "requests" can be addressed to them.

2. Can the International Tribunal issue binding orders to States?

26. Turning then to the power of the International Tribunal to issue binding orders to States, the Appeals Chamber notes that Croatia has challenged the existence of such a power, claiming that, under the Statute, the International Tribunal only possesses jurisdiction over individuals and that it lacks any jurisdiction over States. This view is based on a manifest misconception. Clearly, under Article 1 of the Statute, the International Tribunal has criminal jurisdiction solely over natural "persons responsible for serious violations of international humanitarian law committed in the territory of the former Yugoslavia since [1 January] 1991". The International Tribunal can prosecute and try those persons. This is its primary jurisdiction. However, it is self-evident that the International Tribunal, in order to bring to trial persons living under the jurisdiction of sovereign States, not being endowed with enforcement agents of its own, must rely upon the cooperation of States. The International Tribunal must turn to States if it is effectively to investigate crimes, collect evidence, summon witnesses and have indictees arrested and surrendered to the International Tribunal. The drafters of the Statute realistically took account of this in imposing upon all States the obligation to lend cooperation and judicial assistance to the International Tribunal. This obligation is laid down in Article 29 and restated in paragraph 4 of Security Council resolution 827 (1993). Its binding force derives from the provisions of Chapter VII and Article 25 of the United Nations Charter and from the Security Council resolution adopted pursuant to those provisions. The exceptional legal basis of Article 29 accounts for the novel and indeed unique power granted to the International Tribunal to issue orders to sovereign States (under customary international law, States, as a matter of principle, cannot be "ordered" either by other States or by international bodies). Furthermore, the obligation set out – in the clearest of terms – in Article 29 is an obligation which is incumbent on every Member State of the United Nations *vis-à-vis* all other Member States. The Security Council, the body entrusted with primary responsibility for the maintenance of international peace and security, has solemnly enjoined all Member States to comply with orders and requests of the International Tribunal. The nature and content of this obligation, as well as the source from which it originates, make it clear that Article 29 does not create bilateral relations. Article 29 imposes an obligation on Member States towards all other

Members or, in other words, an "obligation *erga omnes partes*". By the same token, Article 29 posits a community interest in its observance. In other words, every Member State of the United Nations has a legal interest in the fulfilment of the obligation laid down in Article 29 (on the manner in which this legal interest can be exercised, *see* below, paragraph 36).

As for States which are not Members of the United Nations, in accordance with the general principle embodied in Article 35 of the Vienna Convention on the Law of Treaties, they may undertake to comply with the obligation laid down in Article 29 by expressly accepting the obligation in writing. This acceptance may be evidenced in various ways. Thus, for instance, in the case of Switzerland, the passing in 1995 of a law implementing the Statute of the International Tribunal clearly implies acceptance of Article 29.

27. The obligation under consideration concerns both action that States may take only and exclusively through their organs (this, for instance, happens in case of an order enjoining a State to produce documents in the possession of one of its officials) and also action that States may be requested to take with regard to individuals subject to their jurisdiction (this is the case when the International Tribunal orders that individuals be arrested, or be compelled under threat of a national penalty to surrender evidence, or be brought to The Hague to testify).

28. The Prosecutor has submitted that Article 29 expressly grants the International Tribunal "ancillary jurisdiction over States". However, care must be taken when using the term "jurisdiction" for two different sets of actions by the International Tribunal. As stated above, the primary jurisdiction of the International Tribunal, namely its power to exercise judicial functions, relates to natural persons only. The International Tribunal can prosecute and try those persons who are allegedly responsible for the crimes defined in Articles 2 to 5 of the Statute. With regard to States affected by Article 29, the International Tribunal does not, of course, exercise the same judicial functions; it only possesses the power to issue binding orders or requests. To avoid any confusion in terminology that would also result in a conceptual confusion, when considering Article 29 it is probably more accurate simply to speak of the International Tribunal's ancillary (or incidental) mandatory powers *vis-à-vis* States.

29. It should again be emphasised that the plain wording of Article 29 makes it clear that the obligation it creates is incumbent upon all Member States, irrespective of whether or not they are States of the former Yugoslavia. The Appeals Chamber therefore fails to see the merit of the contention made by one of the *amici curiae*, whereby the obligation under discussion would be incumbent solely upon the former belligerents, i.e., States or Entities of ex-Yugoslavia. This view seems to confuse the obligations stemming from the Dayton and Paris Accords of 21 November and 14 December 1995, which apply only to the States or Entities of the former Yugoslavia, with the obligation enshrined in Article 29, which has a much broader scope. It is evident that States other than those involved in the armed conflict may have in their possession evidence relevant to crimes committed in the former Yugoslavia, or they may have instituted proceedings against persons accused of crimes in the former Yugoslavia. Similarly, suspects, indictees or witnesses may live on their territory or evidentiary material may be located there. The cooperation of these States with the International Tribunal is therefore no less imperative than that of the States or Entities of the former Yugoslavia.

Nor does the Appeals Chamber see any merit in another possible contention: that since the International Tribunal is essentially intended to exercise functions that the national courts of the successor States or Entities of the former Yugoslavia have failed or are failing to discharge, it is essentially with regard to those States and Entities that the International Tribunal may exercise its primacy; hence, it is with respect only to them that the International Tribunal may demand the observance of Article 29, and consequently, issue compelling orders. The International Tribunal is not intended to replace the courts of any State; under Article 9 of the Statute it has concurrent jurisdiction with national courts. National courts of the States of the former Yugoslavia, like the courts of any State, are under a customary-law obligation to try or extradite persons who have allegedly committed grave breaches of international humanitarian law. It is with regard to national courts generally that the International Tribunal may exercise its primacy under Article 9, paragraph 2, or, if those courts fail to fulfil that customary obligation, may intervene and adjudicate. The fact that the crimes falling within its primary jurisdiction were committed in the former Yugoslavia does not in any way confine the identity of the States subject to Article 29; all States must cooperate with the International Tribunal.

30. While it does not accept the foregoing argument, the Appeals Chamber does see some merit in the distinction drawn by the Prosecutor in her Brief between "States located on the territory of the former Yugoslavia" and "third States which were not directly involved in the conflict and whose role, then as now, is that of concerned bystanders". Unlike the aforementioned *amicus curiae*, the Prosecutor does not draw any legal consequence from this distinction. According to her, the distinction may only have practical value in that "[t]he mandatory compliance powers expressly conferred by Article 29(2) of the Statute will rarely, if ever, need to be invoked with respect to such third States". Whether these mandatory powers will need to be invoked with regard to third States is, of course, a matter of speculation. The Appeals Chamber accepts however the practical difference between the two categories of States: those of the former Yugoslavia are more likely to be required to cooperate in the ways envisaged in Article 29. As the former belligerent parties, they are more likely to hold important evidence needed by the International Tribunal.

31. Having clarified the scope and purport of Article 29, the Appeals Chamber feels it necessary to add that it also shares the Prosecutor's contention that a distinction should be made between two modes of interaction with the International Tribunal: the cooperative and the mandatory compliance. The Appeals Chamber endorses the Prosecution's contention that:

> [A]s a matter of policy and in order to foster good relations with States, . . . cooperative processes should wherever possible be used, . . . they should be used first, and . . . resort to mandatory compliance powers expressly given by Article 29(2) should be reserved for cases in which they are really necessary.

In the final analysis, the International Tribunal may discharge its functions only if it can count on the bona fide assistance and cooperation of sovereign States. It is therefore to be regarded as sound policy for the Prosecutor, as well as defence counsel, first to seek, through cooperative means, the assistance of States, and only if they decline to lend support, then to request a Judge or a Trial Chamber to have recourse to the mandatory action provided for in Article 29 [. . .]

4. Legal remedies available in case of non-compliance by a State

33. What legal remedies are available to the International Tribunal in case of non-compliance by a State with a binding order for the production of documents or, indeed, any binding order?

As stated above, the International Tribunal is not vested with any enforcement or sanctionary power *vis-à-vis* States. It is primarily for its parent body, the Security Council, to impose sanctions, if any, against a recalcitrant State, under the conditions provided for in Chapter VII of the United Nations Charter. However, the International Tribunal is endowed with the inherent power to make a judicial finding concerning a State's failure to observe the provisions of the Statute or the Rules. It also has the power to report this judicial finding to the Security Council.

The power to make this judicial finding is an inherent power: the International Tribunal must possess the power to make all those judicial determinations that are necessary for the exercise of its primary jurisdiction. This inherent power inures to the benefit of the International

Tribunal in order that its basic judicial function may be fully discharged and its judicial role safeguarded. The International Tribunal's power to report to the Security Council is derived from the relationship between the two institutions. The Security Council established the International Tribunal pursuant to Chapter VII of the United Nations Charter for the purpose of the prosecution of persons responsible for serious violations of international humanitarian law committed in the territory of the former Yugoslavia. A logical corollary of this is that any time a State fails to fulfil its obligation under Article 29, thereby preventing the International Tribunal from discharging the mission entrusted to it by the Security Council, the International Tribunal is entitled to report this non-observance to the Security Council.

34. The aforementioned powers have been incorporated by the International Tribunal into its Rules. According to Rule 7 *bis*:

(A) In addition to cases to which Rule 11 [Non-compliance with a Request for Deferral], Rule 13 [Non Bis In Idem], Rule 59 [Failure to Execute a Warrant or Transfer Order] or Rule 61 [Procedure in Case of Failure to Execute a Warrant], applies, where a Trial Chamber or a Judge is satisfied that a State has failed to comply with an obligation under Article 29 of the Statute which relates to any proceedings before that Chamber or Judge, the Chamber or Judge may advise the President, who shall report the matter to the Security Council.

(B) If the Prosecutor satisfies the President that a State has failed to comply with an obligation under Article 29 of the Statute in respect of a request by the Prosecutor under Rule 8 [Request for Information], Rule 39 [Conduct of Investigations] or Rule 40 [Provisional Measures], the President shall notify the Security Council thereof.

In the light of the above, the adoption of Rule 7 *bis* is clearly to be regarded as falling within the authority of the International Tribunal. This conclusion is also supported by the fact that so far, either at the request of a Trial Chamber or *proprio motu*, on five different occasions the President of the International Tribunal has reported to the Security Council a failure by a State or an Entity to comply with Article 29. The Security Council, far from objecting to this procedure, has normally followed it up with a statement made, on behalf of the whole body, by the President of the Security Council and addressed to the recalcitrant State or Entity.

35. It is appropriate at this juncture to illustrate the power of the International Tribunal to make such a judicial finding. When faced with an allegation of non-compliance with an order or request issued under Article 29, a Judge, a Trial Chamber or the President must be satisfied that the State has clearly failed to comply with the order or request. This finding is totally different from that made, at the request of the Security Council, by a fact-finding body, and *a fortiori* from that undertaken by a political or quasi-political body. Depending upon the circumstances the determination by the latter may undoubtedly constitute an authoritative statement of what has occurred in a particular area of interest to the Security Council; it may set forth the views of the relevant body on the question of whether or not a certain State has breached international standards. In addition, the conclusions of the bodies at issue may include suggestions or recommendations for action by the Security Council. By contrast, the International Tribunal (i.e., a Trial Chamber, a Judge or the President) engages in a judicial activity proper: acting upon all the principles and rules of judicial propriety, it scrutinises the behaviour of a certain State in order to establish formally whether or not that State has breached its international obligation to cooperate with the International Tribunal.

36. Furthermore, the finding by the International Tribunal must not include any recommendations or suggestions as to the course of action the Security Council may wish to take as a consequence of that finding.

As already mentioned, the International Tribunal may not encroach upon the sanctionary powers accruing to the Security Council pursuant to Chapter VII of the United Nations Charter. Furthermore, as the Appeals Chamber has stated above (paragraph 26), every Member State of the United Nations has a legal interest in seeking compliance by any other Member State with the International Tribunal's orders and requests issued pursuant to Article 29. Faced with the situation where a judicial finding by the International Tribunal of a breach of Article 29 has been reported to the Security Council, each Member State of the United Nations may act upon the legal interest referred to; consequently it may request the State to terminate its breach of Article 29. In addition to this possible unilateral action, a collective response through other intergovernmental organizations may be envisaged. The fundamental principles of the United Nations Charter and the spirit of the Statute of the International Tribunal aim to limit, as far as possible, the risks of arbitrariness and conflict. They therefore give pride of place to collective or joint action to be taken through an intergovernmental organization. It is appropriate to emphasise that this collective action:

(i)   may only be taken after a judicial finding has been made by the International Tribunal; and

(ii) may take various forms, such as a political or moral condemnation, or a collective request to cease the breach, or economic or diplomatic sanctions.

In addition, collective action would be warranted in the case of repeated and blatant breaches of Article 29 by the same State; and provided the Security Council had not decided that it enjoyed exclusive powers on the matter, the situation being part of a general condition of threat to the peace.

37. It should be added that, apart from the cases provided for in Rule 7 *bis* (B), the President of the International Tribunal simply has the role of *nuncius*, that is to say, he or she shall simply transmit to the Security Council the judicial finding of the relevant Judge or Chamber.

C. Whether The International Tribunal Is Empowered To Issue Binding Orders To State Officials

1. Can the International Tribunal subpoena State officials?

38. The Appeals Chamber dismisses the possibility of the International Tribunal addressing subpoenas to State officials acting in their official capacity. Such officials are mere instruments of a State and their official action can only be attributed to the State. They cannot be the subject of sanctions or penalties for conduct that is not private but undertaken on behalf of a State. In other words, State officials cannot suffer the consequences of wrongful acts which are not attributable to them personally but to the State on whose behalf they act: they enjoy so-called "functional immunity". This is a well-established rule of customary international law going back to the eighteenth and nineteenth centuries, restated many times since. More recently, France adopted a position based on that rule in the *Rainbow Warrior* case. The rule was also clearly set out by the Supreme Court of Israel in the *Eichmann* case.

2. Can the International Tribunal direct binding orders to State officials?

39. The Appeals Chamber will now consider the distinct but connected question of whether State officials may be the proper addressees of binding orders issued by the International Tribunal.

Croatia has submitted that the International Tribunal cannot issue binding orders to State organs acting in their official capacity. It argues that such a power, if there is one, would be in conflict with well-established principles of international law, in particular the principle, restated in Article 5 of the Draft Articles on State Responsibility adopted by the International Law Commission, whereby the conduct of any State organ must be considered as an act of the State concerned, with the consequence that any internationally wrongful act of a State official entails the international responsibility of the State as such and not that of the official. The Prosecutor takes the opposite view. According to her, the power of the International Tribunal to address compulsory orders to State officials is based on substantially two grounds: first of all Article 7, paragraphs 2 and 4, and Article 18, paragraph 2, of the Statute. It is the Prosecutor's contention that these provisions show that: "State officials acting in their official capacity may be bound by decisions, determinations and orders of the Tribunal". In particular, Article 18, paragraph 2, by providing that, "the Prosecutor may, as appropriate, seek the assistance of the State authorities concerned", envisages that State officials may be directly addressed by the International Tribunal. The other argument put forward by the Prosecutor is substantially based on a syllogism. The major premise is that the International Tribunal, under Article 29, must be endowed with the power to issue compelling orders to States. By the same token, it is also entitled to issue such orders to individuals, because an international criminal court exhibiting the attributes of the International Tribunal "cannot possibly lack the power to direct its orders to individuals. Otherwise its powers would be wholly inferior to those of the national criminal courts over whom it has primacy". The minor premise of the syllogism is that, of course, State officials are individuals, although they act in their official capacity. The conclusion of the syllogism is that the International Tribunal must perforce be endowed with the power to address its orders to State officials.

40. The Appeals Chamber wishes to emphasise at the outset that the Prosecutor's reasoning, adopted by the Trial Chamber in its Subpoena Decision, is clearly based on what could be called "the domestic analogy". It is well known that in many national legal systems, where courts are part of the State apparatus and indeed constitute the judicial branch of the State apparatus, such courts are entitled to issue orders to other (say administrative, political, or even military) organs, including senior State officials and the Prime Minister or the Head of State. These organs, subject to a number of well-specified exceptions, can be summoned to give evidence, can be compelled to produce documents, can be requested to appear in court, etc. This is taken for granted in modern democracies, where nobody, not even the Head of State, is above the law (*legibus solutus*).

The setting is totally different in the international community. It is known *omnibus lippis et tonsoribus* ["to all bleary-eyed and hair-cutters", that is, to everybody, Horace, *Satirae* 1.7.3] that the international community lacks any central government with the attendant separation of powers and checks and balances. In particular, international courts, including the International Tribunal, do not make up a judicial branch of a central government. The international community primarily consists of sovereign States; each jealous of its own sovereign attributes and prerogatives, each insisting on its right to equality and demanding full respect, by all other States, for its domestic jurisdiction. Any international body must therefore take into account this basic structure of the international community. It follows from these various factors that international courts do not necessarily possess, *vis-à-vis* organs of sovereign States, the same powers which accrue to national courts in respect of the administrative, legislative and political organs of the State. Hence, the transposition onto the international community of legal institutions, constructs or approaches prevailing in national law may be a source of great confusion and misapprehension. In addition to causing opposition among States, it could end up blurring the distinctive features of international courts.

41. It is therefore only natural that the Appeals Chamber, in order to address the issue raised above, should start by enquiring into general principles and rules of customary international law relating to State officials. It is well known that customary international law protects the internal organization of each sovereign State: it leaves it to each sovereign State to determine its internal structure and in particular to designate the individuals acting as State agents or organs. Each sovereign State has the right to issue instructions to its organs, both those operating at the internal level and those operating in the field of international relations, and also to provide for sanctions or other remedies in case of non-compliance with those instructions. The corollary of this exclusive power is that each State is entitled to claim that acts or transactions performed by one of its organs in its official capacity be attributed to the State, so that the individual organ may not be held accountable for those acts or transactions.

The general rule under discussion is well established in international law and is based on the sovereign equality of States (*par in parem non habet imperium* [an equal has no authority over another equal]). The few exceptions relate to one particular consequence of the rule. These exceptions arise from the norms of international criminal law prohibiting war crimes, crimes against humanity and genocide. Under these norms, those responsible for such crimes cannot invoke immunity from national or international jurisdiction even if they perpetrated such crimes while acting in their official capacity. Similarly, other classes of persons (for example, spies, as defined in Article 29 of the Regulations Respecting the Laws and Customs of War on Land, annexed to the Hague Convention IV of 1907), although acting as State organs, may be held personally accountable for their wrongdoing.

The general rule at issue has been implemented on many occasions, although primarily with regard to its corollary, namely the right of a State to demand for its organs functional immunity from foreign jurisdiction (*see* above, paragraph 38). This rule undoubtedly applies to relations between States *inter se*. However, it must also be taken into account, and indeed it has always been respected, by international organizations as well as international courts. Whenever such organizations or courts have intended to address recommendations, decisions (in the case of the Security Council acting under Chapter VII of the United Nations Charter) or judicial orders or requests to States, they have refrained from turning to a specific State official; they have issued the recommendation, decision or judicial order to the State as a whole, or to "its authorities". In the case of international courts, they have, of course, addressed their orders or requests through the channel of the State Agent before the court or the competent diplomatic officials.

42. The question that the Appeals Chamber must therefore address is as follows: are there any provisions or principles of the Statute of the International Tribunal which justify a departure from this well-established rule of international law?

43. [On the basis of the aforementioned principles, the Appeals Chamber finds that], both under general international law and the Statute itself, Judges or Trial Chambers cannot address binding orders to State officials. Even if one does not go so far as to term the obligation laid down in Article 29 as an obligation of result, as asserted by one of the *amici curiae*, it is indubitable that States, being the addressees of such obligation, have some choice or leeway in identifying the persons responsible for, and the method of, its fulfilment. It is for each such State to determine the internal organs competent to carry out the order. It follows that if a Judge or a Chamber intends to order the production of documents, the seizure of evidence, the arrest of suspects etc., being acts involving action by a State, its organs or officials, they must turn to the relevant State.

44. The Appeals Chamber considers that the above conclusion is not only warranted by international law, but is also the only one acceptable from a practical viewpoint. If, *arguendo*, one were to admit the power of the International Tribunal to address compelling orders to State officials, say, for the production of documents, there are two hypothetical situations which

could result in the failure of the addressee to deliver the documents without undue delay and a consequent request by the International Tribunal for his appearance before the relevant Trial Chamber. It may be that the State official has been ordered by his authorities to refuse to surrender the documents; in this case, what would be the practical advantage of his being summoned before the International Tribunal, as was indicated in the *subpoena duces tecum* under discussion? Clearly, the State official would be unable to disregard the instructions of his Government: *ad impossibilia nemo tenetur* [no one may be obliged to do something impossible]. Even the advantage of having the State official explaining publicly in court that his State refuses to surrender the documents is one that could be obtained by making public the official response of the relevant State authorities, declining to comply with Article 29. On the other hand, it may happen that a State official, on his own initiative, refuses to hand over the documents although his superior authorities intend to cooperate with the International Tribunal; this, for instance, may occur if that official places on the national legislation concerning his tasks and duties an interpretation different from that advocated by his superior authorities. In this and other similar cases the Appeals Chamber fails to see the advantage of summoning such official before the International Tribunal. It is for his State to compel him, through all the national legal remedies available, to comply with the International Tribunal's order for the production of documents (*see*, however, the exception that the Appeals Chamber envisages below, at paragraph 51). Clearly, as State officials are mere instrumentalities in the hands of sovereign States, there is no practical purpose in singling them out and compelling them to produce documents, or in forcing them to appear in court. It is the State which is bound by Article 29 and it is the State for which the official or agent fulfils his functions that constitutes the legitimate interlocutor of the International Tribunal. States shall therefore incur international responsibility for any serious breach of that provision by their officials.

45. Whilst from a legal viewpoint the International Tribunal is barred from addressing orders to State officials as such, the Appeals Chamber accepts that it might prove useful in practice for the Registrar of the International Tribunal to notify the relevant State officials of the order sent to the State. This notification would serve exclusively to inform State officials who, according to the Prosecutor or defence counsel, may hold the documents, of the order sent to the State. If the central authorities are prepared and willing to comply with Article 29, this practical procedure may speed up the internal process for the production of documents.

D. Whether The International Tribunal May Issue Binding Orders To Individuals Acting In Their Private Capacity

1. Is the International Tribunal empowered to subpoena individuals acting in their private capacity?

46. Neither Croatia nor the Prosecutor denies that the International Tribunal may issue binding orders in the form of subpoenas (that is, under threat of penalty), to individuals acting in their private capacity. However, the Appeals Chamber deems it necessary to consider this matter with particular reference to the question of whether or not State officials may be subpoenaed *qua* private individuals. Furthermore, there seems to be disagreement about the remedies available to the International Tribunal in case of non-compliance.

47. The Appeals Chamber holds the view that the spirit of the Statute, as well as the purposes pursued by the Security Council when it established the International Tribunal, demonstrate that a Judge or a Chamber is vested with the authority to summon witnesses, to compel the production of documents, etc. However, the basis for this authority is not that, as the International Tribunal enjoys primacy over national criminal courts, it cannot but possess at least the same powers as those courts. Such an argument is flawed, for the International

Tribunal exhibits a number of features that differentiate it markedly from national courts. It is, therefore, tantamount to a *petitio principii*: only after proving that the essential powers and functions of the two types of courts (the International Tribunal and national courts) are similar, could one infer that the International Tribunal has the same powers as national courts to compel individuals to produce documents, appear in court, etc. As stated above, the International Tribunal's power to issue binding orders to individuals derives instead from the general object and purpose of the Statute, as well as the role the International Tribunal is called upon to play thereunder. The International Tribunal is an international criminal court constituting a novelty in the world community. Normally, individuals subject to the sovereign authority of States may only be tried by national courts. If a national court intends to bring to trial an individual subject to the jurisdiction of another State, as a rule it relies on treaties of judicial cooperation or, if such treaties are not available, on voluntary interstate cooperation. Thus, the relation between national courts of different States is "horizontal" in nature. In 1993 the Security Council for the first time established an international criminal court endowed with jurisdiction over individuals living within sovereign States, be they States of the former Yugoslavia or third States, and, in addition, conferred on the International Tribunal primacy over national courts. By the same token, the Statute granted the International Tribunal the power to address to States binding orders concerning a broad variety of judicial matters (including the identification and location of persons, the taking of testimony and the production of evidence, the service of documents, the arrest or detention of persons, and the surrender or transfer of indictees to the International Tribunal). Clearly, a "vertical" relationship was thus established, at least as far as the judicial and injunctory powers of the International Tribunal are concerned (whereas in the area of enforcement the International Tribunal is still dependent upon States and the Security Council).

In addition, the aforementioned power is spelt out in provisions such as Article 18, paragraph 2, first part, which states: "The Prosecutor shall have the power to question suspects, victims and witnesses, to collect evidence and to conduct on-site investigations" (emphasis added); and in Article 19, paragraph 2: "Upon confirmation of an indictment, the judge may, at the request of the Prosecutor, issue such orders and warrants for the arrest, detention, surrender or transfer of persons, and any other orders as may be required for the conduct of the trial" (emphasis added).

48. The spirit and purpose of the Statute, as well as the aforementioned provisions, confer on the International Tribunal an incidental or ancillary jurisdiction over individuals other than those whom the International Tribunal may prosecute and try. These are individuals who may be of assistance in the task of dispensing criminal justice entrusted to the International Tribunal. Furthermore, as stated above, Article 29 also imposes upon States an obligation to take action required by the International Tribunal *vis-à-vis* individuals subject to their jurisdiction.

2. Classes of persons encompassed by the expression "Individuals acting in their private capacity"

49. It should be noted that the class of "individuals acting in their private capacity" also includes State agents who, for instance, witnessed a crime before they took office, or found or were given evidentiary material of relevance for the prosecution or the defence prior to the initiation of their official duties. In this case, the individuals can legitimately be the addressees of a subpoena. Their role in the prosecutorial or judicial proceedings before the International Tribunal is unrelated to their current functions as State officials.

50. The same may hold true for the example propounded by the Prosecutor in her Brief: "a government official who, while engaged on official business, witnesses a crime within the jurisdiction of the [International] Tribunal being committed by a superior officer". According

to the Prosecutor: "It cannot be argued that the official concerned is immune from orders to testify as to what was seen". In this case, the individual was undoubtedly present at the event in his official capacity; however, arguably he saw the event *qua* a private individual. This can be illustrated by the example of a colonel who, in the course of a routine transfer to another combat zone, overhears a general issuing orders aimed at the shelling of civilians or civilian objects. In this case the individual must be deemed to have acted in a private capacity and may therefore be compelled by the International Tribunal to testify as to the events witnessed. By contrast, if the State official, when he witnessed the crime, was actually exercising his functions, i.e., the monitoring of the events was part of his official functions, then he was acting as a State organ and cannot be subpoenaed, as is illustrated by the case where the imaginary colonel overheard the order while on an official inspection mission concerning the behaviour of the belligerents on the battlefield.

The situation differs for a State official (e.g., a general) who acts as a member of an international peace-keeping or peace-enforcement force such as UNPROFOR, IFOR or SFOR. Even if he witnesses the commission or the planning of a crime in a monitoring capacity, while performing his official functions, he should be treated by the International Tribunal *qua* an individual. Such an officer is present in the former Yugoslavia as a member of an international armed force responsible for maintaining or enforcing peace and not *qua* a member of the military structure of his own country. His mandate stems from the same source as that of the International Tribunal, i.e., a resolution of the Security Council, and therefore he must testify, subject to the appropriate requirements set out in the Rules.

51. Another instance can be envisaged, which, although more complicated, is not unrealistic in States facing extraordinary circumstances such as war or the aftermath of war. Following the issue of a binding order to such a State for the production of documents necessary for trial, a State official, who holds that evidence in his official capacity, having been requested by his authorities to surrender it to the International Tribunal may refuse to do so, and the central authorities may not have the legal or factual means available to enforce the International Tribunal's request. In this scenario, the State official is no longer behaving as an instrumentality of his State apparatus. For the limited purposes of criminal proceedings, it is sound practice to "downgrade", as it were, the State official to the rank of an individual acting in a private capacity and apply to him all the remedies and sanctions available against non-complying individuals referred to below (paragraphs 57–59): he may be subpoenaed and, if he does not appear in court, proceedings for contempt of the International Tribunal could be instituted against him. Indeed, in this scenario, the State official, in spite of the instructions received from his Government, is deliberately obstructing international criminal proceedings, thus jeopardising the essential function of the International Tribunal: dispensation of justice. It will then be for the Trial Chamber to determine whether or not also to call to account the State; the Trial Chamber will have to decide whether or not to make a judicial finding of the State's failure to comply with Article 29 (on the basis of Article 11 of the International Law Commission's Draft Articles on State Responsibility) and ask the President of the International Tribunal to forward it to the Security Council.

3. Whether the International Tribunal may enter into direct contact with individuals or must instead go through the national authorities

52. Two more questions must be considered by the Appeals Chamber: the means by which the International Tribunal enters into contact with individuals, and the legal remedies available in case of non-compliance by individuals.

53. The Appeals Chamber will make two general and preliminary points. Firstly, a distinction should be drawn between the former belligerent States or Entities of ex-Yugoslavia and third

States. The first class encompasses States: (i) on the territory of which crimes may have been perpetrated; and in addition, (ii) some authorities of which might be implicated in the commission of these crimes. Consequently, in the case of those States, to go through the official channels for identifying, summoning and interviewing witnesses, or to conduct on-site investigations, might jeopardise investigations by the Prosecutor or defence counsel. In particular, the presence of State officials at the interview of a witness might discourage the witness from speaking the truth, and might also imperil not just his own life or personal integrity but possibly those of his relatives. It follows that it would be contrary to the very purpose and function of the International Tribunal to have State officials present on such occasions. The States and Entities of the former Yugoslavia are obliged to cooperate with the International Tribunal in such a manner as to enable the International Tribunal to discharge its functions. This obligation (which, it should be noted, was restated in the Dayton and Paris Accords), also requires them to allow the Prosecutor and the defence to fulfil their tasks free from any possible impediment or hindrance.

54. Secondly, the implementing legislation of the International Tribunal's Statute enacted by some States provides that any order or request of the International Tribunal should be addressed to a specific central body of the country, which then channels it to the relevant prosecutorial or judicial agencies. It may be inferred from this that any order or request should therefore be addressed to that central national body.

Clearly, these laws tend to apply to the relations between national authorities and the International Tribunal the same approach that they normally adopt in their bilateral or multilateral treaties of judicial cooperation. These treaties are, of course, between equal sovereign States. Everything is therefore placed on a "horizontal" plane and each State is concerned with its sovereign attributes when it comes to the fulfilment of prosecutorial or judicial functions. It follows that any manifestation of investigative or judicial activity (the taking of evidence, the seizure of documents, the questioning of witnesses, etc.) requested by one of the contracting States is to be exercised exclusively by the relevant authorities of the requested State. This same approach has been adopted by these States vis-à-vis the International Tribunal, in spite of the position of primacy accruing to the International Tribunal under the Statute and its "vertical" status alluded to above. However, whenever such implementing legislation turns out to be in conflict with the spirit and the word of the Statute, a well-known principle of international law can be relied upon to prevent States from shielding behind their national law in order to evade international obligations.

55. After these general remarks, the Appeals Chamber emphasises that a distinction should be drawn between two classes of acts or transactions:

(i)   those which may require the cooperation of the prosecutorial or judicial organs of the State where the individual is located (conduct of on-site investigations, execution of search or arrest warrants, seizure of evidentiary material, etc.); and

(ii) those which may be carried out by the private individual who is the addressee of a subpoena or order, acting either by himself or together with an investigator designated by the Prosecutor or by defence counsel (taking of witness statements, production of documents, delivery of video-tapes and other evidentiary material, appearance in court at The Hague, etc.).

For the first class of acts, unless authorized by national legislation or special agreements, the International Tribunal must turn to the relevant national authorities. This is subject to an exception which relates to the States or Entities of the former Yugoslavia: in their situation, for the reasons set out above, some activities such as, in particular, the conduct of on-site investigations, may justifiably be carried out by the International Tribunal itself.

With respect to the second class, the International Tribunal will normally turn, once again, to the national authorities for their cooperation. However, there are two situations where the International Tribunal may enter directly into contact with a private individual:

(i) when this is authorized by the legislation of the State concerned;

(ii) when the authorities of the State or Entity concerned, having been requested to comply with an order of the International Tribunal, prevent the International Tribunal from fulfilling its functions. This might arise in the above example (paragraph 49) of a State official who witnessed a crime or acquired possession of a document prior to becoming a State official, or in the other cases of State officials mentioned above (paragraph 50). In these examples the State authorities may be able, pursuant to their legislation or practice, to prevent the individual from testifying or delivering a particular document.

In the above-mentioned scenarios, the attitude of the State or Entity may jeopardise the discharge of the International Tribunal's fundamental functions. It is therefore to be assumed that an inherent power to address itself directly to those individuals inures to the advantage of the International Tribunal. Were it not vested with such a power, the International Tribunal would be unable to guarantee a fair trial to persons accused of atrocities in the former Yugoslavia. As was forcefully stated by the Prosecutor before the Appeals Chamber:

> So, if theoretically, [a State enacted] legislation barring access to its citizens for the purpose of compelling them to give evidence, we would say that in international law that legislation is invalid. We would then assert the Tribunal's entitlement to reach out directly to the individual by issuing an order to that effect, presumably permitting the individual to obey the higher order of international law, even in disobedience to his own domestic law. I think it would be counterproductive to suggest that we are at the mercy of using a State machinery when its citizens may be more willing than their government to discharge their obligations to this institution.... [If] there are reasons to believe that the witness would be willing to comply but the State, either because of its legislation or its attitude, if it has not enacted legislation, is not willing to assist, ... we would have every entitlement to reach out directly, by mail might be the preferable, more prudent, course than sending members of our personnel to an unfriendly territory for that simple purpose.

56. In the two aforementioned situations the International Tribunal may directly summon a witness, or order an individual to hand over evidence or appear before a Judge or Trial Chamber. In other words, the International Tribunal may enter into direct contact with an individual subject to the sovereign authority of a State. The individual, being within the ancillary (or incidental) criminal jurisdiction of the International Tribunal, is duty-bound to comply with its orders, requests and summonses.

4. The legal remedies for non-compliance

57. The second question which the Appeals Chamber will now consider is that of the legal remedies available for non-compliance by an individual with a subpoena or order issued by the International Tribunal. Here, a distinction needs to be made between:

(i) the sanctions and penalties that can be imposed by the authorities of the State where the individual is located; and

(ii) those that can be imposed by the International Tribunal.

The first set of sanctions or penalties is enumerated or hinted at in a number of implementing laws of States: these laws provide that, in case of non-compliance with an order of the International Tribunal, the national authorities shall apply the same remedies and penalties provided for in case of disregard of an order or injunction issued by a national authority. In addition, as demonstrated in the valuable survey submitted by *amicus curiae*, most States, whether of common-law or civil-law persuasion, generally provide for the enforcement of summonses or subpoenas issued by national courts. It is plausible that, in those States, the national authorities will be ready to assist the International Tribunal by resorting to their own national criminal legislation.

58. The Appeals Chamber holds the view that, normally, the International Tribunal should turn to the relevant national authorities to seek remedies or sanctions for non-compliance by an individual with a subpoena or order issued by a Judge or a Trial Chamber. Legal remedies or sanctions put in place by the national authorities themselves are more likely to work effectively and expeditiously. However, allowance should be made for cases where resort to national remedies or sanctions would not prove workable. This holds true for those cases where, from the outset, the International Tribunal decides to enter into direct contact with individuals, at the request of either the Prosecutor or the defence, on the assumption that the authorities of the State or Entity would either prevent the International Tribunal from fulfilling its mission (*see* above, paragraph 55) or be unable to compel a State official to comply with an order issued under Article 29 (*see* above, the case mentioned in paragraph 51). In these cases, it may prove pointless to request those national authorities to enforce the International Tribunal's order through national means.

59. The remedies available to the International Tribunal range from a general power to hold individuals in contempt of the International Tribunal (utilising the inherent contempt power rightly mentioned by the Trial Chamber) to the specific contempt power provided for in Rule 77. It should be added that, if the subpoenaed individual who fails to deliver documents or appear in court also fails to attend contempt proceedings, *in absentia* proceedings should not be ruled out. The Prosecutor contended in her oral submissions that it would be "hypothetical and speculative in the extreme to contemplate a trial *in absentia* on a charge of contempt". By contrast, counsel for Croatia conceded in their oral submissions that *in absentia* proceedings would be admissible, provided they met "the requirement of due process" and amounted to what in United States courts is called "civil contempt", "which would not be imposing 'criminal penalties', but could nonetheless compel someone by even imprisonment until they decided to comply with the court's order".

The Appeals Chamber finds that, generally speaking, it would not be appropriate to hold *in absentia* proceedings against persons falling under the primary jurisdiction of the International Tribunal (i.e., persons accused of crimes provided for in Articles 2–5 of the Statute). Indeed, even when the accused has clearly waived his right to be tried in his presence (Article 21, paragraph 4 (d), of the Statute), it would prove extremely difficult or even impossible for an international criminal court to determine the innocence or guilt of that accused. By contrast, *in absentia* proceedings may be exceptionally warranted in cases involving contempt of the International Tribunal, where the person charged fails to appear in court, thus obstructing the administration of justice. These cases fall within the ancillary or incidental jurisdiction of the International Tribunal.

If such *in absentia* proceedings were to be instituted, all the fundamental rights pertaining to a fair trial would need to be safeguarded. Among other things, although the individual's absence would have to be regarded, under certain conditions, as a waiver of his "right to be tried in his presence", he should be offered the choice of counsel. The Appeals Chamber holds the view that, in addition, other guarantees provided for in the context of the European Convention on Human Rights should also be respected.

60. Of course, if a Judge or a Chamber decides to address a *subpoena duces tecum* or *ad testificandum* directly to an individual living in a particular State and at the same time notifies the national authorities of that State of the issue of the subpoena, this procedure will make it easier for those national authorities to assist the International Tribunal by enforcing the orders

in case of non-compliance. If, by contrast, the Judge or Chamber decides not to notify those national authorities, the only response by the International Tribunal to an individual's failure to obey the subpoena will, necessarily, be resort to its own contempt proceedings.

E. The Question Of National Security Concerns

1. Whether the International Tribunal is barred from examining documents raising national security concerns

61. Croatia has submitted that the International Tribunal does not have the power to judge or determine Croatia's national security claims. Relying upon the *Corfu Channel* case, Croatia contends that "[t]he determination of the national security needs of each State is a fundamental attribute of its sovereignty". Both the Trial Chamber in the Subpoena Decision and the Prosecutor take the opposite view. The Trial Chamber, at the end of its extensive treatment of this delicate matter, concludes that:

> [A] State invoking a claim of national security as a basis for non-production of evidence requested by the International Tribunal, may not be exonerated from its obligation by a blanket assertion that its security is at stake. Thus, the State has the onus to prove its objection.

The Trial Chamber goes on to suggest that:

> [F]or the purpose of determining the validity of the assertions of a particular State relating to national security concerns, the Trial Chamber [seized with the criminal case in question] may hold *in camera* hearings, in a manner which accords with the provisions of Sub-rule 66 (C) and Rule 79. Furthermore, with a view to…the secrecy of the information it may initially conduct an *ex parte* hearing in a manner analogous to that provided for in Sub-rule 66 (C).

In her Brief, the Prosecutor has among other things averred that the Croatian position would "prevent the [International] Tribunal from fulfilling its Security Council-given mandate to effectively prosecute persons responsible for serious violations of international humanitarian law and thus, defeat its essential object and purpose. The effective administration of justice would be severely prejudiced".

62. The Appeals Chamber holds that the claim submitted by Croatia must be dismissed, on three grounds.

Firstly, reliance upon the *Corfu Channel* case is inapposite. It is true that the International Court of Justice confined itself to taking note of the British refusal to produce, on account of "naval secrecy", the naval documents requested by the Court. However, this request had been made on the strength of Article 49 of the Statute of the International Court of Justice and Article 54 of its Rules; the first of these two provisions, of course more authoritative, was undoubtedly couched in non-mandatory terms. The situation is different with the International Tribunal: Article 29 of its Statute is worded in strong mandatory language. More pertinent precedents include the so-called *Sabotage* cases brought before the United States – German Mixed Claims Commission in the 1930s, the *Ballo* case decided by the Administrative Tribunal of the International Labour Organisation in 1972; the *Cyprus* v. *Turkey* case, decided by the European Commission on Human Rights in 1976, and the *Godinez Cruz* case, decided by the Inter-American Court of Human Rights on 20 January 1989. These cases show that there have been instances in which States have complied with judicial requests for the production of sensitive or confidential documents. The scrutiny of documents in those cases was undertaken by the judicial body *in camera*. In the *Cyprus* v. *Turkey* case, where the State in question had refused to comply with the request, the international body made a judicial finding of such refusal and reported it to the competent political body.

63. Secondly, a plain reading of Article 29 of the Statute makes it clear that it does not envisage any exception to the obligation of States to comply with requests and orders of a Trial Chamber. Whenever the Statute intends to place a limitation on the International Tribunal's powers, it does so explicitly, as demonstrated by Article 21, paragraph 4 (g), which bars the International Tribunal from "compelling" an accused "to testify against himself or to confess guilt". It follows that it would be unwarranted to read into Article 29 limitations or restrictions on the powers of the International Tribunal not expressly envisaged either in Article 29 or in other provisions of the Statute.

64. Croatia has argued that, as the Statute operates within the framework of customary international law, there was no need for its drafters to restate therein the principles of State sovereignty, national security and the "act of State doctrine". These principles are firmly anchored in the Statute – so the argument goes – and there was "absolutely no need to provide explicit exemptions for that in the Statute". The Appeals Chamber takes the view that, in the context of national security, this argument is inapplicable.

Admittedly, customary international rules do protect the national security of States by prohibiting every State from interfering with or intruding into the domestic jurisdiction, including national security matters, of other States. These rules are reflected in Article 2, paragraph 7, of the United Nations Charter with regard to the relations between Member States of the United Nations and the Organization. However, Article 2, paragraph 7, of the Charter provides for a significant exception to the impenetrability of the realm of domestic jurisdiction in respect of Chapter VII enforcement measures. As the Statute of the International Tribunal has been adopted pursuant to this very Chapter, it can pierce that realm.

Furthermore, although it is true that the rules of customary international law may become relevant where the Statute is silent on a particular point, such as the "act of State" doctrine, there is no need to resort to these rules where the Statute contains an explicit provision on the matter, as is the case with Article 29. Considering the very nature of the innovative and sweeping obligation laid down in Article 29, and its undeniable effects on State sovereignty and national security, it cannot be argued that the omission of exceptions in its formulation was the result of an oversight. Had the "founding fathers" intended to place restrictions upon this obligation they would have done so, as they did in the case of Article 21, paragraph 4 (g). Article 29 therefore clearly and deliberately derogates from the customary international rules upon which Croatia relies.

In short, whilst in the case of State officials the Statute clearly does not depart from general international law, as stated above (paragraphs 41 and 42) in the case of national security concerns the Statute manifestly derogates from customary international law. This different attitude towards general rules can be easily explained. In the case of State officials there is no compelling reason warranting a departure from general rules. To make use of the powers flowing from Article 29 of the Statute, it is sufficient for the International Tribunal to direct its orders and requests to States (which are in any case the addressees of the obligations laid down in that provision). By contrast, as the Appeals Chamber will demonstrate in the following paragraph, to allow national security considerations to prevent the International Tribunal from obtaining documents that might prove of decisive importance to the conduct of trials would be tantamount to undermining the very essence of the International Tribunal's functions.

65. Thirdly, as was persuasively submitted by the Prosecutor, to grant States a blanket right to withhold, for security purposes, documents necessary for trial might jeopardise the very function of the International Tribunal, and "defeat its essential object and purpose". The International Tribunal was established for the prosecution of persons responsible for war crimes, crimes against humanity and genocide; these are crimes related to armed conflict and

military operations. It is, therefore, evident that military documents or other evidentiary material connected with military operations may be of crucial importance, either for the Prosecutor or the defence, to prove or disprove the alleged culpability of an indictee, particularly when command responsibility is involved (in this case military documents may be needed to establish or disprove the chain of command, the degree of control over the troops exercised by a military commander, the extent to which he was cognisant of the actions undertaken by his subordinates, etc.). To admit that a State holding such documents may unilaterally assert national security claims and refuse to surrender those documents could lead to the stultification of international criminal proceedings: those documents might prove crucial for deciding whether the accused is innocent or guilty. The very *raison d'être* of the International Tribunal would then be undermined.

66. An important consequence follows from the foregoing considerations. Those instruments of national implementing legislation, such as the laws passed by Australia and New Zealand, which authorise the national authorities to decline to comply with requests of the International Tribunal if such requests would prejudice the "sovereignty, security or national interests" of the State, do not seem to be fully in keeping with the Statute.

2. The possible modalities of making allowance for national security concerns

67. Having asserted the basic principle that States may not withhold documents because of national security concerns, the Appeals Chamber wishes, however, to add that the International Tribunal should not be unmindful of legitimate State concerns related to national security, the more so because, as the Trial Chamber has rightly emphasised, the International Tribunal has already taken security concerns into account in its Rules 66 (C) and 77 (B).

The best way of reconciling, in keeping with the general guidelines provided by Rule 89 (B) and (D), the authority of the International Tribunal to order and obtain from States all documents directly relevant to trial proceedings, and the legitimate demands of States concerning national security, has been rightly indicated by the Trial Chamber in the Subpoena Decision, where it suggested that *in camera*, *ex parte* proceedings might be held so as to scrutinise the validity of States' national security claims. The Appeals Chamber, while adopting the same approach, will now suggest practical methods and procedures that may differ from those recommended by the Trial Chamber.

68. First of all, account must be taken of whether the State concerned has acted and is acting bona fide. As the International Court of Justice pointed out in the *Nuclear Tests* case, "one of the basic principles governing the creation and performance of legal obligations, whatever their source, is the principle of good faith. Trust and confidence are inherent in international cooperation, in particular in an age when this cooperation in many fields is becoming increasingly essential". The degree of bona fide cooperation and assistance lent by the relevant State to the International Tribunal, as well as the general attitude of the State *vis-à-vis* the International Tribunal (whether it is opposed to the fulfilment of its functions or instead consistently supports and assists the International Tribunal), are no doubt factors the International Tribunal may wish to take into account throughout the whole process of scrutinising the documents which allegedly raise security concerns.

Secondly, the State at issue may be invited to submit the relevant documents to the scrutiny of one Judge of the Trial Chamber designated by the Trial Chamber itself. Plainly, the fact that only one Judge and he or she alone undertakes a perusal of the documents should increase the confidence of the State that its national security secrets will not accidentally become public.

Thirdly, to ensure maximum confidentiality, if the documents are in a language other than one of the two official languages of the International Tribunal, in addition to the original documents the State concerned should provide certified translations, so that there is no need for the documents to be seen by translators of the International Tribunal.

Fourthly, the documents should be scrutinised by the Judge *in camera*, in *ex parte* proceedings, and no transcripts should be made of the hearing.

Fifthly, the documents that the Judge eventually considers to be irrelevant to the proceedings, as well as those the relevance of which is outweighed, in the appraisal of the Judge, by the need to safeguard legitimate national security concerns, should be returned to the State without being deposited or filed in the Registry of the International Tribunal. As to other documents, the State concerned may be allowed to redact part or parts of the documents, for instance, by blacking out part or parts; however, a senior State official should attach a signed affidavit briefly explaining the reasons for that redaction.

Finally, one should perhaps make allowance for an exceptional case: the case where a State, acting bona fide, considers one or two particular documents to be so delicate from the national security point of view, while at the same time of scant relevance to the trial proceedings, that it prefers not to submit such documents to the Judge. In this case, a minimum requirement to be met by the State is the submission of a signed affidavit by the responsible Minister: (i) stating that he has personally examined the document in question; (ii) summarily describing the content of the documents; (iii) setting out precisely the grounds on which the State considers that the document is not of great relevance to the trial proceedings; and (iv) concisely indicating the principal reasons for the desire of the State to withhold those documents. It will be for the Judge to appraise the grounds offered for withholding the documents. In case of doubt, he may request a more detailed affidavit, or a detailed explanation during *in camera*, *ex parte* proceedings. If the Judge is not satisfied that the reasons adduced by the State are valid and persuasive, he may request the Trial Chamber to make a judicial finding of non-compliance by the State with its obligations under Article 29 of the Statute and ask the President of the International Tribunal to transmit such finding to the Security Council.

69. It goes without saying that it will be for the relevant Trial Chamber to decide whether to adopt any of the aforementioned methods or procedures or to provide for other practical arrangements or protective measures, if need be in consultation with the interested State.

As referenced in the *Blaškić* decision, Rule 7 *bis* ICTY Rules and Procedure of Evidence (RPE) (the same provision exists also in the ICTR RPE) allows a Trial Chamber or permanent judge to *advise* the President of the Tribunal, or the Prosecutor to *persuade* the President, that a State has failed to comply with an obligation to cooperate under the Statute, at which point the President is required to notify the Security Council. Article 87(7) of the Rome Statute states that:

Where a State Party fails to comply with a request to cooperate by the Court contrary to the provisions of this Statute, thereby preventing the Court from exercising its functions and powers under this Statute, the Court may make a finding to that effect and refer the matter to the Assembly of States Parties or, where the Security Council referred the matter to the Court, to the Security Council.

In both cases, then, the court may not directly enforce its requests or orders for assistance, but is instead dependent for its ultimate power on what is essentially a political body. Accordingly, although the power of these courts to demand cooperation from States is based in law, the force of this law is necessarily contingent, and these courts must work in the shadow of these limitations. It is for this reason that the former chief Prosecutor of the ICTY and ICTR, Carla Del Ponte, said that her prosecutors had to use their 'wits and will power to prosecute the highest-ranking individuals' they could and that the work of the tribunals 'took place along the edge of the divide between national sovereignty and international responsibility, in the grey zone between the judicial and the political.'[1] Moreover, it is why the Prosecutor of the ICC has sought, as much as possible, to obtain state referrals of cases rather than using his *proprio motu* powers to initiate investigations so as to insure maximum cooperation from the subject state. At the same time, while cooperation with the tribunals has been far from perfect, what is remarkable is the extent to which these courts have been able to succeed in their work with relatively few appeals to the Security Council or the Assembly of States Parties (ASP), demonstrating that the mere threat of such a referral, combined with other mechanisms to obtain cooperation (ranging from moral suasion and a commitment to the law to pressures applied by the international community), can succeed in persuading States to provide support for investigations and prosecutions of perpetrators.

Cooperation need not only come from States, however. The following case demonstrates the importance of assistance from international organizations as well.

ICTY, Prosecutor v. Dokmanović, Trial Chamber, Decision on the Motion for Release by the Accused Slavko Dokmanović, 22 October 1997

Slavko Dokmanović was the President of the Vukovar municipality in eastern Croatia during 1991 and part of 1992. He was indicted for crimes against humanity and war crimes committed against non-Serbs from the Vukovar Hospital. At the time of his arrest, Dokmanović was residing in Serbia but he was lured across the border into Croatia by investigators from the Office of the Prosecutor (OTP) who told him that he could meet with officials from UNTAES – the United Nations Transitional Administration for Eastern Slavonia, Baranja and Western Sirmium – about obtaining compensation for his lost property in Croatia. When he arrived in Croatia, he was arrested by members of UNTAES and taken to The Hague. Dokmanović committed suicide in detention after his trial but a few days before the judgment was to be handed down by the Trial Chamber.

33. The Trial Chamber finds it established that the arrest of the accused was executed at the Erdut base when UNTAES removed him from the vehicle and handcuffed him. Investigators from the OTP immediately thereafter informed him of his rights and the nature of the charges pending against him. It is thus necessary to determine the authority of the forces involved in the operation to make such an arrest. Such a determination can only be made by the examination of two separate but closely related issues. First, the power conferred on bodies other than States to arrest persons indicted by the International Tribunal and, secondly, whether the mandate of UNTAES allows for its involvement in such an arrest process. It is also necessary to discuss briefly the respective roles played by the OTP and the forces of UNTAES in the arrest of Mr. Dokmanović.

1. Examination of the Statute and Rules

34. The Defence contends that Article 29 of the Statute, in conjunction with Rule 55 of the Rules, prescribes the sole method for securing the presence of accused persons before the International Tribunal. Since the accused was residing in the FRY at the time of his arrest, the Defence asserts that the FRY bore sole responsibility for his arrest and transfer to The Hague

---

[1] Carla Del Ponte and Charles Sudetić, *Madame Prosecutor: Confrontations with Humanity's Worst Criminals and the Culture of Impunity* (New York: Random House, 2009), 7.

for trial. Any other method of proceeding, in the view of the Defence, is in violation of the Statute, Rules and principles of international law. The Trial Chamber, however, finds that the mechanism prescribed in Rule 59 *bis* provides an alternative procedure to that contemplated by Article 29 and Rule 55, and that the circumstances of the present case merited the utilisation of this alternative.

35. The Statute of the Tribunal was adopted by the United Nations Security Council in Resolution 827, on 25 May 1993. This resolution requires that all States cooperate with the Tribunal and take all necessary measures under their domestic law to implement the Statute and comply with those orders issued by a Trial Chamber under Article 29 of the Statute. Article 29 sets out the general obligation of all States to cooperate with the Tribunal and afford it complete judicial assistance. In addition, Article 29, paragraph 2 (d) and (e), provides that States must comply with orders for the arrest or detention of persons and their surrender or transfer. The Report of the Secretary-General emphasizes that the establishment of the Tribunal on the basis of a Chapter VII decision "creates a binding obligation on all States to take whatever steps are required to implement the decision. The Report also states that "an order by a Trial Chamber for the surrender or transfer of persons to the custody of the International Tribunal shall be considered to be the application of an enforcement measure under Chapter VII of the Charter of the United Nations." However, neither the terms of the Article itself, nor the Report of the Secretary-General, provide that this duty of States precludes the arrest and transfer of accused persons by other methods.

36. According to Rule 59 *bis*, once an arrest warrant has been transmitted to an international authority, an international body, or the Office of the Prosecutor, the accused person named therein may be taken into custody without the involvement of the State in which he or she is located. This Rule was adopted by the Judges of the Tribunal at the Ninth Plenary session in January 1996, in accordance with Article 15 of the Statute, which grants the Judges the power to "adopt rules of procedure and evidence for the conduct of the pre-trial phase of proceedings, trials and appeals...and other appropriate matters." The procedure established by Rule 59 *bis* is valid and fully supported by the terms of the Statute.

37. Article 19, paragraph 2, of the Statute confers upon the Judge who has confirmed the indictment in any given case the authority to issue such orders and warrants for arrest, detention, surrender or transfer of persons, and any other orders as may be required for the conduct of the trial. This power, phrased in discretionary terms, clearly indicates that the Article does not contemplate that arrest warrants may only be directed to States. Rule 59 *bis*, therefore, can be regarded as giving effect to this Article when a decision has been made by the confirming Judge that it is "required" that entities other than States receive and execute warrants for the arrest, detention and transfer of accused persons. Judge Riad directed the arrest warrant in the present case to UNTAES, upon the motion of the Prosecution. The Prosecution stated that it had reason to believe that the accused was in the territory of Eastern Slavonia, which was being administered by UNTAES in accordance with a resolution of the Security Council. Thus, the Judge considered that such an order was required, pursuant to Article 19, paragraph 2, of the Statute, and the mechanism established by Rule 59 *bis* was thereby triggered.

38. Article 20, paragraph 2, is the most specific provision of the Statute regarding the procedure to be followed after the confirmation of an indictment and lends additional weight to Rule 59 *bis*. The plain language of this Article only contemplates that an accused person shall be taken into custody, informed of the charges against him, and transferred to the International Tribunal. No mention is made of States, nor is any limitation placed upon the authority of an international body or the Prosecutor to participate in the arrest process.

39. The FRY has failed to pass implementing legislation that would permit it to fulfil its obligations under Article 29. It has taken the position that its constitution bars the extradition of

its nationals to the Tribunal, and thus legislation which provides for the surrender of Yugoslav nationals would be unconstitutional. However, [t]here exists in international law a universally recognized principle whereby a gap or deficiency in municipal law, or any lack of the necessary national legislation, does not relieve States and other international subjects from their international obligations; consequently, no international legal subject can plead provisions of national legislation, or lacunae in that legislation, to be absolved of its obligations; when they do so, they are in breach of those obligations. The approach taken by the FRY is also in direct conflict with Rule 58 of the Rules, which provides that the obligation to surrender accused persons shall prevail over any national legislation.

40. However, as established above, Article 29 is obligatory in terms of conduct and is not a statement of exclusivity. It became clear with the commencement and continuation of the functioning of the Tribunal that several States were not fulfilling their obligations with regard to the arrest and transfer of indicted persons. This is evident from the utilisation of the procedure established by Rule 61 of the Rules on five occasions. The Judges, therefore, adopted Rule 59 *bis* within the parameters of Articles 19 and 20 of the Statute to provide for a mechanism additional to that of Rule 55, which, however, remains the primary method for the arrest and transfer of persons to the Tribunal. Such an interpretation of the Statute is fully consonant with its object and purpose as the constitutive instrument of an international judicial body intended to take effective measures to bring to justice those persons responsible for serious violations of international humanitarian law. Without the presence of those persons indicted by the Tribunal in The Hague, it is not possible for their guilt or innocence to be established and the functioning of the Tribunal is substantially impeded. Although the Rules cannot extend the powers of the Tribunal beyond those envisaged in the Statute, the enactment of a Rule that clearly is not in violation of the Statute and comports with its spirit can only be regarded as legitimate.

41. An interpretation of Rule 55 – grounded in Article 29 of the Statute – which assumes exclusivity, fails to take into account the provisions of Rule 59 *bis* of the Rules. It is axiomatic that a rule cannot be rendered meaningless by a restrictive interpretation of other provisions of the same instrument. Rule 59 *bis* is clear in its terms and is supported by the Statute of the Tribunal. It must, therefore, be considered to be valid and supplementary to Rule 55. Indeed, Rule 59 *bis* explicitly provides that it applies "notwithstanding Rules 55 to 59", indicating further that what was contemplated was an additional mechanism.

42. Furthermore, the FRY has failed or refused to execute the warrants which remain outstanding for the arrest of the three co-accused in the Indictment against Mr. Dokmanović. Considering this failure, the utilisation of the procedure for arrest contemplated by Rule 55 would very well have been an exercise in futility. In addition, when the warrant for the arrest of Mr. Dokmanović was issued, it was reasonably believed that he was residing in the area of Eastern Slavonia. Indeed, the evidence shows that he was in fact resident in Eastern Slavonia until July 1996, when he moved to Sombor in the FRY. Under these circumstances, the utilisation of the procedures of Rule 59 *bis* was appropriate. Although the arrest warrant was issued in April 1996, UNTAES did not itself receive it until July 1996, by which time the accused was no longer residing in Eastern Slavonia. Thus, UNTAES arrested Mr Dokmanović when he subsequently re-entered the area under its administration.

COMMENTARY

Cooperation from states, international organizations, and even NGOs can become complicated when the needs and interests of those entities depart from those of the international criminal tribunal. Certain organizations, for example, might prioritize the provision of humanitarian assistance or reconciliation efforts over accountability. Moreover, to the extent these organizations continue to operate in an ongoing conflict being investigated by an international tribunal, they may have particular security needs that prevent them from openly cooperating with prosecutors and investigators.

Both the ad hoc tribunals and the ICC have devices that allow States and organizations to provide confidential lead evidence to the tribunals. Rule 70 of the ICTY and ICTR RPE and Article 54(3)(e) of the Rome Statute allow parties to provide information confidentially which cannot be disclosed to any other party but which also can only be used as lead evidence, and not as direct evidence, in an investigation. A difficulty arose in the ICC's first trial of Thomas Lubanga Dyilo, however, when the Prosecution discovered that within the information provided confidentially under Article 54(3)(e), there was potentially exculpatory information that it was required to disclose to the defence under Article 67(2) of the Statute. When the Prosecution could not persuade the providers of the confidential information to allow him to turn this information over to the defence, the court suspended the case until a solution could be found. In the end, the trial could proceed only when the providers agreed to the disclosure of the potentially exculpatory materials to the court and ultimately to the defence.[2] In reaction to this episode, the ICC Prosecutor announced that he would seek to reduce any reliance in the future on confidential lead evidence.

In relation to sensitive State material – such as material covered by national security interests mentioned towards the end of the *Blaškić* excerpt above – interesting novel solutions have been envisaged by the STL RPE (see in particular Rules 118–19). Disclosure of such material may only be made with the consent of the provider. If such consent is given, the Prosecutor can present the information as evidence, and the Judges may admit it, and may order that access to the sources of this information be limited. When the provider does not consent to the disclosure of the information, but the Prosecutor is under an obligation to disclose (exculpatory) material, the Prosecutor will have to apply to the Pre-Trial Judge. The Prosecutor will *not* provide him with the original information or any detail about its origin, but will submit a list of proposed counterbalancing measures – measures which remedy the fact that material which should have been disclosed cannot actually be disclosed and, therefore, will ensure that the rights of the other party are respected. It is for the Pre-Trial Judge to rule on the matter and order the necessary counterbalancing measures, if need be, such as provision of the information in summarized or redacted form, identification of similar information, or withdrawal of specific charges. An alternative procedure is to resort to a Special Counsel, a person appointed by the President from a confidential list of persons approved by the provider of the confidential information. This Counsel is entitled to review the information and to then advise the Pre-Trial Judge on the most appropriate counterbalancing measures. Since no trial has yet taken place before the Special Tribunal for Lebanon (STL), only time will tell how this procedure plays out in practice.

---

[2] See *Prosecutor* v. *Thomas Lubanga Dyilo*, Judgment on the Appeal of the Prosecutor against the Decision of Trial Chamber I entitled 'Decision on the Consequences of Non-Disclosure of Exculpatory Materials Covered by Article 54(3)(e) agreements and the Application to Stay the Prosecution of the Accused, Together with Certain Issues raised at the Status Conference on 10 June 2008', Appeals Chamber, 21 October 2008.

3

SURRENDER AND ARRESTS

(A) RELATIONS BETWEEN INTERNATIONAL TRIBUNALS AND DOMESTIC COURTS

The surrender and arrest of fugitives represents a particular and critical form of state cooperation. While impediments in the investigation phase can often be overcome by finding other sources of evidence, a State's failure to surrender or arrest an accused can become an insurmountable barrier to accountability. Among the international criminal tribunals, only the Special Tribunal for Lebanon (STL) permits trials in the absence of the accused.

The ad hoc tribunals and the ICC all allow for the issuance of an arrest warrant based on essentially a showing of probable cause by the prosecution ('reasonable grounds for believing that a suspect has committed a crime within the jurisdiction of the Tribunal', (Rule 47 of the ICTY and ICTR Rules of Procedure and Evidence (RPE)), and 'reasonable basis to believe that a crime within the jurisdiction of the court has been or is being committed', (Article 53(1)(a) of the Rome Statute)). Unlike the ad hoc tribunals, the Pre-Trial Chamber at the ICC will issue a summons to appear rather than an arrest warrant if the prosecution cannot show that an arrest warrant is 'necessary [...] to ensure the person's appearance at trial' or to ensure that the suspect does not obstruct the investigation or continue committing crimes. (See Article 58 of the Rome Statute). As set out in the *Dokmanović* case above, the rules were revised at the ICTY and ICTR to allow those courts to direct arrest warrants to international bodies as well as states. The Rome Statute appears only to allow arrest warrants to be transmitted to States (Article 89(1)). Following an arrest or surrender, an accused at the ad hoc tribunals would have to await trial to determine his fate. At the ICC, however, Article 61 requires that there be held a confirmation hearing within a 'reasonable time' following the accused's surrender to the court. At the hearing, the defence is permitted to challenge the evidence of the prosecution and to present evidence of its own. The charges will be confirmed if the prosecution can present 'sufficient evidence to establish substantial grounds to believe that the person committed the crime charged'. Given the complexity and often lengthy duration of the cases at these tribunals this procedure is a salutary mechanism to ensure that there is a sufficient basis to hold the accused for trial.

Although surrenders from a State to an international tribunal might resemble an extradition, they are critically different. As defined in Article 102 of the Rome Statute, an extradition is a surrender from one State to another State pursuant to a treaty or agreement whereas a surrender is 'the delivering up of a person by a State to the Court, pursuant to this Statute'. Rule 58 of the ICTY and ICTR RPE states that '[t]he obligations laid down in Article 29 of the Statute shall prevail over any legal impediment to the surrender or transfer of the accused or of a witness to the Tribunal which may exist under the national law or extradition treaties of the State concerned'. This provision does not explicitly address whether the rule of specialty that ordinarily applies in extradition cases, whereby an accused can only be tried for the crimes for which he is surrendered and no others, is also relevant to surrenders. The ICTY has had occasion to address this question, as seen in the *Martić* case below. Another issue that has arisen in relation to arrests is whether there can be a remedy for an arrest that either is illegal or violates the suspect's human rights. That question is taken up in the *Nikolić* case below.

Cases

ICTY, **Prosecutor v. Martić,** *Trial Chamber, Decision on the Prosecution's Motion to Request Leave to File a Corrected Amended Indictment, 13 December 2002*

Milan Martić became the highest Serbian official within the Serb breakaway republic in Croatia from 1991 to 1995. He was initially charged in July 1995 with war crimes in connection with the shelling of Zagreb in May of that year. After his surrender to the ICTY in 2002, the prosecution successfully amended the indictment to include crimes against humanity and war crimes charges from the entire period of the war. Martić then complained, inter alia, that this expansive amendment violated the rule of specialty. He was eventually convicted and sentenced to 35 years' imprisonment.

(d) The rule of specialty

29. The Defence has invoked the rule of specialty in support of its rejection of the proposed amendment to the Indictment. This argument is without merit. The Defence rightly argues that the rule of specialty applies in the domain of extradition.

30. The rule of specialty protects the extradited person against prosecution for offences for which the extradition has not been sought. It serves to prevent that the requested state would lose its authority to decide whether it grants extradition under the existing treaty and statute provisions for each and every of the offences for which the extradition is sought. It reflects the equal positions of States in their extradition relations with other States.

31. The relation between the Tribunal, being established under Chapter VII of the Charter of the United Nations, and States is not the same as the relation between equal states. States are under an obligation of International Law to co-operate with the Tribunal, which includes a duty to arrest and transfer accused persons upon the request of the Tribunal. States would therefore not be in a position to object to the prosecution of a transferred accused before the Tribunal on other charges falling within the jurisdiction of the Tribunal than those that were brought against him when that person was transferred. Therefore an accused, who was arrested and transferred by a State under Article 29 of the Statute of the Tribunal would not have the possibility to invoke the principle of specialty for any such offence. The Tribunal is under no obligation to seek, and never sought, the consent of a state that has arrested and transferred an accused when confirming an indictment that enlarges the scope of the charges brought against the accused.

Inexplicably, even though the Rome Statute explicitly distinguishes between surrenders and extraditions, it nonetheless adopts the rule of specialty in Article 101(1):

A person surrendered to the Court under this Statute shall not be proceeded against, punished or detained for any conduct committed prior to surrenders, other than the conduct or course of conduct which forms the basis of the crimes for which that person has been surrendered.

Pursuant to Article 101(2), the State in question can waive specialty and allow the court to proceed on broader charges. In light of the structure of the ICC and the nature of the cases addressed by the court, it is hard to understand the justification for including the rule of specialty in the Statute. Given the investigatory and evidentiary challenges faced by the ICC, it is extremely likely that the prosecution will develop evidence of additional charges in ongoing cases. So long as the defence is given an opportunity to defend the charges and there are no inordinate delays, it seems unreasonable not to include the charges in the case against the accused.

ICTY, Prosecutor v. Nikolić, *Appeals Chamber, Decision on Interlocutory Appeal Concerning Legality of Arrest, 5 June 2003*

Dragan Nikolić was the commander of the Sušica Camp, controlled by Bosnian Serb forces, in the Vlasenica area of eastern Bosnia and Herzegovina. Nikolić was the first person indicted by the ICTY for crimes against humanity and war crimes for the treatment of Bosnian Muslims and other non-Serbs at the camp who were subjected to murder, rape, torture, forcible transfer and sexual violence. In April 2000, Nikolić was living in the Federal Republic of Yugoslavia (FRY) when he was seized by unknown individuals and driven into Bosnia and Herzegovina where he was delivered to the Stabilisation Force (SFOR), the multinational military force in Bosnia, which promptly placed him under arrest and took him to The Hague. There, he challenged the manner by which he was arrested. Nikolić ultimately pleaded guilty and was sentenced to 23 years' imprisonment, which was reduced by the Appeals Chamber to 20 years' imprisonment.

2. The Appeal concerns a decision issued by Trial Chamber II on 9 October 2002 on the legality of the Accused's arrest by the Stabilisation Force (respectively, "Impugned Decision" and "SFOR"). The Accused, indicted by the International Tribunal for crimes against humanity and war crimes on 1 November 1994, was arrested by SFOR on or about 20 April 2000 in Bosnia and Herzegovina. In the Impugned Decision, the Trial Chamber found that the Appellant was "allegedly illegally arrested and abducted from the territory of FRY by some unknown individuals and transferred by them to the territory of Bosnia and Herzegovina" and that "neither SFOR nor the Prosecution were involved in these acts". It also determined that since the Accused had ' "come into contact with SFOR", SFOR was obliged to arrest, detain and transfer him to the Hague'. It found that the Accused's abduction involved neither a violation of the sovereignty of Serbia and Montenegro that could be attributed either to SFOR or to the Office of the Prosecutor ("OTP" or "Prosecution"), nor a violation of the Accused's human rights or the fundamental principle of due process of law. For all these reasons, it concluded that there did not exist a "legal impediment to the Tribunal's exercise of jurisdiction over the Accused".

3. The question presented in this appeal is whether the International Tribunal can exercise jurisdiction over the Appellant notwithstanding the alleged violations of Serbia and Montenegro's sovereignty and of the Accused's human rights committed by SFOR, and by extension OTP, acting in collusion with the unknown individuals who abducted the Accused from Serbia and Montenegro. [. . .]

(a) Preliminary Considerations

17. The essence of the Defence's position is that SFOR, and by extension the OTP, acted in collusion with the individuals who took the Accused from Serbia and Montenegro to SFOR

in Bosnia and Herzegovina. SFOR knew that the accused had been kidnapped. By taking the Accused into its custody, SFOR effectively accepted that kidnapping in breach of Serbia and Montenegro's sovereignty and the Accused's human rights. Therefore, jurisdiction must be set aside.

18. The Appeals Chamber observes that the basic assumption underlying the Defence submissions is that setting aside jurisdiction by the International Tribunal is the appropriate remedy for the violations of State sovereignty and/or human rights that allegedly occurred in this case. That assumption requires further scrutiny. For, if the setting aside of jurisdiction is not the appropriate remedy for such violations, then, even assuming that they occurred and that the Defence is correct that the responsibility for the actions of the Accused's captors should be attributed to SFOR, jurisdiction would not need to be set aside. Thus, the first issue to be addressed is in what circumstances, if any, the International Tribunal should decline to exercise its jurisdiction because an accused has been brought before it through conduct violating State sovereignty or human rights. Once the standard warranting the declining of the exercise of jurisdiction has been identified, the Appeals Chamber will have to determine whether the facts of this case are ones that, if proven, would warrant such a remedy. If yes, then the Appeals Chamber must determine whether the underlying violations are attributable to SFOR and by extension to the OTP.

19. Before turning to these issues, however, the Appeals Chamber wishes to clarify that what is at issue here, is not jurisdiction *ratione materiae* but jurisdiction *ratione personae*. Jurisdiction *ratione materiae* depends on the nature of the crimes charged. The Accused is charged with war crimes and crimes against humanity. As such, there is no question that under the Statute, the International Tribunal does have jurisdiction *ratione materiae*. In this case, jurisdiction *ratione personae* depends instead on whether the Appeals Chamber determines that there are any circumstances relating to the Accused which would warrant setting aside jurisdiction and releasing the Accused. It is to this determination that the Chamber now turns.

(b) Under what circumstances does a violation of State sovereignty require jurisdiction to be set aside?

20. The impact of a breach of a State's sovereignty on the exercise of jurisdiction is a novel issue for this Tribunal. There is no case law directly on the point, and the Statute and the Rules provide little guidance. Article 29 of the Statute, *inter alia*, places upon all States the duty to cooperate with the International Tribunal in the investigation and prosecution of persons accused of committing serious violations of international humanitarian law. It also requires States to comply without undue delay with requests for assistance or orders issued by Trial Chambers, including the arrest or detention of persons. The Statute, however, does not provide a remedy for breaches of these obligations. In the absence of clarity in the Statute, Rules, and jurisprudence of the International Tribunal, the Appeals Chamber will seek guidance from national case law, where the issue at hand has often arisen, in order to determine State practice on the matter.

21. In several national cases, courts have held that jurisdiction should not be set aside, even though there might have been irregularities in the manner in which the accused was brought before them. In the *Argoud* case, the French Court of Cassation (Criminal Chamber) held that the alleged violation of German sovereignty by French citizens in the operation leading to the arrest of the accused did not impede the exercise of jurisdiction over the accused; it would be for the injured State (Germany) to complain and demand reparation at the international level and not for the accused. The *Cour de Sûreté*, the lower court, had actually noted that the State concerned (Germany) had not lodged any formal complaint and that ultimately, the issue was dealt with through diplomatic means. In *Stocke*, the German Federal Constitutional

Court (Bundesverfassungsgericht) endorsed a ruling by the Federal Court of Justice (Bundesgerichtshof) rejecting the appeal of the accused, a German national residing in France, claiming that he was the victim of an unlawful collusion between the German authorities and an informant who had deceptively brought him to German territory. The Court found that, even though there existed some decisions taking the opposite approach, according to international practice, courts would in general only refuse to assume jurisdiction in a case of a kidnapped accused if another State had protested against the kidnapping and had requested the return of the accused. In *United States* v. *Alvarez-Machain*, the Supreme Court of the United States held that the abduction of an accused who was a Mexican citizen, though it may have been in violation of general international law, did not require the setting aside of jurisdiction even though Mexico had requested the return of the accused.

22. On the other hand, there have been cases in which the exercise of jurisdiction has been declined. In *Jacob-Salomon*, an ex-German citizen was abducted on Swiss territory, taken to Germany, and held for trial on a charge of treason. The Swiss Government protested vigorously, claiming that German secret agents had been involved in the kidnapping, and sought the return of Jacob-Salomon. Though it denied any involvement of German agents in Swiss territory, the German government agreed (without arbitration) to return Jacob-Salomon to the Swiss Government. More recently, in *State* v. *Ebrahim*, the Supreme Court of South Africa had no hesitation in setting aside jurisdiction over an accused kidnapped from Swaziland by the security services. Similarly, in the *Bennet* case, the House of Lords granted the appeal of a New Zealand citizen, who was arrested in South Africa by the police and forcibly returned to the United Kingdom under the pretext of deporting him to New Zealand. It found that if the methods through which an accused is brought before the court were in disregard of extradition procedure, the court may stay the prosecution and order the release of the accused.

23. With regard to cases concerning the same kinds of crimes as those falling within the jurisdiction of the International Tribunal, reference may be made to *Eichmann* and *Barbie*. In *Eichmann*, the Supreme Court of Israel decided to exercise jurisdiction over the accused, notwithstanding the apparent breach of Argentina's sovereignty involved in his abduction. It did so mainly for two reasons. First, the accused was "a fugitive from justice" charged with "crimes of an universal character...condemned publicly by the civilized world". Second, Argentina had "condoned the violation of her sovereignty and has waived her claims, including that for the return of the appellant. Any violation therefore of international law that may have been involved in this incident ha[d] thus been removed". In *Barbie*, the French Court of Cassation (Criminal Chamber) asserted its jurisdiction over the accused, despite the claim that he was a victim of a disguised extradition, on the basis, *inter alia*, of the special nature of the crimes ascribed to the accused, namely, crimes against humanity.

24. Although it is difficult to identify a clear pattern in this case law, and caution is needed when generalising, two principles seem to have support in State practice as evidenced by the practice of their courts. First, in cases of crimes such as genocide, crimes against humanity and war crimes which are universally recognised and condemned as such ("Universally Condemned Offences"), courts seem to find in the special character of these offences and, arguably, in their seriousness, a good reason for not setting aside jurisdiction. Second, absent a complaint by the State whose sovereignty has been breached or in the event of a diplomatic resolution of the breach, it is easier for courts to assert their jurisdiction. The initial *iniuria* has in a way been cured and the risk of having to return the accused to the country of origin is no longer present. Drawing on these indications from national practice, the Appeals Chamber adds the following observations.

25. Universally Condemned Offences are a matter of concern to the international community as a whole. There is a legitimate expectation that those accused of these crimes will be brought to justice swiftly. Accountability for these crimes is a necessary condition for the

achievement of international justice, which plays a critical role in the reconciliation and rebuilding based on the rule of law of countries and societies torn apart by international and internecine conflicts.

26. This legitimate expectation needs to be weighed against the principle of State sovereignty and the fundamental human rights of the accused. The latter point will be addressed in Part (c) below. In the opinion of the Appeals Chamber, the damage caused to international justice by not apprehending fugitives accused of serious violations of international humanitarian law is comparatively higher than the injury, if any, caused to the sovereignty of a State by a limited intrusion in its territory, particularly when the intrusion occurs in default of the State's cooperation. Therefore, the Appeals Chamber does not consider that in cases of universally condemned offences, jurisdiction should be set aside on the ground that there was a violation of the sovereignty of a State, when the violation is brought about by the apprehension of fugitives from international justice, whatever the consequences for the international responsibility of the State or organisation involved. This is all the more so in cases such as this one, in which the State whose sovereignty has allegedly been breached has not lodged any complaint and thus has acquiesced in the International Tribunal's exercise of jurisdiction. *A fortiori*, and leaving aside for the moment human rights considerations, the exercise of jurisdiction should not be declined in cases of abductions carried out by private individuals whose actions, unless instigated, acknowledged or condoned by a State, or an international organisation, or other entity, do not necessarily in themselves violate State sovereignty.

27. Therefore, even assuming that the conduct of the Accused's captors should be attributed to SFOR and that the latter is responsible for a violation of Serbia and Montenegro's sovereignty, the Appeals Chamber finds no basis, in the present case, upon which jurisdiction should not be exercised.

(c) Under what circumstances does a human rights violation require jurisdiction to be set aside?

28. Turning now to the issue of whether the violation of the human rights of an accused requires the setting aside of jurisdiction by the International Tribunal, the Appeals Chamber recalls first the analysis of the Trial Chamber. The Trial Chamber found that the treatment of the Appellant was not of such an egregious nature as to impede the exercise of jurisdiction. The Trial Chamber, however, did not exclude that jurisdiction should not be exercised in certain cases. It held that:

> in circumstances where an accused is very seriously mistreated, maybe even subject to inhuman, cruel or degrading treatment, or torture, before being handed over to the Tribunal, this may constitute a legal impediment to the exercise of jurisdiction over such an accused. This would certainly be the case where persons acting for SFOR or the Prosecution were involved in such very serious mistreatment.

29. This approach, the Appeals Chamber observes, is consistent with the dictum of the U.S. Federal Court of Appeals in *Toscanino*. In that case, the Court held that "[we] view due process as now requiring a court to divest itself of jurisdiction over the person of a defendant where it has been acquired as the result of the Government's deliberate, unnecessary and unreasonable invasion of the accused's constitutional rights". A Trial Chamber of the International Tribunal in *Dokmanović* also relied on this approach. Along the same lines, the ICTR Appeals Chamber in *Barayagwiza* held that a court may decline to exercise jurisdiction in cases "where to exercise that jurisdiction in light of serious and egregious violations of the accused's rights would prove detrimental to the court's integrity".

30. The Appeals Chamber agrees with these views. Although the assessment of the seriousness of the human rights violations depends on the circumstances of each case and cannot

be made *in abstracto,* certain human rights violations are of such a serious nature that they require that the exercise of jurisdiction be declined. It would be inappropriate for a court of law to try the victims of these abuses. Apart from such exceptional cases, however, the remedy of setting aside jurisdiction will, in the Appeals Chamber's view, usually be disproportionate. The correct balance must therefore be maintained between the fundamental rights of the accused and the essential interests of the international community in the prosecution of persons charged with serious violations of international humanitarian law.

31. In the present case, the Trial Chamber examined the facts agreed to by the parties. It established that the treatment of the Appellant was not of such an egregious nature as to impede the exercise of jurisdiction. The Defence has not presented to the Appeals Chamber any alternative or more comprehensive view of the facts that might show that the Trial Chamber erred in its assessment of them. Nevertheless, the Appeals Chamber, in fairness to the Accused, has *proprio motu* reviewed all the facts of this case. Upon this review, the Appeals Chamber concurs with the Trial Chamber that the circumstances of this case do not warrant, under the standard defined above, the setting aside of jurisdiction.

32. In the circumstances, the evidence does not satisfy the Appeals Chamber that the rights of the accused were egregiously violated in the process of his arrest. Therefore, the procedure adopted for his arrest did not disable the Trial Chamber from exercising its jurisdiction.

33. Thus, even assuming that the conduct of Accused's captors should have been attributed to SFOR and that the latter was as a result responsible for a breach of the rights of the Accused, the Appeals Chamber finds no basis upon which jurisdiction should not be exercised.

COMMENTARY

In light of the gravity of the cases pursued by the international tribunals, it seems that it would be a rare circumstance where the violations of an accused's human rights during arrest should lead to dismissal of the case. It is much more likely that the remedy for the mistreatment of the accused will come either in a separate action (for monetary damages or to hold those who committed the mistreatment accountable) or through a reduction of sentence. There is precedent for this approach at the ICTR. In the *Media* case, accused Jean-Bosco Barayagwiza was convicted of genocide and crimes against humanity charges. The Trial Chamber reduced his sentence from life imprisonment to 35 years (later reduced to 30 years by the Appeals Chamber) in recognition of Barayagwiza's lengthy pre-trial detention without charge. Previously, the Appeals Chamber found that the violation of Barayagwiza's rights did not warrant dismissal of the indictment, but did justify the remedy of financial compensation (if he were acquitted) or reduction of sentence (if convicted).

(B) INTERSTATE RELATIONS

Issues related to the respect for State sovereignty and the fundamental rights of the accused can of course arise also in inter-State relations. In the past few years, attention has increasingly focused on so-called 'extraordinary renditions', the practice of forcibly transporting a person, usually suspected to be involved in terrorist activity, from one country to another without relying on normal legal procedures, coupled with secret detention and at times torture or other inhuman treatment. This kind of practice intuitively raises a host of cooperation and human rights questions that are more and more often being dealt with by domestic courts.

Italy, Adler and 32 others (Abu Omar *case*), *Milan Single Judge, Verdict of 4 November 2009, Reasons Filed on 1 February 2010*

Nasr Osama Mostafa Hannsa, also known as Abu Omar, was an Egyptian Muslim cleric active in Northern Italy. In 1993, he was being investigated by Italian prosecutors for the crime of 'association in furtherance of domestic or international terrorist aims or of subversion of the democratic structure of the state' and other related offences.

On 17 February 2003, unbeknownst to prosecutors and police officers involved in the case, US CIA agents and at least one Italian Special Operative agent from the *carabinieri* (ROS, Reparti Operativi Speciali) kidnapped him in Milan (Italy). He was taken to the Aviano air force base, then flown to Ramstein air base in Germany, and from there to Cairo (Egypt). He was then detained in Egypt for about one year. During his brief release in 2004, Abu Omar claimed that he had been tortured by the Egyptian secret services.

The Italian prosecutor started investigating this kidnapping and related crimes (such as obstruction of justice through misleading the investigations and disseminating false information). The investigations led to charges against Niccolò Pollari, director of the Italian Military Intelligence Service (*Sismi*) and 32 other individuals, including Italian and US intelligence officers. The case soon became extremely complicated because the Italian Government requested part of the evidence – relating to the relationships between Italian and US intelligence services – to be sealed because of national security interests. This prompted a series of challenges that culminated in a Constitutional Court ruling (Judgment No. 106 of 2009). The court found that 'judicial authorities [...] are free to investigate and adjudicate, [but may not] use as evidence material that relates to the relationships between Italian and foreign intelligence services, even though this material may be connected to the kidnapping. [...] State secrets do not, therefore, relate to the crime of kidnapping – which can be evaluated by the ordinarily competent judicial authority – but rather to two other areas. First, the relationship between Italian and foreign intelligence agencies; second, the organization and operations of *Sismi*, specifically the directives and orders issued by its director to members thereof, even in the case that these relationships, directives and orders are connected to the criminal act itself.'

The accused are subject to the rules relating to the circulation and execution of arrest warrants among the 27 Member States of the European Union (Judgment, Part 1, p. 45). The trial proceeded without the presence of the US agents. This was on the basis of a provision of Italian criminal procedure allowing *in absentia* proceedings when the judge is satisfied that the defendants have notice of the charges and voluntarily choose not to appear for trial. Counsel was appointed for all defendants who did not appear; the defendants are entitled to retrial should they choose to appear in the future.

The responsibility of US defendants for kidnapping. [...][1]

As far as the kidnapping of Abu Omar is concerned, it is first necessary to assess the alleged criminal conduct of the 26 Americans listed as accused. For all of them, at the end of his case, the Prosecutor requested conviction to various terms of imprisonment [...], depending on the degree of their responsibility. The requests of the Prosecutor are justified on the evidence

---

[1] Part 2, p. 70.

[referred to above] both in relation to the conduct and its legal characterization for all of the accused. [...] The Judge only notes that the limits imposed on discovery in this case – and related prohibitions on the use of material – do not actually shield members of the friendly intelligence services. Rather, the limits are prejudicial for the American defendants who are limited in making their case (even in theory) in relation to their conduct and in convincingly supporting their submissions, if any. The conclusion is, therefore, that there is enough evidence to prove the occurrence of extremely serious acts, from a factual and a legal perspective. However, [due to the existence of state secrets on the matter,] only foreigners can be found responsible for these acts, since their conduct was not covered by the protection available to Italians working in the intelligence services.

The result is that there are serious and unambiguous elements that prove the criminal responsibility of all members of the CIA structure operating in Italy in 2003 for the alleged crime. The following facts are proven with certainty on the basis of a large amount of documentary and testimonial evidence.

a) The kidnapping or 'extraordinary rendition' [in English in the original throughout the judgment] of Abu Omar, which occurred in Milan on 17 February 2003, was planned and implemented by a group of CIA agents. The group, following what had been decided by the competent political authority, operated in Milan and in Northern Italy until February 2003 when the act was perpetrated, and then left the territory of Italy in the following days or months.

b) Such operation was planned and implemented with the organizational and operational support of the CIA heads for Italy in Milan and Rome, with the assistance of the US Commander at the Aviano Air Base and with the relevant support of Luciano Pironi, agent of the ROS, who had been specifically enlisted for this operation.

c) The kidnapping of Abu Omar was organized despite the fact that he was, during that period, under investigation by the Milan police and Prosecutor's Office for serious crimes related to terrorism, without the competent authorities (police and Prosecutors) being aware of anything with regard to the planned kidnap. The operation was actually organized assuming that these [Italian] authorities would never be made aware of it.

d) The authorization by the highest US intelligence authorities in Italy (Castelli, Russomando, Medero, De Sousa and Lady) allows the inference that the operation was carried out with the knowledge (and maybe with the benevolent inaction) of the national intelligence authorities. This inference, however, is impossible to prove through the evidence because of the state secret status that was imposed by the executive branch on the matter. [...]

f) All American defendants can be deemed to have participated in the crime of kidnapping, though some of them only carried out preliminary activities relating to the identification of the target and his daily routine, or other activities in the preparation of the kidnapping. There is no doubt that kidnapping is a complex crime, which requires a multitude of acts [...] All of these acts must be taken in furtherance of the end result of violently depriving somebody of his personal liberty. The mens rea required is basic intent; the crime is a continuous offence. There is therefore no doubt that the crime is perpetrated even by persons assisting in its commission as well as assisting in the continuation of its effect after the initial deprivation of liberty. For this reason, those who knowingly prepared the operation and made its continuation possible must be considered responsible for the crime.

g) In this respect, there is no doubt as to the absolute awareness of all defendants of the fact that they were carrying out an unlawful activity. Regardless of the mens rea of each defendant, and of the excuse of performance of a legal duty (issues that are discussed below), there is no doubt that Mr. Lady (as the chief organizer of the kidnapping) and the others under his orders or who were in contact with him, knew very well that the activity they had engaged in was unlawful, due to its modalities, its secrecy, and because of the invasion of another jurisdiction. Even admitting (as a pure hypothesis, and not conceded) that the CIA agents had counted upon complacent Italian agents, the fact that they were acting clearly and seriously in contrast to the Milan police and prosecutors, resolves any doubt as to whether they knew that their conduct was unlawful (see, for instance, the admissions by Lady in the above-mentioned interview in the magazine 'GQ', and the statements of Pironi on this issue).

h) Furthermore, it cannot be doubted that 'extraordinary rendition' is a practice that has been knowingly carried out by the US administration and its agents since 2001, including in 2003. This is shown by the results of the investigations of the Council of Europe, the European Parliament and the European Court of Human Rights, results to which one should add the recommendations and resolutions adopted by these organs and filed by the Prosecutor [...], as well as the witness testimonies of Dick Marty [from the Council of Europe] and Claudio Fava [of the European Parliament] at trial. [...]

i) This element is also borne out by the documents submitted during closing arguments by Counsel for Medero. The fact that Counsel submitted as evidence at trial the whole anti-terrorism legislation issued by the Bush administration during the years in question allows a careful and valuable reading of the legal basis for the so-called 'extraordinary renditions' and permits a careful and penetrating analysis. Counsel for Medero submitted this documentation to support its defence arguments. However, the documentation does not leave any doubt as to US legislative intent (and, consequently, as to executive actions taken to carry out that intent) to allow, and in fact to promote, 'apprehension' of suspected terrorists also outside US territory, following a defensive and offensive policy without boundaries against terrorism [...]

j) In this sense, far from justifying the CIA agents' conduct within Italian territory (as is shown below), these norms allow the activity in question to be put in its proper context, providing the background for the alleged acts (the 'American War') and supporting the finding that they did occur.

Following this reasoning, Counsel for the American defendants – in particular Counsel for Medero and others with detailed argumentations and written pleas – raised the objection that the conduct of the CIA agents is excused on the basis of Article 51(2) of the Penal Code (fulfillment of a legal duty)[2] [...] Since the time of the original discussion on the applicability of Article 51 for collaborators (even as expressed in the abrogated Article 40 of the Military Penal Code for Peace-time), for orders issued by the [fascist] Italian Social Republic [between 1943 and 1945] or by the German invader, it was assumed that such orders were not legally binding and could therefore not be used to excuse the agents [...] This case law is based on the fact that 'order of a public authority' must be understood as being an act legitimately issued by an authority acting lawfully as to the subject-matter and the territorial scope. Such a conclusion has been confirmed throughout the years by countless decisions dealing with relationships of a public nature, thus excluding orders based on private relations. Thus, the excuse in question does not operate – and cannot be invoked by the agents – when orders are issued by a 'non-public authority' – and legitimate authority must be understood as the only authority completely competent to issue such orders. In such circumstances, the agents cannot even invoke as an excuse that they honestly believed that they were performing a legal duty. The issue would rather be one of ignorance of law on behalf of the agent, ignorance that – in a case like the present one – clearly cannot be invoked. For the foregoing reasons – and what was said in relation to the mens rea of kidnapping – the conduct of the members of the CIA group organizing and implementing the kidnapping may not be considered justified under Article 51 of the Penal Code, which refers to an obligation stemming from a binding [non-sindacabile] order.

---

[2] Article 51(2) reads: 'If an act constituting a crime is committed upon orders of a public authority, the official who issued the order is liable for the crime.'

Article 51 is inapplicable to the instant case, since there is no legitimate order from a public authority to which reference can be made. Even less convincing is the defence based on a duty flowing from a legal norm. In this case, too, the norm in question would have to be issued by an authority legitimately competent to issue it. The argument of the defence would make it extremely simple for members of non-Italian police or other security agencies to penetrate the territory of Italy and commit any kind of crime, knowing that they could invoke this excuse [. . .] Thus, regardless of the existence of legal rules and legitimately issued orders binding them, such agents in question may not expect that their conduct (if characterized as a crime) be excused so as to exclude their criminal responsibility. Such norms or orders were issued by authorities who were not competent within the Italian territory and could not, therefore, be operative within this territory. For these defendants, as discussed below and in light of the foregoing, the judge holds that the 'necessary obedience' they owed to their leaders with respect to what they had been ordered to do should [only] be considered in mitigation.

The judge then considered in more detail the positions of Joseph Romano, Sabrina De Sousa, Jeff Castelli and Ralph Henry Russomando, whose defence teams had contested part of the evidence gathered by the Prosecutor. He reached the conclusion that the evidence allowed a conviction for all of them. After disposing of other procedural challenges, the Judge ruled on immunities claimed by Counsel for various defendants.

It is now necessary to deal with the issues relating to the diplomatic or consular immunities of some of the US defendants, with regard to whom evidence of criminal liability has so far been discussed. It is clear that the existence of these immunities may shield criminal liability in the ways and within the limits provided for by the applicable laws. The laws relevant to the instant case are:

- The Convention on Diplomatic and Consular Relations (Vienna, 18 April 1961 and Vienna, 24 April 1963), with the annexed protocols;
- Law n. 804 of 9 August 1967 (ratification and implementation of the above-mentioned conventions and protocols thereto).

Scholars and the limited case law on the matter (see, for instance, Supreme Court, Penal Section, Judgment No. 16659 of 2003) uniformly interpret the aforementioned articles as imposing precise boundaries on diplomatic and consular immunities – in other words, they agree that different types of immunities apply to diplomatic agents, on the one hand, and to consular agents, on the other.

i)   As for diplomatic agents, the immunity from jurisdiction – criminal, civil and administrative – is absolute for conduct in the exercise of their functions. Such immunity continues even after the end of the diplomatic mission in which these agents were engaged.

ii) As for consular agents, their immunity is more limited and excludes 'serious crimes' – that is, intentional crimes punishable by no less than five years' imprisonment (see Article 3 of Law 804/67, which clarifies and interprets Article 41 of the Consular convention).[3] Of

---

[3] Article 41 of the Convention reads: 1. Consular officers shall not be liable to arrest or detention pending trial, except in the case of a grave crime and pursuant to a decision by the competent judicial authority. 2. Except in the case specified in paragraph 1 of this article, consular officers shall not be committed to prison or be liable to any other form of restriction on their personal freedom save in execution of a judicial decision of final effect. 3. If criminal proceedings are instituted against a consular officer, he must appear before the competent authorities. Nevertheless, the proceedings shall be conducted with the respect due to him by reason of his official position and, except in the case specified in paragraph 1 of this article, in a manner which will hamper the exercise of consular functions as little as possible. When, in the circumstances mentioned in

course, this is also only applicable to crimes committed in the exercise of the agents' functions.

iii) For both diplomatic and consular agents to be able to enjoy immunity, a written notification by the sending State is necessary [...]

From the analysis of the aforementioned provisions, the following is clear: if a person with absolute diplomatic immunity (viz., Head of Mission or accredited member of the diplomatic mission, as well as technical and administrative staff of the mission) is charged in criminal proceedings in Italy, that person may not be prosecuted, whether this is during his or her stay in Italy or after he or she has left the country. This applies when the crimes perpetrated are to be understood as acts committed in the exercise of that person's functions. The 'diplomatic functions' of a mission in foreign territory are, according to Article 3 of the Vienna Convention:

(a) Representing the sending State in the receiving State;

(2) [sic] Protecting in the receiving State the interests of the sending State and of its nationals [...]

There cannot be any doubt that, as indicated above, if a duly accredited member of the diplomatic mission carries out activities in the receiving State and this activity is carried out to 'protect...the interests of the sending State', the member may not be subjected to criminal prosecution, may not be tried and may not be convicted, even if the activity amounts to a crime.

The same immunity in criminal matters applies to those individuals exercising consular functions, but with the important limitation foreseen by Article 3 of the previously mentioned Law 804/67. Thus, when the crime committed by the consular agent is a crime punishable by no less than five years' imprisonment, the agent may be tried and convicted even if he or she committed the crime in the exercise of his or her functions.

In the instant case, therefore, the function exercised by the staff of the US Embassy in Rome and the Consulate in Milan who participated in the planning and organization of the crime must be assessed. Further, an assessment should be made as to whether the acts charged can be deemed to fall within the scope of the diplomatic functions exercised.

The issue of consular immunities arises for the five defendants who are members of the US diplomatic staff in Italy charged with kidnapping Abu Omar:

1. Jeffrey Castelli, US Embassy counselor in Rome, CIA head in Italy;

2. Robert Seldon Lady, consul at the US Consulate General in Milan, CIA head in Milan;

3. Ralph Henry Russomando, first secretary at the US Embassy in Rome, CIA agent [...];

4. Betnie Medero, second secretary at US Embassy in Rome, CIA agent;

5. Sabrina De Sousa, second secretary at US Embassy in Rome, CIA agent, and later consular employee in Milan.

As regards the latter, it should be noted that she left the US Embassy in Rome in 2001 and came back to Italy that same year, as consular employee in Milan, together with Robert Seldon Lady. For these reasons, she did not enjoy absolute diplomatic immunity at the time of the events. She could only avail herself, if at all, of the more limited immunity pertaining to consular staff. The same type of immunity was clearly enjoyed by Lady, the principal organizer of the kidnapping and consular head in Milan.

paragraph 1 of this article, it has become necessary to detain a consular officer, the proceedings against him shall be instituted with the minimum of delay.

The other three defendants (Castelli, Russomando and Medero) were undoubtedly members of the US Embassy diplomatic staff in Rome. Total immunity from jurisdiction on the basis of the cited legal provisions must therefore be accorded to them.

In this sense, there can be no doubt that the activity carried out by all mentioned defendants fell within their diplomatic or consular functions. Contrary to the Prosecutor's pleadings on the question, and as a logical inference from the position of Romano discussed above, the 'extraordinary renditions' by CIA agents – though a crime in Italy – can and must be characterized as falling within the ambit indicated by Article 3 of the Vienna Convention ('Protecting in the receiving State the interests of the sending State . . .').

US political authorities, as mentioned above, issued norms and directives that not only legalized, but also undoubtedly imposed that type of activity and conduct on members of the US secret services. Thus, there can be no doubt about the fact that the ambit of the protection of US interests in the world in general and in Italy in particular included the acts in question. The fact that this function was not exercised on the basis of clear treaty language and that, therefore, no clarity on the intentions and the conduct exists, is irrelevant for the legal provision in question. It should further be noted that – due to the secrecy surrounding the relationships between Italy and the USA – this Judge may not deny the possibility that agreements existed between the two governments aimed at allowing such conduct.

On the basis of the foregoing, it cannot be eschewed – and should actually be inferred – that the conduct of US diplomatic and consular agents in the case were activities within their functions, even where they can be characterized as criminal. All US diplomatic agents – Jeff Castelli, Ralph Russomando and Betnie Medero – must therefore be deemed to be outside of our jurisdiction for the period in question.

Let us know turn to the activities carried out by Robert Seldon Lady and Sabrina De Sousa. These persons, as discussed above, were working only as consular employees in Milan during the period in question. For this category of people, the law does not provide immunity from 'serious crimes', as undoubtedly the crime of kidnapping under Article 605 of the Penal Code is, since the maximum term of imprisonment foreseen for kidnapping is 10 years. For the foregoing reasons, Robert Seldon Lady and Sabrina De Sousa must be considered fully responsible for the crime charged.

As for the Italian intelligence officers, the fact that the Government had asserted privilege based on State secret barred the judge from dealing with them as regards the kidnapping, but not for obstruction of justice. The judge therefore proceeded to assess their responsibility for the latter crime, convicting and sentencing two of them to three years' imprisonment. Further, in examining the amount of damages to be paid by the convicted persons, the Judge made the following remark on the gravity of the crime, at p. 142:

It must be highlighted that the harm incurred by Nasr Osama Mostafà Hassan and his wife Ghali Nabila appears to be extremely serious in both financial and non-financial terms (i.e., moral damages as well as other types of damage identified by Italian case law). The violations of human rights suffered by Abu Omar, (but not only by him), under our Constitution and the European Convention [on Human Rights] appear to be very serious, and adequate evaluation is required. The infringement of the right of each person as such to the integrity of his or her body and soul (to be considered as the whole of thoughts, feelings and emotions harboured by each person) constitutes conduct of exceptional gravity, especially if this person is suspected of serious crimes or is being detained for purposes of serving a sentence or on remand. This conduct cannot be tolerated wherever it occurs, but especially in a country that the victim has chosen as a place of freedom and refuge. It is irrelevant that the person was suspected of serious crimes against the country that was hosting him. The fight against terrorism, just like the fight against any other crime that can be planned or committed, must be carried out according to proper domestic and international legal forms, avoiding any inhumane and degrading treatment, as the judgments of domestic and international tribunals on this matter teach us (see in particular the ECHR judgment n. 37291/06 of 28 February 2008 on torture). For these reasons, it is surprising that Counsel for Pollari – though very elegantly and covertly – tried to use the serious terrorist-related accusations against Abu Omar to detract from the amount of harm suffered by him. As stated before, *the fact that the victim is an accused or a suspect makes the damage more serious* when inflicted by the State (or by its agents) that is responsible for protecting him by guaranteeing a fair trial.

COMMENTARY

On 4 November 2009, the Italian judge convicted in absentia the US CIA agents and other officials charged, with the exception of those benefiting from diplomatic immunity. He also convicted several Italians, except for those whose conduct had been covered by the state secret privilege urged by the Italian Government. The verdict is, however, not final; it has been appealed by both the Prosecutor and several accused on matters of law and fact.

An issue to bear in mind while reading this judgment is that Italian prosecutors do not act pursuant to instructions or directive by the executive branch of government – they are independent and are legally obliged to open a file and investigate any crime within their competence as soon as they are apprised of it. Thus, they could not just drop a case: doing so would place them at risk of prosecution for failure to comply with the duty to investigate and prosecute.

Was the judge right in convicting (some of) the accused even though their actions might be explained through information that he could not access, because of the imposition of confidentiality for State secrets? In other words, does a reasonable doubt exist because there might be secret evidence out there that the Government refuses to share?

Compare this judgment with others dealing with kidnapping abroad, such as the US Supreme Court decision in *Alvarez* v. *Machain* 504 U.S. 655 (1992). That decision affirmed the jurisdiction of a US federal court to try a defendant who was forcibly abducted in Mexico, pursuant to a US government plan, and brought back to the US for trial despite the existence of an extradition treaty between the USA and Mexico. Would a US judge have been guided by similar legal principles as the Italian judge if the roles in *Alvarez* v. *Machain* had been reversed?

The Vienna Convention on Consular Relations states that '[i]f criminal proceedings are instituted against a consular officer, he must appear before the competent authorities'. Were some of the accused, or the US Government, in violation of this provision in the instant case?

4

TRIAL PROCEDURES

The statute of the first international tribunal to be established after Nuremberg, the ICTY, did not specify much about the procedural model to be adopted. However, the statute, which had been drafted at the UN by lawyers from common law countries, clearly opted for the adversarial model, also perhaps because of the Nuremberg precedent. For instance, no provision was made for an investigating judge tasked to gather evidence both against and in favour of suspects or accused; instead, the task of investigating and prosecuting persons responsible for the crimes falling under the tribunal's jurisdiction was granted to the prosecution, on the assumption that the defence would then seek exculpatory evidence; in addition, no procedural rights were conferred on the victims, except that of appearing as witnesses, if called to testify by one of the parties.

It was left to the judges to flesh out the procedural model in formulating the ICTY Rules of Procedure and Evidence (RPE). The rules that were adopted for the ICTY (and then for the ICTR) are largely adversarial. Investigations and trials are primarily party led, witnesses are generally called and cross-examined by the parties, and the judges largely act as referees and neutral arbiters of the law and facts. Because there is no jury, hearsay is admissible. It is true that the judges are free to ask questions of witnesses and even call their own witnesses, but otherwise the trials resemble common law proceedings.

The judges at the ad hoc tribunals have the power to amend the RPE and have done so frequently (44 times at the ICTY, fewer at the ICTR). Many of the changes that have been adopted have sought to expedite trials and have incorporated certain civil law features into the proceedings (allowing evidence to come in more expeditiously and giving the judges more control over the scope and pace of the trials). Perhaps the most significant and controversial change has been to allow into evidence more written testimony of witnesses. Under ICTY Rule 92 *bis*, witness statements or testimony that do not pertain to the acts and conduct of the accused (but which, for example, establish that the crimes occurred) can come into evidence entirely in written form. Pursuant to Rule 92 *ter*, a witness can affirm his written statement in lieu of his direct examination, and can then be subject only to cross-examination viva voce.

The procedural model at the ICC is more complex. The investigative phase is plainly common law adversarial, with the parties responsible for uncovering witnesses and evidence. The trial is, however, even more of a mix of common law and civil law aspects than even the latest incarnation of the rules at the ad hoc tribunals. For example, victims are given a formal role at the ICC and are represented during the trial process. There has been considerable litigation about who may be designated as a victim in a case and the scope of their role at trial. In addition, there is some evidence that the judges may be asserting a more active role in the proceedings, as is suggested in the *Lubanga* excerpt below.

As the international tribunals have adopted more civil law devices, two related questions must be considered. First, are the changes being made simply for the sake of expediency, or because international criminal law prosecutions by their nature require a particular combination of rules from the different procedural systems? Second, when procedural mechanisms deriving from different systems are put together, do they still make sense? For example, the admission of written statements in the civil law system is generally grounded in the fact that the statements are taken under oath by a neutral investigative magistrate. The written statements admitted into evidence at the ad hoc tribunals generally have no such protections. The danger in picking and choosing procedural elements is that taken out of context they lose their essence. On the other hand, international criminal trials are unlike any domestic trial and therefore require procedural rules that take into account the particular challenges of these cases.

Cases

ICTY, **Prosecutor *v.* Limaj et al.**, *Trial Chamber, Decision on the Prosecution's Motions to Admit Prior Statements as Substantive Evidence, 25 April 2005*

Fatmir Limaj, Isak Musliu and Haradin Bala, all members of the Kosovo Liberation Army, were indicted by the ICTY for crimes against humanity and war crimes for their alleged role in the operation of a camp in Llapushnik in Kosovo where Serbs and Albanians suspected of collaborating with Serbs were imprisoned, abused, tortured and murdered. At trial, several insider witnesses who had previously provided favourable evidence for the prosecution recanted their evidence. Ultimately, Limaj and Musliu were acquitted while Bala was convicted of war crimes, including murder and torture, and sentenced to 13 years' imprisonment, a judgment that was later upheld by the Appeals Chamber. The following excerpt is from a decision during the trial.

1. By motions, the Prosecution is seeking the admission, as substantive evidence, of video recordings (with transcripts) of the interviews given to representatives of the Office of the Prosecutor ("OTP") by two witnesses, Ramadan Behluli and Shukri Buja, who were called to testify for the Prosecution in the present case and gave oral evidence inconsistent in some material respects with what they had previously said in the course of the interviews. The video-recordings and the transcripts were admitted into evidence solely for the purpose of assessing the credibility of the witnesses. By these motions, the Prosecution seeks to rely on the contents of the video-recordings as substantive evidence.

2. The circumstances which give rise to the motions by the Prosecution for the admission of the two video-recordings are not usual. They have some relevance to the outcome of the motions. Both Ramadan Behluli and Shukri Buja had been interviewed at some length by representatives of the OTP. The interviews had been conducted quite independently of each other on 25 and 28 April 2003, well before this trial. In their respective interviews, each of the two witnesses gave quite detailed accounts of events and circumstances material to this trial.

3. When called to give evidence as a Prosecution witness, each of the two witnesses gave oral evidence which differed in some respects from what had been said by the witness during the earlier interview with the OTP. Further, in other respects, the evidence of each witness given in this trial omitted matters which had been mentioned by the witness during the earlier interview with the OTP. The differences and omissions were, generally, material to the Prosecution case. The effect was that the oral evidence given by each witness during examination-in-chief was significantly less favourable to the Prosecution than the earlier interview with the OTP.

4. In respect of each of the two witnesses, the Prosecution moved, in the course of examination-in-chief, for leave to cross-examine the witness on the ground of hostility. The Chamber was persuaded, in the particular circumstances applicable to each witness, that it appeared that the witness was not prepared to speak the truth at the instance of the Prosecution, *i.e* the party who had called the witness. Each witness was treated as "hostile" and leave was given to the Prosecution to cross-examine on the previous interview. This was done at some length. Each witness was also cross-examined, both generally and with respect to the previous interview, by Defence counsel.

5. Each witness readily agreed that he had been interviewed by the OTP in April 2003 and, subject to a few particular issues, each witness accepted the relevant video-recording as depicting what had transpired during that witness' interview. Each witness also accepted that he had (generally) sought to tell the truth during the interview. Each witness maintained, however, that he now believed that what was said in the April 2003 interview was mistaken in some respects.

6. By the process of cross-examination by Prosecution and Defence counsel, the material differences between the evidence given by the witness before the Chamber, and what had been said at the interview with the OTP in April 2003, were identified. Explanations were given by each witness for the differences and these explanations were tested by cross-examination.

7. It is in this context that the Prosecution then moved, in respect of each of the two witnesses, that the video-recording (with transcript) of the April 2003 interview by the OTP with that witness should be received in evidence, not only for the purpose of assessing the credit of the oral evidence given by that witness in the trial, but also as evidence of the truth of what was said during the April 2003 interview of that witness, *i.e* as substantive evidence.

8. These procedural and evidentiary issues would not have arisen in a civil legal system. While detailed procedures inevitably vary between jurisdictions, in general terms, in a civil system, witnesses would be called and questioned under the control of the court rather than of the parties, and the court would have available to it any previous statements of the witness. While the procedure and evidentiary system of this Tribunal represents an attempt to blend elements of both civil and adversarial systems, it remains primarily adversarial. Hence, in contrast to the position normally found in a civil system, it is the parties who, in turn, call and question "their" respective witnesses, who are then cross-examined by the other party (or parties). Further, the Tribunal does not normally have before it any previous statement of a witness, although an inconsistent previous statement may be put to a witness by an opposing party in cross-examination. It is in this adversarial or common-law context that the notion arises of a witness who is "hostile" to the party who calls the witness.

9. At common law the traditional position is clear. Where a witness is declared to be "hostile" by the court, and leave is given to cross-examine a party's own witness on a previous inconsistent statement, the contents of that previous inconsistent statement may only be received in evidence and used for the purpose of assessing the credit of the witness and deciding whether or not to accept all or any of the evidence given orally in the trial by the witness. Unless the witness, in oral evidence, changes his position and adopts as true what was said in the previous inconsistent statement, the contents of the previous inconsistent statement may not be received and used as substantive evidence in the trial.

10. Thus, the traditional common-law position is that neither the April 2003 interview of Ramadan Behluli, nor that of Shukri Buja, could be received and used as substantive evidence in the trial in the present circumstances. Essentially, it is the position of each witness that while he sought to answer the questions put to him by the OTP in April 2003 honestly, he now realises that in some respects he was mistaken in his answers and the true position is that detailed in his oral evidence given before the Chamber.

11. The primary submission for the Defence is in keeping with the traditional common-law position. It is argued that the only "evidence" of each witness is that given orally before the Chamber. The effect of the evidence of each of the witnesses is that the previous interview contains identified errors. How the errors occurred has been explained and the present belief of the witness has been detailed in oral evidence together with the reasons advanced by the witness for now holding his present belief.

12. The Prosecution essentially submits that the Chamber is in a somewhat unique position, especially because the previous interviews were video-recorded, of being able to evaluate not only whether each of the two witnesses is now telling the truth when he says that his present belief is that his April 2003 interview contains the identified errors, even though he then thought his answers were true, but also whether his present oral account of the material issues is true or the account given to the OTP in April 2003. In support of its motions, the Prosecution submits that the traditional common-law position should not be followed because it is founded heavily on the common-law's objection to hearsay evidence, whereas hearsay, at least if apparently reliable, is admissible before this Tribunal, and because the procedure and evidence applied in this Tribunal is a blending of both civil and adversarial systems.

13. The submissions of both the Prosecution and Defence accept that there is no provision of the Rules which expressly deals with the question raised whether a previous inconsistent statement of a witness may be admitted in evidence in the present circumstances, and if so for what purposes. Nor does the Statute provide any clear guidance. The parties point to the absence of any general principle of law governing the matter. Essentially, the Defence submits that there is no general principle of law *allowing for* the admission of prior inconsistent statements as substantive evidence, while the Prosecution contends that there is no general principle favouring the adoption of a rule *against* their admission into evidence. [. . .]

17. [. . .] Rather, it is necessary to turn to the general rules of evidence and the jurisprudence applicable to hearsay evidence. It is well settled in the Tribunal's jurisprudence that hearsay evidence is admissible under Rule 89(C) provided that it is relevant and has probative value. Where hearsay evidence is sought to be admitted to prove the truth of its content, a Chamber must be satisfied that the evidence is reliable for that purpose, and in doing so, may consider both the content of the evidence and the circumstances under which it arose. As formulated by the Appeals Chamber, a "piece of evidence may be so lacking in terms of the indicia of reliability that it is not 'probative' and is therefore inadmissible."

18. As has been noted earlier, the traditional common-law position is that evidence of the prior inconsistent interviews of Ramadan Behluli and Shukri Buja could only be admitted for the purposes of impeaching the witnesses' credibility but not to prove the truth of their content. This position, however, cannot be accepted as determinative in the present case for several reasons. First, the traditional common-law position is strongly derived from its aversion to hearsay, which is inadmissible in most situations as substantive evidence. As discussed above, such objection has not the same force before this Tribunal as hearsay evidence may be received as substantive evidence provided that it is relevant and sufficiently reliable so as to be considered probative. A further justification which is often advanced for the traditional common-law position is that typically the factual determination of a case will be made by a jury. The difficulty of evaluating and weighting hearsay evidence, as against inconsistent oral testimony given in the presence of the jury, has been perceived traditionally to be too complex for a jury. This objection is of limited force in this Tribunal where the factual determination is to be made by a bench of three judges.

19. Moreover, in many common-law jurisdictions, there has been a profound change of attitude to the admissibility of hearsay evidence, especially in circumstances such as the present. In the United Kingdom, Section 119 of the Criminal Justice Act of 2003, which is anticipated

to come into effect in the near future, provides that a prior inconsistent statement by a witness "is admissible as evidence of any matter stated in it of which oral evidence by that person would be admissible." In the United States federal system, the hearsay limitation does not apply to prior statements made by witnesses under oath and such statements are capable of being used as substantive evidence. Further, a growing number of State jurisdictions in the United States are permitting the use of unsworn prior inconsistent statements for their substantive value and not merely for impeachment purposes. Section 60 of Australia's Uniform Evidence Act of 1995 which applies in federal jurisdiction as well as in the state courts of New South Wales and Tasmania is set out below.[1] In the view of the High Court of Australia, this provision is intended to allow for prior inconsistent statements to be admitted for the truth of their contents. There is provision to similar effect in the State of Queensland. It appears, therefore, that the traditional common-law position with respect to hearsay evidence is undergoing fundamental change in many leading jurisdictions. The effect of this change is to remove what had been the fundamental obstacle to the admission in evidence of a prior inconsistent out-of-court statement of a witness who is called to give evidence in a trial.

20. There is a further way in which Rules of this Tribunal bear on the present issue. As originally drafted, the Rules of this Tribunal reflected the view that the evidence of a witness was the oral testimony given by that witness. Progressively, by process of amendment, there has been a shift away from that view towards an acceptance that, at least in some situations, the evidence of a witness may be received although not given orally before the Tribunal. Thus the Rules no longer provide for the invariable view that the evidence of a witness must be given orally. In the present case, therefore, a critical issue is whether Rule 89(C) would allow the receipt, as substantive evidence, in the present circumstances, of the video-recordings of the April 2003 interviews of the two witnesses.

21. It is necessary, therefore, to examine whether the prior interviews given by Ramadan Behluli and Shukri Buja fulfill the criteria under which they may be admitted as hearsay evidence for the truth of their contents, *i.e* whether they are relevant and of sufficient reliability to be accepted as probative (Rule 89(C)). The prior interviews are highly relevant to the present case, in particular as they relate to the position of Fatmir Limaj as a KLA commander in the relevant geographic area during the time material to the Indictment. [...]

25. For the reasons given, the Chamber is persuaded that, in the very particular factual circumstances presented in this case, the two video-recordings are relevant and sufficiently reliable so as to have probative value in this trial. Therefore, under Rule 89(C), they *may* be admitted as evidence for the truth of their contents, *i.e.* as substantive evidence.

26. However, the word "may" in Rule 89(C) indicates that it is a matter of discretion whether to admit either or both of the video-recordings. Many of the matters already discussed also have a relevance to the exercise of this discretion. We will not discuss them further. On balance they favour the exercise of the discretion to admit the two video-recordings.

27. The Defence, however, argues against the exercise of discretion to admit, especially on the basis that this would lead to an erosion of the standard and burden of proof, and "is guaranteed to lead to miscarriages of justice." On analysis, this line of argument appears to be based on an unexpressed premise that all hearsay evidence is unsatisfactory and should be inadmissible. That evidence is in form hearsay does not necessarily deprive it of probative value or render it unsatisfactory. Its admissibility is firmly established by the jurisprudence of this Tribunal. As discussed earlier, while this is contrary to the traditional view of the common law, it is in keeping generally with the position in civil law jurisdictions and now in a growing

---

[1] [18] Section 60 of Australia's Uniform Evidence Act of 1995 provides: "The hearsay rule does not apply to evidence of a previous representation that is admitted because it is relevant for a purpose other than proof of the fact intended to be asserted by the representation."

number of common-law jurisdictions. Extensive experience in such jurisdictions suggests that the admission of hearsay evidence, per se, will not lead to miscarriages of justice as is submitted. It will be important, however, to evaluate with care the reliability of any hearsay evidence which has been admitted before reliance is placed on it for the purpose of establishing guilt.

28. It is also submitted by the Defence that to admit these video-recordings as substantive evidence is undesirable in principle because this would allow the Prosecution, in effect, to "cherry pick" its way through the evidence, relying only on that which most favoured its case, and to ignore the contrary oral evidence given by each of the two witnesses in the trial. This submission involves weighty issues that are at a watershed between civil and adversarial systems. The more that the Rules and jurisprudence of this Tribunal are altered to incorporate features of a civil law approach, the more issues of this nature will present difficulty. Because of the nature of the source of the difficulty, there is, and there can be, no universal or absolute principle which determines the answer in all cases. The particular circumstances presented by each case will be material. A just result in these circumstances must be sought.

29. Despite the amendments that have been made to the Rules with respect to the form of admissible evidence, oral evidence remains the primary and normal standard. It would not appear to be in the interests of justice for a practice to develop by which the Prosecution could readily seek to brush aside the oral evidence given in court of a Prosecution witness in favour of a disavowed earlier account of the witness. It is not the intended purport of this decision that an earlier account or statement of a witness should be admitted in evidence, as of course, at the instance of the party calling the witness to give oral evidence.

30. The present case illustrates, however, that there may be circumstances where an earlier inconsistent account of a witness may well assist the Chamber to evaluate not only the credit of a witness and the truthfulness of his or her oral evidence, but also whether he or she was being truthful in the earlier account and whether what was then said remains reliable despite the contrary oral evidence.

31. In the present case, both witnesses were considered by the Chamber to be hostile or adverse to the Prosecution, that is the witnesses appeared not to be prepared to tell the truth in oral evidence before the Chamber, when examined by the Prosecution. This involved an evaluation by the Chamber, *inter alia*, of the demeanour of each witness, the oral evidence of the witness to that stage, the terms of the previous account and the circumstances in which it was made. In accordance with long-settled common law principles, much more than some material difference between the oral evidence and a previous account was required before the conclusion could be reached by the Chamber that apparently a witness [...] was not prepared to tell the truth in his oral testimony. Further, the formality and thoroughness of the earlier interview by the OTP of each witness, and the care taken to record the previous interview in a way which greatly facilitated its evaluation by the Chamber, were also material matters that influenced the decisions that each of these witnesses was "hostile".

32. While the Prosecution had an indication that each witness had changed his position in the final proofing immediately before each witness was called to give evidence, the circumstances did not indicate to the Chamber that the Prosecution was seeking to ignore its responsibilities by calling a witness, who was in truth clearly opposed to its case, as a mere device to seek to tender the earlier inconsistent interview of that witness. Such conduct may well have warranted a refusal to exercise the discretion, under Rule 89(C), to admit the video-recordings.

33. Contrary to the thrust of this Defence submission, the outcome of this trial will not be determined by the way in which the Prosecution may choose to rely on aspects of the evidence in support of its case in its closing submissions. It will be for the Chamber to determine what weight, if any, it will eventually attach to either or both of these video-recordings when it comes to assess all the evidence at the final stage of the trial. Both the oral evidence of each

witness and the earlier account on the video-recording will be before the Chamber. It will remain a most significant feature of this aspect of the evidence that each of the witnesses has changed his position and disavows his earlier account. That will demand the most careful scrutiny by the Chamber.

For these reasons, it appears to the Chamber that in these particular circumstances the interests of justice are in favour of the exercise of the discretion to admit both video-recordings as substantive evidence. The Chamber is persuaded that the video-recording of the 25 April 2003 interview of Ramadan Behluli and the video-recording of the 28 April 2003 interview of Shukri Buja, together with the transcripts of each video-recording, should be accepted as substantive evidence, *i.e.* as evidence of the truth of their contents, pursuant to Rule 89(C).

Although the Trial Chamber in the *Limaj* case accepted into evidence the prior inconsistent statements of Behluli and Buja, in the Judgment the Chamber returned to a more common law perspective of the evidence and virtually disavowed any reliance on the prior statements of the key insider witnesses:

In any event, while the Chamber accepts that as a matter of principle, prior inconsistent statements may possibly have some positive probative force, at least if they corroborate other apparently credible evidence adduced from other witnesses during trial, the Chamber is not persuaded in this case that the prior inconsistent statements of these two witnesses can safely be relied upon as the sole or principal basis for proof of a material fact. In the case of these two witnesses, this is especially so because each witness, in oral evidence, disavowed, in very material respects, what previously had been stated in the interview.[2]

Perhaps this is a reminder that no matter what procedural model is adopted at the international tribunals, those working at the tribunals have roots in their own domestic procedural system and may have a tendency to interpret and apply the rules through the lens of their own experiences.

ICC, Prosecutor *v.* Lubanga Dyilo, *Trial Chamber, Decision Regarding the Practices Used to Prepare and Familiarise Witnesses for Giving Testimony at Trial, 30 November 2007*

Thomas Lubanga Dyilo was allegedly a commander of the Forces Patriotiques pour la liberation du Congo (FPLC) in the Democratic Republic of the Congo (DRC). After the DRC referred cases relating to the war there to the ICC, Lubanga was charged with war crimes for his role in enlisting and conscripting child soldiers under the age of 15 years. The trial is ongoing. In this decision, the Trial Chamber considered whether the prosecution should be permitted to 'proof' its witnesses, meaning prepare its witnesses immediately before their testimony in court. In the part of its decision preceding this excerpt, the court found that the Victim and Witnesses Unit could engage in a practice of 'witness familiarisation', meaning that it would explain to the witness the procedures of the trial, show the witness the courtroom, and allow the witness to read his or her prior statement. In this excerpt, the court then considers whether, in addition to these measures, the prosecution would be permitted to meet with the witness to go over his or her testimony.

---

[2] *Prosecutor* v. *Limaj et al.*, Trial Chamber, Judgment of 30 November 2005, para. 14.

37. To further its argument that "witness proofing" should be allowed, the prosecution, in written submission, provided a section specifically citing jurisprudence from national and international courts, which it claimed endorse[s] a well established practice of witness proofing.

38. In beginning its analysis of this area, the Trial Chamber draws particular attention to the Pre-Trial Chamber's discussion of Article 21 of the Statute in its decision of 8 October 2006. This Chamber fully recognises that the present matter must be settled by reference to the sources of applicable law laid out in that provision.

39. Turning first to the national jurisprudence relied upon by the prosecution, the Trial Chamber notes that the various terms and definitions used nationally, as well as the lack of any coherent jurisprudence, render it difficult to determine the extent to which witness proofing can be considered an established practice in this sense.

40. In general, the prosecution's citations of national practice do provide some examples of the permissibility of contact between counsel and witnesses before trial. However, most do not directly deal with the substance of what that contact should entail. The Chamber observes, following consideration of the authorities provided, that the 'New South Wales Barrister's Rules' from Australia, and the 'Crown Policy Manual – Witness' from Canada do seem to provide support for the practice of engaging in some kind of question and answer session with the witness directly prior to their evidence in court, although coaching witnesses or putting suggestions to them would not be permissible.

41. However, the Trial Chamber does not consider that a general principle of law allowing the substantive preparation of witnesses prior to testimony can be derived from national legal systems worldwide, pursuant to Article 21(l)(c) of the Statute. Although this practice is accepted to an extent in two legal systems, both of which are founded upon common law traditions, this does not provide a sufficient basis for any conclusion that a general principle based on established practice of national legal systems exists. The Trial Chamber notes that the prosecution's submissions with regard to national jurisprudence did not include any citations from the Romano-Germanic legal system.

42. A further clarification may be necessary in light of previous submissions by the prosecution that it intended to follow the law of England and Wales closely on this subject and the Pre-Trial Chamber's assertion that the law of England and Wales prohibited the practice of witness proofing. In the Trial Chamber's view, whilst the accepted practice in England and Wales allows a witness, for the sole purpose of refreshing his memory, to read his witness statement prior to giving evidence, it permits neither substantive conversations between the prosecution or the defence and a witness nor any type of question and answer session to take place prior to the witness giving evidence.

43. Turning to the practices of international criminal tribunals and courts, the prosecution submitted that the practice of witness proofing is here permissible, endorsed and well established. The Trial Chamber notes, as has been established by recent jurisprudence from the International Criminal Tribunals of the former Yugoslavia and Rwanda, that witness proofing, in the sense advocated by the prosecution in the present case, is being commonly utilized at the ad hoc Tribunals.

44. However, this precedent is in no sense binding on the Trial Chamber at this Court. Article 21 of the Statute requires the Chamber to apply first the Statute, Elements of Crimes and Rules of the ICC. Thereafter, if ICC legislation is not definitive on the issue, the Trial Chamber should apply, where appropriate, principles and rules of international law. In the instant case, the issue before the Chamber is procedural in nature. While this would not, ipso facto, prevent all procedural issues from scrutiny under Article 21(l)(b), the Chamber does not consider the procedural rules and jurisprudence of the ad hoc Tribunals to be automatically applicable to the ICC without detailed analysis.

45. The ICC Statute has, through important advances, created a procedural framework which differs markedly from the ad hoc tribunals, such as, for example, in the requirement in the Statute that the prosecution should investigate exculpatory as well as incriminatory evidence, for which the Statute and Rules of the ad hoc tribunals do not provide. Also, the Statute seemingly permits greater intervention by the Bench, as well as introducing the unique element of victim participation. Therefore, the Statute moves away from the procedural regime of the ad hoc tribunals, introducing additional and novel elements to aid the process of establishing the truth. Thus, the procedure of preparation of witnesses before trial is not easily transferable into the system of law created by the ICC Statute and Rules. Therefore, while acknowledging the importance of considering the practice and jurisprudence at the ad hoc tribunals, the Chamber is not persuaded that the application of ad hoc procedures, in the context of preparation of witnesses for trial, is appropriate.

46. A final argument advanced by the prosecution in support of its position was that the practice of witness proofing helps the Trial Chamber to establish the truth by furnishing all involved in the trial with a complete picture of the case and it enables a more accurate and efficient presentation of evidence.

47. Since one of the principal goals of the work of the Court is to establish the truth, any available means should be considered. However, whilst some aspects of a proofing session could potentially help the Court arrive at the truth in an efficient manner, many others may well prove detrimental.

48. The prosecution submitted that "witness proofing" would involve providing written statements to a witness a few days prior to their testimony; meeting with the witness at that time to remind the witness of their duty to tell the truth; discussing with the witness during this meeting information which may inform a decision about the protection of the witness; addressing the area of the witness statement that will be dealt with in Court; and showing the witness any potential exhibits for his comment prior to testimony.

49. Addressing the particular elements, the Trial Chamber considers that during the witness familiarisation process the Victims and Witnesses Unit are under an obligation to remind witnesses of their duty to tell the truth and to implement any protective measures which may be necessary. Thus, the elements left for consideration under the topic of "witness proofing" include providing a witness with his written statements, and any discussions with the witness on the content of their statements to the extent that they may be addressed in court, as well as any potential exhibits which may be provided during the witness' testimony.

50. The Trial Chamber considers that allowing a witness to read his past statements will aid the efficient presentation of the evidence and help the Trial Chamber to establish the truth. Witnesses may well have given their original statements a year or more in advance of their in-court testimony. The Trial Chamber is aware that it can be difficult to remember events in their exact detail and the order in which they occurred, particularly when those events were traumatic. Thus, greater efficiency may be achieved by providing past statements to a witness in advance to assist that witness with his recollection. Overall, this process will clarify for the witness events that occurred some time previously.

51. However, with regard to any discussion on the topics to be dealt with in court or any exhibits which may be shown to a witness in court, the Trial Chamber is not convinced that either greater efficiency or the establishment of the truth will be achieved by these measures. Rather, it is the opinion of the Chamber that this could lead to a distortion of the truth and may come dangerously close to constituting a rehearsal of in-court testimony. While the Trial Chamber notes the prosecution's undertaking that it will take all steps to limit any pre-trial rehearsal during a "proofing session", it is not persuaded that this is practically achievable. A rehearsed witness may not provide the entirety or the true extent of his memory or

knowledge of a subject, and the Trial Chamber would wish to hear the totality of an individual's recollection.

52. Finally, the Trial Chamber is of the opinion that the preparation of witness testimony by parties prior to trial may diminish what would otherwise be helpful spontaneity during the giving of evidence by a witness. The spontaneous nature of testimony can be of paramount importance to the Court's ability to find the truth, and the Trial Chamber is not willing to lose such an important element in the proceedings. The pro-active role of judges under the Statute and Rules will help to ensure that witnesses are not "revictimized" by their testimony, whilst also preventing any improper influence being applied to the witness.

COMMENTARY

This decision addresses an enormous divide among procedural cultures. As the court's decision suggests, there is no consensus on this question even among common law lawyers. Most American lawyers would consider it almost malpractice not to carefully prepare their witnesses before trial (and it is striking that the decision does not address practices in the United States, perhaps because the USA is not a State Party). Other practitioners, however, consider it unethical to have too much contact with their witnesses before they testify. A question to consider is whether the solution arrived at by the ICC, which is different from the approach adopted by the ad hoc tribunals, is well suited to these particular kinds of cases.

QUESTIONS

1. When Carla Del Ponte, at the time ICTY and ICTR Prosecutor, tried to persuade countries to condition their aid to Serbia on the surrender of the accused Slobodan Milošević to the ICTY, then UN Secretary-General, Kofi Annan, sent her a letter suggesting that she was overstepping her role. Given the need of the tribunals to persuade Nation States to cooperate with their investigations, and their limited ability to obtain enforcement, what is the appropriate role of the actors at these courts in encouraging such cooperation?

2. To what extent may procedures at the international tribunals take into account the difficulties of investigators in obtaining evidence and witnesses in war crimes cases?

3. How should policy makers balance the need to try international criminal cases efficiently and expeditiously against the rights of the victims to have a full accounting against the rights of the accused? To what extent do the procedures that are crafted for these tribunals reflect judgments about what the tribunals should accomplish?

FURTHER READING

Cassese, *International Criminal Law*, 336–77.

Annalisa Ciampi, 'The Obligation to Cooperate', in A. Cassese *et al.* (eds), *The Rome Statute of the International Criminal Court: A Commentary* (Oxford: Oxford University Press, 2002), 1607.

Robert Heinsch, 'How to Achieve Fair and Expeditious Trial Proceedings before the ICC: Is it Time for a More Judge-dominated Approach?' in C. Stahn and G. Sluiter (eds), *The Emerging Practice of the International Criminal Court* (Leiden; Boston: Martinus Nijhoff Publishers, 2009), 479.

Bert Swart, 'Arrest and Surrender', in A. Cassese *et al.* (eds), *The Rome Statute of the International Criminal Court: A Commentary* (Oxford: Oxford University Press, 2002), 1639.

INDEX